Advances In Consumer Research

volume XXI

Chris T. Allen   Deborah Roedder John
EDITORS

1994 Copyright © ASSOCIATION FOR CONSUMER RESEARCH

All rights reserved. No part of this publication may be reproduced, stored in a retrieval system or transmitted, in any form or by any means, electronic, mechanical, photocopying, recording, or otherwise, without prior written permission of the publisher.

International Standard Book Number (ISBN): 0-915552-32-9

International Standard Serial Number (ISSN): 0098-9258

Chris T. Allen and Deborah Roedder John, Editors

Advances in Consumer Research, Volume 21

(Provo, UT: Association for Consumer Research, 1994)

Preface

The twenty-first Annual Conference of the Association for Consumer Research was held at the Stouffer Nashville Hotel in Nashville, Tennessee on October 7-10, 1993. This volume contains the papers which were presented at these meetings.

Thirty-three members of the Association were on the Conference Program Committee. These individuals contributed many ideas that affected the development of the conference, and served as the review board for selection of special sessions. Many of them also rose very early on Saturday morning in Nashville to help host a welcome breakfast for all who were attending their first ACR Conference. Another 202 members of the Association served as reviewers for competitive papers; many of these persons also chaired sessions or offered discussant comments on papers in Nashville. One of the great pleasures of coordinating an ACR Conference is the opportunity it affords to work with literally hundreds of devoted and caring consumer researchers. We thank all of our paper reviewers and Program Committee members for their many contributions to the success of the 1993 Conference.

Our colleagues submitted 157 competitive papers and 70 special session proposals for review: 78 and 39 of these, respectively, were accepted for presentation in Nashville, and for inclusion in this volume. Over 500 people attended the conference and the most frequent complaint we heard in the hotel hallways was that there were "too many" interesting sessions, which made it hard to choose just one session to attend at any particular time. Of course, this is just the complaint that you *do* want to hear as a conference program coordinator. We are very grateful to all those consumer researchers who submitted papers and made presentations in Nashville. As always, their intellectual products contained in this volume are the true lasting contribution of an ACR Conference.

Several other persons deserve special thanks for various contributions: we thank Keith Hunt for always being there with an answer; Jeff Inman for his assistance in matching competitive papers and reviewers; Jim Muncy and Steve Barnett for their concerted efforts in constructing the physical product that is now in your hands; Dennis Scanio of Centaur Studios in St. Louis, Missouri for creating the original art that you see on the cover; and numerous doctoral students from Minnesota and Cincinnati for diligent service in a variety of tasks.

Co-chairing an ACR Conference is a once-in-a-lifetime experience. It is an extremely gratifying experience because one gets to observe firsthand the tremendous intellectual energy that such a conference generates. From our experience we would observe that ACR is alive and well, and we hope that our efforts have contributed in some small way to preserving the vitality of the Association. Our final and most sincere thanks then must go to Terry Shimp, for giving us this opportunity to serve ACR.

Chris T. Allen
University of Cincinnati

Deborah Roedder John
University of Minnesota
1993 Program Co-chairs, and
Proceedings Co-editors

Conference Committee

PRESIDENT
Terence A. Shimp
University of South Carolina

CONFERENCE CHAIRS
Chris T. Allen, University of Cincinnati
Deborah Roedder John, University of Minnesota

PROGRAM COMMITTEE

Craig Andrews, Marquette University
Sharon Beatty, University of Alabama
Merrie Brucks, University of Arizona
Richard L. Celsi, California State University-Long Beach
Amitava Chattopadhyay, McGill University
Janeen Arnold Costa, University of Utah
Valerie S. Folkes, University of Southern California
Gary Gaeth, University of Iowa
James Gentry, University of Nebraska
Elizabeth C. Hirschman, Rutgers University
Chris Janiszewski, University of Florida
Noreen Klein, Virginia Polytechnic Institute & State University
Donald R. Lichtenstein, University of Colorado-Boulder
Barbara Loken, University of Minnesota
John G. Lynch, Jr., University of Florida
Scott B. Mackenzie, Indiana University
Mary Ann McGrath, Loyola University

Robert Meyer, University of Pennsylvania
Joan Myers-Levy, University of Chicago
Thomas O'Guinn, University of Illinois, Urbana-Champaign
Richard L. Oliver, Vanderbilt University
Cornelia Pechmann, University of California, Irvine
Brian T. Ratchford, State University of New York, Buffalo
Peter H. Reingen, Arizona State University
Marsha L. Richins, University of Missouri, Columbia
Debra Scammon, University of Utah
Itamar Simonson, Stanford University
Ruth A. Smith, Virginia Polytechnic Institute & State University
Douglas M. Stayman, Cornell University
Craig Thompson, University of Wisconsin, Madison
H. Rao Unnava, Ohio State University
Melanie Wallendorf, University of Arizona
Russell S. Winer, University of California, Berkeley

SPECIAL THANKS TO

Jennifer Gregan-Paxton, University of Minnesota
H. Keith Hunt, Brigham Young University
Jeff Inman, University of Southern California
Jeffrey Jass, University of Minnesota
Christopher Joiner, University of Minnesota

Susan Kleiser, University of Cincinnati
Susan Powell Mantel, University of Cincinnati
James Muncy, Valdosta State University
Arti Sahni, University of Cincinnati

REVIEWERS

Aaron Ahuvia
Joseph W. Alba
Dana Alden
Mark I. Alpert
Paul Anderson
Alan Andreasen
Eric J. Arnould
Nancy Artz
April Atwood
Gary J. Bamossy
Hans Baumgartner
William O. Bearden
George Belch
Michael A. Belch
Russell W. Belk
James R. Bettman
Barbara Bickart
Gabriel J. Biehal
Abhijit Biswas
Peter Bloch
Paul Bloom
Paula Fitzgerald Bone
David M. Boush
Sheri Bridges
Terry Bristol
Julia M. Bristor
Susan Broniarczyk
George Brooker
Steven P. Brown
Claus Buhl
Alvin C. Burns
Goutam Chakraborty
Dipankar Chakravarti
Murali Chandrashekaran
Joel B. Cohen
Catherine A. Cole
Larry D. Compeau
T. Bettina Cornwell
Carolyn Costley
Joseph A. Cote
Eloise Coupey
Elizabeth H. Creyer
Ayn Crowley
John Deighton
Rita Denny
Rohit Deshpande
Ravi Dhar
Laurette Dube
Pam Scholder Ellen
Basil Englis
Sevgin Eroglu

Marla Felcher
Edward F. Fern
Eileen Fischer
Robert J. Fisher
Jonathan Frenzen
Marian Friestad
Sarah Gardial
Hubert Gatignon
Linda L. Golden
Ronald C. Goodstein
Cathy Goodwin
Jill A. Grace
Donald Granbois
Paul E. Green
Flemming Hansen
Curtis P. Haugtvedt
William J. Havlena
Scott A. Hawkins
Susan E. Heckler
Deborah D. Heisley
Paul Herr
Robin A. Higie
Ron Hill
Jacqueline C. Hitchon
Morris B. Holbrook
Douglas B. Holt
Martin I. Horn
Michael J. Houston
Daniel J. Howard
Cynthia Huffman
Wes Hutchinson
Easwar Iyer
Bernard Jaworski
Eric J. Johnson
Annamma Joy
Lynn Kahle
Frank Kardes
Harold H. Kassarjian
James Kellaris
Kevin Lane Keller
Robert F. Kelly
Robert J. Kent
Jerome B. Kernan
Tina Kiesler
John Kim
Susan Schultz Kleine
Robert E. Kleine III
Richard Kolbe
H. Shanker Krishnan
Zarrel V. Lambert

Michel Laroche
John L. Lastovicka
Roxanne Lefkoff-Hagius
Donald R. Lehmann
James H. Leigh
Therese A. Louie
Jordan Louviere
Tina M. Lowrey
Richard J. Lutz
Debbie MacInnis
Carole Macklin
Thomas J. Madden
Durairaj Maheswaran
Prashant Malaviya
Tamara F. Mangleburg
Haim Mano
Howard Marmorstein
Charlotte Mason
Michael Mazis
James H. McAlexander
Leigh McAlister
Edward F. McQuarrie
Raj Mehta
Geeta Menon
Timothy P. Meyer
David Mick
Paul Miniard
Andrew Mitchell
Lois A. Mohr
Todd A. Mooradian
David J. Moore
Christine Moorman
John Mowen
James A. Muncy
Patrick E. Murphy
John P. Murry, Jr.
Sunder Narayanan
Prakash Nedungadi
Rick Netemeyer
Carl Obermiller
Cele Otnes
Julie Ozanne
Thomas J. Page
C. W. Park
Pallab Paul
Teresa M. Pavia
James W. Peltier
Lisa Penaloza
Laura Peracchio
Ivan Preston

Chris P. Puto
William J. Qualls
Akshay Rao
S. Ratneshwar
Joseph O. Rentz
Randall L. Rose
William T. Ross
Michael L. Rothschild
J. Edward Russo
Alan G. Sawyer
Charles M. Schaninger
John A. Schibrowsky
David W. Schumann
Linda M. Scott
Richard Semenik
Murphy A. Sewall
John Sherry
Allan D. Shocker
L. J. Shrum
Carolyn Simmons
Surendra N. Singh
Daniel C. Smith
Robert E. Smith
Stephen M. Smith
Michael Solomon
Susan Spiggle
Han Srinivasan
Debra Stephens
Barbara Stern
Brian Sternthal
David M. Stewart
Jeffrey J. Stoltman
Patricia Stout
Elnora W. Stuart
Suresh Subramanian
Mita Sujan
David M. Szymanski
Alice M. Tybout
Joel E. Urbany
Alladi Venkatesh
Meera Venkatraman
Madhubalan Viswanathan
Beth Walker
Wanda T. Wallace
John Walsh
Brian Wansink
Marc Weinberger
Albert R. Wildt
Newell D. Wright
Manjit Yadav
George Zinkhan

Table of Contents and Conference Program

Preface iii

ACR Conference Committee and Reviewers iv

Table of Contents and Conference Program vi

Presidential Address
Academic Appalachia and the Discipline of Consumer Research 1
    Terence A. Shimp, University of South Carolina

Fellow's Award 8
    Richard P. Bagozzi, University of Michigan

ASSOCIATION FOR CONSUMER RESEARCH ANNUAL CONFERENCE

OCTOBER 7-10, 1993
STOUFFER NASHVILLE HOTEL
NASHVILLE, TENNESSEE

THURSDAY, OCTOBER 7

ACR EXECUTIVE BOARD MEETING
10:00 - 5:00

REGISTRATION
4:00 - 8:00

RECEPTION
5:30 - 7:30

FRIDAY, OCTOBER 8

JCP EDITORIAL BOARD MEETING
7:30 - 8:30

REGISTRATION
8:00 - 11:50 and 2:10 - 5:30

SESSION 1
8:30 - 10:00

1.1   *Special Session*: Perspectives on Consumer Health Issues: Theoretical, Methodological, and Policy Insights

Chair: Christine Moorman, University of Wisconsin-Madison

Session Summary
Perspectives on Consumer Health Issues: Theoretical, Methodological, and Policy Insights 12
    Christine Moorman, University of Wisconsin-Madison

Analyzing the Effectiveness of Fear Appeals: A Longitudinal Study
  Lauren Goldberg Block, New York University
  Punam Anand, Columbia University

Consumer Use of Nutritional Information: Results of Two In-Store Observational Studies
  Catherine A. Cole, University of Iowa
  Siva K. Balasubramanian, Southern Illinois University

Women and Abortion: A Phenomenological Analysis 13
  Ronald Paul Hill, Villanova University
  Maggie Jones Patterson, Duquesne University
  Kate Maloy, University of Pittsburgh

Exploring the Effects of Consumer Characteristics on Health Behaviors
  Christine Moorman, University of Wisconsin-Madison

1.2   Special Session: Measuring and Judging Emotional Aspects of Consumption Experiences

Chair: Laurette Dubé, Université de Montréal
Discussants: Robert A. Westbrook, Rice University
        Douglas M. Stayman, Cornell University

Session Summary
Measuring and Judging Emotional Aspects of Consumption Experiences 15
  Laurette Dubé, Université de Montréal

*Conceptual Issues in the Structural Analysis of Consumption Emotion, Satisfaction, and Quality: Evidence
in a Service Setting* 16
  Richard L. Oliver, Vanderbilt University

The Structural Characteristics of Positive and Negative Service Encounters: Experience and Memory
  Marian Friestad, University of Oregon

*Capturing the Dynamics of Consumers' Affective States and Their Effect on Consumer Satisfaction in
Service Delivery Environments*
  Laurette Dubé, Université de Montréal
  Michael S. Morgan, Cornell University

1.3   Special Session: The Proof of the Pudding is in the Eating: The Role of Product Experience in Consumer Decision Making

Chairs: Goutam Chakraborty, Oklahoma State University
       Gary J. Gaeth, University of Iowa
Discussant: John Deighton, University of Chicago

Session Summary
The Proof of the Pudding is in the Eating: The Role of Product Experience in Consumer Decision Making 23
  Goutam Chakraborty, Oklahoma State University
  Alice Wright, California State University, Long Beach

Framing Effects of Advertising and Direct Experience on Attribute Importance
  Alice Wright, California State University, Long Beach
  Richard Lutz, University of Florida

The Joint Effect of Product Experience and Advertising: An Attribute Level Analysis
  Goutam Chakraborty, Oklahoma State University

Multiple Product Experiences and the 'Rebound' Effect
    Gary J. Gaeth, University of Iowa
    Irwin P. Levin, University of Iowa
    Jennifer Castellucci, University of Iowa
    Shailesh Sood, University of Iowa

1.4   *Special Session*: Decision Difficulty and Uncertain Preferences: Implications for Consumer Choice

Chair: Ravi Dhar, Yale University

Session Summary
Decision Difficulty and Uncertain Preferences: Implications for Consumer Choice 24
    Ravi Dhar, Yale University

Is More Choice Always Better?
    Eric J. Johnson, University of Pennsylvania
    Eldar Shafir, Princeton University

How do People Make Emotionally Difficult and Stressful Decisions
    James R. Bettman, Duke University
    Mary Frances Luce, Duke University
    John W. Payne, Duke University

Dynamic Instability in Arriving at a Difficult Decision
    Chip Heath, University of Chicago
    Radhika Puri, University of Chicago

Context Effects in Consumer Choice Among Menus
    Ravi Dhar, Yale University
    Drazen Prelec, MIT

1.5   *Competitive Paper Session*: Gift Exchange, Families, and Spending Patterns

Chair: Tamara F. Mangleburg, Florida Atlantic University
Discussant: Donald H. Granbois, Indiana University

In-Laws and Outlaws: The Impact of Divorce and Remarriage Upon Christmas Gift Exchange 25
    Cele Otnes, University of Illinois, Urbana-Champaign
    Kyle Zolner, University of Illinois, Urbana-Champaign
    Tina M. Lowrey, Rider College

Keeping the Family Together: How We Survived the Divorce 30
    Myra Jo Bates, University of Nebraska-Lincoln
    James W. Gentry, University of Nebraska-Lincoln

Consumer Spending Patterns: Dimensions and Dichotomies 35
    Patricia Ann Walsh, University of Connecticut
    Susan Spiggle, University of Connecticut

Discussant's Comments
Consumer Learning and Coping Behaviors in Transitory Situations 41
    Donald H. Granbois, Indiana University

1.6 *Competitive Paper Session*: **Knowledge, Involvement, and Expertise**

Chair: Roxanne Lefkoff-Hagius, University of Maryland
Discussant: Wes Hutchinson, University of Florida

The Relationship Between Knowledge and Search: It Depends 43
    Carol A. Fiske, University of South Carolina
    Lisa A. Luebbehusen, University of South Carolina
    Anthony D. Miyazaki, University of South Carolina
    Joel E. Urbany, University of South Carolina

Exploring the Relationships Between Means-End Knowledge and Involvement 51
    Michael S. Mulvey, Pennsylvania State University
    Jerry C. Olson, Pennsylvania State University
    Richard L. Celsi, California State University, Long Beach
    Beth A. Walker, Arizona State University

Recovering Forgotten Information: A Study in Consumer Expertise 58
    Elizabeth J. Cowley, University of Toronto

1.7 *Special Session*: **Neglected Classics: Three Intellectual Traditions in the Sociology of Consumption**

Chair: Douglas Holt, Pennsylvania State University

Session Summary
Neglected Classics: Three Intellectual Traditions in the Sociology of Consumption 64
    Douglas Holt, Pennsylvania State University

The Impact of Modernity on Consumption: Simmel's <u>Philosophy of Money</u> 65
    Douglas Holt, Pennsylvania State University
    Kathleen Searls, Pennsylvania State University

Consumption and the Production of Social Order: Baudrillard's Early Work
    Fuat Firat, Arizona State West

Consumption and Social Stratification: Bourdieu's <u>Distinction</u> 70
    Paul F. Anderson, Pennsylvania State University
    Douglas E. Allen, Pennsylvania State University

FRIDAY, OCTOBER 8

SESSION 2
10:20 - 11:50

2.1 *Competitive Paper Session*: **Price Perceptions and Deal Proneness**

Chair: Dhruv Grewal, University of Miami
Discussant: Leigh McAlister, University of Texas, Austin

Perceived Price Fairness: A New Look at an Old Construct 75
    Marielza Martins, University of Illinois, Urbana-Champaign
    Kent Monroe, University of Illinois, Urbana-Champaign

Price Awareness of Consumers Exposed to Intense Retail Rivalry: A Field Study 79
    Kathleen Seiders, Texas A&M University
    Carolyn L. Costley, University of Miami

Promotion Heterogeneity and Consumer Learning: Refining the Deal-Proneness Construct 86
    Caroline M. Henderson, Dartmouth College

2.2   Special Session: Emerging Views of Attitudes: Conceptual and Empirical Perspectives on Attitude Strength

Chairs: Ida E. Berger, Queen's University
                Linda F. Alwitt, DePaul University

Session Summary
Emerging Views of Attitudes and Attitude Process: Conceptual and Empirical Perspectives on Attitude Strength 95
    Ida E. Berger, Queen's University
    Linda F. Alwitt, DePaul University

Creating Strong Attitudes
    Curtis P. Haugtvedt, Ohio State University

Attitudinal Ambivalence & Attitude Strength: A Better Understanding of the Indifference-Ambivalence Dimension
    Joseph R. Priester, Ohio State University
    Richard E. Petty, Ohio State University

The Structure and Impact of Attitude Strength
    Ida E. Berger, Queen's University
    Linda F. Alwitt, DePaul University

Expanding Our View of Strength
    Clark Leavitt, Ohio State University

2.3   Special Session: Knowing More Than We're Told: Inferences From Advertising Claims

Chairs: Carolyn J. Simmons, LeHigh University
                Gita V. Johar, Columbia University
Discussant: John G. Lynch, Jr., University of Florida

Session Summary
Knowing More Than We're Told: Inferences From Advertising Claims 96
    Carolyn J. Simmons, LeHigh University
    Gita Venkataramani Johar, Columbia University

Effects of Advertising Common (but previously neglected) Attributes on Consumer Inference Making
    Sandra J. Burke, Georgetown University
    Youjae Yi, University of Michigan
    Sandra Milberg, Georgetown University

Knowing More (or Less) Than We Can Know: Involvement and Deceptive Inferencing from Advertising
    Gita V. Johar, Columbia University

Inference, Confidence, and Uncertainty: A Protocol Analysis
    Frank R. Kardes, University of Cincinnati

2.4 Special Session: "This Note's for You ... :" Negative Effects of the Commercial Use of Popular Music

Chairs: Basil G. Englis, Rutgers University, New Brunswick
Greta E. Pennell, Rutgers University, New Brunswick
Discussant: Wanda T. Wallace, Duke University

Session Summary
"This Note's for You ....:" Negative Effects of the Commercial Use of Popular Music 97
Basil G. Englis, Rutgers University
Greta E. Pennell, Rutgers University

Using 'Revolution:' A Case Study in Intentionality, Cooptation, and Resistance
Linda M. Scott, University of Illinois, Urbana-Champaign

How Meaning is Attached to Popular Music Through its Association with Youth Subcultures
Elizabeth Blair, Ohio University

When 'Hits' Strikeout: Loving the Song but Hating the Product
Greta E. Pennell, Rutgers University
Basil G. Englis, Rutgers University

2.5 Competitive Paper Session: Phenomenological Accounts of Consumer Experience

Chair: Robert E. Kleine III, Arizona State University
Discussant: Larry D. Compeau, Clarkson University

The Halcyon Days of Youth: A Phenomenological Account of Experiences and Feelings Accompanying Spring Break on the Beach 98
Laura A. Williams, Louisiana State University
Alvin C. Burns, Louisiana State University

Unfulfilled Promises and Personal Confessions: A Postpositivist Inquiry into the Idealized and Experienced Meanings of Consumer Technology 104
Craig J. Thompson, University of Wisconsin-Madison

Possessions and Identity in Crisis: Meaning and Change for Victims of the Oakland Firestorm 109
Shay Sayre, California State University, Fullerton

Discussant's Comments
Redefining Self: Interpreting the Interpretations of Three Diverse Experiences 115
Larry D. Compeau, Clarkson University

2.6 Special Session: Mental Accounting and Consumer Spending

Chairs: Suzanne O'Curry, DePaul University
Chip Heath, University of Chicago
Discussant: Eric J. Johnson, University of Pennsylvania

Session Summary
Mental Accounting and Consumer Spending 119
Chip Heath, University of Chicago
Suzanne O'Curry, DePaul University

Budgeting for Expenses: Mental Accounts for Consumer Purchases Have a Categorical Structure
Chip Heath, University of Chicago
Jack Soll, University of Chicago

Income Source Effects
    Suzanne O'Curry, DePaul University

Mental Accounting and the Sunk Cost Effect: A Field Experiment
    Peter Nye, Northeastern University

2.7   *Competitive Paper Session*: Time Pressures and Time Styles

Chair: Haim Mano, University of Missouri, St. Louis
Discussant: Edward F. McQuarrie, Santa Clara University

Consumer Responses to Time Pressure: A Qualitative Study with Homeowners in Foreclosure 120
    Barbara L. Gross, University of Southern California

The Effect of Stress on Price Sensitivity and Comparison Shopping 126
    Linda K. Anglin, Mankato State University
    J. Kathleen Stuenkel, University of Wisconsin-LaCrosse
    Lawrence R. Lepisto, Central Michigan University

The Dynamism of Personal Timestyle: How We Do More in Less Time 132
    Frank Denton, University of Wisconsin-Madison

FRIDAY, OCTOBER 8

LUNCH
12:00 - 2:00

BUSINESS MEETING

PRESIDENTIAL ADDRESS
Terence A. Shimp
"Academic Appalachia and the Discipline of Consumer Research"

FRIDAY, OCTOBER 8

SESSION 3
2:10 - 3:40

3.1   *Special Session*: Community and Consumption

Chairs: Brenda Gainer, York University
                     Eileen Fischer, York University
Discussant: Craig Thompson, University of Wisconsin, Madison

Session Summary
Community and Consumption 137
    Brenda Gainer, York University
    Eileen Fischer, York University

In Search of Community in the Consumer Research Literature
    Eileen Fischer, York University
    Julia Bristor, University of Houston

Community as Shared Cognitions
   Ajay K. Sirsi, Arizona State University
   James C. Ward, Arizona State University
   Peter H. Reingen, Arizona State University

Consumption and Gendered Communities
   Brenda Gainer, York University

3.2 *Special Session*: Toward a Renaissance of Goals in Consumer Research on Attitudes and Decision Making

Chair: Hans Baumgartner, Pennsylvania State University
Discussant: W. Fred van Raaij, Erasmus University

Session Summary
Toward a Renaissance of Goals in Consumer Research on Attitudes and Decision Making 138
   Hans Baumgartner, Pennsylvania State University

Consumer Goal Structures and the Effects of Goals and Goal Structures on Involvement and Behavioral Intentions
   Rik Pieters, Erasmus University
   Hans Baumgartner, Pennsylvania State University
   Doug Allen, Pennsylvania State University

The Role of Self-Schemas and Action Control in the Regulation of Goal-Directed Behaviors: The Case of Exercising
   Richard P. Bagozzi, University of Michigan

Reactions to Self Versus Other Goal-Directed Behavior: The Influence of Feedback on Perspectives and Future Intentions
   Therese A. Louie, University of Washington

3.3 *Special Session*: A Later Mover Advantage? The Impact of Order of Entry and Brand Features on Consumer Preferences

Chairs: Jennifer Aaker, Stanford University
             Stephen M. Nowlis, University of California, Berkeley
Discussant: Allan D. Shocker, University of Minnesota

Session Summary
A Later Mover Advantage? The Impact of Order of Entry and Brand Characteristics on Consumer Preferences 139
   Jennifer Aaker, Stanford University
   Stephen M. Nowlis, University of California, Berkeley

Attacking a Market Pioneer: Consumer Response to Differentiated Late Entry and Defensive Imitation
   Gregory S. Carpenter, Northwestern University
   Donald R. Lehmann, Columbia University
   Kent Nakamoto, University of Colorado, Boulder
   Suzanne B. Walchli, Northwestern University

The Effect of Differentiating Product Features on Brand Choice
   Stephen M. Nowlis, University of California, Berkeley
   Itamar Simonson, Stanford University

The Third Mover Strategy
   Jennifer Aaker, Stanford University

3.4 *Special Session*: What Not to Forget About Memory Research: The Role of Expectations and Organization in Memory

Chairs: Susan E. Heckler, University of Arizona
Karen Finlay, University of Guelph

Session Summary
The Role of Expectations and Organization in the Encoding and Use of Memory-Based Information: What Not to Forget About Memory Research 140
    Susan E. Heckler, University of Arizona

The Impact of Memory Structure on Recall and Choice: Remembering When Remembering is Difficult
    Karen Finlay, University of Guelph
    John N. Bassili, University of Toronto
    Andrew A. Mitchell, University of Toronto

Lyrics and Melodies in Advertising: The Impact on Consumer Memory and Evaluations
    Wanda T. Wallace, Duke University

The Influence of Expectations Created by Advertising Context on Picture Processing
    Prashant Malaviya, University of Illinois, Chicago
    Jolita Kisielius, Northwestern University
    Brian Sternthal, Northwestern University

The Impact of Expectancy and Motivation on Recall and Evaluation of Product Information
    Susan E. Heckler, University of Arizona
    Laura A. Peracchio, University of Wisconsin, Milwaukee

3.5 *Competitive Paper Session*: Values, Materialism, and the Environment

Chair: Susan Schultz Kleine, Arizona State University
Discussant: Clifford Schultz, Columbia University

Empirical Relationships Between Cognitive Style and LOV: Implications for Values and Value Systems 141
    Roger P. McIntyre, East Carolina University
    Reid P. Claxton, East Carolina University
    David B. Jones, LaSalle University

How Green is My Value: Exploring the Relationship Between Environmentalism and Materialism 147
    Bobby Banarjee, University of Massachusetts, Amherst
    Kim McKeage, University of Massachusetts, Amherst

Paradigms of the Self and the Environment in Consumer Behavior and Marketing 153
    Annamma Joy, Concordia University
    Lisa Auchinachie, Concordia University

3.6 *Special Session*: The "Masculine Mystique": Men's Involvement in Gift Giving, Gift Receipt and Gift Occasions

Chair: Cele Otnes, University of Illinois, Urbana-Champaign
Discussant: Russell W. Belk, University of Utah

Session Summary
The 'Masculine Mystique': Men's Involvement in Gift Giving, Gift Receipt and Gift Occasions 158
    Cele Otnes, University of Illinois, Urbana-Champaign

Men in Mourning: Gift Receipt and Funeral Planning from the Male Point of View
    Kina Mallard, Union University

The Pleasure and Pain of Being Close: Men's Mixed Feelings About Participation in Valentine's Day Gift Exchange Activities 159
     Cele Otnes, University of Illinois, Urbana-Champaign
     Julie Ruth, University of Washington
     Constance C. Milbourne, Leo Burnett U.S.A.

A Toast for the Host? The Male Perspective on Gifts that Say 'Thank You' 165
     Margaret Rucker, University of California, Davis
     Anthony Freitas, University of California, Davis
     Jamie Dolstra, University of California, Davis

3.7   *Competitive Paper Session*: **Affect and Emotion in Advertising**

Chair: Richard Semenik, University of Utah
Discussants: Susan L. Holak, City University of New York, Staten Island
               William J. Havlena, Fordham University

Death by Nostalgia: A Diagnosis of Context Specific Cases 169
     Stacey Menzel Baker, University of Nebraska-Lincoln
     Patricia F. Kennedy, University of Nebraska-Lincoln

Measuring Multiple Emotional Responses to a Single Television Commercial 175
     Jon D. Morris, University of Florida
     James S. McMullen, University of Florida

Exploring the Role of Individual Differences in Affect Intensity on the Consumer's Response to Advertising Appeals 181
     David J. Moore, University of Michigan
     William D. Harris, Quinnipiac College
     Hong C. Chen, Grand Valley State University

FRIDAY, OCTOBER 8

SESSION 4
4:00 - 5:30

4.1   *Competitive Paper Session*: **Consumer Inferences**

Chair: Gabriel Biehal, University of Maryland
Discussant: Susan M. Broniarczyk, University of Texas, Austin

Consumer Inferences and Family Branding Strategies: A Demonstration of Category-Based Induction 188
     Christopher Joiner, University of Minnesota
     Barbara Loken, University of Minnesota

Brand Names and Consumer Inference: The Effect of Adding a Numeric Component to a Brand Name 195
     Teresa Pavia, University of Utah

Consumer Inference as Part of Product Comprehension 201
     Timothy R. Graeff, Middle Tennessee State University
     Jerry C. Olson, Pennsylvania State University

4.2 *Competitive Paper Session*: On Informing the Consumer

Chair: Craig Andrews, Marquette University
Discussant: Christine Moorman, University of Wisconsin, Madison

Effects of a Role Model and Fear in Warning Label on Perceptions of Safety and Safety Behavior 208
    Mark A. deTurck, State University of New York, Buffalo
    Robert A. Rachlin, State University of New York, Buffalo
    Melissa J. Young, State University of New York, Buffalo

Nutritional Information Research: A Review of the Issues 213
    Eve M. Caudill, University of Illinois, Urbana-Champaign

Miscomprehension and Believability of Information Presented in Print Advertising 218
    Richard F. Beltramini, Arizona State University
    Steven P. Brown, Southern Methodist University

4.3 *Special Session*: Behavioral Research Using Scanner Data

Chairs: Amitava Chattopadhyay, McGill University
         Emine Sarigollu, McGill University
Discussant: Scott A. Neslin, Dartmouth College

Session Summary
Behavioral Research Using Scanner Data 224
    Amitava Chattopadhyay, McGill University
    Stephen J. Hoch, University of Chicago
    Glen Mayhew, Washington University
    Scott A. Neslin, Dartmouth College
    Emine Sarigollu, McGill University
    Russell S. Winer, University of California-Berkeley

Real-Time, Real-World Pricing and Promotion Experiments
    Stephen J. Hoch, University of Chicago

An Empirical Measure of Willingness to Pay for Innovation in Frequently Purchased Nondurables
    Glen Mayhew, Washington University
    Russell S. Winer, University of California-Berkeley

Relationship Between Ad Content Information and Brand Sales
    Amitava Chattopadhyay, McGill University
    Emine Sarigollu, McGill University
    Gerald Gorn, University of British Columbia

4.4 *Special Session*: Real-Time Ad Processing: Tracing Dynamic Responses

Chair: Douglas L. MacLachlan, University of Washington

Session Summary
Real-Time Ad Processing: Tracing Dynamic Responses 225
    Douglas L. MacLachlan, University of Washington

Process Tracing of Physiological Responses to Dynamic Commercial Stimuli 226
    Piet Vanden Abeele, Catholic University of Leuven
    Douglas L. MacLachlan, University of Washington

Testing a Dynamic Model of Affective Responses to Advertising
   Joel B. Cohen, University of Florida
   Michel Tuan Pham, University of Florida
   G. David Hughes, University of North Carolina, Chapel Hill

Affective Patterns in Advertisements and Consumer Reactions
   Dan Padgett, Pennsylvania State University
   Hans Baumgartner, Pennsylvania State University
   Mita Sujan, Pennsylvania State University

Attentional Cycling Patterns in Over-Time Measures of Ad Processing
   Esther Thorson, University of Missouri-Columbia

4.5   *Special Session*: Research on the Phenomenon and Treatment of Addiction: A Multi-Disciplinary Perspective

Chair: Michal Ann Strahilevitz, University of Illinois, Urbana-Champaign
Discussants: Elizabeth Hirschman, Rutgers University, New Brunswick

Session Summary
Research on the Phenomenon and Treatment of Addiction: A Multi-Disciplinary Perspective 233
   Michal Ann Strahilevitz, University of Illinois Urbana-Champaign

Addiction in Light of Some Recent Learning Experiments
   Drazen Prelec, MIT

Distinctions and Commonalities in the Experiences and Recovery Processes of Various Addictive Behaviors
   Michal Ann Strahilevitz, University of Illinois, Urbana-Champaign

Informant Brokerage and Social System Therapy: Improving Service Delivery in the Treatment of Chemical Dependency
   John Sherry, Jr., Northwestern University

4.6   *Competitive Paper Session*: That Pervasive Need for Cognition

Chair: H. Shanker Krishnan, Indiana University
Discussant: Robert J. Kent, University of Delaware

Need for Cognition and the Effects of Repeated Expression on Attitude Accessibility and Extremity 234
   Stephen M. Smith, Ohio State University
   Curtis P. Haugtvedt, Ohio State University
   Richard E. Petty, Ohio State University

Evidence of a Relationship Between Need for Cognition and Chronological Age: Implications for Persuasion in Consumer Research 238
   Harlan Spotts, Northeastern University

Need for Cognition, Advertisement Viewing Time and Memory for Advertising Stimuli 244
   James W. Peltier, University of Wisconsin-Whitewater
   John A. Schibrowsky, University of Nevada-Las Vegas

4.7 *Special Session*: **The Wild West in the Consumer Imagination**

Chair and
Discussant: Terrence H. Witkowski, California State University, Long Beach

Session Summary
The Wild West in the Consumer Imagination 251
    Terrence H. Witkowski, California State University, Long Beach

Somewhere West of Laramie: A Case History of Meaning Transfer
    Ronald A. Fullerton, Providence College

Consuming the West: Reading the Western Film
    Thomas C. O'Guinn, University of Illinois, Urbana-Champaign

Consuming the West: Consumer Behavior at a Western Stock Show
    Lisa Penaloza, University of Colorado, Boulder
    Michelle Detry, University of Colorado, Boulder
    Sylvia Allegretto, University of Colorado, Boulder
    Kathy Garcia, University of Colorado, Boulder
    Christine Page, University of Colorado, Boulder

FRIDAY, OCTOBER 8

RECEPTION
5:30 - 7:30

Live Music by the Craig Duncan Band

SATURDAY, OCTOBER 9

WELCOME BREAKFAST FOR FIRST-TIME ATTENDEES
7:30 - 8:30

REGISTRATION
8:30 - 11:50 and 2:10 - 5:30

SESSION 5
8:30 - 10:00

5.1 *Special Session*: **Heightened Self-Consciousness: The Intended and Unintended Consequences of Marketing Activities**

Chairs: Lauren G. Block, New York University
           Gavan J. Fitzsimons, Columbia University

Session Summary
Heightened Self-Consciousness: The Intended and Unintended Consequences of Marketing Activities 252
    Lauren G. Block, New York University
    Gavan J. Fitzsimons, Columbia University

Targeting a Stigmatized Identity: Elderly Consumers' Responses to Age Segmentation Cues
    Kelly Tepper, University of Kentucky

(In)Significant Others: When Who We See Affects What We Buy
    David Wooten, Columbia University

The Non-Target Market Effect: Associated Feelings of Acceptance, Alienation or Apathy?
    Jennifer L. Aaker, Stanford University
    Jay Dean, Young & Rubicam

Marketing, Consumption, and the Pursuit of Beauty in Popular Culture
    Gavan J. Fitzsimons, Columbia University
    Lauren G. Block, New York University
    Morris B. Holbrook, Columbia University

5.2 *Special Session*: Emergent Understandings of Relationships Between Consumption, Production, and the Family

Chair: Deborah Heisley, UCLA
Discussant: James Gentry, University of Nebraska

Session Summary
Emergent Understandings of Relationships Among Consumption, Production, and the Family 253
    Deborah Heisley, UCLA

The Structural Dimensions of the Inter-generational Transfer of Possessions
    Deborah Heisley, UCLA
    Deborah Ann Cours, UCLA
    Melanie Wallendorf, University of Arizona

Family Businesses and Recursive Relationships: The Impact of Production and Consumption on Family Structure
    Elizabeth Gilster, University of Arizona

The Family VCR: Ordinary Family Life with a Common Textual Product
    Thomas C. O'Guinn, University of Illinois
    Timothy P. Meyer, University of Wisconsin
    Mary E. McNeil, Bradley University

5.3 *Special Session*: Recent Developments in Social Marketing

Chair: Alan R. Andreasen, Georgetown University
Discussant: Gary Bamossy, Vrije University

Session Summary
Recent Advances in Social Marketing 254
    Alan R. Andreasen, Georgetown University

Defining Social Marketing: Implications for Practice and Research
    Alan R. Andreasen, Georgetown University

Using Psychographic Research to Develop Campaigns in the Area of Substance Abuse Among Canadian Youth
    James H. Mintz, Program Promotion, Health and Welfare Canada

Race, Ethnicity and Social Marketing
    Steven Rabin, Porter/Novelli

Changing AIDS-Risk Behavior
    Jeffrey D. Fisher, University of Connecticut
    William A. Fisher, University of Western Ontario

A Stage Model for Behavior Change
    James O. Prochaska, Cancer Prevention Center, University of Rhode Island

Using Theory-Based Community Interventions to Reduce AIDS Risk Behaviors: The CDC's AIDS Community Intervention Demonstration Project
    Martin Fishbein, University of Illinois and Centers for Disease Control and Prevention

Communication for Child Survival: Evaluation of HEALTHCOM Projects in Eight Countries
    Robert Hornik, University of Pennsylvania

The Role of Skills in Facilitating Protective Behaviors: Results from Research on HIV
    Susan Middlestadt, AIDSCOM Project, Academy for Educational Development

5.4   *Special Session*: **Behavioral Perspectives on Bundling Research**

Chair: Donald R. Lehmann, Columbia University
Discussant: C. Whan Park, University of Pittsburgh

Session Summary
Behavioral Perspectives on Bundling Research 255
    Rajan Krish, University of Arizona
    Pallab Paul, University of Denver
    Joydeep Srivastava, University of Arizona

The Impact of Bundle Type, Price Framing and Familiarity on Evaluation of the Bundle
    Bari A. Harlam, University of Rhode Island
    Aradhna Krishna, Columbia University
    Donald R. Lehmann, Columbia University
    Carl Mela, Columbia University

The Effects of Incremental Savings, Perceived Quality, and Perceived Sacrifice on Evaluations of Both Focal and Add-On Products Used to Form Product Bundles
    Ajit Kaicker, Valdosta State College
    William O. Bearden, University of South Carolina
    Joel E. Urbany, University of South Carolina

Developing Augmented Product Bundles: Effects of Framing on Perceived Value and Choice
    Dipankar Chakravarti, University of Arizona
    Rajan Krish, University of Arizona
    Pallab Paul, University of Denver
    Joydeep Srivastava, University of Arizona

5.5   *Competitive Paper Session*: **Zajonc's Legacy**

Chair: Alan G. Sawyer, University of Florida
Discussant: Timothy B. Heath, University of Pittsburgh

A Study of the Concept of Affective Choice Mode for Consumer Decisions 256
    Banwari Mittal, University of Miami

Mere Exposure and the Cognitive-Affective Debate Revisited 264
    Marc Vanhuele, Groupe HEC

The Mere Exposure Effect: Is It a Mere Case of Misattribution 270
    Angela Y. Lee, University of Toronto

5.6   Competitive Paper Session: **Building a Better Radio Ad**

Chair: George Belch, San Diego State University
Discussant: Martin I. Horn, DDB Needham Worldwide

A Test of Prescriptive Advice from the Rossiter-Percy Advertising Planning Grid Using Radio Commercials 276
    Robin Higie Coulter, University of Connecticut
    Murphy A. Sewall, University of Connecticut

Incidental Learning from Radio Advertisements With and Without Curiosity-Arousing Questions 282
    Rhonda Gibson, University of Alabama at Birmingham
    Huiuk Yi, University of Alabama
    Dolf Zillmann, University of Alabama

Music and Radio Advertising: Effects of Tempo and Placement 286
    George Brooker, Central Washington University
    John J. Wheatley, University of Washington

5.7   Special Session: **Agent Decision Making: Understanding and Predicting the Preferences of Others**

Chairs: Patricia M. West, University of Texas at Austin
                Christina L. Brown, Northwestern University
Discussant: John Deighton, University of Chicago

Session Summary
Agent Decision Making: Understanding and Predicting the Preferences of Others 291
    Patricia M. West, University of Texas at Austin
    Christina L. Brown, Northwestern University

Predicting Preferences: An Examination of Agent Learning
    Patricia M. West, University of Texas, Austin

Effect of Accountability on Advertisers' Predictions of Consumer Response to Ads
    Christina L. Brown, Northwestern University

Mapping the Outcomes of Consensus and Collaboration in Industrial Marketing Relationships
    Deborah J. Salmond, University of Baltimore
    Jeffrey R. Edwards, University of Virginia
    Robert E. Spekman, University of Virginia

SATURDAY, OCTOBER 9

SESSION 6
10:20 - 11:50

6.1   Competitive Paper Session: **An Advertising Potpourri**

Chair: Sunder Narayanan, University of Illinois, Urbana-Champaign
Discussant: David W. Stewart, University of Southern California

An Exposé on Green Television Ads 292
    Easwar Iyer, University of Massachusetts, Amherst
    Bobby Banerjee, University of Massachusetts, Amherst
    Charles Gulas, University of Massachusetts, Amherst

A Re-Examination of the Relative Persuasiveness of Comparative and Noncomparative Advertising 299
    Paul W. Miniard, University of South Carolina
    Michael J. Barone, University of South Carolina
    Randall L. Rose, University of South Carolina
    Kenneth C. Manning, University of South Carolina

African American Vernacular English in Advertising: A Sociolinguistic Study 304
    Jennifer Edson Escalas, Duke University

Discussant's Comments
"An Advertising Potpourri": Some Comments and A Unifying Theme 310
    David W. Stewart, University of Southern California

6.2 *Competitive Paper Session*: **Innovation and Cultural Dynamics**

Chair: Harold H. Kassarjian, UCLA
Discussants: Lydia Price, New York University
                 Niraj Dawar, INSEAD

Consumer Choice as an Evolutionary Process: An Operant Interpretation of Adopter Behavior 312
    Gordon R. Foxall, University of Birmingham

Exploring Cultural Differences in Consumer Decision Making: Chinese Consumers in Montréal 318
    Kathleen Brewer Doran, McGill University

India's Changing Consumer Economy: A Cultural Perspective 323
    Alladi Venkatesh, University of California, Irvine

6.3 *Special Session*: **Recent Developments in Social Marketing (Continued)**

6.4 *Special Session*: **Managing Attention**

Chairs: Merrie Brucks, University of Arizona
              Barbara Bickart, Rutgers University-Camden
              Chris Janiszewski, University of Florida

Session Summary
Managing Attention 329
    Chris Janiszewski, University of Florida
    Barbara Bickart, Rutgers University-Camden

Shelf-Management Experiments: Brand Versus Category Space Elasticity
    Stephen J. Hoch, University of Chicago
    Xavier Dreze, University of Chicago
    Mary E. Purk, University of Chicago

Using Information Display to Sustain Attention: Encouraging Consumers to Look Longer
    Chris Janiszewski, University of Florida

Managing Brand Image Transfer: How Display Structure Affects Attention to Cues
    Barbara A. Bickart, Rutgers University-Camden
    Lauranne Buchanan, Arizona State University West
    Carolyn J. Simmons, LeHigh University

Competitive Interference at the Point of Purchase
    Raymond R. Burke, Harvard Business School

6.5 *Special Session*: For the Smell of it All: Functions and Effects of Olfaction in Consumer Behavior

Chair: Deborah J. Mitchell, Temple University
Discussant: Susan C. Knasco, Monell Chemical Senses Center

Session Summary
For the Smell of it All: Functions and Effects of Olfaction in Consumer Behavior 330
    Deborah J. Mitchell, Temple University

There's Something in the Air: Ambient Odor and Consumer Decision Making
    Deborah J. Mitchell, Temple University
    Barbara E. Kahn, University of Pennsylvania
    Susan C. Knasco, Monell Chemical Senses Center

Olfactory Stimuli as Advertising Executional Cues
    Pam Scholder Ellen, Georgia State University
    Paula Fitzgerald Bone, West Virginia University

Memory Effects of Imagery Processes in Olfactory and Visual Modalities
    Dipankar Chakravarti, University of Arizona
    Deborah J. MacInnis, University of Arizona
    Gayathri Mani, University of Arizona

6.6 *Special Session*: Consumption of Heroes and Heroes of Consumption

Chairs: Steven VanderVeen, Calvin College
         Jolita Kisielius, Northwestern University
Discussant: Sidney J. Levy, Northwestern University

Session Summary
The Heroes of Consumption and the Consumption of Heroes 331
    Steven VanderVeen, Calvin College

The Consumption of Heroes and the Hero Hierarchy of Effects 332
    Steven VanderVeen, Calvin College

Heroes of Consumption: A Phenomenological Explication of Shopper as Hero
    Mary Ann McGrath, Loyola University
    Cele Otnes, University of Illinois, Urbana-Champaign

Enhancing Brand Equity via Brand Endorsers: Tapping into the Hero
    Jolita Kisielius, Northwestern University
    Joseph Cherian, University of Illinois, Chicago

6.7 *Competitive Paper Session*: Insights About Persuasion and Impression Management

Chair: Howard Marmorstein, University of Miami
Discussant: H. Rao Unnava, Ohio State University

The Persuasive Effects of Evaluation, Expectancy and Relevancy Dimensions of Incongruent Visual and Verbal Information 337
    Charles S. Areni, Texas Tech University
    K. Chris Cox, Texas Tech University

Using Conversation Theory to Investigate Conclusion-Drawing: Implications for Persuasion 343
    Mark Toncar, Kent State University
    James M. Munch, University of Texas at Arlington
    Michael Mayo, Kent State University

Consumer Reaction to Company-Related Disasters: The Effect of Multiple Versus Single Explanations 348
    Brian K. Jorgensen, University of California, Los Angeles

---

SATURDAY, OCTOBER 9

LUNCH
12:00 - 2:00

PRESENTATION OF AWARDS

ACR FELLOW ADDRESS
Richard P. Bagozzi
"Future Developments in Consumer Behavior"

SESSION 7
2:10 - 3:40

7.1   *Special Session*: **The Power, Potential, and Perils of Meta-Analysis: A Workshop on Integrative Reviews**

Chair: Kent B. Monroe, University of Illinois, Urbana-Champaign
Discussant: Steven P. Brown, Southern Methodist University

Session Summary
The Power, Potential, and Perils of Meta-Analysis: A Workshop on Integrative Reviews 353
    Steven P. Brown, Southern Methodist University

What Do Data Really Mean?
    Frank L. Schmidt, University of Iowa

Meta-Analysis for Model Estimation
    Donald R. Lehmann, Columbia University

Validity Threats in Meta-Analysis
    Murali Chandrashekaran, University of Cincinnati
    Beth A. Walker, Arizona State University

7.2   *Competitive Paper Session*: **Gender Issues**

Chair: Newell Wright, Western Carolina University
Discussants: Janeen Arnold Costa, University of Utah
                    Carole Macklin, University of Cincinnati

An Investigation of the Influence of Gender on the Hedonic Responses Created by Listening to Music 354
    Kathleen T. Lacher, Auburn University

Babes in Toyland: Learning an Ideology of Gender 359
    Greta Eleen Pennell, Rutgers University

Social Comparison and the Beauty of Advertising Models: The Role of Motives for Comparison 365
    Mary C. Martin, University of Nebraska-Lincoln
    Patricia F. Kennedy, University of Nebraska-Lincoln

Discussant's comments
Gender Issues: Gender as a Cultural Construct 372
      Janeen Arnold Costa, University of Utah

7.3   **Special Session: "The Play's the Thing:" Elements of Drama in Advertising and Their Effects on Audience Response**

Chair: Basil G. Englis, Rutgers University, New Brunswick
Discussant: William D. Wells, University of Minnesota

Session Summary
"The Play's the Thing:" Elements of Drama in Advertising and Their Effects on Audience Response 374
      Basil G. Englis, Rutgers University

Stylistic Context in Advertising: The Supporting Role of Physical Evidence in Commercial Dramaturgy
      Michael R. Solomon, Rutgers University, New Brunswick

'Once Upon a Time ...:' Advertising Drama and Audience Empathy
      Barbara B. Stern, Rutgers University, Newark
      Basil G. Englis, Rutgers University, New Brunswick

Allegorical Drama in Advertising: Its Use and Effects
      George Jura, University of Wisconsin, Madison
      Jacqueline C. Hitchon, University of Wisconsin, Madison

Discussant's Comments
Effective and Ineffective Drama Advertisements 375
      William D. Wells, University of Minnesota

7.4   **Special Session: Biases in Social Comparison: If You Are One In a Million, There are 4,000 People Just Like You**

Chairs: Geeta Menon, New York University
              Vicki G. Morwitz, New York University
Discussant: Stephen J. Hoch, University of Chicago

Session Summary
Biases in Social Comparison: If You Are One In a Million, There are 4,000 People Just Like You 379
      Geeta Menon, New York University
      Vicki G. Morwitz, New York University

How Managers View Their Markets: False Consensus and Overconfidence in Marketing Managers' Predictions of Consumer Behavior
      Deborah J. Mitchell, Temple University
      Eric J. Johnson, University of Pennsylvania

Judgments of Behavioral Frequencies of Self and Others: The Impact of One on the Other
      Geeta Menon, New York University
      Priya Raghubir, New York University
      Norbert Schwarz, University of Michigan

Do Polls Reflect Opinions or Do Opinions Reflect the Polls? The Impact of Political Polling on Voter Attitudes, Intentions and Behavior
      Vicki G. Morowitz, New York University
      Carol Pluzinski, New York University

7.5 Competitive Paper Session: Public Policy and Ethical Issues

Chair: Mark I. Alpert, University of Texas, Austin
Discussant: Michael A. Belch, San Diego State University

Consumer Research Standards & Public Policy Formulation: The Case of Mickey Mouse & Old Joe 380
    Claude R. Martin, Jr., University of Michigan

The Mammography Guidelines Controversy: What Do Women Think? 387
    Sharyn M. Sutton, National Cancer Institute
    Ellen J. Eisner, National Cancer Institute
    Diane L. Bloom, University of North Carolina
    Paul N. Bloom, University of North Carolina

Ethical Concerns in Marketing Research 392
    Jane Sojka, Washington State University
    Eric Spangenberg, Washington State University

7.6 Special Session: "5" Calories or "Low" Calories? How Consumers Use Numerical and Verbal Product Information

Chair: Madhubalan Viswanathan, University of Illinois, Urbana-Champaign
Discussant: J. Edward Russo, Cornell University

Session Summary
"5" Calories or "Low" Calories? How Consumers Use Numerical and Verbal Product Information 397
    Madhubalan Viswanathan, University of Illinois, Urbana-Champaign

Representation of Numerical and Verbal Information in Memory
    Terry L. Childers, University of Minnesota

Processing of Numerical and Verbal Information: Implications for Consumer Memory and Judgment
    Madhubalan Viswanathan, University of Illinois, Urbana-Champaign

Numerical and Verbal Information: Implications for Persuasion
    Nancy Artz, University of Southern Maine
    Alice M. Tybout, Northwestern University

7.7 Competitive Paper Session: Consumer Complaining and Satisfaction

Chair: Maryon F. King, Southern Illinois University
Discussant: Valerie S. Folkes, University of Southern California

Customers Complain — Businesses Make Excuses: The Effects of Linkage and Valence 399
    Donna J. Hill, Bradley University
    Robert Baer, Bradley University

The Effect of Motivation to Process on Consumers' Satisfaction Reactions 406
    Barry J. Babin, University of Southern Mississippi
    Mitch Griffin, Bradley University
    Laurie A. Babin, University of Southern Mississippi

Does Satisfaction with Multi-Attribute Products Vary Over Time? A Performance Based Approach 412
    Vikas Mittal, Temple University
    Jerome M. Katrichis, Temple University
    Frank Forkin, Research Data Analysis, Inc.
    Mark Konkel, Consumer Attitude Research, Inc.

SATURDAY, OCTOBER 9

SESSION 8
4:00 - 5:30

8.1 *Competitive Paper Session*: **Old and New Models of Consumption**

Chair: Ruth Ann Smith, Virginia Polytechnic Institute and State University
Discussant: Russell W. Belk, University of Utah

'Tea and the Viennese': *A Pioneering Episode in the Analysis of Consumer Behavior* 418
    Ronald A. Fullerton, Providence College

Object-Subject Interchangeability: A Symbolic Interactionist Model of Materialism 422
    Reid P. Claxton, East Carolina University
    Jeff B. Murray, University of Arkansas

A Cross-Cultural Look at the 'Supposed to Have It' Phenomenon: The Existence of a Standard Package Based on Occupation 427
    Cecelia Wittmayer, Dakota State University
    Steve Schulz, Fort Hays State University
    Robert Mittelstaedt, University of Nebraska-Lincoln

8.2 *Special Session*: **Negotiation: An Interdisciplinary Approach**

Chair: Kim Corfman, New York University

Session Summary
Negotiation: An Interdisciplinary Approach 435
    Rami Zwick, University of Pittsburgh
    Harish Sujan, Pennsylvania State University

An Analysis of Team Versus Solo Negotiations
    Leigh L. Thompson, University of Washington
    Susan E. Brodt, University of Virginia
    Erika Peterson, University of Washington

Raising Expectations for Success in Future Negotiations: The Influence of Optimism and Positive Mood
    Harish Sujan, Pennsylvania State University
    Timothy Graeff, Middle Tennessee State University
    Rami Zwick, University of Pittsburgh

The Negotiation Process: The Role of Agenda Setting, Power, and Expectations for Future Interactions
    Shankar Ganesan, Virginia Polytechnic Institute and State University
    David Brinberg, Virginia Polytechnic Institute and State University

An Empirical Investigation of the Expectation of Future Bargaining Interaction on Process and Outcome Efficiency
    P.V. (Sundar) Balakrishnan, Ohio State University
    Charles Patton, Ohio State University

8.3 *Special Session*: **Memory, Product Familiarity and Categorization Influences on the Composition of Consideration Sets**

Chair: Prakash Nedungadi, Indiana University
Discussant: S. Ratneshwar, University of Florida

Session Summary
Memory, Product Familiarity and Categorization Influences on the Composition of Consideration Sets 436
    Kalpesh Kaushik Desai, University of Texas, Austin
    Wayne D. Hoyer, University of Texas, Austin

Influence of Category Breadth and Product Familiarity on the Structural Characteristics of Consideration Sets
    Kalpesh Kaushik Desai, University of Texas, Austin
    Wayne D. Hoyer, University of Texas, Austin

The Effect of Consumer Experience on Consideration Sets for Brands and Product Categories
    Michael D. Johnson, University of Michigan
    Donald R. Lehmann, Columbia University

Where We Are 'Out to Lunch' on Consideration Sets
    Stephen Holden, ESSEC
    Leila Hamzaoui, ESSEC

8.4 *Special Session*: **Meet the Editors**

Journal of Consumer Psychology	Dipankar Chakravarti, Editor
Journal of Consumer Research	Brian Sternthal, Editor
Journal of Marketing	Rajan Varadarajan, Editor
Journal of Marketing Research	Barton A. Weitz, Editor
Marketing Science	Robert Meyer, Associate Editor

8.5 *Competitive Paper Session*: **New Models of Consumer Judgment**

Chair: Sevgin Eroglu, Georgia State University
Discussant: Thomas J. Madden, University of South Carolina

Sequential Phases of Judgment and the Value Representation of Product Alternatives 437
    James R. Bailey, Rutgers University, Newark
    Robert S. Billings, Ohio State University

Incorporating Perceptions of Financial Control in Purchase Prediction: An Empirical Examination of the Theory of Planned Behavior 442
    Arti Sahni, University of Cincinnati

The Effects of Country of Origin, Brand, and Price Information: A Cognitive-Affective Model of Buying Intentions 449
    Wai-Kwan Li, University of Illinois, Urbana-Champaign
    Kent B. Monroe, University of Illinois, Urbana-Champaign
    Darius K-S Chan, University of Illinois, Urbana-Champaign

8.6   Competitive Paper Session: **Interpersonal Influences and Consumer Socialization**

Chair: Jill A. Grace, University of Southern California
Discussant: Jonathan Frenzen, University of Chicago

The Role of Hispanic Ethnic Identification on Reference Group Influence 458
    Cynthia Webster, Mississippi State University
    James B. Faircloth, III, Mississippi State University

Predicting Buyers' Selection of Interpersonal Sources: The Role of Strong Ties and Weak Ties 464
    Pamela Kiecker, Texas Tech University
    Cathy L. Hartman, Utah State University

Cohort Generational Influences on Consumer Socialization 470
    Aric Rindfleisch, University of Wisconsin-Madison

8.7   **Meeting of the 1994 ACR Conference Committee**

Chairs: Frank R. Kardes, University of Cincinnati
             Mita Sujan, Pennsylvania State University

SATURDAY, OCTOBER 9

JCR EDITORIAL BOARD MEETING
5:30 - 7:00

GRAND OLE OPRY PERFORMANCE
9:00 - 12:00

SUNDAY, OCTOBER 10

SESSION 9
8:30 - 10:00

9.1   Competitive Paper Session: **Cognition and Choice**

Chair: Terry Bristol, Oklahoma State University
Discussants: Elizabeth H. Creyer, University of Iowa
             William T. Ross, Jr., University of Pennsylvania

A Conceptual Model of the Role of Situational Type on Consumer Choice Behavior and Consideration Sets 477
    Indrajit Sinha, University of Michigan

Alternative Models of Cognitive Processes Underlying Consumer Reactions to Conjunction Categories 483
    Moonkyu Lee, University of Colorado at Denver
    Francis M. Ulgado, Georgia Institute of Technology

Consumption Schemata: Their Effects on Consumer Decision Making 489
    Albert Wenben Lai, University of Wisconsin-Madison

9.2 *Special Session*: Innovations in Defining and Measuring Brand Image

Chair: Martin Roth, Boston College
Discussant: Susan Nelson, Landor Associates

Session Summary
Innovations in Defining and Measuring Brand Image 495
   Martin Roth, Boston College

Good Life Images and Brand Name Associations: Evidence from Asia, America, and Europe 496
   George M. Zinkhan, University of Houston
   Penelope J. Prenshaw, University of Houston

A Comparative Analysis of Four Research Techniques for Measuring Brand Image
   Martin S. Roth, Boston College

Using the Zaltman Metaphor Elicitation Technique to Understand Brand Images 501
   Robin Higie Coulter, University of Connecticut
   Gerald Zaltman, Harvard Business School

9.3 *Special Session*: The Dark Side of Consumer Behavior: Examinations of Impulsive and Compulsive Consumption

Chair: Meryl Gardner, University of Delaware
Discussant: Christine Wright-Tsak, Young and Rubicam

Session Summary
The Dark Side of Consumer Behavior: Examinations of Impulsive and Compulsive Consumption 508
   Brian Wansink, Dartmouth College

Antecedents of Eating Bouts: When You Can't Eat Just One
   Brian Wansink, Dartmouth College

Validation of an Impulse Buying Tendency Scale
   Wendy Martin, University of Alabama
   Seungoog Weun, University of Alabama
   Sharon E. Beatty, University of Alabama

Two Forms of Compulsive Consumption: Comorbidity Between Compulsive Buying and Binge Eating
   Ronald J. Faber, University of Minnesota
   Gary A. Christenson, University of Minnesota
   James Mitchell, University of Minnesota

9.4 Not Scheduled for Sunday Morning

9.5 *Competitive Paper Session*: Mood Effects

Chair: D. Maheswaran, New York University
Discussant: Ronald C. Goodstein, UCLA

An Examination of the Effects of Context-Induced Mood States on the Evaluation of a 'Feel-Good' Product:
The Moderating Role of Product Type and the Consistency Effects Model 509
   John Hadjimarcou, Kent State University
   Lawrence J. Marks, Kent State University

The Influence of Mood and Gender on Consumers' Time Perceptions 514
    James J. Kellaris, University of Cincinnati
    Susan Powell Mantel, University of Cincinnati

Phenomenological Insights In Mood and Mood-Related Consumer Behaviors 519
    Jacqueline J. Kacen, University of Illinois at Urbana-Champaign

Discussant's Comments
Mood Effects in Consumer Behavior: A Unifying Theme 526
    Ronald C. Goodstein, University of California, Los Angeles

9.6   *Special Session*: **The Effects of the New Food Label on Consumer Decision Making**

Chair: Gary T. Ford, American University
Discussant: Alan Andreasen, Georgetown University

Session Summary
The Effects of the New Food Labels on Consumer Decision Making 530
    Gary T. Ford, American University

Antecedents of Dietary Consumption Behavior
    Alan Levy, U.S. Food and Drug Administration

Health Claims in the Presence of Consistent and Inconsistent Nutrient Information: A Laboratory Investigation
    Gary T. Ford, American University
    Manoj Hastak, American University
    Anusree Mitra, American University
    Debra J. Ringold, University of Baltimore

The Case of the Implied Nutrient Claim: Can Context Influence the Meaning of Ingredient Statements
    Sandra J. Burke, Georgetown University

9.7   *Competitive Paper Session*: **Scale Development and Validation**

Chair: Patricia M. Anderson, Quinnipiac College
Discussant: Thomas J. Page, Michigan State University

Assessing Viewer Judgment of Advertisements and Vehicles: Scale Development and Validation 531
    Tammi S. Feltham, Wilfrid Laurier University

An Examination of the Psychometric Properties of a Conservation-Oriented Consumption Scale 536
    Katryna Malafarina, University of Minnesota
    Jeffrey Jass, University of Minnesota

Socially Desirable Responses in the Measurement of Need for Cognition 543
    James M. Hunt, Temple University
    Karen M. Stevens, Temple University
    Anindya Chatterjee, Temple University
    Jerome B. Kernan, George Mason University

Discussant's Comments
Comments on Scale Development and Testing 547
    Thomas J. Page, Jr., Michigan State University

SUNDAY, OCTOBER 10
SESSION 10
10:20 - 11:50

10.1 *Competitive Paper Session*: **Determinants of Preference for Aesthetic Products versus Services**

Chair: Robert J. Fisher, University of Southern California
Discussant: Lois A. Mohr, Georgia State University

Consumers' Response to Waiting Time: New Segmentation Bases are Required for Service Industries 548
    Marie Marquis, Université du Québec à Montréal
    Laurette Dubé, Université de Montréal
    Jean-Charles Chebat, Université du Québec à Montréal

The Effect of Arousal Seeking Tendency on Consumer Preferences for Complex Product Designs 554
    Dena Cox, Indiana University
    Anthony Cox, Indiana University

Judging the Attractiveness of Product Design: The Effect of Visual Attributes and Consumer Characteristics 560
    Molly Eckman, Colorado State University
    Janet Wagner, University of Maryland

10.2 *Special Session*: **Ethical Issues in Consumer Research**

Chair: Jacob Jacoby, New York University
Discussants: William L. Wilkie, University of Notre Dame
    Craig Smith, Georgetown University

Session Summary
Ethical Issues in Consumer Research 565
    Jacob Jacoby, New York University

Ethics in Consumer Research: An Overview and Prospectus 566
    Morris Holbrook, Columbia University

Ethical Issues Concerning the Deception and Debriefing of Subjects in Consumer Research
    Daniel Toy, Chico State University
    Lauren Wright, Chico State University
    Jerry Olson, Pennsylvania State University

Ethical Issues in the Conduct and Dissemination of Consumer Research
    Jacob Jacoby, New York University

10.3 *Special Session*: **Films as Texts for Interpreting Deviant Consumer Behavior**

Chair: Elizabeth C. Hirschman, Rutgers University, New Brunswick
Discussant: Craig Thompson, University of Wisconsin, Madison

Coming of Age in a Material World: Juvenile Delinquency and Adolescent Angst 572
    Debra Lynn Stephens, Villanova University
    Ronald Paul Hill, Villanova University

Women as Commodities: Prostitution as Depicted in The Blue Angel, Pretty Baby, and Pretty Woman 576
    Elizabeth C. Hirschman, Rutgers University, New Brunswick
    Barbara B. Stern, Rutgers University, Newark

10.4   **Not Scheduled for Sunday Morning**

10.5   *Special Session*: **The Influence of Affective Context on Advertising Effectiveness**

Chair: Douglas M. Stayman, Cornell University
Discussant: Paul W. Miniard, University of South Carolina

Session Summary
The Influence of Affective Context on Advertising Effectiveness 582
    Douglas M. Stayman, Cornell University

The Influence of Affect in Persuasion: The Amount of Processing versus the Type of Processing
    Douglas M. Stayman, Cornell University

The Impact of Emotional Valence and Intensity on Ad Evaluation and Memory 583
    Karen Russo France, University of Pittsburgh
    Reshma H. Shah, University of Pittsburgh
    C. Whan Park, University of Pittsburgh

Advertising's Influence on Standards of Comparison: The Moderating Role of Mood
    Meryl P. Gardner, University of Delaware
    David W. Schumann, University of Tennessee

10.6   *Special Session*: **Individual and Situational Influences on Purchase Goal Specification**

Chair: Stephen Holden, ESSEC
Discussant: Robert Meyer, University of Pennsylvania

Session Summary
Individual and Situational Influences on Purchase Goal Specification 589
    Stephen Holden, Ecole Supérieure de Sciences Economiques et Commerciales

The Effects of Imaging Consumer Experiential Knowledge on Goal Specification
    Cynthia Huffman, University of Pennsylvania

Consumer Consideration Sets and Choice Across Nominal Product Categories: The Role of Individual and Situational Goals
    S. Ratneshwar, University of Florida
    Cornelia Pechmann, University of California, Irvine
    Allan D. Shocker, University of Minnesota

Measuring the Influence of Situational and Enduring Involvement on Consumers' Decision Goals
    Beth A. Walker, Arizona State University
    Mark Houston, Arizona State University

10.7   *Competitive Paper Session*: **Compulsion, Neuroticism, and Anxiety**

Chair: Meera Venkatraman, Suffolk University
Discussant: L. J. Shrum, Rutgers University

Compulsive Buying Tendency as a Predictor of Attitudes and Perceptions 590
    Allison Magee, Arizona State University

Neuroticism, Affect and Postpurchase Processes 595
    Todd A. Mooradian, College of William and Mary
    James M. Olver, College of William and Mary

Anxiety Associated with Social Issues: The Development of a Scale to Measure an Antecedent Construct 601
    Trina Sego, University of Texas at Austin
    Patricia A. Stout, University of Texas at Austin

AUTHOR INDEX 607

PRESIDENTIAL ADDRESS
Academic Appalachia and the Discipline of Consumer Research[1]

Terence A. Shimp, University of South Carolina

In this city whose music tradition personifies much about the glitter and individuality of the late-twentieth century, it would be tempting to draw parallels between country music and the practice and scholarship of consumer behavior. I intend to draw parallels, but not between Nashville and consumer behavior.

I turn instead to the east of Nashville, to the area of Tennessee that is part of the region and culture of what is broadly called Appalachia. Although there is no consensus on the exact boundaries of the Appalachian region (Philliber 1981), one widely accepted specification includes all of West Virginia plus parts of 12 other states—New York, Pennsylvania, Ohio, Maryland, Virginia, Kentucky, Tennessee, North Carolina, South Carolina, Georgia, Alabama, and Mississippi. The area many Americans typically identify as Appalachia consists of portions of four states known as Central Appalachia: southern West Virginia, eastern Kentucky, eastern Tennessee, and western Virginia (Raitz and Ulack 1991). It is this Appalachia to which I refer hereafter.

Appalachia is prized for its physical beauty. The area is perhaps even better known for its economic depression, isolation, and backwardness. Coal miners, hillbillies, moonshine, rundown homes, dilapidated vehicles, and runny-nosed children are all part of the caricature and, sadly, the reality of this region. The word Appalachia is, in fact, virtually synonymous with poverty, as personified by the so-called "war on poverty" in the 1960s during Lyndon Johnson's administration. The image and reality of Appalachia confront most thinking and caring Americans with particular shame and indignity, because the richness of this country surrounds the poverty of this subsegment of its people.

Lest I confuse you into thinking that this address deals with poverty and rural plight, let me quickly note that this is not my purpose. Rather, my reference to Appalachia is strictly metaphoric. This metaphor provides me with a springboard for characterizing the discipline of consumer research, as I see it, and for discussing and evaluating some of the pressures for change.

I hasten to note that the Appalachian metaphor is imperfect. Certainly, the discipline of consumer research is not impoverished; this hall is filled with dozens of individuals who would perform with distinction in any of the social or behavioral sciences.

PARALLEL BETWEEN CONSUMER RESEARCH AND APPALACHIA

In what sense, then, is the metaphor appropriate? Answering this question requires a brief review of one aspect of the history of Appalachia. Appalachia, unlike other areas in the United States, has a rather unique pattern of in- and out-migration: more people have left the hills than have been attracted to Appalachia. Most of the people who live in Appalachia were born and raised there. These are people who knew no other way of life, who enjoyed, or at least tolerated, their existence, and who were unwilling or unable to leave. They never knew prosperity or security for long. The bad times inevitably chased away the good in a sad twist on Gresham's law of currency. Above all, however, these mountain people maintained a deep sense of pride and an indomitable spirit.

Then there were those who sought better opportunities elsewhere. They learned the three Rs in elementary school—reading, riting, and rithmetic—and traveled a fourth R, a road with a route number, away from their homes and toward more economically vibrant cities: Akron, Cleveland, Chicago, Detroit, Pittsburgh, or more recently, Atlanta, Birmingham, Charlotte, Houston, and so on. These out-migrators sought a better life for themselves and their families. The beautiful hills and valleys of Kentucky, Tennessee, Virginia, and West Virginia could no longer support these wanderers. On to the big city, on to jobs in the mills and automobile plants, and on to a life of fulfillment and economic sustenance, or so they hoped.

We have in this description a parallel for the discipline of consumer research. On the one hand, we can remain in our academic Appalachia and be content with who we are and what we are. We can study consumers for the sake of understanding and appreciating consummatory activities without concern with whether outsiders are aware of our work or like what we do. Many in this audience will never leave the hills of academic Appalachia. Along with the proud people of West Virginia, their implicit motto is *montani semper liberi*, which translates into "mountaineers (are) always free." Consumer researchers, in accord with this philosophy, should always be free—to do exactly what we want to do, regardless of the implications (if any) that our work might have.

The other alternative is to seek a way out of academic Appalachia, to head for another venue, one less idealistic and more pragmatic. Forsake the mountains, forego the freedom. As a discipline, we are being told that there is a road that will take us away from our quaint and possibly indulgent existence. It is not a road with a route number, like the ones traversed by actual Appalachian people on their way to the industrial Midwest or Northeast. This road does not have a number, but rather a name: Route Relevance.

Route Relevance is not a new road. Scholars before us in psychology and elsewhere have been urged to take Route Relevance. Earlier decades of social psychologists, for example, were told to take Route Relevance toward a life of greater social impact (for a variety of views, see Bevan 1982; Blank 1988; Duetsch 1980; Gergen 1973; Masters 1984; Mayo and LaFrance 1980; McGuire 1973; Miller 1969; for a similar perspective in the marketing literature, see also Dawson 1971).

What is Route Relevance for consumer researchers and the business schools in which most reside? Why are we being told to take Route Relevance? Where does it lead, what does it promise?

BACKDROP: BUSINESS SCHOOLS AND RELEVANCE

In the Beginning

Research conducted in B-schools until the 1960s was largely very pragmatic and atheoretical. It dealt with mundane business problems. In a sense, it *was* relevant.

Then the famous, or perhaps infamous, Ford Foundation (Gordon and Howell 1959) and Carnegie Corporation (Pierson 1959) reports were published. Both reports criticized research in business schools for being excessively descriptive, lacking in

---

[1] I appreciate the helpful comments of Chris Allen, Mike Barone, Randy Rose, Elnora Stuart, and Joe Urbany. David Sprott deserves recognition for his diligent library work. Most of all, I am indebted to my wife and friend, Judy, for bearing with me while I fretted over having to deliver this speech.

analytical rigor, and failing to produce theoretical generalizations. In as bitter a blow as imaginable, Gordon and Howell (1959, p. 6) proclaimed:

> "What passes as the going standard of acceptability among business schools is embarrassingly low, and many schools of business do not meet even these low standards."

Influenced by these reports, business-school professors moved in the direction of increased sophistication and, in a sense, became *less* relevant. We in marketing and consumer behavior turned away from business practitioners and toward fellow scholars around campus for theoretical ideas, analytical tools, and perhaps even our source of approbation.

We became part of academic Appalachia, a community of relatively isolated scholars doing our own thing and doing it well. We sharpened our skills and honed our craft; we even attracted into the fold scholars from other disciplines and benefitted greatly by their addition. No more could we be accused of being atheoretical, unsophisticated, or purely descriptive. Very few people outside of academic Appalachia knew, or cared, what we were doing, however. We were up in the hollows of the Appalachian hills doing our own thing.

And Now: A War on (Alleged) Poverty in Academic Appalachia

But the situation began changing in the mid-to-late 1980s. The economy deteriorated, American corporations became less globally competitive, and jobs were lost. The conditions were ripe for attack, and attacked we were. The B-school became the whipping boy of critics in the mass media. Detractors caricatured B-school research as trivial and largely irrelevant (e.g., Byrne 1990; Porter and McKibbin 1988). The criticism was not restricted to B-schools. Some cynics aimed their sights more generally at the academy at large and alleged that American institutions of higher education were neglecting their teaching duties and conducting irrelevant research (e.g., Anderson 1992).

Criticism also came from within our own academic Appalachia. Wells (1993) in "Discovery-Oriented Consumer Research" referred repeatedly to the crisis of relevance inherent in consumer research. Lutz (1991) had pretty much said the same thing in his outgoing editorial as *JCR* editor. So had Sheth (1992, p. 348) in a review of the consumer behavior literature when he said:

> My retrospective analysis leads me to conclude that this impressive output in consumer research has had, unfortunately, an equally unimpressive impact among marketing practitioners, policy makers, and the peer disciplines.

The call for greater relevance is now an inescapable element of the consumer research landscape. We are being urged to leave academic Appalachia, to travel Route Relevance, and, in today's vernacular, to "get a life."

WHITHER ROUTE RELEVANCE?

It is easy for critics to claim that consumer research needs to be more relevant. It is not quite so easy to mount a counter-argument. Who wants to be irrelevant? Or, as Jacoby (1985, p. 158) pointedly stated,

> [I]f one chooses to do work that has no relevance, one cannot later complain too loudly if one's work is not taken seriously—even if by other scholars.

However, before we as a discipline too readily accept relevance as a worthy road out of academic Appalachia, we must first consider where that road might take us. I do not claim to have all the answers, but I think the following comments will move us closer to engaging in meaningful dialogue.

Relevance: Of What, To Whom?

Relevance is, by its very nature, an inherently vague concept that lacks semantic validity and suffers nonuniform usage. (For general commentary related to these points, see Zaltman, Pinson, and Angelmar 1973, p. 43 and Bagozzi 1980, pp. 118-119.) Users of the term appear to supply the concept with three implicit properties: They first have in mind a target, insofar as relevance naturally suggests some specific outcome or use for someone. Relevance also implies, albeit somewhat less directly, a certain form of contribution, such as research results having actionable implications for managers. A third property is the suggestion of a time frame, which typically is expected to be a contribution that is realizable sooner rather than later.

But precisely what do critics mean when they say consumer research should be more relevant? And relevance for whom: marketing managers (which managers? which industries? which business types?), public policy officials, consumers themselves, society at large?

Figure 1 attempts to place the concept of relevance in broader perspective. The figure identifies various types of outputs that are generated by consumer research/scholarship and also distinguishes plausible constituencies. Four research products are classified as empirical (P_E), theoretical (P_T), methodological (P_M), and critical (P_C). Only the last requires comment. Consumer researchers engaged in critical scholarship provide probing commentary on issues of managerial or societal importance. While this form of scholarship pales in its occurrence compared to more conventional consumer research, it certainly represents a legitimate and needed output (Shimp 1993). The relevant constituencies, or markets, for consumer research include businesspeople (M_B); fellow academics (M_A); educational audiences (M_E) at undergraduate, masters, and doctoral levels; public policy officials (M_{PP}); and society at large (M_S).

The concept of relevance is greatly expanded and transfigured when considered in this fashion. What most critics probably have in mind when encouraging B-school professors and consumer researchers to journey Route Relevance is to make our research more applicable to the needs of business. Based on this perspective, cells R1-R4 in Figure 1 are the most prized output from our intellectual factories. However, Figure 1 makes it clear that a variety of other forms of relevance are no less important.

Academic Relevance. It could be argued that relevance to fellow academics—cells R5-R8 in Figure 1—is of utmost importance. This may seem self-indulgent, but in actuality it is purely pragmatic: a discipline and its association cannot be sustained unless its members are intellectually satisfied. This requires, first and foremost, that published articles examine interesting phenomena and raise provocative questions. Moreover, these articles must attain the conventional standards that positivistic consumer researchers demand (cf. Cook and Campbell 1979) and fulfill the trustworthiness criteria interpretive researchers expect (cf. Wallendorf and Belk 1989; see, however, Holt 1991 for an alternative perspective).

Teaching Relevance. In this era of ever-increasing importance attached to teaching, consumer research must also be relevant to the needs of the various student groups who take consumer behavior courses. The needs of doctoral students are most easily satisfied

FIGURE 1
Product-Market Perspective on Relevance

Relevance Markets	Consumer Research Products			
	P_E	P_T	P_M	P_C
M_B	R1	R2	R3	R4
M_A	R5	R6	R7	R8
$M_{E \cdot U,M,D}$	R9	R10	R11	R12
M_{PP}	R13	R14	R15	R16
M_S	R17	R18	R19	R20

inasmuch as their expectations are closely aligned with their professors'. Undergraduate and master-level students typically have educational interests, however, that are more similar to those of the business employers they shortly will pursue for jobs. Hence, the critic likely would argue that truly relevant consumer research (translation: that which is relevant for business) also is relevant for students. This would seem to suggest that research relevant to academics is less relevant to all non-doctoral students than is research that is relevant to businesspeople. A challenge to this argument would assert that relevance for academics is also relevance for students inasmuch as bright, competent, and energetic teachers/researchers are capable of showing how academic consumer research is applicable to the needs of business and hence to the needs of students. The parties to this debate would not readily reach agreement.

Public-Policy and Social Relevance. The framework in Figure 1 further recognizes that a full-service consumer research discipline also would generate products that fulfill the relevance needs of public policy officials and society at large. These empirical, theoretical, and other research/scholarship products need not be the same as those that achieve relevance for business constituencies. In fact, relevance for public policy officials would be expected to address questions that are different from, if not diametrically opposed to, the types of questions that are relevant for businesspeople. Being relevant to society at large, including consumers themselves, would involve conducting social marketing research along the lines discussed by Andreasen (1993), would address the dark side of consumer behavior as confronted by Hirschman (1991), and, in general, would force the discipline to "think big" in the words of Richins (1993).

Is Consumer Research Irrelevant to Managers?

The foregoing discussion has identified the various forms of relevance that a full-service consumer research discipline would have to satisfy. Let me relax this sweeping conceptualization and, in so doing, address only the issue of managerial relevance. Putting aside the broader issue of whether consumer research *should* be managerially relevant (cf. Holbrook 1985, 1986, 1989; Jacoby 1985; Pechmann 1990), the present emphasis is one of whether consumer research *is* managerially relevant.

What requirements must managerially relevant consumer research satisfy? First, in the terminology of the validity network schema (Brinberg and Hirschman 1986; Brinberg and McGrath 1985; Lutz 1989), the substantive domain vis-a-vis the conceptual and methodological domains must receive relatively high priority in the inception of a research project if that project is to have relevance. Stated more prosaically, relevant consumer research would study issues that confront marketing managers.

Methodological suitability is a second fundamental requirement. Research methods must be up to the task of generating findings that managers can depend on when making decisions. Advocates of managerial relevance would argue against laboratory research and would generally oppose the use of student subjects (cf. Wells 1993). They may claim that external validity is paramount, but their argument would fail to recognize that external validity is an issue of generalizability and not of relevance per se (cf. Calder, Phillips, and Tybout 1981; Cook and Campbell 1979; Lynch 1982). To wit, a trivial finding may generalize across populations, and in that sense possess external validity. An important finding may be highly relevant to a particular organization but have no relevance whatsoever to other organizations.

Hence, if managerial relevance is to become a key aim for consumer researchers, then the standard Cook and Campbell (1979) desiderata (internal, construct, statistical conclusion, and external validities) that have guided experimental consumer research and provided direction for more recent interpretive work (in the guise of trustworthiness criteria) would have to be adjusted to include an expanded role for relevance. But this necessarily would require some hard tradeoffs. Clearly, internal validity might often be sacrificed. So, contrary to intuition, would external validity—one company's relevance is another's irrelevance. Managerially relevant research—that is, research capable of contributing to the solution of managerial problems or directing specific actions—might ultimately take the form of consulting projects. But, as Herbert Simon (1967, p. 8) instructed:

> The managers themselves are far more qualified than outsiders, whether professors or not, to handle the short-run, practical problems that require intimate knowledge of the business.

Do We Really Want to Travel Route Relevance?

In making the above statements, it may appear that I am taking a decidedly "feline," Holbrookian position (Holbrook 1985, 1986, 1989) and opposing the countervailing "canine" views introduced by Jacoby (1985), Pechmann (1990), Lutz (1991), and Wells (1993). This is not the case. I see merit on both sides of the issue.

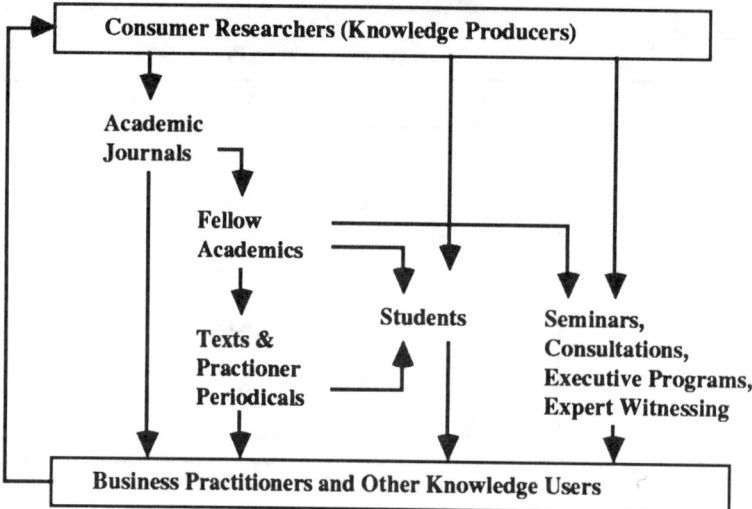

FIGURE 2
Diffusion Process for Academic Research

However, my challenge to the advocates of managerial relevance is threefold:

First, as discussed above, managers are not the only target market that should command the intellectual attention of consumer researchers. (See Wilkie 1981 for an insightful discussion of the drawbacks of excessive emphasis on managerial relevance.)

Second, in calling for more (managerially) relevant research, there has been a tendency to place the blame on alleged methodological deficiencies (e.g., laboratory experiments with student subjects) rather than criticizing researchers for their failure to adequately address the substantive domain. The method is *not* the problem. Surely there is a legitimate role for laboratory experimentation in contributing to the understanding of real-world problems and processes (cf. Henshel 1980; Mook 1983). Duetsch (1980, p. 98) perhaps has stated it most eloquently:

> [T]he research setting does not determine the relevance of the research conducted in the setting (the ideas or theory determine the relevance).... Research of no theoretical significance can be done anywhere—in the laboratory, a school, or a factory. Similarly, research of considerable theoretical significance can be done in a school, factory, or community as well as in the laboratory.

There is a third reason why the plaint of irrelevance is simplified. The critics of academic research (e.g., Anderson 1992; Byrne 1990) contend that only a small number of people read academic articles, and this, supposedly, is because these articles are pretentious, too difficult to read, or deal with trivial topics. What the critics fail to acknowledge is that the knowledge diffusion process does not end with the printing of a journal. Journals such as *JCR* are not typically read by managers, public policy officials, or the public at large. But articles in journals are not hypodermic needles that are intended to be infused directly into the veins of ultimate users. The knowledge diffusion process is more involved than this.

Figure 2 depicts the alternative ways by which the theoretical, empirical, and methodological products of academic journal articles might ultimately influence business practitioners and other users of academic consumer research. As noted, it is a rarity for practitioners to be directly influenced by the output of journal articles. Yet publications in *JCR* and in other consumer research outlets reach students who later become practitioners. These publications also filter down to practicing managers via textbooks, practitioner-oriented periodicals, seminars, consultations, executive programs, and expert witnessing. The knowledge diffusion process is far from immediate, but gradual progress is all that should be demanded in view of the inherent complexity of the phenomena studied in the substantive domain of marketing and consumer research.

Because there are multiple channels of distribution that carry the output of academic consumer research, it is disingenuous to chastise academic articles on the ground that no one reads them or their content is too obscure. A legitimate claim of irrelevance is not to be obtained from attacks on journal obscurity anymore than it can be derived from criticisms of the methods used in conducting consumer research.

AN ALTERNATIVE: THE CONCEPT OF REPRESENTATION

All said, I nonetheless think that most consumer researchers would like to consider our work as potentially capable of having impact outside the academy. Yet, as educators and scholars we do not wish to serve a particular master. The term relevance fails to capture this duality, because inherent in its usage is the expectation that academic consumer research *will* serve someone's needs. Relevance has effectively lost any impartiality it once may have possessed. Due to this value-ladenness, a different concept of academic-practitioner relations is needed—a concept that captures our desire to have impact while simultaneously maintaining, in the words of Pollay (1986), our independence as scholars of the marketplace rather than servants to marketing practitioners.

I would like to introduce an alternative concept, a concept I will call *representation*. To fully explicate this concept, I first need to provide some brief historical context. In particular, it is my belief that much consumer research (including some of my own) has done little more than test theories borrowed from other disciplines. (See Cohen and Miniard 1993 and Olson 1981 for further development of this point.) The consumer has been a virtual afterthought. A consumption-like topic (e.g., an advertising context) is selected to legitimize the undertaking as consumer research. In actuality, any other behavioral domain would have been appropriate, because the borrowed theory is typically omnibus in its explanatory intention and robust in its prior empirical support. The result is that the theory test may contribute to a better understanding of another discipline's theory, but only incidentally is the outcome a better understanding of actual consumer behavior or development of original consumer theory (cf. Olson 1981; Sheth 1992; Wells 1993).

Representation as used here is similar to the principle and practice of representationalism in art, which involves the depiction of an object in a recognizable manner (Bernheimer 1961).[2] Art according to Plato was imitation. My usage of representation captures a similar idea, namely that consumer research needs to focus far greater emphasis on imitating, or representing, the consumer behavior that occurs within the milieu of actual marketplace phenomena. As such, the concept is fully in agreement with other consumer researchers' views about the need for increased attention to substantive issues (see Brinberg and Hirschman 1986; Kernan 1979; Lutz 1991; and Wells 1993) and implicitly also pays tribute to Cialdini's (1976) concept of full-cycle research.

Representation does not eschew the use of other discipline's theories. It does, however, subordinate these theories to the role of instruments rather than the primary objects of empirical inquiry.

The ultimate objective of representation-based research is the development of theory about actual consumer behavior that may serve the needs of *all* markets interested in consumer research: academics, students, businesspeople, public policy officials, and society at large (see Figure 1). Representation thus converges with relevance insofar as both concepts are fundamentally concerned with impact. It, however, diverges from relevance in that representation recognizes its impact via the theories, concepts, and methods that evolve from research, whereas the traditional concept of relevance expects the findings from specific research undertakings to have actionable implications for end users. Moreover, the concept of representation, unlike that of relevance, fully accepts legitimate roles for laboratory research and other forms of research that some may consider impractical.

The concept of representation is idealistic in that it takes the position that the fundamental and abiding purpose of consumer research is to acquire understanding and knowledge of consumer behavior. Shelby Hunt (1991, p. 31) stated this position compellingly when describing the role of scholarly marketing research:

> The prime directive for scholarly research is the same for marketing as for all sciences: *to seek knowledge*.... At some times, the knowledge may assist marketing managers in making decisions. At other times, the knowledge may guide legislators in drafting laws to regulate marketing activities. At still other times, the knowledge may assist the general public in understanding the functions that marketing activities perform for society. Finally, at the risk of 'waxing philosophical', the knowledge may simply assist marketing scholars in *knowing*, a not inconsequential objective.

The concept is pragmatic in that it endorses a close relationship between consumer researchers and practitioners. It fully accepts the value of working with practitioners, as well as with consumers themselves, to generate ideas about consumer issues and actual problems practitioners confront in their interactions with consumers. Wendell Garner (1972, p. 942) said as much when addressing the American Psychological Association two decades ago:

---

[2] Appreciation is extended to Kent Grayson, Northwestern University Ph.D. student, for introducing me to the concept of representationalism in art.

It is self-evident that the scientist doing applied research must maintain effective communication with the problem solvers, the people who apply the knowledge. I want to argue that it is just as valuable for the scientist doing basic research to have communication with the people who have problems that need solution.

My argument that representation is a more worthy pursuit for consumer researchers than relevance is not at odds with Bagozzi's (1992, p. 355) position that "we should resist the temptation to overmanage the direction of the field." The concept of representation offers a general approach to research, but it makes no effort to specify the types of issues or marketplace phenomena that consumer researchers should study. This determination must be made by each researcher on the basis of her or his personal and institutional utility functions. I also share Jacoby's (1985, p. 162) view that one is in an untenable position when arguing for a dominated research strategy. My position is not that other approaches (e.g., pure theory testing) are inappropriate. Rather, the point is that they have dominated consumer research and that more balance is needed at this juncture in the development of the discipline.

BACK TO APPALACHIA

I want to return to the Appalachian metaphor for several closing thoughts.

First, the discipline of consumer research may now be experiencing some of the malaise that characterizes the economic depressed situation in Appalachia. Are we growing and getting better? Are young, creative, and bright people continuing to be drawn to the field? Is consumer research regarded with respect in colleges of business and elsewhere on campus? Are we even taken seriously by our nonbehavioral colleagues in marketing departments? My position is that the answer to all of the above will be affirmative so long as we employ a representation style of inquiry. In so doing we will address interesting questions about the incredibly dynamic and exciting marketplace in which consumer behavior occurs, and we will be developing insight into a consumer behavior that has a face rather them merely illuminating other disciplines' faceless theories.

A second closing thought returns me to the earlier point about generations of people leaving the mountains of Appalachia in pursuit of more prosperous lives in industrialized urban centers. Because those most likely to leave were the young and economically mobile, Appalachia suffered deeply from out-migrations. As a discipline dedicated to interdisciplinary research, we must assure that we retain our young and mobile by not mandating a certain form of research and stifling intellectual creativity. This likely will mean that those of us who are older (and tenured) will have to fight battles with college administrators, who ever-increasingly are insisting on managerially relevant research. We will have to convince them that the real issue is whether the research is representative, not relevant per se, and whether it holds promise of eventually impacting business practitioners and other important constituencies through any of the multiple channels of influence represented in Figure 2.

Third, consumer researchers need not depend on other disciplines to provide us with research grist or approbation for what we do. We have a lot of important things of our own to study. The mundane stuff we study (cf. Kassarjian 1978) is the stuff that determines in large part whether people are happy or sad, whether they have jobs or not, and whether they honor or destroy the environment. All we need do is turn to our own substantive domain to generate interesting ideas that will keep us gainfully occupied for as long as the marketplace remains dynamic.

Fourth, just like the infamous late-nineteenth century conflict between the Hatfields of Logan County, West Virginia and the McCoys across the river in Pike County, Kentucky (who fought and died for 15 years over the disputed ownership of a pig), the field of consumer research has had its periods of internecine throes: interpretivists versus positivists and critics versus adherents of laboratory research. Just as the Hatfield versus McCoy conflict led to no positive outcome, the same can be said when arguing for a dominated research methodology.

As a discipline, we need not tolerate any bias against laboratory research, ethnographic studies, or any other form of research on the ground that the method lacks relevance. The issue, rather, should be one of evaluating whether the subject matter is worthy of studying (i.e., is it representative?) and determining whether the method is suitable for tackling the question at hand. The discipline of consumer research is best served when alternative paradigms are accepted and respected. West (1991, p. 39) captured this philosophy when characterizing the persona of the independent-minded inhabitants of Appalachia:

> Despite strong Calvinistic influences, and unlike Puritan New England, the mountaineers never tried to force their beliefs on others. No one was persecuted for holding different beliefs, nor for disbelief. No 'witches' were burned. One might be a church member or one might not. One might even be an outspoken unbeliever. That was a free man's right.

Finally, we consumer researchers, just like the Appalachians characterized in the next passage (Best in Ergood and Kuhre 1991, p. 3), must be careful that we are not defined by someone else for their interests:

> [T]he worst thing that has happened to Appalachians in the past is that we have been deprived of our identify. We have been defined by missionaries for their purposes; coal, timber, and railroad barons for their purposes; government bureaucrats for their purposes; and lately by middle-class radicals for their purposes.

The beauty of the discipline is that we have been free to examine most any topic related to the phenomena of consummatory activities. We must be more representative in what we study. By being representative we will truly move toward better understanding actual consumer behavior. We will have impact, because our theories will have value for the various constituents who are interested in consumer research.

We need not, however, relinquish our freedom.

I say in closing, *montani semper liberi!* Hopefully, so too will consumer researchers!!

It has been my honor to serve as ACR president. Thank you very much.

REFERENCES

Anderson, Martin (1992), *Imposters in the Temple*, New York: Simon & Schuster.

Andreasen, Alan R. (1993), "A Social Marketing Research Agenda for Consumer Behavior Researchers," in *Advances in Consumer Research*, Vol. 20, eds. L. McAlister and M. L. Rothschild, Provo, UT: Association for Consumer Research, 1-5.

Bagozzi, Richard P. (1980), *Causal Modeling in Marketing*, New York: John Wiley & Sons.

_____ (1992), "Acrimony in the Ivory Tower: Stagnation or Evolution?," *Journal of the Academy of the Marketing Science*, 20 (Fall), 355-359.

Bernheimer, Richard (1961), The Nature of Representation: *Phenomenological Inquiry*, New York: New York University Press.

Bevan, William (1982), "A Sermon of Sorts in Three Plus Parts," *American Psychologist*, 37 (December), 1303-1322.

Blank, Thomas O. (1988), "Reflections on Gergen's 'Social Psychology as History' in Perspective," *Personality and Social Psychology Bulletin*, 14 (December), 651-663.

Brinberg, David and Elizabeth C. Hirschman (1986), "Multiple Orientations for the Conduct of Marketing Research: An Analysis of the Academic/Practitioner Distinction," *Journal of Marketing*, 50 (October), 161-173.

_____ and Joseph E. McGrath (1985), *Validity and the Research Process*, Sage Publications: Beverly Hills, CA.

Byrne, John A. (1990), "Is Research in the Ivory Tower 'Fuzzy, Irrelevant, Pretentious'?" *Business Week*, October, 62-66.

Calder, Bobby J., Lynn W. Phillips, and Alice M. Tybout (1981), "Designing Research for Application," *Journal of Consumer Research*, 8 (September), 197-207.

Cialdini, Robert B. (1980), "Full-Cycle Social Psychology," in *Applied Social Psychology*, Vol. 1, ed. L. Bickman, Beverly Hills, CA: Sage Publications, 21-47.

Cohen, Joel B. and Paul W. Miniard (1993), "The Case of Theory Development: Overcoming the Myopia of Theory Testing," University of Florida, Working Paper.

Cook, Thomas D. and Donald T. Campbell (1979), *Quasi-Experimentation: Design & Analysis Issues for Field Settings*, Boston: Houghton Mifflin Company.

Dawson, Leslie J. (1971), "Marketing Science in the Age of Aquarius," *Journal of Marketing*, 35 (July), 66-72.

Duetsch, Morton (1980), "Socially Relevant Research: Comments on 'Applied' versus 'Basic' Research," in *Advances in Applied Social Psychology*, Vol. 1, ed. R. F. Kidd and M. J. Saks, Hillsdale, NJ: Lawrence Erlbaum Associates, 97-112.

Ergood, Bruce and Bruce E. Kuhre (1991), "Why Study Appalachia," in *Appalachia: Social Context Past and Present*, 3rd. ed., eds. B. Ergood and B. E. Kuhre, Dubuque, IA: Kendall/Hunt Publishing Co.

Garner, Wendell R. (1972), "The Acquisition and Application of Knowledge: A Symbiotic Relation," *American Psychologist*, 27 (October), 941-946.

Gergen, Kenneth J. (1973), "Social Psychology as History," *Journal of Personality and Social Psychology*, 26, 309-320.

Gordon, Robert A. and James E. Howell (1959), *Higher Education for Business*, New York: Columbia University Press.

Henshel, Richard L. (1980), "The Purposes of Laboratory Experimentation and the Virtues of Deliberate Artificiality," *Journal of Experimental Social Psychology*, 16, 466-478.

Hirschman, Elizabeth C. (1991), "Secular Mortality and the Dark Side of Consumer Behavior: Or How Semiotics Saved My Life," in *Advances in Consumer Research*, Vol. 20, eds. R. H. Holman and M. R. Solomon, Provo, UT: Association for Consumer Research, 1-6.

Holbrook, Morris B. (1985), "Why Business Is Bad for Consumer Research," in *Advances in Consumer Research*, Vol. 12, eds. E. C. Hirschman and M. B. Holbrook, Ann Arbor, MI: Association for Consumer Research, 145-156.

_____ (1986), "Whither ACR? Some Pastoral Reflections on Bears, Baltimore, Baseball, and Resurrecting Consumer Research," in *Advances in Consumer Research*, Vol. 13, ed. R. J. Lutz, Provo, UT: Association for Consumer Research, 436-441.

_____ (1989), "Aftermath of the Task Force: Dogmatism and Catastrophe in the Development of Marketing Thought," Association for Consumer Research *Newsletter*, September, 1-11.

Holt, Douglas B. (1991), "Rashomon Visits Consumer Behavior: An Interpretive Critique of Naturalistic Inquiry," in *Advances in Consumer Research*, Vol. 18, eds. R. H. Holman and M. R. Solomon, Provo UT: Association for Consumer Research, 57-62.

Hunt, Shelby D. (1991), *Modern Marketing Theory*, Cincinnati: South-Western Publishing Co.

Jacoby, Jacob (1985), "The Vices and Virtues of Consulting: Responding to a Fairy Tale," in *Advances in Consumer Research*, Vol. 12, eds. E. C. Hirschman and M. B. Holbrook, Ann Arbor, MI: Association for Consumer Research, 157-163.

Kassarjian, Harold H. (1978), "Presidential Address, 1977: Anthropomorphism and Parsimony," in *Advances in Consumer Research*, Vol. 5, ed. H. K. Hunt, Ann Arbor, MI: Association for Consumer Research, xiii-xiv.

Kernan, Jerome B. (1979), "Presidential Address: Consumer Research and the Public Purpose," in *Advances in Consumer Research*, Vol. 6, ed. W. L. Wilkie, Ann Arbor, MI: Association for Consumer Research, 1-2.

Lutz, Richard J. (1989), "Positivism, Naturalism and Pluralism in Consumer Research: Paradigms in Paradise," in *Advances in Consumer Research*, Vol. 16, ed. T. Srull, Provo Utah: Association of Consumer Research, 1-8.

_____ , "Editorial," *Journal of Consumer Research*, 17 (March), no page numbers.

Lynch, John G., Jr. (1982), "On the External Validity of Experiments in Consumer Research," *Journal of Consumer Research*, 9 (December), 225-239.

Masters, John C. (1984), "Psychology, Research, and Social Policy," *American Psychologist*, 39 (August), 851-862.

Mayo, C. and M. LaFrance (1980), "Toward an Applicable Social Psychology and its Contribution to Public Policy Sciences," in *Advances in Applied Social Psychology*, Vol. 1, eds. R. F. Kidd and M. J. Saks, Hillsdale, NJ: Lawrence Erlbaum, 81-96.

McGuire, William J. (1973), "The Yin and Yang of Progress in Social Psychology: Seven Koan," *Journal of Personality and Social Psychology*, 26, 446-456.

Miller, George A. (1969), "Psychology as a Means of Promoting Human Welfare," *American Psychologist*, 24 (December), 1063-1075.

Mook, Douglas G. (1983), "In Defense of External Invalidity," *American Psychologist*, 38 (April), 379-387.

Olson, Jerry C. (1982), "Presidential Address, 1981: Toward a Science of Consumer Behavior," in *Advances in Consumer Research*, Vol. 9, ed. A. A. Mitchell, Ann Arbor, MI: Association for Consumer Research, v-x.

Pechmann, Cornelia (1990), "Responses to President's Column, September 1989," Association for Consumer Research *Newsletter*, June, 5-7.

Philliber, William W. (1981), *Appalachian Migrants in Urban America: Cultural Conflict or Ethnic Group Formation*, New York: Praeger Publishers.

Pierson, Frank C. (1959), *The Education of American Businessmen: A Study of University-College Programs in Business Administration*, New York: McGraw-Hill Book Company.

Pollay, Richard W. (1986), "The Distorted Mirror: Reflections on the Unintended Consequences of Advertising," *Journal of Marketing*, 50 (April), 18-36.

Porter, L. W. and L. E. McKibbin (1988), *Managment Education and Development: Drift or Thrust into the 21st Century?* New York: McGraw-Hill Book Company.

Raitz, Karl B. and Richard Ulack (1991), "Regional Differences," in *Appalachia: Social Context Past and Present*, 3rd. ed., eds. B. Ergood and B. E. Kuhre, Dubuque, IA: Kendall/Hunt Publishing Co.

Richins, Marsha (1993), "Thinking BIG in Consumer Research," presentation at American Marketing Association Doctoral Consortium, August 6, University of Illinois, Urbana-Champaign, IL.

Sheth, Jagdish N. (1992), "Acrimony in the Ivory Tower: A Retrospective on Consumer Research," *Journal of the Academy of Marketing Science*, 20 (Fall), 345-353.

Shimp, Terence A. (1993), "Two Brief Messages: Get More Critical and Be More Thankful," Association for Consumer Research *Newsletter*, June, 2-4.

Simon, Herbert A. (1967), "The Business School: A Problem in Organizational Design," *Journal of Management Studies*, 4 (February), 1-16.

Wallendorf, Melanie and Russell W. Belk (1989), "Assessing Trustworthiness in Naturalistic Consumer Research," in *Interpretive Consumer Research*, ed. E. Hirschman, Provo, UT: Association for Consumer Research, 69-84.

Wells, William D. (1993), "Discovery-Oriented Consumer Research," *Journal of Consumer Behavior*, 19 (March), 489-504.

West, Don (1991), "Freedom in the Mountains," in *Appalachia: Social Context Past and Present*, 3rd. ed., eds. B. Ergood and B. E. Kuhre, Dubuque, IA: Kendall/Hunt Publishing Co.

Wilkie, William L. (1981), "Presidential Address: 1980," in *Advances in Consumer Research*, Vol. 8, ed. K. B. Monroe, Ann Arbor, MI: Association for Consumer Research, 1-5.

Zaltman, Gerald, Cristian R. A. Pinson, and Reinhard Angelmar (1973), *Metatheory and Consumer Research*, New York: Holt, Rinehart and Winston Inc.

ACR Fellow Speech
Richard P. Bagozzi

What I would like to talk about are three areas that have much potential for growth in consumer research in the years ahead. Before I do this, however, let me begin with a caveat. Since the inception of the ACR, the accomplishments I think we should be most proud of are those done by researchers in information processing, and to a slightly lesser extent by researchers in human judgment and choice. This is the heart of our field and the things I plan to talk about are not meant to detract from these accomplishments, but only to add to them. In fact, the information processing tradition in the ACR has produced fundamental contributions to basic knowledge and not only to substantive and applied consumer research. We need to continue this tradition. Another area we should take pride in is the general work done in qualitative research. This includes recent work in post modern aspects of consumption, ethnographic research, feminism, revival of interest in motivation research, and related areas. Our current and past editors of the JCR have done much in recent years to create an intellectual climate of diversity in the field. I am not aware of any field that has such a wealth of different ideas coexisting. Let us hope this continues, too. My comments to follow are not meant to take away from these developments. So let me turn now to three areas for future growth in the field.

When I mention the first area, many of you are likely to react with some skepticism. Nevertheless, I think there is a need for more research in the general area of personality in consumer research. By personality research, I'm not talking about the traditional theories and approaches. These were put to rest years ago by Walter Mischel's 1968 book and by Hal Kassarjian and colleagues in a series of articles.

By personality research, I mean research that is better grounded in individual differences, such as found in recent developments in the self concept and also in recent work in emotions in psychology. There has been a rebirth of sorts in personality research during the past few years which has resulted in better conceptualizations and better measurements that are only now starting to be looked at by consumer researchers. This work focuses on traits and states, as well as temperament.

When I say that there is room in the field for more research into personality, it is important to add that I am not particularly sanguine about personality, per se. Rather the real potential for the newer and better personality concepts lies not so much in their power as main effects or predictors but instead as moderating variables. Personality variables offer the most promise in conjunction with tests of hypotheses from the information processing tradition, for example. The best research using personality in consumer research has incorporated it as part of theory development and testing from other areas. For instance, the need for cognition, a scale developed a while back by Cacioppo and Petty, has recently been used by Curt Haugtvedt and colleagues to help explain the persistence of attitudes and the resistance of attitudes to change. Current research with the need for cognition shows that personality variables have promise when used to complement or qualify the effects of persuasive communication on information processing. Maybe we shouldn't be too surprised to find that consumer behavior can be explained by the interaction of individual difference and situational variables. The task for the future is to develop sound theories behind the interactions.

I used the need for cognition as an example of an individual difference variable that has been used successfully largely because researchers have found a role for it within the context of a well-developed information processing theory; namely, the elaboration likelihood model. In its shorter version, the need for cognition is an 18-item scale. Actually, I think we are likely to see a movement away from the use of a large number of items to measure unidimensional personality concepts. The success of unidimensional scales with many items, such as the need for cognition, is likely to become a rarity. One reason is that researchers often do not have the luxury of being able to administer large scales within the context of their studies. Besides, why use 30 items when 8 to 10, say, might suffice? A second reason is that scales of 20 items or more often contain so much random error, and even systematic error, that it is unreasonable to expect unidimensionality.

In fact, more and more, we are finding that scales originally designed to reflect unidimensional constructs are multidimensional. Often the dimensions have been found to be more interpretable and to replicate better than the total scales. A good example of this is the self-monitoring scale which recently has been used in consumer research. The self-monitoring scale, a 25-item inventory, was originally devised to place people along a continuum from low to high self-monitors. The low self-monitoring individual guides his or her behavior on the basis of relevant inner resources such as values, feelings, attitudes, or dispositions. They are concerned that their own actions are accurate reflections of their underlying values and attitudes. By contrast, the high self-monitoring individual typically strives to be the type of person called for by each situation in which they find themselves. They are concerned about adjusting their actions to fit the interpersonal demands of the social situation. Internal states, such as attitudes, do not necessarily correspond to actions. Well recently, research has challenged this unidimensional representation. Instead, three distinct dimensions of self-monitoring have been found to underlie the scale. One of these is extraversion, a second is other directedness, and the third is acting ability. Researchers have found that these dimensions are not only correlated at low levels amongst themselves but two of them are even negatively correlated at times. Summing items across these dimensions obviously obscures the existence of distinct senses of self-monitoring. And in theory testing, because the dimensions frequently have distinct antecedents or lead to differential consequences, the use of the total scale can lead to misleading conclusions. Another scale used recently by consumer researchers, the self-consciousness scale, has also been found by psychometricians to be multidimensional. Researchers have found three distinct subcomponents: private self-consciousness, public self-consciousness, and social anxiety. We are likely to see greater attention paid to the subdimensions of these and other scales in the years ahead. We also need to re-examine past research based on the total summed scales to see if the conclusions drawn are really valid.

Very recently in personality research there has been a new movement that proposes a general hierarchical conceptualization of personality constructs. The framework proposes 4 alternative levels of abstraction. This movement has been led by the psychometrician Herbert Marsh and a few other psychologists (see also Bagozzi and Heatherton, 1994).

The first level in the hierarchy is the most abstract level or molar level of analysis and is, in fact, the traditional approach. Here all the items of a scale are added together to form a single construct. This has been labeled the *total aggregation* model in the literature, to indicate that an aggregation occurs across all items. In fact, if the scale is multidimensional, the aggregation will be across both items and dimensions. Needless to say this is a crude representation of personality constructs. The total aggregation approach is the one analyzed by Mischel, Kassarjian, and colleagues and found to be so lacking.

The other three levels in the hierarchy are less abstract and allow for multidimensionality. In the *partial aggregation* model we find a more molecular conceptualization of personality. Here each component of personality is represented as a separate indicator of a single higher order construct. Aggregation occurs across items but within dimensions. This point of view appears in current research in the JPSP on state self-esteem, among other constructs. The partial aggregation model has real advantages over the traditional total aggregation model with respect to the evaluation of reliability. Its major disadvantage is that it blurs the distinctions among multiple dimensions should these exist.

This is where the third conceptualization of personality in the hierarchical model comes to the fore. This approach has been termed the *partial disaggregation* model in the literature. Here each component or dimension of a construct is represented as a separate latent variable indicated by unique composites of subscales. In the past few months there has been an explosion of articles and papers using this approach in personality research—most of them in the psychology literature. It has been applied to self-esteem, self-monitoring, self-consciousness, and other personality traits and states. Some forthcoming research has used it in the modeling of emotions as well. The approach arose as a result of developments in psychometrics, but importantly, many researchers have found it especially useful in hypothesis testing and substantive research.

The fourth approach to the representation of personality constructs is labeled the *total disaggregation* model in the literature. This is the most atmostic of the four approaches. Here each individual item in a scale is modeled as a separate indicator of each dimension, where the items and dimensions are hierarchically organized. This approach has been applied with some success to the self-monitoring scale and to the need for cognition scale.

In sum, personality research has promise in consumer research but only if we use wellformed concepts and measures within the context of theory testing. One or more of the four levels in the inerarchical conceptualization of personality can be useful, depending on the researcher's purposes. There is a need to move away from the unidimensional scales and focus more closely on their subcomponents. But even this will only take us so far and is likely to be a transition to the next stage in personality research. Because most of the scales have been developed as unidimensional representations, it is likely that the subdimensions found empirically will be incomplete. The next phase in personality research should strive to better specify theoretically what the components are and then develop specific measures corresponding to them. Until we do this, the use of personality is likely to be a hit or miss affair in consumer research.

The second area for future growth in the field is the exploration of *cross-cultural* dynamics. This is an exciting, wide-open area. But we need to be careful. There is a tendency to take one theory developed in one culture and then apply it in another, searching for differences and commonalities. This approach helps us discover generalities and distinctions and might even lead to important serendipitous discoveries now and then. But it isn't enough and it isn't the way to build a foundation for research in the area. Culture isn't important unless we can specify what it is within and between different cultures that produces the commonalities and differences. Something is to be learned by taking existing theories and measures from one culture into another. But more progress will be made when we identify theoretical differences and develop measures valid across cultures. Many of our existing theories may generalize fully, or as a matter of degree, but there is a need to conceive of theories that explicitly address or incorporate cultural differences.

Cross-cultural research is possible for researchers from all points of view: information processing, human judgment and choice, attitude theory, and so on. To illustrate my points, I would like to take again the example of personality research, particularly the self concept. William James (1890) was an earlier theorist to define the self as an object of self-perception and self-knowledge (Smith, 1992). For him, the "empirical self or me" was the concept most central to personal experience. James maintained that the empirical self has three main divisions: the material self (i.e., one's body and possessions), the social self (i.e., the impression one conveys to others), and the spiritual self (i.e., one's inner or subjective being). Today the study of the self has a rich tradition in both psychology, where the self-concept is represented by such labels as self-schemas (e.g., Markus, 1977) and self-esteem (e.g., Fleming & Courtney, 1984), and sociology, where the self-concept is investigated as part of social-identity theory or role-identity theory, (e.g., Stryker, 1987).

We can think of the self-concept as a cognitive appraisal of the attributes about oneself (Hattie, 1992). The self-concept both mediates and regulates behavior. This is put nicely in the following quote from a recent article by Markus & Wurf in the *Annual Review of Psychology*: "The self-concept interprets and organizes self-relevant actions and experiences; it has motivational consequences, providing the incentives, standards, plans, rules, and scripts for behavior; and it adjusts in response to challenges from the social environment" (Markus & Wurf, 1987, pp. 299-230; see also Markus & Nurius, 1986).

For purposes of the talk today, I would like to draw on a number of articles by Triandis and especially a recent article by Markus & Kitayama in the *Psychological Review*. These researchers have found that two construals of the self can be identified in people, depending on the culture within which one has been raised (Markus & Kitayama, 1991; see also Triandis, 1989). The first, the *independent self-concept* is common in many Western cultures and is characterized by an emphasis on personal goals, personal achievement, and appreciation of one's differences from others. People with an independent self-concept tend to be individualistic, egocentric, autonomous, self-reliant, and self-contained. They place considerable importance on asserting the self and are driven by self-serving motives. The individual is the primary unit of consciousness, with the self coterminous with one's own body. Relationships with others frequently serve as standards of self-appraisal, and the independent self takes a strategic posture vis-à-vis others in an effort to express or assert one's internal attributes. One's personal attributes are primary and are seen as relatively stable from context to context. Emphasis is placed on displaying or showing one's attributes (e.g., pride, anger). The normative imperative is to become independent from others and discover one's uniqueness.

By contrast, the *interdependent self-concept* is common in many non-Western cultures and is characterized by stress on goals of a group to which one belongs, attention to fitting in with others, and appreciation of commonalities with others. People with an interdependent selfconcept tend to be obedient, sociocentric, holistic, connected, and relation oriented. They place much importance on social harmony and are driven by other-serving motives. The relationships one has are the primary unit of consciousness, with the self coterminous with either a group or the set of roles one has with individuals across multiple groups. Relationships with others are ends in and of themselves, and the interdependent self takes a stance vis-à-vis others of giving and receiving social support. One's personal attributes are secondary and are allowed to change as needed in response to situational demands. Emphasis is placed on controlling one's attributes (e.g., avoiding the display of anger). The normative imperative is to maintain one's interdependence with others and contribute to the welfare of the group.

The categories of independent and interdependent selves are, of course, ideal types and some variability is to be expected within any particular culture characterized by one or the other. Nevertheless, the distinctions are very real. Triandis (1989) describes how cultures shape either an independent or interdependent self. Markus and Kitayama (1991) argue that independent and interdependent selves have specific consequences for the acquisition and experience of cognition, emotion, and motivation. However, the ideas are so new that very little cross-cultural research can be found testing the existence of differences in the self-concept and their implications.

I would like to briefly mention one forthcoming study comparing the self-concepts of Japanese and American consumers (Abe, Bagozzi, and Sadarangani, 1994). The researchers began with the self-consciousness scale and found the following cultural differences. Japanese consumers had conceptualizations of the self that were more integrated and less distinct than Americans in the sense that self-images of private and public self-consciousness were more strongly associated in memory for them. The Japanese experienced higher levels of social anxiety than Americans, but lower levels of private self-consciousness. The researchers then related the dimensions of self-conscious to other personality scales recently used in consumer research. One of these was the attention to social comparison information scale, which is itself a refinement in the self-monitoring scale. The researchers found that attention to social comparison information was positively related to public self-consciousness and social anxiety, but unrelated to private self-consciousness. This was true for both Americans and Japanese. Although the authors did not point this out, these findings demonstrate my earlier point that components of personality scales often exist, in this case self-consciousness, and more importantly they function differently both within and across cultures. The researchers also investigated the action control scale, which also has been used by consumer researchers in the past. They found that action control was negatively related to public and private selfconsciousness and social anxiety for both Americans and Japanese. In addition, action control was more strongly and negatively correlated with social anxiety for Japanese, as opposed to American, consumers.

Research like this is interesting, as far as it goes, in that it points out important boundary conditions for measures of the self-concept and its relationships to other constructs of interest both within and across cultures. The next step I hope the authors take is to show how these differences relate to decision making and choice in the marketplace. Cross-cultural research has potential for both providing a testing ground for our theories and suggesting refinements in our theories; maybe even leading to new theories.

The first two areas for future research I mentioned—personality and cross cultural research—complement the core of our field and even provide avenues for enhancing the examination of the core. But they are likely to remain at the periphery. The third and final area for growth I wish to speak about is more fundamental. Moreover, there is opportunity for researchers in information processing and human judgment and choice to make contributions and push their ideas further in this area. The area I am referring to is the general notion of *volition* or will in consumer research.

For purposes of discussion it is useful to think about consumer action as taking place in two stages. The first might be labeled simply *decision making*. Here the reasons for acting are considered and a decision, plan, or intention to act is formed. By reasons for acting, I mean the consumer's assessment of product attributes and the consequences of consumption, the evaluation of these, comparisons of alternatives, and their integration in memory. This aspect of consumer behavior is, of course, where the most progress has been made in the field. A neglected aspect of decision making, however, is the study of how the reasons for acting get transformed or are translated into a commitment and plan to act. We need more research into the motivational processes leading up to volition. How exactly, and when, do judgments, attitudes, and preferences lead to intentions? We have left these processes unexplored but instead have assumed that intentions follow automatically upon attitude or preference formation. The missing mechanisms here seem to lie in particular affective and emotional processes and the coping responses the consumer works out in relation to them. More work is needed in this aspect of consumer decision making.

The issues I want to focus upon in the final minutes concern the processes *following* a decision or intention to act. We might label this aspect of consumer behavior *self-regulation* or *action control* (Bagozzi, 1992). Now for some products and services the translation of intentions into action is straightforward. We evaluate alternative brands, make a choice, and acquire the product immediately or almost immediately thereafter. The situations I want to address are those where the final act of consumption occurs after a gap in time and when impediments can thwart one's plans. Here future consumption in the mind of the consumer is problematic and, in fact, is a goal or objective to be reached. The question is how does the consumer enact his or her intentions? What are the processes of goal pursuit that lead to success or failure?

Well, it is useful to think of the processes as occurring in three stages: the consumer has to first initiate action, second sustain goal pursuit, and third terminate action. Let us look at the first stage. Here hesitations to act must be overcome. These reside largely in internal impediments such as fear of failure or a questioning whether the goal is really worth it. In this first stage appraisals are made about the means needed to achieve the goal. A decision maker assesses his or her self-efficacy with respect possible means to the end. In other words, the consumer evaluates how confidently he or she can perform the means. Judgments are made also about the likelihood that each means, if performed, would lead to goal attainment. And finally the emotional significances of the means are appraised. The initiation of goal pursuit will be a function of the integration of self-efficacy, instrumental beliefs, and affect toward alternative means.

Once the means are set into motion, the effort must be sustained if the goal is to be reached. In this second stage, the instrumental acts are monitored to see if they begin and end when they are supposed to do so, whether they achieve their objectives, whether new contingencies, impediments, or facilitating factors must be incorporated into decision making. Corrections to plans are made and commitment waxes or wanes, depending upon the situation, one's motivation, and judgments made in regard to progress toward the goal.

The final stage of goal pursuit is *termination* of goal pursuit. One issue here is when to abandon one's efforts when the goal is unattainable. Another is when do conditions require a change in goals. And even when a goal has been achieved, termination is sometimes an issue when the consumer cannot disengage from goal pursuit. We see this in the extreme in excessive dieting or over doing things in exercising or in general through various compulsive consumption behaviors. The subfield of customer satisfaction also addresses issues related to termination of goal pursuit that haven't been given much consideration to date.

The processes transforming an intention into goal attainment are obviously complex. No one study will be able to look at the entire sequence of decision making and goal pursuit. But many opportunities exist for investigating each of the subprocesses, and over time we should be able to gain a better picture of how volition functions in consumer decision making and action. This is an area where researchers from the information processing tradition can help shed light.

Let me give a brief example. Julius Kuhl, a German psychologist, has studied the activation of intentions (e.g., Kuhl, 1992). The probability that a given intention will be activated is a non-linear function of the importance, time pressure, and subjective competence associated with the intention. Kuhl found that people differ with respect to the processing of intention-related memory structures. State oriented individuals exhibit a highly generalized and inflexible tendency of decoupling perception and action that is accompanied by excessive reflections about past failures or future possibilities and alternative courses of action. This makes it difficult for state-oriented individuals to initiate new, non-automatized actions. By contrast, action-oriented people reveal processes that serve the recoupling of perception and action in order to realize a chosen intention. In his experiments, Kuhl found that action and state oriented individuals differed with respect to the activation of explicit intention representations in memory. In situations where the execution of intentions had to be postponed, action-oriented subjects deactivated declarative representations of prospective intentions when they were irrelevant to the current task. In contrast for state-oriented subjects, explicit representations of the postponed intentions persisted in a state of increased subthreshold activation. These results were found in a design based on recognition tasks and response time.

Many of the findings and the general experimental approach found in the information processing literature in consumer research are applicable to the study of volition. Information processing theory has much to offer concerning the formation, storage, retrieval, and activation of intentions. It can help us learn also about how goals are represented and integrated with decision making. The research on human judgment and choice can help in understanding how the means for goal pursuit are decided upon and how goal pursuit is guided or altered. These and many other questions remain to be explored. I believe the study of volitional processes needs to be added to the core of consumer research. Thank you very much.

REFERENCES

Abe, S., Bagozzi, R.P., & Sadarangani, P. (1994). An investigation of construct validity and generalizability of the self-concept: Self-consciousness in Japan and the United States. working paper, University of Michigan.

Bagozzi, R.P. (1992). The self-regulation of attitudes, intentions, and behavior. *Social Psychology Quarterly*, 55, 178-204.

Bagozzi, R.P., & Heathenon, T.F. (1994). A general approach to representing multifaceted personality constructs: Application to state self-esteem. *Structural Equation Modeling*, 1, 35-67.

Fleming, J.S., & Courtney, B.E. (1984). The dimensionality of self-esteem: II. Hierarchical facet model for revised measurement scales. *Journal of Personality and Social Psychology*, 46, 404-421.

Hattie, J. (1992). *Self-Concept*, Hillsdale, NJ: Erlbaum.

James, W. (1890). *The Principles of Psychology* (2 vols.). New York: Holt.

Kuhl, J. (1992). A theory of self-regulation: Action versus state orientation, self-discrimination, and some applications. *Applied Psychology: An International Review*, 41 (2), 97-129.

Markus, H. (1977). Self-schemas and processing information about the self. *Journal of Personality and Social Psychology*, 35, 63-78.

Markus, H.R., & Kitayama, S. (1991). Culture and the self: Implications for cognition, emotion, and motivation. *Psychological Review*, 98, 224-253.

Markus, H., & Nurius, P. (1986). Possible selves. *American Psychologist*, 41, 954-969.

Markus, H., & Wurf, E. (1987). The dynamic self-concept: A social psychological perspective. *Annual Review of Psychology*, 38, 299-337.

Smith, M.B. (1992). William James and the psychology of self. In M.E. Donnelly (Ed.), *Reinterpreting the Legacy of William James* (pp. 173-187). Washington, DC: American Psychological Association.

Stryker, S. (1987). Identity theory: Developments and extensions. In K. Yardley & T. Honess (Eds.), *Self and identity: Psychosocial perspectives* (pp. 83-103). New York: Wiley.

Triandis, H.C. (1989). The self and social behavior in differing cultural contexts. *Psychological Review*, 96, 506-520.

Session Overview
Perspectives on Consumer Health Issues: Theoretical, Methodological, and Policy Insights
Christine Moorman, University of Wisconsin-Madison

Using health as a context for gaining insight into consumer behavior issues offers a number of opportunities. First, health information and health behaviors are inherently uncertain. This is the case because of the long time horizons associated with health outcomes which makes the effectiveness of health behaviors difficult to evaluate, because most consumers lack the expertise to evaluate the veracity of health information, and because conflicting messages are often available in the marketplace and media. Second, health is an interdisciplinary area (Moorman and Matulich 1993). Research, as a result, tends to offer insights relating to various physiological, psychological, and social dimensions of health. These perspectives require consumer researchers who study health phenomena to accept a multidimensional view of consumer behavior and to integrate often conflicting perspectives when creating theory.

The session explored several themes. The first is the role of motivation in consumers' decision to engage in uncertain behaviors (like health behaviors). Focusing on "protection motivation" which arouses, sustains, and directs health activities, Block and Anand suggested that the motivation to engage in health behaviors depends in part on consumers' readiness to act. Moorman investigated the effect of health values on consumers' health behaviors, comparing the activating effect of health values to the effect of health motivation described in Moorman and Matulich (1993). Hill et al. deconstructed the abortion experience in terms of factors predisposing pregnant consumers to undergo this procedure. Finally, Cole and Balasubramanian addressed the issue of the role of motivation to process nutrition information, finding that as motivation increases so does inspection of nutrition panels.

A second theme is the role of control in health decisions. Moorman identified two types of health control — behavioral control and health locus of control — and investigated their interaction in health outcomes. Block and Anand examined the impact of a third type of control, termed perceived efficacy, that refers to the extent to which consumers perceive that following the recommended health behavior will be efficacious in ameliorating the harm. Hill et al. explored the effect of perceived control (i.e., responsibility) over the decision to abort as it relates to post-abortion experiences. Finally, Cole and Balasubramanian found that as consumers become more knowledgeable, they perceive greater control over their health. Paradoxically, the control that this knowledge affords is actually a detriment to further health actions.

A third issue contained either explicitly or implicitly in these four studies is the impact of gender on health issues. By selecting mammography and abortion decisions, Block and Anand and Hill et al. addressed gender-specific health decisions, although clearly there are inputs from and impacts on men in the case of abortion decisions. Moorman examined the effects of gender on health behaviors and the extent to which gender and health motivation interact to influence health behaviors. Similarly, Cole and Balasubramanian noted the effects of gender on nutrition information use.

Another theme implicit in the session is the difference between prevention-oriented health behaviors and those that are detection-oriented or curative-oriented. Two of the studies, Cole and Balasubramanian and Moorman, focused on preventive health behaviors and assessed the types of consumer characteristics that correlate with them. Block and Anand focused on mammography screening, which is both preventive (to the extent that it reduces mortality rates if cancer is detected) and curative (because it detects disease already present). Finally, Hill et al. also highlighted consumers' attitudes toward prevention — in this case, birth control activities — that are reported as failed by over 80% of the study's informants.

The final theme relates to the important policy implications indicated by these studies. Three of the studies have direct implications for the design and implementation of health promotion campaigns. Block and Anand's study provided insights into creating more effective public service advertisements aimed at persuading women to follow mammography recommendations. Cole and Balasubramanian suggested that nutrition information should be designed to increase consumers' motivation to process nutrition information and to minimize nutrition knowledge's negative effects. Moorman indicated the importance of attending to individual differences when designing health programs. Finally, Hill et al.'s study may have indirect policy implications because it provided a perspective on the decision makers' view of the abortion experience that informs public policy and it gave insight into the deeply personal and conflicted nature of this act.

REFERENCE

Moorman, Christine and Erika Matulich (1993), "A Model of Consumers' Preventive Health Behaviors: The Role of Health Motivation and Health Ability," *Journal of Consumer Research*, 20 (September), 208-228.

Women and Abortion: A Phenomenological Analysis

Ronald Paul Hill, Villanova University
Maggie Jones Patterson, Duquesne University
Kate Maloy, University of Pittsburgh

ABSTRACT

The purpose of this paper is to broaden our understanding of this controversial topic by examining abortion from a consumer-behavior perspective. To accomplish this goal, the results of a phenomenological study are briefly described based on abortion versus birth decisions concerning 92 different pregnancies. Interview data provide widespread support for most parts of three a priori themes, and suggest that women use a different moral standard when making birth versus abortion decisions than the public debate suggests.

INTRODUCTION

Abortion is the most frequently performed surgical procedure in this country, with approximately 1.6 million abortions performed annually (Davis 1985; Olasky 1992). Twenty-five percent of all pregnancies are terminated in this manner, and approximately 20 percent of all U.S. women have had a legal abortion (Mueller and Major 1989). As noted by Stotland (1992; p. 2078), the "heat of the conflict [over abortion] tends to melt boundaries between medicine and philosophy, between church and state, between demonstrated fact and personal belief." Issues of fertility and sexuality are highly charged in all societies, and abortion represents a symbolic "meeting place" for some of our most contentious views of these topics (McDonnell 1984). Unfortunately, this "heat" has reduced the many different opinions and attitudes on abortion to just two antithetical positions - pro-life and pro-choice (Maloy and Patterson 1992).

Several scholars believe that pro-choice and pro-life positions, which depict abortion in good versus evil terms, fail to capture the complexity of the issue and the ambivalence of the American public in general and consumers of abortion services in particular (Maloy and Patterson 1992; McDonnell 1984). For example, a *New York Times*/CBS News Poll found that only 31 percent of those surveyed fully supported either pro-life or pro-choice views (Dionne 1989). The remaining 69 percent believed that abortion should be legal depending upon the circumstances faced by the woman. The remainder of this paper addresses this issue through a review of the history of abortion in this country, and a brief discussion of the results of a recent phenomenological investigation.

A BRIEF HISTORY OF ABORTION

The term "abortion" is derived from the Latin word "aboriri," which translated literally means "to perish." The oldest known reference to abortion is in Chinese medical texts that date back to around 2737 B.C. (David 1988). Within the American colonies and the United States, abortion was legal from 1607 to 1828. Under the common law of this period, abortion was allowed as long as it was performed with the consent of the woman and before she was "quick with child" (quickening marked the time when the first movements of the child were felt by the woman, which occurs approximately at the end of the first trimester). However, even after quickening, abortion usually was considered only a misdemeanor.

The earliest legislation dealing specifically with the legal status of abortion in the United States was passed in the states of Connecticut and New York during the 1820s and was designed to protect the health of women with unwanted pregnancies from damage by abortion (David 1988). Despite these laws, abortionists continued to operate publicly and typically were acquitted by juries. However, after the founding of the American Medical Association in 1847, an organized drive was launched to professionalize medical training and gain public acknowledgment of the status of physicians. Physicians sought to discredit midwives and all practitioners who did not share their standards. The issue of abortion helped consolidate and focus this movement, and physicians launched an antiabortion campaign in opposition to "greedy" abortionists, whose lack of medical training allegedly put women at risk.

By 1900, as a result of this movement, states throughout the United States enacted legislation that made abortion illegal unless there was a threat to the woman's health as determined by a physician (Ginsburg 1989). Thus, women seeking to terminate pregnancies for social or economic reasons were forced to seek more dangerous illegal abortions (Messer and May 1988). Typical descriptions of this era are summarized by Gloria Steinem (in Bonavoglia 1991, p.x-xi):

There were stories of sexual abuse; for instance, a woman who had been forced to have sex with the abortionist before he would operate. There were stories of race and class hatred; for instance, a woman who had been bargained with—she could have a legal abortion, but only if she agreed to be sterilized. There was humiliation at the hands of those in power; for instance, men on a hospital board who made a young woman describe in detail how she got pregnant—and then denied her a legal abortion anyway.

By the 1960s, several environmental influences emerged simultaneously, and they heavily influenced the movement to legalize abortion. This decade of social upheaval resulted in "the successful culmination of the family planning movement..., the `sexual revolution,' the civil rights and antiwar movements, the movement for `zero population growth,' and, of course, the rebirth of the women's movement" (Staggenborg 1989, p. 211). Further, advances in medicine removed many of the threats to a pregnant woman's life, such as tuberculosis and cardiovascular and renal diseases, leaving few legitimate rationales for the performance of abortion by physicians. With its "cover story" gone, the medical profession questioned its legal position and began an active campaign to liberalize abortion laws (Glendon 1987).

Two landmark opinions by the United States Supreme Court in 1973, *Roe v. Wade* and *Doe v. Bolton*, struck down all state restrictions, and opened the door for "abortion on demand" during the first two trimesters of a pregnancy (Luker 1984). In the more famous of the two decisions, *Roe v. Wade* (410 U.S. 113), the Court held that "[the] right of privacy...founded in the Fourteenth Amendment's concept of personal liberty...is broad enough to encompass a woman's decision whether or not to terminate her pregnancy." Since this right was deemed "fundamental," the states could intervene only to protect the health of the woman (e.g., after it becomes more dangerous for the woman to have an abortion than to carry the fetus to term) or the health of the fetus after it becomes viable (Linton 1989).

Many women's organizations greeted these decisions with elation, but Catholic and pro-life forces accused the Court of "opening the doors to the greatest slaughter of innocent life in the history of mankind" (Rubin 1982, p. 88). Subsequent efforts by those opposed to *Roe v. Wade* to amend the Constitution to change or overturn this decision were unsuccessful and largely have been abandoned. However, a parallel strategy to gain passage of state abortion statutes that are as restrictive as possible under the framework of *Roe v. Wade* has met with limited success (Annas 1989). For instance, the Court, in its recent ruling involving *Planned Parenthood of Southeastern Pennsylvania v. Casey*, let stand requirements that women seeking abortions be offered state-issued literature on fetal development, observe a 24-hour waiting period, and, for those under the age of 18, obtain permission from either one parent or a judge (*Philadelphia Inquirer* 1992).

SUMMARY OF STUDY RESULTS

Consistent with a priori expectations, the women in this study expressed that they experienced conflict during the decision-making process. Further, this ambivalence was typically associated with bonding between the woman and the fetus, which was a function of the informant's awareness of the physical changes happening within her and her embracing of these changes. Finally, these women often experienced a feeling that they had no choice regarding their abortion decisions; instead they felt that others' (including partners and health professionals) were making the choice for them. Contrary to predictions, the feeling of lack of choice exacerbated women's conflicting emotional reactions.

With regard to the abortion experience, the data revealed that a common hope among the informants was that abortion would transport them from their current discomfort and return them to their physical and emotional states that existed before their pregnancies. Consistent with expectations, the women who were conflicted about the abortion decision had more difficulty during and negative reaction toward the abortion procedure. Also, the treatment received by informants from abortionists impacted their abortion experiences. As predicted, poor or neglectful treatment led to negative reactions, both physical and emotional, during their procedures, and good treatment led to more positive experiences. This was the case for both legal and illegal abortions.

A priori expectations suggested the existence of both positive and negative reactions following an abortion. One reaction that informants revealed was a feeling of personal responsibility for the decision to abort, which interestingly occurred even if women felt that the decision to abort was not left to them. Further, longer-term negative reactions tended to exist among informants who experienced poor treatment during illegal abortions, conflict over the meaning of abortion, bonding with the fetus prior to their abortions, and ambivalence concerning the degree to which they wanted their pregnancies. Finally, results indicated that social support following the abortion was far less important in reducing post-abortion trauma than was a woman's sense that her right to choose during the decision-making process had been preserved.

In total, this research revealed (1) that a wide gap exists between the language of the public debate and that of private decision making; (2) that the language of private decision making reflects a moral standard used frequently by women yet virtually ignored in the public debate; and (3) that women who take charge of their own decisions cope better with the emotional aftermath, whether their decision is for birth or for abortion.

REFERENCES

Annas, George J. (1989), "*Webster* and the Politics of Abortion," *Hastings Center Report*, 19 (March/April), 36-38.

Bonavoglia, Angela (1991), *The Choices We Made*, New York: Random House.

David, Henry P. (1988), "Overview: A Brief History of Abortion and Studies of Denied Abortion," in *Born Unwanted: Developmental Effects of Denied Abortion*, eds. Henry P. David, Zdenek Dytrych, Zdenek Matejcek, and Vratislav Schuller, New York: Springer Publishing, 9-30.

Davis, Nanette (1985), *From Crime to Choice: The Transformation of Abortion in America*, Westport, CT: Greenwood Press.

Dionne, E. J. (1989), "Poll on Abortion Finds the Nation Is Sharply Divided," *New York Times*, April 26, A1.

Ginsburg, Faye D. (1989), *Contested Lives: The Abortion Debate in An American Community*, Berkeley, CA: University of California Press.

Glendon, Mary Ann (1987), *Abortion and Divorce in Western Law*, Cambridge, MA: Harvard University Press.

Linton, Paul Benjamin (1989), "*Roe v. Wade* and the History of Abortion Legislation," *American Journal of Law & Medicine*, 15 (2&3), 227-233.

Luker, Kristin (1984), *Abortion & The Politics of Motherhood*, Berkeley, CA: University of California Press.

Maloy, Kate and Maggie Jones Patterson (1992), *Birth or Abortion? Private Struggles in a Political World*, New York: Plenum Press.

McDonnell, Kathleen (1984), *Not an Easy Choice: A Feminist Reexamines Abortion*, Boston: South End Press.

Messer, Ellen and Kathryn E. May (1988), *Back Rooms: Voices From the Illegal Abortion Era*, New York: St. Martin's Press.

Mueller, Pallas and Brenda Major (1989), "Self-Blame, Self-Efficacy, and Adjustment to Abortion," *Journal of Personality and Social Psychology*, 57 (6), 1059-1068.

Olasky, Marvin (1992), "Victorian Secret: Pro-Life Victories in 19th-Century America," *Policy Review*, 60, 30-37.

Philadelphia Inquirer (1992), "High Court Abortion Ruling Satisfies Few," December 27, C3.

Rubin, Eva R. (1982), *Abortion, Politics and the Courts: Roe v. Wade and Its Aftermath*, Westport, CT: Greenwood Press.

Staggenborg, Suzanne (1989), "Organizational and Environmental Influences on the Development of the Pro-Choice Movement," *Social Forces*, 68 (September), 204-240.

Stotland, Nada L. (1992), "The Myth of the Abortion Trauma Syndrome," *Journal of the American Medical Association*, 268 (October 21), 2078-2079.

Measuring and Judging Emotional Aspects of Consumption Experiences
Laurette Dubé, Université de Montréal

Retrospective reports of consumption emotions have been found to be powerful predictors of satisfaction judgments and other post-purchase attitudes and behaviors. This special topic session addressed issues related to how one experiences, remembers, and judges consumption emotions and uses them to form satisfaction judgments in the context of service industries. If understanding emotional experiences is important for physical goods, it becomes particularly important for services where much of the consumption process occurs on site.

The first paper presented by Richard L. Oliver reviewed structural representations of consumption emotions and described a field study that provided evidence suggesting that positive and negative affectivity may be the primary dimensions underlying the emotional experience of consumption with arousal as an additional dimension whose directionality of effect may be service specific. In addition, the results supported a two-appraisal model of satisfaction judgments with cognitive (e.g., assessment of functional or comparative outcomes) and affective (e.g., the experienced emotions) processes operating in tandem. In contrast, quality judgments were found to be primarily cognition-driven.

The second paper presented by Marian Friestad investigated memory for very positive and very negative encounters using self-reported data from a national random sample of consumers of a variety of service industries. Results provided partial support for a "mobilization-minimization" hypothesis that proposes a sequential two-stage model of how people respond to and remember consumption emotions. When measured by the ability to re-live the feelings, analyses revealed that memory for positive and negative emotional experiences decayed at a different pace over long-term periods: memory for positive emotions remained relatively stable whereas memory for negative emotions diminished markedly.

The third paper presented by Laurette Dubé and Michael S. Morgan reported a field study that investigated how consumption emotions change during service transactions that extend over time and how momentary experiences "add up" into retrospective judgments. The dynamic modeling of momentary experiences revealed a pattern of habituation for both positive and negative emotions. Results of regression analyses suggest that retrospective reports of consumption emotions are not simple averages of successive momentary states but they also reflect the pattern of change. In addition, the relative weights of momentary states in retrospective judgments varied as a function of their temporal location, with first and last consumption emotions being significantly more determinant than those experienced in the middle of the service process.

The discussants, Robert A. Westbrook and Douglas M. Stayman, provided insightful comments with respects to further conceptual and empirical development in the domain of consumption emotions and their role in satisfaction judgments. Both emphasized the need to inquire into the differentiated nature of positive and negative affect, such as anger, sadness, joy and pride. Westbrook specifically questioned whether positive affect and negative affect have a common meaning across studies, since investigators typically base their measurements on different types of affective experiences. He further suggested the value of examining the other elements of the overall emotional response syndrome, such as cognitive appraisal, facial expression and nonverbal behavior, emotional experience, physiological response and action impulses. Finally, Westbrook suggested that future research inquire into the specific sources of emotional response and their unique effects beyond satisfaction judgments. Stayman highlighted individual and situational factors that may influence consumption emotions. He also raised the need to provide experimental testing for alternative processes that may moderate single and interactive effects of consumption emotions and cognitions in forming satisfaction judgments.

Conceptual Issues in the Structural Analysis of Consumption Emotion, Satisfaction, and Quality: Evidence in a Service Setting

Richard L. Oliver, Vanderbilt University

ABSTRACT

Recent research linking consumer satisfaction and affect has raised issues which require elaboration before models incorporating consumption affect will become useful. Among these are the dimensional structure of affect and the role these dimensions play alongside consumption cognition (e.g., expectancy disconfirmation, quality). Previous affect work using the Izard (1977) typology has been limited due to the heavy emphasis on negative affect, as opposed to positive affect and arousal. In this paper, the contributions of positive and negative affect are examined with reference to affect frameworks based on dimensions of pleasantness and arousal. In a related topic, the hypothesized duality of consumption affect and cognition, with the specific inclusion of quality judgments, will be discussed. Drawing on Oliver (1989), a structural representation of parallel affect and cognitive mechanisms affecting satisfaction is proposed. Both the dimensional and structural suggestions are tested with data from an adolescent health-care setting. Results show that the parallel representation is supported.

INTRODUCTION

Affect as an essential component of purchase and usage is beginning to attract the attention of consumer researchers, particularly within the context of service satisfaction and postpurchase response. This is so because affect is now known to be a more primitive motivational response in living organisms and because it may interact with cognition as both an antecedent and consequent (Lewis, Sullivan, and Michalson 1984). Thus, the role of affect is intertwined with other cognitive postpurchase responses either because the affect state generated in consumption "recruits" certain cognitions (Chattopadhyay and Alba 1988) or because it is a natural outcome of cognitive processes such as attribution (e.g., Weiner, Russell, and Lerman 1979).

Recently, researchers have begun to entertain affective influences in consumer response. Beginning with work in advertising (e.g., Holbrook and Batra 1987), and continuing in the domain of products (e.g., Westbrook 1987), some strides have been made in understanding the role of affect in consumption. Westbrook and Oliver (1991), for example, find that affect co-exists with cognition (e.g., expectancy disconfirmation) in the formation of satisfaction judgments and that both make independent contributions to satisfaction. Other work (Mano and Oliver 1993; Oliver 1992, 1993a; Oliver and Westbrook 1993) elaborates on this phenomenon and illustrates the attribute-specific and cognitive evaluation bases for affect-augmentation (Oliver 1993a) in consumer response. This paper reviews the work to date in the area of product and service postpurchase judgment, identifies specific issues in the work so far, and provides a new test of affect in the context of service satisfaction.

In doing so, the role, if any, of consumption affect in *quality* judgments will be explored. The fields of quality and satisfaction are merging (Oliver 1993b), although causality issues remain to be resolved. Given the newly discovered importance of affect in satisfaction, a reasonable question is the extent to which quality judgments are similarly affected.

In the following discussion, the dependent variable under study is limited to that of satisfaction. Justification for this is the extreme importance of satisfaction as an antecedent to repurchase or repatronage intentions, as a motivator for word-of-mouth, and as a diagnostic measure for managerial action. After describing efforts to conceptualize affect in consumption generally, a test of a conceptual model is performed in the service sector. As noted, service quality and satisfaction are now generating a great deal of interest in the field of services. The present study attempts to add to that literature.

Affect in Product Satisfaction Contexts

Westbrook (1987) is credited with introducing affect to the existing stream of research on the cognitive basis of satisfaction (Oliver 1980). Using Izard's (1977) emotional typology, he was able to show that two affect constructs, consisting of summated positive and negative affect, correlated in the predicted directions with overall satisfaction over two product categories (automobiles and cable TV—a service). Moreover, these relations held up to the introduction of cognition (i.e., expectancy disconfirmation) in regressions explaining satisfaction.

Later, Westbrook and Oliver (1991) performed a dimensional analysis, also using the Izard (1977) scheme, and found that three affective dimensions could be justified as underlying explanations for the satisfaction judgment. Respectively, these were hostility (a constellation of negative affect), pleasant surprise (positive affect and surprise), and interest. Of note is the fact that they were also able to identify emotional segments of consumers such that each segment was characterized with distinctively different emotional profiles. In order of their positive affectivity toward the tested product (autos), the groups could be described as pleasantly surprised, happy/content, unemotional, unpleasantly surprised, and angry/upset.

Later, Oliver (1993a), again using Izard's (1977) framework, provided evidence that the negative affect dimension could be viewed as having three subdimensions based on the attributional agency. Respectively, these consisted of the externally attributed affects of anger, disgust, and contempt, the internally attributed affects of guilt and shame, and the situation-specific affects of fear and sadness. The two positive affects in the Izard scheme, interest and joy were found to be separately processed for a product used in Oliver's study (autos), but not for the service context (course instruction). Oliver was able to show that the positive and negative affect constellations partially mediated attribute experience. That is, attribute experiences appeared to be the underlying causes for the affects reported in consumption.

Mano and Oliver (1993) replicated this finding in the context of the nature of product evaluation. This study differed on a number of dimensions from those described previously. First, the authors used affect items from Mano's (1991) work, based on the PANAS scale of Watson, Clark, and Tellegen (1988), which describes affect on the two dimensions of positive-negative affect and arousal. This two-dimensional space is sectioned into eight octants (see Mano and Oliver 1993) which are represented by two or three indicators. Second, the product/service context was unrestricted as subjects were allowed to select purchases (including services) which satisfied either a high or low involvement situation, as determined by survey instructions. Third, the selected product was evaluated not on the basis of attributes but on whether utilitarian (i.e., functional) or hedonic evaluation was most pertinent, based on the work of Batra and Ahtola (1990). Results showed that positive and negative affect *and* arousal were key dimensions underlying affect, as theory predicted. When input into a causal modeling framework, arousal was found to be a function of higher hedonic evaluation and lower utilitarian evaluation and positive and negative affect were found to be a function of arousal. Positive affect was also a function of hedonic evaluation. Finally, satisfaction was a function of positive and negative affect in the respective directions, and utilitarian evaluation. Once again, satisfaction is shown to be a function of (aroused) affect.

Specific attribute influences as influencing satisfaction through affect are only recently coming under investigation. Early exploratory attempts have been made by Oliver (1992) and Oliver and Westbrook (1993). Oliver used an MDS approach to position overall satisfaction among attribute satisfactions. Results showed satisfaction to be centrally located among two dimensions of attribute space which the author referred to as static and dynamic. Oliver and Westbrook posed specific predictions about which attribute judgments would predict specific positive and negative affects. Their results were encouraging but not consistently significant. Of note is the fact that clusters of consumers were found roughly in accord with those found in Westbrook and Oliver (1991). Replicated clusters of delighted (pleasantly surprised), contented, unemotional, and angry consumers were found as before. However, two new cluster descriptions, described as tentative and guilty/ashamed, were discovered, thus adding further emotional content to the satisfaction response.

Taken together, these investigations point to a consistent pattern of affective response in the satisfaction judgment. Apparently, attribute experience, in addition to having a direct effect on satisfaction, also drives the affective response the consumer has toward the product. Moreover, affective response appears to be well-specified by positive and negative affect *and* arousal which combine into states which describe more complex affects such as delight. This research stream, however, is tentative and would benefit from further corroboration and extension. More specifically, the affect octant approach of Mano (1991) and Watson et al. (1988) requires further testing in consumer (service) contexts if its validity characteristics are to be known. Additionally, the specific attribute constellation commonly referred to as quality has not been framed within the emotion space. In fact, little is known about the psychological interpretation of quality. The next section speaks to that issue.

Quality and Affect

A number of current works propose a linkage between quality and satisfaction (Bitner 1990; Bolton and Drew 1991; Cronin and Taylor 1992; Swartz and Brown 1989; Zeithaml, Berry, and Parasuraman 1993). None, however, explicitly considers affect. In fact, in Swartz and Brown and Zeithaml et al., the "quality" gap between expectations and performance is viewed as surrogate satisfaction, which some have likened to affect or emotion (e.g., Hunt 1977).

In Bitner (1990) and Bolton and Drew (1991), satisfaction is viewed as a function of expectancy disconfirmation. Service quality, in contrast, is positioned as subsequent to satisfaction under the implicit assumption that quality judgments result from satisfying or dissatisfying service encounters. Cronin and Taylor (1992) indirectly tested this assumption across eight service companies. Of note is the finding that, of the two reciprocal paths (satisfaction → quality and quality → satisfaction), only the quality → satisfaction path was significant.

No study, however, has investigated affect in the context of quality. Cadotte, Woodruff, and Jenkins (1987) tested a "feelings" satisfaction model where satisfaction was defined as a constellation of affective adjectives (e.g., warm/cold). Their model showed that service attributes (in a restaurant setting) impacted this feelings criterion only through the disconfirmation concept. Thus, it is not known how quality is affected, if at all, by affect.

Oliver (1993b) has suggested that quality is largely a performance concept. More to the point, quality relies on assessments of "performance excellence criteria" (Zeithaml et al. 1993). These will tend to be exemplary levels of performance characteristics, those on which the service will truly excel. As such, quality judgments are posited to be a direct function of performance and may, likewise, influence satisfaction directly.

A summary model of the concepts discussed above is shown in the Figure.

Hypotheses

The preceding discussion suggests the following hypotheses:

H_1: Affect in service consumption can be described by a dimensionality consisting of positive affect, negative affect, and arousal.

H_2: Positive and negative affect are a direct function of arousal and a positive/negative function of performance, respectively.

H_3: Quality is a direct function of (high) service performance.

H_4: Satisfaction is a function of affect, quality, disconfirmation, and performance.

METHOD

Procedure

Parents of adolescent patients who had convalesced from various ailments in a short-term hospital recovery center over a seven month period were surveyed as to their satisfaction with their child's stay. The count of individual patients in this time period numbered 377, of which 40 were used in pretesting the list of performance attributes (to be discussed). Parents of the remaining 337 patients were sent surveys, of which 65 usable responses were returned in a one month "response window" allowed for the study—representing a response rate of 19.3%. The average respondent was female, a mother of the patient, had some college, and was somewhat upscale with a family income between $30-50,000.

Measures

For the purpose of this study, measures of performance, affect, quality, disconfirmation, and satisfaction were constructed as follows:

Performance. A list of performance features was generated through two procedures. First, the laddering technique (Reynolds and Gutman 1988) was administered to 20 randomly selected parents from the original list of respondents. This approach resulted in a list of 24 key elements of service delivery. Second, the critical incidence technique (Bitner, Booms, and Tetreault 1990) was administered to a second set of 20 respondents. This resulted in service delivery outcomes which were fully contained in the previous list, thus corroborating the earlier results. In collaboration with the study sponsors, the final list was condensed to 19 delivery features for use in the final study. This outcome list was scored by respondents on five-point bipolar adjective scales (e.g., The nurses would be: rude ... friendly). A summated index was created by aggregating over all outcomes. Note that factor analysis was not used to reduce the dimensionality of the features. Two highly correlated attributes, which would load

FIGURE
Proposed Model Relationships

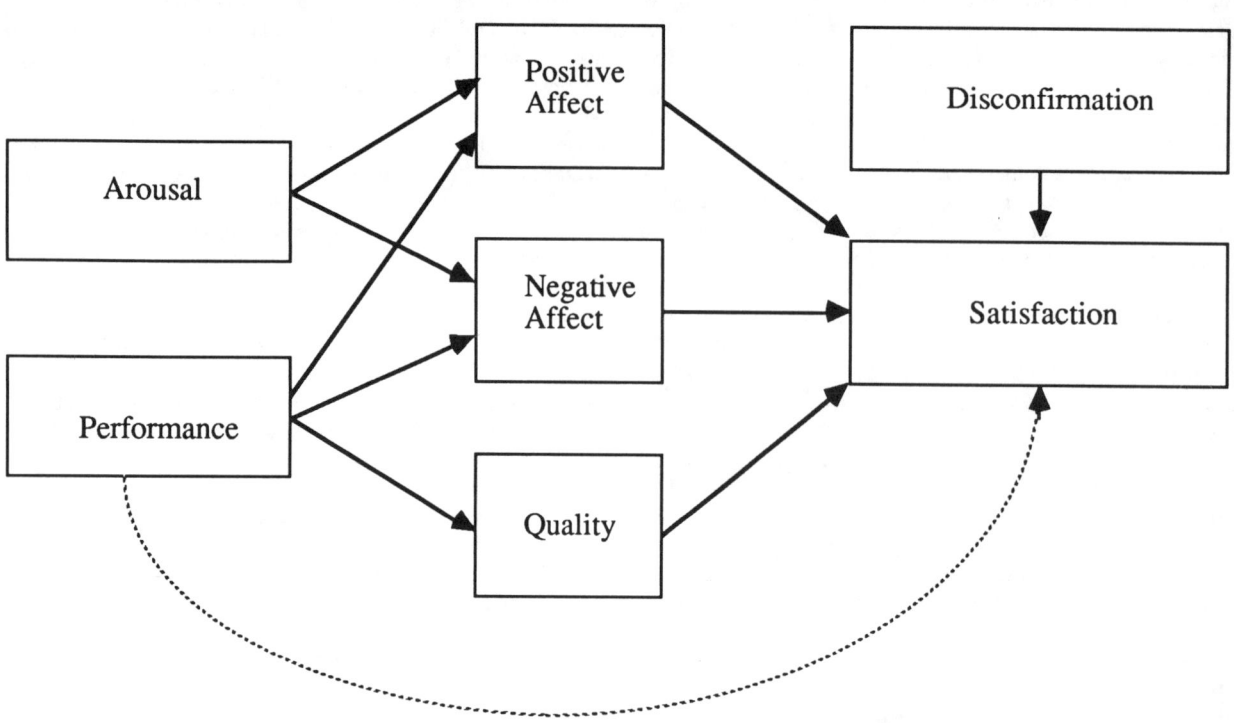

Source: Adapted from Mano and Oliver (1993) and Oliver (1993a,b)

on a single dimension, could have singular, additive impacts on quality or satisfaction. This additivity would be obscured if dimensions were used (Oliver 1993a).

The affects. A set of affects completing the octal dimensional affect solution of Watson et al. (1988) was obtained from their short inventory which measures all eight segments of affect space. Lately, Larsen and Diener (1992) have refined this scale, making it more social and less clinical. The items used in this study were selected from those of Watson et al. and Larsen and Diener so as to provide two items from each octant to represent each of the eight affect categories. All were measured on frequency scales. Respondents were asked to describe "during your experience with the care unit, how frequently you felt" each of the emotions on 5-point scales ranging from "never" (1) to "always" (5).

Quality. Based on work by Garvin (1984), Steenkamp (1990), and Zeithaml (1988), a six-item quality scale was constructed using bipolar adjectives addressing excellence, superiority, value, quality, high standards, and best/worse.

Disconfirmation. Disconfirmation was measured on a disconfirmation scale reported in Oliver (1980). It contains three "better-worse than expected" items sampling benefits, problems, and overall performance.

Satisfaction. Satisfaction was measured using five items from Oliver's Likert-type satisfaction scale used in Westbrook and Oliver (1981), Oliver and Swan (1989), Oliver and Bearden (1985), and other studies. In addition, this scale was augmented with five items reflecting satisfaction with the *child's* experience, specially constructed for this study. Because both parent and child interacted with the service delivery, parents were also expected to reflect satisfying and dissatisfying experiences through the eyes of their child, a form of reflected appraisal.

RESULTS

Dimensional Structure of Affect

Factor analysis of the sixteen affects revealed four factors having eigenvalues greater than unity and explaining 61% of the item variance. This solution, however, contained one variable which did not load at the recommended 0.5 cutoff (annoyed) and one which loaded singularly on the fourth factor (enthused). Thus, the three factor solution, representing fourteen affects, was used to describe the affect structure emerging from this data set. See Table 1.

The results show that the two primary dimensions of positive and negative affect were supported as was the additional dimension of arousal. This corroborates earlier studies of affect in consumption (Westbrook 1987; Westbrook and Oliver 1991; Oliver 1993a), based on the Izard (1977) scheme, and also suggests that the role of arousal has been somewhat neglected in consumer research. Based on these findings, scales of positive and negative affect and arousal were constructed by adding the respective items loading on the factors.

Table 2 shows the descriptive statistics, correlation matrix, and alpha reliabilities of the affect scales and other study variables. This pattern of results is best discussed in terms of the model coefficients, tested here with two-stage least squares (TSLS) due to the recursive nature of the conceptual structure (see the Figure). Table 3 shows the TSLS results of the base model, a submodel of

TABLE 1
Factor Structure of the Affect Items

Variable/Factor Interpretation	1 Neg. Affect	2 Pos. Affect	3 Arousal
Bored	.825	—	—
Gloomy	.803	—	—
Nervous	.669	—	—
Sluggish	.658	—	—
Sad	.529	—	—
Inactive	.522	—	—
Pleased	—	.723	—
Content	—	.691	—
Delighted	—	.684	—
Tranquil	—	.613	—
Calm	—	.594	—
Active	—	—	.794
Surprised	—	—	.761
Lively	—	—	.555
Cum. Variance (%)	31.7	45.1	56.5

TABLE 2
Scale Descriptive Statistics, Intercorrelations, and Reliabilities[a]

Scale	Mean	S.D.	1	2	3	4	5	6	7
1. Neg. Affect	2.88	0.83	.79						
2. Pos. Affect	3.36	0.78	-.45	.73					
3. Arousal	3.03	0.90	-.28	.33	.64				
4. Performance	4.42	0.55	-.30	.45	.11	(*)			
5. Quality	4.47	0.77	-.19	.21	.01	.63	.90		
6. Disconfirmation	3.91	0.78	-.14	.18	.17	.30	.39	.67	
7. Satisfaction	4.28	0.88	-.40	.43	.35	.53	.51	.60	.96

[a]Correlations greater than .25 and .29 in absolute value are significant at the 0.05 and 0.01 levels, respectively. Alpha reliability estimates are shown on the diagonal. (*) = Not intended to be a coherent scale.

quality as a function of the affects, and a model entertaining a direct effect from performance to satisfaction.

These results show that, in accord with Mano and Oliver (1993), both positive and negative affect are a function of the arousal inherent in the service experience. However, the results differ in the present study in that arousal is *negatively* related to negative affect, suggesting that the lack of arousal is a displeasing state. In this context, subjects (i.e., parents) apparently become aroused in anticipation of pleasure—the rehabilitation of their children. Additionally, similar to the results in Oliver (1993a), both positive and negative affect are a function of performance in the predicted direction. Apparently, service consumers do take their affect cues from high and low performance observations.

As expected, quality was also a function of performance ratings. In a second analysis (not hypothesized), the two affects were added to the quality equation. Neither was significant indicating that affect has little relation to the more cognitive quality judgment.

Finally, all predictors of satisfaction were significant in the hypothesized direction when performance was excluded from the regression. Note that the affects contributed to the variance explained despite the fact that two cognitive determinants were also in the equation (disconfirmation and quality). When performance, a third cognitive variable, was added to the satisfaction equation, however, multicollinearity effects were severe. Neither performance, quality, nor positive affect remained significant and satisfaction could be described as a function only of disconfirmation and negative affect.

DISCUSSION

The goal of this study was to provide further evidence of the role and structure of affect in service consumption and to corroborate the combined "two-appraisal" cognitive-affective model of Oliver (1989). Based on prior work, specific hypotheses were proposed and tested. The following discussion focuses, in turn, on the affect structure found in the present study versus that of prior work, the validity of the two-appraisal model in predicting satisfaction, and the relation between quality and satisfaction. Study limitations and future directions round out the discussion.

The Structure of Affect

Prior work (Westbrook 1987; Westbrook and Oliver 1991; Mano and Oliver 1993; Oliver 1993a) has suggested two or three primary affective dimensions underlying consumption. Westbrook

TABLE 3
TSLS Model Results of the Proposed Framework[a]

Dep. Vbl.	Standardized independent variable coefficients						
	Perform.	Arousal	Pos. Affect	Neg. Affect	Quality	Disconf.	R^2
Pos. Affect	.419[b]	.283[a]					.281[b]
Neg. Affect	-.270[a]	-.255[a]					.153[b]
Quality	.634[b]						.402[b]
Quality	.673[b]		-.112	-.037			.410[b]
Satisfaction			.206[a]	-.200[a]	.255[b]	.438[b]	.564[b]
Satisfaction	.170		.153	-.191[a]	.162	.434[b]	.578[b]

[a] $p < .05$, [b] $p < .01$

---

suggested that these may be limited to positive and negative affect whereas Westbrook and Oliver found that arousal may coexist with positive affect and that interest (a low arousal form of affect) may be a third dimension. Later, Oliver found both positive and negative affect dimensions in one sample of respondents and the potential for a third, interest, dimension in a second. In all of these studies, the Izard (1977) DES was used which has no pure arousal elements. In contrast, Mano and Oliver and the present study used the octal representations of Watson et al. (1988). Mano and Oliver found a three-dimensional solution consisting of aroused positive affectivity, negative affectivity, and low arousal; a two dimensional solution showed only the aroused positive and negative factors. The present study supports the separate positive and negative dimensions and, additionally, suggests that arousal may be viewed as a separate third dimension.

Thus, a convergence of findings is beginning to appear suggesting that positive and negative affectivity are the primary dimensions underlying affect in consumption. Moreover, the role of arousal appears to be study-specific. In some samples, it tends to align with positive affect as if to suggest that positive affect is the result (or cause) of such arousal. In others, arousal appears separately, as it did here, or is associated with low arousal states of inactivity or interest. Thus, the role of arousal may be a more interesting phenomenon in consumption, as a research question, than is the valence of affect.

A Two-Appraisal Satisfaction Model

Three studies now exist to provide partial support for a "two-appraisal" representation of the determinants of satisfaction. The two types of appraisal referred to under this interpretation are cognitive judgment, represented here by quality and disconfirmation, and the affect experienced from consumption, represented here by positive and negative affect. Prior to this study, Oliver (1993a) showed satisfaction to be a function of the affects, attribute satisfaction/dissatisfaction (as a proxy for performance), and disconfirmation, and Mano and Oliver (1993) showed satisfaction to be predicted by the affects and utilitarian appraisal (but not hedonic appraisal—which was closely related to affect). Now it is shown that satisfaction is a function of the affects and separate judgments of quality and disconfirmation. In all cases, the affective and cognitive variable sets made significant and independent contributions to satisfaction.

Taken together, the three studies suggest that Oliver's (1989) two-appraisal representation may be a reasonable approach to satisfaction formation. Apparently two mechanisms operate in tandem in consumers' minds, one involving the assessment of functional or comparative outcomes (what the product/service gives me) and one relating to how the product/service influences affect (how the product makes me feel). Oliver did allow for the possibility that cognition influences affect and, in fact, the Oliver (1993a) and Mano and Oliver (1993) findings display such effects. Unfortunately, the quality variable investigated here did not appear to be related to either positive or negative affect.

Quality, Satisfaction, and Affect

Introduction of a direct measure of quality into the satisfaction framework is a recent phenomenon. Previously, Bolton and Drew (1991) provided an indirect (performance-based) quality indicator within a satisfaction framework and showed influences of this quality surrogate on satisfaction. As far as this author is aware, the present study is the first to provide a scaled quality measure that was not performance-attribute based. This measure, which yielded a high alpha reliability of 0.90, was strongly related to satisfaction, although not as strongly as disconfirmation. Moreover, it was more strongly related to performance than any other study variable, indicating that it is a performance-related concept and derives from performance observations as suggested in Oliver (1993b). The data clearly show that it is not affect-based, thus distinguishing quality from satisfaction, which *is* affect-based according to the two-appraisal model. This finding adds support to the quality-influences-satisfaction camp (e.g., Cronin and Taylor 1992) which advocates satisfaction as a superordinate concept to quality.

Future Directions

A number of new research directions are suggested by these results. First, alternative affect schemes beyond those of Izard (1977) and Watson and his colleagues need to be tested to determine if the two and three dimensional interpretations of affect space in service consumption can withstand replication with other theories. Second, much more work on the independent contributions and interplay of affect and cognition in the satisfaction judgment needs to be performed. It appears that the separate contributions of affect and cognition are established; what is missing is evidence on their interaction, causal relationships, and joint dependence on causal agents in satisfaction formation. Thirdly, quality as integral to consumption experience and satisfaction requires greater conceptual and methodological effort if this critical variable is to be properly understood in context. Current writings, particularly in the popular press, assume that quality and satisfaction are isomorphic. It is this author's conclusion that quality is more cognitive and performance-oriented, while satisfaction is a complex summary consumption judgment. More will come of this controversy.

Limitations

Perhaps the greatest limitation of the study beyond the usual caveats regarding static data, small sample restrictions, and measurement error is the possibility that the model as illustrated in the Figure and tested here is mis-specified. It is well-known that alternative model structures will give acceptable fits from the same data set. Of concern to the present study is the temporal ordering of the variables. For example, arousal may be a consequence of affect and not a determinant as suggested in Mano and Oliver (1993), the theoretical source used to frame the present model. Additionally, the observed multicollinearity between performance, quality, and positive affect which attenuated the regression coefficients when all three were resident in the same analysis, suggests that a submodel of effects is operating between the cognitive performance and quality variables and positive affect. Others are advised to thresh out alternative, reasonable interpretations of model structure for testing. This will require samples larger than that used here, especially if multiple indicators are to be employed. Nonetheless, the study findings presented here are offered as early evidence for emerging conceptualizations of affect, quality, and satisfaction in the service area.

ACKNOWLEDGEMENT

Appreciation is expressed to Bob Neydon, Chris Opipari, Mark Stevens, and Terra Travis for their efforts in the design, data collection, and execution of the study. Richard Anton of the Vanderbilt University Medical Center provided valuable assistance in facilitating the sponsorship and conduct of the research. The author also thanks the Center for Services Marketing and the Dean's Fund for Faculty Research of the Owen Graduate School of Management of Vanderbilt University for providing partial support for this project.

REFERENCES

Batra, Rajeev and Olli T. Ahtola (1990), "Measuring the Hedonic and Utilitarian Sources of Consumer Attitudes," *Marketing Letters*, 2 (April), 159-170.

Bitner, Mary Jo (1990), "Evaluating Service Encounters: The Effects of Physical Surroundings and Employee Responses," *Journal of Marketing*, 54 (April), 69-82.

_____, Bernard H. Booms, and Mary Stanfield Tetreault (1990), "The Service Encounter: Diagnosing Favorable and Unfavorable Incidents," *Journal of Marketing*, 54 (January), 71-84.

Bolton, Ruth N. and James H. Drew (1991), "A Multistage Model of Customers' Assessments of Service Quality and Value," *Journal of Consumer Research*, 17 (March), 375-384.

Cadotte, Ernest R., Robert B. Woodruff, and Roger L. Jenkins (1987), "Expectations and Norms in Models of Consumer Satisfaction," *Journal of Marketing Research*, 24 (August), 305-314.

Chattopadhyay, Amitava and Joseph W. Alba (1988), "The Situational Importance of Recall and Inference in Consumer Decision Making," *Journal of Consumer Research*, 15 (June), 1-12.

Cronin, J. Joseph, Jr. and Steven A. Taylor (1992), "Measuring Service Quality: A Reexamination and Extension," *Journal of Marketing*, 56 (July), 55-68.

Garvin, David A. (1984), "What Does `Product Quality' Really Mean?," *Sloan Management Review*, 26 (Fall), 25-43.

Holbrook, Morris B. and Rajeev Batra (1987), "Assessing the Role of Emotions as Mediators of Consumer Responses to Advertising," *Journal of Consumer Research*, 14 (December), 404-421.

Hunt, H. Keith (1977), "CS/D—Overview and Future Research Directions," in *Conceptualization and Measurement of Consumer Satisfaction and Dissatisfaction*, H. Keith Hunt, ed., Cambridge, MA: Marketing Science Institute, 455-488.

Izard, Carroll E. (1977), *Human Emotions*, New York: Plenum Press.

Larsen, Randy J. and Edward Diener (1992), "Promises and Problems With the Circumplex Model of Emotion," in *Review of Personality and Social Psychology*, Vol. 13, Margaret S. Clark, ed. Newbury Park, CA: Sage, 25-59.

Lewis, Michael, Margaret Wolan Sullivan, and Linda Michalson (1984), "The Cognitive-Emotional Fugue," in *Emotions, Cognition, and Behavior*, Carroll E. Izard, Jerome Kagan, and Robert B. Zajonc, eds. Cambridge: Cambridge University Press, 264-288.

Mano, Haim (1991), "The Structure and Intensity of Emotional Experiences: Method and Context Convergence," *Multivariate Behavioral Research*, 26 (No. 3), 389-411.

_____ and Richard L. Oliver (1993), "Assessing the Dimensionality and Structure of Consumption Experience: Evaluation, Feeling, and Satisfaction," *Journal of Consumer Research*, 20 (December), forthcoming.

Oliver, Richard L. (1980), "A Cognitive Model of the Antecedents and Consequences of Satisfaction Decisions," *Journal of Marketing Research*, 17 (November), 460-469.

_____ (1992), "An Investigation of the Attribute Basis of Emotion and Related Affects in Consumption: Suggestions for a Stage-Specific Satisfaction Framework," in *Advances in Consumer Research*, Vol. 19, eds., John F. Sherry, Jr. and Brian Sternthal, Provo, UT: Association for Consumer Research, 237-244.

_____ (1993a), "Cognitive, Affective, and Attribute Bases of the Satisfaction Response," *Journal of Consumer Research*, 20 (December), forthcoming.

_____ (1993b), "A Conceptual Model of Service Quality and Service Satisfaction: Compatible Goals, Different Concepts," in Teresa A. Swartz, David E. Bowen, and Stephen W. Brown (eds.), *Advances in Services Marketing and Management: Research and Practice*, Vol. 2, Greenwich, CT: JAI Press, 65-85.

_____ and William O. Bearden (1985), "Disconfirmation Processes and Consumer Evaluations in Product Usage," *Journal of Business Research*, 13 (June), 235-246.

_____ and John E. Swan (1989), "Equity and Disconfirmation Perceptions as Influences on Merchant and Product Satisfaction," *Journal of Consumer Research*, 16 (December), 372-383.

_____ and Robert A. Westbrook (1993), "Profiles of Consumer Emotions and Satisfaction in Ownership and Usage," *Journal of Consumer Satisfaction, Dissatisfaction and Complaining Behavior*, 6, forthcoming.

Reynolds, Thomas J. and Jonathan Gutman (1988), "Laddering Theory, Method, Analysis, and Interpretation," *Journal of Advertising Research*, 28 (February/March), 11-31.

Steenkamp, Jan-Benedict E. M. (1990), "Conceptual Model of the Quality Perception Process," *Journal of Business Research*, 21 (December), 309-333.

Swartz, Teresa A. and Stephen W. Brown (1989), "Consumer and Provider Expectations and Experiences in Evaluating Professional Service Quality," *Journal of the Academy of Marketing Science*, 17 (Spring), 189-195.

Watson, David, Lee Anna Clark, and Auke Tellegen (1988), "Development and Validation of Brief Measures of Positive and Negative Affect: The PANAS Scales," *Journal of Personality and Social Psychology*, 54 (June), 1063-1070.

Weiner, Bernard, Dan Russell, and David Lerman (1979), "The Cognition-Emotion Process in Achievement-Related Contexts," *Journal of Personality and Social Psychology*, 37 (July), 1211-1220.

Westbrook, Robert A. (1987), "Product/Consumption-Based Affective Responses and Postpurchase Processes," *Journal of Marketing Research*, 24 (August), 258-270.

_____ and Richard L. Oliver (1991), "The Dimensionality of Consumption Emotion Patterns and Consumer Satisfaction," *Journal of Consumer Research*, 18 (June), 84-91.

Zeithaml, Valarie A. (1988), "Consumer Perceptions of Price, Quality, and Value: A Means-End Model and Synthesis of Evidence," *Journal of Marketing*, 52 (July), 2-22.

_____ , Leonard L. Berry, and A. Parasuraman (1993), "The Nature and Determinants of Customer Expectations of Service," *Journal of the Academy of Marketing Science*, 21 (Winter), 1-12.

Session Summary
The Proof of the Pudding is in the Eating: The Role of Product Experience in Consumer Decision Making

Goutam Chakraborty, Oklahoma State University
Alice Wright, California State University

Advertising and product experience are two important ways consumers obtain information about product benefits. Although there is a vast body of research on the role of advertising in consumer decision making, in recent years, interest in research about the role of product experience has intensified. These researchers have investigated the role of product experience from diverse perspectives. This special session brought together researchers studying how product experience influences consumer decision making.

The first paper by Wright and Lutz investigated the role of product experience (trial) in the context of a new product introduction. The authors focused on how the medium of information (Ad, Trial, Ad+Trial and Trial+Ad) "framed" consumers' choice criteria by systematically altering attention and the types of attributes that consumers deemed important during the choice process. Using a candy bar, the authors found that proportionally more search attribute (e.g., price) cognitive responses were mentioned for Ad exposure than Trial, while proportionally more experience attribute (e.g., taste) cognitive responses were mentioned for Trial than Ad. Similar results were found when subjects in a second experiment were asked to list important attributes of a stationary bike. In addition, in the experiment using the candy bar, Ad+Trial led to more important search attributes being elicited, while Trial+Ad led to the elicitation of more important experience attributes.

The second paper by Chakraborty looked at how consumers' evaluations of product attributes are jointly influenced by different types of product experience and direct or indirect claims (through inference) in an ad. The author argued that different types of product experience (shopping or consumption) provide either direct or indirect information about product attributes such as fat-content or flavor. The author reported data from an experiment using real product experience with two brands of electronic typewriters and TV ads. Results indicated that the ad was effective in changing consumers' evaluation of the advertised brand about an attribute when either a direct or indirect claim was made concerning the attribute in the ad and when product experience provided only indirect information concerning that attribute. Results also indicated that, in general, the ad was more effective in the "ad-before" than the "ad-after" experience sequence. However, when a direct claim was made concerning an attribute in the ad and experience provided only indirect information about that attribute, the ad was equally effective in the "ad-before" and "ad-after" experience sequence.

In the first two papers, the focus was on combining information from multiple sources (product experience and ad); the third paper by Gaeth, Levin, Sood, Juang and Castellucci dealt with combining information from multiple product experiences. The authors focused on situations involving mixed product experiences characterized by a product failure followed by a success experience. They reported results from two studies - one using written scenario descriptions of product and service experience and the other using "hands-on" experience with a personal word processor. Results indicated a "rebound effect;" that is, consumers recovered from the failure experience completely after they had the success experience with the same product. This recovery was complete for the more "cognitive" measures such as product quality but not for "emotionally" related feelings such as frustration with the product.

The session discussant, John Deighton, highlighted the commonalties in the three papers and provided insightful comments with respect to each paper. He then presented his thoughts about future research based on an integrative framework having two dimensions - the "salience" and "relevance" of product experience with respect to the claims in an ad.

Decision Difficulty and Uncertain Preferences: Implications for Consumer Choice

Ravi Dhar, Yale University

Most conceptions of rational decision making assume that individual preferences are well defined. This viewpoint of consumers' decision making is inconsistent with the emerging consensus among consumer decision researchers that preferences are often *fuzzy, unstable, and inconsistent*. Consumers are depicted as *constructing* and expressing rankings with respect to possibilities that they have actually considered. An implicit assumption of constructive preferences is that the choice among different alternatives based solely on attribute tradeoffs may be difficult. Decision difficulty does not play a role in normative theory (e.g., MAUT) since it assumes that prior to choice, the decision maker assesses the utility of each possible outcome on each of several dimensions to arrive at the overall attractiveness. In contrast to this view, consumers often arrive at choice situations with no clear idea of their preferences and often find it difficult to face multiple options without becoming confused. Often one does not know which of the two things one wants more, while not being certain that one wants them equally.

Most of the previous research examines difficult decisions within a cost-benefit framework trading off effort and accuracy. The neglected role of *constructive preferences* in creating decision difficulty raises interesting questions. There may be broad classes of problems that cause us difficulty in decision making and are the focus of the present session. One set of problem depends on the *complexity* of the choice situation. Complexity is influenced both by the number of alternatives and the number of attributes used to describe each alternative. A second source of difficulty arises when the choice situation creates emotional stress that may threaten values that are important to us. In such circumstances, the process of decision making is prone to various distortions and errors that can act as powerful barriers to rational thought.

The four papers in the session differ in their degree of process-outcome orientation: the first two papers (Johnson and Shafir; Bettman, Luce, and Payne) make substantive contribution to the *process* by which difficult choices are made. The first paper questions the normative models of economic choice that assume that more choice is better for the individual. They explore situations in which increasing the number of alternatives or features results in decreasing the quality of the choice. They argue that increasing the number of features used in describing an alternative may increase the number of reasons for or against switching. The authors conduct a series of experiments in order to specify both the causes, specific effects, and mediating processes that surround the changes in choice as the number of alternatives that are considered change.

The second paper examines how stress or task related emotional factors influence the manner in which information is processed, an under researched area and shows how its understanding can broaden the impact of decision theory on consumer behavior. The authors propose and test a framework for understanding these effects using mouselab. The results indicate that subjects in the high emotion condition tend to process information both more extensively and by attribute. The studies demonstrate that emotions may alter decision processing by priming coping goals and increasing errors in executing the strategy selected.

The latter two papers are concerned with the outcomes of the choice process (Heath and Puri; Dhar and Prelec). The third paper examines the role of complexity of alternatives on decision instability. The authors propose that the choice process can be viewed as one of sampling relevant information and aggregating that information into a decision. Thus, a choice emerges if the above process results in a stable intention (Montgomery 1983). Two studies that examine the effect of cues on the sampling and the aggregation process are conducted. They find that manipulating both the sampling or the aggregation stage influences the instability of the decision for difficult choice.

The fourth paper examines the role of context in choosing among choice sets or "menus" from which a single item is later selected. The authors question the assumption of rational choice that states that consumer preference among menus is influenced solely by the "utility" of the most preferred item in the menu. The authors show that adding options that are irrelevant may affect the choice among menus when preferences are uncertain. Several potential explanations underlying the observed results are examined.

When taken as a group, the papers in the session should help to highlight some of the promising avenues that are emerging in this important area of research.

In-Laws and Outlaws: The Impact of Divorce and Remarriage Upon Christmas Gift Exchange

Cele Otnes, University of Illinois at Urbana-Champaign
Kyle Zolner, University of Illinois at Urbana-Champaign
Tina M. Lowrey, Rider College

ABSTRACT

While many issues pertaining to gift exchange have been explored, none take into account the changing nature of the American family. Because Christmas giving typically involves immediate and extended family, the high divorce and remarriage rates in America should affect the nature and extent of gift exchange during this holiday. The purpose of this paper is to begin exploring how divorce and remarriage influence gift exchange, by examining givers' motivations when selecting gifts for recipients affected by these changes. We interpret our findings, and offer suggestions for further study.

INTRODUCTION

In recent years, many researchers have noted the inadequacy of the existing "family life cycle" models (c.f., Lansing and Kish 1957; Rich and Jain 1968) to explain patterns of household consumption. Authors including Andreasen (1984) Fellerman and Debevec (1992) and McAlexander (1991) have noted that the growing number of nontraditional households means the influence of status changes such as divorce and remarriage upon consumption patterns must be recognized. Indeed, Glick (1984) notes that in the United States, one half of all first marriages and 60% of all second marriages end in divorce. Nevertheless, "three fourths of all young divorced persons are likely to remarry" (Glick, 1984, p. 7).

For a number of reasons, the issue of how divorce and remarriage affects purchasing patterns is especially salient for researchers interested in gift exchange. Such issues as the amount of income available for gifts (Gerstel 1988), and the ways in which gift-selection tasks are delegated may be different than in intact families. Furthermore, the rates of divorce and remarriage in the U.S.–and the likelihood of consumers being affected by these activities–means their lists of potential Christmas gift recipients may be quite transient.

Likewise, Sherry (1983) notes that such factors as role structure and role incumbency can influence gift exchange within a dyad. Moreover, Otnes, Lowrey and Kim (1993) argue that the study of how roles and motivations affect gift exchange over the life cycle is a worthwhile endeavor. This issue becomes especially important, as one of the functions of gift exchange has been to serve as an agent of social cohesion within the family and community (Cheal 1987). Given the recent changes in the composition of American households, it is worth studying whether gifts still fulfill this purpose in American society.

Thus, our purpose is to begin exploring the issue of how divorce and remarriage influence Christmas gift exchange. Christmas was chosen because it is the occasion during which givers are most likely to include members of their immediate and extended families on their gift lists. As such, the following research questions will be explored:

1. How is the actual list of Christmas gift recipients affected by divorce and/or remarriage?

2. What direct or indirect motivations emerge when givers engage in Christmas gift exchange with divorced or remarried recipients?

METHOD

The data for this study were collected as part of a more general study of gift exchange, and were acquired in two stages. In Stage I, fifteen informants were recruited from a university paper and a local paper in a Midwestern city (pop. 100,000). Fourteen of the informants were middle-class women and one was a white middle-class male. Informants' ages ranged from the early twenties to the late forties. Students were requested not to answer the ads. During November and December 1990, we conducted two in-depth interviews with each informant, and accompanied them on two Christmas shopping trips.

Interviews lasted about an hour and shopping trips ranged from one to two hours in length. Informants chose the sites for shopping trips; these included discount stores, department stores, drugstores and a variety of specialty shops. Interviews were taped and transcribed, and extensive field notes were created after the shopping trips. An incentive of $30 was offered for participation.

Although we did not specifically set out to examine the influence of divorce and remarriage upon gift exchange, the high incidence of relationships characterized by these status changes meant that the topic was worthy of study. Given the transient nature of the American family, we believed incorporating a longitudinal component into our research design would prove rewarding when examining how gift exchange was affected by divorce and/or remarriage. Thus, in Stage II, we asked five of our original informants to participate in a follow-up study during the 1992 Christmas season. All five of these informants were directly or indirectly affected by divorce or remarriage (e.g., either participants in these activities or closely related to a participant). The same research procedures were followed. When combined, both studies resulted in the generation of over 800 pages of text. A more complete description of our informants can be found in Otnes, Lowrey and Kim (1993).

Our data analysis procedure was qualitative. That is, we sought to identify themes or patterns in the text. The first and second authors arrived at our final understanding of the text through an iterative process of interpretation and negotiation. Moreover, the third author–who was not involved in the initial discovery and interpretation of the text for this particular topic–acted as auditor of both the text and of our final interpretation.

FINDINGS

How is the Actual List of Recipients Affected by Divorce and/or Remarriage?

Nine of our original fifteen informants appeared to be involved in gift exchange dyads affected by divorce and/or remarriage. Table 1 lists these recipients, and the overall strategies used by our givers for each. While some recipients were added to the gift list through remarriage in the family, still others were removed, typically after a divorce. Recipients were "lost" after the termination of a marriage and one child was removed because of fights over visitation.

The remaining recipients–typically our informants' own parents and/or children–had been present on Christmas lists prior to divorce or remarriage. However, these status changes had caused

TABLE 1
Summary of Dyads Affected by Divorce and/or Remarriage

Informant	Recipient(s) Affected By Status Change	Type of Status Change Affecting	Informant's Motivation For Giving
Anne	Fiance	Divorce	Compensating
	Fiance's young daughter	Divorce	Assimilating
	Fiance's older	Divorce	Avoidance
	Fiance Ex-wife #1	Divorce	Avoidance
	Fiance Ex-wife #2	Acknowledging	
	New step-nephew	Divorce	Assimilating
	Sister's ex-husband	Divorce	Avoidance
	Sister's children (2)	Divorce	Compensating
Betsy	Father's new wife	Remarriage	Acknowledging
	Sister	Remarriage	Acknowledging
	Sister's stepsons(2)	Remarriage	Assimilating
	Grandmother's husband	Remarriage	Assimilating
Hannah	Father	Divorce	Healing
	Mother	Divorce	Compensating
Jane	Ex-husband	Divorce	Acknowledging
	Husband's new wife	Remarriage	Acknowledging
	Daughter	Divorce	Compensating
	Son	Divorce	Simplifying
	Self	Divorce	Compensating
Karen	Fiance	Divorce	Compensating
	Mother's husband	Remarriage	Acknowledging
Kathy	Mother	Divorce	Compensating
	Father	Divorce	Acknowledging
Laura	Brother	Remarriage	Compensating/Avoiding
	Brother's New Wife	Remarriage	Avoiding*
Rebecca	Ex-husband	Divorce	Avoiding
	Ex-in-laws (3)	Divorce	Avoiding
Rhonda	Stepson	Remarriage	Assimilating

*In this family, single siblings receive gifts, but this activity ceases when they marry. Laura's brother was compensated for his lack of a partner until 1992, when he remarried his ex-wife.

these recipients' relationships with informants to be significantly altered. For example, after many of our informants' parents divorced and/or remarried, the results of these actions changed the roles the giver wished to portray through Christmas gift exchange.

Thus, the impact of divorce and/or remarriage was felt across a wide variety of giver/recipient relationships at Christmas. We now discuss the motivations that emerged, as givers engaged in exchange with recipients affected by these status changes.

Motivations For Exchange

We observed the motivations expressed by givers to those affected by divorce and/or remarriage could be positive, neutral or negative. Positive motivations were designed to *enhance* the relationship between giver and recipient, neutral motives were designed to *maintain* the status quo within the dyad and negative motivations served to actually hinder or *destroy* bonds between the giver and recipient. These categories will now be discussed.

Positive Motivations. Although divorce and remarriage can often result in negative emotions, we nevertheless observed that givers often attempt to express positive motivations when exchanging gifts in a dyad affected by divorce and/or remarriage. Three positive motivations were evident.

Compensation. The motivation for gift-giving in order to somehow "make up" for a loss experienced by the recipient has been observed in other studies (Otnes, Lowrey, and Kim, 1993; Wolfinbarger, 1990). In our study, we observed that compensation emerged for various reasons. For example, some givers feel compelled to make up material losses experienced by a recipient following a divorce. Anne described her fiance as follows:

He's been married and divorced twice. He's practically, in a sense, lost everything that he's had...so I kind of feel like...I want to give him everything that he's always wanted.

That year, Anne showered her fiance with gifts such as a $500 leather trench coat, clothes, toy trucks and a statuette. Through such extravagant gifts, she admittedly attempted to make reparation for material losses experienced through his divorces.

The removal of a spouse from the home can also result in compensation strategies for the children involved. For example, Jane displayed compensation in her gift-giving for her daughter. Jane's ex-husband Bob has custody of their son, while Jane has custody of her daughter. In 1990, Bob was taking "taking their son skiing this year and [he] was going to get all sorts of ski stuff." Jane's compensation to her daughter for this trip was evident through her remark that she was going to buy her daughter "all this stuff," and was going to buy her son "only one game." In 1992, Jane also took her daughter skiing for Christmas, since Bob had taken her son skiing in prior years.

Sometimes divorces can result in a lack of resources or the loss of a previous gift-giving relationship. Without a husband to give her a Christmas present, Jane considered getting herself "something special." We interpret that this type of self-gift (Mick and DeMoss 1990) is compensation for the loss of a significant other with whom to engage in Christmas gift-giving. Furthermore, Jane worried that the lack of presents under the tree might make her young daughter wonder why Santa "forgot" Jane that year:

J: See, I've always bought for myself before so that there'd be presents from Santa.
I: So Santa, that was the reason in the past?
J: Yeah.
I: When you were married, you didn't do that?
J: No.
I: Are you going to wrap it up and everything for yourself?
J: Yeah, probably, so there'll be more under the tree.

Assimilation. Our informants often seemed intent upon using gift exchange to assimilate new relatives acquired through remarriage in the family. The essence of assimilation is that it focused around the giver attempting to enfold new people into the family. This form of gift-giving can be seen as a ritual act of sociability that reinforces group cohesiveness (Johnson 1988). We also observed that recipients could be described as being in various stages of the assimilation process.

For example, Anne is undergoing the first stage of assimilation with Kelley, her fiance's second wife and mother of Connie. The two women have slowly developed a relationship over the past two years. In 1991, Kelley gave Anne and her fiance a Christmas present. This act impressed Anne so much that in 1992, she bought Kelley a nice Christmas present. In this situation, gift-giving has been used to foster goodwill and serve as a symbol between Anne and Kelley that they can co-exist peacefully in the same family.

Various stage of assimilation were displayed when our informants selected gifts for stepchildren. In Anne's case, her sister's stepson was in the first stage. Anne's sister and her husband were denied custody, and Anne was "just getting reacquainted with him" after he turned 18. The hat, gloves, and scarf Anne gave him helped assimilate him into the family.

While Anne's unfamiliarity with her stepson made gift selection a bit difficult, Betsy's and Rhonda's efforts gift selection for stepchildren in the family could be described as routinized. Betsy's sister's stepsons had been part of the family for years, and her gifts to them merely reinforced their successful assimilation. Likewise, the fact Rhonda secured a list from her stepson when purchasing his gifts–and even bought him "gag" gifts–indicates she clearly regards him as "family".

Healing. Divorce and remarriage can often cause rifts within families. Interestingly, gift-giving can be partially responsible for the healing of past wounds. These wounds can be caused by past gift-giving errors or blunders, resulting from the frustration and confusion that divorce can bring to a family. As later gift-giving situations arise, they can become a forum for the repetition of past mistakes, or for the attempt to eradicate these mistakes through improved giving. As such, the actual exchange situation can be a microcosm of the status of the post-divorce relationship as a whole.

Hannah's parents were divorced when she was 13 and her father now lives in another state. Hannah reported in 1990 that she would select "something small" for her father. Indeed, that year she actually chose something for him that *she* collected. Later we learned one of the reasons Hannah apparently put little thought into his gift was because he had consistently "missed the mark" at Christmas and selected things she could not or did not enjoy (e.g. a wool rug that she was allergic to; a bound volume of an author she disliked).

However, in 1992, Hannah reported that the past Christmas, her father had actually had selected something she actually wanted:

Last year he got me this big humongous book which astounded me because my Dad is kind of cheap... He so thrilled me because it wasn't something I specifically asked for and he actually thought about what I might like... I mean I got this and was absolutely thrilled to death.

This gift from Hannah's father clearly seemed to result in a great improvement in their relationship. Hannah noted that "they had not had an argument in over three months and she had even called him [the prior] week (she usually only called at holidays or birthdays)." In fact, for the first time, Hannah anticipated Christmas being "nicer" because of their improved relations. Furthermore, the fact she was actually making a photo collage for her father indicated their relationship was on the mend:

Hannah and her mother had found some frames around the house and were planning to put together collages...with pictures that they had of family and events which would take some time to finish. Hannah said that her father had been very good lately and this was a way of saying "you are still considered family."

Thus, the process involved in Christmas gift-giving can be symbolic of greater rifts that result from divorce. Yet in Hannah's case, gift-giving both exacerbated the problem with her father and served as a vehicle for healing that problematic relationship.

Neutral Motivations

Acknowledgement. Otnes, Lowrey and Kim (1993) observed that Christmas givers often play the role of Acknowledger "to mutually commemorate the existence of relatively superficial social ties between giver and recipient." We observed this role to be most common when our informants offered gifts to recipients who had become "family" through remarriage. Because many recipients were "new" to the family or relatively unfamiliar to our informants, gift selection for them was often problematic. For example, Karen noted that she did not know her stepfather well:

He married my Mom after I moved out. I like the guy, but he's my Mom's husband...and it's sort of like, after a certain amount of flannel shirts and tools...I just don't know what the man wants.

Likewise, Cindy observed, "My stepmom, it's really hard to shop for her. A lot of things I like, she doesn't like." Thus, we interpret one motivation for acknowledgment to stem from the desire to present mere tokens designed to recognize the status of the recipient as a family member.

Interestingly, we also observed givers acknowledging recipients when engaged in reciprocal gift exchange relationships with ex-spouses. For example, Jane mentioned her ex-husband and new wife often got her a gift "from the kids." Likewise, in 1992, she selected a gift of comedy tickets "from the kids" for them. That these gifts are meant as tokens of acknowledgement is evident by the fact neither party was overly concerned these gifts actually pleased the recipient. Rather, Jane chose the tickets because they were something she liked, and discussed how she believed the gifts she received were selected:

J: I think [last year they got her] a heart-shaped thing that smells good that you hang up in the bathroom...That's what they always get me...
I: Is this something you like or something they are into?
J: I think that they're into that.
I: More than you are?
J: Yeah (laughs)

Thus, gifts may be exchanged among ex-spouses for the purposes of acknowledging their role in helping raise children–or possibly to appease the children during the holiday time. This type of acknowledgment supports Gerstel's (1988) statement that "it is parenthood more than marriage that draws together generations of adults" (p. 20). However, these gifts are seldom designed to appeal to the self-concept of the recipient (Belk 1979).

While acknowledgement is typically a "neutral" gift-giving motivation, its existence may also signify a strain in a relationship affected by remarriage. For example, Betsy described the rift between her and her sister, that had developed because her sister refused to attend any family functions if her father's new wife was present:

It's a real problem...And she blames Dad for it, and she blames me for it, and she says that if I would have never let her come to my house, it wouldn't be that way...The worst part is, it's the kids that are gonna get hurt. My kids are being pushed out of her life...And it really, really hurts.

Betsy's unhappiness at her sister's behavior was reflected in the way her Christmas gift selection had changed. In 1990, Betsy described how she loved seeking out unique gifts for her sister. But in 1992, the rift had become so deep that "It's almost like I want to get it over with. Be done with it."

Thus, while the circumstances leading to the acknowledgment in Betsy's case were negative, the fact Betsy was not totally willing to eliminate her sister from her gift list meant that she was attempting to maintain *some* relationship with her.

In summary, we interpret that acknowledgement could stem from one of three motivations in dyads affected by divorce and/or remarriage: 1) presentation of a token recognizing the existence of new family members; 2) serving to recognize the parenting role of an ex-spouse or 3) signify that a relationship had somehow soured because of a remarriage in the family.

Distancing. We also observed that Rebecca had eliminated most, if not all, of the relatives she acquired when married to her ex-husband. However, her son continued to buy gifts for his father, father's sister, and father's parents. Interestingly, all of Rebecca's recipients received gifts from her and her son as a "family thing." Thus, the fact her son selected some gifts for "his" relatives clearly indicated Rebecca no longer considered them to be her family.

Negative Motivations

Even in the best situations, divorce and remarriage are disruptive to families. Thus, it is not surprising some negative emotions were experienced by givers whose relationships with certain recipients were affected by changes in marital status.

Avoidance. It was clear one motive behind the *lack* of gift exchange was our informants' desire to distance themselves from certain recipients. For example, in 1990, Anne had given her fiance's oldest daughter several Christmas gifts. However, by 1992, the relationship between her fiance and this daughter had greatly deteriorated, so much so that Anne reported:

[The daughter] doesn't think of him as a father and always looks at him out of the corner of her eye like, "Maybe all those nasty things my mom told me really are true..." She's already said flat out that she wants nothing more than for him to give her up for adoption.

As a result, Anne had chosen not to give this daughter any gifts in 1992, while at the same time clearly striving to assimilate her fiance's youngest daughter into her new family.

Simplification. We also observed one motivation that apparently was *not* intended to have negative consequences, but its effect upon recipients was often quite devastating. This motivation was one of simplification, in which divorced parents attempted to somehow divide up the gift-giving tasks for their children among themselves. Berman and Turk (1981) note divorced people are often overwhelmed, expressing feelings of "not having enough time to do everything, and of not knowing what to do or how to do it" (p. 180). Clearly, the strategy of simplification was meant to relieve some of the duties during the busy Christmas season. However, in both cases where simplification was attempted, the effect on the children of divorced parents was quite traumatic.

For example, Jane and her husband had split custody of their children–with their daughter living with Jane and their son living with her ex-husband. In addition to practicing compensation for her daughter, Jane also mistakenly assumed she could buy her son only a few presents, since her ex-husband would buy "his big Christmas." However, when Jane's son learned of this plan, she reported:

He just got real sad...and he had tears coming down his face. And when I asked him what was wrong, he said he just couldn't believe I was only going to get him two presents. He said, "You always get my big Christmas." And at first I said, "Well, Dad's only getting [her daughter] one present. And he said, "My Dad's got her several presents...." But he was so sad because he always expects his big Christmas here.

Eventually abandoning her attempt at simplifying gift exchange in 1990, Jane also reported in 1992 she now spent $150 on each child for Christmas gifts.

We also observed that when simplification *was* actually carried out, the consequences could be dire. Hannah described her most traumatic Christmas at age 13, the year her parents divorced:

[Her Dad] walks into the house with these gifts that are humongous, and I said "Who are those for?"...Well, they were not for me. My sister got a new robe, she got jogging shoes, she got a set of cookware...And I got an Andy Gibb album and a picture of my father, and if I wasn't going to put it up, he took the frame back...I went into my bedroom and just cried and cried and cried...And [my Mom said to Dad] "I thought you could have made some effort." And he says, "Well, I thought I'd buy for [Hannah's sister] and you'd buy for Hannah."

While this strategy was no doubt meant to ease parents' logistical and financial burdens of buying for children in two households at Christmas, simplification often had more potentially harmful side effects than any other motivation emerging from our text.

SUMMARY AND CONCLUSIONS

Our study reveals that many of our informants' gift-giving relationships were affected by divorce and/or remarriage. Furthermore, we discovered the motives for exchange with recipients affected by these changes can be positive, neutral or negative. Specifically, the positive motivations we observed were compensation, assimilation and healing; the neutral motivations were acknowledgment and distancing and the negative motivations were avoidance and simplification (which has unintended negative consequences). One might expect gift exchange to be a mechanism by which new family members are recognized. Yet our study also reveals that Christmas gift exchange is also used as a "bridge" between ex-spouses–as well as a means of acknowledging the existence of new spouses of ex-spouses.

Furthermore, our study reveals some gift exchange is clearly used as an attempt to signal to children that relationships between parents in general, and the holidays in particular, are as normal as possible, given the circumstances of divorce and/or remarriage. Finally, it is not too surprising that since changes in marital status often result in trauma for some family members, some negative motivations for Christmas gift exchange surfaced in our study as well.

Given our findings–and given the sizeable number of Christmas gift relationships undoubtedly influenced by divorce and/or remarriage in American culture–it becomes imperative to view gift exchange within the family as a dynamic phenomenon. It is important to realize that even within the same dyad, gift exchange behavior is not necessarily stable over time. Indeed, our paper reinforces the importance of taking into account changes in family status in order to truly understand how gift exchange varies over the life course. Furthermore, the influence of other changes in the lifespan *besides* those related to marital status–e.g., the presence or absence of children in the home; changes in occupational status such as women entering or leaving the workforce–upon gift exchange should also be explored. Such issues may require more innovative and demanding methods of study, such as longitudinal work or the focus upon one family as a case study in changes over the life cycle. However, it is important that research in the area of gift exchange begin to reflect the complexity that is characteristic of American society.

Thus, future research could examine such topics as how gift exchange patterns evolve for dyads across even greater spans of time, and exactly *what* changes in the lifespan contribute to this evolution. Although this paper is exploratory and employs a relatively homogenous sample, hopefully it will lead to greater interest in the topic of how marital status and other changes affect gift-giving behavior across the lifespan.

All informant names have been changed to protect anonymity.

REFERENCES

Andreasen, Alan R., "Life Status Changes and Changes in Consumer Preferences and Satisfaction," *Journal of Consumer Research* 11 (December), 784-794.

Belk, Russell W. (1979), "Gift-Giving Behavior," in *Research in Marketing*, Vol. 2, ed. Jagdish Sheth, Greenwich, CT: JAI Press, 95-126.

Berman, William H. and Dennis C. Turk (1981), "Adaptation to Divorce: Problems and Coping Strategies," *Journal of Marriage and the Family*, 43 (February), 179-189.

Cheal, David (1987), "The Social Dimensions of Gift Behavior," *Journal of Social and Personal Relationships* 3, 423-439.

Fellerman, Rita and Kathleen Debevec, "Till Death Do We Part: Family Dissolution, Transition and Consumer Behavior," in *Advances in Consumer Research*, vol. 19, eds. John F. Sherry, Jr. and Brian Sternthal, 514-521.

Gerstel, Naomi (1988), "Divorce and Kin Ties," *Journal of Marriage and the Family*, 50 (February), 209-219.

Glick, Paul (1984), "Marriage, Divorce, and Living Arrangements," *Journal of Family Issues*, 5 (March), 7-26.

Johnson, Colleen Leahy (1988), "Socially Controlled Civility: The Functioning of Rituals in the Divorce Process," *American Behavioral Scientist*, 6 (July/August), 685-701.

Lansing, John B. and Leslie Kish (1957), "Family Life Cycle as an Independent Variable," *American Sociological Review*, 22, 512-519.

McAlexander, James H., "Divorce, the Disposition of the Relationship, and Everything," *Advances in Consumer Research*, vol. 18, eds. Rebecca Holman and Michael J. Solomon, 43-48.

Mick, David Glen and Michelle DeMoss (1990), "Self-Gifts: Phenomenological Insights from Four Contexts," *Journal of Consumer Research* 17 (December), 322-332.

Otnes, Cele, Tina M. Lowrey and Young Chan Kim (1993), "Gift Selection for 'Easy' and 'Difficult' Recipients: A Social Roles Interpretation," *Journal of Consumer Research*, September, forthcoming.

Rich, Stuart U. and Subhash C. Jain (1968), "Social Class and Life Cycle as Predictors of Shopping Behavior," *Journal of Marketing Research*, 5, 41-49.

Wolfinbarger, Mary Finley (1990), "Motivations and Symbolism in Gift-Giving Behavior," in *Advances in Consumer Research*, Vol. 17, ed. Marvin Goldberg, Gerald Gorn and Richard Pollay, Provo, UT: Association for Consumer Research, 690-698.

Keeping the Family Together: How We Survived the Divorce

Myra Jo Bates, University of Nebraska-Lincoln
James W. Gentry, University of Nebraska-Lincoln

ABSTRACT

Stem families have received very little attention in consumer research, though they constitute one of the fastest growing household types. A phenomenological study of stem families was undertaken, with the following themes being found: increased importance of kinship networks (including in-laws) in socialization and family processes; increased influence of offspring in decision processes as they are given "adult status" earlier; and a sense of family both in trying to maintain continuity with the original nuclear family and in developing a new identity for the stem family.

INTRODUCTION

Consumer research has focused little attention on single-parent households; Ajhuba and Stinson (1993) found five Marketing studies on the subject, indicating a gap in the literature. The growing number of single-parent households in the U.S. suggests a need for exploration of this topic. The purpose of this paper is to examine the themes discovered in a study of divorced mothers and to describe consumption-oriented ways in which they maintained a feeling of belongingness (family connectedness) with their children during the separation and divorce process. Factors relevant from a consumer behavior viewpoint include changes in consumption patterns, changes in consumer decision processes linked to the divorce process, family member role transformations, and altered standards of living.

BACKGROUND

The U.S. divorce rate is creating stem family households at an unprecedented pace[1]. In 1992, nearly 1.2 million couples divorced. Of ever-married Americans, approximately 26% have divorced at some time, and about one-third of the civil cases in the U.S. Court System deal with family relations (DeWitt 1992). It is estimated that two-thirds of first marriages will end in divorce (Martin and Bumpass 1989). From 1960 to 1990, the proportion of children, at any given time, living in stem families rose from 9% to 25%; thus a majority of all children will spend some part of their childhood with an absent parent.

The percentage of single-parent households (the Census Bureau term) increased from 5.5% in 1970 to 9.3% in 1990. Divorce is a process affecting all family members (Bohannan 1970), and the presence of children may well complicate the parental transition from being married to being single. During the divorce process, custodial parents need to emphasize a feeling of family for their children as they make the transition from nuclear family to stem family.

The work of McAlexander, Schouten, and Roberts (1993) is very insightful in terms of consumption and de-acquisition processes associated with divorce, but it focuses on the divorcing couple and omits the children. With an average of one child per divorcing couple (London and Wilson 1988), we assert that the McAlexander, Schouten, and Roberts (1993) study comprises only part of the phenomenon as actually observed in our society.

---

[1] We will use "stem family" in lieu of single-parent family reflecting the fact that, while there may be only one parent in the household, there is another who may influence the child(ren).

METHOD

Previous divorce research shows the importance of qualitative methods for discovering the intricacies of the divorce process (Buehler 1987; Kitson, Babri, and Roach 1985; Kitson and Raschke 1981; McAlexander, Schouten, and Roberts 1993). In order to identify themes used by parents to aid children in coping with divorce, we organized a phenomenological study of divorce and how parents reassure and help their children realize that they still are a family, albeit a changed family. Use of the phenomenological method has been successful in past studies for eliciting ideas relevant to the subject of interest (Thompson, Locander, and Pollio 1990).

The Sample: Fourteen divorced, custodial mothers, were interviewed. These interviewees, located through the personal networks of the authors, reside in three medium-sized Eastern Nebraska and Western Iowa cities. A diverse set of respondents was used to obtain as wide a range of circumstances as possible, resulting in a wide age range for the mothers and their children. Of the 14 mothers, 11 have been married and divorced once; two are currently remarried and 12 are still divorced; one has had three marriages, and another has had two marriages, both resulting in divorce. Two mothers are graduate students; one is of retirement age and has never worked outside the home; 13 are in the workforce; three are grandmothers. The children's ages range from four to 42. Marriage duration was from six to 44 years, with the modal range being nine and 16 years.

The common factor qualifying a respondent was custody of the children. The incidence of divorcing fathers gaining custody of their children is increasing as, in 1990, 14% of fathers and custody, up from 10% in 1980 (Bernstein 1992). The study was not intended to be limited to women only; an attempt to use fathers fitting the parameters failed as none were found. Thus, because of circumstances, this study focused on divorced mothers.

Data Collection: Data were collected during informal sessions in which respondents talked freely about their experiences. These interviews were conducted at the respondent's home, her place of work, or a neutral site agreed upon by both parties. Due to the exploratory nature of this study, it was felt that a single interview with each respondent would be sufficient for the discovery of parental themes. The interviewing author has been divorced and could empathize with respondents and identify with some of the issues presented. Early interviews were less structured than the later ones, and were intended to pinpoint themes used by parents in maintaining a feeling of family as the children progressed through the divorce process. Interviews later in the process were also loosely structured, while at the same time the interviewer was more aware of the nature of individual themes. This helped the interviewer remain focused while allowing respondents freedom to express their own ideas. No respondent was asked to reveal anything that would make her uncomfortable and what was discussed was freely given. Near the end of all interviews, each respondent was asked if she could think of anything of importance that was not dealt with during the session. All dialogues were taped for later transcription and analysis. To ascertain accuracy, copies of the paper in progress were distributed to interviewees for their comments and suggestions which were then incorporated into the final version of the study.

Data Evaluation: Input from colleagues not involved in data gathering has proven valuable in previous ethnographic research (Hill 1991; Mick and Buhl 1992). The interviewing author provided the co-author with partial transcripts and comprehensive notes of each interview for separate evaluation and analysis. If necessary, the co-author could listen to the taped recording of each interview. Written and verbal feedback was given the interviewer for evaluation and was used in subsequent interviews. The authors also communicated on a regular basis concerning the contents of the interviews, and ideas were exchanged throughout the process. This exchange occurred after each interview and was especially beneficial in the identification of themes. At all times, the respondents were given the liberty to express themselves freely. Questions addressed to respondents were very general in nature at the beginning of the interview, gradually becoming more specific. For example, the mothers were asked about people who helped them cope with the divorce process and, after the sources were identified, the mothers were then asked how specific people helped.

The fundamental purpose of the interviews was to uncover themes in family belongingness. After several interviews, the basis for some of the themes began appearing, and gradually these themes became apparent to the interviewer. When no new themes were forthcoming, the interviewing process was stopped. These themes represent increased levels of interaction between the stem family and their kinship networks, an age-related role transformation on the part of the children, and "sense of family" notions (activities involving parent and child with special attention to holidays and rituals). These themes will be discussed in the following section of this paper.

THEMES

Each respondent used different activities to maintain a feeling of family belongingness for her children. These activities, while individualized along family lines, were quite similar thematically across the diversified sample. The ages of the children did not appear to be related to the general behavior of the mothers. At one time the nuclear family had been the source of togetherness and now the stem family had to become that source. The stem family replaced the nuclear family as the basic unit of togetherness in the child's life.

Kinship Networks

In this study, the mother's kinship networks are the people with whom she has regular or semi-regular contact. The network includes relatives, ex-in-laws, friends, and co-workers who become important in helping the mother and children cope with the divorce process. The children's kinship network includes the same people as the mother's network but also adds the father as a member.

Mother's Parents: For divorced mothers, the role of intergenerational influence tends to increase with the breakdown of the nuclear family. Women are under greater time pressures (Weiss 1975), being responsible for all aspects of maintaining a home, raising children, and, often, the family's sole financial support (Weitzman 1985). Child care appears to be the dominant consumer domain where kinship networks enter. The provision of babysitting, minding sick children, and checking on latch-key kids by others allows mothers to cope with their numerous responsibilities. Increased network interaction also provides opportunity for socialization in the extended family.

The women studied here used kinship networks to help with children as they progressed through the divorce process. For some, the mother's parents are prominent, frequently increasing their role in their daughters' lives after divorce. Janice[2], whose parents helped "a lot," noted that her parents stayed close in case she or her daughters needed anything. They waited three years after her divorce before taking their first vacation, and even then, they telephoned her at least twice a week. Barbara, divorced over 20 years, stated "My mother has been my pal. She's not just a mother, she's my buddy." She and her mother live in the same neighborhood. Deanna reported that her parents minded her children when they were too sick for day care or school.

Mother's Siblings: Siblings of the divorced mothers also assisted. Peggy told of the relationship between her bachelor brother and her teenage son. "He (the brother) would take him to basketball games... They would always go out to Denny's after the games." Jane's sister brought her children over so the cousins could play together.

Non-Family: Non-related people also provide support. A neighbor, new to the area, helped Lori, who stated, "for some reason we just clicked." Co-workers and other friends assisted. Janice received "a lot of support from the people I work with." Much non-family help was in the form of moral support—another adult to whom the mother could turn for conversation and time out from the children. Others gave more tangible aid. Jeri described two friends as "family... Somebody extra to call." She left her children in the care of these friends rather than with their father when she went on business trips.

Ex-In-Laws: The role of in-laws was not uniform. In some cases, they were distant from the original nuclear family and maintained this distance after the divorce. "His family never chose to become involved or have contact while we were married" (Jane). Her children are not close to their grandparents, so the divorce was not disruptive of any established interactions between them. Peggy noted that "they were not the Grandmotherly and Grandfatherly type" and she remarked that the grandparent/grandchild relationship "hasn't changed" since her divorce.

In Donna's family, the in-laws were connected to the mother only through the child's father. "I talk to them occasionally." This father sees his parents rarely, usually when taking his daughter on holiday visits, thus limiting the child's contact with her grandparents.

In contrast, some stem families had extensive contact with their in-laws. Cheryl's ex-mother-in-law was instrumental in helping to give her family a feeling of continuity through her divorce, as she included Cheryl and her sons in family get togethers. She, Cheryl, and the children regularly attended church together and, even now, since Cheryl has remarried, they continue to share coffee on Saturday mornings. Kelly talked of her daughter's relationship with her ex-in-laws, stating that "She is very close to them, and I am too... I don't call her 'ex-mother-in-law'." Long-term ties with an ex-husband's family were also noted. Paula, divorced from her son's father for nearly 20 years, stated, "I am still friends with them... I still see them two times a year." Paula's son is also close to his father's parents and visits with them at least once a month. In these cases, the in-laws are clearly a part of the kinship network.

The Father: The father's role in the kinship network varies. Some fathers, who had good relationships with their children before the divorce, maintained this relationship afterwards. Jeri and her ex-husband had a joint custody arrangement, so both parents remained active in their children's lives. Kelly's daughter regularly sees her father and her half-siblings from his previous marriage. As noted above, Kelly remains close to her ex-in-laws and this closeness may help explain some of the father's close relationship with his daughter.

---

[2]Names of respondents have been changed to preserve their privacy.

Some fathers had a minimal role in their children's lives prior to the divorce but the divorce acted as a catalyst in changing this role. Mindy's daughters received telephone calls from their father after going away to college. He had shown little interest in them before they moved away from their home. Erica described her ex-husband as a "workaholic" who had little time for his children during the marriage. He has since re-established contact with the three oldest children. The youngest is still "very, very bitter."

For some families, the father disappeared totally from the lives of the stem family. Barbara has not seen nor heard from her ex-husband in over 20 years. Her youngest daughter has no memory at all of her father.

In summary, expanded kinship networks appear to be the rule in the case of stem families. Clearly, the study of household decision making becomes more complicated when members of the extended family play a greater role than that found in nuclear families. The presence of children in the family of divorce creates a greater likelihood of continued contact with one's ex-in-laws. Several mothers noted the roles of in-laws in the socialization of their children. Some parental control or influence about consumer choices could be transferred to kinship members who may hold different views from the mother. The McAlexander, Schouten, and Roberts (1993) study spoke little on the subject of ex-in-laws other than noting that some divorced people did get help from their ex-spouse's family. On the surface, one might assume that the study of stem families would be simplified due to the elimination of one adult from the household; instead, it appears that a thorough understanding of the consumer decision processes of stem families will be much more difficult to obtain due to the expanded kinship network associated with divorce. The stem mother may feel obligated to accept or accede to the advice and information given to her by kinship members about specific products or services. In the decision making process, the role of the ex-husband may be fulfilled by extended family members or friends adding a dimension not previously present before the divorce.

Equalization Of Roles

Frequently, with the death of a parent, children are told that they are expected to fill the vacated role (most commonly, a young man or boy is told that he is now "the man of the family"). We find such role impositions to be less prominent in the case of divorce, no doubt due to the existence of the estranged spouse. However, we do find a tendency to elevate the status of older (teenage or adolescent) children to that of friend and peer.

For mothers of younger children, the transformation of the child into a more adult-like person was not an issue. Donna thinks that her relationship with her ten year old daughter, Becky, would not be any different if she were still married to Becky's father. "Her father didn't ever have enough to do with her, so from the time she was a baby, I was the one who raised her... Maybe we've grown closer." Becky is still quite young and Donna considers herself to be a mother more than a friend. The transition for Deanna's two boys also has not occurred because she thinks they are still too young (eight and four). Kelly feels that the divorce may have slowed this process for her daughter. "I'd say she's been slower . . . She's not in a hurry."

The mothers with grown or nearly grown children speak of them as friends. Margaret's youngest son is now her "very best friend," the transition occurring when she started listening to what he had to say. "The clue is you listen. Even if you don't agree or you don't understand what he's talking about, you listen." For Erica, "This process was accelerated by the divorce . . . We did become more friends," and the process was fastest with her youngest son, the child most affected by the divorce.

As children mature, they gradually acquire adult status. This happens in all families, but our belief is that this process is more rapid in stem families than in nuclear families. [We have no comparable information on nuclear families, so our belief is somewhat inferential in nature.] We found that single parents seek adult companionship and may fill the void left by a spouse with relationships with older offspring (teenagers and adolescents, as opposed to adult children). Mindy and her children chat informally and talk about anything and everything. She doesn't think that this would be happening if she were still married; she would chat with her husband instead. In her mind, these sessions are an adult way of communicating and getting in touch with her children.

The subtle encouragement of children to become more peer-like may operate in the form of a self-fulfilling prophecy, resulting in the adult-like behaviors being observable earlier in children of stem families. Of her twin sons, now 10, Lori notes, "The thing that has really changed is that they are on their own so much that they have to be responsible for themselves . . . If they don't want hot lunch, they have to pack their own lunch." She thinks that they are more mature from being on their own so much and responsible for their behavior. She expects more out of them as far as chores, etc. as they grow older. "I've never talked down to them, even when they were two."

Just as divorce may result in more reliance on kinship networks, there appears to be greater reliance on offspring in consumer decision making in the stem family. While family decision-making research has paid some attention to intergenerational influence (Berey and Pollay 1968; Childers and Rao 1992), and reverse socialization processes (Ekstrom, Tansuhaj, and Foxman 1987), the standard perception of household decision making (based on nuclear families) is one dominated by fathers and mothers. As attention shifts to stem families, awareness of more joint parent-child decision making is critical (Roberts, Voli, and Johnson 1992). Attempts to market solely to the parent may well result in opportunities missed.

Sense of Family

The third theme to emerge from this study was sense of family. The mothers endeavored to give their children a feeling that, no matter what had happened to the parents' marriage, the children still belonged to a family. Their particular family may have a different structure, but it is a family nonetheless.

Sense of family appeared in three ways. First, there was an attempt to hold on to vestiges of the past and preserve family structure. Second was a need to go forward and seek a new family identity. Finally, holidays provided a bridge between the past and the future.

Holding On To The Past: There were different ways in which the mothers held on to the past and maintained family structure. Continuing some of the nuclear family rituals helped bridge the transition to stem family. In general, some everyday activities were not changed drastically. Peggy continued sharing evening prayers with her son. Kelly stated that family rituals between her and her daughter are the same as when she was married.

The mothers felt that it was important for the family to get together sometime during the day. Eating meals together was very common. "We always have dinner together ... There's been a few occasions when that hasn't happened and my children say, `What, we're not having dinner together?'" (Jane). She feels that sharing mealtime is important for a cohesive environment and nothing is allowed to intrude (TV, etc.) during dinner. It is family sharing time. For Erica, eating together was also important, but in her case it became eating out. "Oddly, one of the things we started doing was eating out." For Jeri the family meal was breakfast, as this was the best time of the day for the family to gather.

The mother's religious beliefs were important in maintaining a sense of family. Cheryl, as reported above, continued in the same church, attending with her ex-mother-in-law. Barbara would make "adventurous trips out of walking to church." Six mothers noted that regular attendance in church was important to them and they tried to instill this same feeling into their children with mixed results. Those with older children (Barbara and Mindy) reported that their children's attendance dropped as they approached and reached adulthood.

Pets have become part of that which is sacred (Belk, Wallendorf, and Sherry 1989; Tuan 1984), and can be linked to the past. Kelly's daughter "always had an animal wherever we moved," not necessarily the traditional dog or cat, but a bird, a mouse, or some other animal. Deanna and her sons kept the family dog and she associated this animal with the divorce. Erica added a dog after her divorce.

For some, living in the same house is important. Mindy is distressed because she must sell her home once monetary child support ceases. This house is where her children grew up and, now that they are almost grown, she can no longer afford to remain there. Conversely, Margaret is looking forward to selling her home. She finances her youngest son's college education, with no aid from his father, and upon his graduation, she plans to travel and tend to her own needs.

In cases where the family had to move, the mother provided some type of continuity for the children. Peggy sees to it that her son has a basketball hoop wherever they live. She also enrolls him in parochial school so "no matter where we lived he always, at least, went to the same school. I always felt that that was one plus." She felt that the same school, the same car pool, and the same set of friends give him a sense of security. When Donna changed homes, she set up her daughter's room right away with many of the same furnishings, except for a new bedspread and a more "grown up" dresser. The important thing for her was to establish the child's private space.

Going Forward: Building a new family identity was also accomplished in different ways. Erica's account of eating out is an example. She maintained the old sense of family through eating together, but in a different setting. Donna had a portrait of her and her daughter taken shortly after the divorce which she hung in her home telling her daughter, "That's our family now."

Trips and vacations are another way to cement a new family identity. Day trips are common for the stem families. Donna noted, "During the summer we go out to Chalco Hills Lake and . . . she usually rides her bike and I walk." Cheryl and Mindy rented cabins at a state park for summer retreats with their children. Deanna vacationed with her sons to prove that they could manage a long trip on their own. "Against everybody's suggestions, I took the kids on a vacation to Colorado Springs . . . We had a ball. It was fun." She would repeat the experience if finances allowed. Janice takes her daughters west where they try always to attend a rodeo, ride horses, and sit for a family portrait posing, in costume, as characters of the Old West. "I decided that maybe what we needed was to completely get away and just really be on our own, so that's what we did . . . We discovered it really pulled us together a lot more."

Being the most visible parent, these mothers interact a great deal with their children. They play Nintendo together (Kelly and Donna); they shop together (Kelly); they attend children's functions (Barbara, Kelly, Paula, Peggy, Janice, and Jane); they share quiet conversation (Mindy); and they have bedtime sharing (Peggy). Time together helped both mother and child make the transition from nuclear family to stem family.

Holidays: Rook (1985) called attention to the role of ritual(s) in consumer behavior. From a marketing perspective, holidays are a period of ritual consumption, from a Christmas tree, to special menus (Wallendorf and Arnould 1990), to birthday cards and gifts. For the stem families, holidays acted as a bridge between holding on to the past and going forward to develop new family identities. Children generally have contact with both parents, individually, thus reminding them of their "old" family. Stem mothers may incorporate both old and new rituals during a holiday season, giving the children a chance to look forward.

Peggy emphasized both Christmas and Thanksgiving. "We always went and cut a live Christmas tree . . . always made Thanksgiving and Christmas dinners even though I thought at the time it would be easier to go out to eat." Paula and her son, too, made a special trip to get a Christmas tree. "He and I would always go get the Christmas tree." Upon bringing it home, they would decorate it together. Janice stated, "I always take the girls' picture in the fall for the Christmas cards." Cheryl celebrates Christmas with her family a week early and then observes the actual holidays with her ex-mother-in-law and her family. Margaret did not remember any holiday not associated with her ex-mother-in-law. "Holidays and birthdays were almost a mandatory family attendance." One result of this is, now that her children are grown, they do not "make so much of birthdays."

Mindy keeps only a few presents under her tree and hides the rest. Every year before attending Christmas Eve services, she excuses herself, returns to the house, and places the rest of the gifts under the tree, making it look as if someone had delivered more while the family was out. One year she did not "have to go to the bathroom" and her kids kept asking if she had something to do inside. Arranging for a neighbor to bring out the presents was her way of "keeping ahead of them." Mindy's children are all high school age and above, and this incident, occurring with older children, demonstrates an enduring aspect of some rituals. Even as old as the children were, Mindy perceived their discomfort when she deviated from expected behavior.

Jeri describes Christmas as time for her family to gather, but "that can take several forms." She is flexible timewise, and the holiday schedule varies from year to year. Donna has difficulty in establishing holiday rituals because her daughter's visitation schedule changes yearly. Lori has never planned a holiday celebration. "Holidays have always been a mess because I work holidays."

Birthdays followed Christmas and Thanksgiving as the most celebrated time. In Jane's family the birthday person chooses the dinner menu "within reason," and they share the birthday dinner. "We always share birthdays together. No one makes any plans for birthdays." Mindy's family celebrates for two days. "We open a present the night before . . . A couple of years ago, it was my birthday and the day before when I got home from work in the garage door they had put streamers that said Happy Birthday." For her children, Mindy's birthday is as important as their own. Barbara's family extended birthday celebrations to include two parish priests. They made homemade gifts for these men and had a birthday picnic in their backyard. Barbara described the priests as part of the family and "the kids thought that was just great."

Holidays logically fall under the "sense of family" category. Menus (Margaret, Jane, Patsy), gift giving (Barbara, Mindy), and rituals (Mindy, Paula, Patsy, Jane) serve as a bridge between the nuclear family and the stem family. In this study, more attempts to hold on to the past during the holiday season were found than trying to create a new identity. This result differs somewhat from the findings of McAlexander, Schouten, and Roberts (1993), who found more evidence for the disposition to break free and for development of new individual identities. The presence of children in the stem families seemed to place more emphasis on the maintenance of family continuity, though in a reconstituted manner.

FOOD FOR THOUGHT

This study does not attempt to identify all themes or processes experienced by the stem family as it re-establishes itself as a family unit with a new structure, but it does provide some ideas as to how single mothers proceed through the process. The interviews revealed that mothers from different backgrounds appear to have common themes used to maintain a sense of family for their children.

This paper is an exploration into the behavior of stem families. It is an attempt to identify themes that can be examined from a marketing perspective. The 14 interviews provide a first step in developing a body of knowledge applicable to this segment of the population. The themes identified provide a foundation on which to base future study.

Future research is needed in the area of consumer decision making in the stem family. Two areas may be of particular interest. First, the process itself is affected by all the people involved. The extent of the influence of the kinship system needs to be examined. In appearance the stem mother may be solely responsible for the family, but for practical purposes some of this responsibility may be shifted to her kinship network. Second, product categories of stem family purchases are of interest to marketers. Stem family trips, eating out more often, and changes in residence indicate consumption patterns which may have different meanings for the stem family as opposed to the nuclear family.

This study was limited to mother-headed families, but as more fathers are granted custody of their children as a result of divorce, they too should be examined. There is also a need for intrafamily data gathering to gain insight into shared experience (Mick and Buhl 1992). As the number of stem families increases, marketers need to understand the behavior of this segment of the population. Some of this understanding may come with increased comparison to nuclear families.

REFERENCES

Ajhuba, Roshan and Kandi Stinson (1993). "Female Headed Single Parent Families: An Exploratory Study of Children's Age in Family Decision Making," *Advances in Consumer Research*, 20, Forthcoming.

Belk, Russell W., Melanie Wallendorf, and John F. Sherry, Jr. (1989), "The Sacred and the Profane in Consumer Behavior: Theodicy on the Odyssey," *Journal of Consumer Research*, 16 (June), 1-38.

Berey, Lewis A. and Richard W. Pollay (1968), "The Influencing Role of the Child in Family Decision Making, *Journal of Marketing Research*, 5 (February), 70-72.

Bernstein, Aaron (1992), "When the Only Parent Is Daddy," *Business Week*, 3294 (November 23), 122, 127.

Bohannan, Paul (1970), "The Six Stations of Divorce," in *Divorce and After*, Paul Bohannan, (Ed.) Garden City, NJ: Doubleday and Company, Inc., 24-35.

Buehler, Cheryl (1989), "Initiator Status and the Divorce Transition," *Family Relations*, 36 (January), 82-86.

Childers, Terry L. and Akshay R. Rao (1992), "The Influence of Familial and Peer-based Reference Groups on Consumer Decisions," *Journal of Consumer Research*, 19 (September), 198-211.

DeWitt, Paula Mergenhagen (1992), "Breaking Up Is Hard To Do," *American Demographics*, October, 52-58.

Ekstrom, Karin M., Patriya S. Tansuhaj, and Ellen R. Foxman (1987), "Children's Influence in Family Decisions and Consumer Socialization: A Reciprocal View," *Advances in Consumer Research*, 14, 283-287.

Kitson, Gay C., Karen Benson Babri, and Mary Joan Roach (1985), "Who Divorces and Why: A Review," *Journal of Family Issues*, 6 (September), 255-294.

_____ and Helen Raschke (1981), "Divorce Research: What We Know; What We Need to Know," *Journal of Divorce*, 4 (Spring), 1-37.

Kron, Joan (1983), *Home Psych: The Social Psychology of Home and Decoration*, New York: Clarkson N. Potter.

London, Kathryn and Barbara Foley Wilson (1988), "D-I-V-O-R-C-E," *American Demographics*, October, 23-26.

McAlexander, James, H., John W. Schouten, and Scott D. Roberts (1993), "Consumer Behavior and Divorce," in *Research in Consumer Behavior*, Russell W. Belk (Ed.), Forthcoming.

Martin, Teresa Castro and Larry L. Bumpass (1989), "Recent Trends in Marital Disruption," *Demography*, 20 (February), 37-51.

Mick, David Glen and Claus Buhl (1992), "A Meaning-based Model of Advertising Experiences," *Journal of Consumer Research*, 19 (December), 317-338.

Roberts, Scott D., Patricia K. Voli, and KerenAmi Johnson (1992), "Beyond the Family Life Cycle: An Inventory of Variables For Defining the Family as a Consumption Unit," *Developments in Marketing Science*, Vol. IV, Ed. Victoria L. Crittenden, San Diego, CA: Academy of Marketing Science, 71-75.

Rook, Dennis (1985), "The Ritual Dimension of Consumer Behavior," *Journal of Consumer Research*, 12 (December), 251-264.

Thompson, Craig J., William B. Locander, and Howard R. Pollio (1990), "The Lived Meaning of Free Choice: An Existential-Phenomenological Description of Everyday Consumer Experiences of Contemporary Married Women," *Journal of Consumer Research*, 17 (December), 346-361.

Tuan, Yi-Fu (1984), *Dominance and Affection: The Making of Pets*, New Haven, CT: Yale University Press.

Wallendorf, Melanie and Eric J. Arnould (1991), "'We Gather Together': Consumption Rituals of Thanksgiving Day," *Journal of Consumer Research*, 18 (June), 13-31.

Weiss, Robert (1975), *Marital Separation*, New York; Basic Books.

Weitzman, Lenore J. (1985), *The Divorce Revolution: The Unexpected Social and Economic Consequences for Women and Children in America*, New York: The Free Press.

Consumer Spending Patterns: Dimensions and Dichotomies

Patricia Ann Walsh, University of Connecticut
Susan Spiggle, University of Connecticut

ABSTRACT

Investigating consumer spending behavior, we present a set of related constructs derived from an analysis of interview data. These constructs form four dichotomous pairs—present/future orientation, control system/ no control system, experience of struggle/ no experience of struggle, and context dependent /independent. This conceptualization forms the basis for the design of a broader study of higher order consumer choices.

Recently two intellectual leaders in consumer research (Andreasen 1993; Wells 1993) issued guidelines for steering the future direction of inquiry in the field. Both noted the current dearth of research on questions involving consumer budget allocation decisions. These questions are important, not only for expanding the scope of consumer research, but they have important macroeconomic implications.

This paper presents findings and analysis from a preliminary investigation into the savings and spending patterns of young adults. By examining financial allocation decisions—higher order choices—we move beyond consumer researchers' focus on the brand level decisions made by individuals. Consumer behavior inquiry typically neglects the broad question of how individuals make financial resource allocation decisions. Thus, no established set of constructs, propositions, or models exist for guiding research on this question.

Therefore, we designed an inductive study with three goals: to gain theoretical insights into our informants' experiences in making money decisions; to develop constructs for guiding additional inquiry; and to specify initial relationships between the constructs.

DATA AND METHODS

As a first step toward realizing these goals, we conducted eight semi-structured, open-ended interviews with third and fourth year undergraduate students. The interviews covered a range of savings and spending decisions and elicited descriptions of specific incidents (Thompson et al. 1989).

We chose undergraduates for two reasons. (1) They have established a degree of financial responsibility, control, and independence, thereby allowing us to intercept a specific and important developmental stage—the point at which patterns of money management are crystallizing. (2) Unlike older consumer groups, they make a wide range of independent consumption and expenditure decisions. Thus, we avoid the data collection and decision complexities of joint budget constraints, financial planning, and decision making in this initial phase of research.

Maximizing variations in comparison, for this paper we report on an analysis of spending decisions of four informants with markedly different patterns. We collectively coded and analyzed the transcripts of these four interviews. We read and re-read each transcript a number of times looking for similarities and differences between and within informants, identifying dimensions for every expenditure made by each informant. We produced a tabulation for each incident discussed. In a hermeneutical procedure, we then reanalyzed each transcript using this set of dimensions looking for commonalities in experiences across a diverse set of decisions. Finally, we synthesized this conceptualization into an integrated framework.

THE INFORMANTS

We present brief case study descriptions of experiential issues for four informants concerning their expenditures. For each informant we focus on their experiences across a range of spending situations.

David

David, a junior majoring in vocal performance, attempts to exert deliberation and control in his spending, although he allows himself some latitude for impulsive and "unneeded" indulgences.

During the interview he described various expenditures in which he exhibits impulsivity or maintains control. The context and definition of the purchase shape his degree of control and source of funds for his monetary outlay. He segregates his financial resources into three categories—cash in the bank, cash in the pocket, and a credit card. For David, each of these accounts permits him differing degrees of freedom and responsibility.

> If I have cash on hand, I would tend to buy impulsively. If I do not have cash on hand I am much more careful...I wait until I really need it instead of going and wasting money.

> In having the extra cash in the bank ... it prevents impulsive buying...when you have cash you can afford to wait.

In these passages David expresses his definition of different forms of cash. He defines cash in the bank as a reserve—liquidity available for meeting various financial obligations. By retaining it in the bank, he resists temptations to spend on unneeded purchases. However, he frequently carries a designated amount of pocket cash for indulging in impulsive spending. By restricting the amount, he creates boundaries on this type of spending. One of the ways he reduces his pocket cash is to carry his credit card.

> ...if I go to a restaurant, like I would use a credit card simply because I don't feel like having...to carry around three hundred dollars...just so you could spend say sixty, seventy, dollars to go to a really nice restaurant, and you don't have to take out that money and need an extra forty dollars...I would probably spend it if I had it...I'd spend it and I'd rather not spend it.

By using the credit card here, David restricts his cash-in-the-pocket, thus decreasing temptation to indulge in impulsive spending. David uses this control strategy in the context where costs are both not predefinable and of sufficient magnitude that residual cash in pocket exceeds his usual designated amount.

However, David's system for control sometimes fails. In another passage he describes a special occasion—special both in regard to the context and failure of control.

> ...for Valentine's Day my girlfriend and I...I was planning to go somewhere with her and...I took some money...say a hundred dollars, and I wanted to use all that money. I just wanted to spend that one day and use one hundred dollars only. And the night before I went and bought flowers, and I was very careful. And at the restaurant it came to about fifty dollars and that was well within our means...But then I went and used the

credit card on that motor inn...and that kind of blew that for me...I had the cash with me for most of the weekend and knowing that it was marked for a specific purpose, that's what kept me from spending it, the cash I mean...It was in my pocket, but I knew that it was for a certain point in the future.

This passage illustrates the failure of David's strategy. Normally he uses the credit card to control spending, but here it facilitated impulse. The Valentine occasion provided a special context for David's experience and consequent behavior. In this context David experienced the confluence of three dimensions—extraordinary occasion, calendar-defined timing, and romantic expressive desire. Despite his careful planning, in this context he exceeded his boundaries, departing from his normal behavior.

David defines himself as a spending realist.

I'm kind of a realist. If I know that I can't afford something, or if it's out of my range, I just don't have the desire for it.

But occasionally David permits himself some indulgences that remain within his boundaries for control. Unlike the Valentine indulgence which he defined as "[blowing] that for me", the purchase of Metropolitan Opera Tickets falls within a predefined comfort range for indulgent spending.

I go to the Met whenever I can...maybe 4 or 5 times a year...I enjoy spending my money on the seats...they range from $20 to $110 and we can get standing room tickets for $9 to $12...and sit in $110 seats [after intermission]...[for] Pavorotti and Kathaleen Battle.

Attending the Met represents a special context for David—with two important dimensions. Attendance is intricately related to his self identity as a musical aficionado, and it includes good value, an important consideration for David across a wide range of purchases.

In contrast with the Met, a periodic expenditure, where David exercises deliberation, planning, and concern with good value, he occasionally buys compact discs. These purchases depart from his routine and desired patterns.

If I buy a CD lately, I would usually buy it on my credit card...only because to buy a CD I'd have to go to the ATM and take out $20...which would involve planning so,...I would buy them with my credit card because it would be an impulsive purchase. The reason is...the Public Library has...85% of what I want to hear...and, I, uh, tape it.

David attempts to resist purchasing CDs because he has an alternative means for getting recordings of the music. He resists the temptation by refusing to allocate pocket cash for this purpose—a strategy we see recurring in his interview. As in the Valentine case he gives in to the impulse to spend where he had deliberately restricted his pocket cash as a strategy to control impulse. In these two cases the credit card enabled the purchase of unplanned indulgences.

In summary, David described spending money for such items as dating, listening to music, paying bills and parking tickets, groceries, gasoline, stereo, and a racing bike. Throughout the interview David expressed concern for value and a desire to manage his financial resources with deliberation. To this end he creates boundaries that function as control strategies. Although sometimes he violates the boundaries, typically on impulses, his spending remains within a manageable range. In a dialectical fashion the credit card functions both to maintain and exceed his boundaries, depending on the context. Finally, he noted that he allows himself to indulge in a few big ticket items—extraordinary purchases—when his earnings are greater.

Melissa

Melissa, a senior business major, attempts to exert spending deliberation and control, like David. However, she frequently exceeds a manageable range of spending comfort. Varied contexts induce different spending strategies. For example, she variously shows a strong sense of obligation to spend, great spending restraint, or spending indulgence.

Obligation to spend. In the context of social obligations, she plans by saving in advance, departing from her typical patterns.

I set aside a lot of my CO-OP money for my parents' twenty-fifth wedding anniversary. I just banked my first three paychecks...and it was a good thing that I did that, too. Otherwise, I probably would have spent it...I wanted to pay off a credit card bill that was quite high and is still quite high. And, instead, I chose to put the money away and spend it on my parents...it meant a lot to them for me and my brother and sister to throw this [party]...and now I'm glad that I didn't spend it paying off my own debts.

Melissa described a similar incident of putting money aside for another social obligation—expenses for bridal shower, bridesmaid dress, rehearsal dinner dress, and bachelorette party for a friend. These examples, involving social commitments where she cannot control the timing of the spending, contrast with her typical spending patterns.

Spending restraint. She described a different pattern in two other purchases.

For the past five years of my life I walked past a Brookstone Store...and I'm just dying to get this foot massager, but its two hundred dollars and [it] feels so good on my feet and I just want this so much...You sit in the chair and put your foot on [it] and it's the best thing in the world. But it was two hundred dollars and I didn't have the money...I eventually broke down and bought it. I had to do a lot of careful consideration. I was not going to pay my bills for the next month if I bought this.

Melissa finally purchased it after five years when a friend working there offered to use his employee discount to help her buy it. She exhibited temporary restraint in another purchase.

I bought a wet suit for water skiing. And I really liked this wet suit because of its neon colors and the way that it looked on my body...I've been meaning to get one for a long time just because everybody had one. But every time we walked in the store these wet suits are like three hundred dollars...I couldn't justify spending that much money...This one particular wet suit was there for two seasons and was marked down considerably...[it] was on sale so I whipped out my charge card and charged it. When I was skiing that day...I felt more enthusiastic, I felt good about myself and I felt thin in this beautiful wet suit...Then later on that night...I realized how ridiculous it was that I just blew, like, almost three hundred dollars on a wet suit that I will probably wear once this summer and then never again for the rest of my life.

These purchases differed in several ways from the previous two. (1) Melissa purchased the wet suit and foot massager for herself, not others. She expected much personal pleasure from both based on their strong hedonic and sensory elements. (2) Calendar-defined timing did not impose a deadline on these expenditures, allowing her to engage in the transactions at her discretion. In the context of these purchases, when a deal became available Melissa spontaneously acquired these items. These acquisitions followed a long period of restraint, despite intense desires. During this period Melissa adapted to the idea of ownership of these items (Hoch and Loewenstein 1991), even consuming the benefits of the foot massager in frequent in-store trials. However, she made no specific plan to execute the purchases. As a result, she did not pre-allocate resources for their acquisition.

Spending indulgence. More typical of Melissa are instances where she indulges herself, employing no attempt to exercise willpower. She described "blowing" the balance of her CO-OP earnings (funds not allocated to her parents' anniversary party) and recurrent indulgences.

> I made ten thousand dollars and it's all gone. I really had a good time...I went on a lot of trips, I spent a lot of money, and I have a lot of suits...I was very spontaneous with my money. I had no problem just going out to dinner...I had no problem going out to happy hour any day of the week, and plus, trips I took to Atlantic City, Boston, New York...I am sort of disappointed I blew all my money away, but hey, at least I had a good time doing it.

> When I go to bars...I'll probably end up spending about twenty dollars an evening...occasionally when I come home from bars and I am very hungry, I have been known to purchase a pizza and eat it, or stop at Subway and get a steak and cheese...or Petro Pantry, or Store 24 to get a bean and beef buritto with cheese.

Contextual similarities between the preceding purchases include: funds available for discretionary spending, strong urges to indulge in personal, routine extravagances, and pursuit of hedonic and experiential gratification. Here we see Melissa indulging herself in a wide variety of recurrent purchases without exercising restraint. This pattern occurs across both low cost and high cost purchases and represents how Melissa's desires expand to fill available means.

In summary, Melissa's pattern of expanding desires to spend available money echoes David's (spending more when he was earning more). However, David's stereo and racing bike represent a few infrequently purchased goods, whereas Melissa's CO-OP expenditures represent a recurrent array of extravagances. Furthermore, during the period of more normally constrained income, she regularly indulges herself in consumables.

Melissa's highly varied and seemingly inconsistent patterns involve deliberation and spontaneity, restraint and indulgence, and responsibility and its neglect. However, the context of spending for Melissa shapes her behaviors consistently. Social obligations in the face of calendar-defined timing and extraordinary purchases dictate responsibility and restraint. Nonetheless, her typical spending behavior is driven by desire for immediate gratification through hedonic and experiential consumption—trips, going out, food. To the extent that available funds and credit permit, she generally shows no deliberation, no restraint, and no fiscal responsibility—routinely maintaining high outstanding credit card balances. Consequently, we see her ambivalence toward money.

> Now I am starting to realize that I am hitting the real world next...May, and I won't have any money to support myself...I wish we never had anything called money. ...Money can cause a lot of problems, it's good and it's bad, I guess I just have a lot of mixed feelings on money.

Jason

Jason, a senior marketing major, routinely expends all of his available resources, including cash, credit cards, and parental permissiveness. In fact, Jason does not limit his spending to available resources, but engineers fiscal extensions.

> My mother works at a credit union...so if I happen to get down to a low amount, I'll say Ma, can you give me about $500, and she can just add it right into that checking account because she's right there. It's much easier.

> If my bike breaks, or if the ring guy just happens to show up the very last day and this is the last day he's going to be on campus and I have to buy my class ring that day, I just write out the check and call my mother that night and say could you place $170 in the account...and it's done, there's no—it's very easy.

> I got carried away...kinda kept going, maxing [credit cards] out right away...They wouldn't let me charge anymore. I was to my limit.

> I get a new credit card in the mail...when one expires or something, I'll just get a new one.

Gaining expanded lines of financing triggers cyclical buying sprees for Jason. Typical items that Jason purchases on such a spree include cross training sneakers, basketball sneakers, jogging sneakers, jeans, and large stocks of school supplies and personal care items.

In addition to buying sprees where Jason spends freely, he also regularly spends freely on "relaxation necessities," Jason's term for leisure and entertainment expenditures. These include:

> ...not your daily necessities, but you still need them...well, party materials, like beer and stuff, going out, relaxation, the movies, maybe going away for the weekend...when it comes to partying...three to four times a week going out to the bars...I spend maybe $15 to $20 [per night].

The above passages in Jason's interview reflect two different spending patterns—cyclical and continual. In both cases he defines items purchased as necessities. In fact, Jason defines everything that he buys as necessary, frequently using the terms, necessities, I need, and essentials. As a consequence, he does not exercise restraint; he buys everything he "needs" and "needs" everything he buys. Thus, Jason never struggles with mounting willpower over desire. Desires are realized as needs.

Jason accumulates money in a cyclical fashion, also.

> I normally just cash [my] check...kinda just keep that in a sock and spend it as needed. Sometimes my money flow catches up and then I blow a large amount on a weekend and then I'm right back to nothing, so I'm having trouble getting ahead.

> One year I worked all semester, I'd worked all summer. I set aside all my money for that spring break and I just decided not to go...I guess as soon as I had all that money I didn't want to spend it...I saved about $700.

This incident of saving up for a particular purchase was a departure from his current typical behavior. (Although he did describe one similar incident of saving up to purchase golf clubs when he was in high school). However, when spring came Jason choose not to spend the money on a spring break trip.

> And then I was like ooph I gotta like withdraw all that money? And then I said, I can't do that. I've got to leave it in there, I saved it this long, I'm just going to keep it a little bit longer.

Obviously, Jason did not "need" a spring break that year. (He did however, "need' one his senior year—his last opportunity). Additionally, Jason hesitated to break his $700 accumulation, treating it as a threshold. Shortly thereafter a need compelled him to tap the fund.

> I had $700 and I...needed basketball sneakers. I needed a pair for indoors, and the outdoor season was coming up. So I took my old indoor sneakers and transferred them to outdoor status and bought new indoor sneakers. And so that was about $110. And then I spent—I kept buying little—it just went fast.

Once Jason crossed the threshold, he dribbled the rest away much like his sock money accumulation. But with his "sock money" he never accumulates a sufficient amount to constitute a critical threshold. He accumulates it over time and blows it at once.

In summary, Jason rarely exercises willpower over spending money. He avoids conflict (Hoch and Lowenstein 1991; Thaler and Shefrin 1981) between willpower and desire by defining strongly desired objects and social/leisure activities (going out) as necessities. Such a definition silences the voice of the foresighted planner (Thaler and Shefrin 1981), short-circuiting inner debate over the purchase decision. Further, he expands available sources of money to meet these needs. Although he described a prior incident of planning and saving, his current patterns reflect a short time horizon of immediate gratifications, where the shortsighted doer (Thaler and Shefrin 1981) dominates.

Susan

Susan, a senior majoring in business, rarely experiences struggle between willpower and desire—an outcome of her ability to moderate desires and to manage her money resources through careful planning and control. Her purchases are typically deliberate and contemplative, yet she does not believe she deprives herself. A Valentine trip to Boston with her boyfriend represents an exception to her normal experience.

> Although I don't have a great amount of money right now, I'm going anyway (giggle)...there's a part of me saying you shouldn't go cause you don't have a lot of money to spend in Boston, but I'm going anyway (giggle). I'm sort of torn, but I want to go, so—I'm not a frugal person in the sense that if I want to do something, I will do it, unless I'm absolutely broke...I don't spend money just foolishly, like go to the store and buy something I don't need, but if I want something.

Here we see Susan's deliberative style, even in the face of the conflict between willpower and desire. The particular context of this decision—joint decision making (with boyfriend), extraordinary occasion (trip to Boston), and a timing mismatch between sources and uses of funds for the trip—generated this unusual conflict.

> I just weigh the pros in the sense that you know it will be fun, you get away from here which is always a good thing—(giggle)—go to Boston...versus, you know it's going to be expensive and I don't get paid this coming week, so I'll get paid next week so, you know, I'll go for the weekend and get paid [next] Thursday...so that's good, but I'd rather get paid this Thursday, so I'd have it and wouldn't have to take it out of the bank.

For Susan, this conflict is not about using the money to go. She regrets having to withdraw money from an account, rather than being able to pay for it with cash already received from a paycheck.

More typically, Susan does not experience conflict because she regularly saves and budgets, indicating a strong sense of deferred gratification. For example, Susan allocates a specific amount for spending during the semester.

> I've been going to school for four years, so I kind of know how much I spend in a semester. You know I haven't lived off campus before—this is my first year. So I always paid my fee bills in the beginning, and then I didn't have to worry about rent or anything like that...I always knew what I spent, like $700 a semester, or something like that...You know that's how much I usually spent. I just know how much I spend.

Susan also designates a specific amount of money for spending during the week.

> I don't spend more than twenty dollars during the week, like just going out, or you know just little purchases.

This twenty dollar limit covers routine, weekly expenditures. Additionally, Susan may also buy hosiery, shoes, or birthday gifts during the week—expenditures she covers easily by maintaining a sufficient precautionary savings balance.

> I like the security of knowing that if I wanted to go and buy something that was more expensive, like a stereo, or something like that...if I wanted to go and buy it, I could ... [my roommate] had to worry about whether she's going to meet the rent payment. I mean, she just spends, but I could not do that because I like to have the security of knowing that if something happened and I needed money, it would be there...[security means] avoiding bad circumstances and taking part in good ones.

Susan described a large, extraordinary expenditure that she was able to make due to her foresight. Her savings patterns provided sufficient funds for her to take part in a good circumstance.

> The most money I've ever spent on anything was France. It was a couple of thousand dollars for tuition and expenses and travelling when I was there, and it would probably be the most substantial money that I've ever spent...my parents said if you think you have the money, and I did have the money, and they said, do you think this is really what you want to do, and I knew it was...it was...the best experience I ever had, travelling around Europe, and you do spend a lot of money, but it was worth it...I wouldn't rather have the money, I'd rather have the experience.

Overall, Susan is moderate, in control, deliberate, and contemplative. She erects boundaries that she easily maintains through her

FIGURE

	PRESENT ORIENTATION/ NO CONTROL SYSTEM	FUTURE ORIENTATION/ CONTROL SYSTEM
CONTEXT DEPENDENT/ STRUGGLE	MELISSA	DAVID
CONTEXT INDEPENDENT/ NO STRUGGLE	JASON	SUSAN

foresight and ability to delay gratification. Thus, when she wants something, she is able to buy it without conflict, because the money is available. Several factors contribute to this availability. (1) She works in an office during the summers and whenever she chooses during the semester. She also has several part-time jobs at school. Together, earnings from these jobs allow her financial independence. (2) She manages this income through established patterns of savings, planning, and budgeting. (3) She exercise deliberation when spending, avoiding impulse, frivolity, and unplanned purchases. However, she buys what she wants, experiencing no deprivation.

DISCUSSION

Our description of four informants reveals four rather different patterns of spending behavior. In addition to the differences between them, we also found interesting variations within each individual.

We identified and dichotomized four dimensions by comparing and contrasting experiential differences between and within the informants. We arrayed them across the four dichotomous dimensions—struggle/no struggle, context dependent/context independent, system of planning/no system of planning, present/future orientation. When we sorted the informants along each of these dimensions, we discovered that two of these dimensions coincide: (1) struggle and context dependence, and (2) system of planning and temporal orientation.

Struggle and context. We found that individuals who experienced struggles did so only when they behaved one way in a given context, and another way in other contexts. For example, Melissa struggled with the wet suit and foot massager decisions (personal, hedonic, time maneuverable, non-recurrent), but not with her parents' anniversary party or a friend's wedding (social obligation, calendar-defined timing), nor the more recurrent personal indulgences (routine, extravagant, funds available).

David experiences struggle in specific, but different contexts than Melissa. Typically, David attempts to plan and exert control over his purchases. He experienced struggle in the context of control failure (Valentine's Day and CDs). Alternatively, neither Jason nor Susan generally experience struggles. Their planning and control, or lack thereof, is consistent across varied contexts. Jason spends all of his available resources and more with little deliberation. Susan makes rational spending choices, planning for purchases and controlling her desires.

System of planning and temporal orientation. Further, we found that the individuals whose consumption is focused in the present generally lack established systems of planning and control over money. Jason and Melissa have large appetites for the immediately gratifying, particularly for recurrent self-indulgences. These present-oriented patterns eclipse attempts to regulate spending behaviors. Consequently, they have been unable to establish *systems* of regulation. Therefore, they live at the limit of present resources and have no accumulation of money from which to draw in the future. This lack of a system for planning and controlling spending then leads to recurrent feelings of deprivation.

In contrast, Susan and David have established systems for planning and controlling spending, even though David experiences periodic failures. Both are future oriented and routinely able to forgo spontaneous consumption whims. Their typical patterns of control, embodied in established systems, enable them to both resist and indulge in desires. This moderated behavior permits occasional indulgences that provides them with little sense of deprivation. Their ability to monitor their spending permits them to accumulate money which in turn facilitates future choices.

Summary. We found substantial variation in spending behavior across and within four informants. We discovered four related dimensions that capture these variations in behavior. Our conceptualization of the intersection of these four dimensions leads to a pairing of the dimensions and forms a fourfold space. We have placed the informants in the quadrant best characterizing their behavior. (See figure).

In effect, we can view these individuals as falling along continua of each dimension. For example, we can array Jason-Melissa-David-Susan along a dimension capturing the degree to which they have an established, effective system of control. Collapsing the dimensions into dichotomies, however, allows us to present the interrelationships of the dimensional pairs.

CONCLUSION

This initial investigation produced the conceptual groundwork to guide the data collection and analysis of a broader project on savings and spending behavior. The constructs and their provisional relationships suggest strategies for collecting additional data. They indicate specific questions to ask informants (for example, describe some decisions in which you felt conflicts about spending money, and some in which you did not). Further, they provide guidelines for selecting additional informants, using theoretical sampling (Strauss 1987), to maximize variations on these dimensions.

In this preliminary study of higher order choices we focused on young adults in college. We have recently conducted additional interviews with non-student young adults as part of investigating a broader socio-demographic range to establish the applicability (or modification) of these dimensions and determine their usefulness in formulating a model of spending behavior.

REFERENCES

Andreasen, Alan R. (1993) "The Future of the Association for Consumer Research: Backward to the Past," Presidential Address in *Advances in Consumer Research*, Vol. 20, eds. Michael Rothschild and Leigh McAlister, Provo, UT: Association for Consumer Research.

Hoch, Stephen J. and George F. Loewenstein (1991), "Time-inconsistent Preferences and Consumer Self-Control," *Journal of Consumer Research*, 17 (March), 492-507.

Strauss, Anselm L. (1987), *Qualitative Analysis for Social Scientists*, Cambridge University Press, Cambridge.

Thaler, Richard H. and Hersh M. Shefrin (1981), "An Economic Theory of Self-Control," *Journal of Political Economics*, 89 (2), 392-410.

Thompson, Craig J., William B. Locander, and Howard R. Pollio (1989), "Putting Consumer Experiences Back into Consumer Research: The Philosophy and Method of Existential-Phenomenology," *Journal of Consumer Research*, 16 (Sept.), 133-146.

Wells, William D. (1993), "Discovery-oriented Consumer Research," *Journal of Consumer Research*, 19 (March), 489-504.

Consumer Learning and Coping Behaviors in Transitory Situations
Donald Granbois, Indiana University

Consumer research usually concentrates on consumers in typical settings, perhaps reflecting the field's Marketing heritage, where standard segmentation concepts such as family life cycles or children's developmental stages dominate. Little is known of behaviors of people in transition between stages or of people living in nonstandard households. These situations require people to learn new roles in the face of uncertainty as to what is effective and appropriate behavior. The three studies of divorced consumers and young adults living away from home for the first time contribute insights into consumer spending and money management problems and practices during these transitory periods. What remains to be learned are the processes consumers use to develop needed new behaviors, and the determinants of the apparent variability of their success in these endeavors.

ATTRIBUTES OF THE THREE STUDIES

Each study reports preliminary results of on-going projects, and each, therefore, is an ideal candidate for conference presentation, where suggestions from audience members are available for the researchers to consider as their projects proceed. They are alike also in their use of a phenomenological approach.

To those trained in more conventional methods, hallmarks of this somewhat free-wheeling, seemingly unstructured approach are no familiar theoretical orientation, no hypotheses, no formal sampling methodology, no formal analytical or statistical scheme for dealing with data collected, and no discussion of findings in light of hypothesis-testing and correlation with earlier findings. Since these missing aspects often provide the major focus of a discussant's critique, a different strategy is obviously called for here. Comments will therefore be limited to interpreting the coping and learning behaviors reported and to offering some suggestions for framing future research questions.

USES OF GOODS

Each study presents the results of intensive study of a very small number of subjects (four, fourteen and fifteen) whose verbatim responses provide first person descriptions of their uses of goods. Verbatim reporting and the researchers' finely detailed interpretations provide insights into how consumers expect products to serve specific social and individual needs. Goods and the acts involving them were found to have important symbolic meanings and social purposes, especially as other family members and significant others are involved. However, these meanings and purposes were obviously not always clearly understood. Subjects found themselves in stressful settings, where they either did not know appropriate consumer norms or perceived them to be in conflict, or where they saw their own behavior as norm-violating.

Some subjects appeared to use money and goods deliberately to deceive themselves as to the appropriateness and efficacy of their own behavior. Others used goods to enhance, correct, modify or sever relationships with others. Goods sometimes enhanced satisfaction for themselves or others and sometimes were used deliberately to deny satisfaction to others. Goods and money were sometimes used with good intentions, but in ways that observers might feel to be detrimental to smooth interpersonal relations or that may actually be damaging to the development of "good" practices by others (Jason's mother provides funds to him with this effect).

GOODS AND SATISFACTION

Subjects appeared to evaluate their own behaviors in terms of self-evalation of performance. Many incidents reported consideration of whether an act led to an increase in the subject's own satisfaction. What is not clear, and what constitutes an important research avenue suggested by many of the incidents reported here, is the factors that determine when normative behavior actually does lead to enhanced satisfaction.

Indeed, several incidents are shown where *deviant* behavior led to great satisfaction. For example, Susan judged her trip to Boston with her boyfriend to be highly satisfying, even though she believed this act deviated from her usual frugal, careful spending of money. How could this self-defined "irrational" behavior lead to such a high level of pleasure?

BEHAVIOR TYPOLOGIES

Authors of each of the studies identify behaviors, name them and suggest some of their functions for the subjects studied and for these subjects' relationships with others. Three themes for coping with divorce, a valenced classification of gift-giving behaviors, and a conceptual scheme for classifying student spending and saving behaviors are proposed and illustrated. We are not sure of the universality nor of the completeness of these constructs, nor are we given much insight into possible individual differences among divorced persons' behaviors, nor of sensitivities of these constructs to situational variables. Not all divorces are alike, surely, and many more college student situations exist beyond those studied here. Nonetheless, the concepts and classifications are provocative, offer insights into the stresses and uncertainties faced by the subjects studied, and provide incentive for developing further understanding of these really not-so-unusual situations.

SURVIVING DIVORCE

Identifying members of broken families as survivors highlights the belief that, though exceedingly common (the majority of marriages now end in divorce, we are told), divorce is viewed as a crisis requiring heroic actions. Subjects in two of the studies felt the need for extraordinary behaviors, many involving products, to adapt to new family structures and relationships. Many such behaviors were exploratory and, apparently, were sometimes considered incorrect by those affected by the breakup of the marriage.

Bates and Gentry provide a less traumatic picture of divorce than that hinted at in the Otnes, Zolner and Lowrey study. Bates and Gentry show mothers to be quite resourceful and inventive in discovering ways to structure life with their children and members of their extended families so as to preserve traditional behaviors developed by the intact family. Their findings provide a good start toward defining the central concept, the "feeling of family," that divorced mothers try to preserve or construct.

Relatives, including in-laws, apparently also feel the need to respond as if to a crisis situation with a repertoire of behaviors that help the mother maintain a family-like setting for children. Kinship networks appeared to be strengthened by divorce, if anything, and the strong matriarchical flavor of these extended networks brings to mind the sort of structure often associated with African-American families. Children were encouraged (or even forced) to mature more quickly and to learn adult consumer roles while still under their mother's care. One can speculate that this anticipatory learning of adult consumer roles may help better prepare children for real consumer roles later. Furthermore, closer relationships between the custodial parent and children seemed to result.

Strangely, all of these adapting behaviors and resulting strengthening of relationships cast an almost positive light on the consequences of divorce. Surely that is not the intention of Bates and Gentry's interpretation. One consequence of their finding that divorced parents enhance the sense of family by preserving past behavior suggests divorce may encourage the preservation of customs and rituals, including ethnic and other specialized behavior.

Otnes, Zolner and Lowrey, on the other hand, show one of the consequences of divorce to be a confusion over proper behavior with respect to gift-giving. Goods were apparently often used in ways intended to manipulate and modify relationships and to communicate shifts in sentiment that were not easily verbalized. As in the Bates and Gentry study, the researchers provide a strong feeling that conventional family structure and life are still normative, as in the comment,

> Some gift exchange is clearly used as an attempt to signal to children that relationships between parents in general, and the holidays, in particular, are as normal as possible, given the circumstances of divorce and/or remarriage.

However, whereas Bates and Gentry's subjects interpreted sustained marriage as the norm and divorce as a crisis outcome and therefore used goods effectively to restore as much "normalcy" as possible, subjects here attempted to use gifts to adapt to new relationships forced by divorce, but some of these efforts were not very successful.

SPENDING PATTERNS

Walsh and Spiggle adapt the admirable strategy of selecting consumer subjects at an important turning point, namely college students living on campus and learning new roles as independent consumers, while still closely associated with and in varying degrees still dependent upon their parents. During such turning points, where students are learning new social roles and experimenting with new consumer behaviors, the learning process is nearer the surface and perhaps more easily discussed by subjects, since it has not become habitual and taken for granted. The subjects displayed quite different patterns of adaptation to their separation from parents. While many of these behaviors reflect realistic adaptation to their new freedom and new responsibilities for managing their own affairs, it is distressing to find some confusion and downright conflicting behaviors as David's, who said he used credit cards both to limit spending and to facilitate impulsive and even foolish spending. David's behavior could develop into careful money management, but (more likely) it could lead to ultimate financial disaster.

Melissa characterized some of her own behavior as somewhat irrational, yet found these "foolish" purchases led to high satisfaction levels. Jason's mother engaged in enabling behavior that fostered his belief that money comes from banks, in much the same way big city children are said to think milk comes from supermarkets. Jason rationalized foolish purchases as necessities, and seems headed toward troubles in marriage, since marriage often founders when one or both partners handle economic matters poorly. Thus, the study indirectly ties into the two investigations of economic and consumption aspects of divorce by suggesting dysfunctional behaviors young persons may bring into marriage.

Like the adults adapting to divorce, who tried to use goods in mostly positive ways to increase satisfaction (to maintain or restore "normalcy" or to help establish a new set of workable relationships) some of the students' behaviors clearly represent successful budgeting strategies. However, all four students also learned that immediate gratification sometimes can come from irrational, nonprescribed behaviors that they themselves hardly approve.

Clearly, much further study of these attempts to develop adaptive behaviors is required. The three studies reported today have made an important start toward suggesting questions and directions for this on-going investigation.

The Relationship Between Knowledge and Search: It Depends

Carol A. Fiske, University of South Carolina
Lisa A. Luebbehusen, University of South Carolina
Anthony D. Miyazaki, University of South Carolina
Joel E. Urbany, University of South Carolina[1]

ABSTRACT

While consumer behavior researchers have discussed the relationship between knowledge and external search behavior extensively, little consensus has emerged regarding the direction and form of that relationship, and little discussion has been offered as to why different relationships emerge. We review the literature in an attempt to reconcile these varying findings, concluding that the knowledge-search relationship is moderated by a number of factors, including the particular dimensions of knowledge and search under consideration. Further, we present a preliminary discussion of how characteristics of the task environment likely moderate the effects of knowledge on search. Research directions are also considered.

Three of the top ten most frequently cited articles in the *Journal of Consumer Research* between 1974 and 1989 (Brucks 1985; Bettman and Park 1980; Johnson and Russo 1984) address the impact of consumer knowledge on search behavior and information processing, suggesting substantial interest in the topic (cf. Cote, Leong, and Cote 1991). There exists an empirical inconsistency in this literature, however, that merits a close look. While many studies have found positive effects of knowledge on search (e.g., Brucks 1985; Srinivasan and Ratchford 1991), several others have found negative effects (see the summary in Beatty and Smith 1987), and still others suggest an inverted-U relationship (cf. Bettman and Park 1980; Johnson and Russo 1984). We explore this inconsistency with the aim of providing an account for different findings in light of the many different operationalizations of the knowledge and search constructs. We conclude that, while general directional (i.e., positive or negative) predictions are typically made regarding the effects of knowledge on search behavior, the nature of this relationship appears to depend significantly upon the conceptual and operational definitions of knowledge and search, as well as a host of what can be called task or market characteristics (Moore and Lehmann 1980).

We begin by briefly reviewing conceptual accounts of the potential effects of knowledge on external search. We then discuss some general conclusions from the empirical literature and develop a preliminary model describing how knowledge-search effects may be moderated.[2]

CONCEPTUAL TREATMENT AND EMPIRICAL EVIDENCE

Before examining the literature, it is useful to distinguish between two components of knowledge which appear in discussions of the knowledge-search relationship. Punj and Staelin (1983) discuss a dimension of knowledge that pertains to the quantity of directly relevant brand information held in memory (i.e., the elements of the "relevant alternative by attribute" matrix; p. 368). Although they refer to this dimension of knowledge as Usable Prior Information or Usable Prior Knowledge, it may be more appropriate to refer to it as Brand Knowledge (BK), since it is concerned with direct information about brands (or alternatives) currently available in the market of interest (see Brucks' [1986] reference to "brand facts" and "personal product usage").

A second dimension of knowledge described by Punj and Staelin (1983) is Prior Memory Structure, which refers to "the consumer's knowledge of the buying process as well as knowledge associated with [the product category] in general" (p. 368). To distinguish this more general knowledge construct from specific brand knowledge, we label it Product Category Knowledge (PCK).[3] Thus, consumers high in PCK know more about important attributes and their interrelationships, know what questions to ask, can disregard irrelevant information, are better able to comprehend new information, and can process information faster (Alba 1983; Alba and Hutchinson 1987; Bettman 1979; Brucks 1985, 1986; Chi 1981; Punj and Staelin 1983). There are two reasons for distinguishing BK from PCK. First, the two constructs may have different effects on search behavior. Second, while BK and PCK likely develop in tandem over time, there are many situations in which existing PCK is relevant to a search problem, yet BK is not (e.g., when a consumer moves to a new market or several new brands have been introduced since the last purchase). Below, we briefly review the different explanations of the knowledge-search relationship and then consider how the distinction between BK and PCK provides further insight into the empirical results.

Positive Relationship

The positive knowledge-search relationship reflects a *facilitating effect* of knowledge: more knowledgeable consumers have better developed cognitive structures in place which improve their efficiency in (i.e., lower their cost of) gathering and processing new information (cf. Alba and Hutchinson 1987; Chi 1981; Punj and Srinivasan 1989). In addition, such consumers have more cognitive resources which can be devoted to search, enhanced abilities to encode new information, and knowledge of what questions to ask in the search process (Brucks 1985). A number of studies have identified primarily positive effects of knowledge on search behavior and tend to focus on PCK rather than on BK (Brucks 1985; Duncan and Olshavsky 1982; Jacoby, Chestnut, and Fisher 1978; Srinivasan and Ratchford 1991; Urbany, Dickson, and Wilkie 1989).

Negative Relationship

Brand knowledge (i.e., information about specific brands or alternatives) provides the most straightforward account of a nega-

---

[1]The authors (listed in alphabetical order) would like to thank Paul Miniard, Mike Barone, and two anonymous reviewers for constructive comments on earlier drafts.

[2]Note that a formal meta-analysis of this literature would be difficult, if not impossible, to interpret given the noncomparability of measures used across studies (see Table).

[3]Note that PCK contains components of both declarative knowledge and procedural knowledge (cf. Anderson 1976). Our sole purpose here is to distinguish specific knowledge about brands from all other kinds of knowledge, as Punj and Staelin (1983) intended.

TABLE
Summary of Measures in Knowledge-Search Studies

KNOWLEDGE MEASURES

	Brand Knowledge	Product Category Knowledge	Mixed
Subjective	None	<u>Self-rating in general: (2 examples)</u> 9-pt single-item question: "How much do you feel you know about CD players?" 7-pt scale of knowledge level for stereos, 1=very low, 7=very high. <u>Self-rating relative to the population: (2 examples)</u> Self-rating of previous knowledge of automobiles compared to the rest of the population (5-pt scale), reported # of cars owned, reported # of cars ridden in. 7-pt "Rate your knowledge of this product as compared to the average person." 1="One of the LEAST knowledgeable", 7= "One of the MOST Knowledgeable." <u>Other:</u> Whether the consumer had previously used the same product type.	<u>Self-rating:</u> 7-pt self-report measure of the DM's opinion on how good a buy s/he would have received at the beginning of the purchase decision. 6-pt Likert-type: "I felt quite knowledgeable about this product category before I began shopping for it." 3 A-D items measuring perceived ability to judge technical products, distinguish good from bad brands, and knowledge. <u>Experience:</u> 6-pt A-D scale: "I do most of the bread shopping for my household." Depth of purchase experience: # of new/used cars bought in last 10 yrs. Width of purchase experience: # of different makes of cars owned by the DM in last 10 yrs # new cars purchased in past 10 years, excluding current purchase. For "self-assessed familiarity": information search experience, usage experience, and ownership status.
Objective	Free recall: "Please list as many brands of CD player as you can." Manipulation of uncertainty: Low uncertainty group was told previous year's price rank-ordering of stores. True/false statements.	Free recall: "Please list as many attributes and features of CD players as you can." Free response regarding knowledge of terminology, available attributes, criteria for evaluating attributes, perceived covariance between attributes, and factors of usage situations for the product that determine attribute importance. Matching terminology to definitions 15 question MC scale to measure objective knowledge of cameras (9 or above=expert).	17-item scale incorporating obj. knowledge of prices, brand info., attribute relationships, and self-reported knowledge. Self-reported ownership/past search behavior "How many times have you [activity] in the last 3 years?" Distinguish between expert and non-experts by using Ss who are undergrad students majoring in pharmacy and who had recently taken a course on non prescription drugs as the experts, and undergrad students not majoring in that field as the non-experts. "Have you bought anything from the bakery in the last month?" Memory probes to elicit existing product knowledge by free recall: "I want you to think about purchasing a (product). Now, tell me everything that comes to mind about (product)."

SEARCH MEASURES

	Time	Activity/Outcome	Index
Subjective	<u>Search time:</u> 6-item scale for perceived search effort: ("I spent a lot of time talking with sales people ...") "When did you buy (product), which month and which year?" "How long before actually buying a (product) did you people think or talk of buying it; was it a short time, or many months or what?" <u>Deliberation time:</u> Measured as whether it took days, weeks, months, or years for the information search process.	Media search: # of TV/radio ads, # of newspaper/magazine ads. Interpersonal search: # of friends, relatives, neighbors consulted. Neutral sources: # of consumer reports or neutral sources consulted. # of 9 different search activities that were undertaken, # of dealers visited, # of cars test driven.	Various indices (both weighted and unweighted), have been constructed using combinations of the following: Unaided recall questions about types & sources of info. or advice sought. Aided recall questions about whether the buyer had consulted friends or neighbors; read books, pamphlets, magazine or newspaper articles; studied newspaper or magazine ads; or watched TV commercials on the product more carefully than a year earlier. Mail order catalogues, Consumer reports, interpersonal sources, store visits, & advice from salespeople. Consultation of acquaintances, salespeople, dealer visits. Retailer search: Hrs. spent searching inside retail stores, # phone calls made to retailers, # brands or models examined. # brands considered, actual shopping time, # stores shopped, # trade sources consulted. Expert opinion, reading brochures, discussion with spouse, auto show, & discussion with children.
Objective	Difference between time spent processing an extrinsic information screen and the time spent processing an intrinsic information screen.	Observed behavioral measures for # brands searched, # attributes searched, & total # of info. acquisitions. # stores shopped in a computerized marketplace. <u>Depth of search</u> - total # info. values acquired, # different brands acquired, # different dimensions acquired, & decision time. Surprise recall task after exposure to brand X attribute matrix.	None

tive knowledge-search relationship. Punj and Staelin (1983) propose that if both internal and external brand knowledge are useful in helping a consumer make a choice, then "the more information obtained prior to active search, the less the need for external search, and vice versa" (p. 368). Evidence consistent with this *de-motivating effect* is provided by a number of researchers (Bettman and Park 1980; Kiel and Layton 1981; Moore and Lehmann 1980; Punj and Staelin 1983; see also Green, Mitchell and Staelin 1977).[4] A second general explanation for a negative knowledge-search relationship is a *selective search effect*, driven by PCK (cf. Brucks 1985). This suggests that consumers high in PCK can identify and focus their search on important attributes and appropriate alternatives relatively quickly (Brucks 1985; Claxton, Fry, and Portis 1974; Johnson and Russo 1984; Newman and Staelin 1972; Srinivasan and Ratchford 1991).

The Inverted-U

Combinations of the previously described effects could account for an inverted-U relationship. It is reasonable to suggest that the leftmost portion of the inverted-U curve reflects a segment of consumers who effectively limit their search because they know too little to even begin the process of search and, potentially, in "blissful ignorance," apply heuristics that do not require extensive information about brand alternatives (cf. Olshavsky and Granbois 1979; Park and Lessig 1981; Urbany et al. 1989). This *heuristic effect* is consistent with the inverted-U relationship proposed recently by Rao and Sieben (1992), which suggests that both novices and experts will limit their search of intrinsic information, but for different reasons: experts because they know extrinsic cues are sufficiently diagnostic in judging performance (assuming that these cues are, in fact, diagnostic), and novices because they have difficulty understanding the intrinsic information.[5] Although low-knowledge consumers possess little brand knowledge (and would presumably be motivated to acquire some to aid in the decision process), they lack the necessary general product information (PCK) that facilitates learning the brand information. Further, confidence in using particular heuristics (e.g., buy at Sears, or judge quality using price) may mitigate uncertainty associated with a lack of knowledge (Urbany et al. 1989).

It is important to consider that both brand knowledge and product category knowledge are acquired through experience with the product category, and are thus integrally related in most circumstances. Therefore, another explanation for an inverted-U relationship would be that the effects of PCK which produce the upward slope (facilitating effects such as lower search costs, greater capacity for search, and knowing what questions to ask) are overridden by the negative effects of PCK (selective search and informed use of heuristics), as well as the de-motivating effects of BK, by the time consumers reach some moderate level of overall knowledge. Of course, even when BK is essentially zero, the opposing effects of PCK may still elicit a curvilinear relationship between knowledge and search (Brucks 1985).

---

[4]The de-motivating effect of prior brand knowledge is contingent on the consumers' (re)entrance to a market which has not changed a great deal (i.e., the BK is not obsolete).

[5]Intrinsic cues are associated with the actual physical and/or performance attributes of a product, while extrinsic cues are product-related attributes apart from the physical product (Rao and Monroe 1988).

Moving to the downward slope of the inverted U, experts are more likely to be knowledgeable about the relationship between surrogate cues (whether extrinsic or intrinsic) and brand performance in a market. To the extent that surrogate cues are truly correlated with performance, highly knowledgeable consumers will attend more to those extrinsic cues relative to searching for intrinsic brand information, e.g., specific feature evaluations (Rao and Monroe 1988; Rao and Sieben 1992; see also Park and Lessig 1981; Srinivasan and Ratchford 1991). This would presumably reduce the amount of search for intrinsic brand information. This heuristic effect may also be applied to the case where consumers know (or believe they know) correlations among intrinsic attributes, and as a result only need to search a certain subset of attributes (e.g., materials used or type of construction).

ANALYSIS

To assess in more depth the relationships described above, we attempted to enumerate all the studies which have specifically examined the knowledge-search relationship since Katona and Mueller's (1955) classic work. Twenty-five papers were identified in the major journals and conference proceedings and were categorized according to the knowledge construct assessed (PCK vs. BK vs. mixed), measure of search behavior (search time vs. activities/outcomes), and direction of the knowledge-search relationship observed. Our objective in the review was to identify commonalities among studies which had identified positive, negative, or inverted-U relationships. (A table summarizing the studies is available from the authors upon request.) The following conclusions were reached.

1. Studies obtaining positive knowledge-search effects tend to use measures which appear to capture product category knowledge. Four of the five studies cited earlier as identifying positive effects of knowledge on search, while varying in methodology, have in common knowledge measures that appear to predominantly capture general product category knowledge, and not specific brand facts. Brucks (1985) took both objective and subjective measures of prior knowledge, but placed subjects in a purchase task in an unfamiliar marketplace (i.e., no brand names), which eliminated brand knowledge as an influence on search, and found that more knowledgeable subjects obtained more attribute information in complex purchase situations. Srinivasan and Ratchford's (1991) measures of (non-brand specific) subjective knowledge also positively affected search, although the effect was modeled to operate through perceived benefits of search. The knowledge measures used by Duncan and Olshavsky (1982) and two of three used by Urbany et al. (1989) addressed general, rather than brand-specific knowledge (e.g., ability to judge, knowledge of important attributes). Further, the product categories examined in those studies (automobiles, televisions, and appliances) are purchased infrequently, suggesting that brand knowledge may need replenishing in new purchase situations.

2. Studies obtaining negative knowledge-search effects tend to use measures of some type of purchase "experience." Srinivasan and Ratchford (1991) illustrate these findings well, as they find search-reducing effects of both positive past experience (satisfaction) and amount of general experience (number of previous purchases). Similar effects of past experience have been found (Bennett and Mandell 1969; Green et al. 1977; Katona and Mueller 1955; Moore and Lehmann 1980; Punj and Srinivasan 1989; Punj and Staelin 1983; see also Reilly and Conover 1983). A consistent theme throughout most of these studies is that satisfaction with previous purchases demotivates search by focusing the consumer's attention on known brands (see, e.g., Kiel and Layton 1981;

Newman and Staelin 1971, 1972; Srinivasan and Ratchford 1991). Clearly, satisfied consumers may have a store of brand knowledge which is sufficient to discourage search, while dissatisfied consumers have greater motivation to seek new alternatives (see also Punj and Staelin 1983).

In all, however, it is difficult to determine whether some measures of purchase experience have captured satisfaction, brand knowledge, product category knowledge, or some aspect of procedural knowledge. Further, it is not entirely clear why some measures of experience (e.g., number of cars previously purchased) reduce search when they may be highly correlated with measures of PCK (which, under some circumstances, appears to affect search positively; Srinivasan and Ratchford 1991). Finally, Beatty and Smith's (1987) results do not fit the pattern described here, as they find consistent negative effects of knowledge on search using what appear to be general PCK measures similar to those discussed in the previous section.

3. Studies obtaining inverted-U effects find varying attention to intrinsic information. The primary commonality across the three studies which clearly identify inverted-U effects (Bettman and Park 1980; Johnson and Russo 1984; Rao and Sieben 1992) is that in each study low knowledge consumers apparently processed information regarding intrinsic attributes less than moderate knowledge consumers and relied more on extrinsic or surrogate cues (e.g., brand name, place, price) in decision or judgment tasks. Presumably, the costs of assessing intrinsic attribute information are relatively high for such consumers. At the other extreme, high knowledge subjects rely more on existing BK or use extrinsic cues because they simply hold more information in memory and/or are more efficient in identifying diagnostic extrinsic information. Moderately knowledgeable consumers are better able than low knowledge and more motivated than high knowledge consumers to search intrinsic information (cf. Bettman and Park 1980).

4. Measurement approaches are quite diverse. The Table presents a categorization of the wide variety of approaches that have been used to measure knowledge and search in this literature. We classified the knowledge measures on the basis of objectivity (cf. Brucks 1985) as well as the component of knowledge captured (product category knowledge vs. brand knowledge vs. mixed). In general, measures which directly tested consumers' knowledge of the product category were classified as objective, while those that were more indirect, capturing consumers' beliefs about how much they know, or surrogates of knowledge such as purchase experience, were classified as subjective. Classifying PCK and BK was sometimes quite difficult, necessitating the "mixed" category (e.g., Rao and Sieben 1992). Measures were classified as capturing PCK if they appeared to assess knowledge of the product category in general, and not knowledge about brands. A relatively large number of measures fit in the PCK group, while only a few capture brand knowledge exclusively.[6]

Like the knowledge measures, the search measures were also classified on the basis of objectivity (where objective refers primarily to researcher-controlled measurement and subjective refers to participant reports of search activities). In addition, we distinguished among time-based, activity-based, and indexed measures of search. As can be seen, the search measures are also very diverse, with most studies relying on self-reported measures of search. Note that time-based measures potentially confound the impact of knowledge on search since more-experienced consumers may be able to search more efficiently and therefore obtain more information in less time than less-experienced consumers. Similarly, an index loses information since an experienced consumer may search differently across these activities than an inexperienced consumer, yet yield the same index score. (For example, experience may lead to searching more brands on fewer, more diagnostic attributes vs. fewer brands and more attributes.) Due to the diversity of search measures used, compounded by the multiple operationalizations of knowledge, few generalizations can be made concerning the effects of employing particular types of search measures.

THE KNOWLEDGE-SEARCH RELATIONSHIP: ON WHAT DOES IT DEPEND?

While the patterns described in the previous section provide some insight, it becomes apparent that our inability to discern a more consistent set of findings is a function of tremendous variation in the types of measures used. We contend that the effect of knowledge on search behavior depends upon the particular components of knowledge and search that are studied. In addition, a number of factors associated with the market or task environment (e.g., number/complexity of alternatives; Beatty and Smith 1987; Moore and Lehmann 1980; Payne 1982) will likely moderate the relationship between knowledge and search, an important consideration which has not been raised in the literature. The remainder of the paper provides an overview of these issues and consideration of research directions.

The model presented in the Figure is a preliminary attempt to organize these factors. It is not intended to be a comprehensive model of search, but is instead designed to illustrate the factors which may influence the knowledge-search relationship. First, we represent brand knowledge and product category knowledge separately, acknowledging that they are likely to be correlated (i.e., they often develop simultaneously). Market stability (Moore and Lehmann 1980) is incorporated to recognize the fact that, on the whole, the more stable a market is from one purchase occasion to the next, the more relevant BK and PCK the consumer will have for an upcoming purchase decision. Brand knowledge (the relevant information the consumer has about available brands) will generally reduce search (no matter how search is defined) because it effectively reduces the need for additional information.[7] Product category knowledge (the relevant information the consumer has about the product category) is analogous to Punj and Staelin's (1983) memory structure, and covers most of the dimensions of knowledge defined by Brucks (1986), which tend to be nonbrand-specific in nature. The PCK-Search path has the potential to be generally positive in direction (cf. Alba and Hutchinson 1987),

---

[6] Since product category knowledge and brand knowledge may be highly correlated in certain instances, it is likely that even measures which appear to capture one component still capture the other to some degree.

[7] There are some interesting complexities regarding brand knowledge that we do not address here. For example, BK may be filled up in different ways — i.e., a consumer may know a little about a lot of brands or vice versa, such that two consumers who have equivalent "amounts" of BK may search very differently. Further, it is also true that a small amount of relevant BK may be sufficient to limit search for two types of consumers: (1) those who are knowledgeable about a brand or brand(s) which they know provide satisfactory performance (cf. Srinivasan and Ratchford 1991), and (2) those who apply simple heuristics to solve the purchase decision problem in spite of limited knowledge about brands (or, perhaps more accurately, because of limited brand and product category knowledge). Generally speaking, though, consumers higher in BK should gather less information in a subsequent purchase.

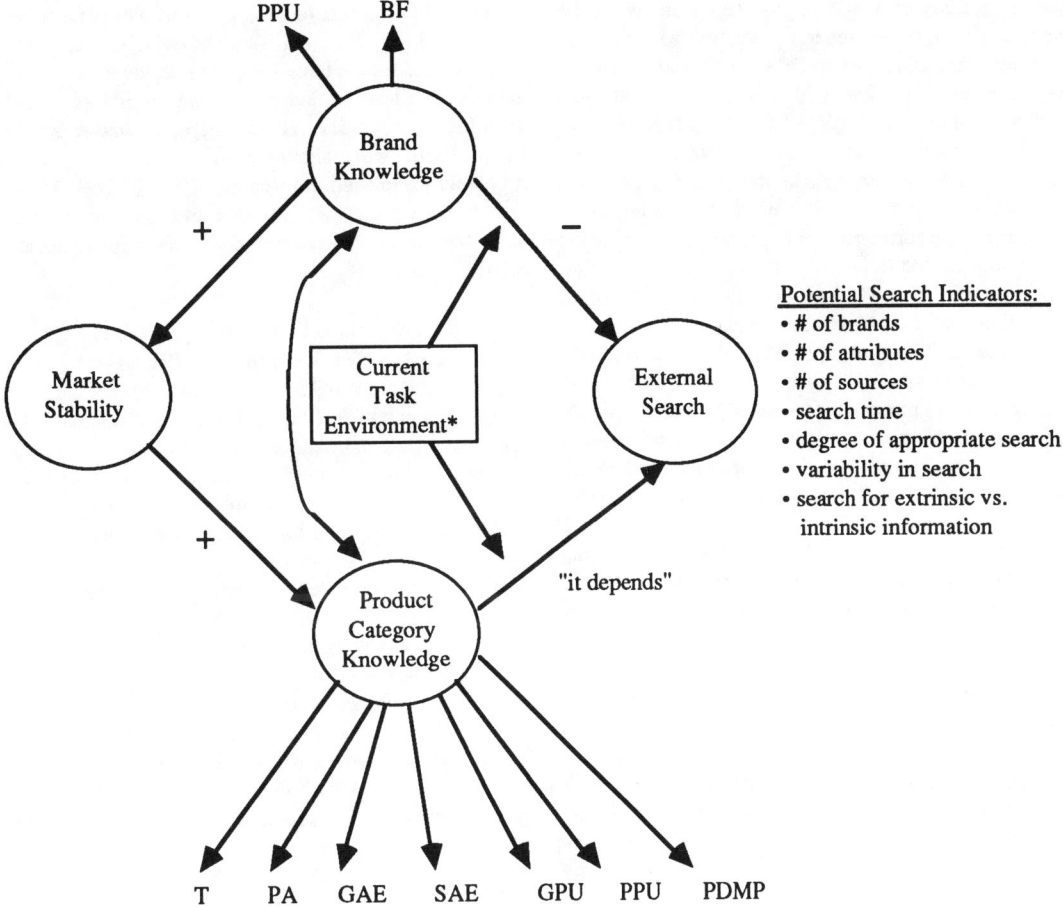

although Brucks (1985) notes logically that negative or curvilinear paths are also possible (thus, "it depends").

The Figure also acknowledges that search may be defined a variety of ways. Economists and managers are likely to be interested in the number of brands/models searched as the key dependent variable (cf. Hauser and Wernerfelt 1990; Stigler 1961), while other researchers tend to be interested in measures relating to the type and amount of information obtained (e.g., Bettman and Park 1980; Brucks 1985), the amount of search "activity" undertaken (Duncan and Olshavsky 1982; Srinivasan and Ratchford 1991), and the consumer's tendency to rely on extrinsic vs. intrinsic cues in search and decision-making (Rao and Sieben 1992). There is no generally "correct" measure of search, and choice of dependent measure appears to be driven by research objectives and/or a desire to be comprehensive. As discussed below, however, the direction of the PCK-Search relationship appears to depend upon how search is defined.

Task Environment and Search Measures

The discussion of how task environment may moderate the knowledge-search relationship focuses on the PCK-search relationship and is initially presented with a focus on a limited number of search measures for reasons of expediency and space. In many cases, variations in the task environment actually reflect variations in the costs and benefits of search (e.g., greater brand differences = greater benefit to search; Stigler 1961). Evidence that the costs and benefits of search may interact in determining search behavior (Axell 1974; Urbany 1986) provides the impetus to consider these potential moderating effects.

Assuming that BK is "empty" enough to create a need for considering external information (i.e., holding BK constant across consumers),[8] the generally positive effect of knowledge proposed by Alba and Hutchinson (1987) is likely moderated by the series of factors listed under task environment in the Figure. The moderating effects, however, are complex and highly dependent upon the search measure used. The most general prediction which can be made is that consumers with greater PCK will better know the outcome they seek, and therefore will tend to search attribute information which is more diagnostic in predicting brand performance. An initial contingency, then, is that the effect of PCK on the *number of attributes searched* depends upon how many attributes are diagnostic (i.e., how many attributes need to be examined in order to predict brand performance confidently). The larger the number of attributes needed to assess performance, the stronger will be the positive effect of PCK on the number of attributes searched. The relationship is also contingent, however, upon the degree to which the attributes are correlated. The more highly correlated the attributes are (such that information about one attribute predicts values of others), the more likely it is that highly knowledgeable consumers will be able to focus in on a small number of diagnostic attributes to assess performance, and potentially reduce their attribute search relative to less-knowledgeable consumers.

Now, consider the impact of PCK on the *number of brands searched*. The traditional cost-benefit model suggests that the cost of gathering information about an additional brand (which is generally lower for highly knowledgeable consumers) will be weighed against the predicted benefit of searching that additional brand (i.e., how much additional utility is likely to be gained by searching it). The effect of knowledge on the number of brands searched depends in part upon the degree of perceived differences in brands (where knowledge should more strongly determine search when there are substantial gains to search), the number of brands available (see discussion below), as well as the number of attributes which are diagnostic (e.g., when fewer attributes are diagnostic, more-knowledgeable consumers can zero in on them, which effectively reduces their cost of evaluating a given brand, and potentially increases the number of brands searched).

Brucks (1985) identified an interesting set of contingencies which illustrates the above arguments. She found that more knowledgeable subjects searched more attributes, but only in a more complex purchase scenario (i.e., where search tended to focus on brands with more attributes diagnostic of performance). Further, she found no effect of knowledge on the number of brands searched. This latter result could have been due (in part) to the fact that only six brands were available in the experimental scenario (three simple, three complex). While we suspect that adding more brands would have moderated the effect of knowledge on the number of brands considered, predicting the precise effect is difficult, as it depends upon the complexity of the purchase situation (e.g., the number of diagnostic attributes). That is, with a large number of brands available, more knowledgeable consumers may have sampled more brands in the simple purchase scenario (because they could easily assess each brand). In the more complex purchase scenario, however, more knowledgeable subjects may have allocated more effort to assessing each of the complex brands and, therefore, may have searched fewer brands than less knowledgeable subjects.

---

[8]Note that BK may itself moderate the PCK-search relationship. PCK (roughly representing the cost of search) may increase search to the extent that BK is relatively empty, where "empty" means a relatively small amount of BK in memory. In short, PCK may facilitate search when BK is relatively dated, but may have limited impact to the extent that BK is full of relevant information.

This small sampling of the potential contingencies illustrates the difficulty of specifying interactions. It is conceivable that all the moderating factors can be linked more explicitly to more general theoretical constructs (e.g., ability and motivation), although we have found this to be a difficult exercise as well. The complex nature of the interactions suggests that the most fruitful research approach will be to carefully define the pieces of the puzzle to examine in sequential fashion. It appears that an important thrust of the future work should be the examination of issues using relatively controlled environments where both knowledge and search can be assessed carefully and the task environment controlled or measured. Two methodological approaches are described briefly below.

FUTURE RESEARCH

Controlled Experimentation. Brucks (1985), Moore and Lehmann (1980), and Rao and Sieben (1992) illustrate experimental approaches which allow for the a priori assessment of knowledge and the controlled measurement of search behavior. These studies distinguished more-knowledgeable from less-knowledgeable consumers via pre-search measurements of knowledge. The advantage of this approach is that subjects bring into the experiment their own natural expertise—as such, observing behavioral differences between different knowledge groups suggests that such differences may be representative of the marketplace. However, a disadvantage is that knowledgeable consumers may differ systematically from less knowledgeable people on other characteristics which influence search behavior (e.g., involvement in the product category). To remedy this, one option is to place subjects in an experimental context in which they learn the information environment from scratch and are tested to assess their levels of knowledge (prior to engaging in a search task). This approach allows knowledge to be manipulated in specific ways and also allows complete control of the information environment to assess potential moderators. Finally, computer-based search tasks allow for objective assessment of search behavior.

In-Market Exploration. Through surveys of recent purchasers of major durables, a greater understanding of the sources used in search and the lower-than-expected search activity for such major purchases has emerged. However, since most of these surveys have occurred after the purchase, the results are potentially confounded by respondent memory, desire to appear rational, post-hoc justification of behavior, and information obtained after the purchase. Assessment of knowledge prior to search becomes particularly muddy, given the level of knowledge acquired through the recent search and purchase process. One approach to better understanding the evolution of search in the marketplace and the impact of knowledge on this process would involve identifying a panel of potential purchasers before or as they begin the search process, administering measures of knowledge prior to search, and following them through the search process. The difficulties inherent in this approach (identification of participants, recruitment into the panel, obtaining unobtrusive measures) most likely explain why it has not been pursued. However, a rigorous in-market exploration can greatly enhance our understanding of the overall search process and the impact of knowledge on this process.

Conclusion

This paper seeks to convey a relatively simple point about a complicated research domain—that general statements about the effect of knowledge on search behavior are currently not possible. The effect depends upon the component of knowledge and the dimension of search behavior under study, as well as a number of task environment factors (which may themselves interact). It seems fairly certain that extending this literature requires a careful assessment of these contingencies.

REFERENCES

Alba, Joseph W. (1983), "The Effects of Product Knowledge on the Comprehension, Retention, and Evaluation of Product Information," in *Advances in Consumer Research*, Vol. 10, eds. Richard P. Bagozzi and Alice M. Tybout, Ann Arbor, MI: Association for Consumer Research, 577-580.

Alba, Joseph W. and J. Wesley Hutchinson (1987), "Dimensions of Consumer Expertise," *Journal of Consumer Research*, 13 (March), 411-454.

Anderson, John R. (1976), *Language, Memory, and Thought*, Hillsdale, NJ: Lawrence Erlbaum Associates.

Axell, Bo (1974), "Price Dispersion and Information - An Adaptive Sequential Search Model," *The Swedish Journal of Economics*, 76 (March), 77-98.

Beatty, Sharon E. and Scott M. Smith (1987), "External Search Effort: An Investigation Across Product Categories," *Journal of Consumer Research*, 14 (June), 83-95.

Bennett, Peter D. and Robert M. Mandell (1969), "Prepurchase Information Seeking Behavior of New Car Purchasers - The Learning Hypothesis," *Journal of Marketing Research*, 6 (November), 430-433.

Bettman, James R. (1979), *An Information Processing Theory of Consumer Choice*, Reading, MA: Addison-Wesley.

Bettman, James R. and C. Whan Park (1980), "Effects of Prior Knowledge and Experience and Phase of the Choice Process on Consumer Decision Processes: A Protocol Analysis," *Journal of Consumer Research*, 7 (December), 234-248.

Brucks, Merrie (1985), The Effects of Product Class Knowledge on Information Search Behavior," *Journal of Consumer Research*, 12 (June), 1-16.

Brucks, Merrie (1986), "A Typology of Consumer Knowledge Content," in *Advances in Consumer Research*, Vol. 13, ed. Richard J. Lutz, Provo, UT: Association for Consumer Research, 58-63.

Chi, Michelene T. H. (1981), "The Role of Knowledge on Problem Solving and Consumer Choice Behavior," in *Advances in Consumer Research*, Vol. 8, ed. Kent B. Monroe, Ann Arbor, MI: Association for Consumer Research, 569-571.

Claxton, John O., Joseph N. Fry, and Bernard Portis (1974), "A Taxonomy of Prepurchase Information Gathering Patterns," *Journal of Consumer Research*, 1 (December), 35-42.

Cote, Joseph A., Siew Meng Leong, and Jane Cote (1991), "Assessing the Influence of *Journal of Consumer Research*: A Citation Analysis," *Journal of Consumer Research*, 18 (December), 402-410.

Duncan, Calvin P. and Richard W. Olshavsky (1982), "External Search: The Role of Consumer Beliefs," *Journal of Marketing Research*, 19 (February), 32-43.

Green, Richard, Andrew Mitchell, and Richard Staelin (1977), "Longitudinal Decision Studies Using a Process Approach: Some Results from a Preliminary Experiment," in *Contemporary Marketing Thought: AMA Educators' Proceedings*, Vol. 41, eds. Barnett A. Greenberg and Danny N. Bellenger, Chicago: American Marketing Association, 461-466.

Hauser, John R. and Birger Wernerfelt (1990), "An Evaluation Cost Model of Consideration Sets," *Journal of Consumer Research*, 16 (March), 393-408.

Jacoby, Jacob, Robert W. Chestnut, and William A. Fisher (1978), "A Behavioral Process Approach to Information Acquisition in Nondurable Purchasing," *Journal of Marketing Research*, 15 (November), 532-544.

Johnson, Eric J. and J. Edward Russo (1984), "Product Familiarity and Learning New Information," *Journal of Consumer Research*, 11 (June), 542-550.

Katona, George and Eva Mueller (1955), "A Study of Purchase Decisions," in *Consumer Behavior: The Dynamics of Consumer Reaction*, ed. Lincoln H. Clark, New York: New York University Press, 30-87.

Kiel, Geoffrey C. and Roger A. Layton (1981), "Dimensions of Consumer Information Seeking," *Journal of Marketing Research*, 18 (May), 233-239.

Moore, William L. and Donald R. Lehmann (1980), "Individual Differences in Search Behavior For a Nondurable," *Journal of Consumer Research*, 7 (December), 296-307.

Newman, Joseph W. and Richard Staelin (1972), "Prepurchase Information Seeking for New Cars and Major Household Appliances," *Journal of Marketing Research*, 9 (August), 249-257.

Newman, Joseph W. and Richard Staelin (1971), "Multivariate Analysis of Differences in Buyer Decision Time," *Journal of Marketing Research*, 8 (May), 192-198.

Olshavsky, Richard W. and Donald Granbois (1979), "Consumer Decision Making—Fact or Fiction?" *Journal of Consumer Research*, 6 (September), 93-100.

Park, C. Whan and V. Parker Lessig (1981), "Familiarity and Its Impact on Consumer Decision Biases and Heuristics," *Journal of Consumer Research*, 8 (September), 223-229.

Payne, John W. (1982), "Contingent Decision Behavior," *Psychological Bulletin*, 92 (2), 382-402.

Punj, Girish and Narasimhan Srinivasan (1989), "Influence of Expertise and Purchase Experience on the Formation of Evoked Sets," in *Advances in Consumer Research*, Vol. 16, ed. Thomas K. Srull, Provo, UT: Association for Consumer Research, 507-514.

Punj, Girish N. and Richard Staelin (1983), "A Model of Consumer Information Search Behavior for New Automobiles," *Journal of Consumer Research*, 9 (March), 366-380.

Rao, Akshay R. and Kent B. Monroe (1988), "The Moderating Effect of Prior Knowledge on Cue Utilization in Product Evaluations," *Journal of Consumer Research*, 15 (September), 253-264.

Rao, Akshay R. and Eric M. Olson (1990), "Information Examination as a Function of Information Type and Dimension of Consumer Expertise: Some Exploratory Findings," in *Advances in Consumer Research*, Vol. 17, eds. Marvin E. Goldberg, Gerald Gorn, and Richard W. Pollay, Provo, UT: Association for Consumer Research, 361-366.

Rao, Akshay R. and Wanda A. Sieben (1992), "The Effect of Prior Knowledge on Price Acceptability and the Type of Information Examined," *Journal of Consumer Research*, 19 (September), 256-270.

Reilly, Michael D. and Jerry N. Conover (1983), "Meta-Analysis: Integrating Results from Consumer Research Studies," in *Advances in Consumer Research*, Vol. 10, eds. Richard P. Bagozzi and Alice M. Tybout, Ann Arbor, MI: Association for Consumer Research, 509-513.

Srinivasan, Narasimhan and Brian T. Ratchford (1991), "An Empirical Test of a Model of External Search for Automobiles," *Journal of Consumer Research*, 18 (September), 233-242.

Stigler, George J. (1961), "The Economics of Information," *Journal of Political Economy*, 69 (June), 213-225.

Urbany, Joel E. (1986), "An Experimental Examination of the Economics of Information," *Journal of Consumer Research*, 13 (September), 257-271.

Urbany, Joel E., Peter R. Dickson, and William L. Wilkie (1989), "Buyer Uncertainty and Information Search," *Journal of Consumer Research*, 16 (September), 208-215.

Exploring the Relationships Between Means-End Knowledge and Involvement

Michael S. Mulvey, Pennsylvania State University
Jerry C. Olson, Pennsylvania State University
Richard L. Celsi, California State University, Long Beach
Beth A. Walker, Arizona State University

ABSTRACT

This research investigates the cognitive basis for involvement. We propose that the means-end knowledge about a product that is activated in a situation creates perceptions of personal relevance or feelings of involvement. We demonstrate the feasibility of this approach by describing the means-end knowledge of consumers at three levels of involvement.

Why do some consumers seem to care more about some products and brands and not others? Why are some consumers highly motivated to seek information about certain products, or to buy and use these products in particular situations? These questions concern consumers' involvement, a key concept for understanding consumer behavior.

Involvement refers to consumers' perceptions of personal relevance for an object, activity, or event (cf. Bloch and Richins 1983). To date, however, most research on consumer involvement is at too high a level of abstraction to explain *why* people perceive a product to have personal relevance. In the typical measure of product involvement, such as Zaichkowsky's (1985) Personal Involvement Inventory (PII), consumers give direct ratings of their interest in a product, or their perceived importance of a product. Such measures indicate the overall level of consumers' overall involvement with the product, but they do not indicate the cognitive basis of that personal relevance. This would require measures of consumers' knowledge (beliefs) concerning *how* and *why* a product is personally relevant.

Celsi and Olson (1988) suggest that the perceived personal relevance of a product is determined by the activated cognitive structure of means-end associations that link people's knowledge about product attributes and benefits with their self-knowledge about important needs, goals, and values. In this paper, we describe an initial attempt to measure the cognitive basis for involvement by measuring the means-end knowledge structures that represent consumers' perceptions of personal relevance.

MEANS-END THEORY

A means-end chain is a simple knowledge structure that links product attributes to the consequences produced by these attributes (Gutman 1982). Olson and Reynolds (1983) described a means-end chain with six levels of attributes, consequences, and values, ordered from less to more abstract (see figure 1).

For example, a couple may decide to deposit money at a small, local bank because it is nearby (concrete attribute) and provides friendly, personal service (functional consequence). Personalized service is seen as important because the couple wants to establish a trusting relationship with the company responsible for managing their money (psychosocial consequence), in order to satisfy their need for security (terminal value). A means-end chain is the cognitive representation of the connection between a person's knowledge about a product (salient attributes and benefits) and their self knowledge (important psychological and social consequences and values). Thus, the end consequences of some means-end chains can be quite abstract—e.g., a person's life goals and personal values.

The means-end approach is based on the assumption that consumers see products as means to important ends. This means that the personal consequences produced by a product are more important (more self-relevant) than the characteristics of the product itself. A product is self-relevant to the extent a consumer sees it as instrumental in achieving important consequences or values. When means-end knowledge is activated from memory or formed in a situation, the person perceives the product to be personally relevant and feels involved with it (Celsi and Olson 1988). Thus, means-end knowledge structures are the cognitive basis for involvement. They also account for how and why consumers feel involved with a product in a particular situation.

Since researchers have not measured the product-related knowledge that underlies involvement, we conducted a simple study to demonstrate the usefulness of means-end theory in representing personal relevance. In particular, we wanted to explore two broad issues about the content and structure of consumers' product knowledge:

Content. How does the means-end knowledge about a product differ between more and less involved consumers? Are there systematic differences in knowledge about attributes, consequences, or values?

Structure. Do more involved consumers have a more complex network of knowledge compared to less involved consumers? Do the interrelationships differ at the attribute, consequence, or value levels?

METHODOLOGY

To examine these issues, we identified three groups of consumers with very different levels of involvement (low, moderate, and high) and compared their means-end knowledge structures about tennis rackets. We measured subjects' involvement with the *activity* of *playing* tennis because most people's self-relevance is focused on playing tennis, not on tennis products. We measured subjects' product knowledge about tennis rackets because this is the most critical product for playing the sport.

Subjects were 58 people from a University community, selected on a convenience basis. This group consisted of 23 women and 35 men, ranging in age from 18 to 51—90% were between the ages of 20 and 22. All but four of the subjects were college students.

We measured subjects' involvement with playing tennis using Zaichkowsky's (1985) Personal Involvement Inventory (PII scores can range from 20-140). Based on their PII scores, we assigned subjects to three, nonoverlapping involvement groups—Low (PII=20-60; n=17), Medium (PII=70-110; n=21), and High Involvement (120-140; n=19). Most people in the low involvement group were novices who played tennis only infrequently and were uninterested in the sport. People in the medium involvement group played tennis occasionally to frequently and were moderately interested in the sport. People in the high involvement group played competitively on a daily basis and were highly committed to the sport (in fact, several were on the university tennis team). Thus, the three involvement groups represented a wide range of involvement

FIGURE 1

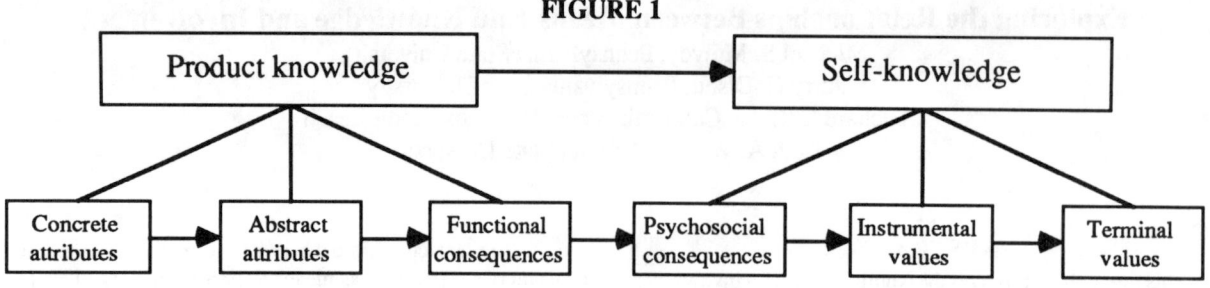

TABLE 1
Listing of Means-End Concepts

Attributes	Consequences	Values
appearance modern	comfort	belonging
brand name company reputation	concentrate	fun and excitement

grip
  grip size
	confidence	impress others
		  prestige, status
		  avoid embarrassment

head size
  large sweet spot
	control
	  racket won't slip
		play my best

material
  flexibility
	exercise	value
		  value for money
		  spend money wisely

price
  not spend too much
	feel
	  fit hand
		winning
		  competitiveness
		  score more points

pros use	not tired or injured	

strings
  string tension
	play better
	  improve play
	  better swing
	  powerful shot
	  accurate shot	

weight	play more	

	quality/durability
	  last a long time
	  won't break
	  reliable	

	satisfied with choice get the right one	

from quite low to extremely high. Three to four weeks after completing the PII, we assembled subjects in small groups of 5 to 10 to measure their means-end knowledge about tennis rackets.

We used a self-administered questionnaire developed by Walker and Olson (1991) to elicit people's means-end knowledge. Essentially, this paper-and-pencil procedure allows subjects to administer the laddering "interview" to themselves. First, subjects wrote down the product features they thought people in general consider when purchasing a tennis racket. Next, they were asked to identify the characteristics that they, personally, would consider when buying a tennis racket for their own use. Of these, they checked the four most important choice criteria in their purchase decision.

Next, subjects completed a self-administered laddering "interview" for each of the four choice criteria. The procedure began by writing the reason the first choice criteria was important to them (often this was a functional consequence of some sort). Then they wrote why that answer was important (what does this get you?). This usually produced a higher-ordered consequence. This pattern of writing why each answer was important continued until subjects could go no further (they reached the end of the means-end chain). This self-administered laddering procedure produced four means-end chains for each subject consisting of two to five levels each.

ANALYSIS

We used a computer program called "Laddermap" (Gengler and Reynolds 1992) to help analyze the laddering responses. The analysis began with a content analysis to reduce subjects' idiosyncratic responses to a common set of meanings. Two independent judges conducted the content analysis, and disagreements were resolved in discussions with a third judge. We identified 26 concepts that summarized all the attributes, consequences, and values mentioned in the laddering responses. Table 1 lists the final means-end concepts, along with examples of the verbatim responses that make up each concept.

Next, we examined the connections between the attribute, consequence, and value concepts. These linkages are often called implications. An implication is the perception of a causal or instrumental relationship between two concepts (a red car implies a fast acceleration). A means-end chain is merely a sequence of causal implications—an attribute implies a consequence which implies another consequence which implies a value. Two types of relationships between concepts are possible—direct and indirect implications. For example, a means-end chain A→B→C contains two direct implications (A→B and B→C), each of which was explicitly stated by a consumer in the laddering interview. In addition, the means-end chain includes an indirect implication between A→C, which was not actually mentioned by a consumer, but is implied by the two direct associations. We combined both types of implications to produce a 26 x 26 implications matrix for each involvement group (available from the first author). The implications matrix accounts for all the direct and indirect relationships between a set of means-end concepts, and thus accounts for the aggregate cognitive structure of the group.

Although some subjects mentioned the same concept or implication more than once, we counted each unique concept and association mentioned by a subject only once. This avoided overweighting associations mentioned by verbose respondents who might mention an association between two concepts several times in the four ladders. Thus, each unique link in a means-end chain received equal weight in the implication matrix.

The aggregate implications matrix for each involvement group was converted to a cognitive structure map by the Laddermap program. The program produces a graphic representation of the key attribute, consequence, and value concepts and the associations between them. Figures 2, 3, and 4 present the cognitive structure maps for the low, medium and high involvement groups, respectively. To simplify the maps, we present only those connections mentioned by at least two consumers.

The format for the cognitive structure maps was suggested by Gengler, Klenosky and Mulvey (1992). Each means-end concept is represented by a circle. White circles represent attributes, grey circles represent consequences, and black circles represent values. The area of the circles are proportional to the percentage of subjects who mentioned the concept. The thickness of the line segments is proportional to the percentage of subjects who linked the concepts (both direct plus indirect associations).

A good cognitive structure map should account for most of the concepts and associations elicited by the laddering procedure and should be easy to interpret (a minimum of crossing lines). The cognitive structure map for low involvement consumers accounted for 70% of all direct and indirect relations, while the maps for medium and high involvement consumers account for 82% and 80% of the relationships, respectively.

RESULTS AND DISCUSSION

The purpose of this research was to explore differences in means-end knowledge structures for consumers with different levels of involvement. We examined both the *content* and *structure* of means-end knowledge. Content refers to the specific means-end concepts mentioned by subjects, while structure refers to the interrelationships between concepts. Both are necessary to understand the cognitive structure basis for involvement.

Content of Means-End Knowledge

First, we examined whether the total number of unique concepts mentioned across the four ladders varied with level of involvement. An analysis of variance revealed a significant main effect of involvement (Hi=9.8, Med=8.1, Lo=8.0; $F[2,55]=3.61$, $p<.05$). A Scheffe test revealed significant differences between high involvement and both low and medium involvement, but no differences between low and medium levels of involvement. This result suggests that high involvement consumers activate more product-related knowledge during decision-making than do medium and low involvement consumers.

This difference in knowledge content was reflected in the average length of the means-end chains. High involvement subjects had somewhat longer chains on average than did low and medium involvement subjects (Hi=3.4, Med=2.8, Lo=2.8; $F[2,55]=8.18, p<.01$). This suggests that high involvement subjects have better defined (more complex or more complete) means-end chains than less involved consumers do.

Next, we looked for differences in the types of knowledge concepts used to make decisions about tennis racquets. We found no overall differences in the average number of attributes mentioned as choice criteria by subjects. Neither were there any differences in the average number of values linked to those product attributes. Perhaps because tennis racquets have a limited number of observable attributes, tennis players, regardless of their involvement, "know" use about the same amount of attribute information. Likewise, perhaps there is a limited number of values which one can satisfy in playing tennis, whether one is an involved or casual player.

Consumers did mention differing numbers of intermediate level, consequence concepts in their laddering "interviews." High involvement subjects mentioned more unique consequences than the medium and low involvement consumers who did not differ (Hi=4.1, Med=2.8, Lo=3.1; $F[2,55]=4.98$, $p<.01$). This suggests that highly involved subjects may have a better understanding of how specific product attributes influence their playing (functional consequences), and how these consequences will help them achieve their end goals (values). Essentially, the product knowledge structure for the highly involved subjects (see Figure 4) is more "interconnected" and "complex" as reflected in the greater number of linked consequences and the longer means-end chains. The more complex means-end chains of highly involved consumers may be due to their greater "product familiarity," as they play more frequently and thereby learn which product attributes provide personally relevant consequences.

Finally, we examined whether specific means-end concepts at the attribute, consequence, and value levels were mentioned more often by a specific involvement group. Logistic regression was used to model the probability that a person would mention a certain concept, given their level of involvement. Model fit was evaluated using the -2 Log L statistic. Differences between the levels of involvement were evaluated using the Maximum Likelihood Estimates (see SAS 1992).

As would be expected, we observed more differences between involvement levels at the consequence level. For instance, *quality/durability* was much more likely to be mentioned by low involvement consumers than high involvement consumers (82% versus 42%; $p<.05$). On the other hand, high involvement consumers were more likely to mention *comfort* in their means-end chains than moderate and lower involvement consumers (53% versus 18% and 23%; $p<.05$). High involvement consumers also mentioned *feel* more often than less involved consumers (58% versus 29% and 32%) and they mentioned *concentrate* more often (26% versus 6%

FIGURE 2
Hierarchical Value Map - Low Involvement

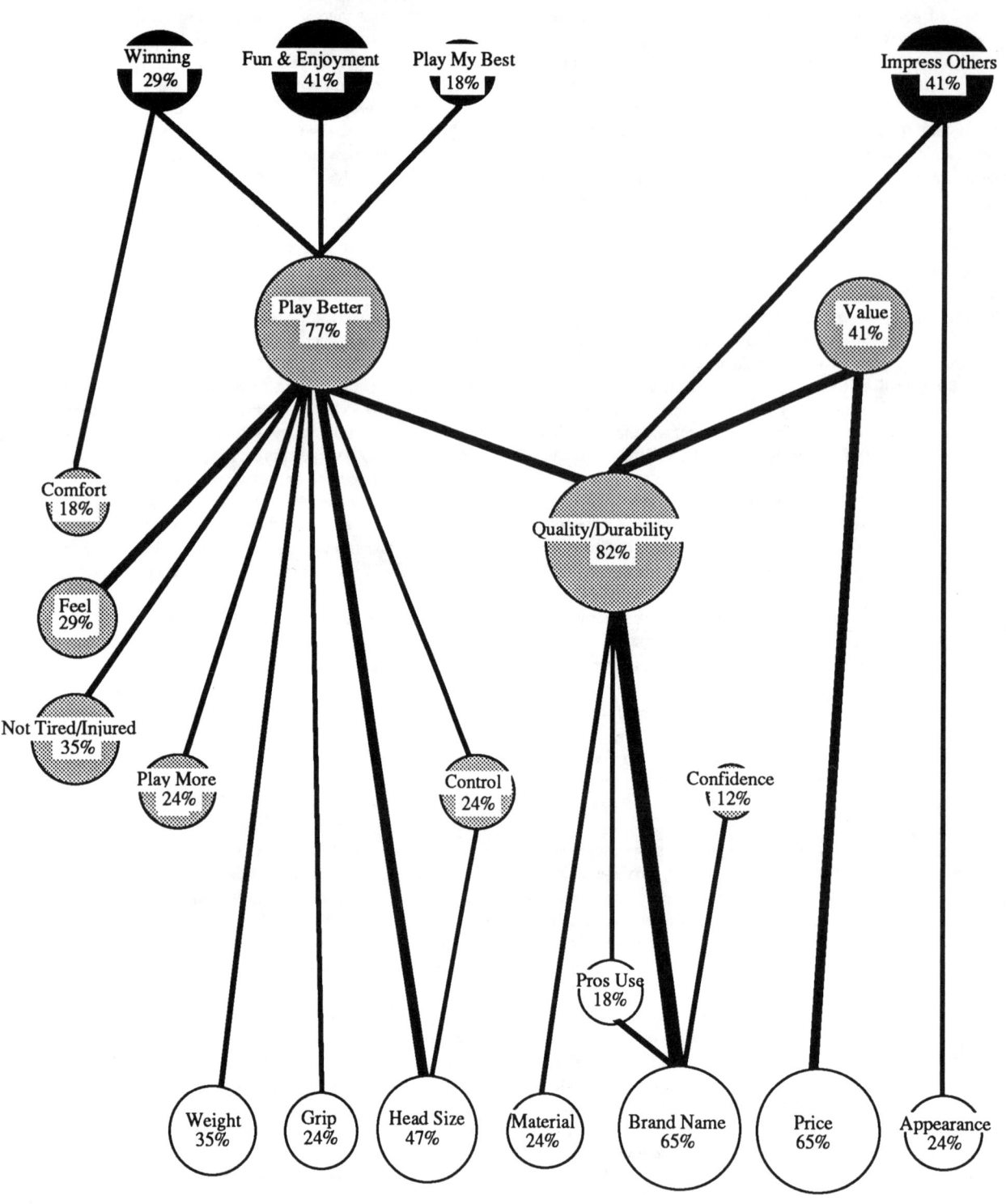

and 5%; p<.15 in both cases). The attribute *racket material* was mentioned more often by highly involved consumers than less involved consumers (p<.05). *Head size* and *brand name* also differed in levels of mention (p<.15). Finally, at the value level, *play my best* was mentioned more often by highly involved consumers (52.6%) than low involved consumers (17.7%; p<.15).

Structure of Means-End Knowledge

Next, we compared the structural linkages between means-end concepts in the cognitive maps for the three involvement groups (see Figures 2, 3 and 4). The overall knowledge structures for the three involvement groups are similar in many respects, but there are interesting differences in meaning at the level of individual means-

FIGURE 3
Hierarchical Value Map - Medium Involvement

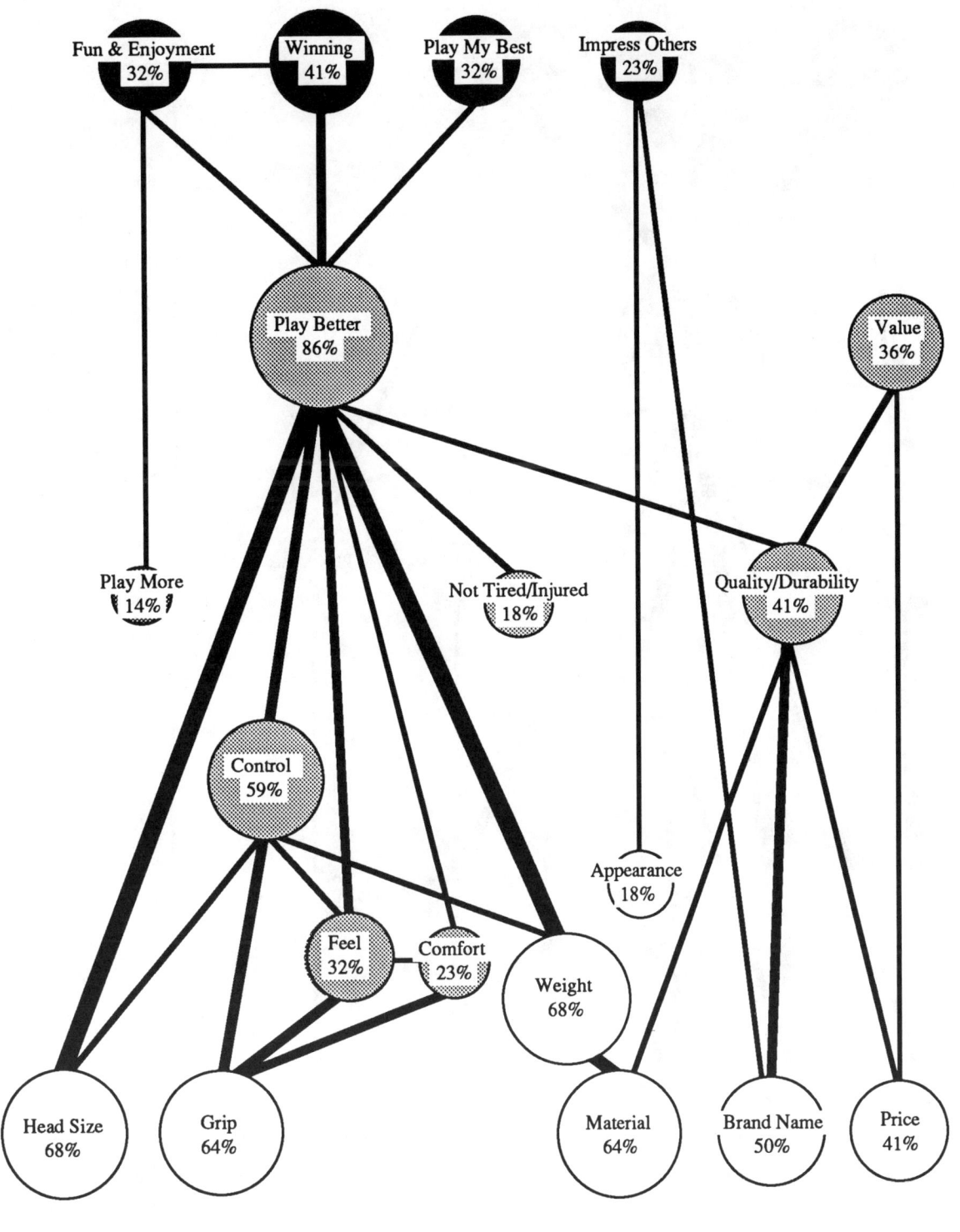

end chains. For example, low involvement consumers seem to have a simple means-end hierarchy: they use *brand name* as the main cue to infer racket *quality and durability*. High involvement consumers, in contrast, are less likely to use brand name as a cue for quality. This does not necessarily mean that quality is less important to highly involved consumers. Rather, unlike low involvement consumers who think about "quality" as a global, abstract attribute, highly involved consumers understand and articulate the specific meaning of what constitutes a high quality tennis racket. Thus, high involvement consumers consider the *head size*, *grip* and the *material* when evaluating a racket. Compared to their lower involvement counterparts, high involvement consumers link these at-

FIGURE 4
Hierarchical Value Map - High Involvement

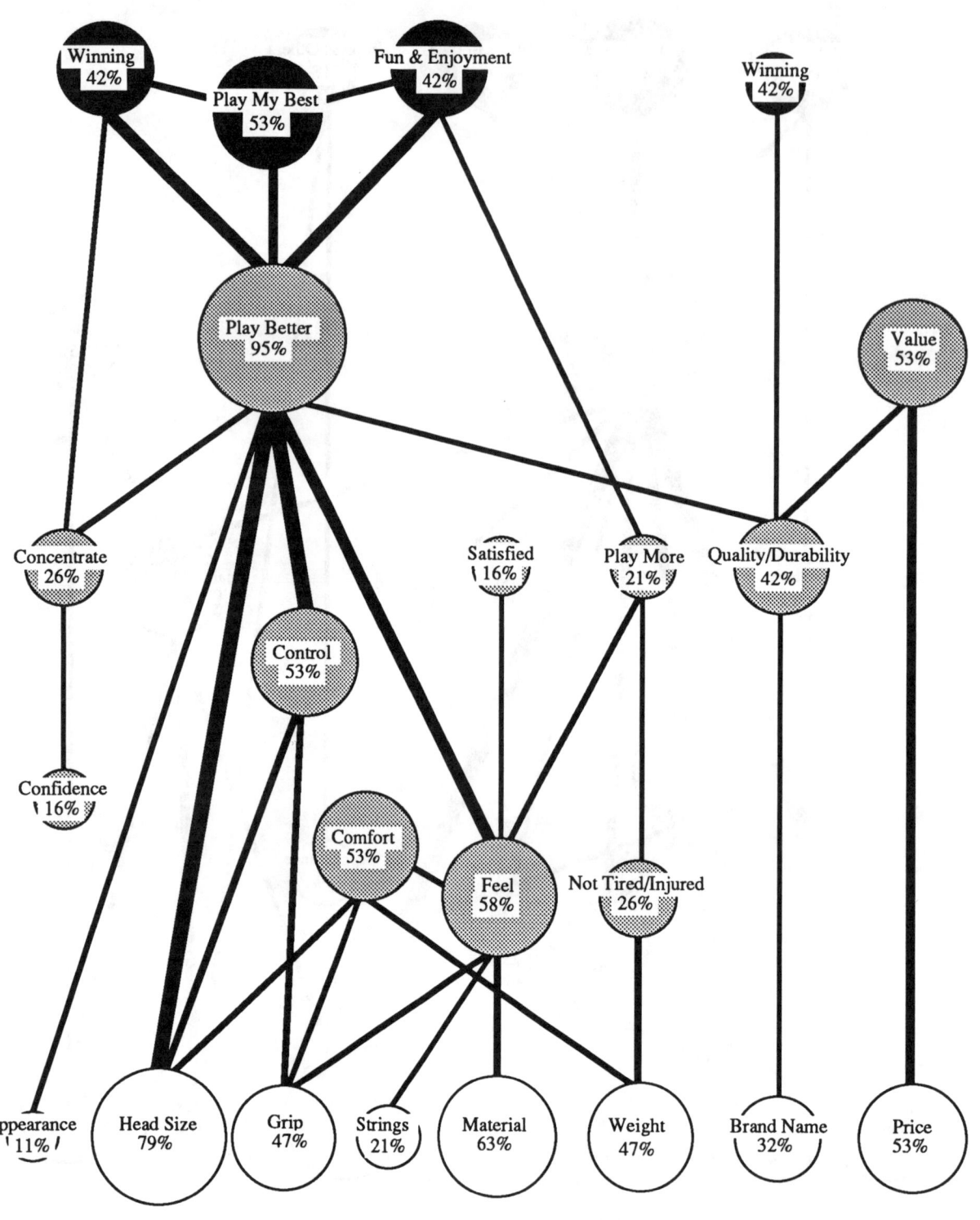

tributes to the benefits of *comfort*, racket *feel* and *ability to concentrate*. These factors in turn, are seen as instrumental in achieving their key goal of *playing their best*.

The content and structure of the other means-end chains vary across levels of involvement, reflecting different levels and types of expertise. For example, low involvement consumers have a simple means-end chain associated with the attribute, *low weight*. They view *low weight* as a means of *playing better*, so they can satisfy their end goal of *fun & excitement*. In contrast, high involvement consumers have a more complex chain of meaning associated with racket weight. First, *low weight* is seen as a means of making play more *comfortable*, which produces better *control*, which allows them to *play better* so they can *win*, the end goal or value. A second means-end chain linked *weight* to *avoiding injury*, which allows the person to *play more* and to experience *fun & excitement*. Although these same concepts also appear on the low involvement cognitive map, they are not connected to product attributes; thus the meaning is not the same. The same pattern occurs with other consequences such as *confidence, feel* and *comfort*.

As mentioned earlier, the thickness of the lines on the map represents the number of subjects who associated the linked concepts. Not only do high involvement consumers have more relationships between salient concepts, but these relationships are stronger. This phenomenon is particularly evident in the relationships between *play better* and the values of *winning, play my best*, and *fun & excitement*. The greater number of lines represented on the maps of high involvement consumers reflects the greater complexity of their means-end knowledge structures compared to lower involvement consumers.

Although this cross-sectional study did not explore the development of means-end chains over time, the results are suggestive. Apparently, the knowledge structures of highly involved consumers have evolved to the point where most concepts are interrelated. The rather subtle implications between many product attributes and functional consequences (*feel, control, comfort*) are appreciated by involved experts. In addition, end goals and values tend to be interconnected for the high involvement consumer. We could speculate that highly involved consumers form a "unit" of self-relevant goals and values associated with playing tennis such as *winning, play my best*, and *fun & excitement*. Perhaps the entire means-end structure relating product-knowledge to these personally-relevant consequences is activated for use during decision-making.

Implications for Future Research

The objective of this paper was to explore means-end knowledge structures associated with different levels of involvement. Of course, the specific results have limited generalizability due to the subject group, the sample size, and the particular product and activity we examined. Our goal is to generate interest in studying involvement from a means-end perspective and stimulate future research aimed at understanding the cognitive basis for involvement.

The means-end knowledge structures provide much richer data about personal relevance or involvement than do broad measures such as PII, which fail to provide insight into the underlying reasons for involvement. It is possible for consumers to have equal levels of involvement (measured by the PII), but perceive the self-relevance of the product in completely different ways. Knowledge of the basis for perceived self-relevance is useful for many marketing applications. For instance, advertisements that communicate an entire chain of meaning, rather than isolated facts and concepts are likely to be more effective (Gengler 1990, Reynolds and Rochon 1990, Young and Feigin 1976).

The present study is cross-sectional. Further research is required to investigate how personal relevance (the relationship between consumers and products) develops over time. We need to understand the evolution of involvement in terms of how product and self knowledge become linked with experience. This will require longitudinal designs and individual-level analyses. Rummelhart and Norman's (1978) work on cognitive learning could be useful in designing such a study.

Finally, researchers should investigate how consumers use their means-end knowledge in tasks such as making decisions. Do they use individual concepts in a means-end chain as choice criteria, or do they treat the entire means-end chain as a single "unit" of meaning? Hayes-Roth (1977) suggested that complex knowledge structures may become "unitized," so that an entire means-end network of meaning could be represented by a "short-hand" representation of the meaning. If so, abstract concepts such as *quality*, *play better*, and *value* may be used as umbrella concepts that "stand for" the whole means-end chain of related concepts. The challenge to researchers is to describe the unitization process, uncover the conditions under which unitization occurs, and develop methods of decomposing the unitized meaning. Once this is done, we will have the means to develop a better understanding of how general concepts as *quality* and *value* are used by consumers in decision making.

REFERENCES

Bloch, Peter H. and Marsha L. Richens (1983). "A Theoretical Model of the Study of Product Importance Perceptions," *Journal of Marketing*, 47(Summer), 69-81.

Celsi, Richard L. and Jerry C. Olson (1988). "The Role of Involvement in Attention and Comprehension Processes," *Journal of Consumer Research*, 15(2), 210-224.

Gengler, Charles E. (1990). *An Architectural Perspective on Advertising Strategy*, unpublished doctoral dissertation, University of Texas-Dallas.

Gengler, Charles E., David B. Klenosky and Michael S. Mulvey (1992). "A Note on the Representation of Means-End Study Results," working paper, Rutgers University, Camden, NJ, 08102.

Gengler, Charles E. and Thomas J. Reynolds (1992). *Laddermap: Software Tool for Analyzing Means-End Data, Version 3.11*.

Gutman, Jonathan (1982), "A Means-End Chain Model Based on Consumer Categorization Processes," *Journal of Marketing*, 46(2), 60-72.

Hayes-Roth, Barbara (1977). "Evolution of Cognitive Structures and Processes," *Psychological Review*, 84(3), 260-278.

Olson, Jerry C. and Thomas J. Reynolds (1983). "Understanding Consumers' Cognitive Structures: Implications for Advertising Strategy," in *Advertising and Consumer Psychology*, eds. Larry Percy and Arch Woodside, Lexington, MA: Lexington Books.

Reynolds, Thomas J. and Jonathan Gutman (1988). "Laddering Theory, Method, Analyses and Interpretation," *Journal of Advertising Research*, 28(1), 11-31.

Reynolds, Thomas J. and John P. Rochon (1990). "Means-End Based Advertising Strategy: Copy Testing Is Not Strategy Assessment," *Journal of Business Research*, 22(2), 131-142.

Rummelhart, David E. and Donald A. Norman (1978). "Accretion, Tuning and Restructuring: Three Modes of Learning," in *Semantic Factors in Cognition*, ed, J.W. Cotton and R.L. Klatsky, Hillsdale, NJ: Lawrence Erlbaum, 37-53.

SAS (1992). *SAS/STAT User's Guide, Volume 2*, Version 6, 4th Edition, Cary, NC: The SAS Institute.

Walker, Beth A. and Jerry C. Olson (1991). "Means-End Chains: Connecting Products With Self," *Journal of Business Research*, 22(2), 111-118.

Young, Shirley & Barbara Feigin (1975). "Using the Benefit Chain for Improved Strategy Formulation," *Journal of Marketing*, 39(July), 72-74.

Zaichkowsky, Judith Lynne (1985). "Measuring the Involvement Construct," *Journal of Consumer Research*, 12(3), 341-352.

Recovering Forgotten Information: A Study in Consumer Expertise

Elizabeth J. Cowley, University of Toronto

ABSTRACT

Consumer knowledge about a product class influences learning and remembering; processes active at both encoding and retrieval affect the designation of importance and ultimately, the accessibility of information. For the expert, more elaborate schema allows them to use their prior knowledge to more deeply encode information, and to access the information later with a rich network of cues. For the novice, the processes at encoding are less important. It is the processes at retrieval which influence whether or not information is remembered. The processes do not act independently, there is evidence of an interaction between encoding and retrieval processes. A study is presented which demonstrates the effects of knowledge on remembering product information.

INTRODUCTION

Information that is determined to be important to a theme (Alba and Hutchinson 1987; Anderson and Pichert 1978) or the accomplishment of a goal (Voss, Greene, Post and Penner 1983) is better recalled than information determined to be less important. The assignment of *importance* or *relevance* may be made at encoding or at retrieval. Evidence exists supporting both the encoding explanation (Alba, Alexander, Hasher and Caniglia 1981; Ausubel 1963; Ausubel 1968), and the retrieval explanation (Anderson and Pichert 1978; Anderson, Pichert and Shirey 1983; Mandler and Johnson 1977; Pichert and Anderson 1977). Alternatively, research in cognitive psychology emphasizes the interaction between encoding and retrieval as critical in determining what information is recalled (Craik and Lockhart 1972; Tulving 1983; Tulving and Thomson 1973).

The explanation offered in this paper is that some consumers assign importance at encoding, while others assign importance at retrieval. The difference between these consumers is the degree of product knowledge or expertise. The ability to assign importance at encoding requires the consumer to have previous knowledge which will facilitate learning, while the ability to assign importance at retrieval requires an elaborated schema which provides an orderly search for important information. The expert is skilled in distinguishing between important and unimportant information, as well as between relevant and irrelevant information (Alba and Hutchinson 1987). The novice, on the other hand, focuses on surface details (Chi, Feltovich and Glaser 1981), and peripheral cues (Brucks 1985).

The Encoding Hypothesis

The encoding hypothesis posits that processes operative during the encoding of the information ultimately affect what information is learned and remembered. Anderson, Pichert and Shirey (1983) offer three mechanisms responsible for this effect. First, the schema directs the attention of the processor to specific details in the text (see Spilich, Voss, Chiesi and Vesonder 1979). Second, the schema provides a framework or a scaffolding which facilitates the collection of information significant to the schema (Ausubel 1963; Chiesi, Spilich and Voss 1979; Spilich, Voss, Chiesi and Vesonder 1979). Third, the schema equips the processor with rules and applications which allow for elaboration through the generation of inferences (see Alba and Hutchinson 1987).

Support for the encoding hypothesis is offered by Chiesi, Spilich and Voss (1979). They provide evidence that a more developed schema serves as a framework for organizing information as it is encoded. The presence of a framework allows for comprehension of more complex information (experiments three and five). Subjects with more elaborate knowledge structures perform better on tests of recall. The processes active during encoding appear to have had less influence on subjects with less developed schemas.

The Retrieval Hypothesis

The retrieval hypothesis proposes that the schema influences processes responsible for the retrieval of the information. The schema may provide: a guide for an orderly search through memory (Alba and Hutchinson 1987); plausible details for reconstruction if information is missing (Anderson, Pichert and Shirey 1983); and rules for editing less important information (Anderson and Pichert 1978). The more complex the schema directing the search, reconstruction or editing, the more pronounced the effect.

Anderson and Pichert (1978) demonstrate support of the retrieval hypothesis. Subjects given a perspective (either a burglar or a homebuyer) prior to reading a story which describes a home and its contents, were required to recall information from the original perspective and later from the other perspective. The information recalled with the first perspective is interpreted as an indication of encoding effects. The information recalled with the other perspective is interpreted as an indication of retrieval effects. Subjects were found to *edit* the information they initially acquired since they recalled additional information relevant to the second perspective. The design does not effectively manipulate encoding, and therefore does not test for the effects of the processes active at encoding. Implicit in the paradigms used in the study of either the retrieval or the encoding processes, is the assumption that the processes are independent. Evidence in cognitive psychology suggests that the processes are *not* independent. The external and cognitive environment at encoding determines the characteristics of the memory trace, which influences the ability to retrieve the original information (Tulving 1983; Tulving and Thomson 1973). The encoding/retrieval paradigm (Thomson and Tulving 1970; Tulving and Osler 1968) requires that both encoding and retrieval be manipulated for the individual processes and the interaction to be understood (Tulving 1983). To properly assess the processes influencing the *importance* designation, both encoding and retrieval must be manipulated.

In summary, there are three ways that schemas may affect the encoding of information; by directing attention, by providing a scaffolding and by encouraging inferential elaboration. There are also three ways that schemas affect retrieval; by supporting an orderly search, by aiding in the reconstruction of missing information and by providing rules for editing. There is also evidence of an interaction between the encoding and retrieval; *encoding specificity* for example. Encoding, retrieval and their interaction must be considered when studying recall.

The previous discussion indicates the degree of elaboration of the knowledge structures allows for the processes at either encoding or recall to influence recall. Consumers with different levels of prior knowledge, and therefore different degrees of elaboration in these knowledge structures, will be differentially influenced by the processes active at both encoding and retrieval.

The difference in knowledge structures and their influence on recall, is discussed in the next section.

EXPERTISE

Expert-Novice Differences

The results of a series of studies examining chess experts by Chase and Simon (1973) caused a shift in focus from the differences in search strategies as a source of expertise to the differences in the quantity, content and organization of localized knowledge. Experts are characterized as having more domain specific information (Chi, Glaser and Rees 1982; Mitchell, Dacin and Chi 1993) which is more organized than the domain specific knowledge held by the novice (Alba and Hutchinson 1987; Chi, Feltovich and Glaser 1982; Fiske, Kinder and Larter 1983). Consequently, the expert will have a more comprehensive schema for the domain when compared to the novice.

Lurigio and Carroll (1985) used semistructured interviews, sorting tasks and decision settings to evaluate the structure of expert and novice probation officers' schema and its influence on decision making. They found that expert probation officers integrated new experiences by rejecting less useful information and enriching the present schemas with more useful information. Spilich, Vesonder, Chiesi and Voss (1979) found that high knowledge subjects offered information which was not present in their earlier verbal protocols when later questioned. They attribute this finding to the expert's elaborate schema which facilitates discrimination between more and less useful information. This ability to discriminate facilitates the *editing* demonstrated by Anderson and Pichert (1978).

H_1: Experts will edit (provide information in the second recall which was previously unrecallable) more than will novices, when they are given a second retrieval context.

H_2: Experts will edit based on importance, novices will be less able to do so.

Encoding versus Retrieval Processes

Knowledge can be represented as hierarchical, with highly inclusive concepts subsuming more specific information. Availability of the appropriate specific information will improve assimilation of incoming information (Ausubel 1960; Ausubel, Robbins and Blake 1957). This suggests that encoding will be facilitated with a more elaborate knowledge structure which contains more specific information. However, encoding information at a specific level may influence the ability to retrieve the information. For instance, if information is encoded with a general schema (shopping for a bicycle), then all information relevant to shopping for a bicycle will be considered as important. If the information is then retrieved with a specific schema (shopping for a trendy bike or shopping for a durable bike), the retrieved information will differ depending on what is important for a trendy bike in one instance, and what is important for a durable bike in the other. This is *editing*.

Conversely, if information is encoded with a specific schema which assigns importance on the basis of that schema, and retrieved with a different specific schema, then changing the assignment of importance will be difficult. Thus, less information will be recalled (Cowley 1993). It is the expert that possesses both general and specific schema. The expert will better be able to provide information important to the situation if allowed to encode with a general schema, than if asked to use different specific schema. The novice will always use a general schema to encode information, therefore there will differ less in their performance.

H_3: Experts will edit more when information is encoded with a general context and retrieved with a specific context, than if encoded and retrieved with a specific context. There will be less difference in editing performance for novices.

Demonstrating that information can be recovered by providing a different retrieval context is evidence of the influence of the processes active during retrieval (Anderson and Pichert 1978; Anderson, Pichert and Shirey 1983; Pichert and Anderson 1977). A change in the influence of the retrieval condition by changing the encoding condition evidences an interaction between encoding and retrieval.

Summary

The expert will edit more often than the novice. The information edited by the expert will be important to the second retrieval context. Editing provides evidence of the influence of the processes active at retrieval (the retrieval explanation). The evidence is that the designation of importance is made at retrieval.

The expert will edit more if allowed to encode information with a general context, than if provided a specific context. Variation in the magnitude of the influence of the retrieval processes as a result of a manipulation of the encoding condition evidences an interaction between encoding and retrieval.

METHOD

In order to understand the influences of the processes active during encoding and retrieval, two different conditions are used. Retrieval is manipulated in both conditions by providing two different usage contexts on two separate recall occasions. Encoding is manipulated between subjects. In one condition subjects encode with a context, in the other condition they do not. The context condition is a replication of the procedure used in Anderson and Pichert (1978) which manipulates retrieval within subjects. In the no context condition subjects are provided usage contexts at retrieval only.

Subjects and Design

Sixty Six undergraduate students[1] of an eastern university were randomly assigned to one of two encoding conditions: context or no context. Those assigned to the context condition were given a usage context before being instructed to read a story slowly and carefully. Those assigned to the no context condition were not given a usage context, they were just asked to read the story slowly and carefully. Students were allowed to take as much time as they wanted to read the story once. Reading time varied between 1.5 and 3 minutes.

Recall was measured twice. Once for an image related context, and again for a function related context[2]. Consequently,

---

[1] Four of the subjects did not understand the instructions and one subject guessed the hypotheses of the study, their data was is not included in the analysis.

[2] The image related context was operationalized by instructing the subjects to imagine that they have recently joined a bicycle club, that the club meets for rides on weekend afternoons. They have been to one meeting, and they like the people in the club very much, but they noticed that everyone has a trendy, stylish bike. They are going shopping for a new bike. The functional usage context is operationalized by instructing the subjects that they want a bicycle to get them from point A to point B. That they do not need anything fancy, just something durable and reliable. They are also concerned for their safety on the street.

the design contained two between subject factors; 2 context conditions; context, no context x 2 knowledge levels; expert and novice, and one within subjects factor; image and functional contexts.

Subjects were designated as expert, intermediate or novice on the basis of their subjective and objective knowledge, familiarity and experience scores. Only experts and novices are used in this analysis, this is discussed in the *Measure of Expertise* section.

Stimulus

Product information was embedded in a story. The story was 340 words and contained 61 idea units. The product information was presented as though it was being seen in a bicycle shop. There were four different types of bicycles mentioned in the story that fall into two general usage contexts; image related and functional. Terminology in the story was not technical, any less familiar terms were explained in nontechnical language. Attributes and benefits were stated, there were no abstracted comments included (ie. the bike is fun to ride). The story was pretested to ensure an equal amount of important information for each context[3]

Measures of Expertise

To properly capture all of the dimensions of expertise, four measures were taken; experience, familiarity, subjective knowledge and objective knowledge. The experience measure was a self report measure of how often the subject rides a bicycle as indicated on a ten point scale anchored with *never* and *very often*. Familiarity was measured on a ten point scale anchored with *novice* and *expert*. The subject was asked to indicate how familiar they felt they were about bicycles. The subjective measure of expertise was taken as an indication of the amount of information the subject held with respect to bicycles on a ten point scale anchored with *novice* and *expert*. Finally, objective knowledge was a raw score of multiple choice questions, definitions and the number of accessible brands.

The coefficient alpha for the sum of these four measure was .93. All of the correlation coefficients were significant ($p < .0001$)[4]. The measures were standardized and summed as the criterion for knowledge class. The pretest scores were added to the sample and an adjusted thirds split was performed[5]. Of the sixty one subjects in this sample, there were 21, 22 and 18 subjects were designated as novice, middle and expert subjects respectively[6].

---

[3] Twenty students at an eastern university participated in this pretest. Each student read the story and rated the importance of each idea unit to one or the other of the usage contexts. Each idea unit was rated on a five point scale anchored with *not at all important* and *very important*. There were 14 ideas important to the image perspective only and 15 ideas important to the functional context only. There were 9 ideas rated as uniquely important to each perspective, but not as highly. The remaining 14 idea units were irrelevant to either of the two usage contexts. An analysis of importance clusters revealed that the ideas were either uniquely important to a perspective or of little importance. No ideas units were important to both perspectives.

[4] The raw scores for the four measures of expertise were correlated as follows;

	Subjective	Objective	Familiarity	Experience
Subjective	1.00			
Objective	.76	1.00		
Familiarity	.88	.77	1.00	
Experience	.78	.71	.72	1.00

[5] The sample was split such that two subjects with the same score were assigned to the same group.

Procedure

Subjects were randomly assigned to either the context or no context conditions. Subjects in the context condition were given the image context. All subjects read the stimulus information and spent the next twelve minutes working on a task of logical inference (French, Ekstrom and Price 1963).

At the time of the first recall, subjects in the no context condition were given the image related usage context, while subjects in the context condition were instructed to think back to the original story about the bicycle shop. All subjects were instructed to write down everything they could remember about the story[7].

Following the first recall task subjects spent five minutes working at the Surface Development Test (French, Ekstrom and Price 1963) which requires that subjects mentally "fold" a two-dimensional figure to match a three-dimensional representation.

Subjects were then told that people can sometimes remember information that they thought they had forgotten if they were given a new perspective with which to think about the information. They were asked to think back to the original story with the following context in mind, they were then provided with the functional usage context. They were asked to recall all of the information again.

Finally, subjects completed a questionnaire gathering the expertise measures, asked what they believed the experimental hypotheses were, thanked for there participation, debriefed and awarded 1.5 bonus marks in their introductory Commerce course.

Dependent Measures

The recalled statements were compared to the idea units from the story. If the subject included enough information to indicate some memory of the idea, credit was given. However, if any of the information was incorrect, credit was not given. Idea units unrelated to those in the story are not included in this analysis[7].

There are four dependent variables. The EDITING variable is the number of idea units included in the second recall that were *not* included in the first recall. The EDITING variable is subdivided into IMPORTANT, RELATED and IRRELEVANT variables. The IMPORTANT variable is the number of edited idea units that are *very important* to the new context[8]. The RELATED variable is the number of idea units rated as *somewhat less important* to the new usage context[9]. The IRRELEVANT variable is the number of idea units remembered in the second protocol which are not related to the new usage context.

RESULTS

Replication

Anderson and Pichert (1978) found that when subjects were given a perspective at encoding and then given a new perspective at the time of the second recall, they remembered 7.1% more of the information *very important* to the new perspective. This translates to approximately one extra idea unit. When the conditions are

---

[6] The mean rating of subjective expertise for the experts was 5.85 of 10, and 1.45 for the novices, is significantly different ($p = .0001$).

[7] If they were told that they could not remember the exact words, but they could remember the meaning, to write down a sentence or part of a sentence that was as close to the original as possible.

[8] A second judge blind to the hypotheses of the study rated 40% of the protocols. 93% of the idea units were identified by both judges.

[9] As deemed by the pretest.

TABLE 1
Mean Number of New Idea Units by Importance in the Second Recall

	Very Important	Related	Total Important	Irrelevant	Total
Expert	1.6**	1.1*	2.7*	.06	3.3
Novice	0.6	0.3	0.9	.03	1.2

* significantly different than the novice at p < .01
** significantly different than the novice at p < .05

TABLE 2
Mean Number of New Idea Units Present in the Second Recall, but not in the First Recall
(by condition)

	Context			No Context		
	Editing	Important to new cue	Related to new cue	Editing	Important to new cue	Related to new cue
Expert	2.3	0.6	0.9	3.9	2.2	1.2
Novice	1.0	0.4	0.1	1.7	1.0	0.7

pooled, subjects participating in this experiment remembered an average of 1.05 idea units *very important* to the new context (IMPORTANT variable), 0.65 new idea units were *related* to the new context (RELATED variable), and .46 new idea units were irrelevant to the new context. Consequently, this study replicates the results reported by Anderson and Pichert (1978).

Hypothesis One

The first hypothesis states that experts edit more than novices. The hypothesis is supported if the expert includes more idea units in the second recall which were not in the first recall than does the novice. The results support the hypothesis, experts provide an average of 3.3 new idea units in the second recall that were not present in the first recall, while novices recall only 1.2 new idea units. This difference is significant ($t = 4.5, p < .0001$). Hypothesis one is supported, the expert edits more than the novice.

Hypothesis Two

The second hypothesis states that the edited idea units provided by the experts will be important to the second retrieval cue. This hypothesis is supported (see Table One). The expert provides 2.7 idea units which were not included in the first recall protocol. The edited idea units are either *very important* or *related* to the second retrieval cue, while the novice provides .9 edited idea units (significantly different from zero, $p < .001$). The difference in performance between the expert and the novice is significant ($t = 3.6, p < .002$).

The expert edits based on the importance of the information. This supports the first portion of hypothesis two. However, the novice also edits based on importance. The finding that both novices and experts edit important information demonstrates that the processes active at retrieval influence what is recalled. The designation of importance occurs at retrieval, this is clear because the edited information is important to the second retrieval context, and not to the first retrieval context.

Hypothesis Three

The third hypothesis states that the expert will provide more information important to the new context in the no context condition than in the context condition. This hypothesis is supported as the new important and related information provided by the expert is 1.5 idea units in the context condition and 3.4 in the no context condition, the difference is significant ($t = 2.45, p < .01$). The difference in performance between the two conditions lies primarily in the information that was very important to the new usage context ($t = 2.57, p < .024$), not in the information related or somewhat less important to the new context ($t = 1.08, p < .29$).

There is a difference for the expert between the context condition and the no context conditions, which suggests that the interaction of the processes active at encoding and those active at retrieval is influential in the designation of importance, and what is ultimately recalled. The provision of a context at encoding does not facilitate the influence of the retrieval process (demonstrated by editing), this suggests that an encoding context may interfere with retrieval for the expert.

There is no difference in the editing performance of the novice between encoding and retrieval conditions. This suggests that although the processes active at retrieval are somewhat influential (see hypothesis one), the processes active during encoding do not affect what is recalled.

The interaction of encoding and retrieval processes appear to be influential in learning and remembering for the expert, but not for the novice. This is consistent with the work of Chiesi, Spilich and Voss (1979).

DISCUSSION

The study presented in this paper demonstrates that experts recall different information in different situations and the information edited by experts for a new situation is important to the that context. This supports the retrieval hypothesis. With the data collected in this study it is impossible to determine whether the schema guides the search through memory or conducts the reconstruction of the original information.

The enhanced performance of the expert in the retrieval condition suggests that encoding with a general context and retrieving with a specific context facilitates editing. The provision of a context at encoding does not facilitate the ability to edit at retrieval.

The difference in editing between context and no context conditions supports the interaction hypothesis in the case of the expert.

The novice is less able to draw different information from memory in varying situations. An explanation of the inability of the novice to distinguish between the important and the unimportant given a situation could be put forth. Though the usage contexts were straight forward, and the product category is not completely unfamiliar to most students, novices are certainly less able to identify the important aspects of product information when compared to experts. The editing performance of the novice does not vary between conditions. This suggests that the processes active during encoding do not effect the accessibility of information at retrieval. As there is no evidence of the encoding explanation, there can be no evidence of an interaction between encoding and retrieval. Future research might investigate the presence of an interaction when the processes at encoding are active in the establishment of the importance of the information.

Results presented in an earlier paper suggest that experts recall more information when provided with a specific context at encoding (Cowley 1993). However, when editing is considered, it appears that a general context at encoding is more facilitating for the expert.

The contribution of this paper is to demonstrate that experts and novices differ in their ability to edit product information given different usage contexts. Also, that the processes active at both encoding and retrieval are important for the expert.

REFERENCES

Alba, Joseph W. (1983), "The Effects of Product Knowledge on the Comprehension, Retention, and Evaluation of Product Information," *Advances in Consumer Research*, 11, 577-580.

Alba, Joseph, Susan G. Alexandra, Lynn Hasher and Karen Caniglia (1981) "The Role of Context in the Encoding of Information," *Journal of Experimental Psychology: Human Learning and Memory*, 7, 283-292.

Alba, Joseph and Lynn Hasher (1983) "Is Memory Schematic?," *Psychological Bulletin*, 90, 203-231.

Alba, Joseph and J. Wesley Hutchinson (1987), "Dimensions of Consumer Expertise," *Journal of Consumer Research*, 13, 411-454.

Anderson, Richard C. and James W. Pichert (1978), "Recall of Previously Unrecallable Information following a Shift in Perspective," *Journal of Verbal Learning and Verbal Behavior*, 17, 1-12.

Anderson, Richard C., James W. Pichert and Larry L. Shirey (1983), "Effects of the Reader's Schema at Different Points in Time", *Journal of Educational Psychology*, 75 (2), 271-279.

Anderson, Richard C., Rand J. Spiro and Mark C. Anderson (1978), "Schemata as Scaffolding for the Representation of Information in Connected Discourse," *American Educational Research Journal*, 15, 433-440.

Ausubel, David P. (1960), "The Use of Advance Organizers in the Learning and Retention of Meaningful Verbal Material", *Journal of Educational Psychology*, 51 (3), 267-272.

Ausubel, David P. (1963), *The Psychology of Meaningful Verbal Learning*, New York: Grune and Stratton.

Ausubel, David P. (1968), *Educational Psychology: A Cognitive View*, New York, U.S.: Holt, Rinehart and Winston, Inc.

Ausubel, David P., Lillian C. Robbins and Elias Blake Jr.(1957), "Retroactive Inhibition and Facilitation in the Learning of School Materials", *Journal of Educational Psychology*, 48 (3), 334-343.

Bartlett, F.C. (1932), *Remembering: An Experimental and Social Study*, Cambridge, England: Cambridge University press.

Brucks, Merrie (1985), "The Effects of Product Class Knowledge on Search Behavior," *Journal of Consumer Research*, 12, 1-16.

Chase, William G. and Herbert A. Simon (1973), "Perception in Chess," *Cognitive Psychology*, 4, 55-81.

Chi, Michelene T.H., Paul J. Feltovich and Robert Glaser (1981), "Categorization and Representation of Physics Problems by Experts and Novices," *Cognitive Science*, 5, 121-152.

Chi, Michelene T.H., Robert Glaser and Ernest Rees (1982), "Expertise in Problem-Solving" in *Advances in the Psychology of Human Intelligence*, Vol.1, Robert Sternberg (Ed.), Hillsdale, NJ:Erlbaum, 7-75.

Chiesi, Harry L., George J. Spilich and James F. Voss (1979), "Acquisition of Domain-Related Information in Relation to High and Low Domain Knowledge", *Journal of Verbal Learning and Verbal Behavior*, 18, 257-273.

Cowley, Elizabeth J. (1993), "Recall: Will Does the Expert Always Remember More?," American Psychological Association Proceedings, in press.

Craik, Fergus I.M. and Robert S. Lockhart (1972), "Levels of Processing: A Framework for Memory Research", *Journal of Verbal Learning and Verbal Behavior*, 11, 671-684.

Fiske, Susan T. (1982), "Schema-Triggered Affect: Applications to Social Perception" in *Affect and Cognition*, Margaret Syndor Clark and Susan T. Fiske (Eds.), Hillsdale, NJ:Erlbaum, 55-78.

Fiske, Susan T., Donald R. Kinder and Michael W. Larter (1983), "The Novice and the Expert: Knowledge-Based Strategies in Political Cognition," *Journal of Experimental Social Psychology*, 19, 381-400.

French, J.W., R.B. Ekstrom and L.A. Price (1963), *Kit of Reference Tests for Cognitive Factors*. Princeton, N.J.:Educational Testing Service.

Lurigio, Arthur L. and John S. Carroll (1985), "Probation Officers' Schemata: Content, Development and Impact on Treatment Decisions," *Journal of Personality and Social Psychology*, 48, 1112-1126.

Mandler, Jean M. and Nancy S. Johnson (1977), "Remembrance of Things Parsed: Story Structure and Recall," *Cognitive Psychology*, 9, 111-151.

Mitchell, Andrew A., Peter F. Dacin and Michelene T.H. Chi (1992), "Differences by Expertise in the Content and Organization of Knowledge for a Product Class", Working Paper.

Pichert, James W. and Richard C. Anderson (1977), "Taking Different Perspectives on a Story," *Journal of Educational Psychology*, 69, 309-315.

Postman, Leo and Karen Stark (1969), "Role of Response Availability in Transfer and Interference," *Journal of Experimental Psychology*, 79, 168-177.

Spilich, George J., Gregg T. Vesonder, Harry L. Chiesi and James F. Voss (1979), "Text Processing of Domain Related Information for Individuals with High and Low Domain Knowledge," *Journal of Verbal Learning and Verbal Behavior*, 18, 275-290.

Thomson, Donald M. and Endel Tulving (1970), "Associative Encoding and Retrieval: Weak and Strong Cues," *Journal of Experimental Psychology*, 86, 255-262.

Tulving, Endel (1983) *Elements of Episodic Memory*, New York: Oxford Press.

Tulving, Endel and S. Osler (1968), "Effectiveness in Retrieval Cues in Memory for Words," *Journal of Experimental Psychology*, 77, 593-601.

Tulving, Endel and Donald M. Thomson (1973), "Encoding Specificity and Retrieval Processes in Episodic Memory," *Psychological Review*, 80, 352-373.

Voss, James F., Terry R. Greene, Timothy A. Post and Barbara C. Penner (1983), "Problem Solving in the Social Sciences" in G.H. Bower (Ed.), *The Psychology of Learning and Motivation: Advances in Research Theory*, Vol.17, NY: Academic Press.

Voss, James F., Gregg T. Vesonder and George J. Spilich (1980), "Text Generation and Recall by High-Knowledge and Low-Knowledge Individuals," *Journal of Verbal Learning and Verbal Behavior*, 19, 651-667.

Summary of Session
Neglected Classics: Three Intellectual Traditions in the Sociology of Consumption
Douglas B. Holt, Pennsylvania State University

This session was organized to begin to address the gap that exists between the theoretical orientations predominant in consumer research and the orientations that shape how consumption is viewed in the social sciences outside of ACR. In particular, the session focuses on intellectual traditions that currently hold sway in the sociology of consumption. While sociology was critical in the early development of marketing and consumer research concepts in the 1950s, the discipline has had little influence on consumer research in the last two decades. This is ironic since it is really in the last two decades that sociology has begun to attend to consumption with increasing theoretical sophistication.

In this session, three key works from the sociology of consumption were selected as exemplars: Georg Simmel's *Philosophy of Money*, Jean Baudrillard's first three books describing the rise of the consumer society, and Pierre Bourdieu's *Distinction* (a reference list is available from the organizer upon request). These works are widely considered to be seminal contributions to the sociological understanding of consumption but, surprisingly, have had negligible impact on consumer research (as measured by citations in *Advances in Consumer Research* and the *Journal of Consumer Research*).

Doug Holt began the session with an overview specifying the nature of the theoretical gap that currently exists in the "new" consumer research. This research tradition's dual goals—to examine consumption at the level of meaning and to take a more macro/molar perspective than currently exists—have only been partially realized. Most of this research is still "micro" in that it does not consider how consumption is socially structured, nor how the act of consumption serves to reproduce and/or transform such structures. In addition, research that has taken a more structural stance draws predominantly from idealist traditions and thus seldom examines the equally-important material dimension of structure.

The three authors discussed in the session offer different approaches to addressing this theoretical gap: Simmel describes how structural shifts from premodernity to modernity altered the nature of consumption, Baudrillard describes how consumption has become the central mode through which society is structured in late/post modernity, and Bourdieu describes how consumption acts as a subtle mechanism through which social stratification is perpetuated.

Since two of the papers are included in this proceedings volume, only the presentation that isn't included—Baudrillard's early works presented by Fuat Firat—will be discussed. Baudrillard is critical in the development of the sociology of consumption for two reasons: he was the first to argue for the centrality of consumption in modern social life (versus Marx' emphasis on production) and he was the first to articulate a comprehensive conception of the consumption system as a system of signs (and thus is the grandfather of semiotically-oriented consumer research). Further, Baudrillard describes the act of consuming as a productive activity in which consumption meanings are cultivated through the educated organization of one's lifestyle, foreshadowing recent research on how consumers manipulate meanings. Ultimately, Baudrillard is interested in using this account of modern society as a tool for critical analysis. At the center of this critique is his observation that human and material values are constructed and transformed within the semiotic web of consumption and so have fewer and fewer material references. Baudrillard's portrait of modern social life poses a number of complex problems for human identity, social change, and certainly also for the manner in which social scientists attempt to understand consumption.

The Impact of Modernity on Consumption: Simmel's *Philosophy of Money*

Douglas B. Holt, Pennsylvania State University
Kathleen Searls, Pennsylvania State University

ABSTRACT

This paper is intended to demonstrate the relevance and usefulness of a classic work in sociology, Georg Simmel's *The Philosophy of Money*, for contemporary consumer research. First, we synopsize Simmel's discussion of the impact of modernity on the nature of consumption: his view of consumption, how consumption was structured in pre-modernity, the relation of modernity to the rise of money exchange, and finally how the changes associated with modernity changed the way in which consumption was structured. In the second half of the paper, we use this Simmelian conception of consumption in modernity to shed new light on two important concepts in consumer research—consumption goals and lifestyles.

Sociologists, influenced by Marx and Weber, often view social change through the lens of production. Thus, descriptions of modernity and explanations of its emergence typically are concerned with economic structure. More recently, however, sociologists have come to view consumption as an important constituent element of modernity (cf. Baudrillard's early work as described in this session), and historians and sociologists have suggested that changes in consumption played a key role in the rise of modernity (McCracken 1988).

While sociologists have only recently begun to explore this relationship, in 1900 Georg Simmel published what is now regarded as a brilliant statement of the role of exchange and consumption in modern society. Unfortunately, *The Philosophy of Money* did not receive a complete English translation until 1978, so it had little impact on previous debates concerning modernity. In the past decade, however, Simmel's work has come to be recognized as a classic treatment of this issue and has served as a rich resource for social scientists concerned with consumption (e.g., Rochberg-Halton 1986; Miller 1987; Featherstone 1991).

This paper introduces Simmel's argument regarding the structural impediments to consuming brought about by modernity. First, we develop Simmel's unique understanding of consumption. We then discuss Simmel's description of the social structuring of consumption in modernity as compared to the pre-modern era and the personality types that evolved to adapt to these structural changes. Finally, we speculate on how Simmel's understanding of modern consumption can be used to extend and critique prominent research streams in contemporary consumer research.

CONSUMPTION, MONEY, AND MODERNITY

Consumption as the Path to Cultivation

Consumption, for Simmel, lies at the heart of the process through which people become cultivated—that is, grow to become participating, reflective members of society. This is because consumption provides a site, par excellence, for what Simmel believed to be the key to cultivation—the interaction between subject and object (Miller 1987; Rochberg-Halton 1986). Subjectivity—the specifically-human capacity for self-reflection, which allows for the self-conscious construction of action and identity—is not naturally endowed; it only develops through the creative tension provided by interaction with objects (including people) extant in the world. For Simmel, consumption provides a vital forum for this subject-object interaction. Through consumption, people come to understand, imbue meaning in, and act upon objects encountered in the world. Consumption provides people the opportunity to refine themselves through interaction with objects in the world. In addition, by confronting, adapting, and integrating alternative world-views substantiated in consumption objects, people not only realize their potential as unique human beings; they also become well-socialized members of a society. Consumption, then, for Simmel, is a profoundly moral activity beholden to the normative ideals of cultivation of the individual, both as a unique personality and as a citizen contributing to the well-being of society.

The Structuring of Consumption in Pre-Modernity

Simmel describes the ideal-typical characteristics of modern versus pre-modern societies in order to examine historical shifts in the social structuring of consumption. Pre-modern and modern societies each pose particular opportunities and challenges for people to become cultivated through consumption. In the pre-modern world, where systems of exchange were based on barter or payment in labor, two primary impediments to consumption existed. First, the overdetermined network of social constraints in premodernity left little room for the pursuit of individuality through consumption. Economic and social relations were naturally intertwined and geographically isolated. Long-term, local relationships based on tradition, kinship, and a diffuse set of social obligations permeated all social interaction, resulting in consumption oriented to propriety rather than individual development. Second, since most production was local, driven by historical needs and regionally specific resources, there was a relatively limited array of goods available for consumption. In this pre-modern economic and social system, the range of consumption objects (important vessels of "objective culture," in Simmel's terminology) to which one was exposed was narrow, resulting in fewer opportunities for the creative tension of subject-object interaction.

But pre-modern economies also uniquely facilitated cultivation through consumption in particular ways. Since the absolute quantity of consumption objects was relatively low and their production local, these objects were readily assimilable by consumers. The objective culture reflected in these goods represented that of the local trading area, which was relatively insulated from the goods representative of vastly different values. Thus, the merging of objective and subjective culture, necessary for consuming in its ideal form, was not problematic for pre-modern consumers.

Modernity as the Rise of Money Exchange

In *The Philosophy of Money*, Simmel argues for a conception of modernity with a more inclusive sweep than the production-focused portrayals of Marx and Weber, characterizing modernity as the increasing abstraction and objectification of social life (Miller 1987). Whereas pre-modern economic relations were local, long-lasting and direct, relations in the modern world become distanced and impersonal. Money, for Simmel, is both a causal agent and an exemplary symbol of these newly impersonal relations. Money is the most abstract and impersonal of things because, particularly in its most advanced stages (e.g., paper money), it is a form with all specific contents removed. Money has value only in terms of its ability to represent other valued things: "Money is the reification of the general form of existence according to which things derive their significance from their relationship to each other" (Simmel 1978, 128). Through the successful employment of its abstract, quantitative, and objective characteristics, money forced similar shifts throughout the entire system of exchange, and consequently, throughout all social relations. Money can be unarbitrarily counted, divided, transferred to unknown others and used by social unequals for heterogeneous purposes. It supports the disinterested stance of the rational actor by replacing diffuse interpersonal ties with an abstract, emotionally distant, quantifiable value (Coser 1977, 193-194). Thus, through money, socio-economic relations become increasingly distanced through the medium of goods. This shift in the socio-economic relations has permeated all aspects of society including, and in particular, the nature of consumption.

In addition to his focus on the impersonal, abstract nature of money exchange, Simmel (like Durkheim, Marx, and Weber) was also interested in money's relationship to industrialization and the division of labor. Simmel describes how economic specialization, which is enabled by the rise of money exchange, accelerates the objectification of social life in modernity. As workers cease to have a direct, holistic relation to the fruits of their labor, the goods produced increasingly become perceived as purely objective, autonomous creations—as objects whose existence is separate from the subjects who produced them, and thus, also from those who will consume them. While his analysis of the rise of specialization in the workforce does not differ significantly from other accounts, Simmel's contribution is to provide an expansive description of its implications well beyond production into the realm of consumption.

The Structuring of Consumption in Modernity

The Philosophy of Money is particularly concerned with examining how these characteristics of modernity—abstraction, objectification, rationality—have transformed peoples' ability to become cultivated. Since consumption is critical in this endeavor, Simmel spends considerable time explicating the relationship between modernity and consumption. Like pre-modernity, the modern era structures consuming in ways that both facilitate and constrain peoples' ability to become cultivated.

The abstraction of social life in the modern era resolves the two dominant constraints of pre-modern times—the intensity of social obligation and the narrow range of available consumption objects. Simmel (like Marx) viewed modernity as a period in which tradition-bound social obligations rapidly dissolved. Freedom of action increased due to the impersonal relations between people that resulted from the abstract character of money exchange. In a monetarized society, persons may be under obligation to many more people than was previously possible, but these obligations are almost entirely anonymous. This allows individuals more autonomy than was previously possible, which the convertibility of money allows them to pursue unfettered. Monetization offers greater possibilities for cultivation because in such anonymous relations, consumption is no longer controlled by local propriety. Thus, the liberating effect of the money economy provides individuals the freedom to articulate the self in the medium of things (Miller 1987, 73-76). Likewise, through the growth of money exchange and the division of labor, the volume of consumption objects available to the average consumer increased dramatically in modernity. This quantitative change vastly expanded consumers' opportunities to confront others' values through the world of goods.

But while modernity resolved some of the previous structural limitations on consumption, these changes also imparted a whole new set of impediments, which include: objectification, rationalization, and proliferation. These structural changes present significant new hurdles to become cultivated through consumption.

Objectification and the Fragmentation of Social Life. Consumption, for Simmel, requires the integration of consumer and consumption object; and so the greater the symbolic distance experienced between self and object, the more difficult it is for the consumer to successfully integrate products. The specialization of labor in modern societies increases subject-object distance both directly and through its indirect consequences on the objects produced. As workers have direct impact on a smaller and smaller percentage of the product, they find it increasingly difficult to "find themselves expressed in the work" (Simmel 1978, 455). That is, the product of their labor becomes increasingly objectified—viewed as something external to its producers, a given element of society whose subjective creation is obfuscated. Ironically, as labor becomes increasingly specialized in modernity, the products of that labor become increasingly commodified. To achieve the production efficiencies possible through the division of labor requires mass production of similar goods. Since these products are no longer directly suited to consumers' needs, they require more intensive work on the part of the consumer to become integrated. Thus, by virtue of the increased separation of workers from products and the increased commodification of available goods, modern products confront consumers as something foreign, something which they may buy with money, but which they will have to invest considerable symbolic and material effort to claim as their own.

Rationalization and the Quantification of Social Life. The rise of money exchange not only increased subject-object distance, it also changed the very manner in which consumers experience consumption objects. In pre-modern society, consuming was an idiosyncratic activity, influenced by the local nature of production and the personalities of producer and consumer. Of central importance were the qualities (material and symbolic uses) of the thing consumed; barter and then money (in its early stages) were merely media of exchange that allowed one to acquire these desirable qualities. However, the abstraction and quantification of all marketable items that results from money exchange eventually led to the transformation of consumption itself. Money's single trait—that it is able to reduce all quality and individuality inherent in things to a common exchange value—transformed the goals of consumption.

Whereas consumers traditionally viewed consumption objects in terms of their particular qualities, money exchange has reoriented consumer perceptions toward viewing objects quantitatively based on their exchange value. The diffusion of money exchange infuses the goods that are exchanged with different properties than in a barter system. Goods become quantified and rationalized. Things are no longer valued for their particular characteristics in isolation from other goods. Rather, goods take on value as a result of their comparability, through monetary exchange, to the universe of goods available. Goods become valued for what they are worth, rather than for what they are. In this exchange environment, consumption increasingly becomes a calculative rather than an emotional endeavor. Objects lost their distinctive character, to be replaced by traits which are quantifiable such as scarcity, relative expense, and newness. Value, which began as a qualitative assessment an object's ability to further the individual's efforts at his own cultivation, is now reduced to an amount, a quantity. This rationalizing process reached its evolutionary peak at the point where people came to view the means to consume (money) as the desired end in itself.

The Proliferation of Objective Culture. The rise of the money economy is accompanied by an enormous increase in "objectified" consumption objects. Simmel argues that individuals in modern society become overwhelmed by this increase. Unlike pre-monetarized societies where the connection between good and self is virtually inalienable, in modern society people are not able to appropriate these goods in such a way that they become instrumental to their life project. Instead, in their efforts to keep up with the proliferation of objective culture, consumers spread themselves too thin, and so do not allow for sufficient interaction with the object necessary for self-development. In modernity, then, consumers often become instruments of objective culture, rather than the opposite.

Modern Personality Types

Consumers in modernity must adapt to these changing social-structural conditions. Simmel offers discussions of a number of "social types"—personality types that have developed in response to the rise of the money economy. These personalities—"the Cynic" (Simmel 1978, 256), and the person burdened with the "Blase Attitude" (Simmel 1971, 329-330)—describe consumers' inability to interact meaningfully with objective culture.

The cynic is one who protects his personal sense of integrity by adopting the rationalizing, valueless mentality of modern life. The cynic understands, accepts, and participates with relish in the calculating character of the money economy. The cynic "...considers the downward movement of values part of the attraction of life..." (Simmel 1978, 256). He is alive to this possibility and finds delight in the many and varied pleasures, stimulations, and objects available for purchase.

The person afflicted with the blase attitude understands the calculative forces shaping modern exchange relations. But he does not accept this condition and so is unable to participate in any meaningful fashion. Rather than re-orient his personality around the value-less nature of the modern economy, he essentially commits emotional suicide by donning "..indifference toward the distinctions between things." (Simmel 1971, 329). Because all aspects of social life are perceived as monochromatic and generally "not worth getting excited about" (Simmel 1978, 256), this individual is unable to interact significantly with objective culture.

Ultimately, then, Simmel expresses his doubts as to whether persons can successfully adapt to the structural shifts of modernity. Simmel found that the inability to develop subjectively significant relationships with the objects of material culture led people to develop a sense of oppression, the social world becoming experienced as anti-individualistic at the same time that it's multitude of opportunities seem to invite creative and individualizing acts. Rather than offering opportunities for self-completion, objective culture developed into a remote and confrontative structure, one which forces the individual to shape his personality in accordance with the dictates of the material world and the materially-oriented way of being (Levine 1986).

A MACRO-HISTORICAL VIEW OF CONSUMER RESEARCH: WHAT SIMMEL MIGHT SAY

A mainstream sociologist surveying consumer research would likely be bewildered by the field's lack of comparative-historical vision. Although comparative-historical approaches were influential in the early development of marketing thought (Jones and Monieson 1990) and are experiencing something of a resurgence presently (Tan and Sheth 1986; Lavin and Archdeacon 1989; Smith and Lux 1993), the historical and situational specificity of many key concepts in consumer research remains unacknowledged (a few notable exceptions notwithstanding—e.g., Arnould 1989). Based on the assumption that the properties of social phenomena are similar to invariant natural phenomena, key consumer research concepts—e.g., exchange, perceived risk, reference group, lifestyle, attitude, values, satisfaction, search—are described as timeless concepts with universal application.

In contrast to this assumed invariance, Simmel's macro-historical analysis of money describes the transitory nature of key consumer research constructs such as desire, goals, exchange, and consumption. In this paper, we have developed Simmel's understanding of how the structural characteristics of consumption were altered by the rise of money exchange. To demonstrate that Simmel's historical perspective can deepen our understanding of consumption, in this section we offer a Simmelian interpretation of two key consumer research concepts—(consumption) goals and lifestyle.

The Commodification of Ends

Consumer research has been heavily influenced by a neo-classical economic conception of action, which examines the means by which people pursue their interests. Such research typically treats the ultimate ends or goals of consumption as subjectively-derived entities exogenous to the research domain. Instead, rational action is taken as a point of comparison to examine the means (or processes or decision heuristics) through which people pursue a given goal. In consumer research, this economic orientation is found in the heavy emphasis given the processes of consumer decision-making (or choice or buyer behavior).

In addition to the attention devoted to means, a growing body of what has been termed symbolic consumer research (Hirschman 1981) describes the ends that people attain through consumption: for example, communicating to self and others (Levy 1959; Mick and DeMoss 1991), sacred experiences (Belk, Wallendorf, and Sherry 1989), and hedonically-satisfying experiences (Holbrook and Hirschman 1982). This research has often been positioned as diametrically-opposed to the cognitive-rationalist assumptions of economically-oriented research in that it emphasizes the subjective, emotional, lived-experience of consuming (e.g. Holbrook and Hirschman 1982; Belk, Wallendorf, and Sherry 1989). Like the means-oriented research, this research stream also often seems to portray a world of universal, invariant constructs, albeit a different set than those discussed in the economic realm.[1] Thus, although one would expect to find a number of useful linkages between theoretical depictions of consumers' means and consumers' ends, instead we are faced with two seemingly-incommensurable sets of constructs that typically "talk past" one another.

Through its longitudinal examination of consumption as a socially-structured mode of action, *The Philosophy of Money* offers an interesting linkage between these two previously-divergent paradigms. Simmel demonstrates that, in modernity, the rational mode of thinking structures not only consumers' means, but the ends that they pursue as well. Consumption objects can be both subjectively-valued in terms of their particular characteristics as perceived by the consumer ("qualitative" value in Simmel's terms) and relatively-valued in terms of their exchange value as set by the market ("quantitative" value). Simmels' conception of qualitative ends here closely parallels the phenomenological orientation of symbolic consumer research, but the conception of quantitative valuing is for the most part missing in the study of ends.

When consumption objects enter the money economy, they become subject to quantitative valuing in addition to, or instead of, qualitative valuing. Goods are appraised in terms of exchange value to the degree that they are exchangeable. Thus, as the market for a good becomes more developed (and thus the good more

---

[1] A notable exception to this characterization is an article by Celsi, Rose, and Leigh (1993), which seeks to link the recent American predilection for high-risk leisure activities to conflicts imposed by modernity on the Western dramaturgical conception of self.

"liquid"), consumption is increasingly structured around quantitative as opposed to qualitative ends. Thus, when Simmel (1978, 443) describes the pervasiveness of the "calculating character of modern times," he is not chiefly interested in the rationalizing character of decision-making so much as the encroachment of means-focused rationality into structuring the goals that people pursue. In the extreme, Simmel observes that means actually become perceived as ends. Thus, we witness such phenomena as shopping as a leisure experience, acquisition as a valued goal, and bargaining and getting the best deal as enjoyable aspects of consuming. In particular, money itself—the ultimate means—becomes a goal rather than a medium.

Here, then, Simmel demonstrates an important and previously unexamined causal relationship between consumers' means and ends. How would one continue to research this relationship in contemporary Western societies? While exchange, and the resultant quantification of ends, has diffused into virtually every nook and cranny of society, there are still a number of consumption categories where the quantification of ends is contested. That is, there exist competing systems of value in these categories that are powerful enough to compete with the market's commodification of the good. For example, consider the consumption of religion, high art, education, and the family. In each of these categories, ideological struggles have persisted that attempt to fend off the redefinition of value by market forces, although these efforts are not always successful (e.g., O'Guinn and Belk 1989). These consumption categories provide fertile grounds for studying the relationship between the impact of market rationalization on ends and other institutional and subjective dimensions of consuming (e.g., Zelizer 1986).

Lifestyles as Strategies for Consuming in Modernity

In consumer research, lifestyles have often been conceptualized as a-historical patterns of consumer preference—elective differences in consumption unrelated to the society in which they are situated. This psychologization of a social concept is fraught with theoretical problems (Holt forthcoming). Simmel's analysis of the impact of modernity on consumption provides an historically-sensitive approach that serves to address some of these weaknesses. Lifestyles can be viewed as the strategies that consumers have constructed to pursue cultivation in the face of the structural impediments posed by modernity as delineated above. Here, we develop a Simmelian interpretation of lifestyle types prevalent today in the United States, arguing that they embody three distinct strategies for consuming in modernity—passive acquiescence, activist insulation, and reflexive alienation.

Passive Acquiescence: Materialism. A materialist lifestyle is one in which the value of consuming is found in the acquisition and ownership of desired consumption objects (Richins and Dawson 1992). Locating value in acquisition and ownership embodies a lifestyle strategy that acquiesces to the quantification of social life in modernity. Materialists accept the conversion of ends to exchange values and, thus, their tastes are structured by these quantitative goals.

Materialism is perhaps the easiest consumption strategy to adopt psychologically because it is harmonious with the structural shifts imposed by monetization (although many people are economically limited in their participation). As such, it is probably the least "strategic" of these strategies, since materialism offers a natural progression for consumers socialized in rationalized modes of thought and exposed to extreme quantities of goods that they are unable to assimilate. Materialism allows consumers to manage the proliferation of consumption objects by ignoring the substantive contents of these objects. With materialism, assimilation is no longer a problem since the specificities of the object are no longer important. The only requirement is that one become knowledgeable of and involved with the exchange values of objects.

While materialism may be the most accessible lifestyle in modernity, Simmel would likely argue that it is ultimately an illusionary solution to modernity's obstacles. Materialism promotes a unidimensional interaction with objective culture, one in which objects are perceived as interchangeable economic entities. So even if consumers are able to integrate objects into their lives through materialism, the result is diametrically opposed to the type of cultivation that Simmel describes. Instead of the well-rounded person who emerges from interacting with a variety of qualitatively-different value systems embodied in consumption objects, consumers who incorporate modernity's quantifying impulse as the foundation of their lifestyle emerge with a narrowly-cast self-understanding driven by exchange value. As research on materialism has pointed out, this leads to the quantification of perceptions of self-worth (Richins and Dawson 1992).

Activist Insulation: Voluntary Simplicity, Consumption Communities, and Subcultures. Unlike materialism, which cedes to the structural changes of modernity, a number of other lifestyles actively confront modernity's proliferation of consumption objects by limiting the universe of goods one must assimilate. Through voluntary simplicity—in which people attempt to limit the material goods used in consumption—consumers have more opportunity to become engrossed by and competent in the limited avenues of consumption and thus achieve the level of subject-object interaction that Simmel associates with cultivation. Subcultures (groups bound by a cohesive moral order organizing all of the experiences of its participants) and consumption communities (less-encompassing than sub-cultures, where one's consumption activities are dominated by interests in a single arena of consumption [adapted from Boorstin 1973]) are lifestyle types in many ways similar to voluntary simplicity. Like voluntary simplicity, both act to limit the volume of objective culture in the universe of ones interests. But, in addition, subcultures and consumption communities also seek to address the fragmentation of modern social life by imposing coherence across the activities in which one engages. By orienting all activities to a single moral order (in the case of the subculture) or consumption category (in the case of the consumption community), these strategies create the sense of holistic personality that has been fragmented in modernity.

While Simmel would no doubt view these activist strategies as superior to materialism, he might also observe that their varying degrees of insularity poses some of the same restrictions on cultivation that he describes in pre-modernity. Limiting one's universe of consumption objects also necessarily limits the span of culture that one will experience in those goods. The proliferation of objective culture is in part a reflection of the increased diversity and complexity of the world to which we are exposed as communication and markets have become globalized. Choosing to limit this range results in limiting our cultivation to a narrower set than exists in the world.

Reflexive Alienation: Slackerism. In recent years, a reflexive awareness of modernity's impediments has grown, and with it a realization that the strategies used in the past to deal with these impediments (activist insulation of various stripes beginning in the 1960s, materialism in the 1980s) have met only a modicum of success. These persons feel that activist efforts to overcome modernity's impediments are futile and they are unwilling to accept what they perceive as the false consciousness of materialism. Burdened with a deep sensitivity to the modern predicament and the perception that there is little that they can do about it, these consumers gravitate to a distanced, cynical, playful, and ironic sensibility in their consumption that reflects their sense of alienation. This skeptical posture toward consumption's rewards, once limited to fringe areas of counter-culture and academe, has grown significantly in the 1990s. Numerous mass media sources have recently claimed that this consumption strategy is emblematic of the post baby-boom generation who are termed "generation x" (the title of a popular book) and those who participate in this lifestyle have often been termed "slackers" (after an independent film of the same name).

CONCLUSION

Simmel's examination of how the structural changes associated with modernity impact consumption offers a radical departure from the predominant research traditions in consumer research. Most consumer research focuses on the individual consumer in his/her current situation. Little attempt is made to understand the social conditions that lead the consumer to consume in a particular manner, nor to understand how these conditions that impact consuming have changed over time. So while consumer research has crafted immensely-detailed descriptions of consumers' behaviors, these depictions are of consumers as atomistic, encapsulated individuals who live outside of time, having no history themselves and being unaffected by the historical changes imparted by others.

To complement our microscopic depiction of consumption, Simmel asks us to stand back and look at consumption as a historically-located mode of activity that is significantly enabled and constrained by social and cultural structures. Mapping Simmel's approach onto current consumer research streams, then, yields a number of interesting insights. Most generally, this mapping forces us to acknowledge that the key constructs of many important paradigms—rational action, materialism, symbolic consumption, lifestyle—are modes of action that have arisen as adaptations to broad socio-historical forces. This acknowledgement has, in itself, significant implications for these paradigms. Our knowledge of these constructs will remain attenuated until we place them in their historical context. To do this requires giving up the assumption of invariance and, instead, describe how and why these constructs change across groups and over time. At the workbench level, what is required is a theoretically-informed historical-comparative tradition in consumer research, one that does not simply describe the histories of particular consumption phenomena, but that also raises the level of analysis to relate these particular descriptions to broader social-cultural changes.

REFERENCES

Arnould, Eric (1989), "Toward a Broadened Theory of Preference Formation and the Diffusion of Innovations: Cases from Zinder Province, Niger Republic," *Journal of Consumer Research*, 16 (September), 239-267.

Belk, Russell, Melanie Wallendorf, and John Sherry (1989), "The Sacred and Profane in Consumer Behavior: Theodicy on the Odyssey," *Journal of Consumer Research*, 16 (June), 1-38.

Boorstin, Daniel (1973), *The Americans: The Democratic Experience*, New York: Random House.

Celsi, Richard, Randall Rose, and Thomas Leigh (1993), "An Exploration of High-Risk Leisure Consumption through Skydiving," *Journal of Consumer Research*, 20 (June), 1-38.

Featherstone, Michael (1991), *Consumer Culture and Postmodernism*, Newbury Park, CA: Sage.

Hirschman, Elizabeth and Morris Holbrook, eds. (1981), *Symbolic Consumer Behavior*, Ann Arbor: Association for Consumer Research.

Holbrook, Morris and Elizabeth Hirschman (1982), "The Experiential Aspects of Consumption," *Journal of Consumer Research*, 9 (September), 132-40.

Holt, Douglas (forthcoming), "In Search of the Style in Lifestyle: A Socio-Cultural Critique" in *Advertising and Consumer Psychology*, eds. Lynn Kahle and Larry Chiagouris, Lawrence Erlbaum.

Jones, Brian and David Monieson (1990), "Early Development of the Philosophy of Marketing Thought," *Journal of Marketing*, 54(1): 102-113.

Lavin, Marilyn and Thomas Archdeacon (1989), "The Relevance of Historical Method for Marketing Research," in *Interpretive Consumer Research*, ed. Elizabeth Hirschman, Provo, UT: Association for Consumer Research, 60-68.

Levine, Donald (1986), *The Flight From Ambiguity: Essays in Social and Cultural Theory*, Chicago: University of Chicago Press.

Levy, Sidney (1959), "Symbols for sale," *Harvard Business Review*, 37(4), 117-124.

McCracken, Grant (1988), *Culture and Consumption: New Approaches to the Symbolic Character of Consumer Goods and Activities*, Bloomington: Indiana University Press.

Mick, David Glen and Michelle DeMoss (1990), "Self-Gifts: Phenomenological Insights from Four Contexts," *Journal of Consumer Research*, 17 (December), 322-332.

Miller, Daniel (1987), *Material Culture and Mass Consumption*, New York: Basil Blackwell.

O'Guinn, Thomas and Russell Belk (1987), "Heaven on Earth: Consumption at Heritage Village, USA," *Journal of Consumer Research*, 16(2): 227-238.

Richins, Marsha and Scott Dawson (1992), "A Consumer Values Orientation for Materialism and Its Measurement: Scale Development and Validation," *Journal of Consumer Research*, 19 (December), 303-316.

Rochberg-Halton, Eugene (1986), *Meaning and Modernity: Social Theory in the Pragmatic Attitude*, Chicago: University of Chicago Press.

Simmel, Georg (1971) *Georg Simmel: On Individuality and Social Forms*, ed. Donald N. Levine, Chicago: University of Chicago Press.

Simmel, Georg (1978/1900), *The Philosophy of Money*, trans. Tom Bottomore and David Frisby, London: Routledge.

Smith, Ruth Ann and David Lux (1993), "Historical Method in Consumer Research: Developing Causal Explanations of Change," *Journal of Consumer Research*, 19(4): 595-610.

Tan, Chin Tiong and Jagdish Sheth, eds. (1985), *Historical Perspectives in Consumer Research: National and International Perspectives*, Provo, UT: Association for Consumer Research.

Zelizer, Viviana (1985), *Pricing the Priceless Child*, New York: Basic Books.

Consumption and Social Stratification: Bourdieu's *Distinction*

Douglas E. Allen, Pennsylvania State University
Paul F. Anderson, Pennsylvania State University

BOURDIEU'S THEORY OF CONSUMER TASTE FORMATION

Bourdieu rejects the traditional notion that what he calls "tastes" (that is, consumer preferences) are the result of innate, individualistic choices of the human intellect. He argues that this "Kantian aesthetic" fails to recognize that tastes are socially conditioned and that the objects of consumer choice reflect a symbolic hierarchy that is *determined and maintained by the socially dominant in order to enforce their distance or distinction from other classes of society*. Thus, for Bourdieu, taste becomes a "social weapon" that defines and marks off the high from the low, the sacred from the profane, and the "legitimate" from the "illegitimate" in matters ranging from food and drink, cosmetics, and newspapers; on the one hand, to art, music, and literature on the other. (While it is sometimes thought that Bourdieu tends to focus on consumer preferences for products that have an obvious or recognized aesthetic component (e.g., clothing, home furnishings, entertainment, cultural activities, etc.), he also extends his analysis to the most mundane and functional items of consumption. This can be seen, for example, in his interpretation of working class selections in the realm of leisure activities and food (see Bourdieu 1984 Chapters 3 and 7)).

Bourdieu's analysis of consumption behavior is a straightforward extension of his broader sociological project. While Bourdieu's work defies easy classification within the confines of Anglo-American sociology (Bourdieu and Wacquant 1992), it does share some affinities with conflict theory. However, Bourdieu's approach seeks to transcend the traditional structure/agency (objectivist/subjectivist) dichotomy that has long bedeviled British and North American social theory. The so called structure-agency issue seeks to make the explanation of human behavior problematic by asking how the institutional and structural properties of society interact with human agency (that is the human being's autonomous ability to act on the basis of independent cognitive processes) to produce the behavior (action) that defines the explanandum of sociology. The structuralist extreme is best represented by Marx and Durkheim who seek to explain human action by structural (e.g., class) and institutional (e.g. religious) factors that lie outside the reach of consciousness. The social phenomenology of Schutz and the ethnomethodology of Garfinkel reflect the extreme subjectivist (agency) view in which the sociologist seeks to understand behavior by grasping the objects of thought that constitute the common sense knowledge and thinking of social actors. Bourdieu seeks to transcend the traditional opposition of structure and agency by recognizing that:

> On the one hand, the *objective structures* which the sociologist constructs in the objectivist moment, by setting aside the subjective representations of the agents, *are the basis of subjective representations* and they constitute the *structural constraints* which influence interactions; but, on the other hand, these representations also have to be remembered if one wants to account above all *for the daily individual and collective struggles which aim at transforming or preserving these structures* (Bourdieu 1990, pp. 125-26, emphasis added).

Thus, for Bourdieu, the relationship between structure and agency is dialectical rather than oppositional. He conceives of the consumption realm (as well as all sociologically relevant sites of investigation) as a *field* (*champ*) of power relations. The field is a multidimensional space of positions or locations in which a person's coordinates are determined by both the amount and composition of the types of "*capital*" that they possess. The most important forms of capital are *economic* and *cultural* capital. The former corresponds to the individual's economic resources while the latter includes such factors as: 1.) cultural knowledge, skills, experiences, abilities; 2.) linguistic competence, modes of speech, vocabulary; and 3.) modes of thought, factual knowledge, world views, etc. The most important fact about cultural capital is that it is generally acquired unreflectively via socialization in one's family, social class, neighborhood, sub-culture, etc. Moreover, it is reinforced by the institutional forces (e.g., schools, churches, welfare systems, parole boards, etc.) that one is exposed to as a result of the locational accident of one's birth.

Bourdieu conceptualizes the field as a site of *struggle* in which individuals and groups seek to maintain or alter the distribution of the various forms of capital that are specific to it. With respect to the consumption field, the main object of struggle is the definition of legitimate, middlebrow, and popular culture. On this view, those who possess large amounts of economic or cultural capital (or both) are "*dominant*" and will seek to impose a hierarchy of taste or preference on those with less capital (the "*dominated*").

Within the consumption field, social classes (what Bourdieu calls "*classes on paper*") may be discerned. Classes on paper are not *real groups* because they lack a strong group identity and are not mobilized for action in the struggle over economic and cultural capital. Classes on paper are made up of individuals who happen to occupy similar positions in multidimensional "capital space" (i.e., they possess similar amounts and types of capital). As a result, they will have experienced similar material and cultural conditions and will have submitted to similar types of conditionings. This means that members of these classes will "have every chance of having similar dispositions and interests, and thus of producing similar practices and adopting similar stances" (Bourdieu 1991, p. 231). Thus, for Bourdieu, a "class on paper" is a *taxonomical device* that has no independent ontological existence. It is a theoretical construct that allows one to explain and predict the actions of those it classifies (including their potential to form into real groups—e.g., labor unions).

It can be seen, then, that Bourdieu's notion of class owes much to Weber. Like Weber, Bourdieu sees "class" as a theoretical construction that allows one to characterize the *propensities* of people with similar social conditionings and similar material conditions of life. Thus, the *structuralist* element in Bourdieu's theory would allow one to refer to the "objective" *life chances* of individuals in specific social classes. As long as we remain at a sufficiently high level of statistical aggregation, it is legitimate to speak of the of various social classes.

This can be demonstrated by using the available data on occupational groupings as a weak surrogate for social class. Featherman and Hauser (1978) present tables that show the outflow percentages from father's occupation to son's current occupation for the 1962 and 1973 OCG surveys. If we take as an example the outflow figures from upper manual to upper nonmanual, we see that in 1962 approximately 24.7% of the sons of upper manual workers had positions in the upper nonmanual category. By 1973 this percentage had increased to 30.9%. Thus, in a very rough way, these figures reflect the occupational opportunity structure for these men in the early 1960s and 1970s. Sons from upper manual origins entering the labor force in the 1960s and early 1970s could be said to have between a 25 and 30 percent chance of attaining an upper nonmanual position. (According to data from the NORC General Social Survey published by Hout (1988), this figure held steady at about 30% over the years 1972-1985.)

Thus, *structural* constraints in the form of economic and cultural resources, educational opportunities, supply and demand conditions, etc., could be said to limit the occupational mobility of men from upper manual origins. (They are limited in the sense that, for example, men from upper nonmanual origins are about *twice* as likely to attain upper nonmanual positions in all three data sets. Indeed, path analytic analyses of mobility table data confirm the continuing role of father's occupation in determining the destinations of sons across the occupational structure.) Thus, structural factors impinge on social class members in the form of statistical life chances. Structural elements determine the opportunity set within which individual actors live out their lives and produce the *practices* which we come to associate with specific class locations.

Of course, structural factors can only be used to "explain" the statistical probabilities or tendencies of actors in the aggregate. Thus, structuralist analyses have tended to leave opaque the mechanisms linking structure and practice at the individual level. Bourdieu seeks to remedy this lacuna with a "bridging" concept that he refers to as "*habitus*". Habitus is a Latin term that refers to a habitual or typical condition, state, or appearance. Bourdieu uses the word to refer to an "open set of dispositions" of individual actors that is constantly modified or reinforced through experience (Bourdieu and Wacquant 1992, p. 133). These dispositions generate individual practices, perceptions, and attitudes—but only in the context of a specific situation. That is, the habitus triggers reactions and influences perceptions in the context of a specific *field*. Moreover, such dispositions are said to be *transposable* in that they are "capable of generating a multiplicity of practices and perceptions in fields other than those in which they were originally acquired" (Bourdieu 1991, p. 13).

While the habitus is sufficiently "open" to allow for human agency, it is nevertheless the product of social conditioning. The dispositions that constitute a "*class habitus*", for example, are learned in the family, school, and neighborhood and unavoidably reflect the material conditions and social conditionings that one experiences as the result of one's location in "capital space". Thus, individuals from working class backgrounds have every chance of experiencing similar life conditions and have every likelihood of generating similar perceptions, practices, and attitudes. One's class origin is not, therefore, a structural straight jacket that determines with certainty one's actions. But, on the other hand, there is a certain probability that persons exposed to similar life experiences will display similar "lifestyles" and behaviors. The habitus, then, acts as a flexible explanatory tool that seeks to mediate between the determinism of structure and the obvious openness of individual action.

On Culture Vultures and Class Warriors: Marketing and Class Reproduction

Having developed the bare bones of Bourdieu's perspective, the remainder of the paper will focus on specific applications of the theory to consumer behavior. As noted above, Bourdieu sees the consumption *field* as a site of struggle over the definitions of legitimate, middlebrow, and popular culture. In his view, the socially and economically dominant in any society seek to maintain a strict hierarchy of cultural forms so that all judgments in the consumption sphere are subject to the hegemony of "legitimate" (i.e., dominant) cultural tastes. This is accomplished *without conscious direction or coercion* because a person's class habitus presents each individual with a preexisting set of "natural" classifications that constitute his or her unreflective definition of reality. Thus, in western industrialized societies, classical music, opera, legitimate theater, books on philosophy, knowledge of foreign languages, modern art collections, and subscriptions to academic journals are just a few of the cultural forms that are unquestionably (and unquestioned) elements of the legitimate or dominant culture. While members of the middle and working classes may eschew such cultural forms (indeed, they may well view them with suspicion or disdain), their position at the pinnacle of the cultural hierarchy goes unchallenged. As a result, those who can appropriate elements of legitimate culture as their own have the power to define the status of all other cultural forms.

This power goes unrecognized, of course, because it appears to be the natural state of "how things are". In particular, the autodidact, the parvenu, and the middlebrow will assume that legitimate cultural forms attain their position as the result of disinterested, objective, and autonomous (Kantian) judgments flowing from a special "knowledge" of such things. Indeed, Bourdieu argues that cultural hegemony is maintained by the dominant because the middle and working classes mistake the arbitrary and socially structured judgments of these classes for choices that require special cultural knowledge. Thus, the door is open for enterprising marketers to offer mobility aspirants (particularly among the middle classes) what has come to be known as "middlebrow" culture. Invariably, such cultural forms are "knock-off" versions of the "legitimate" forms that have been appropriated by the dominant. As a result, a whole "industry" has emerged that specializes in providing palatable versions of legitimate culture and the "knowledge-tools" necessary to appropriate (and appreciate) said forms. Examples include "best-loved classics" on compact discs, the various "great books" programs, the Book-of-the-Month Club, "supermarket" encyclopedias, books on wine appreciation and selection, and foreign language tapes. More specific illustrations would surely include Hirsch's *Cultural Literacy*, *American Heritage Magazine*, the Durants' *The Story of Philosophy*, *An Incomplete Education*, Emily Post's *Etiquette*, *Where There's a Will There's An "A"*, and a plethora of public and commercial broadcasting programs (and books) designed to make science, technology or philosophy accessible to the "average man" (e.g., Nova, The Body in Question, *The Tao of Physics*, *Zen and the Art of Motorcycle Maintenance*, etc.).

The foregoing is just one set of examples that can be used to contrast Bourdieu's approach with the traditional Warnerian model of social class and consumption. Clearly, the latter takes a classic structural-functionalist approach to consumption differences across social classes. For Warner and his followers in marketing, different classes simply have different tastes, preferences and economic resources. The Warner model tends to classify choice behavior rather than attempt an explanation of the deep sociological roots of class preferences. In contrast, Bourdieu sees consumption behavior as one manifestation of (non-Marxian) class conflict with complex implications for cultural hegemony and the often hidden forces that produce what appear to be mundane apolitical product choices.

On Misrecognition

For Bourdieu, the singular mistake made by dominated *class fractions*, particularly the petite bourgeoisie, is to associate *culture* with *knowledge*. Lacking the *lived experiences* that produce the elite habitus, the petite bourgeoisie *misrecognize* what are essentially arbitrary aesthetic selections for special knowledge of what counts as "legitimate" and "illegitimate" in the cultural sphere. The oft repeated (and frequently caricatured) bromide: "I don't know much about art, but I know what I like", perfectly captures the insecurity of those who have been led to believe that culture equals knowledge. Indeed, as the endless cinematic retelling of the Pygmalion myth ("My Fair Lady", "Pretty Women", "Working Girl", "Educating Rita", etc.) seeks to remind us, the only thing that separates the street vendor from the princess is a little cultural capital and a few elocution lessons.

Unfortunately, in their discussions of art consumption, some consumer researchers are also prone to misrecognize the arbitrary nature of aesthetic judgments. For example, one prominent Warnerian (with a strong psychological bent) suggests that a lack of appreciation for legitimate culture represents a kind of sociopsychological pathology (Levy 1980). While recognizing the psychological and social conditioning that leads people to reject legitimate culture, he, nevertheless, *reveals a tacit commitment to the arbitrary cultural hierarchy imposed by the dominant class fractions*:

> To lack aesthetic appetite is a form of starvation, afflicting personalities whose lives are generally ungratifying, whose family relationships are strained or hateful, or whose emotional tone is desperate, depressed, and deprived (Levy 1980, p. 33).

Levy suggests that the "pathological extremes" among those who reject legitimate culture "often reveal dynamics at work in more moderate instances" (Levy 1980, p. 33). On this view, the majority of people who eschew the aesthetic realm do so because of an interaction between a negative self-concept and their perception that the arts are "hopelessly beyond them" (Levy 1980, p. 33). Indeed, Levy reveals his full commitment to the culture-equals-knowledge equation when he claims that:

> The reality of the obstacles to aesthetic appreciation is great. Some high art simply cannot be understood *by that half of the population that has below average intelligence*—an intellectual basis for elitism that may never disappear (Levy 1980, p. 35, emphasis added).

Of course, the assertion that the appreciation of certain kinds of art requires an intelligence level found lacking in half of our citizens not only reinforces elitism, but it also reveals a misrecognition of the arbitrary and class-based nature of society's aesthetic hierarchy. Thus, consumer researchers who are themselves under the spell of the Kantian aesthetic are unlikely to advance our understanding of cultural consumption.

Consumption and Education

It is perhaps understandable that some consumer researchers and arts marketers should misconstrue the linkage between "intelligence" and the aesthetic disposition. The well established correlation between educational credentials and arts consumption can easily lead one to the conclusion that the appreciation of "difficult" art requires the intellectual capacities of those who are able to attain advanced educational certification (Bourdieu 1984). Unfortunately this equation rests on the premise that the "intellectually gifted" in society attain their status because our educational systems are *impartial, fair and objective judges of individual worth*. Hence it is easily concluded that the "best and the brightest" attain the rank, stature, and aesthetic perceptions that are "appropriate" to their intellectual endowments. However, it is now axiomatic among sociologists of education that *western educational institutions are one of the most important agencies of class reproduction* (e.g., Bourdieu and Passeron 1977; Willis 1977, London 1978; Giroux 1983, 1988, 1992; Giroux and Simon 1989; Valli 1986; MacLeod 1987; Brint and Karabel 1989; Weis 1990). As argued elsewhere (Anderson 1991), rather than acting as "social mobility escalators" for the "more talented" members of ethnic/racial minorities and the white working and middle classes, the educational system has a strong tendency to reproduce the existing social order by devaluing the cultural capital of dominated groups. By *judging, classifying, and tracking* students from dominated class fractions on the basis of the *alien* standards of the dominant, schools perpetuate the extant status hierarchy. Moreover, the educational system insures that its reproductive practices will be misrecognized because it makes its judgments on what *appear* to be "objective" and "meritocratic" criteria. It is only rarely recognized that said criteria reflect the (arbitrary) cultural capital of the dominant.

If, as Bourdieu (1984) argues, the cultural, educational, and linguistic field is a site of struggle over the definition of "legitimate" knowledge, aesthetic taste, and appropriate modes of speech (e.g., Bourdieu 1991), then the school is one of the chief instruments that allow the dominant to carry the day. Indeed, path analysis of contemporary mobility tables show that the ability of high status fathers to produce sons who are disproportionately represented in high status occupations is no longer the result of some type of "direct inheritance" (ascription). Instead, the primary effect of father's occupation and education is on *son's educational attainment*, and it is the educational attainment of the son that has the major impact on his occupational destination (Hout 1988). Indeed, Hout (1988) finds that the *college degree* is one of the most critical factors in occupational attainment. Thus, it is the ability of high status fathers to insure that their sons achieve a college education that is one of the principal factors in class reproduction.

The Aesthetic Disposition as a "Relationship" to Culture

Against this backdrop we may find it instructive to explore Bourdieu's (1984) analysis of the micro and macro processes that generate a disposition toward legitimate art among the highly educated. First, as noted above, the class-based vetting practices of schools insure that a disproportionate number of those attaining high educational credentials will have a relationship of *comfortable familiarity* with legitimate culture. On Bourdieu's view, this is acquired unreflectively in virtue of the fact that one is raised in the dominant class. Beyond this, higher education has a tendency (especially important for students from middle or working class cultures) to encourage "legitimate autodidacticism". That is, teacher expectations and peer pressure encourage the acquisition of cultural experiences and knowledge that are not directly related to the school curriculum. As Bourdieu (1984) puts it:

> The educational institution succeeds in imposing cultural practices *that it does not teach* and does not even explicitly demand, but which belong to the attributes attached by status to the position it assigns, the qualifications it awards, and the social positions to which the latter give access (p. 26).

Thus, museum attendance, theater going, recreational reading of "the classics", as well as the development of interests in cinematic genres and directorial styles, foreign travel, and avant-garde music may become a natural and everyday part of one's experience outside the official curriculum.

The "gratuitous" acquisition of cultural interests and experiences by the educated may be contrasted with the autodidacticism of the petite bourgeoisie. This has important implications for consumer research since the latter often constitute the potential target market for both "legitimate" culture and its pale imitations. Bourdieu (1984) notes that autodidacticism can only be understood in relation to the educational system which offers "(very unequally) the possibility of learning by institutional stages in accordance with standardized levels and syllabuses" (p. 328).

> Because he has not acquired his culture in the legitimate order established by the educational system, the autodidact constantly betrays, by his very anxiety about the right classification, the arbitrariness of his classifications and therefore his knowledge... [However,] the absences, lacunae, and arbitrary classifications of the autodidact's culture only exist in relation to a scholastic culture which has the power to induce *misrecognition* of *its arbitrariness* ... (Bourdieu 1984, p. 328, emphasis added).

Thus, once again, because the autodidact mistakenly identifies culture with knowledge, s/he does not know "how to play the game of culture as a game" (Bourdieu 1984, p. 330). On Bourdieu's view, upwardly mobile members of the middle classes are likely to take culture too seriously by displaying a reverence for legitimate art that is lacking in those whose appreciation for culture has been acquired unreflectively in the environs of the home or the educational system. The petite bourgeoisie assume that the "cultivated" possess an immense store of knowledge that is the source of their aesthetic dispositions. Thus they fail to see that, in reality, *the dominant aesthetic amounts to a "relation" to culture rather than a fund of special knowledge.*

CONCLUSIONS

Following Bourdieu, it has been argued that consumer preferences and aesthetic dispositions have deep roots in a class-based hierarchy that is imposed on society by the culturally dominant. Indeed, the Kantian notion of "taste" as an innate faculty residing within the human intellect is *itself* a device that allows those who are endowed with the "right" quantity and quality of cultural capital to determine society's notion of "appropriate" and "inappropriate" food, clothing, leisure activities, housing, literature, art, etc. In opposition to Kant, Bourdieu argues that such judgments are (in one sense) the *purely arbitrary* preferences of the dominant social classes who are in a position to dictate the cultural standards that separate the high from the low, the legitimate from the illegitimate, and the sacred from the profane. Unfortunately, the arbitrary nature of the cultural hierarchy is *misrecognized* by dominated class fractions because the latter are *taught* that cultural and artistic judgments flow from some type of "special knowledge". In reality, however, the cultural selections of the dominant are the result of a "comfortable familiarity" acquired through family and class socialization and the "legitimate autodidacticism" encouraged by institutions of higher learning. Moreover, the well documented class bias of the educational system insures that the dominant will be able to maintain their hegemony in the cultural field by limiting access to the means by which legitimate culture is appropriated.

Bourdieu argues that simple denunciations of the nature of the cultural hierarchy are inefficacious. What must be changed are the conditions that allow the hierarchy to exist. Thus, we must work to universalize "*the conditions of access* to what the present offers us that is most universal" (Bourdieu and Wacquant 1992, p. 84). In his opinion, if we can say that "high" art is superior to kitsch, it is because the former is only accessible if one masters (via the "socialization" processes described above) the cumulative history of previous artistic productions. Thus, *in this sense*, we can say that "legitimate" culture is more universal. But, the conditions of appropriation of universal culture are not equally distributed.

Bourdieu argues that the conditions that allow one to access universal culture include: the freedom from economic necessity, a distancing from practical urgency, the availability of "*skholè*" or the leisure time necessary to invest in cultural capital, and the elimination of the reproductive functioning of the educational system. Whether marketing and consumer research will have a significant role to play in the universalization process is not clear since Bourdieu has given few details of the practical steps necessary to implement this project. What is clear, however, is that consumer researchers bear responsibility for their complicity in activities that help to sustain the extant hierarchy.

Thus, as noted earlier, marketers unreflectively maintain the cultural hierarchy through their attempts to offer mobility aspirants "knock-off" versions of "legitimate" cultural forms. In effect, marketers both profit from the misrecognition of the dominated *while reinforcing said misrecognition*. In the nonprofit arena, marketers assist in the reproductive activities of sub-baccalaureate educational institutions and mistakenly assume that their efforts to "open the doors" of museums and art galleries to "*le peuple*" will somehow enrich the cultural lives of the masses. Unfortunately, they fail to realize that this amounts to little more than "liberal chic" that is inefficacious in either transforming the hierarchy or in universalizing the conditions of access to legitimate culture.

REFERENCES

Anderson, Paul F. (1991), "The Hidden Injuries of Social Class: Implications for Consumer Research," paper presented at the Association for Consumer Research Conference, Chicago, IL.

Bourdieu, Pierre (1984), *Distinction: A Social Critique of the Judgment of Taste*. Cambridge, MA: Harvard University Press.

_____ (1990), *In Other Words*. Stanford, CA: Stanford University Press.

_____ (1991), *Language and Symbolic Power*. Cambridge, MA: Harvard University Press

_____ and Jean-Claude Passeron (1977), *Reproduction in Education, Society and Culture*, London: Sage.

_____ and Loïc Wacquant (1992), *An Invitation to Reflexive Sociology*. Chicago: The University of Chicago Press.

Brint, Steven and Jerome Karabel (1989), *The Diverted Dream*, New York: Oxford University Press.

Coleman, Richard P. (1983), "The Continuing Significance of Social Class to Marketing," *Journal of Consumer Research*, 10 (December), 265-280.

Featherman, David L. and Robert M. Hauser (1978), *Opportunity and Change,* New York: Academic Press.

Giroux, Henry A. (1983), "Theories of Reproduction and Resistance in the New Sociology of Education: A Critical Analysis," *Harvard Educational Review*, 53 (August 1983), 257-293.

_____ (1988), *Teachers As Intellectuals*, New York: Bergin & Garvey.

_____ (1992), *Border Crossings*, New York: Routledge.

_____ and Roger I. Simon (1989), *Popular Culture, Schooling, and Everyday Life,* New York: Bergin & Garvey.

Hout, Michael (1988), "More Universalism, Less Structural Mobility: The American Occupational Structure in the 1980s," *American Journal of Sociology*, 93 (May), 1358-1400.

Levy, Sidney J. (1980), "Arts Consumers and Aesthetic Attributes," in *Marketing The Arts*, ed. Michael P. Mokwa, William M. Dawson, and E. Arthur Prieve, New York: Praeger, 29-45.

London, Howard B. (1978), *The Culture of a Community College,* New York: Praeger.

MacLeod, Jay (1987), *Ain't No Makin' It,* Boulder, CO: Westview.

Martineau, Pierre (1957), *Motivation In Advertising,* New York: McGraw-Hill.

_____ (1958), "Social Classes and Spending Behavior," *Journal of Marketing,* 23 (October), 121-130.

Ross, Dorothy (1991), *The Origins of American Social Science,* New York: Cambridge University Press.

Valli, Linda (1986), *Becoming Clerical Workers,* Boston: Routledge & Kegan Paul.

Warner, W. Lloyd (1962), *American Life,* rev. ed., Chicago: University of Chicago Press.

_____ (1963), *Yankee City,* New Haven, CT: Yale University Press.

_____ and Paul S. Lunt, (1941), *The Social Life of a Modern Community,* New Haven, CT: Yale University Press.

_____, Robert J. Havighurst, and Martin B. Loeb (1944), *Who Shall Be Educated?* New York: Harper & Brothers.

_____ and Associates (1949a), *Democracy in Jonesville,* New York: Harper and Row.

_____, Marchia Meeker, and Kenneth Eells (1949b), *Social Class in America,* Chicago: Science Research Associates.

Weis, Lois (1990), *Working Class Without Work,* New York: Routledge.

Willis, Paul (1977), *Learning to Labor,* New York: Columbia University Press.

Perceived Price Fairness: A New Look at an Old Construct

Marielza Martins, University of Illinois at Urbana-Champaign
Kent B. Monroe, University of Illinois at Urbana-Champaign

ABSTRACT

The value of a product is postulated by Monroe (1990) to be a tradeoff between the perceived benefits, or quality, offered by the product, and the sacrifice, both monetary and non-monetary, perceived as necessary to acquire it. The price-quality relationship research stream has identified brand, level of advertising and store image as variables affecting perceived product quality (Dodds et al. 1991), but so far no variable has been shown to moderate perceived sacrifice assessments. This paper suggests that perception of price fairness, a concept derived from equity research, may be a variable moderating perceived sacrifice and perceived product value, and therefore willingness to buy.

INTRODUCTION

Pricing research has traditionally viewed consumer judgments of price fairness in terms of consumers' relationships with sellers. Conspicuously absent from the present formulation of perceived price fairness is the notion that lateral relationships between customers may be another source of such perceptions. However, Monroe and Petroshius (1981) posit that price perception is essentially a comparative process. Since consumers do share product information, as evidenced by "word-of-mouth" communications research, it is likely that product price will also be discussed and compared.

Firms increasingly rely on the use of various forms of price promotion, such as off-invoice discounts, rebates, coupons, volume buying incentives, discounts to members of particular organizations, or preferred customer cards. Moreover, while some promotions may be available to all customers, others may be limited to consumers possessing particular characteristics. For instance, handicapped passengers may be allowed to purchase bus tokens at a special low price not available to other customers. As a consequence, many sales may result in different net prices being charged different customers. These practices are already so widespread that Marn and Rosiello (1992, p.87) claim that "at any point in time, no item sells at exactly the same pocket price to all customers."

Such price differences may lead consumers to engage in interbuyer price comparisons that generate perceptions of price fairness. The objective of this paper is to describe how this neglected aspect of the perceived price fairness construct may ultimately affect perceptions of monetary sacrifice and value, and therefore, willingness to buy.

Price Fairness and the Principle of Dual Entitlements

The pricing literature in consumer behavior recognizes that customers may respond differently to prices than the traditional economic approach, embodied in the downward sloping demand curve, proposes they do. For instance, pricing research has examined several constructs that are related to price perceptions, such as reference prices and the price-quality relationship.

Among such constructs, researchers have advanced the notion that price acceptability is affected by perceptions of the equity, or fairness, of market prices. According to Kamen and Toman (1970), "consumers have some preconceived ideas about what is a fair price for a given item," and are unwilling to spend more than that amount for the particular item.

Underlying this notion is transaction utility theory, which posits that consumers derive both acquisition and transaction utility from their dealings in the marketplace. While acquisition utility reflects the utility derived from possessing the product, transaction utility reflects the difference between the "fair" price consumers expect to pay and the actual market price encountered. This difference may be positive, giving buyers an extra incentive to complete the purchase process, or negative, dampening consumers' willingness to buy (Thaler 1985).

The Principle of Dual Entitlements

Kahneman et al. (1986) show that, indeed, consumers do form perceptions of the fairness of market prices. Furthermore, these individual perceptions may be based on community norms of fairness, reflected by the principle of dual entitlements. On one hand, this principle suggests that consumers may accept price increases they perceive as being justified by rising sellers' costs and resist price increases that are perceived as resulting in higher profits for sellers. In other words, buyers may see as fair the practice of passing cost increases on to consumers, while the practice of increasing profits at the expense of consumers may be seen as unfairly exploitative. On the other hand, consumers may perceive higher levels of sellers' profits resulting from cost reductions as fair. In other words, sellers may not need to share savings resulting from cost decreases with buyers. As a result of the dual entitlements principle, "it is fair for prices and profits to only ever increase, because it is consistent with this norm of fairness for sellers to pass on cost increases and not cost decreases" (Kalapurakal et al. 1991, p.789).

Equity Theory

The principle of dual entitlements may be an outcome of the compensatory function of prices (Lynn 1990), which is explained in terms of equity theory. Equity theory is a social comparison theory in which individuals evaluate the ratio of the investments they make to a particular exchange to the profits they derive from it, relative to the investments and profits allocated to their exchange partners. Equity theory posits that, for an equitable exchange relationship to exist, the parties involved have to obtain equal ratios of perceived profits, or gains, to perceived investments, or losses. Moreover, according to Homans (1961), equity needs not necessarily be concerned with the outcomes achieved by parties *directly* involved in an exchange. Instead, *indirect* exchange partners, such as two customers buying from the same seller, would also have a right to expect that their common direct partner, the seller, would apportion their individual outcomes by following the rule of equal gain-loss ratios.

Proposition 1: Buyers may take into account the prices paid by other customers for the same products they acquire.

Whenever the ratio comparison reveals unequal gain-loss ratios being allocated to the parties involved in an exchange, an inequitable exchange exists. While the party with the relatively larger gain-loss ratio is perceived as receiving unfair advantages, the party with the relatively smaller gain-loss ratio is perceived as receiving unfairly disadvantageous terms (Adams 1965).

Following the postulates of cognitive dissonance theory, or the "existence of nonfitting relations among cognitions" (Festinger 1957, p.3), equity theory further suggests that inequity results in feelings of distress and tension to the parties in an inequitable exchange relationship. These tension feelings, which Adams (1965) posited to be proportional to the magnitude of the inequity being experienced, would motivate the parties to an inequitable exchange to restore equitable terms. While disadvantageous inequity, a loss, is posited to result in anger on the part of the short-changed individual, advantageous inequity, a gain, leads to guilt on the part of the benefiting individual. According to Lynn (1990), price may be the mechanism utilized by exchange partners to restore equity to inequitable market exchanges.

However, Adams (1965, p.274) suggested that equity "must fail of realization to a greater extent when it is favorable to an individual before he reacts than when it is to his disadvantage." Therefore, a perceived disadvantageous inequity, or loss, elicits greater motivation to reduce inequity than a perceived advantageous inequity, or gain, of the same magnitude. In fact, there is little empirical evidence supporting the fact that feelings of guilt would also lead to equity restoration attempts (Deutsch 1985).

In the pricing context, perceptions of price fairness, like perceptions of exchange fairness, depend on the gain-loss ratio of exchange partners, where the gain, from the consumer's perspective, may be defined as the product to be received, and the loss, as the price to be paid. Perceived disadvantageous price inequity may be experienced by a customer who either pays a higher price and receives a product equivalent to that received by other customers, or who pays the same price but receives less product, either in terms of quantity or quality. Perceived advantageous price inequity, on the other hand, may result from either paying the same price and receiving more product than others, or paying a lower price and receiving an equivalent product.

Prospect Theory

Tversky and Kahneman (1979) propose that perceptions depend on the contextual framing: there is an asymmetry in the way consumers respond to losses vis-à-vis the way they respond to gains. A loss generates a larger response, in absolute terms, than a gain of the same magnitude, and is posited to be more salient in individuals' minds. As a result, disadvantageous inequity, a loss, is likely to be perceived more negatively than advantageous inequity, a gain, is perceived positively, even when of equivalent magnitude. Therefore:

Proposition 2: A perceived disadvantageous price inequity likely will generate a more unfavorable customer response than a perceived advantageous price inequity of the same magnitude generates a favorable customer response.

In other words, when two customers compare the prices they are offered for a particular product, the customer who is offered the higher price will experience a greater decrease in his/hers willingness to buy the product than the customer who is offered the lower price will experience an increase in willingness to buy the product.

EXTENDING THE PRICE-QUALITY RELATIONSHIP TO ACCOUNT FOR PERCEIVED PRICE FAIRNESS

The Price-Quality Relationship

Product quality is one of the most important concepts in marketing strategy, as it is believed to be positively related to competitive advantage (Schnaars 1991). Buyers judge product quality in terms of overall product superiority as compared to substitute products in their evoked sets (Zeithaml 1988). To perform this judgment task, buyers need to evaluate product attributes.

Attributes can be either *intrinsic*, i.e., those that cannot be changed without changing product composition, such as flavor, or *extrinsic*, i.e., those that, when changed, do not alter product composition, such as price. Furthermore, attributes can be classified as 1) *search* attributes, those attributes for which quality can be evaluated before purchase; 2) *experience* attributes, those that can only result in a quality assessment after purchase and use; and finally, 3) *credence* attributes, those for which no quality evaluation can be made by the uninformed buyer, who therefore has to either rely on someone else's evaluation to assess product quality (Steenkamp 1989), or utilize other attributes as indicators of the quality level reflected by the credence attribute.

Buyers face some constraints in their evaluations of intrinsic attributes. First, different types of intrinsic attributes moderate the quality assessment process, and only search attributes lead to a quality assessment prior to purchase. Second, buyers possess limited cognitive abilities, and therefore, even search attributes may not lead to a quality assessment before purchase if buyers are overloaded with information. Finally, the search and evaluation process entails a cost in terms of time, money and effort spent, and therefore buyers may perceive the cost of searching and evaluating new product attributes as too high relative to the perceived benefits derived from this process. As a result, several products and attributes may not even be taken into consideration.

Since not all intrinsic product attributes lead to a quality assessment before purchase, buyers may also rely on extrinsic attributes, which are not directly related to product performance, as quality indicators. Buyers may also choose to rely on extrinsic attributes as a summary measure of product quality level so as to escape information overload or to help make an assessment. Therefore, extrinsic attributes such as price, store name, brand name or advertising intensity may have an impact on buyers' assessments of product quality through their role as quality signals.

Monroe (1990) suggests that buyers internalize the price attribute in terms of perceived price, which may influence perceived product quality and perceived product sacrifice. The ensuing quality-sacrifice comparison results in an assessment of product value. When perceived value is positive, buyers are more likely to purchase the product, otherwise they may continue to search or refrain from buying.

It is interesting to note that, so far, no variable has been identified in the pricing literature as affecting buyers' perceptions of sacrifice, although perceptions of price fairness seem to play such a role in buyer-seller relationships. Buyers seem to compare sellers' costs to the price compensation they are entitled to, resisting price increases perceived as unfair by withholding product demand, i.e., by decreasing their willingness to buy the product, while allowing price increases perceived as fair.

Competitive Upgrade Pricing

Recent events in the software market lead us to believe that perceptions of price fairness indeed would have an influence on perceived sacrifice, perceived value and willingness to buy, even in indirect buyer-seller interactions, represented by lateral customer relationships. Some software companies (Borland, Microsoft) have recently introduced a new pricing policy, the so called competitive upgrade pricing, which allows customers switching from competitors' products to pay the same price offered to those who bought previous versions to upgrade to a new version of the software.

Past patrons complained bitterly, arguing that software companies should demonstrate "gratitude" for their past patronage by charging them a different price for product upgrades than they charge switching customers. What is interesting is that some buyers perceive the upgrade price charged them to be "fair in relation to the product users receive" (Martens 1991), i.e., to be fair in terms of perceived product benefits, and actually suggest that the company either lower the price quoted to past patrons, or *increase the price charged to switching customers*! Therefore, consistent with the propositions of equity theory, which suggests that two potential ways to reduce inequity may be to either decrease the losses of the short-changed individual or increase the losses of the individual experiencing an unfair advantage:

Proposition 3: A decrease (increase) in the perceived price paid by the customer will have a similar reducing (increasing) effect on his/hers perceptions of monetary sacrifice as an equivalent increase(decrease) in the perceived price paid by someone else.

This scenario is also consistent with Holbrook et al.'s (1984) finding that prices may play an ego-expressive role, in the sense that it affects the consumer self-concept. Finding and paying a low price for a particular product may lead consumers to feel smart and competent as shoppers, while paying a high price could cause them to feel resentful (Schindler 1989).

Another interesting observation resulting from complaints on the competitive upgrade pricing policy is the fact that perceptions of disadvantageous price inequity may result in reduced willingness to buy on the part of the customer. For instance, one customer stated that

"The policy of charging those who have Word For Windows Version 1.1 (such as myself) the same price as someone who has Word Perfect or Ami Pro is an insult to us. Frankly, if Microsoft is going to act this way, I am going to get a new word processing package. Not because I can't afford the price, but because I will not let someone ... all over me."

Therefore,

Proposition 4: A perceived disadvantageous price inequity, or a loss, increases buyers' perceptions of sacrifice and decreases buyers' perceptions of value and willingness to buy, while a perceived advantageous price inequity, or a gain, reduces buyers' perceptions of sacrifice, and increases buyers' perceptions of value and willingness to buy, as compared to a perceived equitable price.

Perceptions of fairness necessitate a comparison between the gains and losses achieved by two or more parties. According to Homans (1961, p.76), a man wonders if he is "getting as much as other men in some respect like me would get in circumstances in some respect like mine." Furthermore, for the purpose of establishing how equitable is the treatment they receive, individuals only compare themselves to those perceived to possess similar status or abilities. For instance, Merton (1957, p.242) notes that "some similarity in status attributes between the individual and the reference group must be perceived or imagined, in order for the comparison to occur at all." In pricing research, a relevant ability is the ability to pay the required monetary price to obtain a desired product. Therefore, we may infer that individuals compare themselves to those perceived as possessing similar monetary resources, i.e., similar incomes. Individuals who are perceived to possess a different income level may be quoted or pay different prices without this differential price necessarily resulting in perceptions of price inequity.

Proposition 5: When an individual compares the price he/she is offered for a particular product to the price someone else is offered for the same product and finds a discrepancy, perceived price inequity is more likely to result if their income levels are similar than if their income levels are different.

Anedoctal evidence suggests that better pricing terms may be offered to individuals generally considered as possessing lower incomes without provoking a distress response on customers to whom such price promotions are not extended. For example, most customers do not seem to perceive as inequitable the practice of charging senior citizens, children or students, all perceived as low income groups, a special, lower price than they are charged for the same products. In a sense, customers are accepting a decrease in the losses sustained by students, children and seniors as a way of restoring equity, since such groups are generally perceived as making additional sacrifices as a result of their low income status.

However, this "generosity" may have limits. Galston (1980) distinguishes natural needs, those basic means required for the attainment of urgent and universally desired ends, from luxury needs, those means which exceed such requirements. He ascribes "moral priority," worthy of distributive equity (distribution of rewards according to contribution) and even equality (distribution according to need), to natural needs only (Deutsch 1985, p.43).

For product categories other than basic necessities, it seems that not even the same price can be offered to individuals with lower incomes without provoking distress responses in some customers. In Martins and Monroe's (1993) experiment, subjects objected strongly to welfare recipients being given lower prices for imported bottled water.

Proposition 6: More favorable pricing terms offered to consumer groups generally perceived as low income on product categories considered basic necessities, such as food or transportation, are more likely to be perceived as fair by other customers than equally more favorable pricing terms offered to those groups on non-necessary products.

From equity theory, we can also infer that different prices can be offered to those customers possessing higher incomes without being accompanied by perceptions of inequity. For example, higher income customers qualify for gold credit cards, and therefore lower interest rates, i.e., better pricing for credit, than lower income customers. Preferred customer cards, in some cases, entitle card holders to better pricing terms. However, no known empirical evidence exists indicating whether other customers believe such arrangements to be unfair. Further, there is no known empirical evidence indicating whether the customers given preferential status feel the situation is inequitable.

IMPLICATIONS

Equity research postulates that exchange relationships are perceived by parties involved as either fair or unfair (Adams 1965; Adams and Freeman 1976). Past pricing research concerned with perceptions of price fairness have mainly focused on relationships between buyers and sellers. However, given that equity theory points out indirect exchange relationships as significant sources of fairness perceptions, lateral customer relationships would also seem to be a likely source of price fairness evaluations. Yet, concern with this aspect of the price fairness construct is conspicuously absent from price perceptions research.

However, there seems to be some evidence that customers do pay attention to the prices paid by other customers. Hence, it becomes important to examine the role that perceptions of price fairness resulting from differential pricing strategies will play in consumers' perceptions of product sacrifice, value and willingness to buy.

A confirmation of the significance of this aspect of the price fairness construct implies a need for reevaluation of past price-perceived quality research, in terms of whether the prices utilized in those studies were perceived to be fair. Inconsistent or weak findings may very well be explained by this addition to the price-perceived quality model.

Instances of consumer decision research other than those investigated in pricing also should be scrutinized for the presence of analogous perceptions of fairness. Non-price promotion research would seem to be a reasonable area to look for the presence of similar perceptions of fairness. Further, generalizable measures of fairness perceptions need to be developed. Finally, a typology of situations that lead to fairness assessments on the part of consumers needs to be constructed.

For managers, the addition of this construct to the price-perceived quality model would mean a reevaluation of prices offered to customer segments in terms of whether segments to whom the offer will not be extended perceive the price offer to be fair. Finally, a better understanding of customers' perceptions of price fairness would help managers develop strategies that reduce perceived unfairness and therefore promote product value. Indeed, the rationale for American Airlines' restructuring of prices in the Spring of 1992, was to reduce the perceptions that airline pricing was not fair. The objective of their price structure was to reduce the perception of inequitable prices for similar levels of service.

REFERENCES

Adams, J. Stacy (1965), "Inequity in Social Exchange," in Leonard Berkowitz (ed.), *Advances in Experimental Social Psychology*, 2, New York: Academic Press, 267-299.

Adams, J. Stacy and Sara Freedman (1976), "Equity Theory Revisited: Comments and Annotated Bibliography," in Leonard Berkowitz and Elaine Walster (eds.) *Advances in Experimental Social Psychology*, 9, New York: Academic Press, 43-90.

Deutsch, Morton (1985), *Distributive Justice: A Social-Psychological Perspective*, New Haven, CT: Yale University Press.

Dodds, William, Kent Monroe, and Dhruv Grewal (1991), "Effects of Price, Brand, and Store Information on Buyers' Product Evaluations," *Journal of Marketing Research*, 28 (August), 307-319.

Festinger, L. (1957), *A Theory of Cognitive Dissonance*, Evanston, IL: Row, Peterson.

Galston, William (1980), *Justice and the Human Good*, Chicago, IL: The University of Chicago Press.

Holbrook, Morris, Robert Chestnut, Terence Oliva and Eric Greenleaf (1984), "Play as a Consumption Experience: The Roles of Emotions, Performance, and Personality in the Enjoyment of Games," *Journal of Consumer Research*, 11 (September), 728-739.

Homans, G.C. (1961), *Social Behavior: Its Elementary Forms*, New York: Harcourt, Brace & World.

Kalapurakal, Rosemary, Peter Dickson and Joel Urbany (1991), "Perceived Price Fairness and Dual Entitlement," in *Advances in Consumer Research*, 18, Rebecca Holman and Michael Solomon (eds.), Provo, UT: Association for Consumer Research, 788-793.

Kamen, J. and R. Toman (1970), "Psychophysics of Prices," *Journal of Marketing Research*, 7 (February), 27-35.

Kahneman, Daniel, Jack Knetsch and Richard Thaler (1986), "Fairness as a Constraint on Profit Seeking: Entitlements in the Market," *American Economic Review* 76 (September), 728-741.

Lynn, Michael (1990), "Choose Your Own Price: An Exploratory Study Requiring an Expanded View of Price's Functions," in *Advances in Consumer Research*, 17, Marvin Goldberg, Gerald Corn and Richard Pollay (eds.), Provo, UT: Association for Consumer Research, 710-714.

Marn, Michael and Robert Rosiello (1987), "Managing Price, Gaining Profit," *Harvard Business Review*, 70 (September/October), 84-94.

Martens, Dana (1991) "Upgrade Price Unfair," *CompuServe Message* #109391 (29-OCT-91).

Martins, Marielza and Kent Monroe (1993), "The Effect of Perceived Price Fairness on Buyers' Perceptions of Sacrifice and Willingness to Buy," presented at the *Marketing Science Conference*, St. Louis, MO, March 12-14.

Merton, R.K. (1957), *Social Theory and Social Structure*, Glencoe, IL: The Free Press.

Monroe, Kent (1990), *Pricing: Making Profitable Decisions* (2nd. ed.), New York: McGraw-Hill Publishing Co.

Monroe, Kent and Susan Petroshius (1981), "Buyers' Perceptions of Price: An Update of the Evidence," in *Perspectives in Consumer Behavior*, 3rd ed., T. Robertson and H. Kassarjian (eds.), Glenview, IL: Scott Foresman, 23-42.

Schindler, Robert M. (1989), "The Excitement of Getting a Bargain: Some Hypotheses Concerning the Origins and Effects of Smart-Shopper Feelings," in *Advances in Consumer Research*, 16, Thomas Srull (ed.), Provo, UT: Association for Consumer Research, 447-453.

Schnaars, Steven P. (1991), *Marketing Strategy: A Customer-Driven Approach*, New York: The Free Press.

Steenkamp, Jan-Benedict (1989), "A Model of the Quality Perception Process," *Product Quality*, Assen/Maastricht, The Netherlands: Van Gorcum, 99-129.

Thaler, Richard (1985), "Mental Accounting and Consumer Choice," *Marketing Science*, 4 (Summer), 199-214.

Tversky, Amos and Daniel Kahneman (1979), "Prospect Theory: An Analysis of Decision Under Risk," *Econometrica*, 47 (March), 263-291.

Zeithaml, Valarie (1988), "Consumer Perceptions of Price, Quality, and Value: A Means-End Model and Synthesis of Evidence," *Journal of Marketing*, 52 (July), 2-22.

Price Awareness of Consumers Exposed to Intense Retail Rivalry: A Field Study

Kathleen Seiders, Texas A&M University
Carolyn L. Costley, University of Miami

ABSTRACT

Following the simultaneous market entry by 3 supermarket chains, we conducted a field study to explore consumer responses to this intensified retail competition and price warfare. We investigated consumers' use of price for store choice and the accuracy of their perceptions about retailer price positioning. A content analysis of pricing tactics determined that communications to consumers changed substantively after the entry event. Price basket comparisons among all chains indicated distinct actual pricing positions. Finally, a consumer survey provided evidence that price played an unusually prominent role in store choice decisions and that consumers had very accurate perceptions of market pricing.

Consumers are increasingly confronted with intense marketplace competition. Saturation, overstoring, and a rapid proliferation of new formats have changed the competitive dynamics in many retail markets. As established chains defend marketshare against low cost/low price operators, price warfare has become prevalent. The impact of price-focused competition on consumer perception and retail patronage is relevant across a number of marketing contexts.

Prior research on consumers' responses to retail price positioning spans two literature streams — pricing and retail selection. The influence of various price factors on consumer price perceptions has been examined extensively. Areas of study include types of price appeals (Della Bitta, Monroe, and McGinnis 1981; Mobley, Bearden, and Teel 1988); the use of reference prices (Grewal and Compeau 1992; Liefeld and Heslop 1985; Mazumdar and Monroe 1992; Urbany, Bearden, and Weilbaker 1988); and the magnitude of price discounts (Berkowitz and Walton 1980; Leigh and Varadarajan 1991). Retail patronage literature addresses the patterns of consumers' purchasing behavior and the determinants of store choice (Spiggle and Sewall 1987; Black 1984). Consumers' retail selection processes traditionally have been examined using estimation models to identify and rank determinant attributes (Arnold, Oum, and Tigert 1983; Louviere and Gaeth 1987; Craig, Ghosh and McLafferty 1984). Attributes determined to be the most critical for patronage decisions include convenient location, price, assortment, service, product quality, and shopping environment.

An issue which has not received significant attention within either the pricing or patronage literature is the nature of consumer responses to intensified competitive environments characterized by price battling. We present research focusing on the following question: how does increased competitive rivalry, with widespread price warfare, affect consumers' price sensitivity and price perceptions? To capture the realism of marketplace dynamics, we investigated consumers' response to competitive turbulence in a field setting. We focused on a critical incident which forced a stable competitive environment into disequilibrium and price jockeying.

To establish that price battling occurred, the first stage of the study examined changes in retailers' pricing behaviors. We measured changes in consumer-directed communications (about price) before and after the pivotal event. We also measured the actual price position of competitors—as opposed to the implied advertised price positions—just after entry but before price adjustments and again after the market had a chance to adapt (seven months later). In the second stage we evaluated consumer responses in terms of 1) their use of price for store selection and 2) their perceptions of retailers' actual price positions.

Reseach Context: Simultaneous Entry of Retail Chains

Within a 4-week period in the winter of 1991, a southwestern city (approximately 100,000 population) saw three major supermarket chains enter a market previously served by three competing chains. The established competitors were Appletree (3 stores), Kroger (2), and Winn-Dixie (2); the newcomers were Albertson's (2), H.E.B. Pantry (3), and Randall's (1).

Typically, when a firm enters a market, its objective is to change consumers' buying patterns. New entrants must attract consumers to their stores for trial and continued patronage. Entrenched firms must minimize erosion of market share (customer share; dollar share) by retaining existing customers. The phenomenon of simultaneous entry of multiple firms with multiple locations magnifies the challenges for both the new entrants and the entrenched chains. This event appropriately represents the type of competitive shift central to this study.

STAGE 1: CONTENT ANALYSIS OF PRICING TACTICS

Evaluating retailers' communications to consumers—before and after the critical event of chain entry—required a longitudinal perspective. We conducted a 12-month content analysis of print advertisements to 1) note the content changes in pricing communications, 2) measure the emphasis on various types of messages, and 3) delineate differences in the approaches of the 6 supermarket chains. All supermarket advertisements in the city's only daily newspaper were catalogued. The approximately 600 advertisements (3000 pages) included both promotional inserts and in-paper ads. Exhibit 1 displays the data.

Seven categories of retail pricing practices, representing the most frequently used price tactics, structured the content analysis. The categories are described as follows:

1. Weekly/Biweekly Specials: sale-priced items, both national and private- or store-label brands, representing all store departments.
2. Weekend/2-Day Specials: selected, high-turnover items offered at dramatically deep discounts.
3. Storewide Price Reductions: store- or category-wide "permanent" reductions.
4. Competitive Price Comparisons: retailer's price on particular items compared to competitors' higher prices.
5. Discount/Rebate Offers: programs awarding percentage discounts for minimum purchases over consecutive periods.
6. Coupon Redemption: manufacturer coupons redeemed for double value and acceptance of competitors' store coupons.
7. Product Giveaways: merchandise free-of-charge with minimum or required purchase of other specified items.

The frequency counts reported in Exhibit 1 correspond to the number of mentions of a particular category by an individual chain. No more than one count per category was recorded from a single

EXHIBIT 1
Frequency of Retailer Price Communications

Time Period	Chain	Weekly/Bi-Weekly Specials	Weekend Specials	Price Reductions	Competitive Price Comparisons	Discount/Rebate Offers	Coupon Redemption	Product Giveaways	Total
I. Sep/Oct/Nov 91	Appletree	20	--	--	2	3	2	--	27
	Kroger	15	--	--	4	10	4	--	33
	Winn-Dixie	13	--	--	--	--	--	--	16
Period Total		48	--	--	6	13	6	8	76
% of Total		63	--	--	8	17	8		100
II. Dec 91/Jan/Feb 92	Appletree	20	7	2	--	--	4	4	35
	Kroger	16	--	2	--	5	4	6	29
	Winn-Dixie	12	--	--	8	--	6	2	22
	Albertson's	13	--	--	--	--	--	--	19
	HEB Pantry	13	--	--	13	--	5	6	26
	Randall's	24	10	--	4	8	17	8	47
Period Total		98	17	2	21	7	15	18	178
III. Mar/Apr/May 92	Appletree	20	8	3	--	--	6	8	42
	Kroger	18	4	--	--	10	4	3	42
	Winn-Dixie	12	--	10	10	--	6	--	32
	Albertson's	15	--	5	4	--	4	--	28
	HEB Pantry	13	--	12	--	--	10	--	24
	Randall's	25	14	--	--	2	10	6	57
Period Total		102	26	18	26	12	24	17	225
IV. Jun/Jul/Aug 92	Appletree	21	6	--	--	14	6	3	50
	Kroger	16	3	--	--	5	--	3	27
	Winn-Dixie	12	--	2	8	--	--	--	20
	Albertson's	15	--	--	11	--	3	--	31
	HEB Pantry	13	--	--	13	--	--	--	26
	Randall's	24	10	10	--	--	11	4	59
Period Total		101	19	12	32	19	20	10	213
9 Month Total		301	62	32	80	38	59	45	616
9 Month % of Total		49	10	5	13	6	10	7	100

advertisement. Exhibit 1 is divided into 4 time periods of equal duration. Time period I was prior to the multiple entry event; Periods II, III, and IV were subsequent to entry.

Changes in Price-Oriented Communications

Two content analysis categories—Weekend or 2-Day Specials and Storewide Price Reductions—were non-existent prior to the entry. Competitive Price Comparisons were minimally existent with only three mentions by Winn-Dixie. Weekend Specials were introduced by Appletree and Randall's, the market's highest-priced competitors. These specials were advertised on Fridays and Saturdays, independently of regular weekly specials advertised on Wednesdays and Sundays.

Storewide Price Reductions first occurred after the critical point and were used more for positional than for promotional purposes. While Randall's and Kroger used the tactic to adjust to lowered market prices, Winn-Dixie used store-wide reductions to maintain its Everyday Low Price (EDLP) positioning image.

Competitive Price Comparisons represented the most directly combative attempts to establish EDLP supremacy. Frequency of these advertisements increased as competition among the chains intensified. Price comparisons accounted for 4% of total mentions in Period I, increasing to 12% in Periods II and III and to 15% of total mentions in Period IV. The comparative ads varied along two factors: the object of the attack (a single competitor or a set of competitors), and the length and content of the printed price lists (e.g. 75 items across-categories; 20 produce items; 30 items from a customer's "shopping list"; 150 items comprising an entire product category). H.E.B. Pantry, Albertson's, and Winn-Dixie, the chains which employed this tactic, complemented comparative newspaper advertising with in-store signage listing competitors' prices adjacent to store unit-prices. Because of recent interest in consumers' use of reference prices (Biswas and Blair 1991; Grewal and Compeau 1992; Monroe, Grewal, Compeau 1991; Urbany, Bearden, and Weilbaker 1988), it may be especially rewarding to examine consumers' responses to this prominent use of comparative price ads.

Retailer Coupon Redemption practices qualitatively changed after the entry event. Kroger offered double redemption prior to the market attack, and both Appletree and Randall's adopted the tactic in Period II. Albertson's introduced the practice of honoring all competitors' store coupons at face value (Period II). The EDLP chains (HEB Pantry, Albertson's, Winn-Dixie) eschewed double couponing in their advertising, warning consumers of the double coupons/higher prices trade-off.

Weekly Specials, Discount and Rebate Programs, and Product Giveaways remained relatively stable as competition intensified with only two exceptions. One exception was the increasingly deeper discounting of weekly specials between Periods II and IV by Randall's, Kroger, and Albertson's. In addition to chainwide weekly specials, these chains tailored sales specifically to the local market (e.g., "prices available only at ___ stores."). A second exception was Appletree's Period IV launch of a major program encouraging customer loyalty by awarding customers 10% discounts on consecutive weekly purchases.

Summary. Numerous price-based communication changes occurred as a result of multiple chain entry and increased competitive intensity. Tactics changed with the introduction and extensive use of major new pricing initiatives. Message content changed as advertising became more and more promotional and directly competitive. Specifically, bold pricing tactics such as storewide reductions, competitive comparison ads, and price-slashed specials seized prominent roles. Individual chains battled for differentiation by creating tactical portfolios intended to fortify various price images.

The cumulative effect of retailers' continuing and concerted shifts in price emphasis was an environment of full-blown price warfare.

Price Basket Comparisons

We compared price baskets among the supermarket chains in order to rank competitors in terms of actual price position. These rankings may then be used to evaluate the accuracy of consumer perceptions of the various chains' price positions.

Basket prices were collected and calculated in December of 1991, when the new chains first entered the market, and again in July of 1992. The second appraisal coincided with the related consumer survey. The price basket, designed to cover all major supermarket categories, is commonly used in private market studies. Of the 126 items, 76 are packaged national brand groceries, 15 are general merchandise, and 35 are commodities and perishables. Basket prices are presented in Table 1. Item categories have been aggregated into one Total Basket price.

Results show that all chains remained consistent in their pricing over the 8-month period with the exception of Winn-Dixie, which attempted an EDLP repositioning using highly advertised storewide price reductions. H.E.B. Pantry was the market price leader; Albertson's and Winn-Dixie (in the July survey) trailed by only 2%, an imperceptible distinction (Tigert 1985, 1989). Kroger prices were approximately 6% above H.E.B. Pantry's. Randall's and Appletree shared the high-end of the price spectrum at 15% and 18% above, respectively. It thus appears that there were four distinctly different price positions in the market. This provides empirical evidence of the price variation in the market and confirms the fierce conflict among the 3 EDLP chains for perceived price position leadership.

STAGE 2: CONSUMER RESPONSES

Our content analysis provided evidence that retailers increased price promotion and price positioning activity after three new chains entered the market. The chains varied in their tactics to attract and retain customers. Because of the emphasis on price in general, and the relative emphasis on price comparisons in particular, it would be reasonable to expect consumers to pay more attention to price. This prompts us to express three general hypotheses. 1) Consumers will reevaluate what constitutes "low" price. 2) Consumers will become more price sensitive, re-ordering the importance of choice determinants, giving greater weight to price and lesser weight to other attributes. 3) Consumers will accurately evaluate actual price positions. These expectations guided the empirical second phase.

Evaluation of Low Price

It is likely that the extremely low prices produced by price warfare would change consumers' perceptions of all prices. In other words, consumers' concept of "low" price conforms to the context. Adaptation-level theorists posit that when new information varies over a wider range than consumers' internal reference ranges, it changes those reference ranges (Monroe, Grewal, and Compeau 1991). We would, therefore, expect consumers' standards to change following price warfare. A previously "low" price might no longer be perceived as such. We expect this change to manifest itself in consumers switching to lower-priced stores.

Consumers might be persuaded to switch to the new low price stores unless loyalty keeps them from it. Research has shown, however, that consumers' store loyalty is divided at best (Steenkamp and Wedel 1991; Keng and Ahrenberg 1984). Thus, we don't expect that loyalty will override price sensitivity in this price warfare environment.

TABLE 1
U.S. Retail Grocery Basket Price Comparisons

Supermarket Chain	Price Comparisons				
	July 1992[a]	% Above Low Price Leader	December 1991[b]	% Above Low Price Leader	% Increase
H E B Pantry	$296.67	—	$298.25	—	<.5>
Winn-Dixie	$303.25	2.2	$323.17	8.4	<6.2>
Albertson's	$303.34	2.3	$300.64	.8	.9
Kroger	$313.90	5.8	$310.70	4.2	1.0
Randall's	$341.81	15.2	$340.10	14.0	.5
Appletree	$352.02	18.7	$351.81	18.0	.1

NOTE:
[a] July, 1992: Coincided with consumer survey.
[b] December, 1991: Followed entry of new chains.

Reweighting Determinant Attributes

It is likely that rampant price communications will cause consumers to place relatively more importance on price than on other attributes for determining store patronage. Previous research suggests that attribute determinacy is indeed subject to market dynamics. Arnold, Oum, and Tigert (1983) used a multinomial logit model to identify and rank determinant attributes in store choice decisions across a variety of conditions. Logit coefficients consistently were highest on convenient location, low price, assortment, fast checkout, courteous service, shopping environment, best weekly specials, and meat quality (in approximate rank order).

Increased price variation may also cause attribute reweighting. In a study of context effects on parameter estimates, Eagle (1984) found that expanded variation of one attribute among stores increased that attribute's impact on market share. Consequently, the impact of unchanged attributes decreased. This reinforces our expectation that attribute reweighting will occur when price variation increases as in our price warfare scenario. We expect price to increase in importance for store choice.

Accuracy of Perceived Retailer Price Positions

For consumers to perform inter-store price comparisons usually requires that they retain price information in memory for later recall. Mazumdar and Monroe (1992) note that it is difficult to simplify retailers' price comparisons because there are few printed price lists and advertisements feature a small proportion of merchandise. Furthermore, advertisements often report only sale prices, leaving consumers uninformed about retailers' "everyday" price levels.

While inter-store price comparison is usually a complex consumer task, the price comparison tactics employed in our study context greatly simplified it. Extensive comparative price advertising and in-store signage offering comparative price data facilitate inter-store price comparisons for consumers. Print ads listing items and various retailers' prices allow consumers to compare stores without having to remember prices while they shop around. So, while research has shown that shoppers normally make limited use of price and price status information (Dickson and Sawyer 1990), simplifying the task may change that. We expect that an increased percentage of shoppers will use price information for store choice in this environment where comparative advertising and signage were pervasive.

Being exposed to so much comparison price data and the increased likelihood of using price data should make consumers knowledgeable about retailers' price behavior. Comparative price messages not only should affect consumers' perceptions of retailers' price positions (Urbany, Bearden and Weilbaker 1988), but should make them more accurate judges of actual price positions.

Survey Method

A survey of area consumers was conducted in July of 1992, approximately 8 months after the entry of the supermarket chains. Using random-digit dialing, we completed telephone interviews with 500 primary household food shoppers (approximately 80% response rate). Here, we report on the questions related to consumer price perceptions and store choice attributes.[1]

Respondents were asked their primary and secondary reasons for shopping the chains they reported to shop the most frequently. We expected for responses to these open-ended questions to show price to be particularly determining of store choice. We also expected that other choice attributes would show decreased importance.

Other questions asked respondents to identify the supermarket chain with the highest prices and the chain with the best or lowest prices. We asked respondents to identify the superior chain on each attribute (e.g., price, location, assortment) rather than to rate each chain on all attributes. This neutralizes halo effects of store image on all attributes (Arnold, Oum, and Tigert 1983). We expected respondents' perceptions of the chains' price positions to be fairly accurate. Consumers' ranking of the chains should reflect the ranking designated by the price basket comparison survey.

---

[1] "Which food store has the lowest overall prices?" "Which food store has the highest overall prices?" "Please tell me the single most important reason why you shop at the store where you shop most often for groceries." "Please tell me the second most important reason..."

TABLE 2
Results From Consumer Survey

A. Most Important Reason For Choosing Store Where Respondent Shops Most Often

Reason For Store Choice	Most Important (%)	Second Most Important (%)	Total Percent of Respondents
Price	28	23	51
Location	33	15	47
Assortment	8	16	24
Familiarity	8	6	14
Service	4	10	14

B. Most Important Reason For Choosing Store: Customers Who Shifted Patronage vs. Those Who Did Not

	Shifted Patronage			Did Not Shift Patronage		
Reason For Store Choice	Most Important (%)	Second Most Important (%)	Total Percent	Most Important (%)	Second Most Important (%)	Total Percent
Price	29	25	54	26	19	45
Location	34	14	48	31	17	48
Assortment	10	17	27	06	13	19

C. Perceptions Among All Respondents: Supermarket Chain With Lowest Prices

	Albertson's (%)	Appletree (%)	HEB Pantry (%)	Kroger (%)	Randall's (%)	Winn-Dixie (%)
Lowest	13	3	27	17	3	22
Highest	3	37	1	10	42	3
Lowest/Highest	5.38	.09	26.7	1.71	.07	6.79

D. Perceptions Among Chain's Primary Shoppers: Chain With Lowest Prices

	Albertson's (%)	Appletree (%)	HEB Pantry (%)	Kroger (%)	Randall's (%)	Winn-Dixie (%)
Lowest/Best	52	17	91	48	21	87

RESULTS

Evaluation of Low Price

Assorted evidence suggests that consumers became sensitized to price and probably reformulated their concepts of "low" price. Consumers' reevaluation of low price would likely be manifested by erratic or shifting patronage behavior. When asked to identify which chain they primarily patronized prior to the entry event and which chain they patronized afterwards, over 50% reported shifted patronage. Those who shifted patronage said that price was particularly important to their store choice (Table 2 Part B). This suggests that reconceptualization of "low" price probably triggered behavioral changes.

An impetus to reevaluate the market and gain new price knowledge would logically follow from a redefinition of what constitutes "low prices." The accuracy of consumers' perceptions about retailers' price positions (Table 2 Parts C and D) indicates that they were very knowledgeable. The evidence indicates that consumers paid attention to price information in this market.

Choice Determinacy

Table 2 contains the results used to evaluate our expectations about consumer responses. Result (A) shows the five primary choice determinants for this market and the percentages of respondents choosing these attributes as the primary or secondary reasons for store choice. Because the list of determinant attributes is partial, percentages presented in the table do not total 100%. Price is only 5% below location/convenience as a primary determinant. The combined percentage, used to evaluate overall attribute importance, is 4% higher for price than for location (p<.05).

To judge the importance of these results, we compared them to other markets that were similarly measured. Chicago and Ohio markets (Tigert 1985, 1989)—larger markets than ours—were affected by the entry of only one (Chicago) or 2 (Ohio) new chains. Competitive structure, therefore, was relatively less altered than in our study context where the number of competitors literally doubled. These studies reported the following:

	Reason for Store Choice	Most Important	2nd Most Important	Total
Chicago	Location	52%	11%	63%
	Prices	16%	15%	30%
	Assortment	5%	13%	19%
Ohio	Location	42%	12%	54%
	Prices	17%	16%	33%
	Assortment	11%	19%	30%

Comparing the Chicago and Ohio studies to our results (Prices: 28% 23% 51%) reveals a substantially higher consumer awareness of price in our turbulent market. Fifty-one percent of our respondents—compared to 30% and 33% of Chicago and Ohio respondents—reported that price was the first or second most important determinant of their store choice. This suggests that price sensitivity has increased as a result of intensified competition and price warfare.

The shift in the weighting of determinant attributes, represented primarily by the location/price dyad, is also apparent from these results. Location was important to 63% and 54% of respondents in the comparison studies, but to only 47% in our study.

Additional support for the magnified role of price is contained in Part (B) of Table 2. Respondents who shifted their patronage allocated more importance to price as a choice determinant than those who did not shift (54% versus 45%) (p<.01). The difference is most pronounced in the "second most important attribute" category (25% versus 19%). The weighting for location was stable across the two groups. Consistent with past research, location continued to dominate, yet price became relatively more important in the store choice decision.

Perceived Price Positioning

Respondents' perceptions of the highest and lowest-priced chains in the market are contained in Parts (C) and (D) of Table 2. Part (C) captures price perceptions for the total sample, and Part (D) reports perceptions for the individual chains' primary shoppers. Both analyses are required because the chains have differential market shares and primary shopper perceptions are needed to capture true strengths and weaknesses. A Lowest Priced/Highest Priced Ratio combines the two mentions for the total sample, providing a more refined overall measure of perceived price position. A summary of the results follows:

Respondent Ranking of Chains: From Lowest- to Highest-Priced

Total Sample	Low/High Ratio	Primary Shoppers
H.E.B. Pantry	H.E.B. Pantry	H.E.B. Pantry
Winn-Dixie	Winn-Dixie	Winn-Dixie
Kroger	Albertson's	Albertson's
Albertson's	Kroger	Kroger
Appletree	Appletree	Randall's
Randall's	Randall's	Appletree

We compared these rankings with the Price Basket Survey results in Table 1 (July 1992) to gauge the accuracy of consumers' perceptions of retailers' price positions. Respondent rankings are highly accurate, particularly the more sensitive Ratio and Primary Shopper measures. H.E.B. Pantry is the indisputable price leader; Appletree and Randall's cluster as the highest-priced competitors. Primary shopper perceptions of price image for H.E.B. Pantry and Winn-Dixie are notable, at 91% and 87%, respectively. Examination of the data in Table 2 shows the primary respondent misperception to be Winn-Dixie's price differentiation from Albertson's. In fact, the prices of the two chains are virtually indistinguishable. Their communication strategies however, as indicated by the content analysis, were very different.

DISCUSSION

Price warfare's influence on consumer behavior merits investigation. The *Wall Street Journal* (12/8/92) described the "new breed of thrifty consumer, who willingly treks from supermarkets to warehouse clubs" as having a "frugality habit." The speculation underlying this study is that retailers, by placing extreme emphasis on price through a variety of initiatives and communication tactics, are advancing price sensitivity among consumers.

While controlled laboratory experiments are capable of isolating and testing relationships between variables, a common concern is that freely varying factors in the marketplace may obscure those relationships. In the field study reported, we are able to explore consumer behavior in a dynamic, "noisy" setting that cannot be simulated. We attempted to evaluate the effects of changed competitive structure (particularly price warfare) on consumer responses.

Under "real world" conditions, consumers appeared to change their reference point for "low" price. Those who switched stores said that price was particularly important to their store choice. This is consistent with reference price research based on adaptation, prospect and assimilation theories. Changes in advertised reference prices apparently caused consumers to adjust their price standards.

Increased price variation also caused price to gain relative importance in determining store choice. Price became a more important attribute both within this market context and when compared to other markets of lower competitive intensity. This provides field study support for Eagle's laboratory findings that increased variation in one attribute enhances that attribute's impact on market share (1984).

Accurate knowledge of actual price positions in the marketplace indicates that consumers paid attention to the increased price advertising. Behavior changes reportedly based on price indicate that the increased advertising changed consumers' price sensitivities. This addresses Urbany, Bearden, and Weilbaker's recommendation to examine the accuracy and effects of consumers' price expectations (1988).

Retailer use of competitive comparative price advertising was a particularly intriguing market phenomenon. Conceptual relevance of this practice stems from the current activity in reference price research. Of practical interest is the potential effectiveness of the format. Supermarket chains apparently are dedicating substantial resources to support this type of advertising. An interesting correlation in this study is the heavy usage of competitive comparison advertising by the perceived price leaders, H.E.B. Pantry and

Winn-Dixie. Albertson's adopted the comparison ad format midstream, using it with less frequency than the other two EDLP chains.

While field research benefits from external validity, it sacrifices control over relevant variables—such as nonprice promotions, service enhancements, etc.—which contribute to consumer store choice decisions. Relative lack of comparative data with which to evaluate the results was another drawback. It might be useful to pursue more elaborate survey methodologies that could capture variation in consumer price sensitivity in diverse competitive retail contexts.

REFERENCES

Arnold, Stephen J., Tae H. Oum, and Douglas J. Tigert (1983), "Determinant Attributes in Retail Patronage: Seasonal, Temporal, Regional, and International Comparisons," *Journal of Marketing Research*, 20 (May), 149-157.

Berkowitz, Eric N. and John R. Walton (1980), "Contextual Influences on Consumer Price Responses: An Experimental Analysis," *Journal of Marketing Research*, 17 (August), 349-373.

Biswas, Abhijit and Edward A. Blair (1991), "Contextual Effects of Reference Prices in Retail Advertisements," *Journal of Marketing*, 55 (July), 1-12.

Black. William C. (1984), "Choice Set Definition in Patronage Modeling," *Journal of Retailing*, 60 (Summer), 63-85.

Craig, C. Samuel, Avijit Ghosh, and Sara Lafferty (1984), "Models of the Retail Location Process: A Review," *Journal of Retailing*, 60 (Spring), 5-36.

Della Bitta, Albert J., Kent B. Monroe, and John M. McGinnis (1981), "Consumer Perceptions of Comparative Price Advertisements," *Journal of Marketing Research*, 18 (November), 416-427.

Dickson, Peter R. and Alan G. Sawyer (1990), "The Price Knowledge and Search of Supermarket Shoppers," *Journal of Marketing*, 54 (July), 42-53.

Eagle, Thomas C. (1984), "Parameter Stability in Disaggregate Retail Choice Models: Experimental Evidence," *Journal of Retailing*, 60 (Spring), 101-121.

Grewal, Dhruv and Larry D. Compeau (1992), "Comparative Price Advertising: Informative or Deceptive?," *Journal of Public Policy and Marketing*, 2 (Spring), 52-62.

Keng, Kau Ah and S.C. Ehrenberg (1984), "Patterns of Store Choice," *Journal of Marketing Research*, 21 (November), 399-409.

Leigh, James H. and P. Rajan Varadarajan (1991), "Consumers' Behavioral Responses to Alternative Price Promotions: A Field Study in a Fast-Food Retailing Context," in *Proceedings of the 1991 Symposium on Patronage Behavior*, ed. William R. Darden, Robert F. Lusch, and J. Barry Mason, 133-145.

Liefeld, John and Louise A. Heslop (1985), "Reference Prices and Deception in Newspaper Advertising," *Journal of Consumer Research*, 11 (March), 868-876.

Louviere, Jordan J. and Gary J. Gaeth (1987), "Decomposing the Determinants of Retail Facility Choice Using the Method of Hierarchical Information Integration: A Supermarket Illustration," *Journal of Retailing*, 63 (Spring), 25-48.

Mazumdar, Tridib and Kent B. Monroe (1992), "Effects of Inter-Store and In-Store Price Comparisons on Price Recall Accuracy and Confidence," *Journal of Retailing*, 68 (Spring), 67-89.

Mobley, Mary F., William O. Bearden, and Jesse E. Teel (1988), "An Investigation of Individual Responses to Tensile Price Claims," *Journal of Consumer Research*, 15 (September), 273-279.

Monroe, Kent B., Dhruv Grewal, and Larry D. Compeau (1991), "The Concept of References Prices: Theoretical Justifications and Research Issues," presented at the Association for Consumer Research, Chicago,IL. October 19, 1991.

Spiggle, Susan and Murphy A. Sewall (1987), "A Choice Sets Model of Retail Selection," *Journal of Marketing*, 51 (April), 97-111.

Steenkamp, Jan-Benedict and Michel Wedel (1991), "Segmenting Retail Markets on Store Image Using a Consumer-Based Methodology," *Journal of Retailing*, 67 (Fall), 300-319.

Tigert, Douglas J. and Stephen J. Arnold (1989), "Hypermarket: The Meijer Story in Columbus, Ohio," *Babson College Retailing Report*, Wellesley, MA.

_____ , Lawrence J. Ring, Stephen J. Arnold, and Terry Cotter (1985), "Stealing from the Outer Rings: The Cub Super Food Warehouse in South Chicago," *Babson College Retailing Report*, Wellesley, MA.

Urbany, Joel E., William O. Bearden, and Dan C. Weilbaker (1988), "The Effect of Plausible and Exaggerated Reference Prices on Consumer Perceptions and Price Search," *Journal of Consumer Research*, 15 (June), 95-110.

Promotion Heterogeneity and Consumer Learning: Refining the Deal-Proneness Construct

Caroline M. Henderson, Dartmouth College

ABSTRACT

Researchers have had difficulty clearly defining a segment of deal-prone consumers. One problem with such research is use of an atheoretical and one-dimensional definition of deal-proneness which fails to recognize promotion heterogeneity. Using scanner panel data for two product categories, we find distinct segments that respond to different forms of promotion. On the basis of these results, we develop a theory of promotion learning: that consumers learn to respond in an increasingly complex fashion to their promotion environment. We then develop suggestions for testing this hypothesis.

INTRODUCTION

One popular research area has centered on consumers who respond to promotion—the identification of the "deal-prone" consumer (Webster 1965; Carman 1969; Blattberg et al. 1978; among others; see review by Blattberg and Neslin 1990). The deal-proneness studies to date have failed, however, to provide managers with a coherent view of the consumers most sensitive to promotion. One reason for this may be that deal-proneness should be seen as specific to individual types of deals. We propose refining the construct of deal-proneness through recognition of promotion heterogeneity.

Three empirical questions are addressed:

1) Do segments exist which vary in response to certain types of promotion?
2) Are such segments clearly identifiable in the population?
3) Do the segments vary by product category?

We then use this analysis to build a theory of promotion learning. In the final section we present suggestions for testing this theory.

Deal-Proneness

The construct of deal-proneness, first used by Webster (1965), refers to the consumer tendency to respond to sales promotion. The construct is typically measured by behavior; the deal-prone are those who buy promoted brands—redeem coupons, buy special packs, stock up when price is reduced, or otherwise take advantage of promotions. Difficulties in identifying the deal-prone may be explained by the impossibility of comparing across different studies. Deal-proneness can be specific to individual product categories and to individual types of deals. Yet most identified deal-proneness studies (Blattberg and Neslin 1990) deal with very restricted types of promotions (typically coupons) and a restricted number of product categories. To our knowledge, only Schneider and Currim (1991) measure deal proneness with a heterogeneous set of promotions.

Generalizations across categories can be dangerous; Carman's (1969) measure of deal-proneness produces different results for the two product categories in his study. The Blattberg, Peacock and Sen (1976) segments also show differences among the categories used. Such differences should be expected; product categories differ in motivations to use deals (financial expense, social risk, among others) and in the cost of using promotions (deal availability). If these two factors combine to make deal-proneness category-specific, all single-product studies will be potentially contradictory.

Generalizing across deal types may also be ill-advised. Dodson, Tybout, and Sternthal (1978) provide a compelling analysis of the value of studying promotions as separate types of stimuli. The authors argue that different types of deals should elicit different types of *behavior*, consistent with the precepts of economic utility theory and self-perception theory. For example, deals requiring substantial consumer effort for a small economic gain should lead to the attribution that a brand is purchased because it is preferred not because of its promotion. Deals requiring less effort relative to gain should be effective in undermining consumer brand loyalty. This theory predicts that price-off promotions, an example of the second type, encourage less loyal behavior than coupons, which involve more consumer effort. While the Dodson study's empirical findings support this theory, the study does not analyze consumer segments. Thus, the findings may actually show that different *consumers* are susceptible to different kinds of promotion.

To follow this line of reasoning, it may be possible to identify the attributes of promotion to which consumers differentially respond. Such bases should include the fundamental appeal of promotions or the costs of responding to them. The literature has developed theoretical explanations on these two issues.

A basic economic theory of deal-proneness is that consumers are motivated by a promotion's savings but must trade off such savings against a promotion's costs—particularly the cost of time spent taking advantage of the promotion (Blattberg, Buesing, Peacock and Sen 1978; Narasimhan 1984). While all consumers are intrinsically motivated by possible savings, they are heterogeneous with respect to time costs and thus vary in their deal-proneness. (Narasimhan (1984) shows additionally that those consumers having the lowest costs are also the most price elastic.) Blattberg, Eppen and Lieberman (1981) stress the importance of inventory holding costs which will also vary across the population and lead to varying degrees of deal-proneness. Previous researchers have used this approach to generate hypotheses that identify the deal-prone by relating demographic variables to the consumer's promotional costs. For example, Narasimhan (1984) hypothesizes that heavy usage, unemployment, higher education, and absence of children reduces the cost of using coupons. Thus, promotions can be seen to motivate by providing a basic economic utility but differences in the costs of using promotions may account for heterogeneity of response.

We propose to refine this view further by building on the Dodson, Tybout and Sternthal (1978) observation that all deals are not equivalent. In this approach each deal may be described by its attributes—the cost/benefits pattern uniquely pertaining to the type. As Figure 1 illustrates, promotional types may vary considerably in such attributes. For example, coupons may provide large economic incentives but incur more "time preference" costs due to the extensive pre-use activities required. Many deal pack offers force stockpiling by providing extra product; price-off offers may require purchase of multiple units to attain full savings, etc. Figure 1 is not intended to show a fully-formed theory of promotional differences, simply to suggest that cost/benefit patterns are sufficiently varied to require separate investigations for each promotional type. To illustrate, a consumer with high time costs who is sensitive to price may bypass coupons yet still buy price-off products. Thus, consumer segments which respond only to certain types of promotion may be found. Such segments should also be category-specific. If such segments are found, deal-proneness should be considered multidimensional across deal types.

FIGURE 1
An Illustration of Promotion Attributes

Promotion Attribute	Selected Promotion Types			
	Coupons	Price-off	Deal Pack	Retail Feature
Economic Incentive	++	++	+	+
Time Preferences/Consumer Skill:				
Clipping	—			
Maintaining collection	—			
Newspaper reading	—			—
Pre-planning	—			—
Store switching	—			—
Price comparisons		—	—	—
Inventory:				
Stock-up costs		—	—	
Holding costs		—	—	

METHOD

Two separate scanner panel data bases were used. Data set 1 covered 28 weeks of consumer purchases in a "northeast scanner market"—a metropolitan area of about 250,000 population. This market included three major grocery chains, with a total of fifteen stores. These stores kept a complete scanner record of all purchases made by the 2463 members of the panel—coverage amounting to 85 percent of the all-commodity-volume of the area. Data included purchase records and panel demographics. Available promotional variables included price changes, deal packs, coupons and two types of local advertising; retailer advertising was for weekly price specials and manufacturer advertising carried coupons.

Two product categories were studied to mitigate some of the weaknesses of single-product studies. We analyze purchases of bathroom tissue ("paper") and caffeinated instant coffee ("coffee"). These two product categories provide an interesting contrast. Private label and generic brands are purchased less frequently in coffee than paper. Paper is more likely to be promoted to the trade, and coffee promoted directly to the consumer. The average interpurchase time for paper is 19 days, for coffee it is 43 days.

Data set 2 covered 24 months of consumer purchases from a separate scanner market and included purchase records only for the coffee category. The data were analyzed for instant coffee and provided a replication of the analysis done with data set 1. The categories are equivalent and the time periods roughly comparable, although there are geographic differences in the consumer panels. There are also a few differences in the variables available for study. Data set 2 includes price changes and deal packs in common with data set 2. Coupons, however, are analyzed as store coupon and manufacturer coupons. Retailer advertising, called features, in data set 2 is also comparable but, in addition, a display variable was available.

Proneness Measures

A common measure for deal-prone behavior is percentage of purchases made on deal (Montgomery 1971, Wierenga 1974) and adjusted for the relative prevalence of deals (Webster 1965, Carman 1969). Percentage of purchase measures were the primary measures selected for this study. To develop these measures, the data files were combined and summarized to profile the consumers purchasing each of the product categories (1292 coffee purchasers making 4910 purchases and 2198 paper purchasers making 23727 purchases in a static sample for the 28-week period in data set 1). The percentage of total category purchases representing deals was computed for four types of promotional conditions: *Deal Packs* (special packages including extra product, reusable containers, or premarking with a price discount.), *Retail Ad/Feature* (retail advertising in local newspapers), *Manufacturer Ad* (manufacturer advertising, including coupons, in local newspapers), *Coupon* (purchase was made using a coupon from any source), *Display* (Data set 2 only—special display within the store).

As percentage of purchase measures, these variables assume that purchase samplings for each consumer represent an overall behavior pattern. Data set 1 is limited by a six-month time frame, since, on average, there are only four purchases of coffee per buyer. We have assumed that use of a coupon on five out of ten purchases is equivalent to use of a coupon on one out of two purchases. Thus, we separate deal-proneness from frequency of category usage. While this small sample size may tend to overstate degrees of brand loyalty among infrequent purchasers, a period of six months has been used previously to study loyalty (Johnson 1984). This time frame should introduce no systematic bias in promotional usage. Data set 2 covers a two-year period and is not subject to this potential weakness.

A fifth measure of deal-prone behavior—*Price Change*—was computed as the difference, measured in dollars, between the price paid on the purchase and the average shelf price during the week preceding the purchase. (A value of -.05 indicated that the brand had been discounted five cents.) As this value captures both promotional and nonpromotional price changes, it represents the consumer's response to lowered price. This operationalization avoids imputing promotional price changes from sales data (see, for example, Guadagni and Little 1983). Price changes for paper were computed from average shelf prices across all color combinations of a particular brand-size. Coffee price changes were identified for each brand-size.

The promotion variables are not highly correlated across the population. One exception is a .55 correlation in the coffee category between price change and retail ads. The decision to analyze each product category separately was substantiated by cross-category correlation. For example, the highest correlation was .26 for percentage of coupon purchases between the two categories in data set 1.

Analysis

Two random samples of 320 each (the maximum allowable because of computer constraints) were drawn from each category's consumers. To ensure that these samples did not differ in any way, mean values were compared across all variables in both samples from each category. The variables were standardized and used to create a Euclidean distance dissimilarity matrix, which then was clustered by two algorithms: nearest neighbor and minimum squared error (Schlaifer 1981). The dendrograms were analyzed to find the most suitable number of clusters using both the "elbow" and "intuitive" (Calantone and Sawyer 1978) rules.

Analysis procedure follows the three-step process needed to assess the strength of a cluster solution (Punj and Stewart 1983). This process tests that the cluster solution is 1) different from what could be obtained by a random assignment to groups (F-test across cluster variables); 2) reliable (cross-classification between samples); and 3) related to differences between individuals (F and chi-square tests across non-clustering variables).

In the second step, the output was analyzed for split-half stability by classifying each individual with a discriminant function developed from each sample's cluster analysis (as recommended by Calantone and Sawyer 1978). The ability of each sample's function to correctly classify its own and the other sample was tested by the percentage of correct classification across samples according to the proportional chance criterion (Morrison 1969).

The third test of the cluster results—generalizability—involves the relationship between the clusters and demographics and purchase behavior variables. Consumers in each category were first classified into a cluster with the discriminant function generated from one of the samples of 320. 1276 out of 1292 coffee purchasers and 2196 out of 2198 paper purchasers were successfully classified. Next, all available demographics and purchase variables were analyzed across the groups using F-tests for continuous variables and chi-square tests for nominal or ordinal data.

Data set 2 was used to replicate the analysis in data set 1. The same series of steps were performed on the instant coffee category.

RESULTS

Data Set 1

Five clusters were developed for each sample in each product category, using the minimum squared error cluster analysis. The nearest neighbor algorithm did not yield interpretable results—a common problem when cluster boundaries are not completely clear (Schlaifer 1981). As no strong elbow could be found to select an optimal number of clusters, the final number of clusters was selected judgmentally to provide usable results with an adequate number of consumers per cluster and a clear pattern within the cluster. As Table 1 shows for the entire data base of consumers in each category, the clusters have significantly different mean values on each promotion variable. The paper clusters can be described as:

Cluster 1: *Deal Packs* (13 percent of the sample)
This group has almost three-quarters of its purchase concentrated in deal pack merchandise. The group is very low on all other variables.

Cluster 2: *Retail Ads* (5 percent)
This small group appears to have a very high percentage of purchases (almost one-third) that coincide with the retail featured brand.

Cluster 3: *Coupons* (9 percent)
Over half of this group's purchases are made with a coupon.

Cluster 4: *Manufacturer Ads/Coupons* (1 percent)
This tiny group appears most responsive to manufacturer ads as well as coupons.

Cluster 5: *No Response* (72 percent)
The majority of the consumers in the paper category do not appear to be deal-prone.

The coffee cluster results are somewhat different:

Cluster 1: *All Promotion* (4 percent)
This segment is responsive to four of the five types of promotion measured. One-third of customer purchases are made with a coupon, over three-quarters are the retail featured brand, and, on average, the group saves $0.24 on the regular price of the brand. Seventeen percent of purchases also are made during the week of a manufacturer ad for the brand. Deal packs, however, are not an important part of purchasing.

Cluster 2: *Deal Packs/Coupons* (15 percent)
This group is similar to the paper deal pack segment with the addition that over one-third of their purchases are made with a coupon.

Cluster 3: *Manufacturer Ads/Coupons* (9 percent)
This group also approximates a paper segment (cluster 4), as it has a very high percentage of purchasing coinciding with manufacturer advertising.

Cluster 4: *Coupons* (32 percent)
The coupon group is the largest of the coffee clusters. These consumers use a coupon on almost two-thirds of their coffee purchases but do not appear particularly responsive to other forms of promotion.

Cluster 5: *No Response* (40 percent)
Although smaller in size, this group is equivalent to paper cluster 5 in showing little response.

Split-half clustering yielded similar groups for the two samples. Sizes of the clusters were quite comparable and means were not significantly different between samples. Clusters emerged in the same order for coffee and with one reversal (clusters 2 and 3) in paper. This cluster structure is internally reliable since two samples for each category could be used for fairly accurate cross-classification for members of the other sample on the clustering variables. (On average, 72 percent of paper consumers and 81 percent of coffee consumers were accurately cross-classified, compared with accurate reclassification on the same sample of 91 percent for each and with the proportional chance criterion of 55 percent for paper and 29 percent for coffee.) Such results are impressive given the sensitivity of cluster analysis to minor variations in data sets (for example, Funkhouser 1983). (Detailed study results are available from the author upon request.)

TABLE 1
Cluster Variable Means
(Data Set 1)

Paper	N	Cluster 1 (280)	Cluster 2 (104)	Cluster 3 (208)	Cluster 4 (26)	Cluster 5 (1,578)
Deal packs*		.74 [1]	.05	.01	.03	.03
Price change*		.0498 [2]	.0496	.0512	.0516	.0505
Retail ads*		.02 [1]	.29 [3]	.01	.01	.02
Manufacturer ads*		.00 [1]	.08	.08	.35	.03
Coupons*		.01 [1]	.10	.57	.15	.04

Coffee	N	Cluster 1 (50)	Cluster 2 (192)	Cluster 3 (111)	Cluster 4 (408)	Cluster 5 (515)
Deal packs*		.02	.79	.12	.05	.02
Price change*		-.24	-.01	-.00	-.02	-.00
Retail ads*		.75	.01	.02	.06	.01
Manufacturer ads*		.17	.02	.57	.04	.02
Coupons*		.36	.39	.43	.65	.06

*Significant at .95

Notes:
[1] To be read, "74% of cluster 1 purchases involved deal packs." The values shown for retail ads, manufacturer ads, and coupons are also percentages.
[2] To be read, "the average cluster 1 purchase involved a price increase of $.0498."
[3] Underlining is used to highlight the variables defining the clusters.

TABLE 1A
Coffee Replication Results
(Data Set 2)

Instant Coffee	N	Cluster 1 (669)	Cluster 2 (55)	Cluster 3 (565)	Cluster 4 (149)	Cluster 5 (23)
Deal packs *		-.00	-.00	.00	.00	.28
Price change *		.00	-.00	-.00	-.00	-.00
Features *		.02	.63	.16	.57	.12
Store Coupons *		.00	.77	.10	.14	.07
Manufacturer Coupons *		.06	.19	.42	.28	.16
Display *		.01	.21	.08	.47	.10

Data Set 2 - Replication

Results for the instant coffee category are shown in Table 1a and can be described as:

Cluster 1: *No Response* (46 percent)
This cluster is comparable in size and purchasing pattern to cluster 5 in data set 1.

Cluster 2: *Coupon/Feature/Display* (4 percent)
This cluster is somewhat unique compared with data set 1. A variety of promotions, with the exception of price changes, are used.

Cluster 3: *Manufacturers Coupon* (39 percent)
This cluster is comparable to cluster 4 in data set 1.

Cluster 4: *All Promotion* (10 percent)
Although the size of this segment is larger than cluster 1 in data set 1, the cluster is similar in using of a variety of promotions.

Cluster 5: *Deal Purchases/Coupons* (2 percent)
A much smaller cluster than cluster 2 in data set 1, this cluster has a similar tendency to buy the brand in special packaging.

This analysis reveals a number of similarities with data set 1 (Table 2).

DISCUSSION

The clusters were found to have statistically significant differences on brand loyalty, demographics, and other purchase vari-

TABLE 2

Data Set 1			Data Set 2		
Cluster	Size	Description	Cluster	Size	Description
1	4%	All promotions	4	10%	All promotions
2	15%	Deal packs/coupons	5	2%	Deal packs/coupons
3	9%	Manufacturer ads/coupons	2	4%	Coupons/feature/display
4	32%	Coupons	3	39%	Manufacturer coupons
5	40%	No response	1	46%	No response
Total	100%		Total	100%)	

ables, as shown in Tables 3 and 4. These tables show that consumers who are sensitive to nearly every type of promotion (coffee cluster 1) are also very loyal. They achieve savings through a combined strategy of coupons, price-offs, and large package sizes; they are older and nonworking, presumably able to incur the extra stock-up and holding costs associated with the combination of brand loyalty with deal proneness. This finding validates the importance of distinguishing loyalty, promotion usage, and brand choice in segmentation studies, as initially conceived in Blattberg and Sen (1974). These results disagree with the position of Hackleman and Duker (1980, p. 172) that deal-proneness "by definition" involves low brand loyalty; these results suggest that certain deal-prone consumers are high in brand loyalty.

Nonresponders to promotion (paper cluster 5 and coffee cluster 5 in data set 1 and cluster 1 in data set 2) are likely to buy in small quantities. These consumers are susceptible to private labels. Responding to sales promotion and buying private labels or generics appear to be antithetical consumer strategies, in distinction to the Wierenga results (1974). Consumers do not appear to switch between major brands on deal and private labels, which do not offer deals but are frequently priced lower. Instead, those with the highest percentages of private label purchases are only infrequent users of major brand promotions.

To provide a multivariate classification of the clusters, five-group discriminant analysis was performed for each product. For both categories the discriminating power of the independent variables was statistically significant using the proportional chance criterion. The paper functions reclassified 82% of the data base compared with a proportional chance classification of 55%. For coffee, the functions correctly classified 43% of a holdout sample, a significant improvement beyond a proportional chance of 29%. The functions indicate that promotion segments can be successfully identified with demographics and purchase behavior variables. Of the two variable types, knowledge of purchase habits—particularly brand loyalty—may be the more helpful in identifying groups of deal-prone consumers. Since purchase habits can be category specific, it may not be realistic to generalize segments across product categories.

To explore this issue of generalizability, clusters were compared across the two categories. The cross-classification in Table 5 was developed for the two categories by making certain assumptions about similarities in cluster description. Cluster 5—nonresponsive consumers—were roughly equivalent. Coffee cluster 2 was equated with paper clusters 1 and 2 as referring to a "non-coupon" response. Coffee cluster 1 appears to have no counterpart in paper. This most highly deal-sensitive segment is only a small percentage of the market and is only found for the one product category.

Using these assumptions we classified 37 percent of consumers as belonging to an equivalent deal-prone cluster in each category. The 37 percent is indistinguishable from a random assignment of 36 percent. Thus, knowledge of a consumer's deal-proneness in one category provides no information for classification in another category. This is support for the importance of category-specific research.

Although a no-response segment (cluster 5 in both) is found in both categories, its size varies; almost three-quarters of the paper consumers, but fewer than one-half of the coffee consumers, are non-responsive. This discrepancy might be explained by the relative importance of promotion in these two categories. The coffee industry has led in consumer promotion, particularly in the form of coupons, while the paper industry tends to use trade deals (Quelch 1982). While trade deals can affect consumers when the product is advertised, displayed, or reduced in price, market areas studied in this research show such pass-throughs as being primarily replaced by "everyday low pricing." The net effect is more availability of promotional opportunities for coffee purchasers than for paper buyers. The relative importance of these categories on the shopping list may also be a factor. Coffee, although less frequently bought, costs more than the paper product. Price may motivate consumers to take advantage of deals. Such considerations may shift the costs and benefits of specific types of promotion depending on category.

CONCLUSIONS AND FUTURE RESEARCH: PROMOTION LEARNING PROCESS

The research has shown that promotion heterogeneity should be recognized in the deal-proneness construct. Distinct and identifiable segments can be developed which isolate consumers who respond only to particular forms of sales promotion. These results can be replicated in a second data set. Extending this work, researchers might analyze wider varieties of markets and product categories.

Our research, although largely descriptive, also sees the need for more theory building in the area of deal-proneness. Our empirical findings can provide a basis for generating one such theory. Two noteworthy findings are: the most deal-prone consumers in each product category are older; and, in the coffee category, both ends of the response spectrum are quite brand loyal. In tying these threads together, we speculate on the evolution of deal-proneness segments.

We hypothesize that consumers will change—becoming more or less willing to trade their time for economic gains, becoming more price-sensitive, or learning better use of promotion information. Such changes may occur through several mechanisms: the consumer's changing economic environment or circumstances, or adult socialization processes—as they learn new shopping styles that revise their expectations. Therefore, consumer response to individual promotion types may vary over time. The question is—how can change patterns be predicted? Figure 2 illustrates this process.

Economic incentives and inventory costs may change in a relatively predictable fashion over time. All things being equal, we might expect economic incentives of promotions to become less

TABLE 4
Cluster Description
(Data Set 1)

Paper	Cluster 1	Cluster 2	Cluster 3	Cluster 4	Cluster 5
N	(280)	(104)	(208)	(26)	(1,578)
Average units purchased*	4.2	4.0	6.1	5.2	4.2
Number of purchases* (total)	10.5	7.7	7.0	7.5	12.2
Average elapsed time* (days)	19.0	23.4	23.9	24.0	17.4
Average packages purchased*	1.6	1.6	1.7	1.4	1.4
Total volume*	41.8	28.5	42.4	38.6	49.8
Amount used per day* (units)	.25	.18	.26	.26	.27
Average inventory* (units) [1]	3.5	3.2	5.1	4.1	3.6
Price/roll* (average)	.25	.28	.26	.25	.27
Price/package* (average)	.71	.69	.94	.96	.84
Store loyalty index [2]	.059	.057	.059	.061	.056
Brand loyalty index* [2]	.023	.028	.019	.023	.026
Size loyalty index* [2]	.159	.168	.172	.176	.170
Private label/generic* (%)	.75	.05	.01	.05	.08
Number in house*	3.2	2.6	2.7	2.8	3.1
Number of children*	1.1	.8	.6	.7	.9
Total coupons used* (10 products)	6.8	8.6	16.2	7.7	7.3
Paper coupons used*	.2	.9	4.1	1.5	.6
Average brand switching* (%)	.49	.56	.54	.51	.46
Age:*					
8-24	.08	.12	.04	.00	.07
25-30	.18	.14	.12	.27	.13
31-35	.16	.14	.17	.19	.16
36-40	.16	.13	.08	.04	.12
41-50	.14	.14	.14	.12	.18
51-65	.18	.22	.26	.19	.24
65+	.10	.13	.19	.19	.11
	1.00	1.00	1.00	1.00	1.00
Education:*					
Non-high school graduate	.09	.07	.05	.15	.06
High school	.36	.35	.37	.31	.40
Some college	.26	.22	.19	.19	.21
College graduate	.13	.25	.21	.12	.18
Post graduate	.11	.09	.10	.12	.09
Other	.05	.03	.09	.12	.06
	1.00	1.00	1.00	1.00	1.00
Own Home	.71	.68	.79	.81	.76
Income:*					
Under $10,000	.21	.15	.13	.08	.13
$10,000 - $14,999	.14	.19	.19	.15	.15
$15,000 - $19,999	.18	.26	.17	.23	.17
$20,000 - $24,999	.18	.09	.20	.15	.21
$25,000 - $29,999	.10	.12	.10	.15	.12
$30,000 - $34,999	.09	.06	.08	.12	.08
$35,000 and over	.09	.14	.13	.12	.13
	1.00	1.00	1.00	1.00	1.00

*Significant at .95 (F-test or chi-square)

Notes:

[1] Average inventory is computed for each consumer as:

$$\frac{\text{purchases [average unites—[elapsed time (amount used)] + purchase]}}{\text{number of purchases}}$$

Where amount used $= \dfrac{\text{total units—last units purchased}}{\text{elapsed time first to last purchase}}$

Note that average units purchased is assumed to be the beginning inventory.

[2] The loyalty indices are computed as follows for each consumer:

$$\text{brand loyalty} = \frac{\sum_i (\text{percent purchases of brand i})^2}{\text{total number of brands}}$$

TABLE 3
Cluster Description
(Data Set 1)

Coffee	Cluster 1	Cluster 2	Cluster 3	Cluster 4	Cluster 5
N	(50)	(192)	(111)	(408)	(515)
Average jars purchased*	1.3	1.0	1.1	1.0	1.0
Number of purchases* (total)	2.4	3.0	2.8	4.8	3.9
Average elapsed time* (days)	52.1	50.5	51.9	40.5	41.2
Total volume* (ounces)	22.5	19.5	15.7	34.4	26.0
Amount used per day* (units)	.08	.03	.03	.04	.04
Price/jar* (average)	3.46	3.31	2.86	3.13	2.76
Average ounces*	9.6	6.7	6.0	7.2	6.2
Store loyalty index*	.29	.32	.31	.29	.31
Brand loyalty index*	.033	.030	.029	.028	.032
Size loyalty index*	.19	.17	.17	.17	.18
Private label/generic* (%)	.04	.01	.04	.01	.07
Number in house*	3.5	2.8	3.0	3.1	3.1
Total coupons* (10 products)	11.7	8.2	10.7	13.8	5.3
Instant coffee coupons*	1.1	1.2	1.1	2.9	.4
All coffee coupons*	3.7	2.9	3.7	5.5	1.8
Average brand switching* (%)	.20	.20	.22	.30	.25
Purchases with price change* (%)	.60	.03	.04	.09	.08
Age:*					
18-24	.02	.07	.06	.04	.08
25-30	.08	.14	.08	.09	.15
31-35	.14	.15	.12	.13	.17
36-40	.12	.13	.07	.11	.10
41-50	.18	.13	.26	.21	.18
51-65	.26	.22	.24	.30	.24
65+	.20	.16	.16	.12	.09
	1.00	1.00	1.00	1.00	1.00
Education:*					
Non-high school graduate	.08	.09	.05	.08	.09
High school	.44	.37	.42	.44	.40
Some college	.18	.20	.25	.20	.22
College graduate	.10	.18	.14	.14	.17
Post graduate	.08	.08	.11	.08	.08
Other	.12	.09	.03	.08	.05
	1.00	1.00	1.00	1.00	1.00
Own Home	.90	.77	.76	.81	.72
Employment:*					
Full-time	.22	.37	.33	.31	.42
Part-time	.26	.20	.14	.25	.16
Not employed	.52	.44	.52	.44	.42
	1.00	1.00	1.00	1.00	1.00
Income:*					
Under $10,000	.12	.17	.17	.15	.16
$10,000 - $14,999	.16	.18	.14	.15	.15
$15,000 - $19,999	.12	.14	.23	.18	.17
$20,000 - $24,999	.28	.20	.22	.19	.18
$25,000 - $29,999	.12	.13	.09	.14	.13
$30,000 - $34,999	.08	.08	.05	.10	.09
$35,000 and over	.12	.10	.11	.10	.12
	1.00	1.00	1.00	1.00	1.00

*Significant at .95 (F-test or chi-square)

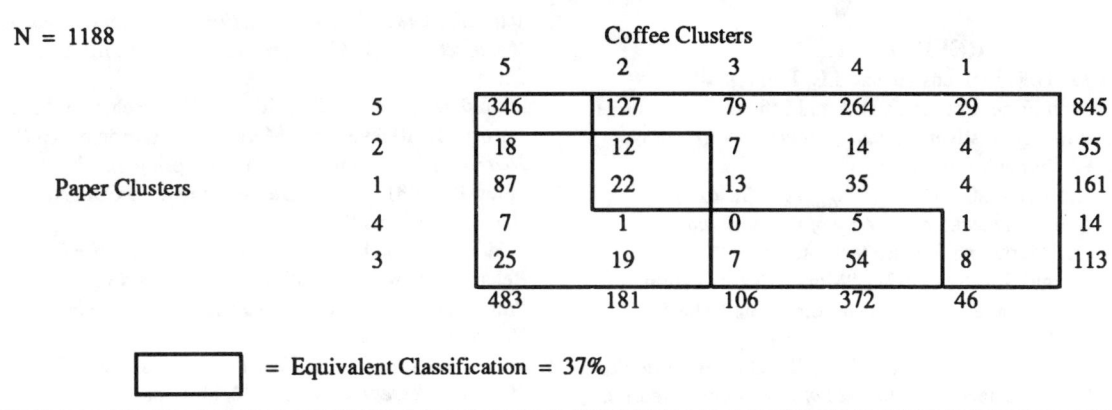

TABLE 5
Cluster Membership Across Categories
(Data Set 1)

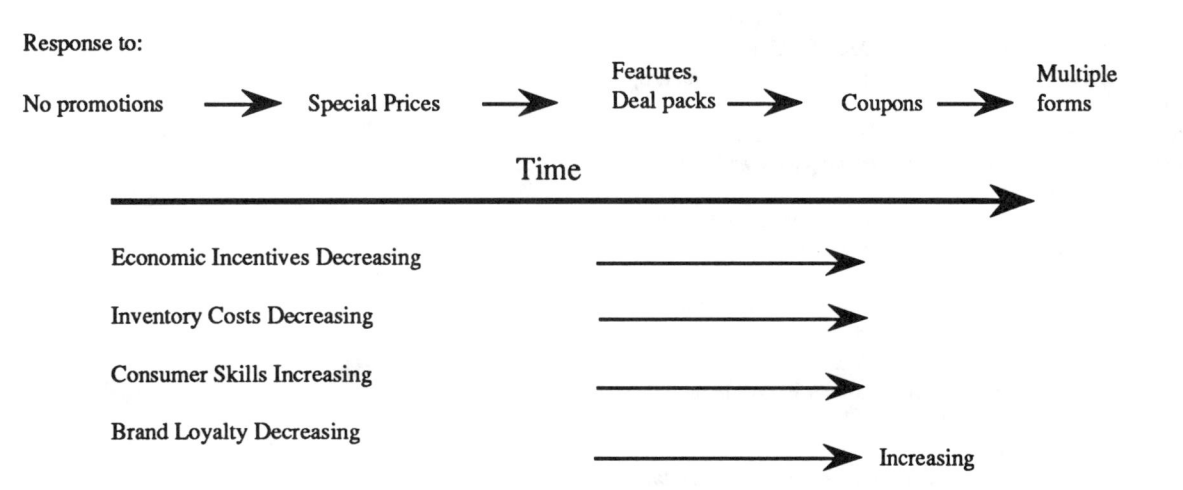

FIGURE 2
Promotion Learning Process

important to consumers as their own economic status becomes more secure with time. Similarly, inventory holding costs may become less salient as home sizes increase, etc. Thus, the economic attractiveness of promotions may diminish eventually, but may be easier to take advantage of—in an inventory sense. Since these mechanisms may balance out, they provide no clear average changes over time.

The attributes loosely grouped under "time preferences," however, are a set of consumer skills at which consumers can learn to become more proficient. We therefore predict that consumers will learn such skills and begin to respond to complex forms of promotion. Non-responsive consumers might select brands without considering available coupons, ads, price cuts or other promotions. The learning process might begin with consumer behavior requiring a slight adaptation—making the regular purchase under a price-off or feature condition. Consumers might then move slowly to take advantage of promotions requiring more effort as they become increasingly adept. Consumers are "rewarded" for their successful usage of promotion and thus an operant conditioning mechanism (Rothschild and Gaidis 1981) may serve to escalate a consumer's involvement with promotion. At this point, promotion-sensitivity may increase to the level at which offers for brands other than the regular brand are attractive. Thus, brand loyalty is undermined. At the end of this continuum is the stereotypical "price shopper"—one who always uses coupons and rebates and switches easily. This view is supported by Demsetz (1962), who shows a relationship between consumer experience with a product category and price paid. Consumers who have been in the market longer buy less expensive brands. At this extreme point, however, we might further hypothesize that brand loyalty could again strengthen. Presumably a consumer with the skills to identify and take advantage of multiple forms of promotion might successfully use these skills to take advantage of deals for preferred brands without needing to switch.

This study cannot provide a real test of the hypothesis since we cannot track the different stages in an ordered progression over time. We strongly suggest that future research be directed toward an over-time research design, such as utilized by Calantone and Sawyer (1978), that tracks such changes as they occur. If confirmed, the promotion learning hypothesis may provide a unifying explanation for deal-proneness studies and measures previously not comparable. It is most important for marketers to gain insight into primary demands for sales promotion, plus knowledge of the points at which they can influence this demand.

REFERENCES

Bearden, W.O., D.R. Lichtenstein and J.E. Teel (1984), "Comparison Price, Coupon, and Brand Effects on Consumer Reactions to Retail Advertisements," *Journal of Retailing*, Vol 60, #2, Summer, pp. 11-34.

Beem, E.R. and H.J Shaffer (1981), *Triggers to Customer Action—Some Elements in a Theory of Promotional Inducement*, Marketing Science Institute.

Blattberg, R.C. and S.K. Sen (1974), "Market Segmentation Using Models of Multidimensional Purchasing Behavior," *Journal of Marketing*, Vol. 38, #4, October, pp. 17-28.

_____, P. Peacock and S.K. Sen (1976), "Purchasing strategies Across Product Categories," *Journal of Consumer Research*, Vol. 3, #3, December, pp. 143-154.

_____, T. Buesing, P. Peacock, and S.K. Sen (1978), "Identifying the Deal-Prone Segment," *Journal of Marketing Research*, Vol. 15, #3, August, pp. 369-377.

_____, and S.A. Neslin (1990), *Sales Promotion: Concepts, Methods and Strategies*, Englewood Cliffs, New Jersey: Prentice-Hall.

_____, G.D. Eppen and J. Lieberman (1981), "A Theoretical and Empirical Evolution of Price Deals for Consumer Nondurables," *Journal of Marketing*, Vol. 45 #1, Winter, pp. 116-129.

Calantone, R.J. and A.G. Sawyer (1978), "The Stability of Benefit Segments," *Journal of Marketing Research*, Vol. XV, August, pp. 395-404.

Carman, J.M. (1969), "Some Insights into Reasonable Grocery Shopping Strategies," *Journal of Marketing*, October, pp. 69-72.

Dodson, J.A., A.M. Tybout, and B. Sternthal (1978), "Impact of Deals and Deal Retraction on Brand Switching," *Journal of Marketing Research*, Vol. 15, #1, February, pp. 72-81.

Densetz, H. (1962),"The Effect of Consumer Exposure on Brand Loyalty and the Structure of Market Demand," *Econometrica*, January.

Funkhouser, G.B. (1983), "A Note on the Reliability of Certain Clustering Algorithms," *Journal of Marketing Research*, Vol. XX, February, pp. 99-102.

Guadagni, P.M. and J.D.C. Little (1983), "A Logit Model of Brand Choice Calibrated on Scanner Data," *Marketing Science*, Vol. 2, #3, Summer, pp. 203-238.

Hackleman, E.C. and J.M. Duker, (1980), "Segmenting the Deal Prone Consumer Using Consumption Volume," in R. Bagozzi, et al, eds., *Marketing in the 80's*, American Marketing Association, pp. 172-175.

Johnson, T. (1984), "The Myth of Declining Brand Loyalty," *Journal of Advertising Research*, Vol. 24, #1, February/March, pp. 9-17.

Montgomery, D.B. (1971), "Consumer Characteristics Associated with Dealing: An Empirical Example," *Journal of Marketing Research*, Vol. 8, #1, February, pp. 118-120.

Morrison, D.F. (1969), "On the Interpretation of Discriminant Analysis," *Journal of Marketing Research*, Vol. VI, May, pp. 156-163.

Narasimhan, C. (1984), "A Price Discrimination Theory of Coupons," *Marketing Science*, Vol. 3, #2, Spring, pp. 128-146.

Punj, G. and D.W. Stewart (1983), "Cluster Analysis in Marketing Research: Review and Suggestion for Application," *Journal of Marketing Research*, Vol. XX, May, pp. 134-148.

Quelch, J.A. (1983), *Trade Promotion by Grocery Products Manufacturers: A Managerial Perspective*, Marketing Science Institute.

Rothschild, M.L. and W.C. Gaidis (1981), "Behavioral Learning Theory: Its Relevance to Marketing and Promotions," *Journal of Marketing*, Vol. 45, #2, Spring, pp. 70-78.

Schlaifer, R. (1981), *Users' Guide to the AQD Collection*, Harvard Business School.

Schneider, L.G. and I.S. Currim (1991), "Consumer Purchase Behaviors Associated with Active and Passive Deal-Proneness," *International Journal of Research in Marketing*, Vol. 8, #3, pp. 205-222.

Webster, F.E. (1965), "The Deal-Prone Consumer," *Journal of Marketing Research*, Vol. 2, #2, May, pp. 186-189.

Wierenga, B. (1974), *An Investigation of Brand Choice Processes*, Rotterdam University.

Emerging Views of Attitudes and Attitude Processes: Conceptual and Empirical Perspectives on Attitude Strength

Ida E. Berger, Queen's University
Linda F. Alwitt, DePaul University

Attitudes occupy a very important position in consumer theory serving as both dependent measures of the effects of marketing stimuli and as independent variables or inputs to consumer decision making. Consequently, consumer researchers have historically been very receptive to new developments in attitude theory or new conceptualizations of the attitude construct. This special topic session explored the implications of an exciting, though potentially controversial, emerging "view" of attitudes.

Over the last decade researchers in social cognition and consumer behavior have been examining "qualitative properties" of attitudes. These properties have included attitude accessibility (Fazio in press; Alwitt and Berger 1992), confidence (Berger 1992), affective-evaluative consistency (Berger 1993; Chaiken et. al. in press), conviction (Abelson 1988), extremity (Judd 1989), ambivalence (Zanna et. al. in press) and many others. Most of these "properties" gauge or tap the strength with which an attitude is held. Attempts to bring structure to this burgeoning list of strength properties have led to a new 'view' of the attitude construct and a new perspective on attitude processes. A growing number of theorists now suggest that attitudes have both a valence and a strength dimension. (See Petty and Krosnick in press.)

Although some consensus exists regarding the importance of considering attitudes in this light there is considerable controversy over how best to measure and model this new aspect of a well researched construct. This session invited researchers to discuss the antecedent processes that lead to variability in attitude strength as well as the cognitive and behavioral consequences of attitude strength, defined in a number of different ways. Researchers considered the structure of the attitude strength construct and the implications of strength in the cognitive representations of consumer brands.

Using Petty and Cacioppo's Elaboration Likelihood framework Curt Haugtvedt discussed some of the antecedent processes that lead to strongly held attitudes. The series of experimental results that he reviewed used the ELM to understand some of the consequences of attitude strength. In particular he showed how elaboration can be used to create attitudes that are both persistent over time and resistant to counter persuasion.

The second paper by Joe Priester and Richard Petty introduced the theoretical and practical implications of examining attitude ambivalence. They discussed the theoretical limitations of considering attitudes as a single bi-polar construct and described the benefits of broadening our perspective to include both positive and negative dispositions. Importantly, their empirical work showed that attitude ambivalence is related to other measures of strength, but in a non-linear way.

The third paper by Ida Berger and Linda Alwitt presented a general view of the attitude strength construct and introduced the notion of attitude conviction. The paper presented the results of a study that operationalized this self-reflective dimension of attitude strength in two consumer relevant domains (environmentally safe products and convenient products). The results showed that attitude conviction is domain and not individual specific and that it is related to some, but not all cognitive measures of attitude strength.

In the fourth paper Clark Leavitt extended the notion of "strength" to the entire cognitive representation of a brand, not just the attitude. Drawing on the results of three empirical studies he concluded that an aspect of strength is the likelihood that an object will be a part of a motivated behavioral sequence. He showed that the likelihood of being chosen is greater when the object is automatically brought to mind by component cues of various sorts (including situational cues). He further suggested that the notion of image or image-schema is a more congenial framework than is attitude.

Ida Berger concluded the session by suggesting a framework that could integrate the four papers. She argued that the papers could be seen in terms of whether they considered antecedents of strength (elaboration for instance), the structure of strength itself (ambivalence, conviction) or consequences of strength (resistance etc.). She suggested that the research challenge is to understand more fully the relationships within this kind of framework.

Summary
Knowing More Than We're Told: Inferences from Advertising Claims

Carolyn J. Simmons, Lehigh University
Gita Venkataramani Johar, Columbia University

Advertising presents products in the most favorable light, emphasizing positive attributes and describing them in ways that maximize their attractiveness. In turn, consumers bring their expectations, knowledge, and information needs to bear on their interpretation of ads. Inferences are an important part of this interpretive process. This session examined the inferences that consumers make in response to common advertising practices and the impact of these inferences on subsequent judgment and behavior. Taken together, these papers (a) contribute to work on contingent models of inference making, recognizing the moderating roles of involvement and knowledge, (b) recognize a range of consequences of incomplete or ambiguous information, including effects on attitude confidence, attribute importance, and product category perceptions, and (c) address methodological issues relevant to understanding when inferences are generated.

The first paper by Sandra Burke, Sandra Milberg, and Youjae Yi examined the effects of claims about attributes which are inherent to the product category, but which are not emphasized by competitive brands (e.g., Mazola corn oil has no cholesterol). Among those who believed the claimed attribute to be atypical of the product category, such claims increased the probability of brand choice and the perceived importance and typicality of the attribute. These subjects also reported believing that brands not making the claim did not possess the attribute.

The second paper by Gita Venkataramani Johar primarily examined claims with *incomplete comparisons* (e.g., this brand is better) and *inconspicuous qualifications* (e.g., qualifications in small print). The inconspicuous qualification was deceptive only under low involvement. Deceptive inferences from incomplete comparisons appeared to be made by some low and high involvement subjects; however, response times revealed that such inferences were made at the time of processing the ad only under high involvement.

The third paper by Frank Kardes examined the effects of set size, valence of information, and instruction set (encouraging consideration of unmentioned attributes or not) on consideration of unmentioned attributes, inferences, brand evaluations, and confidence and uncertainty about evaluations. Positive information increased positive inferences, while negative information increased negative inferences, with the greatest number of negative inferences being made when subjects were encouraged to consider unmentioned attributes. No effects were found for set size. Positive inferences had a stronger impact on evaluations than did negative inferences, whereas negative inferences had a stronger impact on confidence than did positive inferences.

In his concluding discussion, John Lynch addressed methodological issues relevant to the measurement of deception, including designs for determining whether an inference not made at encoding is made at the time of choice, the tradeoffs in using response times versus closed- and open-ended questions to detect inferences, and the use of baseline control conditions to detect inferences. He also identified a number of questions raised by the papers regarding potential mediators (attribute diagnosticity, inferences versus discounting, etc.) and moderators (sparseness versus denseness of information environment) of observed effects.

"This Note's for You[1] ... :" Negative Effects of the Commercial Use of Popular Music

Basil G. Englis, Rutgers University
Greta E. Pennell, Rutgers University

Music is a prominent promotional tool and a hallmark of effective television advertisements. However, despite much recent attention by consumer researchers, the effects of music on consumer behavior remain poorly understood. The assumption guiding most marketers' use of music, as well as consumer research on its effectiveness, has been that well-liked (or disliked) music elicits pleasurable (or aversive) responses in a reflex-like manner. According to this model using well-liked music in a commercial should translate into positive attitudes toward the product, brand, and the ad itself. However, inconsistency in the early empirical findings and recent work concerning the meaningfulness of music, point to a need for more sophisticated models of how music influences listeners' reactions to its use as a promotional tool.

For many people music is heavily imbued with meaning. And, this meaning is an important determinant of how music is experienced. Therefore, understanding how music influences consumer behavior is predicated on understanding what that music means to the individuals who create and consume it. It is important to note, however, that meaning is not an inherent property of the music, but rather arises as a result of listeners' active and reflective interpretive processes.

This panel considered how music acquires "deeper" levels of meaning and how this meaning influences consumer behavior. We also brought together interpretive and experimental methods, as well as idiographic and nomothetic approaches to investigate the meanings that listeners attach to music and how these meanings influence their responses to advertising messages. Finally, work that employed several distinct levels of analysis, ranging from broad socio-historical, to subcultural, to highly individualistic perspectives, was presented.

Linda M. Scott—Using "Revolution:" A Case Study in Intentionality, Cooptation, and Resistance

This paper explored the question of intentionality through a historically situated textual analysis of the Nike "Revolution" campaign. The objective is to understand the role of commercial intention (actual and inferred) on consumer's perception of cooptation. Oral histories taken from the advertisement's creative team, as well as internal documents covering the negotiations over the rights to use the song were used to examine intentionality. The negotiation of intentionalities was explored in the conflict between the creative team's intentions and those of Yoko Ono, Michael Jackson, and the Beatles.[2] Consumers' letters were used to illustrate their resistance to the "cooptation" of this song. This was related to the conflict between the song's socio-historical meaning and the inferred intention behind its use (using "the revolution" to sell shoes). The analysis of these letters suggest that, contrary to the assumptions of Critical Theory, consumers are not uncritical and passive passive receivers of commercial messages.

Elizabeth Blair—From Subculture to Mass Culture: Hegemony Theory Revisited

One way that music acquires meaning is through its association with and use by a culture. This presentation examined the transformation of the subcultural meanings attached to music when it is "adopted" by marketers and advertisers. Hegemony theory was used to explain how musical meaning evolves as its association with a particular subculture is expanded to a larger social sphere, thereby preserving "mass" culture and its inherent power structure. Although the meanings associated with marginalized or "lower" subculture products change, the group's status does not. The aim of this presentation was to document the hegemonic process at work by analyzing examples of the cooptation of rap and heavy metal music. Field interview data were presented to illustrate how this process is perceived and experienced by members of originating subculture.

Greta E. Pennell and Basil G. Englis—When "Hits" Strikeout: Loving the Song but Hating the Product

This presentation described an empirical study designed to test the hypothesis that a well-liked piece of music, when placed in the context of a commercial communication, may result in a negative effect on the product (target of the persuasive message). We take the perspective that "meaningfulness" is highly individualistic. Therefore, we index the meaningfulness of the music used in this study at an individual level. However, our experimental paradigm for studying the effect of music in television advertising allows us to generalize beyond the case of a single individual or advertisement. In-depth, one-on-one interviews revealed that participants disliked "their" music being used for the purpose of advertising, and this effect was moderated somewhat by the experimental context. Also, participants demonstrated very poor product recall when meaningful music was used as background in the ads.

Wanda T. Wallace—Discussant

The concluding discussion highlighted the convergent conclusions of the papers. This point is especially important in light of the diversity of research methods represented in the panel. Additional research should examine the different ways meaningfulness evolves and the possible role that different types of meaningfulness play in determining music's effectiveness in an advertising context. For example, is the negative effects reported in these papers limited to music whose meaning is derived from lyrical content? Or would consumers also react negatively to the commercial use of music that is meaningful because it is associated with a meaningful past, and personal event? Finally, Wallace suggested that additional research is needed regarding possible positive effects of the commercial use of meaningful music.

---

[1] Neil Young (1988), *This Note's For You*, Reprise Records. "... Ain't singin' for Pepsi; Ain't singin' for Coke; I don't sing for nobody; makes me look like a joke; this note's for you ..."

[2] The Nike research was supported by a grant from the Smithsonian Institution.

The Halcyon Days of Youth: A Phenomenological Account of Experiences and Feelings Accompanying Spring Break on the Beach

Laura A. Williams, Louisiana State University
Alvin C. Burns, Louisiana State University

ABSTRACT

Hedonic consumption and self-gifts are both fields of consumer research which call for exploratory investigation. This study provides phenomenological insight into hedonic experiences as a form of self-gifts in the highly social context of Spring Break trips to the beach. Content and interpretive analyses found support for three dimensions of self-gifts: social-self, specialness, and exchange. Experiences of gregariousness, bonding, hedonism, play, and shopping subsist within these dimensions. In addition, strong feelings of freedom, exhilaration and relaxation accompany these experiences, while feelings of delight, melancholy, exhaustion, remorse and closeness follow. Aspects related to self-gifts and hedonic consumption are discussed and future research areas are suggested.

INTRODUCTION

"One thing that I'll always remember is waking up at 7am to the sound of the blender. Every morning, one of my friends who is a morning person would wake up early and have daiquiris ready for all of us by 7:30 am." (f, 20)

Approximately 10 years ago, consumer researchers were introduced to qualities inherent in experiential consumption (Hirschman and Holbrook 1982, Holbrook and Hirschman 1982). Among other factors, experiential consumption is characterized by leisure time usage, hedonic response to surroundings, play activities, and heightened feelings, all of which result in fun, enjoyment and pleasure. In other words, experiential consumption transpires in a phenomenological setting where individuals are affected by distinct outcomes of consuming rather than buying (Holbrook and Hirschman 1982). In accordance with Holbrook and Hirschman's suggestion that hedonic consumption, play and feelings afford a rich texture for the description of experiential consumption situations, we report a study couched in a fertile experiential setting, imbued with excessive and self-indulgent behaviors and geared toward fun and pleasure where there is strong social support for such excesses. It is also a situation where participants, because of their immoderation, undergo profound emotional experiences which are translated into strong personal feelings.

Relatively few studies have been devoted to understanding experiential and/or hedonic consumption. Consequently, our attempt is an exploratory venture utilizing the phenomenological research method of critical incidents. Against this backdrop, our purposes for this study were five-fold. First, we sought to investigate hedonic consumption in a highly social setting. Second, we set out to test the efficacy of self-gift themes as a typology for describing this consumption context. Next, we endeavored to expand the typology to include feelings, and, fourth, we wished to determine relationships between experiences and feelings. Last, we hoped to explore the presence of individual differences in this consumption experience/feelings framework.

SELF-GIFTS AND HEDONIC CONSUMPTION

Hedonic consumption is largely experiential (Hirschman and Holbrook 1992). It is characterized by multisensory input, emotional arousal as the major motivation for consumption, strong emphasis on the pleasure principle, and consuming behavior as opposed to buying behavior. An area of phenomenological research which has discovered widespread presence of hedonic consumption is self-gifts, or instances of self-directed consumption where a person buys something for him/her-self. Mick and DeMoss (1990a, 1990b) have investigated instances of self-gifts and found them to coexist in three dimensions. One dimension involves self-communication where the gift serves to symbolically enhance self-concept, self-esteem, or otherwise strengthen one's identity. A second theme involves exchange whereby consumers adhere to self-contracts, and the purchase of a gift is a self-reward, perhaps for reaching a milestone. The third dimension is entitled specialness and concerns uncommon consumption related to escape, discovery, or achieving perfection. Mick and DeMoss (1990b) have further defined self-gifts as: (1) personally symbolic self-communication through (2) special indulgences that tend to be (3) premeditated and (4) highly context bound. This definition signals that self-gift feelings are saturated with hedonics, and in fact, Mick and DeMoss (1990b) conclude that self-gifts are a pregnant domain within which to study hedonic consumption.

SELF-COMMUNICATION AND SELVES

Self-communication is complicated by the existence of multiple selves. That is, it is believed that a person is made up of a multiplicity of selves, with certain selves relevant under specific circumstances. For example, Belk (1984) notes at least four selves as: individual, family, community, and group. Although Belk (1988) speaks largely of possessions as manifestations and extensions of the self, it seems reasonable to expand his claim to include experiential consumption. Thus, experiences reflect and serve to define the individual as to some relevant self. Our first task, then, involved identifying which self is relevant to hedonic consumption in a social context. Accordingly, our focus fell on the social-self, or that part of oneself that is displayed to others. Stated differently, we would expect socially shared experiential consumption to be symbolic communication expressing or otherwise shaping facets of the social-self.

METHOD

Hedonic consumption and the phenomenology of self-gifts were explored in the context of a Spring Break trip to the beach. For the purposes of this study, Spring Break is a social context defined as a set of experiences that extends over a specific period of time. Since homogenous samples facilitate the identification of themes in exploratory research (Calder 1977), a convenience sample of undergraduate students at a large Southern university was used as informants in this study.

A preliminary questionnaire was administered to 67 undergraduate students to determine if a Spring Break trip depicted an incidence relevant to the study of hedonic consumption and self-gifts. Respondents were asked to recall and describe a Spring Break trip in detail. Their descriptions were to include where they went, who they went with, who paid for the trip, and their motivations for taking the trip. Forty-seven students took trips to destinations other than home, thirty-two of which paid for most or all of the expenses of the trip. In addition, all students taking Spring Break trips to the beach described partaking in some form of hedonic consumption. Therefore, the preliminary investigation suggested that Spring

Break was a viable context for the study of hedonic consumption and self-gifts.

A critical incidence technique was used to solicit the recall of students' most memorable Spring Break trip (see Mick and DeMoss 1990). Student informants were asked to describe in detail (including specific experiences related to where, when, who, how, and why) their most memorable Spring Break trip. They were given a page and a half to write their descriptions. Informants were then asked to describe their feelings during and after the trip. Next, informants were asked to specify the year the trip was taken, the percentage of the trip that they financed out of their own funds, how long (in number of days) the trip lasted and the length of time spent planning the trip. In addition, a series of direct questions measured the degree to which students felt their Spring Break trip was a self-gift. Finally, informants indicated their gender, age, enrollment classification, and employment status.

RESULTS

Informant Profile

A total of 43 usable descriptions were obtained. The reduced sample consisted of students who went on a Spring Break trip to the beach and who classified the trip as a self-gift. Twenty males and twenty-three females ranging in age from 20 to 33 were the informants. All informants described a Spring Break trip to the beach which lasted from 3 to 9 days and cost an average of $300. Seventy percent of the informants paid for most of the expenses out of their own funds, and 88% of the respondents planned their trip an average of 4 to 8 weeks ahead of time.

When asked what best described their Spring Break trip, 49% of the informants felt that Spring Break was a way to escape and discover new and exciting things, and 40% felt that Spring Break was a deserving reward for their work and sacrifices leading up to it. Informants overwhelmingly indicated that their trip included self indulgent activities (91%). In addition, most felt that Spring Break trips similar to theirs are mainly for college students. Eighty-four percent of the informants felt that all college students should have at least one Spring Break trip similar to the one they described, but only 12% felt that Spring Break helped them identify with their fellow college students. The fact that most informants felt that all students should have a Spring Break like theirs, while very few felt that it helped them to identify with college students, lent credence to our argument that *social-self* communication is functioning. Group affiliation was not a prime motivation for our informants, however the social context did seem to be an integral component.

Content Analysis and Tabulations

Content analysis was conducted by coding the experiences and feelings described by students. The authors independently reviewed the questionnaires and compiled lists of mentioned experiences and feelings. They then jointly agreed on a categorization scheme of the predominant experiences and feelings. Definitions of the resulting experiences, concurrent feelings and reflective feelings are listed in Table 1. Experiences are the activities that informants participated in during the Spring Break trip. Concurrent feeling are the emotions that informants felt while on their Spring Break trip, and reflective feelings are the emotions they felt after returning from their Spring Break trip.

Once the experience and feelings categories were agreed upon, the authors jointly judged the descriptions for evidence of the themes. Two PhD students served as independent judges for 25% of the descriptions. Overall interjudge reliability (Perreault and Leigh 1989) for the two PhD students was .79 (.89 for experiences, .75 for concurrent feelings, and .73 for reflective feelings). Averaged with the authors, interjudge reliability for experiences (.82), concurrent feelings (.73), and reflective feelings (.75) equaled .76. All of the above reliabilities meet the acceptability requirement for interjudge reliability in content analyses (Kassarjian 1977).

The frequencies and associated percentages of the reported occurrence of experiences, concurrent feelings, and reflective feelings are listed in Table 2. On average, informants reported 3.3 of the 5 experiences, 2.3 of the 7 concurrent feelings, and 1.5 of the 7 reflective feelings.

Experience Themes

Since all respondents identified their Spring Break trip as a self gift, Mick and DeMoss's (1990b) self-gift typology was applied with the modification of a social-self communication dimension. Two experiences were found to depict social-self communication: bonding and gregariousness. Bonding experiences are those activities that are conducted with close friends. Bonding activities were very evident in informants' descriptions; for example, practically all informants went on the trip with friends. To illustrate, one respondent indicated, "My most vivid memory of this week was when all six of us were on the beach one night talking. We just sat around for hours and talked." (f, 22) The second experience, gregariousness, describes activities that involve social interactions with strangers, or people other than informants' close friends. Gregariousness was identified in over one-half of the written descriptions. Informants wrote about various opportunities to meet others.

"My favorite part were the nights, because there was no scorching sun, but lots of girls (and guys) on the beach having parties. We met tons of girls; I met more girls this Spring Break than I ever can recall." (m, 21)

The specialness dimension is described by Mick and DeMoss (1990b) as the extra meaningful and potentially sacred aspects of a self-gift. In this study, specialness was represented by the experience of hedonism. Hedonism in a social context describes activities done in excess, or extraordinary self indulgences. Informants gave very detailed descriptions of incidents of hedonism which included sunbathing for hours, consuming immense amounts of alcohol, avoiding sleep, and participating in excessive behaviors. The following informants' descriptions attest to hedonism.

"One of the most memorable times during the trip was when my friend had too much to drink and he passed out in our room. A bunch of us got together and picked him up and carried him about a 100 yards to the girls room that we just met that day. All of the girls were sleeping, so we put him in the living room right next to two girls. We left but decided that wasn't enough, so we went back in and stripped him of his clothes. He didn't wake up until the next morning. When he did, he had about 8 girls staring at him." (m, 22)

"Our greatest accomplishment was a beer drinking record. Dusty, Harry, Jim, Rene, Tom, Eric, and I guzzled a total of 75 beers in 53 minutes - then passed out for the rest of the day." (m, 21)

Finally, the third dimension of self-gifts is exchange (Mick and DeMoss 1990b). Exchange is represented in this study by two experiences: playing and shopping. Incidences of play were found in over one-half of the written descriptions. Informants talked of participating in numerous beach and water sports including volleyball, football, frisbee, sailing, snorkeling, and bungi jumping.

TABLE 1
Definitions of Experiences and Feelings

Experiences	Description
Gregariousness	⇒ Meeting people other than those traveling with you ⇒ Social interactions with strangers
Bonding	⇒ Traveling with others ⇒ Activities conducted with close friends
Hedonism	⇒ Any activity done in excess ⇒ Activities may include: sunbathing for hours; drinking immense amounts of alcohol; repetitive bar hopping; neglecting sleep
Play	⇒ Energetic activities ⇒ Activities may include: all forms of beach and water sports; sight-seeing
Shopping	⇒ Retail purchases ⇒ Visiting malls or shopping centers
Concurrent Feelings	**Description**
Halcyon	⇒ Happy, joyful, carefree
Relaxed	⇒ Tranquil and peaceful
Unfettered	⇒ Free and unconstrained ⇒ No rules ⇒ No worries
Irresponsible	⇒ Reckless ⇒ Out of control
Exhilaration	⇒ Elation, extreme happiness ⇒ Captivated, enthralled
Camaraderie	⇒ Closeness, togetherness
Energy	⇒ Energetic, awake, athletic ⇒ Strong, powerful
Reflective Feelings	**Description**
Melancholy	⇒ Sad, depressed, unhappy
Renewed	⇒ Rejuvenated, refreshed
Changed	⇒ Different person ⇒ Matured ⇒ Independent ⇒ Responsible
Delight	⇒ Happy, ⇒ Satisfied, Fulfilled
Exhaustion	⇒ Physical fatigue, tiredness
Remorse	⇒ Embarrassment ⇒ Guilt
Closeness	⇒ Increased intimacy of friendship

Shopping activities were much less prevalent, accounting for only about one out of five cases. Most shopping experiences revolved around mall shopping. One informant wrote,

> "The highlight of the break was a shopping trip to the outlet mall...about 40 minutes away. It was especially exciting for me because they had a particular store...that I love (but usually have to scrape savings to buy anything). Everything was on sale, so I bought up big and saved heaps. I was in the store for about 3 hours." (f, 22)

Concurrent Feelings

Having mapped the experiences into the self-gift dimensions, we next turned to analysis of the feelings informants said accompanied these experiences. As seen in Table 2, a feeling of being unfettered, that is, a feeling of freedom from restraints and restrictions was noted in about 6 out of 10 cases. In the words of two informants,

> "It is a blast to be able to go away from home without anyone telling you what to do or having any obligations for a week straight. It was one of the best feelings of freedom a human being could probably ever experience." (m, 23)

TABLE 2
Incidences of Experiences and Feelings

Experiences	Frequency	As a Percentage of Respondents* Mentioning Experience
Hedonism	40	93%
Bonding	40	93%
Gregariousness	28	65%
Play	23	54%
Shopping	11	26%
Total	142	

Concurrent Feelings	Frequency	As a Percentage of Respondents* Mentioning Concurrent Feeling
Unfettered	26	61%
Carefree	22	51%
Exhilaration	21	49%
Relaxed	15	35%
Camaraderie	6	14%
Energy	4	9%
Irresponsible	4	9%
Total	98	

Reflective Feelings	Frequency	As a Percentage of Respondents* Mentioning Reflective Feeling
Delight	17	40%
Melancholy	15	35%
Exhaustion	11	26%
Remorse	9	21%
Closeness	7	16%
Renewed	3	7%
Changed	2	5%
Total	64	

* n=43

"I felt like there was no tomorrow. We drank and ate what ever we wanted, stayed out all night, slept on the beach during the day. I felt crazy, as if there were no limits." (f, 21)

At the same time about one half of our informants recalled a feeling of being free of cares and everyday worries during their Spring Break. For example, one informant wrote, "I felt...like I didn't have a care in the world. There was nothing to do except drink and hang out." (m, 22) There is the possibility that being unfettered and being carefree really tap the same feeling. That is, while our judges could distinguish informants' words and classify them into these two categories reliably, it is conceivable that the semantic differences are artifacts, and a feeling of freedom (from restrictions and cares) is the underlying emotional response. When we combined the unfettered and carefree feelings categories into one, 77% of our informants experienced the feeling of freedom, the predominant concurrent feeling.

A separate feeling of exhilaration was observed. About one half (49%) of our informants indicated that they felt elated, thrilled, overjoyed, or otherwise extremely happy during their Spring Break. In this informant's words, "I felt exhilarated. I was having a wonderful time. It was wild to see all the different, shocking events that would take place." (m, 21) In contrast, informants also noted a relaxed feeling. About one out of three commented on the sensation of relaxation. For example, one informant wrote, "We had so much fun just relaxing and 'goofing off'." (f, 22) The remaining concurrent feelings themes (irresponsibility, camaraderie, and energy) were found to be in low incidence. That is, while they were present, they were experienced by only a few informants, and did not constitute primary feelings themes.

Reflective Feelings

Reflective feelings revealed an interesting profile. Informants indicated primary reflective feelings of delight and melancholy. Forty percent indicated a delightful feeling of happiness, satisfaction and/or fulfillment after their Spring Break. "I felt very happy. It was the most fun that I ever had up to that point." (m, 21) About one-third reported lament at having to "return to the real world;" they were melancholic about "leaving paradise". One informant described his feelings, "I felt sad because I didn't want to leave. I was with my closest friends and I wish we could've stayed forever." (f, 22) Also, about 1 out of 4 recounted feelings of extreme physical exhaustion as a result of their nonstop activities and probably due to a lack of sleeping accommodations. "I felt very worn out and ready to leave the beach. I was out of money and in need of a good nights' sleep." (m, 22) Occasionally, informants told of 4, 8, 12 or even 20 sharing the same motel room; others told of sleeping in cars, in hotel patios, or on the beach.

"We partied til the sun came up, then we all played on the beach all day long. That night we still hadn't found a place to sleep so we crashed on the patio of a Days Inn Hotel. I believe the guys slept in the car. We repeated another day of fun in the sun the following day. The next morning the beach patrol ran us off the beach because we weren't supposed to be on the beach sleeping. So we drove home as the sun came up." (f, 22)

Two other reflective feelings warrant mention. First, a feeling of closeness to the friends who shared Spring Break experiences was noted by about 16 percent of our informants. "I felt closer to my friends and I felt nostalgic because I had a lot of fun memories to reflect upon." (f, 22) At the same time, 21 percent noted remorse in the form of guilty feelings or embarrassment at what they had done. "I felt terrible. Physically I was exhausted and sunburned. Emotionally, I was worried about my poor judgment and lack of morals during my break." (m, 21) However, both closeness and remorse may be under reported. Given our finding of very high incidence of bonding experiences, the low closeness feeling seems anomalous. This feeling may be too personal to have been elicited by the relatively impersonal methodology. Similarly, it seems reasonable to assume that informants would refrain from telling about guilt or embarrassment for the same reason.

Interestingly, reflective feelings of renewal or change were almost nonexistent. Our informants generally did not indicate that they felt rejuvenated or recharged, and only in rare instances did they feel that the experiences had profound effects on their lives, beliefs, or cognitions.

Relationships between Experiences and Feelings

Our attention next turned to seeming connections between Spring Break experiences, concurrent feelings and reflective feelings. A series of cross-tabulations was run to determine associations: (1) within and (2) between experiences, concurrent feelings and reflective feelings. The within analyses were aimed at refining our dimensions, while the between analyses were intended to further our understanding of the dynamics under study. In these analyses, we omitted the low incidence feelings of irresponsibility, energy, renewal, and change. In all Chi Square tests, any p value of .10 or less was considered significant due to the exploratory nature of our study and the small sample size.

Within experiences, bonding and gregariousness were found to be positively associated ($p < .05$), and this result corroborated our claim that both reflect social-self communication. At the same time, play and shopping were highly associated ($p < .01$), supporting Hirschman and Holbrook's (1982) point that the personal resource of time is part of the exchange process in experiential consumption. The only within-feelings association found was between relaxation and camaraderie ($p < .10$), but we chose to retain these feelings as separate categories in the absence of theoretical support for combining them.

We found that the social-self communication dimension of self-gifts (both bonding and gregariousness) was accompanied with feelings of being unfettered or free from constraints and restrictions ($p < .05$). This concurrent feeling of freedom was associated with reflective feelings of melancholy and closeness to friends ($p < .01$ and $p < .05$, respectively).

On the other hand, the exchange aspect of self-gifts (play) was accompanied by a feeling of exhilaration ($p < .10$). Interestingly, the exchange dimension (play and shopping) was negatively associated with the reflective feeling of remorse ($p < .05$). That is, informants who participated in self-gift exchange did not feel guilty or embarrassed about their behavior. Exchange (play) was also associated with the reflective feeling of closeness to one's friends ($p < .10$). In addition, the reflective feeling of closeness was positively associated with the concurrent feeling of camaraderie ($p < .05$).

Hedonism, or the specialness dimension of self-gift giving, demonstrated no systematic association with specific concurrent or reflective feelings. However, this result was to be expected given that almost all informants reported hedonic experiences.

Individual Differences

Our last set of analyses concerned exploring possible individual differences in experiences or either of the two sets of feelings. We investigated differences by gender and found that females shopped more than males. Thus, experiences and feelings differed very little by gender.

Discussion: Getting What I Deserve and Unfettering My Social-self

"I stayed drunk for 4 days, barely ate, and enjoyed a lot of company from people all over the country." (m, 21)

We need not go into great detail as to what goes on during Spring Break on the beach. The nonstop parties at Daytona Beach, South Padre Island, Ft. Walton Beach, and elsewhere are an integral part of college student folklore. (One of our informants, not used in the study, told us that his fraternity created its own beach and had a week-long party in a city far distant from any ocean or gulf beach. Interestingly, his description was identical to those informants we analyzed.)

However, it is evident to us that, on one plane of self-gift giving, Spring Break serves an important role of reward to oneself for hard work and effort. Play and shopping serve as compensation for the sacrifices students believe they have made. These activities, especially play, are accompanied with strong feelings of exhilaration. When Spring Break is over, college students have no guilt attached to these indulgences. In fact, despite being physically drained, they regret that the break could not go on, and they retain warm feelings of delight and closeness. It appears that satisfactory repayment has been received.

On another level, Spring Break is blatantly hedonic, as virtually all informants narrate stories of extreme self-indulgences ranging from laying on the beach all day to drinking all night. But to us, the interesting phenomenon is not hedonism per se. Rather, it is the social context which allows the social-self almost complete freedom to express itself. We would argue that the social context liberates the social-self. In fact, the strong norm of Spring Break is to act in an unconstrained manner. The experiences of bonding and gregariousness occur solely in the context of peers. There are no parents, teachers, or authority figures to impose judgment or serve as reminders of the restrictions that these students have had to endure as they strive to express their "selves" in "acceptable" ways. When freed of these conventions and in the safe company of peers, expression of the social-self is unfettered, and the experience of social-self communication is a delightful memory even though it may later be accompanied by some guilt or embarrassment.

On the last plane of interpretation, Spring Break has earmarks of sacredness (Belk, Wallendorf, and Sherry 1989). Students participate in a ritual pilgrimage to a location befitting their excesses. Such extravagance may come only once per year and can only be experienced by students. Informants often commented that a Spring Break trip to the beach is sacred because it is a "one time thing". So it is understandable that they look back on the experience with melancholic feelings, knowing that the context is unique, short-lived, and will probably happen only once in their lives.

SUMMARY

Hedonic consumption and self-gifts are both fields of consumer research which call for exploratory investigation. Our study provides phenomenological insight into hedonic experiences as a form of self-gifts in the highly social context of Spring Break trips. Content and interpretive analyses found support for Mick and DeMoss's (1990b) three dimensions of self-gifts. Along with the experiences associated with these three dimensions, a host of feelings themes emerged to describe the consequences of this hedonic gift-giving context. Associations within experience themes and among experiences, concurrent feelings, and reflective feelings reveal their dynamics at least provisionally. Consequently, we offer a tentative interpretative analysis of hedonic experiences and feelings.

We are aware of the sample size, sample representativeness and generalizability limitations of our exploratory study. In addition, we acknowledge the potential limitation of social response bias associated with informants' reports of sexual experiences. Finally, future research in this area should expand the methodology to include informant interviews and participant observation.

This study highlights the need to investigate self-gift behavior in contexts other than product consumption. Our evidence suggests that a variety of hedonic consumption experiences may also be considered self-gifts. Additional exploratory and descriptive research is necessary to extend these findings and to test our conclusions.

REFERENCES

Belk, Russell W. (1984) "Cultural and Historical Differences in Concepts of Self and Their Effects on Attitudes toward Having and Giving," in *Advances in Consumer Research*, 11, Editor Thomas C. Kinnear, Provo, UT: Association for Consumer Research, 754-760.

Belk, Russell W. (1988) "Possessions and the Extended Self," *Journal of Consumer Research*. 15 (2), 139-168.

Belk, Russell W., Melanie Wallendorf, and John F. Sherry, Jr. (1989) "The Sacred and the Profane in Consumer Behavior: Theodicy on the Odyssey," *Journal of Consumer Research*, 16 (1), 1-38.

Calder, Bobby J. (1977) "Focus Groups and the Nature of Qualitative Marketing Research," *Journal of Marketing Research*, 14 (August), 353-364.

Hirschman, Elizabeth C. and Morris B. Holbrook (1982) "Hedonic Consumption: Emerging Concepts, Methods, and Propositions," *Journal of Marketing*, 46 (Summer), 92-101.

Holbrook, Morris B. and Elizabeth C. Hirschman. (1986) "The Experiential Aspects of Consumption: Consumer Fantasies, Feelings, and Fun," *Journal of Consumer Research*, 9 (September), 132-140.

Kassarjian, Harold H. (1977) "Content Analysis in Consumer Research," *Journal of Consumer Research*, 4 (1), 8-18.

Mick, David Glen and Michelle DeMoss. (1990a) "To Me from Me: A Descriptive Phenomenology of Self-Gifts," *Advances in Consumer Research*, 17, Editor Richard Pollay et al., Provo, UT: Association for Consumer Research, 677-682.

Mick, David Glen and Michelle DeMoss. (1990b) "Self-Gifts: Phenomenological Insights from Four Contexts," *Journal of Consumer Research*, 17 (December), 322-332.

Perreault, William D., Jr. and Laurence E. Leigh. (1989) "Reliability of Nominal Data Based on Qualitative Judgments," *Journal of Marketing Research*, 26 (May), 135-148.

Unfulfilled Promises and Personal Confessions: A Postpositivist Inquiry into the Idealized and Experienced Meanings of Consumer Technology

Craig J. Thompson, University of Wisconsin-Madison

ABSTRACT

Marketing promotions frequently portray consumer technologies in idealized terms that promise to easily resolve everyday problems, eliminate inconveniences, save time and enable consumers to achieve their full potential. This paper uses a postpositivist research approach to explore the symbolic meanings and personal dilemmas that arise when the promises of technology fail to materialize. A hermeneutic analysis is presented of a consumer's experience of being disappointed with consumer technology. Next, these personal meanings are situated in a broader context of cultural meanings that reflect an idealization of technology and its empowering properties. This idealization is then discussed with respect to its potential societal effects and its implications for consumer research.

INTRODUCTION

Technology is such a ubiquitous feature of modern life that we often fail to notice the extent to which our experiences are shaped by encounters with technological artifacts. Historical and sociological analyses have documented that technological developments often exert a pervasive influence on the course of societal development (Hill 1988; Romanyshyn 1989). For example, traditional gender based divisions between housework and employment in the "public" sphere have arisen through multiple transformations in technological systems that shifted the household from a site of production to a more "privatized" unit of consumption and that also reduced the physical demands of household maintenance (Cowan 1983).

In concert with the societal influences exerted by technology, marketers have long portrayed consumer technology as both a magic elixir for the tribulations of everyday life and a means to unleash the "true" inner potential of its user. Since the early 1900's, producers of consumer technologies have invested considerable promotional effort to establish the value of these products in the "consumer mind" (Ewen and Ewen 1982; Stern 1993). These promotional activities serve to intertwine modern conceptions of the good-life with the ideal of technological progress and its promise of empowering individuals to do more things, in less time, with more satisfying results, than ever before.

For purposes of this paper, the relevant point is that the promotion of consumer technologies reflects a longstanding cultural view that technology is a tool for enhancing productivity and creating a better way-of-life by controlling nature (Firat and Venkatesh 1993). Within the context of this cultural view, a relevant question is what meanings and personal dilemmas emerge for consumers when the promise of technology fails to materialize. The psychological and sociological consequences that arise from disparities between culturally prominent ideals and consumer realities have been frequently explored in regard to idealized standards of physical attractiveness (Pollay 1986; Richins 1991; Wolf 1991). The idealization of technology also conveys a series of standards about personal efficiency and achievement that may become problematic for consumers who are unable to realize them.

The present paper seeks to explore the symbolic meanings that emerge when a person experiences a disparity between the idealized and actual benefits of consumer technologies. This research approach is consistent with the postpositivist emphasis on developing richer understandings of how consumer experiences emerge in specific cultural contexts (Hirschman and Holbrook 1992). From a postpositivist perspective, personal meanings are not "subjective" in the sense of being idiosyncratic to the perspective of an individual. Instead, personal meanings emerge within a broader cultural context and, as such, they are "scripted" by culturally shared meanings (Foucault 1972).

This postpositivist orientation portrays the "subject," not as a sovereign center of self-chosen meanings, but rather as a participant in a web of cultural discourses and meanings (Dreyfus and Rabinow 1982). In accord with this postpositivist view, the interpretive strategy will be to first articulate the personal meanings a consumer experiences when "technology" fails to provide its anticipated benefits. Next, these personal meanings will be situated within a broader socio-cultural context.

THE PERSONAL MEANINGS OF AN UNREALIZED TECHNOCRATIC IDEAL

The text for this postpositivist consideration was derived from a phenomenological interview with "John", a thirty-four year old, male graduate student and a subsequent "member-check" dialogue used to assess the adequacy of the interpretation and to clarify and elaborate the issues it identified. The interview was conducted in accord with the conventions of existential-phenomenological research (Thompson, Locander, and Pollio 1989) and interviews were audiotaped, with the participant's permission. The interview began by asking if there was any technological product that stood out as being important in John's daily routine. From that point, the course of the interview was largely set by the participant with the interviewer's ensuing questions aimed at evoking more thorough descriptions and/or seeking clarifications of expressed meanings.

The interview was interpreted through a circular process whereby partial understandings of the text were continually reassessed and modified in light of the developing understanding of the whole. The interpretive focus was on highlighting patterns and interrelated meanings which constituted the narrative structure of the text. Two primary evaluative criteria for hermeneutic research are that it provides a coherent and insightful understanding about the text being interpreted and is demonstrable in terms of the text itself (Hirschman and Holbrook 1992; Thompson, Locander and Pollio 1989).

John chose to discuss his recent purchase and usage experiences with a computer printer. During the interview, frequent references were also made to experiences with his personal computer. In a post-interview discussion, John noted that he was unable to meaningfully discuss his experiences of the computer printer without reference to his personal computer. For John, the computer printer and personal printer formed a gestalt-like product constellation in which meanings of the one product where grounded by meanings of the other (see Solomon 1988).

John, who was on educational leave from his duties as an officer in the United States military, had purchased a personal computer upon entering graduate school. For two years, he relied on printers available at the University. After beginning work on his graduate thesis, he purchased a computer printer for home use. John's opening description focused on its technical attributes and capabilities:

J: Well it's made by Toshiba. It is a letter quality printer but it has the capability to go to a dot matrix format, I guess so you can go to a faster speed. It is relatively fast for a letter quality printer and it is fairly adaptable to whatever type of [computer] terminal you are using. Oh, one that I didn't mention is the quality of the printing output which is important.

As the interview unfolded, it became clear that John's computer printer experience involved a range of meanings that extended beyond the scope of this initial technical focus:

J: I knew I could buy the Toshiba [printer] from a catalogue and trust the quality of the product we got. I could have done that with Brother and one or two other brands and not been too concerned about the quality I was going to get in.

I: What was it about those brands that you trusted?

J: I had personal experience in using Brother printers. With the Toshiba, I was able to actually physically see the product in a local store. If I had not been able to see the product and the craftsmanship that went into it then I wouldn't have put quite so much trust in the name. I'm sure I would have been more cautious. I probably wouldn't have bought it.

I: Can you describe the craftsmanship that went into the Toshiba?

J: The way the features were designed. I don't know really how to explain it. Uh...I think it was appearance. Things that may not matter a whole lot in terms of usage or the final product but are at least a surface indicator of the quality that went into the product, the guts of the machine. You hope that if it appears to be a high quality product on the surface that internally the parts will be of equal quality.

Rather than relying on abstract technical criteria, John's assessment of quality was driven by a perceptually-based (and rather aesthetic) intuitive appraisal of its craftsmanship. The "guts of the machine" were understood as a somewhat mysterious realm whose nature must be inferred from surface appearances that "may not matter a whole lot in terms of usage." The references to "trust in the name" and his "hope" that surface appearances reflected the quality of its internal parts also suggest that John's preference for the Toshiba was based more on an interpersonal consideration than an evaluation of technical capabilities. That is, John hoped that the Toshiba corporation would not violate his trust by building a product whose external appearance of quality was deceptive.

This sensitivity to interpersonal concerns permeated John's experiences with computer technology, beginning with the task of shopping for a viable alternative:

J: When I go to computer stores, I can't help but feel that what they try to sell you is based on some inane capability of the computer. I think there really is a mismatch between what we [John and his wife] were looking for and what retailers look for. There was no real good understanding of what we wanted.

John described the local retailers' knowledge of computers and computer printers in the following way:

J: They pull out the brochure with all the feature data like how many words per second and say this looks like a nice printer and with the Toshiba, they showed me how easily the paper loaded in. I didn't feel that there was a lot of in-depth knowledge about the printer. They weren't specifically attuned to the printer. That's what I generally found. A lot of general knowledge about the printer and PC's but not much specific knowledge about how to use it. I would have bought from a dealer if I thought there would have been some sort of service relationship with that person. I would have been willing a pay a premium to that person if, when I had software or hardware problem, I could go back and ask questions.

Within the text of the interview, in-depth knowledge referred to a practical understanding of how to resolve unforeseen problems and technical impediments to operation. In not being "attuned" to the computer printers, local computer retailers were understood as only having a precursory and general knowledge of technical features. During the interview, John described becoming so frustrated with the local retailers, due to their apparent lack of in-depth knowledge, that he saw no basis on which to build a "service relationship." In the absence of this relationship, John made his purchase by catalogue and, thereby, in isolation from an immediately available source of help and social support.

A primary rationale used in promoting consumer technologies is that they increase personal efficiency by liberating consumers from practical inconveniences (Cowan 1983; Ewen and Ewen 1982). For John, the lure of convenience also provided an explicit motivation for purchasing a computer printer:

J: There were a number of reasons for us finally buying a printer. For one thing, my wife is a nurse and she has to make up forms to organize her shift but, since she didn't have access to a printer, she had to rely on me to get things printed up at school. And then too, I found that after I finished my coursework, I wasn't coming into the office everyday and I certainly wasn't staying there ten hours a day anymore. So it was certainly was more convenient for me to work at home.

This promise of increased convenience and control, however, did not readily materialize:

J: Just to get the thing [the printer] on line it took us a couple of days. We ran into all kinds of problems. The assembly wasn't all that difficult. It was the programming that was the problem. Programming it to the computer, It was frustrating. I had to get "Mike" [a friend described as being a computer expert] to help......At that time it was very frustrating. You feel like, you know, what your dad went through before Christmas trying to put something together.

For John, these programming problems magnified the absence of a "service relationship" with a local retailer. With respect to the manufacturer's primary source of assistance—the instruction manual— John described it as unclear, unhelpful and probably written by "someone who knew English out of a Japanese-English dictionary and nobody ever cleared it up." To become a meaningful and useful tool, the printer needed to be situated within a helpful interpersonal relationship. In this regard, the programming problems served a positive function by providing a pretext for establishing a helpful relationship with "Mike" in which operational questions could be answered and the feeling of being alone with uncooperative technology alleviated.

In seeking to characterize his frustration with the printer, John offered an archetypic image of technological befuddlement: the hapless father struggling to assemble gifts on Christmas eve. A useful hermeneutic strategy is to attempt to understand such a metaphoric image within the context of the experience being described. For the typified father, the Christmas eve activity of assembling gifts is an *end* rather than a means: the father is not *playing* with the toys but is engaged in a serious functional task. When completion of the task is frustrated by "technical difficulties," the archetypic father too becomes frustrated.

For John, learning to use technology was experienced as a frustrating struggle. This experience also evoked feelings of personal disappointment and a begrudging resignation over the eventual prospect of "spending time" on the computer printer:

J: To be quite honest with you, my actual experience with using the printer has not been as I much as I had hoped it would be at this point but I anticipate being able to use it down the line. I know that I don't know everything there is to that printer and, in that way, I feel disappointed but I don't think I attribute that to the printer so much as I haven't put the time into learning it. You know, I've spent plenty of time with everything else working with a computer and I ought to expect that on the printer.

By discounting the playful aspects of computer technology, John's primary criterion of product satisfaction became highly utilitarian:

J: I guess I have a very functional orientation toward the computer. I think a computer is a facilitator of work. It's a different level of a tool. I'm not going to buy a $2000 PC just to play games on.

I: How do you feel about the idea of playing with the printer?

J: I look forward to getting the fonts out of it that I want. I see a computer as a means not as an end. There are a lot of people out there where a computer is just an end. Being a tool is just a by-product of the fact that it is fun and they can spend all day at the computer. I'm not that type of person, I like to get what I want out of the printer and then go.

The paradox of his functional orientation is that it had not facilitated his understanding of how to fully utilize the capabilities of the printer and, thereby, receive its utilitarian benefits. In this context, John experienced disappointment and a pervasive sense of uncertainty about the purchase itself:

J: If I didn't have the dissertation coming down the line, it would be a disappointing purchase because of the amount of money I spent for that type of printer versus the utility I have gotten out of the machine. But knowing I've got the dissertation coming down the line, at least in the long term, it's not disappointing. It's disappointing to me at this point because I haven't had the opportunity to use it nor do I feel that I know all of its capabilities.

I: It seems like you are experiencing some uncertainty?

J: I think so. Always until you get to know the product well, there is some uncertainty. Just like with the VCR, you spend a lot of money to buy features and if you don't know all the features you aren't sure if it's disappointing because the features aren't worth the time and effort you put into it.

Summary and Cultural Considerations

Four major bi-polar themes emerge from John's understanding of home computer technology: 1) being isolated/being helped; 2) being accomplished/being frustrated; 3) knowing how to use technology to its full capability/not knowing how to use technology to its full capabilities; 4) working with technology/playing with technology.

When considering the broader implications of John's experiences of a computer printer, the obvious caveat is than any conclusions based on a single case study must be offered in a spirit of "discovery" rather confirmation. Further, it is necessary to distinguish between the aspects of his experiences that were clearly idiosyncratic to his unique circumstances and those that have more potential to reflect culturally shared meanings. In regard to idiosyncratic factors, much of John's disappointment with computer printer arose from his relative lack of expertise with computer systems. As such, the meanings expressed by John cannot be taken as "general meanings" about computer technology. The issue of concern to the present paper, however, is what do consumers experience when anticipated "technological" benefits of increased efficiency and enhanced capabilities do not materialize. In regard to this issue, John's specific case can be used to gain insight into this more general experience of technology as an unfulfilled promise.

Within Western culture, a constellation of "technocratic" meanings have been closely associated with the development of an industrialized, technological society but that transcend any specific form of technology (see Habermas 1972; Heidegger 1977; Romanyshyn 1989). These technocratic meanings include the idolization of efficiency, the desire for complete control over the environment (and the self), and an incessant quest for increased technical capabilities (power). These meanings seem to be reflected in John's understanding of the computer printer as a functional tool that could increase his productivity and make his life more convenient.

As noted by Heidegger (1977), technocratic thinking directs human actions toward an ideal that has pervaded Western culture since the enlightenment: the perfectly functioning machine or system. While the ideal of an optimally functioning technical system is readily imagined, it is far more difficult to attain in the rough terrain of everyday life. Personal efficiency can be derailed by a number of factors: fatigue, boredom, preoccupation with other concerns, a need for unconstrained play and relaxation, technological breakdowns, or as in John's case, not understanding the technology being used. If a person remains understands these "inefficiencies" from a technocratic viewpoint, the inability to realize the hyper-productive potential of our technological equipment could be experienced as a troubling personal inadequacy.

This technocratic orientation can also result in a sense of dehumanization and/or feelings of personal inadequacy (Ellul 1964). That is, individuals may come to understand themselves as a stockpile of productive capacity to be maximized through the use of technological equipment. The ideal of an optimally productive system then becomes the relevant standard by which actions are judged. Conversely, the uncontrolled, unroutinized, emotional and playful aspects of human life come to be seen as inefficiencies that should be reduced or eliminated. These consequences seem relevant to John's experience of being disappointed with the computer printer. For John, time spent "playing" with the computer printer—even to learn its operation—represented a disliked inefficiency; as such, he drew little satisfaction from actually having solved the dilemma nor from the fact that his inability to operate the computer printer served as the impetus for a meaningful and helpful interpersonal encounter; rather, his focus remained squarely fixed on the unproductive use of time.

John assumed the ultimate responsibility for the disappointing performance of his technological product. In so doing, John "confessed" to his lack of understanding and his failure to devote more time to learning about the printer's capabilities. As noted by Foucault (1980), the act of confessing is an important ritual by which a person expresses his/her allegiance to cultural values that are taken to be true and beyond question. In these terms, the cultural prominence of the technocratic perspective may serve to insulate it from self-reflective criticisms. For example, John could have blamed the computer printer for being overly complex or he could have dismissed his original expectations as being unrealistic. These alternative narratives, however, would have, in the first case, directed attention away from his own individual actions and, in the second, rejected the technocratic ideal itself. When technology is understood from a technocratic viewpoint, consumers may be predisposed to believe that they have failed technology rather than questioning the cultural idealization of technology.

This predisposition may be reinforced by the continual use of technocratic themes to promote consumer goods. In the idealized world of the commercial, the person who has mastered technology has mastered the world. In one sense, this idealization of technology is not all that different from that given to other forms of consumer products. From cigarettes to blue jeans, an implicit promotional promise is that these products can somehow improve their user. In the case of technological products—and products that attempt to shroud themselves in a "technical" cloak—these claims have additional claim to plausibility that derives from our cultural faith in the liberating power of technology.

CONCLUSION

Whereas the twenty-first century had once been foreseen as a utopian "age of leisure," the more common modern-day experience is one of having to do more activities, at a faster pace, than ever before (Schor 1992). The products created to "save" time have ironically become implicated in a cultural time "shortage;" in a dialectical fashion, the accelerated speed of our technological equipment seems to have accelerated the pace of our lives. This contemporary state of affairs lends an almost prophetic ring to Heidegger's concern that technocratic thinking could ensnare human experience within its own demands for speed and efficiency. In seeking to realize the ideals of control and efficiency, individuals become susceptible to the paradox of being controlled by the very technological products that are purported to enhance personal control and freedom.

From a Heideggerian perspective, the problems and potentially dehumanizing qualities of technology do not ensue from the inherent features of technological equipment but rather reside with the technocratic thinking that guides its usage. For example, the development of computer and communication technologies such as fax machines, cellular phones, computer communication networks afford vast opportunities for social interaction and creative enterprise. At the same time, these same technologies can exert a demand to accomplish and/or produce more in a reduced time frame, can blur the boundary between home and work, and can isolate the individual by creating a more self-contained and autonomous work environment.

Another dilemma potentially posed by the technocratic perspective derives from its dualistic and dominating orientation (Habermas 1972; Romanyshyn 1989). The technocratic model of selfhood is the autonomous "individual" who exists apart from nature and controls it. The analyses and critiques offered by ecological activists have demonstrated that this technocratic model has encouraged a long history of sacrificing the environment in the cause of dualistically based interests and priorities (King 1990). It is becoming increasingly evident that this technocratic conception is not a viable description of our relationship to our ecological surroundings. From acid raid to ozone depletion, human life and health is inexorably tied to the ecological health of the planet. Rather than understanding ourselves as technocratic managers of environmental resources, ecological activists have been advocating a cultural view in which we see ourselves as fundamentally embedded in an encompassing ecological system and where sustainability assumes priority over efficiency. Such a change in cultural perspective, however, would also entail a dramatic change in how technology is understood.

The accelerating pace of technological innovations and the continued cultural prevalence of technocratic themes creates a need for more a systematically developed understanding of the effects this "cultural condition" exerts on social relationships, individual self-concepts, the perceived pace of everyday life, and consumer perceptions of satisfaction and dissatisfaction. Such an understanding would be valuable from a managerial standpoint in terms of helping to better specify the meanings that inspire the acceptance, rejection, or resistance to technological innovations.

From a more macro-standpoint, the socio-cultural consequences of technocratic thinking also warrant further exploration. For example, it may be that our cultural "faith" in technology may also give rise to a sense of false security in regard to our ability to manage and correct the very problems created by technological advancement. Whether in regard to one's body or the environmental protection, the significance of protecting these biological systems may be moderated by a sense that a "technological cure" can eventually be found to undo whatever damage they incur.[1] The faith in technological cures could perhaps play a shaping role in current public policy debates that are directly or indirectly tied to "consumer behaviors"—such as the "management" of old-growth and rain forests, commercial development of wetland areas, the determination of acceptable levels of environmental pollution and the pace at which natural resources are "harvested."

As McCracken has noted (1988), consumer products, and the meanings ascribed to them through advertising, are a primary vehicle through which cultural values, beliefs and meanings are transferred to the experiences of the individual. This cultural function would also seem to impose a responsibility upon consumer researchers to more fully address the relationships between technocratic ideals, the experienced meanings of consumer technologies, consumers' self-concepts and our cultural orientations toward "nature."

---

[1] A variant of this theme can be seen, for example, in the record grossing film *Jurassic Park*. While offering an explicit moral that human beings cannot fully control nature, its basic premise was that the power of scientific technology could overcome any natural obstacle, even extinction.

REFERENCES

Cowan, Ruth Schwartz (1983), *More Work for Mother*, New York: Basic Books.

Dreyfus, Hubert L. and Paul Rabinow (1982), *Michael Foucault: Beyond Structuralism and Hermeneutics*, Chicago: University of Chicago.

Ellul, Jacques (1964), *The Technological Society*, New York: Vintage.

Ewen, Stuart and Elizabeth Ewen (1982), *Channels of Desire*, New York: McGraw-Hill.

Firat, A. Fuat and Alladi Venkatesh (1993), "The Making of Postmodern Consumption," in *Consumption and Marketing: Macro Dimensions*, eds. Russell W. Belk and Nikhilesh Dholakia, Boston, MA: PWS-Kent, forthcoming.

Foucault, Michel (1972), *The Archeology of Knowledge*, New York: Pantheon Books.

_____ (1980), *The History of Sexuality: An Introduction, Volume 1*, New York: Vintage.

Habermas, Jurgen (1971), *Knowledge and Human Interests*, Boston, MA: Beacon Press.

Heidegger, Martin (1977), "The Question Concerning Technology," in *Martin Heidegger: Basic Writings*, ed. David Krell, 287-317.

Hill, Stephen (1988), *The Tragedy of Technology*, London: Pluto Press.

Hirschman, Elizabeth C. and Morris B. Holbrook (1992), *Postmodern Consumer Research: The Study of Consumption as Text*, Newbury Park, CA: Sage.

King, Ynestra (1989), "Healing the Wounds: Feminism, Ecology and Nature/Culture Dualism," in *Gender/Body/Knowledge*, eds. Alison Jaggar and Susan Bordo, New Brunswick, NJ: Rutgers University Press, 115-144.

McCracken, Grant (1988), *Culture and Consumption*, Bloomington, IN: Indiana University Press.

Pollay, Richard (1986), "The Distorted Mirror: Reflections on the Unintended Consequences of Advertising," *Journal of Marketing*, 50 (April), 18-36.

Romanyshyn, Robert D. (1989), *Technology as Symptom and Dream* London: Routledge.

Richins, Marsha (1991), "Social Comparison and the Idealized Images of Advertising," *Journal of Consumer Research*, 18 (June), 71-83.

Schor, Juliette (1992), *The Overworked American: The Unexpected Decline of Leisure*, New York: Harper-Collins

Solomon, Michael R. (1988), "Mapping Product Constellations: A Social Categorization Approach to Consumption," *Journal of Psychology and Marketing* 5 (Fall), 233-258.

Stern, Barbara (1993), "Feminist Literary Criticism and the Deconstruction of Ads: A Postmodern View of Advertising and Consumer Responses," *Journal of Consumer Research*, 19 (March), 556-567.

Thompson, Craig J., William B. Locander and Howard R. Pollio (1989), "Putting Consumer Experience Back Into Consumer Research: The Philosophy and Method of Existential-Phenomenology," *Journal of Consumer Research*, 17 (September), 133-147.

Wolf, Naomi (1991), *The Beauty Myth: How Images of Beauty are Used Against Women*, New York: Anchor Books.

Possessions and Identity in Crisis: Meaning and Change for Victims of the Oakland Firestorm

Shay Sayre, California State University, Fullerton

ABSTRACT

This study chronicles the experiences of residents evacuated in conjunction with the Oakland residential fire (October 1991) in order to better understand what happens to self definition in the wake of an involuntary disposition of personal possessions. Computerized text analysis is used to analyze interview transcripts within the context of a disaster culture.

Changes in the meanings attributed to physical possessions following the fire are examined for their relationship to the transformation of identity which occurred for victims who lost their homes. The study also develops the notion of 'absence,' which emanated from the transcripts, for its contribution to the disaster literature.

"If we are what we own, then who are we when own nothing?" A paraphrase of William James' notion that we are the sum of our possessions, this question, posed by a disaster victim, illustrates the confusion surrounding loss of personal possessions to natural forces. Involuntary disposition (Young and Wallendorf 1989) of personal possessions eliminates the material and social source of identity for disaster victims, forcing them to transfer meaning to new possessions, and often to recast meanings of possessions destroyed.

The notion that people regard possessions as extensions of themselves has been studied by Belk (1988), whose research indicates that the relationship established by an attachment to an object by its owner is an important source of identity. Loss of possessions [the things we call ours] often results in a lessening of self (Goffman 1961). When possessions are destroyed, the question of what happens to the self is of great importance to those who study behavior.

During the largest residential fire in US history, 3354 homes and 456 apartments were destroyed and 5,000 people were left homeless. For those who lost their possessions, the October, 1991 fire changed their lives. This study uses the experiences of evacuees from the Oakland fire to understand the nature of change in the meaning of possessions lost, and possessions retained during the time of disaster. This event was chosen because of the availability of a unique opportunity to chronicle disaster through news media, personal interviews, diaries, photographs, videotapes, and letters prepared during and after the event, and neighborhood meetings and workshops held following the disaster. The relationship between disaster and possessions can be understood best in the frameworks of meaning, attachment and loss as presented below.

Possessions and Meaning

According to Furby (1978), possessions are multidimensional in nature. Her cross-cultural investigation points out that possessions take on meaning from the society in which they are used. A possession can be a physical entity that signals to others one's self-definition attainment. Abelson & Prentice (1989) suggest that possessions can transcend the physical property dimension when they are expressed as ideas and beliefs. Wicklund and Gollwitzer (1982) suggest that the construction and preservation of a self-definition depends heavily on a person's use and possession of objects as symbols of completeness. For self-symbolizing to begin, they argue, feelings of incompleteness needs to exist; fire victims take on such characteristics.

Most material culture receives meaning through association with specific use and contexts; Kleine & Kernan's (1991) paradigm is ideal for illustrating how individuals understand meaning as a perception or interpretation of an object, idea, or belief in a particular context.

Attachment, Loss and Possessions

According to Rudmin and Berry (1987) *attachment* is a central factor for understanding property ownership. Ball & Tasaki's (1992) definition of attachment as "the extent to which an individual uses an object to develop and maintain a cognitive structure of self" where self is an organization of knowledge, is most appropriate for studying disasters.

The *loss* literature is exhaustive. Loss through disaster has been found to disrupt one's sense of ability to find meaning in experience. Especially significant for this study is Weiner's (1985) finding that by embodying ancestral links, objects may be the basis of an individual's present social identity such that loss of the object would constitute a danger to the viability of the person.

When a familiar pattern of relationships has been disrupted, when symbols of identity are lost, possessions may change significantly in their subjective meanings (McAlexander, Schouten and Roberts 1993). The aspect of loss central to an understanding of the relationship between possessions and identity is one of loss of self, a natural correlate to the construct of possession centrality to self.

Possessions and Identity

Sartre (1943) defined identity as the totality of a person's being, having and doing. Personal identity as it relates to disaster victims is understood to mean their ideas and beliefs (being), objects (having) and activities and lifestyle (doing). Belk's (1987) notion of 'extended self' is useful for understanding the relationship between identity and the relevance of objects. This study assumes that the meaning associated with identity is group-dependent, sociologically determined, and culturally based.

STUDYING A FIRESTORM

Findings from the research literature on natural disasters emphasize the importance of examining disaster through a social framework. Bolin (1989) suggests that social responses to natural disaster flow from pre-disaster characteristics of the impacted individuals and social groupings. A systems approach to disaster analysis, where networks of social units exist within a material environment (Jasnowski 1984), is used for this study.

Person-object relations among fire victims were determined through a qualitative process using in-home and work location interviews. Interview materials were transcribed, entered into computer-readable files, and analyzed using a text-analyzing software to select and organize interview and journal material by key word. The purpose of analysis was to identify patterns of association between the meaning of objects and identity in a variety of references made about the fire. Concepts were allowed to emerge from the data in a holistic and cultural construct.

The Place and the People

The affected area located in the hilly, affluent section of Alameda County, California, is bordered by a regional preserve and the UC Berkeley campus to the northwest, chaparral peaks of about 1500 feet to the north and east, and expensive older homes completely surround the southern portion. Residents worked in nearby Oakland, Berkeley or San Francisco in mostly professional capacities. Homes ranged in price from $250,000 to three million dollars; the average price of the homes lost in the fire was $375,000. An active seismic area, the Hills were rocked in the 1989 earthquake and pose a constant state of disaster alert, it is considered to be a "disaster subculture" (Hannigan & Kueneman 1978), which is a group living in a constant state of danger. Members of the upper socio-economic strata, residents were professionals and executives who preferred a suburban lifestyle but who also enjoyed the convenience of urban activity and culture. This profile suggests that material possessions may have played a significant role in the lifestyles of these pre-fire residents.

Sixty-nine residents were selected for their willingness to act as informants and for their ability to represent the ages, gender, and occupational groups of people evacuated during the firestorm. Seven were renters, 12 lived in college dorms, and the balance were homeowners.

Disaster Subcultures

After the fire, two distinct sub-cultures emerged, separating informants who were able to return to their homes from those who were not ["There is *them*, the people who didn't lose their homes, and there is *us*, the people who did. And not one of them can know what we have lost."] Differences in language, activity and emotions were obvious among members of the two informant sub-groups. One informant said that after the fire, residents of the Hills were no longer co-survivors, they had become 'the residents' and 'the victims'. [Both terms were adopted for use in this text.] "Residents talk about being inconvenienced by the fire; victims stare in emotional agony,' said one male. The victims became a subculture of isolation, unable to communicate with anyone but other victims. One victim who had also survived the holocaust, said that losing everything set him apart from the rest of the world, and that only others who had gone through the experience understood.

Where residents who returned home claimed to feel guilt, victims testified to experiencing feelings of anger (Kubler-Ross 1975) at the termination of the long-term relationship, attachment, and caring they felt for their possessions. Depression, referred to in much of the disaster literature as post-traumatic stress disorder (see Bravo 1990), was apparent in the testimony of many victims. One woman said, "It's hard to grasp the meaning of 'all gone.' Just like my condo and my things, I am 'all gone' most of the time. I just can't get it together."

Nowhere were differences between residents who returned home and victims more apparent as in the transformation in meanings ascribed to objects after evacuation. Informants who returned home expressed a heightened sense of attachment to their belongings. Asked how the meaning of their possessions had been altered as a result of the evacuation, most 'near misses' said that the experience of packing up had increased their general awareness of the meaningfulness of their possessions ["I realized I didn't have a handle on what was really valuable, and that I was going to take a better inventory."].

Others said the evacuation process had enhanced the personal value of many items, and enabled them to recognized the vulnerability of material possessions to disaster and loss. A female informant said after she returned home and unpacked the car, she thought about how important her spoons were because it took so much time to collect them. Another female said that once she returned, she appreciated her things much more, and interjected, "Of course they're, just material things, but they mean a lot to me, they are the summary of my life." The least fortunate were 'near misses' whose homes survived, but not those of their neighbors. One woman said that while she had her possessions, she lost the surroundings that gave the possessions meaning, that they (possessions) all seemed out of context after the fire.

None of the men and women interviewed admitted to placing less emphasis on the importance of possessions as a result of the evacuation and threat of fire, although one college student reflected, "It was stupid that all this stuff was so important. It's really just stuff. But at the time, it was real important."

The Notion of Absence

For people returning home, objects reverted to their utility function, their former use-value. For victims, however, objects had lost their former use-value and assumed a much more powerful meaning as signifiers of *absence*. The term "absence" was used by informants to denote a state of not being present, and implying a lack of something. Testimony taken from victims who could not return home indicates that certain possessions became signifiers for absence. Semantics of their references revealed a distinction between absence and loss; many informants referred to feeling an 'absence of' things, and to things as being 'missing' rather than being lost.

The use of this term *absence* allows the research to shed inappropriate connotations of the term *loss*, which implies grief from something 'never again to be found.' Indeed, insurance enabled most victims to replace their lost possessions. However, the language used by victims suggests that what they suffered was an absence of symbols of their former lives, and that it was this absence that was so disabling.

With no tangible attributes to contribute to the 'layers of meaning' for absent and lost items, possessions assumed labels and dimensions that were symbolic of the shared reality of the victim subculture. Absent material possessions became concepts, taking on idiosyncratic associations that were unique to the discourse of victim survivors. A search was made of the transcripts using their words to signify concepts [concept-set] and then to count the mentions of those concepts in conjunction with either absence or loss referents. Seven specific sets of possessions absent emerged from the data through frequency of mention. The number of occurrences of each concept-set appears in Table 1. This notion of absence is the major construct developed in this paper and the following sections will illustrate this construct in the context of the absence of possessions as concept-sets.

The Absence of Things

Kopytoff (1986) noted that the world of things lends itself to an "endless number of classifications, rooted in natural features and cultural and idiosyncratic perceptions (p. 76). Many informants grouped all objects into single classification—'things.' Things that received meaning through use and context were rendered meaningless in the absence of that context. For instance, a woman's tea set had no meaning without her afternoon ritual that took place in the living room.

Absence of Home/Absence of Personal Space

The importance of the home as an extension of self (Belk 1991, McCracken 1989) is well documented as it relates to status (Hayward 1978), memories (Saegert 1985), territory/place (Hummon 1986) and self-expression (Sadalla et al 1987). Defined as 'action territory' by Bakker & Bakker-Rabdau (1973), home is the place a person claims as his/her own. A house provides an important building block of identity because it reflects history, special interests, strengths and weaknesses. According to one woman's journal:

TABLE 1

Concept Set	Mentions
'things,' possessions, objects	184
house, home	157
work, hobby	133
ashes, charred, burned	121
past, former life	118
neighborhood, community	32
lifestyle, routine	27
space, territory	19
identity	13

"A home is not just a structure containing a collection of objects, it's the environment in which I feel most comfort, most secure. It's my retreat from the world, my pause from life."

Homes were occasionally referred to as 'children': "Our home was our third child, nurtured, loved, encouraged to rise to its highest potential." Or as 'lovers': "This home we searched for so long, loved like a lover, chose simply to be with." And as a 'friends': "My house was my best friend and I miss him." For others, home signified relationships. The leader of a women's group summed up countless stories: "For many women, the loss of their homes represented memories from many years of marriage and raising children. Many women were widowed or divorced, and for them losing their home represented the finality of their relationships."

Similar in nature to an absence of home is the absence of personal space and territory, as expressed by one woman:

"What's missing is my territory, my space. I am still me, but many of the things that identify my purpose and creativity are not there. My territory had my markings, my routines, my responsibilities, my purpose clearly defined."

Loss of Work, Absence of Hobby

Conceptualized as property by Hallowell (1982), work is an example of the subjective dimension of possessions. Architects and writers, painters and photographers saw the death of their productivity when the fire removed all traces of renderings, manuscripts, art and negatives. For them, replacement was not possible. A musician lamented:

"I lost my museum. My work. 100 musical scores. All that is left is a surreal setting. I am now a museum, my work is gone. My work is my life chronicle. My identity was tied to my work, what I produced. My musical expression is all gone as if it were never wrenched from my soul."

A writer who lost the manuscript for her novel said "the Chinese burn messages to the dead at funerals, and being Chinese, I must believe that my book was meant to be a message to the dead."

For others, the absence of hobbies was devastating. A male informant who had 8000 tools and parts in his shop asks, "How much of my identity is tied up in what I can make, fix or modify with tools and a few parts?"

Absence of the Past

Past life emerged from the transcripts as an important possession by informants who felt that by losing all the records, photos, belongings that chronicled their lives, they lost themselves. They have a sense of non-existence before the fire. Reminiscent of Sartre, one man made the connection thus:

"I talk to myself about the elusive relationship between material and sentiment, and the mystery that sentiment might be contained and fused with tangible objects. The fire took everything I had, but it also took everything I was."

Two female informants expressed the sentiments of many others.

"We became orphans without a past. Like we had amnesia, like we didn't exist before the fire. I got new clothes, but they weren't like the old ones. The new ones were sad colors not bright ones, And they were long skirts instead of short ones. I had become another person—the former person was lost in the fire."

Absence of Neighborhood and Community

For many informants, one of their most prized possessions was the Hills neighborhood. Among the attributes mentioned as being missed were the status, the view, the convenience, the stability, the character, the familiarity, the activity and the feeling of belonging that the Hills embodied.

An interesting phenomenon was noticed by a man who recalled that after the fire "all over the neighborhood, Weber grills were standing. We should have designed our houses like the Weber." Adopted by survivors as the 'symbol' of their neighborhood, the Weber was featured in many photographs, drawings, and journal entries portraying the fire's aftermath.

Absence of Lifestyle and Routine

Often possessions were characterized by informants as the way they lived their lives. The findings of Kleine and Kernan (1991) were confirmed by much of the testimony indicating that objects take on the most significance as part of a set, and that their meaning is derived from the contextual set to which they belong. Similarly, one woman said what she sensed first was the disappearance of a regular system of objects that organized her life and "contributed to a smooth flow of daily functions: a pen, a pad, addresses and phone numbers; a nail, a hammer to drive it; a map, a pair of glasses to read it."

Many informants spoke about the absence of their ability to socialize in the same fashion as before the fire. Missing were their routines, their ways of conducting everyday life: "I'm not myself without my morning run along Hiller, my couch-nap in the afternoon, people dropping in for coffee, or our parties on the deck at night." A professor said she missed the "lifestyle of Oakland's urban-edge community that has disappeared from the face of the earth."

The Emergence of Sacred Items

Almost immediately after the fire, victims returned to reclaim whatever they could from the ashes that were once their homes. The experience caused victims to re-define certain possessions so that

TABLE 2

Category	Sub-culture	Pre-Evacuation Meaning	Post-Evacuation Meaning
Utility	Resident	Use-value	Confirmation of former value;
	Victim	Use-value	Symbolic of absent items valuable for maintaining routine/lifestyle; sacred when recovered from ashes
Representational	Resident	Symbolic of past and relationships	Enhanced value; acknowledged vulnerability
	Victim	Symbolic of past and relationships	Lost items became symbols of missing past; sacred when recovered; both were sources of grief and despair
Self-symbolic	Resident	Extenders of self	Re-validation of importance; guilt; enhanced appreciation
	Victim	Extenders of self.	Lost items were symbols of missing past; perceived as death of self; rescued items treasured, symbols of former self
Leisure/ Action/ Lifestyle	Resident	Indicators of status.	Confirmation of importance
	Victim	Indicators of status.	Lost items were symbols of missing past; sources of continuing despair; rescued items became sacred
Assets	Resident	Monetary value	Status-quo when insured; enhanced when not insured
	Victim	Monetary value	When lost, intrinsic qualities not compensated for by insurance; replaced items diminished in value

they had new meanings, and to elevate the status of fire artifacts to that of 'sacred.' In their discussion of sacred items, Belk, Wallendorf and Sherry (1989) tell how objects become sacred when they are separated from the profane, and when their value is associative/symbolic rather than practical/non-symbolic.

In this instance, objects' resilience to the fire delivered them to a state of reverence for many victims who embraced charred artifacts as symbols of their past lives. For most, possessions recovered became possessions prized. An informant admitted to having placed the artifacts from the ashes in a glass case: "They are all we have left of our past lives." Calling themselves the 'ashes crew,' victims combed their land for their 'melted histories', recovering "a drapery of crystal stemware, a stamp pad fused shut, a gutted camera crammed with irretrievable images."

Fire relics had a very high subcultural commodity value among victims, and as such were instruments of communication and therapy. Utilized by therapists to help victims work through loss trauma, relics were important for one workshop participant whose set of fused and knurled silver facilitated personal catharsis. Fire relics were also incorporated into sculpture and mixed media pieces created for the Fire Art Project, which was sponsored by the art community for exhibition in venues throughout the Bay Area to commemorate the one year anniversary of the fire.

The Signification of Possessions and Self

Almost without exception, possessions removed during the evacuation had their meanings enhanced by virtue of either the unpacking process or their destruction. Informants' testimony verify the notion of past research that the level of significance of objects is dependent upon the level of change in physical form. This research found three levels of form-based meaning. 1) Objects that were returned in their original form had their meanings only slighted enhanced. 2) Lost possessions were re-conceptualized and became the most significant symbols of the victims' lost identity. Loss of past as possessions had the specific implications for causing Post Traumatic Syndrome, or despair. 3) Objects that were recovered from the ashes enjoyed the greatest degree of change in meaning for most fire victims——a spoon, worthless before the fire, became a sacred item that represented the totality of a victim's past life and former identity. In Table 2, Dittmar's (1991) classification scheme is used to compare the meaning inherent in physical possessions retained by residents who returned home with the change of meaning attributed by victims to physical possessions that were lost.

Besieged by the trauma of absence and loss, victims expressed the need to re-examine their relationship with possessions. For many, the absence of possessions allowed them the opportunity to reflect on how their things impacted upon their identities. One informant said she was so wrapped up in her material possession that she did not realize they were beginning to own her. She wondered if she had any identity apart from her possessions. Figure 1 is an attempt to conceptualize the transformation of identity that victims reported by comparing the proportions of commodity importance of pre and post fire possessions for self identification.

FIGURE 1

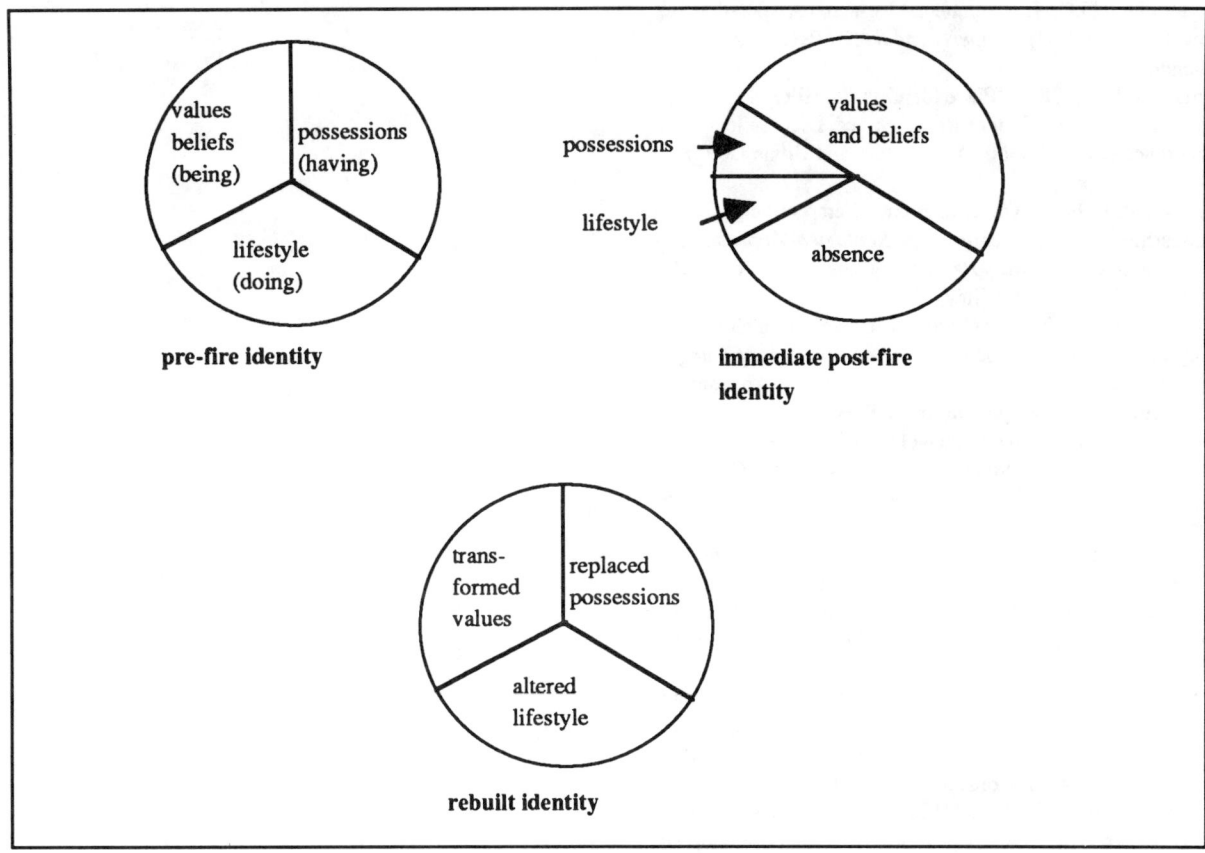

This figure is not intended to represent quantifiable segments but rather to approximate the importance of each aspect of identity to the whole unit.

Conclusion

What role does absence play in the victims' rebuilt identity? To what extent is the new identity a reaction to the post-disaster circumstances? How do gender and age variables affect the personal rebuilding process? These and other questions may be more thoroughly addressed by follow-up research.

The firestorm text used in this preliminary research generated the notion of 'absence,' a concept new to the disaster literature. Results of this study suggest that absence and loss of possessions from involuntary disposition cause a corresponding change in personal identity. Further research is needed to expand and generalize the notion of absence, and to develop the concept of identity signification following natural disaster.

REFERENCES

Abelson, R. P. & Prentice, D. A. (1989), Beliefs as Possessions: A Functional Perspective, in *Attitude Structure and Function*, eds. A. Pratkanis, S. Breckler and A. Greenwald, Hillsdale NY: Erlbaum, 361-381.

Bakker, Cornelis and Marianne Bakker-Rabdau (1973), *No Trespassing: Explorations in Human Territoriality,* San Francisco: Chandler & Sharp.

Ball, Dwane and Lori Tasaki (1992), "The Role and Measurement of Attachment in Consumer Behavior," *Journal of Consumer Psychology* 1 (2), 155-172.

Belk, Russell (1987), "Identity and the Relevance of Market, Personal and Community Objects," in *Marketing and Semiotics*, ed. Jean Umiker Sebeok, New York: Mouton de Gruyter.

_____ (1988),"Possessions and the Extended Self," *Journal of Consumer Research,* 15 (September), 139-168.

_____ (1991), "The Ineluctable Mysteries of Possessions," In To Have Possessions: A Handbook on Ownership and Property [Special Issue], ed. F. W. Rudman, *Journal of Social Behavior and Personality* 6 (6), 17-55.

Belk, Russell, John Sherry and Melanie Wallendorf (1989), "The Sacred and Profane in Consumer Behavior," *Journal of Consumer Research* 16, 1-38.

Bolin, Robert (1989), "Natural Disasters," in *Psychological Aspects of Disaster*, eds. R. Gist and B Lubin, New York: John Wiley & Sons.

Bravo, Milagros, Martiza Rubio-Stipec, Glorisa Canino, Michael Woodbury and Julio Ribera (1990), "The Psychological Sequelae of Disaster Stress Prospectively and Retrospectively Evaluated," *American Journal of Community Psychology* 18 (5), 661-679.

Dittmar, Helga (1991), "Meanings of Material Possessions as Reflections of Identity: Gender and Social-Material Possessions in Society," *Journal of Social Behavior and Personality* 6 (6), 165-186.

Furby, Lita (1978), "Sharing: Decisions and Moral Judgments About Letting Others Use One's Possessions." *Psychological Reports* 43 (2), 595-609.

Goffman, Irving (1975), *Frame Analysis.* Harmondsworth: Penguin.

Hayward, D.G. (1978). "An Overview of Psychological Concepts of Home." *Priorities for Environmental Research.* Washington D.C.: Environmental Research Association.

Hallowell, Peter (1982), *Property and Social Relations,* London: Heinemann.

Hummon, D. M. (1986), "Place Identity: Locality of the Self." In *Built Form and Culture Research.* ed. D.G. Saile, Lawrence KS: School of Architecture and Urban Design, 34-37.

Jasnowski, M. (1984). "The Ecosystemic Perspective in Clinical Assessment and Intervention." In *Ecological Approaches to Clinical and Community Psychology,* eds. W. O'Connor & B. Lubin, New York: Wiley, 41-56.

Kopytoff, Igor (1986), "The Cultural Biography of Things: Commoditization as Process," in *The Social Life of Things: Commodities in a Cultural Perspective,* ed. A. Appadurai, Cambridge: Cambridge University Press.

Kleine, Robert and Jerome Kernan (1991), "Contextual Influences on the Meanings Ascribed to Ordinary Consumption Objects." *Journal of Consumer Research* 18 (December), 311-324.

Kubler-Ross, Elisabeth (1975), *Death: The Final Stage of Growth.* Englewood Cliffs NJ: Prentice-Hall.

McAlexander, James, John Schouten and Scott Roberts (1993), "Consumer Behavior and Divorce," *Research in Consumer Behavior* (forthcoming).

McCracken, Grant (1989), "Homeyness:' A Cultural Account of One Constellation of Consumer Goods and Meanings." In *Interpretive Consumer Research.* ed. E. C. Hirschman, Provo UT: Association for Consumer Research, 168-183.

Rudman, F.W. and J. W. Berry (1987), "Semantics of Ownership: A Free-Recall Study of Property," *The Psychological Record* 37, 257-268.

Sadalla, E.K., B. Vershure & W.J. Burroughs (1987), "Identity Symbolism in Housing." *Environment and Behavior* 19, 569-587.

Saegert, S. (1985), "The Role of Housing in the Experience of Dwelling." In I. Altman & ed. C.M. Werner, *Home Environments.* New York: Plenum Press, 287-309.

Sartre, Jean-Paul, (1943), *Being and Nothingness: A Phenomenological Essay on Ontology,* New York: Philosophical Library.

Weiner, A. (1985), "Inalienable Wealth," *American Ethnologist* 12 (2), 210-227.

Wicklund, Robert and Peter Gollwitzer (1982), *Symbolic Self-Completion,* Hillsdale, NJ: Lawerence Erlbaum.

Young, Melissa and Melanie Wallendorf (1989), "Ashes to Ashes, Dust to Dust: Conceptualizing Consumer Disposition of Possessions." *American Marketing Association Winter Educator's Conference Proceedings,* Chicago: American Marketing Association.

Redefining Self: Interpreting the Interpretations of Three Diverse Experiences
Larry D. Compeau, Clarkson University

At first blush, the three papers in this session offering a descriptive tour of three unique experiences would seem to have very little in common. The first paper by Laura A. Williams and Alvin C. Burns examines the reckless and exhilarating experience of "spring break" as recounted by college students. Shay Sayre, in the second paper, investigates the horrible and unfortunate experience of surviving a firestorm. Finally, Craig Thompson shares some insight regarding the experience associated with embracing new technology, a computer printer. Thus, it seems fairly safe to conclude that these three experiences appear to have little common ground. Collectively, the papers provide us with an emotional roller coaster of seemingly unrelated experiences. However, we can step back from each of these experiences and explore them together in an interpretive fashion. Thus, what is offered in this analysis is a synergistic integration of these diverse papers based on a loose interpretive method, rather than a specific critique or summary of results.

The notion of collectively interpreting interpretations is novel to consumer research, but can be compared to other integrative review techniques such as meta-analysis. In general, interpreting the interpretations attempts to address the same issue; namely, what can the discipline learn from a collection of studies as opposed to a single study? While a meta-analysis might require many studies to accurately assess certain relationships, the nature of interpretive analysis (e.g., richness, depth) would be better preserved by attempting to integrate the results of a few papers.

A brief summary and critique of each paper is offered followed by a synergistic interpretation of their collective findings.

THE SPRING BREAK EXPERIENCE

Williams and Burns offer an engaging description of the emotional experiences that college students enjoyed during a spring break excursion. The study highlights the hedonic experiences in which the students choose to engage as part of the overall "spring break" experience. Students experience feelings of happiness, joy, and elation in a free and unconstrained environment. Excessiveness and over-indulgence in almost all behavior is commonplace as students report feeling carefree, reckless and out of control.

The methodology however, is constraining in that students were required to write about their descriptions and were approached long after their actual spring break experience. Thus, additional insight might be gained if students were interviewed during spring break. The authors also restricted their sample to only those students who considered their spring break vacation as a self-gift. It would also seem that contrasting those students who did not qualify on the self-gift criterion with the students in this sample would be meaningful. Did they enjoy the experience any less? Is there no self-communication involved? Can one consider a gift as earned, as a self-reward even if he or she does not pay for it? Unfortunately, we are not provided with the details of how the students were approached about this self-gift determination so it is difficult to speculate as to any differences.

Surprisingly, shopping was an activity in which some students engaged during spring break. One student reported her shopping trip to the mall as the highlight of her spring break trip. It is curious and most intriguing that in the context of "sex, drugs, and rock'n'roll," a student would even mention going to a mall, much less note that it was the highlight of her spring break. It would be tempting to dismiss this result as an artifact of the method, but the excerpt from the student's written narrative does not seem to point in that direction. The notion that shopping is so significant for this person that it can overshadow the many other "wild and crazy" events that were described seems astounding. Further investigation of the significance of shopping embedded in a seemingly more absorbing and thrilling context is warranted.

A most illuminating theme uncovered was labelled as "unfettering my social-self." Students appear to use the spring break context to liberate, and thus, redefine self. In other words and as the authors note, "the social context liberates the social-self." Students freely choose to go to spring break and thus, are active participants in liberating their social-self and engaging in behavior in which they would not normally embrace. They free themselves from the everyday restrictions imposed by self and others. In doing so, they allow themselves to temporarily lose their normal "self" and extend and create a new self that is unconstrained and liberated. Thus, they temporarily redefine self.

When spring break is over, however, they don't simply shed this temporary self in its entirety, and return to their previous self. Although they return to a position much closer to their previous self, self is nonetheless, permanently altered as a result of the experience. Thus, the students refer to being a different person, more mature, independent, and responsible (quite ironic given their acknowledgement that their behavior during spring break was generally irresponsible).

Thus, we get a peek at the hedonic experiences of students during that notorious excursion referred to as "spring break." Although the reputed excessive and over-indulgent behavior is confirmed, more importantly, the significance for self is uncovered and the process of self-redefinition is depicted.

THE FIRESTORM EXPERIENCE

The agony of losing all of one's possessions is captured with Sayre's account of victimization from the Oakland firestorm. Her description of the emotional experiences of despair and agony the victims suffered is a vivid example of the pervasiveness of emotional losses that can occur as a result of our inability to control nature.

Two forms of losses occurred for these residents. First, there was a loss of self. Victims speak of a lessening of self as a result of a loss of possessions. But, the possessions not only define self, they also define the community in which the self resides. Thus, the victims also speak of loss of community. Without the possessions, victims not only lose self, but because others all around them also have lost all of their possessions, they lose their community as well. It is the community however, which in turn helps to define self. This point is well illustrated by a women labelled as a 'near miss,' a person whose home survived in the face of the destruction of her neighbors' homes. She relates that it was the surroundings that gave the possessions meaning and thus these same possessions were now 'out of context.'

The lack of choice is a critical contextual frame in which this victimization occurs. The residents had no voice; they were not willing and active participants. This experience was plunged into their everyday lives without consideration. Consider the difference in the experiences these victims relate about their loss of home versus the experience of simply moving to a different home. In the latter instance, some level of choice is usually involved and thus, self can be preserved and moved along with most of the other possessions. Moreover, one is given a chance to contemplate the significance of the experience before it actually happens and thus, self can be adapted to the different context in a slow and deliberate fashion. Victims of the firestorm however, simply find themselves in a totally new context, stripped of all of their possessions and are forced to adapt, immediately.

Another important contribution is the notion that possessions can be replaced, but not their significance or meaning. The notion of absence versus loss is an important distinction that highlights that items lost can be replaced but the absence of the meaning of those items endures. Thus, Sayre's paper highlights the vast distance between functionality and meaning. Functionality can occur across many different contexts and appears to have a more universal understanding that transcends contexts and even objects. Personal significance and meaning on the other hand appears to be highly context bound and individualistic. The example of the woman and her tea set illustrates this interpretation. Although the tea set survived, it was rendered meaningless without the afternoon ritual that accompanied it. Although the tea set's functionally remained unchanged, its personal meaning and significance was loss due to the changing context. This context focused approach to the difference between function and meaning appears to be a particularly fertile area for future research.

Finally, it is striking that so little discussion was available on the loss of photographs. Many of the other possessions the victims talked about were often cited in terms of their ability to preserve and remind victims of particularly important concepts or events, thus serving a purpose similar to photographs. An interesting question is whether the lack of these possessions suggests a loss due to the victims' inability to recall or reconstruct past events (Berger 1991).

These people are truly victims. This transformation of identity was not embraced, it was endured as it was thrust upon them without warning, without any opportunity to escape. Without choice, they were forced to undergo a redefinition of self through the "involuntary disposition" of their personal possessions. This total loss of all of their possessions acts to constrain and reduce self. They lose a permanent part of self which may never be regained.

Comparatively, the permanent redefinition of self in response to the loss of all of one's possessions would seem to loom larger than the more temporary redefinition to include excessive behavior, or the less traumatic redefinition associated with the inability to master a product (discussed in Thompson's paper). Thus, the event that precipitates this more substantial redefinitions of self would seem to hold greater significance in the newly redefined self. For example, the firestorm experience would seem to have greater significance in the redefined self of the victims, and their everyday lives, than the spring break experience would have for the students. Self is so much more substantially altered as a result of the firestorm. Thus, the firestorm may actually take on a defining line of change for the victims. That is, the victims may divide their lives into two parts, before the firestorm and after the firestorm. Events, relationships with others may be divided and redefined as qualitatively different "before" and "after." It might be most fruitful to revisit these victims in a few years to examine this potential theme.

THE TECHNOLOGY EXPERIENCE

Thompson offers a glimpse into the everyday experience of embracing a new technology, a computer printer. The whole experience seems to be much less arresting than the students' experiences at spring break or the experiences of the victims of the firestorm. However, it is important to note that these latter two events are rare in the normal course of a person's life, whereas interacting with new technology seems to be a common experience for many consumers.

Central to Thompson's interpretation is the concept of the "technocratic" ideal, a belief that consumer technology is a tool for enhancing productivity and creating a better way-of-life by controlling nature (as might have been believed by the victims of the firestorm). Thus, as this technocratic ideal is embraced, emotions are viewed more as "inefficiencies to be reduced or eliminated." Concomitantly, any unproductive use of time in not tolerated, culminating in a idealization of self as a "perfectly functioning machine." Thus, it is likely that when the technology fails to deliver these benefits, there may be some impact on self as the reality of the experience conflicts with the ideology.

In this particular instance, the promised benefits of increased efficiency via the liberation from practical inconveniences and greater control eludes one consumer, "John." Thus, John experiences frustration, personal disappointment and a "begrudging resignation" over spending time with the newly purchased computer printer when it fails to perform as he had expected. Nonetheless, he pledges his allegiance to the technocratic ideology by "confessing" any failure to be solely his own.

For John, there exists a "before" and "after" set of experiences that appear to contradict each other. Prior to any consumption of the printer, he deliberately chooses to be liberated from the practical conveniences that are seemingly apparent when one does not own a computer printer. He becomes a willing participant in the purchase and consumption of the computer printer. After the purchase however, he becomes a victim of the very technology that seemed to promise freedom. He is forced to confront the technology and attempt to wrestle it into subservience, with little success, in contrast to the promises and the ideology. Thus, in his eyes he is not up to the task, and he fails. The printer now acts to constrain his abilities and his experiences. As Thompson elucidates,

> In seeking to realize the ideals of control and efficiency, individuals become susceptible to the paradox of being controlled by the very technological products that are purported to enhance personal control and freedom.

Thus, John also redefines self. John comes to know self as different then before the experience. Before the experience John viewed himself as more knowledgeable, capable and accomplished at interfacing with technology. Now he has redefined himself as inadequate to this interfacing task. His view of self is somewhat diminished. He is forced into either preserving self at the cost of his technocratic ideology or sacrificing self to preserve the technocratic ideology. He chooses the latter.

REDEFINING SELF

Beyond the methodological link to phenomenology, what contribution do these papers offer collectively that is not obtainable individually? In other words, can the findings from these studies offer any synergistic interpretation that expands their contribution at a higher, more abstract level of understanding? By using an interpretive methodology (Ricoeur 1976) based loosely on existential phenomenology (Giorgi 1975; Thompson, Locander and Pollio 1989; Valle and King 1978; Wertz 1983) and reader-response theory (Culler 1975; Fish 1980; Iser 1978), the papers can be considered text that can be interpreted - an interpretation of the interpretations. Thus, a synergistic integration of the papers is offered based on this analysis.

The following three quotes from the Thompson, Williams and Burns, and Sayre papers respectively, illustrate the distance in the emotional experiences found in these three studies:

> To be quite honest with you, my actual experience with using the printer has not been as much as I had hoped it would be....

TABLE
Contextual Characteristics

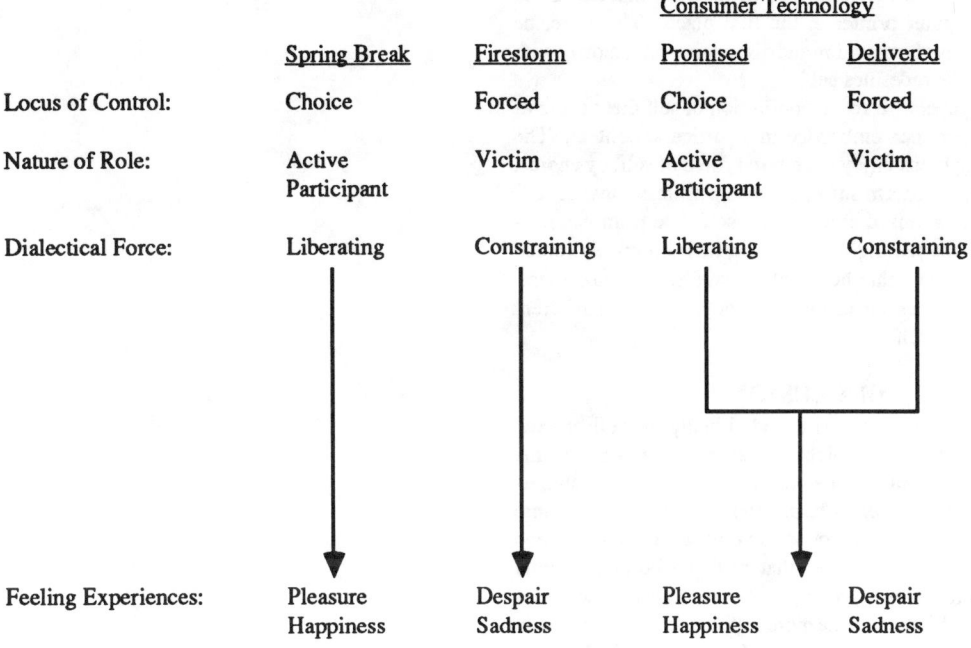

I stayed drunk for four days, barely ate, and enjoyed a lot of company from people all over the country.

It's hard to grasp the meaning of 'all gone.' Just like my condo and my things, I am 'all gone' most of the time. I just can't get it together.

In the first instance we are presented with an example of a person forced to deal with the mundane experience of mastering a technologically-oriented product, and who in the end experiences frustration and disappointment due to an inability to conquer the machine. In the second instance, we catch a glimpse of a person, a student, who experiences pleasure and happiness as he willingly escapes the mundane. And finally, the third quote illustrates the despair and sadness experienced by a victim of a firestorm as she attempts to cope with a very non-mundane loss of all of her possessions - an grossly unwanted deviation from the mundane.

Yet, in each instance the participants relate the experiences to self. In the first instance, the participant confesses to personal failure and redefines self as *not the self he thought he was*. The second quote illustrates a participant breaking away from "normal" self and engaging in experiences normally not allowed to occur, i.e., *temporarily losing self by choice*. Finally, for the victim of the firestorm there is a *forced permanent loss of self*. In all three instances, participants redefine "self" as a result of their experiences. One way to better understand any synergy among these different experiences is to focus on the contexts in which these experiences take place.

The Table highlights characteristics of the contexts in which these experiences are embedded. The context of "spring break" involves an active and willing participant who chooses to engage in the experiences. Thus, the students "escape," by choice, from their normal everyday lives. They are active participants who choose to escape and, in essence, liberate themselves from self, others and their normal lived-world, and consequently enjoy feelings of pleasure and happiness. Thus, the personal meaning and significance of the spring break experience is embedded in these contextual characteristics. Williams and Burns note that a group of students who could not go to the beach, created their own beach, far from any shore. The description offered by an informant who attended this version of spring break was "identical to those informants we analyzed." Thus, it appears that the "mental" escape can occur without a "physical" escape.

The victims of the firestorm stand in stark contrast to the willing participants of spring break. There is no choice here. The victims lose everything they own and are forced to redefine self or seemingly lose self altogether. They find self to be reduced, constrained by the lack of their possessions which previously allowed them to identify and continuously reconstruct self. Consequently, they experience feelings of despair and sadness over a loss that seems much greater than just the physical loss of "things." They have lost more than the presence of their possessions. They have lost meaning, they have lost personal significance, they have lost reminders and definers of relationships with self and others. They have lost self.

In the context of Thompson's examination of computer printer consumption, we can see similar elements, albeit with much less intensity, identified in the experiences of the students on spring break and the victims of the firestorm. The contexts of the "before" and "after" experiences compare with the spring break and firestorm experiences respectively. That is, John is promised (consistent with the technocratic idealogy) that he will be able to escape the constraints imposed upon him by the inconveniences of not owning a computer printer, promises of experiences similar to what the students enjoyed during spring break. Thus, John willingly chooses to become an active participant in embracing this technology so he can enjoy its benefits. However, John soon feels forced into making this technology work for him when the benefits do not materialize so easily. Similar to the firestorm victims, John becomes a victim of the very technology that was promised to liberate him. He feels betrayed, trapped, constrained and forced to redefine self or in the alternative, abandon the very technocratic idealogy that led him to purchase the computer printer in the first place. Therefore, he experiences feelings of frustration and disappointment, mostly with himself and thus, he redefines self.

In all three papers we see a redefinition of self that occurs as a result of an experience embedded in a particular context. The students on spring break enjoy a temporary loss of self, by choice. The victims of the firestorm suffer a forced permanent loss of self. John, relishes the promised extension of self, free from inconveniences - a choice he willingly makes; but, he is ultimately forced to recognize and accept that he is not the self he thought he was. Thus, the context frames the experiences and provides for different significances for the self.

CONCLUSION

The three papers in this session, individually and collectively, provide a vehicle through which we can better understand the significance of the context of consumers' experiences and its relationship in redefining self. The phenomenological insights into experiences of hedonic consumption, involuntary disposition, and technological interaction suggest that self can be significantly altered and redefined as meaningful events transpire within a particular context. Moreover, the more self is redefined, the greater the import attached to the significance of the events which stimulated this self redefinition. That is, events which precipitate more traumatic, involuntary, permanent changes in self will take on greater significance and meaning as part of that self redefinition.

REFERENCES

Berger, John (1991), *About Looking*, New York, NY: Vintage International.

Culler, Jonathan (1975), *Structuralist Poetics: Structuralism, Linguistics, and the Study of Literature*, Ithaca, NY: Cornell University Press.

Fish, Stanley (1980), *Is There a Text in This Class?*, Cambridge, MA: Harvard University Press.

Giorgi, Amadeo (1975), "An Application of Phenomenological Method in Psychology," in *Duquesne Studies in Phenomenological Psychology*, Vol. 2, eds. A. Giorgi, C. Fischer, and E. Murray, Pittsburg, PA: Duquesne University Press.

Iser, Wolfgang (1974), *The Implied Reader: Patterns of Communication in Prose Fiction from Bunyan to Beckett*, Baltimore, MD: Johns Hopkins University Press.

Ricoeur, Paul (1976), *Interpretation Theory*, Fort Worth, TX: Texas Christian University Press.

Thompson, Craig J., William B. Locander, and Howard R. Pollio (1989), "Putting Consumer Experience Back into Consumer Research: The Philosophy and Method of Existential-Phenomenology," *Journal of Consumer Research*, 16 (September), 133-46.

Valle, Ronald and Mark King (1978), An Introduction to Existential-Phenomenological Thought in Psychology," in *Existential-Phenomenological Alternatives for Psychology*, eds. Ronald Valle and Mark King, New York, NY: Oxford University Press, 6-17.

Wertz, Frederick J. (1983), "From Everyday to Psychological Description: Analyzing the Moments of Qualitative Data Analysis," *Journal of Phenomenological Research*, 14 (Fall), 197-242.

Mental Accounting and Consumer Spending
Chip Heath, University of Chicago
Sue O'Curry, DePaul University

Consumers obtain income from a variety of sources and incur many types of expenses. The tendency to categorize both income and expenses is pervasive, and can have a profound impact on patterns of spending, as well as other uses of money. Subjective feelings of wealth, response to sales promotions, self-control problems, and post-purchase evaluations are just a few of the consumer issues addressed by mental accounting.

Heath and Soll showed that consumers tend to set budgets for classes of expenses and monitor expenses against the appropriate budget. They stop purchasing items in the category when total expenses during a particular time period exceed the category budget. Within a class of expenses, purchases differ in their prototypicality. For example, a movie is a prototypical entertainment expense, while a hardback novel is less protoypical. The purchase of a prototypical item decreases future expenses in a category more than the purchase of a less prototypical item with an equivalent monetary price.

Experiments showed that a current expense lowers future expenses within the same category but has little effect on other categories of expenses. Within a category, the effect of one expenditure on another is a function of their similarity. The experiments control for other factors such as satiation and income effects.

O'Curry demonstrated a tendency to assign income to different accounts. Most consumers are familiar with the injunction to "buy something special for yourself" that accompanies many gifts of money. From a normative standpoint, gifts of money, earnings from work, tax refunds, and income from all other sources should be spent the same way.

The first experiment examined differences in spending when income is derived from price decreases compared to cash income. If the gain of real income is the same in both cases and price ratios are unaffected, the pattern of spending should also be the same, except for an increase in quantity purchased when prices fall. However, price decreases may be perceived as a gain to the budget for the product class, rather than as a gain to overall wealth. This experiment demonstrated that consumers may be more likely to buy higher quality or complementary goods when an increase in income is derived from a price decrease rather than an increase in money income. Consumers may also code income and expenses by how "serious" or "frivolous" the source of income or category of expense is. The second experiment demonstrated a tendency for consumers to spend income from frivolous sources on frivolous uses.

Nye tested the hypotheses that (1) the category to which an expense is assigned will affect the consumer's effort to "recover" that expense and (2) sunk costs may be most salient soon after they are incurred. These hypotheses were tested in a natural field setting, in which subjects incurred genuine out-of-pocket costs. Subjects purchased coupon booklets offering a variety of discounted products and services from local merchants. The price of the coupon booklet (sunk cost) was manipulated. A second manipulation encouraged subjects to recategorize the booklet price as a charitable contribution rather than as an investment. Greater coupon usage by subjects who paid the higher price indicated a sunk cost effect. When subjects were able to categorize the booklet price as a charitable contribution rather than an investment, the sunk cost effect was eliminated. The sunk cost effect was strongest immediately after the coupon booklet was purchased. Subjects paying the higher price tended to recover their investment quickly.

Eric Johnson concluded the session with a discussion of the papers and suggested directions for further work.

Consumer Responses to Time Pressure: A Qualitative Study with Homeowners in Foreclosure

Barbara L. Gross, University of Southern California

ABSTRACT

Consumer responses to time pressure are examined in the context of home mortgage foreclosure. The study presents the results of depth interviews with homeowners in foreclosure, yielding descriptive data relevant to both behavioral and affective responses. Themes relate to the experience of foreclosure time pressure, responses that exacerbate time pressure, and decision making under time pressure. A classification of responses is presented, with responses suggested to be contingent upon the degree or intensity of both objective time pressure (clock/calendar time) and subjective time pressure (perceived urgency). In general, a curvilinear relationship between time pressure and productivity is inferred.

INTRODUCTION

Although it has long been recognized that time pressure affects consumer behavior (Howard 1963, Howard and Sheth 1969), little research has specifically examined consumer behavior under conditions of time pressure. Those few studies that do exist have examined it in artificial contexts.

The purpose of the present study is to examine responses to *time pressure* in actual situations faced by actual consumers. The context of *foreclosure* provides an opportunity for such analysis and is dramatic because responses are crucial to future living standards and quality of life. *Depth interviews* are used to gain insight into behavioral and affective responses to time pressure (McCracken 1988).

Foreclosure is a statutorily defined process whereby a lender seeks recovery from a borrower in default on a real property loan. The process is characterized by deadlines and time pressures (Figure 1). In California, it extends over approximately four months and culminates in the lender selling the property at public auction (trustee's sale). However, by taking timely action—such as to secure more favorable financing or sell the home—a homeowner may prevent ultimate foreclosure.

TIME AND CONSUMER BEHAVIOR

The effect of time on human behavior has been studied across the behavioral sciences and the relevance to consumer behavior is fairly well recognized (Jacoby et al. 1976, Gross 1987, Hirschman 1987). It follows that time pressure influences purchasing and consumption.

Subjective Time

A long tradition of research in psychology demonstrates that temporal perception is affected by internal/psychological states and situational influences. Further, work in sociology, anthropology, and philosophy demonstrates variation across cultures and social structures. Thus, the experience of time is largely subjective. Stroud (1955, p. 175) observed 38 years ago that: "We have had for a century or more ample evidence that physical and psychological time [are] by no means identical."

The existence of varied and subjective temporal perception/ orientation implies differential perceptions of time pressure and varied responses to it. As suggested by Hawes (1980, p. 446):

Appropriate conceptualization of time pressure [is] as a multifaceted, subjective phenomenon varying across different groups of people in different ways at different times.

Time Pressure Effects on Consumer Behavior

Consumer researchers have advanced surprisingly little analysis of time pressure effects. Howard and Sheth (1969) included time pressure as an exogenous variable in *The Theory of Buyer Behavior* and commented that little was known about it at that time. Twenty years later, Iyer (1989) observed that research is still sparse. However, in addition to limited work in consumer behavior, contributions are found in the psychology and organizational decision making literature.

Both theory and empirical evidence suggest that decisions made under time pressure are likely to suffer in quality. Friend (1982) demonstrated a strong negative relationship between time pressure and performance on a problem solving test, and Bettman (1979) proposed that available time regulates the amount of information that can be processed. Bruner et al. (1956) proposed that choices made under time pressure are likely to be poorly informed, and Jacoby et al. (1976) cite experiments demonstrating positive relationships between time pressure and selective exposure to information. Bronner (1982) found demand for additional information to be dramatically reduced under time pressure, and Wright (1974) found time pressured consumers to place disproportionate emphasis on negative product information and discrediting evidence.

In contrast, Latham and Locke (1975) found that productivity may increase with time pressure and inferred that motivation to complete a task may be enhanced when available time is reduced. However, beyond a certain threshold, motivation may give way to futility (Janis and Mann 1977), suggesting a curvilinear effect. Isenberg (1981) found support for a curvilinear relationship between time pressure and performance, with effects mediated by the nature of the task. Well-learned tasks are suggested to be associated with a monotonic relationship whereas tasks requiring creative problem solving demonstrate a curvilinear effect.

Time Pressure and Foreclosure: Exacerbating Effects

In addition to statutory time constraints, various correlates of foreclosure serve to exacerbate experienced time pressure. First, foreclosure is unfamiliar. The homeowner typically is unacquainted with the process and with available courses of action. Second, decisions pertaining to foreclosure are critical. The financial and even emotional well-being of the homeowner are at stake. Third, the homeowner is presented with alternatives that conflict both with one another (e.g., sell versus obtain additional financing versus declare bankruptcy) and with the homeowner's own desires. Finally, the homeowner is inundated with solicitations and presented with myriad similar offers within each category of alternative. Given these realities, it follows that decisions made during foreclosure *should* be made with great care and substantial time *should* be devoted to them. However, the exigencies of foreclosure necessitate quick and decisive action.

RESEARCH DESIGN

The paucity of consumer research on perceived/experienced time pressure suggests that a qualitative research design is appropriate—one that emphasizes discovery rather than confirmation (Lutz 1989). The present study seeks to contribute theoretical grounding and incorporate perceptual, subjective, and experiential aspects into the conceptualization of time pressure (Kaufman and Lane 1990).

FIGURE 1
Foreclosure Time Line

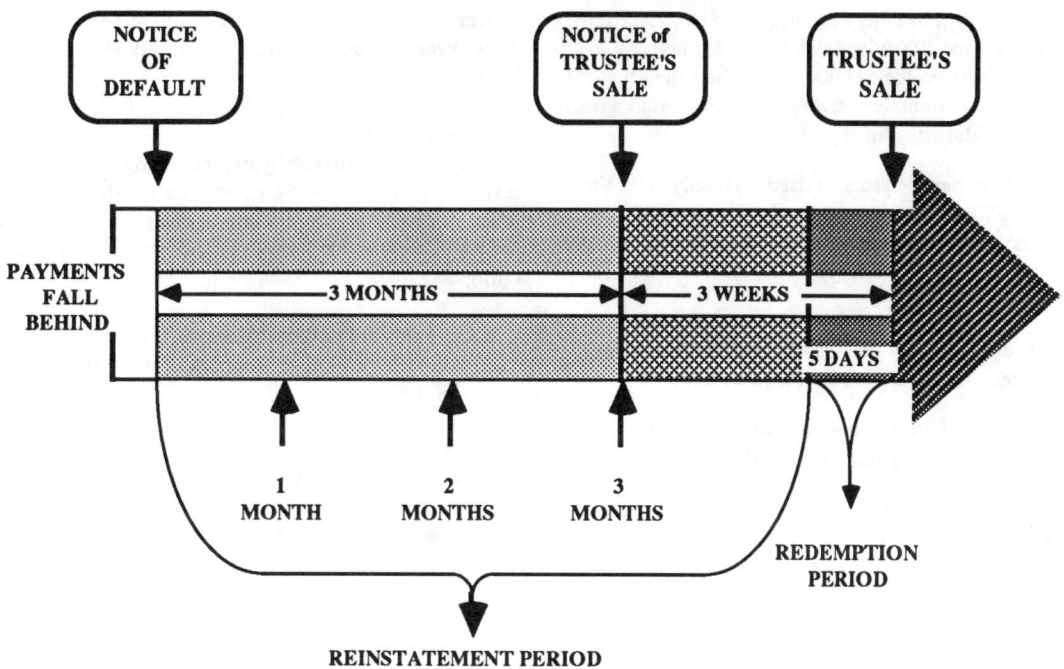

Sample

Data were obtained through interviews with homeowners identified as having received a Notice of Default at least three months prior. Homeowners were contacted by mail and invited to participate in a study on the topic of foreclosure. The response rate to the mailing was 16 percent—substantially higher than anticipated considering the extraordinary pressures facing homeowners in foreclosure. A sample size of 15 was deemed adequate to provide rich, descriptive data.

Nine women, five men, and one married couple participated. Most had been long-time residents, all were residents of middle-income neighborhoods, and all had accumulated substantial equity prior to entering foreclosure. Defaults were precipitated by job loss, business failure, disability, and high risk financing. Several sold their homes, refinanced, or acquired short-term financing as remedies to foreclosure. The majority stalled the foreclosure by declaring bankruptcy.

Data Collection and Analysis

The time line diagram served as an interview guide, orienting the homeowners in time and facilitating spontaneous discussion of time pressure. Informants were asked to "start at the beginning" and to "help me to understand what it has been like." Interviews were loosely structured and nondirective.

An iterative and emergent approach was used in conducting interviews (Strauss and Corbin 1990, Schouten 1991). Data collection and preliminary analysis proceeded concurrently and this aided in refining the direction of the interviews. Subsequently, informants were contacted for follow-up interviews for purposes of updating and clarifying, exploring emergent themes, and validating conclusions. Seven informants completed one follow-up, three completed two, one completed three, and the married couple completed four. Total interview time per informant ranged from one to four hours (mean = 2.3 hours). Verbatim transcripts were supplemented by interview notes and transcripts were content analyzed.

Validation

Feedback was obtained by submitting conclusions back to informants (member checks). Most agreed with conclusions reached by the author and conclusions that were questioned were re-examined. Validation was further facilitated by expert checks with six foreclosure professionals, and by information gleaned through extensive reading and through attending more than 40 seminars on the business and legal aspects of foreclosure.

RESULTS: THE EXPERIENCE OF FORECLOSURE TIME PRESSURE

Interviews with homeowners in foreclosure reveal a pervasive concern with time. As expected, the experience of time pressure was largely subjective.

Perception of Inadequate Time

A virtually universal theme was the inability of homeowners to effect preferred resolutions within the foreclosure period. A number were still in the process of working out a solution and expressed that timing was crucial. Homeowners typically contended with multiple difficulties and demands.

Candace: You think "there's this deadline and we've got to get things done."

Rhonda: The most important thing is time. . . . I knew I had to solve the foreclosure and I felt like I was running out of time.

Norman: Ninety days goes by in a hell of a hurry when it comes down to selling [a house].

Al: [The hardest part is] everything happening at one time. . . . I'm so busy I don't even have time to think.

Time Pressure and the Grave Consequences of Foreclosure

Homeowners discussed concerns that exacerbated the perceived time pressure. Informants were disquieted by concerns over lost investment, altered lifestyle, damaged credit, housing availability, and the effects on their children. To the extent that they worried over these consequences, they also expressed greater concern over impending deadlines.

Rhonda: I've lived here 24 years. I raised my family here. You feel like "am I going to lose everything that I've worked for all my life?" The combination of . . . you might lose your home, and you don't want to lose what you've invested in, it feels like a disaster impending.

Donna: It's scary to know you may not have a place to live, especially when you're responsible for [a child].

Vanessa: You see all these homeless people on the street and it's real scary. . . . It's everything that you do and [all] that you think about.

Valerie: I understand that my credit is going to be ruined. I won't ever be able to buy another house.

"Buying" Time

A number of informants obtained reprieve by borrowing additional funds or by declaring bankruptcy. Nevertheless, they continued to feel time pressure. Such interim solutions "bought time" but failed to provide a decisive resolution.

Chuck and Connie: [The new loan] will take us out of foreclosure but the payments will be higher than before. So it's kind of like buying time.

Candace: [We declared] bankruptcy to stop [the foreclosure] . . . [but] it only stopped it for a short time.

Rhonda: As soon as I put [the loan] money in the bank, it was a relief. It gave me a breather. . . . But then my next thought was "now my payment is doubled and I still don't have a job. I still have to pay back that money." I would say that I bought about six months.

RESULTS: TIME PRESSURE EXACERBATED— DELAY AND PANIC

Although acutely aware of time restrictions, informants reported much delay and mismanagement of time. This exacerbated time pressure.

Denial

Informants typically were loath to accept the reality of foreclosure and initially disregarded the urgency. Several described their reaction as "denial." Most perceived the foreclosure as incongruent with their own self concepts, and several spoke of harboring unrealistic expectations as to the likelihood of restoring financial stability. Some were reticent to accept the alternatives as limited and persisted in opposing what was finally conceded to be the most suitable option.

Rhonda: To deny the reality is your first natural reaction. I was mentally postponing the truth. You want to stay in denial.

Lauren: I didn't become really concerned about my finances until . . . I was [already] about three months behind on my payments. . . . I was in denial.

Candace: I think you *can* see it coming. . . . but you just don't accept it. . . . I try to put it out of my mind. I feel that I have to. People in our position can get very sick. I'm protecting myself.

Procrastination

Informants universally expressed that they had been slow to respond to foreclosure. Some volunteered that they had procrastinated in responding to circumstances preceding the commencement of foreclosure and viewed their overdue responses as precipitating default.

Rick: I saw my income dropping off last year. I should have tried to sell my house at that time. I procrastinated. That was my fault.

Informants reported that the tendency to delay compounded the time pressure and resulted in a reduced number of viable options.

Valerie: It was May when I [first] couldn't pay the mortgage . . . but then I didn't really do anything all summer. It was about the end of August when I put [the house] up for sale.

Al: By the time I tried to borrow money I was already too far behind.

Paul: I talked to two [investors]. They aren't interested [now]. I waited too long.

Rick: I procrastinated because I didn't really think about how little time I had or how much time I needed.

Confusion

Informants expressed confusion with regard to the foreclosure process and the timing and sequence of events. This led to delay, exacerbating the time pressure.

Rhonda: It's totally strange to you and you don't know how to deal with it . . . [or] what to do first.

Norman: I never have been clear on how much time I had or what I can do.

Alice: This whole thing has made me so confused. I've made a lot of mistakes.

Panic

Sometimes the urgency precipitated a sense of panic. It was anticipated that this might prompt hasty decisions. However, most who expressed panic still delayed action.

Rhonda: It threw me into a panic. I was frantic. But I still didn't act fast enough. I still procrastinated. I really don't think you *can* act too fast.

Some expressed relief that they had avoided a panic response.

Alice: This [hard money] lender was really scamming me. They had a sucker . . . a desperate person. I was in a panic. But then [I realized] "I can't make these payments! I'll be back in foreclosure."

Rhonda: You don't want to do anything in panic that you'll end up sorry for. You don't want to just give your house away if you don't really have to.... That's what can happen if you sell under pressure.

RESULTS: DECISION MAKING UNDER FORECLOSURE TIME PRESSURE

Interviews suggest substantial variance in decision quality. Further, individual informants' decision making styles varied over the duration. Early choices frequently limited and even dictated later alternatives.

Decision Quality: Rational and Irrational Behavior

The urgency of foreclosure sometimes propelled homeowners to timely and appropriate action. A few chose a course of action by ascertaining the alternatives and weighing the consequences. As such, time pressure did not preclude rational decision making.

Lauren: I did my homework and I feel like I made an informed decision.... I talked to several attorneys, and several investors, and several lenders....

On the other hand, several volunteered that they had exercised poor judgment and made unreasoned decisions. The pressures of time interfered with their usual rationality.

Norman: I didn't know what the hell I was doing. I was desperate.... I just fell for the first hustle that came along. It was desperation. It was stupidity.

Chuck: You don't always make the best decisions when you're under so much pressure.

Motivation, Focus, and Determination versus Futility

The time pressure of foreclosure characteristically incited intense motivation. Urgency was accompanied by heightened energy, facilitating the search for solutions.

Lauren: It was scary because I was facing losing my house, but it also motivated my determination to want to save it and keep it. It's like the stress gets me more motivated.... The urgency motivated me to action.

Glenda: We'd lie awake at night worrying about losing the house, worrying about what to do next. We called [investors]. ... We tried to refinance. We tried to sell. We begged our lenders for more time.... We listed the house, and then we tried to sell it ourselves.

Al: I got more intent, more determined. I wanted to find a way.

Further, after charting a course of action, energy was focused and homeowners determinedly pursued their chosen paths.

Lauren: I was focused because I knew what the deadline was and I *had* to stay focused. It was about ... staying focused on what I had to do.

Rhonda: Determination—that's the good thing. After you get over the hurt and the disappointment and the humiliation, you start to fight back. You focus and you start fighting for yourself.... You don't think about anything else. I'm so focused, so determined.

Bill: I didn't just sit back and wait. When the house didn't sell, I took it off the market and tried another real estate agent. I've gone through three realty companies. I've dropped the price. I've raised the commission.... Now I'm dealing with investors.

Al: Going through foreclosure is a crisis, and this is crisis management.

On the other hand, as the foreclosure progressed and time pressure intensified, the heightened motivation and productivity sometimes gave way to futility.

Rick: This house is going to be auctioned off. I can't stop the foreclosure now. I'm just going to wait for them to evict me. I'm going to have to just swallow my pride and live with the fact that I lost my house.

Donna: I worked really hard for a long time to try to save my house, to try to scrape together money to make up my payments. And then I thought "this is *stupid*. This isn't working. I'm not going to be able to do it." I started to see it as inevitable that I would lose my house.

Stereotyped Behavior versus Creative Problem Solving

Interviews suggest that homeowners under foreclosure time pressure frequently engage in stereotyped behavior, pursuing familiar but inappropriate strategies. For example, several who attempted to sell their homes persisted in treating the situation as "real estate as usual," thereby disregarding the exigencies of selling under foreclosure time constraints.

On the other hand, some eventually identified and attempted to effect creative solutions. The pursuit of unique and nonconventional alternatives demonstrates a capacity to engage in innovative behavior despite the pressures of time.

Glenda: We have a friend who is going to buy our house. Whatever the balance is that we owe, that will be the price. We'll rent it back [by paying his] mortgage payment.

Bill: [An investor] will buy the house for what I owe and pay off the loans. It's better than going to foreclosure sale and being evicted.

Information Use versus Disregard

Informants displayed tremendous variance in propensity to obtain and use information. Some actively sought input and advice while others disregarded counsel even from professionals whom they had hired.

Lauren: The thing that I did know to do was to ask a lot of questions, find out what other people have done or what other people could do for me, and not trust one point of view.... I wanted to get some education and make decisions based on knowing the way this works.

Chuck: We've tried to get information from different sources. The Small Business Administration, ... companies that do credit repair, ... acquaintances who have been through this, . . . lenders and investors.

Several expressed that the influx of information in the form of solicitation heightened their confusion.

Rhonda: You're flooded with telephone calls and letters and people at your door day and night.... I personally found it very confusing and emotionally upsetting.

Norman: I've got a whole stack of letters. I've been trying to sort through them but there are so many it's a full-time job.

Homeowners overwhelmed by the number of solicitations ignored potentially useful information.

Chuck and Connie: Sometimes we got too many letters at once and we just tossed them.... You start to feel overwhelmed. You don't even want to look at them.

Candace: When the foreclosure first started, we'd get a stack of letters every day.... Most of the stuff I threw in the trash. There was too much.

TOWARD A CLASSIFICATION OF TIME PRESSURE RESPONSES

Based on interviews with homeowners in foreclosure, it is suggested that responses to time pressure are contingent upon the degree or intensity of both *objective time pressure* (clock time, calendar time) and *subjective time pressure* (perceived urgency). Figure 2 presents a proposed classification.

The classification suggests a generally curvilinear relationship between time pressure and productivity. It is inferred that productivity (i.e., effectiveness, efficiency, activity, deliberation) is enhanced when the intensity of *either* objective or subjective time pressure is defined as "moderate" and the intensity of the other is defined as "high." In comparison, when *both* objective and subjective time pressures are defined as "moderate," the urgency is less acute and productivity suffers. Finally, when *both* are defined as "high," the urgency may be experienced as so intense that productivity gives way to panic or even futility.

Quadrant 1 represents the condition under which both objective and subjective time pressures are classified as "moderate." In the foreclosure context, it corresponds to the relatively early stages. The homeowner is aware of deadlines but may fail to acknowledge the urgency. He or she perceives that there will be adequate time to effect a resolution without immediate attention or singular effort.

As shown, Quadrant 1 is associated with *denial, procrastination,* and *stereotyped behavior.* Consumers may deny the magnitude of time pressure, procrastinate appropriate action, and/or engage in behavior that is familiar but not appropriate given time constraints. Homeowners in foreclosure may ignore deadlines, harbor delusions of having "plenty of time," and repudiate the necessity for timely and inventive action. For example, they may defer obtaining a new loan, put off trying to sell, or persist in demanding full market value rather than pricing to achieve a timely sale.

Quadrant 2 represents a "moderate" degree of objective time pressure and a "high" degree of subjective time pressure. Although it is still relatively early in the foreclosure process, the homeowner experiences deadlines as imminent, perceives intense urgency, and is compelled to proceed toward resolution.

This quadrant is primarily associated with *heightened energy, motivation,* and *creative problem solving,* and secondarily associated with the possibility of *panic.* In general, enhanced productivity is suggested. Homeowners in foreclosure may experience significant urgency, motivating a vigorous search for information and alternatives. This urgency also may facilitate heightened energy, providing the stamina required to effect a timely resolution. Alternatively, the urgency may compel the homeowner to panic, prompting hasty and ill-considered actions.

Quadrant 3 represents a "high" degree of objective time pressure but only a "moderate" degree of subjective time pressure. It is now relatively late in the foreclosure process and the homeowner has identified a viable course of action. Although the situation will require sustained effort and attention to time constraints, there is perceived to be an acceptable probability of resolution.

As shown, Quadrant 3 is associated with *directed energy, focus,* and *determination.* Consumers are focused on well-defined objectives, are determined to implement their plans, and have directed their energies toward chosen strategies. Extraneous activity is abandoned as the individual strives to obtain maximum results from limited time. In the case of foreclosure, homeowners have identified a viable course of action and are focused on implementation. For example, efforts may be directed toward consummating a home sale or obtaining a new loan.

Finally, in Quadrant 4 both objective and subjective time pressures are "high." It is late in the foreclosure process and the homeowner is acutely aware that there may be inadequate time to effect a satisfactory resolution.

This quadrant is associated with *panic* or *futility.* Homeowners may make a concluding effort to avoid the ultimate foreclosure—perhaps by committing to a "hard money" loan or by contracting to sell at a "forced sale" price. Alternatively, they may conclude that it is "too late" and simply give up.

IMPLICATIONS AND DIRECTIONS FOR FUTURE RESEARCH

This qualitative study has contributed a degree of richness and holistic perspective to the current understanding of time pressure in consumer behavior. However, the study has necessarily examined time pressure in only one rather exceptional context. It is recommended that future work investigate time pressure in other "real life" consumer contexts such as Christmas shopping, shopping while caring for small children, and shopping where store hours are restricted. Broadening the focus will aid in validating the findings presented herein and contribute additional insight into the experience of time pressure.

Second, there already exists a small but growing body of experimentation employing time pressure as an independent variable. It is suggested that the objective and subjective time pressure constructs that define the quadrants of Figure 2 be operationalized and utilized as independent variables in future experimental designs. The curvilinear relationship between productivity and time pressure observed in this exploratory study may then be formally tested in various consumer contexts.

Third, the classification in Figure 2 suggests a number of variables and relationships that merit specific study. For example, it is suggested that homeowners in foreclosure tend to procrastinate when both objective and subjective time pressures are defined as "moderate." Future research might explore this prediction in other consumer contexts or even pursue a phenomenological understanding of procrastination.

Finally, while legislation to protect homeowners in foreclosure has sought to safeguard defaulting borrowers from the consequences of panic, interviews with homeowners suggest that denial and procrastination are more probable responses. Rather than acting hastily, homeowners in foreclosure are likely to delay. Efforts to validate this conclusion and clarify its consequences may foster public policy directly benefiting homeowners/borrowers.

FIGURE 2
Classification of Responses to Time Pressure

Degree of Subjective Time Pressure / Perceived Urgency

Degree of Objective Time Pressure	MODERATE	HIGH
MODERATE (early in the foreclosure process)	**1** • Denial • Procrastination • Stereotyped Behavior	**2** • Heightened Energy • Motivation • Creative Problem Solving • (Possible Panic)
HIGH (late in the foreclosure Process)	**3** • Directed Energy • Focus • Determination	**4** • Panic • Futility

REFERENCES

Bettman, James R. (1979), *An Information Processing Theory of Consumer Choice*. Reading, MA: Addison-Wesley.

Bronner, Rolf (1982), *Decision Making Under Time Pressure: An Experimental Study of Stress Behavior in Business Management*. Lexington, MA: Lexington Books.

Bruner, Jerome S., Jacqueline J. Goodnow, and George A. Austin (1956), *A Study of Thinking*. New York: John Wiley & Sons.

Friend, Kenneth E. (1982), "Stress and Performance: Effects of Subjective Work Load and Time Urgency," *Personnel Psychology*, 35 (Autumn), 623-633.

Gross, Barbara L. (1987), "Time Scarcity: Interdisciplinary Perspectives and Implications for Consumer Behavior," in *Research in Consumer Behavior*, Vol. 2, Jagdish N. Sheth and Elizabeth Hirschman, eds. Greenwich, CT: JAI Press, 1-54.

Hawes, Douglass K. (1980), "The Time Variable in Models of Consumer Behavior," in *Advances in Consumer Research*, Vol. 7, Jerry C. Olson, ed. Ann Arbor, MI: Association for Consumer Research, 442-447.

Hirschman, Elizabeth C. (1987), "Theoretical Perspectives of Time Use: Implications for Consumer Behavior Research," in *Research in Consumer Behavior*, Vol. 2, Jagdish N. Sheth and Elizabeth Hirschman, eds. Greenwich, CT: JAI Press, 55-81.

Howard, John A. (1963), *Marketing Management: Analysis and Planning*, Revised Edition. Homewood, IL: Richard D. Irwin.

_____ and Jagdish N. Sheth (1969), *The Theory of Buyer Behavior*. New York: John Wiley & Sons.

Isenberg, Daniel J. (1981), "Some Effects of Time-Pressure on Vertical Structure and Decision-Making in Small Groups," *Organizational Behavior and Human Performance*, 27 (February), 119-134.

Iyer, Easwar S. (1989), "Unplanned Purchasing: Knowledge of Shopping Environment and Time Pressure," *Journal of Retailing*, 65 (Spring), 40-57.

Janis, Irving L. and Leon Mann (1977), *Decision Making: A Psychological Analysis of Conflict, Choice, and Commitment*. New York: Free Press.

Kaufman, Carol J. and Paul M. Lane (1990), "The Intentions and Extensions of the Time Concept: Contributions from a Sociological Perspective," in *Advances in Consumer Research*, Vol. 17, Marvin E. Goldberg, Gerald Gorn, and Richard W. Pollay, eds. Provo, UT: Association for Consumer Research, 895-901.

Latham, Gary P. and Edwin A. Locke (1975), "Increasing Productivity with Decreasing Time Limits: A Field Replication of Parkinson's Law," *Journal of Applied Psychology*, 60 (August), 524-526.

Lutz, Richard J. (1989), "Editorial," *Journal of Consumer Research*, 16 (June, September).

McCracken, Grant (1988), *The Long Interview*. Newbury Park, CA: Sage Publications.

Schouten, John W. (1991), "Selves in Transition: Symbolic Consumption in Personal Rites of Passage and Identity Reconstruction," *Journal of Consumer Research*, 17 (March), 412-425.

Strauss, Anselm and Juliet Corbin (1990), *Basics of Qualitative Research: Grounded Theory Procedures and Techniques*. Newbury Park, CA: Sage Publications.

Stroud, John M. (1955), "The Fine Structure of Psychological Time," in *Information Theory in Psychology: Problems and Methods*, Henry Quastler, ed. Glencoe, IL: Free Press, 174-207.

Wright, Peter (1974), "The Harassed Decision Maker: Time Pressures, Distractions, and the Use of Evidence," *Journal of Applied Psychology*, 59 (October), 555-561.

The Effect of Stress on Price Sensitivity and Comparison Shopping

Linda K. Anglin, Mankato State University
J. Kathleen Stuenkel, University of Wisconsin-LaCrosse
Lawrence R. Lepisto, Central Michigan University

ABSTRACT

Stress is a common issue for many consumers yet little attention has been paid to the role of stress in consumer research. This paper empirically examines the role of chronic stress on price sensitivity and comparison shopping. Results indicate that measures of time consciousness, life events, and marital satisfaction have a positive and significant effect on price sensitivity and comparison shopping. The need for novelty was also positively related to both behaviors, while locus of control contributed only to the price sensitivity equation.

INTRODUCTION

The role of stress in the day-to-day lives of people has received extensive coverage in the lay press and in academic research. While stress has been shown to be a potent issue in the lives of many people, little has been done to examine the role of stress in consumer behavior. The purpose of this paper is to study empirically the effect of stress on price sensitivity and comparison shopping.

STRESS

The issues of stress are extremely complex due in part to the conceptualization of stress. A clear delineation has not been made in the literature between stress and stressors. Morse and Furst (1979) note that although Seyle coined the term "stressor" for causative factors in 1950, other researchers since then have failed to differentiate between factors and reactions (stress) thus leading to the current situation where both the cause and result are called "stress". Adding to the confusion, stressors can be classified as physical, social and psychological (Morse and Furst 1979); and in terms of intensity and duration (Schafer 1978). While physical stressors are external factors such as drugs, food, and noise; social stressors or life-change events result from the interaction of the individual with his/her environment (e.g., death of a loved one, divorce, job loss, or financial difficulty). Psychological stressors are intense emotions (e.g. worry, anger, or fear) that are brought on by physical or social stressors. Stress intensity reflects a continuum from the 'little hassles of daily life' to the more intense pressures such as death or divorce. Finally, duration refers to how long the pressure exists. Short-term stressors (e.g., last minute shopping) are acute or momentary conditions, while chronic stressors (e.g., managing career and household, income conditions, or family strains) last over a longer period of time.

Maes, Vingerhoets and Heck (1987, p. 546) define stress as "a state of imbalance within a person, elicited by an actual or perceived disparity between environmental demands and the person's capacity to cope with these demands." This definition suggests that stress can be examined in consumer behavior as a situational influence (Lepisto, Stuenkel and Anglin 1991). When examined from the *interactionist approach*, stress can be included as a person-bound variable (a predisposition or stressor brought to the situation) or as a response to some situational cue (even not in the presence of a stress-related predisposition).

While acute stressors could be considered to affect some specific aspects of consumer behavior, more chronic stressors may affect those behavioral characteristics that tend to be more enduring in the consumer (e.g., their price sensitivity or tendency to comparison shop). In addition, situational (acute) stress can be avoided by avoiding the issue whereas chronic stress is more permanent and, therefore, present in all situations. Three types of stressors were selected for inclusion in this study: life events and marital satisfaction (chronic social stressors) and time consciousness (chronic psychological stressor).

Correlates of Stress

Life Events. It is widely accepted in the social science literature that life status changes have a profound psychological effect on individuals (see, for example, Hendrix, Steel, and Schultz 1987). While these effects are generally deemed as detrimental to a person's well-being, these more chronic stressors, may actually diminish the effects of daily hassles (Caspi, Bolger and Eckenrode 1987). These researchers suggest that experience in coping with major life events provides the individual with feedback on effective and ineffective ways to cope with stress. Such experiential learning may then carry over to subsequent stressors and coping strategies on the daily level.

While consumer behavior may be less dramatic in context, elevated stress levels induced by life status changes can have important potential effects on buyer behavior. Andreasen (1984) suggests that stress may lead to increased dissatisfaction with life in general and with product and service choices in particular, and this can lead to changes in consumption behavior or cause consumers to cling to present patterns of behavior as a means of coping.

Marital Satisfaction. Considerable research has documented an association between marital stress and occupational stress (Burke 1986); marital stress and depression, psychological symptoms, self-dissatisfaction, self-reported health, and activity scope (Chiriboga and Dean 1978); and marital stress and the consumption of alcohol (Bromet et al. 1988).

It is clear that the role of marital satisfaction as a stressor has been widely documented under a number of conditions. Even though no study has addressed the role of marital satisfaction as a stressor in the consumer behavior literature, it does appear likely, given its wide spread effect, that marital satisfaction would also act as a stressor in a consumption situation.

Time Consciousness. In keeping with the framework of situational influence, Belk's (1974) temporal characteristic relates to stress due to time constraints. Time and stress are related when a disparity between environmental demands and the person's capacity to cope with these demands exists. This disparity of demands and available time is common in such situations as two-income households (Burke 1986, Lewis and Cooper 1987) and in persons experiencing job-related stress. In contrast, for older consumers, the excess of available time associated with retirement is often found to be stressful (Palmore et. al., 1979).

Coping With Stress

When a consumer is in a stressful situation, efforts are made to cope with that stress. In general, coping is seen as being either problem-focused or emotion-focused (Folkman and Lazarus 1988). Problem-focused coping is done when individuals address a problem directly by gathering new information and/or learning new skills. On the other hand, emotion-focused coping focuses on managing the emotions aroused by the stressor. According to Scheier, Weintraub, and Carver (1988), individuals manage emotion by seeking social support (moral support, sympathy, or understanding).

The literature generally identifies coping in response to acute (vs. chronic) stress as inhibiting effective decision making and information processing (e.g. Goldberger and Breznitz 1982; Janis and Mann 1977). However, it is important to note that stress does not always have a negative impact. In some situations stress can be an energizer resulting in increased motivation (Kahn et al. 1964) or an incentive that forces a person to be more thorough and complete (Janis and Mann 1977). Chiriboga and Dean (1978) suggest that stress (measured as life events) may well be associated with long-term growth. In Sjoberg's 1981 life situation study, "instrumental actions" (toward a goal) tended to be deeper in intention, and also tended to be carried out in somewhat more tense and unpleasant moods.

Stress and Price Sensitivity

According to Monroe (1973), "Price perception research has progressed from single-cue studies to investigations where the influence of several other variables has been examined. However, many of these studies have not considered adequately the influence of the specific context or situation on the price perception task" pp. 49. Belk (1975) suggests that adaptation-level theory provides a framework from which to study contextual influences on buyers' perception of price.

The adaptation level (AL) provides a frame of reference to which behavior is relative (Helson 1964). According to Monroe (1973), focal stimuli, when applied to pricing, refers to the stimuli to which a consumer directly responds, whereas the contextual stimuli are all other stimuli in the situation which provide the context within which the focal stimuli are judged. Although, in a pricing context, AL has been typically defined as a reference price, some difficulty has been encountered in trying to establish an exact definition of reference price (McConell 1968; Olander 1970; Shapiro 1968).

Thus according to Monroe and Petroshius (1981) the concept of situational influence can be used to evaluate price perception because it has been established that consumers judge prices differently depending on the context prevailing at the time and the predisposition (e.g., being more or less stressed) the buyer brings to the purchase situation.

Having established that price perception should be studied situationally and that stress can be viewed as a situational influence (Lepisto, Stuenkel, and Anglin 1991), it would follow that the degree to which consumers are predisposed to be stressed can affect their perception of price. The manner in which the individual responds to stress constitutes the coping mechanism. When shopping, a stressed consumer may search for a lower price to serve as an indicator of a good purchase decision which will increase the consumer's inner sense of control and self-confidence (problem-focused coping). On the other hand, stressed individuals may use low prices to serve as public indicators of good shopping habits (emotion-focused coping). Given this reasoning, the following hypothesis has been developed:

H1: Consumers experiencing higher stress levels will demonstrate a higher level of price sensitivity.

Stress and Comparison Shopping

Individuals shop for more complex reasons than simply acquiring a product. Diversion from routine activities, exercise, sensory stimulation, social interactions, learning about new trends, and even acquiring interpersonal power have been reported as nonpurchase reasons for shopping (Bellenger and Korgaonkar 1990; Tauber 1972). Given these differing motivations for shopping, Moschis (1976) observed that shoppers possessing different orientations and motivations for shopping also demonstrate different information needs.

While many factors influence the amount of external search performed by the consumer, the major determinants of the degree of external search include costs vs. benefits of information, the choice situation (such as the difficulty of the choice task, and time pressure) and individual differences (such as in-store vs. prior processing, abilities, and concern with optimality of the choice) (Bettman 1979). From this description, it would appear that comparison shopping also can be viewed in a situational context. Specifically, from Belk's (1974) view of situational influence, a consumer's mood and antecedent state can have a major influence on purchase decisions, including a consumer's decision to comparison shop. Therefore, the level of stress a consumer brings to the shopping situation may impact their propensity to comparison shop.

Comparison shopping and search are forms of information seeking. Information seeking, a major component of problem-focused coping (Ashford 1988), enhances the predictability of a situation and this is thought to help individuals avoid future difficulties, deal with present ones, and increase their sense of control and confidence. Consistent with this idea is Tauber's (1972) identification of shopping as an arena where consumers derive satisfaction from finding exactly what they have been looking for, and that satisfaction serves two types of motivations, namely a sense of achievement and mastery over the choice environment. As such, comparison shopping may reflect growth in consumer decision making.

When considering emotion-focused coping, consumers may view shopping as role enactment which describes the motivation to identify with and assume a culturally prescribed role regarding the conduct of shopping activity. Generally, these roles prescribe normative behavior, such as careful product and price comparisons, searching for optimum value, etc. Thus, these shoppers seek ego-enhancement by adding satisfying shopping roles to existing self-concepts (Westbrook and Black 1985).

Chiriboga and Dean (1978) suggest that the readjustment demands of the life events fall within the capabilities of the organism to cope, stress may well be associated with growth. The data implies that stressors may be associated with long-term growth and development in certain situations. As such, comparison shopping may reflect growth in consumer decision-making.

H2: The higher the level of stress, the greater one's propensity to comparison shop.

Individual Characteristics

Although it is reasonable to assume that higher levels of stress have an overall negative physiological and psychological effect on individuals, it would seem likely that these effects vary from person to person and are mediated by specific individual difference variables. In this regard, two such predispositions were selected for inclusion, locus of control and need for novelty.

Locus of Control. Locus of control refers to an individual's subjective perception of a reinforcing event and evaluation as to whether or not that event is contingent upon ones own actions. Externals interpret an event as "luck, chance, fate, as under the control of powerful others, or as unpredictable: while internals interpret an event as contingent on one's "own behavior" or "own relatively permanent characteristics" (Rotter 1966). Numerous studies have documented the moderating effect of locus of control on stress (Caldwell, Pearson, and Chin 1987; Morgan et al. 1986). Common findings suggest that internals experience less distress in response to stressors than externals and achieve better outcomes to the stressful situations than do externals (Parkes 1984) due to more use of task-centered coping mechanisms (Anderson 1977).

Thus stressed internals would be more likely to perceive comparison shopping and searching for lower prices as positive activities leading to a positive outcome. Stressed externals, on the other hand, would be more likely to perceive comparison shopping and searching for lower prices as useless activities since externals do not believe that their own behavior affects the outcome.

Need for Novelty. Joachimsthaler and Lastovicka (1984) report that optimal stimulation level and personality traits (locus of control) directly affect consumer exploratory behavior. Hirschman (1980) suggests that novelty seeking serves as a means of self-preservation. The individual may find it useful to create a "bank" of potentially useful knowledge. Because the future is unknowable and unexpected, consumption problems are almost inevitable; the consumer may wisely decide to seek information that is not "useful" now, but may assume great importance in the future.

A second complementary explanation for novelty seeking is that it functions to improve problem-solving skills (problem-focused coping). That is, the consumer may seek information pertaining to presently adopted products and consumption situations in an effort to improve his/her performance. Additionally, individuals with high stimulation ideals may seek information because of a genuine desire to explore something unfamiliar, while individuals with low stimulation needs may seek information to reduce the risk of trying an unfamiliar product (Raju 1980; Price and Ridgway 1982).

A stressed consumer may be more predisposed to engage in novelty seeking in order to enhance the predictability of future situations and maintain a sense of control and confidence. By "banking" product information a consumer may feel more confident about making good decisions under all circumstances.

METHODOLOGY

Sample

The data for this study were taken from the national Adult Longitudinal Panel, Central Michigan University. Of the 28,000 surveys mailed, 4,131 adults responded for a 15 percent response rate. Due to missing data, the effective sample size was reduced to 3031 for this analysis.

Measures

Indicators of Stress. Measurement scales and their respective descriptive statistics can be found in Table 1. All scales were factor analyzed for psychometric properties. Selected indicators of stress include time pressure, marital satisfaction, and the occurrence of major life events. Perceived control over one's time was measured using a three item Time Consequences Scale. Marital Satisfaction, an index of 10 items, reflects one's satisfaction with different facets of marriage including communication, conflict resolution, financial position, parental responsibility, and relationships (Olson, Fournier and Druckman 1981)

The third indicator of stress, the presence of life change events during the past 12 months, was measured via the commonly used Social Readjustment Rating Scale (Holmes and Rahe 1967). The original scale containing 43 events was reduced to 42. This study added the events without weighting each event because previous findings suggest both approaches generate similar correlations with behavior (Grant et al. 1978; Zimmerman 1983).

Price Sensitivity. Price sensitivity was evaluated using a three-item scale that assessed the degree to which consumers prefer and search for lower prices.

Comparison Shopping. One's propensity to comparison shop was measured via six items which reflect the extent to which one compares products and prices.

Individual Characteristics. Locus of Control was measured using items adapted from Rotter's scale (1966) for internal versus external control. Five items reflecting one's desire to try new and different products were used to operationalize one's Need for Novelty.

Analysis

Five independent variables were used in two multiple regression analyses with price sensitivity and comparison shopping as the dependent variables. Correlations among the independent variables are reported in Table 2.

RESULTS

The regression results, summarized in Table 3, indicate that both price sensitivity and comparison shopping are related positively to the three measures of stress. As people experience increased conflict from how they manage their time and incur more stress producing events, the more likely they are to be price sensitive and the greater their likelihood to engage in comparison shopping. While one would expect increased marital satisfaction to indicate a less stressful situation, it too contributed significantly to the regression equations. As the need for novelty increases, so does ones price sensitivity and their propensity to comparison shop. Although locus of control acted as a mediating variable for price sensitivity, it was not a significant variable in the shopping equation.

DISCUSSION

Findings tended to support the notion that consumers in high stress situations would demonstrate higher levels of price sensitivity and comparison shopping. Specifically, those individuals that suffered from time pressures and a high number of life status changes tended to spend more time comparison shopping and were more price sensitive. While intuitively this may seem backwards, an examination of coping patterns suggests that stressed individuals engaging in either problem-focused or emotion-focused coping would tend to gather information, although for different purposes.

Marital satisfaction, on the other hand, did not perform as expected. Although the relationships between marital satisfaction and comparative shopping, and marital satisfaction and price sensitivity were significant, the expected direction of each relationship was different. It was expected that high degrees of marital satisfaction would result in less stress for the individuals and, therefore, less comparison shopping and less price sensitivity—negative relationships. However, weak positive relationships were found indicating that high marital satisfaction contributed to a greater propensity to comparison shop and a greater propensity to be price sensitive than high levels of marital stress. This surprise may be due in part to the nature of marital satisfaction. Chiriboga and Dean (1978) found that marital stress was the only one of nine preoccupation measures to consistently and universally result in a decline in all measures of psychosocial adjustment and that the magnitude of the relationships were in each case strong. Moreover, the effects of marital stress did not vary over time as did all other measures of negative preoccupation. In light of this finding, it is possible that marital stress actually constitutes a high enough level of stress to cause an individual to engage in coping mechanisms that are not as constructive as emotion- or problem-focused coping. In either case, information seeking and processing would be impaired to such a level that even moderate levels of comparison shopping and price sensitivity may seem high in comparison.

TABLE 1
Measurement Scales

	Range	Mean	S.D.	alpha
Life Events*	0-22	3.17	2.72	—
Marital Satisfaction*	8-56	42.34	10.03	.83
Time Consciousness	3-21	17.53	4.69	.55
I feel rushed to do the things I have to do.				
I frequently do two things at once.				
Daily responsibilities take up most of my energy.				
Locus Of Control	6-42	14.49	7.03	.80
I feel I am not in control of my life.				
I feel that whether or not I am successful is just a matter of luck and chance, rather than my own doing.				
I feel that others are running my life for me.				
I have a hard time finding a meaningful direction for my life.				
I have difficulty making plans for the future (for example, marriage or career plans).				
I have a hard time knowing what to do when I have a problem.				
Novelty Seeking	7-49	29.72	7.42	.81
I usually buy new products before my friends do.				
I like to try new products when they come on the market.				
When I see a new brand on the shelf I often buy it just to see what it's like.				
I often try new brands before my friends and neighbors do.				
I like to try new and different things.				
Price Sensitivity	3-21	14.52	4.65	.76
I shop a lot for specials.				
I find myself checking the prices in the grocery store even for small items.				
I usually watch the advertisements for announcements of sales.				
Comparison Shopping	6-42	32.46	6.86	.80
I carefully compare prices before buying items.				
When I shop, I usually go to several different stores to get the best prices.				
I carefully evaluate most products before I buy them.				
When I buy products, I can usually identify the best available.				
Before I buy more expensive things I always compare what different stores offer.				
I typically pick brands that have the best warranties.				

*Please see original source for scale items.

Locus of control served to mediate the relationship between stress and price sensitivity. Interestingly, the relationship was positive indicating that externals were more likely to be price sensitive than internals. This specifically supports the notion that searching for and finding a lower price serves as social support for emotion control. No significant relationship was found between locus of control and comparison shopping. On the other hand, novelty seeking resulted in a significant and positive relationship with price sensitivity and comparison shopping. Consumers are likely to seek out new products that will help reduce their stress. Those suffering from time pressures might seek time-saving products while those suffering stress from a divorce or lost spouse might seek out new products that would make life easier for them.

Future research can take direction from suggestions offered in the stress literature. Specifically, research needs to be done to develop methods of measuring stress in a consumer behavior

TABLE 2
Correlations Among The Independent Variables

	Life Events	Marital Satisfaction	Time	Locus Control	Novelty	Price Sensitivity
Marital Satisfaction	-.15					
Time	-.01	.06				
Locus of Control	.13	-.45	.05			
Novelty	.07	.03	.10	-.02		
Price Sensitivity	.05	.01	.38	.08	.22	
Comparison Shopping	.03	.09	.81	.08	.19	.52

TABLE 3
Summary of Multivariate Regression

	Dependent Variables Raw Regression Coefficients[a]	
	Price Sensitivity	Comparison Shopping
Independent Variables		
Time Consequences	.68 (28.99)	1.15 (76.63)[b]
Life Events	.09 (2.29)	.08 (3.03)
Marital Satisfaction	.05 (2.45)	.03 (2.10)
Mediating Variables		
Locus of Control	.09 (4.58)	ns
Novelty	.21 (12.18)	.13 (12.03)
F-ratio	156.89	904.32
Adj R^2[c]	.26	.68
n	3031	3031

Notes: a) All regression coefficients are significant at p<.05
b) Values in parentheses are t-ratios
c) All Adj R^2 are significant at p<.0001

context. While a variety of measurement approaches are available (and used for this study), it is still not clear which scales will be most appropriate for consumer research. In addition, measures addressing consumer coping mechanisms should also be developed.

Once scales have been developed, the roles of chronic and acute stress must be differentiated. This is a very complex issue that must be examined from a temporal perspective. Chronic stress would be expected to relate more to long-term lifestyle changes while acute stress would likely cause more defined short-term alterations in behavior. While existing literature places a high degree of importance on the role of temporal factors, most empirical studies have looked at stress as a static variable, and have overlooked the adaptive capacities of consumers.

REFERENCES

Anderson, C. R. (1977), "Locus of Control, Coping Behaviors and Performance in a Stress Setting: A Longitudinal Study," *Journal of Applied Psychology*, 62, 446-451.

Andreasen, A. (1984), "Life Status Changes and Changes in Consumer Preferences and Satisfaction," *Journal of Consumer Research*, 11, 784-794.

Ashford, Susan J. (1988), "Individual Strategies for Coping with Stress During Organizational Transitions," *The Journal of Applied Behavioral Science*, 24 (1), 19-36.

Belk, R.W. (1975), "Situational Variables and Consumer Behavior," *Journal of Consumer Research*, 2 (December), 157-164.

Bellenger, D.N. and P. K. Korgaonkar (1980), "Profiling the Recreational Shopper," *Journal of Retailing*, (Fall), 77-82.

Bettman, James R. (1970), "Information Processing Models of Consumer Behavior," *Journal of Marketing Research*, 7, 370-376.

(1979), *An Information Processing Theory of Consumer Choice*, Reading, MA: Addison-Wesley.

Bromet, Evelyn J., Mary Amanda Dew, David K. Parkinson and Herbert C. Schulberg (1988), "Predictive Effects of Occupational and Marital Stress on the Mental Health of a Male Workforce," *Journal of Organizational Behavior*, 9, 1-13.

Burke, Ronald J. (1986), "Occupational and Life Stress and the Family: Conceptual Frameworks and Research Findings," *International Review of Applied Psychology*, 35, 347-369.

Caldwell, Robert A., Jane L. Pearson, and Raymond J. Chin (1987), "Stress-Moderating Effects: Social Support in the Context of Gender and Locus of Control," *Personality and Social Psychology Bulletin*, 13, 5-17.

Caspi, Avshalom, Niall Bolger, and John Eckenrode (1987), "Linking Person and Context in the Daily Stress Process," *Journal of Personality and Social Psychology*, 52 (1), 184-195.

Chiriboga, David A. and Hannah Dean (1978), "Dimensions of Stress: Perspectives From A Longitudinal Study," *Journal of Psychosomatic Research*, 22, 47-55.

Folkman, S. and R. Lazarus (1980), "An Analysis of Coping in a Middle-Aged Community Sample," *Journal of Health and Social Behavior*, 21, 219-239.

Goldberger, L. and Breznitz (1982), *Handbook of Stress: Theoretical and Clinical Aspects*, New York: The Free Press.

Grant, I., H. Sweetwood, M. Gerst, and J. Yager (1978), "Scaling Procedures in Life Events Research," *Journal of Psychosomatic Research*, 525-530.

Helson, Harry (1964), *Adaptation-level Theory*, New York: Harper & Row.

Hendrix, W., R. Steel and S. Schultz (1987), "Job Stress and Life Stress:Their Causes and consequences," *Journal of Social Behavior and Personality*, 2, 291-302.

Hirschman, Elizabeth C. (1980), "Innovativeness, Novelty Seeking, and Consumer Creativity," *Journal of Consumer Research*, 7 (December), 283-295.

Holmes, R. and R. Rahe (1967), "The Social Readjustment Rating Scale," *Journal of Psychosomatic Research*, 11, 213-218.

Janis, I. and L. Mann (1977), *Decision Making: A Psychological Analysis of Conflict, Choice, and Commitment*, New York: Free Press.

Joachimsthaler, Erich A. and John L. Lastovicka (1984), "Optimal Stimulation Level-Exploratory Behavior Models," *Journal of Consumer Research*, 11 (December), 830-835.

Kahn, R. L., D. M. Wolfe, R. P. Quinn, J. D. Snock, and R. A. Rosenthal (1964), *Organizational Stress*, New York: Wiley.

Lepisto, L., J. K. Stuenkel, and K. Anglin (1991), "Stress: An Ignored Situational Variable," *Advances in Consumer Research*, 18, eds. Rebecca H. Holman and Michael R. Solomon, Association for Consumer Research, 296-302.

Lewis S. N. and C. L. Cooper (1987), "Stress in Two-Earner Couples and Stage in the Life-Cycle," *Journal of Occupational Psychology*, 60, 289-303.

Maes, S., A. Vingerhoets, and E. Van Heck (1987), "The Study of Stress and Disease: Some Developments and Requirements," *Social Science Medicine*, 25, 567-578.

McConnell J. Douglas (1968), "An Experimental Examination of the Price/Quality Relationship," *Journal of Business*, 41, 439-44.

Monroe, Kent B. (1973), "Buyers' Subjective Perception of Price," *Journal of Marketing Research*, 10, 70-80.

and Susan M. Petroshius (1981) "Buyers' Perceptions of Price: An Update of the Evidence" in *Perspectives in Consumer Behavior*, 3rd ed., eds. Harold H. Kassarjian and Thomas S. Robertson, Glenview, IL: Scott Foresman and Company 43-55.

Moschis, George P. (1976), "Shopping Orientations and Consumer Uses of Information," *Journal of Retailing*, 52, 61-70.

Morgan, Charles H., Owen, Dean W., Jr., Miller, Arden, and Watts, Martha L. (1986), "Variations in Stress Responses as a Function of Cognitive and Personality Variables," *Psychological Reports*, 59, 575-583.

Morse, D.R. and M.L. Furst (1979), *Stress for Success*, New York: Van Nostrand Reinhold.

Olander, Folke (1970), "The Influence of Price on the Consumer's Evaluation of Products and Purchases," in *Pricing Strategy*, eds. Bernard Taylor and Gordon Wills, Princeton, NJ: Brandon Systems Press, 50-69.

Olson, D., D. fournier and J. Druckman (1981), Marital Satisfaction Sub-Scale from *ENRICH*, Family Social Science, University of Minnesota.

Palmore, E., W. P. Cleveland, J. B. Nowlin, D. Ramm, and I. C. Siegler (1979), *Journal of Gerontology*, 34 (6), 841-851.

Parkes, Katharine R. (1984), "Locus of Control, Cognitive Appraisal, and Coping in Stressful Episodes," *Journal of Personality and Social Psychology*, 46, 655-668.

Price, Linda L. and Nancy M. Ridgway (1982), "Use Innovativeness, Vicarious Exploration and Purchase Exploration: Three Facets of Consumer Varied Behavior," *Proceedings of the American Marketing Association*, 56-60.

Raju, P.S. (1980), "Optimum Stimulation Level: Its Relationship to Personality, Demographics, and Exploratory Behavior," *Journal of Consumer Research*, 7 (December), 272-282.

Rotter, J. B. (1966), "Generalized Expectancies for Internal versus External Control of Reinforcement," *Psychological Monographs*, 80.

Schafer, Walt (1978), *Stress, Distress and Growth*, Davis, CA: Responsible Action.

Scheier, Michael F., Jagdish K. Weintraub and Charles S. Carver (1986), "Coping with Stress: Divergent Strategies of Optimists and Pessimists," *Journal of Personality and Social Psychology*, 51 (6), 1257-1264.

Shapiro, Benson (1968), "The Psychology of Pricing," *Harvard Business Review*, 46, 14-8, 20, 22, 24-25, 160.

Sjoberg, L. (1981), "Life Situations and Episodes as a Basis for Situational Influence on Action," in *Toward a Psychology of Situations: An Interactional Approach*, ed., David Magnusson, New Jersey: Lawrence Erlbaum Associates, 259-274.

Tauber, E.M. (1972), "Why Do People Shop?," *Journal of Marketing*, (October), 46-49.

Westbrook, Robert A. and William C. Black (1985), "A Motivation-Based Shopper Typology," *Journal of Retailing*, 61 (1), 78-103.

Zimmerman, M. (1983), "Weighted Versus Unweighted Life Event Scores: Is there a Difference?," *Journal of Human Stress*, (December), 30-33.

The Dynamism of Personal Timestyle: How We Do More in Less Time
Frank Denton, University of Wisconsin–Madison

ABSTRACT

A dynamic model of personal timestyle is developed. It proposes a reciprocal relationship between an individual's timestyle and his or her close referents, built on satisfaction or dissatisfaction with time-allocation decisions. The model also describes a set of adaptive timestyle tactics that consumers use to alter their timestyles and achieve personal homeostasis. If one's timestyle is satisfying to his or her personal relationships, there is reinforcement of the timestyle. If one's timestyle is dissatisfying to his or her own needs or to personal relationships, adaptive timestyle tactics are utilized to restore satisfaction. The model offers a new dimension for future research on time and consumer behavior.

The modern intensity of daily human activity ultimately collides with the cold, hard, immutable barrier of time.

As a fundamental variable of individual and group activity (McGrath 1988), time has been examined in a variety of disciplines (economics, household economics, psychology, sociology, anthropology, communications), orientations (past, present, future), activity levels (monochronic, polychronic) and uses (income, obligation, planning). Kaufman, Lane and Lindquist (1991b) offer a concise taxonomy of time concepts.

Consideration of time in consumer behavior is anchored in Jacoby (1976), who integrated literature from economics, sociology, home economics, psychology and marketing and outlined a "terminological system" for consumer research. That work was updated and expanded in an interdisciplinary overview by Gross (1987) and in a comprehensive framework for time allocation offered by Feldman and Hornik (1981).

Most of the work on time and consumer behavior has explored specific effects of time on people and situations, for example: transportation (Cherlow 1981), women's roles (Anderson, Golden, Umesh and Weeks 1989; Hunt and Kiker 1981), taxation and the household (Leuthold 1981), church attendance (Azzi and Ehrenberg 1975), household technology (Oropesa 1993) and shopping (Holman and Wilson 1980; Marmorstein, Grewal and Fishe 1992).

Theory development has been slower, primarily through borrowing from psychology, economics, social psychology and sociology (Hirschman 1987). For example, Etgar (1978) uses an economic approach to include the value of time in his model of the consumption process. Feldman and Hornik (1981) offer an array of time constructs, a framework for time-allocation decisions and a consolidated time-use model encompassing myriad factors internal and external to the consumer.

A key issue in understanding the role of time in contemporary consumer behavior is time scarcity, real or perceived. In her survey of the literature on time scarcity, Gross (1987) concludes that, while time has become an important variable in consumer behavior, relatively little is known about the nature and behavior of time-pressured consumers.

Time scarcity, or the perception of it, is an increasingly important factor in American lifestyle. In one study, 33 percent of adults said they don't accomplish all they intend to each day, 21 percent said they have "no time for fun anymore," and 50 percent (70 percent of those earning $30,000 per year or more) said they would sacrifice a day's pay for an extra day off each week (Hymowitz 1991). A Harris survey found Americans believe their leisure time declined 37 percent between 1973 and 1989 while the workweek increased from 41 to 47 hours, and a Yankelovich Clancy Shulman poll reported 73 percent of women and 51 percent of men felt they had too little leisure time (Gibbs 1989).

The responsible forces are unclear. An economic theory based on rising aspirations poses that, in a consumption-driven economy, people work harder to buy more goods and thus have less leisure time to enjoy them. In the tradition of Galbraith (1958), this view has roots in seminal work by Becker (1965) and Linder (1970). The modern proponent is Schor (1991), who estimates that, compared to 1969, the average employed American in 1987 worked an additional 163 hours a year, or the equivalent of one month. She talks of a "treadmill" and "a profound structural crisis of time."

An alternate theory, from sociologists using time-diary studies beginning in 1965 (Juster and Stafford 1985), is that Americans have more free time than a generation ago, but that television has more than absorbed that extra time. In addition, Robinson contends that modern lifestyle is harassed by a perception of "overchoice," an excess of leisure and consumption alternatives (Robb 1992). Thus, with television consuming so much time and with so many choices for the few remaining hours, this view is that people *perceive* they have less time and thus feel pressured and stressful. Robinson found that 35 percent of women and 25 percent of men say they are constantly under stress, trying to accomplish more than they can handle (Hymowitz 1991).

Existing models of consumer time use do not accommodate these stresses and resulting adaptive or coping behaviors. While they may acknowledge that an individual's temporal considerations and decisions can change over time, the models stop short of explaining the dynamism of contemporary time use. For example, Feldman and Hornik (1981) organize environmental and consumer variables into a static decision model. In real life, as perceptions of time scarcity increase, time-allocation decisions intensify, and people find themselves managing their time as carefully as their money. Each day can become a strategic challenge, with one trying to fit a modern set of needs and goals to the finite resource of time. This paper proposes a dynamic model of the time pressures on consumers and of the range of tactics they use to adapt to such pressures.

CONSUMER TIMESTYLES

Feldman and Hornik (1981) introduced the concept of "timestyle" to characterize the allocation of time among the activities involved in the consumption of goods and services. Anderson et al. (1989) called timestyles perhaps the most promising approach to time in consumer behavior: "The way time is distributed provides a behavioral caricature of the individual, a kind of activity autograph, articulating and affirming the individual's personal priorities and constraints within various role contexts" (p. 346).

Time-diary studies have used as many as 99 classifications of time activities (Juster and Stafford 1985), but functional taxonomies vary around seven (Anderson et al 1989) to ten (Hill 1985). This paper will include eight, to permit separate categories for two activities which seem to be consuming more time: shopping (Schor 1991, p. 107-138) and media use (Hill 1985, p. 135-138). *Market work* is paid labor, including commuting. *Sleep* can vary significantly. *Domesticity* is defined as personal and household maintenance. *Family* includes primary attention to one's partner, children and any other family members. *Shopping* is for both necessity and pleasure. *Media use* is a category when it is the dominant activity, normally television-watching and newspaper-reading. *Religion*

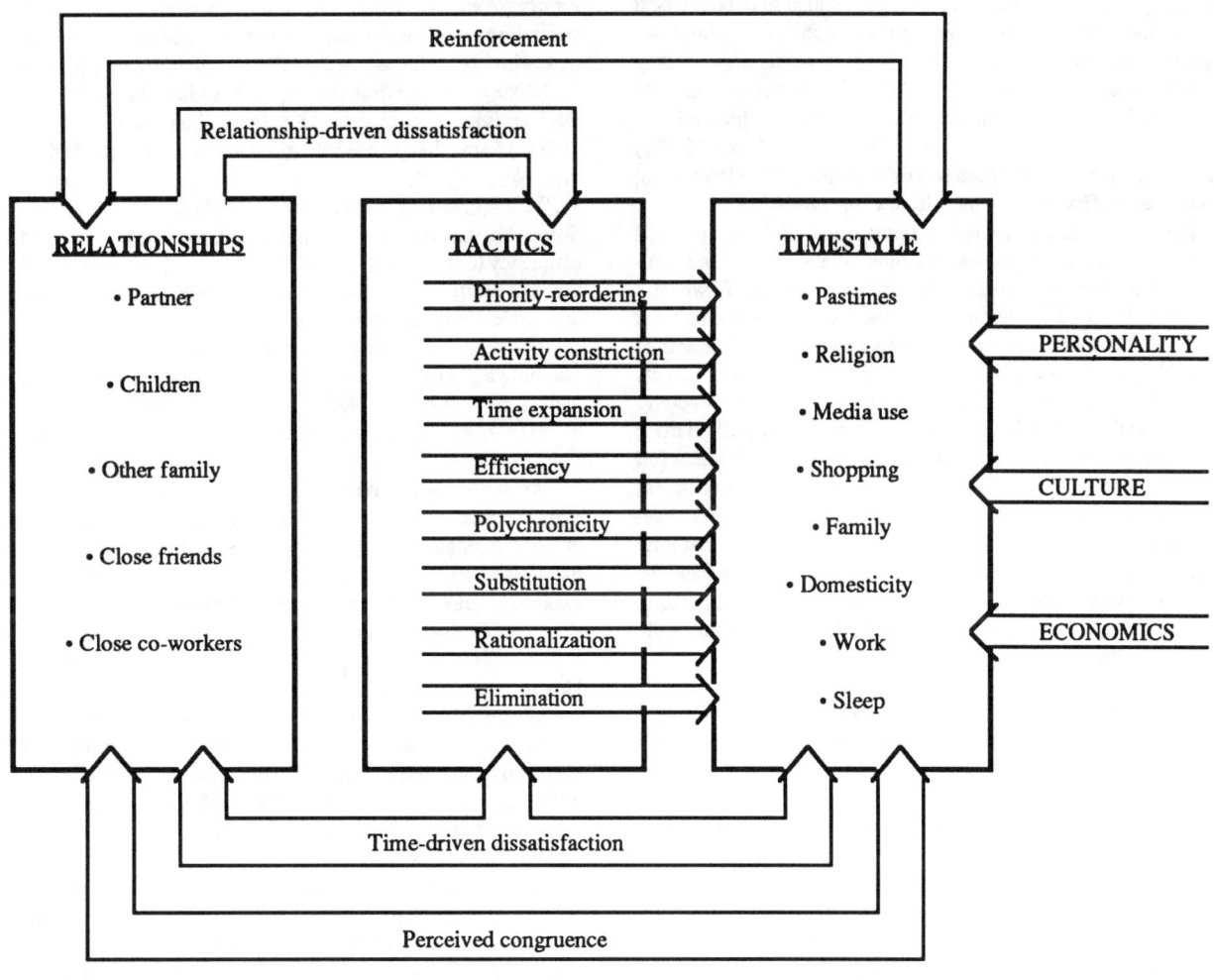

FIGURE 1
Dynamic Timestyle Model

includes church attendance and other religious observances. *Pastimes* are hobbies, entertainment (other than TV), recreation and other leisure activities.

Many authors have focused on what has been considered discretionary time, essentially the last five sets of activities above, on the assumption that necessities like the first three sets require relatively inflexible amounts of time (Hendrix, Kinnear and Taylor 1979). Here, all the activity sets will be considered discretionary, not only because of changes in technology (e.g., home PCs) and lifestyles (e.g., working mothers), but also because this dynamic model recognizes innovation and ingenuity in timestyles. From this perspective, the day is 24 full hours.

Timestyle should be differentiated from lifestyle, which is how one lives. In the context of consumer behavior, lifestyle has been seen primarily as a person's overt consumption behaviors. Both concepts may be seen more broadly. In a larger context, lifestyle expands to consider one's cultural connections, values, personality, roles and relationships with other people and groups (Loov and Miegel 1989). Similarly, as a subset of lifestyle, timestyle in a dynamic context must be seen to include more than allocation of hours and minutes. Rather than being merely how one allocates time, it is how one uses time to satisfy one's own goals and needs, including antecedent influences such as culture and economics (Gross 1987), and how time allocation affects other aspects of one's lifestyle.

CONCEPTUAL MODEL

A conceptual model of the dynamism of consumers' timestyles is depicted in Figure 1. In the model, a consumer's timestyle is altered continually by personal relationships and by a range of adaptive and coping tactics. One is inclined to arrange and rearrange his or her environment and behavior so as to minimize aversion and maximize gratification (Zillman and Bryant 1985). Seen as a dynamic, the process in the model enables the consumer to manage his or her timestyle to maintain functional homeostasis while satisfying needs and goals within a larger lifestyle.

This discussion assumes a weekday, though the model would work equally well for a weekend, with adjustments in the contents of the constructs and processes. For example, for most people on a Sunday, work would shrink, all the other activities—notably religion, sleep and pastimes—would expand, and relationships would be limited to family and closest friends. The dynamics would continue, though perhaps with less intensity.

The Effect of Personal Relationships

A key component of the dynamic nature of timestyle is the effect of personal relationships. Almost all consumers have a reference group of people—family, close friends, close coworkers—who are so much a part of that person's daily activities that they affect his/her timestyle. Certainly, this small group of referents includes cohabitants, but it also includes significant others who, in the course of ordinary daily activities, routinely make overt or covert demands, directly or indirectly, on the individual's time. Commonly, this is the spouse or child, but it also may be the best friend demanding companionship or the close coworker who slows or speeds one's pace of work. These are not idle acquaintances; they are people who are authorized, by relationship or circumstance, to exercise influence on the individual's time. In their hierarchy of social structures and time, Lewis and Weigert (1981, p. 436-437) identify interaction time, when two or more people are interacting directly, as the first overlay on self time, or time alone.

Many, if not most, of a person's time-allocation decisions will affect one or more important personal relationships, and conversely, those relationships will affect the decisions. Lewis and Weigert (1981, p. 437) refer to "time embeddedness" as the fact that all acts of social time are temporally fitted inside of other acts of social time. In the present context, one person's timestyle affects others'. For example, work constricts the time one can devote to children; the four or five hours necessary for a round of golf give rise to the "golf widow" characterization; reading demands one's full attention, at the possible expense of family time; habitual tardiness may draw resentment from close coworkers; two-earner households may perform less housework, provoking dissension among the members. On the other hand, one's close referents also have the power to support her or his timestyle, through the use of positive reinforcement. Figure 1 shows the reciprocal influence of timestyle and relationships.

P1: If a consumer's timestyle is congruent with his or her close personal relationships, the timestyle decisions are reinforced.

At the bottom of Figure 1, emanating from timestyle, is timestyle-driven dissatisfaction, that is, a person's negative feelings that his or her timestyle has not accomplished personal goals or filled appropriate needs. Such feelings might be reified in a number of ways; Schor (1991, p. 11-13) outlines social, as well as psychological and physiological, consequences of time scarcity and pressure.

P2: If an individual's timestyle is incongruent with close personal relationships, dissatisfaction will be created within the relationships.

The Effect of Adaptive Timestyle Tactics

While personality, other antecedent influences and personal relationships will shape one's timestyle, there exists a set of tactics to craft, or finesse, the operation of timestyle. Adaptive timestyle tactics refers to a set of personal heuristics one learns or develops to manage time demands during a finite period of time and achieve acceptable homeostasis. Some of them operate through the help of other people or technology, and others reflect simple decision-making and behavior changes. Timestyle tactics should be carefully differentiated from symptoms of time scarcity, for example, rushing, stress, impatience, tardiness. Instead, these are specific devices one can use to adapt one's time resource to his or her needs and goals, or vice versa. Eight time tactics are used:

- *Priority reordering*, simply deciding one activity is more important than another. Feldman and Hornik's (1981) framework for time allocation implies prioritizing. An extreme example is refusing a promotion or a new job because of greater time requirements (Hymowitz 1991).
- *Activity constriction*, devoting less time to an activity. One common example is sleep, once considered inelastic: Thirty-eight percent of Americans say they have cut back on sleep to make more time (Hymowitz 1991).
- *Polychronicity*, doing more than one thing at a time. A common example is watching television while eating, cooking or sewing, but there are many others, such as shopping while socializing, eating while driving and reading the newspaper while riding an exercycle. Kaufman, Lane and Lindquist (1991a) found that people intentionally plan polychronic time use.
- *Efficiency*, getting the most accomplished in the least time. Some, but not all, labor-saving appliances have facilitated efficiency (Schor 1991, p. 83-105), and time also can be freed through carefully organized chores and errands, for example, and tactically timed commutes.
- *Substitution*, replacing one way of satisfying a need or pursuing a goal with another way. As an example, Feldman and Hornik (1981, p. 415) mention fulfilling a need for entertainment and sociability by playing cards rather than going out to the movies.
- *Time expansion*, or buying time, paying others to perform activities one could perform oneself. Examples are child care and home repair and maintenance. The latter is a reversal of the do-it-yourself trend, which was more to save money, at the expense of time, when money seemed more important.
- *Rationalization*, devising superficial or secondary reasons to justify activities. One might carve out time for a softball league under the guise of fitness, when the real goal is sociableness. Schroeder (1989) found little correlation between people's stated value of an activity and the time they spend on that activity: People say they place low value on TV watching and high value on talking with their children, but they devote far more time to the former.
- *Elimination*. One might forego a career for children or vice versa, but a more common example would be dropping the last activity on the priority list, such as a hobby or recreation. For example, many Americans have let their weekday newspaper subscriptions lapse, and the biggest proportion of these have cited time constraints (Bogart 1989, p. 65, 91).

These tactics function when time-related dissatisfaction appears, whether directly from one's timestyle or from the relationship impact of that timestyle. As Figure 1 shows, a person might be satisfied with her or his timestyle, until it conflicts with a relationship, resulting in relationship-driven dissatisfaction. Whichever the source of the dissatisfaction, the principle of homeostasis calls for action to counter the negative state (Schwarz and Bless 1991).

P3: If one is dissatisfied with one's timestyle, adaptive time tactics are utilized.

P4: If one's personal relationship is dissatisfying because of timestyle, adaptive time tactics are utilized.

One might have activity-driven dissatisfaction salved by a relationship, which then positively reinforces the timestyle—for example, a person disappointed that family demands forced cancellation of a golf game might feel better about that time-allocation decision after a rewarding afternoon with the children.

When dissatisfaction enters the domain of coping and adapting tactics, the individual seeking satisfaction, or homeostasis, is faced with new timestyle decisions, seeking to recreate what Feldman and Hornik (1981, p. 413) call "an optimal combination of satisfaction based on the suboptimization of various needs essential to his/her sense of well being." While it would be rare for one to completely reconfigure one's allocation of time, partial restructurings are common, perhaps even daily, occurrences. In the largest sense, an individual will consider the influences, constraints, goals, needs and resources outlined in the comprehensive models of time allocation (e.g., Feldman and Hornik 1981, p. 414). But at the daily, operational level of time decisions, one will choose from among one or more of the set of eight tactics. They differ in application, personal and resource cost, duration, durability, consciousness and consequence.

P5: Adaptive tactics change one's timestyle.

DISCUSSION

Much of the consideration of time in consumer behavior has treated time as a variable in the study of other consumer phenomena and avoided conceptual development in the area of time scarcity (Gross 1987, p. 40). This model explores the dynamism and functionality of time-constrained behavior itself. While other time-allocation models are useful for their comprehensiveness or their interdisciplinary integration (Gross 1987), this dynamic timestyle model makes four contributions.

First, it offers a level of analysis closer to the rhythm, pacing and function of a consumer's daily life. Time perspectives have been categorized as short or long on a temporal-horizon dimension and as micro or macro at the level of analysis (Gronmo 1989); this model applies at the short micro level of daily life events. It explains how people make the best use of their available time, advancing beyond economic arguments that time is a resource and consumers seek to minimize its expenditure (Hirschman 1987). Understanding this adaptive dynamism provides an important theoretical link at the individual level of analysis, between structural models and the consumer's functioning lifestyle.

Second, the model proposes a reciprocal relationship between an individual's timestyle and his or her close personal relationships. Gronmo's (1989) concept of "social time," can be seen as mere interaction time, synchronizing one's own activities with those of others (Hirschman 1987, p. 72). The present model works at a much deeper level, extending and reifying Lewis and Weigert's (1981) concept of "time embeddedness." In addition to simple coordination of schedules, that perspective encompasses the longer-term time embeddedness of shared lives. While research is sparse, the consumer decision-making literature recognizes that people make decisions in a social context, including feelings of accountability to others, such as family members (Bettman, Johnson and Payne 1991, p. 63-64). From an experiential perspective, Hirschman (1987, p. 76) suggests that activity prioritization is a function of intrinsic personal rewards from the activity and extrinsic social obligations to participate in the activity.

Third, this dynamic model proposes a set of adaptive timestyle tactics that consumers use to alter their timestyles. Hendrix and Martin (1981) explored the concept of temporal incongruence, suggesting that it is caused by a consumer's inability to match his or her needs with the time available, but they did not venture into corrective or adaptive actions that might restore congruence. Most people apparently do not consciously allocate their time in a planned and systematic fashion (Hirschman 1987; Robinson 1977), but they do "make time" for activities that are important to them (Marks 1977). This model shows how time is "made."

Fourth, the present model adds an understanding of the dynamism of personal timestyle. Other approaches see time allocation as a set of straightforward tradeoffs, minimizing time expenditures and maximizing economic benefit (Hirschman, p. 57, 76) or as structured and static (Feldman and Hornik 1981). While the latter note that a person may have different time-related needs at different times (p. 413), their model is more analytic and relational than it is dynamic.

Taken together, these contributions offer a new dimension to research on time and consumer behavior. Previous investigations, exploring specific effects of time on consumers and consumption situations, have assumed that individuals' timestyle decisions are made unilaterally in stable, enduring patterns. The present model proposes that, in everyday practice, timestyle is dynamic, constantly changing, challenged by an ever-churning array of endogenous needs and goals and exogenous obligations and opportunities. As these forces conflict and compete and as time pressure, incongruence and dissatisfaction increase, the consumer works harder to adapt and cope, invoking tactics individually and in combination, trying to match activities, timestyles and relationships to achieve resolution and personal homeostasis.

The model contributes to future research in two ways. First, the tactics themselves, as they are used to liberate time, should be investigated for their direct and indirect effects on consumers' behavior. Second, studies using time as an independent variable should consider the dynamism of individual timestyles and close referents. In some cases, for example, cross-sectional research may be misleading; longitudinal studies may better reflect meaningful changes in this new dimension of time-driven behavior.

Existing time-diary data can measure changes in timestyle, but because of the social and introspective concepts and questions of awareness, methods beyond surveys and self-report will be required. Pointing out that time-budget data can be broad but shallow, Gronmo (1989) concluded that, in order to capture more complex variables, researchers may need to combine time-budget data with qualitative methods, such as depth interviews, observation and historical and case studies. To fully explore the present model, such methodology should include the individual's close referents and should work at several temporal levels, from the consumer's longer-term needs, goals and obligations to the dynamics of his or her daily timestyle.

Finally, to the practitioner, this model of dynamic timestyle offers insights into consumer behavior and marketing phenomena and opportunity. Activity constriction can help retailers understand why, despite the national passion, many people are finding shopping a chore or stressful. Time expansion explains the interest in some new services, such as on-site automobile oil change. When people have car phones, dual-picture TV sets and now even TV receivers within a PC window, they are exercising polychronicity. Renting videotapes, rather than going to the theater, is substitution. Efficiency is achieved through drive-up fast-food windows, fax machines and coffee makers with timers. While male business travelers are lonely and bored on extended trips, women are more energized, productive and stimulated, apparently because the business duty frees them from the multiple pressures at home (Trost 1992)—an example of rationalization? Newspapers trying to staunch the loss of weekday circulation must understand that reading is a solitary, time-consuming activity which is not amenable to polychronicity or efficiency but which is subject to substitution (television) and elimination.

REFERENCES

Anderson, W. Thomas, Jr., Linda L. Golden, U.N. Umesh and William A. Weeks (1989), "The Five Faces of Eve: Women's Timestyle Typologies," in *Advances in Consumer Research*, Vol. 16, ed. Thomas K. Srull, Provo, UT: Association for Consumer Research, 346-353.

Azzi, Corry, and Ronald Ehrenberg (1975), "Household Allocation of Time and Church Attendance," *Journal of Political Economy*, 83 (February), 27-56.

Becker, Gary (1965), "A Theory of the Allocation of Time," *Economic Journal*, 75 (September), 493-517.

Bettman, James R., Eric J. Johnson and John W. Payne (1991), "Consumer Decision Making," in *Handbook of Consumer Behavior*, eds. Thomas S. Robertson and Harold H. Kassarjian, Englewood Cliffs NJ: Prentice-Hall, 50-84.

Bogart, Leo (1989), *Press and Public: Who Reads What, Where, When and Why in American Newspapers*, second edition, Hillsdale, NJ: Erlbaum.

Cherlow, Jay R. (1981), "Measuring Values of Travel Time Savings," *Journal of Consumer Research*, 7 (March), 360-371.

Etgar, Michael (1978), "The Household as a Production Unit," in *Research in Marketing*, Vol. 1, ed. J.N. Sheth, Greenwich, CT: JAI Press, 79-98.

Feldman, Laurence P., and Jacob Hornik (1981), "The Use of Time: An Integrated Conceptual Model," *Journal of Consumer Research*, 7 (March), 407-419.

Galbraith, John Kenneth (1958), *The Affluent Society*, Boston: Houghton Mifflin.

Gibbs, Nancy (1989), "How American Has Run Out of Time," *Time*, April 24, 58-67.

Gronmo, Sigmund (1989), "Concepts of Time: Some Implications for Consumer Research," in *Advances in Consumer Research*, Vol. 16, ed. Thomas K. Srull, Provo, UT: Association for Consumer Research, 339-345.

Gross, Barbara L. (1987), "Time Scarcity: Interdisciplinary Perspectives and Implications for Consumer Behavior," in *Research in Consumer Behavior*, Vol. 2, ed. Jagdish N. Sheth and Elizabeth C. Hirschman, Greenwich, CT: JAI Press, 1-54.

Hendrix, Philip E., Thomas C. Kinnear and James R. Taylor (1979), "The Allocation of Time by Consumers," in *Advances in Consumer Research*, Vol. 6, ed. W.L. Wilkie, Ann Arbor, MI: Association for Consumer Research, 38-44.

_____ and Claude R. Martin (1981), "Temporal Incongruency in Consumer Behavior," in *Advances in Consumer Research*, Vol. 8, ed. K.B. Monroe, Ann Arbor, MI: Association for Consumer Research, 182-186.

Hill, Martha S. (1985), "Patterns of Time Use," in *Time, Goods and Well-Being*, eds. F. Thomas Juster and Frank P. Stafford, Ann Arbor, MI: Institute for Social Research, University of Michigan.

Hirschman, Elizabeth C. (1987), "Theoretical Perspectives of Time Use: Implications for Consumer Behavior Research," in *Research in Consumer Behavior*, Vol. 2, ed. Jagdish N. Sheth and Elizabeth C. Hirschman, Greenwich, CT: JAI Press, 55-81.

Holman, Rebecca H., and H. Dale Wilson (1980), "The Availability of Discretionary Time: Influences on Interactive Patterns of Consumer Shopping Behavior," in *Advances in Consumer Research*, 7, ed. J.C. Olson, Ann Arbor, MI: Association for Consumer Research, 431-436.

Hunt, Janet C., and B.F. Kiker (1981), "The Effect of Fertility on the Time Use of Working Wives," *Journal of Consumer Research*, 7 (March), 380-387.

Hymowitz, Carol (1991), "Trading fat paychecks for free time," *Wall Street Journal*, Aug. 5, B1.

Jacoby, Jacob, George J. Szybillo and Carol Kohn Berning (1976), "Time and Consumer Behavior: An Interdisciplinary Overview," *Journal of Consumer Research*, 2 (March), 320-339.

Juster, F. Thomas, and Frank P. Stafford, eds. (1985), *Time, Goods and Well-Being*, Ann Arbor, MI: Institute for Social Research, University of Michigan.

Kaufman, Carol Felker, Paul M. Lane and Jay D. Lindquist (1991a), "Exploring More than 24 Hours a Day: A Preliminary Investigation of Polychronic Time Use," *Journal of Consumer Research*, 18 (December), 392-401.

_____, Paul M. Lane and Jay D. Lindquist (1991b), "Time Congruity in the Organization: A Proposed Quality-of-Life Framework," *Journal of Business and Psychology*, 6, 1 (Fall), 79-106.

Leuthold, Jane H. (1981), "Taxation and the Consumption of Household Time," *Journal of Consumer Research*, 7 (March), 388-394.

Lewis, J. David, and Andrew J. Weigert (1981), "The Structures and Meanings of Social Time," *Social Forces*, 60 (December), 432-462.

Linder, Staffan B. (1970), *The Harried Leisure Class*, New York: Columbia University Press.

Loov, Thomas, and Fredrik Miegel (1989), "The Notion of Lifestyle: Some Theoretical Considerations," Report No. 15, Lund Research Papers in the Sociology of Communication, University of Lund, Lund, Sweden.

Marks, Stephen R. (1977), "Multiple Roles and Role Strain: Some Notes on Human Energy, Time and Commitment," *American Sociological Review*, 42 (December), 921-936.

Marmorstein, Howard, Dhruv Grewal and Raymond P.H. Fishe (1992), "The Value of Time Spent in Price-Comparison Shopping: Survey and Experimental Evidence," *Journal of Consumer Research*, 19 (June), 52-61.

McGrath, Joseph E. (1988), *The Social Psychology of Time: New Perspectives*, Beverly Hills, CA: Sage.

Oropesa, R.S. (1993), "Female Labor Force Participation and Time-Saving Household Technology: A Case Study of the Microwave from 1978 to 1989," *Journal of Consumer Research*, 19 (March), 567-579.

Robb, Christina (1992), "Where Has Our Free Time Gone? Experts Say It's Squandered on Television," *Wisconsin State Journal*, March 1, 6D.

Robinson, John P. (1977), *How Americans Use Time: A Social-Psychological Analysis of Everyday Behavior*, New York: Praeger.

Schor, Juliet B. (1991), *The Overworked American: The Unexpected Decline of Leisure*, Basic Books.

Schroeder, Jonathan E. (1989), "What Time Means to Others: Expectations of Behavior Based on Time Use Information," in *Advances in Consumer Research*, Vol. 16, ed. Thomas K. Srull, Provo, UT: Association for Consumer Research, 354-358.

Schwarz, Norbert, and Herbert Bless (1991), "Happy and Mindless, but Sad and Smart? The Impact of Affective States on Analytic Reasoning," in *Emotion and Social Judgments*, ed. J.P. Forgas, Oxford: Pergamon.

Settle, Robert B. (1980), "A Discussion of 'Time' Research," in *Advances in Consumer Research*, Vol. 7, ed. J.C. Olson, Ann Arbor, MI: Association for Consumer Research, p. 448-450.

Trost, Cathy (1992), "Long business trips energize women more than men, a survey says," *Wall Street Journal*, July 28, p. A1.

Zillmann, Dolf, and Jennings Bryant (1985), "Affect, Mood, and Emotion as Determinants of Selective Exposure," in *Selective Exposure to Communication*, eds. Dolf Zillman and Jennings Bryant, Hillsdale NJ: Erlbaum.

Community and Consumption
Brenda Gainer, York University
Eileen Fischer, York University

This session directed attention toward the phenomenon of community, often considered to be of immense social importance, yet curiously neglected within our discipline. It focussed on some of the reasons for that neglect and some of the ways in which consumer research might move forward, building on work that has already been done in our own discipline and elsewhere. It highlighted unresolved issues in the study of community and consumption, as well as demonstrating that not only a range of theories but a range of methods will be useful in advancing this line of inquiry.

The paper by Eileen Fischer and Julia Bristor examined the reasons for which the consumption/community link has received inadequate attention. They suggested that our neglect of non-individual level phenomena stems from the biases of our dominant perspectives and theories. The goal of most consumer behavior studies has been to explain how individual cognition, perception, or traits influence individual behavior. When units of analysis other than the individual have been considered, dominant theories have cast group or community level phenomena as the product of rational self-interest maximizing behavior; a perspective which is consistent with a Western or agentic orientation. Their paper drew on theories and research from a range of disciplines to develop a new framework for thinking about the relationships between community and consumption.

The paper by Ajay Sirsi, James Ward, and Peter Reingen focussed on communities defined by their shared consumption patterns, and developed an innovative way of both defining communities and studying them. They drew on ethnographic fieldwork to identify groups who share common food consumption habits, and through intensive semi-structured interviews developed causal maps showing cognitive structures related to foods for members of the groups. Using computer software developed specifically for the project, they were able to identify the nature and extent of shared cognitions related to food consumption which form the basis for the consumption communties they identified. Their results suggested a viable way of defining the boundaries of and linkages between communities, as well as the variation in both beliefs and behaviors that we might expect within consumption communities.

The paper by Brenda Gainer examined variations between the communities that men and women appear to form through a variety of consumption related activities, as well as differences in the social processes surrounding consumption directed at the formation of community. She noted that psychological theory and empirical studies indicate that community is important to women, and that they use consumption to forge bonds of sorority. Based on participant observation and long interviews regarding same-sex shared consumption with male and female informants, she suggested that men also use consumption to build masculine communities; however, it appears that the consumption activities they choose, as well as the communities men constitute, differ from those of women in systematic ways.

The concluding discussion by Craig Thompson emphasized the importance of pushing the boundaries of our discipline beyond the individual level of analysis in order to increase our understanding of consumer behavior. The study of community and its relationship to consumption is crucial to this task.

Toward a Renaissance of Goals in Consumer Research on Attitudes and Decision Making
Hans Baumgartner, Pennsylvania State University

In spite of the importance of the notion of goal-directed action for understanding consumer behavior, surprisingly little consumer research has been devoted to the study of goals. The purpose of this special session was to bring together a number of researchers with interest in goals in an effort to stimulate work in this area. Three papers were presented which covered a broad range of issues in the areas of attitudes and decision making but which were tied together by a common focus on the goal construct.

In the first paper, Pieters, Baumgartner, and Allen dealt with the issue of modeling goal structures, and they also investigated the effects of goals and their structure on involvement and behavioral intentions. It is often assumed that goals are organized in a hierarchical fashion, with lower-level, subordinate goals serving as means to attain higher-level, superordinate goals as ends (e.g., Bettman 1979), but very little empirical research has tried to model explicitly the presumed hierarchical structure of goals. In his presentation of the paper, Rik Pieters proposed a methodology for eliciting and analyzing sequences of linked subordinate and superordinate goals, and he illustrated the method with an exploratory study of the goals underlying consumers' weight loss behaviors. In addition, he presented some preliminary evidence on the usefulness of taking a structural perspective on goals by showing that the linkages between goals contain important information about consumers' involvement with weight loss and their behavioral intentions to engage in specific weight loss behaviors.

In the second paper, Rick Bagozzi addressed the issue of self-regulation in goal-pursuit and in particular discussed the role of self-schemas and action control in the self-regulation of goal-directed behavior (cf. Markus 1977; Kuhl 1985). In the context of a study dealing with exercising, he hypothesized that self-schemas would moderate the attitude-intention, subjective norm-intention, and action control-behavior relations. Specifically, he argued that people with strong exercise self-schemas would activate intentions in response to subjective norms and behavior in response to action control urges. People with weak exercise self-schemas, on the other hand, were hypothesized to activate intentions in response to attitudes. The results of a longitudinal study supported these conjectures.

The third paper by Therese Louie dealt with the implications of the motivated tactician view of consumers for research on judgmental heuristics and biases (cf. Fiske and Taylor 1990). One well-known judgmental bias is the so-called hindsight phenomenon, wherein people feel that they would have been able to predict future outcomes better than they actually could have (e.g., Fischhoff and Beyth 1975). Past research seems to suggest that motivational factors do not have a significant influence on the occurrence of the bias, but this might be due to the lack of personal relevance of the tasks used in most judgmental contexts. In a study set in an investment context, Louie looked at hindsight bias as a function of (a) how involved consumers were in the event for which they made predictions and (b) whether their goals were met or not. The results of the study showed that in goal-related settings the occurrence of the hindsight bias was influenced by motivational mechanisms which are triggered depending on whether or not a goal objective has been attained.

Fred van Raaij served as the discussant for the session and pointed out several fruitful avenues for future research. Given the paucity of work on motivational phenomena, the study of consumers' goals seems to offer great potential for consumer behavior research, and it is hoped that this session will contribute to a renaissance of goal concepts in work on attitudes and decision making.

[References available on request]

A Later Mover Advantage?
The Impact of Order of Entry and Brand Characteristics on Consumer Preferences

Jennifer Aaker, Stanford University
Stephen M. Nowlis, University of California, Berkeley

With the increasing number of brands in the marketplace, many researchers have begun to examine how new brands in a product category can most effectively compete against established incumbents. However, while many have speculated about the optimal marketing strategies used by later movers (vs. first movers) in a product category, few have explicitly and empirically addressed the issue of later mover strategies from a consumer decision making perspective. This session examined behavioral reasons that might account for why later movers sometimes have an advantage over a pioneer. The goal of the session was to build a stronger link between research in consumer decision making and work on innovation-based strategies. Each paper addressed this theme from a different perspective.

The first paper, by Gregory S. Carpenter, Donald R. Lehmann, Kent Nakamoto, and Suzanne B. Walchli focused on the conditions under which a first mover may be at a disadvantage relative to later movers in a product category. Because the first mover has the opportunity to shape the consumer's ideal point, it is often highly associated with a particular competitive position. As a result, the first mover may actually be at a disadvantage due to strategic inflexibility and the inability to reposition. Specifically, the authors analyzed consumer response to a market scenario where a pioneer was attacked by a differentiated brand, and responded by introducing a product line extension or a flanker brand (vs. imitating the differentiated later mover).

The second paper, by Stephen M. Nowlis and Itamar Simonson, examined the innovation-based strategy of offering new product features (e.g., an autofocus feature offered by a brand of binoculars), a strategy used by both later entrants and pioneers that reposition. The authors hypothesized that a new feature would increase the market share of a brand more when (1) the brand's price is higher than the competition, (2) the brand's quality reputation is lower than the competition, (3) the brand has limited features, (4) buyers do not expect to receive feedback after purchase about the actual performance of the new feature, and (5) buyers need to provide reasons to support their choices. Based on the first two predictions, they further hypothesized that the addition of a feature would reduce the price elasticity of a low-quality but not of a high-quality brand.

The third paper, by Jennifer Aaker, examined the impact of order-of-entry and perceptual positioning strategies on consumer preferences and choice. Based on theoretical insights from consumer decision making research, Aaker tested a series of experimental hypotheses regarding the conditions under which second and third movers could most effectively compete against an established pioneer. In addition, strategic implications for the first mover reactions and later mover positioning strategies were discussed.

The discussant, Allan Shocker, offered his perspective on each of the papers and suggested areas for future research.

The Role of Expectations and Organization in the Encoding and Use of Memory-Based Information: What Not to Forget about Memory Research

Susan E. Heckler, University of Arizona

Much research has been reported in psychology and marketing which examines memory structures and how to facilitate memory performance. One criticism that has been raised regarding this stream of research is that, while theoretically interesting, it does not contribute greatly to the understanding of consumer behavior, since memory measures have often been shown to be uncorrelated with choice behaviors. In response to this criticism, researchers interested in memory issues have endeavored to expand their research efforts to clarify and demonstrate the relationships between memory and consumer judgment or evaluation. This session linked two streams of memory-related research by examining a number of mechanisms which affect the development of memory structure *and then* identified the impact of this memory organization on subsequent evaluation and choice.

The first paper, by Karen Finlay, John Bassili and Andrew A. Mitchell, extended research conducted to understand how memory structure impacts choice processes. Different memory structures (i.e., organization of information and links among items in memory) were induced using multiple expectancy manipulations. Their study compared the effect of this organizing mechanism to that of differential levels of cognitive effort at the time of choice. The results of the research showed that an enhanced memory structure can overcome the effects of low motivation and opportunity to exert cognitive effort when subjects are making decisions. The findings of the research indicate that advertisers may have a means to overcome factors outside of their control which negatively affect consumers' propensity to recall information. By presenting choice related information about a target object at encoding in a manner which induces *memory structure*, positive effects on recall and choice may result.

Wanda Wallace of Duke University presented a paper which utilized another mechanism to develop memory structures, and again, related this memory-based information to evaluation and buying intentions. The opening claim of this paper was that memory can be quite good even though the respondent has not processed the meaning or implications of the message. Such a scenario predominately occurs when the structure of material facilitates surface processing and provides adequate memory cues for both encoding and retrieval. Music is one example of such structure. For novel, lyrical ads, recall of the brand name and of the ad is equivalent for sung and spoken versions of the ad; however, recognition of ad claims is worse in the sung than in the spoken version.

Next, Jolita Kisielius, Prashant Malaviya and Brian Sternthal reported an investigation of the influence of the advertising context in choosing pictures that accompany print advertising copy. Results showed that a target camera ad presented along with ads for *competing cameras*, leads to enhanced target judgments when specified unique features are highlighted in the pictorial portions of the ad. However, when the camera ad is presented with ads from *other product categories*, judgments are enhanced if the pictures depicted other people, occasions or objects in conjunction with the camera.. These results tend to support the notion that judgments involve generation of product information and discrimination of products from alternatives. When the pictures and the context complement each other in performing these two functions, judgments are enhanced.

In the final paper in the session Susan Heckler and Laura Peracchio reported the results of a study which manipulated the expectedness of pictorial elements in advertising *together with* individuals' motivation to process the information. Their work related the resulting processing activities to the development of memory and evaluative judgments for the products depicted in the ads. Results of the study showed that interesting interactions occur between the two factors. For example, subjects who were in a low motivation to process condition found the unexpected information difficult to comprehend, but formed more positive evaluations of the products being advertised than subjects more highly motivated to process. It appears that providing a setting in which motivation to process is moderate may lead to the most positive product judgments, as both pictorial and verbal advertising information were processed, but elaborative counterarguing with claims was not induced.

Empirical Relationships Between Cognitive Style and LOV: Implications for Values and Value Systems

Roger P. McIntyre, East Carolina University
Reid P. Claxton, East Carolina University
David B. Jones, La Salle University

INTRODUCTION

Human values serve as vehicles by which culture is handed from one generation to another and as guideposts by which the paths of individual lives are charted. Values have been variously defined as enduring beliefs about preferred conduct or end states of being (Rokeach 1973); as conceptions of desirable influences on the ways people select behavior and evaluate their world (Schwartz and Bilsky 1987); and as society's goals represented within the individual (Beatty, Homer, and Kahle 1988). More narrowly, the study of values offers a richer, fuller picture of both the consumer and consumer motivation. Accordingly, values often provide the basis by which markets are segmented.

Cognitive style refers to the Jungian (1971) psychological type theory which most often classifies people according their modes of information intake on one hand, and their modes of information processing and decision making on the other. This paper contends that cognitive style is an antecedent condition that affects the formation of human values. Because cognitive style defines individual differences in the perception and processing of information and in resulting patterns of decision making, the overall inference is that cognitive style is an immediate and stable influence on human values and value systems. Empirical relationships between cognitive style and items from the List of Values (LOV) scale (Kahle 1983; Veroff, Douvan and Kulka 1981) will be offered in support.

Responding to the call for more complex measures of values that include provision for the effects of fundamental differences among individuals (Richins and Dawson 1992), this paper suggests that cognitive style is a major individual difference variable that may contribute to improved measures of values and value systems. In hierarchical terms, cognitive style is believed to affect value systems and values, which in turn affect beliefs, attitudes, and behaviors.

VALUES AND THEIR MEASUREMENT

Values are central to individual human lives and to society as a whole (Rokeach 1973). Values are cognitive representations of the biological, interpersonal, and social demands placed upon each of us as human beings (Schwartz and Bilsky 1987). People use culturally learned values to create and assess conditions of morality and competence, to guide social interplay, and to help rationalize beliefs, attitudes and behaviors (Rokeach 1973).

In response to the subjectivity of earlier value scales (e. g., Allport, Vernon and Lindzey 1960), Milton Rokeach in 1973 introduced the *Rokeach Value Survey* (RVS). The RVS measures 18 instrumental and 18 terminal values. Instrumental values pertain to ideal modes of behavior. Terminal values pertain to ideal end states of existence. In the RVS, all 18 items in each set are ranked according to their importance to the respondent. Difficulty arises, however, in the ranking of such a large number of values. People rank middle values less reliably than more extreme ones. RVS also ignores a number of widely-held values, and questions have arisen about the superiority of interval- and ratio scaling to the RVS method of rank ordering (Beatty, Kahle, Homer and Misra 1985).

An alternative to the RVS was subsequently developed based on the work of Feather (1975), Maslow (1954) and Rokeach (1973). *The List of Values* (LOV), developed by Kahle (1983) and Veroff, Douvan and Kulka (1981), modifies the terminal values of RVS into a smaller nine-item subset. LOV asks respondents to identify their two most important values from the nine-value list.

The LOV scale has exhibited validity comparable to RVS while offering greater parsimony. LOV has also been found to provide a higher percentage of items that respondents said influenced their lives, although both LOV and RVS are susceptible to social desirability bias. Finally, the LOV scale offers the advantage of greater ease of administration and completion (Beatty et al. 1985; Kahle, Beatty, and Homer 1986).

The Values and Life Style (VALS) methodology was developed at SRI International by Mitchell (1983). Based on the need hierarchy of Maslow (1954) and the social character concept of Riesman, Glazer and Denney (1950), VALS incorporates 32-36 questions pertaining to general and specific attitudes and demographics. Respondents are ultimately classified into one of nine lifestyle groups. In 1989, SRI International introduced VALS 2 to replace VALS. While the VALS system has had a dramatic impact on the business community, its proprietary nature has largely precluded scholarly and scientific attention (Kahle et al. 1986).

All three of the instruments, RVS, LOV, and VALS, show relationships to various forms of consumer behavior. RVS values were found to predict mass media usage, for example (Becker and Conner 1981). Another study found LOV to offer greater utility in predicting consumer trends than VALS (Kahle et al. 1986).

An inherent difficulty arises in the body of work just cited. Simply stated, people are almost never guided by just one value (Micken 1992). While consumers are often segmented using their top-ranked LOV value, for example, such an approach conflicts with Rokeach's concept of an overall hierarchy of individual, ordered values (Kamakura and Novak 1992). A number of researchers have supported the investigation of value systems in preference to single values. Pitts and Woodside (1983, p. 38) indicate that "single values are salient only in the context of the entire value system." Similarly, Schwartz and Bilsky (1987) argue that research should focus on value domains as opposed to individual values.

Instead of relying on directly observable value rankings, Kamakura and Novak (1992) report creating value system segments from latent discriminal values. The authors construct value system segments described as having greater abstraction than traditional single values. The greater abstraction of the value system segments purportedly reflects the multiple values affecting a person's behavior. The authors ultimately produce a segmentation map delineated by the nine LOV values which identifies the dimensions underlying the value systems of each segment. Each dimension is prioritized by the worth/utility assigned by segment members. The resulting value system segments and map are reported to have face validity consonant with the psychological structure of values advanced by Schwartz and Bilsky (1987).

Unlike segmentation based on a LOV top-ranked value, Kamakura and Novak (1992) indicate that more abstract values defined by the latent system provide "a better understanding of the motivations that drive the beliefs, attitudes, and behavior of each segment" (p. 120). They recognize that consumer values are "also affected by many other more immediate (but also less stable) environmental influences, such as price, sales promotions, exposure to advertising messages" (p. 130), and state that such influences must also be considered. It is the contention of this paper that cognitive style may be both an immediate *and* stable influence on human values. Cognitive style may therefore affect behavior to the extent that it may affect formation of value systems and values, which in turn affect beliefs, attitudes and behaviors.

Having been led to the study of values by a search for measures of materialism, Richins and Dawson (1992) similarly conclude that values are complex phenomena that require the use of complex measures to complement traditional ranking procedures:

> It is no more reasonable to measure the value of "warm relationships with others" with a single item than it is to measure attitudes toward religion with a single question on a survey (p. 314).

Richins and Dawson recommend that, as an alternative to revising the Rokeach scales, it may be time to develop entirely different measures of values; measures that are "more suited to the usual application of individual difference variables in consumer behavior" (p. 314). One of the most fundamental individual difference variables is cognitive style. As discussed in the next section, the theory of cognitive style offers a logical and compelling starting point for developing new measures of human values.

COGNITIVE STYLE

The Jungian (1971) psychological type theory known as cognitive style is based on three bi-polar axes: extroversion/introversion, sensing/intuiting, and thinking/feeling. The instrument developed to operationalize cognitive style, the Myers-Briggs Type Indicator (MBTI), adds a fourth axis: judging/perceiving (Myers and McCaulley 1985). The four axes produce a somewhat unwieldy 16 psychological types, thus compelling most researchers to use just two axes: sensing/intuiting and thinking/feeling. Placed at right angles, these axes produce the quadrants that delineate cognitive style (Frisbie 1988; Mitroff 1981). An individual's cognitive style results from the combination of favored information intake mode (sensing/intuiting) with the preferred decision making mode (thinking/feeling). The four resulting cognitive styles include: sensory-thinking (ST), intuitive-thinking (NT), intuitive-feeling (NF) and sensory-feeling (SF). Table 1 presents the generalized characteristics of the four cognitive styles.

Sensing/intuiting is the information intake axis. It refers to how individuals learn about their environment. People typed by the MBTI as sensors (S) tend to learn from detailed sensory input such as data and hard facts. Sensors have been found to perceive reality as being concrete and divisible. Not surprisingly, they are pragmatic and oriented toward numbers, details, and other tangibles. In contrast, people typed as intuitors (N) perceive realities that are holistic and often beyond direct sensation. Intuitors tend to rely on conceptualization and imagination, frequently constructing realities based on possibilities and ideals. Discerners of patterns and trends, Ns have been found to be quite comfortable with intangibles (Gould 1991; Mokwa and Evans 1984).

Thinking/feeling is the axis of information processing and decision making. Thinkers (T) tend to rely on conventional deductive logic. Individuals typed as thinkers tend to prefer explanations that are formal and general, the types in which human qualities play a relatively minor role. Tending to see situations in black and white, Ts are relatively more analytical, impersonal, and objective. Classical conceptions of logic and science provide an excellent portrait of typical T traits. On the other hand, people typed as Feelers (F) place relatively more emphasis on human qualities. They often search for justification of circumstances and expression of feeling, and so operate with greater questioning and individuation. Fs have been found to be empathizing, personal, subjective, and accepting of ambiguity. The disciplines of aesthetics, ethics, religion, and politics are rich in F characteristics (Mokwa and Evans 1984).

The tendency toward a particular cognitive style appears to be innate, presumably due to the endurance of genetic influences (Johnson 1992; Myers and McCaulley 1985). The two poles that predominate a particular cognitive style heavily shape the individual's perceptions of the world. The two non-dominant poles play lesser roles in perception shaping. The cognitive styles of greatest contrast (i.e., those which are "opposites") occur in the quadrants diagonal to each other in Table 1. Two people having opposite cognitive styles may interpret the same phenomenon in markedly different ways.

Cognitive style has been shown to influence problem solving (Hellriegel and Slocum 1975), conflict management (Percival, Smitheram, and Kelly 1992), and information processing (Smith and Urban 1978). A number of cases of cognitive style-based differential behavior are reported in the areas of communicating, learning, and decision making (e.g., McCaulley and Natter 1974). With regard to buying behavior, consumers have been found to prefer interacting with salepeople who share the consumer's cognitive style (McIntyre 1991). Cognitive style may also affect other facets of consumer-salesperson interaction (Singh 1990).

PROPOSED RELATIONSHIPS BETWEEN COGNITIVE STYLE AND LOV

Preliminary theoretical support exists for a relationship between cognitive style and values. Kamakura and Novak (1992) state that value systems are important tools for decision making and conflict resolution. The additional likelihood must be considered that values and value systems occur as the *result* of decision making in many instances. Partly because decision making is subsumed by the thinking/feeling axis of cognitive style theory, the major inference is here advanced that cognitive style is often antecedent to the formation of human values.

It is important to remember that LOV modifies the 18 terminal values of RVS into a smaller nine-item subset and asks respondents to identify their two most important values therein. Terminal values deal with the major undertakings of life, i.e., marriage, parenthood, and other avenues of contentment and realization of self such as daily consumption, work and leisure (Kahle et al. 1986). Therefore, terminal values are perhaps the most subjective of all values in a person's life. The relatively subjective nature of terminal values may make them especially sensitive to polarized responses, depending on a respondent's type from the thinking/feeling axis of cognitive style. Said another way, terminal values refer to many personal and interpersonal states. Reactions to such complex and socially oriented areas may well be expected to vary depending on whether an individual's preferred way of processing information and making decisions is more affective (feeling) or cognitive (thinking) in nature. For these reasons, the eight hypotheses which follow are framed in terms of the thinking/feeling axis of cognitive style theory. Accordingly:

H1: Subjects typed as Feelers (F) will have a significantly greater response to "Warm relationships with others" than those typed as Thinkers (T).

TABLE 1
Characteristics of the Four Cognitive Styles

Thinking

ST (Sensory-Thinker)
- Seeks certainty, precision
- Concrete orientation
- Seeks "right" answer
- Detached from work
- Concerned with methods and techniques
- Impersonal perspective
- Technical specialist
- Relies on observation and measurement
- Oriented toward the present

NT (Intuitive-Thinker)
- Relies on ideas and calculations
- Builds interesting alternatives
- Inventive and Imaginative
- Seeks to solve the puzzle
- Focus on alternatives and outcomes
- Theoretical perspective
- Generalist
- Oriented toward future

Sensing ———————————————— *Intuiting*

SF (Sensory-Feeler)
- Relies on and seeks intense personal experience
- Active and experiential
- Seeks to get job done
- Concerned with actions
- Behavioral perspective
- Pragmatic
- Lives in present, here and now

NF (Intuitive-Feeler)
- Relies on feelings and emotions
- Constructs ideal social systems
- Empathetic and idealistic
- Systemic orientation
- Seeks to address the "real" problem
- Concerned with people's problems
- Focus on social impacts
- Takes a socio-personal perspective
- An idealist
- Oriented toward future

Feeling

H2: Subjects typed as Feelers (F) will have a significantly greater response to "A sense of belonging" than those typed as Thinkers (T).

Because few LOV respondents have traditionally selected "excitement" as their top value choice, the category is usually collapsed into "fun and enjoyment" (Kahle and Kennedy 1988). Based on the perceptions that fun, enjoyment, excitement and security are predominantly affective states, the third hypothesis emerges:

H3: Subjects typed as Feelers (F) will have a significantly greater response to "Fun and enjoyment in life/excitement" than those typed as Thinkers (T).

For the individual, the condition of living is ephemeral. Rationally, all life has the same, "non-secure" eventual outcome. As a result, the value of security is similarly perceived as an affective state:

H4: Subjects typed as Feelers (F) will have a significantly greater response to "Security" than those typed as Thinkers (T).

Many areas of life, however, offer relatively greater opportunity for objective (cognitive) evaluation (e.g., successfully mowing a lawn, having a baby, earning a promotion). Theoretically, individuals who prefer to process information and make decisions from a cognitive orientation (Ts) may have a greater preference for values that are more readily demonstrable. Propositon five reflects the many social indicators of accomplishment:

H5: Subjects typed as Thinkers (T) will have a significantly greater response to "A sense of accomplishment" than those typed as Feelers (F).

In social terms, a corollary to Hypothesis 5 may be:

H6: Subjects typed as Thinkers (T) will have a significantly greater response to "Being well-respected" than those typed as Feelers (F).

While contemporary living offers many value-states that may be judged relatively more affective or cognitive in nature, some values strike at the absolute core of human life. Such values, it would seem, may tend to be desirable regardless of one's preferred style of information processing and decision making. Accordingly:

H7: Subjects typed as Feelers (F) will *not* have a significantly greater response to "Self-fulfillment" than those typed as Thinkers (T).

TABLE 2
Comparisons of LOV Dimensions and Cognitive Styles Dominated by Thinking (T) Versus Feeling (F) (N=218)

LOV Dimension	Prediction	Finding	T Mean	F Mean	t value	Prob.
H1: Warm relations with others	F > T	Supported	6.10	6.76	5.79	0.0001
H2: Sense of belonging	F > T	Supported	5.88	6.30	2.92	0.004
H3: Fun & enjoyment /excitement	F > T	Not Supported	6.65 / 6.17	6.70 / 6.14	0.54 / 0.24	ns / ns
H4: Security	F > T	Supported	6.01	6.47	3.16	0.002
H5: Sense of accomplishment	T > F	Partially Supported*	6.79	6.54	-2.31	0.02
H6: Being well respected	T > F	Not Supported	6.43	6.48	0.43	ns
H7: Self-fulfillment	no difference	Supported	6.70	6.66	-0.45	ns
H8: Self respect	no difference	Supported	6.73	6.78	0.50	ns

*To maintain an experiment-wide alpha of 0.05, a Bonferroni-adjusted alpha of 0.006 was necessary for the 8 individual comparisons. No significance is designated by "ns."

H8: Subjects typed as Feelers (F) will *not* have a significantly greater response to "Self respect" than those typed as Thinkers (T).

RESULTS

Methodology

Sample. Because interest focused more on theory testing than application, a student sample proved appropriate (Calder, Phillips, and Tybout 1981). Responses were analyzed from 218 business students at a southeastern university. Some 110 females and 92 males participated. Average age was 22.6 years (range: 20 to 47).

Instruments. The LOV scale and the sensing/intuiting and thinking/feeling portions of the MBTI were administered to the sample. Following the suggestions of Kahle and Kennedy (1988), the excitement value of LOV was collapsed into the fun and enjoyment value, and responses were measured by a 7-point, Likert-type scale where 1 was "Not Important" and 7 was "Very Important." Regarding the MBTI, its validity and reliability as an indicator of cognitive style have been extensively critiqued (e. g., Druckman and Bjork 1991; Johnson 1992).

Results

The goal was to test each of the hypotheses with regard to the thinking/feeling dimension of the MBTI. Accordingly, t-tests were conducted on the LOV means for each hypothesis. To maintain an experiment-wide alpha of 0.05, a Bonferroni-adjusted alpha of 0.006 was necessary for each of the eight comparisons (Hayes 1988, p. 411).

As summarized in Table 2, five of the eight predictions were fully supported and one was partially supported. As predicted, Feelers valued the LOV categories of "warm relationships with others," "sense of belonging," and "security" more than Thinkers. Also as predicted, no significant differences in the valuation of "self-fulfillment" and "self-respect" were found between Feelers and Thinkers. Similarly, Thinkers were found to value "sense of accomplishment" more than Feelers, although this finding did not meet the required alpha of 0.006. Not supported were the predictions that Feelers would value the collapsed category of "fun and enjoyment"/"excitement" more than Thinkers, and that Thinkers would value "being well-respected" more than Feelers.

IMPLICATIONS, CAVEATS, AND FUTURE RESEARCH

Empirical evidence has been presented of a relationship between the thinking/feeling axis of cognitive style theory, as measured by the MBTI, and the values measured by LOV. Four differences in value preference were predicted and either supported or partially supported between subjects typed as either Thinkers or Feelers. In addition, two values were shown not to be statistically different in their valuation by Ts and Fs, as predicted. Two predictions of differential emphasis on values between Ts and Fs were not supported.

Values are culturally learned (Kamakura and Novak 1992; Rokeach 1973). On the other hand, as previously noted, the tendency toward a particular cognitive style appears to be innate. Given the empirical relationships demonstrated by this paper, a resulting implication is that the presumed genetic influence of cognitive style merits careful consideration as a potential antecedent to the formation of values and value systems in many instances. More specifically, the individual's preferred mode of decision making (thinking or feeling) may not only be antecedent to value formation, it may also closely influence the manner of adoption of values and their ultimate prioritization within value systems. Thus, the introduction of cognitive style into research on values and value systems may offer an additional way of building upon the impressive body of work that already exists in this area.

A further implication is the possibility that MBTI may subsume LOV. The thinking/feeling axis of MBTI measures an individual's preferred information processing and decision making mode. If the innate (and therefore antecedent) preference for a decision making mode does influence the adoption and prioritization of values, MBTI may indeed subsume LOV. Deductively, if an influential antecedent to values (i. e., preferred decision making mode) is measured by an instrument (the MBTI), then the possibility exists that the instrument which measures values' antecedents may subsume other instruments which measure values themselves (LOV). Clearly, a considerable amount of additional research would be necessary to support this possibility. It should also be noted that in conducting a 30-month test-retest reliability study on the MBTI, Johnson (1992) found that most changes in cognitive style designation occur on the thinking/ feeling axis. Although 77% of respondents had retained their original T-F preference upon retest, the author indicates that "the problems with stability of type lie chiefly with the T-F preference" (p. 57).

Lastly, it should also be noted that responding to items on the LOV scale is clearly a cognitive activity, the result of processing the content of each item and deciding on an appropriate response to it. Therefore, this paper's hypotheses were confined to potential influences on LOV of the information processing and decision making component of cognitive style (thinking/feeling). Future investigation will need to determine any effects the information *intake* component (sensing/intuiting) may have on responses to LOV, the adoption values, and their prioritization within value systems.

REFERENCES

Allport, G., P. Vernon, and G. Lindzey (1960), Study of Values, Boston: Houghton Mifflin Co.

Beatty, Sharon E., Lynn R. Kahle, Pamela Homer and Shekhar Misra (1985), "Alternative Measurement Approaches to Consumer Values: The List of Values and the Rokeach Value Survey," Psychology & Marketing, Vol 2 (No. 3, Fall), 181-200.

_____, Pamela M. Homer and Lynn R. Kahle (1988), "Problems With VALS in International Marketing Research: An Example From An Application of the Empirical Mirror Technique," in Advances in Consumer Research, 15, Michael J. Houston, ed., Provo, UT: Assn. for Consumer Research, 375-380.

Becker, B. W. and P. E. Conner (1981), "Personal Values of the Heavy User of Mass Media," J. of Adv. Rsrch (21) 37-43.

Calder, Bobby, Lynn W. Phillips, and Alice Tybout (1981), "Designing Research for Application," *Journal of Consumer Research*, 8 (Sept.), 197-207.

Druckman, D., and R. A. Bjork (1991), *In the Mind's Eye: Enhancing Human Performance* (Chapter 5), Committee on Techniques for the Enhancement of Human Performance, National Research Council, Washington, D. C.: National Academy Press.

Feather, Norman T. (1975), *Values in Education and Society*, New York: Free Press.

Frisbie, George R. (1988), "Cognitive Styles: An Alternative to Keirsey's Temperaments," *J. of Psychological Type*, 16, 13-21.

Gould, Stephen J. (1991), "Jungian Analysis and Psychological Types: An Interpretive Approach to Consumer Choice Behavior," in *Advances in Consumer Research*, 28, Rebecca H. Holman and Michael R. Solomon, eds., Provo, UT: ACR, 743-8.

Hayes, William L. (1988), *Statistics*, Orlando, FL: Holt, Rinehart and Winston, 411.

Hellriegel, Don and John W. Slocum, Jr., (1975), "Managerial Problem-Solving Styles," *Business Horizons*, (Dec.), 29-37.

Johnson, D. A. (1992), "Test-Retest Reliabilities of the Myers-Briggs Type Indicator and the Type Differentiation Indicator Over a 30-Month Period," *J. of Psychological Type*, 24, 54-58.

Jung, Carl G. (1971), *Psychological Types*, (H. G. Baynes, trans., rev. R. F. C. Hull), Princeton NJ: Princeton U. Press.

Kahle, Lynn R., ed., (1983), *Social Values and Social Change: Adaptation to Life in America*, New York: Praeger.

_____, and Particia Kennedy (1988), "Using the List of Values (LOV) to Understand Consumers," *Journal of Services Marketing*, Vol. 2 (Fall), 49-56.

_____, Sharon E. Beatty and Pamela Homer (1986), "Alternative Measurement Approaches to Consumer Values: The List of Values (LOV) and Values and Life Style (VALS)," *Journal of Consumer Research*, Vol. 13 (December), 405-409.

Kamakura, Wagner A. and Thomas P. Novak (1992), "Value-System Segmentation: Exploring the Meaning of LOV, *Journal of Consumer Research*, Vol. 19 (June), 119-132.

Maslow, A. H. (1954), *Motivation and Personality*, NY: Harper.

McCaulley, Mary H., Gerald P. Macdaid, and Richard I. Kainz (1985), "Estimated Frequencies of the MBTI Types," *Journal of Psychological Type*, 9, 3-9.

_____ and F. L. Natter (1974), "Psychological (Myers-Briggs) Type Differences in Education," in *The Governor's Task Force on Disruptive Youth: Phase II Report*, Tallahassee, FL: Office of the Governor.

McIntyre, Roger P. (1991), "The Impact of Jungian Cognitive Style on Marketing Interactions," unpublished doctoral dissertation, Arizona State University.

Micken, Kathleen S. (1992), "Materialism Research: Suggestions for New Directions," *Proceedings of the Research Workshop on Materialism and Other Comsumption Orientations*, eds. Floyd Rudmin and Marsha Richins, ACR, Kingston, Ont., pp. 110-112.

Mitchell, A. (1983), *The Nine American Life Styles*, NY: Warner.

Mitroff, I. I. (1981), "Is a Periodic Table of the Elements for Org. Behavior Possible?", *Human Systs. Mgmt*, 2, 3, 168-76.

Mokwa, Michael P. and Kenneth R. Evans (1984), "Knowledge and Marketing: Exploring the Foundations of Inquiry," in *Marketing Theory: Distinguished Contributions*, Stephen W. Brown and Raymond P. Fisk, eds., New York: Wiley, 170-9.

Myers, Isabel Briggs and Mary H. McCaulley (1985), *Manual: A Guide to the Development and Use of the Myers-Briggs Type Indicator*, Palo Alto, CA: Consulting Psychologists Press.

Novak, Thomas P. and Bruce MacEvoy (1990), "On Comparing Alternative Segmentation Schemes: The List of Values (LOV) and Values and Life Styles (VALS), *Journal of Consumer Research*, Vol. 17 (June), 105-109.

Percival, Terrance Q., Verner Smitheram, and Margaret Kelly (1992), "Myers-Briggs Type Indicator and Conflict-Handling Intention: An Interactive Approach," *Journal of Psychological Type*, 23, 10-16.

Pitts, Robert E. and Arch G. Woodside (1983), "Personal Value Influences on Consumer Product Class and Brand Preferences," *Journal of Social Psychology*, 119, 37-53.

Reisman, David, Nathan Glazer, and Revel Denney (1950), *The Lonely Crowd*, New Haven, CT: Yale University Press.

Richins, Marsha L. and Scott Dawson (1992), "A Consumer Values Orientation for Materialism and Its Measurement: Scale Development and Validation," *Journal of Consumer Research*, Vol. 19 (Dec.), 303-317.

Rokeach, M. (1973), *The Nature of Human Values*, NY: Free Press.

Schwartz, Shalom H. and Wolfgang Bilsky (1987), "Toward a Universal Psychological Structure of Human Values," *Journal of Personality and Social Psychology*, Vol. 53 (3), 550-562.

Singh, Jagdip (1990), "A Typology of Consumer Dissatisfaction Response Styles," *Journal of Retailing*, Vol. 66 (1), 86-87.

Smith, August W. and Thomas F. Urban (1978), "Myers-Briggs Personality Orientations and Information Processing Styles: Implications for Management Education and Development," paper presented at the National Academy of Management, MED Session, San Francisco, August 10.

Synder, M. (1976), "The Self-Monitoring of Expressive Behavior," *J. of Personality & Social Psychology*, 30 (Oct.), 526-37.

Veroff, Joseph, Elizabeth Douvan, and Richard A. Kulka (1981), *The Inner American*, New York: Basic Books.

How Green is My Value: Exploring the Relationship Between Environmentalism and Materialism

Bobby Banerjee, University of Massachusetts, Amherst
Kim McKeage, University of Massachusetts, Amherst

ABSTRACT

Environmentalism is enjoying a rebirth of interest in marketing and consumer behavior. This paper explains and clarifies environmentalism, and explores its relationship with another important consumption-oriented value, materialism. In general, the two are negatively related and may be considered competing orientations. Furthermore, the intricacies of the relationship between various aspects of materialism and environmentalism suggest potential marketing strategies for the promotion of "green" products and environmental concern in general.

INTRODUCTION

Environmentalism is enjoying its second wave of interest and renewal as a topic of vital concern. Environmental destruction first became a national issue with the observance of "Earth Day" on April 22, 1970. Promoted in part by increased media attention, the North American public has focused their attention on issues like air and water pollution, depletion of the ozone layer, deforestation, and a host of other environmental topics. The last two decades have seen increased legislation promoting environmentally friendly production processes and products (Landler, Schiller and Smart 1991), new products launched with a specific environmental appeal (Dillingham 1990), increased spending by firms on "Green Advertising" (Iyer and Banerjee 1992), and increased public participation in recycling (Roper 1990).

The volume of academic research on environmentalism has also been immense, notably in the fields of education, sociology and psychology. Although researchers in marketing and consumer behavior first studied environmental issues in the 1970's, their attention has been cyclical. Interest in the environment appears to be reviving in recent years: the last two ACR conferences have seen competitive and special session papers on the environmental impact of consumer behavior and the Summer 1993 AMA conference had a special track on environmentalism. In addition, the *Journal of Public Policy and Marketing* devoted the entire Fall 1991 issue to the environment, and *Psychology and Marketing* and the *Journal of Advertising* are also bringing out special issues on the topic.

One topic that is often discussed in the popular (and alternative) press is the impact on the environment due to consumption. The dominance of consumer motives among North Americans has led to a "throwaway" society due to the proliferation of consumer goods. The dominant paradigm of this consumer culture is materialistic values (Belk 1983; Fournier and Richins 1991; Richins and Dawson 1992). For example, Mukerji (1983, p. 8) defines materialism as "a cultural system in which material interest are not made subservient to other social goals". This perspective of materialism sets the stage for competition between personal consumption goals and more social goals like environmental protection. However, to our knowledge, there are no empirical studies examining the constructs of environmentalism and materialism.

This paper has two purposes. First, we examine the construct of environmentalism and develop a measure of the construct. Despite more than twenty years of research on public concern for the environment, knowledge of what actually constitutes environmentalism is limited (Dunlap 1985, cited in Gray 1985 p. xiii). A precise conceptualization is lacking and construct definition has generally been weak. Thus a major purpose of this paper is to provide a comprehensive picture of environmentalism and its various components.

Second, we examine the relationship between materialistic values and environmentalism. Theoretical work on materialism emphasizes consumption and acquisition of products and services. We expect that these values are incompatible with environmentalism and in this study we explore the relationship between these competing orientations and discuss the appropriate theoretical basis for such a relationship. Specifically, we examine the dimensionality of materialism and environmentalism and their relationships. We also examine the relationship between materialism and pro-environmental intentions and behaviors.

In the following sections we discuss the constructs of environmentalism, review the theoretical background of each construct, and examine the relationship between these two constructs.

THEORY

Environmentalism: Past conceptualization and measurement

Concern for the environment has usually been conceptualized as an attitude (Gray 1985, p. 22). However, this conceptualization is not without problems, in part stemming from researchers' disagreement about the appropriateness of a tripartite (cognition, affect, and conation; Cf. Maloney, Ward and Braucht 1975), versus a unidimensional, evaluative construct (Dunlap and Van Leire 1978). For instance, many "attitudinal" environmental scales include beliefs, knowledge, intentions, and behaviors (Arbuthnot 1977; Arcury et al. 1987; Constantini and Hanf 1972; Horvat and Voekler 1976; Kinnear and Taylor 1973). Other researchers have advocated the elimination of behaviors from the construct (Gray 1985).

Current measures of environmental concern also differ in terms of the substantive issues they address (Van Leire & Dunlap 1981). Much variation occurs due to the domains various researchers include in the "the environment," although attitudes toward air and water pollution, conservation, and wildlife preservation are commonly measured (Balderjahn 1988; Constantini and Hanf 1972; Cutter 1981; Dunlap and Van Leire 1984; Dyar 1975; Kassarjian 1971). However, conceptualizing environmental concern as attitudes toward substantive issues limits the construct to awareness and knowledge of specific environmental problems, especially those promoted in the media. A thorough conceptualization of environmentalism should logically also include a global level of concern.

The existing measures also differ in their theoretical conceptualization. This variation is due to the differing assumptions of what constitutes environmental concern. Past research has measured respondents' expression of concern, their perceptions of the seriousness of environmental problems, their support for legislation, and their involvement with proenvironmental behaviors (Murch 1973).

Environmentalism: A formal conceptualization

For the purposes of this study, the term environmentalism appears most inclusive. Our conceptualization of environmentalism involves the following:

1. Beliefs about the relationship of humanity and nature. Environmentalism embraces the belief that humanity and the biophysical environment are interdependent, rejecting the view that humans are intended to dominate nature (Dunlap and Van Leire 1984).
2. Beliefs about the importance of the environment to the self. This involves personal relevance, interest in environmental issues, and feelings of connectedness with the environment.
3. Beliefs that current environmental conditions are a serious problem facing the world (Murch 1974).
4. Beliefs that some radical changes in current lifestyle and economic systems may be required to prevent environmental damage (Catton and Dunlap 1982)

This conceptualization allows people to vary in their levels of environmentalism based on the strength of their beliefs. Thus, environmentalism can have a variety of behavioral consequences. For instance, product choice and purchase can be influences by environmentalism. Changes in lifestyle and other consumption behaviors, like walking or biking instead of driving, or repairing and reusing products are also possible. Other consequences are activism (e.g. signing petitions), joining environmental organizations, and keeping abreast of current environmental developments.

Materialism

In recent work, materialism has been conceptualized as an economic consumer value (Inglehart 1981; Richins and Dawson 1992) emphasizing the type and quantity of goods consumed. Materialism has also been conceptualized as one end of a materialist-postmaterialist continuum (Inglehart 1981; Knutsen 1990) where post-materialist values stress self-expression, belonging, and quality of life and reject the notion that possessions are the source of happiness. Post-materialistic values downplay monetary and economic rewards, concentrate on social goals, and promote a cooperative approach to problems. Protection of the environment therefore coincides with post-materialist values (Knutsen 1990).

In contrast, an individual with materialist values places a very high importance on worldly goods (Belk 1984). These values can be exhibited in three principal realms (Richins and Dawson, 1992). *Acquisition centrality* refers to the central place of possessions in the lives of materialists. Acquisition as the *pursuit of happiness* refers to materialists' belief that possessions are essential to their happiness. Finally, *possession-defined success* refers to materialists' evaluation that success is measured by the kind of "things" one owns. The products owned by materialists are not only chosen and acquired for their utility value, but also for their status value.

Acquisition and consumption are central motives that drive materialists' behaviors, so they would not hold environmental protection as a core value. The importance of environmental concern to materialists' self-concept should not be as strong as acquiring material goods. Preoccupation with material goods may preclude any major influence (or even existence) of environmental values. For environmentalists, consumption choices are dictated by values and beliefs placing greater emphasis on environmental protection whereas for materialists, possession and consumption *per se* are central values and choices dictated by beliefs that acquisition of goods brings happiness and defines success. Thus, we expect a negative relationship between materialism and environmentalism. Since both environmentalism and materialism can influence consumption behaviors, we also expect a negative relationship between materialism and environmental intentions and behaviors.

METHOD

Environmentalism Measure

Questionnaire items consistent with our conceptualizations were selected and adapted from several existing scales (e.g. Dunlap and Van Leire 1978; Maloney, Ward, and Braucht 1975; Weigel and Weigel 1978). These items were selected based on the domains of environmentalism described earlier. Additional items were also developed to reflect these domains and other domains not specifically measured in prior research (lifestyle changes, economic systems, self-relevance). After initial screening, 29 items remained which formed the environmentalism measure. Intentions to perform pro-environmental activities and environmental behaviors were two additional scales included to check the validity of the environmentalism measure.

Materialism Measures

Materialism was measured using the scale developed by Richins and Dawson (1992). This eighteen item measure consists of three subscales each containing six items dealing with materialism as a sign of success, as a central value, and as a route to happiness.

THE SURVEY

The instrument consisted of the materialism measure, the environmentalism measure, environmental intentions (5 items), environmental behaviors (9 items), and a social desirability scale (12 items). The instrument was part of a battery of personality and other psychological tests given to 309 students at a Northeastern university. All respondents were enrolled in an introductory marketing course and received extra credit for completing the survey. In addition, they were entered into a lottery.

RESULTS: SCALE PROPERTIES

Dimensions of environmentalism

Exploratory factor analysis of the environmentalism measure suggested a three factor structure. Initial analysis using the principal components revealed four factors with Eigenvalues greater than 1, with a simpler and interpretable structure obtained from varimax rotation. The first three factors accounted for 52.1% of the variance and were retained for subsequent analysis. The fourth factor had mixed loadings, and only a few items loaded on this factor, so it was dropped from subsequent analysis. The loadings of the environmentalism scale items are presented in Table 1.

The first factor accounted for the largest percentage of variance (37.8%). Items which comprised this factor dealt with personal interest in environmental issues, importance and personal relevance of environmental conditions. In general, these items measure the level of inherent concern an individual has for the environment. These are intrinsic and personal components of environmentalism, which we labelled *Personal or Internal Environmentalism*. This factor appeared to reflect the first two domains of our conceptualization of environmentalism, i.e. beliefs about the relationship between humanity and nature, and personal relevance of environmental issues.

The second factor accounted for 8.1% of the variance. Items that loaded strongly on this factor were individual perceptions of the severity of environmental problems like air and water pollution, deforestation, and wildlife extinction. This factor appeared to capture the domain of problem recognition discussed earlier and is labelled *Substantive Environmentalism*.

TABLE 1
Exploratory Factor Analysis of Environmentalism Scale Items[a]

Item	Factor 1	Factor 2	Factor 3
I often think about the harm we are doing to our environment.	.74		
The whole environmental issue is very important to me.	.68		
I am a person who cares about the environment.	.68		
I really don't spend much time thinking about the environment. [b]	.66		
I think of myself as an environmentalist.	.61		
I often worry about the effects of pollution on myself and my family.	.60		
I'm really not interested in environmental issues. [b]	.59		
The following problems are extremely serious and need to be addressed immediately:			
Water pollution		.80	
Air pollution		.74	
Ozone depletion		.70	
Deforestation		.69	
Wildlife Extinction		.64	
Global warming		.56	
Pollution control measures have created unfair burdens on industry. [b]			.76
Let future generations solve their own problems. [b]			.66
The benefits of modern consumer products are more important than the pollution that results from their production and use. [b]			.65
The positive benefits of economic growth far outweigh any negative environmental impact. [b]			.65
The current attention to the environment is basically raised by the media and we don't really need to do anything about it. [b]			.64
I really don't see how the destruction of the rainforests in Brazil affects my everyday life. [b]			.60

Note: Only factor loadings greater than 0.40 are displayed.

[a] Scale points were anchored using abbreviations as follows: SA = Strongly disagree, A = Agree, N = Neutral, D = Disagree, S = Strongly Disagree.

[b] Indicates items that are reverse scored.

The third factor accounted for 6.2% of the variance. Items in this factor were convenience, economic trade offs, and external perception of environmental problems (like media attention). These items also included costs and benefits of consumer products with respect to the environment, the role of future generations, and the effects of environmental legislation on industry and the economy. This factor appeared to reflect the economic and lifestyle domain, and we labelled it *External Environmentalism*.

Reliability and Validity

Coefficient alpha for the summed environmentalism scale was 0.92, and for the subscales were 0.88 for internal environmentalism, and 0.81 for external environmentalism.

A preliminary validation check for the measure involved examining its relationship with pro-environmental intentions (r = .62) and self-reported behaviors (r = .47). Table 2 summarizes these correlations, as well as those for the subscales. Intentions were measured based on a five point scale (strongly agree/strongly disagree) with several statements concerning voluntary recycling, contributing to environmental groups, petition signing for environmental protection and generally promoting awareness of environmental issues. Other items measured recycling behaviors regarding glass, paper, cardboard, plastic and cans, and consumption behaviors such as looking for recycled products and packaging, reading labels for environmental safety, reading environmental magazines, and avoiding environmentally irresponsible companies' products.

A number of studies on environmental concern have found that females tended to be more environmentally concerned than males (Arcury et al. 1987; Borden and Francis 1978; Schan and Holzer 1990). Various theoretical explanations have been offered to account for this finding, such as the ecologically benign female role of nurturer and the male-dominated mastery of nature through technological developments (McStay and Dunlap 1982). Consistent with past research, we found that females' environmentalism scores were significantly higher (t=2.01, p<0.05) than males.

Social desirability was tested because environmentalism is a pro-social value. No significant relationship was found between environmentalism and the social desirability scale.

Dimensions of materialism and reliability

Richins and Dawson (1992) found a three factor structure of the materialism measure. An almost identical pattern of results was obtained in this survey, with all but two of the 18 materialism items loading on the factors discussed earlier. These two items had mixed loadings and were excluded from further scale analysis. Coefficient alpha for the summed materialism scale was 0.83, and alphas for the subscales were 0.76 (success), 0.72 (centrality), and 0.68 (happiness). Consistent with the findings of Richins and Dawson (1992) we did not find any significant gender differences in materialism, nor did we discern any social desirability bias.

Environmentalism and Materialism: The Relationship

As discussed earlier, we expected to find a negative relationship between materialism and environmentalism since these are competing values. We found a negative correlation, albeit a small one (r=-0.20, p<0.01) between environmentalism and materialism. This relationship was hypothesized based on the literature which

TABLE 2
Correlation Matrix for Environmentalism*

	Summed Scale	Internal Scale	External Scale	Substantive Scale	Intentions	Behaviors
Summed Scale	1.00	.90	.81	.75	.62	.47
Internal Subscale		1.00	.66	.58	.65	.50
External Subscale			1.00	.47	.47	.38
Substantive Subscale				1.00	.49	.35
Intentions					1.00	.63

*p<.01 for all correlations.

TABLE 3
Subscale Correlations

	Success	Happiness	Centrality
Internal Environmentalism	-.21**	-.14*	-.12*
External Environmentalism	-.27**	-.15**	-.13*
Substantive Environmentalism	-.12*	-.09	-.10
Intentions in Support of Ideology	-.14*	-.16**	-.03
Pro-environmental Consumption	-.22**	-.09	-.03

*p<.05, **p<.01

posits the two constructs as opposite manifestations of an individual's orientation toward consumption. That is, materialism is generally considered to be a pro-consumption value whereas environmentalism is a conservation-oriented, anti-consumption value.

We conducted additional correlational analysis of the respective constructs (see Table 3). The internal and external dimensions of environmentalism were negatively and significantly correlated with all three dimensions of materialism. The strongest correlation was between external environmentalism and materialism as success (r=-0.27, p<0.01). Thus, materialists, especially those who equate material goods with success, appear unconcerned with the environmental consequences of consumption. The internal dimension of environmentalism, most indicative of core values of conservation is also significantly and negatively related to materialism as centrality, which indicates a core value of consumption.

The environmental intentions and behaviors included in the instrument can further illuminate the relationship between materialism and environmentalism. These intentions support more ideological manifestations of environmentalism. We expect that because of materialists' preoccupation with goods, they would be less willing to consider these pro-environmental actions.

The environmental behaviors suggest constraints on consumption of goods, compared to the more ideological actions of petition-signing and contributing money. Since product acquisition and consumption are central values of materialists, they should be less willing to perform these behaviors.

Correlation analysis supported these hypotheses (see Table 3). Materialism was negatively correlated with both intentions that supported ideology (r=-.12, p<.05) and pro-environment consumption patterns (r=-.15, p<.01). Within materialism, the success dimension had the greatest negative correlation with consumption (r=-.22, p<.01). In addition, both success and happiness were negatively correlated with ideology (r=-.14, p<.05 for success; and r=-.16, p<.01 for happiness).

The success dimension appears to be important for designing interventions to bring about behavioral or ideological change to protect the environment. In the ideological domain, this might include framing environmental concern as an appropriate value for successful, self-actualizing consumers. In the consumption domain, it could involve positioning environmentally friendly products as higher status goods, or attempts to discredit non-green competitors as "downscale" or passé. Because of the strong relationship between the success domain of materialism and these indicators of environmentalism, this alignment of environmentalism with status seems to have good potential for Green marketing. In addition, the significant correlation between the happiness domain of materialism and the environmental intentions would indicate that stressing the positive emotional benefits of involvement with environmental issues could also work as a strategy to promote green products to materialists.

DISCUSSION

In general, it appears that environmentalism encompasses at least three domains: a central, abiding concern with conservation issues; a localized concern with specific environmental problems, and a preoccupation with the economic and personal effects of environmental damage. Environmentalism is negatively related to materialism, and the two constructs may be considered competing orientations toward and ethic of conservation, with environmentalism serving as one broader manifestation of post-materialistic concern with broader social goals.

In an attempt to promote environmentally-friendly consumption, marketers may find it more profitable to bring environmentalism to the realm of consumption through products and packaging innovations stressing success, self-actualization, and status virtues of green consumption. This approach may be more effective than to directly challenge the ideology of consumption centrality and efforts to replace it with core environmental values. Marketers and public agencies can attempt to change perceptions of possession-defined success to include products that are less harmful to the environment by stressing either a success and status aspect of environmental responsibility, or the potential positive emotional or social rewards to be gained by a more green lifestyle. This approach is in contrast to commonly used environmental advertising campaigns that evoke negative affect (e.g. fear or guilt) among consumers.

Further research in this area can explore the strength of the relationship between materialism and environmentalism. For example, the product positioning strategies of companies that launch "green" products can be examined to see whether the utilization of status appeals or the potential for emotional and social fulfillment are useful strategies. Furthermore, experiments examining the relative effectiveness of advertising and promotional appeals using these themes could be conducted. It will be interesting to examine whether more upbeat emotional appeals are more effective than the emotional appeals featuring fear and guilt which are now commonly used.

Limitations

This study suffers from several limitations. First, this is an exploratory study in construct definition. More work in scale development and refinement (e.g. test-retest reliability) is required to establish the reliability and validity of the environmentalism scale.

Second, the correlations between environmentalism and materialism and its components are small although in the expected direction. These small correlations could be due to measurement errors. As the measures are refined the correlations may increase. However, even given the small correlations, interventions to promote environmentally friendly consumption or attempts to change public perceptions may be most effective if "green" consumption can be positioned as part of a success-oriented lifestyle. This positioning would appeal to the more materialistic consumers who might be unwilling to be converted to an environmental "ideology."

Third, this study only begins to explore the relationship between materialism and environmentalism. The exact nature of the relationship is not fully explained. For instance, we did not attempt to provide a temporal perspective on the process wherein materialism leads to lower levels of environmentalism or whether high levels of environmentalism lead to post-materialist values. More research is required before a full understanding of the development of these value-configurations is reached.

REFERENCES

Arbuthnot, Jack (1977), "The Roles of Attitudinal and Personality Variables in the Prediction of Environmental Behavior and Knowledge", *Environment and Behavior*, 9 (2), 217-232.

Arcury, Thomas A., Susan J. Scollay, and Timothy P. Johnson (1987), "Sex Differences in Environmental Concern and Knowledge: The Case of Acid Rain". *Sex Roles*, 16 (9), 463-472.

Borden, Richard J. and Janice L. Francis (1978), "Who cares about Ecology? Personality and Sex Differences in Environmental Concern", *Journal of Personality*, 46, 190-203.

Balderjahn, Ingo (1988), "Personality Variables and Environmental Attitudes as Predictors of Responsible Consumption Patterns", *Journal of Business Research*, 17, 51-56.

Belk, Russell W. (1983), "Worldly Possessions: Issues and Criticisms", in *Advances in Consumer Research*, Vol. 10, ed. Richard P. Bagozzi and Alice M. Tybout, Ann Arbor, MI: Association for Consumer Research, 514-519.

Belk, Russell W. (1984), "Three Scales to Measure Constructs Related to Materialism: Reliability, Validity, and Relationships to Measure of Happiness", in *Advances in Consumer Research*, Vol. 11, ed. Thomas Kinnear, Provo, UT: Association for Consumer Research, 292-297.

Catton, William R., and Riley E. Dunlap (1980), "A New Ecological Paradigm for Post-Exuberant Society," *American Behavioral Scientist*, 24(1), 15-48.

Constantini, Edmond and Kenneth Hanf (1972), "Environmental Concern and Lake Tahoe: A Study of Elite Perceptions, Background, and Attitudes", *Environment and Behavior*, 4, 209-241.

Cutter, Susan C. (1981), "Community Concern for Pollution: Social and Environmental Influences", *Environment and Behavior*, 13 (1), 105-124.

Dillingham, Susan (1990), "Hawking Consumer Goods with the Environmental Pitch", *Insight*, (March 26), 40-42.

Dunlap, Riley E. and Kent D. Van Leire (1978), "The New Environmental Paradigm", *Journal of Environmental Education*, 9 (4), 10-19.

Dunlap, Riley E. and Kent D. Van Leire (1984), "Commitment to the Dominant Social Paradigm and Concern for Environmental Quality", *Social Science Quarterly*, 65 (4), 1013-1028.

Dyar, N.A. (1975), "Assessing the Environmental Attitudes and Behaviors of a 7th grade School Population", *Doctoral Dissertation*, University of California at Berkeley.

Fournier, Susan and Marsha L. Richins (1991), "Some Theoretical and Popular Notions concerning Materialism", *Journal of Social Behavior and Personality*, 6, 403-414.

Gray, David B. (1985), *Ecological Beliefs and Behaviors: Assessment and Change*, Greenwood Press: Westport CT.

Horvat, Robert E. and alan M. Voelker (1976), "Using a Likert Scale to measure Environmental Responsibility", *Journal of Environmental Education*, 8, 36-47.

Inglehart, Ronald (1981), "Post-materialism in an Environment of Insecurity", *American Political Science Review*, 75 (December), 880-900.

Iyer, Easwar and Bobby Banerjee (1992), "Anatomy of Green Advertising", *Advances in Consumer Research*, 20, 494-501.

Kassarjian, Harold H. (1971), "Incorporating Ecology into Marketing Strategy: The Case of Air Pollution", *Journal of Marketing*, 35, 61-65.

Kinnear, Thomas C. and James R. Taylor (1973), "The Effect of Ecological Concern on Brand Perceptions", *Journal of Marketing Research*, 10 (May), 191-197.

Knutsen, Oddbjorn (1990), "Materialist and Postmaterialist Values and Social Structure in the Nordic Countries", *Comparative Politics*, 23 (1), 85-104.

Landler, Mark, Zachary Schiller, and Tim Smart (1991), "Suddenly Green Marketers are Seeing Red Flags", *Business Week*, (February 25), 74-75.

Maloney, Michael P., Michael P. Ward, and G. Nicholas Braucht (1975), "A Revised Scale for the Measurement of Ecological Attitudes and Knowledge", *American Psychologist*, 787-792.

McStay, Jan R., and Riley E. Dunlap (1982), "Male-Female Differences in Concern for Environmental Quality", *International Journal of Women's Studies*, 6 (4), 291-301.

Murch, Alan W. (1974), "Who Cares about the Environment? The Nature and Origins of Environmental Concern", in *Environmental Concern: Personal Attitudes and Behavior Toward Environmental Problems*, ed. Arvin W. Murch, New York, NY: Arno Press.

Mukerji, Chandra (1983), *From Graven Images: Patterns of Modern Materialism*, New York: Columbia University Press.

Richins, Marsha, and Scott Dawson (1992), "A Consumer Values Orientation for Materialism and its Measurement: Scale Development and Validation," *Journal of Consumer Research*, 19, (December), 303-316.

The Roper Organization, Inc. (1990), *The Environment: Public Attitudes and Individual Behavior*, a report on the study commissioned by S.C. Johnson and Son, Inc.

Schahn, Joachim, and Erwin Holzer (1990), "Studies of Individual Environmental Concern: The Role of Knowledge, Gender, and Background Variables," *Environment and Behavior*, 22 (6), (March), 73-86.

Van Leire, Kent D., and Riley E. Dunlap (1981), "Environmental Concern: Does it Make a Difference How It's Measured" *Environment and Behavior*, 13 (6), (November), 651-676.

Weigel, Russel H., and Joan Weigel (1978), "Environmental Concern: The Development of a Measure," *Environment and Behavior*, 10 (1), (March), 3-15.

Paradigms of the Self and the Environment in Consumer Behavior and Marketing

Annamma Joy, Concordia University
Lisa Auchinachie, Concordia University

ABSTRACT

This paper is an attempt at a holistic approach to the study of our environmental crisis and the related implications for the field of consumer behavior and marketing. Contemporary literature in consumer behavior and marketing is examined and the inherent underlying assumptions are discussed. The changing perception of self is proposed as being at the root of our ecological crisis. Implications for future research in Consumer behavior and Marketing are discussed.

INTRODUCTION

This paper is an attempt at a holistic approach to the study of our environmental crisis and the related implications for the field of consumer behavior and marketing. Contemporary environmental marketing literature will be examined, not with the traditional "how to" approach, but with the goal of understanding the underlying assumptions that are inherent in the research. Historically, the ecological crisis appears to have developed because the mainstream attitude that pervaded the social sciences, was that some form of human mechanism would operate to insure that humankind adapts to ever increasing environmental devastation (Dunlap, 1980). Latterly, people began to question this assumption together with the underlying assumptions upon which it is based. In this paper, we wish to emphasize the value of looking at nature-as- extended self in terms of addressig some of the key issues regarding the enviornment today.

THE CONCEPT OF SELF

Complicating any discussion of ecology is an epistemological problem- the distinction between self and object (self and other, me and not-me, man and nature and God, etc). Since Descartes, philosophy has made divisions between what may be assumed to belong to the self and what is "really" out there. A discussion of the perceptions of the meaning of nature is important as our orientation towards nature will affect our ideas of what constitute proper behaviour towards it. Neil Evernden (1989) describes three views of nature (nature-as-object, nature-as-self, nature-as-miracle) using post modern theory which is sensitive to binary constructs such as "self and other" and "man and the environment". It might be noted that it is not unlikely that a single person might, in different contexts, hold all of these views simultaneously.

A. Nature-as-Object

Perceiving nature as a collection of objects, whether these are considered important or not, allows people to consider themselves separate from nature and has allowed humankind to assume that they have the collective right to manipulate nature at will. Control of nature is in partnership with economic development. The ecological movement has now challenged this assumption. As early as 1962, Rachel Carson, a biologist, published a book called *Silent Spring* which described the effects of pesticides on the ecosystem.

Resource conservationists typically see nature-as-object and feel that exploitation is necessary but it must be managed. Everden (1989) explains that authors often compose their writing with this type of orientation towards nature since, were they to do otherwise, they would be accused of being unscientific. For instance, Rachel Carson, a sientist had to reject projection (perceiving feelings in nature) and anthropomorphism (acting as if nature in general has human characteristics) to keep her position in the scientific community.

Environmentalism as a term can describe orientations with diverse approaches including diverse epistemologies. Joel Schwartz (1989) describes Hobbesian environmentalism which has a nature-as-object orientation. Hobbesian environmentalism appeals to human self-interest and takes its bearing from our fear of death: unless we treat the environment well, the environment will "seek revenge" and bring about premature death for humankind. Human self-interest requires that we cease to exploit nature so systematically. Nature-as-object is the orientation adopted by our society as an inevitable result of cultural indoctrination and is at the root of the environmental crisis.

B. Nature-as-Self

This orientation considers nature-as-"extended-self" or nature-as-"like-self". It makes sense, then, that this leads to a concern with the relationship of humans and non-humans and considers rights and obligations within nature or even morality of nature. Joel Schwartz (1989) calls nature-as-self orientation, in its extreme form, ethical environmentalism (Kantian morality) and describes how this orientation will effect public policy. He suggests that this moral law asks people to regard as immoral the preference for human interests over those of animals, vegetables and minerals. Anthropocentrism (the preference for our species over others) is held to be no less immoral than the selfish preference for oneself over other people. Ecological egalitarians have even suggested that natural objects be given legal rights and independent standing in the judicial system (Stone, 1972).

Schwartz (1989) points out several problems that may arise for the legal system when one tries to implement this type of orientation. Not all manifestations of nature-as-self are extreme or have manifested themselves in legal proposals.

C. Nature-as-Miracle (Cultural Construct)

Everden (1989) goes on to describe another orientation towards nature: nature-as-miracle. Miracles are commonly understood as something that runs contrary to nature; therefore, nature-as-miracle does not necessarily follow specific "laws". The "nature-as-miracle" orientation is rejected completely by the scientific community as it questions the very basis for scientific study: there are laws of nature which can be proven. Everden (1989) points out that one can never actually prove a causal relationship as it could always change on the next trial but nevertheless we can and, do act as if it were so rather than a matter of probability. Since Descartes, nature-as-object has been the usual orientation for scientific thought and as a result humans have withdrawn from nature and consider themselves separate from it, observers, as it were, apart and looking in.

For the purposes of this study, a number of published articles on ecological consumption and marketing were identified. The underlying framework that informs much of the discussion in consumer behavior and marketing takes the view of nature-as-object. Such a view arises out of the general assumptions of environmental economics that is the source of much of the work done in marketing. A more emergent view is one of looking at nature as extended self. Some suggestions are made regarding the value of such a perspective to marketers.

NATURE-AS-OBJECT (ENVIRONMENTAL ECONOMICS)

In economics, environmental problems are often explained as a failure of the market system, faulty choices of technology or a failure of stewardship.

A. Failure of the market:

For creationists[1], excessive use of environmental resources is explained as a failure of the "invisible hand" of the market. According to them, prices, guide three critical functions of the economy: they match the output of goods and services to consumer desires, they apportion the limited supply of commodities and they prevent waste (Baumol & Oates, 1979).

B. Faulty Choices in Technology:

Another variant is represented by those who think that the matter can be solved by substituting one form of technology for another. Lovins (1971) see environmental problems as deriving from faulty technological choices. He suggests following a soft energy path (SEP) which advocates using only renewable sources of energy. The soft energy path has five important characteristics: renewability, varied and diverse technologies, simple and accessible technologies, matched in scale to end-use needs and matched in source to end-use needs.

C. Failure of Stewardship:

Others believe that environmental problems are a result of a failure of stewardship. Stroup & Shaw (1989) state that when backed by effective liability laws, private property rights tend to work well. Shortcomings in stewardship are a reflection of deficiencies or failures in the operation of the market.

Hull & St. Pierre (1990) describe three ways in which the principles of stewardship are violated: unrestricted access and common goods, mismatched rights and obligations (externalities) and perverse side-effects of government initiatives. Problems occur when users have no incentive to maintain the environmental asset because the cost of using it is little or nothing and, as a consequence the private costs do not equal the social costs. The existence of pollution, environmental degradation or other unintended side effects are explained as "externalities or spillovers".

Hull and St-Pierre (1990) have identified three approaches to achieving environmental goals:

A. Voluntarism ("Green Consumerism")

Voluntary action is characterised by zero government intervention and requires that consumer standards and purchasing patterns change to reflect environmental concernS within the community as a whole. According to Hull and St-Pierre (1990) voluntarism fails in that it simply reflects a shift in consumer tastes and spending habits. In order for voluntarism to be an effective method, these consumer changes must be sufficiently general to produce a visible change in the market and thus, produce a significant gain on behalf of the environment.

---

[1] A creationist can be defined as someone who believes that resources are always unlimited as humans have the capacity to create new resources through technology and inventiveness.

B. Government Intervention ("Command and control")

Government regulation is at the opposite pole of non-intervention and is characterised by government setting standards for such things as pollution emission rates and technologies used. As discussed earlier, government intervention may also have detrimental side effects by committing resources to unsustainable projects.

C. Market Based Approaches

Economists like Hull and St-Pierre (1990) feel that environmental problems are a result of defects in the marketplace that discourage stewardship and management of environmental assets. The failure may lie ultimately in how humans see themselves in relation to the natural environment. The market based approach falls somewhere between voluntarism, and "command and control" in terms of intervention. Assigning stewardship of environmental assets to various groups and introducing pollution taxes are some of the many possible solutions proposed.

Emission charges, user fees and licences have an impact on prices and the cost of production. Others instruments such as accelerated depreciation, favourable rates of borrowing or lowering of taxes improve the rate of return from investments in environmentally friendly technologies. Others improve market standards with rewards for compliance (Hull & St. Pierre, 1990).

NEO-MALTHUSIAN /ECOLOGICAL PARADIGM

The neo-Malthusians have rediscovered a major principle of Malthus' work that maintains that the human species is subject to, not exempt from, ecological constraints. Perhaps what they have rediscovered is the artificiality of defining man always over and against nature rather than as part of nature in which he is interconnected. There may even be some dim sense here of nature as part of the extended self.

Cook and Cook (1988) describe neo-Malthusian beliefs as follows:

> 1) Materials and energy balance constrain production. 2) Affluence is the more productive mother of invention than is growth in population. 3) The ecological paradigm states that real wealth is technology out of nature *but* nature has furnished a large portion of this wealth. 4) The industrial revolution is coming to a close and the population will outgrow the resources on which it depends. 5) Owing to their scarcity, natural resources will become more expensive. Cook (1981:25) feels that this foretells the end of economic growth based on production and that it means the replacement of the "consumer society by a conserver society".

Steady State Economy:

In response to economic creationism, a new ecological paradigm is emerging: the concept of the sustainable or steady-state economy (SSE). Daly (1980) defines SSE by the following four characteristics of which only human population and total stock (all physical things capable of satisfying human wants and subject to ownership) are held constant. "Technology, information, wisdom, goodness, genetic characteristics, distribution of wealth and income, product mix are *not* held constant" (Daly, 1980:99).

RELATED MARKETING ARTICLES

Marketing researchers, like researchers in other disciplines, have found that there is a substantial portion of the population who either believe that there is no crisis or who believe that technology will overcome any present day environmental dilemma (Talarzyk & Omara, 1974; Milstein, 1979).

Redwood (1974) expressed an optimistic view in his paper on industrial adjustment to environmental pressure. He felt that major threats to the environment in North America would be brought under control in ten years by way of technological innovation. Attempts have also been made to profile the opposing segments of "doomsayers" and "creationists" according to demographic, sociopsychological and lifestyle variables.

A. Profiling the Voluntary Simplifier

Five articles were found to relate to the segmentation of a group termed "voluntary simplifiers". The concept of voluntary simplicity came into vogue during the late seventies and has five underlying basic values: material simplicity, self-determination, ecological awareness, human scale and personal growth (Leonard-Barton, 1981). Attempts were made by various researchers to describe those ascribing to a voluntary simplified lifestyle. Demographic, behavioural, attitudinal, and lifestyle variables were all explored.

B. Profiling the Socially Conscious Consumer (SCC)

Other research has concentrated on building a profile of the socially conscious consumer. The socially conscious consumer (SCC) has been defined as someone who "takes into account the public consequences on his or her private consumption or who attempts to use his or her purchasing power to bring about social change" (Webster, 1975:188). A clear understanding of who socially conscious consumers are and how many they number is not yet apparent. Leigh, Murphy and Enis (1988) reviewed eight previous studies on the SCC and they found many conflicting results. For example, some researchers have found that SCCs are alienated while others have found they are not alienated. In terms of demographics, some research has characterised the SCC as middle class whereas others have characterised the SCC as upper class. It seems apparent that twenty years of research on the topic has not led to much in the way of appropriate segmenting variables for the socially conscious consumer.

C. Profiling the Ecologically Concerned Consumer (ECC)

Sixteen articles were found to relate specifically to the our main topic of interest: profiling the ecologically/environmentally concerned consumer. Some researchers consider this segment to be a sub-segment of the socially conscious consumer segment. Estimates of the ecologically concerned consumer population segment size have not been determined. As with the research on the socially conscious consumer, numerous defining variables have been proposed for segmenting the ecologically concerned consumer (Socio-economic, personality, attitudinal, political orientation, race, knowledge, family life cycle, locus of control, lifestyle, gender, etc.). Webster (1975) found that women were more likely than men to exhibit consistent purchase behaviour in relation to their attitudes toward social conscious consuming. On the other hand, both Leigh, Murphy and Enis (1988) and Antil (1984) report conflicting results in their reviews of past research on the socially conscious consumer. Again it seems clear that research on gender as it relates to environmental concern and behaviour has been inconsistent in its findings.

ECOLOGICAL MARKETING

Ecological Marketing has been defined by Henion (1976:1-2) as

The marketing effort of an [organisation]... expended directly or indirectly on behalf of selling or marketing goods, services or ideas whose positive ecological attributes or content constitute a minor or major appeal for the buyer, user, or adopter for the purposes of making, or which tends to result in, a short-term or long-term profit for a profit-making entity.

Articles concerning marketing strategy and ecology can generally be broken down into the elements of the traditional marketing mix: product, promotion, place and price.

Product

Various views of product management within the ecological marketing framework have been discussed. Kellerman (1978:234) states that "the ecological objectives in planning products are to reduce resource consumption and pollution and to increase conservation of scarce resources". Michman (1985) describes product management in the light of our ecological crisis as merely another opportunity to develop new products that will result in additional profits.

Leigh, Murphy and Enis (1989) used a seven layered hierarchical product differentiation scale to analyse the societal benefit of three selected product classes. The seven criteria used, ranked in decreasing order, were ecological impact, societal impact, product performance, product extension, product information, product design and product embellishment. The rationale for the hierarchical nature of this scale is drawn from the long-range perspective of the total welfare to society. As Leigh et al (1989) point out, one must assume that the primary product differentiation criterion is ecological impact as this is the ultimate constraining force on all human activity.

Promotion

For creating awareness, advertising is probably the most economically effective element of the promotional mix (Henion, 1976). Kellerman (1978) describes promotion as a vehicle for expanding the demand for ecologically benign products while encouraging conservation of scarce resources as well as a vehicle by which consumers and producers can be taught to modify their attitudes toward the environment.

The promotional role of ecological marketing is not always easy. Kinnear and Taylor (1973b) found that neutral sources, such as television documentaries, rank much higher than market dominated sources such as advertisement. The neutral sources are seen as not having any hidden motives for providing environmental information.

Henion (1976) feels that, in general, an economic appeal is usually more effective than an ecological appeal but "piggy backing" the two types of appeals should have a synergistic effect. Other articles were found to relate to the effects of environmental product labelling. Early articles, such as Henion (1972) found that shoppers appeared to respond affirmatively to ecologically relevant buying information about detergents. Frizsche and Duer (1982) found that an environmental attribute (aerosol versus non-aerosol) of a product is a very important part of the bundle of attributes which comprise a product but only for a certain segment of concerned consumers.

Three other articles were found to relate to the effects of energy labelling of refrigerators (Claxton & Anderson, 1979; Hutton & Mc Neil, 1979; Anderson & Claxton, 1982). Anderson and Claxton (1982) found that energy information had a significant impact on the purchase of small refrigerators but they felt that this may be related to the possibility of added savings in terms of electricity bills and not motivated by a concern for the good of society.

Brown and Apostolidis (1979) examined the need for product labelling that describes not only content value but societal and ecological benefits of the product. Olney and Bryce (1991) discuss the contemporary problem of consumer responses to environmentally based product claims. They discuss marketing's overuse of environmentally friendly claims and the consumers ever eroding confidence in companies who claim to encourage environmentally sound consumption. They suggest that guidelines must be set up in order that environmentally benign products be easily recognised.

Place

The next set of articles examined concerns the reverse channels of distribution required for materials recycling. These articles outline, firstly, why this is a marketing problem (Guiltinan & Nwokeye, 1974) and, secondly, various ways of implementing recycling systems (Kellerman, 1978). The advantages and disadvantages of each are evaluated. What is an important concern for our purposes is consumer response to various recycling options. It has been found that, first, a consumer must be aware that a problem exists (e.g. over extended landfills) and, second, the consumer must believe that his/her individual efforts to recycle will help contribute to the overall solution to the problem (Henion, 1976).

Frizsche (1974) found that customers of a recycling service were environmentally inconsistent in their purchase behaviour. Kellerman (1978) discusses the development of reverse channel systems for recycling but also suggests that marketers encourage one-stop shopping as well as developing distribution systems that involve more movement of information and less movement of goods and people. Michman (1985) states that the role of distribution management in light of our environmental problems involves emphasis on mass-transportation, containerisation, unit trains and other goods-handling technologies.

Price

Henion (1976) suggests, if the price of each and every product were based on its true full cost, which includes its social and environmental costs, then there would be no need for ecological marketing. In the real world, assumptions of traditional price theory are often violated. Henion also suggests that ecological marketing can convert non-environmetally concerned consumers into environmentally concerned consumers by way of effective education and merchandising.

Early research findings have suggested that ecologically concerned consumers are not always willing to pay a higher price for environmentally benign products (Herberger & Buchanan, 1971; Kerin & Peterson, 1974; Roa, 1974). One study did find a significant relationship between ecological awareness and willingness to pay (Reizenstein, Hills & Philpot, 1974), however a substantial proportion of the population was still unaware of any environmental problem and unwilling to pay for its amelioration. Reizenstein et al (1974) concluded that communication strategies need to be designed to make all segments more aware of environmental problems.

Both Michman (1985) and Kellerman (1978) state that higher prices should be implemented as this will encourage reduced demands for consumer goods. They also suggest that government instituted financial incentives for producers would encourage environmental behaviour. More recently, Hutton and Markley (1991) designed and studied a financial incentive program to reduce air pollution.

NATURE-AS-SELF IN MARKETING:

Belk (1988a) conducted an extensive review of literature on the self and the extended-self. The extended-self includes external objects, personal possessions, persons, places, group possessions as well as body parts and vital organs. The implications of nature as extended-self is that a relationship should exist between the incorporation of an object into one's extended self and the care and maintenance of the object. Several studies, although unrelated to nature specifically, have confirmed this hypothesis (Belk 1988b, 1987). Newer objects or objects that are highly cathected tend to elicit higher involvement than their older counterparts (Richins & Bloch, 1986). Possessions also aid in constructing and maintaining a sense of past which is crucial to a sense of self. The self extends not only into the present material self but forward and backward into time (Belk, 1990). Belk (1988a) suggests that natural wonders can be incorporated into the extended self in order that we enhance feelings of immortality and having a place in the world.

McClelland (1951) suggests that the more control that we exert over an external object the more likely we are to consider it a part of our extended selves. So why do we *not* consider nature as part of our extended self since we exert so much control over it?

Processes of self-extension:

Sartre (1943) suggests three ways in which we learn to regard an object as part of self: control/mastery, creation and knowledge. The implications of this relate to how people can be taught to see nature as extended-self:

Nature can become part of self through appropriating or controlling it for our own personal use. For example, some people may learn to climb mountains making the mountain part of their extended self. Also, making property public might allow individuals to consider a specific part of nature as a component of their extended-self. This theory was confirmed by work done by McClelland (1951).

Giving possessions to others or destroying possessions are also a means by which one exerts a special form of control and is therefore a means of extending the self. This was confirmed in research by Csikszentmihalyi & Rochberg-Halton (1981). It could be that our destruction of nature is simply another way of making it part of the self.

The second way, proposed by Sartre (1943), of incorporating an object into one's sense of self is through creation. Sartre suggests that buying an object is merely another form of creating the object and even the latent buying power of money contributes to sense of self. An example of this may be seen in certain interest groups such as "Friends of the forest" who buy/sponsor trees.

A third way in which objects become a part of self is by knowing them (person, place or thing). People who go "back to nature" will undoubtedly have more contact with nature and thus, it becomes more familiar and less foreign. It is likely that those more familiar with the great outdoors are more likely to consider it part of their extended self.

Belk's (1988a) concept of the extended-self is criticised by some for being a vague and unidentifiable notion. Belk (1989) states that measurement of the concept is in fact possible through an adapted version of Prelinger's (1959) test so the extended-self can, in fact, be useful in both positivistic and nonpositivistic research but favours using qualitative data.

Finally in postmodernism there is a de-naturalising of the natural. Paradoxically, postmodernism while acutely aware of ideology realises that no discourse can stand outside of ideology. The words "nature" and "natural" in this context become problematic because it is assumed that everything is in one sense "cultural" because it is coming to us always mediated by representations which include language. Not only is the word "nature" a difficulty in postmodernist thought, so is the idea of the "self" or "subject" (Flax,1987). In postmodernist thought "subjectivity is represented as something in process, never as fixed and never as autonomous, outside history. It is always a gendered subjectivity, rooted also in class, race, ethnicity, and sexual orientation" (Hutcheon, 1989:39).

Postmodernism is good at foregrounding unacknowledged politics. It dismisses older ideas of a stable, coherent self as belonging to another time and concludes, for example, that this sense of self was simple confirmed by the *representations* of self that were held at that time.

IMPLICATIONS & CONCLUSIONS

Everden (1989) has proposed three ways in which we can view nature: Nature-as-object, nature-as-self and nature-as-miracle. Nature-as-object has been the traditional orientation for the modern Westernised world and appears to have amplified our ecological crisis. Nature-as-self is proposed as an alternative view which should result in humankind taking a more gentle and caring attitude towards the natural environment. Marketing researchers have done a considerable amount of interesting work relating to the issue of the self but have not taken this issue a step further and related it to the environmental crisis.

Marketing is still dominated by and wrestling with the positivist-empiricist method of neo-classical microeconomic theory. Recent work on critical theory with its emphasis on interdisciplinary study and its goal of seeking social change may help move marketing into the postmodern period.

The economics literature argues that the move into the modern period resulted in a nature-as-object orientation. Marketing research has confirmed that a large portion of the general population are adherents to creationist ideas and believe that no crisis exists as technology will always overcome any present day environmental dilemma. This type of thinking, most certainly, makes it difficult for a nature-as-self orientation to evolve. Three groups (voluntary simplifiers, socially concerned consumers and ecologically concerned consumers) were proposed and attempts were made to identify these consumers using a multitude of segmenting variable. No consistent and significant results were found.

Finally, marketing strategy literature in relation to the environment was reviewed and divided into the traditional marketing mix of product, promotion, place and price. As noted earlier, the discipline of marketing seems to be caught up in examining the traditional cleavages. As a result, marketing has fallen behind other disciplines in proposing new paradigms that explain ecological awareness. Marketing needs to look further and deeper than demographics and other segmentation variables in explaining and describing the ecologically concerned consumer. Since social marketing, as defined by Kotler and Zaltman (1971:3-5), involves "influencing the acceptability of social ideas" and is a "framework for planning and implementing social change" it seems reasonable that marketing should be concerned with the issue of ecological awareness and its related implications. Critical theory with its postmodern perspective should become the approach for seeking this type of knowledge. Paradigms and issues of the self need to be examined with both a historical and interdisciplinary approach. Critical theory aims at improving the quality of human life and, as such, it appears to be the appropriate vehicle for investigating environmental marketing and related issues.

It has been reported that consumer confidence in environmental products is failing due to marketing's overuse of environmentally friendly product claims. Critical theory in consumer research attempts to resolve tensions between public and private interests by providing a systematic approach to revealing deception and its consequences as well as providing a way to achieve competitive advantage without contradicting public interest (Murray & Ozanne, 1991).

A theme that keeps recurring in the literature has been the need for consumer education as it has been found that environmental behaviour often hinges on environmental knowledge. It has been previously noted that much of the present day North American values had been taught through the advertising medium. It may now possible to promote new ideas such as nature-as-self through the same medium.

SELECTED REFERENCES

Anderson, C. Dennis & Claxton, John D. (1982) Barriers to consumer choice of energy efficient products. *Journal of Consumer Research*, 9, 163-169.

Awad, Ziyad; Johnston, Roger H.; Feldman, Shel & Williams, Michael P. (1983) Customer attitude and intentions to conserve energy. *Advances in Consumer Research*, 10, 652-654.

Barnaby, David J. & Reizenstein, Richard C. (1975) Attitudes toward energy consumption. *Advances in Consumer Research*, 3, 246-251.

Belch, Michael (1979) Identifying the socially and ecologically concerned consumer segment through life-style research. In Henion, Karl E. & Kinnear, Thomas C. (Eds) *The Conserver Society*. pp 69-81. Chicago: AMA.

Belch, Michael A. (1982) A segmentation strategy for the 1980's: Profiling the socially-concerned market through life-style analysis. *Journal of Academy of Marketing Science*, 10(4), 345-358.

Belk, Russell W. (1989) Extended self and extending paradigmatic perspective. *Journal of Consumer Research*, 16, 129-132.

Belk, Russell W. (1988a) Possessions and the extended self. *Journal of Consumer Research*, 15, 139-168.

Brooker, George (1976) The self-actualising socially conscious consumer. *Journal of Consumer Research*, 3, 107-115.

Claxton, John D. & Anderson, C. Dennis (1979) Energy information at the point of sale: a field experiment. *Advances in Consumer Research*, 7, 277-282.

Durand, Richard M. & Sharma, Subhash (1982) Conservation or energy development: consumer perceptions of alternate solutions to the energy crisis. *Journal of the Academy of Marketing Science*, 10(4), 410-431.

Everden, Neil (1989) Nature in industrial society. In Angus, Ian & Jhally, Sut (Eds.) *Cultural Politics in Contemporary America*, pp151-164. New York: Routledge.

Firat, A. Fuat (1991a) The consumer in postmodernity. *Advances in Consumer Research*, 18, 70-76.

Fritzsche, David J. (1981) An analysis of energy consumption patterns by stage of family life cycle. *Journal of Marketing Research*, 18, 227-232.

Henion, Karl E. (1972) The effect of ecologically relevant information on detergent sales. *Journal of Marketing Research*, 9, 10-14.

The 'Masculine Mystique:' Men's Involvement in Gift Giving, Gift Receipt and Gift Occasions

Cele Otnes, The University of Illinois at Urbana-Champaign

Much of the research on gift exchange behavior has supported the conclusion that gift giving is primarily the domain of women in American culture. However, several sociological trends (e.g., the rise of nontraditional families and increase in single-person households) may cause men to become more involved in gift exchange than in the past. Moreover, many studies of gift exchange have primarily employed women in their samples. Thus, the purpose of this session was to bring together three papers that focused solely upon men's involvement in gift giving, gift receipt and gift occasions. These papers examined men's attitudes and activities towards giving during three separate occasions.

The first paper presented was "Men in Mourning: Gift Receipt and Funeral Planning from the Male Point of View," by Kina Mallard of Union University. In-depth interviews were conducted with fifteen men who had recently experienced the death of a close relative or friend. Mallard explored the following questions: 1) What artifacts, such as cards, flowers, honoraria, meant the most to you?; 2) Which of these gifts did you keep and why?; and 3) What aspects of the funeral do you most remember? Mallard reported that men tended to value intangible gifts more than tangible ones, and tended not to keep gifts that were given at the funeral. Furthermore, many men also regarded the planning of the funeral as a chore, and were careful to consider the desires of the recipient when planning the funeral.

The second paper, "The Pleasure and Pain of Being Close: Men's Mixed Feelings About Participation in Valentine's Day Gift Exchange," by Cele Otnes (University of Illinois), Julie A. Ruth (University of Washington) and Constance C. Milbourne (Leo Burnett, U.S.A.), is published in its entirety in this volume.

The third paper was titled "A Toast for the Host? The Male Perspective on Gifts that Say 'Thank You,'" by Margaret Rucker, Anthony Freitas and Jamie Dolstra of the University of California, Davis. This study was designed to investigate attitudes and practices associated with hospitality gifts. ANOVA results indicated that men expected to pay over $25 for thank-you gifts, and that Asians expected to pay more than other ethnic groups. Many purchases were low-involvement products such as alcoholic beverages. Furthermore, males reported that the status of the host or hostess would clearly affect the type of gift they would bring, with high-status individuals warranting more expensive gifts.

Our discussant for this session was Russell W. Belk of the University of Utah, who provided many thoughtful comments and a thorough analysis of the strengths and weaknesses of each paper. A lively question and answer period followed, that stimulated many ideas upon the role of both men and women in gift exchange occasions.

The Pleasure and Pain of Being Close: Men's Mixed Feelings About Participation in Valentine's Day Gift Exchange

Cele Otnes, University of Illinois at Urbana-Champaign
Julie A. Ruth, University of Washington
Constance C. Milbourne, Leo Burnett, U.S.A.

ABSTRACT

Most studies examining gift-giving employ women in their samples. This study focuses entirely upon men's attitudes toward a salient holiday in America, that of Valentine's Day. Specifically, it expands upon our earlier finding that men have different attitudes toward the holiday and toward Valentine's Day gift-giving than women. By a qualitative analysis of open-ended questions, we examine what men believe about the purpose of Valentine's Day, what they like most and least about the holiday, and why they did or did not participate in gift-giving activities.

INTRODUCTION

In recent years, topics related to gift selection and gift-giving have received increased attention within consumer behavior. However, many of these studies employ women as their primary sample. Studies that have employed samples of both women and men have tended to examine differences between the sexes in a "breadth over depth" manner.

Yet because of the reciprocal nature of much gift exchange in America, men do engage in gift-giving, although perhaps not to as great an extent as women (Caplow 1984). Furthermore, men may approach gift exchange activities in a completely different manner than women. For example, some studies indicate men may have less positive attitudes about gift-giving than women (McGrath 1994) and may view gift-giving in a less altruistic manner, especially during courtship (Belk and Coon 1990).

Thus, the purpose of this paper is to provide an in-depth examination of men's attitudes toward gift-giving at one salient holiday in American culture—Valentine's Day. This holiday was chosen for study because cultural expectations may make it difficult for men, especially those who are romantically involved, to ignore the holiday or to delegate gift shopping to a female as they often do at other occasions (Fischer 1990).

Our own previous research (Otnes, Ruth and Milbourne 1993) revealed men had less positive attitudes about Valentine's Day gift-giving than women. Given this finding, we now investigate precisely why men had more negative attitudes toward Valentine's Day. As such, this paper will focus upon the following five research questions:

1. What do men believe is the purpose of Valentine's Day?
2. What do men like most and least about Valentine's Day?
3. What do men believe is the purpose of giving gifts at Valentine's Day?
4. What do men believe is the purpose of giving cards at Valentine's Day?
5. If men did not give gifts and/or cards, why did they not choose to give them?

METHOD

The data were collected via a survey administered for extra credit to 105 male undergraduates at a large university in the Midwest. Forty-eight respondents completed the survey in the three-day period immediately after Valentine's Day in 1992 (February 15-18). In order to increase the sample size and confidence in our results, an additional fifty-seven respondents completed the survey immediately after Valentine's Day in 1993. Statistical analyses of the quantitative data (including number of gifts given, gifts received, amount spent on cards and gifts, etc.) indicated no significant differences between the two samples. Thus, we pooled the respondents into one sample.

Respondents were given a six-page survey on Valentine's Day gift-giving. We measured the amount spent on Valentine's Day gifts and cards, the number of people who received gifts or cards from the respondent, and the number of items the respondents received.

In addition to scaled responses regarding attitudes toward Valentine's Day, the survey featured six open-ended questions about participation in Valentine's Day gift exchange. These questions parallel the research questions examined in this study, with responses to what men liked most and least about the holiday combined here.

We analyzed our data by grouping similar responses into categories, revealing the emergent patterns of responses for each question (Wolcott 1990). We opted for this approach in lieu of content analysis (Holsti 1969) because it was apparent our units of analysis were the entire responses offered rather than individual words or phrases.

Upon completing this analysis, the first and second authors examined each others' interpretations, making suggestions as to more appropriate themes.

FINDINGS

#1. Men's Beliefs in the Purpose of Valentine's Day

The first open-ended question asked men "What do you believe is the purpose of Valentine's Day?"

To Show Caring/Affection. By far the most prevalent theme among our respondents regarding the purpose of Valentine's Day was to show affection and caring for significant others, as the following responses indicate:

The purpose is showing someone how much you care about them.

Showing your appreciation for those who care most for you. Such as parents, good friends, "significant others" etc.

To let friends, boyfriends, girlfriends exchange objects, which lets the other person know you are thinking and care about them.

These particular responses capture a broad range of significant others for whom affection and caring is felt and shown. Other respondents, however, indicated that expressing romantic love for a significant other was the only true purpose of Valentine's Day:

To let the person know you care about (romantic) them.

To express your love for a significant other, be it a girlfriend, boyfriend.

> To let someone know you care for them. Usually a girlfriend or wife, not really for family.

This finding is somewhat different than the results for women in our previous study, where women included many friends and family members in their Valentine's Day celebration.

The respondents also made it clear that the *type and intensity of emotion* to be shared depends on the type of relationship and/or "significant other." Many made important distinctions between the types of caring and affection that would be shown to different people, with the main distinctions made between romantic partners, family members, and friends.

> Showing friendship to others and in some cases love if the friendship is that intense.

> The purpose is to express deep love with a romantic partner, or convey friendship with those close to you.

> To show that you appreciate that person. Depending on the type of gift, the emotion conveyed can range from soft to strong.

This result is consistent with the theories and findings regarding the categorization of emotions. More specifically, Shaver et al. (1987) observed that people categorize emotional experiences into five basic categories: joy, love, fear, anger and sadness. Variations on each of these "basic" types of emotions are considered to be subordinate-level members of the basic-level category (c.f., Rosch et al. 1976), capturing important differences in emotion type (i.e., relief is categorized as a member of the "joy" category but is different in character from joy) and intensity (i.e., a feeling of bliss is more intense than a feeling of enjoyment). Here, our respondents indicated that different types of affection could be expressed or felt, and could range in character (e.g., love, closeness, friendship) or intensity, depending on the type of relationship with the significant other.

Obligation. A second prevalent theme identified obligation as a primary purpose of Valentine's Day. Respondents also indicated the important role often played by the expectations of a romantic partner:

> Truthfully it has almost gotten to the point of obligation rather than a true expression of one's feelings. Why only give gifts on Valentine's Day?

> Primarily because people feel obligated. The holiday has been blown up so big that it is expected for not only significant others but family, friends, etc.

> Because your significant other will get pissed off if you don't. That is the honest truth.

> To show people you care about them and to keep them from being disappointed.

The obligation to participate is implicit in the "disappointment" or "anger" (Ellsworth and Smith 1988) that would be felt by the significant other if the respondent did not choose to participate.

Response to A Commercial Holiday. Another theme revealing men's negative beliefs Valentine's Day may be described as response to a commercial holiday. Respondents indicated that the "true" meaning of Valentine's Day was somewhat tainted by pressure exerted by business:

> So Hallmark can sell a lot of cards, etc. But it does let people know you care still.

> (Other than to supplement card companies' sales?) To provide your friends/family significant others with some special recognition.

> To show your love and perpetuate a card company Holiday.

Thus, the responses to this question reveal beliefs about the purpose of the holiday that might be best characterized as "mixed." Most respondents indicated that the holiday afforded an opportunity to show caring and affection for significant others. However, many respondents indicated that feelings of obligation, the need to meet significant others' expectations, and pressure exerted by the marketplace detracted from demonstrations of caring for others.

#2. What Men Liked Most/Liked Least About Valentine's Day.

Although we asked the general questions "What did you like most" and "What did you like least" about Valentine's Day, the responses clearly indicated our respondents' preoccupation with aspects of gift exchange.

Liked Best About Valentine's Day. The most prevalent theme emerging with regard to the "like best" question centered around Valentine's Day gifts, as the following responses indicate:

> Just getting a card from my parents and "Significant other."

> I got a rose from a girl I didn't expect to.

> Spending a little too much, but spending it on someone I care about.

> I received my first rose ever.

> When you give your girlfriend the present you got for her it lights up her face and you know you made her happy.

Interestingly, a tendency for men to enjoy gift receipt more than gift-giving emerged. While gift receipt may always be preferred to gift-giving, this finding is consistent with the literature that indicates women are typically regarded more as the "givers" in America, while men are socialized to be the passive recipients of such effort (Caplow 1984; Sherry and McGrath 1989).

Equally as prominent was the tendency for our respondents to describe *self*-gifts as their favorite parts of Valentine's Day. Self-gifts can be defined as special self-indulgences that tend to be premeditated and highly context-bound (Mick and DeMoss 1990). These self-gifts took many forms. The most common was the time men enjoyed with their significant others during the holiday. Some descriptions of time spent together were quite poignant, and reflect how much this self-gift was valued:

> The intimate time I spent with my girlfriend.

> Being with each other and celebrating our first Valentine's Day together.

> It is the first year that I spent this day with this particular person whom I care about.

> I was able to share it with someone I cared about.

The value of time as a gift during courtship was discussed by Belk and Coon (1991; 1993), who note that men often place equal, or more, value upon intangibles as they do upon tangible gifts.

Moreover, we also support Belk and Coon's finding that sex is often viewed as an important gift during courtship. Sex can be viewed as a gift of self. Given that men may celebrate Valentine's Day primarily to commemorate romance, it is not surprising sex was mentioned as a favorite aspect of the holiday.

Another self-gift that emerged could be viewed as compensation for men's *lack* of romantic involvement at Valentine's Day. This gift involved socializing with other friends who were also not involved in a romantic relationship, or attending a special event on Valentine's Day:

Spending the day with other single friends.

I had a Valentine's Day dance and spent it with my friends.

I was with some of my closest friends I got here, and we had a small get-together.

I spent the evening with a good friend of mine, who is also single, and we had a ball.

While the pleasure expressed at participating in these events is no doubt sincere, for some respondents, spending the occasion with friends may have been important in order to help them alleviate the dissonance associated at being "left out" (e.g., single) at Valentine's Day.

A final form of self-gift male respondents reported receiving was their deliberate attempt to celebrate Valentine's Day in a "low-key" fashion. Respondents wrote:

It was relaxing—we had a great time just being with each other.

No frills. Didn't go out of my way to buy something expensive. Just basic.

The fact that I was not obligated to buy anyone a gift.

For me it wasn't overhyped.

Thus, consistent with the responses regarding the purpose of Valentine's Day, being spared from a heightened feeling of obligation was viewed positively by the respondents.

A few males offered responses centering around the emotional fulfillment of Valentine's Day, without the mention of gifts. For example:

Knowing someone cares and wants to spend time with you.

Mutual expression of love and thoughtfulness.

Girlfriend and I expressed true feelings for each other.

The mood got me and my (ex) girlfriend to talk about "things."

Thus, while many of the "like best" responses did focus upon tangible or intangible gifts, some males valued the overall affective state that was achieved.

Liked Least About Valentine's Day. Perhaps it is not surprising that our respondents' most common answer to "What did you like least about Valentine's Day?" was the lack of a significant other. Like other occasions in America (e.g., wedding anniversaries), Valentine's Day can exclude individuals who do not meet (or feel they meet) the criteria for inclusion in the celebration. As such, legitimacy of participation may be a salient issue for respondents who perceive they are excluded from valid participation. Moreover, the emphasis upon romantic love and couples in America may reinforce feelings of inadequacy among those who are not romantically involved.

While many males simply wrote "Didn't have a girlfriend" in their response to the "like least" question, others were more articulate about why this was such a negative aspect of the holiday:

The fact that I didn't, or never have had, someone to celebrate it with.

No current girlfriend to really enjoy the meaning of Valentines' Day.

Not having anyone to spend time alone with.

I just ended a relationship, and I think V-day is for romantic partners. I didn't give anything nor did I expect anything while my dating friends could exchange things.

Furthermore, references to relationships that have ended reveal that for many single males, Valentine's Day can evoke unhappy memories of past romances.

Our assumption that Valentine's Day may be difficult for uninvolved males was reinforced by the emergence of another salient theme among our "liked least" responses, that of the social and psychological pressure emanating from various sources. Men often reported they were subjected to feelings of guilt, obligation or anxiety during the holiday:

The fact that media and society keeps reminding me what day it was and I didn't have a girlfriend.

Buying cards or even thinking that I had to buy something or else I would feel guilty.

The strings that are attached. There's no such thing as a non-committal Valentine's Day gift.

Feeling obligated to get something for a woman I have only seen sporadically for a few weeks. We are hardly a couple, yet I felt I had to get her something.

I disliked the tension I felt from trying to find the right gift.

I wish that people would not resort to "card companies" to show that they care. It is cheaper and just as easy to make a card. It could be as simple or extravagant as they want.

Therefore, even men who did celebrate Valentine's Day often felt manipulated into participating.

Three common patterns also emerged that were unrelated to gift-giving per se. These were: men's inability to be with their significant other; lack of time to celebrate and bad situational experiences (e.g., "Did not like my dinner."). Separation and lack of time probably stem from the nature of the college sample. Likewise, the situational comments did not seem limited to Valentine's Day in particular.

However, two other categories that also emerged less frequently did relate to gift-giving. First was the view of Valentine's

Day (and gifts in particular) as too expensive. A second category that related to gifts is that men complained when they did not receive anything at the holiday:

I didn't get anything for the first time.

The fact that no one was obligated to buy me a gift.

Girlfriend still has not gotten me a card.

Not receiving a gift from my boyfriend, when I went through the trouble of buying him some things.

Thus, the above responses show how strongly Valentine's Day gifts and cards—or lack thereof—figure in men's enjoyment of Valentine's Day. Specifically, most positive aspects related to receiving gifts, while many negative aspects stem from the pressure of giving, costs incurred in gift-giving, or the lack of gifts received. Furthermore, the inability to participate in Valentine's Day because of lack of a significant other was clearly what made many men most unhappy.

#3 Purpose of Gifts

Consistent with the responses regarding the overall purpose of Valentine's Day, one main purpose of gifts was to show caring and affection for significant others: "To show people that I cared and that I was thinking of them;" "I wanted to show her how much I care." As part of this theme, respondents also indicated that the gift itself would help to demonstrate the importance of the person or the strength of feelings:

Because I wanted to make her feel loved and I figured something material would help.

To say that I care enough about the other person that I got her something.

In addition, respondents described feelings beyond caring and affection, by suggesting that enjoyment and surprise were also important aspects of the gift-giving process:

To let those people know I cared about them and to make them happy.

To make my girlfriend smile.

To surprise a good friend at another university.

To show that I really care and because the gifts were entertaining for me too.

Thus, the emotions related to the gift itself were different than those regarding the purpose of the holiday, where responses focused on the love and affection rather than joy experienced by either the giver or recipient.

Obligation. Respondents also indicated that the desire to meet expectations and obligations was a primary purpose of giving gifts. These obligations stemmed from expectations of significant others, desire to avoid negative situations, and the desire for balanced reciprocity (Belk 1976).

Because if there is someone special, it seems sort of expected.

Because if I didn't, I would never hear the end of it.

To perpetuate the holiday and not seem rude. I knew I was getting one so I had to give.

Altruism. Although not as prevalent as the two themes discussed above, a third pattern in the data suggested altruism: "Because I wanted to do something nice for these people;" "Because I wanted to;" "Because it's a nice gesture." This theme is consistent with altruistic motivations that have been reported in other studies of gift exchange (Wolfinbarger 1990; Goodwin, Smith and Spiggle 1990). However, it is interesting that the theme of obligation was more evident than that which expressed the desire to spontaneously give gifts.

#4 Purpose of Cards

The themes that emerged regarding the purpose of cards was consistent with the prevalent themes about gifts: to show feelings of caring and affection and to meet obligations. Yet respondents also indicated that cards had a particular role in expressing thoughts or feelings:

I'm better at expressing my feelings in writing.

Cards can say it a lot better than I can.

To express my thoughts and feelings in a different way that I wouldn't be able to do whether that is serious or humorous.

With respect to feelings of obligation, respondents indicated they felt pressure exerted by individuals or the marketplace to give cards.

Obligation to some, because I like them for others.

Guilt that I had to and common courtesy.

Sent card to grandma because my mom told me to.

Isn't that what card companies say you're supposed to do?

These types of responses are consistent with previous themes, where pressure was exerted from a variety of internal and external sources.

Accompaniment to Gift. Other respondents did not mention the role of expressing feelings but focused on cards as an accompaniment to a gift: "As tags for the gifts;" "It's part of the package." This theme suggests the card can play a fairly functional role in the gift-giving process and implies that some of our respondents have internalized a rule that packages are somehow "bare" without cards attached.

#5 Why Respondents Did Not Give Cards/Gifts.

Our final question asked respondents who did not give cards or gifts this year to indicate why they did not. The fact that the most prevalent reason was lack of a romantic partner reinforces the notion that for men, the holiday is primarily an opportunity to mark romantic relationships rather than to acknowledge the importance of other types of relationships:

I didn't choose to give a gift because I didn't really have anyone (a girlfriend) to give one to.

No girlfriend.

I don't have a girlfriend—so, no point. And I don't need to be reminded that I want one by giving it to a prospective (yet reluctant) Valentine.

For respondents who perceive Valentine's Day as relevant to those besides romantic partners (e.g., parents, siblings, etc.), the nature of the relationship seemed to dictate the rationale for not participating in gift-giving activities: "Grandparents not living. No girlfriend. Dad left. Roommates—don't like them."

Lack of Adequate Resources. A more pragmatic rationale for not giving cards or gifts also emerged. Here, lack of money and time were cited as reasons for not participating.

Laziness more than anything—I wanted to but time and money hindered me.

Too busy and didn't see any reason to.

Didn't have the time to search for the "right" card.

Again, this situation may be due in part to our student sample.

Response to a Commercial Holiday. The notion that business exerts a great deal of pressure to participate emerged again in the reasons for not giving Valentine's Day cards or gifts. Many respondents expressed this belief in a variety of ways, with frequent references to Valentine's Day being a "Manufactured" holiday. One respondent expressed particularly strong feelings:

Giving gifts on Valentine's Day has become a superficial, trendy thing to do. It's mostly brought about by the media's brainwashing, capitalistic attempts at maximizing profits. Giving Valentine's gifts as a sign of love or friendship is OK if you feel strongly about it—but not if you feel you have to because of what society says. The fact that I'm not involved in a relationship at the moment probably had something to do with it, however.

As suggested by the themes that emerged with respect to the purpose of Valentine's Day, for men the role of a romantic partner seems to be critical aspect in determining their satisfaction with, and participation in, gift-giving activities. As suggested by this respondent, the presence of a romantic partner might help offset negative perceptions of the commercial aspect of the holiday. This finding supports our general proposition that people—especially men—who are not involved in a romantic relationship may not feel like valid participants in the holiday.

DISCUSSION

Several themes emerged across the various questions regarding men's beliefs about and participation in Valentine's Day gift-exchange activities. Clearly, many men believe Valentine's Day provides an opportunity to show feelings of caring and affection for significant others. While many respondents indicated that Valentine's Day was most appropriate for romantic partners, others indicated remembering family members and friends. Consistent with the literature on emotions, our respondents made clear distinctions between the types of emotions shared with different types of people: feelings of closeness and friendship for friends, affection for family members, and strong feelings of love for important romantic partners (Smith and Ellsworth 1985; Shaver et al. 1987).

Feelings of obligation to participate, however, were quite prevalent throughout the responses. These feelings of obligation stemmed from pressure exerted by significant others and institutions (e.g., media and businesses). This result may help to explain why one particular theme emerged with respect to what men liked the most about the holiday: being able to celebrate the holiday in a low-key fashion, without feeling obligated to meet the heightened expectations of others.

Finally, although many respondents indicated the holiday included a variety of celebrants, the predominant "significant other" for most men was a romantic partner. Lack of such a partner was clearly the least liked aspect of the holiday for many respondents and was one of the prevalent reasons why men did not give cards or gifts. This result is not entirely consistent with women's activities. In our previous study, women indicated that they gave cards and gifts to many friends and family members.

These results provide important insight in the nature of men's perceptions about gift-giving at Valentine's Day and point to possible explanations for their perceptions of gift-exchange. In particular, men and women may perceive different levels of "appropriate" gift-exchange participation. While women may have been socialized as the primary gift-givers in our society, men may prefer a more "low-key" approach to marking this particular holiday (and perhaps many gift-exchange occasions). However, the predominant theme concerning what men liked most about the holiday dealt with gift receipt itself. These two themes, in combination, suggest that men enjoy receiving gifts but feel pressured into giving gifts. In fact, no respondent expressed a perception that they had received "too many gifts" or "too much" of a gift, whereas many respondents expressed a desire to feel less obligated to give gifts. A potentially controversial conclusion, then, is that the men in this sample wanted to receive gifts but did not want to invest the time, effort, or emotional or monetary investment to reciprocate.

CONCLUSION

This study has provided important insight into men's perceptions of the purpose of Valentine's Day and the purpose of gift-giving, including cards, to mark the holiday. This study is an important departure from other studies about gift-exchange for two primary reasons: (1) it focuses on men's perceptions and beliefs about a particular gift-giving occasion; and (2) it focuses on a holiday, Valentine's Day, that has received less attention than more prominent gift-giving occasions such as Christmas. This paper expands on our earlier finding that men hold less positive attitudes toward the holiday and delves into the reasons behind these less positive attitudes.

The study reveals that men view Valentine's Day as an occasion to show caring and affection toward significant others. However, the holiday is also associated with negatively perceived pressures to participate.

This study suggests the importance of exploring the gift-giving processes for both men and women in order to explore the commonalities of psychological processes and to explore differences in the perceptions that influence gift-exchange processes and activities. In addition, this study suggests an important role of emotions in gift-exchange activity. Our respondents made important distinctions between the types of emotions expressed through gift-giving activity. They also indicated a variety of emotions that may accompany gift exchange—including joy, love, disappointment, guilt, and anger. Investigations of the role of emotions may provide important insights into the "mixed" feelings men experience during gift-exchange, both at Valentine's Day and other occasions.

REFERENCES

Belk, Russell (1976), "It's the Thought That Counts: A Signed Digraph Analysis of Gift-Giving," *Journal of Consumer Research* 3 (December), 155-162.

Belk, Russell and Gregory Coon (1990), "Can't Buy Me Love: Dating, Money and Gifts," in *Advances in Consumer Research*, Vol. 18, eds. Rebecca Holman and Michael Solomon, Provo, UT: Association for Consumer Research, 521-527.

Belk, Russell and Gregory Coon (1993), "Gift Giving As Agapic Love: An Alternative to the Exchange Paradigm Based on Dating Experiences," *Journal of Consumer Research*, 20 (December), 393-417.

Caplow, Theodore (1984), "Rule Enforcement Within Visible Means: Christmas Gift-Giving in Middletown," *American Journal of Sociology* 89 (May), 1306-1323.

Coon, Gregory and Russell Belk (1991), "Men and Women on Dating and Gift-Giving: Same Planet, Different Worlds," in *Proceedings of the Conference on Gender and Consumer Behavior*, ed. Janeen A. Costa, Salt Lake City, UT: Association for Consumer Research, 94-103.

Ellsworth, Phoebe C. and Craig A. Smith (1988), "From Appraisal to Emotion: Differences Among Unpleasant Feelings," *Motivation and Emotion*, 12 (3), 271-302.

Fischer, Eileen (1990), "'Tis the Season To Be Jolly? Tensions and Trends in Christmas Shopping," presented at the 1990 Assn. for Consumer Research Conference, New Orleans, LA.

Goodwin, Cathy, Kelly L. Smith and Susan Spiggle, "Gift-Giving: Consumer Motivation and the Gift Purchasing Process," in *Advances in Consumer Research*, Vol. 17, eds. Marvin Goldberg, Gerald Gorn and Richard Pollay, Provo, UT: Association for Consumer Research, 690-698.

Holsti, Ole (1969), *Content Analysis for the Social Sciences and Humanities*, Reading, MA: Addison-Wesley.

McGrath, Mary Ann (1994), "Gender Differences in Gift Exchanges: New Directions from Projections," *Psychology and Marketing*, 229-224.

Mick, David Glen and Michelle DeMoss (1990), "Self-Gifts: Phenomenological Insights From Four Contexts," *Journal of Consumer Research* 17 (December), 322-332.

Otnes, Cele, Julie A. Ruth and Constance C. Milbourne (1993), "I Like You, I Like Me: The Influence of Gender, Romantic Involvement and Self-Acceptance on Valentine's Day Gift Exchange," presented at the American Marketing Association Winter Educators' Conference, Newport Beach, CA.

Otnes, Cele, Tina M. Lowrey and Young Chan Kim (1993), "Gift Selection for Easy and Difficult Recipients: A Social Roles Interpretation," *Journal of Consumer Research*, 20 (September), forthcoming.

Rosch, Eleanor, Carolyn B. Mervis, and Wayne D. Gray (1976), "Basic Objects in Natural Categories," *Cognitive Psychology* 8 (July), 382-439.

Shaver, Phillip, Judith Schwartz, Donald Kirson, and Cary O'Connor (1987), "Emotion Knowledge: Further Explanation of a Prototype Approach," *Journal of Personality and Social Psychology* 52 (6), 1061-1086.

Sherry, John F., Jr. and Mary Ann McGrath (1989), "Unpacking the Holiday Presence: A Comparative Ethnography of Two Gift Stores," in Elizabeth C. Hirschman, ed., *Interpretive Consumer Research*, Provo, UT: Association for Consumer Research, 148-167.

Smith, Craig A. and Phoebe C. Ellsworth (1985), "Patterns of Cognitive Appraisal in Emotion" *Journal of Personality and Social Psychology*, 48 (4), 813-838.

Wolcott, Harry F. (1990), *Writing Up Qualitative Research*, Newbury Park, CA: Sage.

Wolfinbarger, Mary Finley (1990), "Motivations and Symbolism in Gift-Giving Behavior," in *Advances in Consumer Research*, Vol. 17, eds. Marvin Goldberg, Gerald Gorn and Richard Pollay, Provo, UT: Association for Consumer Research, 699-706.

A Toast for the Host? The Male Perspective on Gifts that Say Thank You

Margaret Rucker, University of California, Davis
Anthony Freitas, University of California, Davis
Jamie Dolstra, University of California, Davis

ABSTRACT

For the most part, previous research on gift giving has focused on major holidays and rites of passage and taken the female perspective. The present study was designed to investigate attitudes and practices associated with "thank-you" gifts and explore the male perspective regarding these small-scale courtesies. Analyses of data from 86 males indicated a substantial level of concern with matching gifts to the value of the hospitality (simultaneous reciprocity) and the value of any previous thank-you gifts (serial reciprocity). There was also some evidence of gender stereotypes and effects of age and ethnicity as well as situational effects on this type of gift giving.

INTRODUCTION

A number of studies have suggested that, at least in contemporary Western societies, women are the primary performers of gift-giving activities (e.g., Cheal 1986, 1988; Fischer and Arnold 1990; McGrath 1989; Sherry and McGrath 1989). From early in life onward, men appear to have less interest in, and are less adept at, providing others with satisfactory gifts (Corrigan 1989; Rucker, Freitas, Murray and Prato 1991). Quite frequently they enlist the aid of mothers, sisters and spouses or some other close female to assume the gift-giving obligations associated with occasions such as birthdays, weddings, Christmas and Hanukkah. Exceptions may include occasions when the recipient is a girlfriend or spouse, such as Valentine's Day (Otnes, Ruth and Milbourne 1993), or when other circumstances impel males into more active gift giving and receiving roles, such as the death of a close family member (Mallard 1992).

While these and other studies of gift-giving have contributed greatly to our understanding of the rules and gender roles involved in prestation, it should be noted that most of this work has been done in the context of major holidays and rites of passage. As previously suggested by Rucker and Dolstra (1993), an examination of gift exchanges associated with more mundane occurrences is necessary for a more comprehensive understanding of the gift-giving system.

The objective of the present study was to examine gift-giving in the context of reciprocity for hospitality and to determine how hosts and guests respond to what Lowes, Turner and Wills (1971) have proposed as a universal moral dilemma—should there be expectations regarding gifts in return for friendship and hospitality. Specifically, it was designed to determine the male perspective regarding this dilemma and speak to research questions that derive from males' relatively agentive orientation (cf Bakan 1966; Carlson 1971; Meyers-Levy 1988) and their economic approach to gift exchanges (Rucker et al. 1991). In addition, effects of age and ethnicity were examined. Because previous literature provided relevant cross-cultural data, and the two subgroups in our sample were relatively large, the majority of the analyses for ethnic differences were between Asian and White respondents.

General aspects of gift-giving that were considered in this study included selection of the product (type and value), how selection varied with sex and status of the recipient, and importance of wrapping the gift. Issues that were more specific to the gift-for-hospitality context included relative emphasis on simultaneous versus serial reciprocity (matching the gift to the style and value of the hospitality offered versus matching a previous gift from the host or hostess) and norms regarding the sharing of gifts.

With respect to type and value of the product selected as a gift, we proposed that males' tendency to take an economic orientation toward gift-giving would be associated with relatively high concern for appropriateness of price; within a given price range, however, there would be selection of some relatively unusual gifts. Some evidence for this proposition was reported by Morsbach (1977). In his study of gift exchanges in Japan, it was noted that for many Japanese gift occasions, exact monetary repayment is the norm. At the same time, although food is the most typical gift, any product can be an appropriate gift if it is easy to determine the market value.

An economic orientation toward gift-giving would also limit interest in elaborate wrapping of gifts since paper and bows are generally discarded and therefore do not typically add to the permanent economic well being of the recipient. In research conducted in a midwestern U.S. city, Caplow (1984) found that men displayed much less interest in wrapping packages than did their wives. Attention to gift wrapping may vary with ethnic identity, however. As noted by Witkowski and Yamamoto (1991), gift packaging is quite important in Asian cultures, particularly in Japan. The authors suggest that one factor prompting the emphasis on packaging may be the cultural norm of first viewing a gift in private.

How status of the host might affect gift selection is more ambiguous. Some authors have suggested that asymmetric gift exchanges occur as a reflection of economic and social differences (Belk 1976, 1979; Bell and Newby 1976; Cheal 1986; Davis 1973; Moschetti 1979). That is, those with lower status or fewer resources give less, at least in terms of tangible objects. As Gouldner (1960) has suggested, intangibles such as gratitude or deference may be appropriate repayment in some instances. In contrast, at least in some situations, those of lower status may make relatively high investments in gifts for their superiors in an attempt to elevate their own status or ingratiate themselves with powerful others (Cohen, 1958; Hurwitz, Zander and Hymovitch, 1968). In particular, in Asian countries such as Japan, business etiquette dictates that those of higher rank are given better gifts (Morsbach 1977).

Sharing of thank-you gifts by host and guests can reduce the gift's economic value to the host by an uncertain amount. Therefore, males may have some reluctance to share such gifts. Asian males may be especially reluctant to engage in sharing of their gifts but for a different reason, i.e., the cultural norm of opening gifts in private. Work by Furby (1978) suggests that age of respondent could also affect sharing norms. In her study, American subjects were found to have a less absolute conviction about the value of sharing and to make more distinctions regarding appropriate conditions for sharing as they grew older.

From an economic perspective, both simultaneous and serial reciprocity should be seen as important. However, in comparing simultaneous with serial reciprocity, we predicted that males would favor the serial reciprocity approach. Simultaneous reciprocity demands what Davis (1973) has referred to as "ingenious pre-estimation" in determining what one will receive so as to match it in value with what one gives. Serial reciprocity, or matching what one receives as a gift now with what one gives on the next occasion, is more likely to produce an economically balanced exchange.

TABLE 1
Stepwise Logistic Regression Analysis of Ethnicity and Giver vs Receiver Role on Type of Gift - Summary Table

Variable	df	Chi-square
Role	1	5.34*
Ethnicity	1	4.42*

*$p < .05$

METHOD

As part of a larger project on gift giving, 86 male college students were asked to participate in a study of experiences with gift giving in return for hospitality. These students were selected from volunteers responding to an announcement on a campus bulletin board.

At the beginning of the research session, respondents were asked to complete a background questionnaire. Items on this questionnaire included age and ethnicity as well as how much they thought should be spent to thank someone for hospitality.

After completing the questionnaire, subjects were interviewed about their gift-giving attitudes and practices. Items in the interview included questions about types of gifts usually given, whether gifts were generally wrapped, whether they were generally shared, and whether status of the host or hostess would affect gift selection. To address the moral dilemma issue raised by Lowes, Turner and Wills (1971), respondents were also asked whether they had experienced any problems related to thank-you gifts and whether there were situations in which a thank-you gift should always be given or never be given. Another interview item asked for a description of a recent experience with gifts given as a token of appreciation.

RESULTS

Analysis of the demographic data indicated that respondents' ages ranged from 16 to 29 with a median value of 21. The ethnic composition of the sample was 50% Asian, 29% White, 8% Hispanic, 6% Black and 7% other. As noted earlier, due to the limited number of Blacks and Hispanics in the sample, the subsequent quantitative analyses for ethnic differences included Asian and White respondents only.

Analysis of the normative data on thank-you gift value was consistent with previously reported results (Rucker and Dolstra 1993). That is, the majority of males felt that such a gift should cost at least $20 or more. Analysis of variance of the normative values by ethnicity of respondent indicated that the difference between what Asian males expected to pay and what White males expected approached significance (p = .06) with Asian respondents reporting higher average values. An ANOVA for ethnicity on what was actually spent was run for the subgroup whose most recent experience with tokens of appreciation involved giving one rather than receiving one. The difference between Asians and Whites was not significant in this analysis, although again the average dollar amount reported by the Asian respondents was higher than that reported by the White respondents.

Analysis of the products respondents reported exchanging most recently indicated that the product most likely to be exchanged was an alcoholic beverage. However, as shown by the stepwise logistic regression results presented in Table 1, there was a significant difference in whether the gift was alcohol or food, depending on whether the respondent described a gift given or a gift received. Gifts given were more likely to be alcoholic beverages while gifts received were more likely to be food. Furthermore, ethnicity of the respondent added significant information to the equation; Asians were more likely to mention food and Whites were more likely to mention alcoholic beverages. This latter finding is consistent with observations by Morsbach (1977) regarding gift giving in Japan; i.e., food is the traditional and still one of the most popular gifts for just about every occasion.

Further qualitative analysis of the interview data suggested that while many males' thank-you gifts were low-involvement purchases of alcoholic beverages, a number of others were rather unusual high-involvement gifts such as an antique iron and automobile parts from Japan. Variety in gift types was more in evidence in the Asian subgroup than the White, again in keeping with Morsbach's observations that in Japan a range of products are acceptable to balance economic obligations. Males in ethnic groups other than Asian seemed either unaware of product-type norms within their culture or felt that cultural stereotypes regarding males' lack of expertise in gift giving allowed more latitude in choosing unusual gifts, especially for other males.

Data on wrapping of gifts indicated that contrary to our prediction, the majority of males felt it was appropriate to identify a thank-you gift as a gift through at least some semblance of decorative packaging. This could be as simple as covering the item in tissue paper or cellophane or placing a bow somewhere on the product.

However, they were also quick to point out how functional considerations influenced this aspect of gift giving. For example, hot or oily foods did not lend themselves to being wrapped and cut flowers, unless boxed, were apt to be damaged by wrapping.

Stepwise logistic regression analysis indicated that Asians and Whites did not differ significantly in their approach to wrapping thank-you gifts. Across ethnic groups, the pragmatic question of ease of wrapping an item appeared to be given priority over cultural norms.

Approximately 60% of the respondents stated they would give a more expensive or at least more labor intensive thank-you gift to someone of higher status than to a peer. The main reasons offered for this difference were need to make a good impression and to reciprocate for a better class of hospitality. A stepwise logistic regression analysis indicated that responses to this status question did not differ significantly by ethnic group.

Over 65% of the respondents reported that whether they were buying for a host or hostess would affect their evaluation of a product as an appropriate thank-you gift. This finding supports previous work indicating that consumers in general tend to be influenced by gender stereotypes in evaluating products as good or bad gifts (Rucker et al. 1991). Again differences between the two ethnic groups were not significant.

Respondents showed less agreement about the appropriateness of sharing thank-you gifts. About one-third of the sample noted that a number of situational conditions would mediate the

TABLE 2
Stepwise Logistic Regression Analysis of Age and Ethnicity on Sharing of Gifts - Summary Table

Variable	df	Chi-square
Age	1	4.14*

*$p < .05$

appropriateness of sharing. For example, the nature of some products, such as the automobile parts, precluded sharing, while the nature of others, such as flowers, invited sharing. Another mediating condition was whether the gift complemented the meal. When situational characteristics offered no guidance on sharing, our respondents uniformly stated that the gift recipient should make the choice to share or not. As shown in Table 2, the stepwise logistic regression for these data showed that there was a significant difference by age but not ethnic identity. The data indicated that the older subjects were less likely to report sharing of thank-you gifts. This finding is consistent with the developmental trend noted by Furby (1978), i.e., older subjects were more aware of exceptions to a general norm of sharing.

Content analysis of recent gift experiences and problems as well as norms provided evidence of both simultaneous and serial reciprocity. A number of respondents described how the gift should match the hospitality. For example, it was generally agreed that a "nice" bottle of wine was appropriate for a formal dinner whereas beer went with a barbeque. At the same time, there was some recognition of the importance of serial reciprocity, including both value and product type. As one respondent put it, after he brought the beer to his friend's dinner, he expected the friend to provide the beer when the dinner invitation was returned. And since he provided better than an inexpensive generic, he expected his friend to do the same. (Fortunately, for the sake of the friendship, his friend provided an upscale import.)

Analysis of the data did not elicit much that could be construed as reflective of a moral dilemma or problem as was proposed by Lowes et al. (1971). Responses focused more on *what* to give rather than *whether* to give in return for hospitality. Respondents were concerned about how to select an item that would be appreciated by the recipient and gave a number of examples of gift failures. These ranged from bringing an alcoholic beverage to someone who did not approve of drinking or was trying to quit, to giving politically and culturally incorrect gifts, such as flowers for a feminist.

The data also gave some additional evidence of gender stereotyping. Two of the males expressed the opinion that if the invitation was from a female, a gift was necessary. On the other hand, one male said he would never do that for fear the girl would misunderstand his intentions. Other circumstances that were mentioned as inhibiting gift giving included frequent hospitality exchanges (in which case, one invitation served to reciprocate another), knowledge that other guests were not bringing a gift, and dislike of the host. For the most part, however, our respondents had no difficulty with the concept of hospitality meriting some tangible token of appreciation.

CONCLUSIONS

There was some limited support for propositions derived from the economic model of male gift giving, primarily in expressed concerns for both simultaneous and serial reciprocity. However, contrary to the initial expectation, there seemed to be more emphasis placed on simultaneous reciprocity than serial reciprocity. With hindsight, it may be that simultaneous reciprocity is less problematic than usual for this type of gift-giving situation. That is, it may be easier to pre-estimate what type of hospitality will be offered than what type of product will be purchased as a present.

Other findings reinforced previous advice to examine situational constraints in a given area of consumer behavior before applying general rules of thumb (cf Belk 1975; Scammon, Shaw and Bamossy 1982; Sherry 1983). For example, type of gifts often precluded the attention to special wrapping that is given to items for other occasions. In addition, the data provided some support for considering not just cross-country differences in analyzing gift giving, but also ethnic identity within the population of any one country. Age was of limited value as an explanatory variable due to restriction in range, but analyses did suggest that additional attention to changes with age in attitudes toward sharing possessions might elicit useful information on both human development and relationships between possessions and social systems.

REFERENCES

Bakan, D. (1966), *The Duality of Human Existence*, Chicago: Rand McNally.

Belk, R. W. (1975), "Situational Variables and Consumer Behavior," *Journal of Consumer Research*, 2, 157-164.

Belk, R. W. (1976), "It's the Thought that Counts: A Signed Digraph Analysis of Gift-Giving," *Journal of Consumer Research*, 3, 155-162.

Belk, R. W. (1979), "Gift-giving Behavior," *Research in Marketing*, 2, 95-126.

Bell, C., and H. Newby (1976), "Husbands and Wives: The Dynamics of the Deferential Dialectic," in *Dependence and Exploitation in Work and Marriage*, ed. D. L. Barker and S. Allen, New York: Longman.

Caplow, T. (1984), "Rule Enforcement Without Visible Means: Christmas Gift Giving in Middletown," *American Journal of Sociology*, 89, 1306-1323.

Carlson, R. (1971), "Sex Differences in Ego Functioning: Exploratory Studies of Agency and Communion," *Journal of Consulting and Clinical Psychology*, 37, 267-277.

Cheal, D. (1986), "The Social Dimensions of Gift Behavior," *Journal of Social and Personal Relationships*, 3, 423-439.

Cheal, D. (1988), "The Gift Economy. New York: Routledge.

Cohen, A. R. (1958), "Upward Communication in Experimentally Created Hierarchies," *Human Relations*, 11, 41-53.

Corrigan, P. (1989), "Gender and the Gift: The Case of the Family Clothing Economy," *Sociology*, 23, 513-534.

Davis, J. (1973), "Forms and Norms: The Economy of Social Relations," *Man*, 8(2), 159-176.

Fischer, E., and S. Arnold (1990), "More Than a Labor of Love: Gender Roles and Christmas Gift Shopping," *Journal of Consumer Research*, 17(3), 333-345.

Furby, L. (1978), "Sharing: Decisions and Moral Judgments About Letting Others Use One's Possessions," *Psychological Reports*, 43, 595-609.

Gouldner, A. W. (1960)," The Norm of Reciprocity: A Preliminary Statement," *American Sociological Review*, 25, 161-178.

Hurwitz, J. I., A Zander, and B. Hymovitch (1968), "Some Effects of Power on the Relations Among Group Members," in *Group Dynamics: Research and Theory* (3rd ed.), ed. Cartwright and A. Zander, New York: Harper and Row.

Lowes, B., J. Turner, and G. Wills (1971), "Patterns of Gift Giving," in *Explorations in Marketing Thought*, ed. G. Wills, London: Bradford University Press.

Mallard, K. (1992), "An Examination of Gift Exchange at Funerals," Paper presented at the annual Association for Consumer Research meeting, Vancouver, B.C.

McGrath, M. A. (1989), "An Ethnography of a Gift Store: Wrappings, Trappings and Rapture," *Journal of Retailing*, 65(4), 421-449.

Meyers-Levy, J. (1988), "The Influence of Sex Roles on Judgment," *Journal of Consumer Research*, 14, 522-530.

Morsbach, H. (1977), "The Psychological Importance of Ritualized Gift Exchange in Modern Japan," *Annals of the New York Academy of Sciences*, 293, 98-113.

Moschetti, G. J. (1979), "The Christmas Potlatch: A Refinement on the Sociological Interpretation of Gift Exchange," *Sociological Focus*. 12, 1-7.

Otnes, C., J. Ruth and C. C. Milbourne (1993), "The Influence of Gender and Self-acceptance on Valentine's Day Gift Exchange," in *Marketing Theory and Applications*, Volume 4, ed. R. Varadarajan and B. Jaworski, Chicago, IL: American Marketing Association, 54.

Rucker, M., and J. Dolstra (1993), "Gifts as Tokens of Appreciation: New Tests for Old Models," in *Marketing Theory and Applications*, Volume 4, ed. R. Varadarajan and B. Jaworski, Chicago, IL: American Marketing Association, 55-56.

Rucker, M., A. Freitas, D. Murray, and H. Prato (1991), "Gender Stereotypes and Gift Failures: When the Sweet Don't Want Sweets," in *Gender and Consumer Behavior*, ed. Janeen Costa, Salt Lake City, UT: University of Utah Printing Service, 244-252.

Rucker, M., L. Leckliter, S. Kivel, M. Dinkel, T. Freitas, M. Wynes, and H. Prato (1991), "When the Thought Counts: Friendship, Love, Gift Exchanges and Gift Returns," in *Advances in Consumer Research*, ed. R. H. Holman and M. R. Solomon, XVIII, Provo, UT: Association for Consumer Research, 528-531.

Scammon, D. L., R. T. Shaw, and G. Barnossy (1982), "Is a Gift Always a Gift? An Investigation of Flower Purchasing Behavior Across Situations," in *Advances in Consumer Research*, Vol IX, ed. A. Mitchell, Ann Arbor, MI: Association for Consumer Research, 531-536.

Sherry, J. F., Jr. (1983), "Gift Giving in Anthropological Perspective," *Journal of Consumer Research*, 10, 157-168.

Sherry, J. F., Jr., and M. A. McGrath (1989), "Unpacking the Holiday Presence: A Comparative Ethnography of Two Gift Stores," in *Interpretive Consumer Research*, ed. E. Hirschman, Provo, UT: Association for Consumer Research, 148-167.

Witkowski, T. H. and Y. Yamamoto (1991), "Omiyage Gift Purchasing by Japanese Travelers in the U.S.," in *Advances in Consumer Research*, Vol XVIII, ed. R. H. Holman and M. R. Solomon, Provo, UT: Association for Consumer Research, 123-128.

Death By Nostalgia: A Diagnosis of Context-Specific Cases

Stacey Menzel Baker, University of Nebraska-Lincoln
Patricia F. Kennedy, University of Nebraska-Lincoln

ABSTRACT

Nostalgia has been a popular subject in a recent stream of research, but the research has not, as of yet, delineated between the different levels of nostalgia and the levels of emotional intensity associated with each. We suggest that there are three types of nostalgia—real, simulated, and collective—and that each has an inherent value to add to marketing. Propositions are presented which may give a more complete understanding of the use of nostalgia as a promotional tool and its role in marketing.

In addition, we suggest a new scale which may be useful in determining the difference between the positive affect associated with the ad and the nostalgic feeling evoked by the ad.

The traditional literature on symbolic consumption has focused on the motivations for a consumer's product choice intentions (e.g. Dichter 1964; Levy 1959). However, in more recent times, the perceptual meaning of objects within certain contexts has begun to receive more attention (e.g. Kleine and Kernan 1991). Within certain contexts, there are layers upon layers of meanings for an object or for objects (Hirschman 1980). This meaning often is derived from an experience from some time in the past. Thus, the meanings of these products can evoke nostalgic feelings.

The purpose of this paper is to examine the nature of "context specific" nostalgia and the implications that nostalgia has for marketing with the focus being primarily on the feelings evoked by products or other stimuli, not just on the products themselves. After briefly reviewing the literature, we suggest three types of nostalgia which may lead to a better conceptual understanding of the construct, and then examine a scale which allows for the examination of the difference between the nostalgia generated by a stimulus and the attitude associated with that stimulus.

In his medical dissertation, Johannes Hofer (1688) referred to "nostalgia" as a fatal disease. An extreme case of homesickness was the diagnosis as the cause of death for what would be recognized today as suicide or an eating disorder. Actually nostalgia was a fairly common diagnosis for extreme depression until the 1950's, when it started being used to refer to more personal emotions (Davis 1979).

From a psychological point of view, nostalgia has been seen as somewhat problematic because the main concern has been with the interpretation of a stimulus within the context in which it was presented (Daniels 1985). In contrast, the sociological perspective examines these reflections on the past to determine the relevance of nostalgia in our present lives (Davis 1979). That is, psychology has focused on nostalgia on an individual level and sociology has focused on nostalgia from a societal level, both fields have tried to determine the worth, or inherent goodness, of nostalgic feelings.

Nostalgia is actually an emotion which is fairly new to the marketing literature (e.g. Belk 1990; Havlena and Holak 1991; Holak and Havlena 1992; Holbrook and Schindler 1991), but marketing practice has increasingly made use of nostalgic cues in positioning. For example, producers of toys which have stood the test of time, games (e.g. Twister), old-fashioned juke boxes, clocks, Coca-Cola coolers, movies, and music have recognized the persuasiveness of nostalgia.

THE MEANING OF NOSTALGIA

For the purposes of this paper, nostalgia will be defined as a sentimental or bittersweet yearning for an experience, product, or service from the past. This is fairly consistent with Belk's (1990, p. 670) definition of nostalgia as "a wistful mood that may be prompted by an object, a scene, a smell, or a strain of music." Although the definitions of nostalgia differ somewhat from author to author, there is still the same underlying theme. When one feels nostalgic, there seems to be a bittersweet quality to the meaning which is associated with a memory from the past. That is, there is a certain amount of sadness in the emotion that is experienced, but there is also happiness in the emotion. This bittersweet quality is, perhaps, best illustrated through the use of a quote from Abraham Lincoln's poem, "Memory."

> "My childhood's home I see again,
>   And sadden with the view;
> And still, as memory crowds my brain,
>   There's pleasure in it too."
>   Abraham Lincoln at the age of 37
>   (Felleman 1936, p. 540)

The bittersweet quality was present as he recalled with fondness the carefree days of his childhood in a home that was symbolic of his fond memories. His recollection gives credence to the suggestion that the geographic area of a person's childhood is often known to be sacred (Belk, Wallendorf, and Sherry 1989).

The Nostalgic Experience

It is not surprising that family and friends are important elements in the nostalgic experience (Holak and Havlena 1992). The smell of freshly baked cinnamon rolls at a nearby bakery may evoke nostalgic feelings of a grandmother. The playing of a song from the past may bring back memories of an earlier time of laughter and friendship with childhood companions.

Objects such as jewelry, antiques, toys, books, and cars also are known to make people feel nostalgic (Havlena and Holak 1991). There is a deeper meaning in a product than just the tangible product itself. Products can help preserve memories. For instance, souvenirs from trips are often gathered so that the experience can be relived and retold to others. Photographs can serve as an "investment in creating a memory bank" (Belk 1990, p. 670). Family heirlooms also preserve memories of loved ones and the heritage of all that the family has done.

Special events such as weddings, holidays, and school-related experiences are often remembered with a feeling of nostalgia (Holak and Havlena 1992) which may be evoked by tangible objects such as the bride and groom from the top of the wedding cake, or a special Christmas ornament. Family vacation spots also tend to make one feel nostalgic (e.g. Disneyland and Walt Disney World). By returning with a souvenir or photo, in the future nostalgic feelings will be generated by considering a time when ordinary tasks were put on hold so that something could be done with special people. Although there is happiness in the emotion, there is also a certain sadness in the emotion, because it may be wished that these events could be relived (Belk, Wallendorf, and Sherry 1989).

Nostalgia permits people to maintain their identity after major transitions in their lives (Davis 1979). It thrives on apprehension or nervousness about change or transitions in life (Davis 1979). For instance, a time which probably evokes the most nostalgia for some women is the time directly proceeding their first marriage as they

TABLE 1
Proposed Levels of Nostalgia

Level	Definition	Example
Real Nostalgia	symbolic of a time with which there is a direct experiencce; an exemplar	a song from college days that makes you feel like you could "conquer the world" again
Simulated Nostalgia	symbolic of a time with which there is no direct experience; a prototype	antiques, replica cars
Collective Nostalgia	symbolic of a culture, nation, or generation	theme parks, hot dogs, a flag, national pastimes

tend then to remember all of the things that happened to them when they were growing up and may go through their childhood possessions as a way of remembering.

This may seem somewhat counterintuitive, as it would be expected that as individuals prepare for changes in their roles, they would look to the future in order to prepare for what was ahead. Although this may be true, a certain amount of nostalgic reflection is probable as one reflects on how it is that s/he got to where s/he is today. To a certain extent, the amount of nostalgic reflection may be dependent on the perceived quality of life in the past. Thus, an individual's perceived quality of life may be an important mediator for nostalgia.

Hirsch (1992) predicted that the use of nostalgia in marketing communications would increase in the coming decade because the more dissatisfied consumers are with life as it is today, the more they will want to revert back to the past. Thus, in hard economic times, nostalgia is a more useful selling tool. The saying "Nostalgia is the ability to remember yesterday's prices while forgetting yesterday's wages" (Source Unknown), is certainly applicable here. That is we tend to remember the good and forget the bad. This gives rise to our first set of testable propositions.

P1: The more drastic the change in a current life role, the more nostalgia, or symbolic reflection, will occur.

P2: The more satisfied individuals are with their perceived quality of life in the past, the more nostalgia, or symbolic reflection will occur.

P3: The more dissatisfied consumers are with current economic conditions, the more consumers will want to revert to the past, hence the more effective messages which evoke nostalgia will be.

Individual and Gender Differences

Meaning arises from the individual, the object, and the context (Csikszentmihalyi and Rochberg-Halton 1981; Kleine and Kernan 1991); it does not arise from the physical object alone. Csikszentmihalyi and Rochberg-Halton (1981) note that, because meaning is usually not associated with the attributes of an object, the meaning that is assigned to a particular object is quite flexible. In addition, symbolic meaning is fairly subjective (Belk 1987); although the tangible product is the same for everyone, its intangible meaning is different (Hirschman 1980).

Each person has a different symbolic meaning which s/he associates with a particular stimuli (Csikszentmihalyi and Rochberg-Halton 1981). Thus, the saying "one person's trash is another person's treasure" has a certain truth to it. Possessions which are highly treasured by one individual may not necessarily be treasured by another (Csikszentmihalyi and Rochberg-Halton 1981).

It makes it easier to make choices among the increasing array of stimuli when one object is more compatible with our thoughts and feelings than another (Levy 1959). Because the emotions that things evoke are symbolic of attitudes, objects serve as a means of individual differentiation (Csikszentmihalyi and Rochberg-Halton 1981).

Davis' (1979) research showed that men tend to be more nostalgia prone than women. However, Sherman and Newman (1977-78) indicated that although there are differences in gender, they found no differences in "nostalgia proneness" between the genders. These authors did find that, although elderly women are just as likely to have cherished possessions as elderly men, there is a difference in the type of objects which are cherished. Women tend to choose items associated with particular memories (e.g. photographs) while men choose consumer items (e.g. cars). The different ways that women and men view ownership of possessions may also be a factor in the type of objects which are cherished (Rudmin 1991). This gives rise to another testable proposition.

P4: Men and women differ in the items which evoke feelings of nostalgia. The differences due to gender will depend on the product category and the time in the person's life that is being considered.

Given the mixed views on gender differences, proposition four is primarily exploratory because so little work has been done in this area. Gender differences are perhaps the result of socialization (Maccoby and Jacklin 1974) which is bound to be ingrained in an individual. Because nostalgia may often be felt for the times when that socialization was taking place, the objects with which males and females choose to associate memories differ. At times when the differences between genders are less noticeable, perhaps males and females associate similar objects with memories.

Nostalgia is a very private emotion (Daniels 1985). It is obvious that there are differences among individuals and genders as to the type of stimuli that will evoke nostalgic reflection. In addition, it appears that there are different levels of nostalgia that can be evoked. These levels will be discussed in detail in the following section.

LEVELS OF NOSTALGIA

Today marketing communications and products use nostalgic references to target baby-boomers and senior citizens (Havlena and Holak 1991). If these nostalgic references are effective, this may impact sales of the types of products which are aimed at seeking a nostalgic association. We suggest that there are three different levels of nostalgic associations which may be elicited. We categorize these as: real nostalgia, simulated nostalgia, and collective nostalgia. These are summarized in Table 1 and will be discussed in more depth in that order.

Real Nostalgia

Real nostalgia refers to a sentimental or bittersweet yearning for the experienced past. This is the level of nostalgia which Baumgartner (1992) discussed when he examined the relationship between the emotion and the original experience and what Davis (1979) referred to as "true nostalgia." Davis (1979) said that true nostalgia can only be experienced if a person has lived through the event.

Stimuli which elicit real nostalgia can evoke very vivid recollections. With episodic memory, if you have a very vivid piece and a dull piece, it is obvious to which you are going to attend (Alba and Hutchinson 1987). Therefore, real nostalgia may be exemplar-based. That is, experience may be needed for the evoking of "real nostalgia."

A song that was popular when an individual was in college brings back a time when s/he thought s/he could conquer the world. That is, the song elicits a very bittersweet emotion which may be called real nostalgia, because the time is very vivid and experience-based. In addition, as a result of the importance and authenticity of the event, another stimulus which may evoke real nostalgia is a photograph of one's college graduation.

Belk (1990) states that, in general, people insist on the authentic stimulus to symbolize their sacred experience. "A similar wedding ring, a photograph of a similar family's Thanksgiving feast, or a car like the one we had in college may provoke a brief nostalgic flashback, but they are clearly inferior to and would hardly be traded for 'the real thing'" (Belk 1990, p. 672).

Simulated Nostalgia

When "the real thing" is not available, it may be possible to elicit simulated nostalgia. Simulated nostalgia refers to a sentimental or bittersweet yearning for the indirectly experienced past and may be remembered through the eyes and stories of a loved one. Simulated nostalgia may be evoked because a loved one did actually experience the times being depicted or by actually being with them when they relived the times.

Stern (1992) discussed a "historical nostalgia" in which there was not a direct experience with the past being described. In fact, Stern suggests that the event being depicted often occurred before birth. However, the images which were idealized, stressed the inherent goodness of the time. Antiques and collector's items are good examples of products which people may own that elicit this simulated nostalgia.

In addition, products from the past are reintroduced or used by consumers to evoke nostalgic feelings from a past of which they may not have even been a part (Havlena and Holak 1991). Even when the experiential component is blocked from awareness, there is still an emotion (Deci and Ryan 1991). Thus, one can feel nostalgic or attach a symbolic meaning to an object when, in fact, the person has never experienced the event which the object represents. Perhaps, simulated nostalgia helps to explain why an individual may feel nostalgic when wandering around in a museum. That is, a person who has not experienced the events depicted in the museum may still feel nostalgic.

Whereas real nostalgia is similar to an exemplar, simulated nostalgia is similar to a prototype, which is an abstract image that is often associated with a certain occurrence. Research shows that people are not accurate historians of their own personal information (Ross and Conway 1986). Therefore, they tend to embellish and perhaps reconstruct events from the past with which they had no direct experience. For example, when a town celebrates its centennial, the people try to reconstruct events from a past with which they had no direct experience and may feel a bittersweet, nostalgic emotion for the reconstructed events. That is, they experience an emotion referred to here as simulated nostalgia.

Collective Nostalgia

Nostalgia can be felt for a representation of a culture (Belk, Wallendorf, and Sherry 1989). Thus, a sentimental or bittersweet yearning for the past which represents a culture, a generation, or a nation may be called collective nostalgia. This is not an individualistic notion, rather, it is a collectivistic notion which makes the emotion more consistent between individuals of a similar background when it is presented in the same context.

Belk (1990) suggests that collective memory is generation specific. This has certain implications for the types of products which people will collect (Davis 1979) and a person's taste in music (Holbrook and Schindler 1989). This might suggest that a generation of people will feel collective nostalgia for a 57' Chevy or the music of Peter, Paul, and Mary, but other generations will have their own symbols which elicit nostalgic reflection.

Collective nostalgia should not be limited to generations, it could also be used to explain similar emotions experienced by members of a culture or members of a country. In the United States, such symbols as baseball, amusement parks, and the American flag and foods such as hot dogs and fried chicken may elicit this nostalgia. This leads to our next set of propositions.

P5a: *The intensity of the nostalgic emotion is dependent upon the level of nostalgia which is evoked (i.e. directness of experience).*

P5b: *The intensity of nostalgia is greatest when a direct experience has occurred.*

P5c: *Although a consumer may not have direct experience with the past that is evoked by advertising, promotional messages, or products, the consumer may still feel nostalgic, but with less intensity, when presented with the stimulus.*

P5d: *The emotion, referred to as collective nostalgia, is more consistent between individuals, but it is less intense than the more private emotions referred to as real nostalgia and simulated nostalgia.*

Imagery Implications

MacInnis and Price (1987, p. 483) stated that "imagery can play an important role in reliving these experiences." Imagery, or a sensory representation of a memory, allows past experiences to be relived. In addition, imagery may help to give symbolic significance to treasured possessions because of the meaning associated with them (Csikszentmihalyi and Rochberg-Halton 1981). Because of imagery, individuals are better able to "picture" in their mind the actual event which has been elicited by a certain stimulus.

Because imagery can help relive experiences, it may suggest "that a consumption experience can live well beyond its typically conceived duration" (MacInnis and Price 1987, p. 483). As has been pointed out (e.g. MacInnis and Park 1991; MacInnis and Price 1987), this has certain implications for repurchase behavior and perceived satisfaction with the original purchase. This leads to our next propositions.

P6a: The more direct the experience, the more vivid the memories.

P6b: The more intense the nostalgia, the easier it is to image being in the past.

Emotion and Affect

As the preceding discussion indicates, nostalgia is a fuzzy and somewhat messy construct because of the different levels or forms in which nostalgic reflections may occur. Therefore, because the emotion or warmth of the stimulus is very closely related to the attitude or amount of positive affect a person has for that stimulus, it is necessary to distinguish between the two constructs. This is consistent with Batra and Ray (1986), who distinguished a general affect, or positivity, for an ad from the feelings associated with the ad. Their findings emphasize the persuasiveness that feeling responses might have. In fact, they found that the feelings associated with an ad influence a person's attitude towards an ad, which further affects brand attitudes. The relationship between nostalgia and affect for an ad can be summarized in the following propositions.

P7a: The feeling of nostalgia evoked by an ad and the general positive affect for an ad are distinct factors.

P7b: If a person does not have positive affect for an ad, nostalgia will not be present.

The importance of examining these issues was pointed out by Stayman and Aaker (1988), who noted that specific feeling states when viewing the ad exposure should be distinguished from specific affective reactions or global affective reactions toward the ad. Further, it has been pointed out that feelings, which are evoked by exposure to an ad, may have different roles. The feelings may be used to develop an association with a particular brand or to set a certain mood for the ad, therefore there are certain conditions when feelings have direct effects and are not entirely mediated by a persons affect for an ad (Stayman and Aaker 1988). As a result, it is necessary to examine these effects further, rather than just looking at the outcome or underlying process.

METHODOLOGY

An exploratory study was conducted in order to test only the last two propositions (7a and 7b). The intent was to establish that, in fact, the feeling of nostalgia which is evoked by an ad is not the same thing, nor is it entirely mediated by a individual's affect for an ad. Although it was believed that the nostalgic feeling a person would associate with an ad would not be entirely mediated by the person's attitude toward the ad, in general, if a person did not like an ad, then nostalgia would not be felt. Therefore, this initial study was designed to examine only these issues. The focus of the study examined nostalgia as a general construct; it did not attempt to determine the differences in the proposed levels of nostalgia, because it was believed that a tighter definition of the nostalgia construct and scales for measurement of the construct were essential before the construct could be broken down into the proposed levels.

The sample for this study consisted of 86 college students, males and females, who were shown a magazine advertisement which the researchers thought would elicit a nostalgic response in at least some of the students. Pretest results with subjects from an undergraduate marketing class revealed that both men and women expressed feelings which were indicative of nostalgic emotions. One female said, "this ad reminds me of time with my Mom" and one male said this "reminds me of the relationship between my mother and my sister."

The ad that was shown was for Lane cedar chests, in which a mother and daughter were discussing how you would know when you are in love. As the subjects looked at this ad, they were asked to mark a series of responses indicating their intensity of affect and intensity of emotion for the ad. That is, they were presented with a series of items that were designed to measure attitude towards the ad and nostalgia evoked by the ad.

As is fairly typical (e.g. Stayman and Aaker 1988), the attitude items where designed to determine the specific affective reactions toward the ad (e.g. This ad is very appealing) and the global affective reactions toward the ad (e.g. I really like the ad) in order to determine the respondent's general affect for the ad. The nostalgia items were developed for the purposes of this study in order to determine the presence of a nostalgic feeling which was evoked by the specific context of the ad which the students were asked to examine (e.g. I think about the past when I look at this ad). There were six attitude items and six nostalgia items which were presented with a 5-point Likert scale measuring the intensity of feeling from strongly agree to strongly disagree. (These items are presented in Table 2).

RESULTS AND DISCUSSION

A principal factor extraction with varimax rotation was performed to determine if nostalgia and attitude were, in fact, different constructs. A factor analysis of the six attitude items and the six nostalgia items revealed that there were two distinct factors evoked by the ad. After varimax rotation, loadings of the variables revealed that there were two distinct factors (as shown in Table 2).

The factor matrix gives initial support to the proposition that the attitude or affect associated with the ad is independent from the nostalgia associated with the ad. In fact, by examining the factor loadings, one can observe that the items separate into attitude (Factor 1) and nostalgia (Factor 2) indicating that the nostalgic feeling evoked by the ad is not entirely mediated by the attitude towards the ad. This distinction may help to understand the nature and possible effect of feelings, whether a feeling is present or not may have a direct effect on the affect for an ad.

The Cronbach's alpha for the items measuring attitude toward the ad was .94 while the Cronbach's alpha for the items measuring nostalgia was .89. Thus, the items in the scales are fairly reliable and may be useful in determining the difference between the affect and the feeling generated by a stimulus in a context specific situation.

The correlation of attitude towards the ad and nostalgia is .69 ($p<.01$), which supports the final proposition that, in essence, stated that if a person does not like an ad, then a nostalgic feeling will not be evoked. The constructs are fairly highly correlated in a positive direction which indicates that nostalgia is more likely to be elicited when an individual is presented with an appealing stimulus.

CONCLUSION

Past efforts in the consumer behavior literature have moved toward a better understanding of symbolic consumption. However, researchers have ignored the importance that people place on their possessions in creating and maintaining their past (Belk 1990). Nostalgia directs people to search among remembrances of persons and places from the past in order to give meaning to them (Belk 1988). In fact, the absence of symbols (such as photographs) may inhibit nostalgia.

In order to determine our self-identity, it is important that we understand the past. Over time we develop a set of symbols which we believe represent the self-identity that we want to project;

TABLE 2
Factor Analysis Results for Lane Cedar Chests Advertisement

	Means**	Loadings Factor 1	Factor 2
I really like this ad.	2.65	.80	.46
I do not think this ad is interesting.*	2.80	.74	.40
I think this ad is convincing.	2.67	.81	.26
This ad is very appealing.	2.65	.87	.30
This ad is easy to forget.*	2.52	.60	.32
This ad is very effective.	2.41	.83	.34
This ad reminds me of an experience from the past.	2.78	.42	.74
This ad makes me think of an experience which I feel sad about because it is over, yet it is a happy memory.	2.41	.27	.78
This ad does not make me have any feelings about the past.*	3.09	.41	.75
I wish I could relive the experience(s) this ad makes me think of.	2.65	.23	.65
I do not think about the past when I look at this ad.*	3.30	.30	.78
I associate this ad with a happy experience, yet it makes me feel sad.	2.93	.25	.46

** 5-point scale from (5) strongly agree to (1) strongly disagree
* reverse coded

---

nostalgic reflections help us to maintain that identity over time. Just as it is important to look to the future and think of where we are going, it is also important to remember where we have been.

The exploratory study outlined in this paper was intended to establish the distinction between nostalgic feelings associated with an advertisement and positive affect for an advertisement. However, generalizability to other situations is somewhat questionable because the nature of the emotion seems to be "context specific."

The propositions outlined in this paper suggest specific directions for future research. Determining the time in a person's life, the time in the economy, or the types of situations or products which elicit nostalgic feelings to members of both sexes when nostalgic cues are most appealing is important to understand when promotional messages are being created. In addition, the different levels of nostalgia may suggest that there are differences in the intensity of the emotions and the vividness of the memories which are elicited, which has certain implications for marketing communications and the expectations of these communications. Future research should also examine the role which mood, the warmth or humor of a stimulus, plays in the affect or emotion felt as a result of exposure to a stimulus.

Possessions and imagery can play an important role in helping individuals to relive their past experiences and to help elicit nostalgic feelings. Therefore, it is important that consumer researchers recognize the importance of nostalgic associations. Nostalgia is becoming a very popular self-diagnosis for individual feelings elicited by certain stimuli, which are presented with the intention of evoking nostalgia. Certainly a diagnosis of nostalgia today is considerably more positive than a diagnosis of nostalgia was in the late 1600's, as our modern day emotion surely beats "death by nostalgia."

REFERENCES

Alba, Joseph W. and J. Wesley Hutchinson (1987), "Dimensions of Consumer Expertise," *Journal of Consumer Research*, 13 (March), 411-453.

Batra, Rajeev and Michael L. Ray (1986), "Affective Responses Mediating Acceptance of Advertising," *Journal of Consumer Research*, 13 (September), 234-249.

Baumgartner, Hans (1992), "Remembrance of Things Past; Music, Autobiographical Memory, and Emotion," in *Advances in Consumer Research*, 19, eds. John F. Sherry, Jr. and Brian Sternthal, Provo, Utah: Association for Consumer Research, 613-620.

Belk, Russell W. (1987), "Identity and the Relevance of Market, Personal, and Community Objects," in *Marketing and Semiotics: New Directions in the Study of Signs for Sale*, ed. Jean Umiker-Sebeok, New York: Mouton de Grouyter.

_____ (1988), "Possessions and the Extended Self," *Journal of Consumer Research*, 15 (September), 139-168.

_____ (1990), "The Role of Possessions in Constructing and Maintaining a Sense of Past," in *Advances in Consumer Research*, 17, eds. Marvin E. Goldberg, Gerald Gorn, and Richard W. Pollay, Provo, UT: Association for Consumer Research, 669-676.

_____, Melanie Wallendorf, and John F. Sherry, Jr. (1989), "The Sacred and the Profane in Consumer Behavior: Theodicy on the Odyssey," *Journal of Consumer Research*, 16 (June), 1-38.

Csikszentmihalyi, Mihaly and Eugene Rochberg-Halton (1981), *The Meaning of Things: Domestic Symbols and the Self*, Cambridge: Cambridge University Press.

Daniels, Eugene B. (1985), "Nostalgia and Hidden Meaning," *American Imago*, Winter, 42(4), 371-382.

Davis, Fred (1979), *Yearning for Yesterday: A Sociology of Nostalgia*, New York: Free Press.

Deci, Edward L. and Richard M. Ryan (1991), "A Motivational Approach to Self: Integration in Personality," in *Perspectives on Motivation*, ed. Richard Dienstbier, 58, 237-286.

Dichter, Ernest (1964), *Handbook of Consumer Motivations: The Psychology of the World of Objects*, New York: McGraw-Hill Book Company.

Felleman, Hazel (1936), "Memory," by Abraham Lincoln, in *The Best Loved Poems of the American People*, Garden City, New York: Doubleday & Company, Inc., 540-541.

Havlena, William J. and Susan L. Holak (1991), "A Time-Allocation Analysis of Nostalgia-evoking Events: Some Exploratory Results," in *VIIth John-Labatt Marketing Research Seminar Proceedings*, ed. Jean-Charles Chabat, Quebec, Canada.

Hirsch, Alan R. (1992), "Nostalgia: A Neuropsychiatric Understanding," in *Advances in Consumer Research*, 19, eds. John F. Sherry, Jr. and Brian Sternthal, Provo, UT: Association for Consumer Research, 390-395.

Hirschman, Elizabeth C. (1980), "Commonality and Idiosyncrasy in Popular Culture: An Empirical Examination of the 'Layers of Meaning' Concept," in *Symbolic Consumer Behavior: Proceedings of the Conference on Consumer Esthetics and Symbolic Consumption*, eds. Elizabeth C. Hirschman and Morris B. Holbrook, New York: Association for Consumer Research and Institute of Retail Management, New York University, 29-34.

Hofer, Johannes (1688), "Medical Dissertation on Nostalgia," Translated from Swiss by C. K. Anspach, *Bulletin of the History of Medicine* (1934), 2, 376-391.

Holak, Susan L. and William J. Havlena (1992), "Nostalgia: An Exploratory Study of Themes and Emotions in the Nostalgic Experience," in *Advances in Consumer Research*, 19, eds. John F. Sherry, Jr. and Brian Sternthal, Provo, UT: Association for Consumer Research, 380-387.

Holbrook, Morris B. and Robert M. Schindler (1989), "Some Exploratory Findings on the Development of Musical Tastes," *Journal of Consumer Research*, 16 (June), 119-124.

_____ and _____ (1991), "Echoes of the Dear Departed Past: Some Work in Progress on Nostalgia," in *Advances in Consumer Research*, 18, eds. R. H. Holman and M. R. Solomon, Provo, Utah: Association for Consumer Research, 330-333.

Kleine III, Robert E. and Jerome B. Kernan (1991), "Contextual Influences on the Meanings Ascribed to Ordinary Consumption Objects," *Journal of Consumer Research*, 18 (December), 311-324.

Levy, Sidney J. (1959), "Symbols for Sale," *Harvard Business Review*, July-August, 117-124.

Maccoby, Eleanor E. and Carol N. Jacklin (1974), *The Psychology of Sex Differences*, Stanford, CA: Stanford University Press.

MacInnis, Deborah J. and C. Whan Park (1991), "The Differential Role of Characteristics of Music on High- and Low-Involvement Consumers' Processing of Ads," *Journal of Consumer Research*, 18 (September), 161-173.

MacInnis, Deborah J. and Linda L. Price (1987), "The Role of Imagery in Information Processing: Review and Extensions," *Journal of Consumer Research*, 13 (March), 473-491.

Ross, Michael and Michael Conway (1986), "Remembering One's Own Past: The Construction of Personal Histories," *Handbook of Motivation and Cognition: Foundations of Social Behavior*, eds. Richard M. Sorrentino and E. Tory Higgins, New York: The Guilford Press, 122-144.

Rudmin, Floyd (1991), "Gender Differences in the Semantics of Ownership: Hazy Hints of a Feminist Theory of Property," *Gender and Consumer Behavior*, ed. Janeen Arnold Costa, Salt Lake City, UT: Association for Consumer Research, 292-302.

Sherman, Edmund and Evelyn S. Newman (1977-78), "The Meaning of Cherished Personal Possessions for the Elderly," *Journal of Aging and Human Development*, 8(2), 181-192.

Stayman, Douglas M. and David A. Aaker (1988), "Are All the Effects of Ad-Induced feelings Mediated by Aad?", *Journal of Consumer Research*, 15 (December), 368-373.

Stern, Barbara B. (1992), "Nostalgia in Advertising Text: Romancing the Past, in *Advances in Consumer Research*, 19, eds. John F. Sherry, Jr. and Brian Sternthal, Provo, UT: Association for Consumer Research, 388-389.

Measuring Multiple Emotional Responses To a Single Television Commercial

Jon D. Morris, University of Florida
James S. McMullen, University of Florida

Research on emotion and advertising has focused on emotional responses in the viewer and include links between emotional responses, recall, attitude-toward-the-ad, and purchase behavior (Holbrook & O'Shaughnessy, 1984; Thorson, 1989). The fact that both positive and negative emotional responses to the same advertisement have been found (Edell & Burke, 1987) suggests that these relationships might be more complex than previously thought. If more than one emotional response occurs within the same commercial, then a measurement of overall emotion may be insufficient to explain the effects of emotion. For example, one McDonald's commercial has a father sharing french fries with his eight-year-old daughter and then feeling left out when she becomes a teenager and shares fries with her friends instead. After watching the entire ad, viewers might describe it as slightly pleasant. This description would miss the fact that more than one emotional response may have been experienced, a very pleasant emotional response to the first part and a slightly sad emotional response to the second half. These multiple responses may or may not turn out to be significant in the long run, but no researchers have yet addressed this problem empirically. If a method is found for detecting multiple emotional responses to a single commercial the next step may be to explore the relationship among the responses.

Some investigators have hypothesized that more than one emotional response occurs either simultaneously (Burke & Edell, 1989; Mitchell, 1986), in sequences (Aaker, Stayman & Hagerty, 1986; Burke & Edell, 1989; Rossiter & Percy, 1991; Yi, 1990), or combines to make new emotions (Batra & Holbrook, 1990; Hill, 1988; Hill & Gardener, 1987; Mano, 1990; Mitchell, 1986) Some have even gone as far as to predict the effects of multiple emotions (Aaker et al. 1986), arguing that sequence effects would occur according to adaptation (Helson, 1964) and assimilation contrast theory (Sherif & Hovland, 1961).

While Edell and Burke (1987) provide empirical evidence of co-occurring multiple emotional responses, other data also point to this phenomenon. Aaker, Stayman, and Hagerty (1986) have shown that the intensity of one emotion, warmth, varies across a single advertisement. Rossiter and Percy (1991) have suggested that intentionally eliciting multiple emotional responses can benefit advertisers. They propose that a sequence of emotions must be present to motivate behavior. In an approach/avoidance construct (Mowrer, 1960) viewers could be motivated to avoid negative stimuli and search out positive stimuli. For instance, a commercial might begin by eliciting a negative emotional response and end by removing the negative stimuli, which would create a "relief" reaction in the viewer. These types of ads have been called poignant commercials (Thorson & Friestad, 1989).

Dimensions of Emotion

Several methods for measuring emotional responses to advertisements have been tested (eg: Izard, 1977; Plutchik, 1984; Mehrabian and Russell 1974, 1977) with the greatest support for the dimensional approach (Holbrook and Westwood, 1989). This approach holds that emotions are dimensional and measurements of response can be plotted in a single three-dimensional space. The axes of the space, the three dimensions that compose each emotion, are named pleasure, arousal, and dominance (PAD). These dimensions are bipolar, so the pleasure dimension, which is also called valence, runs from pleasant to unpleasant. The arousal dimension runs from aroused to asleep, and the dominance dimension runs from in-control to controlled. By finding an emotion's pleasure, arousal, and dominance scores, it can be plotted in the three-dimensional space, and each emotion's position in the space is unique.

Even using Mehrabian and Russell's (1974) PAD framework, however, measurement of more than one response is problematic. To measure emotional responses to parts of an ad, it is necessary to use one of three methods: 1) rely upon the viewer's memory of all of his/her emotional responses and where they occurred in the ad; 2) continuous measure of emotional responses; or 3) stop the ad at the point of measure. Of these three methods, the first can be ruled out because only the memory of an emotional response, not the actual emotional response itself, would be measured. The other two methods are not as easy to judge.

Continuous autonomic measures or physiological measures have not enjoyed wide acceptance in advertising studies. Among the physiological measures available are heart rate (HR), galvanic skin response (GSR), electrodermal activity (EDA), the electrocardiogram (EKG), electromyogram (EMG), electrogastrogram (EGG), electrooculogram (EOG), electroencephalogram (EEG), pupil dilation, eye movement, and facial expressions. While this is a large arsenal of measures, none of these have been widely accepted as useful in advertising research for measuring emotion (Holbrook & O'Shaughnessy, 1984) and any one physiological measure is inadequate to detect a full range of emotional responses (Russell, 1989; Cacioppo & Petty, 1989).

Aaker et al. (1986) developed a warmth monitor that provides a possible continuous measure. To apply their technique to the measurement of PAD, however, would require a separate instrument for each dimension. If we accept the three dimension theory (PAD) of emotion then a single dimension continuous measure would be inadequate or at best cumbersome.

Measurement of an Ad by Halves

Measuring an ad by halves should be sufficient to determine if more than one emotional response occurs. This assumption is based upon research showing that emotional intensity varies by the midpoint and the end of an advertisement (Aaker et al., 1986). In addition, measuring ads by halves will allow for the comparison of each half alone to the ad as a whole. If this research uncovers multiple emotional responses, then a more continuous analysis of advertisements might be warranted.

Measuring ads by halves could be accomplished using several popular verbal measures. Present verbal measures include emotion and adjective checklists such as the Multiple Affect Adjective Check List (MAACL) (Zuckerman & Lubin, 1965) and the Nowlis (1965) Anxiety Scale. These scales are used in many studies in both psychology and advertising, and are reported to have high reliability and validity scores. Some advertising researchers (e.g., Holbrook & Westwood, 1989; Wells, Leavitt, & McCouville, 1971) have attempted to create their own emotion scales, but have not succeeded in convincing their colleagues to adopt their instruments. Advertising professionals have even gotten into the act with scales such as Leo Burnett's Viewer Response Profile (Schlinger, 1979). These verbal measures are not well suited to the present study because they take several minutes to complete. If an ad is to be stopped in the middle, a measurement taken, and the ad then continued, the pause between halves must be as short as possible. If the pause is too long, it is likely that subjects will lose the flow of

FIGURE 1
The Self-Assessment Manikin (SAM)

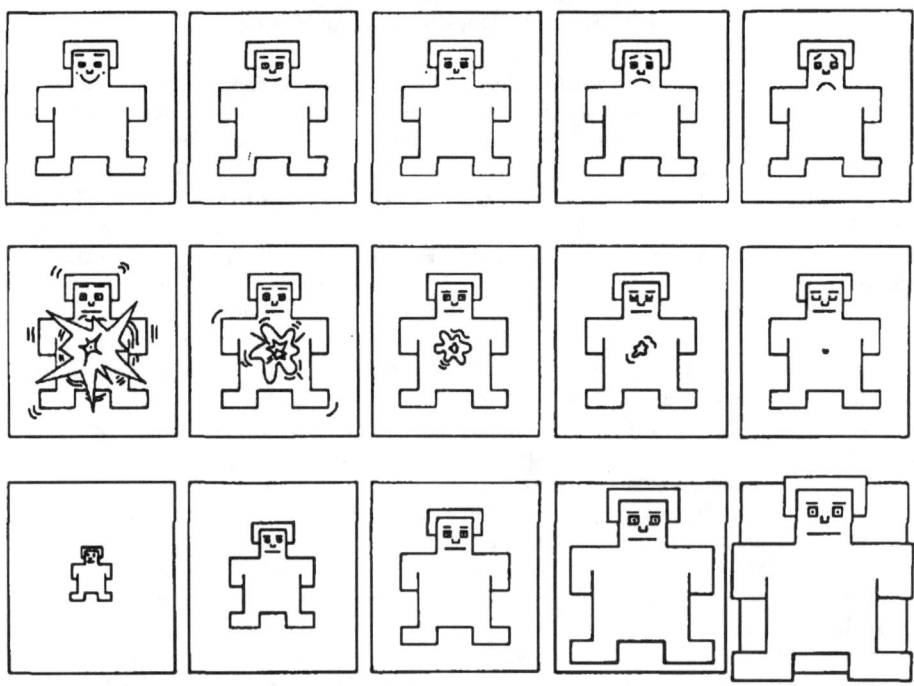

the advertisement, including the emotional responses being measured.

The Self-Assessment Manikin

The Self-Assessment Manikin (SAM) (Lang, 1984) is a graphic character that is used to represent the three dimensions of PAD. Figure 1 is an example of the entire SAM scale. SAM depicts each PAD dimension with a graphic character arrayed along a continuous nine-point scale. The first row of figures is the pleasure scale, ranging from pleasant to unpleasant. The second row is the arousal scale, ranging from aroused to asleep, and the final row is the dominance scale, ranging from controlled to controlling. SAM visually represents Mehrabian and Russell's three PAD dimensions and was designed as an alternative to cumbersome verbal self-report measures (Lang, 1980).

Initially, SAM was compared to PAD by using the catalog of situation employed by Mehrabian and Russell(1974) to standardize the PAD dimensions. The results indicated that SAM "generated a similar pattern of scale values for these situations as was obtained for the semantic differential (Pleasure +.937, Arousal +.938 and Dominance +.660)" (Lang, 1980, p.123). Several studies both in the United States and abroad have validated the SAM scales and demonstrated their effectiveness for measuring emotional responses. Greenwald, Cook and Lang (1989) examined the relationship of affective judgements using SAM and psychophysiological responses based on a dimensional analysis of emotion. Morris, Bradley, Lang and Waine (1992) successfully tested SAM in an advertising context. Thus, SAM presents a promising solution to the problems associated with measuring emotional response to advertising (Morris & Waine 1993).

SAM has been shown to be highly reliable in psychological studies (Hodes, Cook & Lang, 1985) and also highly correlated with traditional measures of PAD (Mehrabian & Russell, 1977) and physiological measures (Lang, Greenwald, Bradley & Hamm, in press). SAM is easy to use and quick, requiring less than 15 seconds. This is of critical importance to the present study. In addition, as a graphic instrument, SAM avoids cultural and language problems suffered by verbal measures (Lang et al., in press). These factors make SAM a good measure for advertising research and a nearly ideal measure for the present study.

METHOD

The primary purpose of this study was to determine if multiple emotional responses to a single advertisement can be detected with a non-verbal measure of PAD.

- $H1$: Two different mean score levels of emotional responses—pleasure, arousal and dominance—will be detected within one television advertisement.
- $H2$: Measurement of PAD mean scores by ad halves using SAM will detect two distinct emotional responses.

Design

This study utilized a 2 x 2 x 4 repeated measures design. The lone between-subjects variable was gender. Within-subjects variables were ad type (2 levels) and presentation mode (4 levels). Table 1 shows the four presentation modes and the measures derived from them.

Stimuli

Forty-one 30-second television advertisements were chosen from a pool of more than 200 commercials collected from several advertising agency reels, the 1989 Clio awards, and some commercials taped from the television in geographic areas other than where the study was conducted. Advertisements known to be currently running or that had been recently run in the study's geographic area were eliminated from the pool. Commercials in the pool were then watched by three judges who were asked to indicate whether they

TABLE 1
Presentation Modes

Mode #	Name	Part of ad shown (see Stimuli)	Time of measurement	Emotional measures derived from mode
1	1st-half-alone	1st 15 seconds	after viewing	response to first half only
2	2nd-half-alone	last 15 seconds	after viewing	response to second half only
3	whole-ad	entire ad	after viewing	response to ad as a whole
4	2nd-half-split	entire ad split in half	after each half is seen	response to first half alone, response to second half after seeing first half, response to ad as a whole

TABLE 2
Means by Presentation Mode

	1st half alone	2nd half alone	2nd half split	Whole ad
Pleasure	6.30	6.37	6.68	6.93
Arousal	5.39	4.98	5.15	5.67
Dominance	5.54	5.69	5.82	5.67
Recall	36.56%	33.66%	49.06%	41.99%

believed the ads would or would not have detectable shifts in levels of Pleasure, Arousal and Dominance. One group, the bi-emotional response ads (bi-ER) included 20 ads that the judges felt (87 % agreement) would elicit two different emotional responses. The second group, the uni-emotional response ads (uni-ER) included 20 ads that the judges felt (93 % agreement) would elicit one emotional response.

On each tape, an ad was shown in one of four presentation modes. These presentation modes were balanced across ads, such that each mode was represented equally often on each tape. For example, on the first tape, ad #1 was shown in mode 3, ad #2 in mode 1, ad #3 in mode 3, etc. Also, across tapes, each ad was seen equally often in each mode, so for ad #1, tape one showed it in mode 3, tape two in mode 2, tape three in mode 1, and tape four in mode 4.

The 40 ads were then randomly ordered for placement on the four experimental tapes. Different versions of each of the 40 ads were randomly ordered for placement on the experimental tapes. Four tapes were made, and the ads were placed in the same order on each tape. This means that effects of ad order should have been the same for all tapes. The break points of the ads came at the 15-second mark unless the scene, jingle, or story made this impractical. In those cases, the break point came at a logical break in the story or scene (as close to the 15-second mark as possible). This was done to allow for easier understanding by subjects who saw only the second half of the ad, and for a less abrupt ending for those who saw only the first half.

Subjects

Thirty-seven subjects, 19 females and 16 males, were recruited from an introductory advertising class. They were primarily freshmen and sophomores and received extra credit in their class for their participation in this study. Subject were randomly assigned to videotape groups. Emotional responses were measured using SAM. The order of the three dimensions was varied to make subjects pay attention to the scale, and to keep them from making the same marks in the same order on every page.

RESULTS

In selecting the television commercials for this study, judges were used to produce two groups (ad types). To determine if the groups were significantly different, each type was analyzed by first-half-alone and second-half-alone presentation modes. A within-subjects MANOVA revealed a type by mode interaction ($F(1/29)=4.66$) for pleasure only. As expected, pairwise t-tests revealed that, for ads which were pre-judged to have more than one emotional response (bi-ER ads), pleasure for the second half was significantly greater than the first half ($t(31)=-2.07$). Ads which the judges felt would elicit the same emotional response throughout (uni-ER ads) showed no difference between halves ($t(31)=0.30$). Pairwise t-tests between types of ads (uni-ER or bi-ER) revealed a significant difference for the first half. Uni-ER ads were significantly more pleasurable than bi-ER ads in the first half ($t(31)=2.34$). No such difference was found for the second-half-alone presenta-

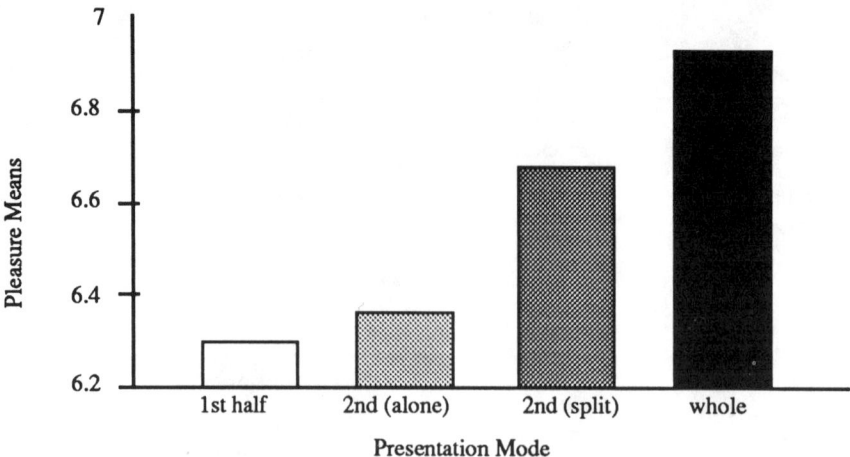

FIGURE 2
Pleasure by Presentation Mode

tion mode (t(31)=-0.04). These results support the premise that ads differed by type in the first half of the commercial. Typically, the second half would be constructed to leave the viewer with a positive feeling about the product. The second half of both presentation types (uni-ER or bi-ER) should be the same.

PAD Results

Mean ratings for pleasure, arousal, and dominance by presentation model are given in table 2. A mixed-model MANOVA was run on the subject means to determine main effects and interactions. No main effects of either gender or ad type were found, nor were any interactions found. Significant main effects for presentation mode were obtained for both pleasure ratings (F(3/87)=6.88) and arousal ratings (F(3/87)=6.45) but not dominance. These results indicate that levels of pleasure and arousal varied depending upon what part of the ad was seen.

To further examine these effects, paired t-tests were conducted on the pleasure and arousal means by mode. Figure 2 illustrates the means by mode for pleasure. The valence results showed that the first-half-alone and second-half-alone presentation modes were significantly less pleasurable than the whole-ad mode (t(31)=-3.93; t(31)=-3.50 respectively) or the second-half-split mode (t(31)=-3.22; t(31)=-2.01 respectively). If the second-half-split mode is considered to be a measure of the entire ad, these results imply that whole ads were more pleasurable than either half alone. For arousal, the t-tests revealed that the first-half-alone and whole-ad presentation modes were more arousing than the second-half-alone mode (t(31)=2.66; t(31)=-3.10). The whole-ad mode was also significantly more arousing than the second-half-split mode (t(31)=2.43). Figure 3 illustrates these results. Thus, in all instances where the first half of the ad was included in the presentation, whether alone, split, or in the whole ad, arousal ratings were higher. Viewing the second half in the absence of the first half produces lower emotion ratings.

Pearson product moment correlations were also calculated to test for relationships between PAD ratings as a function of mode. Overall, pleasure was positively correlated with arousal (r(31)=.4199) and dominance (r(31)=.1570), whereas arousal and dominance were not correlated. Of particular interest are the correlations for the whole-ad presentation mode, because they indicate which halves are most related to the ad as a whole. For the pleasure and arousal dimensions, the correlations revealed that ratings for the whole ad are highly correlated with both the first-half (r(39)=.6425, r(39)=.5568 respectively) and second-half-split modes (r(39)=.6747, r(39)=.3858 respectively). The second-half-alone was also correlated with the whole ad for pleasure (r(39)=.4562) but not for arousal or dominance. The first half was correlated with the second-half-split for all three dimensions (r(39)=.4563, r(39)=.5567, r(39)=.4526 respectively), but the second-half-alone was correlated with the second-half-split only for pleasure and arousal (r(39)=.3160, r(39)=.2659 respectively). Finally, in none of the dimensions were the first and second halves alone correlated.

The first half of the ad seems to be the most important in determining emotional responses to the ad as a whole, because correlations are greater for the first half than the second half in the whole and split modes, and for arousal, the second half is not even correlated with the whole. Furthermore, the correlations with the whole ad are stronger for pleasure than for arousal, signifying that pleasure was the more meaningful dimension for this set of advertisements. Finally, the lack of correlations between the halves suggests that the emotional responses to the two halves are different from each other.

DISCUSSION AND CONCLUSIONS

The results of this study supported both of the stated hypotheses. The first hypothesis predicted that multiple emotional responses would be found within a single advertisement. This was found to be true for both pleasure and arousal, but not for dominance. Subjects reported that they experienced more arousal in the first half than in the second half of the advertisement. Furthermore, they reported that the entire ad was more pleasing than either half. This demonstrates the complexity of emotional responses to television advertising.

The second hypothesis predicted that the technique of measuring emotional responses by ad halves would allow for the detection of multiple emotional responses. The fact that more than one emotional response was found supports this hypothesis. This shows that it may not be necessary to use impractical continuous physiological measures to measure parts of a television commercial.

The Self-Assessment Manikin (SAM) seems to be an effective method for measuring multiple emotional responses. The fifteen seconds given for completing each SAM proved not to be adequate.

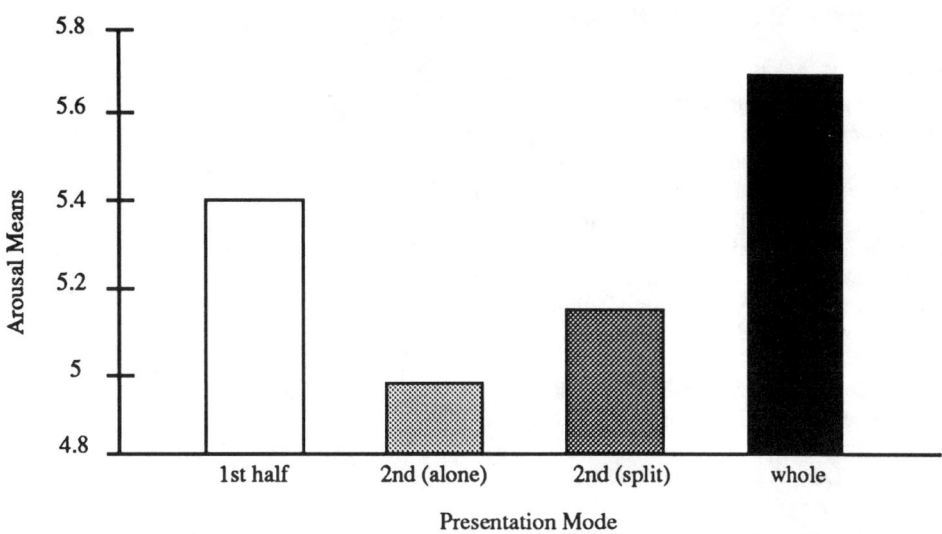

FIGURE 3
Arousal by Presentation Mode

Sequence Effects

By comparing emotional responses from entire commercials to emotional responses from their respective parts, combinations of emotional responses can be evaluated. Although several researchers (Hill, 1988; Hill & Gardener, 1987; Mitchell, 1986) have suggested that emotional responses combine over time, they were not able to determine whether the resulting evaluation would be greater, less, or somewhere between the two emotional responses. The results of this study indicate that, for pleasure, the emotional response to the entire advertisement (mean pleasure in whole ad mode = 6.93, in split mode = 6.68) is more pleasurable than either half alone (first half = 6.30, second half = 6.37). Interestingly, though, this study suggests that if viewers watch the whole ad, it doesn't matter whether more than one emotional response is generated. Overall, levels of arousal and pleasure were the same for ads that elicit more than one emotional response and ads that elicit multiple emotional responses.

Finally, the Self-Assessment Manikin (SAM) was found to be a useful measurement instrument for assessing parts of advertisements, and could be refined even further by using a shorter reaction time. Perhaps a device could be given to each subject to allow them to complete SAM at their own pace and start the next ad segment. Investigators operating within the PAD framework may want to consider SAM as the measuring instrument.

Additional research to determine the relationship between the first half of the commercial and the second half would be interesting. Would changing the first half of the ad affect the second half of the advertisement? What types of changes, on the front end of the commercial, would have the greatest affect on the second half? Multiple emotional responses to the same ad appear to be part of strategy in many advertising campaigns. The results of further study could help assist advertisers in selecting the best combination of stimuli to place in an ad.

REFERENCE LIST

Aaker, D. A., Stayman, D. M. & Hagerty, M. R. (1986). Warmth in advertising: Measurement, impact, and sequence effects. *Journal of Consumer Research*, 12, 365-381.

Batra, R. & Holbrook, M. B. (1990). Developing a typology of affective responses to advertising. *Psychology and Marketing*, 7, 11-25.

Burke, M. C. & Edell, J. A. (1989). The impact of feelings on ad-based affect and cognition. *Journal of Marketing Research*, 26, 69-83.

Cacioppo, J. T. & Petty, R. E. (1989). The elaboration likelihood model: The role of affect and affect-laden information processing in persuasion. In P. Cafferata & A. Tybout (Eds.), *Cognitive and affective responses to advertising* (pp. 127-146). Lexington, MA: Lexington Press.

Edell, J. A. & Burke, M. C. (1987). The power of feelings in understanding advertising effects. *Journal of Consumer Research*, 14, 421-433.

Greenwald, M. W., Cook, E. W. III & Lang, P. J. (1989). Affective judgment and psychological response: Dimensional covariation in the evaluation of pictoral stimuli. *Journal of Psychophysiology*, 3, 51-64.

Helson, H. (1964). *Adaptation level theory*. New York: Harper & Row.

Hill, R. P. (1988). The effects of advertisements on consumers' mood states: An interactive perspective. *Advances in Consumer Research*, 15, 131-134.

Hill, R. P. & Gardner, M. P. (1987). The buying process: Effects of and on consumer mood states. *Advances in Consumer Research*, 14, 408-410.

Hodes, R. L, Cook E. W. & Lang, P. J. (1985). Individual differences in autonomic response: Conditioned association or conditioned fear? *Psychophysiology*, 22, 545-560.

Holbrook, M. B. & O'Shaughnessy, J. (1984). The role of emotion in advertising. *Psychology and Marketing*, 1, 45-64.

Holbrook, M. B. & Westwood, R. A. (1989). The role of emotion in advertising revisited: Testing a typology of emotional responses. In P. Cafferata & A. Tybout (Eds.), *Cognitive and affective responses to advertising* (pp. 353-372). Lexington, MA: Lexington Press.

Izard, C. E. (1977). *Human Emotions*. New York: Plenum Press.

Lang, P. J. (1984). Behavioral treatment and bio-behavioral assessment: Computer applications. In J. B. Sidowski, J. H. Johnson & T. A. Williams (Eds.), *Technology in mental health care delivery systems* (pp. 119-137). Norwood, NJ: Ablex.

Lang, P. J., Greenwald, M. K., Bradley, M. M. & Hamm, A. O. (in press). *Looking at pictures: Affective, facial, visceral, and behavioral reactions.*

Mano, H. (1990). Emotional states and decision making. *Advances in Consumer Research*, 17, 577-584.

Mehrabian, A. & Russell, J. A. (1974). *An approach to environmental psychology.* Cambridge, MA: Oelgesschlager, Gunn, and Hain.

Mehrabian, A. & Russell, J. A. (1977). Evidence of a three-factor theory of emotions. *Journal of Research in Personality*, 11, 273-294.

Mitchell, A. A. (1986). Some issues surrounding research on the effects of "feeling advertisements." *Advances in Consumer Research*, 11, 111-116.

Morris, J. D., Bradley, M., Lang, J. and Waine, C. (1992). Assessing affective reactions to advertisements with (SAM) the Self-Assessment Manikin. Working paper, University of Florida, Gainesville.

Morris, J. D. and Waine, C. (1993). Managing the Creative Effort: Pre-production and Post-production Measures of Emotional Response. Working paper, University of Florida, Gainesville.

Mowrer, O. H. (1960). *Learning theory and behavior.* New York: Wiley.

Nowlis, V. (1965). Research with the Mood Adjective Check List. In S. S. Tomkins & C. E. Izard (Eds.), *Affect, cognitive, and personality* (pp. 221-245). New York: Springer.

Plutchik, R. (1984). Emotions: A general psychoevolutionary theory. In K. R. Scherer & P. Ekman (Eds.), *Approaches to emotion* (pp. 197-220). Hillsdale, NJ: Lawrence Earlbaum Associates.

Rossiter, J. R. & Percy, L. (1991). Emotions and motivations in advertising. *Advances in Consumer Research*, 18, 100-110.

Russell, J. A. (1989). Measures of emotion. In R. Plutchik & H. Kellerman (Eds.), *Emotion: Theory, research, and experience, volume 4, the measurement of emotions* (pp. 83-111). San Diego, CA: Academic Press.

Schlinger, M. J. (1979). A profile of responses to commercials. *Journal of Advertising Research*, 19, 37-46.

Sherif, M. & Hovland, C. I. (1961). *Social judgement: Assimilation and contrast effects in communication and attitude change.* New Haven, CT: Yale University Press.

Thorson, E. (1989). Television commercials as mass media messages. In J. J. Bradac (Ed.), *Messages in communication science: Contemporary approaches to the study of effects* (pp. 195-218). New York: Sage.

Thorson, E. & Friestad, M. (1989). The Effects of Emotion on Episodic Memory for Television Commercials. In A. Tybout & P. Cafferata (Eds.), *Advertising and Consumer Psychology* (pp. 305-324). New York: Lexington Press.

Wells, W. D., Leavitt, C. & McCouville, M. (1971). A reaction profile for TV commercials. *Journal of Advertising Research*, 11, 11-18.

Yi, Y. (1990). Cognitive and affective priming effects of the context for print advertisements. *Journal of Advertising*, 19, 40-48.

Zuckerman, M. & Lubin, B. (1965). *Manual for the Multiple Affect Adjective Check List.* San Diego, CA: Educational and Industrial Testing Services.

Exploring The Role of Individual Differences in Affect Intensity on the Consumer's Response to Advertising Appeals

David J. Moore, University of Michigan
William D. Harris, Quinnipiac College
Hong C. Chen, Grand Valley State University

ABSTRACT

This paper examined the role of the Affect Intensity Measurement scale (Larsen 1984) as an important tool in measuring consumers' response to advertising appeals. The AIM assesses the strength of the emotions with which individuals respond to an affect laden stimulus. The theoretical foundations for the development of the scale are discussed and several studies in both social psychology and marketing focusing on various aspects of the affect intensity construct are reviewed. The theoretical and practical implications of the findings of these studies on the future direction of research in emotional advertising are also presented.

Most researchers in the fields of social psychology, advertising and consumer behavior would readily agree that there are inherent differences in the level of emotional intensity with which individuals respond to an affect-laden stimulus (Aaker and Stayman 1989; Larsen and Diener 1985). The need to recognize the crucial role of emotions in the persuasion process in consumer behavior has been explicitly emphasized by advertising researchers (Allen, Machleit and Sahni 1992; Havlena and Holbrook 1986; Peterson, Hoyer and Wilson 1986). Within the field of marketing it has now been widely demonstrated that the emotions elicited by exposure to an advertising appeal may have a significant influence on attitude toward the ad, attitude toward the brand and consumer decision making (Bagozzi and Moore 1994; Batra and Ray, 1986; Burke and Edell 1989; Edell and Burke 1987; Gardner 1985; Holbrook and Batra 1987; Goldberg and Gorn 1987; Homer and Yoon 1992; Stayman and Aaker 1988). However, most of these studies have seemingly ignored the possibility that differences in the intensity level with which individuals experience their own emotions may have a significant influence on affective and attitudinal responses of the message recipient. Acknowledging this possibility, some marketing researchers have speculated that certain types of individual differences may account for variations in the manner in which consumers respond to emotional advertising messages (Aaker and Stayman 1989; Mackenzie and Lutz 1989). Aaker and Stayman (1989), for example, postulated that the tendency of some individuals to experience their emotions with greater magnitudes of intensity should play a significant role in moderating the affective responses generated by the advertising audience.

Prior research has shown that personality variables such as self-monitoring (DeBono & Packer, 1991; Snyder and DeBono 1985) and need for cognition (Cacioppo and Petty 1982) may significantly influence attitudes and persuasion. For example, Haugtvedt, Petty, Cacioppo and Steidley (1988) have shown that individuals high in need for cognition (N_{cog}) were more influenced by the quality of arguments contained in an advertising appeal for a consumer product than were individuals low in N_{cog} (see also Batra and Stayman 1990). While N_{cog} measures the individual's chronic tendency to enjoy thinking and problem solving activities, there is a surprising lack of research in marketing representing an equivalent measure of an individual's desire for emotional stimulation (Harris and Moore, 1991). In effect, what we still do not know is whether or not individual differences in emotional reactivity may account for a siginficant portion of the variance in consumer response to advertising messages. From an S-O-R perspective, the role of individual differences in emotional reactivity represents the 'black box' in the current state of our knowledge of the manner in which consumers respond to emotional advertising.

The Affect Intensity Measurement scale (AIM) developed by Larsen (1984) has been designed to measure differences in the strength with which individuals experience their emotions in response to identical emotion-eliciting stimuli (Larsen and Diener 1987). The AIM construct is potentially useful in helping advertisers identify the type of individual who may be more disposed to respond favorably to an emotionally charged advertisement as opposed to a cognitively oriented non-emotional appeal. Our objective in this paper is to examine previous research on this important construct and to identify various means by which the AIM can be usefully applied by both theoreticians and advertising researchers who desire to gain increased insight in targeting specific profiles of consumers whose responses to daily events and stimuli may be driven by the intensity of their emotions.

REVIEW OF THE AFFECT INTENSITY LITERATURE

What is the Affect Intensity Construct? Affect intensity has been conceptually defined as "a stable and consistent tendency for some individuals to react more strongly than others to emotion-provoking stimulation, regardless of what specific emotions are evoked" (Larsen 1984, p. 2). In confimation of this theoretical proposition, recent research in social psychology has demonstrated that certain individuals, when exposed to equal levels of affect-producing stimuli, consistently manifest stronger or more intense emotional responses (Larsen and Diener 1985; 1987; Larsen, Diener & Emmons 1986; Larsen et al.1987). Moreover, this emotional reactivity seems to generalize across both positive and negative emotional domains. For example, both laboratory and field studies indicate that when faced with a positive emotion-eliciting event, high affect intensity subjects reported stronger positive affect than those classified as low on the AIM scale (Larsen, Diener & Emmons 1986; Larsen et al.1987). Correspondingly, when faced with a negative emotion eliciting event, these same high AIM individuals reported stronger negative emotional responses than their low AIM counterparts (Larsen, Diener & Emmons, 1986). However, when subjects are exposed to a neutral or non-emotional stimulus or event, these individual differences in emotional reactivity are expected to disappear (Larsen, Diener and Cropanzano 1987). In the Larsen, Diener and Emmons (1986) study, the stimuli were daily life events. In experiment 1 subjects recorded two events per day for 56 consecutive days and rated their affective reactions to those events. In experiment 2 subjects were presented with standardized life event descriptions and asked how they would react emotionally to each of these events. The results of both experiments indicated that high intense subjects responded to the actual and the hypothetical life events with stronger or more intense emotional reactions. Furthermore, this pattern of responses was observed regardless of whether the events elicited positive or negative affective reactions.

The Affect Intensity Scale. The AIM scale (Larsen 1984) is a 40-item instrument designed to capture a broad spectrum of both negative and positive emotional responses (e.g., "Sad movies touch me deeply" and "My happy moods are so strong that I feel like I'm in heaven"). The scale also attempts to capture specific types of physical sensations normally associated with emotional manifestations, such as a pounding heart, sickness in the stomach, or having a shaky voice when talking in front of a group for the first time. Another consideration in the development of the AIM was that the items should reflect intensity rather than frequency of emotional response. Accordingly, the scale avoided items such as "I am very happy quite often" which contains both frequency and intensity dimensions. Instead, items were selected to avoid any confounding of intensity with frequency (e.g., "When I'm happy I bubble over with energy"). Over one, two, and three-month intervals, Larsen and associates have found that test-retest reliabilities of the AIM were .80, .81 and .81, respectively. Meanwhile, the intercorrelation coefficients of the AIM in four separate studies were within the range of .90 to .94 (Larsen and Diener 1987).

The Arousal Regulation Theory of Affect Intensity. Using the underlying principles associated with stimulus intensity modulation (Barnes 1976; Petrie 1967), Larsen and Diener (1987) proposed the following explanation for the existence of individual differences in levels of affect intensity. Within the central nervous system there exists a stimulus intensity modulation mechanism which modulates the individual's responsiveness to sensory stimulation. This mechanism amplifies or augments the effects of stimulation for some individuals and reduces the effects of stimulation for others. As a result, in response to incoming stimulation, the individual who typically reduces stimulation will be relatively understimulated (underaroused) and the augmenter will be relatively overstimulated (overaroused). The reducer should be highly motivated to seek out stronger forms of sensory stimulation, while the augmenter should be inclined to minimize the input of sensory stimulation (Barnes 1976). With respect to the AIM, Diener et al. (1986) suggest that some individuals modulate the intensity of emotional stimuli and therefore tend to manifest stronger or more intense emotional reactions. In contrast, others who may be low on the AIM scale are much less emotionally reactive to equivalent levels of emotion-provoking stimulation. This suggests that when high emotionally intense individuals experience a positive emotional stimulation it tends to be a very strong form of enjoyment. On the other hand, if the emotion is negative it tends to be unbearably unpleasant.

Affect Intensity and Emotional Response to Advertising Appeals. In a program of studies designed to examine the relevance of the affect intensity construct to the field of advertising, Harris (1988) and Moore, Harris and Chen (1993a) tested several hypotheses emerging from the work of Larsen and Diener (1987). One of the issues addressed by Moore, Harris and Chen (1993a) was the extent to which individual differences in affect intensity should moderate the emotional responses generated by message recipients who are exposed to an emotional (versus a non-emotional) advertising appeal. In the first phase of the study 772 psychology undergraduates were administered a battery of individual difference measures, one of which was the AIM scale. Using upper and lower quartile splits, high and low AIM subjects were identified and invited to participate in new experiment two weeks later. This new experiment featured a 2(High vs. Low AIM) x 2(Emotional vs. Non-emotional appeal) between subjects factorial design. The 153 participating subjects were exposed to a 30 minute movie embedded with several TV ads, one of which was the target ad. The emotional version of the ad featured a very moving demonstration of a young child being abused by his parent. The non-emotional ad was a statistical report of the number of child abuse cases reported in a given year in a south western state. In response to the target ad subjects reported the strength of their negative emotions (e.g., anger, sadness, fright) and empathic emotions (e.g, sympathy, concern, compassion). Consistent with the hypotheses of the study, the results showed that high AIM subjects, compared to their low AIM counterparts, manifested stronger affective responses when exposed to the emotional advertising appeal, but showed no differences in emotional response magnitude when exposed to the non-emotional ad.

Parenthetically, this study found that both negative and empathic emotions were manifested in a similar manner by high and low AIM subjects, and these emotions tended to load on the same factorial dimension when factor analysis was conducted. A subsequent experiment (Moore, Harris and Chen 1993, experiment #1) replicated this identical pattern of responses, thus confirming the fact that individuals who express strong negative emotions may also express strong empathy toward the display of suffering experienced by another.

One limitation of the preceding study was the fact that subjects were exposed to only a single version of either an emotional or non-emotional ad. Hence, the generalizability of the findings could be justifiably challenged. To address this limitation, Moore, Harris and Chen (1993a, experiment #2) exposed subjects to three negative emotional ads and three non-emotional ads. Order of presentation was thoroughly randomized. The three negative emotional ads were: (a) a public service ad supplied to our labs by the *Advertising Council* and developed for the Association for Child Abuse Prevention. This ad featured the tear stained face and eyes of a child responding to harsh and condemning words from the angry mouths of adults; (b) a sad and moving public service ad also supplied by the *Advertising Council* on behalf of The United Negro College Fund. This ad featured the disappointment and sadness of two parents and their teenage son when the parents were forced to announce to their son their inability to send him to college; and (c) 'Missing Children'- another PSA featuring the deep emotional anguish of parents whose child is missing and possibly dead. The results of this second experiment (N=90), for the most part, supported the findings of experiment 1, in that, the AIM effect was observed only when subjects were exposed to the emotional ads. Individual differences in affect intensity showed no significant differences in most of the emotional measures associated with the non-emotional ads.

In experiment #3, Moore, Harris and Chen (1993a) exposed subjects to three positive emotional ads and three non-emotional ads in order to confirm the hypothesis that the AIM effect could be manifested across both positive as well as negative emotional responses (Larsen and Diener 1987). Consistent with the findings of other experiments (Larsen Diener and Cropanzano 1987), it was found that in response to the emotional ads, high affect intensive subjects elicited significantly stronger positive and empathic emotions (e.g., amused, joyous, warm, sentimental, compassionate) than did the low AIM subjects. As expected, there were no significant differences in the intensity of the responses of high versus low AIM individuals when exposed to the non-emotional ads.

Affect Intensity and Painful Ad Induced Emotions. One of the interesting issues addressed in the Moore, Harris and Chen (1993a) study was the manner in which high AIM individuals seem to respond when the emotion evoked by the advertising stimulus is unpleasant and or negative. For example, the emotions stimulated in response to the PSAs described earlier tended to be quite unpleasant particularly because these messages focused on some of the more serious issues of life such as child abuse, missing children, lack of money to send children to college and so on. So the research question is this: If high AIM individuals tend to experience the entire spectrum of emotions, positive or negative, with greater magnitudes of intensity, then an unpleasant emotion should be felt with deeper pain and a pleasant emotion should be experienced with greater enjoyment. In keeping with this line of reasoning, Gallagher, Diener and Larsen (1989) proposed that high AIM individuals should manifest a greater tendency to avoid negative stimuli because once these emotions have been aroused, the experience becomes even more intensely unpleasant for high AIM individuals than those who are low on the AIM scale. This suggests that for high AIM individuals, exposure to negative stimulation may be more painful to endure and more difficult to tolerate (Gallagher, Diener and Larsen 1989).

Support for this proposition was derived from the results of Moore, Harris and Chen (1993a, experiment 2. It was found that, in comparison to their low AIM counterparts, high AIM subjects reported that the experience of viewing the three negative emotional ads was more painful and less enjoyable. This may also be explained by the fact that the high AIM subjects tended to demonstrate more 'empathic involvement' in the process of viewing the ads. For example, in response to the item "While viewing the ad I felt I was right there experiencing what the actors were experiencing", high AIM subjects reported significantly higher scores than did the low AIM respondents. These results may help to bolster Gallagher, Diener and Larsen's (1989) view concerning the intensity of the emotions experienced by high AIM individuals.

Affect Intensity and Ad Enjoyment. In an attempt to replicate these findings and to determine whether the level of enjoyment experienced by high versus low AIM individuals will be more intense when exposed to positively toned emotional ads, Moore and Harris (1993b) conducted a new experiment featuring both positive and negative emotional advertising appeals. What was different about this new study was the fact that subjects were exposed to a positive as well as a negative emotional ad within the same experiment. Using this procedure, it was possible to test Larsen, Diener and Cropanzano's (1987) assertion that the same high AIM individuals who report extreme levels of negative affect in response to a given negative emotional stimulus are also capable of experiencing high levels of positive affect in response to positive emotional stimuli. One of the objectives of the study was to examine the relationship between affect intensity and emotional responses. It was predicted that high AIM subjects would manifest stronger emotional reactions than low AIM subjects when exposed to the positive emotional ad as well as the negative emotional ad; in contrast, no significant differences in the intensity of emotional responses were expected to occur in response to the non-emotional ad.

Subjects (N=131) were administered the AIM scale (Larsen 1984) and on the basis of the results upper (N=33) and lower quartiles (N=37) were selected to participate in an experiment three weeks later. The positive emotional ad evoked primarily positive emotions such as joy, happiness and warmth (Aaker, Stayman and Hagerty 1986). This was an ad for special occasion greeting cards by the Hallmark Inc. featuring a joyous but moving wedding scene. The negative emotional appeal was designed to evoke negative emotions such as 'moving', 'sad' and 'sympathetic'. This ad was sponsored by a nationally known disaster relief organization (The Red Cross) and appealed for financial contributions for needy victims of recent disasters around the world. The third type of ad was non-emotional in content, featuring the presentation of factual information about Colgate toothpaste. This ad was selected to serve as a baseline manipulation. Both high and low AIM subjects were not expected to show any significant differences in emotional intensity as well as attitude formation in response to this ad.

The three target ads were embedded among other ads shown during the presentation of a classic TV movie. After viewing the movie subjects were given a second opportunity to view each of the three target ads. Order of presentation was randomized and rigorously followed in order to minimize order effects and carryover biases which could potentially distort the data. At the end of each ad subjects recorded the extent to which they felt each of several emotions, their enjoyment of the ad and their attitude toward the ad.

The results for the three ads were generally consistent with expectations and with prior research (Larsen, Diener and Cropanzanno 1987). High AIM subjects exposed to the *positive emotional* ad scored significantly higher than low AIM subjects on all positive emotions (happy, joyous, warm, moved, and touched). Similarly, for the negative emotional ad, high AIM respondents demonstrated significantly stronger affect intensity on all appropriate measures such as moved, touched, sympathetic and sad. Interestingly, it was found that on such positive measures like happy and warm, there were no significant differences among the high and low AIM subjects who were exposed to the negative emotional ad. Also as expected, high and low AIM subjects exposed to the *non-emotional* ad showed no significant differences on any of the measures of emotional response.

In sum, these results have shown the robustness of the AIM construct, and its test-retest reliability over multiple studies. This study, in particular, has demonstrated that the same high AIM respondents who experienced significantly higher levels of positive emotion in response to a positive advertising stimulus are just as capable of experiencing higher levels of negative emotions when exposed to a negative emotional advertising stimulus. In this respect these findings reinforce Larsen's (1984) theoretical proposition that intensity is a dimension relevant to all emotions, regardless of whether the emotions are positive or negative. Intensity, therefore, refers to the style of emotional experience and expression, rather than its content (e.g., anger, happiness, depression, joy)"(Larsen 1984, p. 1).

Do Cognitive Processes Influence Affect Intensity? As a means of bolstering the psychological underpinnings for the AIM effect, Larsen, Diener and Cropanzano (1987) postulated that individual differences do occur because of the unique manner in which people interpret and process events or experiences in daily life. This general line of reasoning is consistent with the *cognitive appraisal-emotion model* of information processing which contends that the intensity of the emotional response is largely determined by the type of thoughts or cognitive appraisals engaged in by the individual (Epstein 1984; Folkes, Koletsky and Graham 1987; Lazarus 1982; 1984; Roseman, Spindel and Jose 1990). Larsen, Diener and Cropanzano (1987) utilized a theoretical framework proposed by Beck (1967) to predict that a unique pattern of thoughts will be capable of differentiating high and low affect intensity individuals. Accordingly, Larsen et al. (1987) asked subjects to generate verbal protocols in response to a wide range of photograhic slides depicting both negative and positive emotionally provocative scenes. These spontaneous thoughts (called cognitive operations) were organized into the following categories: (a) *Personalization* - thoughts expressing a tendency to exaggerate or overestimate the relevance of a given event or issue to one's personal life (Beck, 1976); (b) *Overgeneralization* - thoughts which suggest that the individual may be using a single event as a basis for making global statements or sweeping generalizations about other relevant issues; (c) *Focus on Emotional Details* - thoughts demonstrating the tendency to be fixated on some specific emotionally provocative detail in a given situation.

The results of the Larsen et al. (1987) study showed that high AIM respondents generated a significantly higher number of cognitive operations than low AIM respondents when exposed to both the positive as well as the negative emotional slides. Also, as predicted, no significant differences in cognitive operations were observed among high and low AIM subjects in response to the neutral (non-emotional) slides (Larsen and Diener 1987; Larsen, Diener and Emmons 1986). These results made an important contribution by proving that high AIM respondents can be identified by the uniqueness in the pattern of their cognitive processing. However, the Larsen et al. (1987) study did not go far enough to demonstrate a relationship between the cognitive operations and the emotional responses of the respondents. Hence, there was only partial and speculative support for the cognitive appraisal-emotion model of information processing.

Within an advertising context, Moore and Harris (1993) extended the Larsen et al. (1987) study by measuring not only the cognitive operations, but also the emotional and attitudinal responses of the message recipients. The results of that study provided support for propositions that Larsen et al. had earlier put forward. First, Moore and Harris (1993) found that the same high and low affect intensity individuals who differed in the magnitude of their emotional responses, also differed in their cognitive operations generated in response to an emotionally charged advertising appeal. This was an important finding since Larsen et al. (1987) did not measure both emotions and cognitive operations within the same study. Second, the results showed that the effect of affect intensity on emotional responses was mediated by the cognitive operations generated by message recipients. In contrast, this mediation effect, as predicted, failed to occur even among high AIM subjects who were exposed to the non-emotional ad condition. This finding, in particular, has provided empirical support for the theoretical speculations advanced earlier by Larsen et al. (1987). The third major finding reported by Moore and Harris (1993) represented a step beyond the model tested by Larsen et al (1987), in that, measures of attitude and intention formation were tested in conjunction with emotions, cognitive operations and emotional responses. The results also showed that both cognitive operations as well as emotions served as the mechanisms through which AIM influenced attitude and intention formation.

The Relationship Between Affect Intensity and Attitude Formation. The theoretical foundation for predicting a direct relationship between affect intensity and attitiude formation has not been specified in the extant literature. In fact, Moore and Harris (1993) is actually one of the first studies to test this relationship (See also Moore, Harris and Chen 1993a; 1993b). Nevertheless, the knowledge which has been gained from the use of other individual difference variables in marketing may serve as guidelines for predicting the relationship between affect intensity and attitude formation. For example, personality variables such as self-monitoring (De Bono and Packer 1991; Snyder and De Bono 1985), and need for cognition (Cacioppo and Petty 1982) have been shown to influence attitudes and persuasion. One recent study by Haugtvedt, Petty, Cacioppo and Steidley (1988) reported that subjects high in N_{cog}, compared to their low N_{cog} counterparts, were more influenced by the quality of arguments presented in the message appeal. This suggests that it was the cognitive effort required to differentiate strong from weak arguments which discriminated the high from the low N_{cog} respondents. In contrast to the N_{cog} construct, AIM is presumed to represent the magnitude of an individual's affective response to emotionally charged stimuli. Hence, it is reasonable to predict that affect intensity should influence attitude formation through the mediating role of emotions or emotionally oriented thoughts. Recent studies conducted by Moore, Harris and Chen (1993a; 1993b) have provided empirical support for this proposition.

Affect intensity as a Representation of Temperament, not Personality. It is very crucial that a distinction be made between affect intensity as a dimension of temperament versus personality. According to Larsen and Diener (1987), personality refers to consistencies in the *content* of behavior while temperament more accurately represents consistencies in the *style* of the behavior manifested by the individual (Strelau 1982). In other words, personality can be defined in terms of what (content) a person does, whereas temperament defines the manner (style) in which a person manifests certain behaviors. To illustrate: When we say that a person scores high on the materialism scale (Richins 1992), we tend to mean that the content of that person's behavior reflects specific actions and attitudes consistent with materialistic values. However, the manner in which various materialists may go about acquiring materialist possessions may differ significantly. Some individuals may pursue their materialistic goals in a rather persistent, deliberate and methodical manner, while others may pursue these goals at a frantic, energetic and vigorous pace. Larsen and Diener (1987) suggests that the characteristic difference between these two behavioral styles (persistent and deliberate versus frantic and vigorous) can be most appropriately defined as the difference in the temperamental characteristic of activity level. Affect intensity therefore represents a dimension of temperament since the style or manner in which an individual responds to a given event or stimulus generalizes across the entire spectrum of emotions, from negative to positive and across a wide variety of situations (Larsen, Diener and Emmons 1986).

The Correlation of AIM and Measures of Lifestyle. According to Eysenck (1967) and Strelau (1982), the characteristics associated with temperament operate in such a way as to regulate emotional arousal. Since this arousal regulation function has been identified as the mechanism responsible for producing variations in the magnitude of affect intensity levels (Larsen 1985), emotional intensity should predictably show a high correlation with specific dimensions of temperament (Larsen and Diener 1987). Given this theoretical perspective, Larsen, Diener and Emmons (1986) found that affect intensity was significantly related to four basic dimensions of temperament: sociability, activity level, arousability and emotionality.

In a more recent study within the field of marketing and advertising, Moore, Harris and Chen (1993a) examined the relationship between AIM and the basic dimensions of temperament as outlined by Larsen and Diener (1987). Each of the four dimensions of temperament was represented by several measures. Examples of these measures are as follows: (a) sociability - "Partying with friends"; (b) activity level - "Jogging alone"; (c) arousability - "Going to an exciting movie at the cinema"; and (d) emotionality - "Enjoyment of scary rides at amusement parks". In addition to these measures, Moore, Harris and Chen (1993a) included other marketing relevant issues such as preferences for TV and radio programs and sensory arousability to olifactory stimuli such as the fragrances of exotic perfumes and the smell of freshly baked bread.

Subjects in this study were 328 undergraduates ranging in age from 19 to 24 years. A questionnaire containing the AIM scale and several lifestyle measures was administered as part of an in-class research activity. For the lifestyle measures, subjects were asked to indicate the extent to which they enjoyed these activities using a 1 - 7 point scale. As predicted, the results were consistent with the findings reported by Larsen, Diener and Emmons (1986). AIM was highly correlated with measures of sociability, in that, high AIM individuals consistently scored higher than their low AIM counterparts on such measures as partying with friends, eating out with friends, singing and dancing and attending entertainment shows. AIM was not significantly related to those activities like jogging and bike riding alone presumably because of the low levels of social and emotional stimulation that these activities can typically offer.

In a similar fashion, it was found that AIM showed a negative but significant relationship to activities such as writing letters to a friend. In contrast, as expected, AIM was very strongly related to emotionally arousing activities like going on a romantic date, listening to romantic emotional music and going to an exciting movie at the cinema. The findings with respect to enjoyment of TV and radio programs should be particularly interesting to both theoreticians and advertising practitioners. For example, AIM showed strong relationships to emotionally arousing programs like TV dramas, soap operas and comedies, but an inverse relationship to programs requiring higher levels of cognitive processing such as local news broadcasts, talk shows and game shows.

DISCUSSION

The review of the influence of affect intensity as an important individual difference construct in the field of social psychology and in the applied context of broadcast advertising has provided us with some degree of insight into the contribution that this construct can make to the theory and practice of advertising and consumer behavior. This review of the extant literature has clearly indicated the test-retest reliability of the AIM scale. This means that advertising researchers may accept, with reasonable certainty, the fact that certain profiles of consumers will respond to emotionally charged advertising appeals with stronger intensity of emotion. Researchers should therefore avoid the possible pitfall of assuming that consumers are all homogeneous in their responses to emotional advertising appeals.

The implications are particularly relevant to advertising researchers. For example, the AIM measurement scale can prove to be a valuable assessment tool when advertisers are pretesting the effect of emotional advertising appeals. In controlled test market conditions using product assessment labs (Clarke 1987), subjects are usually administered a variety of screening questions prior to exposure to the target ads. The AIM can be used in this setting to determine whether a given sample of respondents is unevenly skewed in the tendency to be either high or low in emotional reactivity. Since individual differences in affect intensity seem to influence the respondent's emotional and attitudinal responses to advertising appeals, then advertisers may be well advised to use the AIM to test for sample skewness along this important dimension. Using the results from a biased sample may have far reaching and costly implications for product managers and for the marketing strategies of the firm (Venkatraman, Marlino, Kardes and Sklar 1990).

Another related issue which demands further research is the manner in which high AIM respondents react when the emotions evoked by the advertising stimulus are intensely negative and painful. In two separate studies (Moore, Harris and Chen 1993a; 1993b) it was found that high affect intensity subjects reported that the experience of viewing these ads was more painful and less enjoyable than the intensity of emotions reported by their low AIM counterparts. Furthermore, these high AIM individuals showed a greater tendency to become more empathically involved with the emotions experienced by the actors, thus accounting for a deeper sense of pain felt by these high intensity subjects. Since recent research has shown that high AIM individuals have a greater tendency to avoid negative emotionally charged stimuli (Gallagher, Diener and Larsen 1989), several questions become relevant to advertising researchers. For example, would high AIM individuals show a stronger tendency to develop negative attitudes toward ads which elicit very intense and painful emotions? Furthermore, what are the potential implications for consumers' responses to repeated exposures to such high intensity ads? If high AIM subjects experience their emotions with deeper intensity, it is quite possble that these individuals may also experience satiation and burnout earlier than their low AIM counterparts. Conversely, if the emotions evoked by the ad are pleasant and enjoyable, high AIM subjects may be more tolerant to sustained repetitions of the ad and may therefore be slower than low AIM subjects to experience boredom and burnout. These issues should provide fruitful areas of inquiry for future research.

These questions have relevance to the manner in which advertising practitioners schedule the broadcast of emotional message appeals. A *continuous* pattern of repetitive exposures to a negative emotional appeal may lead to rapid wearout, avoidance or other adverse reactions. A modified pattern of *pulsing* where ads are run for short periods of time, followed by a period of no advertising, may be advisable in order to avoid the possibility of wearout among high AIM message recipients.

More rigorously designed studies need to be conducted to determine the response of high and low AIM individuals across both positive and negative emotionally charged advertising appeals. For the AIM construct to be useful to advertising practitioners further research is needed to demonstrate the relationship between this construct and a wider range of demographic variables. If, in fact, advertisers and management decision makers can establish a reliable correlation between individual differences in affect intensity and identifiable demographic variables, gender, consumer lifestyles, daily activities, media preferences, and buyer behavior patterns, then the AIM construct may prove to be a valuable consideration when conducting research in the area of target marketing and positioning.

REFERENCES

Aaker, David A., and Douglas M. Stayman (1989), "What Mediates the Emotional Response to Advertising? The Case of Warmth," in *Cognitive and Affective Responses to Advertising*, eds. Patricia Cafferata and Alice M. Tybout, Lexington, MA: Lexington Books.

_____ Douglas M. Stayman, Michael R. Hagerty (1986), "Warmth in Advertising Measurement, Impact and Sequence Effects," *Journal of Consumer Research*, 12, (March), 365-381.

Allen, Chris T., Karen A. Machleit and Arti Sahni (1992), "On the Value of Explicitly Incorporating Emotional Experience into the Fishbein attitude Model: An Empirical Assessment", in *Advances in Consumer Research*, Vol. 20.(Eds.) Leigh McAllister and Michael L. Rothschild, Provo, Utah: Association for Consumer Research.

Bagozzi, Richard P. and David J. Moore (1994), "Public Service Advertisements: Emotions and Empathy Guide Prosocial Behavior', *Journal of Marketing*, (forthcoming).

Barnes, G. E. (1976), "Individual Difference in Perceptual Reactance: A Review of the Stimulus Intensity Modulation Individual Difference Dimension", *Canadian Psychological Review*, 17, 29-52.

Batra, Rajeev, and Michael L. Ray (1986), "Affective Responses Mediating Acceptance of Advertising, " *Journal of Consumer Research*, 13, 234-249.

_____ Morris B. Holbrook (1990), "Developing a Typology of Affective Responses to Advertising," *Psychology & Marketing*, Vol. 7, No. 1, (Spring), 65-81.

_____ and Douglas M. Stayman (1990), "The Role of Mood in Advertising Effectiveness", *Journal of Consumer Research*, Vol. 17, 2, (March), 203-222.

Beck, A. T. (1976). Cognitive Therapy and the Emotional Disorders. New York: International Universities Press.

Berlyne, D. E. (1978), "Curiosity and Learning," in *Motivation and Emotion*, 2, 97-175.

Boyle, Gregory J. (1986), "Higher-Order Factors in the Differential Emotions Scale (DES-III)," *Personality and Individual Differences*, 7, 305-310.

Burke, Marian Chapman and Julie A. Edell (1989), "The Impact of Feelings on Ad-Based Affect and Cognition," *Journal of Marketing Research*, 26, 69-83.

Cacioppo, John T., and Richard E. Petty. (1982), "The Need for Cognition," *Journal of Personality and Social Psychology*, 42, 116-131.

Clarke, Darral G. (1987), *Market Analysis and Decision Making: Text and Cases*, The Scientific Press, Redwood City, CA., 112 - 119.

DeBono, K. G., & Packer, M. (1991). The effects of advertising appeal on perceptions of product quality. *Personality and Social Psychology Bulletin*, 17, 2, (April), 194-200.

Epstein, S. (1984). Controversial Issues in Emotion Theory. In P. Shaver (Ed.), *Review of Personality and Social Psychology: Emotions, Relationships, and Health* (pp. 64-88). Beverly Hills, CA: Sage.

Eysenck, H. J. (1967), *The Biological Basis of Personality*, Springfield, IL: Charles C. Thomas.

Folkes, V. S., Koletsky, S., & Graham, J. L. (1987). A Field Study of Causal Inferences and Consumer Reaction: The View from the Airport. *Journal of Consumer Research*, vol. 13, 4, 533-39.

Gardner, Meryl P. (1985), "Mood States and Consumer Behavior: A Critical Review," *Journal of Consumer Research*, 12, 281 - 300.

_____ (1986), "Responses To Emotional and Informational Appeals: The Moderating Role of Context-Induced Moods States," Working Paper, New York University, New York, NY 10003.

Gallagher, Dennis, Ed Diener, and Randy J. Larsen (1989), "Individual Differences in Affect Intensity: A Moderator of the Relation Between Emotion and Behavior," Working Paper, The Department of Psychology, University of Illinois, Urbana-Champaign.

Goldberg, Marvin E. and Gerald J. Gorn (1987), "Happy and Sad TV Programs: How They Affect Reactions to Commercials," *Journal of Consumer Research*, Vol. 14 (December), 387-403.

Harris, William D. (1988), ""Affect Intensity as an Individual Difference Variable in Consumer Response to Advertising Appeals", Unpublished Dissertation, College of Business Administration, The University of Oklahoma, Norman, OK.

_____ and David J. Moore (1991), "Affect Intensity as an Individual Difference Variable in Consumer Response to Advertising Appeals", in Marvin E. Goldberg, Gerald Gorn and Richard W. Pollay (eds.), *Advances in Consumer Research*, Vol. 17, Association for Consumer Research, Provo, Utah, 792-797.

Haugtvedt, Curtis P., Richard E. Petty, John T. Cacioppo and Theresa Steidley (1986), Personality and Ad Effectiveness: Exploring the Utility of Need For Cognition", in *Advances in Consumer Research*, Vol. 15. ed. Michael J. Houston, Provo, Utah: Association for Consumer Research, 209-212.

Havlena, William J. and Morris B. Holbrook (1986), "The Varieties of Consumption Experience: Comparing Two Typologies of Emotion in Consumer Behavior", *Journal of Consumer Research*, 13, (December), 394-404.

Homer, Pamela M. and Sun-Gil Yoon (1992), "Message Framing and the Interrelationships Among Ad-based Feelings, Affect, and Cognition", *Journal of Advertising*, Vol. XXI, No. 1, (March), 19-33.

Holbrook, Morris B. and Rajeev Batra (1987), "Assessing the Role of Emotions as Mediators of Consumer Responses to Advertising," *Journal of Consumer Research*, 14, 404-420.

Larsen, Randy J. (1984), "Theory and Measurement of Affect Intensity as an Individual Difference Characteristic," Dissertation Abstracts International, 85, 2297B (University Microfilms No. 84-22112).

_____ (1985), "Augmenting/Reducing and Emotional Response Intensity," in Emotions, *Personality, and Personal Wellbeing*, M. Clark (Chair), Symposium, American Psychological Association, Los Angeles.

_____ Ed Diener (1987), "Affect Intensity as an Individual Difference Characteristic: A Review," *Journal of Research in Personality*, 21, 1-39.

_____ Ed Diener, and Russell S. Cropanzano (1987), "Cognitive Operations Associated with Individual Differences in Affect Intensity," *Journal of Personality and Social Psychology*, Vol. 33, No. 4, 767-774.

_____ Ed Diener, and Robert A. Emmons (1984), "Affect Intensity as a Dimension of Temperament," in Randy J. Larsen and Ed Diener (1987), "Affect Intensity as an Individual Difference Characteristic: A Review," *Journal of Research in Personality*, 21 (August), 1-39.

_____ Ed Diener, and Robert A. Emmons (1986), "Affect Intensity and Reactions to Daily Life Events," *Journal of Personality and Social Psychology*, Vol. 51, No. 4, 803-814.

Lazarus, R. S. (1982). Thoughts on the Relations Between Emotion and Cognition. *American Psychologist*, 37 (9), 1019-1024.

Lazarus, R. S. (1984). On the Primacy of Cognition. *American Psychologist*, 39 (2), 124-129.

MacKenzie, Scott, B. and Richard J. Lutz (1989), "An Empirical Examination of the Structural Antecedents of Attitude Toward the Ad in an Advertising Pretesting Context," *Journal of Marketing*, Vol. 53 (April), 48-65.

Moore, David J. and Scott Hoenig (1989), "Negative Emotions As Mediators Of Attitudes In Advertising Appeals," in *Advances in Consumer Research*, Vol. XVI, ed.Thomas K. Srull, Provo, UT: Association for consumer Research, 581 - 586.

_____ William D. Harris, and Hong C. Chen (1993a), "Affect Intensity: An Individual Difference Response to Advertising Appeals", Working Paper, The University of Michigan, Ann Arbor, MI 48109.

_____ William D. Harris, and Hong C. Chen (1993b), "Understanding the Role of Affect Intensity in Advertising and Consumer Behavior", Working Paper, The University of Michigan, Ann Arbor, MI 48109.

_____ and William D. Harris (1993), "Do Cognitive Operations Mediate the Effect Of Affect Intensity on Emotional Responses and Attitude Formation?" Working Paper, The University of Michigan, Ann Arbor, MI 48109.

Peterson, Robert, Wayne D. Hoyer and William R. Wilson, eds. (1986), The Role of Affect in *Consumer Behavior: Emerging Theories and Applications*, Lexington, MA: D. C. Heath.

Petrie, A. (1967), *Individuality in Pain and Suffering*, Chicago, IL: University of Chicago Press.

Richins, Marsha L. (1992) "A Consumer Values Orientation for Materialism and its Measurement: Scale Development and Validation", *Journal of Consumer Research*, 19, (December), 303-316.

Roseman, I. S., Spindel, M. S., and Jose, P. E. (1990). Appraisals of Emotion-Eliciting Events: Testing a Theory of Discrete Emotions.*Journal of Personality and Social Psychology*, 19, (5), 899-15.

Snyder, M. & DeBono, K.G. (1985). Appeals to image and claims about quality: Understanding the psychology of advertising. *Journal of Personality and Social Psychology*, 49, (5), 586-597.

Stayman, Douglas M. and David A. Aaker (1988), "Are All the Effects of Ad-induced Feelings Mediated by A_{Ad}?" *Journal of Consumer Research*, 15, 368-373.

Strelau, J. (1982), "Biologically Determined Dimensions of Personality or Temperament?" *Personality and Individual Differences*, 3, 355-360.

Venkatraman, Meera P., Deborah Marlino, Frank R. Kardes, and Kimberly B. Sklar (1990), "The Interactive Effects of Message Appeal and Individual Differences on Information Processing and Persuasion," *Psychology & Marketing*, Vol. 7, No. 2, (Summer), 85-96.

Consumer Inferences and Family Branding Strategies: A Demonstration of Category-Based Induction

Christopher Joiner, University of Minnesota
Barbara Loken, University of Minnesota

ABSTRACT

A useful approach to understanding how consumers evaluate the strength of category-based product attribute statements has been suggested by a recent paper by Osherson, Smith, Wilkie, Lopez, and Shafir (1990) which examined category-based induction and argument strength. The approach is potentially useful as a framework for understanding how consumers evaluate statements about specific properties of family brand categories and individual products within those categories. Our study attempted to demonstrate both the potential and the limitations of the application of these concepts in a marketing environment and provided some support for the usefulness of the concepts, but also raised concerns about the categorization issues underlying their application.

Although categorization theories have recently been used to successfully understand brand extension and family brand management strategies (e.g., Boush and Loken 1991; Park, Milberg and Lawson 1991; Romeo 1991) future consumer research could benefit from more formal and unified sets of propositions. An understanding of how consumers evaluate statements about attributes of a family brand category and individual products within the category, and how these relate to consumers' perceptions of similarity between the family brand, the individual products in the category, and potential new products, would be valuable to marketing researchers and practitioners. Recently, Osherson, Smith, Wilkie, Lopez and Shafir (1990) have proposed a model that is potentially useful for understanding how consumers evaluate the strength of product attribute statements by assessing category-based induction and argument strength (cf. Kardes 1993). Our study is an initial attempt to demonstrate both the potential and the limitations of the application of these concepts in a marketing environment.

The Osherson et al. Framework

Consider an "argument" that contains one or more premises, $P_1...P_n$, and a conclusion, C. Suppose both premises and conclusion have the form "all members of X have property Y," where X is a category and Y is an attribute or property that remains fixed across premises and conclusion (Osherson et al. 1990). An example of a marketing-related categorical argument is the following:

Ivory shampoo is mild
<u>Ivory soap is mild</u>
Therefore, all Ivory health and beauty products are mild

Osherson et al. (1990) propose that the strength of a categorical argument increases as a function of two factors: (a) the degree to which the premise categories are similar to the conclusion category, and (b) the degree to which the premise categories are similar to members of the lowest level category that includes both the premise and conclusion categories (e.g., 'All Ivory health and beauty products' might be the lowest level category which includes the categories 'Ivory shampoo' and 'Ivory soap'). Based on these two factors, the authors developed and found empirical support for a series of propositions relating to categorical argument strength.[1]

A key aspect of the Osherson et al. framework is that categorical arguments can be labeled as *general, specific,* or *mixed*. An argument is general if the categories associated with each of the premises $[CAT(P_1)...CAT(P_n)]$ are all properly included in the category of the conclusion $[CAT(C)]$. For example the argument,

Grizzly Bears love onions
<u>Polar Bears love onions</u>
Therefore, all Bears love onions

is general, since "Grizzly Bears" and "Polar Bears" are included in the "all Bears" category. An argument is specific if any category that properly includes one of $CAT(P_1)...CAT(P_n)$, $CAT(C)$ also includes the others. The following is an example of a specific argument:

Mosquitoes have X
<u>Ants have X</u>
Therefore, Bees have X

Finally, an argument is mixed if it is neither general nor specific. For example the argument,

Flamingoes have X
<u>Mice have X</u>
Therefore, all Mammals have X

is not general because "Flamingoes" are not included in the "Mammal" category and it is not specific because the "Bird" category includes "Flamingoes" but not "Mice" or "Mammals" (Osherson et al., p.186).

In the present research, we selected seven of the original thirteen propositions (Osherson et al. 1990) that we felt would potentially be applicable to studies of existing and new products (e.g., brand and line extensions) that comprise a family brand category. A formal description of each proposition, and an example of each from the present study, are shown in Table 1.

Proposition 1, labeled *premise typicality*, states that the more representative or typical $CAT(P_1)...CAT(P_n)$ are of $CAT(C)$, the more $P_1...P_n$ confirm C. For example, in the following pair of arguments, the first argument "a" is claimed to be stronger than the second argument "b" (assuming that Brand B includes a wide variety of snack foods), because potato chips are more typical of the category snack foods than are granola bars:

---

[1]The framework proposed by Osherson et al. is different from a more recent model (Sloman 1993), not tested here, in that it focuses on the role of categories and perceptions of similarity between categories in assessments of argument strength, rather than on the role of properties or attributes of the categories. Although prior brand research has often classified "categories" such as "Ivory shampoo" as *exemplars* of the family brand category "Ivory products", our alternative interpretation of such products as *categories* is consistent with the conception of categories in the Osherson et al. model. For example, in the Osherson et al. (1990) paper, "grizzly bears" is a more specific category than "bears", even though, alternatively, grizzly bear could be viewed as an exemplar of the bear category.

TABLE 1
Sample Stimuli, Each of Seven Propositions Tested

I. Propositions Involving General Arguments

$P1$ *(premise typicality)*. The more representative or typical CAT (P_1)...CAT (P_n) are of CAT (C), the more $P_1...P_n$ confirm C.

Ex: *(a)   <u>Brand B potato chips are low in sodium</u>
All Brand B snack foods are low in sodium

    (b)   <u>Brand B granola bars are low in sodium</u>
All Brand B snack foods are low in sodium

$P3$ *(conclusion specificity)*. The more specific is CAT(C), the more C is confirmed by $P_1...P_n$.

Ex: *(a)   Brand C windbreakers are machine washable
<u>Brand C trench coats are machine washable</u>
All Brand C outerwear is machine washable

    (b)   Brand C windbreakers are machine washable
<u>Brand C trenchcoats are machine washable</u>
All Brand C products are machine washable

II. Propositions Involving Specific Arguments

$P5$ *(premise-conclusion similarity)*. The more similar CAT(P_1)...CAT(P_n) are to CAT(C), the more $P_1...P_n$ confirm C.

Ex: *(a)   Brand A compact disc (CD) players have soft-touch controls
<u>Brand A turntables have soft-touch controls</u>
Brand A personal stereos have soft-touch controls

    (b)   Brand A compact disc (CD) players have soft-touch controls
<u>Brand A turntables have soft-touch controls</u>
Brand a fax machines have soft-touch controls

$P6$ *(premise diversity)*. The less similar CAT(P_1)...CAT(P_n) are among themselves, the more $P_1...P_n$ confirm C.

Ex: *(a)   Brand C mens' trousers have double-needle stitching
<u>Brand C women's coats have double-needle stitching</u>
Brand C robes have double-needle stitching

    (b)   Brand C men's trousers have double-needle stitching
<u>Brand C men's jeans have double-needle stitching</u>
Brand C robes have double-needle stitching

III. Propositions Involving Mixed Arguments

$P9$ *(nonmonotonicity-general)*. Some general arguments can be made weaker by adding a premise that converts them into mixed arguments.

Ex: *(a)   Brand B tortilla chips are low fat
<u>Brand B pretzels are low fat</u>
All brand B salty snacks are low fat

    (b)   Brand B tortilla chips are low fat
Brand B pretzels are low fat
<u>Brand B chocolate candy is low fat</u>
All brand B salty snacks are low fat

$P10$ *(nonmonotonicity-specific)*. Some specific arguments can be made weaker by adding a premise that converts them into mixed arguments

Ex: *(a)   <u>Brand A microcassette recorders are affordable</u>
Brand A cassette tape players are affordable

    (b)   Brand A microcassette recorders are affordable
<u>Brand A electric typewriters are affordable</u>
Brand A cassette tape players are affordable

IV. Proposition Involving Both General And Specific Arguments

$P11$ *(inclusion fallacy)*. A specific argument can sometimes be made stronger by increasing the generality of its conclusion.

Ex: *(a)   <u>Brand B mixed nuts are packaged for freshness</u>
All Brand B snack foods are packaged for freshness

    (b)   <u>Brand B mixed nuts are packaged for freshness</u>
Brand B frozen pizzas are packaged for freshness.

*indicates that (a) is the "correct" choice (Osherson et al. 1990)

(a): Brand B potato chips are low in sodium
All Brand B snack foods are low in sodium

Is Stronger Than

(b): Brand B granola bars are low in sodium
All Brand B snack foods are low in sodium

Consistent with this proposition, a moderately typical product in a family brand category has been shown to dilute a general family brand belief (i.e., confirm a negative belief) to a greater extent than a less typical product (Loken and John 1993).

Proposition 3, *conclusion specificity*, states that the more specific the category in the conclusion, the stronger the argument. As noted in Table 1, when consumers are given "facts" about Brand C windbreakers and trenchcoats, they should more easily draw conclusions about the more similar, specific subcategory "Brand C outerwear" than about the broader, less specific category "All Brand C products". Proposition 3 is illustrated by the role individual products have in confirming beliefs about brand subcategories (Boush 1993) as compared to the brand category as a whole.

Propositions 5 and 6 are useful in examining how beliefs about individual products (existing or new) in a family brand may confirm beliefs about other existing products or potential brand extensions. Proposition 5, *premise-conclusion similarity* states that the more similar the premise categories are to the conclusion category, the more the premises confirm the conclusion. This proposition can be used to understand the conditions under which an extension of a brand to a new product category will be successful (e.g., Aaker and Keller 1990; Boush and Loken 1991; Park et al. 1990).

Proposition 6, *premise diversity*, which states that the less similar premise categories are among themselves, the more the premises confirm the conclusion, could be used to compare broad versus narrow brand categories (cf. Boush and Loken 1991) and their ability to confirm beliefs about existing or new products. Research on sequential introductions of brand extensions (cf. Keller and Aaker 1992) could also be analyzed within this framework.

Propositions 9 and 10, *nonmonotonicity-general* and *-specific*, demonstrate how an argument is weakened when a new premise is added that introduces a different category to an argument. Learning that another brand's product has a similar attribute as a member of a target family brand should decrease the strength of the consumer's beliefs about the group of products in the target family brand. Thus, in the earlier Ivory products example, addition of the premise that Neutrogena soap is mild should reduce the strength of the argument that All Ivory health and beauty products are mild.

Finally, proposition 11, *inclusion fallacy*, states that a specific argument can sometimes be made stronger by increasing the generality of its conclusion. As shown in the example in Table 1, the conclusion that 'All Brand B products' have a particular attribute should be perceived as stronger than the conclusion that an "atypical" Brand B product has the attribute. If so, this "fallacy" would have implications for communication efforts for certain family brands and individual products.

Prior Knowledge

In the present study, as in Osherson et al. (1990), we attempted to control for effects of *attribute* knowledge (e.g. "machine washable") by using fictitious brands and category attributes whose implications would not affect argument strength (Osherson et al. used obscure biological properties to assure "blank" attributes or properties). Subjects were expected, however, to vary in their knowledge of *categories* used in arguments (e.g. electronics equipment). Therefore, we will examine an exploratory measure of subjects' product category knowledge as a potential mediator of assessments of categorical argument strength.

Prior research suggests that expertise or prior knowledge is associated with richer, more detailed representations of a category in memory (e.g., Alba and Hutchinson 1987). Experts should better understand relations (e.g. similarities) between categories and between category members, and should process similarity judgements (in argument strength choices) more swiftly and accurately than novices (cf. Muthukrishnan and Weitz 1991).

Furthermore, in the present context, experts may form more specific (sub)categories within a hierarchy, thereby influencing their perceptions of the "lowest level category" that includes both premise and conclusion categories; however, such greater specificity among experts (than novices) should not increase their accuracy in responses as long as experts and novices agree that the relevant lowest level category is more general in the "weaker" argument.

In sum, due to their detailed category knowledge structures, experts may be more adept at judging similarities between categories and may more accurately process categorical arguments. On the other hand, while experts are more likely to perceive specific subcategories as their lowest level categories, this skill may not translate into more accurate argument choices. A final possibility is that prior knowledge will actually *interfere* with experts' ability to logically process arguments; that is experts' richer knowledge representations may "overload" the available work space (cf. Wyer and Srull 1986) in memory and interfere with the execution of logical argument processing. Given the tentative nature of these competing hypothetical outcomes, we will treat product category knowledge, as a factor mediating subjects' perceptions of argument strength, as exploratory.

METHODOLOGY

Study Overview and Procedure

Fifty-three undergraduate marketing students completed a questionnaire designed to test the validity of each of the seven propositions in Table 1. Subjects were presented with two arguments and asked to select the argument ("a" or "b") whose conclusion was most believable based on the premises (Osherson et al. 1990).

The first page of the questionnaire contained instructions that were read aloud to the subjects. Subjects were told to assume that the statements above the line were facts and to choose the argument whose facts provided a better reason for believing its conclusion (Osherson et al. 1990). The products were described as fictitious, and an example of the task was presented.

Subjects completed judgements for each of the seven propositions, for each of three product classes: (1) electronics, (2) snack foods, and (3) clothing. The order in which the stimuli were presented was systematically varied: for one-third of the subjects, electronics stimuli appeared first (followed by snack foods and clothing), for another third the snack food stimuli were presented first (followed by clothing and electronics), and for the final third clothing stimuli were presented first (followed by electronics and snack foods). The order in which the propositions were presented was held constant across all three stimulus conditions. However, within each stimulus category set the order in which the seven propositions was presented was randomized. Thus, three different random orders of propositions were used for the first, the second, and the third product categories (regardless of the particular category that appeared in that order). The "expected" (i.e. "correct") answer for the contrasting pair of arguments varied, so that 62% of the time the "correct" answer was "a" and 38% of the time the "correct" answer was "b". Following judgements for the 21 stimuli pairs, subjects reported their perceived knowledge in each of the three product classes.

Stimuli

Three superordinate product categories (electronics, clothing, snack foods) were selected in order that exemplars were familiar to the subject population. For each category, relying on researchers' intuition, we selected specific exemplars that were representative or unrepresentative of the category, and that varied in similarity to one another, depending upon the proposition tested. Finally, product attributes were selected that were general or abstract enough to be applied credibly to a range of products within each category. See Table 1 for examples of questionnaire items.

In developing the stimuli, we used fictitious brands for two reasons. First, we were concerned that prior beliefs about a particular brand name would impair subjects' abilities to evaluate the validity of propositions independently of extraneous factors such as company expertise. Also, while the particular product attributes used should be superfluous to the study findings, we believed that they may, in fact, impact judgements of the validity of conclusions for known brands. The use of fictitious brands made it more likely that subjects would follow the directions to assume the premises were true. Second, using fictitious brands allowed us to use a vast array of products within the category (cf. Osherson et al. 1990). In presenting the stimuli, we stated that the particular brand (e.g. "Brand A") includes a wide range of products (e.g. for the electronics category: computers, fax machines, camcorders, TVs, calculators, clock radios, smoke detectors, stereo and other audio equipment, VCRs, and other electronics equipment).

Measures

For each set of arguments, subjects made two judgements. First, subjects were asked which of the two sets of arguments presented was more believable (Osherson et al. 1990), set "a" or set "b". Second, subjects were asked to rate their confidence in this judgement, on a scale from 0 ("not at all confident") to 10 ("extremely confident"). Since preliminary analyses suggested that confidence ratings for high and low knowledge subjects were similar, results of these ratings were dropped. Finally, subjects were asked to rate their overall (subjective) knowledge for each of the three product categories (electronics, snack foods, and clothing) on three single-item scales from 0 ("not at all knowledgeable") to 10 ("extremely knowledgeable").

RESULTS

Overall Ratings

Results of the choice data, across all subjects, presented in Table 2 (see "Overall" column), indicate support for five of the seven propositions. For propositions 1 (premise typicality), 3 (conclusion specificity), 5 (premise-conclusion similarity), 6 (premise-diversity), and 11 (inclusion fallacy), subjects were significantly ($p< .005$) more likely to select the "correct" set of arguments than the "incorrect" set of arguments, with one exception.

For example, for proposition 1 (premise typicality), subjects were more likely to say that the premises confirmed the conclusion when the premise exemplars were prototypical of the conclusion category. The one exception across these five propositions occurred in the snack foods category for proposition 6. According to proposition 6, the less similar the premise categories are among themselves, the more the premises should support the (specific) conclusion. However, in our study, if Brand B potato chips and Brand B corn chips possessed an attribute ("no cholesterol") then Brand B mixed nuts were also perceived to possess the attribute, more so than if Brand B potato chips and Brand B candy bars possessed the attribute. In retrospect, the particular stimuli selected for this item may have been problematic; the lowest level category that included the premises and the conclusion may have been different than our *a priori* expectations. While we expected the lowest level category to be "snack foods" in the two arguments, our subjects may have felt, for example, that the lowest level category in the first case was "salty snack foods" and "snack foods" in the second.

Results also indicate a lack of support for propositions 9 (nonmonotonicity-general) and 10 (nonmonotonicity-specific). With regard to proposition 9, for two of the three product categories, when a premise was added to a general argument converting it to a mixed argument, subjects were no more likely to judge a conclusion believable than when the premise was not added to the argument. Thus, findings yielded nonsignificant differences between the two sets of argument choices, for the electronics and clothing categories. For the snack foods data, findings were significant, and in the expected direction. With regard to proposition 10, when a premise was added to a specific argument converting it to a mixed argument, again subjects were no more likely to judge a conclusion believable than when the premise was not added. The lack of significant increase in choice for the specific (vs. mixed) argument occurred in all three product categories (electronics, snack foods, and clothing). In fact, for snack foods, findings were actually significant in the reverse direction, supporting the mixed over the specific argument. Possible explanations for the lack of support for propositions 9 and 10 may be that the propositions are not valid for (1) the types of stimuli used in this study (e.g. fictitious stimuli, the particular product categories selected), (2) consumer products, or (3) consumers who are less knowledgeable about the products. It seems unlikely that the artificiality of the stimulus situation would decrease the validity of certain arguments; in fact, by maintaining a high degree of control over the stimuli, we anticipated that the validity of the proposed arguments would be optimized. However, this possibility is raised again later in the discussion section. It also seems unlikely that the particular product categories selected were unusual, since we included three replicates that represented a broad range of product categories. The effects of knowledge on validity judgements are explored next.

Self-Reported Knowledge of the Product Category

Table 2 presents validity judgements for the seven propositions as a function of self-reported knowledge of the product category. Sample respondents were split into two groups, representing high and low knowledge subjects. A median split was used for each of the three product categories (the median self-reported knowledge rating was 6.0 for electronics, 7.0 for snack foods, and 7.0 for clothing).

As the data indicate, results varied depending upon the product category selected. For the electronics category, high knowledge individuals tended to yield stronger overall support for the propositions. As indicated by the number of individuals selecting the "correct" set of arguments, higher knowledge individuals showed significant support for six of the seven propositions (all but proposition 10), whereas lower knowledge individuals showed significant support for only three of the seven propositions.

TABLE 2
Overall, High and Low Knowledge Subjects
Percent (%) "Correct" Response

	Electronics			Snack Foods			Clothing		
	Overall	High	Low	Overall	High	Low	Overall	High	Low
N=	(53)	(30)	(23)	(53)	(32)	(21)	(53)	(23)	(30)
P1	79%**	83%**	74%*	89%**	94%**	81%**	81%**	82%**	77%**
P3	92%**	93%**	91%**	85%**	88%**	81%**	96%**	91%**	100%**
P5	98%**	97%**	100%**	85%**	91%**	76%**	96%**	100%**	90%**
P6	74%**	77%**	70%	28%	28%	29%	79%**	87%**	73%*
P9	55%	60%*	48%	79%**	81%**	76%**	55%	61%	50%
P10	47%	53%	39%	34%	44%	19%	43%	39%	47%
P11	75%**	87%**	61%	94%**	94%**	95%**	89%**	87%**	90%**

* $p<.05$ in chi square analyses of "correct" vs "incorrect" responses
** $p<.01$ in chi square analyses of "correct" vs "incorrect" responses

For the snack foods category, high and low knowledge subjects both yielded support for five of the seven propositions, all but propositions 6 and 10. For the clothing category, high and low knowledge subjects again both yielded support for five of the seven propositions, in this case, all but propositions 9 and 10.

In sum, self-reported knowledge of the product category appeared to influence validity judgements for the electronics but not the snack foods or clothing categories. Thus, the earlier lack of support shown for propositions 9 and 10 cannot be explained solely by differences in subjects' knowledge. While the raw percentages in Table 2 for propositions 9 and 10, for all three product categories, show higher proportions of "correct" responses for high than for low knowledge subjects (with one exception), the overall pattern of significant chi-squares does not show impressive support for these differences.

An examination of the means and standard deviations for the knowledge measures may suggest at least a partial explanation for the different results across the product categories. A ceiling effect in knowledge scores appears to have existed in the snack foods (mean = 6.87, standard deviation = 1.66) and clothing (7.06 and 1.73) categories, but not in the electronics category (5.60 and 2.12). In fact, over 60% of the subjects in the snack foods and clothing categories rated themselves as 7 or above on the 10-point scale. The wider variability and lower overall mean in the electronics (as compared to the snack foods or clothing) category may have generated a "truer" indication of the differences in knowledge between the high and low groups.

DISCUSSION

Summary of Findings and Limitations

Our preliminary investigation indicated support for five of the seven (Osherson et al. 1990) propositions. Propositions 9 and 10, and proposition 6 in the snack food category, were not supported by the data. These mixed results raise a number of issues about the applicability and generalizability of the Osherson et al. propositions to a marketing setting and about the propositions themselves. A closer look at the propositions that were not supported highlights these issues.

Theoretical Implications

As discussed earlier, the characteristics of the specific stimuli used in the testing of the arguments' believability may have affected the proportion of "correct" responses chosen by subjects. In the case of proposition 6 in the snack foods category, subjects' judgements of the lowest level category including products in the conclusion (mixed nuts) and the premises (potato chips and corn chips; potato chips and candy bars) may have had a greater impact on their assessment of argument strength than the diversity of products presented in the premise. In the other two categories, however, this was not the case; the less similar the products in the premises were among themselves, the stronger the argument, as predicted. Future research should examine to what degree differences in consumers' category structures of consumer products influence the strength of categorical arguments. A limitation of the current study was that the stimuli were chosen on the basis of the authors' judgements of similarity and relevant category hierarchies. Future research should include pretests and/or manipulation checks to verify these judgements.

The findings from proposition 10 are interesting and informative as well. Although this proposition was strongly supported in the Osherson et al. study it was not supported in this experiment, and in fact, the findings for the snack foods category were significant in the reverse direction. One possible explanation for the current results is that, in our experiment, including a common "Brand X" label across products introduced a set-size confound. That is, when presented with information about a category consisting of a group of products produced by the same company (a fact that was made salient by the directions and the common Brand X label), subjects may have placed more credence on an argument containing a greater number of premises than one with fewer premises, regardless of the similarity of the products in the premises and conclusion. Further, the expected hierarchical category structure may have been affected by the Brand X label. Rather than think in terms of a category structure such as "All Brand B products, Brand B salty snacks, Brand B potato chips, etc.," subjects may simply have considered the lowest level category to be "All Brand B products". Thus, in proposition 10, the addition of a new premise to a single existing premise (to convert the argument from specific to mixed) may have made the argument stronger. Proposition 9 could be expected to demonstrate evidence of a similar confound, although these arguments involved the addition of a premise to two existing premises rather than just one. In fact, it seems likely that a set-size effect would be more evident under certain conditions, including cases with (1) a small initial number of premises, and (2) a common label across all premises and conclusions (e.g. "Brand B"). With respect to the latter, the stimuli used by Osherson et al. did not have this type of label framing the premises and conclusions of their arguments.

A final issue raised in this demonstration study concerns the validity of the specific-general distinction that is at the core of many of the hypothesized propositions. A fundamental assumption associated with the propositions is that subjects largely agree with each other about facts related to the hierarchical level of different stimulus objects. For example, for one of our marketing stimuli, it was necessary to assume that the majority of subjects conceptualized cassette tape players and microcassette recorders as belonging to the same level category, that "audio products" was at the next level of the hierarchy, and that the category "electronics" was one level above it. Research on the role of context effects in categorization (e.g., Barsalou 1982; Ratneshwar and Shocker 1988), and on goal-derived and ad-hoc categories (e.g., Barsalou 1982, 1983) raises questions about the conditions under which category groupings may change. Depending on what cues were salient to a given subject during the administration of the experiment, a cassette tape player and microcassette recorder may have been included in an intermediate category such as "products that run on batteries," a category that emphasizes different determinant attributes and contains a more diverse set of members than the "audio products" category.

Although an examination of the hierarchical nature of categories and the effects of context seems particularly relevant to the product categories investigated in marketing, similar concerns may arise for the natural object categories described in the original Osherson et al. research. In an example from their paper, subjects were assumed to be in universal agreement on the fact that bees, ants, and mosquitoes were all members of the next level category "insects" rather than another category such as "household pests". Since the propositions of interest are conceptually based on similarity judgements between the premise and conclusion categories, as well as between the premise categories and members of the lowest level category that includes both premise and conclusion categories, lack of consensus about the existence, and hierarchical levels, of the categories may influence expected results. Osherson et al. acknowledge this limitation by stating that greater predictive accuracy for their model of argument strength would require supplementary principles to account for "on-line" categories (p.200). At a minimum, these considerations would suggest that future research involving the application of any categorical argument strength propositions would require pretesting in order to establish how the majority of consumers think about, and represent, the hierarchical levels associated with different consumer categories. Alternative models (e.g. Sloman 1993), or modifications to the Osherson et al. model, which do not assume the existence of these types of stable category structures, should also be researched to see if they provide better explanations of argument strength in a consumer environment.

Managerial Implications

Although further research will be needed to explore the boundary conditions of these propositions and to assess their generalizability to a wider range of product categories, there are a number of potential managerial applications for this approach to analyzing consumers' judgements and decisions. Because the framework includes propositions for general, specific, and mixed arguments, it can be used to investigate a wide range of issues important to marketing management. The categorical argument conceptualization is broad enough to be applied to issues involving current individual products and family brand categories, product category and sub-category relationships, potential brand and/or line extensions, the fortification and dilution effects associated with extension information, and the merits/consequences of broad versus narrow family brands. Although some of the phenomena suggested by the propositions have already been demonstrated in consumer research (e.g., the typicality or "fit" of the extension category) other areas have yet to be investigated. Additionally, by providing a formal, relatively broad framework within which to explore these managerially relevant issues, the categorical argument propositions may provide a unifying approach to tie together some of the different findings in extension and product category research.

REFERENCES

Aaker, David A. and Kevin L. Keller (1990), "Consumer Evaluations of Brand Extensions," *Journal of Marketing*, 54 (January), 27-41.

Alba, Joseph W. and J. Wesley Hutchinson (1987), "Dimensions of Consumer Expertise," *Journal of Consumer Research*, 13 (March), 411-454.

Barsalou, Lawrence W. (1982), "Context Independent Information in Concepts," *Memory and Cognition*, 10 (January), 82-93.

_____ (1983), "Ad Hoc Categories," *Memory and Cognition*, 11 (May), 211-227.

Boush, David M. (1993), "Brands as Categories," in *Brand Equity & Advertising*, ed. David A. Aaker and Alexander L. Biel, Hillsdale, NJ: Lawrence Erlbaum Associates, 299-312.

_____ and Barbara Loken (1991), "A Process Tracing Study of Brand Extension Evaluations," *Journal of Marketing Research*, 28 (February), 16-28.

Kardes, Frank (1993) "Category-Based Induction and Product-Line Coherence," paper presented at the American Marketing Association Winter Educators' Conference", Newport Beach, CA.

Keller, Kevin L. and David A. Aaker (1992), "The Effects of Sequential Introduction of Brand Extensions," *Journal of Marketing Research*, 24 (February), 35-50.

Loken, Barbara and Deborah Roedder John (1993), "Diluting Brand Beliefs: When Do Brand Extensions Have a Negative Impact?" *Journal of Marketing*, 57 (July), 71-84.

Muthukrishnan, A.V. and Barton A. Weitz (1991), "Role of Product Knowledge in Brand Extension," in *Advances in Consumer Research*, Vol. 18, ed. Rebecca H. Holman & Michael R. Solomon, Provo, UT: Association for Consumer Research, 407-413.

Osherson, Daniel N., Edward E. Smith, Osmond Wilkie, Alejandro Lopez, and Eldar Shafir (1990), "Category-Based Induction," *Psychology Review*, 97(2), 185-200.

Park, C. Whan, Sandra Milberg, and Robert Lawson (1991), "Evaluation of Brand Extensions: The Role of Product Feature Similarity and Brand Concept Consistency," *Journal of Consumer Research*, 18 (September), 185-193.

Ratneshwar, S. and Allan D. Shocker (1988), "The Application of Prototypes and Categorization Theory in Marketing: Some Problems and Alternative Perspectives," in *Advances in Consumer Research*, Vol. 15, ed. Michael J. Houston, Provo, UT: Association for Consumer Research, 280-285.

Romeo, Jean B. (1991), "The Effect of Negative Information on the Evaluations of Brand Extensions and the Family Brand," in *Advances in Consumer Research*, Vol. 18, ed. Rebecca H. Holman and Michael R. Solomon, Provo, UT: Association for Consumer Research, 399-406.

Sloman, Steven A. (1993), "Feature-Based Induction," *Cognitive Psychology*, 25, 231-280.

Wyer, Robert S. Jr. and Thomas K. Srull (1986), "Human Cognition in Its Social Context," *Psychological Review*, 93, 322-359.

Brand Names and Consumer Inference: The Effect of Adding a Numeric Component to a Brand Name

Teresa Pavia, University of Utah

Although approximately 10,000 of the 1.35 million Federally Registered trademarks are comprised in part or in whole of a number, the role of numbers in brand names is poorly understood. The different ways manufacturers use numbers in a brand name to communicate explicitly with consumers are discussed. However, in many instances the precise meaning of a number may be opaque to consumers. The effect of a non-explicit, numeric component on consumer inferences is explored with a survey which presented respondents with either a unknown brand with a numeric component or the same unknown brand without a numeric component and asked the respondent to associate a product with the name. The data suggest the addition of a numeric component to a brand name increases the number of technical product associations that consumers make with the name. It appears it may do so by increasing the number of associations made to a particular product (e.g., computers) rather than by significantly increasing the range of product that were evoked.

Firms spend a considerable amount of time and energy developing and protecting their brand names. Consumers rely on brand names to identify products and, in settings where it is difficult to evaluate the intrinsic attributes of a product, may rely on extrinsic attributes such as the brand name for pre-purchase product evaluation (Mazursky and Jacoby 1986).

Research has been conducted on inferential notions drawn from brand names (Chisnall 1974; Peterson and Ross 1972), attitudes towards products attributable to the brand name (Heath, Chatterjee and France 1990; Pavia and Costa 1991; Zinkhan and Martin 1987), and the perceived personalities of various brand names (Alt and Griggs 1988). One branding issue that has received less attention is the use of numbers in the formation of a brand name. A brand name that contains one or more numbers in either written form (e.g., Ten) or digit form (e.g., 10) is referred to as an alpha-numeric brand name. Alpha-numeric brand names may be composed of numbers alone (e.g., 7-Eleven), words and a number (e.g., Hang Ten or Chanel No. 5), letters and numbers (e.g., K2r or A Two Z), or a combination of words, letters and numbers (Formula 44-D). This definition of alpha-numeric brand names includes non-numeric contexts for numerals as well as brand names with explicit numeric meaning.

The role of numbers in brand names is a topical issue for several reasons. First, as of December 1991 there were 1.35 million Federally Registered Trademarks (FRT). Of these, approximately 10,000 are composed in part of a number (see the discussion of FRT and Table 1 for more detail). Second, a review of FRT over the past two years shows the number of such marks is increasing. Third, if the manufacturer intends number in the name to describe some product feature to the consumer it is important to understand if consumers interpret the number as intended. And fourth, if the number does not describe a product feature, but is used symbolically, what sorts of inferences do consumers draw from the number and is the symbolic meaning shared between consumer and manufacturer?

The goal of this paper is twofold. It will provide a taxonomy of explicit uses of numbers in brand names. However, many names were unclassifiable since the number has no apparent meaning. The associations that consumers make in the case of non-explicit numeric meaning were explored with a survey. This survey differed from almost all existing research in this area (the exception is Chisnall 1974) in that it allowed the *consumer* to identify products that go with various brand names rather than rating the brand name with a preselected product. The survey and its subsequent discussion address the different patterns of associations evoked by the addition of a numeric component to a non-numeric brand name and identify questions remaining in this area.

THE "EXCESS" MEANING OF NUMBERS

Outside of the context of branding, researchers have considered the latent or "excess" meaning that people associate with different numbers. Battig and Spera (1962) and Cochran and Wickens (1963) investigated how many free associations subjects could make with the numbers between zero and one hundred. Not surprisingly, 100, 0, 1, 2, and 13 elicited significantly more associations than did other numbers. Knapp and Chen (1964) restricted their investigation to the numbers between one and nine. They found significant correlation of adjectives such as feminine, smooth and powerful with specific digits. Additional support for the deep cultural associations evoked by numbers is found in Menninger (1977) who provided an extensive exploration of number meaning, with special emphasis on how language referring to numbers reflects, and is driven by, the meaning of the number. More recently Schimmel (1993) discussed the history and meaning of various numbers within and across cultures.

Hull (1975) reported that random codes constructed of both numbers and letters were recalled with greater accuracy than codes composed exclusively of random letters. These findings may be related to the cognitive processing of brands. Meyers-Levy (1989) reported that brands formed of words with a high number of associations tend to elicit nondistinctive processing and are somewhat less memorable. This effect was attributed to competing associations triggered during brand name retrieval. Hulls' work suggests the recall of a brand composed in part of a number with a lot of associations may not be predictable.

A PRODUCT BY ANY OTHER NAME

Many studies have shown that, in the absence of other information, consumers may draw inferences about product features or uses from the brand name (Heath Chatterjee and France 1990; Leclerc, Schmitt and Dube-Rioux 1989; Pavia and Costa 1991; Zeithaml 1988; Zinkhan and Martin 1981). For example, new products with brand names judged to be more typical of the product category, such as Polar Bear for ice cream, appear to elicit more favorable attitudes than do new products with atypical names (Zinkhan and Martin 1987).

At a more basic level, researchers have investigated why certain brand names are judged "typical" of a particular product category even though the name itself may not be a word in the consumer's lexicon (Chisnall 1974; Dogana 1967; Peterson and Ross 1972; Sapir 1929). As part of a discussion of the application of these studies to marketing Collins (1977) concluded that "names - even newly invented ones - are never, or rarely, neutral labels" (pg 358). He goes on to suggest that names be selected to "convey the intended 'feeling tone' to the consumer, and so elicit a consumer response in line with the marketing objectives of the brand" (pg. 361).

If brand names are not neutral labels, one may ask what message a particular name is sending to consumers and whether this is an accurate representation of the product. Although alpha-

TABLE 1
Registered Trademarks that Contain At Least One Digit in Which "*" Denotes Any Character String

Numeric part of the trademark	# of registered Federal Trademarks containing this numeric indicator
1*	5819
2*	2801
3*	1957
4*	1365
5*	1237
6*	733
7*	1074
8*	858
9*	832
0*	122
*1	2344
*2	1802
*3	1286
*4	1387
*5	1563
*6	1019
*7	1027
*8	912
*9	717
*0	5078

numeric brand names are given high ratings for "going with" preselected chemical, technical or formulated products (Pavia and Costa 1993), the question of what products consumers are inclined to associate with an alpha-numeric name when left to their own devices remains open. If a consumer's "natural" association with a particular name is wildly variant from the association a manufacturer wishes to establish, it suggests a vigorous and focused marketing campaign may be needed to position the product.

This paper will proceed as follows: first, the actual appearance of numbers in existing trademarks will be examined by looking at Federally Registered Trademarks with the intent to identifying the obvious roles that the numbers play. The discussion will then turn to symbolic roles for numeric components of brand names. Finally, the results of a survey designed to capture the product associations evoked by the addition of a number to a non-numeric, nonsense brand are reported and discussed.

A Review of Federally Registered Alpha-Numeric Trademarks

Table 1 presents the findings from a search of the Registered Federal Trademarks as of December 1991 for all trademarks comprised in part, or in whole, of a digit (this database excludes trademarks registered at only the state level). Table 1 uses standard computer search notation and shows a "*" to indicate "any character string." That is, *1 means a name in which the digit "1" is *preceded* by any character string, but is not followed by any additional characters. So, *1 includes the names "CENTURY 21," but not the trademark "PRODUCT 19." The names identified by 1* are composed in part of a 1 *followed* by any character string; these include "PRODUCT 19" and "8 1/2," but not the trademark "501." Names with more than one digit are double counted; however, over 4600 of the trademarks consist of numbers that are single digits suggesting the number of unique marks is about 10,000.

A review of all of the trademarks containing the single digit 2, or the written word two, was conducted to evaluate the roles that numbers play in a brand name. Seven overlapping roles were identified: an explicit indicator of numeric meaning, an indicator of line extension, an indicator of a sequence of products, a homophone, a part of common speech, an indicator of time or place, and a symbolic rather than literal marker.

The most obvious use for a number in a brand name is for the manufacturer to reinforce a numerically measurable product feature. For examples, consumers may use the brands EYE-PRO 2 HR. GUARANTEE (vision care), and TWO FEET TALL (children's clothing), to understand something about the product, the intended user, or the usage situation. Another common use of a number is to communicate to the consumer that the product is a line extension such as CLOROX 2 (all fabric bleach). Numbers can also be used to indicate the placement of a product within a product line or to indicate product evolution, for example MERCEDES 240SL (automobile).

A homophonic (spelled differently than another word but sounding the same) digit may be used not for its numeric content, but for its aural contribution, although other features may also be relevant. Use of a digit as a homophone may be intended to increase interest, novelty, or recall as in I.C.U.2 (fleecewear), 2-CUTE (girl's clothing), 2-X-S (apparel), and TWO-RIFIC (pizzas).

Sometimes numbers seem to appear in a name simply because they are part of commonly used English phrases or culturally ingrained notions. For example, it is possible that the numeric content of KNIT ONE PURL TWO (sweaters) is less important than the fact that the trademark as a whole is closely associated with knitting. Similarly, when the number indicates time or place, as in 2:7 (religious books), the number appears to be a form of jointly understood shorthand between the producer and the consumer.

In many instances, however, the precise meaning of a number may be opaque to consumers. This may occur when the consumer does not understand the meaning that the manufacturer ascribed to the numeric part of the brand name (e.g., Boeing 747), or it may occur because the numeric part of the brand name was selected to convey a symbolic rather than a literal meaning. To some extent the meaning of the number is irrelevant if the meaning the the producer was trying to convey with the brand name is understood. This leads to the question of what consumers infer from a number in a brand name.

To avoid promotional effects for existing products, the following research presented respondents with either a unknown brand with a numeric component or the same unknown brand without a numeric component and asked the respondent to associate a product with the name. By using an open ended format the survey provided an opportunity to look in detail at the type of associations that were made. It also provided an opportunity to reaffirm existing findings which suggest:

H_1: The presence of a numeric component in a brand name will increase the number of technical, formulated or chemical associations that are made with the name.

METHODS

Respondents were presented with two hypothetical brand names and asked to provide, in an open-ended format, "the product that you think would go best with this made up brand name." Half of the respondents were presented with the two brand names Alustar and Dehax 3000; the other half were presented with the names Dehax and Alustar 4000. This design was selected to provide a contrast between the sorts of products that may be associated with a non-numeric brand name and the same name augmented with a relatively large numeric component. Existing studies suggest that alpha-numeric brand names are accepted for technical, chemical or formulated products (Pavia and Costa 1993), the name Dehax is accepted as a brand name for a laundry detergent (Peterson and Ross 1972), and the name Alustar is accepted as a name for aluminum foil (Chisnall 1974). However, by using an open ended format this study allowed the respondents to identify the product out of all possible products that they felt was most appropriate for this brand name rather than simply rating a the acceptability of a given name for one preselected product.

This study used two different forms of stimuli: a random sample of adults in a populous western county were contacted by mail and exposed to the name in writing, while another sample was contacted by phone and exposed to the name aurally. The telephone portion of the survey was conducted by an independent research organization in which the interviewers were trained for consistent pronunciation of the brand names. The response rate was higher for the telephone portion of the survey, 92%, than it was for the mail portion, 43%. The verbatim open-ended responses from the mail and phone survey were pooled, coded, and like responses were grouped together. The criteria for grouping the answers were to identify 1) groups which permitted unambiguous assignment of responses and 2) groups which would contain no less than 10% of the associations within at least one brand. The assignment to the *a posteriori* groups was performed independently by the author and a trained student auditor. Disagreements were resolved by discussion; there were disagreements on fewer than one percent of the responses. The response groups and the number of responses for each brand may be seen in Table 2.

A group of 43 MBA students unassociated with this research ranked the randomly presented categories as described in Table 2 by level of "technicality." The meaning of "technicality" was left purposefully vague, to allow for the variety of meanings covered in the statement that alpha-numeric brand names are associated with "technical" goods. The presentation of the eight categories in Table 2 appears in the order of least to most technical as rated by this group. With a ranking of 1 indicating the most technical product and a ranking of 8 the least technical, the average rankings were medication 2.2, electronics 2.3, vehicle related 3.2, agriculture 3.4, cleaner/ polish 5.1, personal products 6.1, entertainment/etc. 6.6, and foods 7.0. Although this ranking does not indicate how technical a group is, it provides some indication of the the relative technicality of the groups.

RESULTS

Based on the survey reported above, the first three categories in Table 2 were classified as less technical items from a consumer perspective. Medications, electronics, vehicles or pest control products were clustered together and seen as relatively technical goods. The classification of cleaners is not as obvious. Neither is it clustered with the first four groups, nor is it clustered with personal products, entertainment/clothes/etc. or food. Cleaners will therefore be treated as a somewhat special case.

If cleaners are considered technical products, when the free associations that were evoked by Alustar are compared to those evoked by Alustar 4000 (recall that these names were presented to different respondents), the associations made with Alustar 4000 were more likely to be in technical categories. The increase of technical associations from 74 out of 131 (56%), to 109 out of 130 (84%) is significant at p <0.01. In the case of Dehax and Dehax 3000, the technical associations increased from 97 out of 117 (83%) to 131 out of 141 (93%) which is significant at p<0.025.

If cleaners are considered an ambigious category and are dropped from the analysis, the effect of adding a numeric component to Alustar still leads to a significant increase in technical associations (from 42% to 67% p<.01). The effect on Dehax is significant at p<.03 (from 73% to 88%).

Hypothesis 1 appears to be supported by the data. The net effect of the inclusion of 4000 with the brand Alustar was to move associations away from the less technical food, clothing or personal products and into more technical areas; the inclusion of 3000 with the brand name Dehax decreased the already low numbers of associations with food, clothing and personal products.

Beyond the simple assessment of technical vs. non-technical, these data permit an evaluation of how the flavor, or the nature, of the responses within a category changes with the addition of a numeric component to the name. Table 3 presents the verbatim data to see if the types of associations within a category were different when a number was included in the brand name. The following analysis looks at electronics and vehicles since the net effect of including a number in the brand name was an increase in these categories for both brands.

As Table 3 demonstrates, in the category of electronics the effect of adding the number 4000 to the name Alustar was to increase the number of associations with computers, industrial goods, home electronics and home appliances. With the exception of the industrial carpet cleaner and the satellite equipment, all of these items were mentioned at least once for the name Alustar alone. The net effect of adding 3000 to the brand name Dehax in the category of electronics was similar: the number of computer and home sight/sound systems increased, but no new categories were evoked. In the category of vehicles/vehicle related items, the inclusion of a number in the brand name increased the number of car associations, but did not have any overall effect of changing the sorts of associations that were made. In short, at least within these categories, the net effect of adding a number to a name appears to increase the number of technical associations. It appears to do so by increasing the number of associations made to a particular product rather than by significantly increasing the range of product that were evoked.

TABLE 2
Open Ended Responses for Each Brand in the Given Category
(Absolute number and percentage of column total)

RESPONSE CATEGORIES	Alustar	Alustar 4000	Dehax	Dehax 3000
	n = 131	n = 130	n = 117	n = 141
Foods: cereals, crackers, flour, meat, yeast, etc.	18 % (n=23)	5 % (n=7)	6 % (n=7)	4 % (n=5)
Entertainment/Clothing/Recreation/Shoes: TV show, sports equipment, adult & children' clothes, sheets etc.	10 % (n=13)	5 % (n=7)	2 % (n=2)	1 % (n=1)
Personal Product: shampoo, deodorant, baby wipes, etc.	11 % (n=14)	5 % (n=7)	3 % (n=4)	2 % (n=3)
Cleaner/Polish: kitchen, bath, oven or glass cleaners, solvent, degreaser, etc.	36 % (n=47)	32 % (n=42)	35 % (n=41)	43 % (n=60)
Agriculture/Pest Control: insecticide, weed spray, fertilizer	-	-	17 % (n=20)	9 % (n=12)
Vehicle/Vehicle-Related: car, boat, oil, lubricant, gas additive, etc.	8 % (n=10)	13 % (n=17)	2 % (n=2)	9 % (n=13)
Electronics: TV, VCR, PC, satellite antenna, etc.	10 % (n=13)	24 % (n=32)	4 % (n=5)	13 % (n=18)
Medication: Over the counter cough and cold, prescription drugs, etc.	2 % (n=2)	10 % (n=13)	22 % (n=26)	19 % (n=27)
Other Non-Technical: pet food, trash bags, etc. Technical: nuclear weapons, cellular lines	7% (n=7) (n=2)	5% (n=1) (n=5)	9% (n=7) (n=3)	1% (n=1) (n=1)

DISCUSSION

Alpha-numeric brand names are an important branding option and are currently used by many different firms. There is a considerable number of alpha-numeric brand names currently in use and the understanding that consumers have based on the use of numbers in brand names is just beginning to be understood. The review of the Federally Registered Trademarks suggests that numbers may play a variety of explicit, descriptive roles. For example, numbers may describe the numericity of something in the product (e.g., Product 19 uses 19 to describe the number of different nutrients provided by the cereal). However, when the meaning of the number is not immediately apparent to the consumer, the question of what the consumer thinks the number suggests is open.

The data presented here suggest that when the product feature referred to by the numeric component of the brand name is not readily accessible, consumers are inclined to associate the name with technical goods. This is consistent with other studies, but has provided supporting evidence using a different methodology. The approach of asking for free associations was useful in evaluating the types of associations that were evoked. These data suggest that while the number of associations with technical goods increases when a numeric component is added to the brand name, the types of associations did not change in a readily detectable manner.

One implication of this research for consumer research is that the inclusion of a numeric component in a brand name is an option open to managers, but is not an option without repercussions. This fact appears to be of some concern to manufacturers using alpha-numeric brand names in both explicit and implicit settings. For example, although Product 19 is using the number 19 in a fairly explicit manner, the strong cultural association of numbers with science and technicality, and perhaps practicality over pleasure, led Kellogg's to devote the entire back of the the Product 19 box at one point to the following discussion. "Okay, so we didn't give it the most appetizing name in the world. But you didn't let that fool you. You know these flakes have a terrific taste ... Think of it as your reward for looking past our name."

TABLE 3
Open Ended Responses for Electronics and Vehicle Related Categories

ELECTRONICS

Alustar 10% of all responses	Alustar 4000 24% of all responses
TV (4)	TV (2)
computer (2) unspecified computer product	computer (15) computer peripheral
video tape (2)	videotape camcorder
vacuum (2)	vacuum light, large appliance (4), hair dryer, answering machine
unspecified electronics (2)	unspecified electronics (2)
	industrial carpet cleaner
	satellite equipment
Dehax 4% of all responses	**Dehax 3000** 13% of all responses
computer (2)	computer (6)
computer software	computer software (4)
computer disks	computer disk
remote control	computer product (4)
	stereo equipment
	vacuum
	VCR tapes

Vehicle/Vehicle Related

Alustar 8% of all responses	Alustar 4000 13% of all responses
auto (5)	auto (12)
unspecified car related	car oil, lubricant (4)
airplane, power boat	4000 cc engine
tractor trailer	
gasoline, tires	
Dehax 2% of all responses	**Dehax 3000** 9% of all responses
auto (1)	auto (4)
unspecified car related	car oil, lubricant (7)
	tractor gasoline additive
	tires for race cars

NOTE: a number in parentheses indicates multiple responses.

With regard to the work of Hull (1975) and Meyers-Levy (1989) cited above, the findings here are insufficient to speak to the advantages or disadvantages of alpha-numeric brand names with respect to recall. However, it is interesting to note that in both pairs, respondents were more likely to leave the non-numeric brand name question blank than the alpha-numeric brand name. That is, respondents appeared more likely to associate a product with an unknown alpha-numeric brand name; of the 141 respondents presented with Alustar and Dehax 3000 the responses were 131 and 141, respectively and for Dehax and Alustar 4000 they were 117 and 130, respectively.

At the policy level an additional concern may be that the symbolism and shared cultural meaning of numbers provides an avenue for misrepresentation of one's product. If a number is widely believed to indicate technology, a newer version, an improvement, a longer lasting product, or more power, the brand name may mislead the consumer. It may be difficult to prosecute a producer for a brand name that leads to inappropriate consumer inference if the inference itself is never alluded to in any promotional material. However, it is possible given this and other studies that, even in the absence of a promotional scheme, a consistent strong misconception may be resident in the population based on the brand name alone.

Prior research has demonstrated that consumer may accept certain names with certain types of products. This research extended this work and demonstrated that certain names, particularly those with numeric components, evoke consistent images in consumer's minds. If the product is a technical good it is likely that the images evoked by the brand name will "convey the intended 'feeling tone' to the consumer" (Collins 1977). If the product is not a technical good, a manufacturer should proceed with caution.

REFERENCES

Alt, Michael and Steve Griggs, "Can a Brand Be Cheeky?," *Marketing Intelligence and Planning*, 6, 4 (1988), 9-16.

Battig, William F. and Annette J. Spera, "Rated Association Values of Numbers from 0-100," *Journal of Verbal Learning and Verbal Behavior*, 1, October (1962), 200-202.

Chisnall, P. M., "Aluminum Household Foil in the Common Market: Research for an Effective Brand Name," *Journal of Management Studies*, 11, October (1974), 246-255.

Cochran, Samuel W. and Delos D. Wickens, "Supplementary Report: Rated Association Values of Numbers from 0-100," *Journal of Verbal Learning and Verbal Behavior*, 2, (1963), 373-374.

Collins, Leslie, "A Name To Conjure With," *European Journal of Marketing*, 11, 5 (1977), 340-363.

Dogana, Ferando, "Psycholinguistic Contributions to the Problem of Brand Names," *European Marketing Research Review*, 2, 1 (1967), 50-58.

Heath, Timothy B., Subimal Chatterjee and Karen Russo France (1990). "Using the Phonemes of Brand Names to Symbolize Brand Attributes," *AMA Educator's Proceedings: Enhancing Knowledge Development in Marketing*, Washington, D.C., A. Parasuraman and W. Bearden, American Marketing Association, 38-42.

Hull, A.J., "Nine Codes: A Comparative Evaluation of Human Performance with Some Numeric, Alpha and Alpha-Numeric Coding Systems," *Ergonomics* 18, 5 (1975), 567-576.

Knapp, Robert H. and Rachel J. Chen, "On The Surplus Meaning of Numbers," *Psychological Reports*, 15, (1964), 319-322.

Leclerc, France, Bernd Schmitt and Laurette Dube-Rioux (1989). "Brand Name a la Francaise? Oui, But For The Right Product!," *Advances in Consumer Research*, 16, 253-257.

Mazursky, David and Jacob Jacoby, "Forming Impressions of Merchandise and Service Quality," *Perceived Quality*, J. Jacoby and J. Olsen (Ed.), Lexington Books, Lexington, MA, 1986, 139-154.

Menninger, Karl, *Number Words and Number Symbols*, The MIT Press, Cambridge, 1977.

Meyers-Levy, Joan, "The Influence of a Brand Name's Association Set Size and Word Frequency on Brand Memory," *Journal of Consumer Research* 16, 2 (1989), 197-207.

Pavia, Teresa and Janeen Arnold Costa, "The Winning Number: Consumer Perceptions of Alpha-Numeric Brand Names," *Journal of Marketing* 57, 3, (1993), 85-98.

Pavia, Teresa M. and Janeen Arnold Costa (1991). "Gender Dimensions of the Alphabetic Characters with Implications for Branding," *Gender and Consumer Behavior*, Salt Lake City, UT, J. Costa, University of Utah Press, 173-186.

Peterson, Robert A. and Ivan Ross, "How to Name New Brands," *Journal of Advertising Research*, 12, December (1972), 29-34.

Sapir, Edward, "A Study in Phonetic Symbolism," *Journal of Experimental Psychology*, 12, June (1929), 225-239.

Schimmel, Annemarie, *The Mystery of Numbers*, Oxford University Press, New York, 1993.

Zeithaml, Valarie, "Consumer Perceptions of Price, Quality, and Value: A Means-End Model and Synthesis of Evidence," *Journal of Marketing*, 52, 3 (1988), 2-22.

Zinkhan, George M. and Claude R Martin, "The Additudinal Implications of a New Brand's Name," *Advances in Consumer Research*, A. Mitchell (Ed.), Association for Consumer Research, Ann Arbor, MI, 1981, 467-471.

Zinkhan, George M. and Claude R. Martin Jr., "New Brand Names and Inferential Beliefs: Some Insights on Naming New Products," *Journal of Business Research*, 15, 2 (1987), 157-172.

Consumer Inference as Part of Product Comprehension

Timothy R. Graeff, Middle Tennessee State University
Jerry C. Olson, Penn State University

ABSTRACT

Most consumer research has studied inference-making as a process of "filling in" missing information about a product attribute in order to evaluate a product, or choose among alternative brands. We examine the limitations of this approach, present an expanded view of inference formation as part of the product comprehension process, conceptualize consumers' product-related inferences in terms of the levels of means-end knowledge, and make suggestions for future research.

INTRODUCTION

Inferences are important for understanding consumer behavior. Unfortunately, the dominant approach to studying consumers' inferences has been extremely narrow and has not produced a good understanding of the inference formation process or the types of inferences consumers form. Most consumer research has studied inference-making as a process of filling in missing information about a product attribute in order to evaluate a product, or choose among alternative brands. In this paper, we examine the limitations of this approach. We present an alternative perspective that views inference formation as an integral part of comprehension processes involved in interpreting or making sense of product information. From this perspective, inferences are formed whenever consumers comprehend product information, even when there is no obviously missing information to be filled in. We conclude the paper by identifying several issues for future research suggested by our approach.

THE MISSING INFORMATION PARADIGM

Most of what consumer researchers know about consumer inference has been learned through laboratory experiments based on the "missing information paradigm." In this approach, derived from social psychology, researchers manipulate the amount and type of information given to subjects. In the typical consumer inference experiment, subjects evaluate several brands described by a small set of product attributes (often only two or three). The experiment is set up so that some information is obviously "missing." Some brands are *completely described* in terms of the two or three attributes under study, while other brands are *partially described* by a subset of these attributes.

The usual goal of this research is to determine whether consumers formed inferences about the "missing" attribute. To do so, researchers compare subjects' brand evaluations made under the complete and missing information conditions (Ford & Smith 1987; Huber & McCann 1982; Johnson & Levin 1985; Lim, Olshavsky, & Kim 1988; Simmons & Lynch 1991). Differences in overall evaluations are attributed to the inferences subjects supposedly made about the "missing" attributes. Typically, only these missing attribute inferences are considered.

We believe this view of consumer inference as filling in missing information about specific attributes has produced a limited understanding of (1) the types of product-related inferences consumers form, (2) the circumstance under which consumers form inferences, and (3) the role of prior knowledge in consumers' inference processes.

What Types Of Inferences Do Consumers Form?

In most inference studies, researchers specify *a priori* the product attribute(s) about which consumers are presumed to form an inference (Huber & McCann 1982; Kardes 1988; Simmons & Lynch 1991). Typically, these are the experimentally manipulated "missing" attributes. However, even when researchers have included inferences about product attributes other than those for which there was "missing information," they usually restricted their analysis to inferences about other product attributes. For example, Sujan and Dekleva (1987) had subjects read an advertisement for a product and list the *features* they thought the product might possess (some of these features probably were inferences). But, because subjects were directed to report attributes or features, they may not have reported inferences about more abstract, product-related meanings such as what end states, values, or goals the product may help them achieve.

Other researchers have used more "open" thought listing instructions ("describe what you are thinking about while evaluating these brands"), but they often coded these protocols for inferences about only product attributes (Simmons & Lynch 1991). In one exception, Gardial and Biehal (1986) asked subjects to freely verbalize their thoughts into a tape recorder while choosing between three advertised cameras. In addition to inferences about product attributes, the authors found that subjects formed inferences about product benefits and appropriateness for various users and situations. In fact, less than half of subjects' inferences concerned product attributes.

Such results suggest that consumer researchers have not examined many types of inferences consumers may form while evaluating products. For instance, consumers could make inferences about various attributes or features of a product, how a product works, its uses, its relationship to other products, its appropriateness for certain users or situations, and even its ability to help consumers achieve their goals and values. Consumer researchers need to adopt a broader view of consumer inference that includes these types of product-related inferences.

When Do Consumers Form Inferences?

The missing attribute paradigm used in most consumer inference research seems to imply that consumers form inferences only if they recognize that information about an important attribute is missing (Gardial & Schumann 1990; Huber & McCann 1982). Otherwise, consumers are presumed to use a decision strategy that uses only the available information and does not include inferences (e.g., Burke 1990).

In contrast, we do not see inferences as unusual events that occur only in special circumstances. Rather, we propose that consumers form inferences whenever they comprehend or interpret product information—even if there is no obviously "missing information." To date, however, researchers have not examined the inferences consumers form during ordinary comprehension of product information. We need a conceptual framework for studying consumer inference that accounts for natural inference formation processes.

How Does Prior Knowledge Influence Consumers' Inferences?

Consumers use their prior knowledge activated from memory to form inferences, and different types of inferences require different types of knowledge. Unfortunately, the missing attribute paradigm has focused researchers' attention on how consumers' knowledge effects only attribute inferences. Some research suggests that greater product familiarity and expertise (more product knowledge) is positively related to forming attribute inferences. Kardes, Sanbonmatsu, & Herr (1992) explain this in terms of the missing information paradigm by proposing that the knowledge structures of relative experts contain stronger linkages between attributes, which makes experts more likely to notice the absence of attribute information (and thus more likely to form an inference about a missing attribute) than novices. We need a conceptual framework for studying consumer inference that recognizes the role of product knowledge in forming inferences about aspects of products besides just attributes.

Summary

In sum, past research within the missing information paradigm assumes that consumers form inferences about only specific product attributes for which there is obviously missing information. Little attention has been given to the effects of prior knowledge on other types of inferences besides attributes or features. To expand their vision of inferences, researchers need a broader conceptual framework from which to work. In the next section we develop such a framework to guide the study of consumers' product-related inferences. The framework suggests that consumers form many different types of product-related inferences while comprehending (interpreting) product information, even in situations with no obviously missing information to be filled in.

COMPREHENSION PROCESSES

In much past research, comprehension was viewed as the process by which a person arrives at the *direct* or *literal* meaning of a message. One can find remnants of this narrow perspective in research on comprehension and recall of advertising (Jacoby & Hoyer 1982).

A more modern view, based on Bartlett's (1932) pioneering work on memory, treats comprehension as a *constructive process* of interpretation. Constructive comprehension means that people actively generate or form the knowledge, meanings, and beliefs that represent information in the environment. From this perspective, "meaning" does not reside in the text of a message. Rather, people draw on their prior knowledge to actively *construct*, or *create* the meaning of a message (Bransford, Barclay, & Franks 1972).

Inferences and Comprehension

Most of the meanings that people construct during comprehension are inferences that "go beyond" the information given. People form inferences to construct more complete and more coherent meanings than is possible by only representing the literal information given. Evidence for inferences made during comprehension has come from examining the distortions subjects made in interpreting the information that was originally given to them. Bartlett (1932), for instance, found that subjects did not remember a story as an exact copy of the original text. Rather, subjects comprehended the information by forming inferences that transformed the original information. Researchers have also shown that people do not remember given information verbatim, indicating that the knowledge created during comprehension and stored in memory is not a literal representation of the presented information. Thus, people often cannot distinguish the constructed set of meanings they created largely through inferences from the information that was presented to them (Bransford, Barclay, & Franks 1972).

Inferences and Prior Knowledge

During comprehension, incoming (new) information is interpreted in terms of prior knowledge activated from memory. The activated knowledge acts as a filter or template to guide the interpretation of the new information (Black, Galambos, & Read 1984). The influence of activated knowledge on comprehension is illustrated in a classic study by Bransford and Johnson (1972). Two groups of subjects read a passage describing, in rather general terms, the tasks associated with doing laundry. One group was given a title, "Doing Laundry," along with the information, while the second group received no title. The group that saw the title rated the passage as more comprehensible and exhibited higher levels of recall. Apparently, the title activated subjects' "clothes washing" schema (the contents of which were not measured), and this knowledge enhanced subjects' ability to comprehend (interpret) the information in the passage and recall it later.

Measuring Inferences During Comprehension

Researchers have measured inferences during comprehension with a wide variety of tasks and materials; including simple sentences (Brewer 1977), complex sentences (Harris 1974), and brief stories (Johnson, Bransford, & Solomon 1973). One technique often used to demonstrate inferences during reading comprehension is the "false recognition paradigm." Many studies have found that subjects falsely recognize sentences which contain plausible inferences from the information that actually was presented (Johnson, Bransford, & Solomon 1973). A false alarm is taken to indicate that an inference had been formed during comprehension.

Recently, researchers have recommended using concurrent (think out loud) protocols to directly measure the meanings inferred during comprehension. For example, Collins, Brown, and Larkin (1980) asked subjects to talk about the hypotheses they considered and rejected while reading a short text. Rumelhart (1984) asked subjects five questions (Who?, What?, Where?, When?, and Why?) after reading each new sentence of a story. These think out loud protocols are used to discover subjects' personal interpretations of the stories, including inferences, and how their interpretations change with each additional sentence.

Recently, thought protocol methods have been used by consumer researchers studying advertising comprehension. Mick (1992) argued for an approach that measures the subjective meanings formed by consumers. This approach contrasts with the "traditional view" of advertising comprehension that used "objective" tests of recall for key advertised claims and implicitly assumed verbatim comprehension of message information. To study these personal meanings, Mick had subjects write down their thoughts after reading each new sentence of an advertisement. Many of these subjective meanings were probably inferences.

The most widely used method for studying consumer inferences is the information integration methodology (or functional measurement) developed by Anderson (1982). In the typical consumer inference experiment, subjects evaluate a series of brands described by a small set of attributes. Some brands are completely described by all attributes under study, while other brands are partially described by a subset of these attributes. Researchers compare subjects' evaluations of the completely and partially described brands and draw conclusions (make inferences) about missing attribute inferences. For example, if subjects formed a less favorable evaluation about a partially described brand with missing information than a completely described brand (where that attribute was described as average or moderately desirable), the researcher would conclude that subjects inferred a below average value for the missing attribute.

Unfortunately, information integration methodology has severe problems when measuring inferences. First, this approach does not directly measure whether inferences are actually formed. Second, the approach is designed to measure only a particular inference—the value of a specific missing attribute. It does not measure other inferences subjects might form while evaluating the

FIGURE 1
Product Comprehension Process

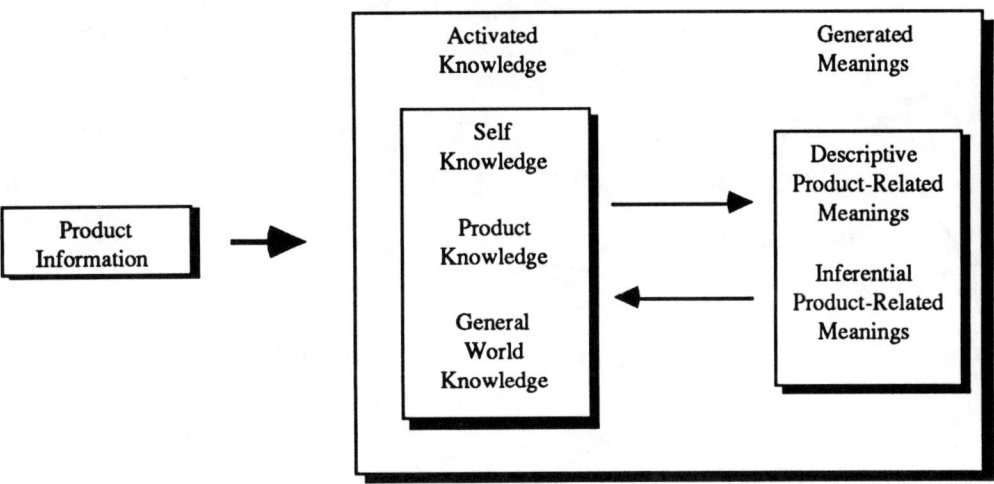

brands. Thus, researchers examining patterns of brand evaluations can conclude only that subjects evaluated the partially described brands "as if" they inferred a certain value for the missing attribute.

In the next section we integrate the ideas presented thus far into a conceptual framework that can guide future study of consumers' product comprehension and inference processes.

A PROPOSED FRAMEWORK FOR CONSUMER INFERENCES

The proposed framework is displayed in Figure 1. The framework treats product comprehension as a constructive process of interpreting product information in terms of activated knowledge and forming new product-related knowledge (meanings and beliefs). The product-related meanings produced during comprehension may be of two broad types. Consumers may form product-related beliefs that merely describe the product information given in the environment (Fishbein & Azjen 1975). For instance, a consumer may "see" that an advertised car is red and represent this as a descriptive belief, "this car is red." Inferential beliefs that go beyond the given product information also may be constructed. In addition to the belief, "this car is red," consumers might infer, "I will be noticed as I drive down the street in this car."

Not all of the meanings consumers form while comprehending product information are necessarily related to products. For example, while considering a purchase, a consumer may comprehend, "it is very hot in this store," or "that salesman reminds me of my uncle." Consumer researchers tend to be particularly interested in the product-related meanings consumers form during comprehension of product information.

The framework also shows that the meanings produced during comprehension (whether descriptive or inferential knowledge) may be integrated with prior knowledge structures in memory. Later, if activated, this knowledge may influence subsequent comprehension and inference processes, and so on, in a continuous, interactive process.

The proposed model is not intended to be a theory of comprehension. Rather, it is a general, conceptual framework that identifies aspects of consumers' product comprehension and inference processes seldom addressed in previous research. Specifically, the framework highlights the role of activated prior knowledge and constructed meanings in the product comprehension process.

Activated Knowledge

The meanings or beliefs consumers form during comprehension are influenced by the knowledge activated at the time of comprehension. For example, Figure 2 displays knowledge concepts which might be contained in a consumer's schema for personal computers.

This product-schema is rather elaborate, containing many different types *of product knowledge*. Some product knowledge concerns concrete computer attributes or features (two disk drives, hard drive, mouse, modem). Other product knowledge is more abstract, relating to overall quality and personally relevant consequences of using personal computers (can run many different programs, good for office or school work). The schema also contains *self knowledge,* including abstract personal goals, consequences, and values (spending time with family, experiencing feelings of accomplishment). Finally, some knowledge is not directly related to personal computers, and can best be described as *general world knowledge* (I learn quickly, Muzak is often played in offices). Attending to information about a personal computer may activate various parts of this knowledge from memory. The activated knowledge allows consumers to construct various types of product-related meanings by inferring a personal computer's attributes, benefits, negative consequences, situational appropriateness, and the abstract, self-relevant goals or values a computer might help them achieve.

Means-End Inferences

Recently, researchers have recognized that consumers may have product-related knowledge at different "levels" of abstraction. At relatively concrete levels, consumers possess knowledge about concrete product attributes and physical characteristics (features). Consumers also have knowledge about more abstract product benefits or consequences of product use, as well as highly abstract knowledge about their own personal goals or values. This knowledge can be modeled as a simple associative network called a "means-end chain" (Gutman 1982). Generic means-end chains linking product-related meanings at various levels of abstraction are of the following form:

$$\text{Attributes} \longrightarrow \text{Consequences} \longrightarrow \text{Values}$$

Means-end chain models of product knowledge are useful in understanding consumer inferences. "Giving meaning to a particu-

FIGURE 2

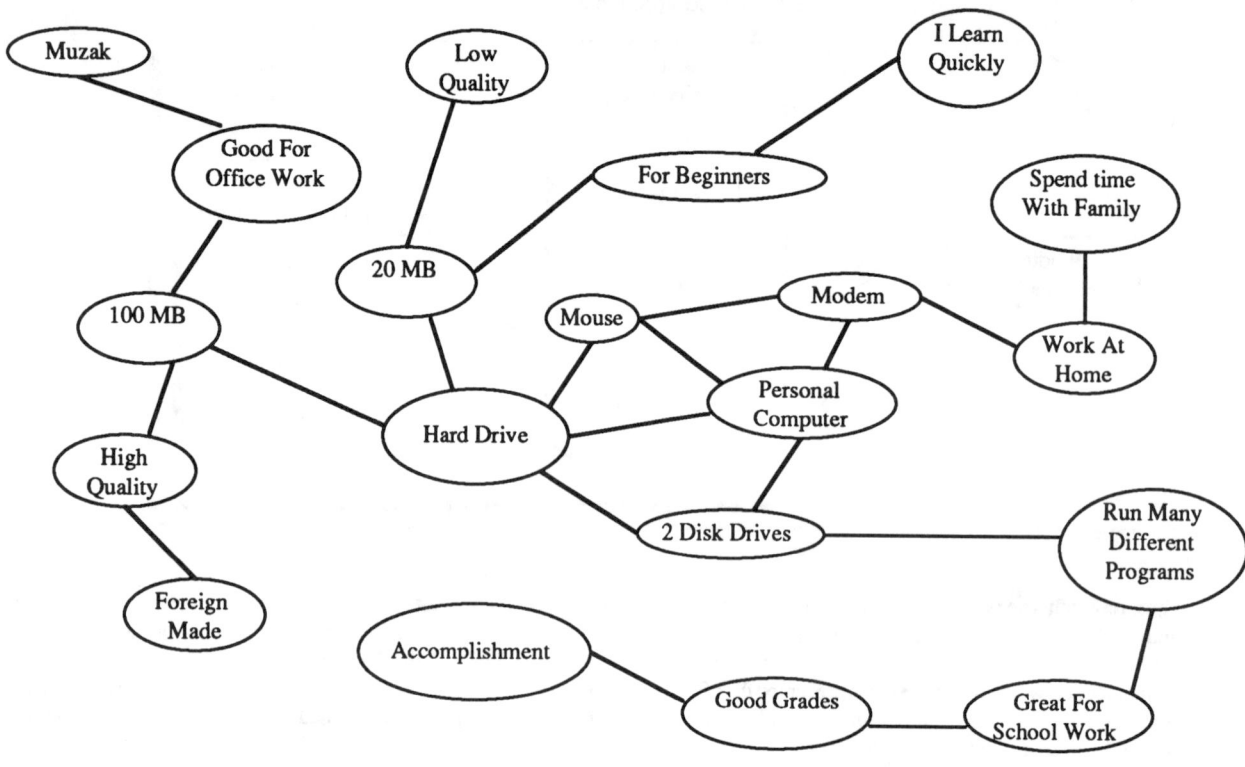

lar brand, defined by specific attributes, essentially depends upon what higher order, more personal elements the defining brand attribute(s) are linked to" (Reynolds & Rochon 1991). During product comprehension, consumers may construct inferential beliefs that certain product attributes are the causal *means* to achieving desired *ends* such as product benefits, or even personal goals or values.

The means-end inferences formed during comprehension are guided by means-end knowledge activated at the time of comprehension. Consider an advertisement stating that a new brand of personal computer has two disk drives and a modem. To comprehend (interpret) this information, a consumer might activate a product-schema for personal computers similar to the one displayed in Figure 2. As previous research suggests, the consumer might infer other attributes such as a hard drive and a mouse. The consumer might also infer meaningful, personally relevant relationships between the advertised attributes and more abstract product-related meanings. Notice that within this product-schema attributes are associated with higher level meanings to form means-end chains. If this knowledge is activated, the consumer might form inferences about concepts similar to those contained in these means-end chains. The consumer may interpret the information about the modem by inferring consequences such as, "I can work at home," and "I can spend more time with my family." One would hypothesize that a meaningful association was formed in memory between buying the computer and the value — spending time with their family. Similarly, consumers may interpret the information about the two disk drives by inferring a means-end sequence of consequences: "that means it can run many different programs," "that would be great for my school work," "I could get better grades," and "I would feel like I had accomplished something."

Note the differences between this view of consumer inference and the predominant view presented in past research. Rather than conceptualizing inferences as filling in missing information about a specific attribute, inferences are seen as an integral (and natural) aspect of the comprehension process of constructing coherent product meanings. To construct personal interpretations of what products mean to them, consumers may infer meaningful, personally relevant associations between a product's attributes and its uses, consequences, appropriateness to various situations and users, and even personal goals or values.

Next, we discuss how the proposed conceptual framework differs from past research in terms of (1) when inferences are formed, (2) whether forming inferences is an automatic or controlled process, and (3) whether all consumers form the same inferences during product comprehension.

When Are Inferences Formed?

As a result of equivocal findings concerning spontaneous missing attribute inferences, researchers have assumed that consumers form inferences only when they notice that information about an important attribute is obviously missing from a brand description. While this assumption may apply to missing attribute inferences, it may not generalize to all types of inferences. The current framework proposes that consumers may form inferences whenever they comprehend product information. Inferences may be formed while comparing two or more brands, as well as evaluating a single brand for which there is no competitive context to create "missing information." In an experimental context, this means that subjects might form inferences while evaluating completely described brands as well as partially described brands.

Is Inference Formation An Automatic Or Controlled Process?

Past research following the missing information paradigm implicitly assumes that inference formation is an intentional, controlled, effortful process. Burke (1990), for example, suggested that consumers form inferences only when the value of more knowledge exceeds the effort (cost) to form the inference. The current framework proposes that inferences can be either automatic or controlled. The automaticity of inference formation is a function of the strength of learned associations between related concepts in memory. The more often consumers activate associations between related concepts, the stronger these associations become, and the more quickly activation spreads between them to form inferences automatically and effortlessly. If cognitive associations between concepts are not strong or frequently activated, inference formation is likely to require cognitive effort.

For example, consumers' product knowledge for cars probably do not contain strong linkages between different brands and their associated yearly maintenance costs. Therefore, inferring the yearly maintenance costs for a certain brand is likely to require considerable cognitive effort and deliberation. On the other hand, consumers' car schemas may contain strong associations between a car's size and its comfort. If so, consumers can quickly and effortlessly infer that a particular small car is uncomfortable.

Do All Consumers Form The Same Inferences?

In nearly every past study, researchers identified *a priori* the specific inference(s) to be measured (usually a belief about a product claim or attribute). For example, studies following the missing information paradigm focused only on inferences about the missing information. We know, however, that inferences are highly influenced by existing knowledge in memory that is activated in the situation. Since no two consumers have exactly the same knowledge (product-schemas) it is not likely they will form the same inferences. In fact, consumers may not form the inference identified *a priori* by the researcher, but still form other types of inferences.

DIRECTIONS FOR FUTURE RESEARCH

The proposed framework views inference formation as a natural aspect of comprehension processing. This perspective offers a number of issues for future research, including the extent to which inferences are formed during product comprehension, the types (levels of abstraction) of product-related inferences consumers form, and the effects of different types of inferences on consumers' attitudes and purchase intentions.

Unfortunately, past consumer inference research has been narrowly focused on missing attribute inferences. Therefore, we lack the theoretical perspective and empirical results to support precise hypotheses and predictions about inference formation in natural situations and settings. At present, we need exploratory, theory-building studies based on the framework presented here. Such research can generate empirical data from which more specific research issues, questions, and hypotheses can be developed and tested in subsequent research.

For the most part, past research has examined the inferences consumers form based on relatively "simple" attribute information presented in highly artificial experimental contexts. Future research should examine the product-related inferences consumers form during comprehension of more complex product information similar to that found in real-world marketing communications (ads, brochures, sales presentations). Perhaps, experiments in natural settings that do not narrowly focus consumers' attention and comprehension processes on a small set of attribute information will reveal that many product-related inferences concern abstract, self-relevant consequences of product use. A means-end chain perspective suggests that consumers are more concerned with what products can do for them, than with their physical attributes and features. This may be especially likely for actual purchase decisions rather than simple product evaluation tasks (often used in consumer research) that have limited consequences.

Past research has demonstrated that positive inferences about product attributes are positively related to consumers' brand attitudes (cf. Kardes 1988). This would be expected from any multiattribute attitude model such as Fishbein's. However, consumer researchers have not yet examined how inferences about more abstract self-relevant product consequences influence consumers' attitudes. Perhaps, inferences about self-relevant product consequences have a greater effect on consumers' brand attitudes and purchase intentions than inferences about concrete product attributes. Researchers have suggested that consumers should be more persuaded by what products can do for them, than their physical attributes and features (Macinnis & Jaworski 1989).

Researchers also need to examine the key factors that influence the amount and types of inferences consumers form during product comprehension. The two most important influences are product knowledge and involvement. Prior research has found that higher knowledge consumers consider attribute information more useful and informative, whereas lower knowledge consumers consider information about more abstract benefits to be more useful and informative (Maheswaran & Sternthal 1990). Gardial & Biehal (1986) found that compared to novices, experts formed more inferences about concrete attributes, but fewer inferences about more abstract self-relevant product consequences. Our framework suggests, as consumers gain product experience, they learn meaningful associations between product attributes and corresponding consequences. More expert consumers, who have well-developed means-end chains in memory, can use this knowledge to form inferences during comprehension of product information. Thus, compared to novices, experts may be more likely to infer means-end associations between attributes and consequences or benefits.

Many researchers, while not setting out to do so, have studied cognitive processes that would be considered inference formation within the current framework. For example, researchers studying decision making have used concurrent verbal protocols to measure the meanings or beliefs consumers form in choosing among products. Many of these beliefs are inferences. For instance, research on substitution-in-use has examined consumers' perceptions of product similarity and typicality for various use occasions (e.g., Ratneshwar & Shocker 1991). Two products may be perceived as similar because consumers believe they are both means to achieving a desired goal within a specific usage situation. These beliefs are inferences.

As another example of inferences in other research contexts, consider Johnson's (1984) studies of noncomparable alternatives. Johnson examined the level of abstraction consumers use when making choices among different product categories. The less comparable the alternatives, the more abstract the concept consumers use in comparing them. Thus, consumers can choose between two television sets based on price, but choose between a new television set and a vacation based on a more abstract consequence such as the entertainment value of each. These beliefs about abstract consequences are inferences.

A final example of inferences in other contexts is given by research on the Elaboration Likelihood Model that examined the effects of level of involvement on the types of cognitive responses consumers form in response to persuasive messages (Petty, Cacioppo, & Schumman 1983). Many of these cognitive responses are inferences. Consumers who are more involved with a particular product or decision situation, are likely to be more motivated during comprehension to interpret the relevant information (Celsi & Olson 1988). Thus, they may form more inferences than consumers who are less involved, and their inferences are likely to be more self-related (more personal consequences). This may help to explain why attitudes formed via central route processes by highly involved consumers are more enduring and more predictive of behavior than attitudes formed through peripheral route processes by less involved consumers.

To obtain a deeper understanding of consumers' inferences, researchers will have to develop new methods for measuring the outcomes of consumers' comprehension processes. We have shown that the information integration methodology has limited utility for understanding consumers' inference processes. Verbal thought protocols have more promise, but we need to develop coding schemes that are sensitive to inferences of varying types. The mean-end chain of attributes, consequences, and values can provide such coding categories.

Inference researchers should also consider other methods for measuring inferences such as personal interviews to follow up on verbal protocols. In a personal interview, researchers can follow up and "probe" to clarify the often cryptic meaning of the thought listings. For instance, researchers can probe to clarify the meaning of protocols (Experimenter: "What were you thinking about when you wrote modem? Subject: "Since this brand has all these other attributes, it probably also has a modem"). Interviews can identify additional inferences not mentioned in verbal protocols (Experimenter: "When you were reading this ad were there any other thoughts you had that you did not write down? Subject: "Yes, I was thinking about how this brand of computer has a color monitor I could use to make color graphs for my class projects."). Interviews can also be used to determine linkages between concepts identified in verbal protocols (Experimenter: "You wrote down homework and grades, what did you mean by that?" Subject: "Because this computer is small and has a modem, I could use it in my dorm room to do my homework, and thus get better grades."). Of course, probing interviews may be better suited for identifying the types of inferences consumers form, not whether consumers spontaneously form these inferences during product comprehension.

CONCLUSIONS

In conclusion, researchers interested in consumer inferences should abandon the narrow view that inferences are formed only by filling in missing information about a specific attribute. Rather, we recommend that researchers adopt a broader view of consumer inference as an integral and ubiquitous aspect of general product comprehension. We can achieve a greater understanding of product-related inferences by viewing them as the constructed personal interpretations of what products and their attributes mean to consumers.

REFERENCES

Anderson, Norman H. (1982), *Methods of Information Integration Theory*, New York, NY: Academic Press.

Bartlett, Frederick C. (1932), *Remembering*, London: Cambridge University Press.

Black, John B., James A. Galambos and Stephen J. Read (1984), "Comprehending Stories and Social Situations," in *Handbook of Social Cognition*, eds. R.S. Wyer Jr. and T. K. Srull, Hillsdale, NJ: Lawrence Erlbaum Associates.

Bransford, John D., Richard J. Barclay and Jefferey J. Franks (1972), "Sentence Memory: A Constructive Versus Interpretive Approach," *Cognitive Psychology*, 3, 193-209.

_____ and Marcia K. Johnson (1972), "Contextual Prerequisites For Understanding: Some Investigations of Comprehension and Recall," *Journal of Verbal Learning and Verbal Behavior*, 11, 717-726.

Burke, Sandra J. (1990), "The Effects of Missing Information on Decision Strategy Selection," *Advances in Consumer Research*, 17, 250.-256.

Celsi, Richard L. and Jerry C. Olson (1988), "The Role of Involvement in Attention and Comprehension Processes," *Journal of Consumer Research*, 15, 210-224.

Collins, Allen, John S. Brown and Kathy M. Larkin (1980), "Inference in Text Understanding," in *Theoretical Issues in Reading Comprehension*, eds. R.J. Spiro, B.C. Bruce and W.F. Brewer, Hillsdale, NJ: Lawrence Erlbaum Associates.

Fishbein, Martin and Icek Ajzen (1975), *Belief, Attitude, Intention, and Behavior: An Introduction To Theory and Research*, Reading, Mass.: Addison-Wesley.

Ford, Gary T. and Ruth A. Smith (1987), "Inferential Beliefs in Consumer Evaluations: An Assessment of Alternative Processing Strategies," *Journal of Consumer Research*, 14, 363-371.

Gardial, Sarah and Gabrial Biehal (1986), "Measuring Consumers' Inferential Processing in Choice," *Advances in Consumer Research*, 14, 101-105.

_____ and David W. Schumman (1990), "In Search of the Elusive Consumer Inference," *Advances in Consumer Research*, 17, 283-287.

Gutman, Johnathan (1982), "A Means-End Chain Model Based on Consumer Categorization Processes," *Journal of Marketing*, 46, 60-72.

Harris, Richard J. (1974), "Memory and Comprehension of Implications and Inferences of Complex Sentences," *Journal of Verbal Learning and Verbal Behavior*, 13, 626-637.

Huber, Joel and John McCann (1982), "The Impact of Inferential Beliefs on Product Evaluations," *Journal of Marketing Research*, 19, 324-333.

Jacoby, Jacob and Wayne D. Hoyer (1982), "Viewer Miscomprehension of Televised Communication: Selected Findings," *Journal of Marketing*, 46(4), 12-26.

Johnson, Marcia K., John D. Bransford and Susan K. Solomon (1973), "Memory for Tacit Implications of Sentences," *Journal of Experimental Psychology*, 98, 203-205.

Johnson, Michael D. (1984), "Consumer Choice Strategies for Comparing Noncomparable Alternatives," *Journal of Consumer Research*, 11, 741-753.

Johnson, Richard D and Irwin P. Levin (1985), "More Than Meets the Eye: The Effect of Missing Information on Purchase Evaluations," *Journal of Consumer Research*, 12, 169-177.

Kardes, Frank R. (1988), "Spontaneous Inference Processes in Advertising: The Effects of Conclusion Omission and Involvement on Persuasion," *Journal of Consumer Research*, 15, 225-233.

_____ , David M. Sanbonmatsu and Paul M. Herr (1992), "The Role of Product Knowledge and Missing Information in Multiattribute Evaluations," *Organizational Behavior and Human Decision Processes*, 51, 76-91.

Lim, Jeen-Su, Richard W. Olshavsky and John Kim (1988), "The Impact of Inferences on Product Evaluations: Replication and Extensions", *Journal of Marketing Research*, 25, 308-316.

Macinnis, Deborah J. and Bernard J. Jaworski (1989), Information Processing from Advertisements: Toward an Integrative Framework," *Journal of Marketing*, 53, 123.

Maheswaran, Durairaj and Brian Sternthal (1990), "The Effects of Knowledge, Motivation, and Type of Message on Ad Processing and Product Judgments," *Journal of Consumer Research*, 17, 66-73.

Mick, David G. (1992), "Levels of Subjective Comprehension in Advertising Processing and Their Relations to Ad Perceptions, Attitudes, and Memory," *Journal of Consumer Research*, 18(4), 411-424.

Petty, Richard E., John T. Cacioppo and David Schumann (1983), "Central and Peripheral Routes to Advertising Effectiveness: The Moderating Role of Involvement," *Journal of Consumer Research*, 10, 135-146.

Ratneshwar, S. and Allan D. Shocker (1991), "Substitution in Use and the Role of Usage Context in Product Category Structures," *Journal of Marketing Research*, 28, 281-95.

Reynolds, Thomas J. and John P. Rochon (1991), "Copy Testing is Not Strategy Assessment, *Journal of Business Research*, 22, 131-142.

Rumelhart, David E. (1984), "Understanding Understanding," in *Understanding Reading Comprehension: Cognition, Language, and the Structure of Prose*, ed. J. Flood, Newark, DE: International Reading Association, 1-20.

Simmons, Carolyn J and John G Lynch (1991) "Inference Effects Without Inference Making? Effects of Missing Information on Discounting and Use of Presented Information," *Journal of Consumer Research*, 17, 477-491.

Sujan, Mita and Christine Dekleva (1987), "Product Categorization and Inference Making: Some Implications For Comparative Advertising," *Journal of Consumer Research*, 14, 372-378

Effects of a Role Model and Fear in Warning Label on Perceptions of Safety and Safety Behavior

Mark A. deTurck, State University of New York, Buffalo
Robert A. Rachlin, State University of New York, Buffalo
Melissa J. Young, State University of New York, Buffalo

ABSTRACT

Subjects examined an oven cleaner containing either a low or high fear appeal in the warning label. Subjects examined the cleaner either alone, or were paired with a confederate (role model). After examining the label, subjects paired with a confederate observed the confederate test the cleaner prior to testing the cleaner themselves. The confederates tested the cleaner in one of three conditions: 1) not wearing safety gloves and getting some of the product on themselves and experiencing a chemical burn, 2) not wearing safety gloves and not getting any cleaner one them, and 3) wearing the safety gloves and not experiencing a chemical burn. Although subjects perceived the oven cleaner to be more hazardous when they read the high fear appeal label, they recalled more information from the low fear appeal warning label. Moreover, the level of fear in the warning did not influence subjects' safety behavior. As predicted, subjects were most likely to wear the safety gloves when they observed the role model wear the safety gloves. Observing the role model suffer a chemical burn when not wearing the safety gloves had almost no effect on subjects' likelihood of wearing the safety gloves.

Students of product safety information have devoted considerable effort toward identifying the message factors that enhance consumers' compliance with product safety recommendations. Despite their efforts, however, the growing literature on the effects of product safety information indicates that product warning labels exert very little influence on consumers' safety behavior (see Lehto & Miller, 1986 for a review). One reason for the apparent lack of effectiveness in product warning labels is the assumption that there is a direct relationship between exposure to a product safety message and consumers' decision to comply with the message's recommendations. Models of consumer information processing of safety information (deTurck, Goldhaber & Richetto, 1992a; McGuire, 1980) suggest that a number of mediating cognitive factors (e.g., comprehension, perception of personal hazard, etc.) may dilute the effects of an otherwise potent warning message.

Situational cues may help determine consumers' decision to comply with a product warning hazard. One salient cue that consumers may rely on is whether others in the situation comply with safety recommendations. The purpose of the current research was to determine whether a product warning label communicating low versus high hazard or the presence of a compliant or noncompliant role model in the situation affected: 1) perceptions of hazard associated with the product, and 2) compliance with the product warning label.

A MODEL OF SAFETY INFORMATION PROCESSING

Consumers possess varying levels of knowledge regarding the safe use of products. Manufacturers draft warning labels to provide consumers with information they may need so as to use a product safely. Whereas some consumers may heed the instructions on a warning label, others may deliberately fail to read it or they may decide not to comply if they do read it. Understanding the circumstances underlying consumers' decision to comply or not comply with product safety messages would contribute significantly to enhancing the quality of safety programs.

Figure 1 depicts a model of consumer information processing related to safety information. According to the model, there is not a direct relationship between exposure to a product safety message and the decision to comply. If we were to calculate the effect of exposure to a warning message and compliance, excluding for the moment psychological and situational cues, based on a .6 correlation (a large effect by social science standards) between adjacent components of the model, the resulting effect of exposure on compliance would be .13 (a relatively small effect).

Two factors which have not received a great deal of empirical attention in previous models of safety behavior are consumer's psychological dynamics and situational cues. At least two psychological factors that have received researchers' empirical attention are product users' information processing objectives and product users' familiarity with a product. Product users' information processing objectives—their reason for attending to product information (form an impression versus memorize)—mediate their attention to product labels, recall of safety information, perception of hazard, and compliance with product safety recommendations (deTurck & Goldhaber, 1989b; deTurck, Goldhaber & Richetto, 1992b).

A consumer's familiarity with a product refers to the extent to which he/she is knowledgeable about the safe use of a product. Consumers' knowledge may come from direct experience with a product, or from exposure to other sources, such as manuals, friends, family members, or the media. Research on familiarity indicates that consumers who are more familiar with a product tend to perceive less hazard associated with a product than their less informed counterparts (deTurck & Goldhaber, 1989a, deTurck, Goldhaber & Richetto, 1992a, 1992b; Godfrey & Laughery, 1984).

By contrast, very little is known about how consumers' safety behavior is affected by situational cues present when they use a product. A consumer's decision to comply with safety recommendations may be based to a lesser extent on safety information, and more on contextual cues when he/she uses a product. One situational cue found to affect individuals' compliance with safety messages is the amount of effort they must exert to comply with the safety recommendations. Wogalter, Godfrey, Fontenelle, Desaulniers & Rothstein (1987) found that people essentially ignored safety recommendations when they were required to exert a substantial amount of effort (walk down a hall 50 feet to use another exit, or to return down the hall they came and use another exit) compared with a less safe alternative requiring little effort (using the door next to the broken one).

Another cue in situations that may affect product users' compliance with safety recommendations is the safety related-behavior of a role model. Consumers do not use products in a social vacuum. Children grow up observing their parents and older peers using products that may pose potential hazards. Family members, friends, or coworkers also collaborate on many projects that may entail using potentially hazardous products and/or engaging in hazardous circumstances. In addition, there are many hazardous situations in our daily routines that involve interacting with others away from formal work projects (e.g., driving in a car).

Despite the fact people may typically avoid using certain hazardous products, or use potentially hazardous products with a great deal of care, they may fail to use hazardous products safely

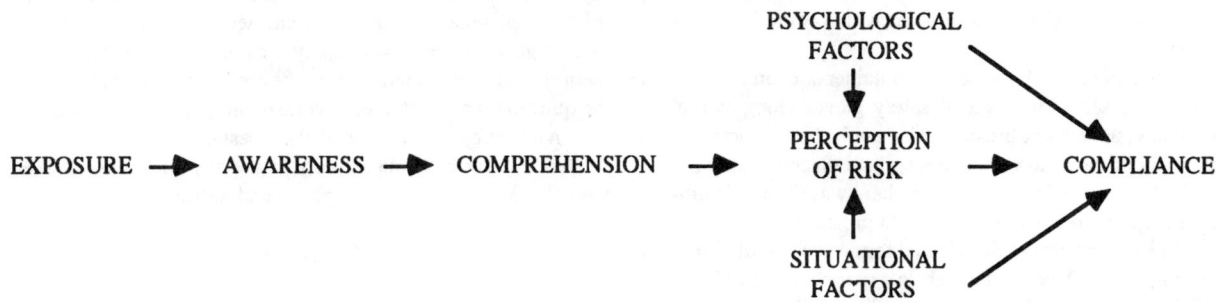

FIGURE 1
A Model of the Effects of Product Warning Labels

when they observe others failing to take proper precautions. A preteen, for example, may believe that smoking is extremely harmful, but decide to smoke because he/she observes some friends smoke, or from observing his/her parents smoke. Similarly, adults may use their safety harnesses when driving their own automobiles, but fail to wear a safety harness when they are a passenger with a driver who does not wear his/her safety harness. Stated differently, product users may rely on role models in a given context as a guide for their own safety behavior rather than their own personal knowledge of a product's potential hazard.

The current model is consistent with models of the attitude-behavior relationship (Fazio, 1986; Fishbein & Ajzen, 1975). These models indicate that the social context exerts a substantial influence on a person's behavior. Although product users may perceive a product or situation to be hazardous, others' behavior in the situation may override their own perception of product hazard, and as a result, they may fail to act prudently when using a product.

Research on helping in hazardous situations suggests that people rely on others' safety behavior when deciding on the degree of hazard posed by certain situations. Latane and Darley (1968) found that subjects working with a confederate would remain in an unsafe environment (smoke-filled room) so long as the confederate remained. In fact, 90% of the subjects remained in the smoke-filled room rubbing their eyes, coughing, and waving the fumes away as they worked. However, when subjects worked alone and the room began to fill with smoke, 75% of them left the room to report that there was smoke. Subjects paired with a confederate obviously relied on the confederate's behavior to determine the hazardous nature of the situation. Similarly, Bryan and Test (1967) obtained results in four experiments indicating that people rely on the conduct of a role model when deciding when to render help to another person. The presence of a helping role model significantly increased incidents of subjects' willingness to help.

Indeed, the social learning literature (Bandura, 1962, 1977) indicates that people often rely on role models' behavior when deciding how they should behave. A great deal of product users' safety behavior may be determined by their observations of how others use a product. Much of the information product users rely on for their own behavior may be a result of vicarious learning rather than direct experience or from product safety information.

Current Study

Subjects were paired with a confederate to test a new product as part of a marketing study. Each confederate-subject pair was given a product (oven cleaner) to examine. The label on the container communicated that there was a either a low or high level of hazard associated with using the product. After examining the product they were asked to test the product to determine its effectiveness. The confederate always tried the product first.

In one condition, the confederate tested the product on a grill without wearing safety gloves. In a second condition, the confederate tested the product while wearing safety gloves. In the third condition, the confederate tested the product without wearing the safety gloves and he/she got some of the cleaner on his/her hand and acted as though he/she got a chemical burn—suffered some discomfort. There were two control conditions (low versus high hazard label) where there was not a confederate present.

It is predicted that the warning label will exert an effect on subjects' perception of hazard associated with the product. More specifically, it is expected that subjects exposed to the higher hazard warning label will perceive there is a greater level of hazard associated with the product than subjects exposed to the lower hazard warning label. However, subjects' compliance with safety recommendations—wearing the safety gloves—will *not* be affected by the degree of hazard communicated in the warning label but by whether or not the confederate complies with the safety instructions in the label.

Results obtained by deTurck, Goldhaber, Richetto, and Young (1992) indicate that high fear appeal warning labels produced greater perceptions of hazard, but that the high fear warning labels were not perceived to be as credible as moderate or low fear appeal labels. To the extent high fear appeal warning labels are not perceived to be as credible as other relevant safety information in a situation, product users should be more likely to comply with other more credible safety cues that are present in the situation such as others' safety behavior. It is assumed that a role model's safety behavior will serve as a credible situational cue that product users will rely on more than safety information in a product label. More specifically, it is predicted that subjects will be more likely to wear the safety gloves when the confederate wears the gloves.

METHOD

Sample

One hundred and twenty-six students (62 females, 49 males, and 15 which did not report gender) from an introductory communication class at the State University of New York at Buffalo were solicited to participate in this study in partial fulfillment of a course requirement.

Procedure

After subjects arrived in the testing site, they were greeted by a research assistant who introduced them to the confederate who was seated in a waiting area and both were escorted to the research laboratory. The participants were then given a written prebriefing statement which told them that the department had been asked by a major manufacturer (no company name was given) to test a new oven cleaning product. After the subject and confederate finished reading the prebriefing statement and had signed the adjoining consent form, they were told that they would have an opportunity to examine and test the effectiveness of this new oven cleaning product. Only one subject participated with a confederate during each session.

On the other side of the room, a container of oven cleaner was set out on a table with a pair of safety gloves along side of it. Additionally, there was a brush (used to apply the product), a wash basin, a roll of paper towels, and a sponge placed nearby on the table. In the corner of the same table, there was a portable hibachi set up on top of a protective covering to protect the tabletop.

Subjects were randomly selected to receive one of two types of warning labels. Two product labels were generated which were identical in every regard except the wording on the warning label. The label was black and white, and contained information regarding the proper use of the product as well as detailed instructions for using the product. Both labels contained a safety warning printed in reverse (white on black) so that it was more salient than the other information on the label. Subjects were randomly assigned to receive either a low or high fear warning label.

Low fear. The low fear warning label read: "Caution: This product may cause minor skin irritation".

High fear. The high fear warning label read: "Danger: This product will cause severe chemical burns to skin".

Both warning labels contained identical additional information regarding what to do if the product came into contact with skin or eyes.

Safety Behavior

The confederate was selected by the research assistant to be the first of the pair to examine and use the product. In all conditions, the confederate examined the jar, and read the product label for approximately one minute. Confederates were instructed to perform one of three safety behaviors.

No Gloves-No Burn. In this condition, the confederate applied a small amount of the oven cleaner to the portable hibachi without wearing the safety gloves as stated on the product label. When testing the oven cleaner, the confederate did not get any of the cleaner on his/her skin and experienced no chemical burn.

No Gloves-Burn. In this condition, the confederate did not wear the safety gloves, and got a small amount of the cleaner on his/her hand while applying it to the grill. The confederate then exclaimed, "Ouch, that burns" and quickly wiped the oven cleaner off using one of the paper towels setting next to the hibachi. The confederate was then instructed to wash his/her hands in the wash basin.

Gloves. In this condition, the confederate wore the safety gloves while applying the oven cleaner to the hibachi and did not get any on his/her skin.

No Confederate (Control). In this condition, subjects examined and tested the oven cleaner without a confederate present.

Dependent Measures

After the confederate finished testing the oven cleaner, he/she was directed to another room to complete a questionnaire while the subject remained to examine and test the oven cleaner. The research assistant remained with the subject and recorded whether the subject wore the safety gloves before applying the oven cleaner to the hibachi.

When the subject finished applying the oven cleaner to the hibachi, he/she was asked to complete a questionnaire. The questionnaire asked the subject to indicate how safe they perceived the product to be on an eight-point scale ranging from 1 (Safe) to 8 (Unsafe). In addition, subjects indicated on an eight point scale from 1 (Certain to Use Safely) to 8 (Uncertain to Use Safely) how certain they would be to know how use the product safely in the future. Questions tested the subjects knowledge of safety-related information regarding the oven cleaner (e.g., what to do if the cleaner gets in eyes, how to apply the product, what safety equipment should be worn while using the product). The final section of the questionnaire contained several demographic questions.

After subjects completed the questionnaire, they were debriefed and given an opportunity to ask any questions. Subjects were thanked for their participation and dismissed.

RESULTS

Perceived Safety

A 2 (fear: low/high) X 4 (role model: none/no gloves-no burn/gloves/no gloves-burn) multivariate analysis of variance was conducted with perceived safety and certainty of safe use as the dependent variables.[1] A main effect was obtained for fear, $F(2,125)=4.25$, $p<.02$. Due to the significant omnibus effect, the univariate ANOVAs were examined to determine the precise effect of fear communicated in the warning on perceived safety and certainty of safely using the oven cleaner. Subjects examining the low fear label reported the product as safer ($M=3.49$) than those subjects who examined the high fear label ($M=4.31$), $F(1,126)=5.26$, $p<.03$. Similarly, subjects in the low fear condition reported feeling more certain about how to use the product safely ($M=2.59$) than subjects in the high fear condition ($M=3.31$), $F(1,126)=5.22, p<.03$.

Recall

A main effect for fear was obtained: Subjects in the low fear condition correctly recalled more facts about the product ($M=7.72$) than subjects in the high fear appeal condition ($M=6.68$), $F(1,108)=7.64$, $p<.01$.

Safety Behavior

As predicted, results from a chi-square analysis revealed that subjects who observed the confederate wear the safety gloves when using the oven cleaner were more likely to wear gloves than in any other condition, even subjects who observed confederates apply the oven cleaner without safety gloves and suffering a chemical burn, $Chi^2 (3),=34.30$, $p<.00$ (Figure 2). The contingency coefficient associated with this effect was .46.

DISCUSSION

As its primary goal, the current study sought to determine the effects of a role model's safety behavior on a naive bystander. Results indicate that although perceptions of a product's hazard may be affected by the product's warning label, compliance with recommended safety behavior is affected by another person's safety behavior in the context and not the warning label. Clearly, subjects followed the confederate's example despite the recommendations in the product warning. These differences cannot be attributed to differential learning from the warning label.

Perhaps the most interesting finding was that observing the role model improperly use the product and get hurt had almost no effect on subjects' subsequent safety behavior. Although research in social learning indicates that when a role model's behavior is punished observers are less likely to engage in the target behavior

---

[1] No main or interaction effects were obtained for gender of confederate or subject; therefore data were collapsed across this variable for all analyses.

FIGURE 2
Percentage of Subjects Wearing Gloves as a Function of Role Model's Safety Behavior

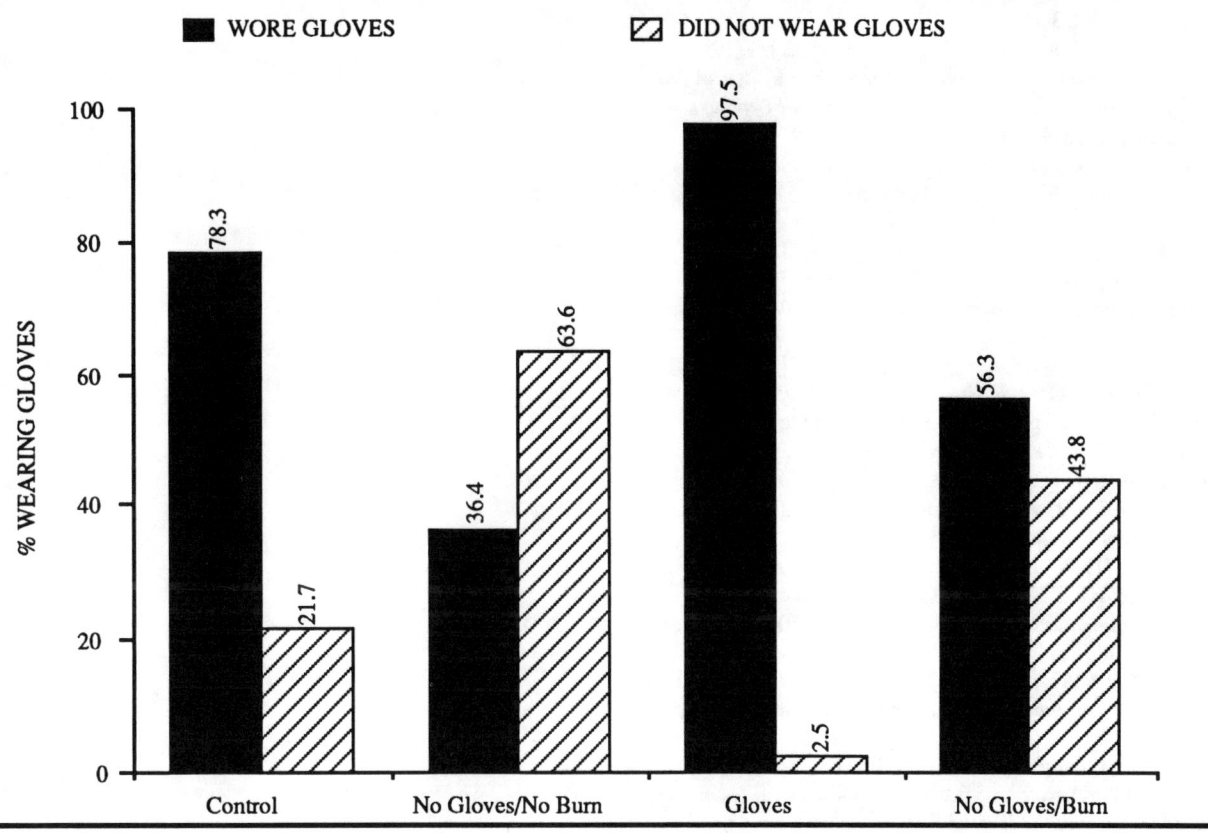

(Walters, Leat & Mezei, 1963; Walters & Parke, 1964), subjects in the current study were not affected by observing the role model get hurt. It may be the case that the current subjects assumed that they would not be as careless as the role model when they tried the product.

It would be useful to extend the current design to determine if well liked role models, e.g., friends or family members, exert more influence on observers' safety behavior than less familiar role models. Well liked role models should exert greater influence over safety behavior than strangers due to the greater affinity between role model and observer and because observers probably spend more time with well liked role models. It would be useful to replicate the current study pairing subjects with a best friend posing as the confederate or a stranger.

In addition, it would be useful to determine if the current effects are robust across a variety of products and/or situations. It is possible that the current effects are limited to products or situations that are somewhat novel to product users. Product users may not be so readily influenced by a careless role model when they are very familiar with a product or situation, although the research reported earlier on familiarity (deTurck & Goldhaber, 1989b, deTurck, Goldhaber & Richetto, 1992a, 1992b; Godfrey & Laughery, 1984) and Latane and Darley's (1968) results from the smoke-filled room study suggest that even with highly familiar hazardous circumstances people are not likely to take proper safety precautions.

Although warning labels may influence product users' perception of a product's hazard, the current findings, as well as previous research results, indicate that it is unreasonable to assume a warning label will directly affect safety behavior. Rather than channeling more resources into increased labeling, greater effort is needed in face-to-face educational programs so as to provide role models for safety behavior. Research on smoking (McAlister, 1989), for example, indicates that educational programs with role models are an effective strategy for deterring smoking. This is not to argue that we should abandon product safety labeling. It is apparent, however, that factors other than the warning labels exert greater influence on safety behavior. It would be more productive if safety researchers did not test the seemingly infinite permutations of passive warning message strategies, but instead, directed their energies toward studying more intrusive warning procedures.

REFERENCES

Bandura, A. (1962). Social learning through imitation. In M.R. Jones (Ed.), *Nebraska symposium on motivation* (pp. 211-269). Lincoln, NE: University of Nebraska Press.

Bandura, A. (1977). *Social learning theory*. Englewood Cliffs, N.J.: Prentice-Hall.

Bryan, J.H., & Test, M.A. (1967). Models and helping: Naturalistic studies in aiding behavior. *Journal of Personality and Social Psychology*, 6, 400-407.

deTurck, M.A., & Goldhaber, G.M. (1989a). Effectiveness of signal words in warnings: Effects of familiarity and gender. *Journal of Products Liability*, 12, 104-114.

deTurck, M.A., & Goldhaber, G.M. (1989b). Effectiveness of product warning labels: Effects of consumers' information processing objectives. *Journal of Consumer Affairs*, 23, 111-126.

deTurck, M.A., & Goldhaber, G.M., & Richetto, G.M. (1989). Effectiveness of product warnings: Effects of language valence, redundancy, and color. *Journal of Products Liability*, 12, 93-103.

deTurck, M.A., Goldhaber, G.M., & Richetto, G.M. (1991). Uncertainty reduction in product warnings: Effects of fear in signal word and hazard statement. *Journal of Products Liability*, 13, 329-338.

deTurck, M.A., Goldhaber, G.M., & Richetto, G.M. (1991). Uncertainty reduction in product warnings: Effects of fear and color. *Journal of Products Liability*, 13, 339-346.

deTurck, M.A., Goldhaber, G.M., & Richetto, G.M. (1992a). Familiarity and awareness: Effects of conscious and nonconscious safety information. *Journal of Products and Toxic Liability*, 14, 341-350.

deTurck, M.A., Goldhaber, G.M., & Richetto, G.M. (1992b). Effectiveness of warnings on alcoholic beverages: Consumers' information processing objectives and level of fear. *Journal of Products and Toxic Liability*, 14, 329-339.

deTurck, M.A., Goldhaber, G.M., Richetto, G.M., & Young, M.J. (1992). Effects of fear-arousing warning messages. *Journal of Products Liability*, 14, 217-223.

Fazio, R. H. (1986). How do attitudes guide behavior? In R.M. Sorrentino & E. Tory Higgins (Eds.), *Motivation & cognition: Foundations of social behavior* (pp. 204-243). New York: Guilford Press.

Fishbein, M., & Ajzen, I. (1975). *Belief, attitude, intention and behavior: An introduction to theory and research*. Reading, MA: Addison-Wesley.

Godfrey, S., & Laughery, K. (1984). The biasing effects of product familiarity on consumers' awareness of hazard. *Proceedings of the Human Factors Society*, pp. 483-486.

Latane, B., & Darley, J.M. (1968). Group inhibition of bystander intervention in emergencies. *Journal of Personality and Social Psychology*, 10, 215-221.

Lehto, M.R., & Miller, J.M. (1986). *Warnings: Fundamentals, design, and evaluation methodologies* (Vol. 1). Ann Arbor, MI: Fuller Technical Publications.

McAlister, A., Ramirez, A.G., Galavotti, C., & Gallion, K.J., (1989). Antismoking campaigns: Progress in the application of Social Learning Theory. In R.E. Rice & C.K. Atkin (Eds.), *Public communication campaigns* (2nd ed., pp. 273-290). Newbury Park, CA.: Sage.

McGuire, W. (1980). The communication-persuasion model and health-risk labeling. In L.A. Morris, M.B. Mazis & I. Barofsky (Eds.), *Product labeling and health risks*, (pp. 99-122). Banbury Report 6, Cold Spring Harbor Laboratory.

Walters, R.H., Leat, M., & Mezei, L. (1963). Inhibition and disinhibition of response through empathic learning. *Canadian Journal of Psychology*, 17, 235-243.

Walters, R.H., & Parke, R.D. (1964). Influence of response consequences to a social model on resistance to deviation. *Journal of Experimental Child Psychology*, 1, 269-280.

Wogalter, M.S., Godfrey, S.S., Fontenelle, G.A., Desaulniers, D.R., & Rothstein, P.R. (1987). Effectiveness of warnings. *Proceedings of the Human Factors Society*, 29, 599-612.

Nutritional Information Research: A Review of the Issues
Eve M. Caudill, University of Illinois, Urbana-Champaign

Similar information disseminated to consumers is often perceived differently, depending on the characteristics of the consumer, the characteristics of the product, and the characteristics of the information itself. For example, previous research indicates that consumers' food purchasing attitudes and behavior are affected by how nutritional information is provided and what information is provided, as well as the individual differences among consumers.

Nutritional information research has traditionally been guided by public policy concerns. Much of the early public policy concerns involved increasing consumers' awareness of the relationship between diet and health. As consumers' interest in health and diet issues began to increase, their interest in the nutritional value of food products increased (Ippolito and Mathios 1991), and researchers turned their attention to the more complex issues involved in consumer acquisition and utilization of the information. (See Table 1).

NUTRITIONAL INFORMATION RESEARCH

Research on nutritional information primarily has involved two general themes: information provision and information acquisition and utilization. This review discusses the research in the context of both these themes, though an underlying goal of most previous research has been to enhance consumers' utilization of nutritional information. Although the utilization construct can be considered from two perspectives, cognitive and behavioral (Bettman 1975), much of the research has focused on cognitive issues, partly because behavioral issues are more complex and difficult to study.

Information Provision

Four areas relevant to information provision will be reviewed: informational aids, information type and format design, information channel, and information viability.

Informational Aids. One concern with nutritional information provision programs has been that consumers do not access nutrition information because of its high processing costs. Researchers have examined, through both field and experimental research, the effect of providing information designed to lower consumers' processing costs. Several field experiments, conducted at point-of-purchase locations, focused primarily on changing purchasing behavior by providing additional or simplified external information (Russo et al. 1986; Muller 1985; Levy et al. 1985; Winett et al. 1991; Patterson et al. 1992).

Russo et al. and Muller conducted similar type supermarket studies; both provided nutritional information on poster boards intended to assist in comparisons across products and nutrients. Russo et al. measured the effect of providing different information matrices ranging from a complete listing of nine nutrients to a summarized nutritional index. Muller measured the effect of several variables including brand name, nutrient importance, and number and order of nutrients. Both studies found that the provision of information per se was the primary factor in behavior change; Russo et al., however, obtained this result only when using a negative nutrient. Davis-Chervin et al. (1985) found similar, though more moderate, results in their information provision program utilizing a cafeteria point-of-choice location.

Levy et al.'s (1985) two year study used shelf markers, which provided simplified and abbreviated brand-specific nutritional information for a variety of different products throughout a number of stores. While this intervention program was able to obtain an overall positive effect on purchasing behavior, a similar study by Patterson et al. (1992), also based in Washington, D.C. and Baltimore supermarkets, was not so successful. Their program showed a modest, to occasionally negative, impact on purchasing behavior. The complexity involved in conducting this type of field study, as well as the potential for an already heightened consumer awareness from previous studies, were suggested as possible reasons for these results.

Finally, Winett et al.'s (1991) mode of information deliverance deviated from previous intervention programs. A computer was used, which interacted with consumers and provided them with feedback concerning their intended purchases. These researchers obtained modest increases in lower-fat food purchases but no changes in higher-fiber purchases.

Overall, these studies indicate that information aids can have a positive, although limited, effect on behavioral change. Design problems can have a major effect on the outcomes of these studies. For example, there is difficulty involved in assessing the comparability of the control and intervention groups. This lack of comparability may be the result of demographic or socioeconomic differences between point-of-purchase locations. Thus, sales response variance could be the result of differences in consumers' ability to process the information or purchase the products.

Several experimental studies indicate that increased cognitive utilization can also result from the use of informational aids. Moorman (1990) combined consequence information (i.e., arousing or emotionally activating information) and reference information (the percentage of nutrient recommended daily allowance), which she embedded into nutritional messages on a package label. Her findings suggest that messages containing consequence information followed by reference information maximize consumer comprehension. Cole and Gaeth (1990) combined a perceptual aid (i.e., additional information on the importance of a nutrient) with cognitive style and age. Their research found the provision of additional information increased consumers' nutrition accuracy ratings, particularly for older consumers. Finally, Viswanathan (1992) provided subjects with summary information which described the nutrient makeup of two products across all available brands. He hypothesized, and in general found, that this type of summary information increased respondents' usage of nutritional information and resulted in increased judgments of product healthiness.

In summary, research has examined the effect of providing informational aids on both the behavior and the cognitive utilization of nutritional information. Because of difficulties in measuring both perspectives simultaneously, researchers have focused on either one or the other. Thus, this research includes two assumptions: 1) consumers will be aware and motivated to read the information when they shop, and 2) consumers will then use the information in their purchasing decisions. Additional research is necessary to assess these assumed linkages between awareness, motivation, and use. Unfortunately, as indicated by previous studies, data are difficult to collect.

Information Type and Format Design. The previous discussion suggests that providing nutritional information per se may not be enough to increase consumers' use of that information. The information used in the format and how the format is designed can also affect these decisions. Research indicates that consumers respond more to information on negative nutrients (e.g., sugar) than to positive nutrients (e.g., vitamins) (Russo et al. 1986; Moorman 1990; Heimbach 1981; Levy et al. 1985; Levy et al. 1991). For

TABLE 1

Source	Nutrients	Product	Dependent Variables
Asam and Bucklin 1973	15 positive and negative nutrients	Canned peas	Perceptions, preferences
Daly 1976	8 negative and positive nutrients	None	Attitudes, purchase intentions
Jacoby et al. 1977	6 negative and positive nutrients	Cereal	Comprehension, information use
Scammon 1977	9 positive and negative nutrients	Peanut butter spread	Nutritiousness, accuracy
Brucks et al. 1984	5 negative and positive nutrients	5 food categories	Processing, information use
Levy et al. 1985	Sodium, calories, fat, cholesterol	14 food categories	Purchase behavior
Muller 1985	8 negative and positive nutrients	5 food categories	Purchase behavior
Russo et al. 1986	9 negative and positive nutrients	6 food categories	Awareness, attitude, knowledge, purchase
Cole and Gaeth 1990	Sodium, sugar, fiber	Cereal	Ability, accuracy
Moorman 1990	Sodium, B6	Hot dogs, margarine	Motivation, ability acquisition
Winett et al. 1991	Fat, fiber	7 food categories	Purchase behavior
Viswanathan 1992	Calories, sodium, fat, fiber	Ice cream bars, cereal	Information use
Geiger et al. 1992	31 negative and positive nutrients	Canned soup	Label format preference
Levy et al. 1992	11 negative and positive nutrients	Cereal; frozen pizza, vegetables, dessert	Format performance/preference
Patterson et al. 1992	5 negative and positive nutrients	8 food categories	Purchase behavior

example, Heimbach found that over half the consumers surveyed reported using nutritional information to avoid consumption of negative nutrients; sugar raised the most concern. Russo et al. (1986) were able to affect purchasing behaviors when information on sugar was provided.

Researchers have found mixed results regarding format complexity. Two studies found consumers preferred the more complex (and complete) information (Asam and Bucklin 1973; Russo et al. 1986), and two studies found that consumers did not respond to more complex information (Muller 1985; Brucks et al. 1984). Scammon examined complexity as a function of adjectival (i.e., preprocessed or simplified) versus numeric (i.e., unprocessed) information and found increased nutritiousness evaluations with the less complex adjectival information. Levy et al. (1991) also found consumers preferred adjectival information; although it did not perform as well as numeric information in nutrition label performance tests.

These mixed findings may be the result of complexity being confounded with amount of information. When researchers provide more complete, complex information, they also increase the information load. Thus, consumers may perceive "more to be better" in their evaluations of nutritiousness, but may find the information too complex to process and use in a purchase decision.

Finally, the order of nutrients can impact the acquisition and use of nutritional information (Muller 1985; Geiger et al. 1991; Levy et al. 1992). Muller ordered nutrients in terms of importance, from most to least, or vice versa, while Geiger et al. and Levy et al. grouped nutrients in terms of whether consumers should include or delete them from their diet. Muller found no nutrient order effect. Levy et al. found consumers rated the grouping format least preferable, calling it "preachy"; while research by Geiger et al. found consumers rated the grouping format useful. Implicit in this research are consumers' perceptions of nutrient importance. For example, Muller's use of relatively unimportant, or unknown nutrients (e.g., phosphorus), may have contributed to his inability to find an individual nutrient effect on purchasing behavior.

Format design has been of particular concern for food regulators (Levy et al. 1992a; Levy et al. 1992b; Levy et al. 1991; Geiger et al. 1991). The Levy et al. studies measured consumers' response to a variety of different formats, which were designed in conjunction with extensive input from external sources (e.g., consumer groups, public hearings). The purpose of their research was to help develop and revise a format most acceptable to consumers in terms of comprehensibility and communication effectiveness. Interestingly, Levy et al.'s 1992 research study found that the label consumers preferred and the label on which consumers successfully performed label use tests were different. This difference suggests the difficulty in designing a format which increases both consumers' motivation to acquire the information and their ability to use the information.

Rather than using predesigned labeling formats, Geiger et al. used consumer input to develop an "ideal" nutrition label. "Ideal" was determined in terms of consumers' perceptions of label usefulness. Contrary to findings by Levy et al. (1991; 1992), Geiger et al. found that consumers preferred a bar graph format.

These studies suggest that the nutrients used in research, the order in which they are placed, and consumers' perceptions of the importance of the nutrients can differentially change consumers' use of the information. We need to be aware of these factors when we design future research programs to change consumers' purchasing behavior (see Russo and Leclerc [1991]) for a discussion on the characteristics that differentiate successful programs from unsuccessful programs). Furthermore, consumers' preference for a particular label format may not necessarily indicate their ability to process and use that information in purchasing decisions.

Information Channels. Nutritional information is typically provided to consumers via package labels, advertisements, or point-of-purchase displays. Researchers have debated the benefits of these different channels in disseminating nutritional information. Some researchers defend the use of advertisements as a source of product information, claiming that advertisements have increased consumers' knowledge of the relationship between diet and health (Calfee and Pappalardo 1991; Ippolito and Mathios 1991; Caswell 1992). For example, market share data has shown that the provision of health claims through manufacturer-produced print advertisements has positively influenced consumers' purchasing behavior (Ippolito and Mathios 1991; Levy and Stokes 1987). Others have warned of the possibility of misleading claims, i.e., the more relaxed regulations for advertising may induce food companies to make claims about relatively unimportant nutrients (Silverglade 1991). Researchers have assumed consumers respond equally to information disseminated through different information channels (see Ford et al. 1992). Interestingly, however, the regulatory agencies do not hold advertisements and labels to the same regulatory standards, thus suggesting these two information channels are not the same. In fact, labels have stricter regulatory standards than do advertisements (Silverglade 1991; Serafino 1992). Implicit in the regulatory differences is that consumers respond differently depending on where they obtain their information; however, this differential response has not been systematically researched.

Usefulness of Providing Information. Much of the earlier research looked at the usefulness of providing nutritional information. Usefulness comes from a more public policy perspective, which is concerned with the necessity of providing this information, that is, do the consumers really need it, and do they really use it in their purchasing decisions. Researchers found that although consumers responded positively to receiving nutritional information (Daly 1976), only certain segments of the population either had the ability (e.g., in terms of education, nutritional concern, or prior knowledge) (Lenahan et al. 1973; Vandenberg 1978) or the motivation to acquire the information (Jacoby et al. 1977).

In summary, research on information provision has found that consumers want nutritional information but whether they use this information is still in question. Research has found that consumers prefer more information, yet we are not sure if consumers actually use all this information or if they just feel more confident when more information is provided. Much of the research has emphasized cognitive utilization (e.g., evaluation of nutritiousness) with less research conducted on the issues of why consumers acquire nutritional information and, then, whether the information is used in purchasing decisions. If our ultimate goal, however, is to change consumers' purchasing behaviors we need to increase our understanding of the link between cognitive utilization and behavioral utilization.

Acquisition and Utilization

Information first has to be acquired for consumers to participate in evaluative or purchase behaviors. Of importance, then, is the issue of motivation. Motivation can be defined as consumers' goal-directed arousal to engage in particular behaviors (see Moorman 1993). Thus, once aware of the information, consumers need to be motivated to acquire the information to form an attitude necessary to change a behavior (Russo et al. 1986).

Motivation and Ability. Moorman's (1990) research suggests that consequence information increases motivation, regardless of consumer differences. In addition, both the lowering of processing costs and the increasing of benefits have been suggested as motivating factors in consumers' use of information (Russo et al. 1986; Russo and Leclerc 1991). Motivation can also be affected by perceptions of nutrient importance.

Deterrents to motivation also exist, including complexity of information, and consumer confusion and disinterest. As previously discussed, a number of research studies have been concerned with the complexity of nutritional information and have sought to reduce this complexity and hence the information processing costs.

Consumer confusion can be attributed to several conditions. The first condition is external to the consumer and is a function of the current state of nutritional information regulation (Caswell 1992; Silverglade 1991). A lack of uniformity in regulatory standards exists between advertisements and labels as well as between some product categories (Caswell 1992). And because products do not all exist under the same regulatory jurisdiction i.e., the USDA regulates meat and poultry products and the FDA regulates packaged food products, the potential exists for different products to exhibit different nutritional profiles.

Confusion can also result from consumers' inability to process nutritional information (Brucks et al. 1984; Moorman 1990; Daly 1976). Consumers' ability, or lack of ability, can change, though, depending on the individual (Moorman 1990, 1993; Levy et al. 1991, 1992; Cole and Gaeth 1990), the product (Brucks et al. 1984), or consumers' perceptions of the nutrient (Muller 1985). Although research on individual differences in the context of nutritional information use has been limited, a number of research studies have included the caveat that these differences have the potential to affect their findings (Ippolito and Mathios 1991; Calfee and Pappalardo 1991; Daly 1976; Jacoby et al. 1977; Heimbach 1981; Vandenberg 1978). There has been no systematic research, however, following up on this concern.

In summary, a number of variables can affect consumers' motivation and ability to acquire and use nutrient information. Many of these issues have not been systematically researched. For example, researchers have not systematically studied issues related to the consumer such as perceptions of nutrient importance or prior knowledge. In previous studies, lesser known nutrients (e.g., thiamine) have been combined with better known nutrients (e.g., vitamin C), perhaps mitigating consumers' response. In addition, prior knowledge should not suggest importance. For example, Moorman (1990) used nutrients familiar to consumers, though she did not measure perceived importance. Prior knowledge and perceived importance are separate issues; prior knowledge would affect ability, while perceived nutrient importance may impact motivation.

GENERAL DISCUSSION AND FUTURE RESEARCH

As this review has summarized, a majority of the studies directly or indirectly have investigated issues related to the acquisition and utilization of nutritional information. However, two areas of additional research would enhance the research already conducted: 1) the further examination of the connection between acquisition and utilization and behavior, and 2) the role of motivation. Although some studies have looked at purchasing behavior, most of the research has assumed purchase and consumption automatically follow the acquisition and utilization of nutrition information. Because the impetus behind much of nutritional information research involves changing consumer behavior, the need exists to confirm this relationship between information utilization and purchase behavior.

Research on two concepts, consumers' individual differences and consumers' differing perceptions of nutrient importance, may increase our understanding of this purchasing behavior. Research involving individual differences has been limited, and researchers disagree on its importance. For example, Moorman's (1990) research suggests that the utilization of information depends on the goals of the individual. Muller (1985) aggregated consumer response, suggesting the unimportance of individual differences.

Conceptually, consumers can be separated into three broadly defined health classifications: those consumers with an overall positive orientation toward their responsibility for their health; those consumers who are interested in specific and idiosyncratic nutrient/health relationships; and those consumers who are not concerned with health issues and see little or no connection between their diet and their health. This assumption of different "health" segments suggests that research results may differ depending on the makeup of the sample taking part in the study and the interaction of this sample with the dependent measures. For example, some consumers indifferent to health issues may show ability, and perhaps motivation, during a research exercise but may exhibit either neutral or negative purchase intentions. Other consumers may be selectively interested in nutritional information, i.e., they may be interested in information on sodium and high blood pressure and may not be concerned about information on fiber.

The above discussion implies that different consumers may have different meaning structures, thereby affecting their perceptions of nutrient information. Venkatesan (1978) has noted that previous research has focused primarily on "what" information or "what" attributes of food products ought to be provided to consumers; however, little attention has been paid to "why" consumers make their purchasing decisions. Why would consumers purchase a food product based on nutritional attributes? We have our assumptions: they do so because they are concerned with their health or with their children's health or because they are concerned with aging or because we've made the processing of this information easier. But we really don't know why.

Not much has changed in nutrition research in this regard; researchers have made little progress linking consumers' attitudes towards nutritional information and purchase and use behaviors. Fifteen years ago Venkatesan (1978) suggested the need for longitudinal research aimed at looking at consumer consumption patterns and, unfortunately, this type of research has yet to be conducted. Phenomenological interviews conducted over an extended period of time would be one method used to study both consumption patterns and meaning structures. This type of methodology enables the researcher to understand an issue from a first-person perspective (cf. Thompson, Locander and Pollio 1989) and allows for more depth of knowledge by the researcher. Because respondents are not prompted by specific questions from the interviewer but, rather, are encouraged to discuss a topic within a flexible set of boundaries, it is expected that respondents will discuss the issues that are of importance to them. This type of methodology could enable the field of nutritional information to gain not only a more in-depth understanding of what variables are affecting purchasing decisions but also why these variables are salient.

Finally, consumers' motivation to search for and use nutrition formats is an important variable and in need of further research. While the majority of the nutritional information research has focused on lowering consumers' processing costs, through the provision of reference materials and easier-to-understand formats, more research should be focused on how to motivate consumers to first pay attention to and then to process and use nutritional information. Ease of processing will not necessarily increase consumers motivation to process the information. Motivation seems to be the driving force behind consumers seeking further information once their attention is gained, and without motivation other consumer characteristics such as ability, cognitive style, or prior knowledge may not be engaged in purchasing situations.

A multi-faceted information provision program may encourage consumer acquisition and use of nutritional information (cf. Russo and Leclerc 1991). Thus, certain types of point-of-purchase signs and advertised health claims may positively motivate consumers to become aware of the nutritional makeup of food products. The provision of packaging labels that are easy to read and comprehend would both encourage attention and facilitate processing. And finally, a concerted effort to bring the information found on labels and in advertising more in sync would create more continuity for consumers and would alleviate some of the confusion generated by varying types of messages.

The type of nutritional information conveyed to consumers is also important. An information message that makes a connection between a nutritional attribute and its health benefit (i.e., a health claim) is more likely to gain consumers' attention than is a lengthy list of ingredients with little relationship to why the consumer should purchase the product. Furthermore, negative nutrients seem to be more motivating to consumers. New labels, required to be on packages by May, 1994, will increase information on negative nutrients, in addition to those previously required (new nutrients for which information is required include calories from fat, saturated fat, cholesterol, sugars, and dietary fiber) (Kurtzweil 1993). Nutrients no longer required are thiamine, riboflavin, and niacin. Also included will be a new dietary reference value called the "Daily Value" which will "help consumers understand the role of individual foods in the context of total daily diet" (p. 13). Finally, health claims will be allowed for six nutrient/disease relationships: calcium and osteoporosis, fat and cancer, saturated fat and cholesterol and coronary heart disease, fiber and cancer and coronary heart disease. The new labels appear to disseminate information in an easily-understood format; however, the amount of information consumers will be confronted with has increased. Whether consumers will be able to assimilate all this information and use it in their purchasing decisions will require further research.

While consumers continue to be interested in the relationship between diet and health in their food purchasing decisions, research has also shown consumers moving away from purchasing based on nutritional attributes (New York Times 1993). Perhaps consumers are becoming disillusioned with the conflicting health information and the bombardment of health related "news" items—although research is needed to investigate these diverging trends. Therefore, as health care costs escalate and the need for consumers to take a more preventive view of their health care increases, continued research is necessary to find ways to more effectively communicate nutritional information to consumers.

REFERENCES

"Americans Found Retreating From Healthy Eating Habits," *New York Times*, 16 April 1993, A, 1

Asam, Edward H. and Louis P. Bucklin (1973), "Nutrition Labeling for Canned Goods: A Study of Consumer Response," *Journal of Marketing*, 37(April), 32-37

Bettman, James R. (1975), "Issues in Designing Consumer Information Environments," *Journal of Consumer Research*, 2(December), 169-177

Brucks, Merrie, Andrew A. Mitchell, and Richard Staelin (1984), "The Effect of Nutritional Information Disclosures in Advertising: An Information Processing Approach," *Journal of Public Policy and Marketing*, 3, 1-27

Calfee, John E. and Janis K. Pappalardo (1991), "Public Policy Issues in Health Claims for Foods," *Journal of Public Policy & Marketing*, 10(Spring), 33-53

Caswell, Julie A. (1992), "Current Information Levels on Food Labels," *American Journal of Agricultural Economics*, 74(December), 1196-1201

Cole, Catherine A. and Gary J. Gaeth (1990), "Cognitive and Age-Related Differences in the Ability to Use Nutritional Information in a Complex Environment," *Journal of Marketing Research*, 27 (May), 175-184

Daly, Patricia A. (1976), "The Response of Consumers to Nutrition Labeling," *Journal of Consumer Affairs*, 10(Winter), 170-178

Davis-Chervin, Doryn, Todd Rogers and Mia Clark (1985), "Influencing Food Selection with Point-of-Choice Nutrition Information," *Journal of Nutrition Education*, 17(1), 18-22

Ford, Gary T., Manoj Hastak, Anusree Mitra, and Debra J. Ringold (1992), "Effects of the New FDA Rules for Food Labels on Disadvantaged Consumers: Unintended Consequences," Marketing Science Institute Research Competition, American University

Geiger, Constance and Ann G. Gallenson (1992), "Nutrition Labeling: In Search of Clarity," *Journal of the American Dietetic Association*, 92(October), 1217

Geiger, Constance, Bonita W. Wyse, C.R. Michael Parent, and R. Gaurth Hansen (1991), "Nutrition Labels in Bar Graph Format Deemed Most Useful For Consumer Purchase Decisions Using Adaptive Conjoint Analysis," *Journal of the American Dietetic Association*, 91(July), 800-815

Heimbach, James T. (1981), "Defining the Problem: The Scope of Consumer Concern with Food Labeling," in *Advances in Consumer Research*, Vol. 8, ed. Kent B. Monroe, Ann Arbor, MI: Association for Consumer Research, 474-476

Ippolito, Pauline M. and Alan D. Mathios (1991), "Health Claims in Food Marketing: Evidence on Knowledge and Behavior in the Cereal Market," *Journal of Public Policy & Marketing*, 10(Spring), 15-32

Jacoby, Jacob, Robert Chestnut and W. Silberman (1977), "Consumer Use and Comprehension of Nutrition Information," *Journal of Consumer Research*, 4(September), 119-128

Kurtzweil, Paula (1993), "Good Reading for Good Eating," *FDA Consumer*, (Special Report), 7-13

Lenahan, R. J., J. A. Thomas, D. L. Call, and D. I. Padberg (1973), "Consumer Reaction to Nutritional Labels on Food Products," *The Journal of Consumer Affairs*

Levy, Alan S., Sara B. Fein, and Raymond E. Schucker (1992a), "More Effective Nutrition Label Formats Are Not Necessarily Preferred," *Journal of the American Dietetic Association*, 92(October), 1230-1234

Levy, Alan S., Sara B. Fein, and Raymond E. Schucker (1992b), "Evaluation of Nutrition Label Formats: FDA Study 2," working paper, Food and Drug Administration, Division of Consumer Studies, Washington, DC,

Levy, Alan S., Sara B. Fein, and Raymond E. Schucker (1991), "Nutrition Labeling Formats: Performance and Preference," *Food Technology*, (July), 116-121

Levy, Alan S. and Raymond C. Stokes (1987), "Effects of a Health Promotion Advertising Campaign on Sales of Ready-to-Eat Cereals," *Public Health Reports*, 102(July-August), 398-403

Levy, Alan S., Odonna Mathews, Marilyn Stephenson, Janet E. Tenney, and Raymond E. Schucker (1985), "The Impact of a Nutrition Information Program on Food Purchases," *Journal of Public Policy and Marketing*, 4, 1-13

Moorman, Christine (1990), "The Effects of Stimulus and Consumer Characteristics on the Utilization of Nutrition Information," *Journal of Consumer Research*, 17(December), 362-374

Moorman, Christine (1993), "A Model of Consumers' Preventive Health Behaviors: The Role of Health Motivation and Health Ability, *Journal of Consumer Research*, 20(forthcoming)

Muller, Thomas E. (1985), "Structural Information Factors Which Stimulate the Use of Nutrition Information: A Field Experiment," *Journal of Marketing Research*, 22(May), 143-157

Patterson et al. (1992), "Evaluation of a Supermarket Intervention," *Evaluation Review*, 16(October), 464-490

Russo, J. Edward and France Leclerc (1991), "Characteristics of Successful Product Information Programs," *Journal of Social Issues*, 47(1), 73-92

Russo, Edward J., Richard Staelin, Catherine A. Nolan, Gary J. Russell, Barbara L. Metcalf (1986), "Nutrition Information in the Supermarket," *Journal of Consumer Research*, 13(June), 48-70

Serafino, James M. (1992), "Developing Standards for Health Claims-The FDA and the FTC," *Food and Drug Law Journal*, 47(4), 335-353

Scammon, Debra L. (1977), "'Information Load' and Consumers," *Journal of Consumer Research*, 4(December) 148-155

Silverglade, Bruce A. (1991), "A Comment on 'Public Policy Issues in Health Claims for Foods'," *Journal of Public Policy & Marketing*, 10(Spring), 54-62

Vandenberg, Robert J. (1978), "Food Label Information: What Consumers Say They Use and What They Actually Use," *Advances in Consumer Research*, Vol. 5, ed. H. Keith Hunt, Ann Arbor, MI: Association for Consumer Research, 484-487

Venkatesan, M. (1978), "Consumer Behavior and Nutrition: Preventive Health Perspective," *Advances in Consumer Research*, Vol. 5, ed. H. Keith Hunt, Ann Arbor, MI: Association for Consumer Research, 513-520

Viswanathan, Madhubalan (1992), "The Influence of Reference Information on the Usage of Nutrition Information," Working Paper, Department of Business Administration, University of Illinois, Urbana-Champaign

Winett, Richard A. et al. (1991), "An Experimental Evaluation of a Prototype Public Access Nutrition Information System for Supermarkets," *Health Psychology*, 10(1), 75-78

Miscomprehension and Believability of Information Presented in Print Advertising

Richard F. Beltramini, Arizona State University
Steven P. Brown, Southern Methodist University

ABSTRACT

Previous research in this area has raised the question of whether or not conclusions based on the forced exposure paradigm are generalizable to more naturalistic settings. In the present investigation the miscomprehension and believability of information targeted toward a student audience are measured under as ecologically valid conditions as operationally feasible. Based upon the results obtained, it appears that some earlier results were indeed well "within the ballpark."

INTRODUCTION

Research on miscomprehension has relied on the "forced exposure paradigm" to estimate the proportion of advertising content that is misunderstood (e.g., Jacoby and Hoyer 1982a, 1989). In this paradigm, study participants are instructed to watch television commercials or read print ads and then answer factual or inferential questions regarding their content immediately afterward. Thus, these studies have assessed miscomprehension rates under conditions unlike those of ordinary advertising exposure, which makes generalization of miscomprehension rates to more naturalistic conditions inappropriate. The present study investigates miscomprehension rates for print advertising under naturalistic exposure conditions and compares these rates to those reported in forced exposure studies.

Also, relatively little attention has been given in previous research to the relationship between miscomprehension and measures of advertising effectiveness. Most existing research has studied deceptive advertising and elicitation of "pragmatic inferences" that mislead consumers regarding the attributes and potentialities of products (e.g., Harris 1977; Harris and Monaco 1978). This research has proceeded from the assumptions that some advertisers encourage miscomprehension and that miscomprehension is positively related to ad believability through the mediation of false inferences (Monaco and Kaiser 1983). The present study explores the relationship between miscomprehension of the factual content of print ads and their perceived believability.

A final limitation of previous research in this area concerns its lack of attention to ensuring the advertising information being assessed is specifically targeted toward an audience of interest to advertisers, and one which is sufficiently defined to permit practical application of the research results. The present study affords that focus by measuring miscomprehension and believability of advertising information among college students, an audience at which millions of dollars are currently directed and which is growing in importance to advertisers.

PREVIOUS RESEARCH

Miscomprehension Rates

The original work on miscomprehension of television commercials by Jacoby and Hoyer (1982a) reported a miscomprehension rate of 29.6 percent for advertising content. This work was criticized by Ford and Yalch (1982) on the basis that methodological characteristics of the study biased the miscomprehension findings upward. Among other things, Ford and Yalch criticized the study's laboratory setting, forced exposure to stimuli, instructions given to study participants, and lack of correspondence between the intended target markets of the advertisements and the study participants whose comprehension was assessed. Jacoby and Hoyer (1982b) responded that the laboratory setting and forced exposure procedure would have the effect of biasing miscomprehension findings downward rather than upward. No subsequent study has directly addressed the external validity questions raised by Ford and Yalch (1982) by assessing miscomprehension rates under ordinary exposure conditions and comparing them to those established in forced exposure studies.

A further criticism leveled against the original Jacoby and Hoyer study concerned inclusion of unequal numbers of true-false items for each ad (i.e., four false and two true). Ford and Yalch (1982) argued that "yea-saying" (i.e., respondents' tendency to answer "true" when uncertain of the correct response) resulted in an overstatement of miscomprehension. Schmittlein and Morrison (1983) reanalyzed the Jacoby and Hoyer data, concluding that if a single index were used to describe the proportion of copy correctly comprehended, that index would be 46 percent.

Despite criticisms of the Jacoby and Hoyer research, subsequent studies have generally found miscomprehension rates consistent with those of the original study. Jacoby, Hoyer, and Zimmer (1983), for example, found miscomprehension rates ranging from 12 to 30 percent, depending on whether the information was presented visually, aurally, or audiovisually (visual presentation resulted in the lowest miscomprehension). Gates (1986) reported miscomprehension rates ranging from 7 to 36 percent for 30-second television commercials. Edwardson, Grooms, and Proudlove's (1981) broadcast journalism study revealed a 37.7 percent miscomprehension rate for newscasts, whereas Hoyer and Jacoby (1985) found a 33.7 percent miscomprehension rate for public affairs programs. Chaiken and Eagley (1976) reported a 38 percent miscomprehension rate, and a 1980 study by Lipstein indicated a 32 percent miscomprehension rate for advertising content. Morris, et al. (1986) found miscomprehension rates as low as 9 percent and as high as 44 percent for true-false items related to print advertisements for blood pressure and arthritis medicines among members of the target market for these products (although only two ads related to a single product category were studied).

Jacoby and Hoyer (1989) concluded that miscomprehension of print ads was between 21 and 37 percent, but have subsequently revised these estimates stating:

> This reanalysis showed that for TV advertising the median miscomprehension rate for individual meanings is 23.3 percent (or, when adjusted for guessing based on the analysis conducted by Schmittlein and Morrison 1983, 14.9 percent). For advertising communications appearing in mass-media magazines, the median miscomprehension rate for individual meanings is 11.8 percent (Jacoby and Hoyer 1990), p. 14).

All of these studies used forced exposure procedures, thus leaving external validity questions unexamined. Consistent with the argument of Jacoby and Hoyer (1982b), it seems reasonable to expect somewhat higher miscomprehension rates under naturalistic exposure conditions relative to those observed in forced exposure studies.

As this review of the miscomprehension literature reveals, varying rates of miscomprehension have been observed under varying study conditions. To integrate these findings as systemati-

TABLE 1
Results of a Meta-Analysis of Miscomprehension Research

Studies of Print Advertisements	N	Observed Miscomprehension Rate
Jacoby, Hoyer and Zimmer (1983)	352	18.8%
Morris, et.al. (1986)	790	20.0%
Jacoby and Hoyer (1989)	1,347	21.4%
	(2,489)	
		weighted mean = 20.6%

Studies of Television Advertisements	N	Observed Miscomprehension Rate
Jacoby and Hoyer (1982)	2,700	29.6%
Jacoby, Hoyer, and Zimmer (1983)	352	26.8%
Morris, et. al. (1986)	696	17.0%
Gates (1986)	168	19.3%
	(3,916)	
	6,405	
		weighted mean = 26.7%

Overall weighted mean = 24.3 % (standard deviation = 5%)

---

cally and precisely as possible, and to provide a benchmark for comparison against the results of the present investigation, meta-analytic techniques were used to generalize across prior studies. First, a sample-size-weighted mean miscomprehension rates was computed across all studies that assessed the miscomprehension of advertising messages. Studies of miscomprehension of message types other than advertising were excluded from the analysis. Results are reported in Table 1.

The overall weighted mean miscomprehension percentage across all studies using advertising stimuli was 24.3 percent, with a standard deviation of 5 percent. Sampling error (computed according to formula derived in Hunter and Schmidt 1990, p. 105) accounted for 44 percent of the observed variance in miscomprehension proportions. Because this was less than the 75 percent that Hunter and Schmidt regard as sufficient evidence of effect homogeneity, the studies were divided into groups of print advertisement and television advertisement studies, and separate analyses were conducted for each group. The weighted mean miscomprehension proportion for print advertisements was 20.6 percent, whereas the proportion for television advertisements was 26.7 percent. Thus, the weighted mean proportion for studies of print advertisements was selected to provide the most appropriate benchmark for comparison against the results of the present research.

Miscomprehension and Believability

Believability is a key attribute for most advertising, since consumers are not likely to respond to advertising in the desired manner if they do not believe what it says. Previous research has indicated that individuals tend to place more credence in two-sided than in one-sided ads (e.g., Settle and Golden 1974; Folkes 1988), that moderate claims are believed more than extreme claims (Beltramini and Evans (1985), and that familiar statements are believed more than unfamiliar statements (Beltramini 1988). Relevant to the investigation at hand, however, Hoyer, Srivastava, and Jacoby (1984) found familiarity to be unrelated to miscomprehension.

A substantial amount of previous research (e.g., Harris 1977; Harris and Monaco 1978; Preston and Richards 1986) has associated miscomprehension with deceptive advertising and attempts by advertisers to foster false beliefs favorable to the advertised product. Jacoby and Hoyer (1982a) maintained that a certain amount of miscomprehension is natural and unavoidable, and that only miscomprehension in excess of that baseline amount should be taken as evidence of deceptive advertising. They pegged that normative baseline at approximately 30 percent. Preston and Richards (1986), however, argued that Jacoby and Hoyer considered only cases in which the literal message of the ad and the meaning that is conveyed to the consumer are identical. They advance the concept of "induced miscomprehension," which they describe as the conveyance of false messages by inference or false implication.

Preston and Richards (1986) also suggested that miscomprehension tends to work in favor of the advertiser. They argued that because consumer expect ads to contain information favorable to the advertiser, they tend to interpret miscomprehended information in a manner consistent with this expectation. This perspective is consistent with theorizing regarding cognitive schemes, which holds that perceptions of, and inferences about, incoming stimuli are influenced by their relation to information contained in the activated schema (Fiske and Taylor 1984). From this perspective, an advertising schema would include the information that advertising messages are favorable to the advertiser. Information that is miscomprehended will be interpreted in a manner consistent with this information, resulting in cognition favorable to the advertiser. Preston and Richards (1986) reanalyzed data from an earlier study (Preston 1967), and found that a far greater proportion of miscomprehended meanings were favorable rather than unfavorable to the advertiser.

These findings related to the *meaning* consumers ascribe to miscomprehended information—to what they thought the ad said. They do not indicate whether consumers *believed* what they thought the ad said. Other psychological theories would suggest that consumers are likely to discount the believability of meanings they ascribe to miscomprehended advertising information. Kelley's (1967) attribution theory, for example, posited that individuals tend to discount the value of information when its source has a potential ulterior motive. Recognizing advertisers' self-interest in conveying positive information, consumers may be skeptical about the believability of advertising messages (Mizerski, Golden, and Kernan 1979; Folkes 1988). It is not clear from this perspective, however, whether miscomprehended material is subject to any greater or lesser discounting than the rest of the ad.

Miscomprehended information may be less believable than correctly comprehended information if it results from cognitive distortion of otherwise plausible facts presented in the ad (e.g., through transpositions of letters or words resulting in altered meanings). Message segments that are interpreted in a manner inconsistent with the context in which they occur are likely to be *less* believable than correctly comprehended information (Neisser 1976). On the other hand, if miscomprehension results from a mismatch between information contained in the receiver's cognitive schemata and the information contained in the actual message, the receiver may interpret the message as consistent with his/her beliefs and prior experience regardless of its actual meaning (Fiske and Taylor 1984), and thus as *more* believable than correctly comprehended information. The first type of error results from non-veridical perceptual encoding of verbal elements in the message, and hence might be described as message-related miscomprehension. The second type results from imposing semantic elements on the message that are not actually contained in it, and thus might be described as schema-related miscomprehension. The present research undertakes an exploratory investigation of the relationship between miscomprehension of advertisements and their perceived believability under ecologically valid study conditions.

Hypotheses

In accordance with the literature reviewed and the research objectives, the following hypotheses were developed for testing:

H1: Exposure to ads under naturalistic conditions will result in higher miscomprehension rates than those typical of forced exposure studies of print advertising (over 20 percent).

H2: There will be no relationship between miscomprehension and perceived believability of advertising information.

METHODOLOGY

To address the criticisms noted of previous research and test the hypotheses under ecologically valid conditions, a mock-up version of a campus newspaper containing a representative mixture of editorial and advertising content was developed. The mock-up was professionally printed and in every way resembled the actual student newspaper. All of the editorial material was actually taken from recent editions of the campus newspaper and reflected current events on campus. Additionally, ten actual advertisements targeted toward students for nationally distributed products were selected for testing based upon similar layouts and amount of information, and were included.

The mock-up newspaper was distributed to two classes of junior level business students entering a large lecture hall before class at a large university. It is typical for students at this university to pass the time before class reading the campus newspaper, so the mock-up newspaper was made available to the students without instructions regarding what to read or attend to. Since free distribution bins are typically located just outside of these classrooms, it was felt that minimal sensitization occurred with distributing the newspapers. In this respect, providing students with the mock-up newspaper resulted in exposure to advertising under as natural conditions as practically possible.

After the class period had begun, the mock-up newspaper was collected and a questionnaire booklet distributed containing four true-false questions relating to the information contained in each ad, and by a ten-item perceived believability scale well validated in other studies (Beltramini 1982, 1988; Beltraminin and Evans 1985; Gould 1988). The true-false questions assessing miscomprehension included two true and two false correct responses for each ad, with the pattern of correct true and false answers randomized across the ten ads. The four items utilized for each advertisement were chosen by the researchers from a larger pool of potential items derived in pretest to achieve consistency of item difficulty and to assure that the items fairly represented information contained in the ads. The items selected were intended to relate to factual material contained in the ads and consist of restatements of that material, more so than merely playing back advertising executions.

A total of 829 usable questionnaires were collected. Comparison of the two classes surveyed showed no significant differences in basic demographic profiles, so the data were aggregated for further analyses.

RESULTS

Miscomprehension rates for the ten ads ranged from a low of 13.2 to a high of 45.5 percent. These observed rates are summarized in Table 2, along with mean believability ratings and correlations between miscomprehension and believability for each advertisement. Although the variability in miscomprehension across test advertisements is substantial, it is consistent with variability shown in previous studies (e.g., Jacoby and Hoyer 1989). Averaging across test advertisements, the overall rate of miscomprehension was 31.5 percent, which is slightly above the 29.6 percent reported by Jacoby and Hoyer (1982b) for forced exposure to television ads and within the range of 21.5 to 36.9 percent reported by Jacoby and Hoyer (1989) for forced exposure to print ads. An item-level analysis similar to that of Jacoby and Hoyer (1990) resulted in precisely the same average miscomprehension figure (31.5 percent) as in the advertisement-level analysis.

In an attempt to reduce confusion regarding whether or not to include "non-comprehension" in calculating miscomprehension, the "don't know" response alternative was not included in the instrument. However, the missing data across items and test advertisements ranged from 3.0 to 31.7 percent, averaging 14.4 percent. If missing data are interpreted as analogous to non-comprehension, the 14.4 percent figure for missing data does in fact approximate Jacoby and Hoyer's (1989) 15.5 percent non-comprehension rate, suggesting a resultant miscomprehension rate of between 31.5 and 45.9 percent (depending on how the missing data are interpreted). This range is approximately 9 to 10 points higher on each end than that of the forced exposure study reported by Jacoby and Hoyer (1989), and higher still than the more conservative item-level results of their 1990 reanalysis. In either case, these results support H1, which predicted that miscomprehension of naturally exposed advertisements would exceed miscomprehension rates reported in a forced exposure studies of print advertising (i.e., 20 percent).

To estimate the effects of guessing on these results, a statistical procedure to correct observed miscomprehension rates for the effects of guessing and yea-saying developed by Schmittlein and Morrison (1983), and subsequently used on the Jacoby and Hoyer (1982) data, was applied. The procedure estimates a parameter representing the proportion of items answered correctly from true knowledge after correcting for guessing and yea-saying. (The procedure is rigorously derived and explained in detail in Schmittlein and Morrison [1983].)

TABLE 2
Miscomprehension and Believability Results

	Average correct pct.	Average Incorrect pct.	Average believability (1)	r(2)
ad 1	71.55	28.45	4.95	-.09*
ad 2	54.50	45.50	4.86	.05
ad 3	80.35	19.65	5.78	-.10*
ad 4	74.55	25.45	3.61	-.10*
ad 5	56.68	43.32	3.78	-.06
ad 6	69.83	30.17	4.66	-.20*
ad 7	58.65	41.35	4.50	-.13*
ad 8	61.40	38.60	4.72	-.00
ad 9	86.80	13.20	4.85	-.14*
ad 10	70.65	29.35	3.94	-.05

(1) where 1 = unbelievable and 7 = believable
(2) correlation between miscomprehension and believability
* p<.05

The analysis indicated that the overall proportion of items answered correctly from true comprehension was approximately 37 percent. Although this figure is seemingly low, it compares with the 46 percent true comprehension figure estimated by Schmittlein and Morrison from the Jacoby and Hoyer forced exposure to television data. Thus, the true comprehension rate for advertising under naturalistic exposure conditions is lower than the forced exposure data.

Table 2 also illustrates an overall average believability rating of 4.57 (where 1=unbelievable and 7=believable), moderately believable. Internal consistencies of the believability scale across the ten test advertisements, measured by Cronback's alpha, ranged from .93 to .96, evidencing unidimensionality. Table 2 also contains the correlation coefficients between miscomprehension and believability, where the number of each study participant's incorrect answers to the true-false items (out of four) were related to their believability ratings for each advertisement. The average correlation was -.08 across the test advertisements, indicating a weak relationship between increasing miscomprehension and decreasing perceived believability of the information contained in the advertisements tested, despite statistically significant correlations in six of the ten cases. Although the relationship is weak, its negative valence suggests a slight tendency to disbelieve miscomprehended information. It should also be noted that the most likely effect of guessing on questions about ad content would be to increase random error, and thus attenuate the strength of the miscomprehension-believability association. Thus, the strength of the "true" relationship is likely to be understated by these results.

DISCUSSION AND IMPLICATIONS

The results of this study suggest that exposure to print ads under naturalistic conditions leads to slightly higher miscomprehension rates than those observed in forced exposure studies. The fact that relaxing experimental controls during ad exposure resulted in moderately higher levels of miscomprehension appears to validate Jacoby and Hoyer's (1982b) assertion that forced exposure in laboratory settings would tend to bias miscomprehension rates downward, rather than upward as implied by Ford an Yalch (1982).

Moreover, the results give a preliminary indication of the magnitude of miscomprehension under one set of naturalistic exposure conditions. The generalizability of the findings is limited by the nature of the sample, setting, and stimuli, but the results do suggest that forced exposure studies slightly understate actual miscomprehension rates for print ads. The point is significant in light of the vigorous criticisms of Jacoby and Hoyer's (1982a) estimates as upwardly biased (Ford and Yalch 1982; Mizerski 1982).

What is perhaps more remarkable about the results is the fact that exposing study participants to test advertisements under naturalistic conditions without instructions regarding what to read or attend to resulted in only slightly greater observed levels of miscomprehension than forcing them to read and attend to advertisements. The results suggest that casual exposure to print advertising can, at least under some circumstances, be effective in conveying intended messages.

The relatively slight increase in miscomprehension rates under more naturalistic exposure conditions provides an additional indication of the amount of miscomprehension that is "normal" or "natural." It would appear that the amount of miscomprehension that should be expected depends to some extent on context and exposure conditions. This is not surprising. However, the relatively slight increase in miscomprehension, given a dramatic change in exposure conditions, lends additional credence to earlier estimates and suggests that the "normative" or "natural" rate of miscomprehension falls within a fairly narrow range.

The low negative correlations observed between miscomprehension and believability suggest that there is a slight tendency to place less credence in meanings that are miscomprehended. Some attenuation in the strength of association between miscomprehension and believability may well have resulted from guessing. However, the negative valence of the relationship may suggest that miscomprehension has the effect of potentially decreasing the believability of the ad overall.

Several caveats must be noted. Exposing study participants to test advertisements under the most naturalistic conditions possible necessarily entailed some relaxation of internal controls. Study participants were free to attend to any of the test advertisements as much or a little as they desired (within the time provided), as they are when naturally exposed to advertising. Thus, without specifically measuring attention to each ad tested there was no assurances that they attended equally to the various test advertisements. This tradeoff was made to preserve the naturalistic conditions, rather than calling undue attention to specific components of each ad, or imposing additional measures to lengthen the completion time for subjects. Still, averaging across study participants and advertisements, the results are not drastically different from those obtained in more tightly controlled studies in which subjects' attention is directed to and focused on each test advertisement for a fixed length of time.

Although the study design provided more ecologically valid conditions for studying miscomprehension, the generalizability of the results is limited by the context. The relative homogeneity, education level, and cognitive abilities of the study participants may not be representative of the larger population, although they do constitute an identifiable and important target market and were, in fact, the intended target market for the test advertisements. Also, even though no instructions were given at the time the newspaper containing the test advertisements was distributed, the fact that they were handed out at all may have somehow influenced how study participants read the contents. Across a total of ten test advertisements and over 800 study participants, however, any such effect is not likely to be large or highly systematic.

Despite these limitations, this exploratory investigation provides a number of implications to both researchers and advertisers. The study has shown that exposure to print advertisements under naturalistic conditions resulted in slightly higher miscomprehension rates than have been reported in previous forced exposure studies. The fact that relaxation of controls on exposure to test advertisements led to only slight increases in observed miscomprehension rates suggests that previously reported "normative" or "benchmark" rates are well "within the ballpark." Contrary to previous critiques, they appear to understate somewhat the amount of miscomprehension that occurs under naturalistic conditions. Statistical integration of prior research findings indicated that information presented in print advertising is miscomprehended less than information presented in television advertising. Correction of the results of studies using both media for the effects of guessing show true comprehension rates to be low regardless of medium or exposure conditions. Estimated true comprehension of print advertisements under naturalistic conditions was 9 percent lower than the estimate for forced exposure to television advertising. However, future research efforts are needed to further explore the relationship between miscomprehension and believability among other media and other samples utilizing naturalistic (versus forced exposure) approaches to enhance the generalizability of research in this area.

REFERENCES

Beltramini, Richard F. (1982), "Advertising Perceived Believability Scale," *Proceedings of the Southwestern Marketing Association*, 1-3.

_____ (1988), "Perceived Believability of Warning Information Presented in Cigarette Advertising," *Journal of Advertising*, 17, 26-32.

_____ and Kenneth R. Evans (1985), "Perceived Believability of Research Results Information in Advertising," *Journal of Advertising*, 14, 18-24.

Chaiken, Shelley and Alice Eagley (1976), "Communication Modality as a Determinant of Message Persuasiveness and Message Comprehensibility," *Journal of Personality and Social Psychology*, 34, 605-614.

Edwardson, M., D. Grooms, and S. Proudlove (1981), "Television News Information Gain from Interesting Video vs. Talking Heads," *Journal of Broadcasting*, 25, 15-24.

Fiske, Susan T. and Shelley E. Taylor (1984), *Social Cognition*, New York: Random House.

Folkes, Valerie S. (1988), "Recent Attribution Research in Consumer Behavior: A Review and New Directions," *Journal of Consumer Research*, 14, 548-565.

Ford, Gary T. and Richard Yalch (1982), "Viewer Miscomprehension of Televised Communication—A Comment," *Journal of Marketing*, 46, 27-31.

Gates, Fliece R. (1986), "Further Comments on the Miscomprehension of Televised Advertisements," *Journal of Advertising*, 15, 4-9.

Gould, S.J. (1988), "Physician Professional Opinion Leadership and Physician Advertising: A Consumer View," *Journal of Health Care Marketing*, 8, 47-57.

Harris, R.J. (1977), "Comprehension of Pragmatic Implications in Advertising," *Journal of Applied Psychology*, 62, 603-608.

_____ and G.E. Monaco (1978), "Psychology of Pragmatic Implication: Information Processing Between the Lines," *Journal of Experimental Psychology: General*, 107, 1-22.

Hoyer, Wayne D. and Jacob Jacoby (1985), "The Public's Miscomprehension of Public Affairs Programming," *Journal of Broadcasting and Electronic Media*, 29, (4), 437-443.

_____, Rajendra K. Srivastava, and Jacob Jacoby (1984), "Sources of Miscomprehension in Television Advertising," *Journal of Advertising*, 13, (2), 17-25.

Hunter, John H. and Frank L. Schmidt (1990), *Methods of Meta-Analysis: Correcting Error and Bias in Research Findings*, Newbury Park, CA: Sage Publications.

Jacoby, Jacob and Wayne D. Hoyer (1982a), "Viewer Miscomprehension of Televised Communication: Selected Findings," *Journal of Marketing*, 46, 12-26.

_____ and _____ (1982b), "On Miscomprehending Televised Communication: A Rejoinder," *Journal of Marketing*, 46, 35-43.

_____ and _____ (1989), "The Comprehension/Miscomprehension of Print Communication: Selected findings," *Journal of Consumer Research* 15, 434-443.

_____ and _____ (1990), "The Miscomprehension of Mass-Media Advertising Claims: A Re-Analysis of Benchmark Data," *Journal of Advertising Research*, 29, (2), 9-16.

_____, _____, and M.R. Zimmer (1983), "To Read, View, Or Listen? A Cross-Media Comparison of Comprehension," *Current Issues and Research in Advertising*, 6, 201-217.

Lipstein, B. (1980), "Theories of Advertising and Measurement Systems," *Attitude Research Enters the 80's*, Chicago: American Marketing Association.

Mizerski, Richard W. (1982), "Viewer Miscomprhension Findings are Measurement Bound," *Journal of Marketing*, 46, 32-34.

_____, Linda L. Golden, and Jerome B. Kernan (1979), "The Attribution Process in Consumer Decision Making," *Journal of Consumer Research*, 6, 123-140.

Monaco, G.E. and D. Kaiser (1983), "Effects of Prior Preference, Inferences, and Believability in Consumer Advertising," in *Information Processing Research in Advertising*, R.J. Harris, ed., Hillsdale, N.J.: Erlbaum.

Morris, L.A., D. Brinberg, R. Klimberg, C. Rivera, and L.G. Millstein (1986), "Miscomprehension Rates for Prescription Drug Advertisements," *Current Issues and Research in Advertising*, 9, 93-117.

Neisser, Ulrich (1976), *Cognitive and Reality*, San Francisco: Freeman.

Preston, Ivan L. (1967), "Logic and Illogic in the Advertising Process, "*Journalism Quarterly*, 44, 231-239.

_____ and J.I. Richards (1986), "The Relationship of Miscomprehension to Deceptiveness in FTC Cases," in *Advances in Consumer Research*, R.J. Lutz, ed., 138-142.

Schmittlein, David C. and Donald G. Morrison (1983), "Measuring Miscomprehension for Televised Communications Using True-False Questions," *Journal of Consumer Research*, 10, 147-156.

Settle, Richard B. and Linda L. Golden (1974), "Attribution Theory and Advertiser Credibility," *Journal of Marketing Research*, 11, 181-185.

Behavioral Research Using Scanner Data

Amitava Chattopadhyay, McGill University
Stephen J. Hoch, University of Chicago
Glen Mayhew, Washington University
Scott A. Neslin, Dartmouth College
Emine Sarigollu, McGill University
Russell S. Winer, University of California-Berkeley

Behavioral research on consumer purchase/choice behavior has often relied on small samples, artificial settings, and measures of behavioral intent rather than actual behavior. Quantitative research on these topics have been criticized for not adequately incorporating behavioral constructs. The purpose of this session was to explore how scanner panel data provides a unique opportunity for consumer behavior researchers to examine a variety of questions in a context that, on the one hand, allows the use of actual field purchase data from a large sample and, on the other, enables the researcher to incorporate behavioral constructs of theoretical and practical importance.

The session consisted of three speakers followed by a discussant. The three speakers focused on very different topics. This is deliberate as our objective was to show the wide range of consumer behavior questions that can be addressed using scanner panel data. The discussant not only critiqued the research presented but built on this diverse range of topics and suggested broad directions for future research.

While the presentations dealt with widely divergent topics, it was clear from the presentations that research based on scanner panel data can contribute to consumer research in three ways: (1) focus on actual behavior rather than surrogate measures such as behavioral intent, (2) enhance external validity and (3) change the conversation.

Though each of the papers presented in the session contribute in all three ways, each paper contributes most strongly on a subset of the three dimensions. Hoch discusses a three-year project focusing on real-time, in-store pricing experiments. His discussion of six experiments that examine consumer's purchase behavior in response to several types of promotions as a function of the consumer characteristics of a store's trading area contribute towards enhancing the external validity of consumer promotion research on the one hand and, on the other, changing the conversation in research on consumer promotions.

The work of Mayhew and Winer focuses on the use of scanner panel data to determine how much consumers are willing to pay for an innovation in the category of frequently purchased nondurables. Their method provides an alternative to survey based methods currently used as inputs to pricing decisions. Thus this paper contributes most significantly in changing the conversation in the domain of research on pricing decisions.

Chattopadhyay, Sarigollu and Gorn focus on the relationship between advertising and sales. Their work extends traditional research in this area which models the link between ad exposure and sales with no regard for the nature of the advertising, by introducing characteristics of the ad in terms of both the mechanical aspects of the ad (e.g., did it involve a direct comparison) as well as consumers' evaluations of the ad (e.g., how persuasive was it considered). Their presentation described some initial findings from a programme of research designed to examine the relationship between the characteristics of advertisements and sales as a function of a variety of market and customer considerations. Thus this research contributes most significantly to a better understanding of advertising effects by focusing on behavior.

To summarize, the presentations provided some insights not only on specific issues in consumer behavior but, more importantly, showed the potential for using scanner data in examining diverse aspects of consumer behavior and contributing to traditional consumer research by enhancing external validity, focusing on behavior, and changing the conversation in specific research domains.

Summary of Special Session
Real-Time Ad Processing: Tracing Dynamic Responses
Douglas L. MacLachlan, University of Washington

Consumer researchers are taking increasing interest in the ways people respond to stimuli presented to them in dynamic fashion such as TV and radio commercials. The purpose of this special session was to demonstrate and encourage continuing research on the processing of dynamic stimuli. Both methodological and theoretical issues were addressed in the session's papers.

The first paper by Piet Vanden Abeele and Douglas MacLachlan, which is included in these proceedings, investigated with a new approach the reliability and validity of a method long used by researchers and practitioners, namely galvanic skin response (GSR). This is a sequel to an article forthcoming in JCR (Vanden Abeele and MacLachlan 1994).

The second paper, by Joel Cohen, Michel Tuan Pham, and David Hughes, used real-time measurement to test predictions of the Cohen and Areni (1991) model of affective responses to advertising. The model distinguishes three phases of affective responses involving increasing levels of affective-cognitive interaction. In the first two phases, affective responses are elicited automatically. In the third phase, affective responses result from elaborative interpretation, which involves the recruitment of additional knowledge. Depending on the kind of knowledge that is accessed during elaborative interpretation, phase-3 affective responses may differ in valence, intensity, and subjective experience from those elicited in the first two phases. Continuous affective responses to a commercial were recorded with a dial-turning instrument (DTI) developed by Hughes (1992) and validated by Pham, Hughes, and Cohen (1993). The commercial was expected to elicit primarily positive phase-1 and phase-2 affective responses. The knowledge accessible for elaborative interpretation was manipulated through a priming task administered in a purportedly unrelated study. The task involved reading and elaborating upon a short news article. A finding of the experiment that the priming manipulation had only local effects supports Cohen and Areni's propositions that (1) Phase-3 affective responses involve the recruitment of additional knowledge, and (2) phase-3 affective responses may differ in valence from spontaneously elicited phase-1 and phase-2 affective responses.

The third paper, by Dan Padgett, Hans Baumgartner, and Mita Sujan, investigated how viewers of television commercials integrate their moment-to-moment affective experiences into an overall emotional evaluation of the ad and Aad. The goal was to determine which characteristics of an extended sequence people use to form a global evaluation. Subjects used a computer based "feelings monitor" to chart their moment-to-moment emotional responses to 30 positive emotional ads, and then indicated their overall emotional reaction and Aad. Consistency of responses in the affect tracing task and the global evaluations allowed ad level analyses. The results revealed subjects use a combination of proxy moments (e.g., mean, peak experience, final moment), magnitude of the linear trend, and duration of the episode to form global evaluations of affective response and Aad. One implication of the findings is that ads which have a goal of liking should end on a high note and arrive there quickly. Also, longer ads have a better chance of eliciting stronger positive reactions than shorter ads, and the peak emotional experience should occur later rather than earlier in the ad.

The fourth paper, by Esther Thorson, examined the results of three studies that observed "cycling patterns" in over-time measures of either intensity or selectivity of attention to TV commercials, news and other programming. The selective attention measure involves videotaping subjects as they watch and analyzing the tapes to determine, for each half second, whether their eyes are oriented toward the TV screen or not. The studies found clear indications of an approximate 60-second cycle of high to low and back to high attention. Results can be interpreted as offering evidence for attention being guided by an internal cognitive model of the environment.

REFERENCES

Cohen, Joel B. and Charles B. Areni (1991), "Affect and Consumer Behavior," in Thomas S. Robertson and Harold H. Kassarjian (eds.), *Handbook of Consumer Behavior*, Englewood Cliffs, NJ: Prentice Hall, 188-240.

Hughes, G. David (1992), "Realtime Response Measures Redefine Advertising Wearout," *Journal of Advertising Research*, 32 (May/June), 61-77.

Vanden Abeele, Piet and Douglas L. MacLachlan (1994), "Process Tracing of Emotional Responses to TV Ads: Revisiting the Warmth Monitor," *Journal of Consumer Research*, 21 (March).

Pham, Michel Tuan, G. David Hughes, and Joel B. Cohen (1993), "Validating a Dial-Turning Instrument for Real-Time Measurement of Affective and Evaluative Responses to Advertising," Marketing Science Institute, Report No. 93-116 (October).

Process Tracing of Physiological Responses to Dynamic Commercial Stimuli

Piet Vanden Abeele, Catholic University of Leuven
Douglas L. MacLachlan, University of Washington

ABSTRACT

Real-time measures of responses to dynamic stimuli such as TV ads are enjoying a resurgence of interest among practitioners and researchers. This paper assesses the reliability and validity of one such measure, galvanic skin response (GSR) in a particular context. Using a different procedure for analyzing the data (i.e., sample average responses within 3-second intervals as the unit of analysis), we determined that GSR is a relatively reliable measure using adequate sample sizes, but that its convergent and discriminant validity in measuring attention is suspect. We conclude that it might be the *pattern* of response, rather than the level, that should be investigated.

INTRODUCTION

Physiological responses keep fascinating consumer researchers as single or as complementary measures of reactions to consumer stimuli (e.g., Kroeber-Riel 1979; Stewart and Furse 1982; Rothschild, Yong, Reeves, Thorson and Goldstein 1988; and Bagozzi 1991). Yet these measures have not to date proved to yield significant and/or easily applicable benefits to the consumer research community. Reasons for the limited success of these measures can be sought in (1) measurement deficiencies (e.g., lack of reliability of such measures as applied in typical marketing research settings), (2) deficiencies in the design of data collection and analysis, and (3) insufficient conceptualization and development of theory.

Although physiological responses are naturally recorded as continuous traces over time, other process tracing approaches involving dial-turning or pencil and paper tasks to measure cognitive and affective responses to dynamic stimuli have also been popular over the years. There is currently a revival of interest in process tracing measures and methods (e.g., Aaker, Stayman, and Hagerty 1986; Boyd and Hughes 1992; Vanden Abeele and MacLachlan 1994). This is a valuable development, because many marketing stimuli are dynamic and, as researchers, we need to understand how people react to such stimuli in real time. There are a number of interesting consumer research questions that might be investigated with continuous process tracing measures. For example, what is the impact of various kinds of dynamically presented stimuli on memory of an ad, on product evaluation, and so forth? Industry practice is ahead of academe in the use of such methods, going back more than fifty years (e.g., Peterman 1940). As academics, one of our roles is to provide basic research on the validity of methods and measures used in practical settings.

Process tracing research raises a number of issues, including (1) what traits to measure, (2) how to measure them, and (3) how to analyze such data. Although many of the process tracing measures require cognitive activity of the respondents in the recording of their reactions (e.g., Aaker et al.'s Warmth Monitor), *physiological* responses involve no cognitive mediation. The latter responses have appeal because of their autonomous, spontaneous, and uncontaminated character.

Our study focuses on a fairly straightforward (in measurement administration) and rather popular physiological measure - epidermal response, also called galvanic skin response (GSR). This measure is known to index physiological arousal and hence to be a potential indicator of the orienting reflex (Ohman 1979; Siddle and Spinks 1979). Orientation or attention is an important precondition for successful processing of externally presented information such as advertising. The attention-getting power of an ad (or specific elements in that ad) is one of the very basic responses of interest to marketers, especially when the target audience is in a situation of low-involvement.

Although a number of other physiological measures have been employed in psychology and consumer research, such as electroencephalographic (EEG) measures (see the debate in *Psychology and Marketing* reviewed by Cacioppo and Petty 1985), GSR has been one of the most used (Bagozzi 1991). However, the interest there has been typically non dynamic, i.e., examining response to a single, non continuous stimulation such as the fear aroused by the picture of an object. In our research we analyze GSR as a continuous response (a "process trace") rather than as a single reaction to a stimulus. The analysis strategy pursued here is to exploit the variances and covariances of measures as computed across commercial stimuli, where stimulus objects are the content of temporal segments of commercials. Although most previous research has looked at *individual* traces, we use the average (over sampled individuals) GSR value within segments of exposure time as the basic unit of analysis. By doing so we can, for example, compare response levels within ads (e.g., where is the peak located?), response levels across ads (e.g., which commercial produces the highest peak?), or response patterns across ads (e.g., does this ad's trace replicate that of another ad?).

Thus, the research reported here is a modest contribution to the literature on process tracing methods. We are examining one trait (attention or orienting response), with one method (GSR), and introduce one particular method of analysis (using the temporal segment as the basic unit of analysis).

RESEARCH ISSUES

The propositions under investigation in our study are the following:

P1: GSR produces reliable sample-average traces.

We propose that GSR reliability can be demonstrated for sample sizes that are of reasonable size for both practical application and consumer research.

P2: GSR is a valid process trace measure of attention or orienting response.

There are several sub propositions underlying this proposition: (1) We propose that traces will be sufficiently valid to distinguish real ad traces from neutral non-ad traces. (2) We propose that GSR correlations will not be affected by the nature of the task set (i.e., whether or not other measures are being taken concurrently). (3) We propose that GSR traces produced in response to commercials will be correlated with constructs theoretically linked to attention (e.g., attention-getting, to be described later). (4) We proposed that there will be appropriate correlation with exogenously assessed properties of temporal segments of ads (to be defined later). Finally, (5) we propose there should be a different response pattern to commercials of different character (e.g. ads selected to be "warm" versus "non warm" or "activating" versus "non activating").

METHOD

Subjects were final-year Belgian business administration undergraduates. The subjects were individually exposed to a videotape of TV commercials and other stimuli in the Consumer Research Lab at Catholic University of Leuven, Belgium. This lab was arranged as a living room in order to put subjects at ease during ad exposure and response measurement.

The treatment to which the respondents were exposed consisted of a videotape containing 12 real TV commercials and multiple insertions of four filler "bogus commercials". The twelve commercials were preselected to represent the extremes on two dimensions, Warmth and Activation, using the same procedure described in Aaker et al. for their dimensions of warmth, information, humor and irritation.

A pretest was performed on a comparable student sample (n=50) who were shown the commercials and asked to give overall ratings on two scales. One of the scales was for Warmth. The other scale was for Activation/Excitement (i.e., for stimulus-induced orienting response). Respondents evaluated 50 commercials, of which 12 were retained, namely three each for the following conditions: (1) high warmth, high activation (denoted WA), (2) high warmth, low activation (Wa), (3) low warmth, high activation (wA) and (4) low warmth, low activation (wa). These twelve ads thus constitute a form of orthogonal design within the study. The scores on warmth and on activation differed highly significantly between the chosen ads at each extreme of the scales; the average warmth and activation ratings of the commercials were nearly (but not perfectly) uncorrelated.

The four "bogus commercials" consisted of a "bouncing ball" animation. A bogus ad was shown after every real ad. This has the advantage not only of allowing us to record the GSR response to "nonsense" material, but also of letting the GSR trace stabilize between commercials. Four videotapes were put together, containing the same real commercials in systematically varied rotations.

Skin response was measured using the ZAK Biosystems EDA/S Module, recording electrodermal conductance at half-second intervals with electrodes affixed on the palms of the non dominant hand. The GSR data handling software is by INTERTEST (Netherlands) and ROGIL (Belgium).

The response to commercials was recorded under one of three conditions. Subjects in the first condition were administered simply the GSR measurement. They were told that we were interested in spontaneous responses to commercials as measured through physiological indexes. Subjects were given time to adjust to the task environment. When their GSR trace had stabilized, they were shown the tape containing the commercials. The sample size in this group was 21 respondents. The measurements obtained from this sample will be denoted as GSR(0), since no other concurrent measure was administered with the GSR.

Subjects in the second condition were given only the task described by Aaker et al., using the instructions for their Warmth Monitor (translated into Dutch). The sample size of this group was 14 respondents. The measures obtained from this group will be denoted as WM(0), since no GSR was administered concurrently.

In the third condition, subjects were given both tasks to perform simultaneously. The subject's dominant hand was assigned the Warmth Monitor task, whereas the non dominant hand was used for GSR measurement. The sample size for this condition was 30 subjects. Two measurements were thus provided by subjects in this condition, which will be denoted as WM(+) and as GSR(+), since in both cases the two measurements were carried out simultaneously.

ANALYSIS

The unit of observation in the study is a three-second segment of a commercial. Each individual's GSR and WM score corresponds to the maximum observed in the corresponding three-second segment. In the case of GSR, the segments have exactly a three second length, as the time axis is strictly controlled in the measurement. In the case of WM, the drawn trace was divided into as many equal sized segments as there were numbers of three-second intervals (i.e., a 30-second commercial would have 10 segments). Note that there may not be a perfect correspondence between real time and distance along the trace for the WM measure.

Temporal segments of all commercials were coded as zero-one dummy variables for a number of format, execution, and content characteristics. These were used as independent variables in one of the analyses to follow.

All individual responses were ipsatized within the respondent; i.e., they were standardized relative to the mean and standard deviation of the individual's GSR and WM responses, respectively. This removes individual differences in the sensitivity of respondents to the two measures (Ben-Shakhar 1985).

In what follows, comparisons are made and correlations computed based on average ipsatized responses (averaged over subjects) to 3-second commercial segments. The twelve real commercials together totaled 110 segments or 330 seconds of programming. The bogus commercials each lasted 10 segments or 30 seconds. For some analyses, we pooled the measures for GSR(0) and GSR(+) into a single series with 220 observations.

RESULTS

Reliability of GSR

Since we use the sample mean as a unit of analysis, reliability will depend on (1) the size of the sample of respondents, (2) the heterogeneity of respondents' reactions, and (3) the domain of variance considered (e.g., all ads or one ad). We base our assessment of reliability on split-sample (i.e., split-half) correlations. Since the error variance (i.e., the sampling variance of the mean GSR score) is known, the typical reliability formula could be used except for the fact that the error variance is heteroscedastic between commercial segments. The "average" reliability can only be computed if an "average" error variance is entered into the reliability formula. This difficulty is avoided if we (randomly) split the sample in half and compute two parallel series for the mean GSR score for each segment for each subsample. Next, we correlate these series and compute the split-half reliability corresponding to the actual sample size used in the study and estimate the sample size required for a given level of reliability, e.g. .90 (Nunnally, 1978). This gives the results shown in Table 1.

Our conclusion regarding reliability of GSR is that it is high enough at the practiced sample sizes for academic research. However, reliability of the measure seems too low to allow confident marketing decisions (e.g., to compare the strength of response at one moment in the ad to that of another). The reliabilities for GSR are still sufficient to carry out research, but they obviously limit the extent to which other variables can be found significantly correlated with GSR.

Validity of GSR

A first way to consider the issue of validity is to compare the responses to real ads with those to bogus ads. The data consist of sample-average 3-second segment GSR scores for bogus ads and also for three ads which run for a total of 10 segments, the same length as the bogus ads. The average GSR trace for both are

TABLE 1
Split-Sample Split-Half Reliability for GSR

Measure	n	Correlation between halves	Split-half R	n for R=.90
GSR(0)	21	.51	.68 [.60]	89.00
GSR(+)	30	.42	.60 [.64]	180.00

Note: The numbers between brackets are obtained when using the average sample-mean variance as an error variance estimate in the reliability formula; the reliability estimates computed on the (arbitrarily) split samples are generally quite close to these values. The "n for R=.90" is the sample size which would be needed for a reliability of .90.

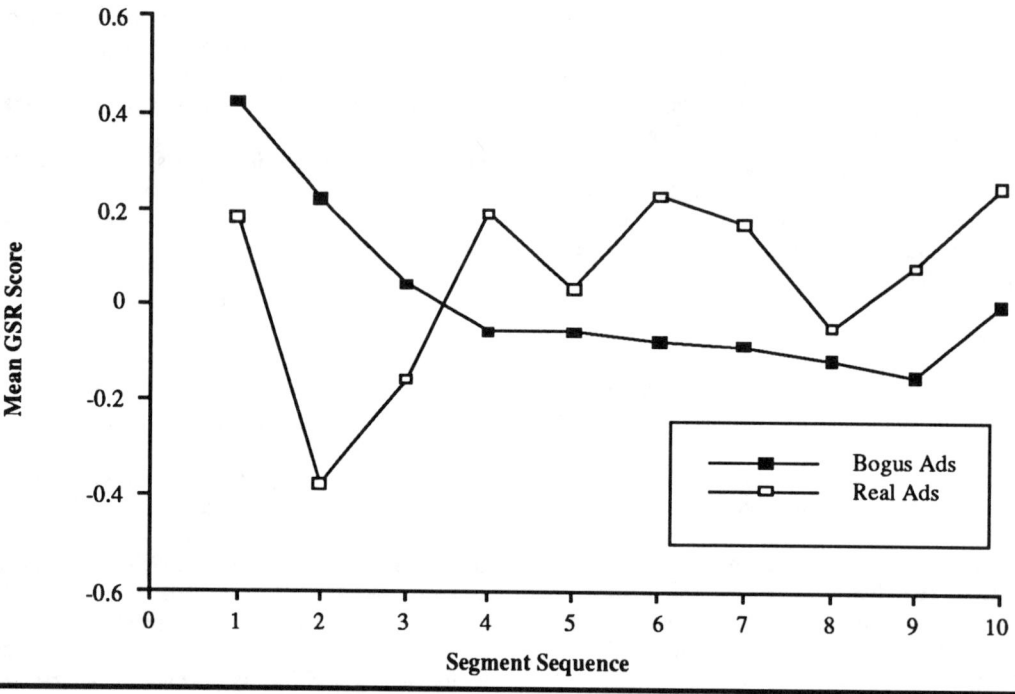

FIGURE 1
Average GSR Score for Bogus Ads and Three Real Ads vs Segment Sequence

portrayed graphically and analyzed by means of a two-way ANOVA. The factors are (1) the type of ad (real versus bogus) and (2) the sequence position of the segment in the commercial (1 through 10). If there is a difference between both GSR traces, this should become obvious in the significant interaction between ad type and segment sequence. A significant interaction implies that the trace differs according to type of ad. Figure 1 shows there is a clear difference in the pattern of GSR according to the type of ad. Each of these traces is of interest in itself, i.e., provides "norms" of the trace to an "average ad" (among the ads we selected) and for the trace to "non-ads". The real ads show a distinctive trace, whereas bogus ads show a typical habituation pattern. These visual conclusions are confirmed by the ANOVA results in Table 2.

From the ANOVA, the sequence effect is marginally significant and the interaction is highly significant.

In Table 3, which is a type of multi-trait, multi-method matrix, we see that GSR(+) and WM(+) are weakly, but significantly correlated at .213. This suggests that there exists a reactivity effect, since other cross-trait measures are not significantly correlated. Thus GSR measures are affected by task set and, to that extent, may not be valid measures when other constructs are being measured concurrently.

Aaker et al. (1986) used evidence that their Warmth Monitor measure (what we have designated WM(0 or +)) correlated with GSR to support their contention that the former is a valid measure, since they hypothesized a domain overlap between "warmth" and whatever is measured by GSR. Our Table 3 also examines GSR's concurrent validity with the warmth measure. However, the correlations between different measures are not significant, even after correcting for attenuation due to lack of reliability (except for the same-sample condition, which could be due to reactivity as noted above). We conclude that there is no strong evidence for concurrent validity of GSR with respect to warmth. On the other hand, this result may provide evidence for discriminant validity of the GSR measure.

We examined convergent validity of the GSR trace by correlating segment averages with another measure of attention-getting power, namely a paper-and-pencil Warmth Monitor-type measure, only specifically a monitor of attention-getting. The latter was administered to a separate sample of 20 students. The correlation

TABLE 2
Effect of Ad Type and Segment Sequence on GSR

Source	df	F-value	Pr>F
Ad type	1	1.77	.190
Segment sequence	9	2.00	.058
Interaction	9	3.29	.003

Note: Dependent variable: GSR(0); R-square: .50; F-value: 2.65; Pr>F(19,50): .0031.

TABLE 3
Correlations Over Measures and Task Sets

	GSR(0)	GSR(+)	WM(0)	WM(+)
GSR(0)	—	.830°	.060°	.100°
GSR(+)	.529 (p=.0001)	—	.070°	.280°
WM(0)	.046 (p=.637)	.052 (p=.588)	—	.910°
WM(+)	.083 (p=.390)	.213 (p=.025)	.825 (p=.0001)	—

Note: T = 110 segments; ° = correlations above the diagonal are corrected for attenuation due to unreliable measurement.

between GSR(0) and this attention-getting measure was 0.23 (p<.05). Although significant, the correlation is not high, thus not providing much evidence of convergent validity for GSR as a measure of attention-getting.

Since we had coded properties of commercial segments, we were able to see if GSR measures distinguished between attention-getting and non-attention-getting characteristics of the commercials. Construct validity of GSR would be supported if GSR were positively correlated with attention-getting characteristics, but were uncorrelated or negatively correlated with non-attention-getting properties.

Deciding whether the results for the segment characteristics offer supporting evidence for our proposition is difficult in the absence of a controlled experimental design. As an approximation to a hypothesis test, we consider the univariate correlations between judged attention-getting power of the segment characteristics and the sample-mean GSR response. An independent panel of judges, consisting of seven management school research assistants, was asked to consider each characteristic as well as the definition of the attention-getting response. They were then asked to predict for each characteristic whether they expected a significantly positive, neutral, or negative correlation with the attention-getting trace (i.e., what we have been calling the attention-getting counterpart to the WM measure); their responses were coded +1, 0, or -1, respectively. Each characteristic was then coded in terms of the sum of the judges' scores, which then could range from +7 to -7. This obviously crude assessment of the attention-getting nature of the segment properties of the ads is probably most valid near the endpoints of the scale, where most agreement occurs among the judges.

The characteristics, their judged attention-getting nature, and correlations with the GSR measure are shown in Table 4.

Because of the high correlation between GSR(+) and GSR(0) series, we pooled both series, to achieve a sample size of 220 observations instead of only 110 for each separate series. The table is divided according to whether the judges on balance agreed that the characteristics were "attention-getting" correlated or not. Only a couple of ad characteristics judged to be positively correlated with attention-getting actually were found to be positively correlated at significant levels. Indeed, several characteristics judged not attention-getting were found to be significantly correlated, only one negatively. Thus there is no real evidence for the construct validity of GSR as a measure of attention provided by this study.

Since several of the properties are not independent in the ads, to study the proposition further, we ran separate dummy-variable regressions with GSR as the dependent variable and with explanatory variables in three groups: ad condition (i.e. warmth/activation category), segment sequence (1st, 2nd, middle, next-to-last, last), and segment properties (specific coded characteristics of the ad execution). Finally, we added the WM measure as a possible covariate. Table 5 contains the adjusted R^2s achieved by adding each set of explanatory variables, in turn.

From Table 5 we see that there is a significant effect of segment position. The maximum variation in GSR that could possibly be explained is the reliability of GSR (either .60 or .68 from Table 1). Segment position explained 7% of the variation in GSR, whereas the numerous segment properties contributed only 12% more to explanation of variation. There was no obvious pattern to the significant coefficients of the segment content, format and execution properties, thus again giving no evidence of construct validity of GSR as a measure of attention. Finally, there was almost no variance explained by the addition of a WM variable, indicating no marginal overlap between the "warmth" construct and whatever is being measured by GSR.

As a final validation method, we examined how GSR differs under different conditions of ad activation and warmth. Figure 2 plots GSR for the four conditions implied by high or low activation

TABLE 4
Pairwise Correlations Between GSR Measure and Segment Properties

Segment Property	Attention Score*	Correlation with GSR	p-value (two-tailed)
Attention-getting			
Emotional experience**	+7	.08	.26
Props (e.g. cartoon fig.)**	+7	.00	.96
Protagonist laughing**	+5	.19	.001
Close-up	+5	.10	.14
Bodily movement	+5	-.09	.19
Three or more scenes	+5	.23	.001
Music**	+4	-.03	.63
Song**	+3	.04	.55
Three or more actors**	+2	-.11	.11
Verbal interaction**	+2	-.06	.34
Product demonstration	+1	.11	.08
Brandname superimp.	+1	.04	.59
Non-attention getting			
Offscreen voice	0	-.05	.51
Two actors**	0	.05	.48
One actor	-1	.00	.95
Two Scenes	-1	-.08	.22
Nonverb. frndly inter.	-1	.07	.30
Inform. text superimp	-1	.12	.08
Product & brand displ.	-2	.18	.01
Product displayed	-3	.13	.05
One scene	-4	-.16	.01
No person	-6	.03	.65

Note: T=220 because we pooled over GSR(+) and GSR(0). *Attention score is an agreement score among independent judges that elements of the ads would be attention-getting. **These properties were viewed by the same judges as being warmth-inducing.

TABLE 5
Regressions of GSR Score on Explanatory Variables

Variable	Adj. R^2
Ad Condition	0.00
Segment Position	0.07
Segment Properties	0.19
WM-dummy	0.20

Note: WM-dummy is defined as WM(+) when dependent variable is GSR(+) and zero elsewhere.

of the real ads and high or low warmth at 5 different points in the ad sequence.

Note that the horizontal axis variable is not continuous real time, but sequence position, from first segment to last. An ANOVA of the same data, Table 6, shows that there is a main (level) effect of activation, a segment sequence effect (as expected), different trace patterns across time for low vs. high warmth commercials, and a three-way interaction. Thus we see there is evidence for a different GSR response depending on type of ad, but only for activation, not warmth.

A number of other analyses of the GSR trace were conducted, including correlations with warmth and format/execution properties within particular ads and with lagged values of dependent and independent variables. However, all results of such analyses were uninformative or inconclusive.

CONCLUSION

A primary suggestion of this study is that the appropriate domain of variation for assessment of reliability and validity of GSR (and other process tracing measures) is across different small

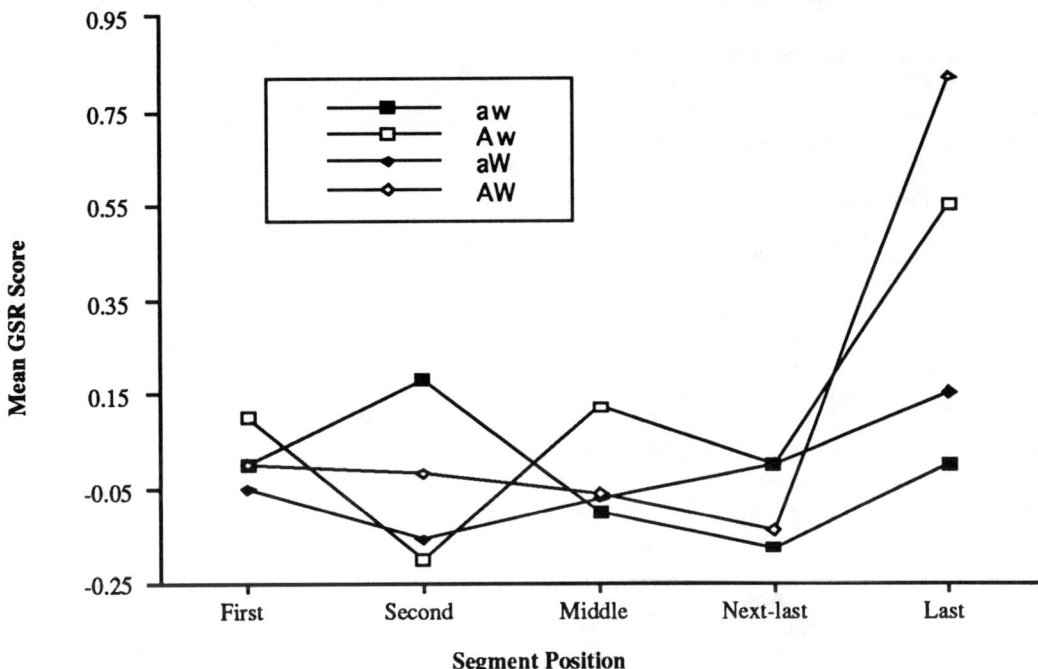

FIGURE 2
Average GSR Score in Activation-Warmth Condition vs. Sequence Position

Note: aw: low activation, low warmth; Aw: high activation, low warmth; aW: low activation, high warmth: AW: high activation, high warmth.

TABLE 6
Effect of Ad Activation, Warmth and Segment Position on GSR Measure

Source	DF	SS	F-value	Pr > F
Activation (A)	1	10.86	11.57	.0007
Warmth (W)	1	0.14	0.15	.6952
Segment Position (P)	4	53.03	14.20	.0001
A*W	1	0.17	0.18	.6715
A*P	4	22.08	5.88	.0001
W*P	4	5.40	1.44	.2189
A*W*P	4	9.28	2.47	.0428

Note: Dependent variable: GSR(0); R-square=.03; F(19,90); F=5.78; Pr>F=.0001.

segments of ads. For this purpose, we suggest that average ipsatized response of subjects within each such segment be the appropriate unit of analysis.

We conclude on the basis of this study that GSR is reliable enough for academic research. However, the GSR score, as we have measured it, does not exhibit evidence of being a valid measure of attention-getting response to dynamic characteristics of TV commercials. At least variation in it cannot be well explained by the variables we have considered in this study. Either we have not measured it well (although we have shown there is a core of systematic variance), or we do not have the right predictors (or have measured the predictors poorly).

An appealing alternative idea is that we should not be considering the level of the GSR trace as the dependent variable of interest, but rather the pattern of that trace. We did find significance of the segment sequence variable in the regressions and found significance of sequence and interaction with sequence in the ANOVAs of Tables 2 and 6.

Future research should be conducted comparing GSR with other attention-getting and similar responses to assess further the convergent and discriminant validity of the measure. But additionally, research should focus on the shape or pattern of the response over commercials.

REFERENCES

Aaker, David A., Douglas M. Stayman and Michael R. Hagerty (1986), "Warmth in Advertising: Measurement, Impact, and Sequence Effects," *Journal of Consumer Research*, 12 (March), 365-381.

Bagozzi, Richard P. (1991), "The Role of Psychophysiology in Consumer Research," in Thomas S. Robertson and Harold H Kassarjian (eds.) *Handbook of Consumer Behavior*, Englewood Cliffs, NJ: Prentice Hall, 124-161.

Ben-Shakhar, Gershon (1985), "Standardization Within Individuals: A Simple Method to Neutralize Individual Differences in Skin Conductance," *Psychophysiology*, 22 (3), 292-299.

Boyd, Thomas C. and G. David Hughes (1992), "Validating Realtime Response Measures," in *Advances in Consumer Research*, Vol. 19, ed. John F. Sherry, Jr. and Brian Sternthal, Provo, UT: Association for Consumer Research, 649-656.

Cacioppo, John T. and Richard E. Petty (1985), "Physiological Responses and Advertising Effects: Is the Cup Half Full or Half Empty?" *Psychology & Marketing*, 2 (Summer), 115-126.

Kroeber-Riel, Werner (1979), "Activation Research: Psychobiological Approaches in Consumer Research," *Journal of Consumer Research*, 5 (March), 240-250.

Nunnally, Jum C. (1978), *Psychometric Theory*. New York: McGraw-Hill, 2nd edition.

Ohman, A. (1979), "The Orienting Response, Attention and Learning: An Information Processing Perspective", in ed. H. D. Kimmel, E. H. van Olst and J. F. Orlebeke, *The Orienting Reflex in Humans*. Hillsdale, N.J.: Laurence Erlbaum, 443-471.

Peterman, J. N. (1940), "The Program Analyzer: A New Technique in Studying Liked and Disliked Items in Radio Programs," *Journal of Applied Psychology*, 24 (December), 728-741.

Rothschild, Michael L., J. Hyun Yong, Byron Reeves, Esther Thorson and Robert Goldstein (1988), "Hemispherically Lateralized EEG as a Response to Television Commercials," *Journal of Consumer Research*, 15 (September), 185-198.

Siddle, David A. T. and John A. Spinks (1979), "Orienting Response and Information Processing: Some Theoretical and Empirical Problems," in *The Orienting Reflex in Humans*, ed. H. D. Kimmel, E. H. van Olst and J. F. Orlebeke, Hillsdale, NJ: Erlbaum, 557-564.

Stewart, David W. and David H. Furse (1982), "Applying Psychophysiological Measures to Marketing and Advertising Research Problems," in *Current Issues and Research in Advertising*, ed. Janet H. Leigh and Claude R. Martin, Jr., 1-38.

Vanden Abeele, Piet and Douglas L. MacLachlan (1994), "Process Tracing of Emotional Responses to TV Ads: Revisiting the Warmth Monitor," *Journal of Consumer Research*, 20 March.

Research on the Phenomenon and Treatment of Addiction: A Multi-Disciplinary Perspective
Michal Ann Strahilevitz, University Of Illinois Urbana-Champaign

Perhaps one of the most controversial subjects examined in the consumer behavior literature is that of addiction. One of the reasons for the controversy may very well be the vast number of disciplines that have studied this topic. The purpose of this session was to present research on the topic of addiction from a variety of perspectives. Our panel included individuals with real world experience in the treatment of addiction as well as prominent researchers from a variety of disciplines (i.e., psychology, anthropology, and economics).

The first paper, presented by Drazen Prelec, discussed work he had done in collaboration with Richard Herrnstein, George Loewenstein, and William Vaughan. Several theories of addiction were discussed including *addiction as a disease, addiction as self medication, the primrose path,* and *the theory of the divided self.* The paper focused on the economic aspects of addiction and examined various diagnostic criteria for identifying potentially addictive commodities. By using learning experiments in a lab setting, the authors illustrated how subjects can be "lured" into making inferior choice patterns evocative of addiction. Based on the results, three diagnostic criteria for identifying commodities that are potentially addictive were inferred: (1) rate dependence (the value per single act of consumption interacts with the frequency of consumption), (2) side-effects (the commodity changes the satisfaction derived from other commodities), and (3) temporal bipolarity (the benefits of the activity are more immediate than its costs).

The second paper, by Michal Strahilevitz, focused on differences and similarities in the experiences and recovery processes of various addictions (i.e., drug addiction, alcoholism, and eating disorders). Based on interpretive material which included interviews with recovering addicts, this paper explored not only the addicts' experiences when engaging in their addictive behaviors, but their experiences when abstaining as well. Themes discussed included: (1) the role of "rock bottom" stories as reference points which stress the loss side of engaging in one's addiction, (2) the fact that many recovering addicts do not consider moderation to be an option, making the decision of how much to consume analogous to a binary choice task (abstain or self destruct), (3) the possibility that the sequential choice process for an addict may be quite different from that of a non-addict (i.e., many alcoholics/drug addicts/compulsive eaters report that saying no to the first drink/hit/bite is much easier than saying no to the second one), and (4) the role of support groups in both adding value to one's abstinence, and creating a sense of community.

The third author, John Sherry, discussed the treatment of alcohol and drug abuse problems from a social systems perspective. Sherry advocated taking a holistic approach to examining chemical dependency. Such an approach requires looking not only at the addict, but also at other structural stakeholders such as the addict's family, peer group, place of employment, treatment agency and voluntary associations, as well as the linkages between (and within) these institutions. Sherry encouraged the use of anthropological methods in studying the treatment of addiction and suggested that the researcher take on the role of "information broker," working in partnership with community psychologists and other key informants. Building on his own experience as a clinician in centers for the treatment of chemical dependency, he discussed some of the problems encountered in the medical world in dealing with alcohol and drug abuse. He illustrated how concepts such as *marketing mix, benefit delivery,* and *segmentation* could be directly applied to improving the service delivery in the treatment of chemical dependency.

Finally, Beth Hirschman (our discussant) shared her own insights on this topic, stressing the importance of further work in this area and reminding us that addictions are common among all classes and walks of life.

Need for Cognition and the Effects of Repeated Expression on Attitude Accessibility and Extremity

Stephen M. Smith, North Georgia College
Curtis P. Haugtvedt, Ohio State University
Richard E. Petty, Ohio State University

ABSTRACT

An abundance of empirical data supports the notion that an attitude's accessibility is a key determinant of the attitude's likelihood of influencing judgment and behavior (see Fazio, forthcoming, for a review). Repeated expression of an attitude has been shown to enhance attitude accessibility, but recent findings suggest that attitude polarization is another possible consequence of this procedure. We conducted a study to determine if these polarization and accessibility effects might be partially mediated by increases in attitude-relevant thought. Consistent with this reasoning, subjects high in their need for cognition (NFC) showed both greater polarization and greater accessibility increases than did low NFC subjects.

INTRODUCTION

Fazio (1986, 1989) has presented a comprehensive view of the role of attitudes in guiding behavior. Fazio defines *attitudes* as object-evaluation associations in memory, and proposes that the primary determinant of whether an attitude will affect behavior is the strength of this object-evaluation association. Attitude strength is thus explicitly defined as the likelihood of attitude activation upon confronting the attitude object. An impressive accumulation of research has supported Fazio's suggestions that attitudes can be automatically activated (e.g., Bargh, Chaiken, Govender and Pratto 1992; Fazio, Sanbonmatsu, Powell and Kardes 1986), that highly accessibile attitudes are more likely to influence judgment and behavior than are less accessible ones (e.g., Fazio, Powell and Williams 1989; Fazio and Williams 1986), and even that highly accessible attitudes provide some adaptive advantages (e.g., Blascovich, Ernst, Tomaka, Kelsey, Salomon and Fazio 1993).

In order to establish the key role of accessibility *per se* in guiding judgment and behavior, and to identify its potential causes, Fazio and colleagues have frequently attempted direct manipulations of attitude accessibility (e.g., Fazio, Chen, McDonel and Sherman 1982). These manipulations have typically involved having subjects express their attitudes repeatedly (e.g., Fazio et al. 1982; Powell and Fazio 1984) and have been successful in that repeated expression shortens response latencies to subsequent attitudinal inquiries and increases the likelihood of automatic activation of the attitude.

These manipulations supposedly affect only attitude accessibility, and leave other aspects of the attitude unchanged. This assumption is critical, since accessibility has been shown to covary with other attitudinal factors (see Raden 1985) that are also hypothesized to reflect strength. If any factor other than accessibility is being manipulated by repeated expression of the attitude, then accessibility cannot be flatly asserted to be the primary causal influence on subsequent judgment and behavior unless the confounding factors are controlled (e.g., as Fazio has done with attitude extremity). It may be that accessibility is but one correlate of the underlying construct of attitude strength, perhaps being a likely consequence rather than a cause of strength.

The assumption that repeated expression affects only an attitude's accessibility has recently come under fire. In a series of experiments, Downing, Judd and Brauer (1992) demonstrated that repeated expression affects the extremity as well as the accessibility of people's attitudes. In their first study, Downing et al. (1992) found increased accessibility and extremity as a function of repeated expression of attitudes on forced-choice, dichotomous response scales. A second study found similar effects of repeated expression on attitudes that were stated aloud in subjects' own words, purportedly free of any constraints. A third study employed nonevaluative responses (i.e., subjects were asked to identify the hues of a number of color ideographs), and found that these responses became more extreme as the number of expressions increased.

The results from Downing et al. (1992) suggest that repeated expression causes subjects to become more extreme in their attitudinal (and nonattitudinal) judgments. Although their results are provocative, they are not without alternative interpretations. First, as noted by Fazio (forthcoming), the dichotomous format used in study 1 removed the possibility of a neutral response. He argues that repeated expression will only change the attitudes of people who are initially neutral and are forced to take a position. Second, the oral response format in study 2 was perhaps not quite so free of constraints as the authors might have it. Fazio (forthcoming) suggests that social norms against repeating oneself over and over again may pressure subjects into varying their responses. Thus, a compelling demonstration that repeated expression can lead to more extreme attitudes must control for these alternative possibilities.

Why would repeated expression lead to more extreme attitudes, anyway? Downing et al. (1992) favor an associative learning model, arguing that the language associated with scale endpoints becomes more strongly associated with the object of judgment. However, an alternative process (also suggested by Downing and his associates) is implied by the work of Tesser and his colleagues (e.g., Tesser 1978; Tesser and Leone 1977; Tesser, Martin and Mendolia, forthcoming). Specifically, it can be hypothesized that repeated attitude expression will often prompt increased thought about the attitude object. Increased thought induces people to increase the evaluative consistency of attributes associated with the object, which polarizes attitudinal judgments (cf. Tesser 1978). Since increased thought about the object's attributes will almost necessarily include additional activation of the object-evaluation link, this process would also be expected to increase attitude accessibility. In the absence of increased thought, repeated expression would still lead to increased accessibility of object-evaluation associations, but might not lead to increased polarization. However, repeated expression paired with increased thought should lead to greater accessibility than repeated expression alone.

An interesting extension of the above reasoning is that situational and individual differences in people's ability or inclination to engage in extended thought about their attitudinal judgments would be likely to moderate the relationship between repeated expression and both extremity and accessibility. For example, if people receive attitudinal inquiries on a variety of unrelated topics in close temporal proximity (as is often the case in repeated expression formats), their ability to think extensively about any given topic is probably minimal. Elaborating on the object of a prior attitudinal inquiry will likely interfere with responses to subsequent questions about unrelated objects. However, if the inquiries are focused on highly related topics, and/or if subjects are given sufficient time between inquiries to ponder their attitudes, thought-induced polarization would be more likely to occur.

Differences in motivation to elaborate should also be important. For example, research suggests that individuals high in their need for cognition (NFC; Cacioppo and Petty 1982) are more likely to generate inferences (e.g., Stayman and Kardes 1992, Study 1) and elaborations (e.g., Cacioppo, Petty, Kao and Rodriguez 1986) in response to persuasive messages than are those low in NFC. Hence, subjects high in need for cognition should be more likely to think extensively about their attitudes than those low in this trait, assuming that the situation allows for a modicum of such elaboration. This would lead to predictable individual differences in the extent to which repeated expression leads to increased accessibility and extremity. Based on the above logic, we designed an experiment to test the following hypotheses:

H1: Attitudes will become more extreme when repeated expressions are called for;

H2: The above effect on polarization will be more pronounced for high NFC subjects than for low NFC subjects, resulting in a 2-way interaction between NFC and time of assessment;

H3: Attitudes will also become more accessible across repeated expressions;

H4: The above accessibility effect will be more pronounced for high NFC subjects than for low NFC subjects, resulting in a 2-way interaction between NFC and time of assessment;

H5: High NFC subjects will generate more elaborations during the interim between attitude assessments than will low NFC subjects; and

H6: The number of elaborations generated will predict the amount of increase in attitudinal extremity and accessibility.

The hypotheses were tested in a simple 2 X 2 design. Subjects, who were classsified as either low or high in NFC on the basis of a median split, privately expressed their attitudes toward recycling at two junctures. The two administrations were approximately 4.5 mins. apart, and attitudes were assessed on four nine-point scales. This methodology (i.e., the use of private expression on multi-response scales) avoids some of the interpretational problems stemming from the use of public expression and dichotomous scales in Downing et al.'s (1992) design. In addition, the questions intervening between the first and second attitudinal inquiries were related to recycling (i.e., they were about pro-environmental behavior in general) and thus would be unlikely to interfere if subjects wished to continue thinking about this topic.

METHOD

Subjects. Subjects were 189 undergraduates at a large midwestern university, who participated for extra credit in a marketing course. They participated in groups of 2 to 5.

Procedure. Subjects were seated in front of MacIIsi computers with color monitors. All questions appeared on the monitor, and responses were taken on Apple Extended keyboards. It was made clear to subjects that they were to respond as *quickly and accurately as possible* to each question. They were first asked to respond to a number of filler items (assessing, e.g., their fear of computers, on 9-point scales) to acquaint them with the computer and the response procedures.

The first set of attitudinal inquiries followed the practice items. Subjects were asked to respond, on 9-point scales with endpoints labeled "1=*strongly disagree*" and "9=*strongly agree*," to the following questions:

1. Recycling is Good
2. Recycling is Foolish
3. Recycling is Desirable
4. Recycling is Valuable

After responding to the four recycling questions, subjects proceeded to answer a series of 58 questions about pro-environmentalism in general.[1] Some examples include, "When I engage in pro-environmental action, I feel like a sucker," "The goal of saving the environment is reachable," "Pro-environmental behavior is too time-consuming," and "Most people are concerned about the environment." Half of these items asked for responses on continuous, 9-point scales (endpoints were the same as for the attitude items); the other half asked for responses on dichotomous ("yes"/"no") scales. In addition, half of the items were framed such that affirmative responses were relatively pro-environmental (e.g., "When I imagine myself engaging in pro-environmental behavior, I feel good"), and half were worded so that affirmative responses were relatively anti-environmental (e.g., "Most people say they will engage in pro-environmental behavior, but don't really intend to do so.").

Next came the second set of attitudinal inquiries on recycling (T2), which were identical to the first set. On average, there was a 4.5 min. gap between the first and second sets of recycling questions, with a range of 2.5 to 8.5 minutes (s.d.=1 minute). NFC scores were negatively correlated with the elapsed time between sets ($r=-.20$, $p<.01$). One way of viewing this result is that, across the 58 intervening questions, high NFC subjects had more accessible attitudes than did low NFC subjects.

After completing the second attitude assessment, subjects responded to a number of questions irrelevant to the present study, then completed the need for cognition scale (short form; Cacioppo, Petty and Kao 1984). Finally, subjects were asked to write on a sheet of paper whatever thoughts they had about recycling while they were doing the experiment.

RESULTS AND DISCUSSION

The first four hypotheses were tested primarily by two repeated measures analyses of variance. A median split was performed on subjects' NFC scores ($M=64.6$) and subjects' placement in this split represented an independent variable in both analyses. The four attitude measures were reasonably interrelated at both administrations ($\alpha=.84$ at Time 1, $\alpha=.85$ at Time 2) and were averaged to form our T1 and T2 attitude measures.[2] The first repeated measures analysis was a 2 (Need for Cognition: Low vs. High) X 2 (Attitude, T1 vs. T2) ANOVA to assess H1 and H2.

The first hypothesis was that repeated expression would lead to greater attitude polarization, as measured by differences between

---

[1] Subjects also completed a brief task involving selective exposure to some pro-environmental or anti-environmental statements. This intervening task did not interact with any of our dependent measures.

[2] The item "recycling is foolish" was reversed prior to averaging to make it directionally compatible with the other measures.

TABLE 1
Average Attitude Responses at T1 and T2, Average Response Latencies at T1 and T2, Total Number of Elaborations, and Correlations Between Accessibility Increases and Attitude Polarization for Subjects Low or High in Their Need for Cognition

	Low Need for Cognition (N=96)	High Need for Cognition (N=93)	Significance of NFC Difference
T1 Attitudes	6.66	6.70	$F = 0.01$
(s.d.)	(3.15)	(3.17)	
T2 Attitudes	6.89	7.71	$F = 3.90**$
(s.d.)	(3.10)	(2.53)	
T1 Accessibility in seconds	4.32	4.10	$F = 0.70$
(s.d.)	(1.84)	(1.71)	
T2 Accessibility in seconds	3.47	2.87	$F = 7.92***$
(s.d.)	(1.68)	(1.19)	
Number of Elaborations	4.84	5.29	$t = 1.35*$
(s.d.)	(2.02)	(2.38)	
Correlation Between Accessibility Increase and Attitude Polarization	$r = .01$	$r = .23**$	$z = 1.52$

* $p < .10$
** $p < .05$
*** $p < .01$

the first (T1) and second (T2) attitude measures. The analysis indicated a significant effect of the repeated variable, $F=6.66$, $p<.05$, supporting H1. As can be seen in Table 1, attitudes were more positive at T2 than at T1. The interaction between NFC and the repeated measure predicted by H2 was only marginal, $F=2.53$, $p=.11$, but the pattern of means is consistent with our hypothesis. The attitudes of low NFC and high NFC subjects were virtually identical at T1 ($F<1$), but the attitudes of high NFC subjects were significantly more positive at T2 than were those of low NFC subjects, $F=3.90$, $p<.05$.

As recommended by Fazio (1990), subjects' response latencies to the four attitude measures at T1 and T2 were submitted to logarithmic transformations prior to averaging. These measures were reasonably reliable ($\alpha=.70$ at T1, $\alpha=.74$ at T2) and were averaged for subsequent analysis. A 2 (NFC: Low vs. High) X 2 (Accessibility: T1 vs. T2) repeated measures ANOVA revealed a main effect of the repeated variable, $F=106.17$, $p<.001$, supporting H3. As can be seen in Table 1, attitudinal responses were more rapid at T2 than at T1.[3] A main effect of NFC also emerged, $F=5.45$, $p<.03$, and indicated that high NFC subjects responded to the attitudinal probes more rapidly than did low NFC subjects. These effects were qualified by a significant NFC by Time (repeated) interaction, $F=4.73$, $p<.05$. Results strongly supported H4, as attitude accessibility was essentially equal at T1, $F<1$, but high NFC subjects responded more rapidly than did low NFC subjects at T2, $F=8.66$, $p<.01$.

Hypothesis 5 was tested by a one-tailed t test comparing the total number of elaborations generated by high vs. low NFC subjects (subjects' elaborations were largely positive and hence were not coded for valence). This comparison was marginally significant, $t=1.35$, $p<.09$ (see Table 1). As expected, high NFC subjects listed more elaborations than did low NFC subjects. Hypothesis 6 suggests that this difference in elaborations should also predict differences in attitude polarization and increased accessibility. To test this hypothesis, we first created change scores for attitudes and response latencies by subtracting T1 attitudes from T2 attitudes, and subtracting T2 latencies from T1 latencies. We then calculated correlations between these two indexes and subjects' total number of elaborations.[4] This analysis revealed negligible correlations, both across all subjects and when calculated within levels of NFC (all rs less than .10).

Downing et al. (1992) reported moderate correlations between subjects' increases in accessibility and the extent to which they exhibited attitude polarization. Consistent with their results, the comparable correlation was modest but significant in our sample, $r(189)=.14$, $p<.05$. Interestingly, this correlation was stronger for high NFC subjects, $r(93)=.23$, $p<.03$, than for low NFC subjects, $r(96)=.01$, n.s. (although this difference was nonsignificant, $z=1.52$, $p=.12$, two-tailed). Since low NFC subjects' attitudes did not change much from T1 to T2, it is not surprising that the two variables were uncorrelated (i.e., range restrictions in this variable make it unlikely that it will correlate with other variables). How-

---

[3] The original means are reported in Table 1. These reactions times are much longer than is typically reported in the attitude accessibility literature, and reflect our use of 9-point response scales in lieu of dichotomous choice items.

[4] In conceptual terms, attitude change and polarization are quite different. However, only 11 subjects held recycling attitudes that were below the scale midpoint, so the change scores essentially represent the same thing. Further, excluding the anti-recycling subjects did not alter the pattern of results in any significant way.

ever, the significant accessibility-extremity correlation for high NFC subjects suggests that different processes may mediate the increased accessibility demonstrated by low and high NFC subjects as a function of repeated attitude expression. It may be that low NFC subjects are gaining in accessibility strictly through the process outlined by Fazio's model. Specifically, their single rehearsal of the object-evaluation association may strengthen this link, leading to faster responses to attitudinal inquiries at T2.

Subjects high in their need for cognition, while also demonstrating an increase in accessibility as a result of the simple rehearsal process suggested by Fazio, may also continue to elaborate on the attitude. This extended elaboration not only strengthens the object-evaluation link, but other associative connections as well (such as those between different attributes of the object; cf. Haugtvedt and Petty 1992; Tesser 1978). As a result, the high NFC subjects get an additional "boost" in attitude accessibility, and their attitudes tend to polarize. Although our data did not provide any direct support for this proposed process, this may be due to weaknesses in our design. For example, our elaborations data were collected at the end of the experiment, several minutes after the second attitude assessment. Many of the thoughts that subjects had during the period between attitude assessments may have no longer been available at this point, as memory traces decayed over time. In addition, although most of the elaborations subjects generated were positive, greater specificity could be obtained by calculating the net positivity of these elaborations, or by analyzing separately those elaborations focused on specific recycling questions and those that reflected attempts to relate the questions to one another (e.g., Meyers-Levy 1991).

The present results replicate and extend earlier findings by Fazio and his colleagues (e.g., Powell and Fazio 1984) and the findings that repeated expression of an attitude increases the attitude's accessibility. We extended this result by demonstrating that the repeated expression effect is somewhat stronger for subjects high in their need for cognition. Second, we have replicated the finding that increased accessibility can sometimes be accompanied by attitude polarization. This result was also found to apply more strongly to subjects high in need for cognition. These results suggest that repeated expression of an attitude may lead to a more complex process than a simple rehearsal of the object-evaluation link, especially for people who enjoy thinking.

REFERENCES

Bargh, John A., Shelly Chaiken, Rajen Govender, and Felicia Pratto (1992), "The Generality of the Automatic Activation Effect," *Journal of Personality and Social Psychology*, 62, 893-912.

Blascovich, Jim, John M. Ernst, Joe Tomaka, Robert M. Kelsey, Kristen L. Salomon, and Russell H. Fazio (1993), "Attitude Accessibility as a Moderator of Autonomic Reactivity During Decision Making," *Journal of Personality and Social Psychology*, 64, 165-176.

Cacioppo, John T., and Richard E. Petty (1982), "The Need For Cognition," *Journal of Personality and Social Psychology*, 42, 116-131.

_____, _____, and Chuan F. Kao (1984), "The Efficient Assessment of Need for Cognition," *Journal of Personality Assessment*, 48, 306-307.

Downing, James W., Charles M. Judd, and Markus Brauer (1992), "Effects of Repeated Expressions on Attitude Extremity," *Journal of Personality and Social Psychology*, 63, 17-29.

Fazio, Russell H. (1986), "How Do Attitudes Guide Behavior?," *The Handbook of Motivation and Cognition: Foundations of Social Behavior*, Eds. Richard M. Sorrentino and E. Tory Higgins, New York: Guilford Press, pp. 204-243.

_____ (1989), "On the Power and Functionality of Attitudes: The Role of Attitude Accessibility," *Attitude Structure and Function*, Eds. Anthony R. Pratkanis, Steven J. Breckler, and Anthony G. Greenwald, Hillsdale, NJ: Erlbaum, pp. 153-179.

_____ (1990), "A Practical Guide to the Use of Response Latency in Social Psychological Research," *Review of Personality and Social Psychology*, Eds. Clyde Hendrick and Margaret S. Clark, pp. 74-97.

_____ (forthcoming), "Attitudes as Object-Evaluation Associations: Determinants, Consequences, and Correlates of Attitude Accessibility," *Attitude Strength: Antecedents and Consequences*, Eds. Richard E. Petty and Jon A. Krosnick, Hillsdale, NJ: Erlbaum.

_____, Jeaw-Mei Chen, Elizabeth C. McDonel, and Steven J. Sherman (1982), "Attitude Accessibility, Attitude-Behavior Consistency, and the Strength of the Object-Evaluation Association," *Journal of Experimental Social Psychology*, 18, 339-357.

_____, Martha C. Powell, and Carol J. Williams (1989), "The Role of Attitude Accessibility in the Attitude-To-Behavior Process," *Journal of Consumer Research*, 16, 280-288.

_____, David M. Sanbonmatsu, Martha C. Powell, and Frank R. Kardes (1986), "On the Automatic Activation of Attitudes," *Journal of Personality and Social Psychology*, 50, 229-238.

_____, and Carol J. Williams (1986), "Attitude Accessibility as a Moderator of the Attitude-Perception and Attitude-Behavior Relations: An Investigation of the 1984 Presidential Election," *Journal of Personality and Social Psychology*, 51, 505-514.

Haugtvedt, Curtis P., and Richard E. Petty (1992), "Personality and Persuasion: Need for Cognition Moderates the Persistence and Resistance of Attitude Changes," *Journal of Personality and Social Psychology*, 62, 308-319.

Meyers-Levy, Joan (1991), "Elaborating on Elaboration: The Distinction between Relational and Item-Specific Elaboration," *Journal of Consumer Research*, 18, 358-367.

Powell, Martha C., and Russell H. Fazio (1984), "Attitude Accessibility as a Function of Repeated Attitudinal Expression," *Personality and Social Psychology Bulletin*, 10, 139-148.

Raden, David (1985), "Strength-Related Attitude Dimensions," *Social Psychology Quarterly*, 48, 312-330.

Stayman, Douglas M., and Frank R. Kardes (1992), "Spontaneous Inference Processes in Advertising: Effects of Need for Cognition and Self-Monitoring on Inference Generation and Utilization," *Journal of Consumer Psychology*, 1, 125-142.

Tesser, Abraham (1978), "Self-Generated Attitude Change," *Advances in Experimental Social Psychology*, Ed. Leonard Berkowitz, San Diego, CA: Academic Press, v. 11, pp. 289-338.

_____, and Chris Leone (1977), "Cognitive Schemas and Thought as Determinants of Attitude Change," *Journal of Experimental Social Psychology*, 13, 340-356.

_____, Leonard L. Martin, and Marilynn Mendolia (forthcoming), "The Role of Thought in Changing Attitude Strength," *Attitude Strength: Antecedents and Consequences*, Eds. Richard E. Petty and Jon A. Krosnick, Hillsdale, NJ: Erlbaum.

Evidence of a Relationship Between Need for Cognition and Chronological Age: Implications for Persuasion in Consumer Research

Harlan Spotts, Northeastern University

ABSTRACT

Originally developed in the persuasion literature by social psychologists, the need for cognition construct has received much interest from researchers in a variety of disciplines. Need for cognition has recently become a topic of interest among consumer researchers examining advertising effects. The research presented in this paper provides evidence of a potential interactive relationship between the primary variables in the ELM that control route to persuasion. Specifically, age-related declines in cognitive ability affect the motivational variable, need for cognition. This points to the possibility that need for cognition may be a dynamic factor that changes over time with respect to age-related cognitive processing changes. Implications for future research in information processing and persuasion are discussed.

INTRODUCTION

Consumer researchers have recently shown increased interest in the construct of need for cognition and its impact on marketing communications within an advertising context. Need for cognition refers to a person's desire to engage in and enjoy effortful cognitive processing, or thinking. The construct has significant effect on the persuasion process as detailed by the Elaboration Likelihood Model (ELM, Petty and Cacioppo 1986).

While age-related issues in consumer research have received less scrutiny, numerous researchers have studied the impact of chronological age on consumer behavior and information processing. Aging has been shown to impact shopping behavior (Lumpkin 1985), information usage (Bearden and Mason 1979, Cole and Houston 1987), and media behavior (Rubin 1986, Davis and French 1989).

Gerontological research has studied the cognitive processing changes that occur with age. Older adults (over the age of 60) appear to have deficits in memory performance, constraints on cognitive resources used in attentional processes, difficulty in discriminating relevant from irrelevant stimuli, and, are slower in learning new information.

Taken together, findings from consumer research and gerontology indicate a potential inverse relationship between need for cognition and chronological age. After a brief review of need for cognition and gerontological research on cognitive processing, two studies are reported that specifically examine the need for cognition and aging relationship. Implications of this relationship on the persuasion process and potential research propositions are then discussed.

LITERATURE REVIEW

Need for Cognition

Drawing from the work of Cohen (1957) and Cohen, Stotland and Wolfe (1955), Cacioppo and Petty (1982) redefined and developed need for cognition as an individual difference variable affecting the persuasion process. Need for cognition reflects an "...individual's tendency to engage in and enjoy effortful cognitive endeavors..."(Cacioppo, Petty and Kao 1984). A series of studies by Cacioppo and Petty (1982; Cacioppo, Petty and Morris 1983, Cacioppo, Petty and Kao 1984, Cacioppo, Petty, Kao and Rodriguez 1986) developed an 18 item scale for assessing a person's need for cognition. Individuals who score high in need for cognition like effortful thinking, such as solving puzzles, extensive deliberation, and thinking abstractly. Those individuals who are low in need for cognition avoid effortful thinking.

In the context of the ELM, need for cognition was developed as an individual difference variable potentially affecting a person's motivation to process persuasive communication. Individuals high in need for cognition are more likely to attend to message argument quality than individuals low in need for cognition (Cacioppo, Petty and Kao 1983); and, exhibit more extensive issue-relevant thinking and stronger attitude-behavior relationships (Cacioppo, Petty, Kao and Rodriguez 1986). Low need for cognition individuals are more likely to engage in peripheral (heuristic) processing than central (systematic) processing (Axsom, Yates and Chaiken 1987).

Need for Cognition and Consumer Research. Using advertising stimuli, Haugtvedt, Petty, Cacioppo and Steidley (1988) replicated the results of earlier need for cognition studies conducted in other disciplines. Not only were attitudes of high need for cognition individuals primarily influenced by strong message arguments, but attitudes of those low in need for cognition were primarily influenced by product endorser attractiveness. These findings were later supported by other researchers (Batra and Stayman 1990, Haugtvedt, Petty and Cacioppo, 1992).

Further studies indicated that attitudes developed by high need for cognition individuals are more persistent than those developed by low need for cognition individuals (Haugtvedt and Petty, 1989). It has also been shown that message content has a moderating effect on message judgments, with more favorable judgments of factual messages observed as need for cognition increases (Venkatraman, Marlino, Kardes and Sklar 1990). Need for cognition had no impact on judgments of evaluative messages.

Additional effects of need for cognition on attitude formation and change processes existed under the following conditions (Haugtvedt, Petty and Cacioppo, 1992): when people are not explicitly told to evaluate the message, and, when people are exposed to relatively short messages in both paced and self-paced situations. Stayman and Kardes (1992) examined memory recall behavior under conditions of implicit and explicit advertising claims. Need for cognition was found to have an impact on retrieval processes under conditions of implicit advertising claims, with recall scores similar to those subjects given explicit advertising claims.

Thus, it becomes clear that need for cognition impacts the processing of information in persuasive messages. It appears to be a factor affecting a person's motivation to process, and in turn, the route to persuasion employed. Given the composition of subjects used in prior research (i.e., primarily young, college-age adults), it seems logical to question the nature of need for cognition in the noncollege, adult population. Is need for cognition a stable personality trait, assumed not to change across lifespan? Or, is it a dynamic construct that varies over time within the individual during different life situations and ages? Little research has focused on changes in a person's level of need for cognition as they age. The next section reviews cognitive processing research in gerontology relevant to this issue.

Gerontological Research in Cognitive Processing

A plethora of research findings have documented a decrease in certain processing abilities as one gets older. Deficits have been found in attentional processes (Hasher and Zacks 1979), memory (Craik 1977), problem solving (Reese and Rodeheaver 1985), and learning (Arenberg and Robinson-Tchabo 1977). It has been acknowledged that older adults tend to slow down in terms of processing time (Hoyer and Plude 1980, Birren Woods and Williams 1980) and utilize less information (Johnson 1990). One explanation for these deficits is related to constraints in cognitive processing resources, which affect the attentional capacity of the older adult (Hasher and Zacks, 1979), alter the available capacity of working memory for cognitive elaboration, and/or affect speed of processing (Salthouse, 1988a).

Hasher and Zacks (1979) proposed a framework that suggested attentional capacity affects the type of processing in which adults engage. The more attentional capacity available for cognitive processing, the more likely it is a person will engage in "effortful" cognitive processes. These types of processes include rehearsal of information and elaborative mnemonic activities requiring excessive attentional capacity that drain resources away from other cognitive operations. The framework differentiates effortful processing with "automatic" processing. The latter are cognitive operations that require little attentional capacity; such as, encoding temporal or frequency of occurrence information, or, activities that were originally effortful, but due to repeated practice require little thought to conduct.

It appears to be evident that age-related changes affect the cognitive capacity of older adults. Salthouse (1988b) conceptualized these limitations in three distinct ways. If cognitive processing occurs through the activation of various nodes in memory, then capacity could be constrained through a decrease in the number of simultaneously active nodes (a reduction in working memory). A second alternative relates to the total number of nodes available for activation at any given time (a reduction in attentional capacity). Finally, the rate at which nodes are activated may slowdown, thus increasing the time required to transmit information (a speed of processing decrement).

To this point in the discussion it seems clear that the consequences of aging on cognitive processing would affect the "ability" variable in the persuasion process as delineated by the ELM. In this context ability is one critical variable affecting route to persuasion. Motivation is the other critical variable. Adults who are low in need for cognition are assumed to have lower motivation to process a message. Thus, under some circmstances they are less likely to process messages via the central route.

In the traditional view of the ELM, the ability variable is not perceived as directly affecting the motivational component. The older adult could be highly motivated to process a message, but deficits in attentional capacity make them more susceptible to distraction; and, consequently messages are processed peripherally. It is possible, however, that ability may indirectly affect the persuasion process through motivation. The concept of interactive effects of variables within the persuasion model is not new. Ratneshwar and Chaiken (1991) found that message comprehensibility had a moderating effect on the impact of source expertise by directly affecting a person's ability to systematically process the message.

In the present research, a scarcity of cognitive resources in older adults may affect their motivation to process a message. In fact, past research has shown that older adults opt to process information differently from younger adults. Johnson (1990) found that retirement-age adults (over the age of 60) were more likely to use a noncompensatory decision strategy in product selection. Younger adults were more likely to use compensatory strategies. It was proposed that older adults were compensating for their reduction in processing capacity by utilizing less cognitively demanding decision strategies.

It is apparent that these deficiencies should impact other variables related to information processing. What is important to highlight is that need for cognition may be a dynamic construct that changes over time in relation to age-related changes in cognitive processing. The focus of this discussion pertains to the relationship between need for cognition, chronological age, and how these factors potentially impact the persuasion process. Specifically, the studies document a decline in need for cognition among older adults. The next section of this paper reports two studies that investigate this relationship. Following this, implications for the persuasion process are presented.

METHODOLOGY

Study 1

Two hundred and thirty-eight adults from local civic groups, senior citizen centers and university staff personnel participated in a self-administered survey. As part of a larger study, each participant completed a number of measures, including the need for cognition scale. While more women than men took part in the study, the percent representation of women to men remained proportionally constant within both the younger and older adult age groups (see Table 1). After accounting for missing data, 201 responses remained for analysis.

Measures. Need for cognition was measured using the 18 item short form (Cacioppo, Petty, Kao, and Rodriguez 1984). Responses were recorded on a seven-point agree/disagree scale. Age was measured by asking respondents to indicate how old they were in number of years. Adults were grouped by ages based on standard practices both in consumer and gerontological research, the cut point being 60 years of age.

Results. The need for cognition scale exhibited adequate reliability (alpha = .81, inter-item correlation = .19). One item assessing the degree to which thinking was used to "make one's way to the top" exhibited unusually low item-to-total correlations. It was dropped from the analysis and the remaining 17 items were summed to create an index (alpha = .81, inter-item correlation = .19). Since a 7 point agree-disagree scale was used, participants could receive scores ranging from 17 to 119. The higher the score, the higher the need for cognition. An examination of the mean level of need for cognition showed older adults had significantly lower levels of need for cognition (t = 9.81, p < .001; see Table 1).

Since both need for cognition and age were measured as continuous variables, regression analysis was employed to investigate the relationship between the two variables. The regression of need for cognition on age was significant ($F_{1,200}$ = 74.887, p < .001) and explained approximately 27 percent of the variance in the dependent variable[1]. The regression weight of -.45 was significant (t=-8.64, p<.001) and in the expected direction. To highlight the relationship between the two variables, age was divided into five categories and regression analysis was used to examine group

---

[1] Initial analysis for both studies examined the impact of gender on the results. gender was not significant in explaining any of the variance in need for cognition and was omitted from the discussion of results.

TABLE 1
Summary Statistics

	Overall Sample		Younger Adults		Older Adults	
	Study 1 (201)	Study 2 (155)	Study 1 (95)	Study 2 (90)	Study 1 (106)	Study 2 (65)
Age: Mean	55	50	34	33	71	69
Range	23-87	20-91	23-59	20-59	60-87	60-91
Education	H.S. Grad	Some College	Some College	College Graduate	H.S. Grad	H.S. Grad
Men	25%	60%	28%	58%	25%	63%
Women	75%	40%	72%	42%	75%	37%
Need for Cog.:						
Mean	81	58.6	92(a)	62(b)	73(a)	54.4(b)
Median	83	60	93	62	68	55.5
Range	40-119	27-84	57-119	36-82	40-99	27-84

TABLE 2
Need for Cognition Scores by Age Decade Regression

	Constant 20-29	b_1 30-39	b_2 40-59	b_3 60-69	b_4 70-79
Study 1					
Weight	91.57	-.24	-.78	-18.19	-18.19
t-value	37.12	-.069	-.19	-5.45	-5.83
p-value	.001	.95	.85	.001	.001
Mean NFC	91.6	91.6	89.2	73.3	72.9
(n)	(34)	(39)	(21)	(44)	(63)
Study 2					
Weight	62.71	-1.41	-2.41	-6.78	-11.52
t-value	34.57	-.62	-.75	-2.93	-4.16
signif.	.001	.54	.46	.004	.001
Mean NFC	62.7	61.3 *+	60.3	55.9 *	51.2 +
(n)	(28)	(48)	(13)	(45)	(21)

differences[2]. The significant regression weights indicate that older adults had lower scores than younger adults.. For adults under the age of 60, 74 percent had need for cognition scores higher than the median; while for adults over the age of 60, 74 percent had need for cognition scores under the median.

Prior research found that education influences need for cognition. Since the two age groups exhibited differences in educational level, this may explain the observed differences in need for cognition. It should be noted, however, that examining the impact of education on the relationship cannot fully equate the two age groups since the educational system in this country has undergone tremendous change over the last 50 years. Also, people continue to educate themselves after they have finished formal schooling through a variety of life experiences.

Respondents indicated the number of years of education they had completed. As can be seen in Table 1, young adults had slightly higher levels of education. Chronological age and education had a strong, negative relationship (r = -.637, p < .001). Education also had a positive relationship with need for cognition (r = .46, p < .001). Hierarchical regression was used to examine the impact of age on need for cognition after accounting for education (see Table 3)[3]. Education explained approximately 21 percent of the variance in need for cognition; chronological age explained an additional seven percent of the variance.

This study provided initial evidence of a relationship between need for cognition and chronological age. A second study using a different methodology gathered additional evidence.

Study 2

One hundred and sixty-five adults participated in a mail survey. Subjects were randomly selected from 10 Massachusetts

---

[2] Age groups do not exactly correspond to age decades due to small cell sizes in the middle of the age range. Subjects in the 40's and 50's decades were grouped together. Additionally, subjects in their 70's, 80's and 90's were combined for the same reason. In the examination of need for cognition scores, the age decades that were combined were not significantly different from each other. Thus, the collapsing of age decades does not substantively change the analysis or results.

[3] The initial analysis included the interaction between need for cognition and age as well as the main effects for each variable. In the first study, this interaction was marginally significant (R^2 change F = 5.2, p < .10) and explained less than 1 percent of the variance in need for cognition. In the second study, the interaction term was not significant.

TABLE 3
Effects of Education and Chronological Age on Need for Cognition

Variable	Beta	t	R^2	R^2 Change	F
Study 1:					
Education	.46	7.01	.21	.21	49.12, p < .001
Education	.24	2.91			
Chronological Age	-.35	-4.30	.28	.07	18.51, p < .001
Study 2:					
Education	.43	5.601	.18	.18	31.37, p < .001
Education	.31	3.809			
Chronological Age	-.24	-2.94	.23	.05	8.99, p < .004

communities. Due to missing data, ten subjects were dropped from the analysis. The need for cognition measure used in Study 1 was again employed. Two modifications were made to the scale. First, the troublesome item from the first study was dropped. Next, a five point response scale was used instead of a seven-point scale. Thus, need for cognition scores could range from 17 to 85.

The average age of adults in this sample was 50. There was a 60/40 split between men and women. The overall proportion of men to women remained relatively constant within both age groups (see Table 1).

Results. The need for cognition scale exhibited adequate reliability (alpha = .91, inter-item correlation = .37). Similar to Study 1, older adults exhibited lower levels of need for cognition than younger adults (t = 5.08, p < .001, see Table 1). The regression weight of -.21 was in the expected direction and significant (t = -4.99, p < .001)

The regression of need for cognition on age was again significant ($F_{1,154}$ = 24.95, P < .001), explaining approximately 14 percent of the variance in the dependent variable. Approximately 57 percent of younger adults scored above the median need for cognition score; while only 26 percent of older adults scored above the median. Investigation of need for cognition across the five age groups highlights the expected relationship (see Table 2).

This sample exhibited a similar relationship between need for cognition and chronological age to that of Study 1 (r = -.45, p < .001). Education again had a positive correlation with need for cognition (r = .425, p < .001). Results of the hierarchical regression indicated that education explained approximately 18 percent of the variance in need for cognition scores, with chronological age explaining an additional five percent.

DISCUSSION

The results of these two studies provide evidence that need for cognition may be affected by dispositional factors inherent in the individual. Specifically, need for cognition may be a dynamic variable that changes with age. This is not to say that everyone over the age of 60 will have low levels of need for cognition. It may be that other factors affect this relationship, such as physical conditioning and/or health, cognitive age, or other physiological/psychological factors.

Education affected need for cognition, which was expected. It is important to note, however, that even after accounting for the impact of education, chronological age had a small, but significant impact on a person's level of need for cognition.

Limitations. While the theoretical basis for the relationship between need for cognition and chronological age is sound, methodological issues may have kept age from having more of an impact on need for cognition. With respect to sampling, Study 1 employed a convenience sample which may have been biased due to self-selection of subjects. However, given the environment in which subjects were recruited (senior citizen centers) the older adults participating in the study may have been in better health than older adults who were unable to travel to the senior center. Since good health has a positive impact on cognitive processing, it could have been possible that no relationship would have been found. A similar argument could be made for the Study 2 sample since the mail survey respondents may have been in better health and consequently had higher levels of processing capacity than nonrespondents. A strength of the study lies in the similarity of results across different data collection methods, scale points and sample composition (women versus men).

It could be argued that since this is cross-sectional research it is subject to all of the associated deficiencies affecting validity. Salthouse (1988) addresses these issues, specifically, as they relate to gerontological research on cognitive processing. Based on extensive reviews of the literature, he concluded that cross-sectional research yields very similar results to longitudinal research.

RESEARCH DIRECTIONS

The implications of these results are important in relation to the motivation and ability variables that control the persuasion process. This highlights the need for further research into the interactive effects of variables controlling the persuasion process. If physiological changes can directly affect the motivational variable in the ELM, then motivation becomes a function of personal relevance and unique individual characteristics. Investigating the following research proposition would be interesting:

P1: *Ability factors in the ELM will have direct effects on route to persuasion (i.e., distraction), as well as indirect effects by affecting motivational factors such as need for cognition.*

Given the results of this study, there are issues that deal specifically with the older adult. According to prior research, need for cognition directly affects a person's motivation to process message arguments in an advertisement. The higher the need for cognition, the higher the motivation; thus resulting in more cognitively effortful central processing. One interesting aspect of the need for cognition and aging relationship would be:

P2: Due to lower levels of need for cognition, older adults are are more likely to process advertisements via a peripheral route than central route to persuasion.

Since level of need for cognition has implications for route to persuasion, a variety of issues arise about message effectiveness, frequency of exposure, and media usage. Many of these issues, as related to age, have been explored in prior research in advertising, but not in the context of the ELM. Prior research has shown that high need for cognition individuals are more likely to attend to, synthesize, and integrate advertising message information into existing knowledge and belief structures. Interesting research propositions relating to need for cognition and chronological age would be:

P3: Given lower levels of need for cognition, older adults should process less advertising information, generate fewer cognitive responses and consequently have weaker and/or nonexistent attitude changes.

Advertising information processed via the central route has been shown to have a greater effect on attitude persistence than processing via the peripheral route; these attitudes are more resistant to counterpersuasion and predictive of future behavior. Individuals low in need for cognition have been shown to process advertisements peripherally. Research may investigate the following:

P4: Older adult attitudes developed through advertising messages may be more transient than those of younger adults due to lower levels of cognitive functioning.

P5: Older adults may experience weak or nonexistent attitude change when exposed to advertising messages, thus retaining the stronger prior attitudes; subsequently, they may be less susceptible to attempts at counterpersuasion than younger adults.

Low need for cognition individuals should be more influenced by peripheral cues (i.e., number of message arguments, source attractiveness and/or credibility, presence of pleasant music, celebrities, etc.) than message content. Thus, the following proposition bears investigation:

P6: Older adults may be more attentive to the peripheral cues (type of models and spokespeople) used in advertisements than younger adults, and consequently more sensitive to their portrayal in advertising.

However, researchers have discussed the possibility that peripheral cues may be processed centrally in some instances. Given the indication that older adults are more likely to use noncompensatory than compensatory decision strategies, peripheral cues may be used in a variety of ways to reduce processing demands. Thus, investigation of the following could be fruitful:

P7: Due to lower levels of need for cognition, older adults may be more likely than younger adults to use peripheral cues in a central manner to reduce demands on their processing capacity resources.

These are just a few of the many research propositions that deserve investigation. It is important to delineate these propositions to guide future research into the processing of advertising information.

CONCLUSION

The research presented in this paper provides evidence of a potential interactive relationship between the primary variables in the ELM that control route to persuasion. Specifically, age-related declines in cognitive ability affect the motivational variable, need for cognition. This points to the possibility that need for cognition may be a dynamic factor that changes over time with respect to age-related cognitive processing changes.

Haugtvedt, Petty and Cacioppo (1992) point out that it is important to identify "... profiles of differences in personal habits and preferences of individuals who differ in need for cognition." Given the rapidly increasing population of adults over the age of 60, it is imperative that consumer researchers delve more deeply into the information processing changes that arise with advancing age and identify those characteristics, like need for cognition, that affect the processing of advertising messages. By doing so, this will produce more effective methods for connecting with this increasing important target market.

REFERENCES

Arenberg, D. and E.A. Robinson-Tchabo (1977). "Learning and Aging," in *Handbook of the Psychology of Aging*, 2nd edition, J.E. Birren and K.W. Schaie (eds.), New York: Van Nostrand Reinhold Company, Inc., 421-449.

Axsom, D., S. Yates and S. Chaiken (1987). "Audience Response as a Heuristic Cue in Persuasion," *Journal of Personality and Social Psychology*, 53, 30-40.

Batra R., and D.M. Stayman (1990). "The Role of Mood in Advertising Effectiveness," *Journal of Consumer Research*, 17, 203-214.

Bearden, W.O. and J.B. Mason (1979). "Elderly Use of In-Store Information Sources and Dimensions of Product Satisfaction/Dissatisfaction," *Journal of Retailing*, 55(1), 79-91.

Birren J. E., A.M. Woods and M.V. William (1980). "Behavioral Slowing with Age: Causes, Organization, and Consequences," in *Aging in the 1980's: Psychological Issues*, L.W. Poon (ed.) Washington, D.C.: American Psychological Association.

Cacioppo, J. T. and R. E. Petty (1982). "The Need for Cognition," *Journal of Personality and Social Psychology*, 42, 116-131.

Cacioppo, J. T., R. E. Petty and C. F. Kao (1984). "The Efficient Assessment of Need for Cognition," *Journal of Personality Assessment*, 48, 306-307.

Cacioppo, J. T., R. E. Petty and K. Morris (1983). "Effects of Need for Cognition on Message Evaluation, Recall, and Persuasion," *Journal of Personality and Social Psychology*, 39, 805-818.

Cacioppo, J. T., R. E. Petty, C. F. Kao and R. Rodriguez (1986). "Central and Peripheral Routes to Persuasion: An Individual Difference Perspective," *Journal of Personality and Social Psychology*, 51, 1032-1043.

Canestrari, R. E. (1963). "Paced and Self-paced Learning in Young and Elderly Adults," *Journal of Gerontology*, 18, 165-168.

Cohen, A.R. (1957). "Need for Cognition and Order of Communication as determinants of Opinion Change," in C.I. Hovland (ed.) *The Order of Presentation in Persuasion*, New Haven, CT: Yale University Press.

Cohen, A., E. Stotland, and D. Wolfe (1955). "An Experimental Investigation of Need for Cognition," *Journal of Abnormal and Social Psychology*, 51, 291-294.

Cole, C. A. and M. J. Houston (1987). "Encoding and Media Effects on Consumer Learning Deficiencies in the Elderly," *Journal of Marketing Research*, 23 (February), 55-63.

Craik, F.M. (1977). "Age Differences in Human Memory," in *Handbook of the Psychology of Aging*, 2nd edition, J.E. Birren and K.W. Schaie (eds.), New York: Van Nostrand Reinhold Company, Inc.

Davis, B. and W.A. French (1989). "Exploring Advertising Usage Segments Among the Aged," *Journal of Advertising Research*, 29(1), 22-29.

Hasher, L. and R.T. Zacks (1979). "Automatic and Effortful Processes in Memory," *Journal of Experimental Psychology: General*, 108(3), 356-88.

Haugtvedt, C. P. and R. E. Petty (1989). "Need for Cognition and Attitude Persistence," *Advances in Consumer Research*, 16, 33-36.

Haugtvedt, C. P., R. E. Petty and J. T. Cacioppo (1992). "Need for Cognition in Advertising: Understanding the Role of Personality Variables in Consumer Behavior," *Journal of Consumer Psychology*, 1(3), 239-260.

Haugtvedt, C., R. E. Petty, J. T. Cacioppo and Theresa Steidley (1988). "Personality and Ad Effectiveness: Exploring the Utility of Need for Cognition," *Advances in Consumer Research*, 15, 209-212.

Hoyer, W. J. and D. J.Plude (1980). "Attentional and Perceptual Processes in the Study of Cognitive Aging," in *Aging in the 1980's: Psychological Issues*, L.W. Poon (ed.) Washington, D.C.: American Psychological Association.

Johnson, M. M. (1990). "Age Differences in Decision Making: A Process Methodology for Examining Strategic Information Processing," *Journal of Gerontology: Psychological Sciences*, 45(2) p75-78.

Lumpkin, J. R. (1985). "Shopping Orientation Segmentation of the Elderly Consumer," *Journal of the Academy of Marketing Science*, 13(2), 271-289.

Petty, R. E. and J. T. Cacioppo (1986). *Communication and Persuasion: Central and Peripheral Routes to Attitude Change*. New York: Springer-Verlag.

Ratneshwar, S. and S. Chaiken (1991). "Comphension's Role in Persuasion: The Case of Its Moderating Effect on the Persuasive Impact of Source Cues," *Journal of Consumer Research*, 18(1), 52-62.

Reese, H.W., and D. Rodeheaver (1985). "Problem Solving and Complex Decision Making," in *Handbook of the Psychology of Aging*, 2nd edition, J.E. Birren and K.W. Schaie (eds.), New York: Van Nostrand Reinhold Company, Inc.

Rubin, A.L. (1986). "Television, Aging and Information Seeking," *Language and Communication*, 6(1/2), 125-137.

Salthouse, T.A. (1988a). "Resource-Reduction Interpretations of Cognitive Aging," *Developmental Review*, 8, 238-272.

Salthouse, T.A. (1988b). "Initiating the Formalization of Theories of Cognitive Aging," *Psychology and Aging*, 3(1), 3-16.

Srull, T., M. Lichtenstein and M. Rothbart (1985). "Associated Storage and Retrieval Processes," *Journal of Experimental Psychology: Learning, Memory and Cognition*, 11, 316-345.

Stayman, D. M. and F. R. Kardes (1992). "Spontaneous Inference Processes in Advertising: Effects of Need for Cognition and Self-Monitoring on Inference Generation and Utilization," *Journal of Consumer Psychology*, 1(2), 125-142.

Venkatraman, M.P., D. Marlino, F.R. Kardes, and K.B. Sklar (1990). "The Interactive Effects of Message Appeal and Individual Differences on Information Processing and Persuasion," *Psychology and Marketing*, 7(2), 85-96.

Need for Cognition, Advertisement Viewing Time and Memory for Advertising Stimuli

James W. Peltier, University of Wisconsin-Whitewater
John A. Schibrowsky, University of Nevada-Las Vegas

ABSTRACT

Need for cognition has been defined as the intrinsic motivation to engage in problem solving activities. It portrays cognitive elaboration as an individual difference variable. Cognitive elaboration has typically been measured via self-reports of cognitive effort. The problem with using self-report measures of cognitive effort is that they are at best subjective and at worst invalid. The current study reports the finding of an empirical investigation examining the relationship between need for cognition, cognitive elaboration, and recall of various advertising stimuli. Results provide support for the notion that higher need for cognition subjects process ads longer and have superior recall for brands and claims.

INTRODUCTION

The study of how involvement affects the way in which people process, evaluate and remember advertising stimuli has long interested consumer researchers (e.g., Celsi and Olson 1988; Greenwald and Leavitt 1984; Petty et al. 1983; Rothschild 1979). Consumer involvement has typically been conceptualized in terms of an individual's motivation to process informational stimuli (e.g., Houston and Rothschild 1978; Richins and Bloch 1986; Zaichkowsky 1985). The predominant viewpoint is that consumers are more likely to engage in "cognitive elaboration" under conditions of high rather than low involvement (e.g., Burnkrant and Sawyer 1983; Celsi and Olson 1988; Greenwald and Leavitt 1984; Petty et al. 1983).

Recent research has been devoted to an individual difference variable with similar cognitive ramifications—the need for cognition (e.g, Batra and Stayman 1989; Cacioppo and Petty 1982; Cacioppo et al. 1983; Cacioppo et al. 1986; Crowley and Hoyer 1989; Haughtvedt et al. 1988; Haughtvedt and Petty 1989). Cacioppo and Petty (1982) defined need for cognition as the "tendency to engage in and enjoy thinking." Cohen et al. (1955) conceptualized need for cognition as "a need to structure relevant situations in meaningful, integrated ways. It is a need to understand and make reasonable the experiential world." Consistent with consumer research on involvement, a positive relationship is hypothesized to exist between the need for cognition and the motivation to expend cognitive effort when processing informational stimuli (e.g., Cacioppo and Petty 1982; Cacioppo et al. 1983; Cacioppo, et al. 1986).

Despite the research pertaining to the need for cognition, relatively little is understood about the relationship between need for cognition and the processing and memory of advertisements. Specifically, higher need for cognition is proportedly related to increased motivation to engage in cognitive elaboration. However, researchers studying need for cognition have measured cognitive elaboration via self-reported measures of cognitive effort (e.g., asking subjects to recall how much effort they used to think about previously seen stimuli). This measure is at best an indirect test of cognitive elaboration, and has resulted in conflicting findings. Moreover, the validity of self-reported techniques to ascertain the nature and scope of cognitive processing has been questioned (Nisbett and Wilson 1977). In addition, virtually no studies have examined the relationship between need for cognition and the cognitive elaboration and memory for advertising stimuli. Studies that have explored related issues in psychology have had conflicting results. Because academic and applied researchers are continually striving to better understand the ways in which consumers process and remember advertising stimuli, further research in this area is warranted.

This study reports the findings from an experiment that investigated the relationship between need for cognition and an objective measure of the cognitive elaboration of advertisements. Specifically, the study examined the impact that need for cognition had on the length of time that subjects viewed print advertisements. In addition, an attempt was made to determine whether the predicted higher ad viewing times for high need for cognition subjects translated into differential memory superiority. Also, the study investigated the degree to which need for cognition affected the processing and recall of different types of advertising stimuli (e.g., characters, products, brands, and claims). Finally, efforts were made to isolate elaboration and memory effects from other possible confounding variables.

CONCEPTUAL FOUNDATIONS

Cognitive Elaboration

Need for cognition theory suggests that individuals who enjoy thinking and problem solving activities are "intrinsicly" motivated to expend cognitive effort. In contrast, individuals characterized as having low need for cognition are considered to be "cognitive misers" (e.g., Cacioppo et al. 1986; Taylor 1981) who view thinking as a relatively unrewarding exercise.

Cohen et al. (1955) conducted the first empirical test of the way need for cognition relates to processing elaboration. Subjects read either ambiguous or structured stories and were asked to rate how interesting and likeable these stories were to them. Subjects also provided post hoc reports of how much effort they expended to understand each type of story. The results did not support a superior self-reported cognitive effort for high need for cognition subjects. Subjects low and high in need for cognition reported similar amounts of cognitive effort devoted to processing the stories. The authors suggested that the measure that they used to assess cognitive effort was insensitive to potential processing differences. A ceiling effect may have been created that artificially restricted the range of felt cognitive effort for high need for cognition subjects.

A similar rationale was offered by Cacioppo and Petty (1982) to explain why they were not able to detect a significant relationship between need for cognition and cognitive effort. They agreed with Cohen et al. that self-reported measures of cognitive effort may not be sensitive enough to detect processing differences. They also suggested that individuals with high need for cognition may find it "easier" to think and to solve problems than individuals with low need for cognition.

Two additional studies concluded that individuals with high need for cognition were more likely to cognitively elaborate informational stimuli (Cacioppo et al. 1983; Cacioppo et al. 1986). In both cases, subjects with high need for cognition reported expending significantly greater cognitive effort to experimental stimuli than their low need for cognition counterparts.

Message Recall

Studies investigating the relationship between need for cognition and message recall have also reported conflicting results.

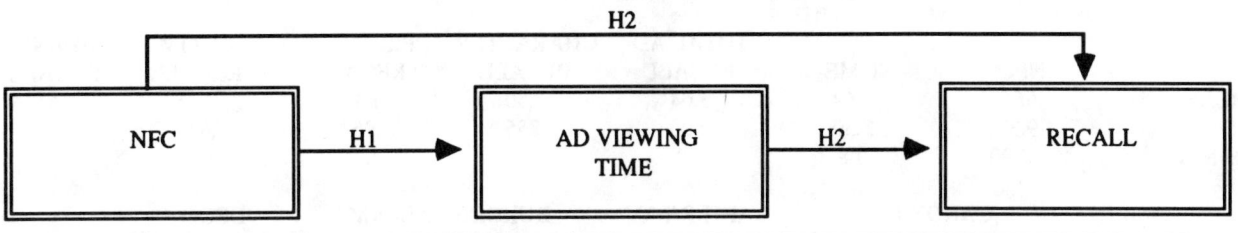

FIGURE 1
NFC and the Elaboration Likelihood Model

Cohen (1957) and Cohen et al. (1955) found no difference in the amount of learning and retention for persuasive messages across high and low need for cognition subjects. However, Cacioppo et al. (1983), and Cacioppo et al. (1986) found that high need for cognition subjects recalled significantly more message arguments than low need for cognition subjects. This finding persisted even after controlling for verbal intelligence (Cacioppo et al. 1986).

The need for cognition studies pertaining to self-reported cognitive elaboration and differential memory have reported mix results. Hypotheses are developed in the next section that try to resolve this conflict by examining need for cognition in terms of advertisement processing time and its subsequent effect on memory for specific ad stimuli.

HYPOTHESES

The willingness to cognitively elaborate informational stimuli is the basic principle behind the need for cognition construct. As discussed, the use of a subjective self-reported level of cognitive effort is at best an indirect measure of cognitive elaboration, and at worst invalid. However, an objective test of the amount of time that an individual spends processing an advertisement is a relatively good surrogate measure of cognitive elaboration (Celsi and Olson 1988). In addition, as compared to self-reported cognitive effort, ad viewing time should be a more sensitive measure of cognitive elaboration because it will significantly reduce or eliminate artificial ceiling effects.

If individuals with higher need for cognition enjoy thinking and problem solving activities more than those with a lower need for cognition, then there may also be a corresponding relationship in the length of time that they process print advertisements.

H1: Need for cognition is positively related to ad viewing time.

H1 postulates that high need for cognition consumers will spend more time processing print advertisements. Researchers studying cognitive elaboration have shown that memory for stimuli is a function of the amount and nature of cognitive activity at encoding (e.g., Jacoby and Craik 1979; Craik and Lockhart 1972; Craik and Tulving 1975). Subsequently, the enhanced ad viewing time predicted for high need for cognition subjects should result in better total recall memory. Previous studies have also concluded that high need for cognition individuals may recall information because of superior verbal intelligence (Cacioppo et al. 1986) and a greater ability to process and solve problems (Cacioppo and Petty 1982). Together, these results suggest that the need for cognition has both a direct effect on recall and an indirect effect via cognitive elaboration (ad viewing time). These relationships are displayed in Figure 1.

H2: Need for cognition is positively related to total ad recall.

No specific predictions are made in H2 regarding how need for cognition is related to differential processing and memory for individual ad stimuli (e.g., characters vs. products vs. brands vs. claims). However, conceptual and empirical research studying the elaboration likelihood model (ELM) offer insight for better understanding how differing levels of need for cognition might influence the degree to which various advertising stimuli are processed and remembered (e.g., Petty and Cacioppo 1981, 1984; Petty et al. 1981; Petty, Cacioppo and Schumann 1983).

Petty and Cacioppo (1981) contend that an individual's level of processing involvement at encoding influences which of two routes to persuasion is utilized—the "central" route (high involvement) or the "peripheral" route (low involvement). Under the central route, individuals are motivated to carefully analyze the content and quality of the persuasive arguments contained in the communication. Alternatively, detailed processing of message arguments is avoided under peripheral processing, and individuals instead focus on other aspects of the communication such as the attractiveness or credibility of the source, music, pictorial stimuli, etc.

The ELM suggests that the enhanced elaboration at encoding for high need for cognition individuals may not translate into superior recall for all aspects of an advertisement. Consistent with the ELM, subjects high in need for cognition should process brands and claims more deeply, and this should translate into superior recall for this information. In contrast, because the test ads used in the current study presented character and product information in "pictorial" form, these more peripherally-oriented stimuli should be recalled better by low need for cognition subjects. Accordingly, H3a and H3b are as follows:

H3a: Need for cognition is positively related to brand and claim recall.

H3b: Need for cognition is negatively related to character and product recall.

An experiment was designed to test the above three hypotheses. It is described below.

METHOD

Procedure

One hundred and thirty students from three introductory marketing classes were recruited to participate in the study. On the day of the experiment, subjects were individually brought into a room and were told that they were going to participate in a concept testing project for a local advertising agency. They were shown four color-illustrated advertisements via a slide presentation. Each test ad contained a character/spokesperson, a product illustration, a brand name, and an advertising claim. Subjects could view these

TABLE 1
Summary Statistics

	NFC*	TIME	TOTAL AD RECALL	CHARACTER RECALL	PRODUCT RECALL	CLAIM RECALL	BRAND RECALL
MEAN	66.7	7.69	3.04	1.50	1.11	.276	.155
SD	9.37	3.50	2.00	.855	.954	.632	.439
RANGE	18-90	0-8	0-2	0-2	0-2	0-2	

	CANDY BAR INVOLVE	AFTER TAN INVOLVE	BURGLAR ALARM INVOLVE	DEOD INVOLVE
MEAN	31.1	35.1	42.4	57.5
SD	13.7	19.9	16.6	10.5
RANGE	10-70	10-70	10-70	10-70

*NFC=Need for Cognition

---

ads for as long or as little as they liked. The amount of time that they viewed each ad was unobtrusively recorded by the experimenter with a stopwatch. After viewing the test ads, subjects went to another room where they were asked to fill out an 18-item need for cognition instrument (Cacioppo and Petty 1984). Upon completion of this task, subjects filled out written protocols asking them to write down as many characters, products, brands and claims that they could remember. Finally, subjects filled out a ten-item involvement scale for each product (Zaichkowsky 1985).

Independent Variables

Need for Cognition: The principle independent variable was the subjects' self-reported level of need for cognition. Numerous studies have concluded that the need for cognition instrument is both valid and reliable (c.f. Haugtvedt et al. 1988). A total summed score across the 18-item need for cognition scale was calculated for each subject. The coefficient alpha found for this measure was .965.

Product Involvement: Need for cognition is a measure of "intrinsic" involvement. A product involvement measure was included as an independent variable to control for the possible effects of "situational" involvement on the processing and memory for the test ads. Using a scale with ten of the inventory items developed by Zaichkowsky (1985), subjects self-reported their involvement for each of the products categories contained in the test ads: candy bars, after tan lotion, burglar alarms, and deodorants. The coefficient alphas for these product involvement measures ranged from .904 to .981. As a note, Zaichkowsky's original involvement scale had twenty items. However, reduced scales have been found to accurately capture the construct (Jain and Srinivasan 1990).

Ad Viewing Time: Advertising viewing time was an observed variable. The experimenter recorded the amount of time that each subject viewed the test ads. It is used as an independent variable to analyze the unique contributions of need for cognition on recall (H2, H3a, and H3b).

Dependent Variables

Ad Viewing Time: Ad viewing time is used an a dependent variable to analyze H1.

Total Ad Recall: A total ad recall score for each ad was calculated as character recall + product recall + brand recall + claim recall.

Character, Product, Brand, and Claim Recall: A recall score was calculated for each of these ad stimuli.

Two graduate assistants were assigned the task of coding the recall responses. A strict coding guide was developed a priori to eliminate scoring subjectivity. Each recall response could receive a score of 0 (incorrect), 1 (partially correct) or 2 (completely correct). The maximum character, product, brand, and claim recall score per ad was two. The maximum total ad recall score per ad was eight. Only ten recall scores had to be resolved through discussion (99.5% agreement).

RESULTS AND DISCUSSION

Table 1 shows the summary statistics for the variables considered in the analysis. The average viewing times across the four test ads ranged from 7.3 to 7.9 seconds. This consistency in means indicates that total viewing time was not dominated by any one ad. Total ad recall averaged 3.04 (on a scale of 0-8), this suggests ceiling and/or floor effects were not a problem (Peltier and Schibrowsky 1991).

The first step in the data analysis was to investigate the correlations of the independent variables to check for multicollinearity. As is evident from Table 2, multicollinearity does not appear to be a problem in this analysis. Additional diagnostics (condition indices, variance proportions, and correlation matrix of regression coefficients) conducted during the subsequent regression analyzes corroborated this conclusion.

A series of regression analyses were conducted to test the hypotheses. Hypothesis 1 predicted that need for cognition would be positively related to ad viewing time. As can be seen from Table 3, H1 was supported. This was true even though product involvement was included in the regression analysis.

Hypothesis 2 predicted that need for cognition is positively related to total ad recall. The data in Table 4 support this hypothesis. The results show that cognitive elaboration at encoding (ad viewing time) and need for cognition were significant predictors of total ad recall. This suggests, as hypothesized, that need for cognition has a direct impact on memory and an indirect impact via cognitive elaboration. It should be noted that product involvement also had a significant impact on total recall.

Hypothesis 3a stated that increased need for cognition would result in higher levels of recall for claims and brands. To test this hypothesis two regression analyses were conducted, one for each of the component recall measures. Tables 5a and 5b show the results of the test of this hypothesis. Note that involvement and ad viewing time were included in the analyses. The results support hypothesis 3a. Need for Cognition was positively related to claim and brand

TABLE 2
Correlations of Key variables

	NFC	INV**	TIME	RECALL
NFC	1.00			
INV	-.04	1.00		
TIME	.18*	.05	1.00	
RECALL	.12*	.18*	.22*	1.00

* Statistically significant p<.05
** INV=product Involvement

TABLE 3
Test of Hypothesis 1

Model: ad viewing time = constant + NFC + involvement

variable	coeff	t-value	p-value
constant	2.740	2.383	.018*
NFC	.068	4.217	.000*
involvement	.010	1.226	.221

* statistically significant p<.05
model overall fit f(2,520)=9.45

TABLE 4
Test of Hypothesis 2

Model: recall = constant + NFC + involvement + time

variable	coeff	t-value	p-value
constant	.070	.109	.913
NFC	.020	2.205	.028*
involvement	.019	4.129	.000*
ad view time	.111	4.542	.000*

* statistically significant p<.05
model overall fit f(3,520)=16.096

recall. This implies that higher need for cognition subjects focused on and better remembered this more "centrally-oriented" information. Furthermore, the significant ad viewing time relationship found for both brand and claim suggest the greater processing effort expended by high need for cognition subjects also contributed to recall superiority.

Hypothesis 3b predicted that increased need for cognition would lead to lower levels of recall for characters and products. It was hypothesized that this "peripherally-oriented" information would be processed more deeply and better recalled by low need for cognition subjects. To test this hypothesis two regression analyses were conducted, one for each of these component recall measures. Tables 6a and 6b show the results of the test of this hypothesis. Note that involvement and ad viewing time were included in the analyses. The results did not support hypothesis 3b. Need for Cognition was not related to character or product recall.

The significant ad viewing time relationships shown in Tables 6a and 6b for these variables provide insight for explaining why low need for cognition subjects did not have superior character and product recall. Specifically, because exposure to the test ads was not fixed across subjects, and was instead self-selected, some of the "additional" elaboration effort expended by higher need for cognition subjects was probably allocated toward processing character and product information. Therefore, while characters and products might receive greater processing effort by low need for cognition subjects in a fixed exposure environment, this was apparently not the case in the variable exposure environment used in the current study.

TABLE 5A
Test of hypothesis 3a: Claim Recall

Model	claim recall = constant + NFC + involvement + time		
variable	coeff	t-value	p-value
constant	-.355	-1.093	.091
NFC	.004	2.052	.041*
involvement	.002	1.166	.244
time	.020	2.480	.013*

* statistically significant p<.05
model overall fit $f(3,520)=4.692$

TABLE 5B
Test of hypothesis 3a: Brand Recall

Model	brand recall = constant + NFC + involvement + time		
variable	coeff	t-value	p-value
constant	-.283	-1.943	.053
NFC	.004	1.960	.050*
involvement	.002	1.763	.079
time	.013	2.355	.019*

* statistically significant p<.05
model overall fit $f(3,520)=4.808$

TABLE 6A
Test of hypothesis 3b: Character Recall

Model	character recall = constant + NFC + involvement + time		
variable	coeff	t-value	p-value
constant	.509	1.822	.069
NFC	.006	1.594	.111
involvement	.006	3.048	.002*
time	.041	3.896	.000*

* statistically significant p<.05
model overall fit $f(3,520)=10.243$

TABLE 6B
Test of hypothesis 3b: Product Recall

Model	product recall = constant + NFC + involvement + time		
variable	coeff	t-value	p-value
constant	.200	.639	.523
NFC	.004	.844	.399
involvement	.009	4.169	.000*
time	.037	3.100	.002*

* statistically significant p<.05
model overall fit $f(3,520)=10.017$

CONCLUSION

The findings from this study suggest that need for cognition has a significant impact on the processing and memory for advertising stimuli. The initial objective of the study was to utilize an objective test of cognitive elaboration to determine whether consumers differ in their intrinsic motivation to process print advertisements. The motivation to engage in cognitive elaboration at encoding was operationalized in this study as the amount of time subjects spent viewing an advertisement. Consistent with expectations, high need for cognition subjects processed test ads significantly longer than those with low need for cognition. This finding provides strong support for the basic premise underlying the need for cognition construct and extends its contextual domain to include the inherent motivation to process advertising-related stimuli. It also suggests that the use of self-reported cognitive effort by previous need for cognition researchers was a valid measure of cognitive elaboration.

Previous studies exploring the relationship between need for cognition and memory have also been in conflict (Cohen et al. 1955; Cacioppo and Petty 1982; Cacioppo et al. 1983; Cacioppo et al. 1986). In addition to testing the motivation to process assumption, a self-selected ad viewing time measure was utilized for the purpose of providing a strong theoretical foundation for predicting and justifying recall differences across varying levels of need for cognition. Consequently, the second objective of the study was to determine the degree to which the predicted higher ad viewing times for high need for cognition subjects translated in superior recall for characters, products, brands, and claims. Using depth-of-processing (e.g., Jacoby and Craik 1979; Craik and Lockhart 1972; Craik and Tulving 1975) and the elaboration likelihood model (e.g, Petty and Cacioppo 1981, 1984; Petty et al. 1981, 1983) as theoretical guides, it was predicted that high need for cognition subjects would spend more time processing the test advertisements, and that their "central" processing effort would result in superior brand and claim recall (supported). In contrast, low need for cognition subjects were predicted to have superior recall for the more "peripherally-oriented" character and product stimuli (not supported). Because greater cognitive elaboration was a major theoretical principle underlying these findings, the strong support found in the study for these hypotheses help resolve the elaboration and memory inconsistencies of previous studies. Furthermore, the findings were present even though other factors were included in the analyzes.

The findings from this study suggest that need for cognition is an important construct that merits future research consideration. Specifically, more research is needed to determine the relationships between need for cognition, product involvement, cognitive elaboration, various measures of memory, and fixed (Broadcast) vs. self-selected (print) exposure media. This suggests that it may be worthwhile to analyze these relationships via structural equations. In addition, the finding that product involvement was a significant predictor of character and product recall, and need for cognition was a significant predictor of brand and claim recall, suggest that these construct should be further investigated to uncover any similarities and differences. Lastly, investigating the relationship between need for cognition and other aspects of information processing, such as decision rules, the number of attributes considered, and the number of brands considered, might also prove to be valuable to consumer researchers.

REFERENCES

Batra, Rajeev and Douglas M. Stayman (1989), "The Interacting Relationship Between Mood, Need for Cognition, and Argument Quality," Paper Presentation Advances in Consumer Research Conference, New Orleans, LA.

Burnkrant, Robert E. and Alan G. Sawyer (1983), "Effects of Involvement and Message Content on Information Processing Intensity," in *Information Processing Research in Advertising*, ed. Richard J. Harris, Hillsdale, NJ: Lawrence Erlbaum Associates, 43.64.

Cacioppo, John T. and Richard E. Petty (1982), "The Need for Cognition," *Journal of Personality and Social Psychology*, 42, 116-131.

_____, _____ and Chuan F. Kao (1984), The Efficient Assessment of Need for Cognition," *Journal of Personality Assessment*, 48, 306-07.

_____, _____, Chuan F. Kao and Regina Rodriguez (1986), "Central and Peripheral Routes to Persuasion: an Individual Difference Perspective," *Journal of Personality and Social Psychology*, 51, 1032-1043.

_____, _____ and Katherine Morris (1983), "Effects of Need for Cognition on Message Evaluation, Recall, and Persuasion," *Journal of Personality and Social Psychology*, 45, 4, 805-818.

Celsi, Richard L. and Jerry C. Olson (1988), "The Role of Involvement in Attention and Comprehension Processes," *Journal of Consumer Research*, 15, 2 (September), 210-224.

Cohen, Arthur R. (1957), "Need for Cognition and Order of Communication as Determinants of Opinion Change," in *The Order of Presentation in Persuasion*, ed. C. I. Hovland, New York: Yale University Press,

_____, Ezra Stotland and Donald Wolf (1955), "An Experimental Investigation of Need for Cognition," *Journal of Abnormal and Social Psychology*, 51, 292-294.

Craik, Fergus I. M. and Robert A. Lockhart (1972), "Levels of Processing: A Framework for Memory Research," *Journal of Verbal Learning and Verbal Behavior*, 11 (6), 671-684.

_____ and Endel Tulving (1975), "Depth of Processing and the Retention of Words in Episodic Memory," *Journal of Experimental Psychology: General*, 104 (3), 268-684.

Crowley, Ayn E. and Wayne D. Howyer (1989), "The Relationship Between Need for Cognition and Other Individual Difference Variables: A Two-Dimensional Framework," in *Advances in Consumer Research*, Vol 16, ed. Thomas K. Srull, Provo, Utah: Association for Consumer Research, 37-43.

Greenwald, Anthony A. and Clark Leavitt (1984), "Audience Involvement in Advertising: Four Levels," *Journal of Consumer Research*, 11 (June), 581-592.

Haughtvedt, Curtis P. and Richard E. Petty (1989), "Need for Cognition and Attitude Persistence," in *Advances in Consumer Research*, Vol 16, ed. Thomas K. Srull, Provo, Utah: Association for Consumer Research, 33-36.

_____, _____, John T. Cacioppo, and Theresa Steidley (1988), "Personality and Ad Effectiveness: Exploring the Utility of Need for Cognition, in *Advances in Consumer Research*, Vol 15, ed. Michael J. Houston, Provo, Utah: Association for Consumer Research, 209-212.

Houston, Michael J. and Michael L. Rothschild (1978), "Conceptual and Methodological Perspectives on Involvement," in *Research Frontiers in Marketing: Dialogues and Directions*, ed. Subhash C. Jain, Chicago: American Marketing Association, 184-187.

Jacoby, Larry and Fergus I. M. Craik (1979), "Effects of Elaboration of Processing at Encoding and Retrieval: Trace Distinctiveness and Recovery of Initial Context," *Levels of Processing in Human Memory*, eds. L.S. Cermak and F.I.M. Craik, Hillsdale, NJ: Lawrence Erlbaum.

Jain, Kapil and Narasimhan Srinivasan (1990), "An Emperical Assessment of Multiple Operationalizations of Involvwmwnr," in *Advances in Consumer Research*, Vol 17, eds. Marvin E. Goldberg, Gerald Gorn, and Richard W. Pollay, Provo, Utah: Association for Consumer Research, 594-601.

Nisbett, Richard E. and Timothy D. Wilson (1977), "Telling More Than We Can Know: Verbal Reports on Mental Processing," *Psychological Review*, 84, 231-259.

Peltier, James W. and John A. Schibrowsky (1992), "The Relationship Between Distractor Similarity and the Recognition of Print Advertisements," in *Advances in Consumer Research*, Vol 19, eds. John F. Sherry and Brian Sternthal, Provo, Utah: Association for Consumer Research, 94-100.

Petty, Richard. E. and John T. Cacioppo (1981), *Attitudes and Persuasion: Classic and Contemporary Approaches*, Dubuque, IA: Wm. C. Brown.

_____ and _____ (1984), The Effect of Involvement on Responses to Argument Quantity and Quality: Central and Peripheral Routes to Persuasion," *Journal of Personality and Social Psychology*, 46, (January), 69-81.

_____, _____ and Rachel Goldman (1981), "Personality Involvement as a Determinant of Argument-Based Persuasion," *Journal of Personality and Social Psychology*, 41, 847-855.

_____, _____ and David Schumann (1983), "Central and Peripheral Routes to Advertising Effectiveness: The Moderating Role of Involvement," *Journal of Consumer Research*, 10 (September) 135-146.

Richins, Marsh L. and Peter H. Bloch (1986), "After the New Wears Off: The Temporal Context of Product Involvement," *Journal of Consumer Research*, 13, (September), 280-285.

Rothschild, Michael L. (1979), "Advertising Strategies for High and Low Involvement Situations," in *Attitude Research Plays for High Stakes*," eds. J.C. Mahoney and B. Silverman, Chicago, IL: American Marketing Association, 74-93.

Taylor, Susan E. (1981), "The Interface of Cognitive and Social Psychology," in *Cognition, Social Behavior, and the Environment*, ed. J. Harvey, Hillsdale, NJ: Erlbaum.

Zaichkowsky, Judith Lynne (1985), "Measuring the Involvement Construct," *Journal of Consumer Research*, 12 (December), 341-352.

The Wild West in the Consumer Imagination
Terrence H. Witkowski, California State University, Long Beach

INTRODUCTION

The North American frontier has inspired imaginations for nearly 500 years, but most evocative of all have been the images produced during the period following the Civil War. This "Wild West" has meant vast expanses and natural wonders, the buffalo and the long-horned steer, and cowboys, Indians, gunfighters, and pioneer settlers. The Wild West has spawned entire genres of literature, painting, music, film, and television as well as popular amusements ranging from Wild West shows to rodeos to cowboy poetry readings. The stagecoach, the warbonnet, the Colt revolver, and the Winchester rifle have become American icons, while sundry other western motifs permeate countless objects of everyday life. Above all, the Wild West has been an idea, a symbol of individualism and unbounded freedom.

The ongoing consumption of the Wild West is a significant phenomenon worthy of study for its own sake. It is deeply embedded in American life and differentiates American consumer culture from other consumer cultures. Yet, the Wild West also has a worldwide following ranging from Japanese tourists in search of authentic dude ranches to the American Indians' Friends Society in Poland. The objective of this special session was to investigate different aspects of this macro phenomenon, as it relates to consumer behavior, from different methodological perspectives—historical, reader response, and ethnographic.

PAPERS PRESENTED

The first paper by Ronald A. Fullerton examined the evolution of the mythology of the West as portrayed in late nineteenth-century dime novels, in Wild West Shows and early movies, and by celebrity heroes including Buffalo Bill, Annie Oakley, and Sitting Bull. The paper then analyzed "Somewhere West of Laramie," the famous and revolutionary 1923 advertisement for the Jordan motor car. This ad exerted enormous power on consumer consciousness because it seamlessly transferred key cultural fantasies about the Wild West to one of the major products of our century, the automobile. Fullerton's explanation introduces a longitudinal dimension to McCracken's theory of meaning movement.

The next paper by Thomas C. O'Guinn used a reader response methodology to investigate the western film, illustrated by John Ford's *The Searchers* and *The Man Who Shot Liberty Valance*. The western has been an enormously successful consumer product because it: (1) attracts a large and diverse set of interpretive communities; (2) works out essential dilemmas such as individuality versus conformity; (3) is an infinitely transferable form; (4) is mythic; (5) is populist; (6) is a game between good guys and bad guys; (7) has a constraining form that yields an open text; (8) illustrates core American values; (9) reveals tensions between adolescence and adulthood; and (10) is great fun.

The third paper by Lisa Penaloza presented ethnographic findings on how animals, humans, and mythic images are marketed, commodified, and consumed at a western stock show. The romance of the Wild West differs greatly from what really goes on at the show: educational seminars on artificial insemination and embryo transfer; pure bred cattle shampooed, blow-dried and carefully "finished" for the show ting; entertainments including a rodeo, mule tiding competitions, and draft horse and dog pulls; and state of the art marketing practices such as video sales pitches and satellite auctions. Nevertheless, romantic images and their associated values—rugged individualism, human independence and mastery over nature, and male dominance—remain as meanings used to market many of these products and services.

DISCUSSANT REMARKS

In his discussant remarks, Terrence H. Witkowski classified the consumption of the Wild West according to different levels of authenticity. *Originals* are material artifacts and other cultural productions that survive from the historical era of the Wild West. *Recreations* are things, services, sounds, and images that attempt to accurately reproduce originals and *interpretations* are things, services, sounds, and images that borrow elements (themes, styles) from originals, but combine and apply them in new ways. Not only has the distinction between the real and the mythical West often been blurred, the social definitions of each of the different levels of authenticity have changed over time.

Heightened Self-Consciousness: The Intended and Unintended Consequences of Marketing Activities

Lauren Block, New York University
Gavan Fitzsimons, Columbia University

With the expansion of consumerism and the consumer movement, considerable attention has been given recently to the potentially serious unintended consequences of traditional marketing activities. Such criticisms are typically focused on the impact of marketing on societal values and cultural norms. Marketing researchers have recently begun to explore the effects of traditional marketing practices on a smaller scale, focusing more specifically on the side effects of standard marketing activities on individuals or subsets of the population.

This session presented four papers that explore how standard marketing practices may affect consumer behavior by influencing the consumer's perceived in-group or out-group status (*perceived self-consciousness*). An underlying assumption in each paper is that perceived self-consciousness can be an intended or unintended byproduct or side effect of marketing strategy.

The Tepper paper raised the issue of self-consciousness in the context of being labelled as an elderly consumer. Tepper demonstrated, using both experimental and qualitative data, that promotion incentives that specifically target elderly consumers with age segmentation cues (e.g., Senior Citizen discounts) unwittingly engender perceived stigma and self-devaluation associated with use of the product.

Wooten addressed how self-consciousness affects purchase intentions among consumers in a numerically rare context. He suggested that self-consciousness mediates the impact of self-felt ethnicity on consumers' choice of food products traditionally associated with their ethnic in-group. Wooten experimentally manipulated social surroundings and then measured consumers' levels of self-consciousness. As consumers became conscious of the potential impact of the marketing activity they were less likely to be influenced by it.

Unlike the Tepper paper, which measured the effects of in-group consciousness on perceived attributions and behavioral intentions, and the Wooten paper, which focused on its effect on purchase behavior, the Aaker and Dean paper dealt with the effects of target marketing on out-group self-consciousness. Aaker and Dean explored the potential impact of targeting on in- and out-group self-consciousness. Based on a series of focus groups and in-depth interviews with consumers, advertising creatives and researchers, they proposed a typology of the situations under which the impact of target marketing on those in the *non* target market can be negative.

The final paper complemented the other three by introducing an interpretive methodology to the study of peripheral impacts of marketing. Block, Fitzsimons and Holbrook used an interpretive approach to study the effects of the beauty ideal on consumers' self-consciousness, as manifested through the products they consume and display. They developed a framework for understanding various types of beauty that correspond to consumers' perceptions of inclusion/exclusion with the beauty ideal. The authors suggest that self-consciousness of one's actual social position vis-a-vis one's desired social position is reflected in the lives of consumers, in pop culture generally, and in motion pictures especially.

Emergent Understanding of Relationships Among Consumption, Production, and the Family

Deborah D. Heisley, UCLA

Although the individual is the focus of most consumer research, the family is recognized by consumer behavior researchers as incredibly important. Most consumer research on the family addresses a priori hypothesized relationships between the family and consumption, focuses on pre-purchase decision making, and frequently misses the contextual richness of the family.

This session presents three empirical papers. Each project uses a qualitative, emergent methodology to attain a rich, complex understanding of consumption and production within the context of households and kinship structures. By focusing on the intergenerational transfer of goods, the American Indian arts and crafts industry, and VCR usage, these papers explicate the complex relationships that occur between consumption, production, and the people that construct and maintain meaning within families.

The first paper, "Structural Dimensions of the Inter-generational Transfer of Possessions," by Deborah D. Heisley, Deborah Cours, and Melanie Wallendorf, concentrates on the intergenerational transfer of goods. Seventeen in-depth interviews indicate that three general models are used by individuals or families to determine the flow of goods through the kinship structure. These models are termed the "immortality of self" model, the "family ties" model, and the "status enhancement of self" model. The immortality of self model and the status enhancement of self model focus on the goods, while the family ties model emphasizes the family relationships that are symbolized by the goods. Each model embraces the complex relationship of several factors. Examples are given of several of the factors operating in each model. When family members employ different models, conflict can occur.

The second paper, "Family Businesses and Recursive Relationships: The Impact of Production and Consumption of Family Structure," by Elisabeth Gilster examines family businesses, specifically the impact of family relationships on industrial consumption activities and of business activities on family structure. Ethnographic data from producers and intermediaries in the Navajo jewelry industry indicate that working with family is generally good for business. Family members foster learning, cooperation, and mutual trust. Being in business together has the effect of strengthening family bonds, but it also creates strains on family relationships. The resultant family situation is likely to have some impact on future industrial consumption activities.

The third paper, "The Family VCR: Ordinary Family Life With a Common Textual Product," by Thomas C. O'Guinn, Timothy Meyer, and Mary McNeil, reports the findings of a study of family consumer behavior as it relates to a common family product, the videocassette recorder. Participant observation, in-depth interviews, viewing questionnaires, and diaries were used in six households for periods from four months to eight years. Their findings indicate a largely individualistic family role structure, strongly influenced by gender and domain authority. They also find the family VCR strongly situated within interpretive communities, with the production and consumption of text an essential aspect of the socially embedded behavior they sought to explore. Finally, they note a distinct disparity between observed and self reported data.

This session goes beyond the typical focus on the interaction of family members surrounding purchase decisions. The focus is on the importance of the kinship structure and the household on negotiating meaning within the complex production and consumption activities which families and households engage in. Emergent, qualitative approaches capture the richness and complexities of these experiences.

Recent Advances in Social Marketing
Alan R. Andreasen, Georgetown University

In my 1992 Presidential Address, I urged consumer researchers to become more involved in social marketing claiming that: "... social marketing is not just good for the soul. It can provide rich intellectual challenges to ACR members of widely varying interests." This session was designed to further these objectives, most particularly, to insure that (a) the problems that consumer researchers choose to work on are responsive to the interests and needs of social marketing practitioners and (b) their research makes use of some of the leading concepts and findings of social marketers in the field.

The first paper in this session by James H. Mintz, Director for Program Promotion, Health and Welfare Canada, described how the federal health department in Canada uses psychographic research to develop campaigns in the area of substance abuse among Canadian youth. The paper described a unique series of tracking studies from 1988 onwards on the awareness, attitudes and behaviors of Canadian Youth as part of Health and Welfare Canada's social marketing campaign to prevent the spread of alcohol/drug abuse and smoking. Several examples were given of how such information influences the design of social marketing messages for youth.

Next was a paper by Steven Rabin, Executive Vice President, Porter/Novelli on race, ethnicity and social marketing. Rabin pointed out that, although many social marketing programs carefully segment markets by race and ethnicity, there is growing uncertainty as to just how we measure these two key variables. He outlined both realities and myths in our understanding of these phenomena and showed how Porter/Novelli has developed a new approach, called Cross Talk, to serve as a framework to deal with these new complexities.

Jeffrey D. Fisher and William A. Fisher, Professors of Psychology at the University of Connecticut and the University of Western Ontario, respectively, described at length their work attempting to change AIDS-risk behavior of adolescents and young adults. They reviewed the AIDS literature on interventions that have targeted risky sexual behavior and intravenous drug use practices. They then described their own work which is based on a highly generalizable model for promoting and evaluating AIDS-risk behavior change in any population of interest. The model holds that AIDS-risk reduction is a function of people's information about AIDS transmission and prevention, their motivation to reduce AIDS risk, and their behavioral skills for performing the specific acts involved in risk reduction. Supportive tests of this model, using structural equation modeling techniques, were reported for populations of university students, gay male affinity group members, and minority inner-city high school students.

James O. Prochaska, Director of the Cancer Prevention Research Center at the University of Rhode Island, next argued that much social marketing work to date dealing with problem behaviors has had very limited success. He suggested that, as a result, there is now a paradigm shift from an action paradigm to a stage paradigm for behavior change. The stage model, which he and his colleagues have spent several years developing, involves progression through five stages: precontemplation, contemplation, preparation, action and maintenance. Different processes of change are used to progress through each of these stages. Applications of the model demonstrate how stage-based social marketing procedures have increased participation rates from 1 to 5% of eligible subjects in action programs to 65 to 75% with stage-matched programs. The model's application to issues of program retention, resistance, relapse, and recovery from high risk behaviors was described.

Martin Fishbein, University of Illinois and Centers for Disease Control and Prevention, next described the development of theory-based community interventions to reduce AIDS risk behaviors by the CDC's AIDS community intervention demonstration project. This intervention is in five urban areas and is designed to increase condom use in a number of ethnically-diverse, high risk populations: men who have sex with men but who do not identify themselves as gay, intravenous drug users (IDUs), female sex partners of IDUs, prostitutes, and street youth. Dr. Fishbein's paper provided an overview of this project and data demonstrating the validity of the theory underlying the interventions.

The final paper was presented by Robert Hornik of the Annenberg School of Communications, University of Pennsylvania. Dr. Hornik described in detail many of the lessons learned from ten HEALTHCOM projects in eight countries. The sixteen interventions (some sites included more than one topic) addressed a variety of child survival related practices, most often the use of oral rehydration therapy and vaccinations. Paired before-after surveys of large representative samples of caretakers of young children were undertaken, supplemented in some sites by time series or control area data. Overall, nine of the sixteen evaluated outcomes indicated substantial success, with absolute increases of 12-24% of the population doing recommended behaviors. There is credible evidence that observed changes were the result of the communications interventions.

The paper also considered why some programs were successful and others were not. Both cross-site evidence and evidence from individual programs support four broad explanations for relative success: (1) ensuring that health communication programs fit with opportunities to put the recommendations into practice: program success was constrained by limitations in complementary delivery of health services; (2) choosing channels that reach audiences; programs were more most successful when they reached 60% or more of the population with their messages which was easiest to do with mass media channels; (3) choosing specific messages that are relevant to the behavior, and (4) building an agency capable of creating a coherent health communication system rather than just producing educational materials. The HEALTHCOM project has shown the possibility of doing large scale social marketing in developing countries effectively, reaching much of the target population and achieving substantial behavior change.

Behavioral Perspectives on Bundling Research
Rajan Krish, University of Arizona
Pallab Paul, University of Denver
Joydeep Srivastava, University of Arizona

Bundling is a pervasive practice in the marketing of products and services. It is the strategy of marketing two or more products and/or services in a single "package" under a single price tag (Guiltinan 1987). The theoretical issues underlying bundling strategies span both the psychology and the economics of consumer value perception. Conceptual insights and empirical evidence on these issues will be useful for understanding more operational questions such as how a specific set of component products should be bundled, presented and priced; how the specific bundle may be evaluated by consumers; the types of bundles that may be the most appealing (e.g., whether or not the component products should be complementary); and how specific consumer characteristics (e.g., expertise and knowledge in the product category) might affect consumers' evaluation of a bundle. Thus the aim of the session was to understand bundling from a behavioral perspective. The session was developed around a set of three papers that broadly examined the effects of bundle type, perceptions of savings, task framing, alternative information presentation formats, and consumer characteristics on consumers' perception of the value of the bundle.

The first paper by Harlam, Krishna, Lehmann, and Mela (1993) examined bundling issues such as the types of products that should be bundled together and the price that should be charged in the context of both durable and non-durable products. Their results indicate that different ways of presenting economically equivalent bundles affect consumers' evaluation of the bundle and consequently purchase intent. They also examined the effect of consumer familiarity with the bundle on the evaluation of the bundle itself. They report that more familiar consumers react differently to the presentation of equivalent bundles than less familiar consumers. Further, more familiar consumers have a higher purchase intent for lower priced bundles than less familiar consumers.

The second paper by Kaicker, Bearden, and Urbany (1993) reported the findings of an experiment that examined the effect of perceived savings of bundle components on overall perceptions of bundle value. Specifically, increasing savings on the focal item increased not only consumer perceptions of value for the focal item, but also increased perceived value for the additional item as well as for the bundle, overall. Similarly, the findings showed that increased savings on the additional item increased perceptions of value for the bundle, but did not affect the perceived value of the focal product. The results indicated that the perceived value of the incremental item and the incremental cost were significant determinants of the perceived value of the focal item and of the overall bundle.

Chakravarti, Krish, Paul, and Srivastava (1993) reported the findings of three experiments which examined how differential bundling and framing of choice alternatives influence judgments and choice. They extended and tested Thaler's (1985) normative principles for integrated and segregated presentation of multiple gains and losses. Their results suggest that segregated presentation of bundle components is preferred to consolidated presentations but that segregation/integration effects on combined value judgments are moderated by the nature of the components involved. Thus, a segregated warranty may make the risk of product failure salient whereas a segregated accessory such as an icemaker may make add-on value more salient. This would produce differential effects on perceived bundle value and choice outcomes. The results thus suggest that the presentation and framing of product and service bundles may influence the salience of product features and consequently consumers' perceived value and choice.

The session concluded with discussant's comments from C. W. Park. He provided a framework integrating the three papers and discussed avenues for future research. Noting that each of the three papers in the session focused on price as the bundling device, he called for research examining bundling approaches using other marketing mix elements (e.g., advertising).

A Study of the Concept of Affective Choice Mode for Consumer Decisions

Banwari Mittal, University of Miami[1]

ABSTRACT

The concept of *Affective Choice Mode* is developed to reflect decision processes for highly involving products that do not lend themselves to extensive information processing. This construct is contrasted with the conventional "information processing mode." The two concepts are then set in a context marked by the consumer involvement in a brand-decision task and potential 'expressiveness' of products. Data from an experimental study based on advertising stimuli for hypothetical brands in four product categories are utilized to empirically test the proposed concepts and their interrelationships.

Consider a consumer buying an alarm clock radio. She inspects several models, noticing many differences among them. Some models have a snooze-alarm control feature, some don't. Some have a battery back-up, others don't. The models also vary on wake-to-music or to-alarm feature, top-mounted versus side controls, push-button versus rotary or sliding switches, lighted alarm-set indicator, automatic FM frequency control, the type of wood grain finish, and the price. She reviews her relative preference for these diverse features, and chooses the model that gives her the best combination of the desired features.

Now consider her buying a dress for an upcoming big social event. Scanning a rack full of dresses in a store, she pulls out a few that seemed nice. One of them particularly caught her eye; she tries it on, and thinks she looks great in it. She tries another one, which she thought made her look too conservative. A third one made her look too sexy. Somehow, the first one looked so right for her; a few more minutes of contemplation about what a great impression she would make donning that dress in the party, and she has made up her mind about that dress.

The above two episodes illustrate two alternative choice modes, termed here, respectively, the *Information Processing Mode*, and the *Affective Choice Mode*. These are explained below.

CONCEPT EXPLICATION AND THEORY DEVELOPMENT

The Information Processing Mode. In his seminal book, *An Information Processing Theory of Consumer Choice*, Bettman (1979) describes the cognitive operations that a consumer performs in a brand decision context. The consumer is thought to acquire information about brand attributes, form evaluative criteria, judge the levels of these attributes in various brands, and employ some judgment rule or heuristic to combine these attribute-levels for overall brand evaluation. MacInnis and Price (1987) refer to the above as "discursive" or "descriptive" information processing, and point out that this has been the traditional focus of consumer information processing research.

The Affective Choice Mode. Zajonc (1980) suggested that the above view of consumer choice appears rather limited, and that not all consumer decisions follow such a path. He argued, "the assumption questioned here is that affect, such as that contained in preferences, is necessarily post cognitive, which implies that a feeling of a preference is generated *upon* the encoding of the specific properties of the object, after the evaluation of their utilities, and after the computation of the individual component utilities into a joint product that represents the overall preference" (Zajonc and Markus 1982, p. 125). Zajonc suggests that affect (i.e., liking) for an object or a brand can occur through other psychological processes which do not entail any elaborate cognitive operations. This alternative mode of preference formation may be termed *Affective Choice Mode (ACM)*.

As one possibility, Zajonc suggests the "mere exposure" theory: when a consumer is repeatedly exposed to a stimulus, s/he develops a positive feeling for the object; this occurs due to sheer familiarity with the object, as one experiences a "glow of warmth, a sense of ownership, a feeling of intimacy." A related mechanism is habituation, which is "repeated use," rather than "repeated exposure". Yet another mechanism is "social reinforcement": teenagers and impressionable adults alike come to develop a preference for specific brands of conspicuous products (Banana Republic clothing) based not on any intrinsic qualities of the brand, but rather on the kind of following the brand has acquired, and on the brand's popularity among one's peers.

In each of the above "explanations" of preference formation, the important idea is that the component features of the object do not play a role as they do in the traditional, IP mode. Rather, it is a *global*, overall view of the object, a "holistic impression" if you will, that constitutes product appraisal. This appraisal can be, and often is, instantaneous, as in "first impressions," or as in "love at first sight." But it can also be the outcome of long term habituation, as in, say, "getting used to a colleague." In either case, the affect felt toward the object can be, and often is, independent of the encoding and processing of any component features or attributes of the object.

In such affective appraisals, the appraiser thinks not as much about the object per se, as about oneself in relation to the object. One asks, for example, how would I look in this hairdo, or does this watch suit my upscale conservative image? In the IP mode in contrast, as for example in buying a personal computer, the focus is on the object without much reference to self-image.

Affective appraisals also differ in how consumers explain their decisions and choices. Preferences formed in the IP mode are explained in terms of the "component" features on which these preferences are based. A personal computer is liked or not liked because of its memory capacity, speed, and connectivity, for example. In contrast, preferences based on cognition-independent affect are explained in overall global terms, e.g., "I liked this dress because its style is good." Or even more notably, they are explained by mere paraphrasing, i.e., *not* explained at all; for example, "I chose this dress because I liked it," or "I liked it because it is so 'cool'." Understandably, in common parlance, love at first sight is referred to as being "blind."

Low Involvement Is Not ACM. In describing the IP mode, Bettman (1979) argues, correctly, that these processes may be used extensively in some cases and only minimally in others. The contingent factor is *Involvement*, the extent to which a decision is risky or important. When the purchase is expensive and/or entails other social or psychological risks, consumer engages in the IP activity extensively. On the other hand, in most low price, low risk or otherwise trivial purchase decisions, the consumer processes sparse product information only cursorily (Mitchell 1981, Laurent and Kapferer 1985). Thus, levels of involvement correspond to the levels of the IP mode.

---

[1]On leave from Northern Kentucky University.

This may lead one to assume that *ACM* occurs in the low involvement decision task environment, and IPM in the high involvement task environment. This assumed low/high involvement and ACM/IPM correspondence is *mis*guided. In our view, ACM and IPM are not opposites but rather simply *different*. The absence or low-level presence of IPM does not in and of itself imply the presence of ACM. In low levels of IPM, sparse, feature specific information may determine the final choice; for example, the brand of salt may be chosen simply by noting whether or not the brand is "iodized." ACM, on the other hand, entails or may entail as much deliberation as a high IPM-based choice. A dress, generally bought in the ACM mode, is by no means a low involvement decision. What matters is not the extent of deliberation, but rather the focus of deliberation: component features in the IP mode, and holistic, self-implicating object impressions in ACM. See Mittal (1988) for further discussion.

Product Expressiveness and ACM. The foregoing postulation is grounded in Park and Mittal (1985) and Park and Young's (1986) distinction concerning "cognitive" and "affective" involvement. According to these authors, cognitive involvement occurs when consumers "process *attribute-based* messages or engage in self-generated cognitive reasoning about message *contents*." Affective involvement occurs, in contrast, when a person identifies a new stimulus with an examplar (i.e., s/he encodes it as similar to something in memory with which an affect is already attached), and then automatically transfers that affect to the brand itself. A person reacts to the stimuli based on prior experiences, emotional experience the stimulus engenders, or social and personality images associated with the product's use, etc. For example, on seeing a particular dress, a consumer may be reminded of a favorite TV star who may have once donned a similar dress; this memory retrieval would then attach the retrieved affect or liking (or disliking) to the present stimulus. More commonly, such "extrinsic" ("extrinsic" to the product, that is) affect-laden exemplars are presented in the brand communications themselves, e.g., an ad featuring a football star in conjunction with the product. This distinction is also echoed in recent social-psychological literature on affective and cognitive types of attitudes (Millar and Millar 1990, Edwards 1990).

Not all products lend themselves to ACM appraisal. This may be because the affect-laden exemplar just does not seem *relevant* to the product category, e.g., featuring Cindy Crawford in an ad for table salt or for a personal computer. What matters most for such products is what the brand does, in *physical* terms, or how the brand performs *objectively*. Park and Young (1986) refer to such products as 'Utilitarian." The other category of products are called "value expressive." These are bought and consumed primarily for the emotional outcomes or the personality image that their use enables the user to express. As a slight departure from this utilitarian/ expressive *dichotomy*, we recognize the presence of the utilitarian function in all products at least to some degree; e.g., a dress has an obvious functional, utilitarian aspect actually, apart from its expressive value. In addition to their varying functional utility, they have less or more expressiveness. Thus, we consider "expressiveness" as an independent characterization of objects (Mittal 1988). It is this "expressive aspect" of products, then, that leads to ACM: the more expressive the product, the more likely it would be appraised via ACM.

Hypotheses. The purpose of the empirical research reported below is to study the concept of affective choice mode and its relationship with related concepts. We expect involvement to be related positively to the IP mode; in contrast, we expect the "expressiveness" to be positively associated with *ACM*. Finally, even though, IPM and ACM do not conceptually imply the opposite of each other, in most empirical situations we would expect the two to be negatively related. Moreover, considering that affective judgments are more readily formed than cognitive judgments, we would model ACM to be negatively influencing IPM rather than the other way around. That is, the greater the extent to which ACM is utilized, the lesser the use of IPM. We turn next to an empirical study to test these expectations.

METHOD

Student subjects from undergraduate business classes were exposed to two advertisements, one for each of the two hypothetical brands of a product category. Four product categories were chosen: shampoo, perfume, pencil, and greeting card— selected due to their (a) pertinence to and familiarity among students, and (b) representation of a broad range of the two antecedent variables— involvement and expressiveness. A priori, pencils were deemed to be low on both, greeting card to be moderate to high on both, shampoo to be moderate to high on involvement and low to moderate on expressiveness, and perfume to be high on both involvement and expressiveness. Also, perfume and greeting card were expected to be processed via ACM, shampoo via the IP mode, whereas both modes were expected to be low for pencils.

Each ad was a color print ad, converted, for purposes of large-group sessions, into a set of 6 to 8 slides with synchronized audio. The ad content for the *two* brands in each product category differed considerably, but in overall terms, both the shampoo ads and likewise both the pencil ads featured their utilitarian attributes (e.g., cleanses oily deposits for shampoo, and easy to sharpen, break resistent for pencils); in contrast, both the perfume and greeting card ads focussed on emotional/personality aspects (e.g., "When You want a certain presence," for perfume, and "fun to send and fun to receive" for cards). The ad content was designed not as a particular treatment, but rather to provide, collectively, adequate variation on the effects they were to generate.

Procedure. Subjects were randomly assigned to one of the four product categories: 21 for shampoo, 21 for pencil, 20 for perfume, and 20 for greeting card, each product run as a separate session. Perfume subjects were all females while the subjects for the other three products were both males and females. (Of the 35 female student subjects available, 20 were drawn randomly and assigned to the perfume condition. The remaining 15 female and all 47 male students were together assigned randomly to the other three products.) The study was introduced as a research sponsored by a local advertising firm interested in testing ads for two new brands. The subjects were told to make up their minds as to which of the two advertised brands they would like to buy. They were also informed that at the end they would be given a free sample of their preferred brand. After being shown the two ads twice (to provide adequate processing opportunity), subjects answered the research questionnaire.

Measures. Measures elicited for the four constructs (Involvement, Expressiveness, IPM, and ACM) are shown in Exhibit 1. Given that the experimental task was brand-decision, *purchase* involvement was the relevant concept, measured here by Mittal's (1989) scale. Expressiveness is measured by the perceived relevance of a set of consumption goals for the specified products. The information processing measures used here are drawn from prior literature (e.g., Laurent and Kapferer 1985). The ACM measures are based on our description of the concept in the foregoing. To supplement the structured measures, respondents were asked two open ended questions: "Why did you prefer this brand?" and "Why did you *not* prefer the other brand?"

Analysis and Results

Factor Analysis. Since the four constructs are measured by

EXHIBIT 1
Measures of the Four Constructs

Purchase-Involvement

1. How important is it to you to make a right choice out of these brands?
    Not at all important (1)/Very important (7)

2. In choosing from among these two brands, how concerned are you about the outcome?
    Not at all concerned (1)/Very concerned (7)

3. In selecting from these two brands, would you say:
    I would not care at all as to which one I buy (1)/I would care a great deal as to which one I buy (7)

4. How important in your life is the brand choice you made in this study?
    Not at all important (1)/Very important (7)

5. In any ways that matter to you how similar or different are these brands?
    Very similar (1)/Very different (7)

Expressiveness

Below are some general goals which you may or may not have had in mind while making your selection of this product. To what extent were these the goals you were seeking or were hoping to satisfy by buying this product? Would you say that you wanted your chosen brand to be:

6. Socially prestigious
    Not at all (1)/Very much (7)

7. Be known to be an expensive brand
    Not at all (1)/Very much (7)

8. Be in fashion or vogue
    Not at all (1)/Very much (7)

9. Should be a brand which I can proudly display
    Not at all (1)/Very much (7)

10. The brand should feel pleasant to my senses
    Not at all (1)/Very much (7)

11. Be something that helps me express my personality
    Not at all (1)/Very much (7)

12. Should set me in good mood when I use it
    Not at all (1)/Very much (7)

13. Be sensually appealing
    Not at all (1)/Very much (7)

14. Be most compatible with how I like to think of myself
    Not at all (1)/Very much (7)

15. Should fit my style
    Not at all (1)/Very much (7)

Information Processing Mode

16. In choosing between these two brands did you consider:
    No information at all (1)/A great deal of information (7)

    And did you:

17. Engage in no feature-by-feature comparison (1)/Engaged in a lot of feature-by-feature comparison (7)

18. Spent hardly any mental effort (1)/Spent a great deal of mental effort (7)

19. How many features of the brand did you consider?
    0 1 2 3 4 5 6 7 8 9

EXHIBIT 1 (CONTINUED)
Measures of the Four Constructs

Affective Choice Mode
Before you made your choice, were you:

20. Weighing good and bad points of the brands (1)/Weighing your *overall* impressions of the brands (7)

21. Thinking more about *the contents* of the brands (1)/Thinking more about yourself as the user (7)

22. In trying to explain your brand choice to someone else, would you say that:
    I could pinpoint in clearcut words my reasons for choosing the brand (1)/I guess I'll just have to say that I chose it "because I liked it." (7)

23. And while making up your mind, were you:
    Contemplating individual features of the brands rather than their *overall* appropriateness (1)/Contemplating overall appropriateness of the brands rather than individual features (7)

---

multiple items, the data were factor analyzed using principal components method. Five factors emerged with eigenvalues >1.0 and 75.8% total variance explained. As Table 1 shows one factor each emerged for involvement, IPM and ACM. Although there are some cross-factor minor loadings, the dominant pattern of item-factor loadings confirms that the measures hypothesized to operationalize a concept cohere. A notable exception is the emergence of two (rather than one) factor for the ten items of expressiveness. The first dimension (expressiveness-I) reflected the public-display aspect (Items 6 through 9 in Table 1); the second dimension (expressiveness-II) captured the aspect of one's inner enjoyment and self-concept congruence (Items 10 through 15 in Table 1). Subsequently, we found a parallel in the self-consciousness literature (e.g., see Scheier and Carver 1980), suggesting that a person's attentional focus can be on either one's private self or public self. In the following analysis, we treat expressiveness as a bi-dimensional construct.

Reliability. The coefficient alpha for internal reliabilities was: .938 for involvement, .885 for Expressiveness-I, .946 for Expressiveness-II, .767 for IPM, and .670 for ACM. The relatively lower reliability for ACM points to the need for further development for this scale.

Protocol Analysis. The two open ended questions ("Why did you prefer the brand you chose?" and "Why did you not prefer the brand you did *not* choose?") were coded independently by three judges. Each sentence was coded in one of the following two categories (see sample coding in Exhibit 2):

(1) *IP Mode Related Thoughts.* This included mention of an intrinsic feature of the brand, or of a consumer benefit whose linkage to intrinsic features is transparent, or reasons that concern a physical outcome from product use, and/or use of any cues for such benefits and outcomes.

(2) *ACM Related Thoughts.* Mention of personality-, personal images, personal enjoyment, or other psycho-social benefits.

The inter-judge agreement was 92% for pencils, 87% for greeting card, 81% for perfume, and 73% for shampoo. The differences were resolved through mutual discussions (with 7% unresolvables dropped). The frequency count in each category served as the measure of protocol-based IPM and ACM scores.

Product scores on the four constructs. Construct scores, computed by averaging the corresponding items in the structured questionnaire, are displayed in Table 2. As expected, pencils were the lowest on involvement and expressiveness, and also on IPM. Shampoo and perfume were moderate and comparable on involvement. Greeting cards scored the highest on involvement and equaled perfume on expressiveness-II (the personal enjoyment factor). On information processing, shampoo and perfume scored about equal, each scoring higher than the other two products. The ACM score for pencils was somewhat higher than one would expect, but it did not differ from the ACM score for shampoo. As expected, perfume and greeting cards both scored higher on ACM than did the other two products.

Also shown in Table 2 are protocol-based scores on ACM and IPM. Based on the reasons for the liked brand, perfume showed more ACM than did shampoo. Greeting card also showed more ACM than did pencils or shampoo. And, shampoos and pencils showed more IPM than did perfumes or greeting cards.

LISREL Estimates of the Model. The model in Figure was estimated by a maximum likelihood, LISREL-IV procedure (Joreskog and Sorbom 1984). The chi-square statistic shows Model 1 to have a poor overall fit (chi-square=9.10, df=3, p=.028). Inspection of the modification indices showed the need to free the causal path from expressiveness-I to IPM. Because expressive products do not lend themselves to being assessed via detailed cognitive operations, this link would seem logical, and if significant, would be expected to be negative in valence. The revised model, Model 1a showed good overall fit (chi-square=.83 (d.f.=2, 'p'=.66). Bentler and Bonnet's (1980) incremental fit index also shows model 1 to be poor but model 1a to have good fit.

Structural Path Estimates. In Models 1 and 1a, all paths are significant except the expressiveness-I to ACM path which is positive in valence (as expected) but falls below statistical significance. Expressiveness-II was positively and significantly related to ACM. Involvement had a positive and significant effect on IPM. Finally, the significance of ACM-to-IPM path (in Models 1 and 1A) provides support for the hypothesized negative association between these alternative choice modes.

Model Estimates Using Protocol Data. The lower panel in Figure presents similar estimates, but with the protocol-based measures for IPM and ACM. As can be seen, Model 1 had good overall fit, as had Model 1a. However, Model 1a was not superior to Model 1 as the chi-square difference between the two was not statistically significant for one degree-of-freedom difference. In terms of the hypothesized paths, again expressiveness-II was but expressiveness-I was not significantly related to ACM. However,

TABLE 1
Factor Pattern Matrix for the Measures of 4 Constructs Using Oblique Rotation (N = 82)

Construct	Items[a]	1[b]	FACTORS 2	3[b]	4	5
Involvement:	1					-.84
	2					-.86
	3					-.79
	4					-.88
	5	.40				-.54
Expressiveness:	6			.82		
	7			.85		
	8			.84		
	9	.32		.54		
	10	.72				
	11	.76				
	12	.82				
	13	.66		.35		
	14	.81				
	15	.73				
IP Mode:	16				.83	
	17		.41		.60	
	18			.32	.68	
	19				.69	-.27
ACM:	20		-.74	.33		-.26
	21		-.73		.33	
	22		-.63			
	23		-.60			
Eigenvalues		9.50	2.26	2.36	1.30	1.28
% variance explained		41.3	12.9	10.3	5.7	5.6

Note: Loadings smaller than .25 omitted
[a] Item Numbers correspond to those in Exhibit 1.
[b] Factor 3 will be termed Expressiveness-I, measured by items 6 through 9; Factor 1 will be termed Expressivness-II, measured by items 10 through 15.

EXHIBIT 2
A Sample of Protocol Sentences Reflecting IPM and ACM

Information Processing Mode (IPM):

1. This brand (of shampoo) manages split ends.

2. The other brand (of shampoo) is designed to remove grease which would dry my hair.

3. I like the idea of changing scents. I would like to try this Innovative product. (perfume)

4. Because it seems like a milder, softer fragrance (perfume).

5. This (pencil) sharpens easy...that is a most important quality.

Affective Choice Mode (ACM):

1. I think this brand (of shampoo) can make me feel better than the other...the other brand makes me a little complicated.

2. (dislike this shampoo brand because) I didn't personally identify with the pictured users.

3. I prefer this (perfume) because it seems moderate, not too flashy...the other brand looked more nontraditionalist.

4. It kind of fits my personality—"When you want a certain presence." I like to stand out and be noticed.

5. This (greeting card) is light and funny and cute...the other brand seemed too serious and I am not a serious person.

TABLE 2
Individual Product Scores on the Four Constructs
Means (S.D.)

	Shampoo (N=21)	Perfume (N=20)	Pencils (N=21)	Greeting Card (N=20)
A. Structured Measures				
Involvement	4.08[a,b] (1.15)	4.62[b] (1.14)	2.26[a,b] (1.01)	5.25[a] (1.22)
Expressiveness—I	2.82[a] (1.36)	4.58[a,b] (1.30)	1.72[a,b] (1.02)	2.98[b] (1.23)
Expressiveness—II	4.33[a,b] (1.08)	5.70[a] (0.99)	1.85[a,b] (1.15)	5.69[b] (0.96)
IP Mode	4.16[a,c] (0.82)	4.12[b,d] (1.08)	2.95[a,b] (1.04)	3.08[c,d] (0.96)
Affective Choice Mode	3.73[a,b] (1.15)	4.38[b,d] (0.98)	3.79[c,d] (1.13)	4.75[a,c] (1.50)
B. Protocol Data				
IP Mode	1.61[a,b] (1.11)	0.45[a,c] (0.68)	1.42[c,d] (0.81)	0.35[b,d] (0.74)
Affective Choice Mode	0.047[a] (0.21)	0.75[a] (0.71)	0.0[a] (0.0)	1.10[a] (0.64)

[a,b,c,d] Variable Means that share any of the superscripts are different at $p \leq .05$ across the corresponding products. For example, involvement mean scores: (1) differ between shampoo and perfume, (2) differ between shampoo and pencil, (3) differ between shampoo and greeting card, (4) differ between perfume and pencil, (5) do *not* differ between perfume and greeting card, and (6) differ between pencil and greeting card. Thus, for each variable, 6 pair comparisons are possible.

---

involvement-to-IPM link was not statistically significant (discussion later). The support for the ACM-to-IPM path was robust. Finally, in Model 1a, the released link of expressiveness-I to IPM was significant and also had a negative sign which is consistent with prior expectations.

Discussion. Some aspects of our research design bear closely on our results. Because the experimental setting virtually ensured a high level of attention to the ads, subjects are likely to have processed information simply because the information *was* presented to them.

The expected relationship of ACM with other concepts was observed. The magnitude of beta for the ACM to IPM link was robust in both but stronger in the protocol data (-.55 versus -.28) Likewise, the expressiveness-II to ACM linkage is stronger for the protocol- than for the structured-measures based data (beta =.49 versus .25). The failure to obtain significant linkage of expressiveness-I to ACM in both estimates is an oddity. A plausible explanation is that the appropriateness of brands for social prestige and public display (which is what expressiveness-I reflects) is judged in the real world from day-to-day observations of brand-users' lifestyles in one's social environment, and the experimental stimuli did not provide for such opportunity.

Finally, the involvement-to-IPM linkage needs a comment. This linkage is significant in direct measure data but not in the protocol data. In direct measures, respondents' real world decision experience (high IP for high involvement product) may have favorably influenced the consistency in the reported involvement and the reported IPM. In the protocols on the other hand, high IPM may have been reported in high as well as low involvement products simply because the information *was* presented. Thus, even a low-involving product like pencil scores high on protocol based IPM (see Table 2); this would appear to be responsible for the nonsignificance of the Involvement—>IPM link in the protocol based analysis.

On the other hand, the failure of this path in this particular analysis may imply that the hypothesis is actually false. As Table 2 shows, the protocol scores on IPM are quite low for the relatively high involvement products perfume and greeting card. Indeed, a major theme of this paper has been that some high involvement products (the ones that are expressive) are appraised not via IPM, but via ACM. The IPM relationship may have been supported in the past due to the inclusion of primarily utilitarian products.

As already argued, IPM and ACM are negatively related but they are not mirror images of each other. Rather, they are distinct

FIGURE
LISREL Estimates of the Relationships

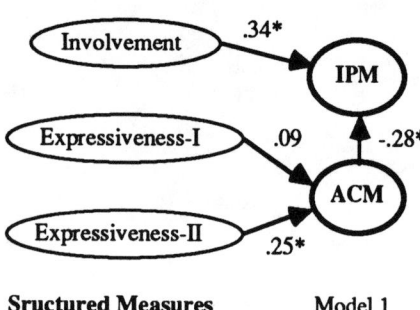

Structured Measures   Model 1

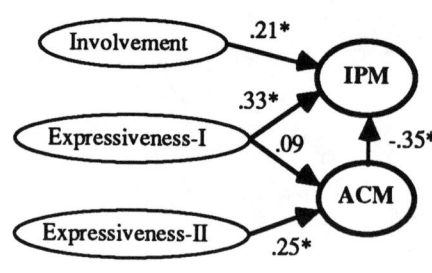

Model 1a

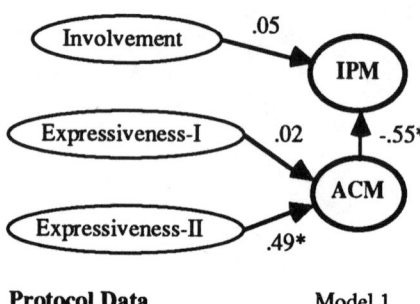

Protocol Data   Model 1

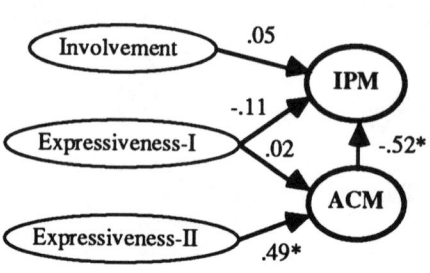

Model 1a

Overall Model fit	Structured Measures		Protocol data	
	Model 1	Model 1a	Model 1	Model 1a
Chi-square	9.10	.83	4.07	2.99
D.F.	3	2	3	2
"p"	.03	.66	.25	.22
Incremental fit	.77	.97	.92	.94
R-Squared (for IPM)	.15	.24	.28	.25
R-Squared (for ACM)	.10	.10	.25	.25

Correlations among the Independent Variables		
Involvement		
Expressiveness-I	.43*	
Expressiveness-II	.68*	.70*

* Significant at 'p'<.05.

concepts. This is because both can exist at low levels (as for a low involvement product, like light bulb) or at high levels (as for someone buying a car if the performance features as well as stylistic aspects of the car are important).

In arguing that when products are highly expressive, the brand is likely to be appraised via ACM, and that information processing is less likely to occur (this being the major theme of the present paper), information processing was defined in a specific way. It was defined as a cognitive algebra performed on a product's intrinsic attributes. Were it to be instead defined more broadly as attention to and encoding of the brand as a whole, then any mental operation performed on the brand (e.g., contemplation of the brand in relation to self, observation of personalities of other brand users, etc.) would qualify as information processing. The processing differences between products that are and are not expressive could not then be studied. Thus, although the definition of information processing is somewhat arbitrarily limited, that limited conception *has* guided much of the consumer decision literature. It is of value to study the boundaries of that limited conception, and to explore choice processes that transcend it. The investigation of ACM in the present paper has been an attempt in this direction.

REFERENCES

Bettman, James R., 1979. *An information processing theory of consumer choice*, MA: Addison-Wesley Publishing Company, Inc.

Edwards Kari (1990), "The Interplay of Affect and Cognition in Attitude Formation and Change," *Journal of Personality and Social Psychology*, Vol. 59 (2), 202-216.

Hirschman, E.C., 1980. "Attributes of attributes and layers of meaning," in *Advances in Consumer Research*, Vol 7, J.C. Olson (ed.), Ann Arbor, MI: Assoc. for Cons. res.

Hirschman, E.C. and M.B. Holbrook, 1982. "Hedonic consumption: emerging concepts, methods and propositions," *Journal of Marketing*, 46, 92-101.

Joreskog, Karl G. and Dag Sorbom, 1984. *LISREL VI: Analysis of Linear Structural Relationships by the Method of Maximum Likelihood*, Mooresville, IN: Scientific Software Inc.

Kroeber-Riel, W., 1979. "Activation research: psychological approaches in consumer research," *Journal of Consumer Research*, 5 (March), 240-250.

Laurent, Gilles and Jean-Noel Kapferer, 1985. "Measuring Consumer Involvement Profiles," *Journal of Marketing Research*, 22, 41-53.

Lutz, K.A. and R.J. Lutz, 1979. "Effects of Interactive Imagery on Learning: Application to advertising," *Journal of Applied Psychology*, 62, 493-98.

MacInnis, Deborah J. and Linda Price (1987). "The Role of Imagery in Information Processing: Review and Extensions," *Journal of Consumer Research*, 13 (March), 473-91.

Millar, Murray G. and Karen U. Millar (1990), "Attitude Change as a Function of Attitude Type and Argument Type," *Journal of Personaity and Social Psychology*, Vol. 59 (2), 217-228.

Mitchell, A.A., 1981. "The Dimensions of Advertising Involvement," ed. K. B. Monroe, *Advances in Consumer Research*, Ann Arbor, MI: Assoc. for Cons. Res., 25-35.

Mittal, Banwari (1989), "Measuring Purchase-Decision Involvement," *Psychology and Marketing*, 6, 147-162.

Mittal, Banwari (1988), "The Role of Affective Choice Mode in the Consumer Purchase of Expressive Products," *Journal of Economic Psychology*, 9, 499-524.

Park C. Whan and Banwari Mittal (1985), "A Theory of Involvement in Consumer Behavior: Problems and Issues," in Jagdish N. Sheth (ed.), *Research in Consumer Behavior*, Vol. 1, Greenwich, CT: Jai Press, Inc. pp. 201-231.

Park, C. Whan and S. Mark Young, 1986. Consumer response to television commercials: The impact of involvement and background music on brand attitude formation. *Journal of Marketing Research*, (Feb.) 11-24.

Raaij, W.F. van, 1984. "Affective and Cognitive Reactions to Advertising," Report No. 84-111, Cambridge, MA: Marketing Science Institute.

Scheier, M.F. and C.S. Carver, 1981. "Private and public aspects of self," L. Wheeler (ed.), *Review of Personality and Social Psychology*, 2, Beverly Hills, CA: Sage.

Solomon, Michael R. (1983), "The Role of Products as Social Stimuli: A Symbolic Interactionism Perspective," *Journal of Consumer Research*, 10 (Dec.), 319-329.

Zajonc, Robert B., 1980. "feeling and thinking: preferences need no inferences," *American Psychologist*, 35 (February), 151-75.

_____, and Hazel Markus, 1982. "Affective and Cognitive Factors in Preferences," *Journal of Consumer Research*, 9 (Septem), 123-31.

Mere Exposure and the Cognitive-Affective Debate Revisited

Marc Vanhuele, Groupe HEC

ABSTRACT

There currently are two interpretations of how affect is generated in the mere exposure effect. Key evidence for and against each interpretation is reviewed and found questionable. A new approach to study the phenomenon is suggested, building on the concept of "perceptual fluency". This approach may give new insights into how and under which conditions low-involvement exposures to stimuli in a consumer behavior context may lead to more positive affect for those stimuli.

INTRODUCTION

The mere exposure effect is introduced in many recent consumer behavior and advertising handbooks as one way in which low-involvement exposures to marketing stimuli can generate more positive affect for those stimuli. Important is that this enhancement has been observed even when those stimuli are not recognized. Although mere exposure has become part of the jargon of our discipline, its implications for consumer behavior are actually unclear. Despite all the research effort psychologists and consumer behavior researchers have devoted to the phenomenon, some authors have questioned its relevance for understanding repetition effects of marketing stimuli (e.g. Cohen and Areni 1991; Petty, Unnava, and Strathman 1991). Two decades of systematic investigations of the effect by psychologists (see Bornstein 1989 for a review) have indeed produced few insights into how and under which conditions it may operate in consumer behavior. The main reason for this knowledge gap may be that we do not have a well-accepted theory of how mere exposure can influence affect. Such a theory would help us transcend the specific manipulations in the existing studies and could lead to more systematic applied research. Unfortunately, the dynamics behind the mere exposure effect are still a matter of debate. The present paper analyzes the strongest evidence advanced by the two camps in this debate. It is argued that this evidence is inconclusive as to what the driving factors behind the mere exposure effect are. In the final section of the paper a possible new direction for future research is suggested that avoids the problems with these previous studies. The main objective of this paper, however, is to activate the debate on the antecedents of affect in the mere exposure effect. A first section introduces the antagonists and their position, and the second section gives a critique of their interpretation of the empirical evidence. The third and final section develops a new interpretation of mere exposure, based on a recent theory of recognition memory.

THE DEBATE: ONE OR TWO EVALUATION SYSTEMS

Zajonc (1968), who introduced the mere exposure effect and the associated research methodology to mainstream psychology, used it as an anchor to develop his theory about the independence of cognition and affect. He demonstrates that exposure to a stimulus is a sufficient condition for the enhancement of affect, and that this enhancement is independent of recognition (Kunst-Wilson and Zajonc 1980). This result is taken as evidence that affect and cognition are under the control of two separate, parallel, and partially independent systems. Moreover, these systems not only function independently but also attend to different stimulus features, labeled "preferanda" and "discriminanda" respectively (Zajonc 1980).

Other researchers challenge this view with the argument that the absence of recognition does not imply the absence of cognition: some other form of cognitive analysis that is not reflected in recognition and cannot be detected with existing methodologies may precede and influence the affective judgments (Lazarus 1984; Tsal 1985). Zajonc replies that this argument cannot be falsified and that therefore "such a theory would have no constraints at all and ... would be quite useless" (Zajonc, Pietromonaco, and Bargh 1982, p. 213). On the other hand, Zajonc from his part fails to specify the circumstances under which affect would be a product of the affective system alone, independently of cognition (like in mere exposure). Another issue is how changes in affect that *are* accompanied by recognition can be explained: can affect also in this case be the product of the affective system alone, or does the presence of recognition imply that affect is a product of (the interaction of) both systems? And if both systems play a role, what determines their respective contributions?

Zajonc's position will be referred to here as the *independence hypothesis*. This hypothesis gained a lot of attention because it challenges the universality of cognitive mediation theories (Obermiller 1985). The competing *cognitive-affective hypothesis* maintains that even in the case of mere exposure, the affective response is the last step in a series of cognitive processes (Anand, Holbrook, and Stephens 1988; Anand and Sternthal 1991).

REVIEW OF EMPIRICAL EVIDENCE

The review and discussion focus on seven studies that are representative for the two positions on the formation of the mere exposure effect. Table 1 gives a brief characterization of the seven studies, which are all seven variations on the same experimental paradigm.

Subjects are exposed to the target stimuli in the first phase of the experiment. Visual stimuli can be presented for a couple of seconds, that is in the case of words long enough to be read and pronounced, or for only a couple of milliseconds, such that subjects have the impression that they saw something without being able to identify what they saw. Auditory stimuli are in three studies presented during a dichotic listening task in which other messages are presented simultaneously with the target stimuli, each group of stimuli being presented to a different ear. In the second phase of the experiment, subjects are asked for affective and recognition judgments for the target stimuli and interspersed distractor stimuli. Only experiments where each subject gave both judgments for all the stimuli are included here, because the relation between these judgments is the issue of the debate.

The target and distractor items are in two studies presented in pairs and subjects are asked to select that item that has been presented previously and that item they like most (the order of these two pairwise choices being counterbalanced across subjects). Another—and for our discussion more interesting—procedure consists of the individual presentation of targets and distractors with a recognition test of the yes/no type and affect measured on a rating scale. The data from this procedure can be analyzed by comparing the average affect ratings in the cells of table 2. One possible comparison is that of the averages for the rows or for the columns of Table 2: one can contrast the ratings of target stimuli to those of distractors, a dimension that is usually referred to as objective familiarity (Obermiller 1985), or focus on subjective

TABLE 1
Description of Reviewed Experiments

	stimuli, exposures	affect rating (R) or paired-choice (PC)
Wilson (1979), Exp. 1	auditory, dichotic	R (1-7 scale)
Kunst-Wilson and Zajonc (1980)	visual, short	PC
Matlin (1971)	visual, long	R (1-7)
Anand and Sternthal (1991)	auditory, dichotic	R (1-7)
Anand et al. (1988)	auditory, dichotic	R (1-7)
Obermiller (1985)	auditory	R (three 1-7 scales)
Seamon et al. (1983)	visual, short	PC

TABLE 2
Familiarity Matrix
(classification of affect by recognition condition)

		Subjective Familiarity	
		"no"	"yes"
Objective Familiarity	no	correct rejection	false alarm
	yes	miss	hit

---

familiarity, that is the difference between stimuli that subjects claim they recognize and those they claim are new. In addition to these contrasts of the marginals of Table 2, the cell values themselves can be compared. Signal-detection terminology is used here to identify those cells (cf., Anand and Sternthal 1991).

Evidence favoring the independence hypothesis

According to Zajonc, the firmest evidence of the independence of affect and cognition in the formation of the mere exposure effect is the finding that increased affect for a stimulus can occur as a result of a previous exposure *even when recognition is only at a chance level* (Zajonc, 1980). He refers to the results of Wilson (1979), where subjects' recognition for target melodies was at a chance level because their attention was focused on a different message during a dichotic listening task, and those of Kunst-Wilson and Zajonc (1980), where a presentation time of only one millisecond for visual stimuli led to the same level of recognition. There are two important problems with the way these date are interpreted, the first with the interpretation of chance recognition, the second with the use of recognition as an indicator of cognition.

Chance Recognition. The results of Zajonc and Wilson are usually cited as strong evidence for the independence position because, unlike in other demonstrations, recognition is not controlled for by a statistical procedure but by an experimental manipulation that apparently removes its effect altogether. The next step in the (implicit) argument is that because recognition is eliminated, it cannot have caused the observed changes in affect for the target stimuli, and those changes must be due to objective familiarity only. In reality, recognition can even in this case be an important determinant of affect. Chance recognition only means that recognition accuracy is at 50 percent, and "perfect" chance recognition means that there was a hit for every miss and a false alarm for every correct rejection. Even with "perfect" chance recognition every item that is a hit can be liked more than a miss, and every false alarm can be liked more than a correct rejection. Thus, even "perfect" chance recognition does not at all exclude the possibility of a "perfect" dependence of affect on recognition.

Recognition and cognition. At the time of Zajonc's and Wilson's experiments, recognition may have been the most sensitive well-accepted indicator of cognitive processing, but no longer. It has been shown, for instance, that items perceived at one point in time facilitate tasks like perceptual identification of semantically related items, lexical decisions, and word-fragment completion, and that these enhancements in cognitive processing can occur without recognition of the previously presented items. These tasks are part of a larger set of so-called indirect memory tests and measure a form of memory that has been labeled implicit, in contrast with explicit memory which is measured with the traditional recognition and recall tests (cf. Richardson-Klavehn and Bjork 1988; Roediger 1990). The results of indirect tests suggest that cognitive processing must have taken place during the exposure to the stimulus and during the indirect memory task, although there is no trace of this in terms of recognition memory. Applied to our discussion, the identification of cognition with recognition, one of the bases of Zajonc's argument, no longer seems justified in light of this recent research. Thus, it is possible that cognitive processing is responsible for the mere exposure effect.

Evidence favoring the cognitive-affective hypothesis

Anand and Sternthal (1991) recast the debate in terms of the objective-subjective familiarity distinction. They argue that in Zajonc's view affective judgments occur "automatically as a function of actual stimulus repetition or objective familiarity", while according to the cognitive model, these judgments depend on the subjective familiarity of the stimulus (p. 294). Translating these ideas into signal-detection terminology, they hypothesize that if objective familiarity is the dominant factor (which they present as Zajonc's position) the following relations should be found (see Table 2): *Affect for hits > Affect for false alarms* and *Affect for misses > Affect for correct rejections*. On the other hand, they consider a finding of *Affect for hits > Affect for misses* and *Affect for false alarms > Affect for correct rejections* as evidence for the dominance of subjective familiarity. In addition, they propose that these four tests can be replaced by one more direct test, namely a comparison of false alarms and misses, that is of stimuli that are subjectively but not objectively familiar and stimuli that are objectively but not subjectively familiar. Higher affect for false alarms would in their opinion support the cognitive-affective hypothesis. This is indeed what they find, which makes them conclude that "these observations imply that affect without recognition involves a cognitive process..." (p. 299).

Anand, Holbrook, and Stephens (1988) also present an explicit comparison of the two positions on the relation between affect and cognition, and also conclude that their "results tend to advance the cognitive-affective model over the independence hypothesis as an explanation for the formation of affective judgments" (p. 399). This conclusion is based on the finding of a significant interaction between objective and subjective familiarity (Figure 1.a), in that affect is more positive for correctly recognized items. This is interpreted as a mediating (or moderating) effect of cognition.

A closer look at these two studies suggests that the evidence in favor of the cognitive-affective model may not be as strong as the authors report in their conclusions.

Noncompeting alternative hypotheses. A first problem with both studies is that the way the hypotheses are operationalized makes them no longer mutually exclusive: accepting one of the competing hypotheses does not lead to rejection of the alternative hypothesis. This is most apparent in Anand and Sternthal's study. They start out with the four inequalities inferred from their basic hypotheses but, instead of evaluating those, they propose another supposedly more direct test. A review of the data in their Table 1, however, indicates that all four inequalities hold (see Figure 2.a) and in all likelihood are statistically significant. Following their rationale, this means that both the independence and cognitive-affective models would be consistent with the data. With respect to the second study, it is obvious from Figure 1.a that there is an interaction between objective and subjective familiarity, which indeed suggests a moderating role for cognition in the generation of affect. This figure presents the data in terms of objective and subjective familiarity. Looking at these results from a different perspective, however, brings the main effect of objective familiarity to the foreground. The two factors in Figure 2.b are objective familiarity and recognition accuracy. The latter, clearly a cognitive factor, does explain the difference between the top and bottom two data points, but leaves the main effect of objective familiarity unexplained. Thus also in this study, both the independence and cognitive-affective hypotheses—at least in the formulation given by these authors—are confirmed.

Mere exposure and subjective familiarity. The previous discussion about the noncompeting hypotheses raises the more general issue of the value of separating the effects of objective and subjective familiarity to compare the independence and cognitive-affective models. Matlin (1971) was the first to analyze the exposure-liking relationships along the two familiarity dimensions (Figures 3a and 3b). She reports the role of subjective familiarity but the important finding from Zajonc's perspective was that of the simple main effects of objective familiarity (Zajonc 1980). It should be stressed that Zajonc acknowledged from the start the importance of subjective familiarity in the creation of affect, even under conditions of limited cognitive processing (like presentation durations of only a millisecond). Thus, the independence hypothesis was not developed to explain the complete pattern of results in the familiarity matrix, but to explain the effect of objective familiarity when subjective familiarity is controlled for. The two studies that defend the cognitive-affective model therefore cannot be considered as evidence against the independence hypothesis. Rather, they show only that subjective familiarity also plays a role. Moreover, the results of those studies actually replicate the finding that subjective familiarity does not really help in explaining the "pure" mere exposure effect. An illustration of those two points is the comparison of the results of Wilson (1979) and Anand and Sternthal (1991). The basic pattern in Figures 2 and 4 is almost the same, which is not surprising because Anand and Sternthal followed Wilson's design as closely as possible (in order to obtain a chance-level recognition). Thus, ironically the same data pattern that is usually considered as the strongest demonstration of the independence of affect and cognition also is interpreted as evidence that even affect without recognition involves a cognitive process. The four interpretation problems raised in the present paper explain this inconsistency.

A comparison of the data patterns across the different studies (see the previous Figures) raises one additional question. Although its experimental design is similar to other studies in this review, the interaction effect found by Anand et al. (Figure 1) is very distinct. How can this be explained? Obermiller (1985) notes that a subject's impression of the accuracy of a recognition response is most likely associated with positive affective feelings, which then may be transferred to the recognized stimulus. In Obermiller's case subjects had higher affect for correctly recognized objectively familiar stimuli only. Anand et al. in addition find higher affect for objectively unfamiliar stimuli that are correctly rejected. The main difference between these studies is that the stimuli in Obermiller's experiment were randomly generated sequences of tones, that probably were difficult to recognize, while Anand et al. analyzed affect for actual musical passages. In addition, Anand et al. pooled the affect ratings for those melodies and the text passages presented to the other ear in the dichotic listening task. As a result, subjects in the latter experiment probably could get a better assessment of their accuracy not only when they claimed they recognized a stimulus, but also when they claimed they did not recognize the stimulus. This may explain the exceptionally high affect for correct rejections.

PERCEPTUAL FLUENCY: A DIRECTION FOR FUTURE RESEARCH

Theories of recognition memory distinguish between two bases of recognition: familiarity and recollection (Mandler 1980). A stimulus can be recognized because it merely looks (or sounds, tastes, smells, or feels) familiar, but this impression can also be confirmed by recollecting details about the context in which it was presented, the thoughts that came to mind during its presentation, the attitudes that were formed etc. Jacoby (Jacoby, Kelley, and

FIGURES

Figure 1a-4a
Affective ratings scored by objective
(old vs. new) and subjective ("old" vs. "new")
familiarity

Figure 1b-4b
Affective ratings scored by objective
familiarity and recognition accuracy
(correct vs. wrong)

Anand, et. al. (1988), Fig. 1.a

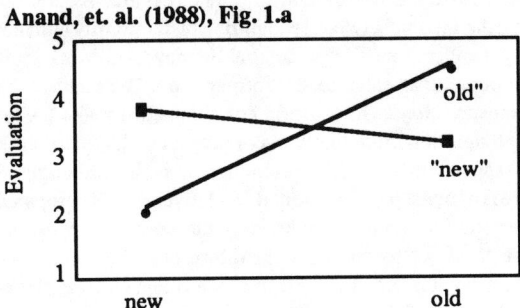

Fig. 1.b

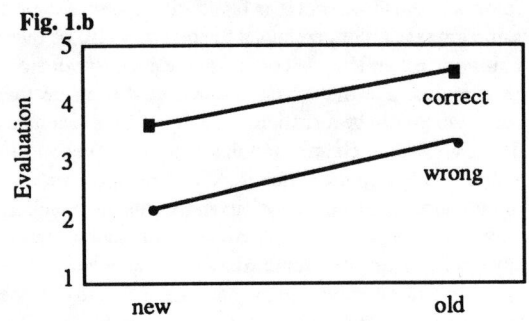

Anand and Sternthal (1991), Fig. 2.a

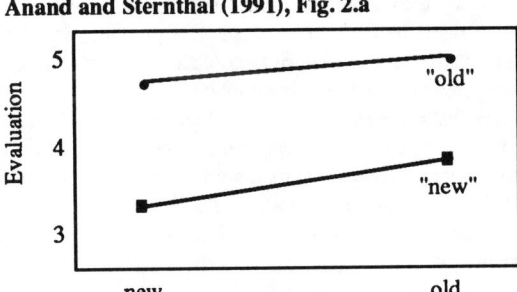

Fig. 2.b

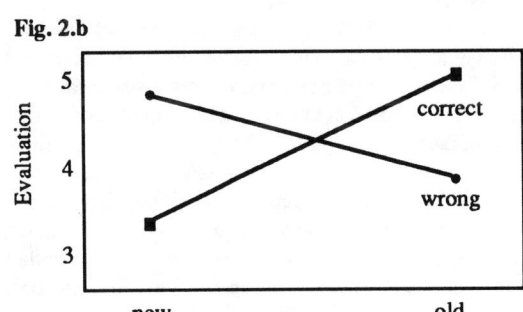

Matlin (1971), Fig. 3.a

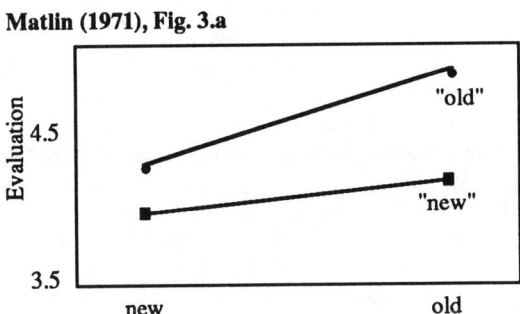

Fig. 3.b

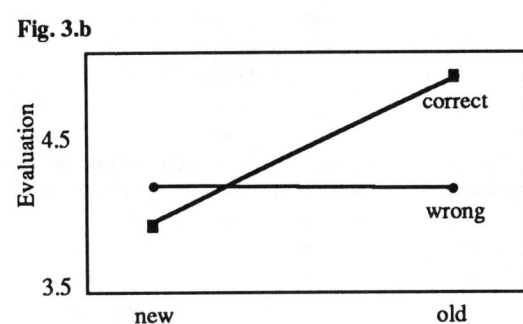

Wilson (1975), Fig. 4.a

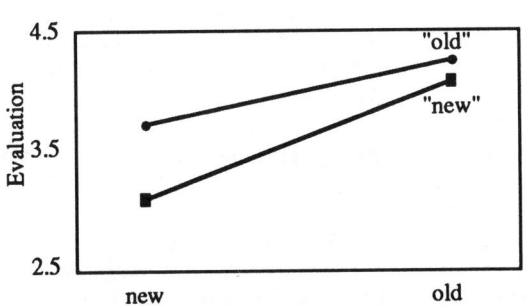

Fig. 4.b

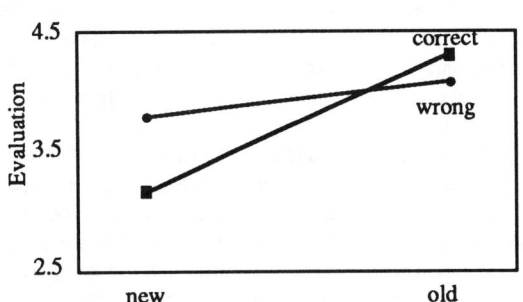

Dywan 1989; Kelley and Jacoby 1990) developed a theory of the antecedents of familiarity that in his opinion also may apply to the mere exposure effect (although he did not test this notion). In short, a previously presented stimulus is easier to perceive than a similar new one, and people are able to make an unconscious assessment of how fluent their perception is. In recognition, they attribute this enhanced perceptual fluency to a previous experience with the stimulus, and thus interpret it as familiarity. Jacoby suggests that the same impression of perceptual fluency may also be interpreted as positive affect and be attributed to some attractive characteristic of the stimulus. For the current discussion, this means that mere exposure would *not* be a sufficient condition for the enhancement of affect, as Zajonc claims, and that a certain level and form of cognitive processing are required. This cognitive processing is apparently more or less unconscious and automatic, much like how affective processing is supposed to operate in Zajonc's framework. In contrast to Zajonc, the same stimulus features may be used for recognition and affective judgments: the difference in these responses is not in what they are based on, but in what fluency is attributed to.

Jacoby's theory may give a cognitive explanation for the creation of affect that applies to low-involvement exposures. In its present formulation it does, however, not account for the fact that affective discrimination of new and old stimuli can be better than discrimination by recognition. This difference in performance is most obvious from the simple main effect of objective familiarity for stimuli that are not subjectively familiar, which was referred to above as a "pure" mere exposure effect (see any of the figures), and from Seamon et al's (1983) comparisons. These authors used paired-choice measures for recognition and affect and observed a "better" performance for affective judgments, in that previously presented stimuli were more often selected as liked than as recognized. Zajonc explains these differences as resulting from a higher *sensitivity* of the affective system. Another explanation, more in line with Jacoby's reasoning, is that people use their assessments of perceptual fluency differently depending on the type of judgment they have to make. Assume that subjects act as if they set some criterion level of fluency that has to be exceeded for a positive response. Because a recognition response is evaluated on accuracy, it would be natural to use a more stringent criterion than for affect where, from the perspective of the subject, no mistakes can be made. Thus, the difference between recognition and affect would be in the level of the *decision criterion* used to interpret perceptual fluency.

From this discussion it appears that the main difference between Zajonc's independence framework and the cognitive-affective model based on Jacoby lies in their account of the different discrimination performance for recognition and affect. For Zajonc, this is also a matter of different sensitivity of the two independent systems involved, while for the framework based on Jacoby, this is a result of two different decision criteria, one for affect and one for recognition, used by the cognitive system. Signal-detection analysis was developed to measure sensitivity of and decision criteria used by detection systems, and it may therefore be possible to develop statistical tests that make a more direct comparison of the independence and cognitive-affective hypotheses than the ones reviewed in the previous sections.

IMPLICATIONS FOR CONSUMER BEHAVIOR AND MARKETING

The framework derived from Jacoby's theory about the attribution of perceptual fluency not only introduces a new perspective on the generation of affect and relationship of affect and recognition, but also can be directly contrasted with Zajonc's conceptualization. Moreover, signal-detection analysis brings new methodological leverage to the debate because it is based on a process model of judgments, which has proven its value in many different contexts.

Demonstrating that the perceptual fluency framework can account for the mere exposure effect not only is theoretically relevant but also has practical utility. The previous section introduced the distinction between recognition by familiarity and recognition by recollection. The perceptual fluency framework implies that conditions that enhance the former should also enhance the mere exposure effect. In contrast, conditions that make the latter type of recognition more likely may make it less likely to observe a mere exposure effect. The argument here is that although mere exposure is a robust phenomenon, it is relatively small compared to the effect of retrieved attitudes, and the contribution of mere exposure to affect formation is therefore probably minor when attitude retrieval is possible. All this means that existing research on the two bases of recognition may help in identifying the conditions that make a mere exposure effect more likely. Interestingly, there seems to be considerable agreement on which factors affect each of the types of recognition (e.g., Gardiner and Java 1991; Jacoby and Dallas 1981). These factors should be examined in a consumer behavior or advertising context.

In conclusion, even if perceptual fluency may not be the full answer to the cognitive-affective debate—maybe no theoretical argument or empirical test can resolve the semantical and philosophical disagreements surrounding this discussion—it at least provides a research agenda for *applied* research on the mere exposure effect.

REFERENCES

Anand, Punam, Morris B. Holbrook and Debra Stephens (1988), "The Formation of Affective Judgments: The Cognitive-Affective Model Versus the Independence Hypothesis," in *Journal of Consumer Research*, 15 (December), 386-391.

Anand, Punam and Brian Sternthal (1991), "Perceptual Fluency and Affect Without Recognition," in *Memory & Cognition*, 19 (3), 293-300.

Bornstein, Robert F. (1989), "Exposure and Affect: Overview and Meta-analysis of Research, 1968-1987," in *Psychological Bulletin*, 106 (September), 265-289.

Cohen, Joel B. and Charles S. Areni (1991), "Affect and Consumer Behavior," in *Handbook of Consumer Behavior*, eds. Thomas S. Robertson and Harold H. Kassarjian, Englewood Cliffs, New Jersey: Prentice-Hall, 188-240.

Gardiner, John M. and Rosalind I. Java (1991), "Forgetting in Recognition Memory With and Without Recollective Experience," in *Memory & Cognition*, 19 (6), 617-623.

Jacoby, Larry L. and Mark Dallas (1981), "On the Relationship Between Autobiographical Memory and Perceptual Learning," in *Journal of Experimental Psychology: General*, Vol.110, No.3, 306-340.

Jacoby, Larry L., Colleen M. Kelley and Jane Dywan (1989), "Memory Attributions," in *Varieties of Memory and Consciousness: Essays in Honour of Endel Tulving*, eds. H.L.Roediger, III and F.I.M. Craik, Hillsdale, NJ: Erlbaum.

Kelley, Colleen M. and Larry L. Jacoby (1990), "The Construction of Subjective Experience: Memory Attributions," in *Mind & Language*, Vol.5, No.1, 49-68.

Kunst-Wilson, William R. and Robert B. Zajonc (1980), "Affective Discrimination of Stimuli That Can not be Recognized," in *Science*, 207 (February), 557-558.

Lazarus, Richard S. (1984), "On the Primacy of Cognition," in *American Psychologist*, 39 (2), 124-129.

Mandler, George (1980), "Recognizing: The Judgment of Previous Occurrence," in *Psychological Review*, Vol.87, No.3, 252-271.

Matlin, Margaret W. (1971), "Response Competition, Recognition, and Affect", in *Journal of Personality and Social Psychology*, 19, 3, 295-300.

Obermiller, Carl (1985), "Varieties of Mere Exposure: The Effects of Processing Style and Repetition on Affective Response," in *Journal of Consumer Research*, 12 (June), 17-30.

Petty, Richard E., Rao Unnava and Alan J. Strathman (1991), "Theories of Attitude Change," in *Handbook of Consumer Behavior*, eds. Thomas S. Robertson and Harold H. Kassarjian, Englewood Cliffs, New Jersey: Prentice-Hall, 241-280.

Richardson-Klavehn, Alan and Robert A. Bjork (1988), "Measures of Memory", *Annual Review of Psychology*, 39, 475-543.

Roediger, Henry L., III (1990), "Implicit Memory. Retention Without Remembering," in *American Psychologist*, Vol. 45, No. 9, 1043-1056.

Seamon, John G., Nathan Brody, and David M. Kauff (1983), "Affective Discrimination of Stimuli That Are Not Recognized: Effects of Shadowing, Masking, and Cerebral Laterality," in *Journal of Experimental Psychology: Learning, Memory, and Cognition*, Vol.9, No.3, 544-555.

Tsal, Yehoshua (1985), "On the Relationship Between Cognitive and Affective Processes: A Critique of Zajonc and Markus," in *Journal of Consumer Research*, 12 (December), 358-362.

Wilson, W.R. (1979), "Feeling More than We Can Know: Exposure Effects without Learning", in *Journal of Personality and Social Psychology*, 37, 811-821.

Zajonc, Robert B. (1968), "The Attitudinal Effects of Mere Exposure", *Journal of Personality and Social Psychology Monograph*, 9, (No. 2, Part 2).

Zajonc, Robert B. (1980), "Feeling and Thinking: Preferences Need No Inferences," in *American Psychologist*, 35 (2), 151-175.

Zajonc, Robert B., Paula Pietromonaco, and John Bargh (1982), "Independence and Interaction of Affect and Cognition", in *Affect and Cognition: the Seventeenth Annual Carnegie Symposium on Cognition*, eds. Margaret S. Clark and Susan T. Fiske, Hillsdale, NJ: Erlbaum, 211-227.

The Mere Exposure Effect: Is It A Mere Case of Misattribution?

Angela Y. Lee, University of Toronto

INTRODUCTION

A number of consumer studies indicate that product evaluations and brand choices are often made under minimal time and with little attention (e.g. Dickson & Sawyer, 1990). Under these conditions, choices may be made based on affective rather than cognitive responses (Baker & Lutz, 1987; MacInnis & Jaworski, 1989) towards the brand. The result of enhanced evaluation under these low levels of processing may be due to a mood congruent effect (eg., Isen, 1984), or it may be due to the mere exposure effect (Zajonc & Markus, 1982).

The focus of this paper is on the latter phenomenon, the mere exposure effect. Over 200 experiments investigating this effect have been published to-date (for a review, see Bornstein, 1989), and while there is still no general consensus as to the underlying mechanism that produces this effect, most explanations involve some form of uncertainty reduction. The purpose of this paper is to discuss the mere exposure effect in light of recent research on implicit memory and to present the results of two experiments which test a misattribution explanation of the mere exposure effect against an uncertainty reduction explanation.

THE MERE EXPOSURE EFFECT

By "mere exposure", researchers refer to a condition which "just makes the given stimulus accessible to the individual's perception" (Zajonc, 1968, p1) and the mere exposure effect is the enhancement of an attitude towards an object as a result of repeated exposures to that object.

Zajonc was one of the first psychologists interested in this effect. Subsequent research has demonstrated the effect across a wide variety of stimuli like drawings, photographs, ideographs, music, using a variety of rating procedures such as ratings of liking, pleasantness, and forced-choice preference judgements (Bornstein, 1989). A number of consumer behavior researchers became interested in the mere exposure effect when the idea that a lot of consumer learning occurs under low involvement conditions was introduced (Krugman, 1965). This subtle repetition effect has since been examined within the context of subliminal effects on brand preference (Hawkins, 1970) and political campaigns (Grush, McKeough & Ahlering, 1978).

It is, however, important to note that not all studies found the mere exposure effect. While most studies have found a monotonic relationship between repetition and evaluation, where evaluation increases with repetition, other studies have found a moderation effect where there is an inverted U-shaped relationship between exposure and affect (eg. Crandall, Montgomery, & Reese, 1973), and a few others have found a novelty effect where repeated exposure leads to a decrease in affect (eg. Cantor, 1968).

In the mere exposure paradigm, the typical experiment has two stages — a study stage and a test stage. Subjects are exposed to stimuli at different levels of repetition in the study stage, and are later asked to evaluate the stimuli amongst other similar but unpresented stimuli. The mere exposure effect is demonstrated by the evaluation enhancement observed for stimuli when they are "old" (presented in the study stage) versus "new" (not presented in the study stage).

A number of different explanations of the mere exposure effect have been proposed (for a review, see Sawyer, 1981). Most of them generally involve some form of uncertainty reduction; these include the two-factor model (Berlyne, 1970), response competition (Harrison, 1968), and expectancy arousal (Crandall, 1970). Other explanations include non-cognitive mediation (Zajonc, 1980), and misattribution (Jacoby & Kelley, 1987).

The uncertainty reduction model posits that organisms prefer stimuli that are predictable. As a stimulus becomes more familiar, it becomes increasingly predictable, less startling, and hence better liked. Berlyne (1966), for instance, argues that any stimulus has a certain amount of arousal potential. The repetition of high arousal potential stimuli will increase liking, whereas repetition of low arousal potential stimuli will lead to the moderation or novelty effect. Berlyne (1970) later adds a second factor to the model, proposing that affect toward a stimulus will become more positive as the stimulus becomes increasingly familiar, until boredom occurs and the frequency-affect curve turns downward.

Zajonc does not really offer a theory that explains the mere exposure effects, rather he argues that a separate affective response system is responsible for the effect, thereby refuting all theories positing that affect is based on cognition (Zajonc, 1980). Zajonc argues that any learning, and therefore the uncertainty reduction mechanism, requires cognition, as demonstrated by recognition. Thus empirical results indicating that enhanced affect can occur in the absence of recognition is supportive of a separate affective response system. This controversy has led to a series of studies which examine whether or not cognition plays a role in the mere exposure effect (eg. Anand, Holbrook, & Stephens, 1988; Obermiller, 1985).

Recent research by cognitive psychologists examining the distinction between explicit and implicit memory has provided a new approach to understanding the mere exposure effect. Jacoby and Kelley (1987), in particular, suggest that the enhanced affect towards a stimulus may be the by-product of a facilitation in information processing as a result of previous exposure to the stimulus.

REPETITION PRIMING AND MISATTRIBUTION

Recent research in memory distinguishes explicit memory, as characterized by conscious recollection of a past event, from implicit memory, which refers to a subsequent facilitation in performance that does not entail explicit retrieval of the experience. Numerous studies have demonstrated that prior exposure to a stimulus can facilitate subsequent performance on various tasks such as lexical decision, perceptual identification, picture naming, etc., without any reference to or conscious recollection of the episode. This facilitation effect is often referred to as 'repetition priming'[1] (for a review, see Schacter, 1989). Jacoby suggests that the facilitation attained in various task performances is due to the fluency in the perceptual identification of the stimulus (Jacoby, Kelley, & Dywan, 1989) as a result of prior exposure. Furthermore, subjects may misattribute this perceptual fluency to sources other than the past experience, and cause them to (mis)judge that the duration of a word being presented is longer (Witherspoon & Allan, 1985), that the background noise accompanying the presentation of a sentence is lower (Jacoby, Allan, Collins & Larwill, 1988), that a statement is true, an argument valid, or a problem easy (Jacoby &

---

[1] In cognitive psychology, the term "priming" refers to the facilitation achieved in a task as a result of prior exposure, while in social cognition the term refers to the manipulation of prior exposure. In this paper, we use the former definition.

Kelley, 1987), and more interesting to us, that a stimulus is more pleasant.

A number of experimental results on repetition priming that are of interest to the present research have been consistently replicated (Tulving & Schacter, 1990). Firstly, repetition priming can be obtained in the absence of recall or recognition. In addition, it has been demonstrated that there is stochastic independence between repetition priming and episodic memory performance like recall and recognition (Eich, 1984; Tulving, Schacter, & Stark, 1982; Schacter, Cooper & Delaney, 1990) in the sense that the performance of an individual on an implicit memory task does not help to predict his/her performance on an explicit memory task, and vice versa. Secondly, different independent variables are found to affect the two types of memory performance differently; in particular, functional dissociations between implicit and explicit memory have been observed in levels of processing manipulations (Jacoby & Dallas, 1981). Finally, repetition priming has also been found to be very sensitive to changes in the particular perceptual feature(s) being processed. Studies have shown that repetition priming effects are attenuated by a change in the surface information available at test (e.g. Roediger & Blaxton, 1987).

The mere exposure effect, like repetition priming, has been observed in the absence of stimuli recognition or recall in a number of studies (e.g. Mandler, Nakamura, & Van Zandt, 1987; Seamon, Brody & Kauff, 1983). The effect is also found to be more pronounced when surface feature processing rather than elaborative processing took place (Obermiller, 1985).

These similarities suggest that the mere exposure effect may be a result of repetition priming. As explained by Tulving, repetition priming is "a nonconscious form of learning that consists in the facilitation of perceptual identification of words and objects" (Tulving, in press). As learning takes place, the uncertainty reduction model may apply. Jacoby, however, goes one step further by arguing that while exposure to a stimulus promotes perceptual fluency, it is the attribution of the cause of this fluency that is critical to the evaluation of the stimulus. When asked to evaluate repeated stimuli, subjects misattribute the cause of the perceptual fluency to affect, rather than to prior exposure, producing the mere exposure effect.

The purpose of the present study is to investigate whether the mere exposure effect is a case of misattribution or of uncertainty reduction.

STUDY 1

As substantiated by research in memory, subjects exposed to a stimulus object develop perceptual fluency for that object. Extending Jacoby's misattribution explanation, subjects evaluating the stimulus are not aware that the perceptual fluency they enjoy while "sizing up" the stimulus comes from prior exposure, and misattribute the ease of processing to affect. So if subjects think they have seen the stimulus object before ("old" in terms of subjective familiarity) when they in fact have not ("new" in terms of objective familiarity), the lack of perceptual fluency may be misattributed as negative affect, resulting in a lower evaluation. On the other hand, if they think they have not seen the stimulus object before ("new" in terms of subjective familiarity) when in fact they have ("old" in terms of objective familiarity), then the perceptual fluency may be misattributed as positive affect, resulting in a higher evaluation. The evaluation thus reflects an effect mediated by subjective familiarity.

On the other hand, Berlyne and other uncertainty reduction advocates believe that the effect is mediated by learning. When the uncertainty that occurs from encountering a stimulus is reduced, subjects will experience enhanced affect. This uncertainty may come from a number of different sources, such as the uncertainty of how to react to the stimulus, the uncertainty of the task they have to do, or the uncertainty of their performance on the task. Therefore, if subjects have been repeatedly exposed to the stimulus, then the learning following exposure, in either conscious or nonconscious form, should result in some uncertainty reduction toward the stimulus. Furthermore, if subjects are informed as to whether or not they have seen the stimulus before, this should also reduce some of the uncertainty that may accompany the task of evaluating the stimulus.

By manipulating both objective familiarity and subjective familiarity, a study can be conducted to examine the processes underlying the mere exposure effect. Objective familiarity is manipulated by frequency of exposure, and subjective familiarity is manipulated by the use of explicit instructions to the subjects that they have or have not been exposed to the stimuli presented for evaluation. For ease of reference, the convenient usage of the terms "old" and "new" will refer to the two states of objective familiarity, and the terms "seen" and "not-seen" will refer to the two states of subjective familiarity.

If the mere exposure effect is entirely due to misattribution, then evaluation of the stimuli should be the same regardless of their being "old" or "new" when evaluation is not contaminated by misattribution of perceptual fluency. In other words, if subjects know whether or not they have encountered the stimuli before, then any perceptual fluency (or the lack of it) will not be misattributed, and evaluation of the stimuli will be unbiased.

H1a   Evaluation will be the same under the "old/seen" condition and the "new/not-seen" condition.

When perceptual fluency occurs ("old") in the absence of subjective familiarity ("not-seen"), then misattribution causes an enhanced evaluation rating. However, when a new stimulus is encountered ("new") in the guise of subjective familiarity ("seen"), then the lack of perceptual fluency is misattributed to a less positive affect.

H1b   Evaluation will be higher in the "old/not-seen" condition than in the "old/seen" condition; and lower in the "new/seen" condition than in the "new/not-seen" condition.

If, on the other hand, the mere exposure effect is due to uncertainty reduction, then evaluation should reflect a main effect of objective familiarity.

H2a   Evaluation will be higher in the "old" condition than in the "new" condition.

For those subjects who are told that they have seen the stimuli before, they should feel more relaxed as a result of some uncertainty reduction towards the stimuli, resulting in higher evaluation.

H2b   Evaluation will be higher in the "old/seen" condition than in the "old/not-seen" condition; and higher in the "new/seen" condition than in the "new/not-seen" condition.

The different predictions of the two models are represented as shown in Figure 1.

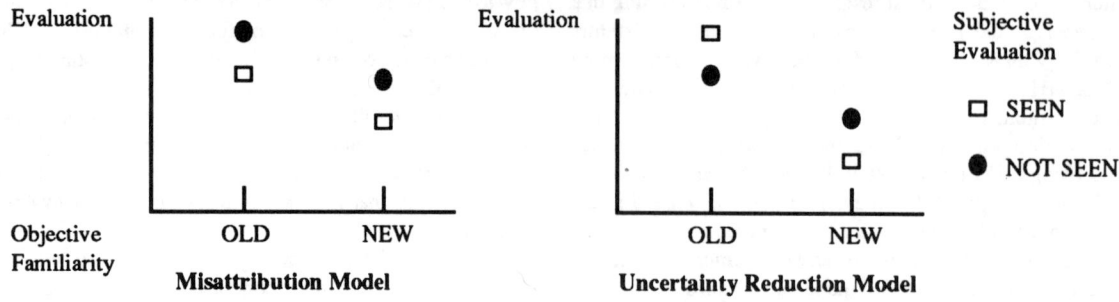

FIGURE 1
Predictions of the Misattribution and the Uncertainty Reduction Models

METHOD

Previous studies have measured subjective familiarity by having subjects report whether or not they had seen the stimuli while also providing evaluations of the stimuli (e.g. Anand et.al., Stephens, 1988; Obermiller, 1985; Wilson, 1979). This creates a number of problems. Firstly, assignment of subjects to this factor is not randomized. Secondly, the results may be due to taking the two measures at the same time. In this study, subjective familiarity is manipulated by informing the subjects that they had either seen or not seen the stimuli earlier and by using stimuli that can only be recognized at chance levels. Complexity of the stimuli was also manipulated, since previous research has sometimes indicated different effects for stimuli with different complexity (e.g. Bornstein, Kale, & Cornell, 1990).

Design

The experiment was a 2x2x2 factorial design with subjective familiarity ("seen" or "not-seen"), objective familiarity ("old" or "new"), and pattern density ("high" or "low") as between-subject factors.

Subjects

Sixty undergraduate students from a large urban university participated in the experiment as partial fulfilment for course credit. The subjects were randomly assigned to the different conditions.

Stimuli

The stimuli were abstract patterns generated by the program Gauss. Ten patterns were made up of 1500 randomly distributed points (high density patterns), with five patterns designated by little squares, and the other five designated by little triangles. Another ten patterns were made up of 800 randomly distributed points (low density patterns), again with five designated by little squares, and the rest by little triangles.

Two high density triangle patterns and two low density triangle patterns were randomly selected to serve as test patterns, and the rest were used as filler patterns.

Abstract patterns were selected for their lack of meaning and distinctive feature. The lack of meaning was intended to minimize within cell variance due to interpersonal differences, while the lack of distinctive feature was intended to ensure a chance recognition for the stimuli. The patterns were pretested for recognition in a forced choice task, and results demonstrated that recognition was at chance level (P(Rn) = 0.5, n = 31).

Two lists consisting of 10 patterns each were developed. List A was made up of 2 high density test patterns, 6 high density filler patterns, and 2 low density filler patterns, with squares and triangles counterbalanced. List B is made up of 2 low density test patterns, 6 low density filler patterns, and 2 high density filler patterns, squares and triangles again counterbalanced.

A total of 25 exposures were presented during the study stage: 3 exposures for each of the test patterns, and 2 or 3 exposures for each of the filler patterns. The sequence of exposures were randomized with the condition that there be no consecutive presentations of the same pattern.

Independent Variables

Objective familiarity was a between- subject manipulation. One half of the test patterns were presented to one group of subjects 3 times, and the other group of subjects 0 times. The reverse was true with the other half of the patterns.

Subjective familiarity was a between-subjects manipulation. Half of the subjects were told that the test patterns were new, and the other half were told that the patterns were old.

Pattern density was a between-subject manipulation. Half of the subjects had high density patterns as old patterns at time of rating, and the remaining half had low density patterns as old patterns at time of rating.

Dependent Measure

Evaluation was measured with a 7-point bipolar scale anchored with "Dislike Very Much" and "Like Very Much".

Procedure

Subjects were presented with a list of 25 patterns at the rate of 8s per exposure, and were asked to indicate whether the patterns were made up of squares or triangles while being exposed to each pattern. At the end of the study phase, the subjects engaged in a distractor task for five minutes. All subjects were then presented with two "old" and two "new" patterns at the rate of 10s per exposure. Half of the subjects were told that the patterns were ones that they had seen earlier, while the other half were told that the patterns were all new. The subjects were asked to evaluate the four patterns on a 7-point scale ranging from -3 to +3, anchored by 'Dislike Very Much' and 'Like Very Much'.

Results

The results were analyzed with a 2x2x2 ANOVA. The predicted main effect was not statistically significant for neither objective nor subjective familiarity. The density of the patterns was highly significant, with low density patterns preferred over the high density patterns ($Mean_{low} = .46$; $Mean_{high} = -.56$; $F(1,232) = 43.12$; $p < .001$). The interaction between objective and subjective familiarity was, however, significant ($F(1,232) = 4.51$; $p < .04$), so was the interaction between density and objective familiarity ($F(1,232) = 11.61$; $p < .001$). The pattern of means indicated a mere

TABLE 1
Mean Rating for Affective Responses By Pattern Density, Exposure, and Instruction

		Subjective Familiarity			
		OLD	NEW	MEAN	MEAN
HIGH DENSITY PATTERNS		(Study 1)		(Study 2)	
Objective	OLD	-.60	-.23	-.42	-.42
Familiarity	NEW	0.27	-.23	0.02	0.29
	MEAN	-.17	-.23	-.20	-.07
LOW DENSITY PATTERNS					
Objective	OLD	1.23	1.30	1.27	
Familiarity	NEW	0.80	0.30	0.55	
	MEAN	1.02	0.80	0.91	

* Higher numbers indicate more positive affective response

exposure effect for the low density patterns, and a novelty effect for the high density patterns.

In light of the interaction between objective and subjective familiarity, separate ANOVAs for old and new patterns were then conducted. With the "old" patterns, there was an insignificant main effect for subjective familiarity, and a significant main effect for density. With the "new" patterns, there was a significant main effect for density ($F(1,116) = 5.04$; $p < .03$), and a significant main effect for subjective familiarity ($Mean_{seen} = .53$, $Mean_{not-seen} = 0.03$; $F(1,116) = 4.43$; $p < .04$), partially supporting hypothesis H2b.

The significant interaction between density and objective familiarity also prompted separate ANOVAs for high and low density patterns to be conducted. With high density patterns, the main effect of objective familiarity was significant, but in the opposite direction of our prediction ($Mean_{old} = -0.42$, $Mean_{new} = 0.02$, $F(1,116) = 2.87$; $p < .10$). The main effect of subjective familiarity was not significant; however, the interaction between objective and subjective familiarity was significant ($F(1,116) = 2.87$; $p < .10$). Subsequent contrasts revealed that the evaluation under the "new/seen" condition was significantly higher than the "old/seen" condition ($F(1,58) = 4.84$; $p < .04$).

For low density patterns, the main effect of subjective familiarity was not significant, nor was the interaction between objective and subjective familiarity. But the main effect of objective familiarity was significant ($F(1,116) = 10.59$, $p < .001$), demonstrating the mere exposure effect, supporting hypothesis H2a in favour of the uncertainty reduction explanation. A comparison between evaluations in the "old/seen" condition and the "new/not-seen" condition shows that the two evaluations were significantly different ($Mean_{old/seen} = 1.23$, $Mean_{new/not-seen} = 0.30$, $F(1,58) = 14.12$; $p < .001$). Hypothesis H1a, which favours the misattribution explanation, was thus not supported. Evaluation in the "old/seen" condition was not significantly different from the "old/not-seen" condition ($Mean_{old/seen} = 1.23$, $Mean_{old/not-seen} = 1.30$, $F(1,58) = 0.50$; $p < .90$); however, evaluation in the "new/seen" condition was higher than in the "new/not-seen" condition as predicted by hypothesis H2b, although the difference was only marginally significant ($Mean_{new/seen} = .80$, $Mean_{new/not-seen} = .30$, $F(1,58) = 2.56$; $p = .11$). When the high density pattern data were included in the analysis, however, the comparison showed a significant subjective familiarity effect on the evaluation of "new" stimuli, as reported above.

Discussion

Clearly the misattribution explanation is not supported by the data. The results are more consistent with the uncertainty reduction explanation, although not all of the uncertainty reduction hypotheses are supported. The mere exposure effect was observed only for low density patterns under the objective familiarity "old" condition, providing evidence for enhanced evaluation following learning. Uncertainty reduction induced by informing subjects that they had seen the stimuli before did not influence evaluation of genuine "old" stimuli, but did produce enhanced evaluation for "new" stimuli. This may represent a ceiling effect achieved in terms of uncertainty reduction when all the stimuli were "old". Informing the subjects that stimuli about to be presented for evaluation were ones that they had seen before, on the other hand, reduced the uncertainty that subjects might have towards unfamiliar stimuli, resulting in an enhanced evaluation.

The novelty effect evidenced in the high density patterns was unexpected, because most studies had reported the mere exposure effect. Bornstein et. al. (1990; Exp.2) found a similar effect when he showed subjects stimuli with varying degrees of complexity. They suggested that when subjects were exposed to both interesting and uninteresting stimuli, evaluations of the two types of stimuli were made relative to each other, so any difference in their evaluations might be contrasted and accentuated, producing an overall decline in the evaluation of the less interesting stimuli. The degree of complexity was varied as a between-subject manipulation in a subsequent study (Exp.3), and the novelty effect for the less interesting stimuli was eliminated.

Since the low density patterns were rated much higher than the high density patterns, a similar stimulus contrast effect might be the reason for the novelty effect observed in the high density patterns in our study. A second study was undertaken to investigate the possibility of a stimulus contrast effect.

STUDY 2

Subjects
Nineteen undergraduate students from the same university participated voluntarily in the experiment.

Procedure
The subjects were again shown 25 patterns generated by the program Gauss, similar to the Study 1, except all the patterns were high density patterns. Subjects followed the same procedure and evaluated two old triangle patterns (at three exposures) and two new patterns (at 0 exposure) at test. Subjects were not told if the patterns were "old" or "new".

Results
A within-subject ANOVA indicated a significant main effect for objective familiarity, in the same direction as in Study 1

(Mean$_{old}$ = -0.42, Mean$_{new}$ = 0.29; $p < .02$.). The novelty effect persists for the high density patterns, in the absence of the more preferred stimuli.

GENERAL DISCUSSION

Developments in cognitive psychology on implicit memory and the results from various studies examining the mere exposure effect (eg., Anand & Sternthal, 1991; Obermiller, 1985) provide sufficient evidence to demonstrate a cognition-mediated mere exposure model. Research has shown that memory of an event can be expressed in terms of a conscious recollection of the event, and in terms of a facilitation in the performance of subsequent tasks. This facilitation, which is independent of recall or recognition of the event, provides evidence that cognitive processing takes place even though the event may not be consciously recollected.

Our data do not provide support for a misattribution explanation. Subjects were informed of the exposure status of the stimuli, and results still showed a preference for the "old" stimuli. It may be argued that even though subjects were aware of the status of exposure, they continued to misattribute the source of perceptual fluency to affective evaluation; although Whittlesea, Jacoby, and Girard (1990) reported a study in which the misattribution from manipulating visual clarity was eliminated when subjects were informed of the manipulation. Nonetheless, this remains a possibility that future research could address. An important lesson is that the mere exposure effect cannot be undone by knowledge of prior exposure. In other words, the consumer's enhanced evaluation for a brand as a result of repeated exposure to the product or to an ad will not be dampened by her/his knowledge that s/he has been repeatedly exposed to the product or the ad.

Furthermore, results from the two studies demonstrate that the mere exposure effect is stimulus-specific. A significant decrease in evaluation of high density patterns is observed with only three exposures, suggesting that evaluation either declined at the second exposure, or that the moderation effect set in at the frequency level of three exposures. When the repetition effect does not behave positively or uniformly across all stimuli, marketers should therefore be cautious in their selection of ad copies, packaging, logos, etc.

It may be interesting to apply the uncertainty reduction model in explaining results found in other mere exposure studies, and to compare their results with those found in the present study. A quick glance at a few studies (Anand et.al., 1988; Anand & Sternthal, 1991; Obermiller, 1985; Wilson, 1979) shows that evaluation is consistently highest for the "hits"[2]. Under the objective familiarity "old" condition, "hits" are rated higher than the "misses"; whereas data in Study 1 showed that evaluations in the "old/seen" and the "old/not-seen" conditions were not different. Bear in mind that a chance (or near chance) level of recognition was manipulated in these studies, which means subjects were faced with having to make a decision that might or might not be correct. The uncertainty of their making a correct decision might add to the anxiety experienced by the subjects. Using the uncertainty reduction explanation, "hits" were evaluated higher than "misses" firstly because the uncertainty towards a stimulus was reduced through a feeling of familiarity. Secondly, in making a recognition response, subjects searched for a match of representation in memory, a "hit" represented situations when a match was successful. Based on a successful match, subjects were more certain of making a correct response, and felt more comfortable with the stimuli, resulting in a higher evaluation. In case of a "miss", subjects failed to find a match in memory, but might not be sure if a match truly did not exist in memory, or that it did, but was simply not accessible. This uncertainty was reflected in a lower rating for the stimuli compared to the situation when subjects were successful in finding a match.

Subjects in our Study 1 did not have the same dilemma. They did not have to perform the recognition task; rather, they were informed that they were going to evaluate patterns that they had either seen or not seen earlier. Subjects were asked during debriefing if they were able to recognize any of the patterns. None of them said they were able to do so. Typically, they said that although they could tell the patterns were different from each other, they were not able to recognize which ones they saw because they all looked similar. The subjects also said they believed the experimenter when told that they had either seen or not seen the stimuli to be evaluated. Consequently, it seems that the instructions and the absence of a recognition task provided the subjects with some certainty that subjects in other studies had not enjoyed. This brought the evaluation in the "old/seen" condition on par with the "old/not-seen" condition.

An alternative explanation could be that telling subjects whether or not they saw the stimuli earlier was not comparable to the feeling of subjective familiarity that subjects relied on to make their recognition responses. So the "old/seen" and "old/not-seen" cells in Study 1 were in fact comprised of both "hit" and "miss" data in the other studies. The external instruction had no effect on evaluation when perceptual fluency was present, and the equivalence in the two cells was an artifact that resulted from combining the "hit" and the "miss" responses.

A more interesting explanation for 'hits' enjoying higher evaluation than 'misses' in other studies may be an issue of the direction of causality. Instead of familiarity mediating recognition and affective responses, recognition responses may be mediated by affective responses, especially when stimuli could only be recognized at chance level. Within the context of implicit memory and uncertainty reduction, it may be argued that implicit learning produces enhanced evaluation, which in turns mediates an explicit memory response. This possibility is currently being tested.

Results from our objective familiarity "new" condition do, however, match the pattern of "false alarm" and "correct rejection" data in Wilson's (1979) study and Anand & Sternthal's (1991) study. Learning could not have taken place when stimuli had not been exposed. That explains the main effect of exposure for these two cells. Between these two conditions, however, subjects in the "false alarm" condition erroneously decided that they had found a match in memory, which made them feel more at ease with the stimulus than those subjects in the "correct rejection" condition who did not find a match, and felt more apprehensive. Subjects in our Study 1 were told that they had seen the stimuli before, even though they had not. This induced sense of familiarity — that they are dealing with "old friends" — is sufficient to boost comfort level which was reflected in their higher rating compared to those who were told that they were going to be dealing with "strangers".

In summary, the mere exposure effect is an important phenomenon to study in understanding consumer behavior, especially under low involvement situations when product evaluations and brand choices are typically influenced by affect. The present study provides additional insight in understanding this phenomenon and suggests how implicit memory may influence the consumer's decision making process.

---

[2] A fourfold classification of actual exposure status and judged status yields "hit" (old item judged as old), "miss" (old item judged as new), "false alarm" (new item judged as old), and "correct rejection" (new item judged as new).

BIBLIOGRAPHY

Anand, P., M.B. Holbrook, & D. Stephens (1988), "The formation of affective judgments: The cognitive-affective model versus the independence hypothesis," *Journal of Consumer Research*, 15, 386-391.

Anand, P., & B. Sternthal (1991), "Perceptual fluency and affect without recognition," *Memory & Cognition*, 13(3) 293-300.

Baker, W.E., & R.J. Lutz (1987), "Levels of processing and levels of explanation," in S. Hecker & D.W. Stewart (Eds.), *Nonverbal Communication in Advertising*. Lexington: Lexington Books, 84-89.

Berlyne, D.E. (1966), "Curiosity and exploration," *Science*, 153, 25-33.

Berlyne, D.E. (1970), "Novelty, complexity, and hedonic value," *Perception & Psychophysics*, 8, 279-286.

Bornstein, R.F. (1989), "Exposure and affect: Overview and meta-analysis of research, 1968-1987," *Psychological Bulletin*, 106, 265-289.

Bornstein, R.F., A.R. Kale, & K.R. Cornell (1990), "Boredom as a limiting condition on the mere exposure effect," *Journal of Personality and Social Psychology*, 58, 791-800.

Cantor, G.N. (1968), "Children's 'like-dislike' ratings of familiarized and nonfamiliarized visual stimuli," *Journal of Experimental Child Psychology*, 651-657.

Crandall, J.E. (1970), "Predictive value and confirmability of traits as determinants of judged trait importance," *Journal of Personality*, 38, 77-90.

Crandall, J.E., V.E. Montgomery, & W.W. Reese (1973), "Mere exposure versus familiarity, with implications for response competition and expectancy arousal hypothesis," *Journal of General Psychology*, 88, 105-120.

Dickson, P.R., & A.G. Sawyer (1990), "The price knowledge and search of supermarket shoppers," *Journal of Marketing*, 54, 42-53.

Grush, J.E., K.L. McKeough, & R.F. Ahlering (1978), "Extrapolating laboratory exposure research to actual political elections," *Journal of Personality and Social Psychology*, 36, 257-270.

Harrison, A.A. (1968), "Response competition, frequency, exploratory behavior, and liking," *Journal of Personality and Social Psychology*, 9, 363-368.

Hawkins, D. (1970), "The effects of subliminal stimulation on drive level and brand preference," *Journal of Marketing Research*, 7, 322-326.

Isen, A.M. (1984), "The influence of positive affect on decision making and cognitive organization," *Advances in Consumer Research*, 11, 534-537.

Jacoby, L.L., L.G. Allan, J.C. Collins, & L.K. Larwill (1988), "Memory influences subjective experience: Noise judgments," *Journal of Experimental Psychology: Learning, Memory and Cognition*, 14, 240-247.

Jacoby, L.L., & M. Dallas (1981), "On the relationship between autobiographical memory and perceptual learning," *Journal of Experimental Psychology: General*, 3, 306-340.

Jacoby, L.L., & C.M. Kelley (1987), "Unconscious influences of memory for a prior event," *Personality and Social Psychology Bulletin*, 13, 314-336.

Jacoby, L.L., C.M. Kelley, & J. Dywan (1989), "Memory Attributions," in H.L. Roediger & F.I.M. Craik (Eds.), *Varieties of Memory and Consciousness: Essays in Honour of Endel Tulving*. Hillsdale: Erlbaum.

Krugman, H. (1965), "The impact of television advertising: Learning without involvement," *Public Opinion Quarterly*, 29 (Fall), 349-356.

Mandler, G., Y. Nakamura, & B.J. Van Zandt (1987), "Nonspecific effects of exposure to stimuli that cannot be recognized," *Journal of Experimental Psychology: Learning, Memory, and Cognition*, 13, 646-648.

MacInnis, D.J., & B.J. Jaworski (1989), "Information processing from advertisements: Toward an integrative framework," *Journal of Marketing*, 53, 1-23.

Obermiller, C. (1985), "Varieties of mere exposure: The effects of processing style and repetition on affective response," *Journal of Consumer Research*, 12, 17-30.

Roediger, H.L., III, & T.A. Blaxton (1987), "Retrieval modes produce dissociations in memory for surface information," in D.S. Gorfein & R.R. Hoffman (Eds.), *Memory and Cognitive Processes: The Ebbinghaus Centennial Conference* (pp.349-379). Hillsdale: Erlbaum.

Sawyer, A. (1981), "Repetition, cognitive responses and persuasion," in R.E. Petty, T.M. Ostrom, & T.C. Brock (Eds.), *Cognitive responses in persuasion* (pp.237-261). Hillsdale: Erlbaum.

Schacter, D.L. (1989), "Implicit memory: History and current status," *Journal of Experimental Psychology: Learning, Memory, and Cognition*, 13, 501-518.

Schacter, D.L., L.A. Cooper, & S.M. Delaney (1990), "Implicit memory for unfamiliar objects depends on access to structural descriptions," *Journal of Experimental Psychology: General*, 119, 5-24.

Seamon, J.G., N. Brody, & D.M. Kauff (1983), "Affective discrimination of stimuli that are not recognized: Effects of shadowing, masking and cerebral laterality," *Journal of Experimental Psychology: Learning, Memory, and Cognition*, 9, 544-555.

Tulving, E. (in press), "Conscious and nonconscious memory: What kind of a difference?" in A. Baddeley and L. Weiskrantz (Eds.), *Attention: Selection, Awareness and Control. A Tribute to Donald Broadbent*. New York: Oxford University Press.

Tulving, E., & D.L. Schacter (1990), "Priming and human memory systems," *Science*, 247, 301-305.

Tulving, E., D.L. Schacter, & H.A. Stark (1992), "Priming effects in word-fragment completion are independent of recognition memory," *Journal of Experimental Psychology: Learning, Memory, and Cognition*, 8, 336-342.

Wilson, W.R. (1979), "Feeling more than we can know: Exposure effects without learning," *Journal of Personality and Social Psychology*, 37, 811-821.

Witherspoon, D., & L.G. Allan (1985), "The effects of a prior presentation on temporal judgments in a perceptual identification task," *Memory & Cognition*, 13, 101-111.

Whittlesea, B.W.A., L.L. Jacoby, & K.A. Girard, K.A. (1990), "Illusions of immediate memory: Evidence of an attributional basis for feelings of familiarity and perceptual quality," *Journal of Memory and Language*, 29, 716-732.

Zajonc, R.B. (1968), "Attitudinal effects of mere exposure," *Journal of Personality and Social Psychology Monographs*, 9(2, Pt.2).

Zajonc, R.B. (1980), "Feeling and thinking: Preferences need no inferences," *American Psychologist*, 35, 151-175.

Zajonc, R.B., & H. Markus (1982), "Affective and cognitive factors in preferences," *Journal of Consumer Research*, 9, 123-131.

A Test of Prescriptive Advice from the Rossiter-Percy Advertising Planning Grid Using Radio Commercials

Robin Higie Coulter, University of Connecticut
Murphy A. Sewall, University of Connecticut[1]

An archive of 570 radio commercial tests of low involvement products is used to evaluate prescriptive advice offered by the Rossiter-Percy Advertising Planning Grid. The Rossiter-Percy Grid is an extension of the established Foote Cone and Belding Planning Grid that managers have long used as a guide to advertising copy strategy. Analyses of the radio commercial tests indicate meaningful differences in the ability of execution formats and copy variables to affect brand recall and preference. These findings suggest that the theoretical underpinnings of the Rossiter-Percy model provide an important basis for understanding the effectiveness of advertising copy strategy decisions.

INTRODUCTION

When deciding the composition of an advertisement, advertising and marketing managers must address a variety of issues, including: the communications objectives, the type of product, the characteristics of the target audience and their purchase motivation. Over the years, many managers have relied upon the Foote Cone and Belding (FCB) Planning Grid to help guide advertising decisions and plans (Vaughn 1980, 1986; Ratchford 1987; Ratchford and Vaughn 1989). Recently, Rossiter, Percy and Donovan (1991; Rossiter and Percy 1987) introduced the Rossiter-Percy Advertising Planning Grid, which builds upon the established FCB Grid. Briefly, the Rossiter-Percy Grid suggests the need to consider two communications objectives: brand awareness (including brand recall and brand recognition) and brand attitude before deciding on the copy variable and execution strategies to be used. The Rossiter-Percy Grid prescriptive copy variable and execution strategies for brand awareness are not product category dependent (i.e., the same advice applies regardless of the product category.) However, according to the Rossiter-Percy model, the execution strategy for the brand attitude communications objective is dependent on two variables: 1) consumer involvement; i.e., perceived risk in choosing the test brand on the next purchase and 2) consumer motivation (informational versus transformational).

The purpose of this article is to determine the extent to which some of the prescriptive advice offered by the Rossiter-Percy Grid is effective in establishing better brand recall and more favorable brand attitude for low involvement products advertised on the radio. We review the prescriptive advice offered by the Rossiter-Percy Grid for establishing better brand recall and the advice for establishing more favorable brand attitude for low involvement informational and transformational motivations. Then, we use an archive of 570 radio commercial tests to examine the extent to which following the advice yields favorable brand recall and brand attitude.

BACKGROUND

Brand Recall and Prescriptive Advice

Studies of television, radio, and magazine advertisements have provided evidence of the importance of copy variables and execution style in achieving favorable brand recall (Duncan and Nelson 1985; Haller 1972; Ogilvy and Raphaelson 1982; Sewall and Sarel 1986; Stewart and Furse 1986). Copy variables that have been hypothesized, or have been shown, to have a positive effect on brand recall include: short main copy line, repetition of the message, use of personal references, and celebrity presenters (Belch 1981; Kahle and Homer 1985; MacLachlan 1984; Rossiter, Percy and Donovan 1991). Other research has shown both positive and negative relationships between humor and brand recall and music and brand recall (Cantor and Venus 1980; Gelb and Zinkhan 1985; Stewart and Furse 1986; Walker and von Gonten 1989; Weinberger and Campbell 1991).

Rossiter and Percy suggest that the attention-getting abilities of some execution factors will facilitate achieving higher brand recall, and consequently they offer the following prescriptive advice for establishing brand recall:

- Associate the category need and the brand in the main copy line.
- Keep the main copy line short.
- Use repetition of the main line copy.
- Include a personal reference.
- Use a bizarre execution.
- Use a jingle (for broadcast ads).

Brand Attitude and Prescriptive Advice

Research has also studied the effects of execution format on brand attitude, brand preference and other measures of persuasion (Diamond 1968; Ogilvy and Raphaelson 1982; Rossiter, Percy and Donovan 1991; Sandage, Fryburger and Rotzoll 1988; Wells, Burnett and Moriarity 1989). As noted, the prescriptive advice offered by the Rossiter-Percy Grid for establishing favorable brand attitude is dependent on two variables: consumer involvement and consumer motivation. The majority of the advertisements in the archive of radio commercials were for low involvement products (as might be expected because of the fleeting nature of the message and the difficulty in providing detailed, specific information via this medium). Thus, our empirical study examines only low involvement products, and we selectively review the low involvement informational and transformational motivations of the Rossiter-Percy Grid. (See Rossiter, Percy and Donovan 1991 for a detailed explanation of high involvement informational and transformational motivations.)

Involvement and Motivations. The involvement dimension of the Rossiter-Percy Grid is defined on the basis of the typical target audience's perceived risk in choosing the test brand on the next purchase. Brand choices in a product category that are "sufficiently low in perceived risk to simply 'try the brand and see'" are referred to as low involvement decisions. Products typically purchased in this manner include aspirin and candy (Rossiter, Percy and Donovan 1991, p.15). In contrast, brand choices in product categories that are "risky enough to be worth processing advertising information at a more detailed level" are referred to as high involvement decisions. Products typically purchased in this manner include insurance and automobiles (Rossiter, Percy and Donovan 1991, p.15).

The motivation dimension of the Rossiter-Percy Grid is based on the work of Katz (1960), Fennell (1978), Wells (1981) and Ratchford and Vaughn (1989) and distinguishes between informational and transformational motives. Rossiter, Percy and Donovan

---

[1] The authors thank Radio Recall Research, Holmdel, NJ for supporting this research.

TABLE 1
Hypothesized Relationships Between Copy Variables and Execution Format and Dependent Variables

Rossiter-Percy Grid	Our Measure	Hypothesized Relationship with Brand Recall	Hypothesized Relationship with Brand Attitude
Number of words in the main copy line	Number of words per message repetition [a]	inverse	no effect hypothesized
	Number of ideas per message repetition [b]	inverse	
Repetition of the main copy line	Number of message repetitions	positive	no effect hypothesized
	Number of brand name mentions	positive	
Use a unique execution	Atypical versus typical format	positive	no effect hypothesized
Problem-solution format [c]	Problem-solution format	no effect hypothesized	positive
Slice-of-life format [d]	Slice-of-life format	no effect hypothesized	positive

[a] Calculated by dividing the total number of words in the commercial by the number of message repetitions in the commercial
[b] Calculated by dividing the total number of ideas in the commercial by the number of message repetitions in the commercial
[c] For low involvement/informational brand attitude strategy
[d] For low involvement/transformational brand attitude strategy

(1991) suggest that informational purchase motives are those motives that can be satisfied by providing information about the product or brand. The authors suggest that these are negatively-reinforcing and include: problem removal, problem avoidance, incomplete satisfaction, mixed approach-avoidance and normal depletion. On the other hand, transformational purchase motives are positively reinforcing and include sensory gratification, intellectual stimulation and social approval.

For products that are purchased as a result of low involvement/ informational brand processes, the Rossiter-Percy Grid prescribes the use of a simple problem-solution format. Here, the negative purchase motivations are addressed by supplying pertinent reasons for brand usage (eg., demonstrating that the consumer "problem" is alleviated through use of the product). For products that are purchased as a result of low involvement decisions and transformational motivations, the Rossiter-Percy Grid prescribes a format that incorporates emotional authenticity; here, the slice-of-life format is recommended because it helps consumers to "put themselves emotionally into the role of using the advertised brand" (Rossiter and Percy 1987, p. 239). To summarize, a problem-solution format is expected to facilitate positive attitude for low involvement/ informational products, whereas the slice-of-life format is expected to be more effective in creating favorable brand attitude for low involvement/transformational products.

THE DATA AND HYPOTHESES

The present study examines an archive of 570 radio commercials for which both brand recall and purchase intention change were measured. The commercials had never been aired, and included 28 low involvement product categories. These commercials were drawn from 1,664 radio commercials tested by an advertising research firm between July 1982 and December 1989.

This archive of radio commercials provides a good opportunity to investigate the viability of several of the prescriptive advertising tactics set forth by the Rossiter-Percy Grid. Because the data were not collected specifically for the purpose of evaluating the Grid, we used surrogate measures when testing the propositions. Table 1 presents the Rossiter, Percy and Donovan variables and our substitutes; the details of our operationalizations are provided in the Classification and Measurement section. Table 1 also reports the hypothesized relationships between the execution elements and formats and brand recall and brand attitude.

PROCEDURE

For each data collection over the seven year period, approximately 100 people were recruited at shopping malls in each of three metropolitan areas (typically, one eastern, one central and one western). The participants were asked to come to a specific location to answer a short survey about their entertainment interests and brand purchase intentions. While subjects were responding to the questions, a "radio" (actually a disguised recorder) was played in the room. Three commercial messages were included in the musical program. The order of the commercials was rotated for different groups of subjects. The procedure is similar to the "semiforced exposure" for television commercials described by Dunn and Ziff (1974). At the end of the session, subjects again reported their brand purchase intentions. The following day, subjects were contacted by telephone and asked if they recalled

TABLE 2
Product Categories and Informational and Transformational Motivations

Informational	Transformational Motives
Medicated skin cream	Shampoo
Analgesics	Non-medicated cream
Stomach medication	Regular soda
Cold medicine	Regular coffee
Antiseptic	Fruit juice
Vitamins	Snack food
Other medicines	Bubble gum
Feminine hygiene	Hard candy
Deodorant	Candy bar
Grooming aids	
Diet soda	
Cereal	
Prepared foods	
Other food	
No sugar gum	
No sugar bubble gum	
Detergent	
Bleach	
Cleaners	

hearing the commercials played while they were completing the questionnaire. Measures of unaided brand recall, category aided brand recall, claimed recall and proven recall were obtained.

CLASSIFICATION AND MEASUREMENT

Product Category Classification and Purchase Motivations

As noted, the Rossiter-Percy Grid distinguishes between low involvement and high involvement product categories. Using the Rossiter, Percy and Donovan (1991) definition of low involvement (trial experience is sufficient) and a listing of products previously identified as low involvement in similar research (Ratchford 1987), two judges independently evaluated the product categories, assigning 28 as low involvement. There was 100 percent agreement between the two judges. Next, using the guidelines based upon the informational and transformational motives, the two judges independently classified the motivations as informational (19 product categories, including 355 commercials) and transformational (9 product categories, including 215 commercials). Again, there was 100 percent agreement between the two judges. Table 2 lists the products included in the analyses and their respective motivations.

Dependent Variables

Brand Recall. The day-after telephone interview was used to establish subjects' level of brand recall. During the interview subjects were asked "Do you recall a commercial for (product category of the test product, for example a pain reliever or a soft drink)?" (which is based upon Burke Marketing Research's definition of category-aided brand recall). For a particular commercial, brand recall is expressed as the percentage of the individuals who correctly named the brand.

Brand Attitude. The data set we used did not include a direct measure of brand attitude. We used a change in brand purchase intention for the product category as a surrogate to assess persuasion and brand attitude. Our reasoning for this is based on the expectation of a positive correlation between purchase intention and brand attitude (Haley and Baldinger, 1991; Ogilvy and Raphaelson, 1982). Subjects completed a measure of purchase intention both prior to and after the exposure to the commercials. At both times, subjects responded to the prompt: "Name the brand that you plan to select when you next make a purchase in each of these five product categories" (the advertised product category and four other product categories which varied over the data collection). The change in purchase intention (post-intention minus pre-intention) for a commercial was used as the measure of brand attitude.

Independent Variables

Two professionals at the research company coded all of the commercials in the archives for copy variables and execution format (discussed subsequently). Any discrepancies in codings were resolved by subsequent discussion between the coders.

Copy Variables. As noted, the Rossiter-Percy Grid suggests that a short main copy line, repetition of the main copy line and the use of a bizarre execution will favorably affect brand recall. The archive did not provide the number of words in the main copy line. Hence, message repetition (i.e., the number of times the main message of the commercial was repeated) was used to compute two surrogate measures — the number of words per message repetition and the number of ideas per message repetition. The assumption herein is that fewer words and ideas per message repetition would have the same positive effect on brand recall as a short main copyline. As shown in Table 1, we used number of words and number of ideas per message repetition as surrogates for the number of words in the main copy line. Additionally, as measures of Rossiter, Percy and Donovan's "repetition of the main copy line", we used number of message repetitions and number of brand name mentions in the commercial.

Execution Format. The radio commercials in the archive were coded by the research professionals as: sing-and-sell playlets (32%), slice-of-life (31%), announcer only (26%), testimonial (8%), and problem-solution (3%) ads. Sing-and-sell playlets use jingles to help gain attention, and slice-of-life commercials employ a common situation related to the product category with "everyday people" in the ad. Announcer only ads are rational, information-intensive advertisements, with virtually no humor or gimmicks. The problem-solution format acknowledges a problem that the consumer might face, and then offers the advertised brand as the appropriate solution to the problem; testimonials employ a spokesperson to discuss positive personal experiences with the brand.

TABLE 3
ANCOVA Results for Brand Recall

Source of Variation	F-value [a]
Covariates	
Number of Words per Message Repetition	11.46**
Number of Ideas in Commercial	9.21**
Number of Ideas per Message Repetition	8.56**
Number of Message Repetitions in Commercial	4.35*
Number of Brand Mentions in Commercial	1.98
Number of Words in Commercial	.23
Format (typical/atypical)	12.01**

[a] The degrees of freedom for all F-tests is 1/549.
** p<.01
* p<.05

For all product categories, Rossiter, Percy and Donovan (1991) predicted that a bizarre execution format would be effective in producing favorable recall. For our purposes, we define "bizarre" as different from the "typical" or "expected" format. Hence, we classified testimonial and problem-solution format ads (11 percent of all ads; i.e., infrequently used) as *atypical*, and announcer only, slice-of-life and sing-and-sell ads (89 percent of all ads; i.e., frequently used) as *typical*.

For products that fall into the low involvement/informational category, Rossiter, Percy and Donovan (1991) posit that the problem solution format would be most effective in achieving favorable brand attitude. Hence, we classified problem-solution and testimonial execution formats *as prescribed*; other formats were classified as *not as prescribed*. The slice-of-life (representing emotional authenticity) format is predicted to be the most effective low involvement/transformational brand attitude strategy. As a consequence, we classified slice-of-life *as prescribed*, and other formats were classified *not as prescribed*.

RESULTS

Brand Recall

To assess whether or not the Rossiter-Percy Grid advice for low involvement product commercials is effective in generating brand recall for radio commercials, we included execution format (atypical/typical) as an independent variable and the number of words, ideas, message repetitions, brand mentions and words and ideas per message repetition as covariates in an ANCOVA. Recall that the commercial is the unit of analysis. Table 3 reports our findings.

The results indicate that the typicality of the execution format, the number of ideas, the number of words and ideas per message repetition, and the number of message repetitions significantly affect brand recall. Specifically, as predicted by the Rossiter-Percy Grid, atypical execution formats achieve a greater brand recall than typical execution formats; the respective adjusted means are 16.2 and 12.0. Also as hypothesized, the fewer the number of ideas per message repetition and the more the message was repeated, the better the brand recall. In contrast to the Rossiter-Percy Grid advice, the number of words per message repetition has a positive effect on brand recall. Although not hypothesized (but necessarily included in the analysis because of the ideas per message repetition variable), the number of ideas in the ad has a positive effect on brand recall. In total, 8.3 percent of the variance in brand recall is explained by the aforementioned variables.

Brand Attitude

To assess the Rossiter-Percy Grid advice regarding brand attitude, we included two factors, product category purchase motivation (informational/transformational) and execution format (as prescribed/not as prescribed) in the ANOVA. The results indicate that the purchase motivation by execution format interaction is significant ($F_{1/566}=24.9$; $p<.001$) and the execution format main effect is significant ($F_{1/566}=13.1$; $p<.001$). The Figure illustrates the interaction effect. As predicted, for low involvement/transformational products, the slice-of-life format outperforms other formats in achieving favorable brand attitude ($\bar{x}_{slice}=3.88$, $\bar{x}_{other}=.31$. For low involvement/informational products, however, the recommended problem solution format was less effective than other formats ($\bar{x}_{problem+testimonial}=1.53$, $\bar{x}_{other}=2.39$). The effect of execution format indicates that across all of the commercials, following the Rossiter-Percy Grid advice results in more favorable brand attitude ($\bar{x}_{as\ prescribed}=3.13$, $\bar{x}_{not\ as\ prescribed}=1.75$). In total, 8.6 percent of the variance in brand attitude is explained by the informational/transformational dimension and the execution format.

Much research has distinguished between recall and attitude change measures (Gibson 1983; Higie and Sewall 1991; Ross 1982; Stewart 1986, 1989). Thus, it is not surprising that the Rossiter, Percy and Donovan Grid did not include the copy variables expected to effect brand recall in their brand attitude prescriptive advice. To empirically determine the validity of this distinction, we included the covariates expected to affect brand recall as covariates in an ANCOVA with product category purchase motivation and execution format (as prescribed/not as prescribed) as independent variables. Consistent with others' findings, this analysis indicates a significant motivation by execution format ($F_{1/549}=30.50$, $p<.001$) and a significant execution format main effect ($F_{1/549}=12.59$, $p<.001$). Among the covariates, only the number of brand mentions significantly affected brand attitude ($F_{1/549}=10.35$, $p<.001$).

DISCUSSION

Researchers have offered guidelines for developing advertisements using a variety of conceptualizations. The effectiveness of

FIGURE 1
Informational/Transformational Motives by Execution Format Interaction on Brand Attitude

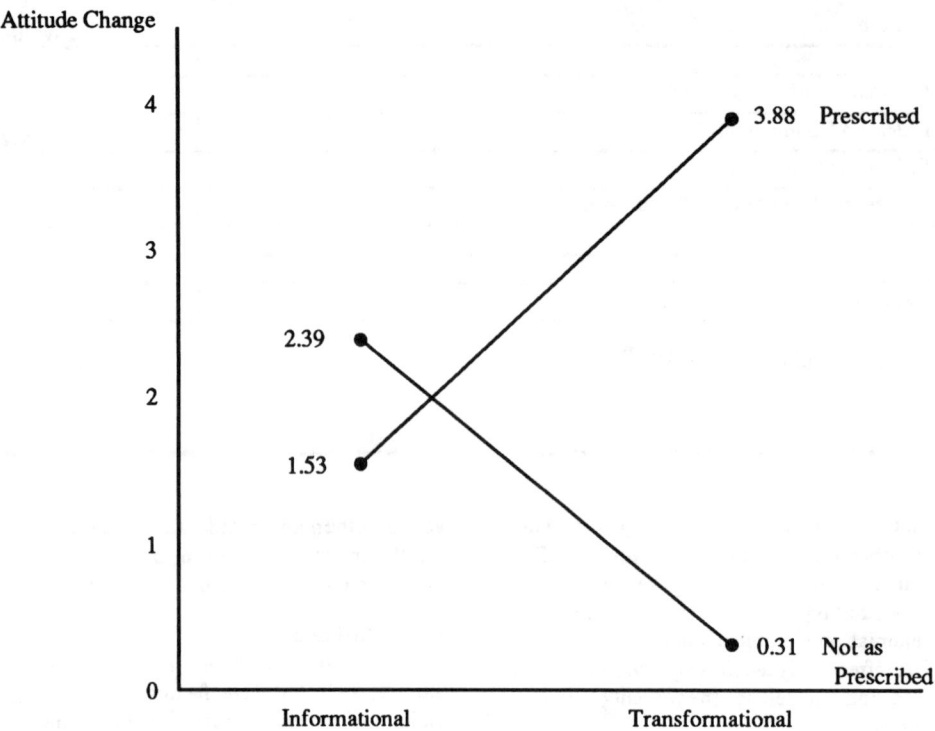

the prescriptive advice, however, has been infrequently tested. Our examination of the low involvement product radio commercial archive provides insights as to the extent to which following the Rossiter-Percy Grid advice produces improved brand recall and brand attitude. Overall, our empirical findings support Rossiter, Percy and Donovan's conceptual formulation. However, for radio commercials, there may be potential refinements to the prescriptive advice.

Brand Recall

Brand recall was enhanced, as expected, by more message repetitions, fewer ideas per message repetition and an atypical execution format. We found that brand recall improved with the number of words per message repetition and the number of ideas in the commercial. In other words, brand recall was facilitated by providing more information. Contrary to expectations, the number of brand name mentions did not promote greater brand recall.

These results have important implications for copy writers. In part, the findings suggest the importance of including information in commercials for low involvement products. In addition, our results indicate that infrequently used execution formats are more effective than frequently used formats. Thus, as suggested by the Rossiter-Percy Grid, unique executions (eg., atypical formats, copy variables or story lines) may be more likely to attract attention and promote brand recall. Finally, the Rossiter-Percy Grid hypothesis that a simple and frequent communication of the main message in an advertisement facilitates brand recall is corroborated by our findings that more message repetitions and fewer ideas per message repetition are effective in establishing greater brand recall.

Brand Attitude

The archive of radio commercials enabled us to examine the extent to which following a recommended execution format for low involvement/informational and low involvement/transformational products would increase brand attitude. As expected, we found that the slice-of-life execution format was a more effective strategy for low involvement/transformational products. However, for low involvement/information products, the prescribed problem-solution (and testimonial) format was a less effective method for generating favorable brand attitude. One possible explanation for these contrary findings is that an atypical format (similar to the brand recall hypothesis) may result in more favorable brand attitude for low involvement/informational motives. It may be that the problem-solution format is less effective for low involvement products than for high involvement products because consumers pay less attention than is necessary to process the message and have an impact on brand attitude.

Summary

Both brand recall and brand attitude models explained approximately eight percent of the variance in the dependent measures. Thus, although the Rossiter, Percy and Donovan prescriptive advice contributes to understanding the communications objectives of a particular commercial, the creativity and originality of the advertising creative staffs may be of significantly greater value. Moreover, our results further support the need to identify and pursue different communications objectives. The empirical evidence indicates that the inclusion of variables expected to promote brand recall (with the exception of number of brand mentions) does not significantly affect brand attitude.

LIMITATIONS AND FUTURE DIRECTIONS

This investigation provides useful insights about the types of commercial strategies that may be effective for low involvement product radio commercials. The theoretical underpinnings of the Rossiter-Percy Grid appear to provide an important basis for understanding the effectiveness of execution format and copy variables. The analyses of this archive of radio commercial tests indicate meaningful differences among the ability of various formats and copy variables to affect brand recall and brand attitude. Nonetheless, other research might seek to propose alternative product classification schemes and related conceptually-based prescriptive advice to investigate commercial strategy effectiveness.

The currently available field data enabled us to assess some of the hypotheses set forth by Rossiter, Percy and Donovan (1991), an important step in determining the efficacy of their advice. Because the data did not have a one-to-one correspondence of the measures detailed by Rossiter, Percy and Donovan, we attempted to meet the spirit of their intentions with the most appropriate surrogate measures. Our preliminary examination suggests that it may be worthwhile to invest in an experimental research design that more rigorously tests the stated variables and operationalizations included in the Rossiter-Percy Grid.

Finally, radio commercials were used to examine the effects of various copy variables and execution formats on brand recall and brand attitude for low involvement products. An obvious extension of this study would be to test the Rossiter-Percy Grid prescriptive advice for high involvement products. Further, a comparison across media might provide additional insights in terms of the most effective execution and copy strategies for specific media and advertising vehicles.

REFERENCES

Belch, George E. "An Examination of Comparative and Noncomparative Television Commercials: The Effects of Claim Variation and the Repetition on Cognitive Response and Message Acceptance." *Journal of Marketing Research* 18, 3 (1981): 333-349.

Cantor, J. and P. Venus. "The Effect of Humor on Recall of a Radio Advertisement." *Journal of Broadcasting* 24, 1 (1980): 13-22.

Diamond, Daniel S. "A Quantitative Approach to Magazine Advertisement Format Selection." *Journal of Marketing Research* 4, 3 (1968): 276-287.

Duncan, Calvin P. and James E. Nelson. "The Effects of Humor in a Radio Advertising Experiment." *Journal of Advertising* 14, 2 (1985): 33-40, 64.

Dunn, Theodore F. and Ruth Ziff. "PREF: A New Copy Testing System." *Journal of Advertising Research* 14, 5 (1974): 53-59.

Fennell, G. "Consumers' Perceptions of the Product-Use Situation." *Journal of Marketing* 42, 2 (1978): 38-47.

Gelb, Betsy D. and George M. Zinkhan. "The Effect of Repetition on Humor in a Radio Advertising Study." *Journal of Advertising* 14, 2 (1985): 13-20, 68.

Haley, Russell I. Haley and Allan L. Baldinger. "The ARF Copy Research Validity Project." *Journal of Advertising Research* 31, 2 (1991): 7-32.

Haller, T. B. "Predicting Recall of TV Commercials." *Journal of Advertising Research* 12, 5 (1972): 43-45.

Higie, Robin A. and Murphy A. Sewall. "Using Recall and Brand Preference to Evaluate Advertising Effectiveness." *Journal of Advertising Research* 31, 2 (1991), 56-63.

Kahle, Lynn R. and Pamela M. Homer. "Physical Attractiveness of the Celebrity Endorser: A Social Adaptation Perspective." *Journal of Consumer Research* 11, 4 1985: 954-961.

Katz, D. "The Functional Approach to Studying Attitudes." *Public Opinion Quarterly* 24, 2 (1960): 163-204.

MacLachlan, James. "Making a Message Memorable and Persuasive." *Journal of Advertising Research* 23, 6 (1983/1984): 51-59.

Ogilvy D. and J. Raphaelson. "Research on Advertising Techniques that Work - and Don't Work." *Harvard Business Review* 60, 4 (1982): 14-16.

Ratchford, Brian T. "New Insights About the FCB Grid." *Journal of Advertising Research*, 27, 4 (1987): 24-38.

_____ and Richard Vaughn. "On the Relationships Between Motives and Purchase Decisions: Some Empirical Approaches." In *Advances in Consumer Research*, Vol. 16, T.K. Srull, ed. Provo, UT: Association for Consumer Research, 1989.

Ross, Harold L., Jr. "Recall versus Persuasion." *Journal of Advertising* 22, 1 (1982), 13-16.

Rossiter, John R. and Larry Percy. *Advertising and Promotion Management*. New York: McGraw-Hill Book Company, 1987.

_____, _____ and Robert J. Donovan. "A Better Advertising Planning Grid." *Journal of Advertising Research* 31, 5 (1991): 11-21.

Sandage, C.H., Vernon Fryburger and Kim Rotzoll. *Advertising: Theory and Practice*. New York: Longman (1988).

Sewall, Murphy A. and Dan Sarel. "Characteristics of Radio Commercials and Their Recall Effectiveness." *Journal of Marketing* 50, 1 (1986), 52-60.

Stewart, David W. "Measures, Methods and Models in Advertising Research." *Journal of Advertising Research* 29, 3 (1989) 54-60.

_____. "The Moderating Role of Recall, Comprehension and Brand Differentiation on the Persuasiveness of Television Advertising." *Journal of Advertising Research* 26, 2 (1986), 43-47.

_____ and David H. Furse. *Effective Television Advertising*. Lexington, MA: D.C. Heath and Company 1986.

Vaughn, Richard. "How Advertising Works: A Planning Model." *Journal of Advertising* 20, 5 (1980): 27-33.

_____. "How Advertising Works: A Planning Model Revisited." *Journal of Advertising*, 26, 1 (1980): 27-33.

Walker, David and Michael F. von Gonten. "Explaining Related Recall Outcomes: New Answers from a Better Model." *Journal of Advertising Research* 29, 3 (1989), 11-21.

Wells, William, John Burnett and Sandra Moriarity. *Advertising: Principles and Practice*. Englewood Cliffs, NJ: Prentice Hall, 1989.

Weinberger, Marc G. and Leland Campbell. "The Use and Impact of Humor in Radio Advertising." *Journal of Advertising Research* 30, 6 (1991), 44-52.

Incidental Learning from Radio Advertisements With and Without Curiosity-Arousing Questions

Rhonda Gibson, University of Alabama at Birmingham
Huiuk Yi, University of Alabama
Dolf Zillmann, University of Alabama

ABSTRACT

Ostensibly while waiting for an investigation to start, respondents were exposed to radio featuring popular music and local commercials. The presentational format of two commercials, one advertising male products, the other female products, was manipulated: Persuasively relevant information was conveyed in declarative or interrogative-declarative form. In the latter form, curiosity-arousing questions preceded the presentation of factual information about products. Following exposure, respondents were subjected to a surprise test on information acquisition. Regardless of salience of products advertised (male products for men, female products for women), the presentation of factual information in interrogative-declarative format, compared to the presentation of that information in purely declarative format, produced superior information acquisition. The significance of the use of questions to gain attention to commercials under conditions of disinterest and distraction is emphasized.

The use of questions in efforts at evoking curiosity, enhancing information acquisition, or prompting desired attitude formation is common in advertising. Textbooks instruct practitioners to help draw consumer attention to their ads by using various types of questions in the headline and throughout the copy (Bolen, 1984; Faison, 1980; Jewler, 1992; Moriarty, 1991). Content analyses indicate that such instruction is followed faithfully: Questions are employed in approximately 20 percent of print ads (Howard, 1989), with utilization higher in more cognitively oriented texts and in magazines read by more highly educated audiences. The most common placement of questions in print advertisements is the headline (Myers and Haug, 1967).

Although there has been limited research on the specific effects of questions in advertising (Moore, Reardon, and Durso, 1985; Howard, 1986, 1989), several studies have investigated the impact of questions on information acquisition (Burnkrant and Howard, 1984; Kantor, 1960; Lumsdaine, May, and Hadsell, 1958; MacLachlan and Jalan, 1985; Tamborini and Zillmann, 1985; Zillmann and Cantor, 1973) and persuasion (Petty, Cacioppo, and Heesacker, 1981; Swasy and Munch, 1985; Zillmann, 1972; Zillmann and Cantor, 1974). It has been shown, for the most part, that the use of questions does indeed enhance information acquisition and persuasion, particularly in messages with strong arguments. Instead of using the format, "This is so and so," for instance, research has shown that it is more persuasive to employ questions such as "Isn't this so and so?" or "This is so and so, isn't it?" Analogously, and more important to the present investigation, research has shown information acquisition to be superior for question-and-answer sequences like "How is it? So and so." than for the purely declarative format "It is so and so." The research, however, has focused almost exclusively on situations of high attention, such as with captive audiences in classrooms or in settings where respondents have been specifically instructed to listen to the radio (Howard, 1986). The impact of questions in situations of low attention, in contrast, has been neglected. Such neglect is surprising, in light of the fact that conditions of semi-attention and incidental learning typify the circumstances under which much advertising is received and processed.

The elaboration likelihood model or ELM (Petty and Cacioppo, 1986), commonly used to examine persuasion and communication processes, suggests that the influence of questions on information acquisition would differ in situations of high and low attention. ELM distinguishes between central and peripheral routes of information processing. Central processing is inferred when attitude change appears to be based on the receiver's diligent consideration of information contained in a message. Processing resulting from less diligent methods implies the *peripheral* route. Central processing is viewed as characteristic of high-involvement and high-attention communication situations—for example, when an issue is of high personal relevance or when there is significant external motivation for processing—and generally results in enhanced recall of processed information. Peripheral processing is viewed as characteristic of low-involvement or low-attention situations and is often illustrated by non-message-oriented processing. For example, under circumstances of low involvement, recipients may focus more on source characteristics, such as credibility or attractiveness, than actual message content.

The ELM suggests, then, that questions, depending on the amount of attention afforded the ad by the message recipient, have varying degrees of influence on the amount of information processed and retained from an advertisement. It is expected that questions, by drawing attention to the message, enhance consideration of the content of this message, but only in low-involvement settings where recipients are not inclined to devote much effort to thinking about the message. When the topic of the message is personally relevant and represents a situation of high-involvement, recipients are considered more likely to process and elaborate the content of a message (Chaiken, 1980; Petty and Cacioppo, 1979; Petty, Cacioppo, and Goldman, 1981). Under these conditions, it would be unlikely that the use of questions could enhance elaboration further. In fact, it has been suggested that for an advertisement of high personal relevance, the presence of rhetorical questions might actually interfere with recipients' thought processes (Munch and Swasy, 1988; Petty, Cacioppo, and Heesacker, 1981).

Given these considerations, for advertisements that use declarative or interrogative-declarative formats, but that present identical factual information, the following hypotheses are proposed:

H_1: For advertised products and services low in salience to recipients, because of minimal interest and motivation to elaborate, questions draw attention to the message, shift processing from peripheral to central, and consequently produce superior information acquisition.

H_2: For advertised products and services high in salience to recipients, because of adequate interest and motivation to elaborate, the attention-getting capacity of questions is immaterial; therefore, a difference in information acquisition should not be expected. In fact, considering the argument by Petty, Cacioppo, and Heesacker (1981) that questions may be distracting under these circumstances, it could be expected that in a situation of high salience, the *declarative* format results in superior information acquisition.

Alternatively, it has been argued (Zillmann, 1972) that individuals, being continually rewarded for providing answers to questions and punished for failure to do so, develop strong habits of responding with answers to questions. This conditioned response tendency is thought to generalize to rhetorically posed questions. They are presumed to foster increased attention and result in a covert linguistic response. It is this covert response, because it focuses information processing on the contiguous, relevant parts of the message, that is expected to mediate superior information acquisition. In situations of poor attention, then, where declarative formats fail to reach the audience, interrogative-declarative formats are thought to play on deep-rooted information-processing mechanisms and trigger attention to the message. The process is perhaps best illustrated by dichotic listening: During experimentation in which competing messages were presented—one to the left, the other to the right ear—respondents were readily induced by questions to one ear to favor the message received on that ear (Zillmann and Cantor, 1973). This process of quasi-mechanically attracting attention should also operate under conditions of sufficient and high attention.

Such reasoning leads to the following hypothesis:

H_3: Regardless of the salience of advertised products and services to recipients, questions, because they prompt a conditioned tendency in individuals to pay attention, produce heightened alertness and enhanced information processing that ultimately results in superior acquisition of question-related information.

METHOD

Overview

Ostensibly while waiting, students listened to two experimental radio advertisements. The advertisements featured declarative or interrogative-declarative formats. They were edited into actual radio programming consisting of both music and actual commercials. Following exposure, students were subjected to a surprise recall test. They completed a questionnaire testing their recall of the information presented in the experimental commercials. In a mixed-measures factorial design, format of message (declarative, interrogative-declarative) and respondent gender (male, female) were independent-measures factors, and product salience (male, female) was a repeated-measures factor.

Respondents

Ninety-five undergraduate students, 42 males and 53 females, were recruited from introductory communication classes. They received class credit for participation in the study.

Procedure

When students arrived at the 22-seat theater, they were asked to sign-in and sit quietly while the session administrator finished preparing the study materials. After two to three minutes, students were informed there would be an additional short delay because a videotape needed for the study had not yet been delivered. They were told that, for their convenience, the radio would be turned on for them while they waited. They were not specifically instructed to listen to the radio.

Four different audio tapes were prepared to sound like a portion of an actual local radio broadcast popular with college students. The exposure material began in the middle of a song, continued with an actual local commercial, then followed with the first experimental advertisement, another song, and the second experimental advertisement, ending with music. One experimental commercial advertised male products, the other female products. The order of the two experimental commercials was altered systematically. However, respondents in each session heard both commercials either in declarative or interrogative-declarative format.

Approximately 30 seconds into the final song, the session administrator shut off the tape and informed students that the study had actually already begun, that exposure to the radio music and commercials was part of an investigation. Respondents were asked to complete a 16-item questionnaire testing their recall of the information presented in the two experimental commercials. They were asked to complete the questions to the best of their ability, even if they had not paid much attention to the broadcast. After completion of the questionnaire, the students took part in an unrelated investigation. They were eventually debriefed and thanked for their participation.

Advertisement Variations

Two 60-second radio commercials for actual local department stores were specially written. The commercials were similar in content and presentation to actual local advertisements heard on the radio. Both the narration and background music were typical of that used in actual commercials.

One commercial featured female-oriented products such as lingerie and women's aerobic wear, whereas the other commercial featured male-oriented products such as men's dress and athletic shoes. This was done to effect a variation in salience. Male products were assumed more salient for men than women. The reverse was assumed to be the case for female products.

Two versions of each of the gender-oriented commercials were prepared. One version presented all pertinent information in statement format. The other presented the same information in a question-and-answer format.

For example, information in the male-products commercial in question-and-answer format was presented as follows:

> What fantastic deal is McRae's offering this week? A special price on Cole-Haan dress shoes for men.
> Why is this deal so special? Because, for a limited time, you can get a pair of these high-quality Italian leather dress shoes for just $109—that's a whopping $70 off the regular price.

The same information was presented in the declarative format as follows:

> McRae's fantastic deal this week is a special price on Col-Hahn dress shoes for men.
> This deal is so special because for a limited time, you can get a pair of these high-quality Italian leather dress shoes for just $109—that's a whopping $70 off the regular price.

Likewise, information in the female-products commercial in question-and-answer format was presented as follows:

> What great lingerie bargains do we have for you this week? A special sale on Vanity Fair robe and nightgown sets.
> And just how ridiculously low are Gayfers' prices? A spectacular 40 percent off! They're regularly $60, but at Gayfers you can get both pieces for just $36.
> How long do these unheard of prices last? Only through Saturday.

The same information was presented in the declarative format as follows:

> We have great lingerie bargains for you this week like a special sale on Vanity Fair robe and nightgown sets.

Gayfers' prices are ridiculously low—a spectacular 40 percent off! They're regularly $60, but at Gayfers you can get both pieces for just $36.

But these unheard of prices last only through Saturday.

Measurement of Information Acquisition

Respondents completed eight questions (five unaided and three aided) for each of the two experimental advertisements. An example of an unaided question is: "Which store advertised specials on men's shoes?" The answer was to be written onto a prompt line. An example of an aided question is: "How much were the athletic shoes on sale for?" One of multiple choices was to be marked. Acquisition of information was tested for the name of the department store, product brand names, store prices, amounts of discount, specific types of bonuses offered, etc. The number of correct responses defined the measure of information acquisition.

RESULTS

The information acquisition scores were subjected to a mixed-measures analysis of variance with presentational format (declarative, interrogative-declarative) and respondent gender as independent-measures factors and product salience (higher for men than women, higher for women than men) as a repeated-measures factor.

The analysis yielded a highly significant main effect for presentational format: $F(1, 91) = 7.60, p < 0.01$. The main effect of product salience approached significance: $F(1, 91) = 3.15, p < 0.10$. The gender main effect was utterly negligible ($F<1$). So were all pertinent interactions ($F<1$), except for the nonetheless negligible interaction between respondent gender and product salience: $F(1, 91) = 1.55, p < 0.25$.

The findings thus reveal a uniform effect of presentational format: Information acquisition in the declarative condition was $M = 2.02$; in the interrogative-declarative condition it was $M = 3.14$. Information acquisition was, therefore, significantly superior in the interrogative-declarative condition.

The significance-approaching main effect of product salience merely indicates that information about male products ($M = 2.85$) tended to be better remembered than information about female products ($M = 2.32$), this tendency applying to both respondent genders.

The absence of interactions is striking and significant from a theoretical perspective. In this context, if credence were given to the $p < 0.25$ interaction between respondent gender and product salience, the effect pattern would still be irrelevant to the theories tested. The rather inconsequential finding would be that men, as might be expected, tended to learn more about the male than the female products advertised ($M = 2.98$ and $M = 2.08$, respectively), but that women failed to learn more about the female than the male products advertised. If anything, women tended to learn more about male than female products ($M = 2.72$ and $M = 2.55$, respectively).

DISCUSSION

The findings give strong support to the proposal that the use of rhetorical question-and-answer sequences for the conveyance of persuasively relevant materials, as compared to the conveyance of such materials in purely declarative form, results in the superior learning of these materials in audiences that are not otherwise motivated to pay close attention. Questions, then, appear to have the capacity to draw attention to a message, and thus engage listeners, when such attention is impaired or lacking for reasons of disinterest or, perhaps more important, distraction and interference from happenings competing for attention. As radio commercials are often received under conditions of poor attentional focus, such as while driving an automobile, during the routine performance of chores, or in the midst of family interactions, the demonstration that questions can help reach an otherwise inattentive audience should be of considerable practical significance.

It should be recognized that the incidental-learning conditions created in this investigation were rather severe. Learning was, first of all, truly incidental in that respondents were not instructed to pay attention to the commercials; respondents were, in fact, led to believe that the radio was played for their entertainment. It must be assumed, in addition, that these respondents were greatly distracted by the research environment and the examination-like investigation in which they were to take part. It should, therefore, not surprise that information acquisition was extremely poor for declarative commercials and, although significantly better, far from perfect for interrogative-declarative commercials.

Regarding formal hypotheses, only H_2 receives unequivocal support. As predicted, the use of question-and-answer sequences produced better information acquisition than the use of statement sequences, and this effect was independent of product salience. This effect pattern is consistent with the assumption of quasi-mechanical responding to questions.

The findings of this investigation give no support to the proposal, suggested by the elaboration likelihood model and expressed in H_1 and H_2, that questions induce different levels of attention and information acquisition in situations of low and high product salience. Counter to prediction, the effect of the use of questions proved to be the same at the two levels of salience. It did not diminish with increased salience, as predicted. Moreover, an effect reversal from low to high salience, as suggested by the distraction rationale (Petty, Cacioppo, & Heesacker, 1981), is without any support from the findings.

It might be argued that such assessment is premature in light of the fact that a variation in salience was assumed rather than empirically demonstrated. It is conceivable that the male and female products involved in the commercials were of similar subjective importance to both male and female respondents. In fact, the nonsignificant interaction between product-gender and respondent-gender could be interpreted as indicating that products failed to exert gender-specific attention-motivating appeal. Moreover, it will be recalled that, if anything, women acquired less information from the female than from the male commercial. Could this mean that to female respondents female products may have been less salient than male products? If so, the experimental findings would not constitute an appropriate test of the ELM, and the findings could not disconfirm predictions based on this model.

In order to eliminate this interpretational dilemma, a post-test was conducted with respondents drawn from the population of respondents for the experiment, but without involving respondents who had taken part in the experiment. Twenty-two respondents were simply asked to rate, on 11-point scales ranging from "not at all" at zero to "extremely" at 10, the subjective importance that various products had to them ("When you go shopping, how important are the following products to you?"). All products of the two commercials, interspersed with yet other products, were presented in a random sequence. For analysis, the ratings were averaged across advertised products within the male and female commercials. A mixed-measures analysis of variance produced a highly significant interaction between product and respondent genders: $F(1, 20) = 119.59, p < 0.001$. It carried with it a significant main effect of product: $F(1, 20) = 19.56, p < 0.001$. The main effect of respondent gender was not significant, however ($p > 0.10$).

The product main effect shows that female products ($M = 2.48$) were deemed less salient than male products ($M = 4.04$) by both men and women. More importantly, the interaction shows salience to differ between genders as had been assumed: For male respondents, male products ($M = 6.40$) were significantly ($p < 0.001$ by t-test) more salient than female products ($M = 1.67$). For female respondents, in contrast, male products ($M = 1.07$) were significantly ($p < .01$) less salient than female products ($M = 3.89$).

These findings, then, vindicate the choice of male products as more salient to men than to women, and of female products as more salient to women than to men. More importantly, they uphold and strengthen the interpretation that, in the effect of interrogative-declarative presentations, product salience was of no consequence. It certainly did not exert the influence on information processing that the elaboration likelihood model projects.

It might prove beneficial in future research to further examine the impact of product salience on the effectiveness of questions in advertising. Such studies could feature commercials advertising products which represent varying levels of salience to consumers, thus providing more specific information about the effectiveness of the interrogative format. It could also be useful to investigate the impact of questions in television advertisements, which, like those heard on the radio, are often consumed in situations of poor attentional focus. Such investigations could help clarify the impact of questions in situations of incidental learning.

REFERENCES

Berger, Ida and Andrew A. Mitchell (1989), "The Effect of Advertising on Attitude Accessibility, Attitude Confidence, and the Attitude-behavior Relationship," *Journal of Consumer Research*, 16 (3), 269-279.

Bolen, William H. (1984), *Advertising*, New York: John Wiley.

Bowers, John W. (1965), "The Influence of Delivery on Attitudes toward Concepts and Speakers," *Speech Monographs*, 32 (2), 154-158.

Burnkrant, Robert E. and Daniel J. Howard (1984), "Effects of the Use of Introductory Rhetorical Questions versus Statements on Information Processing," *Journal of Personality and Social Psychology*, 47 (6), 1218-1230.

Chaiken, Shelly (1980), "Heuristic versus Systematic Information Processing and the Use of Source versus Message Cues in Persuasion," *Journal of Personality and Social Psychology*, 39 (4), 752-766.

Faison, Edmund W. J. (1980), *Advertising: A Behavioral Approach for Managers*, New York: John Wiley.

Howard, Daniel J. (1986), *Question Effects on Information Processing in Advertising*. Unpublished doctoral dissertation, Ohio State University.

_____ (1989), "The Prevalence of Question Use and Question Strategies in Print Advertising," in *Current Issues and Research in Advertising*, Vol. 11, eds. J. H. Leigh and C. R. Martin Jr., Ann Arbor, MI: University of Michigan.

Jewler, A. J. (1992), *Creative Strategy in Advertising* (4th ed.), Belmont, CA: Wadsworth Publishing Company.

Kantor, B. R. (1960), "Effectiveness of Inserted Questions in Instructional Films," *Audiovisual Communication Review*, 8, 104-108.

Lumsdaine, Arthur A., Mark A. May, and R. S. Hadsell (1958), "Questions Spliced into a Film for Motivation and Pupil Participation," in *Learning from Films*, eds. M. A. May and A. A. Lumsdaine, New Haven: Yale University Press.

MacLachlan, James W. and Pradeep Jalan (1985), "The Effects of Questions and Ambiguity on Brand Recall of Advertised Products," *Journal of Advertising* 14 (1), 18-22.

Moore, D. J., R. Reardon, and F.T. Durso (1985), "The Generation Effect in Advertising Appeals," *Advances in Consumer Research*, 13, 117-20.

Moriarty, Sandra E. (1991), *Creative Advertising: Theory and Practice* (2nd ed.), Englewood Cliffs, NJ: Prentice-Hall.

Munch, James M. and John L. Swasy (1988), "Rhetorical Question, Summarization Frequency, and Argument Strength Effects on Recall," *Journal of Consumer Research*, 15 (1), 69-76.

Myers, James H. and Arne F. Haug (1967), "Declarative vs. Interrogative Advertisement Headlines," *Journal of Advertising Research*, 7 (September), 41-44.

Petty, Richard E. and John T. Cacioppo (1979), "Issue Involvement Can Increase or Decrease Persuasion by Enhancing Message-relevant Cognitive Responses," *Journal of Personality and Social Psychology*, 37 (10), 1915-1926.

_____ and _____ (1986), *Communication and Persuasion: Central and Peripheral Routes to Attitude Change*, New York: Springer-Verlag.

_____, _____, and Rachel Goldman (1981), "Personal Involvement as a Determinant of Argument-based Persuasion," *Journal of Personality and Social Psychology*, 41 (5), 847-855.

_____, _____, and Martin Heesacker (1981), "Effects of Rhetorical Questions on Persuasion: A Cognitive Response Analysis," *Journal of Personality and Social Psychology*, 40 (3), 432-440.

Swasy, John L. and James M. Munch (1985), "Examining the Target of Receiver Elaborations: Rhetorical Question Effects on Source Processing and Persuasion," *Journal of Consumer Research*, 11 (4), 877-886.

Tamborini, Ron and Dolf Zillmann (1985), "Effects of Questions, Personalized Communication Style, and Pauses for Reflection in Children's Educational Programs," *Journal of Educational Research*, 79 (1), 19-26.

Zillmann, Dolf (1972), "Rhetorical Elicitation of Agreement in Persuasion," *Journal of Personality and Social Psychology*, 21 (2), 159-165.

_____ and Joanne R. Cantor (1973), "Induction of Curiosity via Rhetorical Questions and its Effects on the Learning of Factual Materials," *British Journal of Educational Psychology*, 43 (2), 172-180.

_____ and _____ (1974), "Rhetorical Elicitation of Concession in Persuasion," *The Journal of Social Psychology*, 94, 223-236.

Music and Radio Advertising: Effects of Tempo and Placement

George Brooker, Central Washington University
John J. Wheatley, University of Washington[1]

ABSTRACT

An experiment examined the effects of music tempo and music placement in a radio ad. Dependent variables included feelings, attitudes, unaided recall, and purchase likelihood. Results showed tempo had expected effects on perception of the music, but no impact on dependent measures; structure of the ad (music placement) showed stronger effects on the dependent variables.

"Music hath charms . . ." as the adage goes. It also has an attraction for marketers. Music has been incorporated in advertising messages at least since the early days of radio broadcasting. In spite of its long history of use, the effects of music in advertising are only now beginning to be explored and understood. The question, "What is the effect of music in a commercial?" is beginning to receive increasing attention.

Those who produce radio commercials are forced to rely largely on their judgment and on trial and error when dealing with the question of whether or how to employ music. If a decision is made to use music, a number of other decisions must be made, e.g., whether it should be familiar or an original composition, classical or popular, its tempo and placement within the ad, its appropriateness for the product or service being advertised, and a host of other considerations. It is apparent that research is needed to address these questions.

Bruner (1990) has reviewed non-marketing as well as marketing studies of music effects. Among his conclusions are the notions that music has emotional meanings for people, and people experience feelings as a response to music. Additionally, when used in marketing situations, music is capable of affecting the behaviors as well as the feelings of consumers. However, advertisers must be aware that music can distract (Park and Young 1986), facilitate (Hecker, cited in Alpert and Alpert 1991), or attract attention (MacInnis and Park 1991) of the listener based on elements such as the music's ability to generate emotion-laden memories, fit with the product, and its context.

A recent observation by Alpert and Alpert (1991) seems like an appropriate starting point for additional research on this topic. They observed that ads could be expected to shift from an affective to a cognitive emphasis as music's role in a commercial changed from strong to weak. This insightful observation suggests the likelihood that the placement of music in a radio commercial and the nature or structure of the musical accompaniment should be key elements affecting success. The research reported in this paper also answers the call of Kellaris and Cox (1987) for an investigation of the affective and cognitive impact of musical and commercial structure in a radio commercial. Attitude toward the ad, attitude toward the brand, message recall, feelings, and purchase intentions toward a brand in a popular product category are examined here. Tempo is the structural element of music which is studied; the position of the music in the commercial relative to the message is the structural element of the commercial which is explored.

Music Structure: Tempo

The studies of tempo cited most often are those of Milliman (1982, 1986). He found traffic in a supermarket moved more slowly when music was slow, and the increased time in the store resulted in increased sales; his later study found people lingered longer over restaurant meals with slow music, but bar bills (rather than food bills) were the elements leading to increased revenue. Bruner (1990) cites several studies where tempo affected perceptions of the music. Specifically, slower music was perceived as sad, faster tempi were perceived as happy. Kellaris and Kent (1991) found tempo affected perceptions of music's appealingness, arousingness, and behavioral intentions toward the music. Alpert and Alpert (1990) manipulated sad vs. happy vs. no music with tempo as one element involved in rating music as sad or happy. They found effects of music on subjects' moods and purchase intent, with sad music having more impact on selection than happy music, and a marginal superiority for sad vs. no music on purchase intention.

The effects of tempo, in summary, are: tempo can affect feelings, attitudes, behavior, perceptions, and stated intentions. Based on the studies of tempo cited, faster music would be expected to have a positive impact on emotion; it should increase the attention given to an ad, and should lead to positive effects on dependent measures in comparison with music in a slower tempo. None of the previous research has examined the effects of tempo, *per se*, on individual products or brands.

Hypothesis 1: Music tempo will influence attitudes, recall, feelings, and purchase intentions, with faster music having positive effects, and slower music having negative effects.

Commercial Structure

The effect of commercial structure (presence of music) is unclear; Sewall and Sarel (1986) found little impact of music in radio commercials on recall, while Hunt (cited in Bruner 1990) found recall was positively affected by the presence of music in radio commercials.

MacInnis, Moorman, and Jaworski (1991) present the viewpoint that advertising execution affects the motivation, opportunity, and ability to process brand information presented in the message. They note several aspects of advertisements which, for example, may lead consumers to increase the attention given to ads. Introducing novel stimuli, using prominent cues, and arousing curiosity are among the ways of increasing the attention-getting aspects of commercials. Many musical executions are novel; depending upon the format, they can be prominent; and music can be used to generate curiosity by being "interesting," surprising, and the like. Additionally, it has already been noted that music affects moods and feelings. It has been found that people, ". . . attend to stimuli that make them feel good" (Isen, *et al.*, cited in MacInnis, Moorman, and Jaworski 1991). Therefore, it is to be expected that consumers will attend to ads containing music which has positive emotional content. In sum, the use of music in commercials has the potential to attract attention and increase the motivation of people to learn about the product or brand being presented.

However, music may also distract from the message. It would seem that music which attracts attention and leads the listener into the message portion of the ad should increase message processing, retention, and recall. Conversely, music which attracts attention will divert some processing capability from the message, reducing ability to process, retain, and recall information. The structure of the commercial may be used to influence these outcomes. Placement of music at the beginning of the message, without a voice-

---

[1] The authors thank Mark S. Lawson for technical assistance in creating tapes and for knowledge in selecting musical pieces.

over, could draw attention and act as a lead-in to the message, increasing message effects. Placement of music in the background of the voice-over could draw some attention from the message, reducing its effects. Although there is no prior evidence regarding attitude toward the ad and attitude toward the brand, these are intervening variables in the buying process; they would also be expected to be influenced similarly by the position of the music.

Hypothesis 2: Music position in an ad will influence, attitudes, recall, purchase intention, and feelings, with music at the start of the message having positive effects, and music as background having negative effects.

METHODOLOGY

The research design was a 2 X 2 factorial with a control group. The factors were slow music/fast music and music-as-introduction/music-as-background to a radio commercial. The control group received a voice-only version of the commercial, without any music.

The test commercial (for ice cream) was the middle commercial in a set of three presented to consumers. The other two commercials were for an airline and a retailer. The placement of the test commercial was intended to avoid primacy and recency effects.

Copy for the test ad was developed professionally, and the announcer reading the copy was on the staff of a major radio station in the Northwest. Versions of all three commercials had been used in a previous research project.

Considerations in selection of music for the test ad included: appropriateness for the product, congruence with the announcer's voice, identifiable differences in tempo between selections, and comparable familiarity of the selections chosen.

Several styles of music were pretested. Ultimately, selections from Vivaldi's "Four Seasons: Summer" were chosen for the slow/fast manipulations. All musical versions of the commercial used material from the first sixty seconds or the last sixty seconds of the piece. Pretesting indicated these differed in tempo (first :60 is slow, 76 BPM; last :60 is fast, 142 BPM); the selections met the subjective criteria and dealt with the familiarity issue by being parts of the same musical work.

Musical versions of the test commercial were created using the sixty second selections as background for the voice portion of the commercial (fast or slow music versions), or with the first thirty seconds of each tempo version as an introduction to the commercial. In the music-as-introduction versions, there were twenty seconds of music prior to the voice message, and the music was faded out over the first ten seconds of the announcer speaking. In all versions, musical volumes were equal (except as it was being faded), and quiet enough to have the announcer's voice dominate the presentation. The text was identical in all three versions.

Information gathered included: preferred types of programming (for a local radio station); unaided recall of products advertised, brand names, and flavor of the ice cream; measures (on 1-10 point scales) of attitude toward the test ad and the brand; a purchase likelihood measure (on a 1-10 point scale) for the test ad product; semantic differential measures (5 point scales) of feelings engendered by the test commercial; manipulation checks; preferred music types (for the local radio station); and demographics (education level, marital status, age, and sex).

The feelings measures included sixteen bipolar adjectives. The measures and the instructions for their use were developed from the work of Edell and Burke (1987). These researchers identified sixty-nine adjectives people had used to describe how ads made them feel. Examination of their list indicated some were polar opposites of the same dimension. The feelings measures used here were put into semantic differential form for ease of response, clarity, and interpretability. Using Edell and Burke's list, polar opposites were paired using Osgood, Suci, and Tannenbaum's (1957) listings of opposites. For those descriptors not presented in Osgood, et al., a thesaurus was used to develop polar opposites.

Feelings were chosen from each of Edell and Burke's three types (upbeat, negative, and warm) in approximately equal numbers. The final set of adjectives was chosen for their apparent unique contributions. (Many of Edell and Burke's descriptors appear highly correlated; they are used as synonyms for each other in a thesaurus.)

Procedure

The study was conducted in and around a small Northwestern community which houses a university. Subjects were adults. An attempt was made to minimize the number of students in the study, but this proved difficult because more than half those over age eighteen in the area were students.

People were run individually in the experiment. Interviewers ascertained that individuals had not participated in the study previously, then led them through the procedure. After warm-up questions and questions about preferred programming, individuals were told they would be listening to some radio ads, and should do so as they would any other ads they would hear on the radio. The particular version of the test ad they heard was determined randomly. A Walkman was used in each case to deliver the three commercials in the set of ads. Following the listening experience, the recall, attitude, purchase likelihood, feelings, and other measures were collected; people were thanked and the interview was terminated.

RESULTS

A total of 100 people participated in the study, with 20 in each treatment condition. The sample was 54% female; most (58%) had some college, with an additional 33% having college degrees or graduate school education. Only 26% were married and 62% were single. Ages ranged from 19 to 75, with a mean age of 27.9 years.

Manipulation checks indicated that fast music was perceived as faster (t=-6.18, 77 d.f., p <.001) and more cheerful (t=1.93, 77 d.f., p <.03) than slow music. Music-as-introduction was somewhat (t=-1.28, 78 d.f., p <.11) more effective than music-as-background in leading people to want to listen to the ice cream ad. A measure of concentration indicated a slight tendency (t=1.15, 78 d.f., p <.13) for those exposed to music-as-background to have more difficulty concentrating on the ice cream ad than those in the music-as-introduction condition.

The differences between the music manipulations and the no-music control group were examined using oneway ANOVA. The presence of music led people to state they had difficulty paying attention to the ad in comparison to the no-music control group. Tests using Duncan's multiple range procedure indicated fast music led to greater reported difficulty concentrating (p <.05) than no music; placement of music in the background of the ad, similarly, made it marginally more difficult (p <.10) to concentrate than no music.

The number of correct unaided recall answers was summed for the questions on type of product advertised, brand name, and flavor for the ice cream ad. This created an unaided recall measure. This measure and the other dependent measures were subjected to a MANOVA with tempo and placement of music as independent variables. The result was significant, and ANOVAs were performed to explore individual results. Mean values for all measures are presented in Table One.

TABLE 1
Mean Values for Dependent Variables*

Variable	Music Position	Tempo		Control
		Fast	Slow	
Unaided Recall	Introduction	2.50	2.55	2.65
	Background	2.00	2.20	
Purchase Likelihood	Introduction	5.25	5.45	5.00
	Background	4.30	3.85	
Attitude Toward Ad	Introduction	6.20	6.25	6.05
	Background	5.20	5.56	
Attitude Toward Brand	Introduction	5.85	5.70	5.10
	Background	5.20	4.72	

TABLE 2
ANOVA on Unaided Recall

Source of Variation	SS	df	MS	F	Sig.
Music Placement (P)	2.950	1	2.950	4.791	.032
Tempo (T)	.504	1	.504	.818	.369
P X T	.252	1	.252	.410	.524
Residual	45.561	74	.616		

TABLE 3
ANOVA on Purchase Likelihood

Source of Variation	SS	df	MS	F	Sig.
Music Placement (P)	31.623	1	31.623	4.259	.043
Tempo (T)	.301	1	.301	.041	.841
P X T	2.162	1	2.162	.291	.591
Residual	594.400	74	7.424		

The first exploration involved the unaided recall measure. Table Two presents the result. This analysis indicates that placement of the music in a radio commercial has a significant impact on unaided recall. Those in the music-as-introduction condition remembered more pieces of information than those in the music-as-background condition.

Duncan's multiple range tests indicated the no-music control group remembered more information than those in the background music condition (p <.05), and the no-music control had a marginally (p <.10) improved recall over those in the fast music condition. ANOVAs also were done on the attitude and purchase likelihood measures. There was a marginal (p <.11) effect of music placement on attitude toward the ad, with music-as-introduction more favorable than music-as-background. Results on attitude toward the brand were weaker still, although the pattern was similar.

The likelihood of purchase ANOVA result is presented in Table Three. Again, placement of the music is the only factor influencing the outcome. Music used as an introduction to the commercial leads to higher purchase likelihood than music-as-background to the ad. The no-music control group did not differ significantly with either music-receiving group on purchase likelihood or the attitude measures (Duncan's test).

The semantic differential measures of feelings engendered by the ice cream commercial were subjected to a factor analysis using principal components with Varimax rotation. The four-factor rotated result is presented in Table Four. Total variance explained was sixty-six per cent.

MANOVA and ANOVA were performed on the "feelings" factors. Only the first factor produced a significant result. The ANOVA for it is presented in Table Five. Once more, only the placement of music in the commercial has a significant effect. In this case, background music developed a negative set of feelings compared with introductory music.

Oneway Analysis of Variance also was performed on the feelings factors to examine the impact of the no-music condition with the music factors. Once more, only the first factor displayed differences at the .05 level. This analysis revealed that both the no-music and introductory music conditions differed from the background music condition which produced more downbeat feelings (pun intended) than the first two. Marginally significant (p <.10) results were found between the no-music group and background music group on the second factor, between no-music and introductory music on the fourth factor, and between no-music and slow music on the fourth factor.

DISCUSSION

This research presents a surprising result: although the earlier differences emerged regarding perceptions of slow/fast on tempo, and faster music was perceived as more cheerful than slow music, tempo had no significant effects on any of the feelings, attitudinal, recall, or purchase likelihood measures for the product. This is a distinct contrast to previous findings that tempo affected behavioral intentions (Kellaris and Kent 1991). However, those behavioral intentions were directed toward the music, itself (e.g., intention to listen to the music again, intention to purchase the music, etc.), not toward a product or brand advertised using music. The Alpert and Alpert (1990) findings regarding perceptions and purchase intention were confounded by the inclusion of other musical elements

TABLE 4
Rotated Factors for Feelings Measures: Principal Factor with Varimax Rotation

feelings	1	2	3	4
irritated-pleased	-.7779	-.1636	-.2195	-.0584
happy-sad	.7724	.2357	.1356	-.0498
good-bad	.7661	.1889	.2747	.0487
interested-indifferent	.7410	.1230	.3404	.1022
cheerful-depressed	.7052	.3705	.0897	-.0511
regretful-rejoicing	-.6555	-.2988	-.1495	.1991
insulted-honored	-.5873	-.1801	-.4267	.1596
affectionate-callous	.2960	.7481	.2069	.2111
sentimental-unemotional	.3399	.7222	.0667	.1996
adventurous-cautious	.1538	.6744	.1134	-.3653
hopeful-pessimistic	.2075	.6108	.3708	-.0245
confident-dubious	.2111	.2070	.8078	-.0766
critical-accepting	-.3762	-.1105	-.6497	-.0358
carefree-worried	.2171	.4936	.6457	-.0247
contemplative-impulsive	-.2257	.0451	-.2424	.7946
calm-nervous	.2673	.0460	.4207	.6196

TABLE 5
Anova on First "Feelings" Factor

Source of Variation	SS	df	MS	F	Sig.
Music Placement (P)	259.200	1	259.200	11.230	.001
Tempo (T)	8.450	1	8.450	.366	.547
P X T	.050	1	.050	.002	.963
Residual	1754.100	76	23.080		

with tempo in a mixed factorial design. Thus, there is no way to determine the unique effects of tempo from their study. From this research, it appears that the effects of tempo are not a direct influence for an individual product. Tempo's effects appear to influence perceptions of the music and attitudes and behaviors toward music, but this influence is not transferred to the product-related elements measured here.

Perhaps some of the difference between the findings of this research and those of Alpert and Alpert (1990) may be ascribed to the fact that they used different musical pieces to change tempo, while this study did not. It is possible that their results reflect the reactions of subjects to the different musical pieces. Alpert and Alpert took great care in constructing their manipulations, but this element was not controlled. Kellaris and Kent's (1991) work used music composed by one of the authors to fit a particular style, and their confirmatory experiment used three musical pieces. Certainly, the confirmatory experiment presents a similar problem of different musical pieces. The original experiment, using music composed for the research, is more problematic. As a new piece, it may be novel, stimulate curiosity, and otherwise increase motivation to pay attention to the ad (MacInnis, Moorman, and Jaworski 1991). However, results were limited to the music, itself; there was no attempt to generalize to other variables.

The Milliman (1982,1986) effects were found with generalized behaviors. Marketing effects were secondary phenomena resulting from the generalized behaviors. Again, different musical pieces were used as stimuli, and the previous comments apply.

Tempo did have some of the anticipated results. Consistent with previous research, faster music was perceived as more cheerful than slower music. Additionally, there was a slight effect of tempo, as the control group had marginally better recall of advertising information than those receiving the fast tempo music. It is not as if tempo has no impact on a commercial's effects. However, the direct effects are somewhat muted and may be in a direction the advertiser does not want to develop. As Alpert and Alpert (1991) have pointed out, commercials which have music dominant tend to be affect-based rather than cognitive-based. The results of this research are consistent with that position, showing lowered information recall with fast music compared to no-music. Advertisers need to be quite specific regarding the objectives of their advertising on the cognitive/affective dimension, recognizing there is apt to be a trade-off here regarding the use of music, especially when a faster tempo is used.

Commercial structure effects were more pronounced and pervasive. Placement of music in the commercial had clearly significant effects on information recall, purchase likelihood, and the joyous-melancholic feelings factor, with the expected directional effects on attitude toward the ad and attitude toward the brand. In all cases, music-as-introduction to the ad generated more positive results than music-as-background to the ad. Marginal differences found on a measure of difficulty in concentrating on the message and measured desire to listen to the ad also favored the music-as-introduction commercial structure. These results are clear in favoring the music-as-introduction structure over music used as background.

These results are consistent with the views of MacInnis, Moorman, and Jaworski (1991): advertising execution does affect motivation and ability to process information. In this study, music acted to distract individuals from the message (in the background condition), restricting ability to process information; it also acted, marginally, to invite attention to the message (in the introduction condition), motivating people to process the message. The multitudinous tasks music can perform in an ad (Scott 1990) are represented further here in developing feelings of joyousness from an introductory position, and in the marginal impact on other feelings based on position and tempo.

The finding of effects of commercial structure on purchase likelihood extends the process closer to its natural conclusion. Obviously, purchase is not examined here, but that is a logical next step. Music has been shown to affect behavior. The behavioral intention effects seen here should be extended in further research.

The Sewall-Sarel/Hunt discrepancy appears to have at least a partial explanation here. Commercials in a straight announcement mode lead to greater recall than commercials using background music; however, commercials using music as an introduction have the same effect; and there is no difference between announcement-only and music-as-introduction. It should be noted that music-as-introduction ads were predominantly text, with music fading for the first ten seconds of the sixty second message, making that ad closely comparable to the announcement-only ad in terms of message content presentation. It could be expected that the message in these two cases will be relatively clear and uncontaminated by other stimuli.

There were no significant interactions found in any of the ANOVAs. Bruner (1990) has suggested the possibility of interaction effects of musical components. This research examined only one musical component (tempo), so examination of component interactions is not feasible. The lack of interactions between music structure and ad structure suggests advertisers may need to concern themselves only with the major elements of the ad without regard for possible negative joint effects. On the other hand, absence of interactions here also may mean there are no synergies to be gained through combined effects, either.

It is worth noting that there was no programming included with the commercial presentations. As a result, there was nothing provided to direct attention away from the ads; indeed, individuals were told they would be listening to radio ads. In addition, this was a highly educated sample. This would seem to be a difficult set of conditions in which to demonstrate differences in variables such as unaided recall; nevertheless, differences were found. This suggests that a more natural listening mode might present even more substantial results. Without having attention directed to messages by researchers, listeners are apt to have their attention directed or diverted solely by the messages presented. This, certainly, is a notion worth further exploration.

The results of this research seem clear. As examined here, the structure of the music was less important than the structure of the ad in determining results. However, since only one element of music structure was examined, these results should be viewed cautiously. Other structural elements of music (e.g., pitch and texture) should be explored. With only a single music piece, it was not possible to manipulate many structural elements.

REFERENCES

Alpert, Judy I., and Mark I. Alpert (1991), "Contributions from a Musical Perspective on Advertising and Consumer Behavior," in R. Holman and M. Solomon (eds.), *Advances in Consumer Research, Vol. 18*, Provo, UT: Association for Consumer Research, 232-238.

_____ and _____ (1990), "Music Influences on Mood and Purchase Intentions," *Psychology and Marketing*, 7 (Summer), 109-133.

Bruner, II, Gordon C. (1990), "Music, Mood and Marketing," *Journal of Marketing*, 54 (October), 94-104.

Edell, Julie A., and Marian C. Burke (1987), "The Power of Feelings in Understanding Advertising Effects," *Journal of Consumer Research*, 14 (December), 421-433.

Kellaris, James J., and Anthony D. Cox (1987), "The Effects of Background Music in Advertising: A Replication and Extension," in S. P. Douglas, et al., (eds.) *American Marketing Assocation Educators' Proceedings, Vol. 53*, Chicago: American Marketing Association, 283.

_____, and Robert J. Kent (1991),"Exploring Tempo and Modality Effects on Consumer Responses to Music," in R. Holman and M. Solomon (eds.), *Advances in Consumer Research, Vol. 18*, Provo, UT: Association for Consumer Research, 243-248.

MacInnis, Deborah J., and C. Whan Park (1991), "The Differential Role of Characteristics of Music on High- and Low-Involvement Consumers' Processing of Ads," *Journal of Consumer Research*, 18 (September), 161-173.

_____, Christine Moorman, and Bernard J. Jaworski (1991), "Enhancing and Measuring Consumers' Motivation, Opportunity, and Ability to Process Brand Information From Ads," *Journal of Marketing*, 55 (October), 32-53.

Milliman, Ronald E. (1982), "Using Background Music to Affect the Behavior of Supermarket Shoppers," *Journal of Marketing*, 46 (Summer), 86-91.

_____ (1986), "The Influence of Background Music on the Behavior of Restaurant Patrons," *Journal of Consumer Research*, 13 (September), 286-289.

Osgood, Charles E., George J. Suci, and Percy H. Tannenbaum (1957), *The Measurement of Meaning*, Urbana, IL: University of Illinois Press.

Park, C. Whan, and Mark S. Young (1986), "Consumer Response to Television Commercials: The Impact of Involvement and Background Music on Brand Attitude Formation," *Journal of Marketing Research*, 23 (February), 11-24.

Scott, Linda M. (1990), "Understanding Jingles and Needledrop: A Rhetorical Approach to Music in Advertising," *Journal of Consumer Research*, 17 (September), 223-236.

Sewall, Murphy A., and Dan Sarel (1986), "Characteristics of Radio Commercials and Their Recall Effectiveness," *Journal of Marketing*, 50 (January), 52-60.

Agent Decision Making: Understanding and Predicting the Preferences of Others
Patricia M. West, University of Texas at Austin
Christina L. Brown, Northwestern University

Michael Solomon (1986) coined the term "surrogate consumer" when referring to individuals who are employed to make decisions on behalf of their clients. We have broadened the concept to include all individuals who make consumption decisions on another's behalf and refer to these people as "agent decision makers." The notion of a "principal-agent relationship" has been examined in marketing from the economic perspective of agency theory. Rather than the incentive and control issues of traditional agent theory, however, this session focused on the ability of well-intentioned agents to fully understand the principals' preferences and perceptions in order to effectively choose on their behalf.

The first paper, by Patricia M. West, described a laboratory experiment examining agents' ability to learn to predict a principal's tastes. Three factors are identified as impacting *agent learning*: 1) how the agent responds to feedback from a principal indicating their evaluation of an alternative; 2) the "latitude of acceptance" of the principal (i.e., *picky* v. *easy-to-please*); 3) the informational value of feedback from the principal. Information theory suggests that not all feedback is equally informative. A *picky* person provides informative feedback when he/she reports liking an alternative. An *easy-to-please* person provides informative feedback when he/she reports disliking an alternative. Subjects are sensitive to differences in the informational value of feedback. Those subjects who focused attention on informative feedback demonstrated higher predictive accuracy. Subjects who viewed mostly preferred alternatives did not learn as well as subjects who viewed either a balance of preferred and nonpreferred, or mostly nonpreferred alternatives.

The second paper, by Christina L. Brown, expanded "agent decision making" to include decisions made by marketers on behalf of consumers. These types of agent decisions are made more complex and problematic by two important features of the marketer's environment: first, marketers are held highly accountable for their decisions and must justify them to others; second, marketers face a more complex set of decision inputs than do consumers. Accountability will change the way the inputs are integrated but may not result in better decisions. This framework was tested on 124 advertising professionals predicting consumer responses to ads in an experiment simulating a typical advertising copy meeting. Results demonstrated that private intuitive responses to ads dominate the decision process regardless of accountability; that accountable decision makers make more systematic, analytical decisions; but that accountability does not always improve decision accuracy. In particular, when market research was not present or was of weak diagnosticity, most decision makers would have made more accurate predictions by relying exclusively on their private intuitive responses to ads.

The third paper, by Deborah Salmond, Jeffery R. Edwards and Robert E. Spekman, examined agent decision making in a business-to-business context. The results from an in-depth field research project were discussed. Key informants on both sides of the buyer-seller relationship participated in interviews and a response questionnaire. Each side reported on its view of the relationship by assessing its own and the other's performance and transaction costs. Successful relationships were ones in which partners had *shared expectations* and were in *consensus* with respect to the management of the relationship. Response surface methods were used to assess the effects of shared expectations and consensus on performance and transactions costs.

The concluding discussion by John Deighton addressed the question of whether the concept of agent decision making could be considered "consumer behavior," arguing positively that the prediction of consumers' behavior was an important part of the West and Brown papers. He also suggested that the notion of agent decision making was useful beyond the consumer behavior context, as evidenced by the business-to-business application in the Salmond et al. paper.

An Exposé on Green Television Ads

Easwar Iyer, University of Massachusetts, Amherst
Bobby Banerjee, University of Massachusetts, Amherst
Charles Gulas, University of Massachusetts, Amherst[1]

ABSTRACT

We present the results from content analyzing 95 green TV ads. Although firm conclusions may be elusive because of sample characteristics, some very striking patterns emerge. For instance most green ads pertain to domestic consumables, are very shallow in their orientation, use women spokespersons and a testimonial format. A significant number of ads also attempt to influence consumer behavior and these tend to be more deep in their orientation. There are a also striking differences between green print ads and green TV ads in terms of their structure, strategy and tactics.

INTRODUCTION

Concern among American consumers for the biophysical environment is not only growing rapidly but is here to stay. According to a comprehensive follow-up study conducted in 1992, The Roper Organization states "... while Americans are somewhat less focused on the environment now — and more worried about recession, unemployment, and rising health care costs, among other economic woes — their environmental concerns have not dissipated. Far from it." (Roper Organization, 1992, p. 1). Another expert who has tracked the publics concern for the environment writes that there is continued interest in the environment and that the "... recent surge in environmental concern is not a passing fad" (Rehak, 1992, p. 251). Witness, for instance, the near doubling of the True-Blue Green segment from 11% to 20% between 1990 and 1992 (List, 1993, Roper Organization, 1992). The True-Blue Green segment consists of the greenest consumers in terms of their environmental attitudes and behaviors (Roper Organization, 1992; 1990). More and more marketers are targeting this segment because of the four advantages it offers: first, this is a large segment even now and for that reason alone is worth pursuing; second, this segment is rapidly growing and therefore it is advisable to develop marketing programs fostering an association with it; third, this segment consists of the most lucrative and desirable consumers in that they are very affluent and highly educated; and fourth, this segment is the leading edge in the innovation adoption process because of its demographic and psychographic characteristics, and therefore will be a strong influence on the trailing segments.

To target the green consumer marketers have responded in different ways, including designing new products (Hinds, 1987), repositioning existing products (Bremner, 1989), creating a new corporate image (Iyer and Banerjee, 1992). Among the different marketing activities, one of the most visible has been the explosion in green advertising, both in print and television media. Unfortunately, this explosion in green advertising has not been accompanied by a corresponding growth in the number of scholarly studies on the subject issue (Kangun, Carlson, and Grove, 1991). Part of the reason for the paucity in scholarly work could be the absence of a framework to categorize green advertising. Iyer and Banerjee (1992) addressed that very question and developed a framework to categorize green print ads. We propose to expand on their framework and present a new scheme to analyze green TV ads.

1.0 The Analytical Framework

Iyer and Banerjee (1992) proposed and used a framework to analyze green print ads. We could not directly apply their framework in our context since we were analyzing TV ads and their framework was developed for print ads. Thus, we had to adapt their original framework to conform to our current needs. A detailed listing of all the categories used in this study is provided in Table 1 following a brief description of a select few.

In terms of the ad's *structure* we were interested in who the *sponsor* was, the type of *product*[2] *promoted*, the degree of *greenness*, and the type of *characters* portrayed. Next, we categorized the advertiser's *strategy*, i.e., the objectives or goals implied in the ad. There were four separate objectives that we identified: first, a sponsor's attempt to *position the product/service as green*; second, a sponsor's attempt to present the *corporate entity as green*; third, a sponsor's attempt to *influence viewers' future behavior*; and fourth, a sponsor's attempt to *enlist viewers' support* either by becoming a member of the sponsoring organization or through a donation to the sponsoring organization. In coding *tactics* we expanded on the scheme used by Iyer and Banerjee (1992) and proposed seven categories. The first category, *zeitgeist*, was used to identify those ads that merely jumped on the green bandwagon; all ads with an *emotional* appeal were placed in the second category; ads emphasizing *financial* aspects were in the third category; the fourth category captured ads using *euphoria* as a tactic; the fifth category, *management*, was used to identify ads in which the sponsoring organization emphasized control or social responsibility; all forms of *testimonials* were classified in the sixth category; and ads using *comparison* as an appeal were placed in the seventh and final category. Lastly, we developed six new categories to identify the substantive *issues* emphasized by sponsors of green television ads. The five issues of *atmosphere, land, water, animal life, and plant life* have been identified and accepted as the most salient ones in environmental marketing (Iyer and Banerjee, 1992; Ottman, 1991). We added a sixth category, *catch-all*, to define those ads that referred to more than one substantive issue. The details of the analytical framework used in this study including the main taxonomy, main categories and sub-categories is provided below.

2.0 The Sample

Our sample was drawn from a large pool of green ads that were recorded by Ogilvy and Mather during 1991-1992 for other purposes. We defined an ad to be green if any part of the ad — headline, copy, or voiceover — referred to any aspect of the biophysical environment — atmosphere, land, water, animal life, or plant life — *and* there was an explicit effort to portray the sponsor or its offering as being sensitive and responsive to any aspect of the biophysical environment. This definition excludes ads that merely allude to nature more as a backdrop than in an active sense. Our definition, in that sense, is somewhat more restrictive than the one generally used in trade circles, although we hasten to note that there is no well accepted definition of green advertising. According to the more

---

[1] We thank Robert Rehak of Ogilvy & Mather for providing the ads analyzed in this study.

[2] In case of a corporate ad, the product being promoted was the company's name/image.

TABLE 1
The Analytical Framework

STRUCTURE	ADVERTISER	Manufacturer/Producer Retailer Corporate - For Profit Corporate - NonProfit Service Organization Others	
	PRODUCT	Durables Household Consumables Personal Consumables Personal Care Services Industrial Corporate Others	
	GREENNESS	Shallow Moderate Deep	
	CHARACTERS	Real People	Male Female Children Mixed
		Cartoon characters Animal dominant No Characters Others	
STRATEGY	PRODUCT/SERVICE CORPORATE VIEWER BEHAVIOR VIEWER SUPPORT		
TACTIC	ZEITGEIST	Mere Statement Bandwagon	
	EMOTIONAL	Fear Guilt Humor Self-Referencing You Make a Difference Nature/Aesthetics	
	FINANCIAL	Coupons Premiums Contests Cause Subsidy	
	EUPHORIA	Health Natural Ingredients	
	MANAGEMENT	Social Responsibility Control	
	TESTIMONIAL	Celebrity Expert J. Doe	
	COMPARISON	Direct & Explicit Indirect & Implicit	
	OTHERS		
ISSUES	ATMOSPHERE LAND WATER ANIMAL LIFE PLANT LIFE CATCH-ALL		

FIGURE 1

ADVERTISER TYPOLOGY

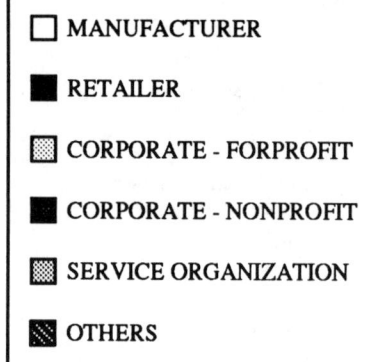
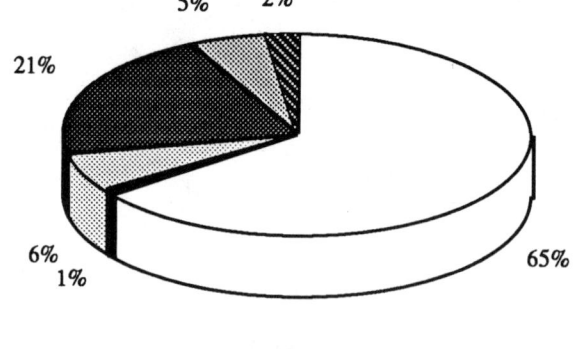

ITEMS ADVERTISED

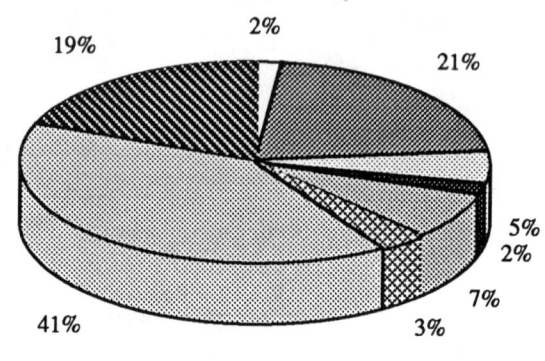

---

inclusive definition, an ad would be green even if the sponsor or its offering was green only by implication without a clear cut claim (Kangun, Carlson, and Grove, 1991). As stated earlier, we were more restrictive and required the claim to be explicit in terms of how the sponsor or its offering interacted with the biophysical environment. One of our motives in adopting a stringent definition was to ensure that the two coders had a high degree of agreement in their independent identification of a green ad. Secondly, it was important to be consistent with the definition used by Iyer and Banerjee (1992) since we were adapting their framework to analyze these TV ads. Moreover, our stringent definition does not pose any problems since its only impact was to limit the size of our sample; in fact some of our conclusions are even more striking because of our stringent definition.

Two viewers independently viewed the entire pool of ads and identified an ad to be green or otherwise. One viewer identified 95 ads as being green; the second viewer identified a subset of only 92 ads as being green. In other words there was complete agreement on 92 ads with only 3 ads being discrepant. Upon discussion they both agreed that there were indeed 95 green ads; these ads constituted our sample.

3.0 Coding : Intercoder Reliability

Two of the researchers served as coders of the ads analyzed in this study. At first they became familiar with the analytical framework by discussing the categories among themselves and with the principal investigator. Next, they identified the green ads to be analyzed from a larger pool of taped ads. This step has already been described. After agreeing on the set of ads to be analyzed, each coder independently categorized each ad. This was followed by a comparison of the two codings. At this stage, differences were resolved through discussion; the final results are based upon the coding categories determined after such discussion. Inter-coder reliability, measured as percentage agreement, varied from a low of 73% (Greenness of Ad) to a high of 96% (Strategy); this procedure and the agreement rates are consistent with those adopted by other researchers doing similar work (Gilly, 1988) and recommended by experts in content analysis (Kassarjian, 1977)

4.0 Descriptive Analyses

Our first step was to analyze the frequency distribution of the four main categories in our taxonomy, i.e., Structure, Strategy, Tactic, and Issues.

4.1 Structure

There were four main categories within structural factors, i.e., Advertiser, Product, Level of Greenness, and Characters Portrayed in an Ad; we analyzed their frequency distribution. The following pie-charts (Figure 1) show that manufacturers, followed by non-profit agencies, were the largest sponsors of green TV advertising and corporations, followed by household consumables, were the most frequently advertised items.

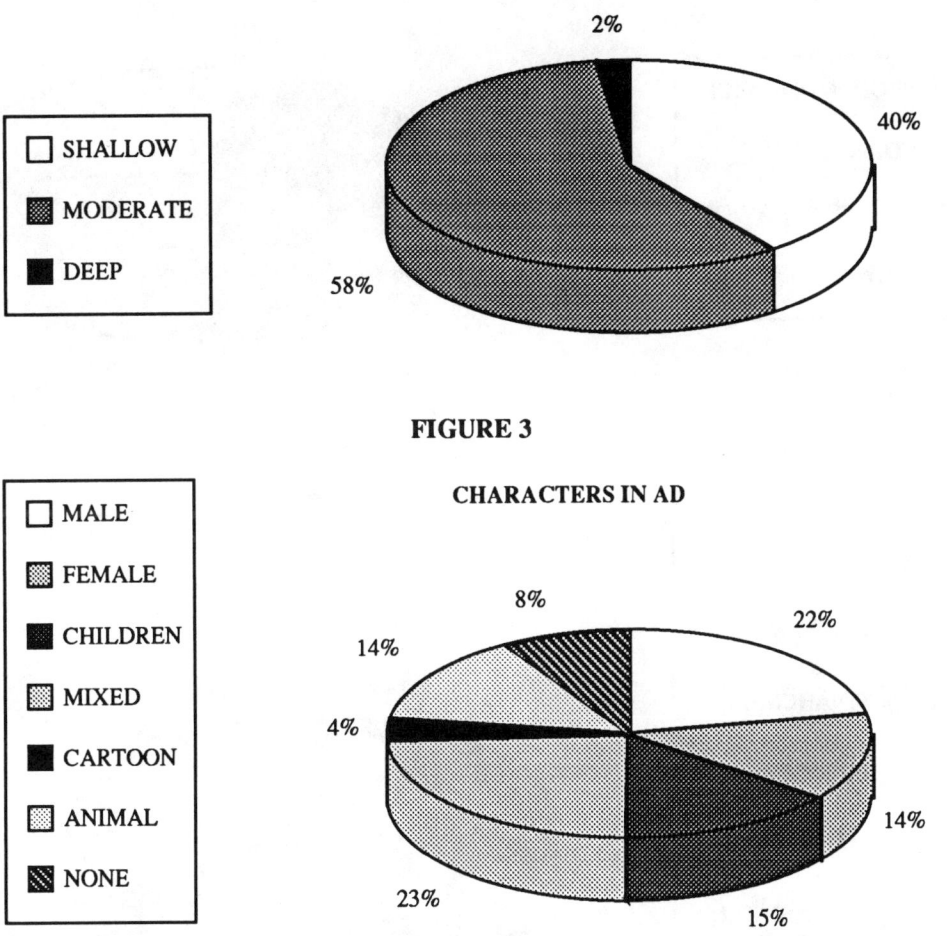

FIGURE 2

GREENNESS

- SHALLOW
- MODERATE
- DEEP

2%, 40%, 58%

FIGURE 3

CHARACTERS IN AD

- MALE
- FEMALE
- CHILDREN
- MIXED
- CARTOON
- ANIMAL
- NONE

22%, 14%, 15%, 23%, 4%, 14%, 8%

Likewise, we analyzed the greenness of an ad as well as the type of characters portrayed in it. We have adapted the concepts of *deep* and *shallow* ecology proposed by Naess (1973) while categorizing the greenness of an ad. The distinction between *deep* and *shallow* ecology is a function of the varying degree of involvement in green behaviors; some are enduring and deep while other are more superficial. For example, driving a small car instead of a big car, thereby expending less energy and causing less environmental pollution, would be considered an example of green behavior. Alternatively, using a bicycle instead of a car —any size car— would also be a symbol of being green. In the context of these two scenarios, downsizing the car would reflect a relatively shallow involvement in a green lifestyle since that choice merely reduces, without completely eliminating, the negative impact on the environment whereas riding a bicycle instead of a car would reflect deeper involvement in a green lifestyle since, presumably, the negative impact on the environment has been eliminated.

Likewise one could conceptualize greenness of an ad being on a continuum varying from shallow to deep. Three categories, rather than a dichotomy, better captures a continuum; therefore we categorized greenness of an ad into three: *shallow, moderate,* and *deep*. The frequency distribution of greenness of an ad is as shown in figure 2. It is quite obvious that there are very few green ads that are deep. This is hardly surprising, since, our expectation, based on Iyer and Banerjee (1992) was that there would be a lot of shallow green ads. It is therefore pleasantly surprising that the vast majority of green ads are at least moderate in their greenness. Two reasons can be offered to explain the unexpected findings. First, television is a medium that is better suited than print to add realism to a depiction; thus one would expect to find more TV ads that are moderate to deep as compared to print ads. Second, the television ads used in this study are more recent than the print ads used by Iyer and Banerjee (1992); with the ever growing public concern and increased government regulation, as discussed earlier, sponsors may have begun to produce more green ads.

The categorization of characters used in an ad is self-explanatory. The motivation to study portrayal of characters stems from Balch (1992) who suggested that the use of children would personalize the concept of conserving for the future. Overall, almost three in four ads use live characters instead of animals or cartoon figures. When "real" people are portrayed in an ad, most often it tends to be male dominant, although female dominant and child(ren) dominant ads are also fairly frequent. It is interesting that child(ren) dominant ads are used fairly frequently (15%) and slightly more so than female dominant ads (14%). Although a longitudinal analysis on a broader sample will be required to test Balch's (1992) hypothesis

FIGURE 4

STRATEGY

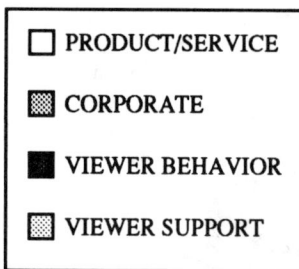
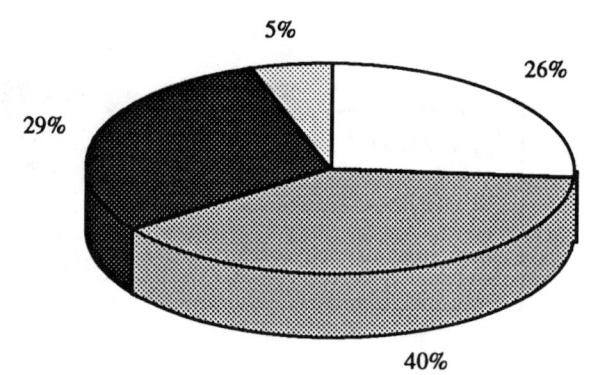

FIGURE 5

TACTIC

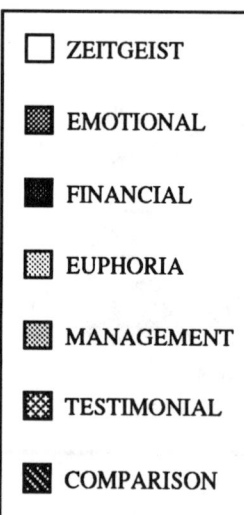
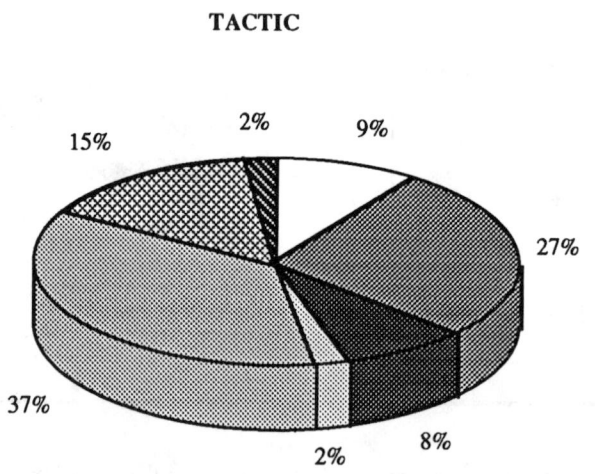

that children best personalize the concept of future, the relatively high frequency of child(ren) dominant ads provides it with oblique support. (Figure 3).

4.2 Strategy

The frequency distribution of the four categories of strategy is shown in figure 4. It is clear that the most dominant strategy was to position the corporation as being green. Changing consumer values and government regulations may have forced corporations to put on a new green face themselves and be consistent with the times.

This was followed by two strategies, i.e., influencing viewer behavior (29%) and positioning the product/service as green (26%), that were used almost equally frequently. Soliciting viewer support came in last (5%).

4.3 Tactics

The frequency distribution of the seven tactics categories is as shown in figure 5. The most frequently used tactic (37%) was the one emphasizing management control and responsibility. This was followed by emotional appeals (27%) and testimonials (15%) with other kinds of appeals being used only sporadically.

4.4 Issues

The frequency distribution of the six categories of issues emphasized in the ads is represented in the pie-chart shown in figure 6. The data suggest that most ads (42%) focused on more than one issue in their message. However, the single issue most frequently addressed was land (27%), implying a primary focus on solid waste disposal. Land was followed by water (12%) and other less frequently used issues. Our finding is consistent with the prevalent belief that land is scarce and that landfills are often abused and misused.

5.0 Themes in Green TV Advertising

The simple descriptive analysis showed that most green ads on TV were sponsored by manufacturers, tended to promote corporate image or personal and household consumables, were typically moderate in depth, and used "real" persons more often than not. This picture gets clarified and new patterns emerge when more detailed analyses are performed. For instance, we cross-tabulated the type of advertiser with the greenness of an ad; we linked the types of issues most often associated with the type of product

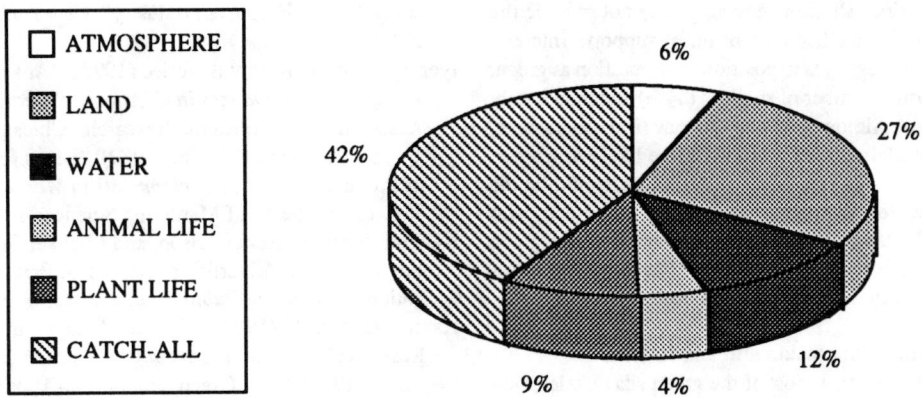

FIGURE 6
ISSUES

advertised, and so on. Likewise we did other cross-tabulations, wherever meaningful, in an effort to relate different factors within the analytical framework. Space limitations precludes us from reporting each and every result; moreover not all the relationships were interesting or revealing. Rather, we have chosen to elaborate upon a few themes that we believe are interesting and worthy of reporting.

5.1 Advertiser & Greenness

The greenness of an ad seemed to vary with the type of advertiser. Manufacturers' ads were generally shallower than those employed by nonprofit organizations. In coming to this conclusion, we hasten to note that quite a significant share (42.6%) of manufacturers' ads were moderately green although it was significantly lower than the proportion of nonprofit corporate ads (95%) that were moderately green. Our sample included ads from nonprofit organizations such as World Wildlife Fund, Greenpeace, and Nature Conservancy. These organizations are household names in terms of being synonymous with green issues; it is, therefore, hardly surprising that they sponsor green ads that are deeper than those of manufacturers.

5.2 Advertiser & Tactics

The result of this cross-tabulation was also very interesting. Most manufacturers (44.2%) adopted management control or social responsibility as their tactic. A typical message would include some mention of how the company was responsible or proactively involved in environmental issues. On the other hand, nonprofit organizations almost exclusively (65%) used emotional appeals. Within the category of emotional appeals, the type "you make a difference" was by far the most frequently used (65%). This result is consistent with the model that businesses, in general, and manufacturers, in particular, are under pressure from consumers, regulators, and activists to show social responsibility, whereas nonprofit organizations, some of which are the very activist organizations bringing pressure on businesses, have to legitimize their existence by appealing to and including consumers in their activist agendas.

5.3 Product & Greenness

The most widely advertised "product" was the corporate entity itself; this was followed by household consumables as the second most frequently advertised product. We found that while corporate ads were moderately green (65%), those for the household consumables were typically shallow (65%). Our result seems to suggest that creation of a corporate image, being amorphous at best, necessitates the use of a message that is at least moderately deep, for otherwise the effort may not produce the desired image. On the other hand, since a product's relationship with the environment is far more tangible, a shallow message might suffice to position it as green. Alternatively, it could be that product managers hesitate using deeper messages lest their product might alienate the mainstream whereas corporate managers, sensing a major permanent trend, adopt deeper messages.

5.4 Product & Tactics

As mentioned earlier, most often the advertised "product" was the corporation itself; in this event, the vast majority (57%) of the ads used management control and social responsibility as the basis of appeal in the message. Household consumables were the second most frequently advertised products; in this case, the form of appeal used most often (45%) was a testimonial. It is interesting to note that a testimonial of an everyday consumer, rather than that of an expert or a celebrity, was the one most commonly (78%) used. This is unlike "regular" advertising in which superstars dominate when testimonials and endorsements are used as a tactic. One of the reasons for the difference could be that superstars are more sensitive to being associated with a green product through their testimonial. Even more interesting was the fact that most often (89%) such testimonials were from women, typically in the role of a homemaker. This could be because most of the testimonials were for household products such as laundry detergents, dishwashing soap, and these products are still perceived to be feminine (Iyer and Debevec, 1989; Debevec and Iyer, 1986).

5.5 Product & Issues

When the corporate entity was the "product" being advertised, most ads (52%) focused on multiple environmental issues, whereas when household consumables were advertised, most ads (55%) focused solely on land as the issue of concern. To borrow a metaphor commonly used in marketing principles courses, some communication programs are like shot-guns and spray their target while others are like rifles and clearly focus on their target. In that vein, it appears that corporate advertising is like a shot-gun and ads for consumables are more akin to a rifle.

5.6 Strategy & Greenness

Of the ads whose primary strategy was to position the product/service as green, the vast majority (64%) were shallow, whereas of all the ads whose primary strategy was to influence viewer behavior or enlist viewer support, the overwhelming majority (94%) were moderately green. It appears that advertisers shy away from positioning their product/services using moderately deep or very deep green messages lest they are viewed as radical thereby alienating the mainstream market. On the other hand, ads used to influence viewer behavior were almost always at least moderately green, if not deep. Moderately deep messages may have to be used to motivate viewers since shallow messages may not provide the impetus needed to influence behavior or enlist support. Interestingly enough, if the strategy was to position a corporation as green, there are about an equal number of shallow (54%) and moderately deep (46%) messages. Although we cannot draw firm conclusions, it would seem that certain corporations are more likely to want to be portrayed as green as compared to others; those would be the ones with the moderately deep green messages. Yet others who might not want to be tagged as a "green corporation" use green messages that are relatively shallow, perhaps fearful of the consequences of using a green message that was deep.

6.0 What's the Point: Conclusion and Limitations

Our analysis showed that most of the green ads on television attempted to position the corporation or a household consumable as green. The corporate ads typically were either shallow or moderate in their greenness and focused on multiple environmental issues in the copy. Ads for household consumables typically tended to be shallow in their greenness and focused almost exclusively on land pollution as the issue of concern. As was expected, most corporate ads used management control or social responsibility as their bases for appeal. Typically, ads for household consumables used testimonials — most often that of an everyday person, very likely a female in the role of a homemaker — as their basis for appeal.

The television commercials studied here differed from the print ads examined by Iyer and Banerjee (1992). The most notable difference was that the TV ads tended to use *zeitgeist* or *bandwagon* tactic far less frequently as compared to print ads. Further, TV ads tended to focus on specific substantive issues and were likely to be at least moderately deep in terms of the greenness of the message. Part of the reason for the differences between green print and TV ads in terms of the tactics and issues emphasized could be the differences between the two media themselves. Television is more amenable to deeper portrayals; after all the amount of dialog in an average TV ad far exceeds the amount of copy in a typical print ad. Further, TV ads are dynamic whereas print ads are static. Yet another factor could be that the TV ads analyzed in this paper were more recent. With increasing pressure on businesses, both from consumers and government, it is possible that corporations are more willing to spend "greenbacks" to improve their corporate or product's "greenness".

Our findings and the themes that we have presented must be tempered by the fact that they were based on a convenience sample. Moreover, the interpretive nature of our analysis, notwithstanding the high inter-coder reliability, warrants caution in reading our conclusions. Further studies along these lines will help in reaching more firm conclusions.

REFERENCES

Balch, George (1992), "Encouraging Recycling in a Demographically Diverse City: Segmenting the Market in Chicago", *Advances in Consumer Research*, Vol. 20, Association for Consumer Research: Chicago, IL.

Bremner, Brian (1989), The New Sales Pitch: The Environment", *Business Week*, (July 24), 50.

Debevec, Kathleen and Easwar Iyer (1986), "The Influence of a Spokesperson in Altering a Product's Gender Image: Implications for Advertising Effectiveness", *Journal of Advertising*, 15 (4), 12-20.

Gilly, Mary C. (1988), "Sex Roles in Advertising: A Comparison of Television Advertisements in Australia, Mexico, and the United States", *Journal of Marketing*, 52 (2), 75-86.

Hinds, Michael de Courcy (1989), "In Sorting Trash, Householders Get Little Help from Industry", *New York Times*, (July 29).

Iyer, Easwar and Bobby Banerjee (1992), "Anatomy of Green Advertising", *Advances in Consumer Research*, Vol. 20, Association for Consumer Research: Chicago, IL.

_____ and Kathleen Debevec (1989), "Bases for the Formation of Product Gender", *Developments in Marketing Science*, Vol. 12, Academy of Marketing Science: Atlanta, GA.

Kangun, Norman; Kent Carlson, and Michael Grove (1991), Environmental Advertising Claims: A Preliminary Investigation", *Journal of Public Policy & Marketing*, 10(2), 47-58.

Kassarjian, Harold (1977), "Content Analysis in Consumer Research", *Journal of Consumer Research*, 3 (June), 8-18.

List, S.K. (1993), "The Green Seal of Eco-Approval", *American Demographics*, (January), 9-10.

Naess, Arne (1973), "The Shallow and the Deep, Long Range Ecology Movement: A Summary, " *Inquiry*, 16, 95-100.

Ottman, Jacquelyn (1991), *Environmental Consumerism: What Every Marketer Needs to Know*, J. Ottman Consulting: New York.

Rehak, Robert (1992), *Greener Marketing and Advertising: Charting a Responsible Course*. Rodale Press.

The Roper Organization (1992), *Environmental Behavior, North America: Canada, Mexico, United States*. A Report on the Study Commissioned by S.C. Johnson and Son, Inc.

The Roper Organization (1990), *The Environment: Public Attitudes and Individual Behavior*, A Report on the Study Commissioned by S. C. Johnson and Son, Inc.

A Re-Examination of the Relative Persuasiveness of Comparative and Noncomparative Advertising

Paul W. Miniard, University of South Carolina
Michael J. Barone, University of South Carolina
Randall L. Rose, University of South Carolina
Kenneth C. Manning, University of South Carolina

ABSTRACT

Recent research has demonstrated that relative measures are more sensitive than nonrelative measures which have traditionally been used in assessing comparative advertising effects. This evidence has been offered as a means of explaining the equivalence of direct comparative and noncomparative ads with respect to persuasion, a typical finding of past research. To more fully substantiate the robustness of these findings, the present study re-examines comparative and noncomparative ads previously found to be equivalent in persuasiveness. As expected, the relative measures used in the current investigation revealed greater persuasion engendered by the comparative ad than by the noncomparative ad. Furthermore, the results provide evidence for a biasing effect, in which a relative encoding frame, once activated, may influence the processing of subsequent noncomparative information.

INTRODUCTION

Since Wilkie and Farris' (1975) suggestions about the potential persuasion advantages of comparative over noncomparative ads, these two forms of advertising have been pitted against each other in numerous investigations. Although comparative ads have been found to outperform their noncomparative counterparts (Demirdjian 1983; Golden 1979; Gorn and Weinberg 1984; Levine 1976), such findings are the exception rather than the rule. Indeed, in some cases, comparative ads have been found to be less persuasive than noncomparative ads (Grossbart, Muehling, and Kangun 1986; Swinyard 1981). Most often, however, comparative and noncomparative ads are reported to produce very similar levels of persuasion (Belch 1981; Dröge 1989; Golden 1979; Goodwin and Etgar 1980; Gorn and Weinberg 1984; Grossbart et al. 1986; Levine 1976; Sujan and Dekleva 1987; Swinyard 1981).

One response to this diversity in empirical findings has been a search for moderating factors (Iyer 1988; Miniard, Rose, and Till 1992a; Pechmann and Stewart 1990; Shimp and Dyer 1978). Iyer (1988), for instance, observed that comparative ads outperformed noncomparative ads when the advertised brand was unknown, but not when the advertised brand was familiar (see Shimp and Dyer 1978 for similar results). Similarly, Pechmann and Stewart (1990) have considered the moderating role played by the relative market shares of the advertised and comparison brands. They found comparative ads outperformed noncomparative ads when a low-share advertised brand was compared to a high-share brand, while the opposite was true when a high-share advertised brand was compared against a low-share brand. When both the advertised and comparison brands possessed moderate shares, direct comparative and noncomparative ads appeared equal in their persuasiveness.

Researchers have also begun to pay greater attention to the measures used to test for potential persuasion differences between comparative and noncomparative ads. One early indication of the importance of alternative measures in assessing persuasion was provided by Gorn and Weinberg (1984). Although persuasion is typically gauged by responses to various belief, attitudinal, and/or intention measures, Gorn and Weinberg reasoned that one possible outcome of comparative advertising is an enhanced association of the advertised and comparison brands. Based on this rationale, they included measures of the perceived similarity between the advertised and comparison brands. Their results supported comparative advertising's associational effect, which has become one of the more consistent findings in the comparative advertising literature (Dröge and Darmon 1987; Johnson and Horne 1988; Pechmann and Ratneshwar 1991; Sujan and Dekleva 1987).

Recently, Miniard, Rose, Manning, and Barone (1992b) have developed the framing correspondence hypothesis as a means of conceptualizing the role of measurement in tracking comparative advertising effects. In the following section, we briefly review this conceptualization and its implications for measuring comparative advertising effects.

THE FRAMING CORRESPONDENCE HYPOTHESIS

Conceptualization

According to the framing correspondence hypothesis, a measure's sensitivity to advertising effects depends upon the degree of correspondence between the encoding frame used during ad processing and the measure's response frame. One characteristic important to both types of frames is whether they are relative or nonrelative in nature.

Comparative ads presenting claims about the advertised brand relative to one or more competitors are likely to lead to the use of a relative encoding frame during ad processing, in which information about the competitor(s) is used as a point of reference. This reference point becomes an integral part of the encoding frame employed during ad processing, as information about the advertised brand will be encoded relative to that regarding the comparison brand. Consequently, the resulting post-message impressions (e.g., beliefs, attitudes, and intentions) stored in memory are themselves likely to be relative in nature.

In contrast, noncomparative ads lack explicit reference points, in that they present information focusing solely on the advertised brand. Unless consumers spontaneously generate their own reference points, a nonrelative encoding frame is likely to characterize ad processing.[1] As a result, the post-message impressions stored in memory are unlikely to be relative in nature.

Similarly, measures can differ in whether they employ relative or nonrelative response frames (cf. Barnard and Ehrenberg 1990; Teas and Wong 1992). Relative measures require judgments using some specified reference point (e.g., "How likely is it that brand A powdered cleaner is safer and gentler than brand B?") which nonrelative measures lack (e.g., "How likely is it that brand A powdered cleaner is safe and gentle?").

The framing correspondence hypothesis predicts that the most sensitive measures of an ad's effects are those that contain a response frame which corresponds to the encoding frame present

---

[1] Evidence germane to this supposition is provided in a study conducted by Walker, Swasy, and Rethans (1986), in which only 10% of subjects exposed to a noncomparative ad reported thinking about how the advertised brand compared to a competing brand(s).

during ad processing. Thus, when an ad is processed with a nonrelative encoding frame and the resultant post-message impressions are stored in a nonrelative fashion in memory, nonrelative measures are expected to yield the most sensitive assessment of the ad's effect. However, when a relative encoding frame is used during ad processing, relative measures with response frames that mirror the encoding frame should prove most sensitive.

Correspondence between encoding and response frames is important for at least two reasons. One reason is suggested by Tversky, Sattath, and Slovic's (1988) compatibility principle. A lack of correspondence between the information stored in memory and a response frame will increase the number of mental transformations and, consequently, the number of errors that arise when transforming stored impressions into a form required by the measure. As a result, when the post-message impressions residing in memory are relative in nature, more transformation errors are likely to occur in response to nonrelative measures, and such errors should undermine the accuracy of such measures in capturing advertising effects.

Further support for the framing correspondence hypothesis can be found in the memory literature. According to the principle of encoding specificity (Tulving and Thomson 1973), the retrieval of information encoded during ad processing should be facilitated when aspects of the encoding context (i.e., cues) are present at retrieval. Comparative ads, which encourage a relative encoding frame during ad processing, provide an association between the advertised and comparison brands. This frame can be recreated through the use of relative measures, which provide an external association between the two brands. This external association serves to cue the retrieval of comparatively framed ad information more precisely than nonrelative measures which do not explicitly specify this association.

In sum, the framing correspondence hypothesis posits that the encoding frame present during ad processing directly influences the nature of the resultant mental representation. The encoding frame is thought to be a function of the particular reference point (if any) activated during ad processing. Identification of the relevant frame (and, for relative encodings, the specific reference point as well) is critical in determining a measure's sensitivity to advertising effects, as measures which employ response frames that correspond to the encoding frame used during ad processing should provide the most sensitive assessment of advertising effects.

Empirical Evidence

Most of our work germane to the framing correspondence hypothesis has been within the context of comparative advertising. We observed that one rather common characteristic of research reporting little difference in the persuasiveness of comparative and noncomparative advertising is their use of nonrelative measures. Yet, as suggested by the framing correspondence hypothesis, measures using relative response frames that correspond to the encoding frame activated by a comparative ad should prove most sensitive to the unique effects of comparative ads. Consequently, we have executed a number of studies that tested for persuasion differences between comparative and noncomparative ads using both relative and nonrelative measures (Miniard et al. 1992b, 1993; Rose et al. 1993). This research has shown relative measures consistently outperform nonrelative measures in revealing persuasion differences in favor of comparative advertising.

While our research suggests that the reliance on nonrelative measures may be one reason that prior investigations have often found direct comparative and noncomparative advertising to be equivalent in their persuasiveness, none of our studies employed ads used in prior studies reporting null findings. Rather, new ads which typically featured an unknown advertised brand compared to a well-known brand, a combination that is quite conducive to the emergence of persuasion differences in favor of comparative advertising (Iyer 1988; Shimp and Dyer 1978), were created and tested.

We sought to overcome these limitations in the present study by re-examining comparative and noncomparative ads previously reported to be equivalent in their persuasive effects. As noted earlier in the paper, Pechmann and Stewart (1990) did not detect persuasion differences between a direct comparative ad and a noncomparative ad when the advertised and comparison brands possessed moderate shares. In their study, persuasion was assessed in terms of subjects' responses to the question, "In the future, when you need to buy [product category], which brand do you think you will actually buy?" However, we wondered whether this single indicator of persuasion, operationalized in a manner that does not correspond to the encoding frame of the comparative ad, might provide a very conservative estimate of any potential persuasion differences between their direct comparative and noncomparative ads. Consequently, we retested the ads from one of the two product categories examined by Pechmann and Stewart in their moderate share condition.[2] We attempted to enhance the odds of detecting persuasion differences by using a set of measures with two important features. First, to maximize the measures' sensitivity to the comparative ad's effects, the measures employed a response frame that corresponded to the encoding frame encouraged by the comparative ad. Second, in addition to asking subjects to choose between the advertised and comparison brands, we also assessed their beliefs, attitudes, and intentions toward the advertised brand relative to the comparison brand. Doing so enabled us to more fully examine the different ways in which advertising may be influential.

METHOD

Subjects and Ads

Sixty-six undergraduate business students were assigned randomly to one of two conditions, in which they were presented with either the noncomparative or direct comparative print ad for Comet brand cleanser used by Pechmann and Stewart (1990). The ads were similar in layout, but differed from one another in several respects. First, the headline in the comparative ad included a reference to a comparison brand, Ajax. Also, the first attribute claim in the comparative ad described Comet as being safer and gentler on surfaces than Ajax. The headline and first attribute claim in the noncomparative ad, on the other hand, made no references to the Ajax brand. Claims regarding the second and third attributes (cleaning ability and use on many surfaces) were noncomparative in nature in both the comparative and noncomparative ads.

Procedure

Subjects were informed that they would be shown an ad for a brand of powdered cleanser. They were also instructed to evaluate the advertised brand with the expectation that, following ad exposure, they would answer questions regarding their impressions of the advertised brand and make a choice between different brands of powdered cleansers. To this end, subjects were presented with two folders, the first of which contained the experimental ad. Subjects were allowed to examine this ad for as long as they wished, after which they were to complete a questionnaire included in the second folder. Subjects were instructed to answer the questions without referring back to the ad.

---

[2] We wish to thank Connie Pechmann for providing us with these ads.

TABLE
Means and Significance Tests

Measure	Ad Condition		p-value
	Comparative	Noncomparative	
"Safeness/Gentleness" Belief	7.00	5.74	.006
"Cleaning Ability" Belief	5.81	5.71	.837
"Use on Many Surfaces" Belief	7.25	5.56	.001
Overall Quality	6.94	6.59	.348
Brand Attitude	7.34	6.41	.015
Purchase Intention	7.16	6.06	.078

Note: Higher scores indicate more favorable responses towards the advertised brand relative to the comparison brand.

Measures

With the exception of a dichotomous choice measure, in which subjects made a choice between Comet and Ajax, all measures employed 9-point response scales. These measures were relative in nature, in that they required subjects to make judgments regarding Comet relative to the comparison brand, Ajax. For example, beliefs regarding the first attribute were assessed through the use of a likelihood measure which asked subjects, "How likely is it that Comet is safer and gentler on surfaces than Ajax?" Similar measures were used to assess subjects' beliefs with respect to the remaining two attributes (cleaning ability and use on many surfaces). Subjects were also asked to indicate their perceptions of the overall quality of Comet compared to Ajax on a scale anchored by "very low" and "very high." Subjects' attitudes towards Comet relative to Ajax were then assessed using the average value ($r = .98$) of two scales, one with the endpoints of "more unfavorable" and "more favorable," and the other, "more negative" and "more positive." Lastly, subjects indicated their intentions to purchase Comet compared to Ajax.

RESULTS

The Table summarizes the cell means and significance tests for the relative measures. Mean differences between ad conditions were tested using one-way analysis of variance (df = 1,64).

Consistent with our earlier findings (Miniard et al. 1992b, 1993; Rose et al. 1993), the current results support the usefulness of assessing comparative advertising effects with correspondent relative measures. As can be seen in the Table, subjects reported significantly ($p<.05$) more favorable beliefs about the advertised brand relative to comparison brand for two (i.e., "safeness/gentleness" and "use on many surfaces") of the three featured attributes following exposure to the comparative ad. Similarly, the comparative ad produced significantly ($p<.05$) more favorable attitudes toward the advertised brand relative to the comparison brand. Relative purchase intentions were also more favorable toward the advertised brand in the comparative ad condition ($p<.1$). Surprisingly, responses to the overall quality measure, although directionally consistent with the responses to the other measures, did not statistically differ across the ad conditions ($p>.1$).

Further evidence of the comparative ad's persuasive superiority was provided by the choice measure. When asked to choose between the advertised and comparison brand, a greater percentage of subjects chose the advertised brand in the comparative (97%) than the noncomparative (80%) ad condition ($\chi^2(1) = 4.54; p<.05$).

DISCUSSION

Although our prior research has suggested that one reason for null findings in the comparative advertising literature was the failure to employ correspondent relative measures, this evidence is limited by its failure to retest the same comparative and noncomparative ads used in published studies reporting no differences in the ads' persuasive effects. To overcome this limitation, we re-examined ads from Pechmann and Stewart's (1990) moderate share condition. These ads were also attractive because they featured a well-known advertised brand, unlike the fictitious advertised brand typically used in the ads examined in our earlier investigations. As such, Pechmann and Stewart's ads afforded a more stringent test of potential persuasion differences by virtue of having to change pre-existing attitudes toward the well-known advertised brand rather than simply influence attitude formation, as in the case of an unknown advertised brand (Iyer 1988; Shimp and Dyer 1978).[3]

The present findings reinforce our earlier findings. By using persuasion measures with response frames that corresponded to the encoding frame encouraged by the comparative ad, we observed significant persuasion differences between the comparative and noncomparative ads. In particular, the comparative ad produced more favorable beliefs, attitudes, and purchase intentions. And when asked to choose between the advertised and comparison brands, more subjects selected the advertised brand following exposure to the comparative ad.

Although we used ads from Pechmann and Stewart's (1990) moderate share condition, self-reported usage data suggest that the advertised and comparison brands featured in these ads were not moderate share brands for the subjects participating in our research. Nearly two-thirds of the subjects reported being current users of the advertised brand, whereas only 15% indicated that they currently use the comparison brand. These relative usage levels are much more in alignment with Pechmann and Stewart's (1990) high-share advertised brand and low-share comparison brand condition.

Interestingly, it has been suggested (Pechmann and Stewart 1990) that high-share brands should rely on noncomparative ads rather than comparative messages in order to avoid potential problems associated with the latter (e.g., providing free advertising for the comparison brand, increasing awareness of the comparison brand, upgrading the comparison brand's image). However, published empirical evidence germane to this situation is limited to Pechmann and Stewart's (1990) findings of noncomparative ads being more persuasive than comparative ads for high-share advertised brands. In contrast, our findings imply just the opposite, at

---

[3]Nearly 85% of the subjects reported having previously used the advertised brand, thus indicating that the vast majority of subjects entered the study with pre-existing attitudes toward the advertised brand based on prior consumption experience.

least within the confines of our study. If both patterns of effects prove robust, future efforts might focus on understanding when each type of advertising might be most effective for high-share brands.

There is another aspect of our findings which we believe is worth emphasizing. Although only the initial attribute claim in the comparative ad described the advertised brand as superior to the comparison brand, a significant effect was observed for the third and final attribute claim (use on many surfaces). Subjects were more likely to perceive the advertised brand as superior to the comparison brand on this attribute after processing the comparative ad, even though the ad did not make any reference to the brand's relative performance on this feature. Perhaps subjects inferred that the absence of harsh abrasives (discussed in the ad as substantiation for the claim involving the safe and gentle attribute) would enable the product to be used on a greater number of surfaces. Whatever the reason, this result in itself is suggestive of the potential for relative encoding frames, once activated, to alter subsequent processing of even noncomparative information. Such findings should be particularly important to public policy officials, since it indicates the possibility for misleading consumers about the relative performance of competing brands even in the absence of any overtly deceptive ad claims.

It is also interesting that this apparent biasing effect of a relative encoding frame was limited to the third featured attribute and did not extend to the second attribute presented in a noncomparative fashion within the ad. The fact that this effect occurred for one attribute but not the other implies that the impact of a relative encoding frame on the processing of noncomparative claims may be moderated by certain factors. Future research may wish to further explore when comparative ads containing noncomparative claims may lead to biased processing.

Limitations

One potential threat to the meaningfulness of our findings is whether they are driven by a demand artifact. Specifically, subjects in the comparative ad condition might infer that the experimenter wants them to perceive the advertised brand as superior to the comparison brand. This inference should become particularly salient when responding to the relative measures. Thus, the persuasion differences suggested by the relative measures may simply reflect subjects' willingness to comply with presumed experimenter expectations rather than the actual impact of the ads themselves.

Although certainly plausible, the pattern of effects observed in our study seem rather incompatible with a demand explanation. In particular, it is not obvious why a demand effect would lead subjects to provide responses that differ significantly for some, but not all, of the relative measures. Presumably, a demand effect, once operative, should alter subjects' responses to all of the measures. Further evidence germane to this demand explanation can be found in Rose et al. (1993).

A more clear-cut limitation of our study is the sole reliance on relative measures. Unlike our earlier investigations, we did not include nonrelative measures to serve as a benchmark. Unknown, then, is how the relative measures' performance would compare to nonrelative measures. By the same token, it would have been desirable to have included the particular measure used by Pechmann and Stewart (1990) in assessing advertising effects. Lacking this, it is impossible to determine whether the different effects observed in their study and our study are due to differences in how persuasion was measured versus the other factors (e.g., subject population, exposure condition, etc.) along which the two studies differed from each other.

REFERENCES

Barnard, Neil R. and Andrew S. C. Ehrenberg (1990), "Robust Measures of Consumer Brand Beliefs," *Journal of Marketing Research*, 27 (November), 477-484.

Belch, George E. (1981), "An Examination of Comparative and Noncomparative Television Commercials: The Effects of Claim Variation and Repetition on Cognitive Response and Message Acceptance," *Journal of Marketing Research*, 18 (August), 333-349.

Demirdjian, Z. S. (1983), "Sales Effectiveness of Comparative Advertising: An Experimental Field Investigation," *Journal of Consumer Research*, 10 (December), 763-770.

Dröge, Cornelia (1983), "Shaping the Route to Attitude Change: Central Versus Peripheral Processing Through Comparative Versus Noncomparative Advertising," *Journal of Marketing Research*, 17 (August), 290-303.

Dröge, Cornelia and Rene Darmon (1987), "Associative Positioning Strategies Through Comparative Advertising: Attribute Versus Overall Similarity Approaches," *Journal of Marketing Research*, 24 (November), 377-388.

Golden, Linda L. (1979), "Consumer Reactions to Explicit Brand Comparisons," *Journal of Marketing Research*, 16 (November), 517-532.

Goodwin, Stephen and Michael Etgar (1980), "An Experimental Investigation of Comparative Advertising: Impact of Message Appeal, Information Load, and Utility of Product Class," *Journal of Marketing Research*, 17 (May), 187-202.

Gorn, Gerald J. and Charles B. Weinberg (1984), "The Impact of Comparative Advertising on Perception and Attitude: Some Positive Findings," *Journal of Consumer Research*, 11 (September), 719-727.

Grossbart, Sanford, Darrel D. Muehling, and Norman Kangun (1986), "Verbal and Visual References to Competition in Comparative Advertising," *Journal of Advertising*, 15 (1), 10-23.

Iyer, Easwar (1988), "The Influence of Verbal Content and Relative Newness on the Effectiveness of Comparative Advertising, *Journal of Advertising*, 17 (3), 15-21.

Johnson, Michael D. and David A. Horne (1988), "The Contrast Model of Similarity and Comparative Advertising," *Psychology and Marketing*, 5 (Fall), 211-232.

Levine, Philip (1976), "Commercials That Name Competing Brands," *Journal of Advertising Research*, 16 (December), 7-14.

Miniard, Paul W., Randall L. Rose, and Brian D. Till (1992a), "An Elaboration Likelihood Model Perspective on Comparative Advertising," *AMA Winter Educators' Conference Proceedings*, Vol. 3, eds. Chris T. Allen, Thomas J. Madden, Terence A. Shimp, Roy D. Howell, George M. Zinkhan, Deborah D. Heisley, Richard J. Semenik, Peter Dickson, Valarie Zeithaml, and Roger L. Jenkins 375-383.

Miniard, Paul W., Randall L. Rose, Kenneth C. Manning, and Michael J. Barone (1992b), "Assessing the Effects of Comparative and Noncomparative Advertising with Relative and Nonrelative Measures: A Test of the Framing Correspondence Hypothesis," Working Paper.

Miniard, Paul W., Randall L. Rose, Michael J. Barone, and Kenneth C. Manning (1993), "On the Need for Relative Measures When Assessing the Persuasiveness of Comparative Advertising," *Journal of Advertising*, forthcoming.

Pechmann, Cornelia and S. Ratneshwar (1991), "The Use of Comparative Advertising for Brand Positioning: Association Versus Differentiation," *Journal of Consumer Research*, 18 (September), 145-160.

Pechmann, Cornelia and David W. Stewart (1990), "The Effects of Comparative Advertising on Attention, Memory, and Purchase Intentions," *Journal of Consumer Research*, 17 (September), 180-191.

Rose, Randall L., Paul W. Miniard, Michael J. Barone, Kenneth C. Manning, and Brian D. Till (1993), "When Persuasion Goes Undetected: The Case of Comparative Advertising," *Journal of Marketing Research*, 30 (August), 315-330.

Shimp, Terence A. and David C. Dyer (1978), "The Effects of Comparative Advertising Mediated by Market Position of the Sponsoring Brand," *Journal of Advertising*, 7 (Summer), 13-19.

Sujan, Mita and Christine Dekleva (1987), "Product Categorization and Inference Making: Some Implications for Comparative Advertising, *Journal of Consumer Research*, 14 (December), 372-378.

Swinyard, William R. (1981), "The Interaction Between Comparative Advertising and Copy Claim Variation," *Journal of Marketing Research*, 18 (May), 175-186.

Teas, R. Kenneth and John K. Wong (1992), "Item Context and the Stability of Entity-based and Attribute-based Multiattribute Scaling Methods," *Journal of Consumer Research*, 18 (March), 536-545.

Tulving, Endel and Donald M. Thomson (1973), "Encoding Specificity and Retrieval Processes in Episodic Memory," *Psychological Review*, 80, 352-373.

Tversky, Amos, Shmuel Sattath, and Paul Slovic (1988), "Contingent Weighting in Judgment and Choice," *Psychological Review*, 95 (3), 371-384.

Walker, Beth A., John L. Swasy, and Arno J. Rethans (1986), "The Impact of Comparative Advertising on Perception Formation in New Product Introductions," in *Advances in Consumer Research*, Vol. 13, ed. Richard J. Lutz, Ann Arbor, MI: Association for Consumer Research, 121-125.

Wilkie, William L. and Paul Farris (1975), "Comparison Advertising: Problems and Potential," *Journal of Marketing*, 39 (October), 7-15.

African American Vernacular English in Advertising: A Sociolinguistic Study

Jennifer Edson Escalas, Duke University

ABSTRACT

In our diverse society, language variation is an important cultural identifier. To understand and target important consumer segments, one must be aware of the dialect they speak. In examining the language used by African Americans in advertising, this sociolinguistic study finds that only 14% of a sample of current television ads with black actors use grammatical features from African American Vernacular English (AAVE), while only 34% used AAVE phonological features. In order to increase our understanding of language as it relates to cultural diversity, a framework based on perceived fit is developed.

CULTURAL DIVERSITY AND LANGUAGE

Cultural diversity is on the rise in America. The most recent census projects minority groups to continue growing, given the higher fertility rates of Asians, Hispanics, and African Americans compared to the rate of whites (Harper 1992). Past consumer research has pointed out that these growth patterns in ethnic subcultures have significant impact for the consumption aspects of American life (Deshpande, Hoyer & Donthu 1986).

One important aspect of culture is language. The Whorfian hypothesis asserts that the structure of the vocabulary and grammar of an individual's language actually shapes that person's view of the world (Hunt & Agnoli 1991). Others have argued that language constitutes the most important instrument of socialization; that reality is filtered, apprehended, encoded, codified and conveyed via some linguistic shape (Smitherman 1991). Regardless of whether one accepts such strong hypotheses, the notion that language is a critical aspect of culture cannot be rejected (Fasold 1991, Gumperz & Hymes 1964).

In relating language to diversity, part of the definition of a subculture may be manifested in linguistic differences (Wolfram 1991). Language evolves and changes continually, with people tending to speak most similarly to those around them. Furthermore, language can serve a unifying function for sociocultural groups (Fasold 1984). Language is a means by which individuals locate themselves in social space. Speech is an act of identity: when we speak, we identify ourselves as belonging to a particular group, be it gender, social class or race (Coates 1986).

THE AFRICAN AMERICAN MARKET

African Americans constitute an important subculture in the U.S. This market segment totals 29.5 million consumers earning over $200 billion, 80% of which is disposable income (Stith 1989). Many subcultures, regions, and social groups in the U.S. have their own unique dialects.[1] This is true for African Americans as well. The dialect spoken by African Americans was called Black Vernacular English by sociolinguists in the '70s and '80s, but has more recently been given the name African American Vernacular English (AAVE) (e.g., Baugh 1991, Smitherman 1991). Vernacular refers to dialects that incorporate nonstandard language forms. Unfortunately, because the phonetic or grammatical features found in vernacular dialects are not taught by formal grammarians to be "proper," they are often stigmatized by American society.

---

[1] The term dialect is used in sociolinguistics as a neutral label to refer to any variety of language which is shared by a group of speakers. Dialects are not deviant forms of language, rather they are simply different systems with distinct sets of language patterns (Wolfram 1991).

AAVE

It has been estimated that a large majority of the African American population uses AAVE. People often quote Dillard, as an expert in this area, who asserted that 80% of African Americans use AAVE to some extent (e.g., Dillard 1972 in Williams & Qualls 1989). Many years ago, people believed AAVE was nothing more than distorted Standard English, spoken by unintelligent or uneducated people. Sociolinguistic research has shown that AAVE is a complex, highly consistent dialect that follows grammatical rules to the same extent as do the more socially accepted forms of English (Wolfram 1991). This is truly a dialect of English, not just slang. Sociolinguistic studies conducted all over the U.S., from major cities to rural areas, from the East Coast to the West, provide strong evidence that there is clearly a common core of linguistic features and structures that define AAVE (Wolfram 1991, Fasold 1991). There are some regional differences, but there exist overriding similarities everywhere AAVE is spoken.

One example comparing AAVE to Standard English (SE) illustrates that widely accepted language forms need not be more consistent than those labeled vernacular: reflexive possessive pronouns. Compared to SE, the AAVE forms are actually more consistent, as follows:

SE	myself	yourself	herself	himself
	ourselves	yourselves	themselves	
AAVE	myself	yourself	herself	*hisself*
	ourselves	yourselves	*theirselves*	

The SE forms are a mixture of possessive pronouns and objective pronouns, while in AAVE they are completely consistent—they are always the possessive pronoun. *Myself* is equivalent to *my book*, as is *yourself* (*your book*), *herself* (*her book*), *ourselves* (*our books*) and *yourselves* (*your books*). However, the SE third person masculine forms are inconsistent: *himself* (compared to **his** book) and *themselves* (**their** books). AAVE's forms (*hisself* and *theirselves*) are actually more consistent than those of SE.

It turns out that language change is guided by logical, evolutionary principles (Wolfram 1991). There are a variety of language influences acting on English, adapting it to carry out communication needs under ever changing physical and social conditions. Some groups adopt changes while others do not, leading to linguistic variety. Vernacular dialects are often the result of these natural processes and thus initiate more internal consistency in language than the rigid forms prescribed by elementary school grammar teachers. And it cannot be said that one form of language has evolved from the other. In some cases dialects cling to older forms than those in prescriptive grammars, while in other cases the dialect form is an evolutionary step forward.

Language Attitudes

In American English, standardness is defined and prestige is achieved by a lack of stigmatized grammatical structures (Wolfram 1991). Vernacular dialects, on the other hand, exhibit the presence of socially obtrusive structures. One example of a frowned upon dialectal feature is the use of double negatives in AAVE, and many other American dialects, (e.g., *They don't want none*), even though this is a widely used form in languages other than English. Since non-standard forms are socially disfavored and of low status, and AAVE contains nearly entirely socially stigmatized variants as its set of unique features, general population attitudes towards AAVE are surely unfavorable. There may, however, be covert prestige in the use of AAVE, especially among African Americans who strongly identify with black culture. In this way, use of AAVE provides status and solidarity. The problem, however, is that covert prestige is relevant only to subculture members as it is unlikely to be understood or valued by the general population.

Fasold (1984) summarized research on how people in general tend to rate speakers of the high and low forms of a language. It has been found that high language forms are considered to be high on status and intelligence, while low forms are found to be high on affect, trustworthiness, and friendliness. Other studies have found Standard English speakers to be judged as more ambitious, competent and self confident, while vernacular speakers were evaluated as higher on personal attractiveness (i.e., good natured, talkative and good sense of humor) (Coates 1987).

Sociolinguistic studies have found an interaction between language attitudes and other preexisting stereotypes. For example, Williams (1974 in Fasold 1984) found that teachers, listening to the same voice track, rated the speaker differently depending on whether a black, white, or Hispanic child was pictured speaking. The teachers' ratings were anchored by their preexisting stereotypes on dimensions that have been shown to correlate with school performance. Extending these findings, people with strong negative stereotypes may find people who use a moderate degree of dialect features to be speaking with a very strong dialect and to possess the negative characteristics that they associate with the stereotyped group.

RELEVANT MARKETING THEORY

The consensus in marketing is that both blacks and whites are offended by the use of vernacular speech. Advertisers who use "black slang" are accused of promoting negative stereotypes. For example, in the 1930s and '40s, advertisers used offensive stereotypes that were perceived as being racist, as in a toothpaste ad that showed a black boy eating a watermelon and declared "Go right ahead, Sambo! Sink those ivories in that luscious watermelon." In another ad from the 1930s, a black "mammy" exclaimed: "Lawsee! Folks sho' whoops with joy oyer Aunt Jemima pancakes" (Alsop 1984).

One of the problems with the current use of AAVE in advertising is that many ads are written by whites and are thus unnatural for the black actors. Blacks are told to speak in a "street style" even if they normally would not speak in that fashion. This has been referred to as the "right-on" school of advertising (Alsop 1984). Obviously such lack of naturalism will be detected by African Americans watching the commercial, leading to unfavorable reactions. It may be that people associate AAVE with negative images because of the correlation between AAVE use and stereotypical presentations.

Actually, much of recent consumer behavior research into black advertising has found that whites are not averse to seeing blacks in ads, while African Americans respond more favorably to ads when black actors are present (Whittler 1989, Pitts et. al. 1989). However, these studies used print ads and television commercials with singing and jingles rather than spoken words. The print ad study found that strong race identifiers, both blacks and whites, used heuristics to process ads with African American actors (Whittler 1989). Specifically, the heuristic was to base one's response on a similar-agree, dissimilar-disagree standard (i.e., strong black identifiers would agree with black actors but disagree with white actors and vice-versa for strong white identifiers), rather than to evaluate the ad's message content. Furthermore, the author states that video and audio presentations of ads may make an actor's race more salient, thus increasing the use of these heuristics.

The television ad study asserted that previous studies using print media lost rich cultural messages that video and audio components of commercials provide (Pitts et. al. 1989). The authors found that TV ads produced by black advertising agencies targeting an African American audience conveyed value themes to black viewers that white viewers failed to perceive. This occurred due to the use of symbols and icons understood only by the distinct black subculture, which possesses a unique complex of behaviors, tradition, language and values. While black respondents displayed more positive affect towards these commercial messages than did comparable whites, the latter group did not respond negatively to the ads.

While marketing studies have often examined the realistic portrayals of blacks in advertising from the viewpoint of it being marketers' social responsibility to erase undesirable stereotypes (e.g., Kassarjian 1969), in today's diverse society, believable incorporation of cultural ad elements provides a benefit for marketers as well: it improves their ability to successfully target important subcultures. AAVE, as an important linguistic cultural element, should create connections to this growing market segment.

SOCIOLINGUISTIC DATA ANALYSIS

In order to assess the degree to which AAVE is used in television advertisements, an exploratory sociolinguistic study was conducted.

Methodology
Selection of Advertisements

Two sources of commercials were used. The first was a collection of 77 commercials produced by black advertising agencies, targeting the African American consumer. These ads, however, date back to the mid 1980s. For the second set, I taped over 100 hours of prime time and sports television from the three major networks, various local and cable stations, including MTV and BET, in the Fall of 1992. To this was added over 20 hours of daytime and BET television from Los Angeles to include geographic diversity. The ads videotaped from television were reduced to a set that included only those ads that prominently featured black actors. These ads were selected for analysis because they featured black protagonists or contained African Americans with speaking parts.

Categorization

In the real world, AAVE features are not categorical. AAVE is made up of a constellation of phonological and grammatical structures. However, because commercials are "standardized" in their language, I took any example to be categorical for this study. Each ad has been placed in just one category, based on the highest feature found in the continuum described below. For example, a commercial featuring a black African American who uses both AAVE vocabulary and mild AAVE phonology would be classified as "mild phonology." The classification system is highlighted in Table 1.

The final three classifications deserve further elaboration. Phonology refers to the sound patterns of language. Here, phonological features were divided into two groups: mild and strong. Mild phonology was essentially a standard Southern dialect, which has undergone a vowel shift moving short front vowels upward (e.g., *bit* becoming like *beet*), long front vowels backward (e.g., *bait* becoming like *bet*), and back vowels forward (e.g., *suit* becoming

TABLE 1

AAVE Form	Classification System	
Singing Only	No spoken English	*Least AAVE*
Can't tell Black	"Standard" English - race indeterminable	
Black Voice	Speaker determined to be black	
Intonation	Speech rhythm, pitch fluctuation	
Vocabulary	Stereotypical words - "Mama" "child"	
Mild Phonology	Standard Southern Dialect	
Strong Phonology	AAVE phonological forms	
Grammar	AAVE grammatical forms	*Most AAVE*

TABLE 2

AAVE Form	1987	1992
Singing Only	19.5%	7.1%
Can't tell Black	16.9%	21.4%
Black Voice	20.8%	23.8%
Intonation	10.4%	2.4%
Vocabulary	5.2%	7.1%
Mild Phonology	11.7%	16.7%
Strong Phonology	14.3%	7.1%
Grammar	1.3%	14.3%
Total:	100.1%	99.9%

like *soot*) (Wolfram 1991). This categorization also included AAVE intonation and vocabulary. G-dropping (e.g., *fishin'*, *runnin'*) was also labeled a mild phonological feature.

Strong phonology included final stop cluster reduction (e.g., *bes* for *best*); /ð/ (the initial sound in *that*) and /θ/ (the initial sound in *thing*) becoming [d] or [t], respectively, at the beginning of a word (e.g., *dat* for *that*), or [f] or [v] respectively, at the end of a word (e.g., *toof* for *tooth*); /ð/, /z/, and /v/ becoming stops mid word (e.g., *sebm* for *seven*); and other specific word examples, such as *ask* becoming *aks*.

AAVE grammatical structures consist of the following forms: present tense third person /s/ absence (e.g., *He play basketball*), plural /s/ absence (e.g., *Those five kid over there*), double negatives, remote time been (e.g., *I been known her* meaning *I have known her a long time*), possessive /s/ absence (e.g., *John book*), copula absence (e.g., *She nice*), and habitual "be" forms (e.g., *He be looking good*, which implies a continuing, habitual form not present in Standard English but found in many other languages).

Results

As mentioned above, the study was conducted on two commercial sets. Because the two data sets are not scientifically comparable, the results are discussed separately.

Television Ads Targeted to African Americans

The first ad set consisted of 77 commercials produced by black advertising agencies in 1987. The product categories for these ads included: deodorant, laundry detergent, cooking oil, beer (and malt liquor), coffee, soft drinks, diapers, toothpaste, shampoo, fast food restaurants, hair relaxant, amusement parks, public service announcements, tires, automobiles, telephone services, auto products, film, and baby food.

The first column in Table 2 displays the tabulation of the degree of AAVE used by the African Americans in this set of advertisements. The percent indicates the proportion of the ads that were coded as using a particular level of AAVE (e.g., 10.4% of the 77 ads from 1987 had AAVE intonation patterns, but no AAVE vocabulary, phonology or grammar). Each ad was only categorized once, depending on the strongest form of non-standard language used.

Obviously, the singing only ads (19.5%) did not feature any spoken language, and so an assessment of AAVE use could not be made. In those ads classified as "Can't tell Black" (16.9%), the unseen announcers had voices that were so standard that the race of the speaker could not be determined. Just over 20% of the time, the voice of the announcer was identifiably black, but the language spoken was standard. The voice was usually male and essentially the classification was based on voice quality alone.[2]

Next, 10.4% of the ads were categorized as "Intonation." In these cases the rhythm of the speech and the fluctuation in pitch were identifiably African American. Some examples include: *I just l•o•v•e our privacy*, and *Looks this g•o•o•d*. Of the ads, 5.2% went beyond simple intonation and included black vocabulary, often stereotypical words. Examples from this ad set include *looks just so*, *kind of sweet on you*, *Mama*, *Baby*, and *Child*. Furthermore, I included such expressions as *Ooowie*, *Mmm mm*, and *Ooow* as vocabulary classifiers.

Mild phonology was present in 11.7% of the ads. Examples of mild phonology include the speech of Lena Horne and Debbie Allen, two entertainer celebrity endorsers featured in these ads. Just over 14% of the ads were categorized as "Strong Phonology."

---

[2] Studies have shown that people are surprisingly good at identifying an unseen Standard English speaker's race, although it is difficult to specify on what basis the judgments are being made (Wolfram 1991).

Some examples of the AAVE phonological features found in this set of ads consist of: *Don't let the smoov taste fool ya* (King Cobra Malt Liquor), *Da new Ford Taurus, Crest toofpaste,* and *Wid every can ah Crisco.*

Finally, it was noticeable that essentially no ads used AAVE grammatical structures. I was liberal in my classification of one ad as having AAVE grammar. This particular ad presented an interview with an employee and was filled with other features of informal English, including repeated use of the phrase *you know*. The employee said things such as *Look atcha, How am I cusomer service if I can't help you when you aks for ma help?* and *I stand there and go diggin' through the merchandise wid 'um*. These are border line, non-prescriptive English grammatical structures, but do not really constitute a full constellation of AAVE. However, this was by far the most realistic portrayal of AAVE speech found in this sampling of advertisements.

General Viewing Television Ads

In the set of ads from 1992, 42 distinct ads had blacks prominently displayed. The product categories for these ads included: beer, diapers, automobiles, laundry detergent, cereal, education and public service announcements, digestive products, credit cards and financial services, orange juice, athletic shoes, department stores, fast food restaurants, telephone services, auto products, toothpaste, games and toys, undergarments, soft drinks, and insurance companies. Although 42 ads may seem to be a small number, ads that were aired repeatedly only count as one ad for this study. Additionally, strict criteria were used to narrow down the selection of ads. Many ads have black actors in a large group of racially diverse individuals but the blacks do not have speaking roles. These ads would not have been included in the sample.[3]

The second column in Table 2 displays the tabulation of the degree of AAVE used by the African Americans in this second set of advertisements. The coding scheme for this sample of commercials followed the same categorization criteria described in Table 1 above. Much of the same vocabulary found in the 1987 sample was present in the 1992 ads. Vocabulary features present uniquely in this collection of ads included *Man* and *Amen*. Words exhibiting strong (AAVE) phonological features are found in the following phrases: *Dinnah basket, I love dis place, Dat's the wildest thing, Dey oughta, o evah hopeto,* and *dis cup*.

Grammatical features included in these ads consisted of one double negative, several irregular uses of the verb *to get*, and one fairly complete constellation of AAVE features. At the end of a K-mart commercial, where many different customers are shown walking through the department store and the viewer is allowed to "eavesdrop" on their conversations, a black woman uses a double negative, subtly and as the ad fades away.

The irregular use of the verb *get*, in the place of *have*, is found in the popular Diet Pepsi campaign, featuring Ray Charles, with the now familiar slogan, *You got the right one baby, Un Huh*. The use of *you got* is either a case of auxiliary verb deletion as in *you've got*, or a correctly formed past tense. However, the prescriptively correct grammatical structure is *you have*. Nevertheless, use of the *got* form is, in terms of descriptive grammar, becoming more and more widespread and accepted across all varieties of English.

In a commercial for Gain detergent, a man is shown to be an entrepreneur, running a landscape business. He says such things as *Lucky for me, I got this green thumb*. Here what is missing is the contracted form of *have*, because his more correct wife responds: *Lucky for me, I've got this little scoop*. The husband also says *specially* for *especially* and *plantin'* with g-dropping. Another commercial, for Sunny Delite, has a group of young boys raiding the refrigerator. They also use the *got* rather than the *have* form, as in: *We got soda*.

There is one case of present tense third person /s/ absence. In a commercial for Budweiser, a group of black men are playing basketball. Curly Neal approaches them, asking to play ball. They respond, *Say what? Wid chu?* To which he says, *No, wid you mama*. Later, after the former Harlem Globetrotter has turned out to be an excellent dribbler and is able to slam dunk, one of the basketball players says, *Man, he deserve one a deese*, referring to the beer, of course.

Finally, a McDonald's ad features three young black men talking about a friend who has recently done well in his job at McDonald's. They greet each other with *Waz up*, a greeting of solidarity, and reply *Nothin' much*. When the young employee calls his mother to tell her about a promotion, he calls her *Mama* and she calls him *Baby*. The friends admit the money he earns allows him to buy *fresh clothes*. When they start teasing him, one says *Don't rip my boy too hard now*. These aren't really AAVE grammatical structures, but I rank this ad high in terms of overall AAVE flavor and use of a symbolic interaction routine, neither of which is captured in my categorization criteria. Again, it is noticeable that plural /s/ absence, remote time been, possessive /s/ absence, copula absence, and habitual "be" forms were not included in a single ad, despite the fact that many of these forms, especially habitual "be," are recognized AAVE structures. The grammatical features highlighted above were very "mild" examples of AAVE.

DISCUSSION AND FUTURE RESEARCH

This paper reviewed the role of AAVE in television's portrayal of African Americans in advertisements. The sociolinguistic analysis showed that the use of AAVE was quite low, with a some phonological features and stereotypical vocabulary items, but very few AAVE grammatical structures. The explanation for the lack of AAVE found in television advertisements is threefold. First, the language attitudes that permeate our society greatly stigmatize vernacular grammatical structures. Second, given the historical portrayal of blacks in commercials, advertisers are especially careful to avoid any ad variable that could be misconstrued as racially insulting. And third, for a majority of products, the individuals who dominate the marketing decision making process are primarily non-African American. Thus advertising that includes black actors is developed based on non-African American conceptions of what it should look and sound like.

This study is not without limitations. First, the coding taxonomy will be difficult to replicate. Second, only a single judge was used, which precludes the reporting of reliability measures. In all, the study suggests that dialectal language variation is under utilized as a cultural targeting mechanism. This is primarily due to a lack of understanding on the part of consumer researchers and marketing practitioners. In order to help remedy this situation, I next propose a framework to guide future research in this area.

Directions for Future Research

In the increasingly diverse American society, marketers must be able to target one subculture without offending another or the general population. An important aspect of reaching diverse groups is to include cultural elements in ad campaigns. Language variation is an important cultural symbol for many potential market seg-

---

[3] A study conducted in 1984 showed that 9% of all ads featuring live actors had African Americans in them, slightly less than the black population of roughly 12% of America (Alsop 1984), although this figure has likely increased since that time.

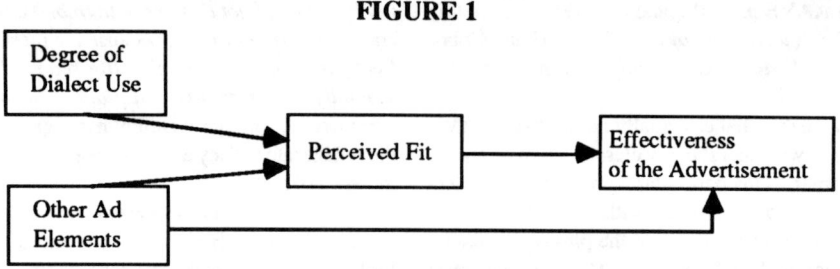

FIGURE 1

ments. Grammar, phonology, and vocabulary vary across ethnic groups, regional groups, class structure, gender and age. In fact, many of the AAVE findings reported above could be replicated for Hispanic advertising or commercials targeting teens. But language variation can evoke strong reactions, from covert prestige to negative stereotypes. In order to understand dialectal differences, a variety of issues must be addressed by consumer behavior research. Figure 1 highlights a framework for the study of the effectiveness of language variation in advertising.

To target a particular subculture, one must relate to its members through realistic cultural messages. In order to create realism, there must be a perceived fit within the cultural aspects of the ad and between these aspects and non-cultural ad features. Thus, reaction to dialect features in ads will be mediated by the perceived fit between linguistic form and other aspects of the advertisement. Language variation should not be examined independently of a wide range of ad elements that impact whether viewers respond positively or negatively to the use of vernacular language features. These ad elements include, but are not limited to, ad setting, communication style, product category, type of persuasion (e.g., informational vs. transformational), media selection, degree of targeting, program context, actors, music, and use of other cultural symbols and values. Perceived fit issues relating to these execution variables will be briefly discussed.

As mentioned above, language variation is not categorical in nature. There are degrees of non-standardness; dialect usage spans a continuum. In normal daily speech, nearly everyone uses some language features that could be described as vernacular. The question is to what extent, what percent of the time are these features used. Therefore fit implies the correct level of vernacular features given other goals for the ad campaign.

Setting is an important variable for perceived fit. Language use changes depending on the environment. In more formal settings, language becomes more formal, more "standard." As familiarity with others increases and the setting becomes more informal, people tend to use more variation in their speech. Thus, when an advertisement's setting is formal, especially in a professional environment, more standard English forms should be used. In a more informal setting, use of vernacular forms can increase, properly reflecting the true usage of language in our society. The degree of formality issue extends to other ad elements as well, including communication style and product category. For example, an ad for insurance using a fear appeal will not be as conducive to dialect use as an ad for a sports-related product in an action driven setting.

Written language is, by its very nature, more formal than spoken language (Stubbs 1983). Therefore, language variation effectiveness depends on the proper choice of media, be it print, radio, or television. Non-standard linguistic forms, which are more informal in nature, are better suited to be heard than read. A content analysis of advertisements in three well known magazines targeting African Americans (*Jet*, *Ebony*, and *Upscale*, April 1993 issues) found no written forms of AAVE phonology or grammar, supporting the notion that written language is more formal than oral speech acts. There were two cases of limited dialect differences in vocabulary: written reference to McDonald's restaurant as "Mickey D's" (*Jet*) and a Nike ad which encourages fathers not to "sweat" their sons (*Ebony*).

The more specifically marketers can target their messages, the more they can use idiosyncratic cultural elements, because fear of offending other groups is reduced. The degree to which advertisers can target their messages depends in part on the product category and media selection. For example, written AAVE vocabulary, phonology and grammar were found in the magazine *Rap Pages* (April 1993), targeted at young Rap fans, primarily black and Hispanic, although only in ads for Rap music (e.g., "Dead enz kidz doin' lifetime bidz"). Obviously, the surrounding text, which is also written almost exclusively in AAVE, plays a major role in what degree of non-standard lect can be used. The same extends to program context in television advertising. For example, given the increasing use of AAVE forms in television programming (e.g. *Fresh Prince of Bel Air, A Different World*), advertising that includes AAVE shown during these programs should be more effective.

Despite the fact that the majority of African Americans speak AAVE, it would be a mistake to assume the black subculture is entirely homogeneous. One subsegmentation strategy is based on the intensity of ethnic affiliation. Deshpande et.al. (1986) found that strength of cultural identification influenced Hispanics' attitudes towards Spanish media. Williams and Qualls (1989) found that strong black identifiers had more favorable attitudes towards black celebrity advertising than weak black identifiers and whites. The hypothesis is that language variation should be more effective for highly intense ethnic affiliators than for those who are weak cultural identifiers.

Finally, marketers must be careful to combine language variation with other cultural ad elements appropriately. The actors must be clear members of the subculture. The cultural symbols and values must be carefully researched and understood. Choices in music selection must also be made sensitively. Each of these cultural elements can backfire when used inappropriately. Alternatively, portrayal of situations that are strongly correlated with ethnic culture need to include dialect features in order to be considered believable. The Budweiser commercial set in the inner city with black actors playing basketball is a case in point. How credible would this ad be, to any viewer, if it used Standard English?

In conclusion, who we are is reflected in how we speak. In order to communicate with and relate to the growing and diverse subcultures in American society, we must understand how language is used across these groups. Use of language variation to target subcultures must be done with sensitivity, because improper use of vernacular English will be rejected by the targeted subculture and may be offensive to other groups who view the ad. An important dimension to the successful implementation of targeted language strategy is the perceived fit between the level of dialect and other ad elements.

REFERENCES

Alsop, Ronald (1984), "Firms Still Struggle to Devise Best Approach to Black Buyers," *Wall Street Journal*, October 25, p. 35.

Baugh, John (1991), "The Politicization of Changing Terms of Self References among African American Slave Descendents," *American Speech*, Summer, v. 66, pp. 133-146.

Coates, Jennifer (1987), *Women, Men and Language: A Sociolinguistic Account of Sex Differences in Language*, New York, NY: Longmen Inc.

Deshpande, Rohit, Wayne D. Hoyer and Naveen Donthu (1986), "The Intensity of Ethnic Affiliation: A Study of the Sociology of Hispanic Consumption," *Journal of Consumer Research*, v. 13, September, pp. 214-220.

Fasold, Ralph (1991), *The Sociolinguistics of Language*, Cambridge, MA: Basil Blackwell, Inc.

Fasold, Ralph (1984), "Language Attitudes," Chapter 6 in *The Sociolinguistics of Society*, Cambridge, MA: Basil Blackwell, Inc.

Gumperz, John J. and Dell Hymes (1964), *The Ethnography of Communication*, American Anthropologist Special Publication, December, v. 66, n. 6, part 2.

Harper, Lucinda (1992), "Census Bureau Lifts Population Forecast, Citing Fertility, Immigration, Longevity," *Wall Street Journal*, December 4, s. B, p. 1.

Hunt, Earl and Franca Agnoli (1991), "The Whorfian Hypothesis: A Cognitive Psychology Perspective," *Psychological Review*, v. 98, n. 3, pp. 377-389.

Kassarjian, Harold H. (1969), "The Negro and American Advertising, 1946-1965," *Journal of Marketing Research*, v. 6, pp. 29-39.

Pitts, Robert E., D. Joel Whalen, Robert O'Keefe, and Vernon Murray (1989), "Black and White Response to Culturally Targeted Television Commercials: A Values Based Approach," *Psychology and Marketing*, v. 6, n. 4, pp. 311-328.

Smitherman, Geneva (1991), "'What is African to Me?': Language Ideology and African American," *American Speech*, Summer, v. 66, pp. 115-132.

Stith, Melvin T. (1989), "Introduction," *Psychology & Marketing*, v. 6, n. 4, pp. iii-iv.

Stubbs, Michael (1983), *Discourse Analysis: The Sociolinguistic Analysis of Natural Language*, Chicago, IL: University of Chicago Press.

Whittler, Tommy E. (1989), "Viewers' Processing of Actor's Race and Message Claims in Advertising Stimuli," *Psychology & Marketing*, v. 6, n. 4, pp. 287-310.

Williams, Jerome D. and William J. Qualls (1989), "Middle-Class Black Consumers and Intensity of Ethnic Identification," *Psychology & Marketing*, v. 6, n. 4, pp. 263-286.

Wolfram, Walt (1991), *Dialects and American English*, Englewood Cliffs, NJ: Prentice-Hall, Inc.

"An Advertising Potpourri": Some Comments and A Unifying Theme

David W. Stewart, University of Southern California

ABSTRACT

This paper offers a discussion of three papers that deal with the affects of advertising content. The discussion briefly reviews the contribution of each paper and the issues for future research raised by each paper. It concludes with a call for more attention to the characteristics and content of the stimuli to which consumers are exposed and to which they respond.

INTRODUCTION

The collection of three papers in this session certainly deserves the title, "potpourri". It is a challenge to identify a unifying theme in such diverse papers. Nevertheless, there is a common theme that is shared by these papers. Before turning to this theme, if is useful to consider each paper. I will consider each paper in alphabetical order, then turn to some unifying themes.

AFRICAN VERNACULAR ENGLISH IN ADVERTISING

An "African American Vernacular English in Advertising: A Sociolinguistic Study" by Jennifer Escalas offers the compelling argument that how something is said is as important as what is said. There is no doubt that specific vernacular or dialects are underrepresented in advertising relative to their frequency of use in the general population. It also almost certainly the case that offering information in a vernacular or dialect that is similar to that used by the message recipient increases the effectiveness of the communication, at least with respect to some measures. It is less clear just which measures of effectiveness may be influenced by the use of familiar vernacular. An interesting set of empirical questions revolve around how the use of familiar vernacular affects such varied measures as attention, recall, memory, likeability, believability, attitude, intention, and actual choice of a product. It may be that vernacular influences some of these measures more than others. It may also be the case that familiar vernacular indirectly affects some measures of advertising effectiveness through direct effects on other measures. For example, likeability for an ad that uses familiar vernacular may in turn influence attitude toward the product, which in turn may influence purchase intention or choice.

A second set of questions that surrounds the use of vernacular or dialect focuses on the effects of such usage on consumers who are do not use the vernacular. Various vernaculars and dialects are often associated with stereotypes which may not be positive. On the other hand, it is useful to recognize that vernacular and dialect play a powerful role in literature, cinema, and theater. Vernacular has been used as a defining characteristic of personalities by such writers as Mark Twain and Tennessee Williams. There may well be circumstances when the use of vernacular or dialect can help define the identity of a product or service among individuals regardless of whether they use the vernacular. This is a relatively unexplored domain, but one might speculate that vernacular is a potentially important component of advertising that uses a dramatic approach (Wells 1989).

AN EXPOSE ON GREEN TELEVISION ADS

The content of advertising is also the focus of the paper entitled "An Expose on Green Television Ads" by Iyer, Banerjee and Gulas. This paper is an interesting effort to examine the rise of "green" marketing as represented in advertising. The authors offer a useful coding system for the content of green advertisements. The coding system captures the structure, strategy, tactics, and issues that compose green advertising. Although the content coding system is offered as an approach for examining the content of green ads, much of it could be readily applied to advertising in general. Indeed, an examination of advertising for green products might well be expanded by considering how advertising for such products differs from advertising in general.

The general conclusion of the authors, that advertising for green products tends to be shallow, associated with domestic consumable products, uses women as spokespersons, and employs testimonials might well describe most television advertising. Stewart and Furse (1986) and Stewart and Koslow (1989) report data on advertising that demonstrates that women are the most frequent and most effective spokespersons in advertising for consumer package goods. Thirty-second, or 15-second commercials almost by definition must be rather superficial. What is surprising about the findings reported by Iyer, Banerjee, and Gulas is that green ads appear to be as superficial as other ads. Perhaps this reflects the nature of the medium; there is only so much depth of information that fits in a 30 or 15 second commercial. Such superficiality may also reflect the conclusion by advertisers that "green" is just one more decision making heuristic that happens to appeal to a particular segment of the market. Yet another explanation for the apparent superficiality of green ads is the desire by advertisers to avoid the appearance of radicalism while still appealing to green sensitivities.

It may be that television, in its present form as an advertising medium, is a superficial medium. The authors suggest that television is more amenable to deeper portrayals than print. This is almost certainly true, but the capability of a medium is different from the realization of that capability. The potential of television as medium for communication, particularly advertising messages remains largely untapped for all products and services.

A RE-EXAMINATION OF THE RELATIVE PERSUASIVENESS OF COMPARATIVE AND NONCOMPARATIVE ADVERTISING

"A Re-examination of the Relative Persuasiveness of Comparative and Noncomparative Advertising" by Miniard, Barone, Rose, and Manning is also focused on the content of advertising, but in a more narrow sense that the other two papers. Miniard, Barone, Rose and Manning are specifically concerned with contrasting the relative effectiveness of advertising that contains comparative claims with advertising that does not contain such claims. These authors are to be commended for using products that are representative of those used by their sample of respondents and for using ads that are relatively representative of real ads for products that actually exist. This adds a dimension of generalizability to their findings that is not always present in advertising research.

The authors report that the relative effectiveness of comparative versus noncomparative claims appears to be a function, at least in part, of whether the measure of effectiveness employed uses a relative scale or an absolute scale. They suggest that a relative scale is a better measure of advertising effectiveness for comparative claims, while absolute measures are better for noncomparative advertising messages. They argue that this difference in the efficacy of measures is a function of the compatibility of measures with differences in the encoding of advertising messages that follows receipt of comparative claims versus noncomparative claims. This is an intuitively appealing proposition but it raises questions about how advertising executions might be compared. If different measures produce differ results based on the nature of the communication, comparisons become an attempt to compare apples and oranges. It is unclear how an execution should be evaluated and selected in such cases.

Miniard, Barone, Rose, and Manning contrast their results with those obtained by Pechmann and Stewart (1990) in an earlier study of comparative advertising. It is not at all clear that such a comparison of the two studies is appropriate. In contrast to the Miniard, Barone, Rose and Manning (MBRM) study, the Pechmann and Stewart (1990) paper focused on the role of attention on advertising response. Thus, unlike MBRM they did not use a forced exposure technique. Indeed, Pechmann and Stewart (1990) report that only 35% of their respondents actually read the ads and their respondents were more likely to read ads that mentioned products they already used. Pechmann and Stewart (1990) measured purchase intention twenty-four hours after advertising exposure rather than immediately following (as MBRM did), they examined comparative advertising for high, low and moderate share brands (MBRM appear to have examined comparative advertising for only a high share brand), and they used rather different measures from those employed by MBRM.

Given the considerable differences in procedures, measures, and foci of the two papers it is not surprising that differences exist in the findings of the two studies. The results offered by MBRM are interesting in their own right, but contrasting the results with a very different study does not appear to be very useful and may obscure some important reasons for the differences that are present.

One other finding of MBRM is intriguing. Their results would appear to suggest that when product attributes are correlated, consumers make inferences from an explicit claim about one of these attributes to the associated but unmentioned attribute. While this finding is intuitive it raises some interesting issues about the ability of advertising to deceive when attributes that are perceived to be correlated by consumers are not actually associated in the context of a given product. This is an issue that deserves further attention from researchers.

CONCLUSION

Taken together the three papers suggest that researchers might well give more attention to the content of advertising to which consumers respond. There is a tendency in much advertising research to hold most of the content of advertising stimuli constant in order to achieve sufficient control to examine specific cognitive processes used by consumers. This is a perfectly appropriate approach when the objective of research is the examination of cognitive processes, but it has the disadvantage of obscuring the variety of advertising stimuli to which consumers are exposed. Greater attention to advertising content as it appears in a more natural environment may well expand both the range of stimuli about which information is available and the types of processes that are discovered to be at work in response to advertising. Unfortunately, only one of the studies, MBRM, examines the relationship of content differences and measures of advertising effectiveness. More attention to advertising content as it relates to advertising's impact on measures of advertising performance would be a welcome contribution to research in the future.

REFERENCES

Escalas, Jennifer (1994), "African American Vernacular English in Advertising: A Sociolinguistic Study," in Chris Allen and Debra Roedder John (Eds.), *Advances in Consumer Research*, Volume 20 (Provo, UT: Association for Consumer Research).

Iyer, Easwar, Bobby Banerjee, and Charles Gulas (1994), "An Expose on Green Television Ads," in Chris Allen and Debra Roedder John (Eds.), *Advances in Consumer Research*, Volume 20 (Provo, UT: Association for Consumer Research).

Miniard, Paul W., Michael J. Barone, Randall L. Rose, and Kenneth C. Manning (1994), "A Re-Examination of Comparative and Noncomparative Advertising," in Chris Allen and Debra Roedder John (Eds.), *Advances in Consumer Research*, Volume 20 (Provo, UT: Association for Consumer Research).

Pechmann, Cornelia and David W. Stewart (1990), "The Effects of Comparative Advertising on Attention, Memory, and Purchase Intention," *Journal of Consumer Research*, 30 (September), 180-191.

Stewart, David W. and David H. Furse (1986), *Effective Television Advertising: A Study of 1000 Commercials*, (Lexington, MA: Lexington Books).

Stewart, David W. and Scott Koslow (1989), Executional Factors and Advertising Effectiveness: A Replication, *Journal of Advertising*, 1989, 18 (3), 21-32.

Wells, William D. (1989), "Lectures and Drama," in Patricia Cafferata and Alice Tybout (Eds.), *Cognitive and Affective Responses to Advertising*, (Lexington, MA: Lexington Books).

Consumer Choice as an Evolutionary Process: An Operant Interpretation of Adopter Behavior

Gordon R. Foxall, University of Birmingham

ABSTRACT

Growth of knowledge in consumer research requires alternative interpretations of consumer choice to the prevailing trait and information processing models derived from structural psychology. Consumer behavior may be construed as environmentally determined, an evolutionary process in which the replication of patterns of choice is explained by the metaprinciple of selection by consequences. The Behavioral Perspective Model of purchase and consumption (BPM) is described and applied to the communication of innovations. The role of interpretation in consumer research is discussed.

SELECTION BY CONSEQUENCES

Structural accounts of human activity assume that observed behavior results from what is happening within the individual (e.g. Hillner 1984). An objection to structural accounts in consumer research is that they continue to dominate inquiry to the exclusion of the other, equally valid element in a complementary approach to behavioral science, selection by consequences (Skinner 1981), which embraces both evolution by natural selection and the evolution of human behavior and cultures. Although any process in which gradual and incremental change occurs over time is frequently described as 'evolutionary' (Faber and Proops 1991), an *evolutionary explanation* requires a causal mechanism to account for historical development (Van Parijs 1980). The principle of selection by environmental consequences is the basis of a range of explanatory mechanisms in the biological, social and psychological sciences (Skinner 1981). Common to all is that the inferred selective operation of the environment is held to determine the continuity of an organism, practice or organization and the class or species to which it belongs. In the neo-Darwinist synthesis, a predisposing genotype contains the potential of an organism to develop and behave, adapt and survive; but, it is, ultimately, the adaptation of the phenotype to the environment that decides it biological fitness, or capacity to reproduce, and - thereby - that of the genetic material to replicate (Dawkins 1986).

The evolutionary explanation of behavior in social science, has been identified by van Parijs (1981) as *operant conditioning*, the procedure in which the rate of a response is determined by the prior consequences of similar behavior (Skinner 1974). Selection by consequences thus applies both to the 'contingencies of survival' that determine the course of natural selection, and to the 'contingencies of reinforcement' that shape and maintain operant behavior. Cultural evolution is a subset of the latter: practices that result in the wellbeing and survival of social groups or organizations are thereby selected and transmitted from generation to generation (Skinner 1981). Dawkins (1988: 33) points out that, whereas in natural selection 'the replicators are the genes, and the consequences by which they are selected are their phenotypic effects', in operant conditioning 'the replicators are the habits in the animal's repertoire, originally spontaneously produced (the equivalent of mutation). The consequences are reinforcement, positive and negative [and punishment]'.

THE BEHAVIORAL PERSPECTIVE MODEL

The operant paradigm appears from time to time in consumer research (e.g. Berry and Kunkel 1970; Nord and Peter 1990) but only recently has it been subjected to a detailed critique that permits its usefulness to a pluralistic consumer research to be gauged (Foxall 1987, 1990). The resulting Behavioral Perspective Model of purchase and consumption (BPM) relates patterns of consumer choice to their differing environmental consequences. Detailed accounts of the derivation and application of the model (Figure 1) are available (Foxall 1990, 1992a, 1992b, 1992c, 1993a). The following is, therefore, only a summary. There are three kinds of effective consequence of consumer behavior. *Hedonic* reinforcement derives from the satisfaction produced by buying, owning and consuming economic goods (Hirschman and Holbrook 1982). *Informational reinforcement* is provided by feedback on the consumer's performance, especially the social status produced by conspicuous consumption. *Aversive* consequences are the costs of consuming: relinquishing money, waiting in line, forgoing alternative products, etc. (Wearden 1988).

The antecedent events that set the scene for consumer behavior form the behavior setting. This consists of all the physical, social and temporal elements that signal the likely consequences of behaving in a particular way. Behavior settings facilitate or inhibit consumer movement and choice and form a continuum from the most open (where consumers are positively reinforced, free to choose their behavior) to the most closed (where agencies other than the consumer largely determine the pattern of pre-purchase, purchase and consumption behaviors). The consumer is represented in two ways: their *learning history* is the cumulative effect of rewarding and punishing outcomes of past behavior; it represents the personal factors influencing consumer choice and primes the consumer's approach/avoidance responses; and *state variables*, moods, ability to pay, deprivation, influence momentary purchase and consumption, etc.

In an evolutionary account of consumer behavior, the learning history which predisposes certain types of activity can be considered the equivalent of the genotype; the pattern of behavior resulting from this predisposition and the selecting environment, the phenotype (Faber and Proops 1991). Since cultural evolution is Lamarckian, the environmental factors (behavior setting, some state variables, consequences) can be most appropriately considered in relation to the rate at which behavior, the phenotype, is repeated. Four broad classes of consumer behavior can be inferred from the pattern of high/low hedonic and informational reinforcement that maintains them (Figure 2). *Maintenance* consists of activities necessary for the consumer's physical survival and welfare (e.g. food) and the fulfilment of the minimal obligations entailed in membership of a social system (e.g. paying taxes). *Accumulation* includes the consumer behaviors involved in certain kinds of saving, collecting, and instalment buying. *Pleasure* includes such activities as the consumption of popular entertainment. Finally, *Accomplishment* is consumer behavior reflecting social and economic achievement: acquisition and conspicuous consumption of status goods, displaying products and services that signal personal attainment. Both types of reinforcer figure in the maintenance of each of the four classes, though to differing extents.

COMMUNICATION OF INNOVATION

Initial versus Later Adopters

These four classes of consumer behavior can be viewed as a hierarchy. The successive lifestyles, which are a function of

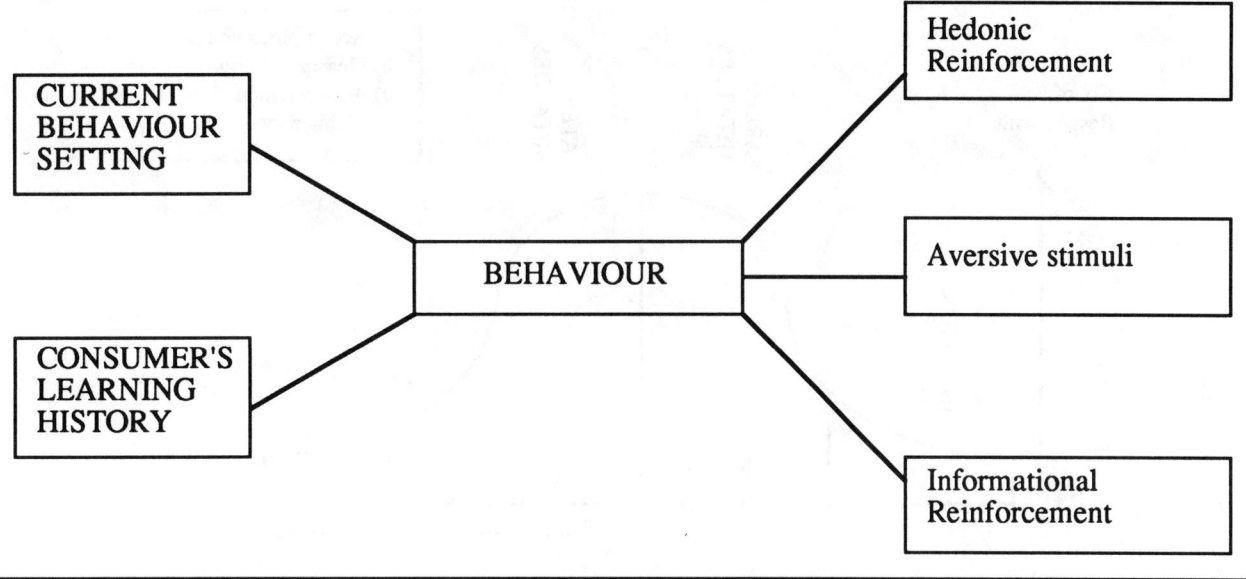

FIGURE 1
Summary of the Behavioral Perspective Model

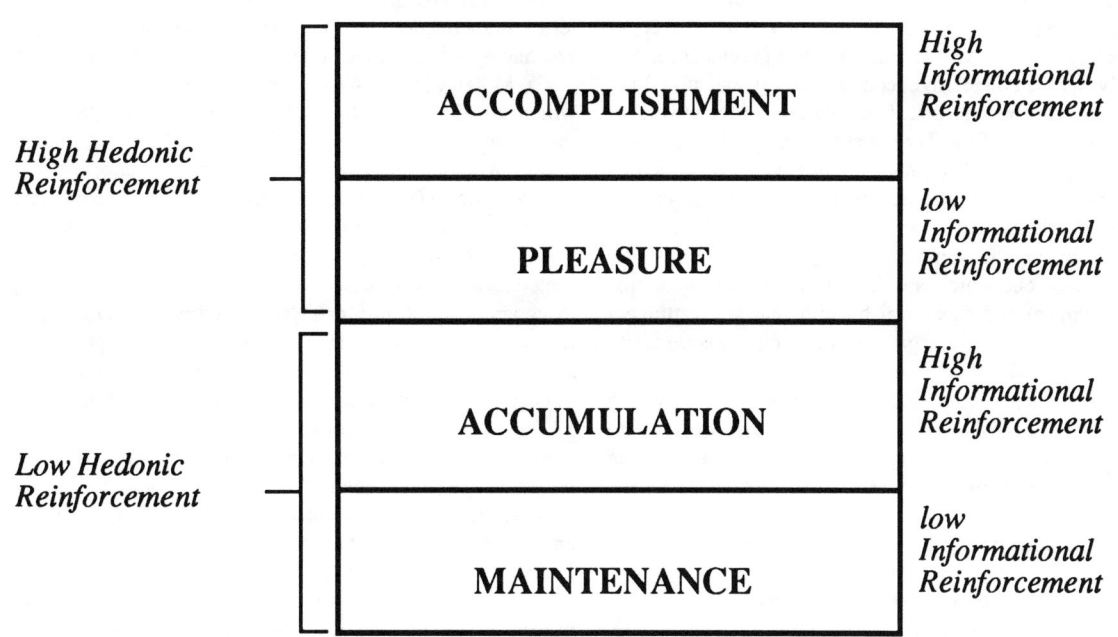

FIGURE 2
Operant Classes of Consumer Behavior

experience rather than age, of many consumers are likely to be characterized by Maintenance, then Accumulation, then Pleasure, then Accomplishment. Figure 3 proposes another sequence, by which the communication of innovations may be interpreted in a behavioral perspective. The rationale for this sequence is most apparent in considering the differences between the initial and later adopters (cf. Midgley 1977; Rogers 1983). The general argument is that initial adopters are drawn from those consumers whose behavior, for the product class/category in question, is described as Accomplishment. This may be a general lifestyle characteristic of this group. They are experienced consumers who have a level of product knowledge and expertise in consumption plus a degree of wealth that allows then to make earlier adoption decisions and to act on them. They are not necessarily older than later adopters but, at least in the product class under consideration, are sufficiently economically socialized to act first. They should, therefore, differ from later adopters on all four explanatory variables posited by the BPM. Initiators, as opposed to later adopters will exhibit differences in the pattern of hedonic and informational reinforcement that maintains their behavior, a learning history that predisposes them towards earlier adoption, a susceptibility to the motivating effect of behavior setting elements that encourage earlier adoption, and the presence of state variables that facilitate earlier rather than later adoption.

FIGURE 3
An Operant Interpretation of Adopter Classes

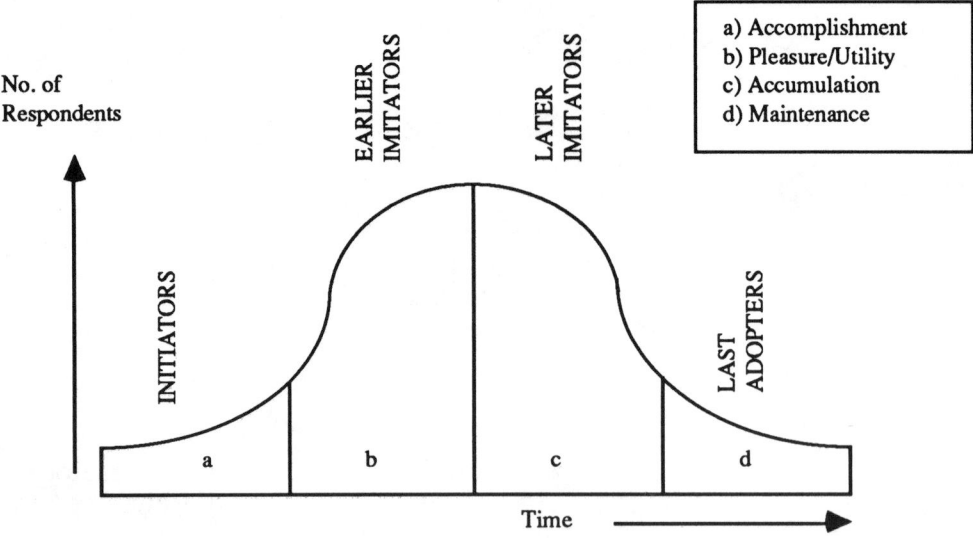

Pattern of Reinforcement. By assuming that Initiators' consumer behavior is characterized by Accomplishment, the model understands that they are susceptible to relatively high levels of both hedonic (pleasurable/utilitarian) and informational (social/symbolic) reinforcement. This is consistent with the evidence. Not only incentives, based on relative economic benefit and utility, but also social recognition and status motivate the first buyers of innovations (Bandura 1986). The rewards of early adoption identified repeatedly in the diffusion literature may be classified as producing primarily economic benefit (hedonic reinforcement) (Rogers 1983; Gatignon and Robertson 1991). Among the sources of economic advantage are some innovation characteristics usually treated separately but which are fundamentally related to the economic, technical and functional benefits that are contingent upon adoption: relative advantage, compatibility, low complexity and low economic risk.

These are elements in the consumer's learning process, which actually refers to a class of economic costs. All are concerned with the costs and benefits of integrating the innovation into an existing physical and social system, particularly with the joint effects (cost reduction and/or the release of synergy) of operating it alongside existing equipment or practices. Economic advantage consists in what has hitherto been described as incentives or hedonic reinforcement (Gatignon and Robertson 1991). Social benefit is the conferral of status, usually through he conspicuous use of the innovation, though sometimes through its highly visible purchase. The prestige which accrues from these consumer behaviors may derive from others' admiration of the economic relative advantages conferred by the innovation but, unless the item is additionally amenable to social observation, it cannot deliver the additional social advantages which corresponds to feedback or informational reinforcement (Gatignon and Robertson 1991). Not only are these sources of economic and social benefit known to be associated with the speedier diffusion of innovations: Initiators perceive greater positive benefit (relative advantage, conspicuousness, compatibility) and lower negative consequences (risk, complexity) than do later adopters.

Learning History. Initiators generally have a shorter decision process than that of later adopters. They are venturesome, impulsive, able and willing to bear risks and make relatively rapid decisions to adopt. The new products they buy are discontinuous innovations, having maximal impact on current consumption patterns. Initiators need less interpersonal influence than later adopters, having less need for others to legitimize their adoption decisions. Midgley (1977: 49) defines innovativeness as 'the degree to which an individual makes innovation decisions independently of the communicated experience of others'. Moreover, initiators are more self-reliant and inner-directed than later adopters (Midgley and Dowling 1978). But their behavior is far from spontaneous and innate. Initiators have greater expertise with the relevant product class, possibly deriving from their heavy use of the product and their opinion leadership (Gatignon and Robertson 1991). Their capacity to recognize atypicality, to think in abstractions, combining product features, to deal with a large number of separate product dimensions, and to examine the environment for new products are also indicative of experience and expertise (Gatignon and Robertson 1991). Their being less influenced than later adopters by interpersonal communications is the result of experience; like any other behavior, it is the outcome of a situationally-determined learning history, the consolidated outcome of contingency-based learning and vicarious adoption with the product class and exposure to the innovation in question mediated by mass communication.

These initial adopters model the new consumption behavior to the less active sections of the population and thereby initiate the market (Rogers 1983). The behavior of the Initiator group is associated with innovations that confer substantial relative advantage over currently-used products and methods, both economic and social. In the terms of the BPM, such innovative adoption is maintained by high levels of both hedonic and informational reinforcement. These consumers can afford to acquire the tangible benefits of innovative products; it he process of consuming them, they enhance their status and prestige (Bandura 1986). Moreover, they can afford to undertake the early adoption of some innovations that fail: event his conveys to others that the adopter has the economic means and socials standing to disregard the occasional loss. They have positive attitudes towards newness and progress, and are more likely than others to be offered credit and, if required, to accept it (Rogers 1983).

State and Setting Variables. Initiators are affluent relative to members of the later adopter categories, risk takers who are eager to try the innovation for its own sake. There is no unequivocal evidence of their being older than other adopters. But they have higher social status, greater upward social mobility, and a more favourable attitude towards credit than later adopters. They also show more extensive social participation, are 'cosmopolitan', have greater knowledge about innovations and display more opinion leadership (Rogers 1983), all of which are likely to be the result of more extensive consumer experience. Most crucially of all, and true of a wide range of product classes including food, personal care items, domestic appliances, computers and computer services (Gatignon and Robertson 1985) is that initiators are already established and heavier users of the product category in question. They are experienced users with a high level of product field expertise, which may account for the absence of communicated experience in their innovative decision making. Moreover, they are likely to have established relationships with retailers or other suppliers and to be able to arrange trial of the new product; the effect is to enlarge their learning history and enable quicker comparisons and decisions to be made.

Categories of Later Adopters

'People who strive to distinguish themselves from the common and the ordinary adopt new styles in clothing, grooming, recreational activities, and conduct, thereby achieving distinctive status' Bandura 1986: 150). But the capacity of an innovation to confer status is closely linked to its exclusivity: as it diffuses, it becomes commonplace. When the product is approaching the end of its life cycle, it has become a routine acquisition, appealing only to those who are tradition bound, economically limited, and so conservative as to try new (to them) products that have been severely tried and tested by preceding adopters. By the time these consumers (the Last Adopters) adopt it, the product has ceased to be an innovation in any radical sense: it may embody continuous improvements of a minor kind but its adoption is unlikely to have an extensive impact on consumption. These consumers, the Laggards, are depicted in the diffusion literature as having no capacity for leadership, including opinion leadership: they are not, therefore, reinforced by high levels of informational reinforcement. What hedonic reinforcement maintains their behavior is similarly of low intensity: only products that cannot fail are assumed.

Between the Initiators and the Last Adopters are the Earlier Imitators (Rogers's 'deliberate' Early Majority), and the Later Imitators (Rogers's 'sceptical' Later Majority). The assignment of these adopter groups respectively to the contingencies maintaining consumer lifestyles marked by Pleasure/Utility and Accumulation is not quite as clear-cut as that of the first and last adopter categories to Accomplishment and Maintenance. But the characterizations are supported by the diffusion literature. The Earlier Imitators are not leaders despite their fairly high level of social interaction: they are not reinforced primarily by informational consequences of their actions. Moreover, their interest is in 'getting it right' when they try new products: they are cautious, taking time to deliberate before deciding. These actions suggest a high level of functional utility, hedonic reinforcement. The behavior of the Later Imitators is negatively motivated. This group adopts an innovation only when it has become economically essential to do so - its members are not seeking hedonic reinforcement, however. When they do adopt the item, it is principally for reasons of social pressure: they must finally adopt in order not to lose the honour or esteem of their fellows. Their adoptive behavior is thus negatively reinforced but by considerations of informational reinforcement. Products adopted by these adopter categories are dynamically-continuous; they embody improvements incorporated by manufacturers who by this time have experience of the market's requirements and may represent considerable extensions of the functional attributes of the innovation. They impact on consumption patterns and are purchased by groups seeking price and utility advantages.

CONCLUSION

This analysis indicates that it is feasible to present an alternative, though complementary, interpretation of consumer choice which attributes its changing topography to environmental rather than intrapersonal determinants. Whether these accounts must remain incommensurable remains to be seen, though the recent growth of cognitive ethology suggests that this is improbable. The paper also demonstrates that it is possible to apply the metaprinciple of selection by consequences to expand the range of interpretations available to consumer researchers. By contributing to an interactionist (person x situation) approach to consumer behavior, the model and its interpretations appear in line with emerging thought on the most appropriate methodological approach to research. Current attention is focused on the empirical correspondence of the model and its testing, the implications of rule-governed, as opposed to contingency-shaped consumer behavior, and the application of the model to the consumption of financial services and asset management (Foxall 1993b).

A broader research theme is the relationship of operant classes to the competitive environment, to develop an ecological analysis of successive operants much as strategic theorists have related industrial structure to its competitive determinants (e.g. Lambkin 1990). Since we are concerned with the population of consumer responses, competition is ultimately between the operant classes or 'species' of consumer behavior, each maintained by its unique combination of environmental consequences (Table 1). What environmental conditions make each of these more likely than the others at a particular time? Why does selection among these variations occur when it does? It is also necessary to propose why not all eligible consumers join the requisite adoption category for a particular innovation, e.g. why not all who have reached the Accomplishment stage even for the product class in question become Initiators.

REFERENCES

Bandura, Albert A. (1986) *Social Foundations of Thought and Action*, Englewood Cliffs, NJ: Prentice-Hall.

Berry, Leon L. and Kunkel, John H. (1970) "In Pursuit of Consumer Theory," *Decision Sciences*, 1, 25-39.

Dawkins, Richard (1986) *The Selfish Gene*, Oxford: University Press.

_____ (1988) "Replicators, Consequences, and Displacement Activities." In A. C. Catania and S. Harnad (eds.) *Selection of Behavior*, NY: Cambridge University Press.

Faber, M. and Proops, L. (1991) "Evolution in Biology, Physics and Economics: A Conceptual Analysis." In Saviotti, P. and Metcalfe, J. S. (eds.) *Evolutionary Theories of Economic and Technological Change*, Chur, Switzerland: Harwood.

Foxall, Gordon R. (1987) "Radical Behaviorism and Consumer Research", *International Journal of Research in Marketing*, 4, 111-129.

_____ (1990) *Consumer Psychology in Behavioral Perspective*, NY: Routledge.

_____ (1992a) "The Behavioral Perspective Model of Purchase and Consumption: From Consumer Theory to Marketing Practice," *Journal of the Academy of Marketing Science*, 20, 189-198.

TABLE 1
Ecological Adaptation of Consumer Operants to the Marketing and Communications Environment

NICHE	MARKETING MIX	CONSUMER OPERANT	SOURCES OF HEDONIC REINFORCEMENT	SOURCES OF INFORMATIONAL REINFORCEMENT	PATTERN OF COMPETITION
Discontinuity	New brand in new product class; Heavy media communication; High price; Exclusive distribution	*Accomplishment*	High relative advantage; Compatibility; Low perceived complexity; Low perceived risk	Conspicuousness; Status enhancement	Between buying innovation, re-using current product, saving
Dynamic continuity	Product improvement in original and new brands; Falling prices; Promotion limited, stressing functional improvements; Expanding range of outlets	*Pleasure/utility*	Very high relative advantage; High compatibility; Lower complexity	Status confirmation	Between buying original innovation (revised), new brand version(s), using old product, saving
Continuity	More suppliers entering; More brand versions showing minor improvements; Low prices; Widespread distribution; Promotion stresses social necessity, compatibility, low complexity; Vicarious learning and trial; Preponderance of buyer-dominated interpersonal communication	*Accumulation*	Avoidance of relative disadvantage of old product/method; Very high compatibility; Very low complexity	Avoidance of low status; Social pressure to conform	Between multiple versions of brands in product class, old method (if available)
Ubiquity	Proliferation of brands; Tendency towards steady state market; Line/brand extensions; Low prices; Commonplace distribution; Promotion minimal (new brand launches); Interpersonal communication to the fore	*Maintenance*	Avoidance of disadvantage of failure to adopt; Economic necessity	Avoidance of ridicule; Conformity to social norms	Between multiplicity of similar brands (old method superseded)

_____ (1992b) "The Consumer Situation: An Integrative Model for Research in Marketing," *Journal of Marketing Management*, 8, 383-404.

_____ (1992c) "A Behaviourist Perspective on Purchase and Consumption." *Proceedings of the European Conference*, F. van Raaij and G. Bamossy (eds.) Amsterdam: ACR.

_____ (1993a) "Situated Consumer Behavior: A Behavioral Interpretation of Purchase and Consumption." In R. W. Belk (ed.) *Research in Consumer Behavior*, 6, JAI Press Greenwich, CT.

_____ (1993b) *The Behavioral Perspective Model of Purchase and Consumption: Refinement, Extension and Evaluation*, Research Centre for Consumer Behavior, University of Birmingham.

Gatignon, Hubert and Robertson, Thomas S. (1985) "A Propositional Inventory for New Diffusion Research," *Journal of Consumer Research*, 11, 849-867.

_____ and _____ (1991) "Innovative Decision Processes." In T. S. Robertson and H. H. Kassarjian (eds.) *Handbook of Consumer Behavior*, Englewood Cliffs, NJ: Prentice-Hall.

Hillner, Kenneth P. (1984) *History and Systems of Modern Psychology*, NY: Gardner.

Hirschman, Elizabeth C. and Holbrook, Morris B. (1982) "Hedonic Consumption: Emerging Concepts, Methods and Propositions," *Journal of Marketing*, 46, 92-101.

Lambkin, M. (990) "Evolutionary Models of Markets and Competitive Structure." In G. Day, B. Weitz and R. Wensley (eds.) *The Interface of Marketing and Strategy*, Greenwich, CT: JAI.

Midgley, David F. (1997) *Innovation and New Product Marketing*, London: Croom Helm.

Midgley, David F. and Dowling, Graeme R. (1978) "Innovativeness: The Concept and its Measurement," *Journal of Consumer Research*, 4, 229-40.

Nord, Walter and Peter, J. Paul (1990) "A Behavior Modification Perspective on Marketing," *Journal of Marketing*, 44, 36-47.

Rogers, Everett M. (1983) *Diffusion of Innovations*, NY: Free Press.

Skinner, B. Frederic (1974) *About Behaviorism*, NY: Knopf.

_____ (1981) "Selection by Consequences," *Science*, 213, 31 July, 501-4.

Van Parijs, Philippe (1981) *Evolutionary Explanation in the Social Sciences: An Emerging Paradigm*, Totowa, NJ: Rowman and Littlefield.

Wearden, John H. (1988) "Some Neglected Problems in the Analysis of Human Operant Behavior." In G. Davey and C. Cullen (eds.) *Human Operant Conditioning and Behavior Modification*, NY: Wiley.

Exploring Cultural Differences In Consumer Decision Making: Chinese Consumers In Montréal

Kathleen Brewer Doran, McGill University

Consumer decision making processes have been widely studied in North America. However, to date, little understanding exists of how culturally-based social influences (Hofstede, 1980; Hofstede and Bond, 1988; Kluckhohn and Strodtbeck, 1961) affect the utility of widely accepted models of consumer decision processes (e.g. Engel, Kollat and Miniard, 1986) in cultures outside North America. Yet this understanding is crucial as the world moves toward a global society. Those studies which do exist, such as Arnould's (1989) study of preference formation in Niger, highlight deviations from North American marketing models. Additional research in this area may show, for example, that cultures with a strong group orientation differ substantially from their more individualistic North American counterparts in types and numbers of search sources consulted. Research in a number of other disciplines (see, for example, Boyacigiller and Adler, 1991) has already begun to expose the American parochialism embedded in fundamental organizational theories, thus leading to the over-generalization of North American-based theory globally. There are a number of ways in which cultural factors such as overall orientation, values, attitudes and beliefs may lead to models which represent alternatives to the classic models of consumer decision making. Possible points of divergence include nearly every phase of the consumer decision making process.

This study was designed as an exploratory interpretive investigation into the role of culture on decision making processes. Participants from a contrasting culture, China[1], were chosen as the basis for the inquiry, both because of their cultural polarity to North Americans and because of their importance—since there is still little research on Chinese consumer behavior despite the vast potential of the Chinese market. The objectives of the study were twofold. First, the study was designed to produce a descriptive examination of the search and choice characteristics of the Chinese expatriate in Montréal. Second, by investigating a group culturally distant from those usually studied, this study was designed to expose areas of disparity between accepted search and choice theories and non-North American populations.

The study assumes that influence applied through culture and socialization may shape individual consumer decision making. Even in North America, where consumer choice patterns have traditionally been considered individual (or possible family) processes, the influence of reference groups is well-known, even if not well-studied. Olshavsky and Granbois (1979) note the importance of social influence on the majority of consumer choice events. Yet reference group is not as strong an influence on consumer decision processes as culture. A number of studies have noted differences in decision processes among various nationalities (e.g. Anderson and Engledow, 1977, Douglas, 1976), but few have attempted to explore the possible cultural implications of these findings (for exceptions see Arnould, 1989; McGuinness, Campbell and Leontiades, 1991). This study attempted to address this gap in the research, as the basis for more culturally-grounded future research.

In spite of the strength of cultural influence, a certain level of adaptation to new purchasing environments is expected, as is acculturation to new cultural situations generally. The current study defines *consumption culture* as a dynamic condition combining an individual's core culture with the consumption setting, including interactions with the prevalent culture at the consumption location. One focus of this study is to determine how culture and marketing environment interact through the study of consumption culture in Montréal.

METHODOLOGY

Participants and Participant Selection

The study employs interpretive techniques and a relatively small sample. Participants for the study were all Chinese nationals currently living in Montréal. All were either graduate students or visiting scholars at one of the four Montreal universities, or were recent graduates of a North American graduate program working in Montréal. Tenure in North America ranged from two months to ten years. Fifteen men and ten women were interviewed and ranged in age from about 23 to 50 years. Slightly over half the participants were married. While most of the participants were students, they were older (average in their 30's) and more experienced than the bulk of the student population and most had significant buying experience in China. The Chinese community in Montréal is thriving and dedicated to preserving Chinese culture for those Chinese now living in the city.

A snowball sample was employed beginning with six individuals personally known to the researcher. At the end of each interview, participants were asked to provide an introduction to one or more of their friends who they felt would be appropriate to the needs of the study. This element of the study became critical as many potential respondents appeared to be somewhat shy and extremely busy with their own school commitments.

Interview Parameters

Whenever possible, interviews were conducted in participants' homes. However, some were conducted in the participants' offices, as some individuals were reluctant to bring a relative stranger into their homes. Nonetheless, exposure to individuals' offices still provided a deeper insight into the respondent than a neutral site would have. Interviews were arranged in advance in person or by telephone, after an introduction from one of the earlier participants. Each session was recorded on audio tape using a palm-sized recorder, after permission was received from the participant. The interviewer took extensive field notes during each interview, and also kept a field journal.

By definition, the study was more etic than emic, since the researcher was neither a member of the Chinese culture nor a participant in the search process. Various procedures were undertaken to ensure high data quality and interpretation (Hudson and Ozanne, 1988; Belk, Wallendorf and Sherry, 1989). For example, defamiliarization exercises were undertaken to help eliminate cultural biases resulting from the cultural differences between the researcher and the sample population. Memoing and external auditors were also employed to help improve the validity of findings.

Interviews were somewhat free-form, although they followed a basic outline, and ranged in length from about 40 minutes to over two hours; slightly over an hour on average. Interview content included background information, cultural information, and a se-

---

[1] For purposes of this paper, "China" and "Chinese" refers to the People's Republic of China and its citizens.

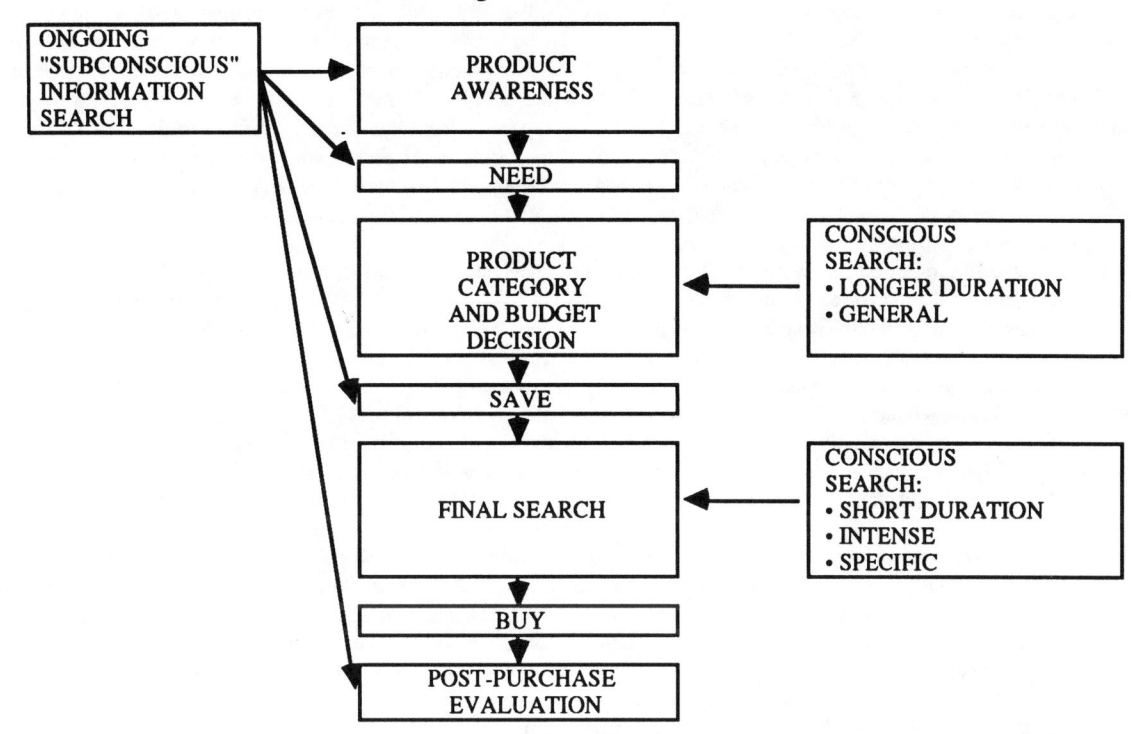

FIGURE 1
Decision Making Process for Chinese in Montréal

ries of questions based on actual situations involving the purchase of consumer electronics. These verbal protocols generally evolved into a more theoretical discussion of beliefs and attitudes concerning various information sources and search strategies. In addition, the researcher used a series of hypothetical situations to help draw out the interviewee, and to help determine how the current living situation might modify normal search patterns. Topics covered included determinants of search, information sources used, beliefs and attitudes concerning those sources, and a discussion of each individual's self-concept and relationship to his or her culture. The focus of the interviews was on information search; however, developing an appreciation for search strategies and rationales required delving into other areas of the consumer decision making process as well. This depth was particularly important in determining the placement of search within the decision making framework.

Consumer Choice Domain

A focus group of graduate students of multiple nationalities was used to help define the product choice for the interviews and to help structure the interview content. The study utilized consumer electronics as the basis for search discussions. While all participants have bought some electronic equipment, not all have bought the same type. Some have bought audio equipment and systems; others have bought video equipment (e.g. television and VCR); and some have experience buying both. Those who had experience with both product categories approached the two searches in an identical fashion, lending viability to the utility of the overall category choice. Some had experience in both their home countries and Canada; these individuals utilized similar, but not always identical, searches, lending credence both to the existence of adaptation and the tangibility of consumption culture.

ANALYSIS AND DISCUSSION

A Description of the Chinese Choice Process

While exhibiting some individual differences, the Chinese participants, as a group, showed remarkable similarity in their choice processes. An overall model of the choice process used by participants in the study is outlined in Figure 1. The model reflects discrete time differences from generally accepted models of consumer search (e.g. Engel, et al, 1986). In addition, the group reflects a distinct system for information search patterns and source choice.

Since the Chinese value thrift highly, attitudes which approve the use of debt are rare. In the current sample, every individual saved in advance to make the purchase; impulse buying for this type of product was unheard of. While several individuals used credit cards for convenience and safety, all paid off their entire balances monthly. This credit consciousness tends to truncate the choice and search process into two distinct stages: a general search, prior to saving, designed to develop a familiarity with the products offered and common price points, and an intense short-term search, following saving, designed to choose and buy the product. The first stage of the search tends to be more leisurely and less directed. It includes visits to and consultations with friends and relatives and store visits (nearly always accompanied by friends). Individuals considering purchase may even borrow an item from a friend to "try it out," though this behavior decreases sharply with exposure to the West. Once a decision is made to buy and a budget selected, search virtually stops (except, perhaps, for accompanying a friend who is shopping) until the desired budget figure has been reached. At that time, in the second stage, an intense search of short duration, usually under a week, is undertaken and the final purchase is made.

Information Search

For the Chinese, information sources are viewed differently than they are in North America, possibly because much less information is available in China than in Montréal. Sources of information used were strongly divided by the type of information sought. The participants made a profound distinction between information perceived as "factual" and that perceived as "evaluative." Within the sample, there were consistent views concerning the three types of information source: personal—generally friends and family; neutral, such as *Consumer Reports*; and marketer-dominated, such as advertising and salespeople. Personal sources were heavily consulted in all areas. However, most participants preferred to use both neutral and marketer-dominated information only for price and availability, although several admitted that they might also use these types of sources to provide details on functions available on various models. Messages which implied an evaluative element were discounted unless they came from personal sources: "I don't trust other people, only my friends or my family. They [store representatives or manufacturers] might try to make me buy something I don't want. But for prices or functions, I ask. They can't lie about that."

In general, store searches occurred in two distinct phases, which coincided with the early, pre-saving search and the final, post-saving search. First, potential buyers wanted to browse stores undisturbed to get a general idea of product choices and price ranges early in the search process. They did not want to interact with salespeople at that time. The other time for store searches was at the time of purchase, after money had been budgeted and saved for the new purchase. One typical participant explained her reactions this way: "when salespeople talk to me, it makes me feel bad. I feel guilty and uncomfortable. I feel I have to buy...I feel pressed and sometimes afraid and I leave the store—even if I want to stay." Self-service, warehouse-type stores, and large electronics specialists were the most popular places to shop since they provided the shoppers with several key ingredients: relative anonymity from aggressive salespeople, large selection at a reasonable price, and an appearance of staying power and success.

One reason for the strong emphasis on both brand and personal sources of information which was mentioned by a number of participants was the need for trust. In addition, only one of the participants was willing to be an early adopter, with the rest preferring to wait until one of their friends or relatives already has a unit of the type desired. Since relationships are so strong, and the perceived importance of the product is so great, the Chinese interviewed often went beyond visiting a friend's home to see a product and actually borrowed the item to try it out. This process was possible because such a high level of trust exists in personal relationships, and having personal hands-on experience with the product before purchase helps build trust (and loyalty) with the manufacturer and product. However, as acculturation increased, borrowing behavior declined dramatically.

Social desirability also played a role for the group, as individuals tried to match their choices to those of their friends. One individual stated his feelings this way, "I want to buy at least as high a quality as my neighbors, but not too high, or I may embarrass them and lose face myself." This same issue of matching levels and social desirability may help to explain why adoption rates are slow at first, and then very rapid. It may be considered socially undesirable to be first, unless several people buy at the same time.

Local reference groups tended to have less impact on process than overall culture. However, reference group had a dynamic impact on information search and product choice outcomes. For example, five acquainted participants had the identical model of Aiwa personal cassette player, based on consecutive recommendations. Other areas where indivdual differences were clear included urban versus rural upbringing and marital status. Those individuals who were raised in rural environments tended to depend even more heavily on friends' recommendations than did other participants in the sample. Married individuals, even those who were physically separated from their spouses, tended to develop a dialogue with their spouses. However, while joint decision making was the norm through the first half of the decision process, it was less apparent during the final choice phase.

Other Search Characteristics

Although the Chinese are thrifty by nature, they value quality very highly. As a result, they choose a model first, then try to find the best price for that model, rather than setting a price threshold first and finding the best model they can for a given price. Functionality was very important to these individuals, who have a highly developed sense of product utility. In their combined views encompassing face, thrift and quality, they try to buy only functions they use, but those functions they do buy should be the best quality. Their attitudes toward products and money appeared to be "prudent practicality." For example, unlike many North Americans, not one of the people involved in the study had a VCR they did not know how to program, or a cassette recorder they didn't know how to use for recording. Many considered that it would be wasteful if they had functions which they considered superfluous. Similarly, they made a strong effort to learn how to use their new equipment when they got it home. Yet, product appearance was also important to a number of participants. Several noted that it was important for the product to have a "good face;" they felt comfortable because the unit was "very pretty; it looks very nice. Having a good look is important."

Brand influence was particularly accentuated in the sample group. Perhaps this aspect was an artifact of the product category chosen, yet in discussions of all types of product categories, brand influence was a major factor. In the case of consumer electronics, in addition to individual brand influence, there appeared to be an element of brand identification with a producing nation; in this case, Japan. Every individual interviewed commented on the perceived superiority of Japanese electronics. With only two exceptions, the participants were willing to wait to buy until they could afford to "buy Japanese." Both of the exceptional cases bought products which consisted of Japanese parts, but which were assembled elsewhere. Representative comments included, "We Chinese may not like the Japanese people very much, but we trust Japanese electronics. They are the best, and having the best is very important to me."

The importance of electronics in the Chinese culture was alluded to by a number of participants. Since ownership of major items such as houses or cars is seldom viable, consumer electronics play an important symbolic role projecting an aura of personal success. Yet appearances within the group seemed more important in China than in Canada. Some professed a sense of being more liberated in Canada, less bound by convention. For this reason, many individuals noted that they felt they might have bought a fancier or more upscale item in China than in Canada. Brand and national origin of products were also considered more important in China than in Canada, though brand and product origin were still very important. "Japanese machinery is [a] fashion in China...[it] shows you have money. Americans don't market as much," was a typical comment which combined the symbolic value of possessing electronic equipment with the quality image associated with specific national origins.

Most participants continued to buy equipment from the same store once an initial purchase had been made. For example, having bought a music system, a consumer would most often return to the same store to purchase a television and VCR, even though he/she would probably visit other stores casually.

Acculturation and Choice Processes

There were trends in acculturation which tended to differ over time. Acculturation appeared to occur along a relatively steady, but shallow, slope as long as an individual had in mind a specific time period to return to China. The rate of acculturation accelerated with the imposition of one of two conditions. First, when landed immigrancy was obtained (even when the plan was still to return), or second, when a decision was made to try to stay in North America, individuals began to acculturate at a greatly intensified rate. One exception to this pattern was the youngest female, who had little experience buying in China and, therefore, appeared to adopt more typically Western strategies right away.

One interesting development was the contrast between those who had come directly to Canada from China versus those who had lived in the United States first. Those who had lived in the U.S. "melting pot" tended to be more assimilated given a consistent period of exposure to the West than those who came directly to Canada where "multiculturalism" encourages more retention of traditional values for immigrants. The "melting pot" sample was more likely to use marketer-dominated and neutral sources, less dependent on personal source evaluations, and less brand conscious. These individuals were most likely to have bought equipment which was not of Japanese origin, or were more willing to do so in the future. However, it is possible that this difference results not from specific differences encountered between U.S. and Canadian culture, but simply from exposure to an additional culture, regardless of its characteristics.

Overall, the more acculturated individuals exhibited less brand consciousness, and were more likely to shop alone, as well as more likely to buy less fancy equipment, but sooner. As individuals became more used to the retail choices in Montréal, the likelihood of frequenting small ethnic stores where they could forgo tax increased. However, this gray market activity had very high perceived risk for most of the sample. In the same light, as acculturation increased, Chinese consumers were likely to shop more stores, as well as use more marketer-dominated and neutral sources of information. Finally, they were more likely to try to "buy the most product for the money" rather than choose the model first, and then try to locate it at the best price.

Study Contributions and Limitations

The current study makes contributions to the literature in four basic areas. First, the descriptive knowledge gained from an interpretive investigation of a population which has not been widely studied can be used to add data to a growing information base on marketing habits in the multinational context. Second, the study reinforces the assumption that massive cultural differences exist between East Asian, in this case Chinese, and North American buyers, and that these differences drive essential distinctions in consumer decision making processes. In other words, culture matters, and the particular dimensions of a culture relate directly to existing patterns of search and choice in a given situation. Third, even in a strongly reinforced subculture such as the Chinese community in Montréal, over time assimilation occurs which reflects the influence of the dominant culture and marketing environment encountered. Last, the study develops the notion of consumption cultures which combine elements of social culture with the marketing environment to create a contextual synthesis in each choice set.

Relationships obviously play an important role in the search and choice processes: the friends who are consulted, the product choices made with reference to appearances within the reference group, the emphasis on developing a brand relationship and the stores patronized over time all represent long-term commitments and relationships for the consumer. As anticipated, satisfaction levels were uniformly high. The search process itself, which emphasizes hands-on experience and personal knowledge of the product through friends and relatives, appears to lead to more realistic expectations, and therefore greater satisfaction.

Based on these results, there is support for the notion of a consumption culture which combines elements of both an individual's deep cultural roots and the marketing environment encountered in any particular choice event. Consumption culture in this sense is evolutionary; it maintains many of the deepest cultural values, while adapting search and choice patterns to the current situation and marketing environment. It is possible that the results of this study reflect normal new immigrant behavior. However, most individuals maintained central behaviors developed in China, at least until a decision was made to remain in the West. Further, many of the participants did not consider themselves immigrants, but temporary visitors, and many of this returning faction were buying items with the intention of bringing them home to China. Nonetheless, even behavior typical of new immigrants lends credence to the concept of consumption culture by showing how the marketing environment may affect purchasing behavior.

The study itself is unquestionably exploratory in nature. The sample size is small, as well as rather homogeneous, since all participants have, or are now working toward, advanced degrees. More importantly, perhaps, there is no control group of North Americans. Yet, because the effects of acculturation mitigate true Chinese buying characteristics, the differences found here may, in fact, understate the extent to which culture influences decision making. Further, while the study provides an illuminating view into the adaptation of one group into a distinctly different environment, it may not fully capture the processes used when in their home environment. Additionally, the study may suffer somewhat from two elements: first, students' somewhat impoverished financial status may have an overly large impact on budgeting as a factor in search procedures; second, the high education level achieved by all of the participants affects the representativeness of the sample for the overall population.

There are, of course, limitations associated with protocol-type analyses (see Nisbett and Wilson, 1977), although there are a number of precedents in this area (e.g. Herr, Kardes and Kim, 1991; Rosen and Olshavsky, 1987). At the exploratory level, however, verbal reports still provide new insights into general modes of behavior. Nonetheless, as noted in Adler, Campbell and Laurent (1989), only through exploration and experimentation can an appropriate methodology for investigating structurally divergent cultures such as the Chinese be developed. Perhaps these self report techniques will lead to new breakthroughs in ways to compare cultures experimentally.

Finally, while an understanding of consumer decision making processes is very important, since this study investigates only one culture it only begins to address the long term needs of cross cultural research in developing generalizable theories for global use. Nonetheless, the varying degrees of acculturation found were strongly related to length of stay in the West, which adds an element of multiculturalism.

CONCLUSIONS AND SUGGESTIONS FOR FUTURE RESEARCH

The results of this study are compelling, yet clearly require a significant body of follow up research. First, researchers must investigate the Chinese in other decision contexts in order to test the robustness of the proposed model. Second, studies need to be undertaken which encompass a number of different cultures with contrasting dimensionalities. Third, the research needs to move beyond exploration into a more confirmatory mode. Fourth, in order to truly explore cultural differences in consumer decision making, studies must be undertaken in situ.

The findings of this investigation show some of the ways in which new immigrants adapt to new cultures from the perspective of consumer decision making processes and particularly external search. Specifically, the study inquires into the existence of a distinct and evolutionary consumption culture. In addition, the analysis of interview information shows broad differences in culture-based search patterns between the Chinese respondents and findings from previous, Western-based investigations.

Cultural differences appear to be more important than national borders when investigating decision making *processes*, but local marketing environments, including current reference group and ambient culture, also have a profound effect, especially on *contextual outcomes*. Therefore, marketers should be careful to think globally in terms of understanding cultural differences, but act locally by understanding the effect of local environment.

REFERENCES

Adler, N., N. Campbell and A. Laurent. 1989. In search of appropriate methodology: from outside the People's Republic of China, looking in. *Journal of International Business Studies*, 20(1): 61-74.

Anderson, R. D. and J. L. Engledow. 1977. A Factor Analytic Comparison of U. S. and German Information Seekers. *Journal of Consumer Research*, 3(March): 185-196.

Arnould, Eric J. 1989. Toward a Broadened Theory of Preference Formation and the Diffusion of Innovations: Cases from the Zinder Province, Niger Republic. *Journal of Consumer Research*, 16(September): 239-267.

Belk, R. W., M. Wallendorf and J. F. Sherry, Jr. 1989. The Sacred and the Profane in Consumer Behavior: Theodicy on the Odyssey. *Journal of Consumer Research*, 16(June): 1-38.

Boyacigiller, Nakiye and Nancy J. Adler. 1991. The Parochial Dinosaur: Organizational Sciences in a Global Context. *Academy of Management Review*, 16(2): 262-290.

Douglas, S.P. 1976. Cross National Comparisons and Consumer Stereotypes: A Case Study of Working and Non-Working Wives in the U.S. and France. *Journal of Consumer Research*, 3(June): 12-20.

Engel, J.F., R.D. Kollat and P.W. Miniard. 1986. *Consumer Behavior*. 5th ed., Hinsdale, Ill.: Dryden Press.

Herr, Paul M., Frank R. Kardes and John Kim. 1991. Effects of Word-of-Mouth and Product-Attribute Information on Persuasion: An Accessibility-Diagnosticity Perspective. *Journal of Consumer Research*, 17(March): 454-462.

Hofstede, Geert. 1980. *Culture's Consequences: International Differences in Work Related Values*. Beverly Hills: Sage Publications.

Hofstede, Geert and Michael Harris Bond. 1988. The Confucius Connection: From Cultural Roots to Economic Growth. *Organizational Dynamics*, 16(Spring): 5-21.

Hudson, L. and J. Ozanne. 1988. Alternative Ways of Seeking Knowledge in Consumer Research, *Journal of Consumer Research*, 14(March): 508-521.

Kluckhohn, F. and F.L. Strodtbeck. 1961. *Variations in Value Orientations*. Evanston, Illinois: Row, Peterson.

McGuinness, N., N. Campbell and J. Leontiades. 1991. Selling Machinery to China: Chinese Perceptions of Strategies and Relationships. *Journal of International Business Studies*, 22(2): 187-207.

Nisbett, R. E. and T. D. Wilson. 1977. Telling More Than We Can Know: Verbal Reports on Mental Processes. *Psychological Review*, 84(3): 231-259.

Olshavsky, Richard W. and Donald H. Granbois. 1979. Consumer Decision Making—Fact or Fiction? *Journal of Consumer Research*, 6(September): 93-100.

Rosen, D. L. and R. W. Olshavsky. 1987 A Protocol Analysis of Brand Choice Strategies Involving Recommendations. *Journal of Consumer Research*, 14(December):440-444.

India's Changing Consumer Economy: A Cultural Perspective

Alladi Venkatesh, University of California, Irvine

ABSTRACT

As India moves from a production oriented mixed economy to a consumer society, there is a need to understand the forces behind this transition. In this paper, I examine a number of cultural and social themes accompanying the consumerist trends in India. Although India remains in the bottom half of the world economies, there is every reason to believe that this is not likely to last long, for many structural changes are evident including the transformation of the middle class which is at the vanguard of the consumer revolution.

INTRODUCTION

This paper examines the changing consumer scene in India. Unlike some of the other Asian countries like Malaysia, Indonesia, Thailand, and Taiwan, where the "consumer revolution" has already forged ahead, or is in progress, India has been a slow starter in this push for change. However, recent trends suggest that a wave of consumerism is spreading to India also. This paper is based partly on my ethnographic field work conducted in Madras, a Southern Indian city of approximately five million people, and partly on a reading of secondary sources. This should be considered work in progress and, therefore, only some initial ideas are presented here. The reader is also referred to other related works undertaken by the author (Venkatesh 1994/95a, 1994/95b; Venkatesh and Swamy 1994/95).

The general presentation in this paper will be thematic or topical rather than analytical, or theoretical. That is, the paper explores several themes instead of a unifying set of research questions or a single theory. Thus this is a thick description of Indian culture and India as a consumer society.

SOME GENERAL COMMENTS

Several authors have pointed out the growing economic and consumer power of India. Many multinational corporations are beginning to invest in India. In this respect, India is no different from many other emerging consumer economies, whether they are in Eastern Europe, Asia or Latin America (Arnould 1989, Belk 1988, Ger and Belk 1990, Witkowski 1993). This fact by itself does not give any special clue to the Indian scene unless one also examines what peculiar circumstances pertain to India. In other words, just because there may be similarities across different markets and cultures on certain dimensions, it does not mean that the content and patterns of the developments are the same. The paper will not provide a comparative analysis of India with other countries where similar developments may be taking place. My experience in India has taught me some important lessons. With the burgeoning of comparative studies, there may be a tendency among researchers to draw quick conclusions about cultures in which they may have only superficial familiarity. Any serious study of different cultures requires some deep knowledge gained through a proper study of the culture. See Arnould (1989) for a good example of writing with great cultural depth and understanding. This can be accomplished by a knowledge of the literature, the economic scene, and important cultural works that reflect the culture in some meaningful terms. A second lesson that I have learnt is that belonging to a particular cultural group does not immediately qualify one to claim scholarly expertise on that group. It certainly helps, no doubt. For example, many of the best works on India are written by non-Indian scholars who have devoted a great deal of time and effort over a period of several years. Their interpretations may be different from those of indigenous scholars but they are nevertheless well-informed and well-founded. Although I am an Indian by birth, I couldn't have gained the knowledge required for my work without doing field work in India for sufficiently long duration (seven months) and studying the relevant literature that provided me with important theoretical insights needed to interpret my empirical observations.

RISING CONSUMERISM IN INDIA

Consumerism is used here in the sense of the development of consumer oriented tendencies, marked by the availability of a variety of manufactured consumer goods and active advertising of the products in various media. Much research exists on the evolution of consumer societies in the West. Although there are some common characteristics in these societies, there are also many differences. The differences are based on cultural variations within each culture. This is the reason why I have proposed a new paradigm for the study of consumerism based on cross-cultural differences. I have labeled this "ethnoconsumerism" (Venkatesh 1994a). Recent cross-cultural work has shown us how the same products may undergo different consumer usages and experiences based on particular cultural norms and practices. The case in point is the motor scooter (dy Pessler 1992). The author describes in great detail the cultural context and experience of the motor scooter in three different cultures, Italy, England and India. The vehicle was marketed as an aesthetic object in Italy, it became a mark of rebellion among punk groups in England, and a family/personal utility transportation in India.

Part of the rising consumerism in India may be cast in the general context of global tendencies in consumerism. Recent work suggests that global diffusion of consumerism has been aided by the expansion of multinationals, the diffusion of telecommunication and satellite technologies, the general dissatisfaction with socialist political regimes and rising economic success in East Asian countries. Certainly, recent moves in India echo these developments.

What is happening in India may also be described in postmodern terms. Indian development does not follow standard chronological sequences observed in some Western societies. Models of social change do not follow any known patterns of change. Modernist methods found in the conventional social sciences have limited value when the objective is to capture change in non-Western cultures. This is because modernist thinking is regimented, very rationalistic and (pseudo)scientifically oriented. Postmodernist thinking accommodates non-linear thinking, and is open-minded when it comes to alternate or non-orthodox patterns. For example, some new technologies in India are diffusing faster than some old technologies. So, one cannot use the historical progression of the West as a model to study India. Indian consumer scene is replete with what might be misinterpreted by the modernist to be contradictions and the juxtaposition of opposites (and therefore, non-natural), but in reality they represent highly symbolic modes of behavior much of which must be understood within the Indian cultural framework.

The Discourse of Consumerism

In this category, we include the rhetoric of consumerism in everyday life. A large part of consumerism depends on advertising. A second aspect of consumerism discourse relates to the everyday patterns of behavior one expects to find in consumerism or commercialism. In India, there is a burgeoning of consumer related articles from branding to lifestyles to fashion in popular media. Newspapers have regular columns devoted to these matters. A number of magazines have appeared in the area of advertising, business, women's fashion that constantly discuss these issues. Much of Indian consumerism is directly dependent on what goes on in feature films and the movie industry. In a country, where the celebrities used to be politicians and public figures, they have been gradually replaced by movie actors and actresses, and business celebrities. Thus the discourse of consumerism can be seen in media, movies, and other entertainment forms.

Televisual Culture

The televisual culture in India is marked by strong consumerism and commercialism. Singhal and Rogers (1989) have already established how influential the television has become as a cultural and entertainment medium. The TV reaches the four corners of India as no other technology has done in the country's history. The next development within the context of television is the consumer advertising. Consumer advertising is burgeoning with the arrival of satellite TV, or more specifically, Star TV. A mix of domestic and multinational brands are advertised on Star TV as for example, Bajaj scooters, Stayfree sanitary napkins, Pepsi's Hostess Chips, McDowell Whiskey, just to name a few. The diffusion of consumerism is further accelerated by the sponsoring of sports, concerts and other entertainment for the public. The participation of industries in the cultural production system is on the increase. To provide a glimpse of the quantitative developments of advertising industry in India here is an excerpt from a recent article (Mulchandani 1992).

"Advertising in the visual medium stands at Rupees 410 crore (US$ 130m)...This market in the next five years is expected to boom going upto Rupees 1500 crore (US$ 480m). Advertising in most developing economies stands at 1.5 to 2 per cent of the total GNP. In India it stands at .1 per cent...The potential for growth is tremendous. And money is flowing freely."

New Technologies / Consumer Electronics

Indian economy is also changing with the advent of new technologies. Ironically, the traditional technologies have not had much impact on Indian consumer. For example, very little of the recent changes in India can be attributed to the telephone or the automobile both of which have existed in India for a long time. These same technologies have had profound impact on Western industrial economies in the last five decades. The telephone system in India is highly underdeveloped and is run by the government. It is indeed the butt of many jokes and ridicule in India. In the case of automobiles, the impact has been minimal because very few Indians could afford the automobile.

On the other hand, there are some other technologies which have made a difference in Indian life, the motor scooter, the television and the VCR, and other household appliances like the refrigerator and the cooking stove. The motor scooter and the motor cycle have become ubiquitous because of their affordability and maneuverability. Many young families and individual professionals, both male and female, use motor scooters as personal transportation.

Much of the revolutionary changes in India can be attributed to the emergence of consumer technologies. The first impact of this is the access to electronic information, and entertainment. More specifically, it has an impact on tastes in music, popular or classical, exposure to various entertainment forms from different cultures. This is also a prelude to what one might call the development of a mass culture society. Another consequence of this is the development of the material culture.

India in the Global technological Context

Singhal and Rogers (1989) have initiated important research on the diffusion of television and VCRs in India with interesting implications for the popular-cultural practices in Indian communities.

Four developments have begun to change the general nature of inquiry relative to technology. First, the rise of postindustrialism and information technologies has sensitized researchers to a radically different technological environment which is not amenable to standard modes of inquiry that were originally developed to investigate material technology. Second, the modern technologies have begun to interconnect the world in unprecedented ways giving a new meaning to the world order. This interconnectedness seems to imply the emergence of a universal language of technology which could potentially bridge cultural differences. Third, the ascendance of Eastern countries such as Japan, Korea and Taiwan as the producers of modern technologies and the accompanying rapid diffusion of modern technologies within those countries, has prompted researchers to view technologies in a non-developmental, culture-specific framework. Thus for the first time in several centuries the sources of some new technologies are no longer located in the Western hemisphere. Finally, as Appadurai (1988) has pointed out in a different context, countries like India which are experiencing new levels of material success have begun to view their cultural practices in a self-conscious, self-reflective fashion without using Western yardsticks of what is acceptable and not acceptable.

These developments stand in contrast to the notions of modernization and Westernization which dominated earlier thinking on the subject (Srinivas 1966) (see next section for a discussion of this issue). Previous research on India has dealt with issues of social change occurring due to modernization and Westernization. While modernization was used as a broad concept dealing with urbanization, social mobility and new media experiences, Westernization was identified with social and cultural patterns dealing with clothing, eating, language and the like. Although these are still valid concepts to analyze contemporary Indian ethos, they can only serve as a back drop.

Recent work by Singhal and Rogers (1989) is an interesting example of the approach that one may use in studying technological change. They have been studying the cultural shifts occurring within the Indian entertainment scene as a result of the arrival of TVs and VCRs. The technological diffusion of both TVs and VCRs has been rather astonishing and cannot be completely explained by economic variables such as disposable income and standard of living. In fact their diffusion pattern is unlike that of some other technologies such as telephone, refrigerator and the automobile. It seems more to do with the patterns of culture than mere economic processes.

One can of course venture an explanation to the Indians' adoption of modern consumer technologies in terms of class ideology and consumption styles as Appadurai (1988) attempted to show with respect to certain aspects of food consumption. But this is not plausible because the historical role that food has played in Indian culture has no parallel in the adoption of technologies. Nevertheless, it is evident from Appadurai's work and the work of more recent authors that one has to look for a contemporary theme to better explain the various cultural shifts. For example, Singer (1989) has insightfully characterized the current Indian cultural scene in terms of "the coexistence of the past and the present." This is in direct contrast to some earlier views which have tended to represent past and present in antagonistic and hierarchical terms. Thus modernization and Westernization were regarded as both superior and antagonistic to traditionalism. This view is beginning to fade because the current research on India seems to suggest that the Indians are shaping their culture in ways different from those of an earlier generation.

The City of Madras–A Transformed Consumer Space

Any one familiar with Madras would immediately recognize it, in spite of its size (Pop: 5 million), as a sleepy town known for its regional (South Indian) cultural forms, temples and traditional norms and practices. Many Indians, and even foreign visitors, have long considered Bombay, Calcutta and Delhi as modern, Westernized, sophisticated cities leaving Madras in a more traditional mold. However, in recent years, we are witnessing some forces of change that are moving Madras closer to the other cities in its profile. Much of this seems to be occurring due to rapid a rise in consumerism. Here is an excerpt from an article (Khandekar 1992):

"After all, what was Madras in the '70s...[I]t] was just a big idli [a local food item]. With its simply dressed people, its lack of red lipstick and bursting *salwar-kameezes* [a traditional north-Indian dress], its pathetic ignorance of sofas and carpets and kabaabs and lichees. It didn't even let girls wear jeans or cut their hair and it only splurged on books, music and sports. Madras was just a mandatory stop to catch up with country cousins...Until thirteen years later, and somewhat fed up with eveteasing [a local Delhi pastime], *chhole-bhature* [a local food item of Delhi], tapestried chairs,..it was time to go back to the big *idli* for a change...The shocks began...Indeed, Madras in the '90s is a stunning revelation. The same girl who dresses demurely for concerts will hop on her two-wheeler in jeans, salwar-kameez or even skirts...Continental and Mughlai restaurants run by the Shettys and Reddys [local restaurateurs]..." (Khandekar 1992).

The significance of changing Madras is that it represents the transformation of the Indian urban scene which for the last five decades was limited to the three cities, Bombay, Calcutta and Delhi. The changing Madras is one more dramatic example of the changing consumer scene in India. As consumer researchers, we are not accustomed to examining the semiotics of geographical spaces to understand cultural transformations and meanings. Gottdeiner's (1985) work in this area is quite instructive, that is, to study consumerism one must also look at the symbolic meanings of spatial arrangements, which include not only consumers, but street signs, shopping environments and many other urban symbolisms and iconic forms.

Specific Factors That Account for Indian Consumerism

In sum, we have identified thirteen different factors to describe India as an emerging consumer society. While these factors are not to be considered exhaustive, they are representative of the movement of India towards a consumer oriented society. The factors are:

- Burgeoning middle class, its changing values and pent up consumer demand,
- Changing women's roles, their labor participation and the changing structure of the family,
- Rising consumer aspirations and expectations across many segments of the population,
- Increased consumer spending on luxury items aided by past savings and the introduction of the credit system,
- New types of shopping environments and outlets,
- Media proliferation, satellite and cable TV, and the thriving film industry,
- Media sophistication and familiarity with English language among media people and a wide segment of the population,
- High degree of consumer awareness and sophistication across different segments,
- The emergence of traveling Indian consumers—immigrants in US and England, overseas workers, tourists, professionals and their exposure to world-wide consumer products,
- Strong domestic consumer goods manufacturing sector,
- Resurfacing of hedonistic cultural elements after centuries of dormant state,
- Entry of multi-national corporations into India, and
- The emergence of the rural consumer sector.

Now we shall address some key cultural and social themes marking recent developments in India.

THE CULTURAL CONTEXT

Anybody studying India cannot take it on its face value. No amount of field work will yield important insights into India unless this is also accompanied by a cultural understanding which can only be obtained by a knowledge of the secondary sources. A society that has an uninterrupted history dating back to more than 3000 years has strong cultural and historical roots that cannot be easily unraveled but must be understood nevertheless. In this seamless web of complexity one has to pick a few important threads as a way to gaining meaning into the cultural presence of India.

One of the first things that we learn from India's socio-cultural history is the role of religion in the daily life of Indians. Hinduism, which is the primary religion of the country, is not an organized theological movement but represents a way of life that has evolved over many centuries. Hinduism represents a complex system of daily practices, rituals, beliefs, and symbolic patterns that overlap various aspects of social life. From cosmological doctrines which define how the physical and spiritual world is constituted to more mundane aspects of life, Hinduism provides the framework to understand all these matters. In spite of the key role played by religion, or perhaps because of it, there is no word for "religion' in the Indian languages. There is only a literal translation for the English word but it does not represent the same reality as the word implies in English. This is because the religious history of the West has no parallel in India. In the West, religion stands in opposition to science, to rationalist thought and in fact to modernity which is the defining philosophical and cultural position of the West in the last four hundred years. Science and religion are understood in oppositional terms, science representing the materiality of life and religion representing its spiritual dimension. Such a distinction is totally absent in Hinduism and in Indian culture where spiritualism and materialism are not considered opposites. In fact, Indians believe that the material world and the spiritual world belong to the same realm of experience. Indians do believe in the notion that life can be both spiritual and materialistic at the same time without any implied antagonism. Similarly, the concept of secularism, another Western idea, is totally absent within Indian cultural scheme except as a borrowed idea from the West. Indians either ignore secularism in their daily lives or wear it like a necessary garb in dealing with the West.

Indians believe that objects have symbolic meanings at three levels, aesthetic, functional and spiritual. In contrast, the Western notion of the objective world extends to its aesthetic and functional dimensions only. What is significant about the Indian experience is the spiritual coloring that is readily accorded to material objects. This is an important part of the Hindu cosmology and must be given serious consideration in the study of Indian consumer culture.

Indian culture must be understood in cosmological terms of how human life is constituted in terms of the universal order, and also in social everyday terms and as part of daily human experience. Indians are conscious of these two dimensions, the transcendental and the phenomenological, and are able to switch back and forth with considerable ease. In the Western context, the transcendental is the religious or the spiritual realm and has been relegated over the centuries to a marginal status, while the phenomenological has become the material realm and has gained considerable social and cultural strength over the former. Indians consider life to be a matter of multiple experiences closely tied to the both the transcendental and everyday aspects of existence. To a Westerner, such an outlook is more likely to produce a lot of contradictions, but, to an Indian, contradictions, oppositions are not to be minded but dealt with as part of the rich experience of human life.

An aspect of Indian cultural life has to deal with time. Time is neither historical nor chronological. Time is essentially cyclical. Similarly, birth and death are not considered two finite events but two stages in one's continuous existence. Thus the time before birth and after death have concrete meanings for many Indians. Because of this, the individual experiences take on different meanings since the Indian is prone to establish associations with people dead and gone.

The concept of self in Indian culture is not a well defined property of a single individual but something which extends and is linked to several others selves. Clearly, it is different from the Cartesian self which establishes the identity of the individual in the West.

MODERNIZATION IN THE INDIAN CONTEXT

Several authors have written on modernization, both as a process and an end-state (Bendix 1967, Gusfield 1967, Inkeles 1969, Schnaiberg 1970, Vajpeyi 1982, Singer 1989). Schnaiberg has studied the change process occurring through modernization, especially in the context of the family. Based on some previous studies, he notes that there is a hypothesized shift from an extended family system to a nuclear family system, consonant with individual mobility (social and geographic). He further postulated changes in the structure of production and consumption functions at home, declining importance of primary groups, greater dependence on impersonal resources (e.g. media) for information, and decline in religious involvement. Schnaiberg conducted a study of 803 Turkish households in the city of Ankara and evaluated them on six dimensions: media usage, extended family ties, declining religiosity, nuclear family role structure, environmental orientation, and production/consumption orientation. Since the study was conducted in a "developing" country, the findings are relevant to us. He found that all these dimensions were correlated with "modernism." At the theoretical level, it means that even in non-Western societies, the process of urbanization and modernization and the impact of new technologies will grossly parallel the developments in Western-industrialized societies. One should not forget that there could be exceptions to this. For example, in Iran, the recent history tells us that modernization over the years had the opposite reaction of pulling the country toward religious formalism.

In the Indian context, the early work of Srinivas (1966) is relevant to us. Srinivas has discussed social change in terms of Westernization, industrialization, urbanization and secularization. Westernization results in the introduction of new institutions (elections, newspapers etc.,) and modifications to old institutions. It introduces such things as Western technology, clothing and eating practices, scientific and rationalistic view points. Modernization is related to Westernization. It is a general term that includes Westernization, industrialization, and secularization. Countries may prefer the term "modernization" to Westernization because it does not have the negative connotation of having to give up what is good within the indigenous culture. Vajpeyi's research (1982) explored the attitudes, opinions, perceptions and beliefs of the Indian elites toward modernization. His findings show that the Indian elites support the idea of social change through modernized developments as long as the traditional value system is not negatively impacted. This view is also confirmed by Singer (1989). In many non-Western societies modernization has become a value-laden term, because its main challenge lies in the discovery of relevant ideology. The urge for modernity is commingled with the urge for identity. In India, the dominant cultural values are hierarchy, holism, continuity and transcendentalism. There is a fundamental religio-social outlook where religion and personal life are neither separate nor antagonistic.

Rural versus Urban Economic Structure

In terms of development theory, India has been regarded as an agricultural economy which is becoming rapidly industrialized. This also means that a large percentage of Indian population lives in rural sector as opposed to urban centers. Currently, the division between rural and urban population distribution is 70% to 30%. While this reveals a large rural bias, it however points to a dramatic shift to greater urbanism because in 1960 the distribution was 85% and 15%. Urban industry, which was barely existent thirty years ago, generates 40% of the national output. While the rural labor force still exists based on historically constructed caste lines as non-competing groups, the structure of the urban labor force is becoming more cosmopolitan. Thus what used to be a caste-based labor force is slowly giving way to class-based one. Of course, even in urban areas, the transformation is not total and is limited to white collar jobs. Lower income people usually belong to lower castes in the caste hierarchy with less education and lower skill levels. It is only at the middle range that things are changing dramatically.

THE CHANGING ROLES OF WOMEN

India is certainly witnessing some of the most significant changes in the economic and social status of women in the urban areas and in the nature of the household structure. For the first time we are able to see trends that transcend the caste hierarchy, to a more class based system. This means that caste hierarchy is disappearing among the upper strata of society. This does not however mean that caste differences are themselves disappearing. In other words, economic prosperity has touched people belonging to different castes, and educational levels are increasing along similar lines. Many women from different castes do attend colleges and universities, and are gainfully employed. This has given them both economic and social status. Many young women, in contrast to what had happened in the yester years, are choosing their marriage partners either directly or through some sort of consensus with their parents. Even though many marriages today are still arranged, men and women exercise equal choice in the decision. The decision remains a family decision more by consensus rather than by an imposition from the parents.

The attitudes of women with respect to marriage, career, economic status, are undergoing so many changes that there seem to be intra-generation differences among women within narrow age categories. By that I mean that it is not merely a difference between a parent and a daughter that one expects to find here, but differences among groups of younger women within narrow range of age categories. Thus, the views and modes of behavior of a thirty year old woman in establishing her own identity, may be radically different from those of a twenty five year old, and the view of a twenty five year old may be different from a twenty year old and so on down to younger age groups. These changes are extremely vibrant and turbulent at the same time.

The joint family system is certainly a major structural arrangement that ensures male domination within the household through traditional gender-based household patterns of behavior. More and more, the joint family system in India is giving way to a nuclear family system. When we combine this shift to nuclear family system with the emergence of career roles for women and their ability to generate independent income for the family, there is no question that women's role in household management and decision making is getting stronger. It does not necessarily mean that the nuclear family system can by itself cause these changes to occur, but it is one of the facilitating factors. The other factors are, career opportunities for women, their income generating power, the presence of the elderly in the household or in close physical proximity, the family's adherence or non-adherence to traditional norms of behavior, and attitudes toward changes that have the potential to alienate the families from traditional patterns causing anxieties in daily lives. Add to this the attitudes of friends and families that are part of the social network. If the attitudes within the social network are progressive (or conservative), the attitude of the families will also be progressive (or conservative). One cannot, therefore, minimize the social interaction effect in these matters.

In a number of cases, in spite of the structural changes, the traditional norms are so strong that both men and women closely adhere to the significations and the symbolic processes inherent in the traditional family system. In other words, even though the joint family system as an empirical reality might be disappearing, family values are still cherished and many old family norms are observed. The families feel that there is a lot that the traditional family patterns offer that need to be preserved. For example, the grand parent-grand child relationship is an absolute necessity in many families. In fact, it is the modification of the joint family behavioral norms and not their total abandonment that has been welcomed both by older grand parents and younger parents, and their children. Many husbands are very pleased and relieved that their wives are working, are pursuing jobs if not careers, generating income for the families, and finding happiness in both domestic as well as outside involvement. In this category of people, it is almost impossible to find young men (or women) wanting to marry young women (or men) who are not currently employed, or by virtue of their qualifications not easily employable. Men are not looking for women who would just tend the home, nor women are looking for men who would be economic liabilities. Both men and women seem to prefer life partners with professional qualifications (a doctor, or an accountant, or an MBA etc.,). Both seem to be convinced that they are entering the marriage as nothing but equal partners. Many housewives in their forties or even older feel a vicarious pleasure in seeing their daughters go to college and develop career aspirations denied to them when they were young. They also feel that female children are no longer a burden in this changing society, females as wage earners can only contribute to the welfare of the family. Within the family context, the attitudes toward women are changing, this even from older women and men from an earlier generation, for they suddenly see the world opening up to a part of their own flesh and blood. In this sense, there is no need to discriminate between a daughter and a son and worry about the liminality of the daughter's' status.

What I have seen among the urban middle class people is that the oppressive element of the Indian family seems to have been taken out and a more healthy version of it seems to have been put in its place. The preservation of the family system at any cost seems to be the motivation for these strategies. Much of this arises from what they learn about the West (whether true or not) that families are breaking apart, older parents are being sent away to the purgatory of nursing homes, detached from their families when there is the utmost need for people to be together. As Indians modernize (whatever the term means) or seem to approximate Western oriented independent behavior, it is important to remind ourselves that the individualistic philosophy of the West is not totally embraced by Indians. If I were to describe how the individualist and collectivist principles are being played out in contemporary modern India, I have to say that collectivism is still the preferred model with various adjustments to individual desires. This principle is the cardinal principle of the difference between India and the West and the indications are that it will remain so even as India is changing.

CONCLUSIONS

In conclusion some salient aspects of India that are both challenging and interesting are described briefly in the following:

a) India is multilingual, that is, it has 16 major languages and ten non-comparable scripts. For consumer researchers and practitioners, multi-lingualism presents some challenging issues of translation, semantic representation in advertising and package design. Even for consumers, the semantic differences create problems of meaning and comprehension.

b) India is multi-cultural. (Here, following Maus, an Indianist himself, we have to emphasize that India is culturally diverse but not culturally heterogeneous (Dumont 1986, p. xiv)). This means that various practices relating to food, clothing, the use of symbolic forms, and rituals have regional as well sub-cultural variations, while they also have many common threads both at the religio-social and semantic levels.

c) Indian society is stratified hierarchically and laterally on the basis of caste. Caste is a social category that is unique to India and cannot be compared to race or class while some of its features may have some resemblance to both of them (Beteille 1991).

d) India is multi-religious. The majority (82%) are Hindus, followed by Muslims (12%), and Christians (4%). The rest include Sikhs, Budhists and Parsis. Religious strife in India has been historically confined to Hindus and Muslims although the recent conflicts involving Sikhs have widened its scope. Although religious symbols are not frequently used, it is not uncommon to find them in the ads.

e) India is witnessing some of the most significant changes in the economic and social status of women. The attitudes of women with respect to marriage, career, and their roles in the family and society are undergoing radical changes and there is considerable literature describing these changes (Liddle and Joshi 1986, Sharma 1986, Wadley 1977). The changing roles of women is accompanied by similar changes in the family structure and household systems (Saradamoni 1992).

f) The clash between traditionalism and modernism, or the blending of the two, is a perennial theme that one discovers while studying India, and is played out in different ways depending on the social and historical contexts. From an etic point of view, one can find Indians who are traditional, or modern, or progressive, or even Westernized, or some combination thereof (Chakraborty 1991, Srinivas 1966). From an emic point of view, similar labels are used by Indians to describe themselves, although the term "Westernized" seems the least favored (based on personal interviews). Indians use a combination of this terminology, to represent the notion that on some aspects of their lives, they are modern, while on some other aspects, they are quite traditional. Among many middle-class Indians this ontological tension exists regardless of age or gender, signifying the fear of a possible loss of cultural identity in moving away from their imagined notions of Indianness.

h) In terms of the contemporary power structure based on political, social and economic means, but leaving the caste aside for a moment, we describe India as a multi-layered society. The layer significant for our study includes a variety of groups, the salaried middle class, professionals (lawyers, doctors, business managers, some bureaucrats, etc.,), small entrepreneurs, educationists and the like. It is this layer that is most significant from the point of view of social change. The changing values within the Indian context that are having an impact on the rest of the society seem to find their most resonance in this class of people. People in this category seem to be very ambitious, work very hard, and want to improve their financial condition. We regard this category of people most important for studying the changing consumer culture.

SELECT REFERENCES
(Please contact author for other references)

Appadurai, Arjun (1988), "How to Make a National Cuisine: Cookbook in Contemporary India," *Comparative Studies in Society and History*, Vol 30, 1.

Arnould, Eric (1989), "Toward a Broadened Theory of Preference Formation and the Diffusion of Innovations: Cases From Zinder Province, Niger Republic," *Journal of Consumer Research*, Vol 16,2, 239-267.

Belk, Russell W. (1988), "Third World Consumer Culture," in E.Kumcu and A.F.Firat eds. *Marketing and Development: Toward Broader Dimensions*, JAI Press.

de Pyssler, Bruce (1992), "The Cultural and Political Economy of the Indian Two-Wheeler," in J.F.Sherry, B. Sternthal eds., *Advances in Consumer Research*, Vol. 19, 437-442.

Ger, Guliz, and Russell Belk (1990), Measuring and Comparing Materialism Cross-Culturally, in J.F.Sherry, B. Sternthal eds., *Advances in Consumer Research*, Vol. 17, 186-192.

Mehta, R and R.W.Belk (1991) Artifacts, Identity, and Transition: Favorite Possessions of Indians and Indian Immigrants to the United States," *Journal of Consumer Research*, 17,4, 398-411.

Schnaiberg, Allan (1970), "Measuring Modernism: Theoretical Empirical Explorations," *American Journal of Sociology*, Vol. 76, 399-425.

Singhal, Arvind and Everett Rogers (1989), *India's Information Revolution*, SAGE (India) Publications

Srinivas, M.N. (1966) *Social Change in Modern India*, Berkeley, University of California Press.

Vajpeyi, D. (1982), "Modernity and Industrial Culture of Indian Cities," *Journal of Asian and African Studies*, Vol. XVIII, No. 1-2, 74-97.

Venkatesh, Alladi (1994/95a - Forthcoming) "Ethnoconsumerism: A New Paradigm for the Study of Cross-Cultural Consumer Behavior," in Janeen Costa and Gary Bamossy (eds.) *Marketing in a Multicultural World: Ethnicity, Nationalism, and Identity*," SAGE Publications.

Venkatesh, Alladi (1994/95b - Forthcoming) "Gender Identity in the Indian Context: A Socio-Cultural Construction of the Female Consumer," in Janeen Arnold Costa ed. *Gender and Consumer Behavior*, SAGE Publications.

Venkatesh, Alladi and Suguna Swamy (1994/95 - Forthcoming), "India as an Emerging Consumer Society: A Cultural Analysis," in R.Belk, G.Ger, and C.Schultz eds., *Consumption in Marketizing Economies* (), JAI Press.

Witkowski, Terrence (1993), "The Polish Consumer in Transition," L. McAlister and M.L.Rothschild eds. *Advances in Consumer Research*, Vol. 20, 13-17.

Managing Attention
Chris Janiszewski, University of Florida
Barbara Bickart, Rutgers University-Camden

The study of attention is an enigma. Grocery retailers and manufacturers highlight the importance of attention every time they negotiate a trade promotion that includes a commitment to an end-of-aisle display. Retailers buy full-page newspaper ads, businesses double the size of their Yellow Page displays and direct marketers construct more inviting envelopes all in the hopes of increasing the attention consumers will devote to their message. Despite the tremendous amount of money spent on buying consumer attention, little to no research is done on attention. The rules developed 50 years ago—make it bigger, make it brighter, make is easier to find and read—seem applicable today. Consumer attention is a competitive process that can only be achieved at the expense of others.

For many businesses, attention is not a competitive process, but a managed process. Grocery retailers are not interested in maximizing attention to a single item in a display, but promoting attention to as many items, in as many product categories, as possible. A mass merchandiser is not interested in simply getting consumers to attend to a feature advertisement in the Sunday newspaper, but in attending to all of the products featured in the ad. A catalog retailer not only wants to encourage the consumer to view merchandise, but to remember the merchandise that is being offered. Businesses seek to manage attention and to know the benefits of managed attention on consumer memory, inference making, belief formation and brand choice. This special topic session brought together a set of papers that investigates how retailers can manage attention and the potential benefits of managed attention from a variety of perspectives and in several contexts.

The first paper by Stephen J. Hoch, Zavier Dreze, and Mary E. Purk, described the results of a series of shelf-management experiments that assessed the sales and profit potential of micro-merchandising. These experiments were conducted in 20 different product categories in 60 Dominick's Finer Foods stores over a period of 4 to 6 months. The results suggest that brand shelf position has a significant impact on sales. Moving an item a couple of shelves up or down changes sales by an average of 40%, while moving it horizontally can affect sales by up to 105%. The number of facings allocated to an item influences sales in two ways. First, it limits the number of units available to the consumer and the probability of out-of-stocks; and second, it affects the amount of attention consumers devote to the item—the more facings, the higher the probability of being in the consideration set. These results suggest a small, but reliable influence of manipulating attention to the product display.

The second paper by Chris Janiszewski reported the results of two studies investigating the influence of display factors on attention in multi-item displays. Queuing theory was used to hypothesize that the amount of attention to a single item in a display would decline as the number of salient, potentially focal items surrounding the item increased. The surrounding items could comprise a visual processing queue and longer queues would encourage the visual system to engage in hurried information gathering. Across 48 four-item displays, distance was used to vary the queue size associated with any focal area. As the queue size associated with an area increased from one to two the amount of time spent viewing that area dropped by 8%. There was no decrease in viewing time associated with increasing the queue size from two to three. Similar results were obtained when this hypothesis was tested using measures of attention to catalog pages.

The third paper by Barbara Bickart, Lauranne Buchanan, and Carolyn Simmons discussed the results of an experiment that showed how display structure can be used to create attention, particularly when display structure holds meaning to the consumer. Specifically, they found that display structure affected consumers' perceptions of value for a familiar brand, but not an unfamiliar brand. The authors suggest that for the familiar brand, the display structure violated consumers' expectations, resulting in increased attention to and processing of contextual information. Thus, the use of an accessible brand attitude as an input to brand judgments (versus other, stimulus-based inputs) was partially contingent on whether the display structure violated consumers' expectations.

The final paper by Raymond Burke examined one specific application of managed attention—the processes by which manufacturers can reduce the effects of competitive activities on a new product introduction. The results of a series of computer-based simulated shopping experiments suggest that when a competitor cuts its price, consumers' attention to an unmerchandised new product drops significantly, while attention peaks when the new product was put on promotion. The results suggest that new products can get lost in the clutter at the point of purchase. Merchandising and promotions may enhance consumer attention, especially in the context of competitive promotions.

The session ended with a demonstration of Ray's newest simulated shopping software, which allows the consumer to select an item from the shelf and view it in three dimensions.

For the Smell of It All: Functions and Effects of Olfaction in Consumer Behavior
Deborah J. Mitchell, Temple University

Marketers have long used odor in a variety of contexts to influence consumer cognition and behavior. Some of these applications have been based on strong evidence regarding the effects of odor; some continue to be based more on intuitive beliefs and assumptions. Marketing applications have tended to fall into three broad categories. First, marketers have capitalized on consumers' tendencies to use scent as an inference cue in certain contexts. Thus, cleansers may be scented with a pine scent, based on the knowledge that consumers infer extra cleansing power from that odor. Here odor is a physical product attribute, added to increase the likelihood that consumers will infer positive product attributes and thus evaluate the product more highly.

A second marketing application of odor has received widespread media and consumer attention: the use of scent strips or scratch-and-sniff attachments in print advertising. Here again odor is emphasized by the marketer as a physical product attribute; product trial based on that attribute is made possible by the scent strip or scratch-and-sniff technology.

Finally, the third general application of odor is distinct in both its orientation and purpose. In the first two applications, product attribute information is inferred or conveyed through scent. The orientation is internal or product-specific; the goal is related to product attribute information. However, the use of ambient odor is not necessarily to communicate product attribute information but rather to provide an atmospheric, or stimulus in the external environment. Here, odor is loaded into the atmosphere of a consumer setting, such as a retail store or mall, with the general intent to influence shoppers.

The widespread and increasing use of odor by marketers has been exceeded perhaps only by the number of claims made about its efficacy in the media. However, most of these claims are not based on psychological theory, nor have they been examined in an academic setting. Fundamental questions relating to the effects of odor on mood, memory, and purchase behavior remain open. In addition, questions regarding how potential effects of odor might vary with its functional application (e.g., ambient odor vs. odor in print advertising) remain largely unaddressed. However, this is beginning to change.

This session brought together researchers from varied empirical and methodological backgrounds, working on primary, different but related, dimensions of olfaction and consumer behavior. In addition, the studies examined different marketing applications of odor, reflecting the diversity in which odor is used in consumer environments. Theoretical implications for a general understanding of olfaction were addressed in the concluding discussion by Susan Knasko.

The first paper, by Mitchell et al., was concerned with ambient odor and consumer decision-making. Two theoretical approaches, one emphasizing odor as primarily an affect inducer, the other focused primarily on odor and cognitive mediation, were examined in the contexts of both static and dynamic consumer choice. Next the Ellen and Bone study, adopting an Elaboration Likelihood Model approach, used marketing applications of odor in scratch-and-sniff advertisements to investigate the effect of olfaction on attitude toward the ad (Aad) and attitude toward the brand (Ab). Finally, Chakravarti et al investigated how product odors may affect memory for those products, and how odor may facilitate or inhibit visual imagery while encoding product information.

The Heroes of Consumption and the Consumption of Heroes
Steve Vander Veen, Calvin College

The archetypal hero, according to Jungian analysis, manifests itself in human behavior. The objective of this session was to show how the archetypal hero manifests itself in consumer behavior and what this might imply for marketing managers.

The first paper by Steve Vander Veen attempted to show that all consumption is ritualistic, all rituals have heroes, and all consumption is the consumption of heroes. Ritualistic behavior has three stages: separation, transition, and incorporation; yet, it also has elements of the heroic adventure: separation, initiation, return. In terms of hierarchy of effects, it is helpful to think of the decision-making process as "dream-do-rationalize-share." However, different consumers emphasize different aspects of the hierarchy of effects at different times. Some consumers may be more "hedonic" and others more rational. Those more rational rely more on heroes outside of themselves (horizontal role shift) and seek "communitas," while those more hedonic rely more on the hero within (vertical role shift) and seek a "peak-experience." Products then become either horizontal or vertical "power enhancers," to either help one "be like Mike" or "just do it" — "it" remaining undefined. Yet, to be heroic, a consumer has to both "do" and "share."

The second paper by Mary Ann McGrath and Cele Otnes reported the findings of a series of qualitative studies. Common to the studies of Christmas shopping, gift-giving, wedding arrangements, etc. was a storytelling format in which the consumer emerged as hero. This paper elaborated and exemplified three shopping scenarios enriched by phenomenological descriptions in which informants conceptualized themselves as victorious protagonists. One scenario described the consumer as a valorous gift-shopper involved in a treasure hunt for the perfect gift. A second scenario described the consumer as vanquishing the retail institution, possessing enhanced powers of observation, discrimination, taste, and judgement. The consumer scans and comparison shops and in the end emerges victorious with the perfect object, frequently at a bargain price. A third scenario described the consumer as a liberator of defenseless objects enslaved in a retail setting. In this context, the object becomes animated, invested with status and significance, and becomes elevated, sacralized, and transformed. Without the shopper, the object would have languished in mundane obscurity.

The third paper by Jolita Kisielius and Joseph Cherian reported on findings of an experiment in which an endorser was personified as a hero by manipulating the endorser's biography. In this experiment, two biographies were compared. In one, the biography was manipulated to represent a credible source. In the second, this same biography was given the added dimension of having periods of separation, initiation, and return. A second independent variable manipulated the relevance of the brand being endorsed; i.e., did the hero endorser utilize the brand pre-separation or post-separation? A third independent variable manipulated the type of endorsement, making it either "rational" or "global." The experiment hypothesized that (i) the more dramatic hero would garner more positive affect, and (ii) the dramatic hero would improve respondents' attitudes toward the product. In terms of interactions, the (iii) influence of the power enhancer was expected be most positive post-separation in conjunction with the more dramatic hero, and (iv) global endorsements used in conjunction with the more dramatic hero were expected to most improve respondents' attitudes toward the product. The more dramatic hero was found to significantly garner more positive affect.

The comments by discussant Sidney Levy pointed out why some consumer behaviorists may not be naturally enamored with myth and meaning in marketing. For one, consumer behaviorists may ask: "What is it?" or "I don't understand it!" Second, they may claim: "Well, I already knew that!" Yet, we all should! Some of the ideas presented were first discussed by Plato. Levy has been discussing myth and meaning in marketing for the last twenty years! Third, they may ask: "Why do we need it?" The answer is that the myths we hear and read about are the things we all feel. Myths tap into the fundamental and pragmatic issues of life. Finally, they may ask: "Is it true? Do I believe it?" Of course, this is what all knowledge ultimately comes down to.

To conclude, consumers are potentially the heroes of consumption if they do and share. For marketing managers, it can be informative to think of consumers as potential heroes, shopping as heroic quest, products as "power enhancers" (either describing or creating roles) or as "damsels in distress," retail institutions as "villains" or "dragons," endorsers as heroes or as "little old men or old crones," etc.

The Consumption of Heroes and the Hero Hierarchy of Effects

Steve Vander Veen, Calvin College

This paper utilizes the Jungian hero archetype to define a consumption archetype. A hero hierarchy of effects is suggested and applied introspectively.

I. INTRODUCTION

Many marketing scholars make distinctions between and among cognitive learning (cognition-affect-conation), behavioral learning (cognition-conation-affect), hedonic consumption (affect-conation-cognition) and other effects hierarchies en route to an attitude (see, e.g., Solomon 1992 and Henderson and Rust 1987). Though Smith and Swinyard (1982) have attempted to integrate and distinguish between trial users and committed users (low order cognition—low order affect—trial purchase—high order cognition—high order affect—commitment purchase) and Hirschman (1988) to compare consumer problem-solving behavior to the heroic quest, all hierarchies presume purchase behavior is the "end all" of conation. But is it? And what does it matter?

This paper utilizes the Jungian hero archetype to define a consumption archetype and a hero hierarchy of effects. This new hierarchy suggests that purchase behavior is not the epitome of conation and, because it is not, the role of promotion has to be looked at differently.

II. ARCHETYPES AND CONSUMER BEHAVIOR LITERATURE

Stern proposed literary criticism as "a branch of humanistic inquiry that may provide an additional way of learning about consumers" (1989, p. 322). Others include Holbrook (1987) and Calder and Tybout (1987). One particular school is that of archetype or myth, which identifies and characterizes forms of text by defining "collective psychological, cultural, and literary thought patterns or archetypes" (Stern, ibid).

This particular school is indebted to Jung and, like Jung, appears to be gaining momentum in an age of postmodernism (Griffin 1989). Manifestations of the myth school can be seem in current discussions of archetypal psychology, process theology, and even consumer behavior, resuming work begun by McCracken and Pollay (as reported in Stern 1989), Olson (1981), Sherry (1987), Walle (1990), and others.

III. THE ARCHETYPES OF SELF AND HERO

William Shakespeare wrote that all the world was a stage, transversed by actors in various stages of life. Thomas and Biddle (1979) went beyond Shakespeare and introduced the world to man's various roles intra-stage. Jung introduced the world to the author-director, actor-manager.

> Thus, throughout the whole cycle of life, the archetype stands behind the scenes, as it were, as a kind of author-director or actor-manager, producing the tangible performance that proceeds on the public (and the private) stage (Stevens 1982, p. 52).

The theory of archetypes is said to have originated with Plato's belief in the soul (Nagy 1991, p. 157). But archetypes are more than spiritual, they are instinctive (biological) as well. Further, archetypes are collective as well as individual, objective as well as subjective.

Jung concluded that there are "certain collective unconscious conditions which act as regulators and stimulators of creative fantasy activity". Insofar, they act like instincts. But they also have a "distinctly numinous character" which can only be described as "spiritual" (Stevens 1982, p. 169).

Archetypes reside in the unconscious. However, they influence conscious behavior through an individuation process (cf. Maslow's self-actualization). Their mode of manifestation is active imagination, a mechanism for resolving conflict between the conscious and the unconscious, which can be tapped via dream analysis (Aziz 1990, p. 25).

A main difference between archetypes and the concept of schemata utilized in cognitive psychology is that archetypes reside in individuals from before the time individuals are born. In fact, it is "the essential role of personal experience...to develop what is already there" (Stevens 1982, p. 16).

Like schemata, archetypes are believed to contain emotions, images, and scripts for action: "Archetypes are systems of readiness for action, and at the same time images and emotions" (ibid, p. 62). Specifically, it may be archetypal complexes that are most closely associated with the cognitive processing concept of schemata (ibid, p. 65).

The archetypal system *in toto* was defined by Jung as "the Self," which "has programmed within it the complete scenario for individual life (ibid, p. 76).

Thus, the hero archetype, as seen in dream and myth ("dream is the personalized myth, myth the depersonalized dream"—Campbell 1949, p. 19) and, for that matter, all of literature and life (in particular, sports—Walle 1990), reflects the archetype of the self; i.e., the travails of the hero are the travails of the self.

> The hero must conquer the same "dragon" to which the psychotic has fallen victim. He is the one who goes alone to seek it out when other, choosing to cling to their present level of security, remain behind. Finally, the hero is the one who undertakes the battle and ultimately is given, because of his sincerity, the strength tho overcome the dragon and take possession of the "treasure hard to attain." The winning of the "treasure hard to attain" is, of course, an allusion on the part of Jung to an experience of the archetype of total unity, the self, the goal of the process of individuation (Aziz 1990, p.29).

"The hero is the man of self-achieved submission" (Campbell 1949, p. 25), submission to the psyche (or self) and submission to the path of the psyche; i.e., death and rebirth, doing and sharing.

> In a word, the first work of the hero is to retreat from the world scene of secondary effects to those causal zones of the psyche where the difficulties really reside, and there to clarify the difficulties, eradicate them in his own case...and break through to the undistorted, direct experience and assimilation of..."the archetypal images"...His second solemn task and deed...is to return then to us, transfigured, and teach the lesson he has learned of life renewed (ibid, pp. 17-20).

IV. THE CONSUMPTION ARCHETYPE

Symbolic of the self archetype is the hero archetype and the now proposed consumption archetype. The consumption archetype can be seen manifested in seemingly eclectic bits of consumer behavior literature and in disciplines as seemingly diverse as anthropology and theology, psychology and sociology via the following three propositions: (i) all consumption is ritualistic, (ii) all rituals have heroes, and (iii) all consumption is the consumption of heroes.

A. All Consumption is Ritualistic

The first proposition of the consumption archetype is that all consumption is ritualistic, meaning that the goal of consumption is some combination vertical and horizontal role shift leading to a unspecified role of roles, a combination of roles, where work=joy. This role shift occurs via the aid of "call finders," or goods which help consumers uncover their role or "calling" in life.

Goffman (1959), e.g., introduced the "dramaturgical perspective" which compared consumers to actors playing different roles with the help of scripts, props, and costumes, initiating the idea of role shift and power finding. Vance Packard spoke dramatically of role shift, saying that we "convert the buying and use of goods into rituals, that we seek spirit satisfactions, our ego satisfactions, in consumption (1960, p. 25). Wright and Snow, e.g., remarked that television commercials "portray nothing less than the transformation of the individual through consumption (1980, p. 3). Schudson noted that products say "buy me and everything will be easier for you"...(1984, p. 6). Levy (1981) reinforced the idea that products stand for something else and that products are consumed with scripts. Rook and Levy (1983) investigated the relation between consumer myths and their enactment in everyday ritualistic behavior. Rook defined ritual as:

> a type of expressive, symbolic activity constructed of multiple behaviors that occur in fixed episodic sequence, and that tend to be repeated over time. Ritual behavior is dramatically scripted and acted out and is performed with formality, seriousness, and inner intensity (1985, p. 252).

Solomon and Anand (1985) connected ritualistic behavior to ritual artifacts (i.e., power finders) or products employed symbolically to operationalize the ritual. Solomon (1983) put forth the idea that products define social roles. Belk (1988) described how products could "extend" self.

Thus products are more than signs or containers of antecedent psychic contents. Products can and must be an expression of a purposeful course that "psychic energy follows," representative of a definite but not yet realized goal (Aziz 1990, p. 16).

Therefore, in defining (and in not defining) social roles, call finders give consumers the power to shape identities (see, e.g., Belk and Mehta 1991, Schouten 1991). When these call finders help provide "self-transcending, extraordinary experiences" (Belk, Wallendorf, and Sherry 1989), or peak-experiences (Maslow 1976), they are vertical in nature and are sacred. When these call finders result exclusively in "communitas," they are profane. In fact, when the

> boon brought from the transcendent deep becomes quickly rationalized into nonentity, the need becomes great for another hero to refresh the word (Campbell 1949, p. 218).

The goal of ritualistic consumption could be described as self-actualization (Maslow 1954), meaning, spiritual consumption (Holbrook 1987, Hirschman 1985), a feeling of achieving the role general, which represents the sum total of all roles consumers play and determines what the consumer does for society and what s/he can expect from it (Thomas and Biddle 1979).

In effect, therefore, it is the role of the hero to help bring what is unconscious to consciousness. In fact, the hero's quest is a vertical ritual of one. Over time, this ritual becomes socialized (cf. Belk 1989, p. 7) via narrative, drama, and myth (Raglan 1936); the ritual becomes collective, horizontal, accepted as rational behavior, and something profane because it acts as a giant leveler. In other words, the ritual of one in the end becomes something very unheroic.

The stages of role shift, again which mimic the self and which are mimicked by the hero, consist of (i) separation, in which a person disengages from a social role or status, (ii) transition, a liminal state of social limbo (Turner 1982) in which a person eventually adapts to fit new roles, and (iii) incorporation, in which a person integrates the self with the new role or status (van Gennep 1908, as reported in Schouten 1991). Again, these stages resemble the stages of problem-solving (cf. Hirschman 1988).

B. All Rituals have Heroes (Because Heroes Start Them)

Lord Raglan (1936) explained that the ability of ritual to confer benefits on whom or on whose behalf the ritual was being performed was enhanced and perpetuated by narrative, drama, myth, and out of myth, heroes. According to Campbell (1949), heroes are personifications of myths, and myths the windows of culture.

Thus, it is the innovation and the socialization of that enacted dream that becomes the context for the hero; i.e., the hero originally separates himself from existing social roles, enters "uncharted territory," conquers it and returns. The hero returns because, as part of the individuation process, a hero "'does not shut one out from the world, but gathers the world to oneself'" (Aziz 1990, p. 41). For this reason, "relationships with objects are never two-way (person-thing), but always three way (person-thing-person)" (Belk 1988, p. 157).

McCracken also saw the connection of heroes to ritualistic behavior, describing North Americans as active consumers of the meaning made available by the celebrity world and admitting that "we have some general sense that rituals play an important part in the process" (1989, p. 317). Further, that "celebrities are seen to have created the clear, coherent, and powerful selves that everyone seeks" (ibid, p. 318).

Thus, a short version of the heroic hierarchy could be simply: dream-do-rationalize-share; i.e., affect—conation (trial)—cognition—conation (share), for "no man is an island" and the utility of possession comes from a utility of sharing.

C. All Consumption is the Consumption of Heroes (to Locate the Self and be Heroic)

Therefore, if all consumption is ritualistic and if all rituals have heroes, all consumption is the consumption of heroes. This proposition parallels the psychological concepts of agency and identity (see Palus, Nasby, and Easton 1990).

Thus, consumers are agents seeking identity. Further, "we believe that a primary way in which people represent their identities is narratively, in the form of stories", and that "versions of the story are told to oneself and to others" (ibid, p. 505).

V. THE HERO'S JOURNEY

As stated above, the hero's journey broadly consists of separation (S), initiation (I), and return (R), but includes more specific adventures. These more specific adventures are outlined by Campbell.

Relative to Separation, first the hero receives the "call to adventure." Here the "familiar life horizon has been outgrown; the old concepts, ideals, and emotional patterns no longer fit" (Campbell

1949, p. 51). It is a time when "destiny has summoned the hero and transferred his spiritual center of gravity form within the pale of society to a zone unknown" (ibid, p. 58). Second, the hero may refuse the call. Third, for those who have not refused the call,

> the first encounter of the hero-journey is with a protective figure (often a little old crone or old man) who provides the adventurer with amulets against the dragon forces he is about to pass (ibid, p. 67).

Fourth, the hero crosses the first threshold. The little old crone or old man represent personifications of the hero's own destiny; in fact, they represent personifications of the hero's own psyche. Finally, the last event of Separation is within "the belly of the whale." It is period of rebirth for the hero, or, as Ursinus and Olevianus (1563) state in the *Heidelberg Catechism*, "the mortification of the old man, and the quickening of the new" (Q&A 88).

Relative to Initiation, the first phase is one of "the road to trials." These trials might include crossing mountains, ditches, or desserts. In fairy tales it is the prince slaying the dragon. A second phase is "the meeting with the goddess."

> This is the crisis at the nadir, the zenith, or at the uttermost edge of the earth, at the central point of the cosmos, in the tabernacle of the temple, or within the darkness of the deepest chamber of the heart (Campbell 1949, p. 109)....Woman, in the picture language of mythology, represents the totality of what can be known. The hero is the one who comes to know (ibid, p. 116).

The third, fourth, and fifth phases of initiation (i.e., "woman as temptress," "atonement with the father," and "apotheosis") are the ones where the hero learns that he and the woman and the father are, in essence, the same. In Jungian terms, all belong to the Psyche. In Christendom, a parallel structure is the Trinity, except that the hero is an "image-bearer" versus God himself.

The final phase is "the ultimate boon." The boon is "simply a symbol of life energy stepped down to the requirements of a certain specific case" (ibid, p. 189).

> The agony of breaking through personal limitations is the agony of spiritual growth. Art, literature, myth and cult, philosophy, and ascetic disciplines are instruments to help the individual past his limiting horizons into spheres of ever-expanding realization (ibid, p. 190).

Regarding Return, the hero brings the "runes of wisdom, the Golden Fleece, or his sleeping princess, back into the kingdom of humanity (ibid, p. 193). But the responsibility is frequently refused. It is Moses refusing to deal with the people Israel after coming down from Mount Sinai. The second phase is "the magic flight." Phase three a rescue from without, if necessary. To finish the monomyth, the hero must

> re-enter with his boon the long-forgotten atmosphere where men who are fractions imagine themselves to be complete. He has yet to confront society with his ego-shattering, life-redeeming elixir, and take the return blow of reasonable queries, hard resentment, and good people at a loss to comprehend (ibid, p. 216).

VI. A CONSUMER'S JOURNEY: BUYING AN MINIVAN

A. Separation

1. The Call to Adventure: Jill and Steve see TV advertisements for minivans. They also notice their friends drive them. Steve is also aware that if the family buys a camper-trailer in the next two years, they have nothing to pull it with. Further, Jill and Steve plan to be youth leaders at their church—a van would be convenient for social activities. Is being a youth director and a family man part of that magical role of roles? In what proportion?

2. Refusal of the Call: Steve balks at the idea of buying a minivan because it is expensive. Jill does not like how "boxy" they look. Minivans would be so hard to clean.

3. Supernatural Aid: But friends convince them that minivans are great for traveling—they keep the kids far apart so there is much less commotion and fighting. Is this a good reason? Is this being a good parent? Would this be fulfilling? But with this in mind, the next trip to grandmother's is unbearable—all three kids seem to be fighting continuously. Jill buys *Car and Driver* and *Consumer Reports*. Jill and Steve start driving through car dealerships on off-hours.

4. The Crossing of the First Threshold: Jill and Steve finally visit a dealer. They visit the dealer and salesperson who sold them their last car, a Sentra. "He's a nice guy and he's not pushy," says Steve. "And he sells a great product—Nissan." Again, the salesperson, Gerrit, is not pushy. He's suggestive. He asks a lot of questions. He seems orientated toward the future. He convinces them to test drive a Quest XE. He gets the keys from the manager.

5. In the Belly of the Whale: Alone for a drive, Jill and Steve attempt to confirm all Jill has read about Nissan minivans. All is confirmed. They are strong believers. But Jill has a little of "doubting Thomas" in her and wants to check out other vehicles. The salesperson at the Plymouth dealership is unfamiliar with the Nissan Quest and compares it with a station wagon! Steve, already satisfied with the Nissan and with Gerrit, is particularly upset. The test drive is also not particularly impressive. Steve has all the ammunition he needs. The salesperson at the Mercury dealership notes that he has never been inside of a Quest, and does not really know how the Quest and the Villager compare. Again, Jill knows more about competitor's minivans than the salesperson. Steve has more ammunition. The salesperson at another Nissan dealership has not seen the Mercury Villager. Ironically, both vehicles were designed by Nissan and built by Ford! The last salesperson of the day "cut to the chase." A seller of Mercury Villagers, this man was all price and stated he was only interested in getting his inventory out-the-door. "This guy ought to work at K-Mart," thought Steve. "Over the next five years what he is saving me is squat. Is he interested in how this vehicle will fulfill my needs? I doubt it."

B. Initiation

1. The Road of Trials: Jill and Steve decide to buy. The next problem is financing. Will Gerrit stand behind them? Jill and Steve wonder what their parents, siblings, friends, and fellow church-members will say. Will the kids be hindered from fighting on long trips? Will the vehicle help Jill and Steve be "successful" youth leaders? Will the vehicle be able to pull a camper through the mountains and hold enough luggage for a "successful" vacation (i.e., will this vehicle not make Steve a better family man but show him he is a good one)? Will this vehicle help Jill and Steve find their role of roles?

C. Return

How will Jill and Steve tell their story and to whom?

VII. APPLYING THE HERO HIERARCHY OF EFFECTS

With Smith and Swinyard, the hero hierarchy makes heavy emphasis on trial purchase for high involvement products, such as automobiles. Trial purchase is, in effect, the period in which the new car buyer is in the "belly of the whale." Here the buyer is and should be "cut-off" from the dealer, the salesperson, from friends, and from advertising for it is here the buyer must decide for himself.

But the hero hierarchy goes further, emphasizing in particular the importance of the "protective figure...who provides the adventurer with amulets against the dragon forces he is about to pass." The car dealer and *Consumer Reports* have to give the consumer reasons for rationalizing the purchase. In addition, the car dealer has to entice the buyer to get into the "belly of the whale." In other words, someone needs to say "Just do it" and someone else need to say "This is why—to be 'like Mike.'" In other words, the Share is emphasized. If marketers are providing consumers with an experience, they also have to provide them some semantics for sharing.

In addition, there are other notables. The car dealership, e.g., represents the "threshold guardian" which can be passed via keys given by the car salesperson. Here must be where the salesperson vs. manager "game" originated in consumer buying situations.

Advertising would seem to play a dual role, either serving as "the call to adventure" or the "gentle divinity" carrying the consumer back across the threshold. Thus, advertising has a particularly difficult role. As caller to the adventure, it would seem to have to be emotionally awakening, an imagination-prompter. Here the spokesperson would be the "little old man or crone." As a gentle divinity, advertising would likely have to be more cognitive, preparing the hero as God prepared Moses to face the people Israel and Pharoah of the Egyptians.

Finally, the hero hierarchy suggests that involvement is highest right after trial purchase. Here the consumer is not only experiencing the product with nearly all of his senses but he is also thinking up reasons to defend his purchase (or non-purchase). This, again, would have implications for advertising: advertising has to enhance involvement at the "call to adventure" and has to assume respondents are already high involved in the initial stages of return. Also, advertising needs to be emotional at the "call" and more rational at "return."

In addition, there are some "macro" implications. The hero hierarchy of effects suggests that in terms of Product Life Cycle, the stages of Maturity and Decline could be characterized by profane and meaningless product use. Also, in terms of the Diffusion of Innovations, late Majority and Laggards would be rational versus "hedonic" users.

VIII. CONCLUSION

So who is this masked man, the hero? The hero is someone who dreams, acts on those dreams, rationalizes his action, and shares the means to his fulfillment. He is heroic for helping others uncover their selves.

Further, few heroes fit all, because self-actualization (cf. the Christian concept of Sanctification) is as much a subjective as an objective process, and there may be as many roads to self-actualization as their are people. Aquinas once wrote that humans are made in the image of God but that since God is infinite He may be mirrored only through a virtually infinite number of humans (cf. Jung's concept of Synchronicity).

Finally, few heroes are forever. When the power of one hero becomes completely rationalized, the sheep seek a new shepherd. Yet without a shepherd, all sheep are astray (cf. Isaiah 53:6).

X. REFERENCES

Aziz, Robert (1990), *C.G. Jung's Psychology of Religion and Synchronicity*, New York: State University of New York Press, 1990.

Belk, Russell W. (1988), "Possessions and the Extended Self," *Journal of Consumer Research* 15 (September): 139-168.

_____, Melanie Wallendorf, and John F. Sherry, Jr., "The Sacred and the Profane in Consumer Behavior: Theodicy on the Odyssey," *Journal of Consumer Research* 16 (June): 1-38.

_____ and Raj Mehta (1991), "Artifacts, Identity, and Transition: Favorite Possessions of Indians and Indian Immigrants to the United States," *Journal of Consumer Research* 17 (March): 398-411.

Calder, Bobby J. and Alice M. Tybout, "What Consumer Research Is..." *Journal of Consumer Research* 14(June, 1987):136-40.

Campbell, Joseph (1949), *The Hero with a Thousand Faces*, Princeton, NJ: Princeton University Press.

Goffman, Erving (1959), *The Presentation of Self in Everyday Life*, Garden City, NJ: Doubleday.

Griffin, David Ray (1989), "Introduction: Archetypal Psychology and Process Philosophy: Complementary Postmodern Movements" in Griffin (ed.), *Archetypal Process: Self and Divine in Whitehead, Jung, and Hillman*, Evanston, IL: NU Press.

Henderson, Pamela W and Roland T. Rust (1987), "An Integrative Physiological Model of Advertising Response," *Research in Marketing* 9: 185-210.

Hirschman, Elizabeth (1985), "Primitive Aspects of Consumption in Modern American Society," *Journal of Consumer Research* 12 (September): 142-154.

_____ (1988), "Consumer Behavior Theories as Heroic Quest," in Srull (ed.) *Advances in Consumer Research* 16, Provo, UT: Association for Consumer Research.

Holbrook, Morris B. (1987) "What is Consumer Research?," *Journal of Consumer Research* 14 (June): 128-132.

Levy, Sidney J (1981), "Interpretating Consumer Mythology: A Structural Approach to Consumer Behavior," *Journal of Marketing* 45 (Summer): 49-61.

Maslow, Abraham (1954), *Motivation and Personality*, New York: Harper and Row.

_____ (1976), *The Farther Reaches of Human Nature*, New York: Viking Press.

McCracken, Grant (1989), "Who is the Celebrity Endorser? Cultural Foundations of the Endorsement Process," *Journal of Consumer Research* 16 (December): 310-320.

Nagy, Marilyn (1991), *Philisophical Issues in the Psychology of C.G. Jung*, New York: State University of New York Press, 1991.

Olson, Jerry (1981), "Presidential Address—1981: Toward a Science of Consumer Behavior," in Mitchell (ed.) *Advances in Consumer Research* 9, Provo, UT: Association for Consumer Research.

Packard, Vance (1960), *The Wastemakers*, New York: D. Mackay.

Palus, Charles J., William Nasby, and Randolph D. Easton (1990), "Executive Identity and the Hero's Story: The Voyage of Dodge Morgan and the American Promise," *Journal of Applied Behavioral Science* 26 (4): 501-527.

Raglan, Lord (1936), *The Hero: A Study of Tradition, Myth, and Drama*, London: Watts and Company.

Rook, Dennis W. and Sidney J. Levy (1983), "Psychological Themes in Consumer Grooming Rituals," in Bagozzi and Tybout (eds.) *Advances in Consumer Research*, Ann Arbor, MI: Association for Consumer Research.

Rook, Dennis W. (1985), "The Ritual Dimension of Consumer Behavior," *Journal of Consumer Research* 12 (Dec): 251-264.

Schouten, John W. (1991), "Selves in Transition: Symbolic Consumption in Personal Rites of Passage and Identity Reconstruction," *Journal of Consumer Research* 17 (March): 412-422.

Schudson, Michael (1984), *Advertising: The Uneasy Persuasion*, New York: Basic Books.

Sherry, John F. Jr. (1987), "Advertising as a Cultural System," in Umiker-Sebeok (ed.) *Marketing and Semiotics: New Directions in the Study of Signs for Sale*, Berlin: Mouton de Gruyter.

Smith, Robert E. and William R. Swinyard (1982), "Information Response Models: An Integrated Approach," *Journal of Marketing* 46 (Winter): 81-93.

Solomon, Michael R. (1983), "The Role of Products as Social Stimuli: A Symbolic Interactionism Perspective," *Journal of Consumer Research* 10 (December): 319-328.

_____ and Punam Anand (1985), "Ritual Costumes and Status Transition: The Female Business Suit as Totemic Emblem," in Holbrook and Hirschman (eds.) *Advances in Consumer Research*, Ann Arbor: Association for Consumer Research.

_____ (1992), *Consumer Behavior: Buying, Having, and Being*, Boston: Allyn and Bacon.

Stern, Barbara (1989), "Literary Criticism and Consumer Research: Overview and Illustrative Analysis," *Journal of Consumer Research* 16 (December): 322-344.

Stevens, Anthony (1982), *Archetypes: A Natural History of the Self*, New York: William Morrow and Company, Inc.

Thomas, Edwin J. and Bruce J. Biddle (1979), "The Nature and History of Role Theory in Biddle and Thomas (eds.) *Role Theory: Concepts and Research*, Huntington, NY: Robert E. Krieger Publishing Company.

Turner, Victor W. (1982), *From Ritual to Theater: The Human Seriousness of Play*, New York: Performing Arts Journal Publications.

Ursinus, Zacharias and Caspar Olevianus (1959, orig. 1563) "The Heidelberg Catechism" in *Psalter Hymnal, Centennial Edition*, Publication Committee of the Christian Reformed Church.

Walle, Alf H. (1990), "Finding the Epic Hero," *Marketing Insights* (Spring): 60-67.

Wright, David E. and Robert E. Snow (1980), "Consumption as Ritual in the High Technology Society," in Browne (ed.) *Rituals and Ceremonies in the Popular Culture*, Bowling Green, OH: Bowling Green University Popular Press.

The Persuasive Effects of Evaluation, Expectancy and Relevancy Dimensions of Incongruent Visual and Verbal Information

Charles S. Areni, Texas Tech University
K. Chris Cox, Texas Tech University

ABSTRACT

Though research on *memory* processes has addressed the influence of incongruency between visually and verbally presented information in advertisements, little is known regarding the effects of visual-verbal incongruency on *persuasion* processes. Moreover, the consumer behavior literature has examined only a subset of the various dimensions of incongruency. A review of the literature on schema theory suggests *expectancy*, *evaluation*, and *relevancy* as important dimensions of visual-verbal incongruency. The persuasion literature further suggests several testable research propositions regarding the effects of each dimension of incongruency.

With the exception of the radio medium, most advertisements present the audience with visual and verbal information. However, until recently, most of the approaches to studying the *persuasive* impact of advertising focused on the impact of product attribute claims (c.f., Lutz, 1975). Fortunately, Mitchell and Olson (1981) introduced a new direction for research by demonstrating that visual elements in ads influence brand attitudes independently of verbal attribute claims.

Subsequent research attempted to identify the various *processes* by which visual elements influence attitude change. Visual information was found to influence persuasion via its ability to: (1) elicit a positive attitude toward the ad (Mitchell & Olson, 1981; Miniard, Bhatla, & Rose, 1990), (2) induce simple judgment heuristics (Petty & Cacioppo, 1981b; Petty, Cacioppo, & Schumann, 1983), and (3) influence brand attribute perceptions (Petty & Cacioppo, 1981b; Edell & Staelin, 1983). However, these studies continued to view visual and verbal elements in advertisements as influencing persuasion *independently* of one another. Yet, most print and television ads are designed so that visual and verbal elements *interact* to produce the overall message (Nylen, 1986), suggesting the need for a more integrated approach.

Research regarding the impact of advertising on *memory* has adopted a more integrated perspective with respect to the impact of visual and verbal elements (Kisielius & Sternthal, 1984; Houston, Childers, & Heckler, 1987; Heckler & Childers, 1992). Houston et al. (1987), borrowing from schema theory, identified the degree of *incongruency* of visual and verbal elements as an important influence on the recall and recognition of various information presented in an ad. Although originating in the memory literature, Heckler and Childers (1992) have recently proposed the incongruency construct as a useful conceptual basis for examining the persuasive effects of visual and verbal advertising components.

While the marketing literature has tended to adopt a unidimensional view, the literature on schema theory suggests multiple dimensions of visual-verbal incongruency. Based on a review of this literature, the present study adds *evaluation* to the *expectancy* and *relevancy* dimensions suggested by Heckler and Childers (1992). Research examining the elaboration likelihood model of persuasion (Petty & Cacioppo, 1981b, 1986) and the heuristic-systematic model of persuasion (Chaiken, 1980, 1987) suggests that the relevancy dimension of visual-verbal incongruency influences the process by which visual elements persuade an audience, whereas the evaluation and expectancy dimensions influence the nature and amount of thought devoted to visual and verbal elements, thereby moderating their persuasive impact. Formal research propositions are derived regarding the role of each form of visual-verbal incongruency in persuasion.

SCHEMA THEORY

The theoretical foundation for much of the work regarding incongruent visual and verbal elements stems from schema theory (Houston et al., 1987). A schema is a cognitive structure that comprises an individual's knowledge about a given domain (Taylor & Crocker, 1981). One of the basic principles underlying all conceptualizations of schemas is that they represent expectations that guide the processing of incoming information from the environment (Schank & Abelson, 1977). For a given knowledge domain, then, incoming stimuli can be thought of as being consistent, inconsistent, or irrelevant to an existing schema (Hastie, 1981).

Early research in the area of schema theory focused on memory for schema congruent and incongruent information (c.f., Hastie, 1981; Srull, 1981). Many of these studies produced apparently conflicting results until Srull (1981) made the distinction between investigations employing re*call* tasks and those entailing *recognition* tasks. He argued, persuasively, that schema incongruent information would be better recalled because it necessitates greater elaboration to resolve the inconsistency, thus creating a larger number of associative links in memory. These associative links, then, provide a greater number of potentially successful cues, increasing the likelihood that the incongruent information will be recalled. However, in recognition tasks the cues are present in the environment, so self-generation is unnecessary. Congruent information is easily linked to the schema representation during encoding, facilitating later recognition.

Houston et al. (1987, p.362) suggest that in the context of processing information in an advertisement, visual elements provide hypotheses or expectations as to the nature of the verbal appeal. These expectations are either confirmed or disconfirmed. They demonstrated that ads presenting incongruent visual and verbal information produced greater recognition and recall when the picture and the brand name were interactive (i.e., related semantically—see Lutz & Lutz, 1977). More importantly, given the purpose of the present study, Heckler & Childers (1992) demonstrated that, in the absence of an interactive picture, recall and recognition of incongruent visual information is superior to that for congruent visual information. Their research is also important because, unlike previous research, it presented a multidimensional view of visual-verbal incongruency. However, a review of the schema theory literature suggests that only a subset of the dimensions of incongruency necessary for understanding persuasion have been identified in the consumer behavior literature.

EVALUATIVE AND THEMATIC DIMENSIONS OF INCONGRUENCY

Several researchers have discussed multiple forms or dimensions on which incoming information can be incongruent with an existing schema. The most basic distinction, however, is between thematic (or *descriptive*) and *evaluative* dimensions of schema incongruency (Felipe, 1970; Wyer & Gordon, 1982; Fiske & Pavelchak, 1986).

Evaluative Incongruency

Srull and Wyer's (1989) model of person schemas includes multiple forms of evaluative incongruity. They identify three types of information that may exist within a schema: specific behaviors, personality traits, and evaluative concepts. If these personality traits are evaluatively consistent, then an overall evaluative concept of the person is formed and the specific behaviors of an individual are linked to the concept. If, on the other hand, the personality traits are evaluatively inconsistent, then an evaluative concept cannot be formed, and the specific behaviors remain linked to disjoint personality traits. Research suggests that individuals elaborate more and have superior memory for evaluatively incongruent information (Wyer & Gordon, 1982; Wyer & Martin, 1986).

The notion of evaluative incongruency can easily be adapted to the context of visual and verbal information in an advertisement. For example, a progressive, college educated, twenty-five year old female might find the photograph of a scantily clad female model in a sports car ad distasteful. However, the verbal claims regarding specific features of the car may, nevertheless, persuade her that the car is an exceptional value. Thus, her evaluations of these two ad elements are ev*aluatively incongruent*; that is, valenced in opposite directions. IN fact, many investigations in the persuasion literature have employed experimental ads in which the evaluative implications of visual (i.e., endorser attractiveness) and verbal (i.e., desirability of product attributes) elements were manipulated orthogonally (Petty & Cacioppo, 1981; Miniard et al. 1991).

Thematic Incongruency

With respect to the processing of visual and verbal information in ads, Heckler and Childers (1992) have discussed *thematic* dimensions of congruity in terms of the consistency of pictorial e ments with the central appeal of the copy. Based largely on the ork of Goodman (1980), thematic incongruency is further separated into *relevancy*, which refers to material pertaining directly to the copy theme, and *expectancy*, which refers to the degree to which incoming stimulus information fits some predicted pattern evoked by the copy theme.[1] The beautiful female model in the aforementioned sports car ad, for instance, would be *expected* but certainly not *relevant*. On the other hand, a recent Honda CRX ad emphasizing the theme of speed and power showed the car taking off vertically like a rocket. This visual element was *unexpected* but *relevant* to the copy which stated, "The Honda CRX...it's a rocket."

This distinction has proven to be useful for understanding the impact of incongruity between visual and verbal information in ads on memory. Visual elements that are highly relevant are recognized and recalled more easily than irrelevant elements, whereas visual elements that are highly expected are more difficult to recall and recognize than unexpected visual elements (Heckler & Childers, 1992). As elaborated below, the distinction between expectancy and relevancy is useful for understanding the role of visual-verbal incongruency in persuasion as well.

To summarize, the literature on schema theory and the marketing literature on advertising suggest relevancy, expectancy, and evaluation as important dimensions or forms of incongruency

between visual and verbal elements of an ad. Although these studies offer insights regarding the impact of each dimension in memory processes, there is very little research explicitly examining the impact of each form of incongruency on the persuasive process. However, several investigations in the advertising and persuasion literature do suggest testable propositions.

VISUAL-VERBAL INCONGRUENCY AND PERSUASION

Independent Effects

Based on a review of the literature on advertising and attitude change, a number of research propositions are derived below regarding the persuasive impact of each dimension of visual-verbal incongruency acting independently of the other two dimensions. hese propositions fall into two categories. The first concerns the influence of each type of incongruency on the d*irection of audience elaboration*. Specifically, the distinction is made between thoughts directed at the *execution of the ad* and thoughts directed at *brand related arguments* (see Lutz, 1985). Next, predictions are offered regarding the *moderating influence* of each dimension on the persuasive impact of *visual and verbal elements* in an ad.

Relevancy. Petty and Cacioppo's (1981a, 1986) development of the Elaboration Likelihood Model (ELM) of persuasion provides insights regarding the persuasive effects of the relevancy dimension of visual-verbal incongruency. The ELM posits that the nature of the attitude change process is dependent upon the level of elaboration the audience devotes to a persuasive communication. The endpoints of the elaboration continuum are associated with two distinct *routes* to persuasion, with high elaboration corresponding to the *central* route and low elaboration representing the *peripheral* route. The central route to persuasion occurs when the individual diligently processes issue or object relevant information, whereas the peripheral route results when the audience associates the attitudinal object with some positive or negative cue in the persuasion context.

Experimental research on the ELM typically entails a manipulation of the audience's level of elaboration. Communication elements affecting attitudes in the low elaboration condition are termed *peripheral cues*, and those influencing attitudes in the high elaboration condition are labeled *central arguments*. Initial research seemed to suggest that information regarding the source of a communication produced attitude change via the peripheral route (i.e., Petty & Cacioppo, 1979; Chaiken, 1980). However, Petty and Cacioppo (1981b) found that the *physical attractiveness* of *visually presented* sources in an ad influenced subjects' brand attitudes for a fictitious brand of shampoo in the high elaboration condition of the experiment. This finding, they reasoned, was due to the *relevance* of the appearance of the models in the ad for evaluating the product. Rather than acting as a simple positive or negative cue, the attractiveness of the models' hair served as a central argument regarding the effectiveness of the shampoo.

Importantly, Petty and Cacioppo's conceptualization of *relevance* differs from that of Heckler and Childers (1992). Heckler and Childers discuss the relevance of visually presented information in terms of the degree to which it *identifies or clarifies the theme* or primary message communicated in an ad, whereas Petty and Cacioppo refer to relevance as the extent to which visually presented information is central to *evaluating the attitudinal object*.

Miniard et al. (1991) provide a more diagnostic assessment of the role of the relevancy dimension, as defined by Goodman (1980) and Heckler and Childers (1992), in persuasion. They manipulated the visual content of an ad for Sunburst, a fictitious brand of soft

---

[1] Heckler and Childers' use of the term relevancy is different from that of Hastie (1981), who labels congruent and incongruent information *relevant*, and reserves the term *irrelevant* for information unrelated to the schema.

drink. The theme of the ad emphasized that the Sunburst was a healthy soft drink. In the relevant visual information condition the ad featured a photo of sliced oranges, whereas in the irrelevant visual information condition the ad presented a photo of three puppies. A manipulation check measure showed that the two photos differed according to how "relevant" and "appropriate" they were, but not with respect to their overall attractiveness. While photo *attractiveness* influenced subjects' attitudes under conditions of low elaboration, photo *relevance* dominated picture-based persuasion in the high elaboration condition. Measures of product attribute beliefs suggested argument based thought mediated the persuasive impact of the picture manipulation in the high elaboration condition.

Taken together, these results suggest that relevancy guides the *route* or *process* by which visual information drives persuasion. The following research propositions follow from this conclusion.

P$_1$: The relevancy dimension of visual-verbal incongruency has a stronger influence on attitude change at higher levels of audience elaboration.

P$_2$: At higher levels of audience elaboration, relevant visual information induces more brand/argument related thought than does irrelevant visual information.

P$_3$: At higher levels of audience elaboration, relevant visual information induces less ad/execution related thought than does irrelevant visual information.

Expectancy. Schema theory suggests that unexpected information "interrupts" the processing of additional information until the discrepancy can be successfully interpreted (Schank & Abelson, 1977). In an advertising context, the presentation of an unexpected visual element would distract the audience from processing additional information in an ad. Since most advertisements present information in order to induce favorable brand evaluations (MacInnis & Jaworski, 1989), the presentation of unexpected visual information would distract an audience from engaging in brand related thought. The audience might instead direct its thought to the ad itself, attempting to resolve the discrepancy by determining the meaning or purpose of the unexpected visual element. An early study by Bither and Wright (1973) provides evidence of such a distraction effect.

Bither and Wright found that for subjects having a low level of self-esteem the congruent version of the ad produced more positive attitude shifts than either the moderately incongruent version or the highly incongruent version. Subjects having either a moderate or a high level of self-esteem formed the most favorable attitudes when they were exposed to the moderately incongruent version of the ad. Additionally, as intended, the manipulation of visual-verbal incongruency induced three levels of self-reported distraction. Although the mediating role of distraction was not assessed, these results suggest that hi*ghly unexpected visual information* distracted the subjects from considering the *highly favorable verbal claims*. When subjects were able to process these claims, they formed positive brand attitudes.

However, Heckler and Childers (1992) demonstrated that while the increased elaboration induced by unexpected visual information enhanced recall and recognition of the visual elements in the ads, *memory* for verbal claims was unaffected. Why, then, did Bither and Wright find that distraction moderated the *persuasive impact* of the verbal claims? This apparent disparity can be resolved by distinguishing between thoughts regarding the *execution of the ad* and thoughts directed at *brand attribute arguments* (Lutz, 1985). The distraction effect produced by unexpected visual information might actually *increase* thoughts about the selection of the copy in an ad (i.e. execution related thought) in order to resolve the inconsistency. Thus, it does not necessarily follow that recall and recognition of verbal information will be inhibited by the presentation of unexpected visual information; it does, however, suggest that thought directed at evaluating the product will be "interrupted" by the presentation of unexpected visual information.

P$_4$: Unexpected visual information induces more ad/execution related thought than does expected visual information.

P$_5$: Unexpected visual information induces less brand/argument related thought than does expected visual information.

Evaluation. The most relevant research regarding the persuasive impact of the evaluation dimension of visual-verbal incongruency stems from Chaiken's (1980, 1987) development of the Heuristic-Systematic Model (HSM) of persuasion. The HSM distinguishes *systematic* processing, an analytic orientation in which the audience accesses and scrutinizes all of the available information to assess its relevance to the judgment task, from *heuristic* processing, which entails the examination of only a subset of the information that allows the use of simple inferential rules to complete the judgment task. An audience member attempts to meet a *sufficiency threshold*, or desired level of confidence, in forming his or her attitude.

In the context of the HSM, evaluative incongruity between two elements of a persuasive communication increases an individual's sufficiency threshold by creating uncertainty regarding the appropriate judgment (Maheswaran & Chaiken, 1991). This uncertainty increases the level of thought devoted to all of the incongruent elements in order to resolve the inconsistency. Maheswaran and Chaiken (1991), for instance, found that subjects presented (verbally) with evaluatively incongruent consumer consensus and product attribute information (i.e., low consensus-strong claims, high consensus-weak claims) devoted more thought to evaluating a fictitious telephone answering machine than did subjects receiving congruent information. More importantly, the increased amount of thought enhanced the persuasive impact of the product claims manipulation. These same principles may be applied to HSM studies involving the presentation of visual *and* verbal information (c.f., Chaiken & Eagly, 1983). Unlike the expectancy dimension, which appears to distract an audience from evaluating the featured product, evaluative incongruency increases the amount of thought devoted to evaluating the product by increasing the audience's uncertainty as to the "correct" attitudinal position.

P$_6$: Visual information that is evaluatively inconsistent with the verbal information in an ad induces more brand/argument related thought than does evaluatively consistent visual information.

P$_7$: Visual information that is evaluatively inconsistent with the verbal information in an ad induces less ad/execution related thought than does evaluatively consistent visual information.

Interaction Effects

For purposes of clarity, the preceding discussion focused on the persuasive effects of each type of visual-verbal incongruency operating in isolation. However, it is quite likely that the visual information presented in a given ad varies on more than one incongruency dimension. Hence, it is important to qualify the persuasive effects presented in Propositions 1-7 with the moderating effects of the other dimensions.

Based largely on the research of Maheswaran and Chaiken (1991), Propositions 6 and 7 asserted that evaluatively incongruent visual and verbal information induces more brand/argument related thought, and less ad/execution related thought. However, most of the HSM studies employing evaluatively incongruent verbal and nonverbal stimulus information have failed to detect, or at least report, "elaboration" effects (Chaiken & Eagly, 1983; Axsom et al. 1987). Perhaps evaluative incongruency al*one* is insufficient for producing these results. Though much more research is needed before all moderating variables are identified, if this "elaboration" effect is driven by increased uncertainty regarding the appropriate judgment, then it should be more pronounced when the evaluatively incongruent visual information is considered equally, or close to equally, *relevant*. That is, a greater level of uncertainty should be created when relevant, rather than irrelevant, visual information is evaluatively incongruent with the attribute claims in the copy of the ad. Thus:

P_8: Evaluatively incongruent visual information tends to induce more brand/argument related thought when it is relevant to the verbal information presented in an ad.

P_9: Evaluatively incongruent visual information tends to inhibit ad/execution related thought when it is relevant to the verbal information presented in an ad.

Maheswaran and Chaiken (1991) found that the presentation of evaluatively incongruent information enhanced the persuasive impact of verbally presented arguments because it was perceived as being more diagnostic of the correct judgment than was the consensus information. However, highly relevant visual information presented in an ad could be perceived as being more diagnostic than verbally presented attribute claims. An obvious example would be an automobile ad emphasizing style as the dominant theme and presenting a photograph of the car. The photograph, if judged to be evaluatively incongruent with the verbal claims, would dominate the audience's assessment of the stylishness of the car, thereby *reducing* the persuasive impact of the verbal claims. Thus, when evaluative incongruency is high, and the visual information in an ad is highly relevant, the persuasive influence of verbally presented arguments may be enhanced or reduced depending on their perceived relative diagnosticity.

A related issue concerns the persuasive impact of relevant visual information. Propositions 1-3 stated that relevant visual information influences persuasion at high levels of audience elaboration by increasing the amount of brand/argument related thought, and decreasing the amount of ad/execution related thought. While a number of exogenous variables induce high levels of audience elaboration, u*nexpected* or *evaluatively inconsistent* visual information may elicit *high levels of elaboration*, potentially moderating the impact of relevant visual information.

The prediction regarding the impact of evaluative incongruency is easily derived from the preceding propositions. Since both high relevance and evaluative inconsistency increase brand/argument related thought (P_1 and P_6, respectively), and decrease ad/execution related thought (P_3 and P_7, respectively), the following propositions also hold:

P_{10}: Relevant visual information tends to stimulate more brand/argument related thought when it is evaluatively incongruent with the verbal information presented in an ad.

P_{11}: Relevant visual information tends to inhibit ad/execution related thought more when it is evaluatively incongruent with the verbal information presented in an ad.

The influence of the expectancy dimension of incongruency on the processing of relevant visual information is more complex. Propositions 2 and 3 state that at high levels of audience elaboration, relevant visual information induces more brand/argument related thought, and less ad/execution related thought, respectively. Further, Propositions 6 and 7 posit a direct effect of expectancy wherein unexpected visual information induces less brand/argument related thought, and increases ad/execution related thought, respectively. Thus, for an audience predisposed to a high level of elaboration, the relationship between relevancy and expectancy is straightforward.

P_{12}: When an audience is predisposed to a high level of elaboration, relevant visual information induces more brand/argument related thought when it is expected.

P_{13}: When an audience is predisposed to a high level of elaboration, relevant visual information induces less ad/execution related thought when it is expected.

Audiences predisposed to a low level of elaboration that subsequently encounter relevant but unexpected visual information, according to Propositions 3 and 4, will engage in m*ore brand/ argument related thought*, and *less ad/execution related thought*. However, the unexpected visual information induces higher levels of elaboration by distracting the audience, which *decreases brand/ argument related thought* (P_5), and *increases ad/execution related thought* (P_4). Since these effects are in direct conflict, for an audience predisposed to a low level of elaboration, the moderating effect of expectancy on the persuasive impact of relevancy is indeterminate.

DISCUSSION

At least two issues must be addressed before the propositions offered above can be examined empirically. The first concerns the conceptualization of evaluation, expectancy, and relevancy as orthogonal dimensions of visual-verbal incongruency, hence the suggestion that each dimension can be manipulated independently of the others in experimental ads (Miniard et al., 1991; Heckler & Childers, 1992). However, given that individuals possess schemas regarding the nature of visual stimuli typically presented in advertising (Wright, 1986), this conceptualization is problematic. For example, ads usually present positive visual stimuli in hopes that they will become associated in some way with the advertised product (Cohen & Areni, 1991). This implies that negatively valenced visual material (i.e., evaluatively incongruent) would be considered unexpected as well. Likewise, advertisers typically employ visual elements that support the verbal claims in an ad (Nylen, 1986). Thus, irrelevant visual material may also be somewhat unexpected. While such interrelatedness does not invalidate the conceptual distinctions drawn here, it should inform both the design and analysis of future empirical work.

CONCLUSION

The notion of schema incongruency provides a conceptual basis for assessing the degree to which visual and verbal elements operate synergistically in an advertising context. While our analysis suggests expectancy, relevancy, and evaluation as key dimensions on which visual and verbal information are related, other dimensions may prove useful for understanding the interaction of visual and verbal advertising elements in persuasion. However, examining the propositions offered above would seem a useful starting point.

REFERENCES

Axsom, D., Yates, S. & Chaiken, S. (1987). Audience response as a heuristic cue in persuasion, *Journal of Personality and Social Psychology*, 53, 30-40.

Bither, S.W. and Wright, P.L. (1973). The self confidence-advertising response relationship: a function of situational distraction, *Journal of Marketing Research*, 10, 146-152.

Chaiken, S. (1980). Heuristic versus systematic processing and the use of source versus message cues in persuasion, *Journal of Personality and Social Psychology*, 39, 752-766.

Chaiken, S. (1987). The heuristic model of persuasion, in *Social Influence: The Ontario Symposium*, Vol. 5, J.M. olson & C.P. Herman (eds.), Hillsdale, NJ: Erlbaum, 3-39.

Chaiken, S. and Eagly, A.H. (1983). Communication modality as a determinant of persuasion: the role of communicator salience, *Journal of Personality and Social Psychology*, 45, 241-256.

Cohen, J.B. and Areni, C.S. (1991). Affect and consumer behavior, in *Handbook of Consumer Behavior*, T.S. Robertson & Kassarjian, H.H. (eds.), Englewood Cliffs, NJ: Prentice-Hall, 188-240.

Eagly, A.H. and Chaiken, S. (1992). *The Psychology of Attitudes*, Fort Worth, TX: Harcourt Brace Jovanovich.

Edell, J.A. and Staelin, R. (1983). The information processing of pictures in print advertisements, *Journal of Consumer Research*, 10, 45-61.

Felipe, A.I. (1970). Evaluative versus descriptive consistency in trait inferences, *Journal of Personality and Social Psychology*, 16, 627-638.

Fiske, S.T. and Pavelchak, M.A. (1986). Category-based versus piecemeal-based affective responses: developments in schema triggered affect, in *Handbook of Motivation and Cognition: Foundations of Social Behavior*, eds. Richard M. Sorrentino and E. Tory Higgins, New York, NY: The Guilford Press, 167-203.

Goodman, G.S. (1980). Picture memory: how the action schema affects retention, *Cognitive Psychology*, 12, 473-495.

Hastie, R. (1980). Memory for information which confirms or contradicts a general impression, in *Person Memory: the Cognitive Basis of Social Perception*, eds. Reid Hastie et al., Hillsdale, NJ: Erlbaum, 155-177.

Hastie, R. (1981). Schematic principles in human memory, in *Social Cognition: The Ontario Symposium*, Vol. 1, eds. E. Tory Higgins et al., Hillsdale, NJ: Erlbaum, 39-88.

Heckler, S.E. and Childers, T.L. (1992). The role of expectancy and relevancy in memory for verbal and visual information: what is incongruency?, *Journal of Consumer Research*, 18, 475-492.

Houston, M.J., Childers, T.L., and Heckler, S.E. (1987). Picture-word consistency and the elaborative processing of advertisements, *Journal of Marketing Research*, 24, 359-369.

Kisielius, J. and Sternthal, B. (1984). Detecting and explaining vividness effects in attitudinal judgments, *Journal of Consumer Research*, 21, 54-64.

Lutz, K.A. and Lutz, R.J. (1977). Effects of interactive imagery on learning: application to advertising, *Journal of Applied Psychology*, 62, 493-498.

Lutz, R.J. (1975). Changing brand attitudes through modification of cognitive structure, *Journal of Consumer Research*, 1, 49-59.

Lutz, R.J. (1985). Affective and cognitive antecedents of attitude toward the ad: a conceptual framework, in *Psychological Processes and Advertising Effects: Theory, Research, and Application*, L.F. Alwitt and A.A. Mitchell (eds.), Hillsdale, NJ: Erlbaum, 45-63.

MacInnis, D.J. and Jaworski, B.J. (1989). Information processing from advertisements: toward an integrative framework, *Journal of Marketing*, 53, 1-23.

Maheswaran, D. and Chaiken, S. (1991). Promoting systematic processing in low-motivation settings: effect of incongruent information on processing and judgment, *Journal of Personality and Social Psychology*, 61, 13-25.

Meyers-Levy, J. and Tybout, A.M. (1989). Schema congruity as a basis for product evaluation, Journal of Consumer Research, *Journal of Consumer Research*, 16, 39-54.

Miniard, P.W., Bhatla, S., and Rose, R.L. (1990). On the formation and relationship of ad and brand attitudes: an experimental and causal analysis, *Journal of Marketing Research*, 27, 290-303.

Miniard, P.W., Bhatla, S., Lord, K.R., Dickson, P.R., and Unnava, H.R. (1991). Picture-based persuasion processes and the moderating role of involvement, *Journal of Consumer Research*, 18, 92-107.

Mitchell, A.A. and Olson, J.C. (1981). Are product attribute beliefs the only mediator of advertising effects on brand attitudes?, *Journal of Marketing Research*, 18, 318-332.

Nylen, D.W. (1986). *Advertising: Planning, Implementation, & Control*, Dallas, TX: South-western Publishing Company.

Petty, R.E. and Cacioppo, J.T. (1979). Issue-involvement can increase or decrease persuasion by enhancing message-relevant cognitive responses, *Journal of Personality and Social Psychology*, 37, 1915-1926.

Petty, R.E. and Cacioppo, J.T. (1981a). *Attitudes and Persuasion: Classic and Contemporary Approaches*, Dubuque, Iowa: William C. Brown Company.

Petty, R.E. and Cacioppo, J.T. (1981b). Issue involvement as a moderator of the effects on attitude of advertising content and context, *Advances in Consumer Research*, 8, 20-24.

Petty, R.E. and Cacioppo, J.T. (1986). *Communication and Persuasion: Central and Peripheral Routes to Attitude Change*, New York, NY: Springer-Verlag.

Petty, R.E., Cacioppo, J.T., & Schumann, D. (1983). Central and peripheral routes to advertising effectiveness: the moderating role of involvement, *Journal of Consumer Research*, 10, 134-148.

Schank, R. and Abelson, R. (1977). *Scripts, Plans, Goals and Understanding: An Inquiry Into Human Knowledge Structures*, Hillsdale, NJ: Erlbaum.

Srull, T.K. (1981). Person memory: some tests of associative storage and retrieval models, *Journal of Experimental Psychology: Human Learning and Memory*, 7, 440-463.

Srull, T.K. and Wyer, R.S. (1989). Person memory and judgment, *Psychological Review*, 96, 58-83.

Taylor, S.E. and Crocker, J. (1981). Schematic bases of social information processing, in *Social Cognition: The Ontario Symposium*, Vol. 1, eds. E. Tory Higgins et al., Hillsdale, NJ: Erlbaum, 89-134.

Wright, P.L. (1986). Schemer schema: consumers' intuitive theories about marketers' influence tactics, *Advances in Consumer Research*, 13, 1-3.

Wyer, R.S. and Gordon, S.E. (1982). The recall of information about persons and groups, *Journal of Experimental Social Psychology*, 128-164.

Wyer, R.S. and Martin, L.L. (1986). Person memory: the role of traits, group stereotypes, and specific behaviors in the cognitive representation of persons, *Journal of Personality and Social Psychology*, 50, 611-675.

Using Conversation Theory to Investigate Conclusion-Drawing: Implications for Persuasion

Mark Toncar, Kent State University
James M. Munch, University of Texas at Arlington
Michael Mayo, Kent State University

ABSTRACT

Kardes' (1988) recent article examining spontaneous inference processes in advertising is one of the most significant studies of conclusion-drawing in persuasion in two decades. Consistent with earlier conclusion-drawing studies, Kardes' approach relies heavily on the use of the logical syllogism as a theoretical basis for exploring persuasion. In this article we explore the value of reconsidering conclusion-drawing from a conversation theory point-of-view. The three target arguments used by Kardes for conclusion-drawing are analyzed and evaluated to highlight important differences between message-based and receiver-based meanings in advertising processing.

INTRODUCTION

In her recent article, Thomas (1992) suggests utilizing principles of everyday conversation to investigate a variety of marketing topics, including issues in both personal selling and advertising. One topic which may potentially benefit from a conversation theory approach is the effects of conclusion-drawing in persuasion. The purpose of this paper is to illustrate how considering a conversation theory approach to conclusion-drawing may help improve our understanding of how conclusion-drawing affects persuasion.

THE PRINCIPLES OF CONVERSATION

Conversation contains a system of implicit and explicit rules (Grice 1975,1978). These rules govern when and how long we talk, the words we use, and expectations of our conversational partners during our talk (Nofsinger 1991). Although many of us are unaware of these principles, socialization processes lead us to follow them nonetheless. We use these rules not only to guide us in our own talk, but to interpret and assign meaning to the talk of others. This system of rules, termed the Cooperative Principle, allows us to say one thing, and be confident that our message will be interpreted as something more, or something different than the literal meaning of the words that we use.

One domain where conversational principles may apply is advertising. Upon hearing an advertising claim that appears to be irrelevant, consumers may change the meaning to make it relevant. For example, to understand and make relevant General Motors' "Heartbeat of America" advertising slogan, consumers are expected to infer meanings that go beyond the literal meaning of the words used. Inferences that go beyond the explicitly stated and logically implied meanings of a claim are termed pragmatic inferences. Claims which require a pragmatic inference to arrive at the intended meaning of the claim are termed pragmatic implications. Decoding of the pragmatic implication using the principles of conversation results in a pragmatic inference by the receiver.

Advertising studies have shown that consumers will pragmatically infer a subjective meaning if it is not explicitly stated or logically implied (Harris 1977; Gaeth and Heath 1987; Bruno and Harris 1980). Further, prior research has demonstrated that consumers confuse pragmatically implied product claims with claims that are directly asserted (Harris 1983; Grunert and Dedler 1985). However, previous research has not applied the principles of conversation to the investigation of advertising effectiveness.

A related area which has received significant research attention concerns the effects of conclusion-drawing on persuasion. A pragmatic inference is one type of inference, and an inference can be thought of as a conclusion.

PERSUASION AND CONCLUSION-DRAWING

The logical syllogism is the most popular argument structure used in marketing to examine conclusion-drawing effects. The syllogistic framework in conclusion-drawing research was first explored in Hovland and Mandell's (1952) classic study. The authors exposed two independent groups of subjects to a communication advocating devaluation of the American dollar. For both groups the communicator outlined the general economic conditions that would make devaluation of a country's currency desirable and then, using a syllogistic argument, demonstrated that these conditions existed in the United States. For the explicit conclusion group, the conclusion to the logical syllogism was clearly stated while for the other group it was not. As it turned out, an explicit statement of the conclusion was a great deal more effective in eliciting opinion change than leaving the conclusion to be drawn by the audience.

To equate level of ability between groups, Thistlethwaite, de Haan, and Kamenetzky (1955) administered a comprehension test to groups so the effects of stating the conclusion or leaving it unstated could be determined with understanding held constant. Thistlethwaite et al. found no significant differences in attitude change between groups.

Linder and Worchel (1970) argued that differences in subjects' levels of motivation to effortfully draw the conclusion may account for Thistlethwaite et al.'s data. To consider this explanation, their procedure required subjects to view a series of seven logical syllogisms projected on a screen in front of them. Syllogisms were sequentially arranged, (i.e., the conclusion of one syllogism served as the first premise of the next one). The final syllogism was:

(First premise): Smoking filtered and unfiltered cigarettes introduces large quantities of tar into the lungs.

(Second premise): Tar released from burning tobacco causes lung cancer.

(Conclusion): Smoking filtered and unfiltered cigarettes causes lung cancer.

Subjects were assigned randomly to one of three conditions. In the high effort conditions, the communication explicitly presented the "correct" conclusion of the first syllogism and subjects were asked to infer the conclusion of each of the remaining six syllogisms. In moderate effort conditions, subjects were given three conclusions and were asked to draw four conclusions themselves. In low effort, five conclusions were generated for subjects and they were asked to generate two. After viewing the syllogisms subjects responded to attitude items including the linkage between smoking and lung cancer. Results indicated acceptance of the target conclusion increased as motivation increased.

Spontaneous Inference Formation

Extending Linder and Worchel's research, Kardes (1988) argued that we know subjects can be induced to draw conclusions

TABLE 1
Conclusion Latencies as a Function of Conclusion Explicitness and Involvement

	Explicit conclusion		Implicit conclusion	
	High involvement	Low involvement	High involvement	Low involvement
Conclusion 1	3886 (n=41)	3641 (n=41)	3832 (n=39)	4112 (n=40)
Conclusion 2	4643 (n=37)	4587 (n=42)	4616 (n=39)	4992 (n=36)
Conclusion 3	5003 (n=43)	4810 (n=41)	4877 (n=41)	4917 (n=38)
Overall mean	4520 (n=48)	4413 (n=48)	4503 (n=48)	4722 (n=48)

NOTE: The conclusion latency means are expressed in milliseconds. TABLE 1 is taken from Kardes (1988) p. 229.

---

by explicitly asking them to do so, but can marketers use advertisements to motivate subjects to spontaneously infer conclusions without explicit prompting from the experimenter?

To test this general proposition Kardes randomly assigned subjects to conditions in a 2 X 2 X 2 between-subjects design with two levels of conclusion explicitness (explicit or implicit), two levels of involvement (high or low), and two levels of measurement order (measurement of response latency first or measurement of evaluation latency first). Subjects were told that they would be asked to evaluate several ads and were given a folder containing four print ads. The target ad contained three sets of arguments and was presented last.

Kardes reasoned that explicit conclusion subjects should respond to inquiries about the relevant conclusions quickly (irrespective of involvement) because they can simply retrieve from memory conclusions provided to them earlier. Implicit conclusion subjects on the other hand should respond to inquiries more slowly when involvement is low, because they should be insufficiently motivated to generate missing conclusions on their own. Kardes' critical test then involves implicit conclusion-high involvement subjects. If these subjects respond as quickly as the explicit conclusion subjects, we can infer that the involvement manipulation was effective in eliciting spontaneous inference formation.

Consistent with his theorizing, Kardes' conclusion latency data (provided above in Table 1), when averaged across the three conclusions ((4520+4413+4503)/3 vs. 4722, $F(1,188)= 5.28$, $p<0.02$), provides support for the hypothesis that when conclusions are omitted, spontaneous inference formation is more likely in high than in low involvement conditions.

Conclusion-Drawing and Attitudes

Consistent with prior research findings of the persuasiveness of explicit conclusions, Kardes reasoned that if the message arguments are compelling, any variable that enhances comprehension should increase persuasion. Since involvement should enhance motivation, Kardes hypothesized and found that brand attitudes are significantly more accessible and favorable (see Kardes' Table 3, and page 230) in the implicit conclusion-high involvement and explicit conclusion conditions than in the implicit conclusion-low involvement conditions.

RECONSIDERING CONCLUSION-DRAWING VIA CONVERSATION THEORY

Interestingly, the data in Table 1 highlight large response time differences between conclusions 1, 2, and 3. This suggests that subjects may have expended different levels of effort or may have assigned differing levels of subjective meaning to Kardes' words in trying to reach "appropriate" conclusions (cf. Mick 1992). Also, because response times are so different between conclusions, Kardes' footnote 3 becomes especially interesting:

"Errors were operationalized as the failure to respond to a target conclusion item within the allotted time period of seven seconds, or pressing the button labeled 'No' (the target questions were always worded in the affirmative direction). Response latencies to questions upon which errors were committed were deleted from subsequent analyses." (Kardes 1988 p., 229).

Given these issues, we decided to reconsider Kardes' conclusion types and their potential meanings from a conversation theory point-of-view.

Conclusion Types

As a first step in reconsidering subjects' inferences we evaluated the structure of the three arguments used in Kardes' research. Then we collected data to improve our understanding of how subjects may have processed these structures. We begin by presenting Kardes' three argument structures.

Conclusion 1: The CT-2000 also features a horizontal disc load, a current track display, and a motorized drawer. Other CD players lack a motorized drawer. Inserting a disc is difficult without one.
(Explicit conclusion) *Inserting a disc is easy with the CT-2000.*

Consistent with past persuasion research on conclusion-drawing, conclusion 1 may best be considered a logical syllogism:

First premise— CT 2000 has a motorized drawer.
Second premise— Inserting a disc is difficult without one.
Conclusion— Inserting a disc is easy with the CT 2000.

Kardes' planned contrast for conclusion 1 revealed that, as predicted, conclusion latencies were faster in the implicit conclusion-high involvement condition and the explicit conclusion conditions than in the implicit conclusion-low involvement condition ($F(1,157) = 4.73, p < 0.04$). Thus, the personal relevance of the message and form of the syllogistic argument influenced subjects' inference processes.

Conclusion 2: All CD players require digital filters, because the decoding of digital sound creates sampling frequency distortions that must be filtered out. Digital filters are expensive and each filter accounts for a large portion of the total price. One advanced filter is sufficient for filtering out sampling frequency distortions and two less advanced filters are no better than one advanced filter. Most CD players have two less advanced filters. The CT-2000 has one advanced filter.
(Explicit conclusion) *The CT-2000 filters out sampling frequency distortions at less cost.*

Conclusion 2 does not conform to the hierarchical steps in a logical syllogism, but could be labeled a compound or "double-barreled" syllogism. The sentences comprising conclusion 2 actually contain two sets of syllogistic arguments. The first sentence contains two major premises: (1) All CD players require digital filters; and (1A) Decoding of digital sound creates frequency distortions. The first portion of sentence two is a second premise to major premise 1: Digital filters are expensive. Sentence three is a syllogistic second premise for major premise 1A: One advanced filter is sufficient for filtering distortions. The last clause in sentence three (i.e., the notion that two less advanced filters are no better than one advanced filter) is a syllogistic conclusion about the ability to filter distortions (i.e., a response to second premise following major premise 1A). Finally, sentence four notes that most CD players have 2 less advanced filters, while sentence five states that the CT 2000 has one advanced filter. These sentences add strength to the issue of number of filters, but offer no undisputed conclusion about filter cost. Therefore, subjects may logically arrive only at the portion of Kardes' conclusion about filtering out distortions.

As is evident in Kardes' explicit conclusion, the author's intent is a dual conclusion about filtering distortions at less cost. Consistent with his results for conclusion 1, the planned contrast for conclusion latencies for conclusion 2 were also significant. Subjects' spontaneous inferences in the implicit conclusion-low involvement conditions were significantly slower than the other three conditions ($F(1,150) = 4.41, p < 0.04$). Thus, even though conclusion 2 is quite obtuse, subjects' conclusion latencies were significantly affected by the treatment variables.

Conclusion 3: Best of all, the CT-2000 brings you a sophisticated laser technology. The purpose of lasers is to reduce distortion from dust and scratches. Most CD players have one laser. The CT-2000 has three.
(Explicit conclusion) *The CT-2000 reduces more distortion from surface irregularities than most CD players.*

Conclusion 3 is not syllogistic. To arrive at a conclusion, subjects must infer the meaning of the argument by employing the maxims of conversational theory. Subjects must pragmatically infer that the greater the number of lasers a CD player has, the greater the reduction in distortion.

The planned contrast for conclusion 3 was not significant. As rationale for his findings, Kardes suggests that because conclusion 3 is presented at the end of the text subjects may have processed these arguments less extensively than earlier arguments. One alternative interpretation for these data resides in conversation theory. If subjects were "required" to pragmatically infer the meaning for conclusion 3 in order to comprehend it, the formation of receiver-based meanings may account for the dramatically slower response latencies shown for conclusion 3. In addition, this deeper level of subjective comprehension processing in response to this conclusion may have rendered Kardes' treatment variables ineffective (Mick 1992).

Pragmatic Inferences

To examine the alternative, subjective meanings that subjects may assign to the above three conclusions, forty-two students were provided a copy of Kardes' three arguments (implicit conclusion version) and were told: "Advertisers and marketers use product claims to sell products. We have provided you with three claims that might be used in advertising. Please write down the meaning of each of these claims." After writing meanings for each of the three arguments subjects were provided with Kardes' explicit conclusions and asked to judge whether their answers matched Kardes' intended meanings or not. Finally, subjects were asked if they did or did not understand each of the three arguments. Subjects were then dismissed. Two researchers coded subjects' responses for the incidence of counterargumentation. Counterarguments were defined as any disagreement with Kardes' intended, syllogistic conclusion. Interjudge reliability was 90% and differences were resolved by discussion. The results are presented in Table 2.

Interestingly, Conclusion 1, the most "logical" argument from a syllogism framework, yields the largest number of incorrect conclusions. This finding suggests that subjects may not typically process advertising claims in a syllogistic fashion. Consistent with Mick's (1992) point-of-view, although the syllogistic information-processing model remains the most widely adopted theoretical basis for persuasion research, the model may over-emphasize message-based meanings while disregarding receiver-based meanings.

Subjects' responses to Conclusion 2 suggest that processing this compound structure results in a good deal of inaccuracy, some problems in understanding and significant counterarguing. Perhaps advertisers desiring to highlight multiple product attributes should exercise caution in developing complex message structures.

Conclusion 3, the most conversational argument, *and* the argument which "requires" the greatest leap or pragmatic inference, is most accurately identified. However, Kardes' data (see Table 1) suggest claims that necessitate a pragmatic inference are significantly deeper levels of processing than syllogistic reasoning (4877 vs. 3832 milliseconds).

Conclusion-Drawing and Attitudes

Differences in the number of counterarguments reported for each conclusion (see Table 2) provides weak evidence that subjects' attitudes may significantly differ in response to the various types of conclusions. The pragmatic inference "required" for conclusion 3 creates twice the level of counterargumentation compared to the logical syllogism form in conclusion 1. Interestingly, this counterargumentation occurred even though no explicit instructions to counterargue were given to subjects. Apparently, the

TABLE 2
Frequency of Subjects Agreement with Kardes' Conclusions

	Types of Agreement		Types of Disagreement	
	Correctly Identified Kardes' Conclusion	Correctly Identified yet Counter-Argued with Conclusion	Incorrectly Identified Kardes' Conclusion	Didn't Understand Facts of the Conclusion
Conclusion 1 (n=42)	21	4	17	0
Conclusion 2 (n=42)	19	8	12	3
Conclusion 3 (n=42)	26	8	8	0

heightened processing involvement required to conversationally infer conclusion 3 activated subjects' need to affectively respond. (Complexity of the compound syllogism contained in conclusion 2 may have required deeper processing as well).

In his recent article examining subjects' levels of subjective comprehension in response to an advertisement for a CD player, Mick (1992) found that deep comprehension levels (receiver-based meanings such as pragmatic inferences) were positively related to both ad credibility and ad attitude when the valence of those meanings were taken into consideration. Also, surface level comprehension (message meanings related to the explicit or asserted message content) was shown to be negatively related to these dependent variables. Given these findings, it would be interesting to reassess Kardes' conclusions to explore whether significant differences exist between conclusion 3 (i.e., a receiver-based conversational implication) and conclusion 1 (i.e., an explicit message-based syllogistic argument).

While it is plausible that Kardes' conclusion 3 did not "work," and his experiment was successful in spite of this, a reexamination of the data from a conversation theory viewpoint offers an alternative, and equally plausible explanation. Because conclusion 3 is non-syllogistic and requires a pragmatic inference, it may have had unmeasured and unintended effects. These effects may be one basis for Kardes' results. He eliminated those subjects who either counterargued or took over seven seconds to respond to a target conclusion item. The mean response latency for conclusion 3 (which elicited significant counterargumentation in our sample) was nearly 5 seconds! Those subjects who processed the message most deeply, and took longer to do so, may have been eliminated from Kardes' study. Similarly, subjects who recognized that conclusion 3 was not substantiated, and counterargued with the conclusion, were also deleted from analysis. In light of the relationship between level of comprehension and attitude discussed above, it appears that Kardes' results may not have been obtained in spite of conclusion 3, but because of conclusion 3!

SUMMARY

Past studies examining persuasion have tended to adopt an objective orientation toward message comprehension (cf. Mick 1992) and studies of conclusion-drawing have relied on use of the logical syllogism as a theoretical basis for persuasion research (Kardes 1988; Linder and Worchel 1970). The syllogistic model and the basic idea that humans have a need to maintain consistency among feelings, thoughts, and actions, will no doubt remain a powerful model for future research (cf. McGuire 1978). Kardes' research clearly illustrates the strength of the syllogistic approach. Both the simple syllogistic structure and the compound syllogism are shown to be consistent with the notion that when subjects possess sufficient ability and motivation, they should be left to draw their own inferences.

A great many advertisements do not conform to the syllogistic structure, however. "Have you driven a Ford Lately?"; "Get Met. It pays."; "We drove our competition into the copier business." These are just a few examples of current advertising messages that have meanings that go beyond the words used, and require the receiver to subjectively assign meaning to the message. This paper suggests that when arguments do not clearly conform to a syllogistic structure, marketers may consider receiver-based models of spontaneous inference processes. A Conversation Theory Framework which considers the role of pragmatic implication may be one promising approach for exploring these structures and their relationships to receivers' advertising processing strategies.

Conversation theory, with its emphasis on the generation of receiver-based meanings for messages, offers a useful method for investigating the subjective interpretations of persuasive communications, and the effects of these self-generated meanings on subsequent attitude structure. The Conversation Theory framework need not be limited to advertising issues, however. Research in the areas of buyer-seller interaction, relationship marketing, and globalization of advertising issues are a few of the areas that could benefit from a conversation theory perspective.

This paper offers evidence that people may process information in a manner that is not syllogistic. Further, through a reexamination of an important paper in the conclusion-drawing literature, we demonstrate that using principles derived from the investigation of everyday conversation offers insights and suggests issues that have not been addressed in the marketing literature. Conversation theory offers a receiver-based approach to understanding the process of social influence and persuasion.

REFERENCES

Bruno, Kristin J., and Richard J. Harris (1980),"The Effects of Repetitions on the Discrimination of Asserted and Implied Claims in Advertising," in *Applied Psycholinguistics*, 1 (August), 307-321.

Gaeth, Gary J. and Timothy B. Heath (1987),"The Cognitive Processing of Misleading Advertising in Young and Old Adults: Assessment and Training," in *Journal of Consumer Research*, 14 (June), 43-54.

Grice, H.P. (1975),"Logic and Conversation," in P. Cole and J.L. Morgan (eds) *Syntax and Semantics: Volume 3. Speech Acts*, pages 41-58, Academic Press, New York, N.Y.

Grice, H.P. (1978),"Further Notes on Logic and Conversation," in P. Cole (ed) *Syntax and Semantics: Volume 9. Pragmatics*, pages 113-128, Academic Press, New York, N.Y.

Grunert, Klaus G. and Konrad Dedler (1985),"Misleading Advertising: In Search of a Measurement Methodology," in *Journal of Public Policy & Marketing*, 4, 153-165.

Harris, Richard J. (1977), "Comprehension of Pragmatic Implications in Advertising," in *Journal of Applied Psychology* 62, Number 5, pages 603-608.

_____ , ed. (1983), *Information Processing Research in Advertising*, Hillsdale, NJ: Lawrence Erlbaum.

Hovland, Carl I. and Wallace Mandell (1952), "An Experimental Comparison of Conclusion-Drawing by the Communicator and the Audience," in *Journal of Abnormal and Social Psychology*, 47 (July), 581-588.

Kardes, Frank R. (1988), "Spontaneous Inference Processes in Advertising," in *Journal of Consumer Research*, 15 (September), pages 225-233.

Linder, Darwyn E. and Stephen Worchel (1970), "Opinion Change as a Result of Effortfully Drawing a Counterattitudinal Conclusion," *Journal of Experimental Social Psychology*, 6 (October), 432-448.

McGuire, William J. (1978), "An Information-Processing Model of Advertising Effectiveness," in *Behavioral and Management Science in Marketing*, ed. Harry L. Davis and Alvin J. Silk, New York: Ronald, 156-180.

Mick, David Glen (1992), "Levels of Subjective Comprehension in Advertising Processing and Their Relations to Ad Perceptions, Attitudes, and Memory," *Journal of Consumer Research*, 18 (March), 411-424.

Nofsinger, Robert E. (1991) *Everyday Conversation*, Sage Publications, Newbury Park, CA.

Thistlethwaite, Donald L. Henry de Haan, and Joseph Kamenetzky (1955), "The Effects of `Directive' and `Nondirective' Communication Procedures on Attitudes," *Journal of Abnormal and Social Psychology*, 51 (July), 107-113.

Thomas, Gloria Penn (1992), "The Influence of Processing Conversational Information on Inference, Argument Elaboration, and Memory," in *Journal of Consumer Research*, 19 (June), pages 83-92.

Consumer Reaction to Company-Related Disasters: The Effect of Multiple Versus Single Explanations

Brian K. Jorgensen, University of California, Los Angeles

ABSTRACT

Following a negative company-related event, such as an airline crash or a food poisoning incident, consumers are likely to be exposed to one or more causal explanations for the event. This paper investigates the extent to which single versus multiple explanations affect consumers' acceptance of the explanation and consumers' anger and blame toward the company. Although the experiment reported here does not demonstrate an effect of single versus multiple explanations on the likelihood or acceptability of an explanation, reactions to single and multiple explanations are shown to operate as predicted by attributional theory.

INTRODUCTION

On December 21, 1988, Pan Am flight 103 crashed into the town of Lockerbie, Scotland, killing all 258 passengers and crew members aboard, as well as a number of people on the ground. All who heard about the disaster wondered how it could have occurred. Was it weather conditions, terrorism, poor security? Who was to blame? Would or could it happen again? As company, government, and media representatives searched for answers, the public tried to make sense of the wide array of causal speculations, explanations, and excuses that filtered through to it.

When large-scale negative company-related incidents occur they can be very important because they have the potential of directly and indirectly affecting large numbers of people. Recent incidents involving bad meat from Jack in the Box Restaurant and syringes in Pepsi cans attest to the high level of publicity that these kinds of incidents can generate. From a marketing perspective, company-related disasters and crises can be particularly damaging when a company's products bear the company name. Brand equity and customer loyalty may drop rapidly if a company is blamed for a serious negative incident.

Consumer behavior scholars have studied consumer attributions following relatively small-scale company-related annoyances, such as defective merchandise (Folkes 1984) and delayed airline flights (Folkes, Koletsky, and Graham 1987). However, consumer reactions to major company-related disasters, such as jet crashes, oil spills, or drug-related scares, have been largely neglected. Further, the tendency of attribution theorists to focus their study on single, as opposed to multiple, causal explanations (Leddo, Abelson, and Gross 1984) seems to have carried over into the consumer behavior literature.

This paper investigates consumer reaction to multiple versus single explanations for image-threatening company-related disasters within a framework of attributional theory and conjunctive explanations. Following a review of the literature, the results of a preliminary experiment in this area are presented. Opportunities for future research are then addressed.

ATTRIBUTIONAL THEORY AND COMPANY-RELATED DISASTERS

Because company-related disasters are highly negative and unexpected, consumers are likely to try to understand the cause of these types of incidents (Bucher 1957; Veltfort and Lee 1943; Weiner 1986). However, members of the general public usually do not have first hand information regarding company-related incidents from which to develop their own causal attributions. Rather, in these situations third party sources, such as the media or company representatives, must generally supply possible or probable causes. The important question then becomes how consumers react to the explanation or explanations that have been offered. Of the various available approaches to the study of attributions, Weiner's (1986) attributional theory is particularly well-suited to the study of consumer reactions to company-related events because Weiner's theory focuses on the consequences of attributions, rather than on the process by which the attributions are made.

According to Weiner's theory, once a person has made a causal attribution, he is expected to experience particular affects or be motivated to perform particular behaviors based on where he determines that the cause falls along three distinct dimensional continuua. These three dimensions are locus, controllability, and stability. The locus dimension addresses the degree to which the cause is internal to or external to the target of the attribution. Thus, for example, an airline accident that is attributed to an improper instruction by an air traffic controller may be considered external to the company, while an accident due to pilot error would probably be considered internal. Controllability concerns the extent to which a cause is within the control of the target entity. Therefore, using the previous example, the air traffic controller problem would probably be considered uncontrollable by the company, while the pilot error problem might be seen as more controllable. Stability reflects the degree to which a cause is something unchanging as opposed to fluctuating or changing over time. Given the infrequency with which they occur, most company-related disasters should tend to be caused by relatively unstable causes, and, therefore, stability is not further considered here.

Weiner's causal dimensions are theorized as influencing various emotional reactions and, ultimately, behavior (Weiner 1986). With particular reference to the company disaster situation, the controllability and locus dimensions, which are somewhat overlapping in most cases, are expected to influence the emotions of anger and pity (Folkes 1984). Behavior is thought to be indirectly affected through the attributionally-induced affective states and resulting attitudes.

EXPLANATIONS OF COMPANY-RELATED DISASTERS

Impression Management

The way in which consumers react to a company-related disaster situation may depend not only on the attributional circumstances underlying the incident but also on the way in which management responds. "Impression management" describes the process by which people, or in this case companies, control others' impressions of them (Leary and Kowalski 1990; Russ 1991). Impression management can be particularly important in response to serious negative events (Schlenker 1980).

One of many approaches that management might take to manage impressions following a company-related disaster is referred to in the crisis management literature as "telling one's own story" (Meyers and Holusha 1986). In other words, management is advised to give its own explanation for what caused the incident. Often, more than one factor may be potentially responsible for a particular incident. For instance, the deaths linked to Jack in the Box hamburgers were eventually traced to both bad meat (an external cause) and improper cooking temperatures (an internal cause). In other cases, until the actual cause or causes are isolated, a number of potential explanations may be available, some of which may be better for the company than others.

The Conjunctive Fallacy and Conjunctive Explanations

Little, if any, of the research stemming from Weiner's (1986) attributional theory has addressed the consequences of multiple attributions. However, in the judgment and inference literature, Tversky and Kahneman (1983) and others have investigated the different effects of multiple or "conjunctive" versus single statements and explanations on people's judgments and predictions. These investigations have centered around what has become known as the "conjunctive fallacy."

The Conjunctive Fallacy. The conjunctive fallacy, or conjunctive error, describes people's tendency to estimate the joint probability of "A and B" to be greater than the probability of "A" or "B" individually, where A and B are descriptions of a person or thing or explanations for an event or action (Tversky and Kahneman 1983). Thus, for example, when asked to judge the likelihood of possible causes of an airline accident, people might consider the conjunction of "sunspot activity and pilot error," to be more likely than "sunspot activity." This tendency is regarded as a fallacy or error because it is statistically impossible for a conjunction of two items to be more likely than either of the items that make up the conjunction.

The robustness of findings of conjunctive errors in various contexts has led to a number of investigations into why people make these types of errors (e.g., Leddo, Abelson, and Gross 1984; Locksley and Stangor 1983; Tversky and Kahneman 1983; Wells 1985; Zuckerman, Eghrari, and Lambrecht 1986). Initially, the conjunctive fallacy was linked to the "representativeness" of the component items (Tversky and Kahneman 1983, Wells 1985). Thus, for example, if pilot error is considered to be a more representative cause of airline accidents than is sunspot activity, then the combination of the two explanations may appear more representative, and thus more probable, than the sunspot cause. Wells (1985) found some support for a representativeness explanation by showing that the combination of representative and unrepresentative statements produced strong conjunctive error effects, while the combination of two unrepresentative or two representative statements produced lower error rates.

Another possible explanation for the conjunctive fallacy is that subjects are misinterpreting the single statements as though they were meant to exclude the conjunctive statements. So, for example, subjects might be interpreting the "pilot error" explanation for an airline accident as "pilot error without sunspot activity." Leddo, Abelson, and Gross (1984) have discounted this explanation, noting that the errors have been found in a between-subjects study, where subjects saw only the single or the conjunctive explanation (Pennington 1984), and that in other studies the statement "A" was replaced with "A, whether or not B," without a weakening of conjunction effects (Locksley and Stangor 1984; Tversky and Kahneman 1983). On the other hand, Morier and Borgida (1984) have found that certain task features in conjunctive problems, such as ranking versus rating the probability of simple and conjunctive statements, can reduce, but not eliminate, conjunctive errors. They have also found that some conjunction problems can be debiased by clarifying wording.

The conjunctive fallacy has also been attributed to improper combination procedures on the part of subjects. Abelson, Leddo, and Gross (1987), have shown that the likelihood of a conjunction can often be approximated by a geometric mean of each of the conjunction's components. Also, Yates and Carlson (1986) have shown that a procedure for summing the likelihoods of conjunction components can predict incidence of errors in some instances.

Conjunctive Explanations. In comparing conjunctive effects across a wide array of studies, Abelson, Leddo, and Gross (1987) find much stronger conjunctive effects in explanation tasks than in other tasks. Further, Locksley and Stangor (1984) find that rare events or outcomes are much more likely to bring about conjunctive errors than common events or outcomes. Presumably, more common events can be more easily explained by single causes.

Since company-related disasters are generally accompanied by explanations, and since these are relatively uncommon events, the conjunctive explanations literature seems highly relevant to the company disaster situation. However, this connection should still be made with some caution. First, the array of possible causes for company-related disasters is much more complex than for the outcomes described in the conjunctive explanation studies. For example, some causes may be insufficient in and of themselves to cause a disaster but may be able to contribute to a disaster in conjunction with another cause. This possibility is not addressed in the conjunctive explanations literature.

Further, the conjunctive explanations literature addresses the effects of conjunctive versus single explanations on judgments of the likelihoods of the explanations. Effects of multiple versus single explanations on affective responses, attitudes, and behaviors are not addressed. Although a more likely explanation may be presumed to be better explanation, and may, therefore, be expected to lead to stronger reactions, this line of reasoning is not yet supported in the literature.

STUDY AND HYPOTHESES

As a preliminary study of single versus multiple explanations, an experiment was designed to study consumer reactions to a company-related disaster, where the disaster is attributed to either an internal/controllable factor, an external/uncontrollable factor, or both an internal/controllable factor and an external/uncontrollable factor (hereafter referred to as "mixed" or "mixed/ambiguous"). Given the robustness of the conjunctive explanation findings, the conjunctive error effect was expected to be observed:

H1: A multiple cause for a negative company-related incident that includes both internal/controllable and external/uncontrollable factors will be judged as more likely than at least one of the single factor causes making up the multiple cause.

Weiner's (1986) attributional theory proposes that when a negative outcome is controllable by the attributional target, greater blame and anger and less sympathy should be expressed toward the target than if the outcome is uncontrollable. Anger and sympathy should, in turn, influence general attitudes toward the attributional target, such that consumers should express more negative attitudes and purchase intentions toward companies connected with negative events where the cause appears to be internal/controllable, as opposed to external/uncontrollable. Therefore:

H2: Consumers will express greater anger, less sympathy, poorer attitudes and purchase intentions, and higher levels of blame toward a company involved in a negative incident to the extent that the cause of the incident is perceived as more internal to and more controllable by company management.

TABLE

Variable	Causal Attribution(s)		
	Internal/ Controllable n = 12	Both n = 12	External/ Uncontrollable n = 12
Controllability	5.42	5.13	3.33
Locus	5.00	3.92	2.46
Stability	2.92	3.04	3.29
Likelihood	0.75	0.67	1.33
Anger	4.67	5.00	3.17
Sympathy	2.50	2.83	3.50
Blameworthiness	5.08	5.08	2.83
Attitude toward Company	-1.52	-1.44	-0.54
Purchase Intention	-2.00	-1.83	-0.17

Although mixed/ambiguous causal attributions, have begun to be used in attributional studies (e.g., Weiner, Graham, Peter, and Zmuidinas 1991), systematic theoretical or empirical analyses of their properties and effects have not yet been carried out. However, Weiner, et al. (1991) suggest that affective and behavioral reactions to mixed attributions should fall within the range between the reactions to each single cause that makes up the mixed cause. How closely the reactions to the mixed attribution mirror those of one or the other of the single attributions may depend to a large degree on the circumstances of the situation. In the present study, the mixed attribution presents a situation where the company that is connected with the negative event is the only volitional entity that can be blamed for the incident. Since blame is generally accorded only to volitional entities (Anderson 1991), the level of blame, as well as the levels of other affective and behavioral responses, should, in this case, be more similar between mixed and internal/controllable attributions than between mixed and external/uncontrollable attributions.

H3: Where the external cause of a company-related disaster is not controlled by a person or entity, the reported levels of affects, attitudes, and blame for a mixed set of explanations should be more comparable to levels for the internal/controllable attribution than to levels for the external/uncontrollable attribution.

Methodology

An experiment was conducted with 36 subjects consisting of 18 adult undergraduate students and 18 adult members of a church group. The subjects were run in two groups on the same day. A vignette approach was chosen because this approach has been widely used in attribution studies of this type and also because company disaster information generally reaches the consumer in the form of a story, such as a news story or a conversation. Following the description of a fatal airliner crash, one of three alternatives was suggested as the possible cause of the crash: (1) bad weather (external/uncontrollable), (2) poor aircraft maintenance (internal/controllable), or (3) bad weather and poor maintenance (ambiguous/mixed). The study design was completely between-subject, with 12 subjects viewing each distinct vignette.

On the experimental cover sheet, subjects were instructed to read the company-related vignette and imagine that they were reading a current news story. They were further instructed not to turn back to the story after they had finished reading it. On the page following the cover sheet, subjects were presented with the vignette. The vignette was followed by a questionnaire, which included a number of dependent measures and manipulation checks. The first question measured subjects' overall reaction to the airline referenced in the vignette on four seven-point semantic differential scales anchored by very unfavorable-very favorable, bad-good, negative-positive, dislike very much-like very much. These scales were averaged for the attitude measure. Next, three questions measured, on seven-point scales, how much anger and sympathy subjects felt toward the airline, if any, and the extent to which subjects felt that the airline was to blame, if at all. A measure of purchase intention was then presented, in which subjects were asked to rate the likelihood that they would choose to fly with this particular airline as opposed to other comparable airlines. This measure was taken on a seven-point scale anchored by very unlikely-very likely.

Finally, subjects responded to manipulation checks designed to test whether the causal dimension manipulations had successfully presented causes that were perceived as either internal/controllable or external/uncontrollable. A six item set of scales was modified from Russell (1982). Two each of the six seven-point items measured the extent to which the subject found the cause to be controllable/uncontrollable, internal/external, and stable/unstable, respectively. Each pair of scales was averaged to arrive at a single scale score for each dimension. The stability measures were taken to assure that the manipulations did not differentially affect stability.

RESULTS AND DISCUSSION

The data were analyzed by one-way ANOVA for each of the manipulation checks and dependent variables. Cell means for each dependent variable are presented in the Table. The results of specific statistical analyses are presented in the Table.

Manipulation Checks

As expected, the causal attribution given had a significant effect on controllability ($F(2,33)=12.25$, $p<.0001$) and locus ($F(2,33)=14.76$, $p<.0001$). Paired tests using the .05 level indicated that for both of these manipulation check variables the external/uncontrollable attribution differed from the internal/controllable and mixed/ambiguous attributions, which did not differ from one another. However, in directional terms, the mixed attribution was situated substantially more midway between internal and external with regard to locus than with regard to controllability. Also as expected, the judged stability of a cause was not significantly affected by causal attribution.

Hypothesis 1

Contrary to expectations, whether the airliner crash seemed due to an internal/controllable, an external/uncontrollable, or a mixed cause had no effect on the judged likelihood that the cause given was indeed the actual cause. Thus, a conjunctive error was not demonstrated in this case. A number of possible reasons for this result can be suggested.

First, unlike nearly all conjunctive explanation and conjunctive error studies, this study was a completely between-subjects study. Thus, while subjects in traditional conjunctive error studies are exposed to both the individual causes and the conjunctive cause, the subjects in this study saw only one or the other. Those studies showing that conjunctive errors are attributable to the way tests are constructed and worded (e.g., Morier and Borgida 1984) support the idea that through debiasing, which can be effected through a between-subjects study, the conjunctive error may be greatly reduced or eliminated.

The results here may also be partly attributable to the fact that the causes making up the conjunctive explanation were judged to be fairly equally likely. Conjunctive errors have usually been found to be more pronounced in situations where one component cause is considered much more likely than the other. Further, studies that trace conjunctive errors to statistically incorrect averaging processes (e.g., Abelson, Leddo, and Gross 1987; Yates and Carlson 1986) also suggest that the errors should be more likely in cases of unequal component causes.

The failure to observe conjunctive error effects may also stem from the complexity of company crisis situations. Consumers may feel ill-equipped to judge for themselves and may, instead, defer to the trustworthiness of the source of the information to determine the likelihood that what is reported is true. If this is the case, future studies should show that both common and unusual causes reported by the same source should be considered equally likely candidates for the true cause.

Hypotheses 2 and 3

Affective measures and blame. According to Weiner's (1986) attributional theory, a negative event that is due to controllable causes should lead to greater anger and blame and to less sympathy than an event that is due to uncontrollable causes. The effect of attribution on anger was significant ($F(2,33)=3.62$, $p<.05$). However, pairwise tests at the .05 level found a difference only between the external/uncontrollable attribution and the mixed attribution. Still, directional results supported both hypotheses 2 and 3 in that both internal/controllable and mixed attributions led to greater anger than did the external/uncontrollable attribution. Although not significant, the results for sympathy were also in the predicted direction.

As expected, the effect of attribution on blame was significant ($F(2,33)=10.52$, $p<.001$). In addition, pairwise tests at the .05 level supported hypothesis 3 in that the higher levels of blame for internal/controllable and mixed attributions were significantly different from the level of blame for external/uncontrollable attributions, although not significantly different from one another.

Attitude and purchase intentions. The effect of attribution on attitude approached significance ($F(2,33)=2.73$, $p<.10$), with a directional indication that attitudes were poorer toward companies connected with negative incidents when the causal attribution was internal/controllable or mixed than when the attribution was external/uncontrollable. The effect of attribution on purchase intention was significant in the expected direction ($F(2,33)=6.23$, $p<.01$). Pairwise tests indicated that external/uncontrollable attributions led to higher purchase intentions than did internal/controllable or mixed attributions.

With regard to purchase intentions, the scenario in the vignettes used here may have resulted in stronger results than would a scenario in which the company-related disaster does not have an effect on the product itself. Whereas an oil spill or chemical leak will not affect the product that is sold at the gas pump or the drug store, an airline crash may signal that the airline is offering an inferior product.

Summary and General Discussion

The results of this study do not lend support to the hypothesis that conjunctive errors play a role in consumer reaction to company disasters, although the study does not rule out the possibility that in other disaster settings conjunctive errors could play a role. The study does, however, support the expectation that consumers' affects, attitudes, and, perhaps, behaviors following a negative company-related incident may be influenced by their understanding of the cause or causes underlying the incident. Also, under the particular circumstances of the vignette presented in this study, consumers' reactions to a mixture of internal/controllable and external/uncontrollable causes were similar to their reactions to a sole internal/uncontrollable cause. However, this result may not necessarily generalize to every case. If, for example, the external cause had been an attribution to a volitional entity, such as a terrorist, the result may have been different, since more blame may have been focussed externally. Also, a greater difference between the likelihoods of the two component explanations may have affected the relative likelihood of the conjunctive explanation, and perhaps other variables as well.

FUTURE DIRECTIONS AND CONCLUSIONS

Consumer reaction to various explanations for company-related disasters is an important area of research that has received little attention. This preliminary research into the area of conjunctive explanations suggests that differences in a company's approach to a disaster situation can have important consequences. The number and types of explanations for a particular incident that reach the consumer may influence emotions, attitudes, and behaviors toward the company.

The research presented here suggests the need for further investigation into a number of different questions regarding single versus multiple explanations for company-related disaster situations. One important research direction would entail an examination of mixed attribution situations where the external cause is controllable by a person or group outside of the company. Another interesting question concerns disaster situations where there is no effect on the company's product, such as in the case of the Exxon Valdez oil spill or the Union Carbide Bhopal incident. A third direction would be the examination of incidents where multiple explanations consist of two internal/controllable or two external/uncontrollable explanations, rather than a mixture of one of each type.

REFERENCES

Abelson, Robert P., John Leddo, and Paget H. Gross (1987), "The Strength of Conjunctive Explanations," *Personality and Social Psychology Bulletin*, 13 (June), 141-155.

Anderson, Norman H. (1991), "Psychodynamics of Everyday Life: Blaming and Avoiding Blame," in *Contributions to Information Integration Theory, Volume II: Social*, ed. Norman H. Anderson, Hillsdale, NJ: Erlbaum, 243-275.

Bucher, Rue (1957), "Blame and Hostility in Disaster," *American Journal of Sociology*, 62 (March) 467-475.

Folkes, Valerie S. (1984), "Consumer Reactions to Product Failure: An Attributional Approach," *Journal of Consumer Research*, 10 (March), 398-409.

———, Susan Koletsky, and John L. Graham (1987), "A Field Study of Causal Inferences and Consumer Reaction: The View from the Airport," *Journal of Consumer Research*, 13 (March), 534-539.

Leary, Mark R. and Robin M. Kowalski (1990), "Impression Management: A Literature Review and Two-Component Model," *Psychological Bulletin*, 107 (1) 34-47.

Leddo, John, Robert P. Abelson, and Paget H. Gross (1984), "Conjunctive Explanations: When Two Reasons are Better than One," *Journal of Personality and Social Psychology*, 47 (November), 933-947.

Locksley, Anne and Charles Stangor (1984), "Why versus How Often: Causal Reasoning and the Incidence of Judgmental Bias," *Journal of Experimental Social Psychology*, 20, 470-483.

Meyers, Gerald C. and John Holusha (1986), *When It Hits the Fan: Managing the Nine Crises of Business*, New York: Mentor.

Morier, Dean M. and Eugene Borgida (1984), "The Conjunction Fallacy: A Task Specific Phenomenon," *Personality and Social Psychology Bulletin*, 10 (June), 243-252.

Pennington, N. (1984), *Technical Note on Conjunctive Explanations*, Unpublished manuscript, Center for Decision Research, University of Chicago.

Russell, Dan (1982), "The Causal Dimension Scale: A Measure of How Individuals Perceive Causes," *Journal of Personality and Social Psychology*, 42 (June), 1137-1145.

Schlenker, Barry R. (1980), *Impression Management*, Belmont, CA: Wadsworth, Inc.

Tversky, Amos and Daniel Kahneman (1983), "Extensional Versus Intuitive Reasoning: The Conjunction Fallacy in Probability Judgment," *Psychological Review*, 90 (October), 293-315.

Veltfort, Helene Rank and George E. Lee (1943), "The Coconut Grove Fire: A Study in Scapegoating," *Journal of Abnormal and Social Psychology*, 38 (April) 138-154. (Clinical Supplement)

Weiner, Bernard (1986), *An Attributional Theory of Motivation and Emotion*, New York: Springer-Verlag.

———, Sandra Graham, Orli Peter, and Mary Zmuidinas (1991), "Public Confession and Forgiveness," *Journal of Personality*, 59 (2), 281-312.

Wells, Gary L. (1985), "The Conjunction Error and the Representativeness Heuristic," *Social Cognition*, 3 (Fall), 266-279.

Yates, J. Frank and Bruce W. Carlson (1986), "Conjunction Errors: Evidence for Multiple Judgment Procedures, Including 'Signed Summation,'" *Organizational Behavior and Human Decision Processes*, 37 (April), 230-253.

Zuckerman, Miron, Haleh Eghrari, and Mark R. Lambrecht (1986), "Attributions as Inferences and Explanations: Conjunction Effects," *Journal of Personality and Social Psychology*, 51 (6), 1144-1153.

Summary
The Power, Potential, and Perils of Meta-Analysis: A Workshop on Integrative Reviews
Steven P. Brown, Southern Methodist University

As its title implied, this special session discussed the power of meta-analysis (e.g., to overcome the limitations and assumptions inherent in statistical significance testing), its potential for testing theory and establishing prior probabilities for particular relationships, and the perils associated with statistical problems such as heteroskedasticity and truncation. The session questioned assumptions often made by researchers regarding error rates in empirical research and the meaning of statistical significance. It also questioned assumptions made about meta-analysis (e.g., that it is useful only for summarizing research results but not for theory development or testing). The session chair Kent B. Monroe of the University of Illinois described the background to the session proposal and introduced the speakers.

The first paper, "What Do Data Really Mean?," was delivered by Frank L. Schmidt of the Department of Management and Organization, University of Iowa. Professor Schmidt, one of the world's leading experts on meta-analysis, described the limitations of statistical significance testing and pointed out ways that meta-analysis overcomes these limitations. He observed that the assumption often made by researchers that error rates in their research approximate the alpha levels specified for Type I error is erroneous. Using examples based on sample sizes typical of consumer research, he showed that Type II error is a much more serious hazard, with rates exceeding .50. He also criticized the assumption that statistically non-significant effects are equal to zero, noting the failure to find an effect may usually be attributable to insufficient power in the study design and that non-significant effects are usually _not_ equal to zero. Professor Schmidt concluded that statistical significance testing is "an addiction" that researchers should fight to break.

The second paper, "Meta-Analysis for Model Estimation," was delivered by Professor Donald R. Lehmann of Columbia University. Professor Lehmann discussed the uses of meta-analysis for establishing prior probabilities regarding the strength of relationships of interest in situations where data are sparse or expensive (e.g., new product forecasting). In such situations, estimates of patterns (e.g., life-cycle shapes) or relations among variables (e.g., advertising to awareness or attitude) often rely on other "relevant" information, usually estimates based on prior studies. He summarized some past work suggesting that generalization across products and situations is the rule rather than the exception. He concluded by suggesting how to perform meta-analysis across studies even when the individual studies do not contain sufficient data to allow for estimation of a relationship on a study-by-study basis.

The session's final paper, "Validity Threats in Meta-Analysis," was delivered by Murali Chandrashekaran of the University of Cincinnati (co-authored with Beth A. Walker of Arizona State University). This paper focused on two statistical threats to validity in regression of effect sizes from meta-analysis on potential moderator variables, namely heteroskedasticity and truncation. The paper proposed a maximum-likelihood estimation technique that yields greater power and efficiency than OLS estimation. A Monte Carlo study compared estimation methods and found the maximum-likelihood technique superior.

Discussion of the three papers was provided by Steven P. Brown of Southern Methodist University. He reviewed a number of assumptions commonly made by consumer researchers (e.g., that error rates approximate alpha rates for Type I error, that Type I error is the type of error that researchers should be most concerned with, that larger effect sizes are in some sense "better," that the null hypothesis is the appropriate test in most studies, and that meta-analysis is useful only for summarizing prior research results but not for developing or testing theory) and reviewed how the papers had shown these assumptions to be shaky at best and more often erroneous. He concluded that the three papers in sequence addressed issues related to the "power, potential, and perils" of meta-analysis as per the session's billing.

An Investigation of the Influence of Gender on the Hedonic Responses Created by Listening to Music

Kathleen T. Lacher, Auburn University

ABSTRACT

This exploratory investigation examines the influence of gender on the creation of hedonic responses to new (first time heard) music. Music evokes sensorial, emotional, imaginal and analytical responses in individuals upon its first hearing and these responses may differ in strength between males and females. Results show that gender does influence the strength of the different responses. Males tended to have a stronger analytical response and females a stronger sensorial response.

INTRODUCTION

Past empirical consumer research studies have examined music as a background feature in advertising (e.g., Alpert and Alpert 1989; MacInnis and Park 1991; Park and Young 1986), its use in classical conditioning (e.g., Bierley, McSweeney and Vannieuwkerk 1985; Gorn 1982; Kellaris and Cox 1989), and the effect of music as a background on purchase behavior (e.g., Milliman 1986, 1982). A group of studies addressing consumer aesthetics have explored the mapping of preference space for consumers who listen to jazz recordings, using multidimensional scaling techniques (Holbrook 1982; Holbrook and Holloway 1984; Holbrook and Huber 1979; Huber and Holbrook 1979).

As noted by Kellaris and Rice (1993), there has been a call for the research community to focus on music attributes (e.g., tempo, rhythm, dynamics, pitch) and how they affect the consumer. Several such studies have emerged. The effects of music tempo, modality and loudness on evaluative measures and behavioral intention have been explored (Kellaris and Kent 1991; Kellaris 1992; Kellaris and Rice 1993). The evaluative measures were intended to capture emotions and were different for each study. These studies found that faster tempos and major modes had a positive effect on behavioral intention. Loudness had a negative influence on women listeners. Kellaris and Altsech (1992) discovered that music loudness had a significant effect on the perception of time duration. The louder the music, the longer was the perceived duration of the music (how long it lasted). These findings are helpful to those who use music to influence consumers via retail atmospherics or marketing communications.

An alternative and complementary approach to understanding music and its influence lies in studying the hedonic responses that are generated in a consumer when listening to music (Lacher 1989). This approach centers on the hedonic consumption paradigm, which states that some products are consumed, not for their utilitarian value, but because they create experiences of feeling, fantasy and fun (Hirschman and Holbrook 1982; Holbrook and Hirschman 1982). It is important not only to identify a product's attributes, but also to identify the subjective responses created by the product, its experiential power, to better understand the entire phenomenon of music, not only as a product in its own right (Holbrook and Anand 1990; Kellaris 1992; Lacher 1989), but also the situational power it exerts in consumer experiences (e.g., shopping, waiting in a doctor's office, watching a television advertisement).

Using the hedonic consumption paradigm as guidance, Lacher and Mizerski (1994) explored the responses and relationships involved in the purchase of music. Their findings show that the four hedonic responses created by listening to music (Lacher 1989) significantly influenced both affect toward the music and the experiential involvement in the music. Those responses are

The Sensory Response

Described by Yingling (1962) as an awareness of the need to approach or withdraw from the source of the music or the source of tension associated with the music, the sensory response is typified by some physical movement, from swaying or the simple tapping of toes, to dancing to the music. Ortmann (1927) recognized the sensory response as the most primitive of the responses to music.

The Imaginal Response

The images, memories, or situations that music evokes are expressed in the imaginal response (Myers 1914). In an instrumental piece of music, an individual may hear passages that reminds one of the ocean or a storm (Gatewood 1927). The lyrics of a piece of music may also trigger images. These images may be specifically tied to the words or symbols, subjectively interpreted from the message (Holbrook and Grayson 1986). The imaginal response captures the fantasy aspect of hedonic consumption.

After a piece of music has been experienced, indexical associations may occur. Indexical associations are defined as the pairing of a musical event and an extramusical object, so that reexperiencing the music will trigger emotion-laden memories of the initial experience (Dowling and Harwood 1986). How many of us have songs that make us remember our first love or prom night? However, indexical associations are not created solely by the music, situational factors are also an issue. Therefore they are different from the imaginal response.

The Emotional Response

The emotional response represents the feelings one experiences when listening to music, such as joy, rage, sadness, or love (Gatewood 1927; Hargreaves 1982; Yingling 1962). The emotional component may be the most influential response since it is regarded as the primary ingredient in music appreciation (Havlena and Holbrook 1986; Holbrook and Anand 1990; Meyer 1956; Sloboda 1985; Yingling 1962).

The Analytical Response

Listening to music requires the discrimination and assimilation of the music elements and provides cognitive stimulation (Hantz 1984). Sloboda (1985) recognizes that people may analyze the music while listening to it. Most listeners have certain expectations about music—how the melody should progress, how the harmonies should be constructed—which are learned through experiencing music.

Cognition seeking (Hirschman 1984) describes the hedonic consumer behavior where an individual seeks pleasure by discerning cause and effect relationships. In his study, Myers (1912) describes a subject who engaged in cognition seeking while listening to music. This subject wanted to analyze the music elements, to see how they progressed and if the progression made sense. The analytical response to music reflects the listener's engagement in the objective, logical examination of the music.

Gender Issues

As suggested by Konecni (1982), gender of the listener may moderate the responses that music creates. Meyers-Levy (1988) used gender to interpret other forms of judgments in the consumer research literature. Holbrook (1986) found gender differences in the aesthetic responses to clothing design features. Studies also show gender sensitivity to the loudness of music (Kellaris and Alstech 1992; Kellaris and Rice 1993) which can affect behavioral intention. Therefore, to better understand the subjective responses that music creates, gender differences should be explored.

The purpose of this study is to examine the effect of gender on all four hedonic responses to music, namely the sensorial, emotional, imaginal and analytical. To date, only the emotional has been addressed (e.g., Kellaris and Kent 1991; Kellaris and Rice 1993). Specifically, the research hypothesis is that gender of the listener will influence the music's ability to evoke the hedonic responses to music.

METHOD

Sample

The sample came from both the Colleges of Business and Arts and Sciences of a southern state university. All of the subjects were given extra credit by their respective instructors for participation in the experiment. The sample consisted of 215 subjects, with 52% male and 48% female. The ages ranged from 19 to 36 years with 95.8% being 24 years of age or younger, placing the sample well within the range of the population of purchasers of rock music described by Miller (1992).

Selection of Music Stimuli

The stimuli used were rock-style songs. This genre of music was deemed most appropriate for the sample population. Original music was used to insure that the responses would be created purely by the music, not by any previous experiences with the music.

The first phase of the materials selection entailed acquiring a pool of songs from which a panel of judges would select two (Mizerski et al. 1988; Pucely et al. 1987). The university student radio station was used as a source of materials with the Assistant Program Director assisting in an advisory capacity. This student had access to all music currently being played on the station and knowledge of what other radio stations in the area were playing. The songs came from albums that had been recently released. The selected songs were not yet being played on the radio in this market during this experiment.

Previous studies (Holbrook 1981; Holbrook and Bertges 1981) have identified four musical features (product attributes) which affect aesthetic judgments. They are tempo, rhythm, dynamics, and phrasing. The pool of songs selected by the investigator was based on the variability of these features among the songs. Good overall production of the songs and the quality of the performance were also criteria for evaluation.

The tempo of a piece of music has been found to be the strongest influence in creating emotional responses to music (Hevner 1937; Holbrook and Anand 1990). Kellaris and Kent (1991) also found tempo to be influential in both the appealingness and arousingness of the music and behavioral intent, with faster tempos creating more positive responses. Since tempo is instrumental in evoking emotional responses and influencing music preferences, it was considered the most important factor for final song selection.

Five judges, each of whom had significant expertise in music, were used to select the final two songs. The judges were instructed to pick one with a fast tempo and one with a slow tempo, and decided on two songs by consensus. The song "Maniac" from the album *Somethin' Bitchin This Way Comes* by the group Lock Up was the fast tempo choice (henceforth, SONG A) and "Marlene Dietrich's Favorite Poem" from the album *Deep* by artist Peter Murphy the slow tempo choice (henceforth, SONG B). To determine the actual tempo of each song, the number of beats occurring within the duration of a minute was measured using a metronome (Garretson 1971). The tempo for SONG A fell between 108 and 112 beats per minute. The tempo category for this speed is Moderato, meaning moderate, but faster than a walking pace (Andante). SONG B fell between 72 and 74 beats per minute, placing it in the tempo category of Adagio, meaning slow and leisurely (Garretson 1971).

The two songs also vary with respect to rhythm and dynamics. For SONG A, the dynamics were a constant forte (loud); the rhythm was steady. Phrasing had a staccato quality, certain notes of the melody were detached. Instrumentation consisted of lead and bass guitars and drums. Voices were male and in the medium register. SONG B had dynamics that ranged from mezzopiano to piano (medium soft to soft). The rhythm was flowing, the phrasing legato (no perceptible interruption between the notes). Instrumentation included a synthesizer and what appeared to be a twelve-string guitar, creating a lush texture. The male solo voice was a low register and singing as one would sing a ballad. The contrast between the musical elements of the two songs would be expected to generate variations in the emotional responses created by the two songs (Sloboda 1985) and facilitate the differentiation of the sensorial, imaginal, and analytical responses.

Experimental Setting

A large conference room, which seats about 40 people, was used. Chairs were comfortable, padded and had arms. Two chairs were at each table. Tables were arranged so that four tables were in each row, two to the right of the aisle and two to the left. There were ten rows in all. Lighting was dimmed to half, making a more informal, comfortable atmosphere while still allowing enough light to answer the questionnaires.

The stereo system was set up in the front of the room. The system components included an amplifier/receiver, a cassette tape deck and two speakers. Settings volume and balance on the stereo playback system remained the same throughout the length of the data gathering.

Music was played as the subjects were arriving. The music picked was the album Court and *Spark* by Joni Mitchell. Its selection was totally arbitrary on the part of the investigator, using intuition to select music that would allow the introduction of test music stimuli to be less of a contrast in the data collection facility. Subjects were encouraged to relax and pretend that a friend had given them some new songs to listen to, in order to get their opinion of them.

Procedure

Because subjects can influence each others opinions by both verbal and nonverbal actions (Kuhn 1980), care was taken to insure the independence of responses among subjects. As subjects arrived they were seated every other seat. Questionnaires were passed out face down.

When the experiment was scheduled to begin, subjects were given instructions on the operation of the experiment. The method used was one advocated by Wapnick (1976) and used by Pucely et al. (1987) and Mizerski et al. (1988). Two songs were played. Each song was played twice. During the first playing, subjects were instructed to listen to the music. When the song played for the second time, the subjects were to answer the questions on the questionnaire that pertained to that song. The questionnaire also included some demographic questions located at the beginning and end of the questionnaire. When the subject finished filling out the questionnaire, the subject was permitted to leave.

The order of the songs was rotated, so that half the sample heard SONG A/SONG B and half heard SONG B/SONG A. This was done so that song order effects on a subject's responses toward the songs played could be analyzed.

Measures Used

The dependent measures used for the experiment were those used by Lacher and Mizerski (1994). In that study, the sensorial and imaginal responses were created and validated using confirmatory factor analysis. The sensorial response was a two item scale comprised of "I was moving some part of my body (head, foot, hand) in rhythm with the music." and "I wanted to dance to the music." The imaginal response scale contained three items: "The song created a picture in my mind"; "The song made me remember something"; and "The song prompted images in my mind." Each item was measured using a six-point scale anchored by "strongly disagree/strongly agree."

The emotional response scales (Asmus 1985) and analytical response scale (Pucely et al. 1987) already existed in the music research literature. The emotional response, which originally contained nine different emotion dimensions, was tested by Lacher and Mizerski (1994) for its applicability to rock music. Results suggested that the six dimensions (and scale items), *Exuberance* (vigorous, vibrant, exuberant), *Patriotic* (heroic, victorious, patriotic), *Amused* (humorous, comical, amusing), *Rage* (hate, anger, rage), *Sad* (sad, blue, depressed), and *Calm* (calm, tranquil, relaxing) were enduring while the other three (*Sedative, Longing,* and *Sensual*) were song specific. The analytical response had two scales consisting of "I wanted to see how the song developed" and "I analyzed the way the song was put together and why it came out the way it did — whether it seemed right and made sense." Again, all items were measured using a six-point scale anchored by "strongly disagree/strongly agree."

Analysis

The two songs were aggregated to produce more generalizable results (Lacher and Mizerski 1994). The constructs were represented by a single indicator created by summating the individual scale items (MacKenzie and Lutz 1989).

RESULTS

Check for Song-Order Influence

Multivariate analysis of variance (MANOVA) was used to determine whether song order had an effect on the nine dependent responses. Results indicate that song order did influence the responses (Wilk's $\lambda=.8619$, Exact F=2.13, hypothesis df=13, error df=173, p<.01, both Pillai's trace and Hotelling's trace confirm Wilk's λ). Song order will be a covariate in the analysis of gender effects on the hedonic responses to music.

Gender Effects

MANOVA was again used to determine whether gender of the listener had any effect on the dependent variables, with song order used as a covariate. Gender did have a significant effect on the nine dependent variables (Wilk's $\lambda=.7942$, Exact F=3.43, hypothesis df=13, error df=172, p<.01, with Pillai's trace and Hotelling's trace confirming Wilk's λ).

While univariate F ratios ignore the intercorrelations among the dependent variables, it is sometimes advisable to perform the calculations to see which of the individual dependent variables may be affected by the independent variables, although it may be likely that no significant differences may be detected on the individual level (Pedhauser 1982). Upon examination, three dependent variables had significant results. Music seemed to evoke in males a stronger response in the emotional dimension *Amused* than in females (F=9.75, p<.01) and in the analytical response (F=7.10, p<.01). Females responded more strongly to the sensorial response (F=4.29, p<.05).

DISCUSSION AND CONCLUSIONS

This exploratory study examined the influence of the gender of the listener on the creation of the four hedonic responses to music. Experimental findings supported the overall research hypothesis. Gender did have an overall effect on music's ability to evoke the responses. Specific individual responses affected were the *Amused* emotional dimension, the analytical response (more strongly felt in males) and the sensorial response (more strongly felt in females).

These findings suggest that males and females respond differently to music. Seeing "how the song developed" and "whether it made sense" may be evoked more readily in males than females. Responding to music through movement (e.g., dancing) is more strongly evoked in females. Why this is so opens avenues to future research. Variables that may influence these differences could be attributed to biological phenomena such as hormonal differences in brain development (Kimura 1992) or social-psychological processes such as sex roles (Meyers-Levy 1988) or a combination of both.

It should be recognized that the generalizability of these findings are constrained by two limitations, sample and stimuli. First, the sample should be expanded to include a larger scope of people, along demographic variables such as age, income, and occupation. Second, different music genres should be tested. It may be that classical music or jazz may evoke different response strengths.

However, knowing that gender affects music's ability to evoke hedonic responses is important for those who produce music as a product and for those who use music to influence consumer behavior. What may appeal to one gender may not appeal to another. As with loudness of music (Kellaris and Altsech 1992; Kellaris and Rice 1993), certain responses may either enhance or detract from a consumer's experience.

In conclusion, evidence from this study suggests that music's ability to create hedonic responses in individuals is influenced by the gender of the listener. These results are in line with other studies that tested gender differences (e.g., Holbrook 1986; Kellaris and Rice 1993). Given the present findings, future research should include different music genres, broader listener base and characteristics, the elements of music that produce the hedonic responses, and biological and social-psychological variables.

REFERENCES

Alpert, Judy I. and Mark I. Alpert (1989), "Background Music as an Influence in Consumer Mood and Advertising Responses," in *Advances in Consumer Research*, Volume 16, ed. Thomas K. Srull, Provo, UT. Association for Consumer Research, 485-491.

Asmus, Edward P. (1985), "The Development of a Multidimensional Instrument for the Measurement of Affective Responses to Music," *Psychology of Music*, 13(1), 19-30.

Bierley, Calvin, Frances K. McSweeney and Renee Vannieuwkerk (1985), "Classical Conditioning of Preferences for Stimuli," *Journal of Consumer Research*, 12(December), 316-23.

Dowling, W. Hay and Dane L. Harwood (1986), *Music Cognition*, New York: Academic Press.

Garretson, Robert L. (1971), *Conducting Choral Music*, 3rd ed., Boston, MA: Allyn and Bacon, Inc.

Gatewood, Esther L. (1927), "An Experimental Study of the Nature of Musical Enjoyment," in *The Effects of Music*, ed. Max Schoen, New York: Harcourt Brace.

Gorn, Gerald (1982), "The Effects of Music in Advertising on Choice Behavior: A Classical Conditioning Approach," *Journal of Marketing*, 46(Winter), 94-101.

Hantz, Edwin (1984), "Studies in Musical Cognition: Comments from a Music Theorist," *Music Perception*, 2(2), 245-64.

Hargreaves, David J. (1982), "Preference and Prejudice in Music: A Psychological Approach," *Popular Music and Society*, 8(3&4), 13-8.

Havlena, William J. and Morris B. Holbrook (1986), "The Varieties of Consumption Experience: Comparing Two Typologies of Emotion in Consumer Behavior," *Journal of Consumer Research*, 13(December), 394-404.

Hevner, Kate (1937), "The Affective Value of Pitch and Tempo in Music," *American Journal of Psychology*, 49(October), 621-30.

Hirschman, Elizabeth C. (1984), "Experience Seeking: A Subjectivist Perspective of Consumption," *Journal of Business Research*, 12, 115-36.

_____ and Morris B. Holbrook (1982), "Hedonic Consumption: Emerging Concepts, Methods and Propositions," *Journal of Marketing*, 46(Summer), 92-101.

Holbrook, Morris B. (1986), "Aims, Concepts and Methods for the Representation of Individual Differences in Esthetic Responses to Design Features," *Journal of Consumer Research*, 13(December), 337-47.

_____ (1982), "Mapping the Retail Market for Esthetic Products: The Case of Jazz Records," *The Journal of Retailing*, 58(1) Spring, 115-29.

_____ (1981), "Integrating Compositional and Decompositional Analyses to Represent the Intervening Role of Perceptions in Evaluative Judgements," *Journal of Marketing Research*, 18(February), 13-28.

_____ and Punam Anand (1990), "Effects of Tempo on Responses to Music," *Psychology of Music*, 18, 150-162.

_____ and Stephen A. Bertges (1981), "Perceptual Veridicality in Esthetic Communication: A Model, General Procedure and Illustration," *Communication Research*, 8(October), 387-424.

_____ and Mark W. Grayson (1986), "The Semiology of Cinematic Consumption: Symbolic Consumer Behavior in Out of Africa," *Journal of Consumer Research*, 13(December), 374-81.

_____ and Elizabeth C. Hirschman (1982), "The Experiential Aspects of Consumption: Consumer Fantasies, Feelings, and Fun," *Journal of Consumer Research*, 9(September), 132-40.

_____ and Douglas V. Holloway (1984), "Marketing Strategy and the Structure of Aggregate, Segment-Specific, and Differential Preferences," *Journal of Marketing*, 48(Winter), 62-7.

_____ and Joel Huber (1979), "Separating Perceptual Dimensions from Affective Overtones: An Application to Consumer Aesthetics," *Journal of Consumer Research*, 5(March), 272-83.

Huber, Joel and Morris B. Holbrook (1979), "Using Attribute Ratings for Product Positioning: Some Distinctions Among Compositional Approaches," *Journal of Marketing Research*, 16(November), 507-16.

Kellaris, James J. (1992), "Consumer Esthetics Outside the Lab: Preliminary Report on a Musical Field Study," in *Advances in Consumer Research*, Vol.19. eds. John F. Sherry and Brian Sternthal, Provo, UT: Associaltion for Consumer Research, 730-734.

_____ and Moses B. Altsech (1992), "The Experience of Time as a Function of Musical Loudness and Gender of Listener," in *Advances in Consumer Research*, Vol.19. eds. John F. Sherry and Brian Sternthal, Provo,UT: Association for Consumer Research, 725-729.

_____ and Anthony D. Cox (1989), "The Effects of Background Music in Advertising: A Reassessment," *Journal of Consumer Research*, 16(June), 113-18.

_____ and Robert J. Kent (1991), "Exploring Tempo and Modality Effects on Consumer Responses to Music," in *Advances in Consumer Research*, Vol.18, eds. Rebecca H. Holman and Michael R. Solomon, Provo UT: Association for Consumer Research, 243-248.

_____ and Ronald C. Rice (1993), "The Influence of Tempo, Loudness, and Gender of Listener on Responses to Music," *Psychology and Marketing*, Vol. 10(1) (January/February), 15-29.

Kimura, Doreen (1992), "Sex Differences in the Brain," *Scientific American*, September, 119-125.

Konecni, Vladimir J. (1982), "Social Interaction and Musical Preference," in Th*e Psychology of Music*, ed. D. Deutsch, New York:Academic Press, 497-516.

Kuhn, Terry Lee (1980), "Instrumentation for the Measurement of Music Attitudes," *Contributions to Music Education*, 8, 2-38.

Lacher, Kathleen T. (1989), "Hedonic Consumption: Music as a Product," in *Advances in Consumer Research*, Volume 16, ed. Thomas K. Srull, Provo, UT: Association for Consumer Research, 367-73.

_____ and Richard Mizerski (1994), "An Exploratory Study of the Responses and Relationships Involved in the Evaluation of, and the Intention to Purchase Music," forthcoming, *Journal of Consumer Research*.

MacInnis, Deborah J. and C. Whan Park (1991), "The Differential Role of Characterisitics of Music on High– and Low–Involvement Consumers' Processing of Ads," *Journal of Consumer Research*, 18(September), 161–173.

MacKenzie, Scott B. and Richard J. Lutz (1989), "An Empirical Examination of the Structural Antecedents of Attitude Toward the Ad in an Advertising Pretesting Context," *Journal of Marketing*, 53(April), 48-65.

Meyer, Leonard B. (1956), *Emotion and Meaning in Music*, Chicago:The University of Chicago Press.

Meyers-Levy, J. (1988), "The Influence of Sex Roles on Judgment," *Journal of Consumer Research*, 14, 522-530.

Miller, Cyndee (1992), "Marketers Find Alternative Way to Appeal to Young Music Lovers," *Marketing News*, October 12, p. 28

Milliman, Ronald E. (1986), "The Influence of Background Music on the Behavior of Restaurant Patrons," *Journal of Consumer Research*, 13(September), 286-89.

_____ (1982), "Using Background Music to Affect the Behavior of Supermarket Shoppers," *Journal of Marketing*, 46(Summer), 86-91.

Mizerski, Richard, Marya J. Pucely, Pamela Perrewe and Lori Baldwin (1988), "An Experimental Evaluation of Music Involvement Measures and Their Relationship with Consumer Purchasing Behavior," *Popular Music and Society*, 12(3), 79-96.

Myers, Charles M. (1914), "Individual Differences in Listening to Music," *British Journal of Psychology*, 7, 68-111.

Ortmann, Otto (1927), "Types of Listeners: Genetic Considerations," in *The Effects of Music*, ed. Max Schoen, New York:Harcourt Brace, 38-77.

Park, C. Whan and S. Mark Young (1986), "Consumer Response to Television Commercials: The Impact of Involvement and Background Music on Brand Attitude Formation," *Journal of Marketing Research*, 23(February), 11-24.

Pedhazur, Elazar J. (1982), *Multiple Regression in Behavioral Research, Explanation and Prediction*, 2nd ed., New York, NY: Holt, Rinehart and Winston.

Pucely, Marya J., Richard Mizerski, and Pamela Perrewe (1987), "A Comparison of Involvement Measures for the Purchase and Consumption of Pre-Recorded Music," in *Advances in Consumer Research*, Volume 15, ed. Michael J. Houston, Cambridge, MA: Association for Consumer Research.

Sloboda, John A. (1985), *The Musical Mind: The Cognitive Psychology of Music*, Oxford: Clarendon Press.

Smith, Patricia Cain and Ross Curnow (1966), "Arousal Hypothesis and the Effect of Music on Purchasing Behavior," *Journal of Applied Psychology*, 50(3), 255-256.

Wapnick, Joel (1976), "A Review of Research on Attitude and Preference," *Council for Research in Music Education*, 48, 1-20.

Yingling, Robert W. (1962), "Classification of Reaction Patterns in Listening to Music," *Journal of Research in Music Education*, 10(2), 105-20.

Babes in Toyland: Learning an Ideology of Gender
Greta Eleen Pennell, Rutgers University[1]

ABSTRACT

This paper examines the subtle, yet powerful ways children are taught a traditional ideology of gender through toy advertising. By integrating hermeneutical and semiotic methods, this research decodes the symbolic language of gender encoded in the toys themselves and their presentation in print advertisements and catalog listings. The themes of females as "babes," living in a fantasy world, that are inferior to males emerged from the analysis. This research demonstrates that children's toys send clear and consistent messages to children that affirm traditional cultural values and preserve traditional relations between the sexes.

By three or four years of age children know whether they are girls or boys, as well as how to use gender as a basis for categorizing the world around them (see Katz 1986 for a review of this research). Abilities, interests, and activities are just a few of the things children classify as being characteristic of either boys and men (daddies) or girls and women (mommies). Understanding how to carve the world on the basis of gender and their own place within such a categorization system marks the development of children's gender identity (Kohlberg 1966; Yorburg 1974). To the chagrin of egalitarian, "politically correct" parents, the relationship that forms between children's understanding of maleness and femaleness (Spence 1985), their own biological sex, and society's gender categories (Sherif 1982) is usually highly stereotyped, embracing a core of traditional ideologies regarding gender and the appropriate roles of men and women.

This paper examines how this ideology is transmitted to children through one of the most ubiquitous aspects of their lives—toys. Integrating hermeneutic and semiotic methods, this research decodes the symbolic language of gender contained in these cultural artifacts. In so doing, the meaning conveyed by these signs is "made opaque" (Goffman 1976 p. 27), highlighting the subtle, yet powerful ways children are taught narrowly defined and stereotypical sex-roles, starting at a very young age.

As early as three years of age children not only differentiate between "girls' toys" and "boys' toys," they clearly prefer same-sex-typed toys (Fagot 1974; O'Brien, Huston, & Risley 1983; Caldera, Huston, & O'Brien 1989). Toys and their advertisements provide children with important information about what it means to be a girl and boy (Chafetz 1974). However, little attention has been given to what children are taught about gender via these media. Most research has focused on either demonstrating sex-typing of toys (Schwartz & Markham 1985; Fisher-Thompson 1990) or on explicating the factors involved in the development of children's preferences.[2]

---

[1] The author would like to thank Elizabeth Hirschman and Eviatar Zerubavel for their comments on earlier drafts.

[2] Some of the factors that have been studied in regard to children's preference for sex-typed toys are parental reaction to sex-typed play (Fagot & Leinbach, 1989), adults toy preferences especially in terms of the toys they purchase for children (Thompson, Molison & Elliot, 1988) and the effect of seeing children of the same or opposite sex playing with the toy (Liss, 1977; Ruble, Balaban, T. & Cooper, J., 1981).

The few studies that have examined the gender lessons encoded in toys and toy advertising have conducted their analysis in terms of either (1) the kinds of toys designed for girls (e.g. dolls, household goods, "beauty aids") and boys (e.g. trucks, erector sets, athletic gear) and what roles these toys prepare children for (Mitchell 1973; Chafetz 1974), or (2) the frequency and ways boys and girls are pictured (typically boys are pictured actively engaged with the toy whereas girls are often shown observing the action) (Chafetz 1974; Schwartz & Markham 1985).

These studies use detailed coding schema within a positivist paradigm to reveal statistically significant sex stereotyping of toys and their presentation in the media. Schwartz & Markham (1985) state that although their findings are robust, they fail to capture the subtle ways in which stereotypical notions of femininity and masculinity are communicated. Their research points to the need for further analysis of toys in order to more fully articulate what children learn about gender.

METHOD

This paper takes a hermeneutical tact to uncover major themes regarding gender symbolized in children's toys. In this approach toys, their packaging, catalog listings and advertisements are treated as cultural texts in which society's dominant ideologies are embedded (Barthes 1968; Geertz 1975; Goffman 1976; Hirschman 1990). While hermeneutics provides the analytical course, semiotics represents the vehicle by which this analytical path is traversed. However, before going into detail about these two facets of the method, I begin with a description of the landscape or interpretive frame in which this quest took place.

Interpretive Frame

As mentioned earlier, advertisements and catalog listings for toys, the toys themselves, and their packaging are all types of texts. The first three of these form the interpretive frame used in this research. In particular, catalog listings from two national department store chains and multi-page, color advertisement supplements from two newspapers were the primary data sources. The catalogs provided 292 pages of descriptions and pictures of over 1,000 different toys including skates, bicycles, and board games. Listings (and advertisements) for electronic games (e.g. Nintendo and Sega Genesis) were excluded from this analysis because they appear to represent a unique "toy" genre and signification system.

Advertising supplements from a state-wide newspaper and from a smaller local newspaper were collected over a two month period (October and November). Only full-color supplements containing two or more pages of toys were included. These data sources provided an additional ninety-seven pages of photographs and descriptions for the season's most popular toys. The complete sample of supplements included advertisements for two national toy store chains, a national discount store chain, a regional discount store chain, and a local grocery/department store chain (i.e. superstore). This is important to note, because together the advertising agencies responsible for creating these promotional materials and the sponsoring corporations act as "auteurs" (Wollen 1985) stamping their collective ideologies into the layout and design chosen. As a result, each store's ad campaign represents a different source, analogous to different informants or to a between subjects design used in other types of research. Examining the juxtaposition of the same toys across a variety of advertisement layouts not only

Hermeneutical Approach

The themes embedded in these texts emerged and evolved through the use of the hermeneutical technique of close reading (Hirschman 1990; Holbrook & Grayson 1986). Close reading involves a detailed examination of a text's elements and record of the themes contained in these elements. In a toy advertisement such details might include the pronouns and adjectives used in the toy's description, the toy's color(s), and/or its position relative to other toys in the picture. These textual details or component parts become the standard against which emerging interpretations of the text as a whole are evaluated. This recursive shift in focus from looking at the text as a whole, to looking closely at its individual parts and back again to the whole is analogous to the interplay between theory and data (Gadamer 1975). Known as the Hermeneutic Circle, it is this oscillation between parts and whole that is the basis of interpretive research, as well as the means by which any degree of "objectivity" in the positivist sense is achieved (Hirschman 1990; Thompson, Locander & Polli 1989).

Close reading was conducted by carefully studying each toy's verbal description and photograph. A log identifying the major signs found on each toy and the themes conveyed by them was kept. Major signs were initially defined as the features distinguishing girls' toys from boys' toys. This included features appearing almost exclusively on toys stereotypically associated with one sex over another, as well as features differentiating the girls' and boys' model of the same toy. In most cases these models were clearly labeled or described as being for a boy or girl (e.g. the Playskool garage "is the perfect place for the little handy*man*") or they were pictured with children of the "appropriate" sex (e.g. the "Weebles Busy Fire Station Ride-on" is always shown with a boy while its counterpart, the "Weebles Busy Playhouse Ride-on" is always riden by a girl). The initial search for differences follows from the procedure Goffman (1976) used to identify "genderisms" in the advertisements he analyzed. In addition, once a major sign and theme began to emerge, notation was made of any exceptions or "counter-examples."

The individual interpretations of the major signs served as the point of entry into the hermeneutical circle in which symbolic meanings and patterns found in individual parts were related to increasingly larger wholes. For example, the themes emerging from treating each toy as an entire text and the individual signs as components were then related to a new whole represented by a particular genre of toy (e.g. baby dolls, games, and "wheels, wings, & moving things"), which themselves became parts to the entire category of toys. In so doing, early emerging themes such as activity/ passivity, and beauty/brawn evolved as the increasingly larger wholes to which they were related suggested other, broader interpretations of the text.

Another part/whole relationship central to this analysis focused on the arrangement of toys in each photograph, the layout of photographs on each page, and the relationship between pages in the catalogs and advertisements. As I will describe later, this particular relationship provided a framework for pulling together several diverse themes such as "girls stuff is simple," and "boys are artists."

Semiotic Analysis

The analytic method used follows closely from the Saussurean tradition of semiology in which the meaning of a sign is determined by its relationship with the other signs within a larger system. In particular, it is difference or contrasting relationships that determine a sign's character (Saussure 1959 p. 121). These polar oppositions or syntactical relationships establish a sign's meaning by defining what it is not. For example, what is meant (signified) by the word (sign) masculine may be difficult to describe, but syntactics suggests that whatever masculine may be, it is *not* feminine. Syntactical analysis helps disembed the ideology of gender from the texts of toys and their advertisements.

However, literacy in a semiotic language requires an understanding of both syntactics and semantics.[3] Therefore, this analysis is not purely structural, but also looks at the semantic levels of symbolic meaning. Semantics refers to the relationship between a sign and its object. The meaning of a sign depends on the objects with which it is associated. To continue with the earlier example of what masculine means, semantic relationships suggest that if masculine is typically used to signify or represent men, aggressive behavior and the color blue then these objects come to define this particular sign (word).

Through these two levels of analyses (syntactic and semantic) I highlight the ways in which a highly stereotypical ideology of gender is encoded in children's toys, and how these messages effect the development of gender identity in girls and boys.

EMERGENT THEMES

Three themes emerged through the course of this analysis (1) Females as Babes, (2) Living in a fantasy world, and (3) The Masculine Supremacy Effect. The cultural importance of these themes is reflected in the non-practical, non-utilitarian, purely conventional, and redundant ways toys are marked with the signs of these messages. In the following section, each theme, complete with examples, is described. In order to highlight the semantic and syntactic relationships comprising these themes, the semiotic quadrangle developed by Eviatar Zerubavel (1987) is used.[4] Based, in part, on Levi-Strauss' (1959) notion that signifieds on the same side of an opposition may be treated as homologous, the semiotic quadrangle graphically represents the semantic relationships from which the themes begin to emerge, as well as the oppositional relationships between signs that brings these themes into sharper focus.

Females as Babes

The primary theme revealed from a close reading of toys and their advertisements was of females (both girls and women) as babes. The double entendre here is intended to reflect this theme's dual and almost inseparable component messages. Being female, femaleness, and femininity means being passive, an object of adornment rather than action, whereas being male and male-related things are active. Secondly, by extending this notion of passivity to dependency and helplessness females are infantilized. Tuchman (1978) has referred to this characterization of women and girls as

---

[3] Although Levi-Strauss (1966) has argued that "the existence of differentiating features is of much greater importance than their content" (p. 75) this emphasis on structure, especially as demonstrated most recently by deconstructionists such as Derrida, ignores the inseparable nature of the semantic and syntactic aspects of signs (Culler, 1975; Zerubavel, 1987).

[4] Greimas (1982) developed a similar tool for mapping the logical structure of a text. However, semantic relationships are represented differently.

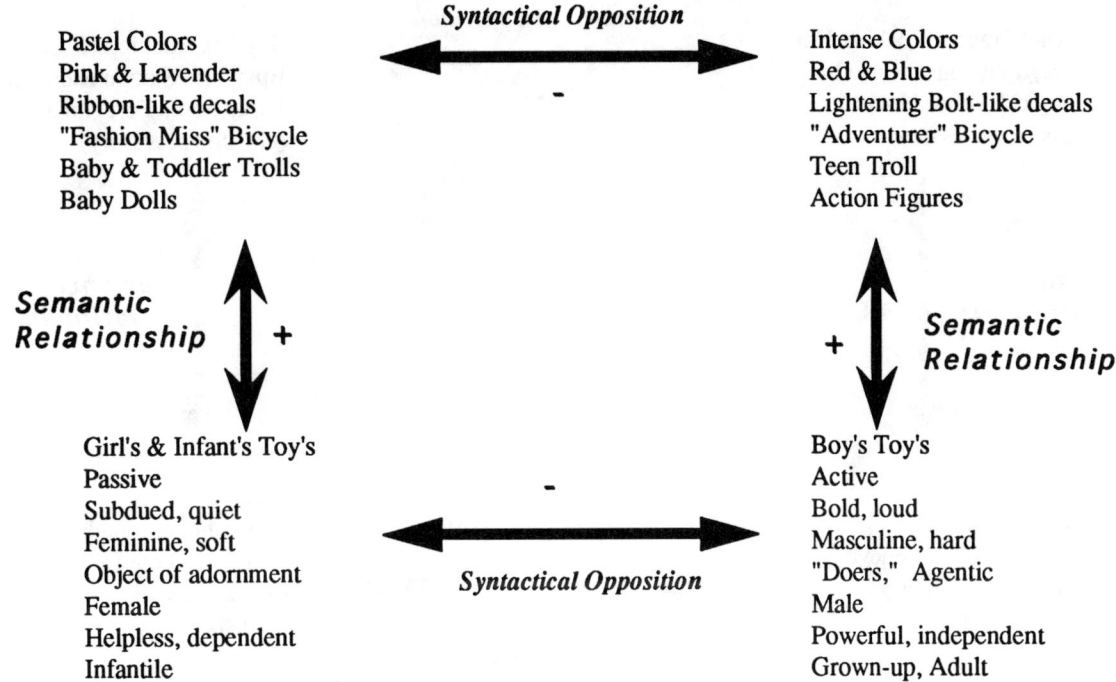

FIGURE 1
Semiotic Quadrangle and Symbolic Representation of "Females as Babes"

child-like adornments needing protection as "symbolic annihilation" (p. 8).

Both of these messages are conveyed by the colors, decals, and names used for girls' and boys' toys, as well as the ways male and female models are posed and pictured in toy advertisements and on toy packaging (See Figure 1). Since this latter means of conveyance has been well-documented by Chaftez (1974), Goffman (1979), and most recently by Schwartz & Markham (1985), this discussion focuses on those signs encoded on the toys themselves.

Color. The most noticeable contrast between girls' and boy's toys is the differential use of colors. Pastels, especially pink and lavender, are used in almost every toy for girls. Toys for boys, on the other hand, use intense colors, such as bold primary colors or dark colors, most noticeably black. Moreover, pastel colors are used exclusively for girl and infant toys, thereby serving as one way being female begins to be equated with being infant-like. Pastel colors are typically described as being "soft" and "gentle." They are the colors of nurseries and bedrooms, places where one is most often quiet and relaxed. Although some work on the psychology of color may indicate that these colors induce a passive state, this explication is not meant to reify this relationship. Instead, the goal is to illustrate how through repeated associations, pastel colors come to represent passivity. In contrast, bright, bold colors represent action.

Decals. One of the most notable uses of of decals for signifying the passive nature of girls and the active nature of boys is found on the "1-2-3 Bikes" by Playskool. These miniature versions of "big-kid" bicycles are designed for children ages two through five years. The girl's model features a two-toned (pink and lavender) ribbon-like decal whereas the decal on the boy's bike resembles a lightening bolt which changes from bright red to orange to yellow. Aestheticians such as Maitland Graves (in Sahlins, 1976 p. 193) suggest that curved, undulating lines symbolize passivity, softness and femininity. In contrast, the straight lines comprising the thunderbolt decal represent boldness, hardness, and masculinity. These decals, indeed the very existence of two different models, indicate, by virtue of their non-utilitarian, arbitrary, and conventional character, the importance of both differentiating between boys and girls, and assuring that they learn the cultural expectations of their respective gender roles.

Toy Names. Both aspects of being a babe are represented in toy names. For example, bicycles designed for girls are named "L.A. Lady," "Fashion Miss," and "Double Take." These bikes feature bags or baskets that can double as a purse, implying that girls need to be or are primarily concerned with how good or well-coordinated they look. Boys' bikes often feature water bottles, suggesting that boys are going to be riding their bikes so hard that they will need to replenish bodily fluids. Their names also signify the active nature of boys such as "Ambush," "Adventurer," and "Mudslinger."

The infantization of females is highlighted by comparing the names of a girl and boy version of a roller-blading doll. The girl doll is "Baby" while the boy doll is "Dude." Even trolls, which originally were genderless, are often "sexed" today. In those cases where the troll is clearly male it is always older, whereas infant and toddler trolls are always female. In fact, virtually every *baby* doll is female. In those few cases (counter-examples) where and infant doll is male it is either a minority (e.g. "Paco, the Mexican boy"), or there is a female version too and the boy doll is rarely included in advertisements for the product. The "Talking Urkel Doll" is not only a minority, but his character (as played on television) is effeminate. Constant association of females with infants sends a clear and consistent message. Girls are babes and therefore they are passive, helpless, dependent beings.

Living in a Fantasy World

The second theme, living in a fantasy world, extends the classic gender distinction of public and private from the worlds of work and home to the more abstract realms of reality and fantasy. Males occupy the public sphere, consequently they need to know how things really work and what they really look like. Preparing

362 / Babes in Toyland: Learning an Ideology of Gender

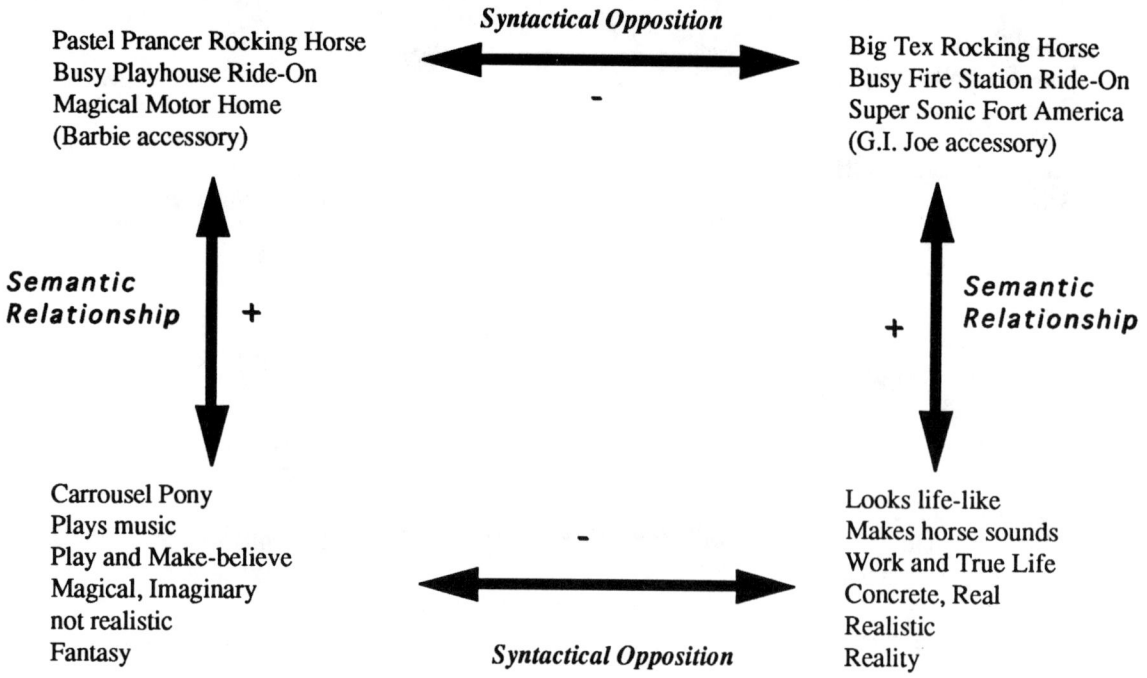

FIGURE 2
Semiotic Quadrangle and Symbolic Representation of "Living in a Fantasy World"

boys for this role is serious business and is symbolized in some way (e.g. color, sounds, amount of detail) in virtually every toy designed for boys. For example, "Big Tex" the spring horse makes life-like sounds in proportion to how "fast" *he* is ridden. It is so important that this message regarding reality and masculinity be received that it is sent simultaneously across multiple channels. The realistic sounding and looking horse is shown being ridden by a boy, *and* the horse itself is described as being male. Opposite "Big Tex" is "Pastel Prancer," a scaled-down replica of a carrousel pony.[5] Although carrousel ponies are also "real" things they are part of the carnival world, a place for amusement and play. In addition, "Pastel Prancer" is a second order representation (a model of a model of a real thing), thereby removing it one step further from the reality of horses as living beasts. Moreover, the soft pinks and lavenders used to color this rocking horse make it even more fantasy and dream-like. Even the colors of "real" carrousel ponies usually are ones that real horses might be (e.g. white, black, brown).

---

[5] Although not included in the previous discussion on the characterization of females as passive and males as active, "Big Tex" and "Pastel Prancer" not only symbolize that distinction but act in ways to create it. The rate sounds are generated by "Big Tex" depends on the activity of the rider. The more active and faster the rider bounces the more sound that is created. Symbolically (because the horse is described as male and because it is depicted more as a boy's toy) the message is that boys are active. Boys are made to be more active because the horse's sounds reinforce the rider's activity. "Pastel Prancer" lacks this reinforcement component. Instead, it plays carrousel music at the same volume and rate regardless of how vigorously the rider rocks it. The music will play even if the rider just sits quietly. According to behaviorist theory, since activity is not reinforced it should extinguish, thereby making girls (because they are more likely than boys to be riding this model) less active and more passive.

Other examples of the syntactical and semantic relationships carrying this theme's message are shown in Figure 2. The colors and names of the girls' toys signify fantasy, dreaminess and a world of pretend. There are "Magic Tea Party" sets, "every little girl's dream horse, Starlight," "Party Kitchens," the "Fantasy Wardrobe Trunk" and for slightly older girls the "Dream Phone Game." Pink and/or lavender comprise the basic color scheme used by all of these toys. Boys' toys do not belong to the world of fantasy. Instead, the names and colors of their toys connect them directly to the real world, such as the "NASCAR Hot Stock Raceway," "Olympic Superstars," and G.I. Joe's newest mode of ground transportation, the "Humvee Replica," a military vehicle introduced during Operation Desert Storm.

The most notable contrast within this theme is the lack of functional detail in toys for girls. Apparently, since girls occupy the private world of fantasy they do not need to worry about the realities of everyday life. Their toys, which replicate this world have very little detail. These differences in detail and realism between toys designed for boys and toys designed for girls is not merely a function of whether or not the toy promotes socialization into a stereotypic gender role. Highly detailed and intricate toys can be found for both girls and boys. However, when comparisons are made between toys within the same price range, or models of the same toys there are usually marked differences in the complexity and detail found in toys for each sex. For example, the "Playskool doll house", "comes completely furnished." However, these furnishings are extremely over-simplified with no moving parts. The garage that is advertised as the counterpart to this house is described as being "ideal for the handyman." In contrast to the doll house its accessories include a car with tires that can be changed, removable engine parts, workshop, a detailed lawn mower and more. Similar discrepancies can be found in other toys. Although girls have dolls that cry, eat, talk, and need potty trained, these functions are uni-dimensional. Dolls that cry, cry one way. In contrast, many toy cars that make engine sounds make more than one type of noise. Just as a "real" car's engine sounds differently when the motor is idling or revving, many toy cars also have different sounds to indicate whether their engines are idling or revving. Toys for boys are more multi-faceted, reflecting the complex, public, real-world that is their dominion.

Masculine Supremacy Effect

Historically, features and attributes associated with males have been evaluated more positively than female or feminine characteristics. Inductive reasoning based on these premises lead one to the general rule that being male is better than being female. This notion has dominated both scholarly thought and the thinking of the general public. Dubbed the "masculine supremacy effect" by Cook (1985 p. 96), in recent years this perspective has come under attack from scholars arguing that difference does not necessarily mean deficit.

In order to counter the effects of a long tradition in which the natural superiority of males was espoused, educators developed curricula to encourage psychological androgyny. The underlying assumption was that a fully functioning, psychologically healthy person was one who was both feminine and masculine. Although progress has been slow, some recent findings suggest that the evaluative tide may be turning (c.f. Eagly, Mladinic, & Otto, 1991; Pennell, 1993) and that stereotypically female things are evaluated at least as positively, if not more so, than male characteristics. However, by returning to Toyland one is bombarded with messages telling children that being male is better than being female.

Toy advertising uses many types of signs to convey the masculine supremacy theme. Using distance to impart a size difference to the boy and girl models of a particular toy that are actually the same size, toy advertisements frequently position the boy's model in the foreground and the girl's model in the background. This makes the girl's toy look smaller than the boy's toy, suggesting that boy things and by extension boys are more important and better than girls and their things. Goffman (1979) maintains that differences in size are so completely associated with differences in social weight—power, authority, rank, and renown—that relative size is routinely used to ensure that the picture's message will be understood at a glance (p. 28).

Toys belonging to the category of arts, crafts & handiwork also symbolize this theme. Items designed for girls suggest, via their names (e.g. "Sew Easy" and "EZ 2 Do Fashion Machine") that the crafts girls are interested in are simple. The woodcraft kits designed for boys, however, are referred to as names like "Master Workshop," and imply that the kinds of things boys do take mastery and skill. Furthermore, boys are not shown in these advertisements doing "crafts," but are only shown painting or doing some other type of "art." Crafts belong to the realm of pop culture, a profane alternative to the true art of high culture. Regardless of whether or not one type of craft or artform is more difficult than the other, the message sent to kids through these names is that girls' stuff is simple and boys' stuff is harder to do. From there it is a small step to concluding that if girls do easy stuff they must not be as smart or as good as boys. Moreover, things that girls are able to do well must not be as difficult or important as the things boys can do.

Finally, sets of action figures designed for boys go by names such as "B.O.T.S.," an acronym for Brains, Originality, Talent, & Strength, "Challenge of the Champions" and "Mighty Men of Valor." All of these figures are themselves males, thereby strengthening the association between being male and being smart, talented, strong, valiant, and a champion. In the case of girls' toys there are no female B.O.T.S. or brave and mighty dolls. The only female dolls that are "champions" are beauty contestant winners.

DISCUSSION

It has been twenty years since Mitchell (1973) and Chafetz (1974) documented the role toys play in socializing children and reinforcing stereotypical notions of femininity and masculinity. During this time numerous groups have worked to raise people's consciousness and loosen the glue holding gender stereotypes together. Yet, children today continue to hold traditional views regarding what it means to be a boy or girl.

This research reveals that children's toys and their presentation in mass media send clear and consistent messages that affirm cultural values and preserve traditional relations between the sexes. The redundancy of these signs and their continued association with either females or males obscures gender's socially constructed nature. Their purely conventional, extra-practical, and non-functional character indicates the importance of these messages for social life. As Goffman (1976) noted "gender expressions are by way of being mere show; but a considerable amount of the substance of society is enrolled in the staging of it" (p. 8).

REFERENCES

Barthes, Roland (1968). *Elements of semiology*. Translated by Annette Lovers & Colin Smith. New York: Hill and Wang.

Belk, Russell, John F. Sherry, Jr., & Melanie Wallendorf (1988). "A Naturalistic Inquiry into Buyer and Seller Behavior at a Swap Meet". *Journal of consumer Behavior*, 14, 449-470.

Caldera, Y.M., Althea C. Huston, & M. O'Brien. (1989). "Social interactions and play patterns of parents and toddlers with feminine, masculine, and neutral toys." *Child Development*, 60, 70-76.

Chafetz, Janet Saltzman (1974). *Masculine/feminine or human? An overview of the sociology of sex roles*. Ithaca, Il: F.E. Peacock Publishers.

Cook, E. P. (1985). *Psychological androgyny*. New York: Pergamon Press.

Culler, Jonathan (1975). *Structuralist poetics*. Ithaca, NY: Cornell University Press.

Eagly, Alice H., A. Mladinic, & S. Otto. (1991). "Are women evaluated more favorably than men? An analysis of attitudes, beliefs, and emotions." *Psychology of Women Quarterly*, 15, 203-216.

Fagot, B.I. & M.D. Leinbach,. (1989). "The young child's gender schema: Environmental input, internal organization." *Child Development*, 60, 663-672.

Gadamer, Hans Georg (1975). *Truth and method*. New York: Crossroad.

Geertz, Clifford (1975). *The interpretation of culture*. London: Hutchinson.

Goffman, Erving (1976). *Gender Advertisements*. New York: Harper Colophon Books.

Hirschman, Elizabeth C. (1990). "Secular immortality and the American ideology of affluence." *Journal of Consumer Research*, 17, 31-42.

Holbrook, Morris B. & Mark W. Grayson. (1986). "The semiology of cinematic consumption: Symbolic consumer behavior in *Out of Africa*." *Journal of Consumer Research*, 13, 374-380.

Katz, Phyllis A. (1986). "Gender Identity: Development and Consequences." In Richard D. Ashmore & Frances K. Del Boca (Eds.), *The social psychology of female-male relations: A critical analysis of central concepts*. (pp. 21-67). Orlando, Fl: Academic Press.

Kohlberg, Lawerence A. (1966). "A cognitive-developmental analysis of children's sex-role concepts and attitudes." In Eleanor Maccoby (Ed.), *The development of sex differences*. Stanford: Stanford University Press.

Levi-Strauss, Claude. (1962). *The savage mind*. Chicago: University of Chicago Press.

Liss, M. B. (1977). "The effects of televised modeling cues on children's sex-typed toy preferences." *Dissertation Abstracts International*, 37, 3581-3582.

O'Brien, M., Althea C. Huston, & Risley (1983). "Sex-typed play behavior in toddlers in a day care center." *Journal of Applied Developmental Psychology*, 21, 866-871.

Pennell, Greta Eleen (1993). You and me as she and he: The meaning of gender-related concepts in other- and self-perception. Unpublished Masters thesis, Rutgers University.

Ruble, Diane N., Terry Balaban, & Joel Cooper. (1981). "Gender constancy and the effects of sex-typed televised toy commercials." *Child Development*, 52, 667-673.

Sahlins, Marshall (1976). *Culture and practical reason*. Chicago: University of Chicago Press.

Saussure, Ferdinand de. (1959). *Course in general linguistics*. New York: Philosophical Library. (Original 1915).

Schwartz, Lori A. & William T. Markham. (1985). "Sex stereotyping in children's toy advertisements." *Sex Roles*, 12, 157-170.

Sherif, Carolyn Wood (1982). "Needed concepts in the study of gender identity." *Psychology of Women Quarterly*, 6, 375-398.

Spence, Janet T. (1985). "Gender identity and its implications for the concepts of masculinity and femininity." In T.B. Sonderegger (Ed.), *Psychology and Gender, Nebraska Symposium on Motivation* (Vol. 32, pp. 59-96). Lincoln: University of Nebraska Press.

Thompson, Craig J., William B. Locander, & Howard R. Pollio. (1989). "Putting consumer experience back into consumer research: The philosophy and method of existential-phenomenology." *Journal of Consumer Research*, 16, 133-146.

Thompson, D. F., K.L. Molison, & M. Elliott. (1988). "Adult selection of children's toys." Poster presented at the annual meeting of the Eastern Psychological Association, Buffalo, NY.

Tuchman, Gaye (1978). "The symbolic annihilation of women by the mass media." In Gaye Tuchman, Arlene Kaplan Daniels & James Benet (Eds.), *Hearth and Home: Images of Women in the Mass Media*, (pp. 3-38). New York: Oxford University Press.

Wallendorf, Melanie & Russel W. Belk. (1989). "Assessing trustworthiness in naturalistic consumer research." In Elizabeth C. Hirschman (Ed.), *Interpretive Consumer Research* (pp. 69-84). Provo, Utah: Association for Consumer Research.

Wollen, Peter. (1985), "The Auteur Theory," in Gerald Mast and Marshall Cohen (Eds.), *Film Theory and Criticism*, Oxford: Oxford University Press, 553-562.

Yorburg, B. (1974). *Sexual identity: Sex roles and social change*. New York: Wiley-Interscience.

Zerubavel, Eviatar (1987). "The language of time: Towards a semiotics of temporality." *Sociological Quarterly*, 28, 343-356.

Social Comparison and the Beauty of Advertising Models: The Role of Motives for Comparison

Mary C. Martin, University of Nebraska-Lincoln
Patricia F. Kennedy, University of Nebraska-Lincoln

ABSTRACT

Social comparison theory itself has enabled marketers to understand better several types of marketing phenomenon, including comparing one's physical attractiveness to advertising models (Martin and Kennedy 1993, 1994; Richins 1991), comparison of material possessions (Richins 1992), and consumer sensitivity to social comparison information (Bearden and Rose 1990). One aspect of the theory that has yet to be systematically studied is the *motive* for comparison. As such, this study examines the role of motives in social comparison. The marketing studies cited have assumed the motive for comparison to be self-evaluation, as originally proposed by Festinger (1954). However, three motives have been identified in the social psychology literature: self-evaluation, self-improvement, and self-enhancement.

After a general discussion of motives, the role of motives with respect to female adolescents comparing their physical attractiveness to that of models in ads is explored. Propositions are presented, highlighting when comparison to advertising models will occur and the differential effects on self-perceptions of physical attractiveness and self-esteem that may occur when motives are taken into consideration.

A study was conducted to determine underlying motives in female adolescents when they compare their physical attractiveness to that of models in ads. The results indicate that both self-evaluation and self-improvement as motives for comparison to advertising models exist in female adolescents, as well as in combination with each other. The study also reveals specific methods suggested for self-improvement, the frequency with which respondents indicated that they were able to discount the beauty of advertising models, and the frequency with which female adolescents aspire to be models. Future research, because these motives were found to exist, should address the propositions presented to determine whether differential effects on self-perceptions of physical attractiveness and self-esteem occur, depending on the predominating motive at the time of comparison.

Social comparison theory has been revitalized in recent years in both psychology (see Goethals 1986) and marketing (e.g. Martin and Kennedy 1993, 1994; Bearden and Rose 1990; Richins 1991, 1992). In marketing, the theory has been used in investigating several phenomenon, including comparing one's physical attractiveness to advertising models (Martin and Kennedy 1993, 1994; Richins 1991), comparison of material possessions (Richins 1992), and consumer sensitivity to social comparison information (Bearden and Rose 1990). While the theory itself has enabled marketers to understand better these marketing phenomena, one aspect of the theory that has yet to be systematically studied is the *motive* for comparison. The marketing studies cited have assumed the motive for comparison to be self-evaluation, as originally proposed by Festinger (1954). However, Wood (1989) showed that social comparison may occur for other reasons, including self-improvement or self-enhancement. The purposes of this study are, therefore, to 1) present an overview of the motives for social comparison; 2) present propositions concerning the role of motives in the context of comparison of physical attractiveness to advertising models by female preadolescents and adolescents; and 3) present the results of a study designed to measure the types of motives that exist when female preadolescents and adolescents compare their physical attractiveness to that of models in ads.

COMPARISON MOTIVES

Festinger's (1954) social comparison theory can be summarized in three fundamental propositions:

1. People have a *drive* to evaluate their opinions and abilities.
2. In the absence of *"objective"* bases for comparison, this need can be satisfied by *"social"* comparison with other people.
3. Such social comparisons will, when possible, be made with *similar* others.

Festinger (1954) proposed accurate *self-evaluation* as the purpose of social comparison. Self-evaluation can be defined as the judgment of value, worth, or appropriateness of one's abilities, opinions, and personal traits.

However, Festinger (1954) considered *self-enhancement* as a comparison motive briefly in his original theory by specifying an ego-enhancement function termed a "unidirectional drive upward." Self-enhancement is defined as an an individual's biased attempts to maintain positive views of him/herself to protect or enhance self-esteem. Thornton and Arrowood (1966), Hakmiller (1966), and Wheeler (1966) found support for the existence of a unidirectional drive upward, a self-enhancement motive, and comparison to others who are dissimilar (i.e. those of superior status) with respect to personality traits. To determine what motives are in existence, studies have generally employed rank-order paradigms. For example, Thornton and Arrowood (1966) employed a rank-order paradigm in which subjects were administered a bogus personality test described as measuring either a positive or negative trait. The subjects received a bogus score on the personality test and then indicated which score in the rank ordering they wished to see. The authors interpreted the results in terms of self-evaluation and self-enhancement as motives for comparison to others.

Social psychologists have shown that social comparison may also occur for reasons of *self-improvement* (see Wood 1989). Self-improvement is defined as an individual's attempts to learn how to improve or to be inspired to improve a particular attribute. Despite the importance of self-improvement demonstrated in research on achievement motivation (Atkinson and Raynor 1974) and observational learning (Bandura 1986), and in the popularity of "how-to" books, few studies have examined the role of self-improvement in social comparison.

In summary, three motives found to exist in social comparison processes include:

1. *Self-evaluation* — an individual's judgment of value, worth, or appropriateness of his/her abilities, opinions, and personal traits.

2. *Self-enhancement* — an individual's biased attempts to maintain positive views of him/herself to protect or enhance self-esteem.

3. *Self-improvement* — an individual's attempts to learn how to improve or to be inspired to improve a particular attribute.

Given that these motives exist, what role do they play in social comparison processes? An individual's motive for social comparison will influence the comparison process by determining *whom* one will select for comparison. Whom one selects for comparison, in turn, determines the *type* of comparison taking place—upward, downward, or similar. For example, all three motives may be served when *upward* comparisons are made. Upward comparisons occur when one makes comparisons with others who are superior or better off in some way. Thus, self-evaluation is served when one evaluates his/herself against a higher standard. Self-improvement is served when one learns from a superior other. Finally, if one assumes similarity on *surrounding* dimensions (those involved in comparisons but not the focal dimension under evaluation), the upward comparison may be self-enhancing (Wood 1989). Conversely, *downward* comparisons occur when one makes comparisons with others who are inferior or less fortunate than oneself. All three motives may be served by downward comparisons, but they most commonly occur for the purpose of self-enhancement. That is, an individual's biased attempts to maintain positive views of him/herself to protect or enhance self-esteem are most commonly achieved by comparing to inferior others. *Similar* comparisons occur when one makes comparisons with others who are similar on the attribute under question or surrounding attributes. Again, all three motives may be served by similar comparisons, but they most commonly occur for the purpose of self-evaluation. Further, a combination of motives may be in operation at one time. For example, self-evaluative comparisons may ultimately lead to self-improvement (Wood 1989).

Self-enhancement may also occur by *avoiding* social comparison. For example, Brickman and Bulman (1977) found that at times people do appear to avoid social comparison deliberately. Avoidance of social comparison will occur when one believes that his or her ability is particularly low or if he or she feels threatened (Friend and Gilbert 1973; Gastorf et al. 1978; Pyszczynski, Greenberg, and LaPrelle 1985; Samuel 1973; Smith and Insko 1987), and will occur even in the presence of comparisons "forced" upon one from the environment (Martin 1986). Avoidance of upward comparisons serves to preserve one's self-esteem (Wood 1989).

MOTIVES FOR COMPARISON AND ADVERTISING MODELS

Studies have found that female preadolescents, adolescents, and college students do compare their physical attractiveness with that of models in ads (Martin and Kennedy 1993, 1994; Richins 1991). While these studies have assumed that the motive for comparison was self-evaluation, it is likely that comparison to advertising models may serve any one of the three motives—self-evaluation, self-improvement, or self-enhancement—depending upon which predominates at the time of comparison.

In the context of advertising, given that advertising models represent an ideal (perhaps unrealistic) image of beauty, the type of comparison that generally occurs will be *upward*. That is, female preadolescents and adolescents will generally consider advertising models to be superior in terms of physical attractiveness. Again, any one of the three motives can be served through upward comparisons. However, it is likely that upward comparisons to models in ads by female preadolescents and adolescents will generally not be *self-enhancing* because similarity on *surrounding* dimensions, such as age (i.e. most models appear to be in their twenties) or context (e.g. the model is not a schoolmate), will not be perceived to exist. Thus, when self-enhancement predominates as the motive for comparison, female preadolescents and adolescents will most likely *avoid* upward comparisons to advertising models in an attempt to preserve self-esteem. Therefore, the first proposition is suggested.

P1: *When self-evaluation or self-improvement predominates as the motive for comparison, female preadolescents and adolescents compare their level of physical attractiveness with that of models in ads; when self-enhancement predominates as the motive for comparison, female preadolescents and adolescents will avoid comparisons of physical attractiveness to models in ads.*

THE RESULTS OF COMPARISON

Social comparison theory has central relevance for dimensions of the self-concept, particularly self-esteem. Comparisons on self-relevant dimensions appear to have special impact on one's self-esteem and feelings (Wood 1989). James's (1984) definition of self-esteem (one's successes divided by one's pretensions) highlights social comparison processes by suggesting that aspirations are often defined by comparison with others, often to the detriment of self-esteem. Also highlighting social comparison processes in self-evaluation and the formation of ego-identity in adolescence, Erikson (1968) wrote, "The individual judges himself in light of what he perceives to be the way others judge him in comparison to themselves and to a typology significant to them; while he judges their way of judging him in light of how he perceives himself in comparison to them and to types that have become relevant to him." The idea that social comparison affects self-esteem was even implicit in Festinger's (1954) original conception of social comparison theory.

Comparison with advertising models may result in changes in *self-perceptions of physical attractiveness* (Martin and Kennedy 1993; Richins 1991). In turn, because the domain of physical attractiveness has consistently been found to be a significant factor in determining self-esteem, changes in self-perceptions of physical attractiveness should affect levels of *self-esteem*. The importance of this domain, unlike others, is unable to be discounted by female preadolescents and adolescents (Harter 1986, 1992; Rosenberg 1986). Therefore, if exposure to advertising with physically attractive models lowers self-perceptions of physical attractiveness, levels of self-esteem will also decrease. However, this study proposes that changes in self-perceptions and/or self-esteem may be influenced by the type of motive predominating at the time of comparison. Therefore, the subsequent discussion will focus on possible differential effects on self-perceptions of physical attractiveness and self-esteem, depending on the predominating motive for comparison. In addition, because it was hypothesized that female preadolescents and adolescents will avoid comparisons to advertising models when self-enhancement predominates as the motive for comparison, the subsequent discussion will focus on the motives of self-improvement and self-evaluation.

SELF-EVALUATION AS A MOTIVE FOR COMPARISON

Information obtained from social comparison is not used for self-evaluation until the age of seven or eight, even though social comparison has been found to occur in children as early as preschool age (Ruble 1983). Further, the ability to make social comparisons develops through several stages or levels. An adolescent's cognitive abilities, subsequent self-evaluation of competence resulting from social comparison, and behavior effects tend to influence the process of social comparison (Ruble 1983). According to Renick and Harter (1989), social comparison information assumes increasingly greater importance in an effort to self-evaluate as levels of cognitive-developmental skills increase. For example, the authors found, in a study of learning disabled (LD) children in grades three through eight, that social comparison processes play an important role in self-evaluation and formation of their perceived academic competence. LD students perceive themselves as becoming less academically competent when they compare themselves to normally achieving students but maintain high self-evaluations of academic competence when they compare themselves to other LD students. Because adolescence is a period of transition, with self-perceptions on dimensions of the self generally unstable until late adolescence, the increasing importance placed on social comparison may reflect an effort to stabilize one's self-evaluation of a particular domain (for example, physical attractiveness).

Richins (1991) hypothesized that exposure to advertising with highly attractive models would temporarily lower female college students' self-perceptions of physical attractiveness. Ads from fashion magazines containing highly attractive models were used, with half of the ads showing a facial close-up and the other half showing full-body images of models in revealing sportswear. Richins compared the self-perceptions of physical attractiveness provided by a group of female college students exposed to ads with highly attractive models and those provided by a group exposed to ads with no models. No significant differences were found between the two groups and the hypothesis, therefore, was not supported. In a similar study, Martin and Kennedy (1993) found only partial support for a lowering of self-perceptions of physical attractiveness in female preadolescents and adolescents. Only in fourth graders were self-perceptions of physical attractiveness lowered after exposure to advertising.

The lack of support for these hypotheses may be related to the motive for comparison. While these studies assumed the motive for comparison was self-evaluation, if self-evaluation as the motive for comparison did not predominate at the time of comparison (rather, self-enhancement or self-improvement predominated), lowered self-perceptions by those exposed to idealized images would not necessarily occur. That is, if one was *not* attempting to judge the value or worth of their physical attractiveness, self-perceptions would *not* be affected. Conversely, if self-evaluation predominated at the time of comparison, comparisons should result in lowered self-perceptions. In turn, changes in self-perceptions of physical attractiveness will affect levels of self-esteem. Therefore, the second proposition is suggested. Congruent with Richins (1991) and Martin and Kennedy (1993), who employed an experimental procedure with one-time exposures to ads, the effects are hypothesized to be temporary.

P2: *When self-evaluation predominates as the motive for comparison, comparisons to models in ads will temporarily lower female preadolescents' and adolescents' self-perceptions of physical attractiveness and self-esteem.*

SELF-IMPROVEMENT AS A MOTIVE FOR COMPARISON

Evidence suggests that self-improvement prompts upward comparisons with others. Feldman and Ruble (1977), for example, found that young children compare themselves to other children to learn how to perform tasks. However, self-improvement as a goal for comparison "may be demoralizing, because one is forced to face one's own inferiority" (Wood 1989, p. 239), depending upon whether an upward comparison is perceived as threatening or inspiring. If the target of comparison is perceived as a noncompetitor, then an upward comparison is considered inspiring, rather than threatening. For example, a junior tennis professional making upward comparisons to Martina Navratilova is likely to be inspired by her as opposed to perceiving her as a threat. However, comparison to a fellow junior player is likely to be threatening (Wood 1989). Thus, under competitive conditions, upward comparisons are perceived as threatening and tend to be avoided (Dakin and Arrowood 1981; Miller and Suls 1977; Knippenberg, Wilke, and deVries 1981). An advertising model is most likely to be perceived as a noncompetitor when self-improvement predominates as a goal for comparison. Again, motives may overlap to some degree, particularly self-evaluation and self-improvement, but if one's goal is merely to learn how to improve or to be inspired to improve his/her physical attractiveness (i.e. self-improvement), the individual's self-perceptions of physical attractiveness should not be affected (as in self-evaluation).

Therefore, when self-improvement is the predominating motive for comparison, self-perceptions of physical attractiveness should not be affected. This is due to the fact that competitive conditions do not exist, causing comparisons to advertising models to be considered inspiring rather than threatening. However, if one is inspired to improve her physical attractiveness, feelings of self-esteem may be enhanced in anticipation of an improvement. Therefore, the third proposition is suggested. Congruent with the second proposition, the effect on self-esteem is hypothesized to be temporary.

P3: *When self-improvement predominates as the motive for comparison, comparisons to models in ads will not affect female preadolescents' and adolescents' self-perceptions of physical attractiveness, but will temporarily raise their self-esteem.*

FEMALE PREADOLESCENTS' AND ADOLESCENTS' MOTIVES FOR COMPARISON TO ADVERTISING MODELS

Given the role that motives play in comparison, the next logical step is to determine which motives predominate when female preadolescents and adolescents compare their physical attractiveness to that of models in ads. As such, a Thematic Apperception Test sketch (TAT), a type of projective technique, was administered to a sample of female preadolescents and adolescents in grades four, eight, and twelve to determine the predominating motive when comparing oneself to advertising models. A total of 143 female preadolescents and adolescents completed the TAT, including 59 fourth graders (nine to ten years old), 51 eighth graders (thirteen to fifteen years old), and 33 twelfth graders (seventeen to eighteen years old).

The use of projective techniques in marketing research, particularly TATs, has been revitalized in recent years. For example, Rook (1985) used TATs to investigate the nature of young adults' personal grooming rituals. Most recently, Mick, DeMoss, and Faber (1992) used TATs to investigate the motivations and meanings of self-gifts. The projective hypothesis (Rappaport 1942) suggests that respondents, in generating imaginative stories about a pictorial stimuli, will reveal unconscious and other hidden aspects of their current concerns, motivations, perceptions of significant others, and view of the world. Thus, for the purposes of this study, the TAT represents an appealing technique in that it can reveal underlying motives. In fact, this story-telling technique was originally used by Henry Murray in his studies of motivation (see Chandler and Johnson 1991). Based on the results of pretests with TATs, which indicated that many responses strayed from the

FIGURE

Susie is reading a magazine at home. She notices how pretty the model in the ad looks. She starts comparing the way she looks to the way the model in the ad looks.

Make up a story about Susie and write it in the space below. In your story tell:
1. what else if happening at the moment
2. why Susie is doing what she is doing
3. what Susie is thinking
4. what will happen next

Tell your story here:

---

subject at hand, the projective sketch used for this study was followed by specific questions about the pictorial stimuli. The sketch and questions are shown in the Figure.

Each TAT was analyzed by two judges to identify the predominating motive—either self-evaluation, self-improvement, or self-enhancement. Inter-rater reliability was .78. Discrepancies in coding were resolved through discussion. The results of the coding are presented in Table 1.

Within each grade, both self-evaluation and self-improvement were common. In many cases, a combination of self-evaluation and self-improvement motives were operating at the same time. Responses indicative of self-enhancement would be characterized by statements such as, "After seeing the model, Susie feels better about the way she looks," or "Susie thinks she's prettier than the model." As such, neither judge found evidence of self-enhancement motives.

Responses that indicated self-evaluation as the predominating motive were further coded into positive or negative instances, with most responses being negative. Some responses that indicated self-evaluation as the predominating motive include:

"Susie wants to look like the model and is upset she doesn't. If she doesn't look like the model she is not beautiful. Susie is unhappy." (a twelfth grader; negative self-evaluation)

"Susie should be able to compare herself but not put herself down. Susie should realize that her body and physical features are just as good as a model's body. Susie is thinking about her future as a model." (a twelfth grader; positive self-evaluation)

"Susie started to compare herself to the model. She is thinking that the model is so much prettier than her. She started to list the things that model has better than her like her hair and her eyes. After she got done doing that, she felt really bad about herself." (an eighth grader; negative self-evaluation)

"There once was a girl named Susie. She was looking at this magazine that had a model she wanted to look like if she looked like a model, but she didn't so she was mad at herself." (a fourth grader; negative self-evaluation)

Several themes also emerged from the TATs. Shown in Table 2 are results in terms of specific methods suggested for improvement of physical attractiveness, the frequency with which respondents indicated that they are able to discount the beauty of advertising models, and frequency with which respondents indicated a desire to be a model. These results show that most of these methods (all except wearing make-up for the first time or changing the make-up currently worn) become more common as one gets older. Some of the responses indicating self-improvement as predominant and methods suggested are as follows:

"Susie's listening to her radio and reading the magazine. She's reading the magazine to find new images for herself or a new

TABLE 1
Female Preadolescents' And Adolescents' Motives for Comparison*

	Grade					
	4th (n=59)		8th (n=51)		12th (n=33)	
	No.	%	No.	%	No.	%
Motive						
(+) Self-Evaluation	6	10.2	5	9.8	2	6.1
(-) Self-Evaluation	38	64.4	40	78.4	24	72.7
Self-Improvement	23	39.0	34	66.7	21	63.6
Combination	12	20.3	22	43.1	11	33.3
None	10	17.0	3	5.9	3	9.1

* Percentages do not add up to 100% as some responses fell into more than one category.

TABLE 2
Additional Results of TAT Coding*

	Grade					
	4th (n=59)		8th (n=51)		12th (n=33)	
	No.	%	No.	%	No.	%
Self-Improvement Methods						
Make-Up	6	10.2	13	25.5	3	9.1
Hairstyle	4	6.8	6	11.8	5	15.2
Clothing	3	5.1	2	3.9	3	9.1
Buying Product in Ad	3	5.1	3	5.9	8	24.2
Dieting	2	3.4	6	11.8	10	30.3
Able to Discount Beauty	7	11.9	11	21.6	4	12.1
Aspirations to be a Model	14	23.7	5	9.8	2	6.1

* Percentages do not add up to 100% as some responses fell into more than one category.

look. She finds a girl in there that she really wants to be. So she goes out and buys the product that the pretty girl is advertising in hopes that she'll end up looking just as good." (a twelfth grader)

"Susie bought a teen magazine at the grocery store. When she gets home she flips through the pages. Then she stops at a page where she sees a beautiful model. Lately she's been trying to find new ways to do her hair and wear her make-up and this photograph gives her a great idea. After staring and daydreaming at the picture she decides to go in her room and try to do her hair and make-up like the model in the picture." (an eighth grader)

"Susie notices how beautiful the model is! She wants to be just as beautiful. She reads about the model to find out how to be that pretty. It says first you have to have make-up. So she walks into the bathroom and takes some of her mom's make-up and puts in on. Then the book says to get on a pretty dress. So she went to her closet and got out her best dress. The last thing the book said was to look in a mirror. So she looked into the mirror and saw how pretty she looked." (a fourth grader)

Though questionable as a method of "improvement," dieting was mentioned most frequently by twelfth graders as a way to improve their physical attractiveness. References were made to eating disorders, including bulimia and anorexia, even by fourth graders. For example, responses include the following:

"Susie is paging through a magazine that has unusually and uncommon beautiful gals. She is looking at the magazine to get ideas for clothing, hoping she can find the right look. Susie is liking what clothes she sees but realizes that she could never look as great as the model and feels very depressed. She would like to buy the clothes so therefore becomes anorexic and dies." (a twelfth grader)

"Susie sits there thinking about how guilty she feels for eating so much. She wishes she could be just like all the girls in the magazine. Feeling very depressed she goes to the bathroom, sticks her finger down her throat and vomits all the food she has eaten." (a twelfth grader)

"She is turning the pages because Susie knows she won't be able to look like the model. But she is thinking how much she would like to look like the model. Next she will probably try to go on a diet to look like the model in the magazine." (an eighth grader)

"Susie asks her mother if she can go on a diet. Her mom says no so she starves herself to get skinny like the model. She thinks she's fatter than anybody else. One day she goes to the movies. She eats a lot of junk food so she goes home and tells her mom that she has to throw up. She goes to the bathroom and sticks her finger down her throat and makes herself throw up because she wants to be pretty and skinny." (a fourth grader)

Table 2 also shows the number of responses indicating that subjects are able to discount the beauty of advertising models. That is, some respondents indicated that being physically attractive is not important or that the beauty of advertising models is unrealistic. For example, some responses are as follows:

"Susie is comparing herself to something she can never be. Advertising promotes bulimia and anorexia and low self-esteem. Susie should feel good about herself for what she is, not how she looks. Some people are gorgeous, yes, but who wants a present that's all wrapping and no gift." (a twelfth grader)

"Well, Susie is comparing herself to this model. She is wishing she could look this way. She is looking at every feature of her. She is thinking how could I ever look that beautiful? It's impossible. So she just turns the page and forgets about what she saw." (an eighth grader)

"Susie thinks that she has to be as pretty as the model. But she doesn't because in her own special way she is special. It isn't the way she look, it's the way she feels inside is what matters." (a fourth grader)

The TATs were also coded as to whether a respondent indicated that she would like to choose modeling as a career. As Table 2 indicates, career aspirations to be a model were most common in fourth graders. For example, responses include:

"Susie is daydreaming about what she would be like if she was a model. Susie is reading the magazine to get some beauty tips. Susie is thinking she could be a model some day. Susie will become very beautiful and become a model." (a fourth grader)

"Susie is thinking she wants to be a model when she gets older but she will not be pretty enough so she can not be a model. Her mother is cooking and Susie tells her mother she wants to be a model but she thinks she is not pretty enough and her mother say she is. And when Susie got older she was a model." (a fourth grader)

Overall, the TAT proved to be successful in uncovering underlying motivations for comparison to advertising models. The greater number of TATs indicating no motive and lacking specificity in terms of methods suggested for self-improvement in fourth graders is most likely due to less ability to verbalize and present thoughts in a written form as compared to the eighth and twelfth graders. The analysis of the TATs also revealed the potential seriousness of female preadolescents and adolescents being preoccupied with physical attractiveness. Given the large proportion of negative self-evaluative responses, the relatively few number of respondents that discount the beauty of advertising models, and the references made to eating disorders, female preadolescents and adolescents may be at risk with respect to maintaining self-esteem, positive self-perceptions of physical attractiveness, and even proper levels of body weight needed to be physically healthy.

CONCLUSION

This study has examined the role of motives in social comparison. Specifically, the role of motives with respect to female preadolescents and adolescents comparing their physical attractiveness to that of models in ads was explored. Propositions were presented, highlighting when comparison to advertising models may occur and the differential effects on self-perceptions of physical attractiveness and self-esteem that may occur when motives are taken into consideration.

The results of a study attempting to determine underlying motives were also presented. The results indicated that both self-evaluation and self-improvement as motives for comparison to advertising models exist in female preadolescents and adolescents. In addition, the study revealed specific methods suggested for self-improvement, the frequency with which respondents indicated that they were able to discount the beauty of advertising models, and the frequency with which female preadolescents and adolescents aspire to be models.

Given that both self-evaluation and self-improvement were shown to be motives in existence when physical attractiveness is compared to that of advertising models, future research should empirically test the propositions put forth. The question of whether self-perceptions of physical attractiveness and self-esteem are differentially affected depending on the predominating motive needs to be answered. An experimental procedure similar to that used by Martin and Kennedy (1993) or Richins (1991) could be used to investigate the differential *short-term* effects. However, a longitudinal study investigating the differential *long-term* effects would be desirable. In addition, the impact of advertising models needs to be assessed when both self-evaluation and self-improvement operate at the same time.

These issues have important public policy and managerial implications as well. First, if the attractiveness of advertising models adversely affects self-perceptions of physical attractiveness and/or self-esteem, what is the ethical responsibility of marketers? Further, if adverse effects do occur, should marketers be proactive by using less attractive or no models in advertising? Does the use of highly attractive models really "work?" For example, for those who have a self-improvement motive, the use of a highly attractive model may both increase the likelihood of purchase and have no detrimental effects on self-perceptions and/or self-esteem. On the other hand, the use of less attractive models in advertising may actually be advantageous. For example, the use of a less attractive model may give rise to a self-enhancement motive, thus increasing purchase intentions as well as self-perceptions and/or self-esteem. Finally, if differential effects on self-perceptions of physical attractiveness and/or self-esteem occur depending on the predominating motive at the time of comparison, perhaps preadolescents and adolescents can be taught how to view advertising (i.e. taught which motive to use) to prevent any adverse effects. These issues, it is believed, are important and deserve increased attention from academic researchers in marketing.

REFERENCES

Atkinson, John W. and Joel O. Raynor eds. (1974), *Motivation and Achievement*, Washington, DC: Hemisphere.

Bandura, Albert (1986), *Social Foundations of Thought and Action: A Social Cognitive Theory*, Englewood Cliffs, NJ: Prentice-Hall.

Bearden, William O. and Randall L. Rose (1990), "Attention to Social Comparison Information: An Individual Difference Factor Affecting Consumer Conformity," *Journal of Consumer Research*, 16 (March), 461-471.

Brickman, Philip and Ronnie J. Bulman (1977), "Pleasure and Pain in Social Comparison," in *Social Comparison Processes: Theoretical and Empirical Perspectives*, eds. J.M. Suls and R.L. Miller, Washington, DC: Hemisphere, 149-186.

Chandler, Louis A. and Virginia J. Johnson (1991), *Using Projective Techniques with Children*, Springfield, IL: Charles C. Thomas.

Dakin, Stephen and A. John Arrowood (1981), "The Social Comparison of Ability," *Human Relations*, 34, 89-109.

Erikson, Erik H. (1968), *Identity: Youth and Crisis*, New York: Norton.

Feldman, Nina S. and Diane N. Ruble (1977), "Awareness of Social Comparison Interest and Motivations: A Developmental Study," *Journal of Educational Psychology*, 69, 579-585.

Festinger, Leon (1954), "A Theory of Social Comparison Processes," *Human Relations*, 7, 117-140.

Friend, Ronald M. and Joel Gilbert (1973), "Threat and Fear of Negative Evaluation as Determinants of Locus of Social Comparison," *Journal of Personality*, 41, 328-340.

Gastorf, John W., Jerry Suls, and John Lawhon (1978), "Opponent Choices of Below Average Performers," *Bulletin of the Psychonomic Society*, 12, 217-220.

Goethals, George R. (1986), "Social Comparison Theory: Psychology from the Lost and Found," *Personality and Social Psychology Bulletin*, 12 (September), 261-278.

Hakmiller, Karl L. (1966a), "Threat as a Determinant of Downward Comparison," *Journal of Experimental Social Psychology*, Supplement 1, 32-39.

_____ (1966b), "Need for Self-Evaluation, Perceived Similarity and Comparison Choice," *Journal of Experimental Social Psychology*, Supplement 1, 49-54.

Harter, Susan (1986), "Processes Underlying the Construction, Maintenance, and Enhancement of the Self-Concept in Children," in *Psychological Perspectives on the Self*, Vol. 3, eds. J. Suls and A.G. Greenwald, Hillsdale, NJ: Lawrence Erlbaum Associates, 137-181.

_____ (1992) "Visions of Self: Beyond the Me in the Mirror," paper presented at the Nebraska Symposium on Motivation, Lincoln, NE.

James, William (1984), *Psychology: The Briefer Course*, Cambridge, MA: Harvard University Press.

Knippenberg, A. van, H. Wilke, and N.K. de Vries (1981), "Social Comparison on Two Dimensions," *European Journal of Social Psychology*, 11, 267-283.

Martin, Joanne (1986), "The Tolerance of Injustice," in *Relative Deprivation and Social Comparison: The Ontario Syposium*, Vol. 4, eds. J.M. Olson, C.P. Herman, and M.P. Zanna, Hillsdale, NJ: Erlbaum, 217-242.

Martin, Mary C. and Patricia F. Kennedy (1993), "Advertising and Social Comparison: Consequences for Female Preadolescents and Adolescents," *Psychology and Marketing*, 10 (November/December), forthcoming.

_____ and Patricia F. Kennedy (1994), "The Measurement of Social Comparison to Advertising Models: A Gender Gap Revealed," *Gender and Consumer Behavior*, Newbury Park, CA: Sage Publications, forthcoming.

Mick, David Glen, Michelle DeMoss, and Ronald J. Faber (1992), "A Projective Study of Motivations and Meanings of Self-Gifts: Implications for Retail Management," *Journal of Retailing*, 68 (Summer), 122-144.

Miller, Richard L. and Jerry M. Suls (1977), "Affiliation Preferences as a Function of Attitude and Ability Similarity," in *Social Comparison Processes: Theoretical and Empirical Perspectives*, eds. J.M. Suls and R.L. Miller, Washington, DC: Hemisphere, 103-123.

Pyszczynski, Tom, Jeff Greenberg, and John LaPrelle (1985), "Social Comparison After Success and Failure: Biased Search for Information Consistent with a Self-Serving Conclusion," *Journal of Experimental Social Psychology*, 21, 195-211.

Rappaport, D. (1942), "Principles Underlying Projective Techniques," *Character and Personality*, 10 (March), 213-219.

Renick, Mari Jo and Susan Harter (1989), "Impact of Social Comparisons on the Developing Self-Perceptions of Learning Disabled Students," *Journal of Educational Psychology*, 81 (4), 631-638.

Richins, Marsha L. (1991), "Social Comparison and the Idealized Images of Advertising," *Journal of Consumer Research*, 18 (June), 71-83.

_____ (1992), "Media Images, Materialism, and What Ought to Be: The Role of Social Comparison," in *Meaning, Measure, and Morality of Materialism*, eds. F. Rudmin and M. Richins, Kingston, Ontario: Research Workshop on Materialism and Other Consumption Orientations, 202-206.

Rook, Dennis W. (1985), "The Ritual Dimension of Consumer Behavior," *Journal of Consumer Research*, 12 (December), 251-264.

Rosenberg, Morris (1986), "Self-Concept From Middle Childhood Through Adolescence," in *Psychological Perspectives on the Self*, Vol. 3, eds. J. Suls and A.G. Greenwald, Hillsdale, NJ: Lawrence Erlbaum Associates, 107-136.

Ruble, Diane N. (1983), "The Development of Social-Comparison Processes and Their Role in Achievement-Related Self-Socialization," in *Social Cognition and Social Development: A Sociocultural Perspective*, eds. E.T. Higgins, D.N. Ruble, and W.W. Hartup, Cambridge, England: Cambridge University Press, 134-157.

Samuel, William (1973), "On Clarifying Some Interpretations of Social Comparison Theory," *Journal of Experimental Social Psychology*, 9, 450-465.

Smith, Richard H. and Chester A. Insko (1987), "Social Comparison Choice During Ability Evaluation: The Effects of Comparison Publicity, Performance Feedback, and Self-Esteem," *Personality and Social Psychology Bulletin*, 13, 111-122.

Thornton, Dorothy and A. John Arrowood (1966), "Self-Evaluation, Self-Enhancement, and the Locus of Social Comparison," *Journal of Experimental Social Psychology*, Supplement 1, 40-48.

Wheeler, Ladd (1966), "Motivation as a Determinant of Upward Comparison," *Journal of Experimental Social Psychology*, Supplement 1, 27-31.

_____ (1974), "Social Comparison and Selective Affiliation," in *Foundations of Interpersonal Attraction*, ed. T. Huston, New York: Academic Press.

Wood, Joanne V. (1989), "Theory and Research Concerning Social Comparisons of Personal Attributes," *Psychological Bulletin*, 106 (2), 231-248.

Yanish, Donna L. and James Battle (1985), "Relationship Between Self-Esteem, Depression and Alcohol Consumption Among Adolescents," *Psychological Reports*, 57, 331-334.

Discussant comments
Gender Issues: Gender as a Cultural Construct
Janeen Arnold Costa, University of Utah

It has been my task to summarize, critique and generally comment upon the first two papers of this session, "An Investigation of the Influence of Gender on the Hedonic Responses Created by Listening to Music" by Kathleen T. Lacher and "Babes in Toyland: Learning an Ideology of Gender" by Greta Eleen Pennell. My initial response to these papers and the presentations is that, while both efforts are in the right direction and contribute to our knowledge of gender and consumer behavior, each is a case of not quite the right amount of information and analysis. By that specifically I mean that Lacher's analysis simply does too little; while, on the other hand, Pennell attempts to accomplish too much. When we are dealing with gender, which is a rich and complex aspect of society, it is important to explicate and analyze fully.

Gender is a cultural construct of elaborate dimensions. All societies take the basic morphological distinction between male and female and extend this differentiation into full-blown gender dichotomies with associated assumptions, stereotypes, and societal expectations. Individual psychology and aspects of personality, social roles involving work, play, the home, and other activities and interactions, responsibilities in production and reproduction, expectations of behavior, even dress and manner of speech, all become gender-typed in the construction of gender roles. As with other aspects of culture, the various dimensions of gender are interrelated, woven into the fabric of society, affecting and affected by virtually all other aspects of human behavior and interaction. Furthermore, this complex set of interrelated features varies significantly in form from one society to the next. To reiterate, then, gender is culturally based, elaborate, and integrated with all other aspects of society.

What this means in terms of Lacher's paper is quite simple: experiments simply may not capture well the sophistication and complexity of gender constructions. Lacher is careful to indicate this study is "exploratory," which is something we must note. However, it is incumbent upon Lacher to push the analysis as much as possible, to do more than is done in the current version of this paper. For example, Lacher indicates we must differentiate between the effects of biology and culture in terms of response and behavior. The extant literature on this topic is vast (cf Ardener 1978, Friedl 1978, Hastrup 1978, Sanday 1981). The analysis would have been well-informed by a perusal of this literature. We would have been able at least to begin sorting the effects of nature versus nurture in the phenomenon under study.

In finding that, essentially, men are more amused and analytical, while women are more sensorial in their hedonic responses to music, the ground is laid for further interesting exploration. Yet, I again suggest that Lacher could push the analysis more at this point. The conclusion is simple; in fact, it is too simple. Given that the experiment yields these findings, I suggest an exploration of why and how this is the case is appropriate now, based again on extant literature and studies. Simply put, there is ample evidence to suggest that, in American society, men are seen both as more capable of and more dedicated to "having fun," as well as more analytical and technical than women (Costa and Pavia 1992, 1993; Cowan 1979; Miller 1983; Pavia and Costa 1993). Similarly, American female gender roles include characterizations and manifest behaviors of women as sensorially connected with their social and physical environments (Bellah et al. 1985; Epstein 1988; Harris 1981; Kitzinger 1985). Lacher could draw on this existing research and findings, thereby contextualizing in an appropriate fashion. People learn gender-appropriate behaviors and responses; relating her findings to what is already known about gender expectations in American society would be fruitful.

Pennell's paper errs in the opposite direction. Gender biases are pervasive and intricately interwoven; still, without de-emphasizing the importance of any particular aspect, we must begin to sort through the biases. In attempting to analyze the infantization and objectification of women, the masculine supremacy effect, and the issue of fantasy versus reality, all within the same paper, we are again reminded of the pervasiveness of the gender dichotomy in American society. We begin, perhaps, to experience the hopelessness of attempting to change gender biases. But what also occurs in attempting to cover these three very important themes within the same necessarily short paper is that each can be treated only superficially. In reality, entire books could be written on each theme. I suggest then, that Pennell consider subsuming one theme under another, or focus on a single theme or on the interrelation of the themes.

Let us consider how such an analysis might work. Is it not possibly the case that the masculine supremacy aspect of gender dichotomization in American society subsumes the other two themes? Males are thought to be, stereotypically and traditionally, superior to females in American society (de Beauvoir 1960; Epstein 1988; Oakley 1972, 1981). Part of that hierarchy is manifest through the infantization of women, and through the objectification of women, both of which are discussed by Pennell. Thus, the male supremacy issue and the infantization/objectification issue are interrelated and could be fruitfully analyzed as such. Furthermore, in the United States, activities in the public sphere traditionally are more valued than those in the private sphere; they are claimed to be more valuable because they generate income and result in increased visibility and "success" for the social unit in question. The public sphere is historically associated with men rather than women (Friedl 1978; Harris 1981; Mitterauer and Sieder 1982). This leads to the simplistic assertion that men work (outside the home) and women don't work (except inside the home, which isn't as valued). It is only a slight step from there to the association of men with reality and women with fantasy. Males are superior, work outside the home, engage in valued activities, deal with reality; females are subordinated in each and all of these ways (Oakley 1972, 1981). So, again, the male supremacy effect can be said to account for this aspect of Pennell's analysis. It is important to remember that my analysis here is hypothetical, however. Given the interrelated nature of gender in society, I would suggest that the superordination or subordination of each of Pennell's themes to one another might be possible. The result of such an endeavor would be richer description and analysis, as well as a more coherent argument.

I have a few final comments about the Pennell paper which are unrelated to my previous discussion. First, I would like to compliment Pennell on the clear explanation of semiotics and hermeneutics; the analysis is useful. However, within the hermeneutic circle, it is necessary to interpret and reinterpret on the basis of what might be called "negative cases." That is, when something within the data does not seem to fit the interpretation, we must return to the interpretation and expand it, reconfigure it, or figure out some way by which we may account for the "negative case" or apparent anomaly in the data. In the data and analysis presented by Pennell, certain such anomalies come to mind, which in turn call for a broader analysis. For example, it is suggested that male children are provided with toys which encourage them to engage in play which is reality-based. Conversely, according to Pennell, female children are asked to use toys which encourage them to engage in fantasy. If we then consider the mutant human action figures, the attempts to play at space travel or at knighthood on the part of boys, how can we expand our analysis to account for these activities which appear to be fantasy-based? A return to the hermeneutic circle might result in an expanded interpretation which looks at each of the activities which is fantasy-based for boys. My initial observation is that these activities are again based in the public sphere and are concerned with physical strength. If further analysis bears out this observation, the "negative cases" can be found to be not really negative cases at all. Instead, they provide further support for the assessment of consumer behavior in toys as related to gender socialization and the male supremacy effect.

In addition, are we not ourselves buying into the gender hierarchy when we suggest that the toys which simulate the kitchen or the sewing machine are fantasy, rather than reality-based (see also Rheingold and Cook 1975, Walum 1977)? Pennell makes an important point that these types of toys for girls are marketed as "easy to do." I would suggest that, in fact, the case points to the male supremacy effect once again. In reality, sewing, cleaning the kitchen and cooking are all difficult, time-consuming tasks. Under the male supremacy assumption, females have to be taught slowly and carefully how to do these things. Thus, names for these toys which include words such as "easy" and "simple" are not talking about the tasks themselves but about the need to make such tasks easy for slow-to-learn females. The male supremacy effect is again affirmed.

Another important point is that socialization into these gender roles is so pervasive that the situation may, indeed, be nearly hopeless in terms of any real change from a critical perspective. Even when parents have reached a point of political consciousness where they attempt to avoid gender-typed toys, it is often the children themselves who demand such toys. A child is gender socialized through marketing, through peers, through adults; and the pressure to conform is immense, if unconscious. A boy may not only desire blue and red toys, but may also refuse to play with—or even own—pink and purple toys. A boy who sees a toy advertised with only girls at play in the ad may refuse to play with that toy merely on the basis of the ad itself. The opposite case, that of girls' refusing to play with boys' toys, is less likely to occur. After all, if it is more desirable to be in the superior position, to be male, then acting like a male through playing with male toys is simply more acceptable than a boy playing with girls' toys.

Well, it is quite clear that much remains to be studied in this sub-area of our discipline. Merely suggesting that men and women, boys and girls, do things differently, behave differently in terms of consumption, is not enough. It is time to stop accepting such a finding as important—the field of gender and consumer behavior has progressed to the point that the response to such a simplistic finding should be, "of course." The questions, the issues for analysis, then become—why, how, and in what way? Let us work to inform ourselves more about this complex phenomenon, avoiding both oversimplification and superficial treatment of an important and intricate aspect of behavior which deserves full recognition and study.

REFERENCES

Ardener, Shirley, editor (1978), *Defining Females: The Nature of Women in Society*, New York: Halsted Press.

Bellah, Robert N., Richard Madsen, William M. Sullivan, Ann Swidler and Steven M. Tipton (1985), *Habits of the Heart: Individualism and Commitment in American Life*, New York: Harper & Row.

Costa, Janeen Arnold and Teresa M. Pavia (1992), "What It All Adds Up To: Culture and Alpha-Numeric Brand Names," *Diversity in Consumer Behavior*, Advances in Consumer Research, Vol. XIX, John F. Sherry, Jr. and Brian Sternthal, eds., Provo, Utah: Association for Consumer Research, 39-45.

_____ (1993), "Alpha-Numeric Brand Names and Gender Stereotypes," *Research in Consumer Behavior*, Vol. 6., Janeen Arnold Costa and Russell W. Belk, editors, Greenwich, Connecticut: JAI Press, Inc., forthcoming.

Cowan, Ruth Schwartz (1979), "From Virginia Dare to Virginia Slims: Women and Technology in American Life," *Technology and Culture*, 20 (January), 51-63.

de Beauvoir, Simone (1960), *The Second Sex*, London: Four Square Books.

Epstein, Cynthia Fuchs (1988), *Deceptive Distinctions: Sex, Gender, and the Social Order*, New York: Russell Sage Foundation.

Friedl, Ernestine (1978), "Society and Sex Roles," *Human Nature*, (April).

Harris, Marvin (1981), "Why Women Left Home," *America Now*, New York: Simon & Schuster, 76-97.

Hastrup, Kirsten (1978), "The Semantics of Biology: Virginity," *Defining Females: The Nature of Women in Society*, Shirley Ardener, ed., New York: Halsted Press, 49-65.

Kitzinger, Sheila (1980), *Women as Mothers*, New York: Vintage Books.

Miller, Jon D. (1983), *The American People and Science Policy: The Role of Public Attitudes in the Policy Process*, New York: Pergamon Press.

Mitterauer, Michael and Reinhard Sieder (1982), *The European Family*, Chicago: University of Chicago Press.

Oakley, Ann (1972), *Sex, Gender and Society*, London: Temple Smith.

_____ (1981) *Subject Women*, New York: Pantheon Books.

Pavia, Teresa M. and Janeen Arnold Costa (1993), "The Winning Number: Consumer Perceptions of Alpha-Numeric Brand Names," *Journal of Marketing*, 57 (3), 85-98.

Rheingold, H.L. and Cook K.V. (1975), "The Content of Boys' and Girls' Rooms as an Index of Parents Behavior," *Child Development*, 46 (2), 459-463.

Sanday, Peggy (1981), *Female Power and Male Dominance: On the Origins of Sexual Inequality*, New York: Cambridge University Press.

Walum, C.R. (1977), *The Dynamics of Sex and Gender: A Sociological Perspective*, Chicago: Rand McNally.

"The Play's the Thing:" Elements of Drama in Advertising and Their Effects on Audience Response

Basil G. Englis, Rutgers University

This panel focused on the analysis of advertising drama, and concerned the effects of the *elements* of drama on consumer experiences of and responses to advertising. Although other researchers have considered the distinction between advertising drama and lecture or argument in advertising, we also need to further disaggregate drama into its constituent elements in order to discover how each element is implicated in the effect of advertising drama on consumers. This panel builds upon previous work in two ways: first, the panel considers the role of specific dramatic elements in advertising, and thus goes beyond the simple contrast of drama with narrative (or other) forms of advertising. Second, it presents hypotheses, and in some instances data, relating elements of advertising drama to consumer responses, thus advancing beyond theoretical analysis of form and content.

Michael R. Solomon—Stylistic Context in Advertising: The Supporting Role of Physical Evidence in Commercial Dramaturgy

This paper argued for the overlooked importance of *stylistic context* in advertising—the physical cues that "place" a product in some real or imagined *setting*. Despite the potential ramifications of executional nuance for advertising effectiveness, surprisingly little research has addressed issues related to the *stylistic context* of advertisements (i.e., information communicated by specific styles of clothing, furniture, housing, and other expressive products used to create settings in these portrayals). In addition to other vital dramaturgical elements such as plot and character, the setting depicts the context (or scene) in which the action will occur. Thus, visual context and consumers' responses to that context are potentially of great import to advertisers, since the information conveyed by an ad's setting can influence the degree to which members of a target market decode meaning and identify with its central characters and intent. Data from a study of professional set designers were presented to address this issue. The strategic applications of advertising context, exemplified by the growing practices of product placement, collaborative advertising, and the presentation of responsible social messages were also discussed.

Barbara B. Stern and Basil G. Englis—"Once Upon a Time ...:" Advertising Drama and Audience Empathy

This presentation began with a theoretical distinction between "plot" and "story" – plot is the key element from which dramatic effects flow. The distinction is memorably captured by E. M. Forster: "'The king died and then the queen died,' is a story. 'The king died, and then the queen died of grief' is a plot." A plot adds the elements of temporal succession, causality, and motive to the recitation of events in a story, imposing unity on a pattern of events structured with a beginning, a middle, and with an end. These requirements form the structural elements that distinguish a classical, plotted drama. In contrast, vignette dramas depict one or more episodes of metonymic association rather than a pattern of chronological progression and causation as found in classical, plotted dramas. Because the audience experiences dramatic events without narrative intrusion, empathy—an identification with and projection of self onto the staged characters—may result. Empathy is often the goal of advertisements that seek to engender consumer identification with a person or object, to the extent that the observer becomes a vicarious participant and may thereby experience a sense of participation in the physical sensations of a product, the lifestyle of the users, or the processual flow of a service experience. An analysis of drama in television advertisements was presented in terms of elements of plot and character, and which distinguished between vignette and classical forms. And, data from an empirical study that contrasted the effects of classical, plotted dramas with vignette dramas on audience empathy with ad characters were presented.

George Jura and Jacqueline C. Hitchon—Allegorical Drama in Advertising: Its Use and Effects

Since Aristotle, allegory has been treated as a particular kind of metaphor—a continuous metaphor, which substitutes a whole series of referents for words or phrases used as singular referents in the text. While metaphors can exist within a poem or even within a single speech act, allegory requires an extended narrative, dialogue, or sequence of dramatic elements (actions, scenes, actors, and so on), which allow it to be understood concurrently with the surface "story." Although allegory can be understood on the surface level, and can even be interesting on this level alone, it is the "higher," figurative level that conveys the intended meaning. While other figures of speech have found widespread use in print advertising, allegory is found mostly in television ads as a result of the properties of the medium, for it alone is able to present a dramatized story using motion, pictures, colors, and sound, in addition to verbal content. Examples of allegorical dramas in advertising were presented, including Apple Computer's Macintosh commercial depicting ... "why 1984 won't be like *1984*," Diet Pepsi's spot with Michael J. Fox as a knight rescuing a female tenant in distress, and Jello's godfather scenario featuring Bill Cosby. Intrinsic to an allegorical drama is stimulation of an elaborate network of associations in the viewer's mind—the deeper meaning of the allegory emerges from the spreading activation of meanings elicited by the surface story. These associative linkages may, for example, be cued by traditional structural forms such as "white-knight-rescues-fair-damsel-in-distress-overcoming-draconian-obstacles" (e.g., the Diet Pepsi ad) or by specific literary allusions (e.g., the Apple Macintosh ad's reference to *1984*).

William D. Wells—Discussant

William D. Wells discussed the papers presented in this session – his comments are published elsewhere in this volume.

Discussant's Comments
Effective and Ineffective Drama Advertising
William D. Wells, University of Minnesota

ABSTRACT

Drama advertisements and studies of drama advertisements confront parallel hazards. Both can: 1) focus on affect instead of effect, 2) focus on the product category instead of on the brand, and 3) "get to" the wrong respondents. This paper describes those hazards and their implications.

INTRODUCTION

The purpose of any advertisement is to state, describe and illustrate the advantages of the product, and to do that in an interesting, engaging and convincing way. The purpose of any research project is to measure what it is supposed to measure, and be sure that users understand what findings really mean.

The burden of this discussion is that drama advertisements and research on drama advertisements confront parallel problems; and, because they confront parallel problems, they can miss the mark in parallel ways.

Specifically, both drama advertisements and research on drama advertisements can overlook critical differences between: 1) affect and effect, 2) brand and product, 3) prospect and nonprospect. When those distinctions are glossed-over, advertisers and researchers are less likely to succeed.

AFFECT AND EFFECT

When people say "that was a great advertisement," they usually mean, "I really liked it, I really enjoyed it, or it really turned me on." They could say the same thing with the same meaning about a great movie, a great concert, or a great play.

Obviously, this use of the term "great" does not necessarily imply effectiveness. Everyone can remember "great" advertisements for products they never buy, and everyone can remember modest notices that sent them off in search of objects they eventually took home. Another way to say this would be to say that an advertisement can be entertaining and ineffective, mundane and still work. (Kamins, 1990; MacKenzie and Lutz, 1989).

This seems especially true of dramas and comedies. Some "great" advertising dramas, and some "great" advertising comedies, are mainly entertainment. Some unpretentious playlets present benefits that make consumers change their minds (Stewart and Furse, 1986).

So, when evaluating advertisements, it is important to be clear about affect and effect. Although that difference may seem obvious, it is easy to overlook.

The Video Storyboard survey (Vadehra, 1993), for instance, asks consumers to name their favorite TV commercials, and publishes a widely-cited list of the "top 25" campaigns. The Video Storyboard report never mentions effectiveness. By omission, it encourages an assumption that "best liked" means best in every way.

Similarly, academic investigators have been known to focus on affect instead of effect. We know that consumers' evaluations of advertisements contain at least two dimensions: an entertainment dimension, tapped by terms like "clever, imaginative, amusing, and original;" and a relevance dimension, tapped by terms like "informative, convincing, effective, and worth remembering" (Aaker and Stayman, 1990; Leavitt, 1970; Schlinger, 1979).

Many researchers who examine "attitude toward the ad" focus on the entertainment dimension and ignore the relevance dimension, or merge entertainment and relevance, or treat relevance as though it were "attitude toward the brand" (e.g., Biehal, Stephens and Curio, 1992; Chattopahdhyay and Nedungadi, 1992; Madden, Allen and Twible, 1988; Minard, Sirdeshmukh, and Innis, 1992; Muehling, Laczniak, and Stoltman, 1991). Even when entertainment and relevance correlate, they convey separate information (Burke and Edell, 1989). Studies that focus on entertainment and submerge relevance have lost track of what advertisements are all about.

A widely-cited Advertising Research Foundation project (Haley and Baldinger, 1991) increases the danger that the spotlight will shift away from relevance. This study measured "liking" of five pairs of TV commercials that had been found to differ, within pairs, in split-cable sales tests. The study found that, on the average (across observations and rating methods) the more effective commercial was the better liked.

Unfortunately, the report called this *weak* correlation, based on *five* observations, a "strong relationship...between the likability of the copy and its effects on sales" (Haley and Baldinger, 1991, page 29). Naturally, "casual listeners" got the message "if you have a good likability score you have a winner" (Cook, 1992, page 7).

The danger is that "liking" will be translated as "entertainment," and entertainment will be viewed as the only element of attitude toward the ad. None of the evidence, including the ARF evidence, supports a conclusion that entertainment is the only element of attitude. Given the authoritative sponsorship and wide distribution of the ARF study, it is most unfortunate that this point was not more clearly made.

PRODUCT AND BRAND

One of the advantages of comedies and dramas is that they tell interesting stories about everyday consumer trials. As attribution theory (Kelly, 1973) would have it, when the same product solves the same problem across actors and situations, consumers are likely to conclude that the magic will work for them (Folkes, 1988).

This inference is especially effective when consumers draw it for themselves. As we all know, consumers are more apt to follow their own inclinations than to yield to pitches forced on them from outside.

The problem is that, unless the advertiser is a near monopolist, the drama or the comedy must hinge upon the brand. It must be Windex, not just any glass cleaner, that sparkles the window. It must be Excedrin, not just any medication, that cures the pain. It must be Old Spice, not just any magic essence, that attracts the opposite sex.

The attribution problem for the advertiser is that product and brand covary. Consumers are liable to conclude that any glass cleaner, any pain reliever, or any after-shave, will do the trick.

When ancient dramatists wanted to be sure that everyone got the message, choruses explained the happenings on the stage. When silent-film producers wanted everyone to understand the dialogue, sub-titles conveyed the actors' words. Today, creative directors use voice-over narratives, interruptive demonstrations, subtitles, and concluding taglines to make sure that everyone gets the point. Although these devices diminish the drama, they are considered worth the cost.

But even with all that assistance, consumers sometimes fail to focus on the brand. They attribute the magic to the product category, and assume that just about any well-known brand will work. Again, that's not what advertisers want. Unless advertisers dominate their categories, they want to unsell competitors' offerings, and sell their own, instead.

Advertising research can also focus on the category when it should be focusing on the brand. Many researchers assume that "attitude toward the brand," measured with scales like "favorable—unfavorable, important—unimportant, and useful—useless" is an adequate dependent variable (e. g., Brumbaugh, 1993; Macinnis and Park, 1991; Stayman and Kardes, 1992).

The problem is, category and brand covary. "Favorable—unfavorable, important—unimportant, and useful—useless" can easily refer to stereos in general, or toothpaste in general, or running shoes in general, instead of the specific object featured in the ad. When this interpretation is even possible, experimenters cannot determine what their findings really mean.

This ambiguity is especially hazardous in research intended to have managerial implications. If a study is intended to measure sales effectiveness, and the dependent variable does not separate brand from product category, the research is liable to assign high scores to the wrong ads.

PROSPECTS AND NON-PROSPECTS

In many product categories, genuine prospects are quite rare. Few consumers are willing and able to buy office copiers, or Mercedeses, or diamond rings. Few are ready to enlist in the armed services, rent a truck, purchase a life insurance policy, or take a Carribean cruise.

Even among frequently-purchased grocery and drug-store items, genuine prospects are rarer than they might seem. Not everyone in the supermarket is about to buy liquid detergent, or glass cleaner, or frozen dinners. Not everyone has headaches "this big."

Moreover, prospects are likely to be different. They have agendas, motives, perceptions, problems, and experiences that non-prospects do not have. Indeed, that's what makes them prospects.

One of the consequences of this uniqueness is that prospects are more likely than non-prospects to be interested in, and attentive to, brand-centered stories. Brand-centered stories carry information that might be useful, and are about consumers specifically like them.

Conversely, non-prospects are more likely to be interested in general-interest stories. Non-prospects pursue "nonbrand" processing strategies, as Gardner, Mitchell and Russo (1985), and many others, have often found (Maheswaran, Mackie and Chaiken, 1992; Petty and Cacioppo, 1986; Petty, Cacioppo and Schumann, 1983).

This means that, when researchers test drama or comedy advertisements on the general population, and the general population contains many non-prospects (as it often does), brand-centered stories are likely to be under-rated, and general-interest stories are likely to be over-rated. When effectiveness is the ultimate dependent variable, this is precisely the wrong result.

An analogous problem infects experiments. Even when subjects are category users, some—possibly, many—have little or no real interest in stereos, or soft drinks, or ball-point pens, or whatever is featured in the ad. That reduces sensitivity to brand-specific information, and inflates sensitivity to everything else (Heslin and Johnson, 1992; Laczniak and Muehling, 1993; Smith, 1993).

Furthermore, when randomization doesn't work perfectly—and it often doesn't in small samples—*non-prospects* can confound outcomes. Because non-prospects are so different, their reactions are almost certain to be different. These different reactions can generate "significant" but false results.

So, when testing or studying drama or comedy advertisements, it is especially important to focus on prospects for the brand. A drama or a comedy that fascinates prospects might not fascinate non-prospects, and the other way around.

Finally, a drama or a comedy can fail because prospects do not buy into it. Prospects know a lot about category users; they are category users themselves. They also know the features of the leading offerings; and the images, myths and allegories that those offerings represent. This knowledge makes them expert critics. Whenever characters, situations, or implications don't "ring true," prospects are likely to tune them out.

Once again, it is critical that prospects, and not non-prospects, be respondents in research on drama and comedy ads. Prospects have feelings, knowledge, intentions, loyalties, resources and experiences that non-prospects do not have. When researchers substitute non-prospects for prospects, this vital background, so critical to accurate assessment, cannot play its proper role in determining the results.

It is especially risky to ask non-prospects—directly or indirectly—whether the advertisement makes them want to buy the brand. If they say "yes," they may be flattering the researcher, or casting votes for ads they like. If they say "no," they may be saying no because they are non-prospects. Had they been prospects, they might have said something else. In both academic and applied investigations, responses from non-prospects can mislabel the ad's effect.

Prospects are especially important in research on advertisements intended to affect drug addiction, compulsive gambling, misuse of credit, eating disorders, driving while intoxicated, and other deviant behavior. There, genuine "prospects" are likely to be very different from ordinary citizens. Dramas that seem virtuous and persuasive to the rest of us—and to the dramas' sponsors—may seem pitifully unrealistic to the at-risk audiences they are designed to reach.

So, dramas and comedies, and evaluations of dramas and comedies, confront parallel problems. Both can: 1) focus on affect instead of effect, 2) focus on the product category instead of on the brand, or 3) "get to" the wrong respondents.

Copy testers, and researchers who study the dynamics of persuasion, should keep those caveats in mind. An involving production is not necessarily an effective advertisement. In both industry and academia, failure to distinguish between "greatness" and effectiveness can lead to spurious results.

SOME UNRESOLVED ISSUES

An understanding that entertainment is not sales effectiveness only opens the discussion. Many substantive and methodological issues remain. Here are just a few:

1. Most observers seem to agree that verisimilitude increases empathy for advertising dramas (Deighton, Romer, and McQueen, 1989; Solomon, 1994). Yet some advertising dramas are surreal, and many are highly exaggerated. Exactly what does verisimilitude mean in this context? Where does fidelity to reality help, and where does it hurt?

2. The same questions could be asked about advertising comedies. The answers would probably be different.

3. Voice-over commentary, interruptive demonstrations, concluding taglines, and other devices that make messages unmistakable seem to interfere with empathy. Can advertising dramatists get both? If not, how should the trade-off be made?

4. How do the "rules" for effective advertising comedies differ from the rules for effective advertising dramas? How do the "rules" for effective print comedies or dramas differ from the rules for effective radio or television comedies or dramas? Surely the rules are not all the same.

5. An allegory differs from a metaphor in that it "requires an extended narrative, dialogue, or sequence of dramatic elements which allow it to be understood concurrently with the surface story." This "'higher,' figurative level conveys the intended meaning" (Jura and Hitchon, 1994). How can advertisers be sure that this "higher, figurative level" does not obscure the advertiser's message?

6. Some researchers believe that positive affect "rubs off" on the brand through a process like classical conditioning (Shimp, Stuart, and Engle, 1991). Does this actually happen, or is the process entirely cognitive? If conditioning occurs, why don't negative reactions to dramas like "Ring Around the Collar" destroy positive brand images? Or maybe they do.

7. Attribution theory suggests that a series of vignettes is likely to be more effective than a single story. Is this suggestion correct? Does it also apply to comedies?

8. Most observers seem to agree that empathy or sympathy "build" during successful dramas (Stern and Englis, 1994). Yet we know that viewers can empathize or sympathize with single photographs. Is empathy instantaneous, or does it build? If empathy builds, how long does optimal empathy take?

9. In an advertising context, are empathy and sympathy the same process? If not, are empathy strategies more effective in some product categories, and sympathy strategies more effective in others?

10. Arousal theory (Berlyne, 1970) suggests that easily appreciated dramas are likely to wear out first. Is this suggestion correct? Does it also apply to comedies?

11. Under what circumstances should dramas portray unrealistic, ideal role-models; and, under what circumstances should dramas portray consumers as they are? The answers for comedies are probably different.

12. "1984" may be the most famous drama advertisement. Was it effective? Did it sell many—or any—Apple computers?

These questions show how little we know about dramas and comedies. Because we know so little, any of these questions could lead to break-through research. And, because we know so little, any dependable finding would make a valuable contribution to our scientific understanding of how advertising works.

REFERENCES

Aaker, David A., and Douglas M. Stayman (1990), "Measuring Audience Perceptions of Commercials and Relating Them to Ad Impact," *Journal of Advertising Research*, 30 (August/September), 7-17.

Berlyne, Daniel E. (1970), "Novelty, Complexity, and Hedonic Value," *Perception and Psychophysics*, 8 (November), 279-286.

Biehal, Gabriel, Debra Stephens, and Eleonora Curio (1992), "Attitude Toward the Ad and Brand Choice," *Journal of Advertising*, 21 (September), 19-36.

Burke, Marian Chapman, and Julie A. Edell (1989), "The Impact of Feelings on Ad-Based Affect and Cognition," *Journal of Marketing Research*, 26 (February), 69-83.

Brumbaugh, Anne M. (1993), "Physical Attractiveness and Personality in Advertising: More than Just a Pretty Face?" In Leigh McAlister and Michael L. Rothschild eds., *Advances in Consumer Research Vol. 20*. Provo, UT: Association for Consumer Research, 159-164.

Chattopadhyay, Amitava, and Prakash Nedungadi (1992), "Does Attitude toward the Ad Endure? The Moderating Effects of Attention and Delay," *Journal of Consumer Research*, 19 (June), 26-33.

Cook, William A. (1992), "Love, Hate and Likability," *Journal of Advertising Research*, 32 (March/April), 7-9.

Deighton, John, Daniel Romer, and Josh McQueen (1989), "Using Drama to Persuade," *Journal of Consumer Research* 16 (December), 335-343.

Folkes, Valerie S. (1988), "Recent Attribution Research in Consumer Behavior: A Review and New Directions," *Journal of Consumer Research*, 14 (March), 548-565.

Gardner, Meryl Paula, Andrew A. Mitchell, and J. Edward Russo (1985), "Low Involvement Strategies for Processing Advertisements," *Journal of Advertising*, 14 (2), 4-12, 56.

Haley, Russell I., and Allan L. Baldinger (1991), "The ARF Copy Research Validity Project," *Journal of Advertising Research*, 31 (April/May), 11-32.

Heslin, Richard, and Blair T. Johnson (1992), "Prior Involvement and Incentives to Pay Attention to Information," *Psychology & Marketing*, 9 (May/June), 209-220.

Jura, George, and Jacqueline C. Hitchon (1994), "Allegorical Drama in Advertising: Its Use and Effects," This Volume.

Kamins, Michael A. (1990), "An Investigation into the 'Match-Up' Hypothesis in Celebrity Advertising: When Beauty May Be Only Skin Deep," *Journal of Advertising*, 19 (1), 4-13.

Kelly, Harold H. (1973), "The Process of Causal Attribution," *American Psychologist*, 28 (February), 107-128.

Laczniak, Russell N., and Darrel D. Muehling (1993), "Toward a Better Understanding of the Role of Advertising Message Involvement in Ad Processing," *Psychology & Marketing*, 10 (July/August), 301-319.

Leavitt, Clark (1970), "A Multidimensional Set of Rating Scales for Television Commercials," *Journal of Applied Psychology*, 54 (5), 427-429.

MacInnis, Deborah J., and C. Whan Park (1991), "The Differential Role of Characteristics of Music on High- and Low-Involvement Consumers' Processing of Ads," *Journal of Consumer Research*, 18 (September), 161-173..

MacKenzie, Scott B., and Richard J. Lutz (1989), "An Empirical Examination of the Structural Antecedents of Attitude Toward the Ad in an Advertising Pretesting Context," *Journal of Marketing*, 53 (April), 48-65.

Madden, Thomas J., Chris T. Allen and Jacquelyn L. Twible (1988), "Attitude Toward the Ad: An Assessment of Diverse Measurement Indices Under Different Processing 'Sets'," *Journal of Marketing Research*, 25 (August), 242-252.

Maheswaran, Durairaj, Diane M. Mackie, and Shelly Chaiken (1992), "Brand Name as a Heuristic Cure: The Effects of Task Importance and Expectancy Confirmation on Consumer Judgments," *Journal of Consumer Psychology*, 1 (4), 317-336.

Minard, Paul W., Deepak Sirdeshmukh, and Daniel E. Innis (1992), "Peripheral Persuasion and Brand Choice," *Journal of Consumer Research*, 19 (September), 226-239.

Muehling, Darrel D., Russell N. Laczniak, and Jeffrey J. Stoltman (1991), "The Moderating Effects of Ad Message Involvement: A Reassessment," *Journal of Advertising*, 20 (June), 29-38.

Petty, Richard E., and John T. Cacioppo (1986), *Communication and Persuasion: Central and Peripheral Routes to Attitude Change*, New York, Springer.

_____, _____ and David Schumann (1983), "Central and Peripheral Routes to Advertising Effectiveness: The Moderating Role of Involvement," *Journal of Consumer Research*, 10 (September), 135-146.

Schlinger, Mary Jane (1979), "A Profile of Responses to Commercials," *Journal of Advertising Research*, 19 (2), 37-46.

Shimp, Terence A., Elnora W. Stuart, and Randall W. Engle (1991), "A Program of Classical Conditioning Experiments Testing Variations in the Conditioned Stimulus and Contents," *Journal of Consumer Research*, 18 (June), 1-12.

Smith, Stephen M. (1993), "Does Humor in Advertising Enhance Systematic Processing?" In Leigh McAlister and Michael L. Rothschild, eds., *Advances in Consumer Research*, Vol. 20, Provo, UT: Association for Consumer Research, 155-158.

Solomon, Michael R. (1994), "Stylistic Context in Advertising: The Supporting Role of Physical Evidence in Commercial Dramaturgy," This Volume.

Stayman, Douglas M., and Frank R. Kardes (1992), "Spontaneous Inference Processes in Advertising: Effects of Need for Cognition and Self-Monitoring on Inference Generation and Utilization," *Journal of Consumer Psychology*, 1 (2), 125-142.

Stern, Barbara B., and Basil G. Englis (1994), "'Once Upon a Time...' Advertising Drama and Audience Empathy," This Volume.

Stewart, David W., and David H. Furse (1986), *Effective Television Advertising: A Study of 1000 Commercials*, Lexington, MA: Lexington Books.

Vadehra, Dave (1993), "My, How TV Spots Have Changed!" *Advertising Age*, 64 (August 16), 16.

Special Session Summary
Biases in Social Comparison: If You are One in a Million, There are 4,000 People Just Like You

Geeta Menon, New York University
Vicki G. Morwitz, New York University

Consumers both shape and are shaped by their social context. They often compare themselves to other people (e.g., their reference group), and their attitudes and judgments are affected by such comparisons. In fact, the literature in psychology and marketing indicates that behavior too is often affected by social influences (e.g., Bearden and Etzel 1982; Bearden and Rose 1990).

There is ample evidence that these social comparisons are prone to biases. We concentrate on three forms of bias, two consensus effects and one uniqueness effect: (a) The *false consensus effect* is the tendency for individuals to falsely assume that other people are similar to them (i.e., "They are like me"). In general, this bias might manifest itself when consumers are asked to provide information about other people. (b) The *"backward" false consensus effect* is the tendency for individuals to falsely assume that they are similar to other people (i.e., "I am like them"). This bias might manifest itself when consumers are asked to provide self-judgements, and information about oneself is not accessible or reliable. Consumers may therefore use information about other people when constructing or estimating their own values. (c) The *false uniqueness effect* is the tendency for individuals to falsely assume that they are different from other people (i.e., "I am unique").

Each of the three papers presented in this session demonstrated one or more of the biases discussed above. In addition, Steve Hoch's comments as discussant helped tie the findings of the papers together. The first paper by Deborah Mitchell and Eric Johnson examined how managers' predictions of their markets suffer from a very large false consensus bias. Additionally, managers are systematically overconfident in their predictions. The second paper by Geeta Menon, Priya Raghubir and Norbert Schwarz illustrated that a respondent's estimate of the frequency of a behavior is subject to false consensus bias. The extent of this bias is moderated by the diagnosticity of the information of oneself in memory. Further, this paper introduces the concept of a backward false consensus effect. This effect is shown to occur when adequate information about oneself is not accessible. Finally, Vicki Morwitz and Carol Pluzinski demonstrated all three biases in a political polling context. Voters surveyed prior to the 1992 U.S. Presidential Election demonstrated false consensus bias when they expected that many others would also vote for the same candidate for whom they intended to vote, despite a preponderance of information available indicating the contrary. In actual voting, however, people had a tendency to switch from their intended vote to the candidate expected to win by the majority (i.e., Clinton). This type of "bandwagon" phenomenon exemplifies the behavioral consequence of the backward false consensus effect. This paper further shows that an overwhelming percentage of voters believe that they are not at all influenced by published political polls. At the same time, they perceive that most other voters are influenced by the same polls, illustrating the false uniqueness effect.

REFERENCES

Bearden, William O. and Michael J. Etzel (1982), "Reference Group Influence on Product and Brand Purchase Decisions," *Journal of Consumer Research*, 9 (September), 183-194.

_____ and Randall L. Rose (1990), "Attention to Social Comparison Information: An Individual Difference Factor Affecting Consumer Conformity," *Journal of Consumer Research*, 16 (March), 461-471.

Consumer Research Standards & Public Policy Formulation: The Case Of Mickey Mouse & Old Joe

Claude R. Martin, Jr., University of Michigan

ABSTRACT

In December, 1991 a consumer research paper "Brand Logo Recognition by Children Aged 3 to 6 Years, Mickey Mouse and Old Joe the Camel," produced a crescendo of demands to make significant changes in public policy, including banning the "Old Joe" advertising campaign. This paper reviews the demands for public policy change and offers a summary of evaluations by four independent reviewers of the study addressing issues of reliability, validity, reporting of convergent results and support for conclusions in the data offered. Serious concern is raised as to its efficacy to underpin major changes in public policy.

INTRODUCTION

In December, 1991 a consumer research paper produced a crescendo of demands to make significant changes in advertising regulation, including the banning of one campaign specifically. The article by Fischer, et al. entitled "Brand Logo Recognition by Children Aged 3 to 6 Years, Mickey Mouse and Old Joe the Camel," appeared in the *Journal of the American Medical Association* [*JAMA*]. In the year following the publication of the articles there was extensive media coverage of calls for banning the ad campaign, including 72 individual wire service stories. While accompanied in the same issue of *JAMA* by two other research articles and three editorials, the Fischer, et al. research was the most cited in demands for a significant change in public policy regarding advertising.

This unusual response to consumer research provoked our interest in reviewing the study on four dimensions: reliability, validity, reporting of convergent results and support for conclusions in the data offered. The objective is to explore whether this research stands the test for changing public policy.

DEMANDS FOR PUBLIC POLICY CHANGES

Shortly after the *JAMA* publication the American Cancer Society, American Heart Association and American Lung Association formally petitioned the Federal Trade Commission to immediately ban the *Old Joe* campaign [Cimons 1992, Dagnoli 1991, Snider 1991]; Senator William Cohen called for the senate to be involved in an effort to ban *Old Joe* Camel [*Scripps Howard News Service*, 1992]; Representative Henry Waxman asked the House Subcommittee on Health and the Environment to recommend strict controls on all advertising and specifically to prohibit the RJR ad campaign [Waxman, 1991]; *Advertising Age* [January, 1992] called upon RJR to drop the *Old Joe* campaign; the attorneys general of 26 states began to lobby for more control over cigarette advertising calling for repeal of a section of the Cigarette Labeling and Advertising act [Zukin 1992 and Levine 1992]; the New York Metropolitan Transportation Authority, citing the research in *JAMA*, banned all tobacco ads on subways, buses and trains beginning in 1993 [Harrigan 1992]; The Surgeon General of the United States, the Secretary of the Department of Health and Human Services, and the American Medical Association demanded that R.J. Reynolds stop using Old *Joe* [*Washington Times* 1992; Brown 1991, Enrice 1992, Horovitz 1992, Fara Warner 1992, Vesey 1992, *U.S. News & World Report* 1992, Lipman 1992, Kong 1992, Roberts 1992, Standora 1992]; a resolution was passed by a committee of the Chicago City Council condemning R. J. Reynolds Tobacco Company for the *Old Joe* ads [*Chicago Tribune* 1992]; there was a parade by physicians and their families through the streets of Chicago to protest *Old Joe* and calling for a ban on the ad campaign [*Reuters News Service* 1992, *Associated Press* 1992]; and the Surgeon General Antonia Novello in collaboration with the American Medical Association launched a nationwide contest among elementary and junior high school students calling for letters, essays, poems or cartoons focused on a theme of "Say No, Old Joe" [*Detroit Free Press* 1993].

It is difficult to quantify the news coverage and subsequent demands for public policy reformulation, including banning *Old Joe*. We reviewed 172 newspaper articles and 71 wire service stories all of which reported on the Fischer, et al. research. To give a flavor for the reporting the following sampling of headlines is offered:

Puffing Camel Rivals Mickey in Kid's Eyes
The Charlotte Observer [12/11/91]

Joe Camel Is Also Pied Piper, Research Finds
The Wall Street Journal [12/11/91]

Most Kids Can Identify Camel Character
The Associated Press [12/11/91]

Study: Camel Cartoon Sends Kids Smoke Signals
The Boston Herald [12/11/91]

To Some, Cartoon Camel Isn't Funny
Seattle Post-Intelligencer [12/11/91]

Ban: Health Groups Say Study Proves All Tobacco Ads Must Be Crushed Out
The Detroit News [12/12/91]

We also reviewed 82 print media editorials and 23 syndicated columnists. Of these editorial efforts there were 32 specific editorial calls for the banning of *Old Joe* and/or a more stringent regulation of tobacco advertising including the *Boston Globe* [December 12, 1991], *Atlanta Journal and Constitution* [December 14, 1991], *Fort Worth Star-Telegram* [December 17, 1991], *Syracuse Herald-Journal* [March 11, 1992], *The News & Observer (Raleigh, N.C.)* [March 12, 1992], *Denver Post* [March 15, 1992], *Philadelphia Inquirer* [March 15, 1992], *San Francisco Examiner* [March 17, 1992], and the *New York Observer* [March 23, 1992].

THE EVALUATION PROCESS

A census of research associations and journals was undertaken to ascertain their research guidelines. These included the fields of statistics, advertising, marketing, economics, sociology and psychology. Input was generated from the *American Statistical Association, American Association for Public Opinion Research, American Economic Review, Journal of Marketing Research, Journal of Marketing, American Marketing Association*, and *American Psychological Association*. Also examined were the "instructions for authors" of the *Journal of the American Medical Association*. This produced a compendium of standards upon which to judge social science/business research:

RESEARCH STANDARDS
Provide sufficient information to judge quality of the results
Built-in Controls
Validity/Reliability
Outcome measures not clearly related to variables of investigation
Full and unambiguous testing hypotheses
Subjects representative of population
Results are generalizable
Convergent results reported and/or discussed
Claims and assertions supported by the research
Reporting or discussion of the limitations of the methodology used
Complete review of the literature
Full details of the treatment of subjects involved
Non-advocacy position by authors
Speculation of authors clearly identified
"Full disclosure"

While there are no formal research guidelines for *Association for Consumer Research,* we perceive that there would be general acceptance of these by most *ACR* members.

The Fischer, et al. article was submitted to four researchers in varying social science fields (marketing, advertising research, consumer behavior and corporate strategy) from differing major universities for their independent reviews. They were not provided with the research standards as discussed above, but rather were asked to independently evaluate each of the three papers on the basis of the usual norms for their disciplines. All four are experienced in analytical techniques and are reviewers for journals in their selected fields. The net result were evaluative comments, both general and specific, concerning the Fischer, et al. research which were then correlated to these standards.

The elements on which the reviewers' focused were: reliability, validity, full disclosure, and support for conclusions in the data offered.

FISCHER, ET AL., DESCRIPTION

Fischer, et al. investigated "brand logo recognition by children aged 3 to 6 years." Children were instructed to match logos with one of 12 products pictured on a game board. Twenty-two logos were tested, including those representing children's products, adult products, and those for two popular cigarette brands (*Camel* and *Marlboro*). The setting for the research were preschools in Augusta and Atlanta, Georgia. A convenience sample of 229 children attending 10 preschools was used. Fischer, et al., claim the children demonstrated high rates of logo recognition and when analyzed by product category, the level of cigarette logos was intermediate between children's and adult products. The recognition of the *Disney Channel* logo and *Old Joe* were described as "highest in their respective product categories" [Fischer, et al., p. 3145]. The *respective categories* are "children's brands" (the Disney logo) and "cigarette brands" (*Old Joe*). The data offered by Fischer, et al. shows hat the *Disney Channel, McDonald's, Burger King, Dominos Pizza, Coca Cola, Pepsi, Nike, Chevrolet* and *Ford* all had higher recognition scores than *Old Joe*. This is not discussed in the research findings by the authors.

INDEPENDENT EVALUATIONS

Marketing Management Reviewer

Overall Evaluation. This paper leads with an advocacy position and then seeks to prove that position, rather than scientifically examining the relation between advertising and smoking behavior. The result is a plethora of citations from anti-smoking advocates and a failure to consider research that has addressed the advertising-smoking relationship and found countervailing evidence. The authors go far beyond their basic methodology, inferring advertising recognition to a simple matching exercise involving children. They ignore the data that shows improvement in cognitive skills to correctly match logos to products among older children in the study.

Specific Comments. The authors cite a series of studies [Aitken, et al. 1987, 1988, 1990; Armstrong, et al. 1990; Chapman and Fitzgerald 1982; Davis 1987; Goldstein, et al. 1987; Levit, et al. 1981; Seldon and Dordoodian 1989; Warner 1987], and then state "Collectively these studies provide compelling evidence that cigarette advertisements are seen by adolescents ....cigarette advertising is causally linked to smoking behavior" [Fischer, et al. p. 3145]. In a recent review of these studies the conclusion is reached that "such studies have not examined the causal link between advertising message recall and smoking behavior" [Mazis, et al. 1992, p. 24]. The advocacy position of the Fischer research team is clear from their conclusion that there is "compelling evidence."

Are-reading of the Leckenby and Plummer article [1983] cited by the Fischer team shows advertising recognition is a complex, multi-variable measurement that is used, among others, to evaluate copy and as a surrogate measure for advertising effectiveness. That is not what they proposed. The methodology simply allows them to have subjects match certain symbols (logos) with product pictures. This is *not* advertising recognition, but simply a matching exercise. The *Old Joe* logo could be very difficult to match to any of the other product categories and the matching may simply reflect the cognitive ability of the participants to match through a process of elimination. Controls for such a possibility are necessary.

The data concerning non-matches needs to reported. In how many instances did participants mismatch the other logos to cigarettes and how many times did they mismatch other cigarette logos to other non-cigarette products? In this vein, how many times were multiple cards incorrectly assigned to the same product? This information is not reported.

In their conclusion, Fischer, et al. [1991] state that "R J Reynolds Tobacco Company is as effective as the *Disney Channel* in reaching six year old children." The authors go far beyond their data and what they studied. The data simply show that six year old children were better than younger children at the task of matching logos to products generally, and that they matched *Old Joe* to cigarettes as a product at a rate not significantly different than they matched the *Disney Channel* to *Mickey Mouse*. The authors fail to show whether there are other matches that are also not significantly different, thus reinforcing the conclusion that six year olds have developed a better cognitive skill for matching.

Advertising Reviewer

Overall Evaluation. This article is very demand ridden. In other words, it is biased to get the results the authors' desire. It was set up not to fail. A classic example follows:

The task is demanding in that the Camel ads *always* show the camel with cigarettes. In the study the cigarette is not present. You are really just asking the subjects "what is missing from this picture?" So if the subjects correctly identify the cigarette, they are identifying what is missing from the picture, a task right out of kindergarten curricula. It is an obvious violation of experimental design protocol to have the stimulus material and the dependent measure be parts of the same image, separated only for the purpose of this study. This makes this study nothing more than a classical conditioning or S-R (stimulus-response) replication. I'm not entirely sure, but I think some higher order primates such as chimpanzees would have done as well. I'm only partially facetious on this.

Specific Comments. Essentially the authors take 3 to 6 year old children, expose them to 22 different brand "logos" and ask them to match them to pictures of 12 different product categories. The basic problems are:

a. The choice set is relatively small. One only has twelve choices. To be more externally valid, one would need more alternative choices, as would be true in a real world setting or information environment. It is also true that give so few choices, it is likely that the children employed some heuristic, choice rules and elimination procedures which may have systematically biased the results. But, given the lack of controls, etc. we simply don't know.

b. To be valid the study should have included not only more alternatives, but more varied ones as well. This would allow us to know whether alternative explanations are likely. For example, what if the authors would have included a picture of a zoo? If subjects would have then matched Old Joe with the zoo, what would these results have meant? There are so many more credible alternative explanations for the data than the authors tested or even acknowledge. I'd suggest they could have used other cartoon characters such as *Green Giant, Pillsbury Dough Boy, Trix Rabbit, Hamburger Helper,* etc. A child may recognize the *Green Giant* at a fairly early age; may even like him, but that doesn't mean he will eat his green beans, broccoli or asparagus.

c. It is possible that subjects are merely responding to context. What is the study would have included elements that also appear in camel ads such as pool tables, guitars, automobiles, etc.? My guess is that you would have high matching rates there as well. Such a finding would support the idea of the results being due to nothing more than "recognizing things often found with *Old Joe*," which means very little beyond some vague context effect.

The authors also play a little loose with their third hand summaries of other's research. They state that "by age six years, half of all children regularly go shopping by themselves" [Fischer, et al. p. 3147]. The attribution for this is to a book by J.U. McNeal [1987, p. 33]. This is *not* an empirical finding. The authors cite and refer to it as if it were research by McNeal supportive of their conclusion. The fact is that it is not; they simply misrepresent it. What is its face validity? The last time you were in K-Mart, Walmart or Target did you notice a lot of kids six and under shopping by themselves?

Consumer Behavior Reviewer

This reviewer did not follow the general format of the others, but rather concentrated on three "major conclusions" of the Fischer, et al. paper.

Conclusion #1. "Children's knowledge of cigarette brands logos is likely the result of their exposure to environmental tobacco advertising..." [Fischer, et al. p. 3148].

a. "Knowledge" is measured by a widely used measure of memory - the recognition test. This measure is believed to capture the most basic form of memory [Krugman, 1982] that need not lead to future behavior. For example, children recognizing the no-smoking symbol would not logically be lead to later smoking cigarettes!

B. On the issue of reliability there is a concern that the recognition task used by Fischer, et al.[1991] to measure knowledge of logo/trade characters is subject to extensive guessing [Mizerski 1982]. Several aspects of the method used in this study would prompt levels of guessing or bias far beyond the levels (8.3%) assumed by the Fischer, et al. [1991, p.3146]. The following are a few major factors:

1. "Each subject's parent signed a parental consent form and completed a short questionnaire about...the use of cigarettes in the home" [p.3146]. It appears that the only product asked about was cigarette use. The very next day, the children were tested! There is a strong likelihood that the topic of cigarettes was discussed with at least some of the children, which would affect the recognition task the following day. This problem is often referred as a "demand artifact" and can impose a serious bias.

2. A "don't know" option was not offered. This has been shown to bias/inflate recognition scores [Mizerski 1982].

C. Remembering a trade character does not necessarily translate to *liking* or *preference*. Indeed, the *negative* aspects of smoking would be expected to have been exposed to these children, and in a more extensive and organized fashion (e.g., in school) as the child ages. Matching a negative symbol (picture of a cigarette - perhaps similar to a no smoking sign) to *Old Joe* may actually reflect the impact of no smoking education. This was found in two studies [Aitken, et al. 1986, 1987] that are cited in the Fischer, et al. article.

D. The use of the McNemar Test, to test for "a significant change in correct responses between two logos (the *Disney Channel* and *Old Joe*) [Fischer, et al., p. 3146] does not appear to be the appropriate statistic. Siegel [1956, p. 63] notes this statistic is used to measure changes in response to the *same* stimulus. The McNemar Test would not be appropriate for use to test for differences between two stimuli (logo vs. trade characters) that are quite different.

Conclusion #2. "It has been shown that children prefer brands that they see advertised. This effect has been shown to even influence their preference of products that they are too young to use, such as lipstick and diet soft drinks " [Fischer, et al. p. 3147].

This study simply does not provide primary data for this point. They cite previously published studies and imply that high recognition scores transmit into preference for brands-and more importantly-product category use.

a. Recognition, even if carefully measured, is *not* a surrogate for preference. Preference is best measured by seeing the choice of a user [See: Zajonc and Markus 1982]. There is some research that uses affect as a measure of preference, but few, if any, would suggest a very rudimentary measure of memory (recognition) is able to assess preference.
b. There is a citation [Goldberg, et al. 1978] that is used as support for the statement, "it has been shown that children prefer brands that they see advertised" [Fischer, et al. p. 3147]. Goldberg, et al. [1978] used a television advertisement in their research, this study did not, it used a logo. Furthermore, an alternative of a tennis ball, which was not advertised, was presented to the children as preferred by their mothers. The tennis ball tended to be the *most* preferred option by children despite exposure to a a televised toy ad. The Goldberg, et al. [1978] research amply demonstrated that even forced exposure to a TV ad for a toy is overcome by parental influence. My conclusion is that the citation cannot be used to support the Fischer, et al. [1991] conclusion.
c. The remaining part of the second conclusion, "this effect has been shown to even influence their preference of products that they are too young to use, such as lipstick and diet soft drinks," relies on a citation from Gorn and Florsheim [1985]. That study *failed to find* any effect of a diet soft drink TV commercial on *preference* - although Fischer, et al. [1991] state it did. Furthermore, the Gorn and Florsheim [1985] study used forced exposure to a television commercial in its methodology, not the different "logo" study offered by Fischer, et al. [1991].

Conclusion #3. "The R J Reynolds Tobacco Company is as effective as the *Disney Channel* reaching 6 year old children" [Fischer, et al. p. 3148].

a. The definition of "effective" and "reaching" is not clear. Simple recognition of the *Disney Channel* cannot imply "effectiveness." Recognition does not imply preference or other choice/behavioral activity-it is only a very basic measure of memory. "Reaching" is equally ambiguous and subject to the same criticism.
b. The sources of recognition of cigarette logos are not necessarily a derivative of advertising. Other possibilities include: (1) experimental bias already discussed under the first conclusion; (2) school based anti-smoking material, already cited by Fischer, et al. [1991]; and (3) various anti-smoking messages and no smoking logos.

Strategic Management & Public Policy Reviewer

Overall Evaluation. A fundamental problem with this study is that there is no basis for its underlying premise that early logo recognition leads to premature smoking.

Specific Comments. This reviewer offered the following more specific comments regarding the Fischer, et al. [1991] study:

1. Recognition of "children's brands" may be understated because of the logos used. Nike, for example, is not particularly a children's product, and the generic name "*Kelloggs*" is not necessarily a good proxy for particular Kellogg's cereals that are promoted to children. Moreover, all but one of the children's logos (*Disney Channel*) include a word as part of the logo, which may tend to reduce correct matching rates among children who cannot yet read.
2. Recognition rates of "adult brands" may be low because of the products used. Children had to match the logo with a product. The adult products included two computers and two television networks, which had to be matched with a television. It seems likely that children would confuse the "product" pictures of a TV and a computer, since the dominant feature of a picture of a computer is the TV monitor. For these reasons, recognition rates of cigarettes compared to other adult products are probably overstated.
3. The key comparison of *Old Joe* and *Mickey Mouse* lacks any control. Given the fact that there is very little difference among six year olds in recognition scores for cigarette brands, it is extremely likely that they would also do quite well on the best known adult logo, *Chevrolet*. In fact, *Chevrolet* is more widely recognized among all children than is *Old Joe*. "*Chevrolet* is as well recognized as *Mickey Mouse*," however, doesn't have quite the same punch. It is suggested that by age 6, kids may be able to recognize most logos.
4. Another factor producing the lack of significant differences in recognition on *Old Joe* and *Mickey Mouse* is sample size. Among 6 year olds, *Mickey Mouse* is more widely recognized, but the difference is not significant in part because there are only 23 6-year-olds in the sample. Sample sizes are larger for the other age groups (e.g., 60 at age 5).
5. The lack of any relationship between children's recognition of cigarette logos and the use of cigarettes in the home is curious. Kids should be more likely to recognize the logo of the brand their parents smoke, at least as long as the logo is on the package. Thus, the Marlboro red roof, the "Camel" name, and the camel and pyramids should be more widely recognized by children from households in which those brands are used.

SUMMARY

The summary of the findings concerning reviews of the Fischer, et al. article [1991] is seen in Table #1.

Using the major disciplinary standards discussed earlier, there are six on which the majority of the reviewers identified errors in the reported research: building in of controls, validity and reliability, outcome related to variables of investigation, reporting and/or discussion of convergent results, support for claims and assertions, an advocacy position by the authors and identification of authors' speculation.

Summarizing some of the key evaluations, on the issue of validity there is no basis offered for the study's underlying premise that early logo recognition leads to smoking. There is no evidence offered by the authors that logo recognition scores are correlates to behavior initiation. The failure of the authors to consider the basic works in recall and recognition [Bagozzi and Silk 1983; Singh and Rothschild 1983; Mizerski 1982; Valentine and Blum 1961; Wells, et al, 1989; and Finn 1988] is disturbing.

The authors go far beyond their basic methodology inferring advertising recognition to a simple matching exercise by children. Leckenby and Plummer [1983], cited by the authors, conclude that advertising recognition is a complex, multi-variable measurement, not the more simplistic matching exercise offered by Fischer, et al. [1991].

Fischer, et al [1991] ignore data showing improvement in correctly match logos to products among older children in the study and likewise do not report on mismatches.

TABLE #1

Fischer, et al., "Brand Logo Recognition by Children Aged 3 to 6 Years," *Journal of the American Medical Association,* Vol. 266 No. 22, December 11, 1991, pp. 3145-3148

RESEARCH STANDARDS	A	B	C	D
Provide sufficient information to judge quality of the results			√	√
Built-in Controls	√	√	√	
Validity/Reliability	√	√	√	√
Outcome measures not clearly related to variables of investigation	√		√	√
Full and unambiguous testing hypotheses	√			√
Subjects representative of population		√		
Results are generalizable	√			√
Convergent results reported and/or discussed		√	√	√
Claims and assertions supported by the research	√		√	√
Reporting or discussion of the limitations of the methodology used	√			
Complete review of the literature	√			√
Full details of the treatment of subjects involved				√
Non-advocacy position by authors	√	√		√
Speculation of authors clearly identified	√		√	√
"Full disclosure"				√

REVIEWERS

The study found that brand logo recognition increased with age, and that by age 6, recognition of Old Joe is comparable to the *Disney Channel* logo. The authors state that recognition of the *Disney Channel* logo and *Old Joe* were "highest in their respective product categories" [Fischer, et al., p. 3145]. They fail to point out in conjunction with the statement that the respective categories were "children's brands" and "cigarette brands" and that the *Disney Channel, McDonald's, Burger King, Dominos Pizza, Coca Cola, Pepsi, Nike, Chevrolet* and *Ford* had higher recognition scores than *Old Joe.*

Among conclusions reached are that "very young children see, understand, and remember advertising" [Fischer, et al., p. 3145]; that "children's knowledge of cigarette brand logos is most likely the result of their exposure to environmental tobacco advertising" [Fischer, et al., p. 3148]; and that "R. J. Reynolds Tobacco Company is as effective as the *Disney Channel* in reaching 6-year old children" [Fischer, et al., p. 3148]. There is nothing in the data reported to substantiate these conclusions.

DISCUSSION

One could question the time and effort spent in appraising an already published article. "After all, isn't this overkill for a mere 7 pages?" In many cases it probably would be so, but here we are dealing with a paper that has the potential to have a major impact on public policy. It was the crescendo of calls for public policy changes regarding advertising, specifically for cigarettes, and demands that a particular advertising campaign be banned that prompted our interest. Indicative of the general acceptance of the research was an accompanying editorial in *JAMA* entitled "Tobacco Marketing: Profiteering From Children." In it, Representative Henry Waxman makes the statement that "the tobacco companies' success at targeting young people is apparent from the data reported in this issue of THE JOURNAL. Old Joe Camel has demonstrated appeal and recognition among youth" [Waxman, p. 3185].

A reviewer of the original draft of this paper commented, "but what impact has occurred as a result of this research?" As recently as August, 1993 there was a strong recommendation of the Federal Trade Commission staff to completely ban the Joe Camel campaign [Wall Street Journal, 8/11/93, pp. B-1-B5]. The Fischer, et al. research was specfically cited as the major underpining for the staff recommendation. The implications for the first amendment and for other "controversial" ad campaigns is all too evident. The following is indicative of the impact of the staff recommendations:

FTC watchers say the move may signal a vigorous new activist mindset at the FTC. 'It is one of the most controversial isues to come before the FTC in recent years because it is such a strong step and such a strong statement,' says Linda A Goldstein, a partner with Hall, Dickler, Lawler, Kent & Friedman, a New York law firm. 'It would be the first time the FTC has ever taken such a Draconian step.' [*Wall Street Journal* [8/11/93, p. B-1]

We submit that when four reviewers from differing disciplines independently evaluated the Fischer, et al. [1991] study they raised significant questions about the quality of it. Particularly disturbing is the advocacy nature of the research and serious questions concerning reliability and validity. Our concern is not with supporting or attacking cigarette smoking or even cigarette advertising. Rather, our concern is with the quality of the research that can impact public policy, as far-reaching as that suggested by the FTC staff, that then can be applied to other product categories. We suggest the need to better codify research guidelines and more rigorously apply them to consumer research.

REFERENCES

Advertising Age, "Old Joe Must Go," editorial page, January 13, 1992

Aitken, P.P., D.S. Leathar, F.S. O'Hagen, and S.I. Squair, "Children's Awareness to Cigarette Advertisements and Brand Imagery," *British Journal of Addiction,* 1987, 82: pp. 615-622

Aitken, P.P., D.S. Leathar, A.L. Scott and S.I. Squair, "Cigarette Brand Preference of Teenagers and Adults," *Health Promotion,* 1988, 2: pp. 219-226

Aitken, P.P. and D.R. Eadie, "Reinforcing Effects of Cigarette Advertising on Underage Smoking," *British Journal of Addiction,* 1990, 85: pp. 399-412

Associated Press, "Most Kids Can Identify Camel Character," New York: December 11, 1991

_____, "AMA Protest Parade Targets Old Joe Ads," Chicago: June 21, 1992

Atlanta Journal and Constitution, "For Kid's Sake, Scrap Cartoon Camel," December 14, 1991

Bagozzi, Richard P. and Alvin J. Silk, "Recall, Recognition and the Measurement of Memory of Print Advertisements," *Marketing Science* (1983) vol. 2 no. 2, pp. 95-134

Boston Globe, "What's Good For R.J. Reynolds," December 12, 1991

Boston Herald, "Study: Camel Cartoon Sends Kids Smoke Signals," December 11, 1991

Brown, David, "Old Joe and Mickey Mouse Nose to Nose," *The Washington Post,* December 11, 1991, p. A-23

Chapman, S. and B. Fitzgerald, "Brand Preference and Advertising Recall in Adolescent Smokers: Some Implications for Health Promotion," *American Journal of Public Health,* 1982, 72: pp. 491-494

Charlotte Observer, "Puffing Camel Rivals Mickey in Kid's Eyes," December 11, 1991, pp. 1-A & 6-A

Chicago Tribune, "Panel OK's Resolution Condemning Old Joe Ads," May 6, 1992

Cimons, Marlene, "Tobacco Foes Seek Federal Injunction," *The News & Observer,* Raleign, NC, March 29, 1992, p. 2G

Dagnoli, Judann, "*JAMA* Lights New Fire Under Camel's Ads," *Advertising Age,* 1991, pp. 3 & 32

Davis, R.M., "Current Trends in Cigarette Advertising and Marketing," *New England Journal of Medicine,* 1987, 316: pp. 725-732

Denver Post, "Joe Camel, Child Molester," March 15, 1992

Detroit Free Press, "Say No to Joe Camel," March 17, 1993, p. 1-E

Detroit News, "Do Your Kids Know Old Joe," December 12, 1991, p. 5

Enrice, Dottie, "Feds Walk A Mile To Ban Joe Camel," *New York Newsday,* March 14, 1992, p. 8

Finn, Adam, "Print Ad Recognition by Children Aged 3 to 6 Years," *Journal of Marketing Research* (May, 1988) Vol. 25, pp. 168-177

Fischer, Paul M., Meyer P. Schwartz, John W. Richards Jr., Adam O. Goldstein, and Tina H. Rojas, "Brand Logo Recognition by Children Aged 3 to 6 Years," *Journal of the American Medical Association,* December 11, 1991, vol. 266, no. 22, pp. 3145-3148

Fort Worth Star-Telegram, "Joe Camel: Brilliant Campaign, Unintended Results," December 17, 1991

Goldberg, M.E., G.J. Gorn and W. Gibson, "TV Messages for Snack and Breakfast Foods: Do They Influence Children's Preference?" *Journal of Consumer Research,* 1978, 5: pp. 73-81

Goldstein, A.O., P.M. Fischer, J.W. Richards, and D. Creten, "Relationship Between High SchoolStudent Smoking and Recognition of Cigarette Advertisement, " *Journal of Pediatrics,* 1987, 110: pp. 488-491

Gorn, G.J. and R. Florsheim, "The Effect of Commercials for ASdult Products on Children," *Journal of Consumer Research,* 1985, 11: pp. 962-967

Harrigan, Susan, "Snuffed Out!" *New York Newsday,* June 27, 1992, p. 5

Horovitz, Bruce, "Most -Advertised Cigarettes Are Teens Choice, Study Says," *Los Angeles Times,* March 13, 1992, p. 16

Kong, Dolores, "Do Ads Lure Youngsters To Drink, Smoke?" *The Boston Globe,* April 27, 1992, pp. 41-44

Krugman, Herbert, "Memory Without Recall, Exposure Without Perception," *Journal of Advertising Research,* Vol. 1 [1982] pp./ 80-85

Leckenby, John and Joseph Plummer, "Advertising Stimulus Measurement and Assessment Research: A Review of Advertising Testing Methods, *Current Issues and Research in Advertising,* James Leigh & Claude Martin, eds., 1983, pp. 135-165

Levine, Andrea C. (Assistant Attorney General of State of New York), letter to Senator John C. Danforth (R-MO.), July 8, 1992

Levit, E.M., C. Coate, and M. Grossman, "The Effects of Government Regulation on Teenage S moking," *Journal of Law Economics,* 1981, 24: pp. 545-569

Lipman, Joanne, "Surgeon General Puts Joe Camel on the Endangered List," *Wall Street Journal Classroom Edition,* April 1992, p. 8

Mazis, M.B., D.J. Ringold, E.S. Perry and D.W. Denman, "Perceived Age and Attractiveness of Models in Cigarette Advertisements," *Journal of Marketing,* Vol. 56 No 1 [1992], pp. 22-38

McNeal, J.U., *Children As Consumers* (1987), Lexington, MA: Lexington Books, pp. 5, 12, 47, 179

Mizerski, Richard, "Viewer Miscomprehension Findings are Measurement Bound," *Journal of Marketing,* Vol. 46 No 4, (1982), pp. 32-34

New York Observer, "Commentary," March 23, 1992

Philadelphia Inquirer, "Pushing Butts to Kids," March 15, 1992

Raleigh News & Observer (Raleigh, N.C.), "Old Joe, 'Friend' of Kids," March 12, 1992

Reuters News Service, "US Doctors Stage Protest Against *Old Joe,*" Chicago: June 21, 1992

Roberts, Selena, "Surgeon General Wants to Snuff Out Joe Camel," *Orlando Sentinel,* May 25, 1992, p. A-4

San Francisco Examiner, "Just Say No to Joe Camel, March 17, 1992

Scripps Howard News Service, "Senator Wants Ban on RJR's 'Old Joe'" March 20, 1992

Seattle Post-Intelligencer, "To Some, Cartoon Camel Isn't Funny," December 11, 1991, p. 9

Seldon, B.J. and K. Dordoodian, "A Simultaneous Model of Cigarette Advertising: Effects on Demand and Industry Response to Public Policy," *Review of Economic Statistics,* 1989, 71: pp. 673-677

Siegel, S., *Nonparametric Statistics,* New York: McGraw-Hill Book CVompany [1956]

Singh, S.N. and M.L. Rothschild, "Recognition as a Measure of Learning from Television Commercials," *Journal of Marketing Research,* Vol. 20 [August 1983] pp. 235-248

Snider, Mike, "Doctors Turn Up The Heat on Smoking," *USA Today,* December 11, 1991, pp. 1-2D

Standora, Leo, "Docs: Time For Old Joe To Become a No-Show," *New York Post,* March 10, 1992, p. 3

Syracuse Herald-Journal, "Luring Kids to Smoke: The Uncool Side of Joe Camel," March 11, 1992

U.S. News & World Report, "An Anti Smoking Campaign Heats Up," p. 14

Valentine, Appel and M.I. Blum, "Ad Recognition and Response Set," *Journal of Advertising Research* , (June, 1961) pp. 13-21

Vesey, Susannah, "Up In Smoke," *Atlanta Constitution,* ("Peach Buzz" column) March 20, 1992

Wall Street Journal, "Joe Camel Is Also Pied Piper, Research Finds," December 11, 1991, pp. B1 & B4

Wall Street Journal, "FTC Staff Recommends Ban of Joe Camel Campaign," August 11, 1993, pp. B1 and B5

Warner, Fara, "Novello Throws Down Gauntlet," *AdWeek's Marketing Week,* March 16, 1992, p. 4

Warner, K.E., "A Ban on Promotion of Tobacco Products," *New Eng land Journal of Medicine,* 1987, 316: pp. 745-747

Waxman, Henry, "Tobacco Marketing: Profiteering From Children," *Journal of the American Medical Association,* December 11, 1991, vol. 266, no. 22, pp. 3185-3186

Webster's Ninth New Collegiate Dictionary, Springfield, MA: Merriam-Webster Inc. (1990)

Wells, William, John Burnett, and Sandra Moriarty, *Advertising: Principles and Practices* (1989) New York: Prentice-Hall Inc.

Zajonc, R.B. and H. Markus, "Affective and Cognitive Factors in Preferences," *Journal of Consumer Research,* Vol. 9 [September, 1982], pp. 123-131

Zukin, Helen E., "Brief Exposures," *Indoor Pollution Law Report,* August, 1992

Washington Times, "Camels 'Old Joe' Creates Young Smokers," letter from Louis W. Sullivan and Antonia C. Novello, March 30, 1992, p. E2

The Mammography Guidelines Controversy: What Do Women Think?

Sharyn M. Sutton, National Cancer Institute
Ellen J. Eisner, National Cancer Institute
Diane L. Bloom, University of North Carolina
Paul N. Bloom, University of North Carolina

ABSTRACT

Medical researchers have begun to question the appropriateness of guidelines (supported by the National Cancer Institute, American Cancer Society, and others) which recommend that women between forty and fifty obtain mammograms every one to two years. This paper reports on the early stages of a consumer research program which seeks to understand how women are responding to this controversy. The findings have implications both for dealing with the current controversy and for improving preventive health programs of all types.

INTRODUCTION

Consumer researchers have been devoting increasing attention to how they can contribute to the resolution of social problems. For example, a subject emphasized in several sessions at the 1992 ACR Conference was how consumer research can be used to improve the effectiveness of preventive health programs.

One preventive health topic that has already been the subject of considerable consumer research is: How can women be persuaded to have regular mammograms? Numerous studies have been done to identify the factors that influence decisions to have mammograms (for reviews, see AMC Cancer Research Center 1992, Rimer 1992); and a number of consumer-research-based intervention programs have been tested and evaluated (Rimer 1992).

Although progress has been made in persuading women to have mammograms, a recent development is viewed by public health officials as threatening this progress. Over the last year, many researchers have begun to question the appropriateness of the existing guidelines for mammography (supported by the National Cancer Institute, American Cancer Society, and others), which recommend that women between 40 and 50 have a mammogram every one to two years and that women over 50 have one every year. The concern is that women under 50 may not benefit from mammograms and may even be harmed by them. Indeed, one randomized clinical trial done in Canada with women between 40 and 50 showed that women who obtained regular mammograms were more likely to die of breast cancer than women who never had mammograms (Miller et al. 1992).

Concern about how women would respond to this controversy over mammograms led the Office of Cancer Communications of the National Cancer Institute to conduct several consumer research studies to generate ideas about how public health officials could best minimize any negative consequences from the controversy. Of particular concern was that women over 50 — who clearly benefit from having mammograms according to clinical trials — would become less inclined to have mammograms.

This paper reports on two focus groups that were conducted to gain an understanding of women's reactions to and thinking about the controversy. Insights from these groups were used to guide the construction of a nationally projectable quantitative survey (Sutton, Eisner, and Johnston 1993), which was completed after the deadline for this conference. Issues are raised in these studies that relate to research in areas such as how consumers respond to risk communications, how consumers react to information that is discrepant with prior knowledge and behavior, and how consumer skepticism works. However, this research was not drawn upon for specific research hypotheses to guide the research reported here because of a desire to take a fresh, exploratory approach in conducting the focus groups.

METHOD

The focus groups were conducted in January 1993 in Richmond, Virginia. Richmond was selected because it was easily accessible to the National Cancer Institute staff (located in Maryland) and because it was not as major a metropolitan area as Washington, Baltimore, or Philadelphia. The first group consisted of ten women ages 40 to 49, and the second consisted of ten women ages 50 to 65. Both groups were recruited to include a mix of individuals who were having regular mammograms and those who were not. No one in either group had ever been told they had (or might have) cancer. In terms of education, all participants had either a high school education or had attended one or two years of college. While the study contained predominantly white women, several African-American women participated. Each group was two hours in length.

The topic guide for the first part of each group followed a sequence of topics, ranging from general perceptions about breast cancer and mammography to personal behaviors with regard to obtaining mammograms. In the second half of each group, participants were asked to read and discuss a "News and Opinion" article adapted from a column published in the *Chicago Tribune* entitled, "Is It a Mammogram or a Mammoscam?" The article addressed a number of issues, including the current controversy about mammograms for younger women. Results of the Canadian study were also reported.

FINDINGS

Summary of General Discussion on Mammography

Women in the focus groups were concerned about a number of health-related problems, including cancer, high blood pressure, Alzheimers disease, arthritis, the general deteriorating effects of aging, and the high costs of health insurance and health care. When the term "breast cancer" came up, some participants immediately thought about other women they have known with the disease. Others thought about losing a breast or dying.

In the course of discussion, group members were asked to indicate how likely they thought they were to get breast cancer on a scale from "1" to "7," where "1" signified "not at all likely" and "7" signified "very likely." As a whole, the group of older women rated themselves as less likely to get breast cancer than did the younger women. Some said they didn't think they were likely to get it because they are healthy; others, because no one in their family had it, or because they have a positive outlook on life.

> "I believe in positive thinking. I put '1' even though my grandmother and my mother had cancer."
> "I've heard that 85% of all illness begins in the mind. I don't know if that's correct, but I believe it."

Although several older women thought they wouldn't get breast cancer because there was no history of it in their families, others who had a family history also seemed to feel exempt from getting the disease. One said, "I gave a '1' even though I had a sister who died of breast cancer. But I'm a healthy person. I just don't feel as if I'm going to get it."

There was a feeling among the older women of having passed a certain "window of vulnerability." Having not gotten breast cancer by the time they were in their fifties, many considered themselves to be safe at this point. As one older woman expressed it, "I [gave myself a low rating] because there isn't any history of it around [in my family] and [because] I've been tested at least 4 or 5 times since I was 40 or 45 years old, and nothing has shown up yet."

By contrast to the older group, the younger women were more likely to choose higher ratings of 4 or 5 simply because they were women and therefore knew themselves to be at risk.

The discussion of susceptibility to breast cancer quickly led to a discussion of mammography. Group members perceived the major advantages of mammograms to be finding breast cancer early while it is more easily curable, knowing whether or not one has breast cancer, and peace of mind. Major disadvantages included cost, pain and discomfort, and the fear of finding cancer.

In both groups, women expressed concern that mammography equipment might not be working properly and could, as a result, give them too much radiation. Several participants mentioned having seen a program on *20/20* about the inaccurate reading of mammograms. There was concern that the individuals who read their mammograms may err and fail to detect early cancers.

Some focus group participants indicated that they had gotten mammograms either because they had found lumps, had other problems (e.g., bleeding) or because their doctors had recommended the test. Others had heard that women over 40 should have mammograms and agreed with that point of view.

Summary of Discussion on Mammography Guidelines Controversy

The crux of the focus group discussion centered around examining participants' reaction to the current scientific controversy over whether women in their forties should be having mammograms, given the findings of several recently published studies. As mentioned earlier, the stimulus for this discussion was a news and opinion article that appeared in the *Chicago Tribune* during December 1992.

As the women discussed the article, several major themes emerged. These key themes are discussed below:

1. The current controversy over mammograms for younger women is generally perceived as positive.

It is interesting to note that none of the women in the focus groups had any knowledge of the mammography age controversy before being exposed to the article. In general, the fact that there was yet another medical controversy going on did not surprise them. Women in both focus groups said they expected the experts to disagree about complex health questions.

"It seems to be the same thing over and over again. It may be necessary; it may not be necessary. It is good; it's not good. It does prove something; it doesn't prove something. And they're still arguing about it. They can't make up their mind whether statistically it's really doing any good."

"There's controversy no matter what it is, whether it's AIDS or whatever. There's always controversy."

As the discussion progressed, it quickly became apparent that this type of debate is viewed in a positive light. Women in the groups believed that disagreement among experts and cancer organizations will prompt more studies on important questions. The following statements and dialogue illustrate participants' view that conflicting ideas are constructive and that disagreement ultimately results in greater truth and certainty:

"I think it's a kind of checks and balance system. Suppose I have my opinion and I think this is the only opinion in town. But then you come along and you've had experiences I wasn't exposed to. To me, when they disagree, it means that someone is trying to improve."

"I think many different organizations are working independently, trying to get information. That's what I like. There are a lot of people gathering information....I see value in it for getting an unbiased opinion."

Controversy was also viewed as positive because it generates media attention. Newspaper and magazine articles remind them to have mammograms, whereas they might not otherwise think about it.

2. Participants are indoctrinated with the concept of early detection.

In both focus groups, the women firmly believed that mammograms detect breast cancer early when it is most curable. Early detection, they said, was the key to survival, as well as to less radical surgical treatment. Even after reading the article, almost all the women said they would continue getting mammograms.

"This is the thing to do. We've heard it for 10, 15, 20 years now, that we should have mammograms. And that's what we do, most of us."

"I do believe there's still something to mammograms....Maybe it has some merit still, even if they can't agree on it. There's got to be some merit to it because they are detecting [breast cancer] and they are saving some people."

3. Women give credence only to the information that confirms their prior beliefs; they disregard conflicting information.

Upon first reading the article, some participants (particularly in the younger focus group) were taken aback by the statement that although mammograms detected more small breast tumors earlier in women in the mammography group, these women did not live longer than individuals in the other group. "Confused," "angry," "scared,""makes you wonder," "makes you feel insecure" were some of the initial reactions to the article. The following comment was typical:

"It doesn't make me feel good. It upsets me. Maybe I've been wasting my time. Here I'm being exposed to low radiation for nothing. I could be giving myself breast cancer. Maybe I have this lump from the last mammogram. Who knows?"

Within a few minutes, however, they were all engaged in "selective distortion," accepting only information consistent with the belief that mammograms save lives. Information which conflicted with their early detection mindset — namely, that more women in the 40-49 age group who had mammograms died of breast cancer than those who didn't have mammograms — was largely disregarded.

Participants used a number of different mechanisms to discount parts of the article that did not fit their prior beliefs. Some participants tried to discredit the Canadian and Swedish studies based on their very limited (and often incorrect) knowledge of research methodology. They questioned, for example, the size and composition of the samples studied. They also wondered what other factors regarding the study participants might have caused more of them who had mammograms to die from breast cancer.

> "I wonder who paid for that independent study. With independent studies they may interview 1,000 women, but what's 1,000 women when you consider how many millions of women there are? I heard one the other day about a survey of children. I was listening to it and I thought, 'I don't agree with that.' This was a survey of [only] 39 children."
> "What kind of women were they? Were they different races? Certain groups might be more susceptible to certain diseases than others. They didn't even bring that up in the article. It says Swedish and Canadian."

Some women discredited the article in and of itself ("It says News and Opinion not News and Gospel!"), while others simply quoted the article selectively.

4. Participants were skeptical about research study findings in general, and foreign studies in particular.

As a whole, participants were not swayed by the research findings reported in the article. Instead, as indicated above, they questioned how the study was conducted (e.g., how many women were in it) as well as other variables that might have affected the results. Participants were particularly skeptical about foreign studies, feeling that women in other countries may be exposed to different environmental factors than American women, thus making them more susceptible to cancer. Likewise, they felt that women from different cultures may have a greater predisposition toward certain diseases such as breast cancer. The following verbatim illustrates participants' unwillingness to accept study results at face value:

> "In so many of these studies, they don't tell you where they [the participants] live, what they do, what their family background is. What kind of study? Where does this come from?"

In both groups, women expressed a desire for additional information regarding how the studies were performed and who the participants were. They wondered, for example, whether the women who got breast cancer were in a higher risk group to begin with, or could have been exposed to any contributing environmental factors. They also speculated on the possibility that some of the women who died of breast cancer had been on birth control pills, while the women who did not get the disease were not.

Overall, it was clear from the discussion that participants did not understand the concept of randomized clinical trials. Members of the focus groups tended to think that differences between the study and control groups were attributable to individual differences, making some women more likely to develop breast cancer than others. Several women said they would like to read the original journal articles, even though they acknowledged the difficulty of understanding such material.

Participants were also wary of research because they believe that research on the same question can generate different answers. The Canadian study is just one study, they said, and they wonder what future studies will reveal. In the absence of more complete and convincing information on the relationship between having mammograms and survival rates for younger women, participants said they are unlikely to change either their behavior or their perceptions regarding mammograms. As one woman put it, "The jury is still out."

5. Participants think that statistics can be manipulated to support any viewpoint.

Also contributing to the skepticism about medical research was the belief that statistics can be used to support any point of view. Conclusions based on statistics were generally not convincing to focus group participants, as the following comment indicates:

> "I feel like now it's become a game of statistics. You can go back and interpret statistics anyway you want to. You can make the numbers work from any angle you want to and they always come out different. Statistics...depend on what point of view the person that's compiling them is trying to come up with. So I have no faith in statistics."

6. Participants think that women in their forties should have more mammograms rather than fewer.

Women in both groups wrestled with the copy point in the article which stated that mammograms would not help women in their forties survive breast cancer. Early detection, they reasoned, should lead to better chances of a cure. The fact that the Canadian study showed that more younger women who had mammograms died from breast cancer than women who did not have mammograms was confusing to them.

In trying to make sense of it, a few participants had brief flashes of fear that the radiation from mammograms might be responsible for the negative outcome in younger women. This fear, however, quickly gave way to another hypothesis, based partly on a sentence from the article stating that breast cancer grows faster in younger women. Participants reasoned that if this is the case, women in their forties need to have more, not fewer, mammograms. If breast cancer starts between mammograms, by the time the next mammogram is scheduled two years later, the cancer could grow dangerously out of control. One woman explained it this way:

> "Cancer grows very rapidly in a young person. But in an older person, it grows very slowly. As everyone was saying, I think it's backwards. When you're 40 you should have one every 6 months. When you get to be 50, you can have that lump in your body for a year or two and it would not grow that rapidly."
> "To me it's disturbing, the fact that all these women are dying from breast cancer between 40 and 49. Maybe they should start mammograms at age 35 and catch it in time. Evidently, it hasn't been caught in time if they're dying from it. It wasn't early enough detection."

To participants, the need to monitor women in this younger age group more closely seemed logical because their bodies are going through vast hormonal changes — changes which could increase the chances of their developing other health problems. In the older focus group, participants mentioned that women in their forties may not be examined as frequently by a physician after their childbearing years, causing early stages of breast cancer to go undetected. One woman put it this way:

> "They'd better get on the stick and start examining these girls even closer than before because that's where the body change comes in...I think that is the time of your life that you pay the least attention to yourself because you're getting the kids in and out of college and in and out of marriage. You're getting them in and out of everything. We've all been through it. It's too busy."

Women in the older group also thought that women in their thirties and forties may be more at risk for breast cancer because they have been exposed to so much more in the way of pollutants, contaminants, and chemicals (e.g., in food) during their lives than women in their fifties. There was discussion, for example, about whether long-term usage of birth control pills could be making women who are now in their forties more susceptible to breast cancer. This seemed logical to participants, since there is some evidence of a linkage between estrogen replacement therapy and breast cancer, and estrogen is also the main ingredient in birth control pills. Overall, there was consensus in the older group that younger women need to have mammograms more frequently.

7. *The fact that mammograms are not 100% accurate does not disillusion women.*

While none of the focus group participants were aware of the guidelines controversy before reading the article, a number of individuals recalled having heard or read something in the news about the accuracy of mammograms. When the subject of accuracy came up, women in both groups noted that they were not surprised to hear that mammograms are not always accurate. They did not expect medical tests to be completely reliable since "nothing is 100% foolproof and "no tests are completely accurate." They were impressed, in fact, that mammograms were accurate most of the time, as the following comment illustrates:

"I used to trust fully that mammograms were going to find breast cancer, and I was just floored when I found out [they weren't completely accurate]... I was going through it like this is God saying I'm O.K. After I got myself psyched up, I come to find out maybe it's 89% accurate. But it's better than not doing it."

Many participants also said that women should do breast self-examinations to increase the likelihood of detecting cancer early.

8. *The motives of mammography equipment owners and doctors are questioned.*

A sub-theme in both groups was lack of trust in the motivations of mammography equipment owners as well as doctors who recommend mammograms or have their own equipment. Some participants wondered whether mammography facilities try to convince women to have mammograms because these tests are necessary and beneficial, or because the facilities need to use the equipment to make money. Analogies were made to heart bypass operations and MRI tests.

"I read that where it's available it seems like there are a great number of by-pass operations, and where it's not available, nobody needs one."

"I've read that doctors recommend tests to support the equipment they have. I read that so many hospitals in a particular area had MRI machines that they couldn't support it, so doctors were pushing these tests."

Although a number of women had stated during the first part of the focus groups that they trust their doctor's advice on tests, some participants also thought that their physicians recommend mammograms to protect themselves from malpractice suits. The following comment was typical:

"I think a lot of tests are recommended or sold just so the doctor can say, 'Well, I did everything; I did the best I could.' It doesn't really mean that you had it because you need it or you fall into a risk group, it's just so the doctor can say, 'I'm free and clear.' He's protecting himself against malpractice."

9. *A change in guidelines would not hurt the credibility of the organizations involved.*

As a whole, participants did not regard a potential change in the mammography guidelines as a major event. Focus group participants believed that physicians' groups and organizations responsible for setting guidelines already meet periodically to review new literature and evaluate current recommendations. They view this reevaluation as constructive and positive, calling it a "safety check." Moreover, they feel reassured that these organizations will "put all their ideas together, research it, and come out with an answer." Some said that the National Cancer Institute and the American Cancer Society have to "pay attention to the new studies because it's contradicting some of their beliefs" and "they have to go back and substantiate their opinion."

It made sense to participants that as the science evolves, experts might need to change the guidelines. Consideration of such a change, however, would not cause the major cancer organizations to lose credibility in these women's eyes.

10. *A change in the guidelines would not change participants' behavior with regard to having mammograms; the choice of whether (or when) to have a mammogram is a personal decision.*

In terms of how a change might affect them personally, all the younger women said they would continue having mammograms in their forties even if the official recommendations were changed. No one said they would follow the recommendations just because they were "official." They described the guidelines as "a jump-start" to get them thinking about whether or not to have a mammogram. Overall, they felt that the guidelines should either remain the same or be made even more protective for women in their forties. One younger woman echoed the thoughts of others in her age group when she said:

"I would go and have one as soon as I can, even if they decided to change the recommendations. I would go either way. I wouldn't wait until I was 50 to have a mammogram because I think that there's enough breast cancer that's been found in that 40 to 49 group for me that I consider early detection to be worthwhile."

Responding in a similar way, women in the older group said that a revision in the mammography recommendations would not affect their own behavior regarding mammograms because having this test was just "the right thing to do."

Women regarded the choice about how often to have a mammogram as a personal one, to be made after considering the available information. As the women put it:

"Statistics are great when reading an article like this, but it has to come down to your individual perception of things. And you and your doctor have to decide whether this is what you want or not. If it gives you peace of mind, then you do it. If you think it's a waste of time, then you don't do it."

"You know, there's an old saying: 'There are two sides to every story, and then there's the truth.' And unfortunately, we never know the truth. I believe the truth is within ourselves."

It should be noted, however, that some younger group members expressed concern that mammograms for their age group would no longer be covered by insurance if the experts ended up changing the guidelines to exclude younger women. Perceiving this as a possibility, some thought that changing the guidelines to exclude women in their forties would be "insensitive" on the part of NCI, since it would leave women paying for mammograms out of their own pocket.

DISCUSSION AND CONCLUSION

As is the case with all focus group studies, the findings from these groups must be interpreted cautiously. Studies in different cities using more diverse subjects and employing alternative stimulus materials (rather than a news story) could clearly produce different results. Nevertheless, the findings do provide several ideas and insights that could be useful for guiding future research on (1) how to design more effective preventive health programs and (2) how to how to handle the current mammography guidelines controversy.

The findings suggest that designers of preventive health programs need to recognize the extreme complexity and unpredictability of consumer decision making about preventive health. Clearly, persuading someone to take a preventive health action involves much more than making them understand their risk of contracting a disease. Many factors seem to influence decisions about behaviors like obtaining a mammogram, including factors like perceptions of the risks associated with screening tests or treatments, concerns about insurance coverage, and negative feelings about doctors. Preventive health programs could benefit from additional consumer research on several of the issues identified in these focus groups, such as:

- Which information sources (e.g., mass media, friends, doctors, government agencies) do individual consumers rely on and trust the most to guide their preventive health behaviors? Is information source reliance related to age, education, ethnic background, health history, and/or other factors?
- How does distrust of health care providers and insurers influence behavior? How can this distrust be reduced?
- How do consumers process information about scientific research on preventive health? How do prior beliefs and habits distort the processing of new information about preventive health behaviors? How do consumers respond to descriptions of research designs and reports of statistical results? How can research findings be presented to consumers so that they understand them accurately?
- What role does "positive thinking" play in leading some consumers to underestimate certain health risks?
- Do consumers overestimate the health risks of preventive health behaviors (e.g., the risk of radiation from mammograms) or treatment (e.g., chemotherapy) relative to the health risks of diseases? How can more accurate risk perceptions be created?

Work that consumer researchers have done on information processing, decision making, perceived risk, and several other topics would seem to have relevance for addressing these issues.

Without additional research, it is premature to offer a recommendation about what should be done about the current mammography guidelines controversy. However, if future research produces similar findings, it would suggest that the guidelines controversy will not have a dramatic impact on the frequency with which women obtain mammograms. The development of strategies to minimize the effects of the controversy may not be necessary.

REFERENCES

AMC Cancer Research Center (1992), *Breast and Cervical Screening: Barriers and Use Among Specific Populations*, Denver, CO: AMC Cancer Research Center.

Miller, Anthony B., Cornelia J. Baines, Teresa To, and Claus Wall (1992), "Canadian National Breast Screening Study," *Canadian Medical Association Journal*, 147(10), 1459-1476.

Rimer, Barbara K. (1992), "Understanding the Acceptance of Mammography by Women," *Annals of Behavioral Medicine*, 14(3), 197-203.

Sutton, Sharyn M., Ellen J. Eisner, and Cecile M. Johnson (1993), "The Mammography Guidelines Controversy," Where Does the Consumer Fit In?" working paper, National Cancer Institute, Bethesda, MD.

Ethical Concerns in Marketing Research

Jane Sojka, Washington State University
Eric R. Spangenberg, Washington State University

ABSTRACT

Although ethical issues in the discipline of marketing have been previously addressed, the expanding domain of the field of consumer research mandates that ethical issues be re-examined. By increasing the scope of consumer research to include social issues, and by utilizing qualitative research methods, researchers are finding themselves closer to their subjects: both in terms of physical proximity and level of intimacy. This paper examines how disciplines outside of marketing have handled sensitive ethical issues and offers general guidelines for consumer researchers to consider when faced with decisions regarding research ethics.

INTRODUCTION

Picture this: As a diligent consumer researcher, you have taken the plea for socially responsible consumer research to heart and are studying people who overspend. In dutifully looking out for your respondents' best interests, you have, of course guaranteed confidentiality of all information exchanged in the interview process. As you interview one respondent, the subject casually mentions that in frustration over his spending habits and indebtedness, he frequently "cuts loose" and takes his frustration out physically upon his child. You find yourself in the uncomfortable and possibly illegal position of knowing more than you want to know. According to the law, you must report child abuse; at the same time you have promised your respondent confidentiality in return for his willingness to share sensitive information. What do you do now?

Consumer researchers may wish the above scenario was a vision from the twilight zone and nothing close to a situation they might encounter. However, non-positivistic paradigms as well as exploration of non-traditional consumer behavior topics have expanded the domain of consumer research. The reality of current consumer research suggests that if researchers have not already experienced similar situations, they soon may. Hence, concerns about ethical research practices which were irrelevant to consumer researchers in the past, should now be addressed.

Leaders in the field of consumer behavior have pleaded for research that will benefit society and its consumers (e.g., Belk 1987). As a result, consumer researchers have actively begun examining social issues such as drug addiction (Hirschman 1992), illicit drug consumption (Rose, Bearden and Teel 1992), homeless people (Hill 1992), and compulsive buying (O'Guinn and Faber 1989). In addition to including social issues, consumer researchers have also begun to utilize a wide cadre of research methods relatively new to our discipline. For example, ethnographic reports (e.g., Wallendorf and Arnould 1991), in-depth interviews (e.g., Schouten 1991), and field research (e.g., Belk, Wallendorf and Sherry 1989)—all well established research methods in other disciplines—have been used to explore new content areas in consumer research.

The effect of both topic and method expansion in consumer research is that researchers are becoming closer—in terms of intimacy as well as physical proximity—to their respondents. It is fairly simple to ask a woman what kind of laundry detergent she uses; it is quite a different matter, however, to ask her why she chose to have breast implants. In this example, the research topic changes the level of intimacy between the consumer researcher and respondent(s). The physical proximity of the respondent-researcher relationship changes as well. Instead of encoding a survey from an anonymous student at a large university, researchers come face-to-face with respondents in a variety of situations. Field work and in-depth interviews usually require interviewing or observing participants on more than one occasion; hence, subjects are viewed less as a sample population and considered co-workers in the investigation of a research question. Hirschman (1993) provides an interesting perspective on this notion in a study examining feminism.

It is beyond the scope of any single paper to generate prescriptions for the ethical dilemmas now facing consumer researchers. Ethical decisions are essentially value judgements which researchers must face according to their own standards. It is our hope, however, that by raising the issues and examining how more mature disciplines (specifically sociology, psychology and anthropology) have addressed similar situations, the field of consumer behavior will benefit in several ways. First, it is important that consumer researchers address ethical issues within the discipline before outsiders—such as the government, or university administrations—address them (Twedt 1963). Second, good research design entails anticipating outcomes: ethical questions arising in the research process should be no exception. By examining how other researchers have handled ethical elements in their work, consumer researchers will begin questioning ethical implications of their own research. Finally, our paper presents ethical guidelines for researchers to consider when designing research. While far from encompassing every situation a researcher may encounter, these guidelines might at least encourage researchers to ask "what if...?," thus raising the awareness of ethical issues in consumer research.

HISTORICAL CONTEXT OF ETHICAL ISSUES IN MARKETING

Ethical issues in marketing research are certainly not new. In 1963, when marketing was "still enough of an art so that it is unlikely that any two practitioners...would proceed exactly alike" (p.48), Twedt (1963) proposed a code of ethics. Although directed primarily at marketing practitioners rather than academicians, the code was prompted by three main issues: (1) the desire to maintain public confidence in marketing research procedures; (2) the need to self-regulate the discipline before outsiders decided marketing research needed regulation; and (3) the concern to maintain a positive public image of marketing in general. Also encouraging ethical research practices, the first volume of *The Journal of Marketing Research* devoted space to an article addressing ethical concerns in marketing research (Blankenship 1964).

Indeed, initial concern about marketing ethics and the reputation of the marketing discipline were probably valid. Steiner (1976) noted that prejudices against marketing date back as far as ancient Greece. Although Farmer (1987) recanted pieces of his criticism of marketing ethics in an international context, the two earlier works in his trilogy were based on the premise that the discipline was largely unethical and unresponsive to major world needs (Farmer 1967; 1977). He lamented that there are still "large numbers of vociferous critics who see nothing good in a field that tries to figure out, among other things, how to influence 10-year olds to demand something they do not need and cannot even use" (Farmer 1987, p. 111). Hence, improving the public image of the marketing discipline is still of concern to marketing professionals: both in industry and academia.

Other ethical issues—such as confidentiality and deception—relevant to current research were also addressed in early literature on marketing ethics (Tybout and Zaltman 1974). However, the changing context of current consumer research raises new implications for both of these issues. Assuming and maintaining respondent confidentiality on even sensitive topics is fairly straightforward; withholding illegal information is an entirely different matter.

Likewise, deceptive research in a laboratory situation is common in consumer research. However, the use of deception in the field poses a different set of issues. Deceptive field research might include quasi-experimental designs such as having a confederate pose as a shoplifter to see how other shoppers react. While existing ethical guidelines frown upon deceit in general, Twedt's (1963) marketing guidelines did not consider deceptive field research. Hence, the broadened domain of consumer research makes it necessary to look beyond marketing guidelines alone for prescriptions to ethical questions.

DECEPTION

Deceptive research, where the true purpose of the experiment is masked, is not only frequently used, but may in fact be necessary in the laboratory to avoid demand artifacts which could influence results (Sawyer 1975). Kelman (1967), however, noted ethical problems in controlled laboratory studies by Bramel (1962; 1963) for example, in which male undergraduates were led to believe they were sexually aroused by photographs of men. Kelman rightly noted that for many persons in this age group, sexual identity is a sensitive issue; self-doubts raised by this experiment could cause lingering effects on the participants in spite of adequate debriefing. Further example of this type of ethical dilemma includes the infamous "Milgram Studies" of the early sixties (e.g., Milgram 1963) involving subjects who thought they had administered electrical shocks to the point of "killing" confederates posing as subjects. Indeed this program of research served as an impetus for psychologists to confront many of the ethical issues now before consumer researchers.

Continuous use of deceptive practices may influence subject pools and ultimately effect research results. In studying how experimental subjects view their responsibility in a research project, Epstein, Suedfeld and Silverstein (1973) found that a higher percentage of subjects who had never participated in an experiment were more concerned about honesty. The authors surmised that previous experience with deceptive research practices may have resulted in experienced subjects less willing to be honest in subsequent research. Hence, even in a laboratory situation, deceptive research techniques may lead to a general distrust of researchers and cast a disparaging tone on the discipline undertaking such work. In consumer research using student populations, for example, we must ask ourselves if the "extra-credit for participation" is in reality a course requirement due to the professor's implicit pressure in acquiring subjects.

The problem of deception becomes more crucial in a field setting where respondents may not be aware of their participation in research. Whether or not researchers choose to reveal their purpose depends upon the research topic, design, and the observed population. In Humphrey's (1970) study of homosexual behavior in public restrooms, it is unlikely he would have obtained the same level of information by revealing his motives. Rather, by posing as a "watch queen," he was able to become part of the group and publish new insights into homosexual behavior.

Some social science researchers maintain that deception is necessary to further the progress of science. Barnes (1979) argued that deception is an integral part of all social relations. For example, individuals don't necessarily "bare their souls" to casual acquaintances. Rather, deception by way of not revealing all details about one's self is an accepted part of human relations.

Sagrin (1973), on the other hand, challenged researchers to respect the rights of people who do not wish to be researched. An extreme example was a group of Viet Nam era U.S. Army deserters given political asylum in Sweden. Although an analysis of the group might have made an interesting research article, they did not wish to cooperate with academic researchers. Their asylum was tentative and, if revoked, could result in dire consequences at the hands of U.S. military command.

Similarly, organizations open to the public (such as Alcholics Anonymous) who willingly welcome individuals trying to overcome addictions may not wish to be used as research venues. While anyone may attend an AA meeting as an addict, feelings and experiences revealed by participants within the context of a chapter meeting are to remain anonymous; the use of any information requires participants' permission (Bissell and Royce 1987). While it might be tempting for a researcher to pose as an addict or even to capitalize on an addiction to gain access to a group, using information gained from restricted organizations is, at best, ethically questionable.

When evaluating the use of deception in the field, researchers should consider several issues. First and foremost, subjects' needs and risks should be the overriding concern in every research project. The role of researchers, according to the American Anthropological Association, is "to do everything in [the researchers'] power to protect their [respondents'] physical, social, and psychological welfare and to honor and respect their dignity and privacy" (Spradley 1980, p. 21). Perhaps the first step for researchers in a phenomenological study should be to mentally reverse roles and ask how they would feel as a respondent participating in the proposed research.

A final point to consider is the effect field work might have on subjects' behavior (Kidder 1981). Will subjects alter their behavior as a result of a non-deceptive investigation? Will the project cause the subjects any inconvenience? Asking permission to observe customers while they shop might change their behavior as well as cause embarrassment. Thus, it might be best to observe them unobtrusively; it is less likely to cause any inconvenience or discomfort. In contrast, locating homosexuals by recording their license plate numbers while they are engaged in supposedly secret homosexual activity poses quite a different situation (Humphreys 1970).

CONFIDENTIALITY

Another issue particularly critical when addressing sensitive topics is respondent confidentiality. Confidentiality means that although the researcher knows who the respondent is, identity or information shared within the research context will not be revealed. Under anonymous data collection procedures, assuring confidentiality is assumed because the researcher is unaware of respondent identity. Obviously, as researchers venture forth into the field in search of more intimate information, maintaining confidentiality becomes more difficult.

Clearly, most researchers agree that the privacy of respondents should be respected (Hill 1993; Spradley 1980). Government legislation such as the 1974 Privacy Act limits the disclosure of records among federal agencies (Alexander 1983).

Furthermore, the success of non-survey research—such as participant observation, field work, and interviews—is largely based on trust between researcher and respondent. Studying social worker/client relations, Johnson (1975) found that establishing trust was one of the most difficult parts of a field project. At least initially, promises of confidentiality may be helpful in establishing trust with respondents so that meaningful and valid data is obtained.

Informed Consent

Informed consent is one method frequently used by researchers to assure respondents of confidentiality. In addition, informed consent is a prerequisite for obtaining funds from the U.S. Public Health Service (1969) and is strongly recommended in the "Ethical Principles of Psychologists and Code of Conduct" (APA 1992).

While it is possible to encourage respondents to share sensitive information about topics such as drinking and sexual behavior without an informed consent (Blair, Sudman, Bradburn, and Stocking 1977), it may be helpful in improving the probability of valid responses. Subsequent research suggests that offering an informed consent to respondents may prompt a halo effect; that is, respondents informed about the research prior to beginning the interview and assured of confidentiality through informed consent, tend toward more positive evaluations of the researcher and the research process in general (Singer 1978).

There are, however, exceptions to the positive effects of informed consent. In laboratory experiments, informed consent may induce biases influencing experimental results (e.g., Gardener 1978; Singer 1984). Also, informed consent may bias field research. For example, Reamer (1979), in a study of juvenile status offenders (youths who have committed offenses that would not be considered crimes if committed by adults, such as running away from home), found that assuring subjects of confidentiality resulted in fewer responses to information about sensitive topics. It appears that promising the youths confidentiality, "primed" them to become suspicious that the information would *not* remain confidential.

Alternative Approaches To Maintaining Confidentiality

Particularly when researching illegal activities or behaviors that might encourage illegal acts, protection of respondent confidentiality becomes an even thornier dilemma. While researchers want to honor their commitment of respect towards subjects' desire for confidentiality, knowledge of illegal activity may place the research and researchers in jeopardy. Van Maanen's (1983) field work on police activities, for example, resulted in court subpoena requesting his field notes. He reports being in "a moral fix" (p. 275). He could obey the subpoena and, via his notes, provide incriminating evidence of police brutality or he could refuse to comply, thus protecting patrol officers with whom he had worked. Had the case not been dropped before going to court, Van Maanen was to face contempt of court charges.

A more radical form of assuring confidentiality offered by Adler and Adler (1993) involves self-censorship on the part of the researcher. While living next door to a drug dealer, the Adlers had opportunity for inside observation of the intricacies of drug marketing activities. Realizing that publication of their findings would legally jeopardize the drug-dealer who had become their friend, they elected to postpone publication of their work until their respondents had changed professions and the researchers had relocated.

Anticipation of potential consequences might also be an alternative to serving jail time. Knerr (1982) suggests researchers take the following precautions to minimize the threat of legal action: (1) desensitize the research through design and statistical techniques rendering the data useless to legal authorities, or (2) store the data with a researcher residing outside the U.S. He noted an ingenious sociologist studying drug peddlers. At the conclusion of each taped interview, the tape was dropped in a mailbox and sent to a researcher in Canada to be transcribed and analyzed; thus keeping the raw data out of reach of a U.S. subpoena.

RECOMMENDATIONS

Just as the "caveat emptor" philosophy in the early days of marketing has been replaced with consumer rights, the focus of ethical research concerns has changed. While early ethical concerns in marketing focused on protecting the image and rights of the marketer, the current emphasis is shifting toward protecting the rights and privacy of respondents. By examining research ethics from other disciplines, we see that there are few absolute answers when dealing with ethical questions; each research project needs to be considered on an individual basis.

One way in which researchers can help each other is by including ethical concerns in their publications. While empirical researchers are always careful to publish 'p' values establishing the "significance" of their results, ethical considerations should be of equal importance. Learning how other consumer researchers have confronted these difficult issues would be helpful for future research purposes and would contribute toward development of additional guidelines.

Below are general guidelines that consumer researchers might wish to consider prior to undertaking a project.

1. *The Welfare of the Subject Takes Precedence Over All Other Research Decisions.* Just as the marketing concept revolves around the customer, so too should consumer research focus on the welfare of the respondent. The simple heuristic—a subject should never be worse-off as a result of participating in a consumer research project—is a reasonable approach. To take this a step further, it would be admirable if researchers could say that their research leaves subjects better off than they were prior to engaging in the research. Perhaps consumer researchers should take a cue from addiction counselors who are strongly encouraged to donate a portion of counseling hours to clients who can't afford to pay. This donation is seen in counseling circles as restitution for making a living off of other people's misfortune. Consumer researchers might consider monetary or in-kind donations to groups who help them achieve personal or professional goals.

2. *Anticipate Potential Ethical Conflicts Prior to Beginning the Research.* When interviewing people on sensitive topics, the researcher needs to be as prepared as possible to handle difficult situations if they arise. For example, in the state of Washington, if child abuse is discovered, the researcher must report it to the police and to his/her supervisor within 24 hours. If a researcher is engaging in research that might uncover such information, alerting his/her department chair prior to the probability is advisable.

3. *Consider the Cost/Benefit of the Research Project.* Do the potential research benefits outweigh risks to the respondent and researcher? For example, if anticipating the possibility of uncovering illegal information, it might be wise to inform the respondent in advance about the researcher's legal obligation. While this might inhibit information flow, less information may be more valuable than contesting a court subpoena. Again, it depends on the research project and respondent pool.

4. *When In Doubt: Pre-Test.* Consumer research often includes pretesting to insure valid results; it is often equally feasible to pretest ethical concerns (Berscheid, Baron, Dermer,

and Libman 1973). If unsure how the sample population might react to an experiment, the researcher could survey a subsample about ethical concerns. For example, researchers could ask addiction counselors (many of whom are recovering addicts) how they would feel if a researcher reported on an AA meeting.

CONCLUSIONS

Our suggestions are far from exhaustive; in fact, it is hoped that other researchers will challenge and expand this list of considerations. By raising ethical issues, the discipline of consumer behavior can hopefully continue to grow and expand to make a positive contribution towards *peace*: "the one which all thought, feeling and ultimately all scholarship should aspire" (Hirschman and Holbrook 1992, p.126). It would be a sad irony if, while striving to make a positive contribution, consumer researchers ethically violate the society they are attempting to improve. Perhaps if the researcher in the opening scenario had considered the issues raised above, he/she would not be wondering what to do now.

REFERENCES

Adler, Patricia A. and Peter Adler (1993), "Ethical Issues in Self-Censorship," in *Researching Sensitive Topics*, eds. Claire Renzetti and Raymond M. Lee, Newbury Park, CA: Sage, 249-266.

Alexander, Lois (1983), "Proposed Legislation to Improve Statistical and Research Access to Federal Regulations," in *Solutions to Ethical and Legal Problems in Social Research*, eds. Robert F. Boruch and Joe S. Cecil, New York, NY: Academic Press, 273-292.

Barnes, J.A. (1979), *Who Should Know What?: Social Science, Privacy and Ethics*. Cambridge: Cambridge University Press.

Belk, Russell W. (1987), "ACR Presidential Address: Happy Thoughts, in *Advances in Consumer Research*, Vol. 14. eds. M. Wallendorf and P. Anderson, Provo, UT: Association for Consumer Research, 1-4.

_____, Melanie Wallendorf, and John F. Sherry (1989), "The Sacred and the Profane in Consumer Behavior: Theodicy on the Odyssey," *Journal of Consumer Research*, 16 (June), 1-38.

Berscheid, Ellen, Robert Steven Baron, Marshall Dermer, and Mark Libman (1973), "Anticipating Informed Consent," *American Psychologist*, 28 (October), 913-925.

Bissell, LeClair and James E. Royce (1987), *Ethics for Addiction Counselors*, Center City, MN: Hazelton Foundation.

Blair, Ed, Seymour Sudman, Norman M. Bradburn and Carol Stocking (1977), "How to Ask Questions About Drinking and Sex: Response Effects in Measuring Consumer Behavior," *Journal of Marketing Research*, 15 (August), 316-321.

Blankenship, A.B. (1964), "Some Aspects of Ethics in Marketing Research," *Journal of Marketing Research*, 1 (2), 26-31.

Bramel, D. A. (1962), "A Dissonance Theory Approach to Defensive Projection," *Journal of Abnormal and Social Psychology*, 64, 121-129.

_____ (1963), "Selection of a Target for Defensive Projection," *Journal of Abnormal and Social Psychology*, 66, 318-324.

Epstein, Yakov M., Peter Suedfeld, and Stanley J. Silverstein (1973), "The Experimental Contract," *American Psychologist*, 28 (March), 212-221.

Farmer, Richard N. (1967), "Would you Want Your Daughter to Marry a Marketing Man?," *Journal of Marketing*, 31 (January), 1-3.

_____ (1977), "Would You Want Your Son to Marry a Marketing Lady?," *Journal of Marketing*, 41 (January), 15-18.

_____ (1987), "Would You Want Your Granddaughter to Marry a Taiwanese Marketing Man?," *Journal of Marketing*, 51 (October), 111-116.

Gardner, Gerald T. (1978), "Effects of Federal Human Subjects Regulations on Data Obtained in Environmental Stressor Research," *Journal of Personality and Social Psychology*, 36 (6), 628-634.

Hill, Ronald Paul (1992), "Homeless Children: Coping With Material Losses," *Journal of Consumer Affairs*, 26 (2), 274-287).

_____ (1993), "A Primer for Ethnographic Research With a Focus on Social Policy Issues Involving Consumer Behavior," in *Advances in Consumer Research*, Vol. 20, ed. Mike Rothschild, Provo, UT: Association for Consumer Research.

Hirschman, Elizabeth C. (1992), "The Consciousness of Addiction: Toward a General Theory of Compulsive Consumption," *Journal of Consumer Research*, 19 (September), 155-179.

_____, (1993) "Ideology in Consumer Research, 1980 and 1990: A Marxist and Feminist Critique," *Journal of Consumer Research*, 19 (March), 537-555.

_____ and Morris Holbrook (1992), *Postmodern Consumer Research*, Newbury Park, CA: Sage.

Humphreys, L. (1970), *Tea Room Trade*. Chicago, IL: Aldine.

Johnson, John M. (1975), *Doing Field Research*, New York, NY: Free Press.

Kelman, Herbert C. (1967), "Human Use of Human Subjects: The Problem of Deception in Social Psychological Experiments," *Psychological Bulletin* 67, 1-11.

Kidder, Lousisett (1981), *Research Methods in Social Relations*, Chicago, IL: Holt, Rinehart and Winston.

Knerr, Charles R. (1982), "What to Do Before and After a Subpeona Arrives," in *The Ethics of Social Research: Surveys and Experiments*, ed. Joan E. Sieber New York, NY: Springer-Verlag, 191-207.

Milgram, Stanley (1963) "Behavioral Study of Obedience," *Journal of Abnormal Social Psychology*, 67, 371-378.

O'Guinn, Thomas C. and Ronald J. Faber (1989), "Compulsive Buying: A Phenomenological Exploration," *Journal of Consumer Research*, 16 (September), 147-157.

Reamer, Frederic G. (1979), "Protecting Research Subjects and Unintended Consequences: The Effect of Guarantees of Confidentiality," *Public Opinion Quarterly*, 43 (Winter), 497-506.

Rose, Randall L., William O. Bearden, and Jesse E. Teel (1992), "An Attributional Analysis of Resistance to Group Pressure Regarding Illicit Drug and Alcohol Consumption," *Journal of Consumer Research*, 19 (September), 1-13.

Sagrin, Edward (1973), "The Research Setting and the Right Not to Be Researched," *Social Problems*, 21 (Summer), 52-65.

Sawyer, Alan G. (1975), "Demand Artifacts in Laboratory Experiments in Consumer Research," *Journal of Consumer Research*, 1 (March), 20-30.

Schouten, John W. (1991), "Selves in Transition: Symbolic Consumption in Personal Rites of Passage and Identity Reconstruction," *Journal of Consumer Research*, 17 (March), 412-425.

_____ (1978), "The Effect of Informed Consent Procedures on

Respondents' Reactions to Surveys," *Journal of Consumer Research*, 5 (June), 49-57.

―――― (1984), "Public Reactions to Some Ethical Issues of Social Research: Attitudes and Behavior," *Journal of Consumer Research* 11 (June), 501-509.

Spradley, James P. (1980), *Participant Observation*. Chicago, IL: Holt, Rinehart and Winston.

Steiner, Robert L. (1976), "The Prejudice Against Marketing," *Journal of Marketing*, 40 (July), 2-9.

Twedt, Dik Warren (1963), "Why a Marketing Research Code of Ethics?" *Journal of Marketing*, 27 (March), 48-50.

Tybout, Alice M. and Gerald Zaltman (1974), "Ethics in Marketing Research: Their Practical Relevance," *Journal of Marketing Research*, 11 (November), 357-368.

U.S. Public Health Service (1969), *Protection of the Individual as a Research Subject*, Washington, D.C.: U.S. Government Printing Office.

Van Maanen, John (1983), "The Moral Fix: On the Ethics of Fieldwork," in *Contemporary Field Research: A Collection of Readings*, ed. Robert M. Emerson, Prospect Heights, IL: Waneland Press, 269-287.

Wallendorf, Melanie and Eric J. Arnould (1991), "'We Gather Together': Consumption Rituals of Thanksgiving Day," *Journal of Consumer Research*, 18 (June), 13-31.

More extensive relevant references available upon request.

Summary of the Special Session
"5 calories" or "low" calories: How Consumers Use Numerical and Verbal Product Information
Madhubalan Viswanathan, University of Illinois, Urbana-Champaign

The objective of this session was to examine how consumers use numerical and verbal magnitude information, where magnitudes refer to product information such as "120 calories" and "high calories" that convey the location of a product along an attribute. The session brought together papers in the area of numerical and verbal information that relate to several facets of consumer memory and decision making to provide a sense of the range of issues involved in this area of research and to bring out the importance of this hitherto neglected area of research to consumer research and practice. Abstracts of papers are included in the proceedings.

The first paper presented by Terry Childers investigated how numerical and verbal information is represented in memory. Competing perspectives about the nature of memory representations of numerical and verbal magnitudes were tested. An experiment used a learning task followed by a speeded recognition task to test alternate hypotheses. The results suggested that numerical and verbal information may be represented in memory in a verbal-like form.

The second paper presented by Madhubalan Viswanathan examined how consumers encode and use numerical and verbal product information. Across several studies, numerical information was found to be recognized faster and more accurately, to be recalled more exactly, and to require less encoding time, when compared to verbal information for a learning task. However, several advantages for numerical information disappeared for a choice or a judgment task. Further, differences in memory for information as well as the relationship between memory and subsequent judgments were found across tasks.

The third paper by Nancy Artz and Alice Tybout presented by Nancy Artz examined the persuasive implications of numerical and verbal information in advertising. Drawing on differences between numerical and verbal information in terms of precision and evaluativeness, numerical claims were argued to require an additional processing step to interpret the evaluative meaning of a claim, when compared to verbal claims. An experiment demonstrated that a subject's ability to perform the additional processing required by numerical claims has consequences for the persuasive effect of such claims.

J. Russo, the discussant, pointed out that the papers presented dealt with whether numerical versus verbal information is (i) the more natural internal representation, (ii) better remembered after learning, choice, or judgment, and (iii) more persuasive. He presented a broad framework within which these papers could be viewed consisting of three elements; stimuli, processing tasks, and performance tasks with a time delay between processing and performance tasks. Using the framework, he pointed out that the stimuli used in the papers varied in familiarity, in presenting one or both modes of information, and in past knowledge that subjects may have about the stimuli; the processing tasks varied in difficulty as well as anticipated and actual effort; the distracter task used in the time delay varied; and the performance tasks used varied within and across studies. Using the general framework as a basis, he pointed out that there could be multiple factors operating between stimuli and performance tasks and that it is difficult to go from "molar" concepts such as numerical and verbal information to underlying processes. He presented two issues with respect to a future agenda, the first pertaining to context specificity versus generalizability and the second pertaining to simultaneous presentations.

REPRESENTATION OF NUMERICAL AND VERBAL INFORMATION IN MEMORY
Terry L. Childers, University of Minnesota

This paper investigated how numerical and verbal information is represented in consumer memory. Competing perspectives about the nature of memory representations of numerical and verbal magnitudes were tested. One perspective tested here was that both numerical and verbal information is represented in memory in an abstract form in terms of the meaning or magnitude conveyed by them. A competing perspective tested was that numerical and verbal magnitudes are represented in their original forms in memory.

The experiment used to test these perspectives involved exposure of subjects to numerical and verbal information describing product attributes during a learning task followed by a recognition task. The mode as well as the meaning or semantic content of the information was manipulated at exposure as well as at recognition. Hypotheses were developed in terms of speed of recognition to test the two perspectives. Specifically, if numerical and verbal information is represented in memory in an abstract form, then recognition speed was predicted to be identical for information at recognition that was *similar in meaning* to information at exposure. If numerical and verbal information is represented in memory in its original form, then recognition speed was predicted to be identical for information at recognition that was *similar in mode* to information at exposure. The results suggested that numerical and verbal information may be represented in memory in a verbal-like form. This research provides insights into the nature of representation of numerical and verbal information in memory and has implications for consumer memory and decision making involving these two modes of information.

PROCESSING OF NUMERICAL AND VERBAL INFORMATION: IMPLICATIONS FOR CONSUMER MEMORY AND JUDGMENT
Madhubalan Viswanathan, University of Illinois, Urbana-Champaign

This study focused on how consumers encode and use numerical and verbal product information. A framework based on differences in how magnitude information is *presented* to consumers (i.e., numerical versus verbal modes of presentations) and, differences in how magnitude information is *processed* by consumers was used to derive hypotheses. Magnitudes presented in numerical versus verbal modes were argued to differ in the degree to which they describe the location of a brand on an attribute in that a verbal magnitude readily conveys its meaning (i.e., the description of the location of a brand along an attribute) whereas a numerical magnitude has to be compared to other information in order to derive meaning from it. Further, the processing of magnitude information was distinguished in terms of either processing a magnitude in terms of its surface features (i.e., surface level processing) or in terms of its meaning (i.e., meaning level processing). This distinction is important for the processing of numerical and verbal magnitudes because differences between numerical and verbal labels in the degree to which the meaning conveyed by them is readily available may lead to different degrees of meaning versus surface level encoding.

Using the framework described above, verbal information was argued to be processed in terms of its meaning to a greater extent than numerical information during learning. During choice or judgment, both types of magnitudes were argued to be processed to a greater extent in terms of their meaning. Hypotheses were derived for differences in encoding, recognition, recall, and judgment between these two modes of information for learning, choice, and judgment tasks. Across several studies, numerical information was found (i) to be recognized faster and more accurately, (ii) to be recalled more exactly, and (iii) to require less encoding time, when compared to verbal information for a learning task. However, several advantages for numerical information disappeared for a choice or a judgment task. Further, a larger degree of recall of numerical information in a verbal form was found following choice or judgment when compared to learning, perhaps because of a greater degree of processing of numerical information in order to make an inference from it in these tasks. Also, a stronger relationship was found following choice or judgment between the evaluative equivalent of numerical information recalled in a verbal (i.e., descriptive) form and subsequent judgments than between the evaluative equivalent of numerical information recalled in a numerical form and subsequent judgments, perhaps because of a greater degree of usage of descriptive information. Implications of this research for the processing of numerical and verbal magnitude information as well as the processing of magnitude information in general were discussed.

NUMERICAL AND VERBAL INFORMATION: IMPLICATIONS FOR PERSUASION

Nancy Artz, University of Southern Maine
Alice Tybout, Northwestern University

This research examined the persuasive implications of numerical and verbal information in advertising. Drawing on differences between numerical and verbal information in terms of precision and evaluativeness, numerical claims were argued to require an additional processing step to interpret the evaluative meaning of a claim, when compared to verbal claims. Consequently, when processors do not have the knowledge required to interpret the evaluative meaning of a numerical claim, they may use contextual cues to a greater extent than when they do have the required knowledge. Therefore, judgments will be influenced by contextual cues to different degrees depending on the availability of knowledge to interpret the evaluative meaning of a numerical claim.

An experiment demonstrated that a subject's ability to perform the additional processing required by numerical claims has consequences for the persuasive effect of such claims. An experimental procedure was used where subjects formed impressions of products using numerical or verbal information. Task demands as well as availability of reference information to interpret numerical information were manipulated. Hypotheses relating to the effects of different conditions on consumer judgment were tested. The results suggest that the processing of numerical claims is similar to that of verbal claims when subjects have reference information and sufficient cognitive resources to interpret the evaluative meaning of numeric claims. However, when subjects are unable to interpret the evaluative meaning of numeric claims, differences in the processing of numeric versus verbal claims are found. Specifically, subjects tended to use contextual cues as a basis for forming their evaluative judgments. This research brings out the importance of studying how consumers process numerical and verbal information in terms of their potential effects on persuasion.

Customers Complain—Businesses Make Excuses: The Effects of Linkage and Valence

Donna J. Hill, Bradley University
Robert Baer, Bradley University

ABSTRACT

Company reactions to customer complaints were examined. A framework, based upon a psychological theory of excuse making (Higgins and Snyder 1990) was advanced. Excuses were classified as either linkage (diminishing the individual's perceived causal role in producing the event) or valence (diminishing the perceived negative consequence of the act). Subjects sent complaint letters to companies who had caused them dissatisfaction. Company excuse responses were categorized according to the excuse framework. The effects of different excuse types were measured. The results showed that valence excuses lead to less perceived harm and less perceived blame than linkage excuses. Valence excuses were also rated more acceptable than linkage excuses. The effects of different kinds of linkage and valence excuses were also examined. The implications for complaint management were discussed.

The decade of the 1980's may be regarded by historians as the decade of customer rebellion (Desatnick 1987). Customers everywhere are demanding that they get what they pay for, whether it is on-time delivery, courteous treatment at the point-of-purchase, or a clean hotel room. Concerned with service and product quality, companies by the scores are adopting customer orientations that consider customer satisfaction the key to long-term profitability. Customer oriented firms are contributing to the customer rebellion by energetically encouraging their customers to complain. As consumers become more vocal about their dissatisfaction, the management of their complaints will play an increasingly important role. Every marketing manager will have to develop approaches for effectively responding to disgruntled customers. Although there is now a large body of literature on consumer complaining behavior, relatively little is known about complaint management. What is known is that a rapid company response, apologies, financial compensation (e.g., coupons, refunds and rebates), demonstrating a genuine interest in relieving the problem, and directly addressing the problem can all help recapture a dissatisfied customer (Folkes 1984; Gilly and Gelb 1977; Clark & Kaminski and Rink 1992; Goodwin and Ross 1992; Krentler and Cosenza 1987).

Garrett, Meyers and Camey (1991) claim that despite the significant advancements that have been made in our understanding of consumer complaints, very little attention has been devoted toward understanding the role of communication (i.e., what is said) in complaint interactions. This is unfortunate since the complaint process is, after all, a communication process. Disappointed consumers communicate their dissatisfaction to company representatives who, in turn, communicate their response. One aspect of the communication process that is worthy of more attention, they maintain, is account analysis. Accounts are excuses or explanations that accused actors give to minimize the severity of their predicament. When things go wrong in an organization, employees may try to soothe disgruntled customers by excusing either their own or their firm's behavior (Bitner 1990). Hill, Baer and Kosenko (1992) contend that managers should be cognizant of the excuse making activities of their employees. Rather than handling complaints in their own haphazard way, front line personnel should be trained in how to verbally respond to complaints.

The study of excuses may help enlighten the complaint management process. The marketing literature has been almost silent about excuse making. It is as if marketers believed that firms do not make excuses for their mistakes. As consumers, however, we know that firms do make excuses. This should come as no surprise. People have a natural tendency to present themselves in a positive light (Goffman 1963) and excuses can help serve that purpose. The desire to put oneself in a good light should be heightened whenever aspersions are cast about one's character, conduct, motives or skill. Not only individuals, but organizations too are vitally concerned with nurturing positive images (Higgins and Snyder 1990); negative perceptions of a firm are hazardous to its long-term viability.

The purpose of the present paper was to explore company excuse making in the face of a customer complaint. Specifically, we advanced a framework for understanding excuses based upon a psychological theory of excuse making (Higgins and Snyder 1990, 1991; Snyder 1985; Snyder and Higgins 1988; Snyder, Higgins and Stucky 1983). A structure for categorizing excuse types is presented and consumer reactions to the different excuse types are measured.

Previous definitions of excuses (Scott and Lyman 1968; Schonbach 1980) have made a distinction between excuses and justifications. Excuses have been considered as explanations as to why one should not be held so completely responsible for unfortunate acts or consequences; justifications have been regarded as attempts to minimize the perceived undesirability of those events. In their psychological theory of excuse making, Higgins and Snyder (1990) have proposed a broad definition of excuses that subsumes under one over arching process the traditional excuse and justification distinction. Higgins and Snyder define an excuse as the "motivated process of (a) diminishing the perceived negativity of esteem-threatening outcomes and (b) shifting causal attributions from sources that are relatively more central to the person's sense of self to sources that are relatively less central" (p.74). Within the traditional framework, excuses shift causal attributions, whereas justifications diminish the perceived negativity of the event.

According to excuse theory (Higgins and Snyder 1990, 1991; Snyder 1985; Snyder and Higgins 1988; Snyder, Higgins and Stucky 1983) excuse making is triggered whenever individuals or organizations perceive themselves to be linked to acts or outcomes that are perceived as undesirable. The tendency to offer an excuse is based upon two independent assessments (linkage-to-act and valence-of-act) that are made whenever individuals or organizations are confronted with information that is threatening to a positive view of oneself. The linkage-to-act assessment represents the degree to which the individual perceives him or herself to be linked (from no linkage to total linkage) to a particular act or outcome. The valence-of-act assessment represents the individual's qualitative assessment of the positiveness of the act or outcome (from positive to negative). Factors that contribute to either the perceived negativity of the event or to a sense of responsibility for the event will enhance the tendency to engage in excuse making. If excuse making is caused by the perception that one is linked to a negative event, then for an excuse to be effective it must temper the negative repercussions of the act by either distancing the excuse maker from the undesirable act (linkage excuse) or by altering the perception that the event was negative (valence excuse). If the individual successfully lessens the perceived negativity of the event, the motivation to cut one's link to the act may decrease. On the other hand, if the individual effectively reduces their perceived connection to the negative event, the need to alter the perceived negativeness of the act will correspondingly diminish.

We propose that there are three types of linkage excuses (Denial, Deflection and Explanation) and two types of valence excuses (Minimization and Justification).

Linkage Excuses. (1) Denial excuses attempt to eliminate the perceived linkage to the act by verbally denying any implication of guilt (e.g., "I didn't do it"). Denials do not repudiate the fact that something wrong occurred. Rather, they deny that they had anything to do with it. (2) Deflection excuses go beyond denial by pointing out who or what was to blame (e.g., "He did it"). By pinning the blame on someone or something else, the excuse-maker can further disconnect him or herself from having any apparent responsibility. (3) Explanations seek to lower the sense of condemnation for the act by identifying extenuating circumstances that contributed to the negative event. With explanation, the accused does not completely deny responsibility for the event but implies that the event is, for the reasons they provide, not a permanent reflection on their motives, skill, character or conduct (e.g, "I had a bad day"). Explanations are successful to the extent that they encourage external attributions for the dissatisfying event.

Valence Excuses. (1) Minimization excuses aim to underestimate the perceived unpleasantness of the event by suggesting that the event was not quite as bad as the complainer describes it (e.g., "its not that bad"). Minimization excuses do not deny that an error has occurred or that the organization is responsible. Instead, minimization excuses assert that the event was not so bad after all. (2) Justification excuses also assume responsibility for the event but go beyond minimization by boldly asserting that not only was the event not so bad but it was, in fact, quite good and that the customer is better off as a result (e.g., "Its better for everyone if you wait your turn"). Justification is the claim that, contrary to the perceiver's opinion, the action taken was a positive one.

In an earlier study (forthcoming), we found considerable support for this excuse classification scheme. In that study, students were asked to write complaint letters to companies who had recently caused them genuine dissatisfaction. Company replies were analyzed in the context of the excuse framework discussed above. Two judges coded excuses in terms of the five different excuse types. We found that 51.9% of the firms who responded to the written complaint letter did so by offering at least one excuse. In fact, companies who gave an excuse averaged 1.45 excuses per letter. The most common excuse type given was deflection excuses (47.4% of all excuses), followed by explanations (30.9%), denials (12.4%), justifications (5.2%) and minimizations (4.1%).

HYPOTHESES

In the present study we examined the impact of the different excuse types that we had collected earlier. Subjects rated each excuse in terms of a) their acceptability, b) the extent to which the excuse maker was blameworthy, and c) the amount of harm experienced by the complaining party. Based upon excuse theory, hypotheses were formed. We propose that linkage and valence excuses should effect consumers differently. Because they challenge the perceived negativity of the event, valence excuses should primarily influence the perceived positiveness of the event.

H1: Valence excuses would cause the event to be perceived as less harmful than linkage excuses.

Linkage excuses do not attack the valence of the act. Instead, they seek to diminish the extent to which one is perceived as connected to that negative event.

H2: The excuse maker should be perceived as less blameworthy after a linkage excuse than a valence excuse.

Specific hypotheses can also be made regarding comparisons between the different valence excuses and different linkage excuses. Justification excuses go beyond minimization excuses by asserting that not only was the event not too bad, but that the customer is actually better off as a result of the company's actions.

H3: Between the two types of valence excuses, justifications should result in less perceived harm than minimizations.

Explanations admit one contributing role in the undesirable event, but deny that this has any bearing on one's ability to do well in the future.

H4: Among the three types of linkage excuses, explanations should result in the highest ratings of blame.

Deflections are more effective than denials because rather than merely disavowing one's association with the negative event, deflections name the culprit who was responsible.

H5: Among the linkage excuses, deflections should result in the lowest ratings of blame.

METHOD

Collecting Organizational Excuses

To test our hypotheses, we used genuine excuses actually offered by businesses to complaining customers. These excuses were collected in a study previously described. In that study, we asked students to write letters of complaint to companies who had recently caused them genuine dissatisfaction. Students complained about a variety of different products and services representing an extensive range of prices ($5.00 - $2000.00). A content analysis of the company responses was conducted to determine the types of excuses provided. The coding scheme consisted of identifying excuse statements and categorizing them by excuse type (denial, deflections, explanations, minimizations, and justification). Two business-school graduate students were trained as coders. After a brief practice session, all company response letters were coded by both judges. The inter-judge reliability for the five excuse types ranged from 71% (deflections) to 98% (denials). When the coders disagreed, a panel of two faculty members jointly categorized the excuse type.

Questionnaire Design and Procedure

Since the excuses we received covered a broad range of products, services and price ranges, we modified the excuses to fit one complaint situation. For this purpose, we created an automobile repair scenario. The scenario described a customer, whose warranty had just expired, seeking service from an automobile dealership. The customer was charged for labor and replacement parts. However, the customer claimed that the repairs failed to fix the car. The customer complained because additional charges will now be incurred to repair what was wrong in the first place. Each excuse that we collected was adapted to this scenario. However, excuses whose meaning was unclear or implausible were eliminated. In cases in which the base message was reiterated by a previous excuse, the most typical excuse of that type was used. A total of 37 statements (types of excuses) was developed in this manner. Table 1 shows each excuse statement used in the present study. Of these 37 excuses, 2 were justifications, 4 were minimizations, 5 were denials, 13 were deflections and 13 were explanations.

A questionnaire was then constructed and administered to a total of 51 junior and senior level business students enrolled in a

TABLE 1
List of Modified Excuses from Company Replies to Customer Complaints

Justification Statements
1. We have a practice of replacing worn parts before they fail. This is good preventive maintenance that helps avoid more costly repairs in the future.
2. Replacing worn parts before they fail helps keep our customers safe.

Minimization Statements
3. Our records indicate that the extra repair only cost you $15.00 in parts and labor.
4. We reviewed our records. The parts we replaced, although they may appeared to be unworn, they actually needed to be replaced to prevent other parts from failing.
5. When in doubt, we have to replace the parts. This policy is necessary because customers would be even more unhappy if a part we did not replace broke shortly after leaving the shop.
6. You should realize that by taking care of the problem before it actually broke saved you from having to come back.

Denial Statements
7. We regret that you thought the original repair work was done incorrectly.
8. We have no record of your car being serviced at our dealership. Could you please supply us with a receipt?
9. Is it possible that your car is experiencing new problems that began after we repaired your car the first time?
10. We're sorry you are unhappy, but we stand by our original work.
11. We did not replace anything that wasn't broken.

Deflection Statements
12. We have shared your concerns with our entire service staff. Concerns like yours helps improve our quality control.
13. The repairs conducted on your car were recommended to be replaced by the car manufacturer. We were only following the guidelines.
14. I have forwarded your comments to the District Service Manager.
15. It's not our fault that the warranty on your car has already expired.
16. Industry wide, we have noticed that suppliers are cutting costs by using inferior replacement parts.
17. I have talked to the manager of the service department about your problem.
18. It's quite possible that the machine that tested the part malfunctioned.
19. Dirt and grime clogged the machine that we used to test your worn parts.
20. Our cashier was instructed not to charge you for the replacement parts.
21. I think the car salesperson mislead you about our repair policy.
22. Under normal use the part would not need replacement after the warranty expired. This car was apparently abused somewhere along the way.
23. Our repair policies conform to strict state and federal regulations.
24. The service manager is directly responsible for service repairs. You need to speak with him.

Explanation Statements
25. We can assure you that our repair policy is accepted industry practice.
26. We tried our best.
27. Its only reasonable to expect a car will need some service from time to time.
28. Please give us another chance, we have hired a new service manager and he may be easier for you to work with.
29. We have an excellent service quality program. Our satisfaction surveys indicate that 99% of our customers are completely satisfied. No one can please everyone.
30. Sorry, but everyone has their own personal preferences. All are customers are different. They expect different things from us.
31. Our mechanic was sick that day and did not perform at his best.
32. We usually don't replace parts unnecessarily. Apparently, this must have slipped past our staff.
33. As you know today's cars are very complex and occasional problems of this sort can't be avoided.
34. We did not mean to replace parts that did not need it. It was an accident.
35. The mechanics that worked on your car were inexperienced but are now more seasoned.
36. Perhaps an inspection oversight occurred.
37. We have increased efforts at training our service staff.

TABLE 2
Mean Ratings for All Excuses

Excuse Items	Harm	Blame	Acceptance
1	3.62	4.31	3.45
2	3.54	3.78	3.98
3	4.53	4.88	3.13
4	3.84	4.56	3.43
5	4.28	4.58	3.34
6	4.76	4.98	2.80
7	4.72	5.17	2.86
8	5.90	6.09	4.70
9	4.68	4.88	3.15
10	6.00	6.02	1.98
11	4.25	4.62	3.03
12	3.37	4.02	4.60
13	4.35	4.39	3.33
14	3.94	4.70	3.45
15	5.51	4.88	2.62
16	5.82	5.62	2.16
17	4.56	5.16	3.64
18	5.26	5.84	2.74
19	5.76	6.08	2.28
20	3.54	4.28	4.90
21	5.54	5.94	2.42
22	5.83	5.16	2.40
23	4.34	4.34	4.34
24	4.98	5.10	3.10
25	4.07	4.62	3.00
26	5.41	5.86	2.29
27	4.54	4.90	3.21
28	4.11	5.17	4.02
29	5.31	5.40	2.35
30	5.56	5.58	1.96
31	5.90	6.35	1.60
32	5.32	5.74	2.70
33	5.06	5.08	2.68
34	5.52	6.32	2.34
35	6.08	6.40	1.80
36	5.44	6.16	3.04
37	4.46	5.08	3.24

marketing course. Subjects were first instructed to read the description of the car repair dissatisfaction incident. Following this reading, each of the 37 excuse statements was presented. Subjects were asked to rate the 37 statements on a scale of 1 (not at all) to 7 (completely) for the following three items: 1) "To what extent was the customer harmed by this experience?" 2) "To what extent was the dealership deserving of blame?" and 3) "To what extent should the customer accept this answer?" Item 1 was chosen to measure the extent that the company response impacted the perceived valence of the dissatisfaction. Item 2, on the other hand, was a measure of the impact on the perceived linkage between the dissatisfying act and the car dealership. Additionally, item 3 assessed how acceptable these excuses were to the rater.

RESULTS

Table 2 shows the average harm, blame and acceptance ratings for each of the 37 different excuses used in the present study. The table shows considerable variation between the different excuses on all three dependent variables (harm, blame and acceptance). Harm ratings ranged from 3.37 ("We shared your concerns with our staff") to 6.08 ("The mechanics were inexperience but are now more seasoned"). Blame ratings ranged from 3.78 ("Replacing worn parts before they fail helps keep our customers safe") to 6.40 ("The mechanics who worked on your car were inexperienced but are now more seasoned"). Acceptance means ranged from 1.60 ("Our mechanic was sick that day and did not perform at his best") to 4.60 ("We shared your concerns with our entire staff").

To test the hypotheses, a series of a priori contrasts were conducted between the different excuse types for each dependent variable. The first hypothesis states that valence excuses would lead to less perceived harm than linkage excuses. Table 3 shows the mean harm, blame and acceptance ratings for the combined valence (minimization and justification) and combined linkage excuses (denial, deflection, and explanation). The table indicates that the customer was perceived as harmed less after a valence (M = 4.11) than a linkage excuse (M = 4.95, t(43) = 6.13, p < .001). Hypothesis 1 was thus supported. According to hypothesis 2, linkage excuses should have resulted in less attributed blame than valence excuses.

TABLE 3
Mean Ratings for Linkage and Valence Excuses

Excuse Typ	Harm	Blame	Acceptance
Valence Excuses	4.11a	4.57a	3.32a
Linkage Excuses	4.95b	5.33b	2.87b

Within each dependent variable (Harm, Blame, Acceptance), means with different superscripts are significantly different from one another, $p < .05$. Ratings were given on the following scale: 1 = not at all to 7 = completely

TABLE 4
Mean Ratings for Five Excuse Types

Excuse Type	Harm	Blame	Acceptance
VALENCE EXCUSES			
Justification	3.59a	4.09a	3.68a
Minimization	4.38b	4.77b	3.14b
LINKAGE EXCUSES			
Denial	5.14c	5.38c	2.57c
Deflection	4.81d	5.05d	3.22b
Explanation	5.11^c	5.59^e	2.63^c

Within each dependent variable (Harm, Blame, Acceptance), means with different superscripts are significantly different from one another, $p < .05$. Ratings were given on the following scale: 1 = not at all to 7 = completely

---

Table 2 indicates that not only was this hypothesis not supported, but the means were in the opposite direction: Linkage excuses resulted in more blame than valence excuses: $M = 5.33$ and $M = 4.57$, respectively, $t(49) = 6.27$, $p < .001$.

Inspection of the top portion of Table 4 indicates support for hypothesis 3. Justifications resulted in less perceived harm ($M = 3.59$) than minimization excuses ($M = 4.38$, $t(49) = 4.84$, $p < .001$).

Between the linkage excuses, it was predicted that explanations would result in the most blame (hypothesis 4) and that deflection would result in the least blame (hypothesis 5). As illustrated in the bottom portion of Table IV, both of these final hypotheses were supported. Explanations resulted in more blame ($M = 5.59$) than denials ($M = 5.38$, $t(49) = 2.05$, $P < .05$). Denials resulted in more blame than deflection: $M = 5.38$ and $M = 5.05$, respectively ($t(49) = 3.18$, $P < .01$).

Although no hypothesis concerning the acceptability measure were made, means tests were also conducted to determine differences in acceptability. Table 2 indicates that valence excuses were perceived as more acceptable ($M = 3.32$) than linkage excuses ($M = 2.87$, $t(49) = 4.18$, $p < .001$). Justifications were the most acceptable excuse of all and differed significantly from minimizations ($M = 3.14$, $t(49) = 3.44$, $p < .001$). Denials ($M = 2.57$) and explanations ($M = 2.63$, ns) were the least acceptable excuses. Both were accepted to a significantly less extent than deflections ($M = 3.22$), $t(49) = 5.45$, $p < .001$ and $t(49) = 3.18$, $p < .01$, respectively (see Table 4).

DISCUSSION AND IMPLICATIONS

This paper presented a framework for studying organizational excuse making based upon a psychological theory of excuses. We have argued that excuses work by "shifting causal attributions" (Higgins and Snyder, 1991, p. 74). Excuses are communication strategies that are aimed at soothing or pacifying dissatisfied customers by providing plausible causal attributions designed to alleviate their displeasure. These attributions, in turn, may moderate the customer's perception of the actual harm done or of who or what was responsible for the bad outcome. The basic premise of this framework is that people will react differently to a transaction outcome depending upon the type of attribution they make. An examination of the effects of the thirty-seven different excuses provides evidence that excuses can have a striking impact on consumers' perceptions. All subjects in our study ware exposed to an identical scenario describing a customer dissatisfied with their automobile service. Yet, widely differing ratings of harm, blame and acceptance were obtained depending on the particular excuse. Thus, different excuses can cast the same situation in vastly different lights.

Using this framework, excuses can be classified as either linkage or valence excuses. Linkage excuses (denial, deflection and explanation) were purported to diminish the extent to which the accused actor was connected to the negative event. Valence excuses (minimization and justification) reduce the perceived negativity of the event.

Results provide support for four of the five stated hypotheses. As we had anticipated, linkage and valence excuses provoked different reactions among our research participants. Valence excuses led to perceptions of less harm than linkage excuses (H1). The least amount of harm was associated with justification excuses (H3). Finally, among linkage excuses, explanations resulted in the highest ratings of blame and deflection excuses resulted in the lowest ratings of blame (H4 & H5).

The combination of reducing the perceived harmfulness and blameworthiness of the event was also associated with higher ratings of acceptability. Even so, the highest mean acceptability rating that we obtained (justification excuses) were still below the mid-point of the rating scale (M = 3.68 on a 7-point scale), indicating that subjects were reluctant to accept any excuse to a great degree. Although it seems likely that lower blame and lower harm ratings caused higher levels of acceptability, it may also be the case that higher excuse acceptability ratings influenced perceptions of harm or blame. An experimental design is needed to examine the causal relationship between these variables.

When faced with an angry customer there is a natural tendency to give an excuse. Our findings indicate that the various types of excuses offered may have different effects. Managers need to be cognizant of this and train employees to respond with excuses in an appropriate manner. Secondly, we suggest that excuses could be combined with speedy response, apologies, compensation and or other forms of financial restitution to improve chances of reinstating a dissatisfied customer. For example, if a customer is complaining about a partially filled bag of chips, the company could respond with an apology for the dissatisfaction, coupons to recapture the customer, and a justification (partially filled bags are better because the chips are more prone to breakage if placed in a smaller bag) to reduce the perceived harm. This type of three pronged response would have a better chance of succeeding in the long run than merely offering coupons. Excuses can serve an additional function of reducing the perceived harm as well as educating the consumer and possibly even modifying future expectations to be more realistic.

The results also suggest that explanations and deflections were not very effective in terms of alleviating perceptions of harm and blame and were not very acceptable. Yet, in our preliminary study, these two types of excuses were found to be, by far, the most common types of excuse responses (deflection represented 47.4% and explanations 30.9% of all excuses). In light of our findings, managers would be wise to re-evaluate their use of these two types of excuses.

Hypothesis 2 was not confirmed by our study. According to hypothesis 2, linkage excuses should have resulted in less attributed blame than valence excuses. Contrary to our expectation, valence excuses resulted in more blame than linkage excuses. Thus valence excuses were more effective than linkage excuses in alleviating both harm and blame. According to excuse theory, valence and linkage should be independent judgements that have a differential impact on perceptions of harm and linkage. However, the present study found that harm and blame ratings for four of the five excuse types were highly correlated (correlations ranged from .64 to .81). Explanations were the one type of excuses where blame and harm were not highly correlated (.26). In retrospect, the correlation between harm and blame should not have been surprising. As harm decreases, it seems natural that there should be a corresponding decrease in blame. Without harm, there is little to find blameworthy. Despite these results, we would still conjecture that linkage and valence are independent. Perhaps this was not the case in the present study because, regrettably, we measured blame instead of linkage. Blame and linkage are two different constructs. Blame is an attribution made after the perceiver assesses and does not accept the validity of the excuse (Shaver 1985; Shaver and Drown 1986; McGraw 1987). Blame is a judgment of disapproval and fault. It involves accusations and criticism. By contrast, linkage reflects the extent to which an internal rather than an external attribution can be made for the cause of an action (Higgins and Snyder 1991). It is independent of the severity of any consequences that action produces and makes no recriminations. From these perspectives, linkage and blame are quite different. Although harm and blame are related, harm and linkage should be independent. For example, consider justifications (valence excuse). Justification excuses represent a high degree of linkage and a low level of blame. The accused admits that the act was internally caused (high linkage) but denies that the action was wrong or the outcome was harmful. By contrast, explanations involve a high degree of harm because there is no denial of the harmful consequences, but seek to provide external attributions (low linkage) for those harmful consequences.

This paper provides evidence that excuses serve a worthwhile function after a dissatisfying experience. Clearly business organizations in our study responded to complaining customers with excuses. They showed an obvious preference for deflections followed by explanations. The results showed that to mitigate the negative effects of the customer's displeasure, events should be managed to make the act appear less disagreeable. These results support findings by Giacalone and Pollard (1987) who found that personnel managers in their study who were accused of breaching the confidentially of an employee could temper the negative repercussions of the breach by down playing the actual harm suffered. Smith and Whitehead (1988) point out, however, that this strategy will be effective only to the extent that the audience for the excuse does not have knowledge regarding the actual negative consequences.

Business should be strategic in their use of excuses. If honored, they can successfully present the organization in a favorable light. Although it has not been fashionable in marketing to talk about organizational excuse making, excuses are not necessarily lies. As Mehlman and Snyder (1985) point out, excuses tend to operate in gray areas where there are few objective yardsticks for measuring the "truth" about varying explanations of events. Garrett, Bradford, Meyers and Becker (1989) argue that organizations *should* give excuses. There is a popular misconception, they maintain, that the company is always wrong and the consumer is always right. Customers have the right to protest or complain, businesses have the right to respond. Organizational excuses fulfill a vital function. They allow the customer to weigh all information before passing judgment. By providing information concerning what went wrong, excuses serve to educate consumers about the complexities of the marketplace. In turn, consumers can use this information to make informed decisions about repeat purchases and how forgiving they should be.

REFERENCES

Clark, Gary L. and Peter Kaminski and David R. Rink (1992), "Consumer Complaints: Advice on How Companies Should Respond Based on an Empirical Study," *Journal of Services Marketing*, 6, (Winter), 41-50.

Desatnick, Robert L. (1987), *Managing to Keep the Customer*, San Francisco CA: Jossey-Bass Publishers.

Folkes, Valerie (1984), "Consumer Reactions to Product Failure: An Attributional Approach," *Journal of Consumer Psychology*, 13, (March), 534-539.

Garrett, Dennis E., Jeffrey L. Bradford, Renee A. Meyers and Joy Becker (1989), "Issues Management and Organizational Accounts: An Analysis of Corporate Responses to Accusations of Unethical Business Practices, *Journal of Business Ethics*, 8, 507-520.

_____, Renee A. Meyers, and John Camey (1991), "Interactive Complaint Communication: A Theoretical Framework and Research Agenda, *Journal of Consumer Satisfaction, Dissatisfaction, and Complaining Behavior*, 4, 62-79.

Giacalone, Robert A. and Hinda G. Pollard (1987), "The Efficacy of Accounts for a Breach of Confidentiality by Management," *Journal of Business Ethics*, 6, 393-397.

Gilly, Mary and Betsy D. Gelb (1982), "Post-Purchase Consumer Processes and the Complaining Consumer," *Journal of Consumer Research*, 9, (December), 323-328.

Goffman, E. *Behavior in Public Places*, (1963), New York: Free Press.

Goodwin, Cathy and Ivan Ross (1990), "Consumer Evaluations of Responses to Complaints: What's Fair and Why," *Journal of Services Marketing*, 4, (Summer), 53-61.

Higgins, Raymond, L. and C. R. Snyder (1990), "The Business of Excuses," in R. A. Giacalone and Paul Rosenfield (Eds.), *Impression Management in the Organization* (pp 73-85).

_____ and C. R. Snyder (1991), "Reality Negotiation and Excuse-Making," in *Handbook of Social Psychology: The Health Perspective*, eds. C. R. Snyder and R. Donelson, New York: Pergamon Press, 79-95.

Hill, Donna, Robert Baer and Rustan Kosenko, "Organizational Characteristics and Employee Excuse Making: Passing the Buck for Failed Service Encounters," in *Advances in Consumer Research*, Vol. 19, eds. John F. Sherry and Brain Sternthal, Provo, UT: Association for Consumer Research, 673-677.

Krentler, Kathleen and Robert Cosenza (1987), "Redress Response and its Effects on Company Impression," *Public Relations Review*, 13, (Fall), 33-45.

McGraw, Kathleen (1987), "Guilt Following Transgression: An Attribution of responsibility Approach," *Journal of Personality and Social Psychology*, 53, 247-256.

Mehlman, Rick C., and C. R. Snyder (1985), "Excuse Theory: A Test of the Self-Protective Role of Attributions," *Journal of Personality and Social Psychology*, 49, 994-1001.

Schonbach, Peter (1980), "A Category System for Account Phases," *European Journal of Social Psychology*, 10, 195-200.

Scott, Marvin B. and Stanford M. Lyman (1968), "Accounts," *American Sociological Review*, 23, 46-62.

Shaver, Kelley (1985), *The Attribution of Blame: Causality, Responsibility and Blameworthiness*, New York: Springer-Verlag.

Shaver, Kelley and Debra Drown (1986), "On Causality, Responsibility, and Self-Blame: A Theoretical Note," *Journal of Personality and Social Psychology*, 50, 697-702.

Smith, Stephanie H. and George I. Whitehead III (1988), "The Public and Private Use of Consensus-Raising Excuses," *Journal of Personality and Social Psychology*, 56, 355-371.

Snyder, C. R. (1985), "The Excuse: An Amazing Grace?" In ed. B.R. Schlenker, *The Self and Social Life* (pp 235-260), New York: McGraw-Hill.

_____ and Raymond L. Higgins (1988), "Excuses: Their Effective Role in the Negotiation of Reality," *Psychological Bulletin*, 104, 23-35.

_____, Raymond L. Higgins, and Rita J. Stucky (1983), *Excuses: Masquerades in Search of Grace*, New York: John Wiley and Sons.

The Effect of Motivation to Process on Consumers' Satisfaction Reactions

Barry J. Babin, The University of Southern Mississippi
Mitch Griffin, Bradley University
Laurie Babin, The University of Southern Mississippi

ABSTRACT

This paper investigates potential moderating effects of the relationship between important explanatory variables and consumer satisfaction. Recent developments in assimilation-contrast theory suggest that involvement may change the satisfaction judgment process. Specifically, as involvement increases so should the likelihood of contrast, resulting in relatively more extreme satisfaction scores. Consistent with this reasoning, experimental results reported here support the moderating ability of involvement. Conversely, the potential priming effect of mood on reference standards is evidenced only under relatively low involvement.

INTRODUCTION

The disconfirmation paradigm provides the most popular theoretical basis for studying consumers' postconsumption reactions (Woodruff, Cadotte, and Jenkins 1983; Woodruff et al. 1991). Clearly, consumer disconfirmation is well established as an important causal agent of consumer satisfaction (Oliver 1980; Swan and Trawick 1981; Churchill and Surprenant 1982). Other variables, such as perceived performance, a priori expectations, and prior attitude, have also been considered as predictors of satisfaction with varying degrees of success (e.g., Westbrook 1980; Churchill and Surprenant 1982; Tse and Wilton 1988). The process with which these variables affect satisfaction is largely consistent with the disconfirmation paradigm's theoretical roots—assimilation-contrast theory (LaTour and Peat 1979). For example, a consumer's subjective evaluation of performance requires a comparative process using some internalized standard as a basis for assimilation or contrast.

Despite the attention the satisfaction construct has received (see Perkins 1991), the number of variables that have been found to relate to consumer satisfaction are few when compared to other key consumer behavior variables (e.g., brand choice). In light of this, some authors have argued for a need to focus more on the invariance of the relationship between antecedent and consequence variables (Westbrook 1987; Westbrook and Oliver 1991). These studies espouse a more molecular position by examining changes in the evaluative process across consumption contexts (Oliver and DeSarbo 1988).

This paper's purpose is to report results of an investigation of the impact of consumers' processing motivations on satisfaction judgments. More specifically, this study examines experimentally the effect of differences in cognitive effort, corresponding to differences in motivational levels, on the satisfaction judgment process. The study's results add to our understanding of consumer satisfaction and provide evidence consistent with previous reasoning that questions the assumption of a linear, monotonic relationship between disconfirmation and satisfaction (Woodruff et al. 1983).

CONCEPTUAL BACKGROUND

Assimilation-Contrast Theory

Attempts at explaining postconsumption reactions using assimilation-contrast logic predate its maturation into the "disconfirmation model" (Anderson and Hair 1972). Using assimilation-contrast rationale, outcomes of consumption experiences are compared to internalized standards (e.g., expectations, performance norms, etc.) that serve as anchors for subsequent evaluations (LaTour and Peat 1979). Two results are possible.

Assimilation occurs if a consumption experience is perceived as consistent with internalized standards. The effect of this process on satisfaction ranges from negligible to modest as long as any discrepancy between a standard and an outcome is small. Thus, a "zone of indifference" results where a consumption outcome is perceived as equivalent to the norm, and the satisfaction response function is relatively nonresponsive to disconfirmation or performance perceptions (Woodruff et al. 1983; Woodruff et al. 1991; Zeithaml, Berry, and Parasuraman 1993). These zones of indifference are consistent with assimilation-contrast based findings in the pricing literature showing zones where consumer preference is nonresponsive to changes in price discounts and promotions (Kalwani and Yim 1992).

Alternatively, *contrast* results if consumer perceptions of the outcome differ notably from internalized standards. The result is substantially higher or lower satisfaction levels (depending on the direction of contrast) than would be observed under assimilation and a more responsive satisfaction function. Under contrast, changes in perceived performance relative to expectations (disconfirmation) will produce changes in satisfaction that are not realized under assimilation.

The Effect of Greater Effort

Due to the pervasiveness of assimilation-contrast explanations of social judgments, a significant amount of research has investigated contextual factors that enhance the likelihood of either reaction (Manis, Nelson, and Shedler 1988; Wedell, Parducci, and Geiselman 1987). One line of research suggests that enhanced cognitive effort, such as that associated with increased involvement or motivation, makes assimilation less likely. Martin (1986) reports a series of studies showing an increased likelihood of contrast when a subject's motivation to form an impression is disrupted. The result is explained in terms of a "set/reset" model (Martin 1986; Martin, Seta, and Crelia 1990). Nondisrupted subjects are better able to "partial out" a convenient standard of judgment and "reset" their frame of reference to provide their "genuine" reaction to a target.

An important implication of the set/reset model is that contrast is more cognitively complex than is assimilation. When one is unable or unwilling to expend a great deal of cognitive effort, he/she is more likely to use the less effortful alternative (assimilation) (Gilbert, Pelham, and Krull 1988). As illustration, one experiment required subjects to form an impression of an ambiguously described person (Martin et al. 1990, experiment 1). Subjects were primed with either a positive or negative concept and either distracted from completing the impression task or allowed to finish it with no distractions. Results showed that subjects in the distraction condition were more likely to rate their impression of the person as positive (negative) following a positive (negative) prime than those not distracted. That is, the supplied reference (prime) had a greater impact when subjects' cognitive effort was attenuated. A second experiment manipulating willingness to expend cognitive effort in place of ability duplicated these results (Martin et al. 1990, experiment 2). Specifically, subjects were more likely to assimilate (give an impression consistent with a prime) when motivation to form the impression was low. Paralleling the earlier result, reliance on the prime was more likely under low involvement conditions despite an individual's characteristics. Thus, a target's actual characteristics appear more predictive of impressions when the ability and/or willingness of subjects to expend cognitive effort is comparatively high. For a more detailed discussion of assimilation and contrast mechanisms compare Herr (1989) and Martin et al. (1990).

Implications for the Satisfaction Judgment

We propose that factors that influence the assimilation-contrast process will also influence satisfaction judgments. This is consistent with conceptual evidence suggesting that the size of "zones of indifference" in satisfaction response functions, where assimilation is a likely result, may vary situationally (Zeithaml et al. 1993). One might expect that under conditions of high (low) involvement the zone of indifference would be relatively small (large) given the associated increase (decrease) in willingness to process information (Petty, Cacioppo, and Schumann 1983).

Thus, the chances of contrast are enhanced as involvement increases and reported satisfaction is expected to be more responsive to differences in outcomes. This rationale is congruous with previous research investigating generalized negativity which found consumer appeal for automobiles was affected by discrepancies from expectations only under conditions of high involvement (Oliver 1976).

P1: Consumer satisfaction is more (less) responsive to disconfirmation under conditions of relatively high (low) involvement.

Priming effects may also influence the satisfaction judgment. The studies cited above (i.e., Martin 1986; Martin et al. 1990) show how simple affective primes can influence assimilation-contrast under certain conditions. These findings are also consistent with elaboration likelihood theory (Cacioppo and Petty 1989). It suggests that primes can influence salient information in a prime-congruent manner under conditions of low ability or unwillingness to process information. Essentially, such primes serve as a cognitive economizer. Thus even if the prime is irrelevant, it can affect the evaluative process.

A prime that may occur naturally in situations involving satisfaction judgments is a consumer's concurrent mood. While mood has been suggested as a nuisance factor sometimes related to consumer satisfaction (Peterson and Wilson 1992), it may be that consumer mood is serving as a prime for subsequent thoughts. Thus the relationship is something more than a nuisance. Peripheral cues like these would be most influential under low motivation and/or low ability to process issue-relevant information. Under these conditions, assimilation may lead to evaluations consistent with the prime (mood). Given sufficient motivation however, consumers are more likely to exert greater cognitive effort diminishing the effect of these primes.

P2: Mood is more (less) highly related to satisfaction under conditions of low (high) involvement.

RESEARCH METHODS

Study Description

An experiment manipulating product category involvement (2 levels) was conducted to test the propositions developed above. This manipulation was accomplished by assigning subjects randomly to one of two involvement conditions. Approximately half of all subjects were assigned to evaluate their last experience at a restaurant and half their last experience at a supermarket. Based on prior discussions with consumers representative of the subjects, the restaurant was assumed to be relatively more involving. This form of manipulation was considered desirable because both restaurants and supermarkets evoke product category involvement magnitudes quite representative of common, everyday consumption experiences. At the same time, it was expected that this manipulation would effectively result in significant differences in involvement.

Specific steps were taken to help insure a wide range of satisfaction scores and avoid ceiling effects commonly inhibiting consumer satisfaction measures (Peterson and Wilson 1992). To accomplish this, subjects were assigned a stimulus to rate based on a favorable or unfavorable image condition rather than allowing them to rate a stimulus of their choice. This approach was used *only* to avoid a severely skewed satisfaction distribution and not to test hypotheses regarding image. Thus, pretesting was conducted to identify restaurants and supermarkets that the subjects would be familiar with, but that would vary in image. Counterbalanced with the involvement manipulation, half of the subjects rated a relatively favorable stimulus and half a relatively unfavorable stimulus.

Subjects in the experiment were 87 undergraduate students residing in a small university town. Prior to beginning each session, subjects were given the opportunity to leave the classroom rather than participate (no subjects chose to leave). The survey booklet cover explained that the research was being conducted to rate consumer reactions to local retail establishments. Subjects first filled out a 4-item mood scale (e.g., "Currently, I am in a good mood" using a 5-point Likert Scale) (Peterson and Sauber 1983). Afterwards, index cards were passed out containing the name of either a favorable or unfavorable restaurant or supermarket. The card instructed subjects to raise their hand if they were either unfamiliar with the retailer on the card or had not been there in the past six months. This procedure resulted in reassignment of four subjects.

Subjects were then instructed to turn the page and respond to the remainder of the survey at their own pace. First, subjects were asked to state how long it had been since they last visited the assigned place and then to describe their last experience there in writing. Next, subjects recorded their reactions to the consumption experience. Disconfirmation was assessed using a 5-point Likert statement (e.g., "The restaurant turned out better than I expected.") (Oliver 1980). In addition, a graphical depiction of disconfirmation was obtained by having subjects indicate on a line how far above or below expectations the experience was. Distances were measured to the nearest tenth of an inch. Five items assessed consumer satisfaction. These items were patterned after previous efforts (Westbrook 1980; Oliver 1980; Holbrook and Batra 1987; Babin, Griffin, and Darden 1993) and contained items using a number of different scaling approaches (e.g., "I was satisfied with my experience at the restaurant," 100-point rating scales, etc.) to avoid common problems associated with measuring satisfaction. Finally, a manipulation check for product category involvement (e.g., "I think restaurant decisions are quite involving" on a 5-point Likert Scale) was administered, and subjects were given a chance to guess the purpose of the study. No subjects were considered either contingency or demand aware based on this analysis. Subjects were then debriefed and dismissed.

Measurement Results

The central dependent measure in this study is consumer satisfaction. Thus, a thorough analysis of the measurement quality of this variable was undertaken. The five items discussed above displayed a high degree of consistency as indicated by coefficient

TABLE 1
Effect Size Estimates

Predictor	η	df	F	p <
Involvement (Inv)	.15	1	1.57	ns
Disconfirmation (DC)	.61	2	29.74	.01
Mood	.08	1	1.20	ns
Inv x DC	.30	2	3.27	.05
Mood x Inv	.29	1	7.11	.05
Mood x DC	.22	2	2.03	ns
Mood x Inv x DC	.29	2	3.25	.05

α (.91). In addition, a maximum likelihood factor analysis was conducted providing evidence of unidimensionality. The χ^2 goodness of fit statistic with 5 degrees of freedom is 3.21 (p > .668), suggesting a good fit to the data. The Goodness of Fit and Comparative Fit indices are .98 and .99, respectively, confirming this result (Bentler 1990). Based on these analyses, the five items were normalized to a constant metric (100 points) and averaged to provide a satisfaction score for each respondent.

Three levels of disconfirmation of expectancies were created using the Likert item described above. Those respondents indicating disagreement (agreement) with the idea that the experience was better than expected were placed in negative (positive) disconfirmation group, while those giving a neutral response were placed in a third (confirmation) group. This classification was validated by a high correlation with the graphical disconfirmation item (r = .64).

The four item mood scale displayed high internal consistency (α = .87), replicating previous results (Peterson and Sauber 1983). Thus those items were summed to obtain a mood score for each individual. In addition, the multiple item measure of involvement displayed an acceptable coefficient α (.76) and was summed to form the appropriate measure.

Manipulation Check

An ANOVA model was conducted to assess the effectiveness of the involvement manipulation. Results show that the involvement manipulation successfully altered involvement scores (F = 6.25; p < .01). The means for each level confirm the direction of the manipulation (11.03 for restaurants and 10.00 for supermarkets with a scale range of 3 to 15). Additional analyses revealed no differences in the frequency of visits or familiarity of the restaurants and supermarkets used in the study.

RESULTS

Because mood is a continuous variable, ANCOVA was used to isolate the effects needed to test both research hypotheses. In the model, satisfaction (DV) is predicted by the two interactions of primary interest (involvement x disconfirmation and mood x involvement) as well as both main effects and the remaining interactions. The main effects and remaining interaction are not relevant to the research hypotheses but are included as control variables. The overall model predicts a significant proportion of the variance in subject satisfaction scores (F = 13.4; p < .0001).

Proposition 1

If the likelihood of contrast is greater under conditions of relatively high involvement, the effect would be captured by the interaction between subject disconfirmation and involvement. As can be seen in Table 1, this interaction significantly predicts subject satisfaction while controlling for all other variables (F = 3.27; p<.05). Further, the mean satisfaction scores by involvement and disconfirmation levels (Figure 1) show that this effect is in the hypothesized direction. Subjects in the high involvement condition displayed more extreme satisfaction scores. It can be inferred that high involvement subjects were less likely to assimilate a performance based on their more extreme reactions to outcomes both above and below expectations. To summarize, involvement appears to satisfy conditions for moderation of the relationship between disconfirmation and satisfaction (Baron and Kenny 1986).

Proposition 2

The second proposition suggests that mood can influence consumer satisfaction under conditions of relatively low involvement. This effect is supported by the significant mood by involvement interaction (F = 7.11; p < .05). Baron and Kenny (1986) recommend separate regression models to analyze the moderating role of a continuous variable. Thus, separate regressions were run for the low and high involvement conditions. Figure 2 depicts this effect graphically. While mood has little impact on satisfaction for subjects in the high involvement (restaurant) condition (β = -.08; B = -.67; p > .10), it significantly affects satisfaction scores for subjects in the low involvement (supermarket) condition (β = .38; B = 2.90; p < .05). A comparison of the raw regression coefficients for each model supports involvement as a moderator of the relationship between mood and satisfaction (F = 3.10; p < .05). Consistent with P2, subject satisfaction scores were unaffected by their reported mood in the high involvement condition, but satisfaction was positively associated with mood in the low involvement condition.

Although not central to tests of the propositions, neither involvement nor mood produced a significant main effect, while disconfirmation did, as supported by numerous previous efforts (Tse and Wilton 1988). The three-way interaction was also significant. Although space limits a detailed discussion, this result, as well as results of contrasts not reported here, suggest that the mood-involvement interaction has varying effects across disconfirmation levels.

DISCUSSION

These results demonstrate that the disconfirmation-satisfaction relationship is not invariant to changes in consumers' processing motivation. Specifically, it appears that as involvement becomes relatively high (low) and consumers are willing (unwilling) to exert correspondingly greater cognitive effort in deliberating consumption outcomes (Petty et al. 1983), contrast (assimilation) becomes more likely. This finding is consistent with intuitive reasoning that consumers are more likely to have extreme reactions to consumption outcomes they perceive as relatively important.

In terms of behavioral outcomes of consumer satisfaction, this might translate into increased brand switching under high involve-

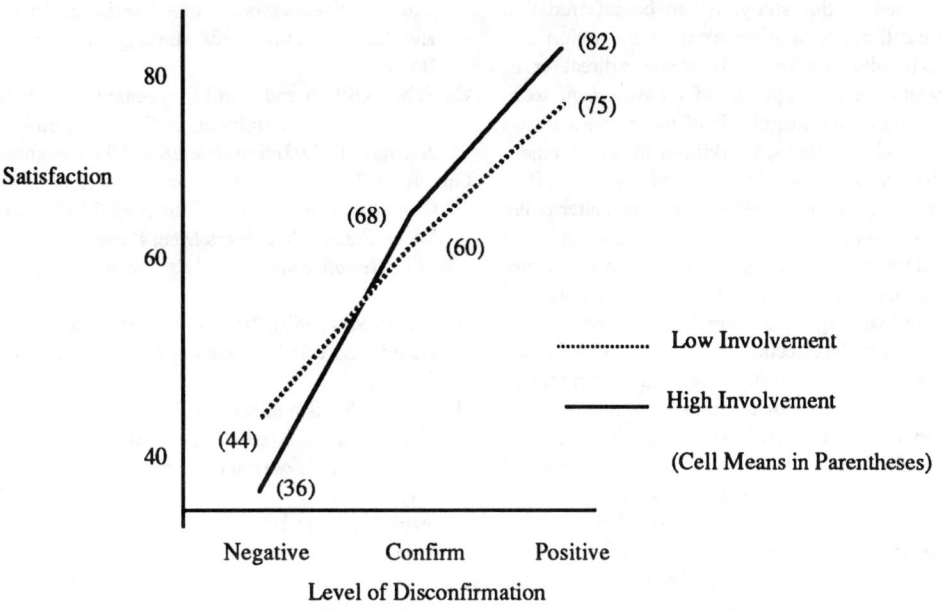

FIGURE 1
The Effect of Involvement and Disconfirmation on Satisfaction

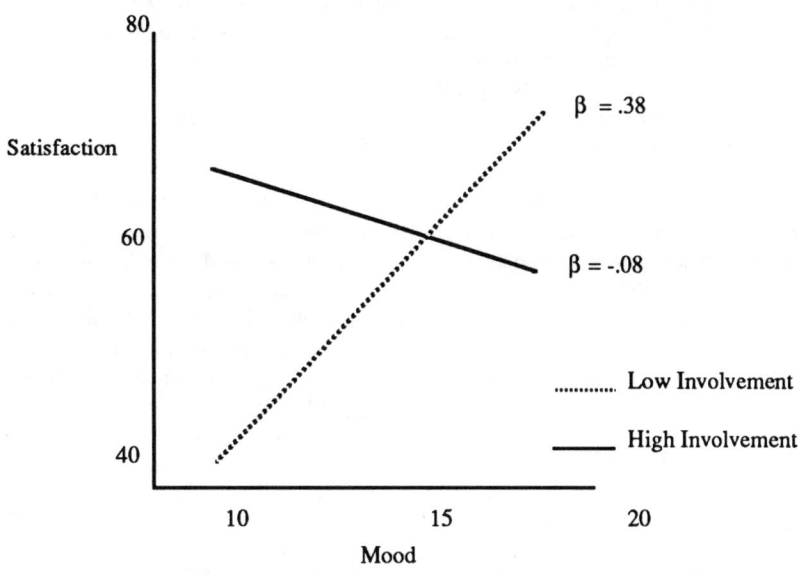

FIGURE 2
The Effect of Mood and Involvement on Satisfaction

ment at the same level of disconfirmation. Alternatively, consumers may be more likely to display brand loyalty as involvement decreases while holding disconfirmation constant. Other behavioral outcomes, such as word-of-mouth and complaining behavior, may also conform to this pattern. Thus, brands that perform superior to norms held by consumers may benefit from encouraging deliberation of the product outcome. Such encouragement may be facilitated by encouraging feedback on product performance using monetary or discount incentives. For example, a new product might be accompanied by a satisfaction survey that consumers could complete and return in exchange for a small monetary incentive. Brands that do not perform well compared to these reference points however, may benefit from satisfaction judgments more conducive to assimilation. This might be particularly important in product classes where the consumer can be expected to hold a favorable expectation (Woodruff et al. 1991).

The study also suggests that internal reference points besides expectations, even those that appear irrelevant to the satisfaction judgment, can influence consumer satisfaction. In this study, subject mood influenced reported satisfaction under low involvement only. It is also conceivable that beyond mood, any emotional traces evoked by recall of the stimulus concerned might influence the satisfaction judgment. If so, satisfaction of consumers under low involvement could be affected by emotions evoked during the communication, purchase, or usage situation so long as they are stored in conjunction with the stimulus.

Further research is needed on these issues. Based on the nature of relationships revealed in this study, it can be inferred that consumer zones of indifference or tolerance in consumption outcomes correspond to involvement levels. However, a direct test of this proposition awaits the development of measurement techniques capable of assessing the magnitude of these zones across consumers and consumption contexts. In addition, the involvement manipulation used here is assumed to have altered cognitive effort based on previous theory (Petty et al. 1983). However, alternative studies that control for product involvement, while manipulating cognitive effort directly, may dissect this effect even more precisely. The involvement manipulation here also could be criticized for encompassing a limited range. However, if a wider range were considered in future studies, the effects found here should be larger.

Additional research is needed to study mood and other factors potentially associated with satisfaction under low involvement. For example, does mood influence satisfaction judgments similarly under conditions of positive or negative affect? Another conceptual area that needs clarification is whether or not the results imply "true" shifts in consumer satisfaction, or does mood simply bias satisfaction measurement? The present experiment is unable to detect the true mechanism but leaves this interesting question for further study. Furthermore, other contextual factors may also prime this judgment. For instance, it is possible that the satisfaction outcome from consumption of one product might influence satisfaction with another consumed concurrently or in close proximity. For example, our satisfaction with one store in a mall may be influenced by our experience with a previously visited retailer.

In conclusion, this paper sought to investigate differences in the disconfirmation model of consumer satisfaction at different, yet comparable, levels of involvement. The results of the study suggest disconfirmation corresponds to satisfaction more strongly as motivation to process increases. This may help explain substantial differences in effect sizes for disconfirmation across studies of consumer satisfaction (cf., Swan and Trawick 1981; Oliver 1980; Tse and Wilton 1988). Further, disconfirmation models of consumer satisfaction may need to consider extraneous variables as potential moderating variables. This study showed how one previously thought nuisance variable, consumer mood, can influence consumer satisfaction at relatively low levels of involvement. More work is needed to reveal additional potential priming and framing effects.

REFERENCES

Anderson, Rolph E. and Joseph F. Hair, Jr. (1972), "Consumerism, Consumer Expectations, and perceived Product Performance," in *Proceedings of the 3rd Annual Conference of the Association for Consumer Research*, Provo, UT: Association for Consumer Research, 67-79.

Babin, Barry J., Mitch Griffin, and William R. Darden (1993), "An Empirical Comparison of Alterative Conceptualizations of Postconsumption Phenomena," *Journal of Consumer Satisfaction, Dissatisfaction, and Complaining Behavior* (in press).

Baron, Reuben M. and David A. Kenny (1986), "The Moderator-Mediator Variable Distinction in Social Psychological Research," *Journal of Personality and Social Psychology*, 51 (July), 1173-1182.

Bentler, P.M. (1990), "Comparative Fit Indices in Structural Models," *Psychological Bulletin*, 107 (March), 238-246.

Cacioppo, John T. and Richard E. Petty (1989), "The Elaboration Likelihood Model: The Role of Affect and Affect-Laden Information Processing in Persuasion," in *Cognitive and Affective Responses to Advertising*, Patricia Cafferata and Alice M. Tybout eds., Lexington, Mass.: Lexington Books.

Churchill, Gilbert and Carol Surprenant (1982), "An Investigation Into the Determinants of Customer Satisfaction," *Journal of Marketing Research*, 19 (November), 491-504.

Gilbert, D. T., B. W. Pelham, and D. S. Krull (1988), "On Cognitive Components of the Social Inference Process: When Person Perceivers Meet Persons Perceived," *Journal of Personality and Social Psychology*, 54 (October), 733-740.

Herr, Paul M. (1989), "Priming Price: Prior Knowledge and Context Effects," *Journal of Consumer Research*, 16 (June), 67-75.

Holbrook, Morris and Rajeev Batra (1987), "Assessing the Role of Emotions as Mediators of Consumer Responses to Advertising," *Journal of Consumer Research*, 14 (December), 404-20.

Kalwani, Manohar U. and Chi Kin Yim (1992), "Consumer Price and Promotion Expectations: An Experimental Study," *Journal of Marketing Research*, 29 (February), 90-100.

LaTour, Stephen A. and Nancy C. Peat (1979), "Conceptual and Methodological Issues in Consumer Satisfaction Research," in *Advances in Consumer Research*, Vol. 6, ed. William Wilkie, Ann Arbor, MI: Association for Consumer Research, 431-437.

Manis, M., T. E. Nelson, and J. Shedler (1988), "Stereotypes and Social Judgment: Extremity, Assimilation, and Contrast," *Journal of Personality and Social Psychology*, 55 (January), 28-36.

Martin, Leonard L. (1986), *Categorization and Differentiation: A Set, Re-set, Comparison Analysis of the Effects of Context on Person Perception*. New York: Springer-Verlag.

_____, John J. Seta, and Rick A. Crelia (1990), "Assimilation and Contrast as a Function of People's Willingness and Ability to Expend Effort in Forming an Impression," *Journal of Personality and Social Psychology*, 59 (January), 27-37.

Oliver, Richard L. (1976), "Hedonic Reactions to the Disconfirmation of Product Performance Expectations: Some Moderating Conditions," *Journal of Applied Psychology*, 61, 246-250.

_____ (1980), "A Cognitive Model of the Antecedents and Consequences of Satisfaction Decisions," *Journal of Consumer Research*, 27 (November), 460-468.

_____ and Wayne S. DeSarbo (1988), "Response Determinants in Satisfaction Judgments," *Journal of Consumer Research*, 14 (March), 495-507.

Perkins, Debra S. (1991), "A Consumer Satisfaction, Dissatisfaction and Complaining Behavior Bibliography: 1982-1990," *Journal of Consumer Satisfaction, Dissatisfaction and Complaining Behavior*, Vol. 4, 194-228.

Peterson, Robert A. and Matthew Sauber (1983), "A Mood Scale for Survey Research," in *Proceedings* of the American Marketing Association's Summer Educators Conference, Chicago: American Marketing Association.

_____ and William R. Wilson (1992), "Measuring Customer Satisfaction: Fact and Artifact," *Journal of the Academy of Marketing Science*, 20 (Winter), 61-71.

Petty, Richard E., John T. Cacioppo, and David Schumann (1983), "Central and Peripheral Routes to Advertising Effectiveness: The Moderating Role of Involvement," *Journal of Consumer Research*, 10 (September), 135-146.

Swan, John E. and Frederick I. Trawick (1981), "Disconfirmation of Expectations and Satisfaction with a Retail Service," *Journal of Retailing*, 57 (Fall), 49-67.

Tse, David K. and Peter C. Wilton (1988), "Models of Consumer Satisfaction Formation: An Extension," *Journal of Marketing Research*, 25 (May), 204-212.

Wedell, D. H., A. Parducci, and R. E. Geiselman (1987), "A Formal Analysis of Ratings of Physical Attractiveness: Successive Contrast and Simultaneous Assimilation," *Journal of Experimental Social Psychology*, 23, 230-249.

Westbrook, Robert A. (1980), "Intrapersonal Affective Influences on Consumer Satisfaction with Products," *Journal of Consumer Research*, 7 (June), 49-54.

_____ (1987), "Product/Consumption-Based Affective Responses and Postpurchase Processes," *Journal of Marketing Research*, 24 (August), 258-270.

_____ and Richard L. Oliver (1991), "The Dimensionality of Consumption Emotion Patterns and Consumer Satisfaction," *Journal of Consumer Research*, 18 (June), 84-91.

Woodruff, Robert B., Ernest R. Cadotte, and Roger L. Jenkins (1983), "Modeling Consumer Satisfaction Processes Using Experience-Based Norms," *Journal of Marketing Research*, 20 (August), 296-304.

_____ , D. Scott Clemons, David W. Schumann, Sarah F. Gardial, and Mary Jane Burns (1991), "The Standards Issue in CS/D Research: A Historical Perspective," *Journal of Consumer Satisfaction, Dissatisfaction and Complaint Behavior*, 4, 103-109.

Zeithaml, Valarie A., Leonard L. Berry, and A. Parasuraman (1993), "The Nature and Determinants of Customer Expectations of Service," *Journal of the Academy of Marketing Science*, 21 (Winter), 1-12.

Does Satisfaction With Multi-Attribute Products Vary Over Time?
A Performance Based Approach

Vikas Mittal, Temple University
Jerome M. Katrichis, Temple University
Frank Forkin, Research Data Analysis, Inc.
Mark Konkel, Consumer Attitude Research, Inc.

ABSTRACT

A multi-attribute approach to study satisfaction is suggested. Linkages between an attribute's performance, goal-fulfillment (Swan 1988), and satisfaction are drawn. Preliminary exploration of automotive industry data suggests the viability of the approach. Results indicate that performance on different attributes contribute differentially to CS, and that an attribute's salience seems to change between pre-purchase evaluations and post-purchase judgement of satisfaction. Research and managerial implications are discussed.

INTRODUCTION

The dominant paradigm of expectation disconfirmation (Oliver 1980) as an explanation of customer satisfaction (CS) has been extended and modified recently by many theorists (c.f Yi 1990). Findings suggest that disconfirmation, expectations and performance affect satisfaction differentially based on factors such as individual response tendencies (Oliver and Desarbo 1988) and product durability (Churchill and Surprenant 1982). While the role of disconfirmation and expectations in satisfaction judgement has been widely studied, relatively little attention has been devoted to the effect of performance on satisfaction (Swan 1988; Yi 1990). Studies examining the impact of performance on satisfaction seem to indicate that product performance has a separate and distinguishable impact on satisfaction irrespective of expectations (cf. Churchill and Suprenant 1982, Swan 1988); however, these studies generally treat performance as a uni-dimensional construct. That is, they either examine performance of a single attribute, or use an overall "index" of performance and relate it to satisfaction. On the other hand, most research considering consumer evaluation of decision alternatives takes the approach that products have multiple attributes with varying performance levels (cf. Wilkie and Pessemier 1972; Bettman, Johnson and Payne 1992). More recently, such a multi-dimensional approach has been taken in a satisfaction context. Oliva et al (1992), have proposed a catastrophe model of consumer satisfaction with service, where specific service attributes are related to overall service satisfaction in order to determine the impact of a particular attributes on satisfaction. This points to both a conceptual and methodological similarity of approach between multi-attribute attitude research and satisfaction research.

This study explores the structure of attribute contributions to overall satisfaction and compares this structure to the self reported importance of attributes in the formation of initial purchase preference attitudes. The purpose of such an exploration is to emphasize the temporal variation in the importance of product attributes in the satisfaction judgement process. That is, this study proposes that there may be a vital distinction between attributes consumers consider important in product choice versus satisfaction evaluation. This is accomplished utilizing a data set from the automotive industry.

PERFORMANCE AND SATISFACTION

Although earlier studies used product performance ratings as a proxy for CS (e.g., Olson and Dover 1976; Anderson 1973), later studies (Oliver and Desarbo 1988; Swan 1988; Churchill & Surprenant 1982) have conceptually distinguished between performance and other moderators of CS such as disconfirmation and expectations. Churchill and Surprenant (1982) demonstrated discriminant validity between performance, disconfirmation, and expectation. An interesting finding has been that performance has an effect on satisfaction that is separate and distinct from, and sometimes stronger than, disconfirmation or expectations (Churchill and Surprenant 1982; Swan 1988). In fact, for a complex durable good (Video disk product) Churchill and Surprenant (1982) found that performance had the largest impact of all variables used to explain satisfaction. They speculated that performance was the dominant factor in determining CS for durable goods.

Swan (1988) proposed an argument about the performance-satisfaction link. He argued that consumers buy products to fulfil their needs/values and the degree to which the needs/values are fulfilled depends on how well the product performs. As product performance increases, the needs/values are better met leading to increased satisfaction. In addition, holding disconfirmation constant, higher satisfaction would result from higher performance (Swan 1988). The relationship was tested for restaurants where satisfaction with food and service was studied separately. Results showed that performance was a significant predictor of satisfaction compared to disconfirmation and expectation. For service satisfaction the results were mixed. The first performance component, time, was not significant while the second performance component, attention, was highly significant. These findings raise the possibility that different attributes of a product impact CS differentially; this is especially true because even for food satisfaction, the "performance index" had a low reliability alpha suggesting the possibility that performance on various attributes regressed separately may have had more explanatory power.

Swan's conceptualization specifies a positive monotonic relationship between performance on an attribute and satisfaction, but one can easily think of situations when a decrease in performance or a fixed level of performance on an attribute leads to increased satisfaction. For instance, in the case of an automobile, weak acceleration may cause higher satisfaction for a customer who is concerned with the control of the vehicle or who has young drivers in the household. Powerful acceleration, on the other hand, may cause higher satisfaction to a driving enthusiast. Similarly, in the case of prescription glasses, the more precise (not higher) the performance, the higher the satisfaction. The reason is that satisfaction may not be linked directly to performance, but to the degree with which performance leads to goal fulfillment (Johnson 1984). Thus, any *level of performance that maximizes goal fulfillment*, should lead to higher satisfaction. This notion is consistent with Johnson's (1984) comparison of non-comparable alternatives; since the performance of different attributes (e.g. trunk space versus. mpg) cannot be directly compared, customers may use a higher level of abstraction (i.e. goal-fulfillment) to determine satisfaction. Thus, the level of performance that maximizes satisfaction varies with the attribute's contribution to customer's goal fulfillment.

MULTI-ATTRIBUTE MODELS

The literature on the multi-attribute nature of products has been developed in diverse marketing areas such as choice modelling (Danes and Cattin 1980), attitude modelling (Wilkie and Pessemier 1973), and consumer information environments (Johnson and Katrichis 1988). Within the literature on choice and attitude modelling an important consideration has been the determination of the salience of attributes in terms of their impact on a choice or formation of an attitude.

Within this literature the issue of the impact of particular attributes on the judgement or choice decision has gone by many names. Myers and Alpert (1968) referred to it as determinance to distinguish it from importance of an attribute to a consumer. For instance, a steering wheel might be an important attribute for your car to have, but because all cars have them, it will not be determinant, or have an impact on brand choice. The term salience is more often used (cf. Day 1972; Wilkie and Pessemier 1973) to make the same distinction, while others simply use the term importance, or decision importance (Bettman et al 1992). Operationally, the difference is generally one of inserting the phrase "to your decision" after the word important in measurement items (Wilkie and Pessemier 1973) when direct methods are used.

Most of the research concerning attribute salience has focussed on pre-purchase decision making (c.f. Bettman et al 1992). Rendering satisfaction evaluations, is, however, a post-purchase phenomenon. Here we assert that salience of an attribute varies temporally as the customer uses the product, and thus attenuates satisfaction judgements over time.

SATISFACTION AND MULTI-ATTRIBUTE PRODUCTS

The process of expectations formation about a product is a learning experience based on previous experiences (Woodruff, Cadotte, and Jenkins 1983) with the particular product or similar products. Part of the learning involves recognizing salient attributes and forming expectations about them (Day 1977). Such an attribute by attribute learning process occurs for not only complex products but also simple products (Day 1977). Bolton and Drew (1991) found that customers accord different weights to the core, facilitating, or supporting attributes while evaluating service satisfaction.

LaTour and Peat (1979) propose a model of satisfaction where overall satisfaction is a linearly additive function of the outcome of attribute level comparisons and each outcome is weighted by its stated importance. Thus, the more important an attribute, the higher its impact on overall satisfaction. The model includes salient attributes, but does not discriminate between different degrees of salience among attributes. Thus in their model, importance remaining constant, all salient attributes should be equally relevant in satisfaction evaluation. However, empirical evidence (Wilkie and Weinreich 1972) shows that importance is a poor criteria for judging the relevance (or salience) of an attribute in the evaluation process. Furthermore, linear compensatory models of satisfaction judgement formation, such as the one proposed by LaTour and Peat, are not only difficult for customers to execute but also require the explicit resolving of difficult value trade-offs (Bettman et al 1992). Additionally, linear additivity of attribute level satisfaction may not hold under the "elimination by aspects" or "frequency of good and bad features" models of judgement formation (Bettman et al 1992). In these respects, the weighted average rule appears to be more of a normative strategy than a realistic strategy for judgement formation.

One can easily conceive of situations where "unimportant" attributes become salient through use of a product and therefore relevant in satisfaction evaluation. A young car driver may be very enthusiastic about the styling of her car (high importance) but be continuously bothered by the leaky engine (salient); more likely this customer will be dissatisfied with her car. Thus, salience of an attribute should be the relevant criteria for a customer's satisfaction judgement. The logic here is that, in the context of satisfaction, more salient attributes will be more "active" in memory and more readily available for processing (Anderson 1990); in other words, memory "nodes" regarding salient attributes will have a higher activation potential and therefore influence the satisfaction judgement.

In addition, the performance (hence contribution to goal attainment) of certain attributes can be known with reasonable certainty (eg. trunk space) before the purchase process; on the other hand, the performance of other "sensory" or "experiential" attributes is uncertain (eg. wind noise) and may only be "discovered" during the post-purchase consumption process. Expectation-disconfirmation regarding attributes that were evaluated with certainty before the purchase process must already be positive or else it would result in strong cognitive dissonance (Festinger 1957); these attributes, though still salient, may not be instrumental in the subsequent satisfaction judgement task.

PROCEDURE

Data from a survey of new-car buyers for the year 1992 was used to explore the above ideas. The survey was conducted among buyers of new domestic (all brands) 1992 model year vehicles purchased in the months January - March 1992. Respondents had used the vehicle for 3-5 months ensuring that they had experience with the various attributes under investigation. Of the 134,833 surveys mailed out, 43,908 (33.5%) were usable returns. For the sake of efficiency, a small random sampling of completed responses yielded a working sample of 1,342 responses for the current study. The mean age of these respondents was between 40-44 years with an average of 4,854 miles on the new car purchased. The average price of the car bought was 19,000 dollars. These numbers indicate that the respondents included in this study are not only representative of the industry, but also that they had driven the vehicle long enough to "explore" the various attributes of the product.

Measurement

Overall satisfaction was measured on a 5 point scale (5 = completely satisfied and 1 = very dissatisfied); attribute level performance was measured on a 5 point scale (5 = excellent and 1 = poor). Pre-purchase salience was assessed via a 5 point scale (5= extremely important, 1=not at all important) in answer to the question "How important was each of the following in your decision?" Attribute level performance was measured for 27 attributes. Of those 27 attributes, pre-purchase importance ratings were available for 9 attributes.

Analysis and Results

Descriptive statistics for attribute level performance and pre-purchase importance are reported in Table 1. Correlations between attribute-level performance and overall satisfaction, and purchase decision importance and overall satisfaction are reported in Table 2. The data show that performance on various attributes was rated differentially with a range of 4.47 to 3.43. All relationships between attribute level performance ratings and overall satisfaction are positive and significant, as are the relationships between pre-purchase importance ratings and overall satisfaction. Further, performance on different attributes was differentially related to overall satisfaction.

TABLE 1
Descriptive Statistics

	Performance		Importance	
	Mean	s.d.	Mean	s.d.
Freedom from stalling	4.47	0.75		
Overall exterior styling	4.47	0.67	4.08	.82
Starting ease	4.45	0.70		
Ease of handling	4.43	0.71	4.28	.69
Appearance of paint job	4.38	0.80		
Water leaks	4.35	0.82		
Smoothness at idle	4.35	0.78		
Braking	4.33	0.78		
Fit of other body panels	4.30	0.79		
Overall interior styling	4.29	0.73	3.95	.78
Durability/Reliability	4.27	0.79	4.47	.67
Fit of doors	4.27	0.86		
Front seat comfort	4.27	0.78		
Fit:chrome trim/moldings	4.27	0.81		
Riding comfort	4.24	0.76	4.14	.75
Power/pickup	4.23	0.81	3.92	.86
Overall workmanship	4.16	0.81		
Ease of shifting gears	4.16	0.89		
Comfort of lap belt	4.16	0.81		
Smooth transmission	4.13	0.89		
Value for the money	4.07	0.89	4.16	.85
Comfort of shoulder belt	4.02	0.96		
Fuel economy/mileage	4.02	0.86		
Quietness	3.97	0.92	3.95	.81
Squeaks/rattles	3.96	0.97		
Cargo capacity	3.94	0.96	3.43	.99
Wind noise	3.89	1.00		
Overall satisfaction	**4.20**	**0.74**		

n=1342

Table 3 shows the rankings of performance ratings in column one, and decision importance ratings in column 2. Column 3 shows the rankings of the correlations between attribute level performance and overall satisfaction, and column 4 shows the relationship between an attribute's decision salience and satisfaction.

Several points are of interest in this table. First, a comparison of columns 2 and 3 seems to indicate that there is some difference between how salient an attribute is in the purchase decision and how much performance on that attribute contributes to overall satisfaction. Most notably, the exterior styling of the vehicle dropped from 5th place in pre-purchase decision importance to 8th place in terms of its relationship with overall satisfaction. This may be because, regardless of the level of exterior styling of the vehicle, it can be assessed with a relatively high degree of certainty prior to the decision to purchase. Once the purchase decision is made, styling remains exactly what it was prior to purchase and is no longer salient in judgements about satisfaction. A similar case could be made for ease of handling. Riding comfort, power/pickup, quietness, and value for the money all increased in salience after the purchase. For the first three attributes it could be argued that this was due to the "experiential" or hedonic nature (Kahneman and Snell, 1990) of the attributes; that is, because they are attributes that the consumer experiences on a fairly regular basis after purchase, they have increased in salience. The increase in value for money is harder to account for but may be due to a difference in a pre-purchase and post-purchase comparison group for consumers. Pre-purchase comparisons of value for the money may be between different price ranges of vehicles. In the pre-purchase choice task, consumers may be asking themselves whether a $25,000.00 vehicle represents as much value for the money as a $15,000.00 vehicle. After the purchase, consumers, if they bought a $15,000.00 vehicle, may be making judgements about the value for the money on $15,000.00 vehicles only.

The simple correlation coefficients between each attribute's performance rating and satisfaction were used as a measure of the attribute's contribution to satisfaction. A simple correlation coefficient was calculated between these correlations and the self reported pre-purchase importance scores yielding a relationship of .77 (p<.05), indicating a much stronger relationship than expected between pre-purchase importance of an attribute and its relationship to overall satisfaction. Visual inspection of the data reveals that the data-point for "Cargo-capacity" is indeed an influential outlier (Everitt and Dunn 1992). As explained earlier and as evidenced by the fact that it ranked last in all categories (Table 3) "Cargo-capacity" appears to be an unimportant and non-salient attribute. We therefore, recomputed the correlation coefficient which was .66 (p<.05), indicating that post purchase salience may be related to pre-purchase salience but that they are somewhat

TABLE 2
Simple Correlation Coefficients Between Overall Satisfaction and Attribute Performance / Pre-Purchase Importance

	Attribute level performance	Pre-purchase importance
Overall workmanship	.637	
Durability/Reliability	.627	.280
Value for the money	.586	.206
Riding Comfort	.558	.327
Squeaks/rattles	.557	
Fit:chrome trim/moldings	.531	
Ease of handling	.526	.253
Fit of other body panels	.522	
Quietness	.521	.224
Wind noise	.506	
Fit of doors	.504	
Ease of shifting gears	.488	
Smooth transmission	.486	
Front seat comfort	.483	
Appearance of paint job	.482	
Smoothness at idle	.479	
Braking	.479	
Overall exterior styling	.473	.255
Power/Pickup	.465	.208
Starting ease	.462	
Overall interior styling	.450	.292
Comfort of lap belt	.441	
Water leaks	.440	
Freedom from stalling	.443	
Comfort of shoulder belt	.420	
Fuel economy/mileage	.382	
Cargo capacity	.326	.078

Note: all correlations are significant (p<.01), n=1342

TABLE 3
Ranks

	Performance Ratings	Importance Ratings	Correlations of Overall Satisfaction w/ Performance	w/Importance
Overall exterior styling	1	5	8	4
Ease of handling	2	2	4	5
Overall interior styling	3	6	6	2
Durability/Reliability	4	1	1	3
Riding comfort	5	4	3	1
Power/pickup	6	8	7	7
Value for the money	7	3	2	8
Quietness	8	6	5	6
Cargo capacity	9	9	9	9

different. The strength of this relationship may also be due in part to a couple of methodological difficulties. First, the 3-5 months driving experience, after purchase may not have given salience the opportunity to change dramatically. Second, and probably more likely, pre-purchase importance was assessed at the same time as performance and satisfaction, and was assessed post-purchase. So some of the salience shifting might already be part of the pre-purchase importance ratings utilized.

One puzzling observation is that despite ranking fourth in performance "Durability/Reliability" (DR) has the highest correlation with overall satisfaction. One possible explanation, is that in recent years the auto-industry has consistently advertised DR (sometimes under the rubric "quality") as a yardstick of satisfaction. Thus, by making DR salient and, in some cases, leading customers to automatically (automatically is used here in an information-processing manner) equate DR (attribute performance) with satisfaction (goal-fulfillment) we may be obtaining a biased result. Another explanation is that information regarding DR was processed at a "deeper" level (Craik and Lockhart 1972).

DISCUSSION

The direct link between goal-fulfillment and satisfaction on an attribute level has not been explored within the CS literature. The current findings, provide justification for exploring this link. Despite the methodological limitations, the notion that an attribute's salience in the purchase decisions is different than salience for satisfaction judgements is supported. This has several implications.

First, we find that information-processing and multi-attribute choice modelling approaches (Bettman et al 1992) can be fruitfully applied to CS research within a goal-fulfillment (Johnson 1984) model. Second, the results offer support for arguments that CS research should not treat complex, multi-attribute products as simple products (Day 1977) or the satisfaction judgement decision as a uni-dimensional decision. Increasingly, scholars are acknowledging the multi-dimensional nature of satisfaction as an affective construct (Westbrook and Oliver 1991). Our findings suggest that satisfaction may also be multi-dimensional vis-a-vis performance and goal-fulfillment of salient attributes.

Third, the approach utilized suggests a need to address the temporal variance inherent in the satisfaction judgement process. Schematic representations (Matlin 1983) of products may evolve over time; judgement heuristics (Bettman et al 1992) or experience based norms (Woodruff, Cadotte and Jenkins 1983) may change over time. The ratings in this study were obtained after only 3-5 months of driving. It is likely, that the relative performance of various attributes and hence their contribution to goal-fulfillment will change over the course of many more months or years. Several managers in the auto-industry have asked the question: Which satisfaction rating should I worry about: the one customers report after using the car for 6 months, or the one customers report with the disposed vehicle, and just before they are ready to buy their next car? Obviously, satisfaction at each point in time is important and has strategic implications for researchers and managers alike. For instance, the satisfaction rating after disposal of the vehicle may be very salient and relevant to the next purchase decision (LeBarbera and Mazursky 1983) and has market share implications (Fornell and Wernnerfelt 1987). The satisfaction after 6 months is crucial because it may well be the summary judgement about a product that is spread via word-of-mouth (c.f. Richins 1983); this has obvious implications for new brands introduced in a market. Fourth, an attribute level view of customer satisfaction is better able to guide managerial resource allocation under a TQM approach. For instance, managers frequently ask the question: What attributes of the product should I enhance to improve CS? This approach provides guidance to managers regarding this issue.

Fifth, the findings suggest that pre-purchase choices may not lead the customer to buy products that will be most satisfying during consumption. Kahneman and Snell (1990) found that there was little or no correlation between the predictions of "hedonic change" that individuals made and the changes they actually experienced after using the product. They phrased the issues as follows: (1) Do people know what will be good for them and (2) do people choose what will be good for them? In particular, they note people's predictions about their own "hedonic experiences" were no better than the predictions made about a random stranger. Such findings, in the context of satisfaction, raise some serious policy and ethical implications. For instance, how might the pre-purchase decision environments be designed to sensitize customers to this sort of "miscalculation?"

LIMITATIONS

The reader should view the results as extremely preliminary and exploratory. Although the dataset used was obtained from "real" customers purchasing real products, it was originally collected for managerial purposes and has drawbacks associated with the practical limitations of such a data set. For instance, all measures utilized were single indicators, so no assessment of measures could be performed. A more complete matching of importance scores and performance scores would have been desirable. This would have enabled us to compare more attributes on their pre and post purchase importance. Also, because measures of pre-purchase importance were taken after purchase, they represent beliefs about pre-purchase importance and as such may not be fully representative of pre-purchase importance. Because the dataset was developed for managerial purposes, the attributes that were included were ones that had been found to be of interest to managers in previous studies. Thus, the attributes represent a mixed bag in the sense that they may not be truly comparable (Johnson, 1984). For instance, some attributes (cargo capacity) are more concrete while other attributes are really consequences of other attributes (eg. riding comfort may a consequence of wind noise, comfort of lap belt, ease of handling etc.). Finally, all the results are based on simple bivariate correlations and as such are somewhat tenuous.

Although the results are supportive, more conclusive empirical evidence for the propositions await. However, the discussion does point to examining CS as a construct that varies temporally across product attributes.

REFERENCES

Anderson, John R. (1990) *Cognitive Psychology and its Implications*. 3rd ed., New York: W.H. Freeman and Company.

Anderson, Rolph E. (1973) "Consumer Dissatisfaction: The Effect of Disconfirmed Expectancy on Perceived Product Performance," *Journal of Marketing Research*, 10, Feb., 38-44.

Bettman, James R., Eric J. Johnson, and John W. Payne (1992) "Consumer Decision Making," in *Handbook of Consumer Behavior*, Thomas S. Robertson & Harold H. Kassarjian (eds.) New Jersey: Prentice Hall.

Bolton, Ruth N. and James H. Drew (1991) "A Multistage Model of Customers' Assessments of Service Quality and Value," *Journal of Consumer Research*, 17, March, 375-384.

Churchill, Gilbert A., and Carol Surprenant (1982) "An Investigation into the Determinants of Customer Satisfaction," *Journal of Marketing Research*, 19, November, 491-504.

Craik, F.I.M. and R.S. Lockhart (1972) "Levels of processing: A framework for memory research," *Journal of Verbal Learning and Verbal Behavior*, 11, 671-684.

Danes, Jeffrey E. and Philippe Cattin (1980) "Multiattribute Choice Models: A Critical Review," in *Advances in Consumer Research*, vol. 8, Kent B. Monroe ed., Association for Consumer Research, Ann Arbor, MI.

Day, Ralph L. (1977) "Extending the Concept of Consumer Satisfaction," in *Advances in Consumer Research*, vol. 6, William D. Perreault, Jr., ed., Association for Consumer Research, Ann Arbor, MI, 149-154.

Day, George (1972) "Evaluating Models of Attitude Structure," *Journal of Marketing Research*, 9, August, 279-286.

Everitt, Brian S. and Graham Dunn (1992) *Applied Multivariate Data Analysis*. New York: Oxford Univ. Press.

Festinger, L. (1957) *A Theory of Cognitive Dissonance*. New York: Harper and Row.

Fornell, Claes and Birger Wernnerfelt (1987) "Defensive Marketing Strategy by Customer Complaint Management: A Theoretical Analysis," *Journal of Marketing Research*, 24, November, 337-346.

Johnson, Michael D. (1984) "Consumer choice strategies for comparing non-comparable alternatives," *Journal of Consumer Research*, 11, 741-753.

_____ and Jerome M. Katrichis (1988) "The Existence and Perception of Redundancy in Consumer Information Environments," *Journal of Consumer Policy*, 11, 131-157.

Kahneman, Daniel and Jackie Snell (1990) "Predicting Utility," in R.M. Hogarth (ed.), *Insights in decision making*. Chicago: Univ. of Chicago Press.

LaTour, Stephen A. and Nancy C. Peat (1979) "Conceptual and methodological issues in consumer satisfaction research," in *Advances in Consumer Research*, vol. 6, William D. Perreault, Jr., ed., Association for Consumer Research, Ann Arbor, MI, 431-437.

LeBarbera Priscilla A. and David Mazursky (1983) "A Longitudinal Assessment of Consumer Satisfaction/Dissatisfaction: The Dynamic Aspect of the Cognitive Process," *Journal of Marketing Research*, 20, Nov., 393-404.

Matlin, Margaret W. (1983) *Cognition*. New York: CBS College Publishing.

Myers, James H. & Mark I. Alpert (1968) "Determining Buying Attitudes: Meaning and Measurement," *Journal of Marketing*, 32, Oct., 13-20.

Oliva, Terence A., Richard L. Oliver, & Ian C. MacMillan (1992) "A Catastrophe Model for Developing Service Satisfaction Strategies," *Journal of Marketing*, 56, July, 83-95.

Oliver, Richard L. (1980) "A Cognitive Model of the Antecedents and Consequences of Satisfaction Decisions," *Journal of Marketing Research*, 17, November, 460-469.

_____ and Wayne S. Desarbo (1988) "Response Determinants in Satisfaction Judgements," *Journal of Consumer Research*, 14, March, 495-507.

Olson, Jerry C. and Philip Dover (1979) "Disconfirmation of Consumer Expectations Through Product Trial," *Journal of Applied Psychology*, 64, April, 179-189.

Richins, Marsha L. (1983) "Negative Word-of-Mouth by Dissatisfied Consumers: A Pilot Study," *Journal of Marketing*, 47, Winter, 68-78.

Swan, John E. (1988) "Consumer Satisfaction Related the Disconfirmation of Expectations And Product Performance," *Journal of Consumer Satisfaction, Dissatisfaction and Complaining Behavior*, vol. 1, 40-47.

Westbrook, Robert A. and Richard L. Oliver (1991) "The Dimensionality of Consumption Emotion Patterns and Consumer Satisfaction," *Journal of Consumer Research*, 18, June, 84-91.

Wilkie, William L. and Edgar A. Pessemier (1973) "Issues in Marketing's Use of Multi-Attribute Attitude Models," *Journal of Marketing Research*, 10, November, 428-441.

Wilkie, William L. and Rolf P. Weinreich (1972) "Effects of the Number and Type of Attributes Included in an Attitude Model: More is *not* Better,' *Proceedings*. 3rd Annual Conference, *Association for Consumer Research*, 1972, 325-340.

Woodruff, Robert B., Ernest R. Cadotte, and Roger L. Jenkins (1983) "Modelling Consumer Satisfaction Processes Using Experience Based Norms," *Journal of Marketing Research*, 20, August, 296-304.

Yi, Youjae (1990) "A Critical Review of Consumer Satisfaction," in *Review of Marketing* 1990, Valarie A. Zeithaml, ed., Chicago: American Marketing Association, 68-123.

"Tea and the Viennese": A Pioneering Episode in the Analysis of Consumer Behavior
Ronald A. Fullerton, Providence College

ABSTRACT

Before Consumer Behavior as a self-aware discipline developed during the 1950s and 1960s, there were sustained episodes of serious study of the phenomenon in both U.S. and Europe. This paper examines one such episode, the consumer research done by Paul F. Lazarsfeld and his colleagues at the University of Vienna during the late 1920s and early 1930s. Particular attention is paid to their study, "Tea and the Viennese". The research combined quantitative and qualitative analyses and evinced an unusually high skill in interpreting consumer experience.

INTRODUCTION

Interest in the history of consumer behavior has risen strikingly during the past decade. The interest embraces both the development of the *discipline* of Consumer Behavior (e.g., Mittelstaedt 1990), and studies of past *behavior* by consumers (e.g., McCracken 1988, Part I; Sheth & Gross 1988). As a discipline with self-awareness and such institutions as regular conferences and journals, Consumer Behavior developed only after 1950 (Mittelstaedt 1990).

There was, however, organized study of consumer behavior on both sides of the Atlantic before World War II (1939-1945). The groups doing it had neither contact with one another nor consciousness of building a discipline; their senses of identity lay elsewhere. In the United States consumer behavior was studied by market researchers, some sociologists (e.g., Lynd 1933), and by university home economists (e.g., Kyrk 1923). In Germany the Society for Consumption Research (*Gesellschaft fuer Konsumforschung*) in Nuernberg developed a dense network of trained consumer observers across the country's cities and towns (Vershofen 1937, 1940).

The focus of this paper is on still another group in Central Europe, the social scientists who clustered about Paul F. Lazarsfeld's Office of Economic-Psychological Research (*Wirtschaftspsychologische Forschungsstelle*) at the University of Vienna from about 1927 to 1934. Drawn partly by Lazarsfeld's (1901-1976) personal magnetism, and partly by the lack of employment for university graduates in those economically depressed years, some of the most talented social researchers of this century worked on the Office's research projects involving consumers. They included several who, like Lazarsfeld, emigrated to the U.S. during the mid-1930s: Hans Zeisel (1905-1992), who excelled at sociology, statistics, market research, and legal scholarship; Herta Herzog, whose research prowess made her one of the most respected figures in the marketing and the advertising communities during the 1950s; and Ernest Dichter (d. 1991), whose flamboyant advocacy of "motivation research" made him the most famous marketing figure since Phineas T. Barnum. Another alumnus, Marie Jahoda, became one of Britain's leading sociologists.

The Work of the Office

Jahoda, Zeisel, and Lazarsfeld wrote *The Unemployed of Marienthal*, a classic of Sociology which analyzed the impact of long-term unemployment. To finance such research—the conservative University administration of that time was not prepared to lavish support upon a group so heavily composed of Jews and Socialists—Lazarsfeld had hit upon the idea of conducting market research for Austrian firms. Market research was still rare in Austria at the time.

Market Research and the Boundaries of Social Research

The Office researchers actually valued market research projects for their own sake as well as for the modest fees that they brought in. Both Lazarsfeld and Zeisel believed (and continued to believe throughout their lives) that market research provided social researchers fine opportunities to explore the richness of human behavior (Abrams 1977; Bartos 1986; Lazarsfeld 1982, p. 20; Zeisel 1967). Lazarsfeld was always interested in why people made the *choices* which they did, whether in everyday products, radio programs, or voting (Coleman 1982, p. 5). In the early 1930s, he had a special interest in determining "to what amount *emotional factors influence use of commodities in addition to [the] purely economic and technical factors which [have] only [been] taken into consideration [by market researchers] until now*" (Lazarsfeld 1934a, emphasis in original).

To Office researchers fired by Lazarsfeld's enthusiasm, the thirty odd market research studies which they conducted on consumers and noodles, vinegar, laundry service, radio programming, movies, milk, shoes, edible fats and other everyday products, were opportunities to expand the bounds of social research with searching examinations of consumer behavior. For each project researchers strove to: "question hundreds of people from all social circles about everything which they have ever experienced or done with a given product" (Herzog 1933, translated by the author[1]),..."seeking to uncover all of the connections among a certain group of consumers and a certain product" (Wirtschaftspsychologische Forschungsstelle 1933). A consumer's purchase of even a mundane product, Lazarsfeld later told American researchers, "has not one reason but a great many" (In Wheeler 1937, p. 82)—whether or not the consumer was consciously aware of these. Reasons typically included promotional and word-of-mouth *influences*, price and product *attributes*, and the consumer's own attitudinal *tendencies* (Wheeler 1937, p. 83). All of these could be uncovered through large-scale intensive interviewing whose results were carefully analyzed from cross-disciplinary perspectives.

A Dynamic Research Atmosphere

For each project the Office sent out several interviewers (most had university degrees) with long questionnaires, to query respondents "selected in such a way as to represent a fair sample of the population involved in the purchase of the particular commodity being investigated" (Lazarsfeld 1934c, p. 101). The interview procedure was described by Lazarsfeld as follows:

> [The interviewer] talks quite freely with the interviewee concerning the latter's experiences in regard to this particular commodity. The interviewer notes everything the interviewee has to say, but at the same time keeps in mind a number of definite questions which he knows to be essential... He asks one of these questions whenever a good opportunity presents itself in the course of the conversation until the whole set is exhausted. In this way the free expression of the interviewee is combined with the set directions established by the basic plan of the investigation. (Lazarsfeld 1934c, pp. 101-102).

As a project progressed there were frequent meetings at which Lazarsfeld exhorted, cajoled, and criticized, stimulating further

---

[1] All translations from the German are by the author.

analysis and effort in both research methods and interpretation of results (Lazarsfeld 1933; Wagner 1989). "The proverbial Austrian sloppiness, of which we all had our share, was... transformed into a flexible, adoptive, and non-hierarchical organization...[in which] improvisation was a permanent feature in all our work" (Jahoda 1983, pp. 347-348; corroborated by Wagner 1989)).

The Office's approach to consumer research, as Zeisel later noted, assured that "All its studies were brilliant, late, and cost more than we could bill our client... The only thing we ever paid for on time was the coffee our researchers needed when they worked on their reports in a lonely corner of a coffeehouse" (Zeisel 1979, p. 13; corroborated by Neurath 1989). The remainder of this paper will elucidate one of these studies, which explored tea drinking among the citizens of Vienna.

"TEA AND THE VIENNESE"

"Tea and the Viennese" was one of the most charming reports produced by Lazarsfeld's Office. He discussed it briefly in several of his early American publications (e.g., Lazarsfeld 1934b, p. 66; 1935, p. 33; Wheeler 1937, p. 275). When Lazarsfeld brought a copy with him to the U.S. in 1934, Rensis Likert liked it so much that he prepared a translation for his students at New York University (Lazarsfeld 1982, p. 34); this has since been lost. The discussion here is based on the 58 page typed German version in the Lazarsfeld Archive at the University of Vienna ("Der Tee und die Wiener" ca. 1932. Hereafter "Der Tee").

Genesis of the Study

The tea study was commissioned by the Viennese firm of Julius Meinl, then a coffee and tea importer, now a well-known grocery chain in the city. Ever alert for new projects, Lazarsfeld had presumably convinced Meinl managers that the Office would be able to discover why some Viennese did drink tea, and how others could be induced to join them.

Tea drinkers were far outnumbered by coffee drinkers in Vienna, following a pattern found across Western Europe generally (Britain's preference for tea was an historical anomaly which has never been explained well). Both beverages had been widely introduced in Europe three centuries before (Becher 1990, pp. 77-87; Schivelbush 1980, Chapter 2). Upper class Viennese drank mostly genuine ("bean") coffee, middle and working class people chicory and grain-based ersatz coffee much of the time (Becher 1990). Coffeehouses were as much a part of Viennese culture on all social levels as were afternoon tea rituals in Britain (See Repplier 1932).

Research Begins

Still, there were tea drinkers in Vienna. A research team co-directed by Lazarsfeld and one Hans Herma, and including among its principle investigators two university graduates named Renee Bittner and Gertrud Falk, began to explore the tea consumption experience from multiple perspectives. The research was done during winter months. Vienna's citizens loved to talk with market researchers at that time (Herzog 1933), and Lazarsfeld's investigators gave many the opportunity to do so. 353 tea drinkers were intensively interviewed about their personal histories as tea consumers. 18% were working class, 47% lower middle class (white and pink collar employees, government bureaucrats, etc.), and 35% higher on the socio-economic scale: "lawyers, teachers, doctors, hoteliers, fur dealers, artists, higher bureaucrats, privy councilors, deputies (*Prokuristen*), bank directors, craftspeople, publishing executives, etc." ("Der Tee", Anhang I).

An additional 288 respondents were queried about their receptivity to different words and phrases which could describe tea, a technique intended to elicit promotable, desirable characteristics of a product ("Der Tee", pp. 13, 32ff).

Finally, in order to derive overall consumption statistics, 1749 Viennese were questioned about "which [warm] beverages they drank and how often" (Ibid., p. 49). Nearly four fifths of those questioned lived in less affluent areas of the city; the rationale for this proportion is not explained in the report.

THE RESEARCH FINDINGS

As expected, only a minority of Viennese described themselves as regular tea drinkers. Usage among the working class was especially low. Meinl was advised that it could best promote sales of its tea by promoting primary demand ("Der Tee" p. 42). Two thirds of the middle and upper-middle class people did report drinking tea occasionally. Even among those who used it, tea was drunk less regularly than coffee. In contrast to coffee, however, whose consumption peaked early in the day, tea drinking increased over the course of the day.

Approximately 30% of the Viennese tea drinkers had learned to drink it as children in households where it was the customary beverage. For example: "When the respondent was still a girl her family found it agreeably cozy (*gemutlich*) during the winter to sit together over cups of tea" ("Der Tee" p. 15).[2] A working class female told an interviewer: "We got tea even when we were still children, especially tea with milk, and *especially when we were sick*. I still today drink milk tea with great pleasure, but the tea must be strong" (Ibid., p. 16).

The great majority of Viennese were socialized into coffee and not tea drinkers, however. "Coffee for breakfast is a family tradition. Vienna is indeed the city of coffee," asserted an upper middle class respondent (Ibid., p. 11). The city's tea drinkers had developed the habit after childhood. Lazarsfeld and his colleagues found that the propensity to try tea increased with age, just as that to drink milk declined. "In most cases—when it is tried at all—tea drinking sets in relatively late and increases...in importance only in stages" (Ibid., p. 12).

Tea Drinking and Rational Decision-Making

Among the Viennese, the choice to try tea was usually made after childhood, during adolescence and adulthood. "Generally speaking this choice is grounded in rational decision-making" (Ibid., p. 12). The choice to drink tea was a conscious one. "*One is not just aroused* [by external stimuli] *to drink tea, he also makes his own decision to do so*" (Ibid., p. 12, emphasis in original). One reflection of such conscious decision-making was that tea drinkers had more words to describe the beverage, and spoke more about its physical characteristics (taste, stimulative properties, ease of preparation, etc.) than did drinkers of milk or coffee.

Much of "Tea and the Viennese" explores the reasons why adolescents and adults made the choice to adopt tea as a regular or fairly regular drink. Lazarsfeld identified two major categories of reasons. One involved personal expansion—decisions which were bound up in conscious choices to expand one's efficacy or horizons. The other, which applied to even more people, involved external occasions which stimulated the choice process.

---

[2] Office reports were rich in such citations, some of them like this summarizing a respondent's comments, others direct quotations from respondents. Both kinds will be seen in this paper. The italicized words, phrases, and sentences follow the interviewers' emphases.

Tea and Personal Expansion

For nearly a quarter of the tea drinkers, the choice was closely linked with important life changes such as asserting independence from parents, getting one's first flat, migrating to the big city, getting one's first adult job, and getting married. Adopting tea was a way of expressing the expanded possibilities inherent in life's turning points and rites of passage.

To apprentices, secondary school pupils, and university students, drinking tea frequently represented emancipation from parental oppression. Here are three examples:

—Her mother did not want to allow her to drink tea...[The mother] was even willing to spare her the work and cook the coffee for her. But she wanted to drink tea because it tasted good to her, because it won't make her fat, because it's cheaper than coffee, and then too *because she wanted to assert her will.* Her mother should drink coffee herself but not try to convince her that [tea] is unhealthy just because she doesn't like its taste. She has drunk tea for many years and will remain with it (Ibid., p. 18).

—Has drunk tea since she was 14. *That is when she came to prevail*, earlier her parents didn't allow it. (Ibid., p. 18).

—Since this respondent has *studied in Vienna* she drinks lots of tea. At home it was supposed to be bad for the health and never allowed. *Even now her mother has no idea that she has tea for breakfast.* (Ibid., p. 18).

Among slightly older people (who presumably got along better with their parents) adoption of tea "was often explicitly associated with new living conditions" (Ibid., p. 19). Some examples follow:

—Earlier, in childhood, only cocoa or milk. Tea only when sick. When she *went to work in the office she got accustomed to it as a breakfast beverage.* On a trip with her boss got used to English breakfasts. Since then... (Ibid., p. 19).

—Since childhood only coffee for breakfast. When he *lived alone* as a university student he got used to drinking tea every night and also on other occasions. (Ibid., p. 19)

—I came from the country, didn't know about tea there. When I came *to Vienna as a servant* I quickly got used to drinking tea and since then have enjoyed drinking it. When I went home to visit, it was in autumn and very cold, I cooked a big pot of tea; it was looked at with astonishment and they said, "Such a thing we don't drink the entire year." (Ibid., p. 19)

—Previously she equated tea drinking with taking medicine. Since her *husband*, who loves tea, always laughed at the face she made [when] she prepared him his tea, she has gotten used to drinking tea. (Ibid., p. 20).

—As a child and young woman never preferred tea, drank it only when forced to do so at social events or when a guest. First liked to drink tea *when she owned her own home.* One can chat pleasantly over tea, it dispels boredom. (Ibid., p. 20).

External Stimuli

Slightly over a third of the tea drinkers had chosen to adopt the beverage because of influences from external stimuli. Such stimuli included travel to and living in areas where tea drinking was the norm, e.g., China, India, and Russia. For example:

—Respondent has made many journeys and has learned to esteem tea, especially in places where there was no *drinking water*. In China and India in particular he has gotten as accustomed as a native to tea. (Ibid., p. 21).

For others, the external influences flowed from social mores and norms, especially those of parts of Vienna's upper middle class refined society. Some had come to view tea as the "modern" drink, a perfect accompaniment to the fashionable cold suppers. A "tea culture" analogous to that of the fussiest Oxbridge undergraduates (Repplier 1932) had developed. "Strikingly often the correct preparation [of the tea], the correct trimmings [to the tea], and the correct side dishes [to serve with the tea] play important roles" (Ibid., pp. 21-22). One upper-middle class respondent explained to an interviewer:

—I am often invited to the M.'s. The tea is exquisite there because the lady of the house *takes great pains with its preparation.* One cannot leave the preparation of tea to common people. They simply cannot understand anything about it. There come into play certain national constants which simply cannot be learned. For me tea adds to the supply reservoir of my best internal charm impulses. Many like tea only out of an imitative quest, but to me tea signifies *joy, festivity.* A thousand charming ideas well up in a social circle after enjoying this noble beverage. After the enjoyment of a fine tea there springs forth a social scintillation which flows over all participants. (Ibid., p. 22).

Finally, some Viennese adopted tea when sick, especially because of its milder impact on their stomachs, then stayed with it whether their stomachs remained sensitive or not:

—Until four years ago this respondent drank coffee at breakfast and during breaks. After his stomach sickness he took tea because coffee caused pains. His wife never drinks tea, she is a real coffee sister. (Ibid., p. 24).

—The respondent has drunk tea for three years, before that coffee. Previously drank tea only now and then as she lay in bed, felt chilled, or had something wrong with her stomach. *Tried tea once and it tasted very good.* It is above all lighter than coffee. She also saw that tea in the coffeehouse and also at home is *cheaper*.

The last respondent was unusual in that she was motivated in part by tea's lower cost. One of the striking findings of Lazarsfeld and his colleagues was that the lower price of tea was seldom mentioned as an attraction—despite the fact that the report was researched during the depths of the Great Depression.

CONCLUSION: LAZARSFELD'S AUSTRIAN LEGACY TO CONSUMER RESEARCH

There is a sense of wonder and excitement about the tea and other Office studies which reflect the best side of the youth of a discipline. These consumers seem so *alive*, pouring out their souls to researchers who understood and appreciated their revelations. The diversity of consumers' experiences with tea, and the complex interplay of emotion and reason which shaped their choices, testify to the power and richness of the consumer research which revealed them sixty years ago. Neither respondents nor investigators were yet jaded; methodologies had not yet hardened into opposed dogmas, allowing the Office researchers to select freely from a wide variety of methods of analysis. The tea study shows the skill of Lazarsfeld and his colleagues in formulating questions and in extracting rich meaning from responses. As Converse (1987, p. 137) argues, Lazarsfeld was almost without peer as an interpreter of social research.

Lazarsfeld, who came to exercise great influence upon social researchers in the United States after emigrating there in 1934, was an important pioneer of psychological "depth" analyses of qualitative research—but also of statistical analysis (his doctorate was in applied mathematics, his four-by-four tables were famous, he invented latent structure analysis). His Viennese studies combined both. Eventually, however, the two approaches diverged in consumer research, as in social research generally. Methodologies became more elaborate, increasing rigor but decreasing inspiration and creativity in interpretation of research. The stereotype of sinister "motivation research" which Vance Packard (1957) concocted from Dichter's boasts, discredited qualitative research for a quarter century. Only during the past decade have we again developed that awareness of the breadth of consumer experience which allows us to appreciate fully Lazarsfeld's Austrian work.

REFERENCES

Abrams, Mark (1977), "Social Research and Market Research: The Case of Paul Lazarsfeld," *Journal of the Market Research Society*, 19 (1), 12-17.

Bartos, Rena (1986), "Hans Zeisel: Forensic Sociologist," *Journal of Advertising Research*, (Feb./Mar), 39-42.

Becher, Ursula A.J. (1990), *Geschichte des modernen Lebenstils*, Munich: C.H. Beck.

Coleman, James S. (1982), "Introduction," in Patricia L. Kendall ed., *The Varied Sociology of Paul F. Lazarsfeld*, New York: Columbia University Press, 3-10.

Converse, Jean M. (1987), *Survey Research in the United States: Roots and Emergence, 1890-1960*, Berkeley: University of California Press.

Herzog, Herta (1933), Speech in German Extolling Value of Market Research. Typewritten ms. Lazarsfeld Archive, Vienna.

Jahoda, Marie (1983), "The Emergence of Social Psychology in Vienna," *British Journal of Social Psychology*, 22, 343-349.

_____, Paul F. Lazarsfeld, Hans Zeisel (1933 [1971]), *Marienthal*, translated by the authors, John Reginall, Thomas Elsaesser, Chicago & New York: Aldine-Atherton.

Kyrk, Hazel (1923), *A Theory of Consumption*, Boston: Houghton Mifflin.

Lazarsfeld, Paul F. (1933), "Gutachtenkurs". Parts I-V. July 20-28. Lazarsfeld Archive, Vienna.

_____ (1934a), Untitled Draft of a Proposal to the U.S. Commerce Department, 2/1/34. Lazarsfeld Archive, Vienna.

_____ (1934b), "The Psychological Aspect of Market Research," *Harvard Business Review*, 13 No. 1 (October), 54-71.

_____ (1934c), "English Wirtschaftspsychologische Forschungsstelle Report," typed manuscript, Lazarsfeld Collection, Columbia's Butler Library, Box 34 Folder 5.

_____ (1935), "The Art of Asking WHY in Marketing Research", *National Marketing Review*, 1, 32-43.

_____ (1982), "An Episode in the History of Social Research: A Memoir," in Patricia L. Kendall ed., *The Varied Sociology of Paul F. Lazarsfeld*, New York: Columbia University Press, 11-73.

Lynd, Robert S. (1933), "The People As Consumers," in *Recent Social Trends in the United States*, vol. 2, New York & London: McGraw Hill, 857-911.

McCracken, Grant (1988), *Culture and Consumption*, Bloomington: Indiana University Press.

Mittelstaedt, Robert A. (1990), "Economics, Psychology, and the Literature of the Subdiscipline of Consumer Behavior," *Journal of the Academy of Marketing Science*, 18 No. 4 (Fall), 303-312.

Neurath, Paul (1989), Interviews with the author, June 12th, 14th, 21st.

Packard, Vance (1957), *The Hidden Persuaders*, New York: McKay.

Repplier, Agnes (1932), *To Think of Tea!*, Boston: Houghton Mifflin.

Schivelbusch, Wolfgang (1980 [1992]), *Tastes of Paradise*, translated by David Jacobson, New York: Pantheon.

Sheth, Jagdish N., & Barbara L. Gross (1988), "Parallel Development of Marketing and Consumer Behavior: A Historical Perspective," in Terence R. Nevett & Ronald A. Fullerton, eds., *Historical Perspectives in Marketing*, Lexington MA: Lexington Books, 9-34."

Der Tee und die Wiener" (ca. 1932). Typed report, Lazarsfeld Archive, Vienna.

Vershofen, Wilhelm (1937), "Absatswirtschaft und Verbraucher". Typed manuscript, Gesellschaft fuer Konsumforschung, Nuernberg.

_____ (1940), *Handbuch der Verbrauchsforschung*, Berlin: Carl Heymann.

Wagner, Gertrude (1989), Interview with the author, June 23rd.

Wheeler, Ferdinand C., ed.(1937), *The Technique of Marketing Research*, New York & London: McGraw Hill. [Lazarsfeld wrote Chapters 3, 4, 11, and 15].

Zeisel, Hans (1979), "The Vienna Years," in Robert K. Merton, James S. Coleman, Peter H. Rossi, eds., *Qualitative and Quantitative Social Research: Papers in Honor of Paul F. Lazarsfeld*, New York: The Free Press, 10-15.

_____ (1967), "Die Wiener Schule der Motivforschung," presented at WAPOR-ESOMAR Conference. Lazarsfeld Archive, Vienna.

Object-Subject Interchangeability: A Symbolic Interactionist Model of Materialism

Reid P. Claxton, East Carolina University
Jeff B. Murray, University of Arkansas

Why do some consumers emphasize the building of human relationships while others emphasize acquisition and possession of material goods? While an impressive amount of consumer research has addressed the definition and measurement of materialism (e.g., Belk 1985; Richins and Dawson 1992), somewhat less attention has been devoted to theoretical explanations of the phenomenon. The purpose of this paper is to draw on the insights of symbolic interactionism to suggest an explanation as to why some consumers are more materialistic than others.

Symbolic interactionism (Blumer 1969; Mead 1934; Solomon 1983) suggests that society is continually produced and re-produced through the individual's interaction with the symbolic representations of surrounding society. As will be explained, symbolic interaction with material and non-material culture enables the individual to develop a sense of self, become socialized, participate in society, and understand the roles and significance of other people. It is this continuous process that permits the individual to fulfill multiple roles without, in the words of Csikszentmihalyi (1982), "falling apart."

The concept of *interchangeability* is introduced to refer to a psycho-social mechanism that permits individuals to selectively substitute the influences of objects and subjects (other people) for each other as necessary to construct, adapt, and maintain self definition. Presumably, an individual who places greater symbolic reliance on objects, as opposed to subjects, is more materialistic.

Understanding the sociology of interchangeability may provide insight into materialism by making more explicit the role of consumption in the individual's adaptation to changing physical and cultural environments. Interchangeability may also offer a dynamic dimension to other theories of self-via-consumption, e.g., extended self (Belk 1988), self-concept (Goffman 1959; Sirgy 1982), and product symbolism (Levy 1959).

This paper has three major sections. The first reviews previous materialism research. The second presents specifics of the interchangeability model. The third discusses materialism from the perspective of interchangeability.

MATERIALISM: REVIEW OF PREVIOUS RESEARCH

Over the last quarter-century, materialism has been generally defined in terms of the role of material objects in affecting terminal goals such as life satisfaction, happiness, and social progress (Belk 1985; Csikszentmihalyi and Rochberg-Halton 1981).

One of the foremost issues pertaining to materialism is whether it is a positive or negative force in society (Belk 1985). History records a number of bases for disapproval of materialism. *Puritanism* faulted materialistic consumption as providing a distraction from spirituality. *Quakerism* condemned the multiplication and acquisition of goods as an affront to simplicity. *Socialist criticism* interprets consumerism as stemming from worker exploitation. Aesthetic snobbery provides an *aristocratic criticism* of materialistic consumption: mass tastes are, by definition, low (Schudson 1991; Will 1991). Materialism has also been classified as a potential source of inter-group conflict (Murray and Ozanne 1991). Materialistic individuals may be more vulnerable to personal dissatisfaction due to a greater tendency to compare their lives with idealized media images of wealth (Richins 1992). In addition, evidence exists that materialistic people tend to be relatively unhappy (Belk 1984), desirous of fast solutions, easily frustrated, and prone to violence (Rudmin 1992).

While materialism is often considered a negative social force, some researchers have postulated that self-denial of material objects may be related to psychological debilities such as eating disorders, masochism, and self-hatred (Belk 1985; D'Arcy 1967; Masson 1976), thereby suggesting that insufficient emphasis on material objects may also be damaging.

From a symbolic interactionist perspective, materialism is neither positive nor negative in society. In fact, from this perspective, defining self through symbolic interaction with objects is a natural and pervasive part of socialization. McCarthy (1984) asserts that human identities reside in objects more than in individuals. One reason this may be true is that objects help orient individuals by "making visible and stable the categories of culture" (Douglas and Isherwood 1979).

Belk (1988) indicates that without insight into the meanings people attach to possessions, attempts to understand consumption behavior are virtually hopeless. Over time, symbolic meaning is transferred from society to objects, then from objects to individuals (McCracken 1986). The acquisition of objects as expressions of self, symbols of security, and symbols of connectedness and differentiation appears to be "a usual and culturally universal function of consumption" (Wallendorf and Arnould 1988, p. 532).

At the social level, objects create a common language necessary for three fundamental social processes: integration, comparison, and differentiation (Weissner 1984). Mass-produced, homogeneous consumer goods provide an avenue of cultural integration across a society (Wallendorf and Arnould 1988). Boorstin (1971) indicates that advertising has become the folk culture of American society, thereby integrating consumption communities. This value-expressive dimension of objects suggests that brand names often produce feelings of community among purchasers (Friedman 1985). Two Japanese automobiles, the Honda Accord and the Honda Civic, provide literal examples of how agreement, harmony, and community can be embodied by objects' brand names.

At the individual level, mass-produced objects provide a way for individuals to embrace cultural values and social integration, while simultaneously demonstrating individual self-expression. Objects become singularized by the individual through transfer of meanings and emotions (Kopytoff 1986; McCracken 1986). Singularized objects come to symbolize the self and thereby become part of self concept. Any loss of these objects is felt not only as loss of face and status, but also more deeply, as actual damage to the conceptualized, or extended, self (Belk 1988). Ultimately, however, the symbolic meaning of singularized objects results from social relationships. Thus individuals derive meaning from, and reproduce culture by, interacting with both objects and subjects.

THE INTERCHANGEABILITY MODEL

Interchangeability and Symbolic Interactionism

Theoretical support for basing self-definition on relationships with interchangeable objects and subjects stems from symbolic interactionism (Blumer 1969; Mead 1934). This perspective rests on three basic tenets: people behave toward objects according to the meanings the objects have for them; such meanings are created by social interaction among people; and, the individual subsequently

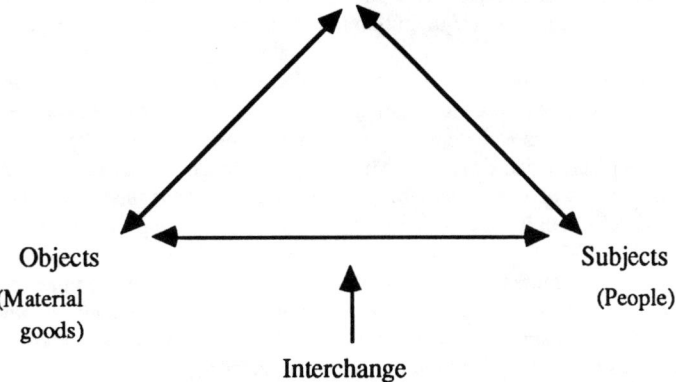

FIGURE 1
The Interchangeability Model

learns such meanings through a dynamic and interpretive process which is applied to everything encountered during the experience of living (Blumer 1969). The applicability of symbolic interactionism to the study of materialism is apparent from the words of Blumer: "[people] live in worlds of objects and are guided in their orientation and actions by the meanings of these objects" (1969, p. 21). For society to be possible, actors must share a strong reciprocity of perspectives made possible largely by objects.

Central to symbolic interactionism is the concept of "self-identity" (Stone 1962). Self-identity is knowledge that the self exists. Self-identity permits communication and other interactions with the self which, in turn, produce "self-definition." Self-definition is a simultaneous recognition of self, and of a beyond-self reality. Knowledge of an alternative reality compels the individual to experience portions of it. Individuals thus act toward the self, becoming the object of their own action. This infers that the self is not a structure, but a dynamic and constant process (Blumer 1969; Mead 1934).

Understanding the self as process means that self-definition must be continually reconfigured as symbolic meanings in the environment change and evolve. For example, as styles and product designs evolve, the meanings of already-owned products change, as do other people's perceptions of the product owners (Kehret-Ward 1982; Mick 1986). Social actors consume objects' symbolism in order to help define social reality and thus ensure that subsequent behavior will be appropriate for the reality defined. The consumer therefore relies on objects' inherent social information to enhance role performances and thus shape self-definition (Solomon 1983).

In sum, as meanings change, the contexts in which individuals define themselves also change. The result is a social process in which the survival of the individual is dependent upon constant adaptation of self-definition.

A Model of Interchangeability

Individuals may experience deficiencies in self-definition stemming from an absence of critical symbols for the identity in question. An example would be a lack of the "speech markers" (e.g., speaking style, technical vocabulary) appropriate to a particular social setting, situation, or occupation. Deficiencies in such symbols result in the tendency to compensate with other symbols within that same "identity area" (Braun and Wicklund 1989, p. 164). Interchangeability in the form of materialism may be used to compensate for feelings of emotional deprivation, dependency, or lowered self worth (Wachtel and Blatt 1990). In such instances, material objects may be directly substituted for human relationships that contribute insufficiently to an affected individual's self-definition.

The interchangeability model (see Figure 1) represents the relationship among subjects, objects, and self-definition. The model suggests that, in some cases, when someone cannot adequately integrate aspects of other people into his or her self-definition, then objects may be substituted, consciously or otherwise. In other words, the respective contributions of subjects and objects to the individual's continuing development may be substitutable for each other at various times.

Subjects (people) *generally* serve to help the individual feel connected to a culture, community, reference group, and family. Objects (material goods), generally help the individual fulfill what is widely regarded as a universal need for personal uniqueness within the culture (Snyder and Fromkin 1980). The interchangeability model shows double-headed arrows extending from self-definition to both subjects and objects. These arrows reflect the two-way, mutually-affecting relationship that exists between us as individuals and the subjects and objects in our lives. As Belk observes, "we may impose our identities on possessions and possessions may impose their identities on us" (1988, p. 141).

The sense of belonging that arises from the individual's relationship with subjects is akin to the concept of *Gemeinschaft* (Tonnies 1957), or mechanical solidarity (Durkheim 1893/1964). These concepts emphasize the shared meanings which produce community identity. The sense of individuality imparted largely from the individual's relationship with objects is commensurate with the concept of *Gesellschaft* (Tonnies 1957), or organic solidarity (Durkheim 1893/1964). These concepts emphasize unique experience and individual interpretation of shared meanings. In many respects, the bonds between the individual and subjects are also forms of sacred consumption, while those between the individual and objects are forms of secular consumption (Belk, Wallendorf, and Sherry 1989), although exceptions occur in both instances.

In the interchangeability model, the degree of contribution by objects and subjects to the creation and rejuvenation of self-definition is never static. In response to certain environmental demands, greater reliance may be placed on objects to help in the adaptation of one's self-definition. In other circumstances, relatively greater reliance is placed on subjects for the preservation and evolution of the sense of self. Further, objects and subjects do not simply make "non-human" and "human" contributions, respectively, to self-definition. Although the model represents a social/material duality, each may contain part of the other, and serve in the other's role at certain times. Such is the case when people are used as objects (objectification), and when objects are viewed as possessing human qualities (anthropomorphism). In other words, the lines of contribution between object and subject to self-definition may sometimes blur.

The horizontal arrow between objects and subjects at the bottom of the model represents the ability of individuals to maintain and modify their self-definition by selectively interchanging either objects or subjects in response to environmental demands. The situationally-determined interchangeability of objects and subjects in the continuing evolution of self-definition is akin to forms of mediating consumption (Hirschman 1990/1991).

A concrete example illustrates many of these points. In rural regions of post-Soviet Russia, being called an "individual" can be a form of social censure. The current economic turbulence has caused pro-collective Russian farmers to rebel against capitalistic measures. Successful, pro-capitalist farmers are described by their less prosperous, pro-collective detractors as being "individuals" who are living only for themselves. Part of the incriminating evidence of such individuality is the pro-capitalist farmers' newly-constructed, two-bedroom single family homes (Hays 1992). Such a situation exemplifies how a relative absence of material possessions tends to negate the perception of human beings as individual entities. In addition, the behavior of the pro-capitalist farmers may be interpreted as their giving stronger emphasis to the objects portion of the interchangeability model in constructing self-definitions. At the same time, their pro-collective counterparts may be viewed as placing greater emphasis on the subjects portion of the model.

EXPLAINING MATERIALISM: THE SOCIOLOGY OF INTERCHANGEABILITY

The interchangeability model prompts a number of consumption related questions about the interrelation among objects, subjects, and self-definition. What happens to self-definition when too much emphasis is placed on objects? On subjects? By suggesting that a life-enhancing self-definition results from both objects and subjects, it is assumed that sufficient resources exist for every individual to draw upon in response to emerging environmental circumstances. In some circumstances, however, objects can be in short supply, as in the crippled economies of the post-Soviet nations. In other circumstances, the availability of subjects can be insufficient, as in the African-American community's need for more black role models.

A legacy of the Industrial Revolution is the potential for an abundance of objects. In many respects, an abundance of objects has permitted the advancement of knowledge, comfort, and other forms of civilization on a scale unprecedented in history. At the same time, a wealth of objects has produced greed, addiction, pornography, and other examples of the dark side of consumption (Hirschman 1990). In identifying the phenomenon of conspicuous consumption, Veblen (1899/1979) described a deleterious aspect of emphasis on objects.

Tournier (1957) similarly described a world in which material things are substituted for people and cited an inability to communicate, relate, and connect as a cause of human objectification. Citing 19th century laws treating women as chattel, Dworkin (1981) argues that women of today are still treated as sexual objects in pornography, prostitution, and rape (Belk 1988).

Yet, modern America still socializes its children to place tremendous emphasis on the ability of objects to forge self-definition. As one example, the Milton-Bradley company targets pre-teen girls for a board game called "Mall Madness." The first player to buy a certain number of items and successfully leave the mall wins. It can be argued that the "born to shop" and "shop 'til you drop," bumper-sticker sense of self encouraged by such products may be demeaning and deleterious to young people. It is also noteworthy that the game's name — Mall Madness — overtly equates shopping and consumption with insanity. It is as if the culture is warning that an emphasis on objects, at the expense of subjects, has dysfunctional consequences. Similarly, millions of young Americans have been encouraged over the years to "go cuckoo for Cocoa Puffs." Not coincidentally, a number of time-honored American shopping themes carry similar associations with mental disease, e.g., moonlight madness sales and the various "Crazy" epithets adopted by discount retailers. The overriding theme of all of these examples is an unbalanced, even irrational, emphasis on the importance of objects in self-definition. Deteriorated human relationships and a weakened social fabric may be unintended results.

While swings in emphasis between objects and subjects in defining the individual occur more or less continuously, interchangeability swings appear to occur in whole societies at more periodic intervals. The decade of the 1980s has been widely characterized as a decade of greed in America, a decade when emphasis was clearly on the contribution of material factors in defining the national self. During the recessionary 1990s, however, the interchangeability pendulum has largely swung from objects to subjects for much of industrialized society, including Japan.

Through the late 1980s and early 1990s, Japan's postwar generations practiced unfettered "consumer one-upsmanship," fueled by the island-nation's great "bubble" economy of spiraling land and equities prices. The bubble burst, however, with the 1992 recession. A freshly sober Japan has awakened to new economic realities. "'Having ridden Japan's economic wave to the crest of excess, the material generation is suddenly growing reflective.... The civilization based on rapid consumption is over'" (Ono 1992, p. A-1). Embarrassed by the "conspicuous consumption of the 1980s: thick gold chains, tinted hair and Remy Martin by the quart," the Japanese are in the midst of a sweeping interchange from objects to subjects in a reconfiguration of national self-identity. According to one 35 year-old Japanese woman:

"Before, I was trying to provide my well-being by arming myself with products." Now, "no matter who [else] spends what kind of money, I don't care.... The crucial thing is to always be able to feel warm-hearted" (Ono 1992, p. A-1).

Popular Japanese magazines that once heralded the newest consumer fads now offer columns on strengthening romantic relationships. In the past, such publications often promoted objectification, counseling women to collect a different man for each purpose: "one with a car, another with money, one as a standby and, of course, one to get serious about." As the pendulum swings from the material to the social, these same magazines are advising women to choose just one man, "preferably the 'uncool but sincere' type" (Ono 1992, p. A-1).

In the western hemisphere, North Americans are variously characterized by marketers as returning to "family values," "cocooning," "burrowing," or a host of other terms referring to greater emphasis on the contribution of other human beings to the construction and maintenance of individual self-definition. While such a trend may be encouraging to some observers, one perspective is that — instead of re-balancing the values of the 1980s — the apparent emphasis on hearth, home, and family in the 1990s may be the latest round of person objectification. As one observer noted,

"I see people having babies as if there were a race on. You've got to have an MBA, a BMW and a baby — it's the accessory of the '90s" (Gannett 1992, p. A-10).

Many marketing practitioners of the 1990s may be offering the themes of hearth, home and family as camouflage for promotion of postmodern conspicuous consumption. Such 1980s status symbols as Waterford crystal, Mercedes-Benz, Volvo, designs by Donna Karan, the MasterCard gold card, Shearson Lehman brokers, and even Money magazine have attempted to reposition themselves in terms of 1990s family values. As noted by Lipman (1992, p. B-1), "...the theme rings especially false for the luxury goods that proudly touted themselves as symbols of conspicuous consumption just a few years back."

CONCLUSION

This paper draws heavily on symbolic interactionism to further consider the important role of material objects in individual self-definition. The establishment and maintenance of a viable sense of self results, in part, from symbolic interaction with subjects *and* objects. Where functional human relationships are lacking, people may turn to the symbolism of objects for portions of self-definition. We contend that the individual may substitute subjects and objects for each other, consciously or not, in the creation and maintenance of self-definition. "Interchangeability" is the term we give to the substitutability between subjects and objects for self-definition purposes.

Our intent is to portray interchangeability and materialism, not as negative and damaging forces motivated by greed and power, but as ways of protecting the self in a class society. In the words of Sennett and Cobb (1972, p. 171):

...the activities which keep people moving in a class society, which make them seek more money, more possessions, higher-status jobs, do not originate in a materialistic desire, or even sensuous appreciation, of things, but out of an attempt to restore a psychological deprivation that the class structure has effected in their lives. In other words, the psychological motivation instilled by a class society is to heal a doubt about the self.

Although improvement of the conceptualization and measurement of materialism is important (and indeed precursive) to theory-building, it is time to move forward and begin to construct explanations. By applying symbolic interaction to a social/material duality, consumer researchers interested in materialism have an additional perspective for further explication of why some people, but not others, emphasize material objects in their lives. Thus the interchangeability model may prove helpful in further explaining some of the complexities and apparent inconsistencies of consumption behavior in real life.

REFERENCES

Belk, Russell W. (1984), "Three Scales to Measure Constructs Related to Materialism: Reliability, Validity, and Relationships to Measures of Happiness," in *Advances in Consumer Research*, Vol. 11, ed. Thomas Kinnear, Provo, UT: Assn. for Consumer Research, 291-297.

_____ (1985), "Materialism: Trait Aspects of Living in the Material World," *J. of Consumer Research*, Vol. 12 (Dec.), 265-280.

_____ (1988), "Possessions and the Extended Self," *J. of Consumer Research*, Vol. 15 (September), 139-168.

_____, Melanie Wallendorf and John F. Sherry (1989), "The Scared and the Profane in Consumer Behavior: Theodicy on the Odyssey," *J. of Consumer Research*, Vol. 16 (June), 1-38.

Blumer, Herbert (1969), *Symbolic Interactionism: Perspective and Method*, Berkeley, CA: University of California Press.

Boorstin, Daniel J. (1973), *The Americans: The Democratic Experience,* New York: Random House, 145-148.

Braun, Ottmar L. and Robert A. Wicklund (1989), "Psychological Antecedents of Conspicuous Consumption," *J. of Economic Psychology,* 10, 161-187.

Csikszentmihalyi, Mihaly (1982), "The Symbolic Function of Possessions: Towards a Psychology of Materialism," paper presented at the 90th Annual Convention of the American Psychological Assn., Washington, D. C.,: Aug. 26, 1982.

_____ and Eugene Rochberg-Halton (1981), *The Meaning of Things: Domestic Symbols and the Self*, New York: Cambridge University Press.

D'Arcy, P. F. (1967), Asceticism (Psychology of)," in *New Catholic Encyclopedia*, Vol. 1, New York: McGraw-Hill, 941-942.

Douglas, Mary and Baron Isherwood (1979), *The World of Goods*, New York: Basic Books.

Durkheim, Emil (1893), *The Division of Labor in Society* (reprinted in 1964, Harmondsworth, New York: Free Press).

Dworkin, A. (1981), *Pornography: Men Possessing Women*, NY: Perigee.

Friedman, Monroe (1985), "The Changing Language of a Consumer Society: Brand Name Usage in Popular American Novels in the Postwar Era," *J. of Consumer Research*, V. 11 (Sept.), 927-938.

Gannett New Service (1992), "People Without Kids Seeking A Voice," *The News-Leader* (Springfield, MO), November 16, p. 10-A.

Goffman, Erving (1959), *The Presentation of Self in Everyday Life,* Garden City, NY: Doubleday Anchor.

Hays, Laurie (1992), "A Tast of Capitalism At Russian Collective Brings Chaos and Strife," *Wall Street Journal*, November 27, A-1.

Hirschman, Elizabeth C. (1990), "Secular Mortality and the Dark Side of Consumer Behavior: Or How Semiotics Saved My Life," *ACR Newsletter* (Dec.), pp. 1-6.

_____, (1990/1991), "Point of View: Sacred, Secular, and Mediating Consumption Imagery in Television Commercials," *J. of Advertising Research* (Dec./Jan.), 38-43.

Kehret-Ward, Trudy (1982), "A Strategy for Understanding the Semiology of Product Choice," paper presented at 1982 Association for Consumer Research Convention, San Francisco, CA.

Kopytoff, Igor (1986), "The Cultural Biography of Things: Commoditization as Process," in *The Social Life of Things: Commodities in Cultural Perspective*, ed. Arjun Appadurai, Cambridge, England: Cambridge University Press, 64-91.

Levy, Sidney J. (1959), "Symbols for Sale," *Harvard Business Review*, 37 (July/August), 117-124.

Lipman, Joanne (1992), "Marketers of Luxury Goods Are Turning From Self-Indulgence to Family Values," *Wall St. Journ.*, Oct 22, B-1.

Masson, J. Joussaieff (1976), "The Psychology of the Ascetic," *Journal of Asian Studies*, 35 (Aug.), 611-625.

McCarthy, E. Doyle (1984), "Toward a Sociology of the Physical World: George Herbert Mead on Physical Objects," in *Studies in Symbolic Interaction*, ed. Norman K. Denzen, Greenwich, CT: JAI, 105-121.

McCracken, Grant (1986), "Culture and Consumption: A Theoretical Account of the Structure and Movement of the Cultural Meaning of Consumer Goods," *J. of Consumer Research*, Vol. 13 (June), 71-84.

Mead, George H. (1934), *Mind, Self and Society*, Chicago: University of Chicago Press.

Mick, David Glen (1986), "Consumer Research and Semiotics: Exploring the Morphology of Signs, Symbols, and Significance," *J. of Consumer Research*, Vol. 13 (September), 196-213.

Murray, Jeff B. and Julie L. Ozanne (1991), "The Critical Imagination: Emancipatory Interests in Consumer Research," *J. of Consumer Research*, Vol. 18 (September), 129-144.

Ono, Yumiko (1992), "Recession in Japan Gives a Generation First Taste of Sobriety: Moderation and Meditation Supplant Gaudy Excess as Party Abruptly Ends: A New Trend: Individuality," *Wall St. Journ.*, December 23, p. A-1.

Richins, Marsha L. (1992), "Media Images, Materialism, and What Ought to Be: The Role of Social Comparison," Proceedings of the *Research Workshop on Materialism and Other Comsumption Orientations*, eds. F. Rudmin and M. Richins, Queen's Univ. and the Assn. for Consumer Research, Kingston, Ont., 202-206.

_____ and Scott Dawson (1992), "A Consumer Values Orientation for Materialism and Its Measurement: Scale Development and Validation," *J. of Consumer Research*, V. 19 (December), 303-316.

Rudmin, Floyd W. (1992), "Materialism and Militarism: De Tocqueville on America's Hopeless Hurry to Happiness," Proceedings of the *Research Workshop on Materialism and Other Comsumption Orientations*, eds. F. Rudmin and M. Richins, Queen's Univ. & the Assn. for Consumer Rsrch, Kingston, Ont., 110-112.

Schudson, Michael (1991), "Delectable Materialism," *The American Prospect*.

Sennett, Richard and Johathan Cobb (1973), *The Hidden Injuries of Class*, New York: Vintage Books (Random House).

Sirgy, M. Joseph (1982), "Self-Concept in Consumer Behavior: A Critical Review," *J. of Consumer Research*, 9 (Dec), 287-300.

Snyder, C. R. and Howard L. Fromkin (1980), *Uniqueness: The Human Pursuit of Difference*, New York: Plenum Press.

Solomon, Michael R.(1983), "The Role of Products as Social Stimuli: A Symbolic Interactionist Perspective," *J. of Consumer Research*, Vol. 10 (Dec.), 319-329.

Stone, G. P. (1962), "Appearance and the Self," in *Human Behavior & Social Process*, ed A. M. Rose, Boston: Houghton Mifflin, 86-118.

Tonnies, Ferdinand (1957), *Community and Society*, trans. by C. Loomis, East Lansing, MI: Michigan State University Press.

Tournier, Paul (1957), *The Meaning of Persons*, trans. by Edwin Hudson, New York: Harper & Row.

Veblen, Thorstein (1899), *The Theory of the Leisure Class*, NY: MacMillan (repr. 1979, Harmondsworth, England: Penguin.)

Wachtel, Paul L. and Sidney J. Blatt (1990), "Perceptions of Economic Neesas and of Anticipated Future Income," *J. of Economic Psychology*, 11, 403-415.

Wallendorf, Melanie and Eric J. Arnould (1988), "'My Favorite Things': A Cross-Cultural Inquiry into Object Attachment, Possessiveness, and Social Linkage," *J. of Consumer Research*, Vol. 14 (Mar.), 531-547.

Weissner, Polly (1984), "Reconsidering the Behavioral Basis for Style: A Case Study Among the Kalahari San," *J. of Archaeological Research*, 3, 190-234.

Will, George (1991), "Consumption Always Treated as Problematic," Gannett Publishing (April 28), syndicated column.

A Cross-Cultural Look at the 'Supposed to Have It' Phenomenon: The Existence of a Standard Package Based on Occupation

Cecelia Wittmayer, Dakota State University
Steve Schulz, Fort Hays State University
Robert Mittelstaedt, University of Nebraska-Lincoln

ABSTRACT

Consumers often buy products for reasons other than the product's functional performance, basing their purchase decisions instead on the symbolic or social significance of the product. In those instances, product ownership/use serves as a form of symbolic communication between consumer and observer, enabling the consumer to use the product for impression management. The idea of product ownership as impression management is closely related to research which suggests a relationship exists between occupation, social class, and consumption of what has been referred to as the standard package. This paper examines the standard package concept and suggests that variations in the standard package exist because of cultural and occupational differences. Further, it suggests that students will acquire the items in their occupational standard package in a particular and fairly predictable order.

INTRODUCTION

Consumers often buy products for reasons other than the product's functional performance, basing their purchase decisions instead on the symbolic or social significance of the product. In those instances, product ownership/use serves as a form of symbolic communication between consumer and observer, enabling the consumer to use the product for impression management (Solomon 1983). The idea of product ownership as impression management is closely related to work by Riesman and Roseborough (1955), which suggests a relationship exists between occupation, social class, and consumption of what they call the standard package. Although Riesman and Roseborough used the term to describe the possessions of American corporate executives, the existence of a standard package has also been noted in other cultures. Therefore, the purpose of this study is to examine the universality of the standard package concept and to ascertain whether variations in the standard package exist because of differences in occupation and/or culture. A brief review of the symbolic interactionist literature is presented and results of an empirical study are discussed. Data to test the hypotheses were collected from working professionals and from college seniors in corresponding majors.

STANDARD PACKAGE VARIATIONS BASED ON OCCUPATION AND/OR CULTURE

Although marketers generally assume that products are used by consumers for need satisfaction, the idea that consumption may be tied to the consumer's self-image is not exactly a revolutionary one. For example, Tucker (1954, p. 139) writes:

> There has long been an implicit concept that consumers can be defined in terms of either the products they acquire or use or in terms of the meanings products have for them or their attitudes toward products.

Symbolic interactionist theory suggests that products are used for impression management, i.e., products have symbolic meanings and product ownership/use serves as a form of symbolic communication between consumer and observer (Solomon 1983).

In general, products with strong communicative properties have high visibility in use, high variability in use, and high personalizability (Holman 1981). Unless a product has visibility in use, observers will not see its purchase, consumption, and/or disposition and the product loses its communicative qualities. Likewise, if a product lacks variability (if it is available to everyone and everyone uses it in exactly the same way), no individual differences are implied by its usage. Generally, high variability is attributed to financial or time constraints on consumption and to the consumer's ability to make small but distinct changes in the product. Finally, products have high personalizability if their use brings to mind a stereotypical image of the frequent user.

However, Solomon and Buchanan (1991) suggest that sometimes products also have symbolic interdependence—together, several products transmit a message that each product alone does not. This is consistent with Riesman and Roseborough's (1955) suggestion that a relationship exists between occupation, social class, and consumption of what they call the standard package. They speculate that a standard package of possessions exists for much of the middle class in the United States. To date, researchers have not empirically established the group of products which make up the standard package, but it is generally assumed to include socially visible products like clothes, cars, homes, furniture, and vacations. Dholakia and Levy (1987b, p. 437) refer to a similar constellation of products as the American Dream, which they define as being able "to own your home, nicely furnished and two cars; to travel and to be a member of local clubs." Further, they contend that the same American Dream exists for a broad spectrum of the American consuming public.

However, this phenomenon is not limited to the American middle class experience; the existence of a standard package has also been noted in other cultures. (See, for instance, Arnould's 1989 discussion of the standard package for natives in the Zinder Province of Niger, Bourdieu's 1984 discussion of the lifestyles of the French petite bourgeoisie, and Paroush's 1965 discussion of priority purchase patterns for Israeli households.) According to Dholakia and Levy (1987b, p. 42), each society develops a set of core products that define its consumption standard or the consumer dream. As Olshavsky and Granbois (1979) point out, ownership of the standard package may not be discretionary; instead, standard package items may be a requisite part of a culturally mandated lifestyle.

The term standard in standard package (and American in American Dream) implies that the same group of products is consistently desired and purchased by all households within a particular society or social class. However, Porter (1967) and Riesman and Roseborough (1955) have suggested that variations in this standard package may exist for different occupations and/or income levels. In a similar vein, symbolic interactionist theory suggests that, since symbolic meanings are learned through a socialization process, individuals with a common history or culture should attach the same or similar meanings to objects and/or actions although that meaning can be expected to shift for different reference groups or subcultures. Indeed, differences do seem to exist in the priority patterns or order of acquisitions for different consumer segments in the United States (Dickson, Lusch, and Wilkie 1983; McFall 1969).

The consequences of an individual's failure to adopt the culturally mandated lifestyle of his/her society are also different for different cultures. For example, collectivity and homogeneity are stressed more in Asian cultures than in western cultures. Compared to American firms, Asian firms demand a higher level of employee commitment plus absolute loyalty and conformity. When an employee doesn't conform, shame is often used as punishment (Terpstra and David 1991, pp. 47-54). In the Asian workplace, public humiliation is not uncommon and is, in fact, socially tolerated (Bond 1989, pp. 278-293). Therefore, the consequences of nonconformity are likely to be more severe in collectivist cultures than in western cultures.

This study is based on two underlying premises: 1) the concept of a standard package is universal; it exists in every culture and 2) consumers are aware of and can identify the culturally mandated standard package for their lives. However, it is unreasonable to suggest that the same standard package exists across cultures. Therefore,

H1a: Different cultural groups will identify different standard packages.

H1b: Different occupational groups will identify different standard packages.

STANDARD PACKAGE IDENTIFICATION BY STUDENTS

Riesman and Roseborough (1955) suggest that the social and organizational upward mobility of a family is made easier by the family's ability to identify subtle differences in standard packages and to adapt their current standard package to a new peer group as the family's breadwinners climb the corporate ladder. However, an individual's anxiety about appropriate and inappropriate product consumption does not begin when he/she contemplates a job promotion; it begins when he/she first imagines him/herself as part of the organization. According to Solomon (1983), an individual's confidence in his/her ability to meet role demands may determine the degree to which he/she depends on material symbols to convince others of his/her abilities.

This premise was supported by Wicklund and Gollwitzer's (1982) study of symbolic self-completion. They found that male MBA students who were least likely to succeed (based on an index of their grades, number of job interviews, and number of job offers) were more likely to try to look successful. They noted that incomplete students (those with lower grades, fewer job interviews, and fewer job offers) were more likely to wear luxury watches and carry expensive briefcases—both associated with successful employment in the business world and therefore part of the businessman's standard package.

In his discussion of product symbolism, Solomon (1983) suggests that role performance is aided when an individual possesses the material symbols or products which are associated with that role. Consequently, consumption of the right products may be less important when role knowledge is high and the consumer has mastered the repertoire of behaviors associated with a social or occupational role. On the other hand, consumption of the right products is very important when the appropriate behavior is either unknown or known only in an idealized sense, i.e., the individual has only a stereotyped view of the role and has not yet had an opportunity to rehearse or experience the appropriate behavior.

Therefore, it seems reasonable that someone who is anticipating (but has not yet achieved) membership in an occupational group will strive to identify the standard package variations that seem most acceptable to that group.

H2a: Students will accurately identify the standard package items for their occupational area.

H2b: Students in different occupational areas will identify different standard packages.

H2c: Students from different cultural backgrounds but from the same occupational area will identify different standard packages.

METHODOLOGY

To assess the components of the standard package across cultures and occupations, information was collected from Asian business professionals, American business professionals, and American public school educators. To assess the level of congruence between working professionals and students, information was also collected from Asian business administration majors, American business administration majors, and American music education majors. All the students were seniors at a major midwestern university. The Asian students were foreign students attending the university on educational visas and generally expected to return to their home countries after graduation. Likewise, the Asian business professionals were in this country temporarily, attending a semester-long management development seminar at the same university. Both the American and the Asian business professionals had worked in their fields for 5-10 years. The public school educators taught in a nearby midwestern community; all had been teaching for at least 5 years.

The products which comprise the standard package for middle-class, midwestern business professionals were established via a convenience sample of 50 business professionals from a variety of career areas (i.e., accounting, marketing and advertising, law, investment management, and corporate management). These professionals were asked to describe, using adjectives and brand names, their cars, homes, vacations, entertainment preferences, hired services, investments, etc. Their responses served as a basis for scoring the possessions described by the other two professional samples and by the three student samples. (See Appendix A for a list of the possessions described by the respondents and for an example of the 5-point coding scheme used to rate the professionals' descriptions.) Student respondents were asked to describe the possessions they thought they would own 5 to 10 years after graduation.

Chi-square goodness-of-fit tests were used to determine whether a significant difference existed between the observed (i.e., student) responses and expected (i.e., professional) responses in each product category. The Chi-square test should only be used if no more than 20% of the expected frequencies are less than 5 and no expected frequencies are less than 1 (Siegel and Castellan 1988, p. 49). Because the sample size for some of the groups was small (N = 13 for the public school teachers, for example) and therefore the expected cell frequencies were small, the 5 coding categories used to describe the American business professionals' possessions were collapsed before the Chi-square statistics were calculated, per the recommendations of Siegel and Castellan (1988, p. 49). Even with the collapsed coding scheme, the SPSSX Chi-square program did issue warnings for some of the Chi-square calculations. (Table 1).

TABLE 1
Sample Sizes

American business professionals	N = 50
Asian business professionals	N = 17
Public school teachers	N = 13
American business administration students	N = 186
Asian business administration students	N = 27
American music education students	N = 14

TABLE 2
Hypothesis 1a
Comparison of Asian Business Professionals to American Business Professionals

	Chi-Square	Probability
First Car	48.23	$p < .0005$
Second Car	27.79	$p < .0005$
Home/Apt.	42.61	$p < .0005$
Vacation	30.51	$p < .0005$
Recreation	.28	$p = .595$
Clothing	30.32	$p < .0005$
Jewelry/Watch	15.23	$p < .0005$
Briefcase/Luggage	35.28	$p < .0005$
Home Furnishings	17.69	$p < .0005$
Personal Computers	3.09	$p = .079$
Home Improvements	1.83	$p = .176$
Investments	6.03	$p = .014$
Hired Services	1.70	$p = .193$
Entertain Friends	4.65	$p = .031$
Entertain Business Associates	2.67	$p = .102$

RESULTS

According to H1a, different cultural groups should identify different standard packages. To test this hypothesis, responses from Asian business professionals were compared to the responses from American business professionals. Of the 15 product categories examined, 10 of the Chi-square statistics were statistically significant; therefore, the hypothesis was supported. The five categories which did not meet the Chi-square cutoff were recreation, personal computer, home improvements, hired services, and entertainment of business associates. (See Table 2 for the Chi-square statistics.)

According to H1b, different occupational groups should also identify different standard packages. To test this hypothesis, responses from American public school teachers were compared to the responses from American business professionals. Here, 13 of the 15 Chi-square statistics exceeded the critical value; therefore the hypothesis was supported. Only the Chi-square values for personal computers and investments were below the critical value. (See Table 3 for the Chi-square statistics.) Together, the results of these two hypothesis tests suggest that an individual's possessions are a function of either his/her culture or occupation. However, support for the remaining hypotheses is less clear-cut.

According to H2a, students should accurately identify the standard package items for their occupational area. This hypothesis was based on symbolic interactionist theory, which suggests that role performance and group acceptance are aided when an individual possesses the material symbols or products which are associated with that role (Solomon 1983). The assumption here is that students will have observed professionals in their career area and will have noted the possessions owned by these professionals. It should be noted, however, that what is predicted here is no difference which involves the acceptance of the null hypothesis, an admittedly weak test.

When the responses from American business administration students were compared to the responses from American business professionals, only two Chi-square statistics—clothing and jewelry—were below the critical value. (See Table 4 for the Chi-square statistics.) Evidently, about all these business administration students have absorbed from observing professionals in their area is how to dress appropriately for the job.

The results of the comparison of music education students to public school teachers were more encouraging. Here, seven of the 15 Chi-square statistics were below the critical value—first car, home/apartment, jewelry/watch, home furnishings, home improvements, investments, and hired services. (See Table 5 for the Chi-square statistics.) However, it should be noted that the music education students used in this project had just returned from eight weeks of practice teaching. Clearly, they'd had the opportunity to observe and absorb the lifestyle of their professional counterparts. Given this recent experience, it is therefore surprising that the Chi-square statistic for clothes was not within the acceptable range. It should also be noted that, unless the business administration students had recently participated in an internship and/or were already working at least part-time in their field, they probably had not had

TABLE 3
Hypothesis 1b
Comparison of American Public School Educators to American Business Professionals

	Chi-Square	Probability
First Car	32.42	p < .0005
Second Car	10.86	p = .001
Home/Apt.	43.87	p < .0005
Vacation	78.00	p < .0005
Recreation	36.32	p < .0005
Clothing	40.56	p < .0005
Jewelry/Watch	60.26	p < .0005
Briefcase/Luggage	61.81	p < .0005
Home Furnishings	30.21	p < .0005
Personal Computers	1.90	p = .168
Home Improvements	18.69	p < .0005
Investments	.15	p = .701
Hired Services	37.92	p < .0005
Entertain Friends	25.09	p < .0005
Entertain Business Associates	74.29	p < .0005

TABLE 4
Hypothesis 2a
Comparison of American Business Administration Students to American Business Professionals

	Chi-Square	Probability
First Car	120.06	p < .0005
Second Car	50.94	p < .0005
Home/Apt.	331.06	p < .0005
Vacation	18.67	p < .0005
Recreation	18.46	p < .0005
Clothing	.56	p = .76
Jewelry/Watch	.55	p = .76
Briefcase/Luggage	9.90	p = .007
Home Furnishings	59.33	p < .0005
Personal Computers	78.93	p < .0005
Home Improvements	32.68	p < .0005
Investments	9.44	p = .009
Hired Services	175.88	p < .0005
Entertain Friends	124.48	p < .0005
Entertain Business Associates	80.05	p < .0005

a similar opportunity for observation and instead may have based their perceptions on somewhat inaccurate information from friends, family, and/or the mass media.

Finally, responses from Asian business administration students were compared to the responses from Asian business professionals. Here, student perceptions were close to reality for 10 of the 15 product categories—second car, vacations, recreation, jewelry/watches, home furnishings, personal computers, home improvements, investments, hired services, and entertainment of business associates. (See Table 6 for the Chi-square statistics.) Without further research, it is impossible to know why Asian business students were more accurate in their perceptions than American business students, but several possible explanations suggest themselves: in general, Asian society may be more homogeneous than American society and therefore fewer differences exist across all the subgroups within that society; Asian business students may have more contact with Asian business professionals and therefore may base their perceptions on what they actually observe while American students may base their perceptions on stereotyped portrayals in the media; and/or the consequences of NOT learning the appropriate standard package may be more severe in collectivist cultures.

According to H2b, students in different occupational areas will identify different standard packages (i.e., their perceptions are not based on a universal standard package for middle-class America; instead their perceptions are based on what they know or what they think they know about their intended profession.) To test this hypothesis, the responses from American music education students were compared to the responses of American business administration students. Only two of the Chi-square statistics did not exceed the critical value—home/apartment and hired services—indicating that the students were anticipating markedly different standard

TABLE 5
Hypothesis 2a
Comparison of American Music Education Students to American Public School Educators

	Chi-Square	Probability
First Car	1.17	p = .280
Second Car	37.27	p < .0005
Home/Apt.	.01	p = .939
Vacation	9.69	p = .002
Recreation	18.75	p < .0005
Clothing	5.72	p = .017
Jewelry/Watch	1.87	p = .171
Briefcase/Luggage	9.75	p = .002
Home Furnishings	1.74	p = .187
Personal Computers	12.00	p = .001
Home Improvements	.59	p = .442
Investments	.16	p = .688
Hired Services	.35	p = .556
Entertain Friends	15.02	p < .0005
Entertain Business Associates	6.21	p = .013

TABLE 6
Hypothesis 2a
Comparison of Asian Business Administration Students to Asian Business Professionals

	Chi-Square	Probability
First Car	30.82	p < .0005
Second Car	.30	p = .583
Home/Apt.	29.10	p < .0005
Vacation	3.54	p = .06
Recreation	.02	p = .879
Clothing	4.10	p = .043
Jewelry/Watch	2.43	p = .119
Briefcase/Luggage	5.15	p = .023
Home Furnishings	1.76	p = .185
Personal Computers	.18	p = .674
Home Improvements	.74	p = .391
Investments	.19	p = .660
Hired Services	3.33	p = .068
Entertain Friends	6.22	p = .013
Entertain Business Associates	1.17	p = .28

packages. Therefore, the hypothesis was supported. (See Table 7 for the Chi-square statistics.)

Finally, H2c suggests that students from different cultural backgrounds but from the same occupational area will identify different standard packages. To test this hypothesis, responses from Asian business students were compared to the responses from American business students. Again, only two Chi-square statistics did not exceed the critical value—home improvements and hired services—indicating that the students were anticipating markedly different standard packages. Therefore, the hypothesis was supported. (See Table 8 for the Chi-square statistics.) This suggests that the Asian students formed their standard-package expectations before they came to this country. If their expectations had been shaped by American media or by contact with American business professionals or American business students, their expectations should have been closer to those of the American business students.

CONCLUSIONS AND IMPLICATIONS

Based on the results of this exploratory study, it appears as though the standard package concept is indeed a universal concept, although variations in that standard package seem to exist because of cultural and/or occupational differences. However, these results do call into question one of the underlying assumptions of this study, namely that consumers are aware of and can accurately identify the culturally mandated standard packages for their lives. Although the American music education students and the Asian business administration students were fairly accurate in their expectations/perceptions (non-significant differences in 7 of the 15 and 10 of the 15 product categories, respectively), the American business students were not (non-significant differences in only 2 of the 15 product categories). As was indicated earlier, however, the accuracy of the music education students may have been enhanced by their recent practice teaching experiences. Had the business

TABLE 7
Hypothesis 2b
Comparison of American Music Education Students to American Business Administration Students

	Chi-Square	Probability
First Car	9.76	p = .008
Second Car	14.83	p = .001
Home/Apt.	4.95	p = .084
Vacation	40.09	p < .0005
Recreation	34.59	p < .0005
Clothing	192.50	p < .0005
Jewelry/Watch	87.18	p < .0005
Briefcase/Luggage	49.40	p < .0005
Home Furnishings	31.87	p < .0005
Personal Computers	256.68	p < .0005
Home Improvements	9.04	p = .011
Investments	39.91	p < .0005
Hired Services	1.64	p = .441
Entertain Friends	413.00	p < .0005
Entertain Business Associates	33.11	p < .0005

TABLE 8
Hypothesis 2c
Comparison of Asian Business Administration Students to American Business Administration Students

	Chi-Square	Probability
First Car	17.43	p < .0005
Second Car	25.62	p < .0005
Home/Apt.	7.79	p = .020
Vacation	71.59	p < .0005
Recreation	44.47	p < .0005
Clothing	330.00	p < .0005
Jewelry/Watch	137.00	p < .0005
Briefcase/Luggage	60.80	p < .0005
Home Furnishings	29.60	p < .0005
Personal Computers	494.99	p < .0005
Home Improvements	5.57	p = .062
Investments	72.57	p < .0005
Hired Services	1.64	p = .441
Entertain Friends	295.00	p < .0005
Entertain Business Associates	55.19	p < .0005

administration students had a similar experience, their accuracy may have also improved.

Aside from the issue of accuracy/inaccuracy in expectations, however, these Chi-square statistics seem to reveal something else about the students. The values of the Chi-square statistics reflect the magnitude of the deviation of their perceptions from the reality of the business professionals. Therefore, when the Chi-square values are arranged in ascending order, they may signal an order of acquisition akin to the priority patterns discussed by Dholakia and Levy (1987a and 1987b) and McFall (1969). In his research, McFall (1969, pp. 54-55) states:

> The priority pattern concept implies that consumers tend to think of their household goods purchases in terms of sets to be acquired in a particular order over time. The acquiring of goods in accordance with a priority pattern is not simply an individual process; it is also a group phenomenon.

One reasonable conclusion that can be drawn from this research is that students will quickly purchase those items which they recognize as an integral part of their occupational standard package (as signaled by the smallest Chi-square values) but will postpone the purchase of items about which they are unsure and/or uninformed. Therefore, students (at least American business students) are likely to acquire clothes and jewelry first, briefcases and retirement plans next (probably because retirement or investment plans are generally furnished by the employer), homes and hired services far in the future. (See Table 9 for the Chi-square statistics of American business administration students arranged in ascending order.) This order also suggests that students are least knowledgeable about

TABLE 9
Ascending Order
Comparison of American Business Administration Students to American Business Professionals

	Chi-Square	Probability
Jewelry/Watch	.55	$p = .76$
Clothing	.56	$p = .76$
Investments	9.44	$p = .009$
Briefcase/Luggage	9.90	$p = .007$
Recreation	18.46	$p < .0005$
Vacation	18.67	$p < .0005$
Home Improvements	32.68	$p < .0005$
Second Car	50.94	$p < .0005$
Home Furnishings	59.33	$p < .0005$
Personal Computers	78.93	$p < .0005$
Entertain Business Associates	80.05	$p < .0005$
First Car	120.01	$p < .0005$
Entertain Friends	124.48	$p < .0005$
Hired Services	175.88	$p < .0005$
Home/Apt.	331.06	$p < .0005$

(and/or have the least experience with) purchasing homes and hiring service providers such as cleaning help, lawn services, etc. Consequently, the real value of this research may lie in the information it provides to marketers about the students' order of product acquisition. This research might also be used to shape the advertising for products in the standard package. Specifically, it points out that how-to-purchase information and/or strong product benefit information should be included in the advertising for some product categories.

REFERENCES

Arnould, Eric J. (1989), "Toward a Broadened Theory of Preference Formation and the Diffusion of Innovations: Cases from Zinder Province, Niger Republic," *Journal of Consumer Research*, 16 (September), 239-267.

Bourdieu, Peter (1984), *Distinction: A Social Critique of the Judgement of Taste*, Cambridge, MA: Harvard University Press, 169-225, 261-317.

Dholakia, Ruby Roy and Sidney J. Levy (1987a), "The Consumer Dream in the United States: Aspirations and Achievements in a Changing Environment," *Journal of Macromarketing*, 7 (Fall), 41-51.

_____ and _____ (1987b), "Effect of Recent Economic Experiences on Consumer Dreams, Goals and Behavior in the United States," *Journal of Economic Psychology*, 8, 429-444.

Dickson, Peter R., Robert F. Lusch, and William L. Wilkie (1983), "Consumer Acquisition Priorities for Home Appliances: A Replication and Re-evaluation," *Journal of Consumer Research*, 9 (March), 432-435.

Holman, Rebecca (1981), "Product Use as Communication: A Fresh Appraisal of a Venerable Topic," in *Review of Marketing*, eds. Ben M. Enis and Kenneth J. Roering, Chicago: American Marketing Association, 106-119.

McFall, John (1969), "Priority Patterns and Consumer Behavior," *Journal of Marketing*, 33 (October), 50-55.

Olshavsky, Richard W. and Donald H. Granbois (1979), "Consumer Decision Making—Fact or Fiction?" *Journal of Consumer Research*, 6 (September), 93-100.

Paroush, J. (1965), "The Order of Acquisition of Consumer Durables," *Econometrica*, 33 (January) 225-235.

Porter Jr., James N. (1967), "Consumption Patterns of Professors and Businessmen: A Pilot Study of Conspicuous Consumption and Status," *Sociological Inquiry*, 37 (Spring), 255-265.

Riesman, David and Howard Roseborough (1955), "Careers and Consumer Behavior," *Consumer Behavior*, ed. Lincoln Clark, New York: New York University Press, 2, 1-18.

Solomon, Michael R. (1983), "The Role of Products as Social Stimuli: A Symbolic Interactionism Perspective," *Journal of Consumer Research*, 10 (December), 319-329.

_____ and Bruce Buchanan (1991), "A Role-Theoretic Approach to Product Symbolism: Mapping a Consumption Constellation," *Journal of Business Research*, 22 (2, March), 95-109.

Tucker, W.T. (1954), *Foundations for a Theory of Consumer Behavior*, New York: Holt, Rinehart and Winston, 133-144.

Wicklund, Robert A. and Peter M. Gollwitzer (1982), *Symbolic Self-Completion*, Hillsdale, NJ: Lawrence Erlbaum Associates, 153-155.

APPENDIX A
Standard Package Coding for American Business Professionals' First Car
(Based on Kiplinger's 1993 New Car Buyer's Guide)

Cars valued over $40,000 = Code 5
Includes Infiniti, Jaguar, Porsche

Cars valued between $30,000—$40,000 = Code 4
Includes Audi, BMW, Cadillac, Lexus, Lincoln, Mercedes Benz, Saab

Cars valued between $20,000—$30,000 = Code 3
Includes Accura Legend, Buick LeSabre/Park Avenue, Chrysler New Yorker/Imperial, Ford Crown Victoria, Honda Accord, Mazda 929, Mercury Marquis, Nissan Maxima, Oldsmobile Cutlass/98, Pontiac Bonneville, Subaru Legacy, Volvo

Also includes Jeep Cherokee, Ford Explorer

Cars valued between $15,000—$20,000 = Code 2
Includes Accura Integra, Buick Century/Regal/Skylark, Chevrolet Cavalier/Lumina, Chrysler LaBaron, Dodge Dynasty, Ford Mustang/Taurus, Honda Prelude, Infiniti, Mazda 626/Miata, Mercury Cougar/Sable, Nissan Altima, Oldsmobile Achieva/Cutlass, Pontiac Grand Prix, Subaru Legend, Toyota Camry/Celica/MR2/Corolla, Volkswagon Cabriolet

Also includes mini-vans like Dodge Caravan, Chevrolet Blazer, Izuzu and most pickups

Cars valued under $15,000 = Code 1
Includes Chevrolet Cavalier/Geo, Dodge Shadow/Colt, Ford Escort/Festiva, Honda Civic, Hyundai, Plymouth Sundance, Pontiac LeMans/Sunbird, Saturn, Toyota Tercel, Volkswagon Fox

Standard Package Identification
Professional Questionnaire

Using adjectives or brand names whenever possible, please describe the possessions/lifestyle of a typical Japanese business professional. If you don't think a category is applicable, write Not Applicable on the blank.

First Car _____

Second Car _____

Apartment/Home _____

Vacations _____

Recreation _____

Clothing _____

Jewelry/Watch _____

Luggage/Briefcase _____

Home Furnishings _____

Personal Computer _____

Home Improvements _____

Investments _____

Hired Services _____

Entertainment with friends _____

Entertain business associates _____

Negotiation: An Interdisciplinary Approach
Rami Zwick, University of Pittsburgh
Harish Sujan, Penn State University

Negotiated exchanges occur frequently not only in business markets but also in consumer markets. In consumer markets the trend is for greater negotiation activity. Product categories such as airline tickets, hotel rooms, and interest rates, that used to be fixed in price, are now negotiable. Despite the real-world importance the consumer behavior literature includes very little on negotiation and the research that has been published is relatively narrow in its theoretical scope. The rich arrays of theoretical paradigms that exist for the study of bargaining and negotiation, for example in behavioral decision theory, economics, social cognition, motivation, and management science research, have scarcely been tapped. A step towards remedying this vacuum was taken through this special topic's session.

The first presentation titled "An Analysis of Team Versus Solo Negotiations," based on work done by Leigh L. Thompson, University of Washington, Susan E. Brodt, University of Virginia, and Erika Peterson, University of Washington, was presented by Susan Brodt. Teams, two or more people working together to achieve a common goal, while negotiating with solo opponents were found to be remarkably effective in increasing the size of the total amount of resources to be divided. However, they were not able to claim a significantly larger share of these resources.

The second presentation titled "Raising Expectations for Success in Future Negotiations: The Influence of Optimism and Positive Mood," based on work done by Harish Sujan, Penn State University, Timothy R. Graeff, Middle Tennessee State University, and Rami Zwick, University of Pittsburgh, was presented by Harish Sujan. Optimists were found to fulfill their expectations for success through a more prosocial route than pessimists. Optimists were also found to be more receptive to a positive mood state than pessimists; the mood caused them to increase their expectations for success.

The third presentation titled "The Negotiation Process: The Role of Agenda Setting, Power, and Expectations for Future Interactions," based on work done by David Brinberg, Virginia Tech, and Shanker Ganesan, S.U.N.Y. Albany, was presented by Shanker Ganesan. The effects of power imbalance, expectations for future interactions and agenda (issue by issue versus multiple issues at the same time) on personal and joint outcomes were reported. The mediating effects of specific negotiation behaviors, aggression, compromise and problem-solving, were also reported.

The final presentation titled "An Empirical Investigation of the Expectation of Future Bargaining Interaction on Process and Outcome Efficiency," based on work done by P.V. (Sundar) Balakrishnan and Charles Patton, Ohio State University, was presented by Sundar Balakrishnan. A new methodology for measuring the process and outcome efficiency of negotiations was first presented. Then the effect of expectations of future interactions on these efficiencies was examined. Lastly, the value of this examination for aiding decisions on sequential versus simultaneous negotiation agendas was discussed.

The session was chaired by Kim Corfman.

Session Summary
Memory, Product Familiarity, and Categorization Influences on the Composition of Consideration Sets

Kalpesh Kaushik Desai, University of Texas at Austin
Wayne D. Hoyer, University of Texas at Austin

The concept of consideration sets is important to marketers because unless the brand (or product) is included in the consideration set, it is unlikely to be chosen by the consumer and since the brands in the consideration set are perceived by consumers as "substitutable," the composition of the consideration set reflects a more precise picture of the nature of competition. This special session deliberated on issues related to the nature of consideration sets by examining how consumers consider certain products depending on the type of product category, the extent of their familiarity with the category, and the "effectiveness" of advertising.

Nedungadi (the chair) started the session by providing a framework which will help researchers to approach this topic from different perspectives. The first paper by Desai and Hoyer examined the influence of the task factor, category breadth i.e, the number of distinct types or variety of brands available in a category and product familiarity, an individual difference factor on the nature of consideration sets. The nature of consideration sets is characterized by (1) the *size* (number of brands in the set), (2) the *variety* (how different the brands in the consideration sets are), (3) the *preference dispersion* (is it concentrated in favor of one or two brands or dispersed equally among all the brands in the set ?), and (4) the *number of reasons* (product benefits, features, and attributes) used by consumer to form the consideration set. The study was conducted in the context of consumer durables (telephones and watches) and consumables (crackers and pretzels). The results showed that category breadth influenced the nature of consideration sets. However, there were no effects of product familiarity and any interaction effects of category breadth and product familiarity. The results indicate that in the growth phase of the product life cycle (when the category breadth is relatively high), it should be easier for a brand to enter the consideration set since consumers' consideration sets in such a stage (main effect of category breadth) is characterized by larger size (willing to consider more brands), greater variety (willing to consider brands of different types), more equal preference dispersion (hence the per brand preference is low). However, the use of a greater number of reasons by consumers makes it difficult for a brand to enter a consideration set in the growth stage since the brand has to perform well on a greater number of "factors" (reasons).

The second paper by Johnson and Lehmann examined the proposition that as consumer experience grows (as when moving from brands to categories), consideration sets become larger through the assimilation of relatively atypical alternatives into a set of more prototypical alternatives. These predictions were tested in the context of consumer nondurables, both at the brand level (soft drinks and candy bars) and category level (beverages, snacks, and lunch products). The results confirmed the proposition of the authors. One other interesting finding was that while set growth is reflected primarily by an increase in set size for soft drinks, the growth for beverages is reflected primarily by the inclusion of a wider range of typical to atypical alternatives. The results indicate that different models for predicting choice may be appropriate at different levels of experience.

The third paper by Holden and Hamzoui reported the findings of a field test that examined: (1) the hypothesis that brand consideration resulting from advertising is conditioned on the cues present in the ads, and on the presence of those same cues at retrieval, and (2) whether there was a relationship between brand awareness (consideration) and the "effectiveness" (recall) measures of advertising. Ads of an existing restaurant (Leonardo's) with the motives of "healthy" and "different" were printed in consecutive weeks (1 insertion a week) in a students' daily newspaper. A week later, in a short intercept survey conducted on campus, subjects tried to retrieve *Leonardo's* with three different cues—"restaurants," "healthy" restaurants," and "different" restaurants (a between subjects factor). Subjects' recall of restaurant *ads* from the newspaper, prompted recall of Leonardo's ad and "proved" recall of Leonardo's ad (provision of details) were then measured. The results revealed that though all the ad recall measures were above the baseline levels, there was no overall influence of advertising, nor any evidence of an effect in the matched ad/cue condition on brand recall (consideration). These results indicate that conceptually, the influence of an ad on brand awareness (unprompted by reference to the ad) is different from brand awareness cued by reference to the ad. The latter is labeled as ad awareness not brand awareness.

S. Ratneshwar (the discussant) brought his expertise in memory, information processing and product strategy to the area of consideration sets. He talked about the possible reasons for the ad being "ineffective" in Holden and Hamzoui paper and why the "category breadth" increases in the Desai and Hoyer paper. He concluded by highlighting the implications of these factors on nature of consideration sets.

Sequential Phases of Judgment and the Value Representation of Product Alternatives

James R. Bailey, Rutgers University
Robert S. Billings, Ohio State University

ABSTRACT

Consumer decisions are presumably driven by stable preferences or attitudes (i.e., value representations), but recent advances call this assumption into question. Because research from a variety of literatures suggests that such values change when processing is thorough and deliberative, this study posits a three-phase process by which *judgment* will influence attribute importance and feature desirability differently than *choice*. Results replicated previous research regarding decision process, and documented bi-directional and polarized change in subjects' value representations of alternatives under judgment, but not under choice.

INTRODUCTION

Consumers presumably possess an underlying constellation of attitudes or preferences that guide judgment of and choice between product alternatives that includes at least two key evaluative components: the *importance* attached to attributes (e.g., the price of an automobile) and the desirability attached to *features* an attribute can assume (e.g., the specific price of $15,000). Both components are implicated in models of decision making. For example, conjunctive and disjunctive models assume feature desirability is compared to a predetermined standard. The lexicographic model posits that alternatives are first compared on the most important attribute. Similarly, the elimination-by-aspects model holds that attributes are weighted according to their importance to determine the order of examination, and then specific features are compared to predetermined minimum criteria. Compensatory models, whether additive or multiplicative, assert that feature desirability is compared within alternatives.

All of these models assume that attribute importance and feature desirability (referred to herein as values or value representations) are activated from memory and applied to alternatives during processing. However, because traditional decision research has emphasized information integration not representation (see Hastie 1991), we know little about the factors that shape such values. The emerging perspective is that they are not stable, but rather are constructed by, among other things, task factors of the decision problem (see Payne, Bettman and Johnson 1992 for a review). One task factor that has been implicated in the malleability of values is response mode.

Response mode effects are strong and pervasive in decision making. One well-replicated effect involves preference reversals as a function of bidding on versus stating a preference for gambles. Another involves differential weighting of predominant attributes as a function preference assessment (i.e., matching or choice; see Tversky, Sattath and Slovic 1988 for a review of both effects). In addition to *outcome*, response mode also affects decision *process*. For example, Schkade and Johnson (1989) demonstrated that response mode influenced the time taken to render decisions, the pattern of information search, and the extent to which alternatives are directly compared.

Although numerous response modes are possible, in multiattribute decisions like those faced most often by consumers, the modes of *judgment* (i.e., the explicit evaluation of alternatives) versus *choice* (i.e., the selection of one alternative from many) have received the most attention. Using an information display board, Billings and Scherer (1988) showed that judgment led to more thorough, less variable, and more interdimensional information acquisition patterns than choice. Controlling for information acquisition and time, Bailey, Billings and Strube (1989) found that judgment led to superior recall of product alternatives when compared to choice.

Several arguments suggest that precisely because of these differences in processing, value representations change under judgment, but not under choice. The following section reviews these arguments by examining the judgmental process in relation to research on attitude change, impression formation, and information integration.

SEQUENTIAL PHASES OF JUDGMENT

What is of primary interest is the nature and degree of value change instigated by the processes involved with judgment versus choice. Understanding this change is predicated on recognizing that judgment is not uniform, but rather entails a sequence of phases, each of which alters values accordingly. Based on literature in this tradition, the sequence can be delineated into three interrelated phases—activation, evaluation, and confirmation—each with its own unique effect.

Activation

Logically, the first cognitive act of decision makers when they become aware of a domain of objects to be judged is to *activate* the relevant constellation of values. However, this is a memory-based process and as such is not comprehensive (Pennington and Hastie, 1986). It stands to reason that the nature of decision tasks would influence recall differentially.

Biased recall. Direct support for the position that the activation of values is less than complete comes from research on the attitute-behavior relationship. Wilson, Dunn, Kraft, and Lisle (1989) reasoned and demonstrated that the lack of attitude-behavior consistency found in some research is due to attitude change caused by processing *reasons* as opposed to *feelings*. Specifically, the more thorough evaluation induced by focusing on reasons led to recalling a biased or incomplete set which was adopted as the new attitude, thereby accounting for the discrepancy between attitudes and behavior. The resulting change was shown to be bidirectional, as some change was positive, some negative.

Because the thorough processing cited by Wilson et al. (1989) parallels that evoked by judgment, it is reasonable to expect biased recall under judgment. However, choice also requires that existing values be activated, and is therefore susceptible to biased recall as well. Nevertheless, there are other potential sources of value change in the judgment process, especially in the evaluation phase.

Evaluation

The partial activation of values should be updated in the next phase, *evaluation*, as decision makers encounter information that reminds them of their original representation. Simultaneously, though, further alterations would occur as trade-offs between attributes and features are considered and previously unknown information is integrated.

Compensatory strategies. One of the central differences between judgment and choice is that the former triggers greater use of compensatory strategies than the latter. Recognizing and employing trade-offs between features may cause decision makers to reevaluate the desirability attached to these features or the importance attached to the relevant attributes. For example, if a decision maker allows the low price of an automobile to compensate for poor gas mileage, the importance of price may increase, whereas the importance of gas mileage may decrease. Similarly, poor gas mileage may become less undesirable, and low price may become more desirable. Overall, the resulting change would be bidirectional, as some trade-offs would lead to positive change and others to negative change.

On the other hand, choice leads to noncompensatory deliberation that proceeds in service of identifying the alternative most harmonious with the initial representation (Tversky 1972). Hence, trade-offs are not emphasized and value representations are less likely to be reevaluated.

Impression formation. Related to a compensation-based explanation is one that concerns the *manner* in which information is processed under judgment versus choice. Judgment requires the formation of overall evaluations of each alternative, where information regarding specific attributes must be combined into a coherent whole. This process is not fundamentally different than that described in research on impression formation. Fiske and Neuberg (1990) have proposed a continuum model where the primary process is *category-based*, which is easy to execute and relies on general distinctions. Category impressions will persist unless the perceiver is motivated to reevaluate them. If so motivated, a more thorough, *attribute-based* process is engaged, where existing impressions will change as they become more individuating. Once again, the resulting change would not be uniformly more positive or negative, but rather some of both (i.e., bidirectional), depending on the individual's perception of the information.

The extension to choice and judgment in a decision situation is straightforward. Choice is more of a category-based process in that it activates but does not reevaluate existing representations, whereas judgment is more attribute-based because existing values are activated and further reevaluated, and new information is integrated.

Confirmation

The third phase—*confirmation*—occurs after the judgment of all alternatives are formed, and the decision maker reviews the value representations employed in the process. The motivation to assess whether judgmental designations reflect underlying value representations arises both from consistency strivings (cf. Festinger 1959) and a desire to avoid post-decisional regret (Janis and Mann, 1977).

Self-generated cognitions. An extensive research program by Tesser (see 1978 for a review) has found that instructing subjects to reflect on their attitudes causes polarization; positive attitudes become more positive, negative attitudes become more negative. The mechanisms implicated in the polarization process include: (a) the generation of beliefs that are consistent with existing cognitions and attitudes, (b) the failure to consider cognitions inconsistent with existing attitudes, and (c) the reinterpretation of ambiguous cognitions about the attitude.

The polarization dynamic is part cognitive and part motivational in that it reaffirms the decision and relieves the decision maker of any anxiety. This strongly resembles the well-documented bolstering effect in choice contexts (Janis and Mann 1976). However, under choice bolstering occurs predominately between chosen and non-chosen alternatives. In contrast, under judgment each alternative is evaluated, and therefore polarization should occur for all alternatives

SUMMARY AND HYPOTHESES

Research from a variety of disciplines support the notion that deliberative processing has a destabilizing effect on values, attitudes, beliefs, or preferences. Therefore, this study predicted that judgment will lead to more thorough processing than does choice and a concomitant change in value representations. Consistent with previous research on decision process (measured by information search on an information display board; IDB), three hypotheses follow:

Hypothesis 1a. Judgment will lead to more information searched than choice.
Hypothesis 1b. Judgment will lead to less variable patterns of information search than choice.
Hypothesis 1c. Judgment will lead to more interdimensional patterns of information search than choice.

This portion of the study served mainly to replicate Billings and Scherer (1988) with consumer-oriented decision stimuli, and is necessary to document the processes purported to influence value representations.

Change in value representations were measured for information displayed on the IDB with pretest and posttest questionnaires. Two hypotheses follow:

Hypothesis 2a. Judgment will lead to more bidirectional change in value representations than choice.
Hypothesis 2b. Judgment will lead to more polarized change in value representations than choice.

METHODS

Subjects and Procedure

Subjects were 33 female and 31 male undergraduates who received extra course credit for participating in a consumer study on automobiles. All subjects were screened for having been involved in an automobile purchase, and completed the pretest questionnaire regarding attribute importance and feature desirability for automobile alternatives.

Upon arriving at the laboratory one week later, subjects were introduced to a practice IDB, given explanations, and allowed to practice. They were then introduced to the test IDB and instructions were repeated. Experimenters then provided two statements designed to manipulate response mode. *Choice* was manipulated by instructing subjects to choose one of the eight automobile alternatives. *Judgment* was manipulated by instructing subjects to judge each of the alternatives on a 7-point scale ranging from *extremely positive* (1) to *extremely negative* (7). No time constraints were placed on the subjects, and they were told to examine as much of the information as they liked. These instructions were identical to the ones used by Billings and Scherer (1988). Following the completion of the task, the posttest questionnaire was administered, and subjects were debriefed.

Materials

The IDB consisted of eight used automobile alternatives listed vertically down the left side, and six attributes listed horizontally across the top of the board. The attributes and the features they could take on were as follows: (a) make: Chrysler, Volkswagen, Ford, Chevrolet, Toyota, Honda, Nissan, Subaru; (b) type: sports, compact, mid-sized, full-sized; (c) mileage: 0-1,000, 1,000-10,000, 10,000-25,000, 25,000-50,000; (d) price: $2,500-5,000, $5,000-7,5000, $7,500-10,000, $10,000-above; (e) features: stereo system, digital display instruments, air conditioning, sun-roof; and (f) color: red, blue, black, brown, green, white, orange, silver. Each feature under type, mileage, price and features was presented twice to cover all alternatives.

TABLE 1
Means and Standard Deviations for Decision Process Variables

Process Variables	Choice	Judgment
Amount		
M	24.521	35.932**
SD	8.473	9.471
Variability		
M	3.324	1.593**
SD	1.796	2.122
Search Pattern		
M	-.001	.026
SD	.454	.579

NOTE: **$p<.001$; For Search Pattern, positive values denote interdimensional patterns and negative values denote intradimensional patterns.

TABLE 2
Means and Standard Deviations for Value Change Variables

Value Change Variables	Choice	Judgment
Polarization		
M	.177	.261*
SD	.112	.175
Bidirectional Change		
M	.768	1.51**
SD	.274	.72

NOTE: * $p<.05$; ** $p<.001$

The pretest and posttest questionnaires were identical and consisted of 38 items (6 attributes and 32 features) responded to on 7-point scales. Attributes were rated on importance, with the endpoints being *extremely unimportant* (1) and *extremely important* (7). Features were rated on desirability using a scale from *extremely undesirable* (1) to *extremely desirable* (7). Filler items were present so that the questionnaire would appear comprehensive and realistic.

RESULTS

Decision Process

Analysis of variance indicated significant effects for response mode manipulations on amount of information search, $F(1, 62)=24.97$, $p<.001$, and variability of information search, $F(1, 62)=11.97$, $p<.001$, but not search pattern, $F(1, 62)=.04$. Inspection of Table 1 indicates that compared to choice, judgment led to more information being disclosed and a less variable search. Though not significant, the search pattern variable was in the expected direction.

A second analysis examined differences in search pattern by treating the first and second halves of the total moves as a repeated measures design. This within-trial analysis revealed no difference by condition ($F[1, 62]=.30$), but across conditions, the search pattern for the first half was significantly more intradimensional ($M= -.398$) than the second half ($M= .123$; $F[1, 62]=101.34$, $p<.001$).

Attribute Importance and Feature Desirability Change

Bidirectional. Bidirectional change was measured by computing the average absolute amount of change in attribute importance and adding it to the average absolute amount of change in feature desirability. Analyses indicated significant effects for response mode, $F(1, 62)=22.78$, $p<.001$. As predicted subjects in the judgment condition altered their value representations more than did subjects in the choice condition (see Table 2).

Polarization. Polarization was measured by the amount of change that resulted when subjects shifted importance and desirability ratings to a more extreme position (either more negative or more positive) from pretest to posttest. Analysis showed a significant effect for response mode ($F[1, 62]=5.15$, $p< .05$), where polarization occurred more in the judgment condition than in the choice condition.

Additional Analysis

The central logic of this paper is that value representations are influenced by thoroughness of information processing. If thoroughness of processing and information search are equivalent, however, then amount of information search should influence attribute importance and feature desirability regardless of response mode condition. Conversely, if the two are not equivalent, then amount of information search should have no impact beyond that of response mode. Finally, information search may relate to depth of processing differently in the two response mode conditions, suggesting an interaction.

To examine these questions, a regression analysis was conducted including amount of information, response mode, and the interaction, and is interpreted in the same manner as a traditional ANOVA. The F-ratios for the effect of response mode on these indexes were, of course, identical to the ones reported previously. Analysis indicated no effect for amount of information ($F[2, 61]=.75$) or the interaction ($F[3, 60]=.66$) for polarization. Further, there was no effect of amount of information on bidirectional change ($F[2, 61]=.50$). However, the effect of the interaction on bidirectional change was only marginally nonsignificant ($F[3, 60]=3.09, p=.08$). This suggests that amount of information search was of little consequence under choice, whereas under judgment it is positively related to bidirectional change.

DISCUSSION

The central hypotheses of this paper were that response mode affects the value representation of decision alternatives as well as decision process. This study replicated previous results regarding decision process, and further demonstrated that the values attached to product alternatives change under judgment but not under choice.

These decision process results replicate Billings and Scherer (1988) regarding amount and variability of information searched, but not search pattern. This lack of effect was probably due to the larger subject pool employed by Billings and Scherer, where 104 subjects completed eight boards each. However, the current experiment did find that regardless of response mode condition, subjects shifted from intra to interdimensional search patterns. By using consumer products as decision stimuli, this study provides convergent validity for the effect of response mode on decision process.

The most important finding of this paper relates to the change of value representations under judgment but not under choice. The three-phase model of judgment proposed to account for this change is in need of further investigation, but it does possess certain empirical and theoretical advantages. First, because the model is phased, it is testable. For example, judgment and choice both require activation of existing values which results in biased recall and consequently bidirectional value change. However, because the evaluation implicated in judgment is much more pronounced than that of choice, after the decision making process is initiated the two should diverge. Second, the confirmation phase acknowledges the conflictual nature of judgment. Choice between alternatives has long been recognized as inherently conflictual (Janis and Mann 1977), but research on judgmental conflict has focused on resolution within alternatives through compensatory strategies. The current model addresses within alternative conflict (evaluation), but more importantly acknowledges between alternative conflict (confirmation) in judgment. Judgment requires explicit evaluations of alternatives, thereby stating that some alternatives are *better* than others. The polarization that accompanies the confirmation phase, then, resembles bolstering in that it reaffirms the representations used to render judgments. Whether intended or not, judgments are recommendations for choice and are not devoid of conflict. Third and most important, the model addresses concerns over the static nature of research on accessing, evaluating and resolving information in judgment (Einhorn and Hogarth 1981). This interpretation assumes that decision makers enter decision situations with a constellation of relevant values, and postulates a dynamic process by which decision makers access those values, consider information, and resolve their judgments. In this way, the three-phase model incorporates and compliments research in the information integration tradition.

A related finding is that bidirectional change is associated with increased information search under judgment but not under choice. Although not statistically significant, the general pattern is worth interpreting. This finding is consistent with a multi-phase model of judgment, as more information search means more evaluation, which equates to more change. In contrast, more information search under choice does not mean more evaluation. Rather, it may simply mean that more information was required to identify an appropriate alternative, or to rule out rival ones (Tversky 1972). Hence, even when judgment and choice are similar in terms of information search, they do not influence value representations similarly. Judgment and choice appear to express fundamentally different purposes to the decision maker, which in turn are manifested in the consideration and value representation of decision alternatives.

Implications and Future Directions

Marketing efforts have been largely concerned with changing consumer attitudes or preferences through persuasion and that once changed, these values will extrapolate to consumer decisions. However, the current data suggest that the relationship between values and the actual decision is moderated by the manner in which the decision is made. Specifically, predecisional preferences should predict decisions under conditions where the underlying value representations remain stable (e.g., choice), but the relationship may diminish when conditions promote reevaluation (e.g., judgment).

Various research questions emerge from these findings. If the thorough decision process evoked by judgment accounts for change in value representations, do other factors that evoke thorough decision process also result in value change? To the extent that factors like importance, personal relevance or accountability encourage judgment-like processing, value change should occur (although the type of change should vary according to type of processing evoked). In general, any circumstances that influence the purpose of decision making may also influence the structure of value representation.

Of course, this effort is not without limitations. For example, the model implies choice evokes deliberation similar to yet less-involved than that of judgment. However, in this study choice served mainly as a comparison condition. Further, the three phases—activation, evaluation, and confirmation—while intuitively appealing, are inferred only by outcome measures. Future research may want to employ thought-listing or verbal protocol techniques for corroborative evidence.

CONCLUSION

As decision makers, consumers bring complex structures of values to any purchase decision, and are moved by individual proclivity and task factors to process the relevant information in any number of ways. Thus far, research has assumed that consumers are untouched by the process used to arrive at decisions. This paper contends that consumers are influenced by the path they take to arrive at decisions, and one manifestation of that influence is a change in value representations.

REFERENCES

Bailey, James. R., Robert S. Billings and Michael J. Strube (1989), "The effects of response mode on the organization of memory," paper presented at the 97th meeting of the American Psychological Association, New Orleans, LA.

Billings, Robert S. and Lisa L. Scherer (1988), "The effects of response mode and importance on decision making strategies: Judgment versus choice." *Organizational Behavior and Human Decision Processes*, 41, 1-19.

Einhorn, Hillel. J. and Robin M. Hogarth (1981), "Behavioral decision theory: Processes of judgment and choice," *Annual Review of Psychology*, 32, 52-88.

Festinger, Leon (1957), *A theory of cognitive dissonance*, Standford: Standford University Press.

Fiske, Susan. T. and S. L. Neuberg (1990), "A continuum of impression formation, from category-based to individuating processes: Influences of information and motivation on attention and interpretation," in *Advances in Experimental Social Psychology*, Vol. 23, ed. Russel Fazio, New York: Academic Press.

Hastie, Reid (1991), "A review from a high place: The field of judgment and decision making as revealed in its current textbooks," *Psychological Science*, 2, 135-138.

_____ and Park, Bernadette (1986), "The relationship between memory and judgment depends on whether the judgment task is memory-based or on-line," *Psychological Review*, 93, 258-268.

Janis, Irving. L. and Leon Mann (1977), *Decision Making: A psychological analysis of conflict, choice and commitment*, New York: Free Press

Payne, John. W., James R. Bettman and Eric J. Johnson (1992), "Behavioral decision research: A constructive processing perspective," *Annual Review of Psychology*, 43, 87-131.

Schkade, David. A. and Eric J. Johnson (1989), "Cognitive processes in preference reversals," *Organizational Behavior and Human Decision Processes*, 44, 203-231.

Tesser, Abraham (1978), "Self-generated attitude change", in *Advances in Experimental Social Psychology*, Vol. 11, ed. L. Berkowitz, New York: Academic Press.

Tversky, Amos (1972), "Elimination by aspects: A theory of choice," *Psychological Review*, 79, 281-299.

_____ , Shmuel. Sattath and Paul Slovic (1988), "Contingent weighting in judgment and choice," *Psychological Review*, 95, 371-384.

Wilson, Timothy D., Dana. S. Dunn, Dolores. Kraft and Douglas. J. Lisle (1989), "Introspection, attitude change, and attitude-behavior consistency: The disruptive effects of explaining why we feel the way we do," in *Advances in Experimental Social Psychology*, Vol. 22, ed. L. Berkowitz, New York: Academic Press.

Incorporating Perceptions of Financial Control in Purchase Prediction: An Empirical Examination of the Theory of Planned Behavior

Arti Sahni, University of Cincinnati

ABSTRACT

While consumer researchers have recognized that financial control over purchase obviously has an impact on purchase, more attention has been devoted to attitude and subjective norms as antecedents of purchase to the neglect of financial capability. The Theory of Reasoned Action has been modified by Ajzen to predict goals, i.e., behaviors that are not completely under a person's control. This modified theory has been termed the Theory of Planned Behavior. It provides a natural framework for explicit consideration of the facilitating and constraining effects of financial capability. This paper adapts and operationalizes the central construct of this modified theory, 'perceived behavioral control', as 'perceived financial control', and offers an initial test of the Theory of Planned Behavior in a consumer behavior context. Hypotheses consider the differential role played by perceived financial control in predicting purchase of an inexpensive and a relatively-expensive product. The results support the Theory of Planned Behavior and highlight the importance of *explicitly* including financial capability when predicting purchase.

Researchers in diverse fields have been interested in predicting human behavior. A theory that has provided useful direction and generated considerable research is the Theory of Reasoned Action (Ajzen and Fishbein 1980; Fishbein and Ajzen 1975). The Theory of Reasoned Action has received substantial empirical support in consumer and social psychology (Sheppard, Hartwick, and Warshaw 1988).

Recently, however, researchers have recognized the limits of the Theory of Reasoned Action. For example, Bagozzi and Warshaw (1990) draw a distinction between goals and behaviors and point out that the Theory of Reasoned Action (henceforth TRA), as its name implies, is concerned with the prediction of 'behaviors' and not goals. They say, "the key assumptions underlying theories of reasoned behaviors are (1) that action is preceded by a deliberative process culminating in a conscious decision to act and (2) that, if the individual tries to act, no impediments are likely to stand in the way, such as ability limitations, lack of money, environmental contingencies, and unconscious habits. Behaviors subject to such impediments (e.g., purchasing a new house, hiring a top lawyer, stopping smoking) may be considered goals" (Bagozzi and Warshaw 1990, page 127). Thus, a major assumption of the TRA is that the behavior being predicted is under the person's complete volitional control.

While the merit of the TRA lies in its parsimonious representation of complex human decision making, the same can also be its drawback. With the increasing interest in goals versus outcomes, this parsimonious nature proves to be a constraining factor. Specifically, the assumption that the behavior being predicted is under complete volitional control is unrealistic, since most behaviors, even mundane ones, pose problems of behavioral control (Ajzen 1985; Ajzen and Madden 1986).

Purchase behavior has been examined frequently in the TRA framework (e.g., Bonfield 1974; Fishbein and Ajzen 1980; Miniard, Obermiller, and Page 1982; Ryan 1982; Warshaw 1980). However, purchase is often only partially under a person's volitional control because of financial constraints. As Sheppard, Hartwick and Warshaw (1988) suggest, "a variety of consumer activities involve limits on the consumer's ability to perform a given intended action or to achieve a certain outcome. Examples include intentions to purchase expensive items (for which the necessary resources may not be available)" (p. 326). Indeed, predicting purchase of many expensive products can be conceived of as a problem of predicting a goal, and not a behavior.

Recently, there have been attempts by various researchers to modify the TRA to allow for prediction of goals (Ajzen 1985, 1991; Bagozzi 1990; Bagozzi and Warshaw 1990; Warshaw and Davis 1984, 1985; Warshaw, Sheppard, and Hartwick, forthcoming). One direct extension of the TRA is the Theory of Planned Behavior (henceforth TPB, Ajzen 1985, 1991), which relaxes the assumption of complete volitional control. The TPB provides a viable framework for investigating situations where consumers may have only limited financial control over their purchases.

This paper has two related purposes. The first is to conduct an empirical test of the TPB in a consumer behavior context. The second involves adapting and operationalizing the TPB to make it more relevant to the needs of consumer research. This operationalization explicitly considers the role of financial capability in predicting purchase—a factor that has been recognized but nevertheless neglected by consumer psychologists.

THE THEORY OF PLANNED BEHAVIOR

According to the TRA, whether a person performs a behavior depends immediately upon his or her intention. Intention in turn is determined by two factors—attitudes and subjective norms. The constructs specified in the TRA are motivational in nature. For example, the stronger the intention to perform a behavior, the more likely it is that the person will try harder to achieve it. But the performance of many behaviors depends not only on motivation but also on non-motivational factors like the person's ability to actually perform the behavior. Various researchers have suggested that notions of ability and behavioral control be included in models that attempt to predict human behavior (e.g., Ajzen 1985; Kuhl 1985; Liska 1984; Sarver 1983; Triandis 1977).

According to Ajzen's TPB, whenever control over a behavior is not complete, intentions will not be sufficient as the sole predictor of behavior. The TPB features a construct called 'perceived behavioral control' to capture non-motivational factors like ability, availability of resources, co-operation of others, environmental contingencies, etc., that may be required in addition to intention in predicting behavior. Perceived behavioral control is defined as "the person's belief as to how difficult or easy performance of the behavior is likely to be—and beliefs about resources and opportunities may be viewed as underlying perceived behavioral control" (Ajzen and Madden 1986, page 457). Thus, if a person believes she/he possesses the required resources and expects few impediments in reaching the goal, the person perceives greater control over the behavior.

Two versions of the TPB have been offered (see Figure 1). According to version 1, perceived behavioral control is an independent predictor of intention.

This suggests that, even if one has a positive attitude towards the behavior and important others would approve of it, one may not form strong intentions to perform the behavior if perceived control is lacking. This version assumes that the effect of perceived behavioral control on behavior is completely mediated by intention, making intention the sole direct antecedent of behavior.

FIGURE 1
Theory of Planned Behavior: Version 1 without broken arrow, Version 2 with broken arrow

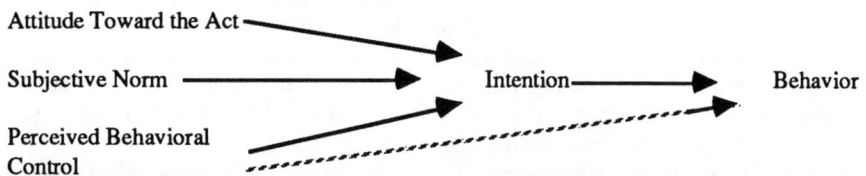

According to version 2, perceived behavioral control, besides having an influence on intention, can also have a direct affect on behavior. This link is proposed because, when it is difficult to perform a behavior, intention will not readily translate to behavior. In such cases, a measure of how easy or difficult a person thinks it would be to engage in the behavior, should provide useful information on the ability of a person to engage in the behavior. Ajzen (1991) offers two reasons for this direct affect. First, if two people have equally strong intentions to engage in a behavior, the one that has less doubts about his ability to achieve it, is more likely to achieve it, perhaps because he is more likely to persevere. Second, because a measure of perceived behavioral control can serve as a substitute for a measure of actual control. In the case that a person from the very outset realistically perceives that it will be problematic for some reason or the other for him to achive the goal, the, even if he sincerely intents to achieve it, it is very likely that he will not be sucessful in his endeavor.

The TPB has received considerable empirical support. According to Ajzen (1991), 16 empirical tests of version 1 have been conducted in the past 5 years and reveal that, "the addition of perceived behavioral control to the model led to considerable improvements in the prediction of intentions; the regression coefficients of perceived behavioral control were significant in every study" (p. 189). Also, 12 empirical tests of version 2 have been conducted and show, "that the combination of intentions and perceived behavioral control permitted significant prediction of behavior in each case, and that many of the multiple correlations were of substantial magnitude" (p. 187).

FINANCIAL CONTROL AND PURCHASE

While consumer researchers have recognized that financial capability has an impact on the purchase of some expensive products, much more attention has been devoted to brand attitude as the primary antecedent of purchase. There could be two reasons for this. One reason could be that, in accordance with the TRA, price, income, and notions of affordability have been treated as external variables whose effect is expected to be mediated by beliefs about the brand or beliefs of important others. However, empirical tests of the TPB in diverse contexts have shown that perceived behavioral control exerts an influence on intention and behavior that is independent of attitudes and subjective norms (Ajzen 1991). Therefore, it might be expected that beliefs about 'financial control' would exert an influence on purchase intention and purchase that is independent of attitude and subjective norm.

A second reason comes from the fact that there is a difference between purchasing a brand from a given product category versus purchasing a given product. Consumer research is predominantly concerned with the former; that is, given a product category, what factors determine brand choice. In this situation the effect of perceived financial control is minimal: beliefs about brands should determine choice of one brand from the consideration set (Hartwick 1983; Warshaw et. al, forthcoming). However, our study is concerned with the likelihood that a person will make a purchase from a general product category. In this situation perceived financial control should be predictive since its effect may not be mediated by beliefs about the product. A measure of whether a person (perceives he) has the required financial resources at his disposal should impact intention to purchase and actual purchase.

When predicting purchase, problems of behavioral control are most likely to be problems of financial control. Therefore, the construct of perceived behavioral control translates to 'perceived financial control' in the consumption context. Thus, the TPB is a framework that allows explicit consideration of the constraining and facilitating effects of financial resources, in combination with the traditional constructs of attitude and subjective norms. As specified in the hypotheses below, financial considerations should improve prediction of both purchase intentions and purchase.

HYPOTHESES

Perceived financial control should enhance prediction of *intentions* for both inexpensive and expensive products. This is possible since perceived financial control has motivational implications for intentions (Ajzen and Madden 1986). The more a person believes s/he possesses the required financial resources for purchase, the more s/he is likely to form strong intentions to purchase. Thus,

H1: Perceived financial control will add explained variance in the prediction of *intention* over and above that provided by attitudes and subjective norms.

According to the TPB, the incremental variance added by perceived behavioral control in predicting *behavior* is inversely related to the degree of control over the behavior (Madden et al. 1992). Hence, when *actual* financial control is relatively high, perceived financial control will add little to the prediction of behavior. In other words, intentions alone will be sufficient to predict purchase because the financial resources required for purchase are under the person's control.

Whenever *actual* financial control in a situation is low, the effect of perceived financial control on purchase will not be entirely mediated by intention. Therefore, "to ensure accurate prediction of behavior over which individuals have only limited control, we must assess not only intention but also obtain some estimate of the extent to which the individual is capable of exercising control over the behavior in question" (Ajzen and Madden 1986, page 456). The rationale for this is that, "holding intention constant, the effort expended to bring a course of behavior to a successful conclusion is likely to increase with perceived behavioral control. For instance, even if two individuals have equally strong intentions to learn to ski, and both try to do so, the person who is confident that he can master this activity is more likely to persevere than is the person who doubts his ability" (Ajzen 1991, p. 184). Thus,

H2: Perceived financial control will add explained variance in the prediction of *behavior*, but this effect would only be expected for relatively-expensive products.

METHODOLOGY

Sample and Procedure

To identify product categories that would allow for a test of the hypotheses, informal one-on-one interviews were conducted with undergraduate students. The students were asked to supply events, and activities associated with those events, that they would consider inexpensive versus relatively-expensive. They also supplied dollar amounts corresponding to each activity in each event category. On the basis of these interviews, 'celebrating the completion of mid-term exams by going out to dinner, a sporting event, or a rock concert' was chosen as the inexpensive scenario; 'buying a gift/dinner for someone for Valentine's day' was chosen as the relatively-expensive scenario.

The study was described as a survey being conducted by the University to determine students' spending habits and activities. Respondents were undergraduate students enrolled in an introductory marketing class during the winter term. Data were collected at two time periods. At time 1, the students indicated their attitude, subjective norm, intention and perceived financial control for both scenarios. The total number of responses obtained was 154. At time 2—two weeks later—behavioral self-reports were solicited for the mid-term celebration and Valentine gift scenarios. Of the 154 students who had participated at time 1, 117 (76%) participated at time 2. The respondents were given class participation credit.

Questionnaire

To anchor the cost aspect of the scenarios, actual dollar ranges that were obtained from the one-on-one interviews were mentioned in the measures. For example, intention for the Valentine scenario read "I intend to buy dinner/ a present (in the range of $25-$50) as a Valentine's day gift". For the mid-term scenario it read "I intend to celebrate the completion of mid-term exams by going out to dinner, a sporting event, or a rock concert, where I might spend $10-$25".

All the constructs were measured on 7-point scales. Attitudes were measured by 7 items: pleasant/unpleasant, boring/interesting, good/bad, unfavorable/favorable, enjoyable/unenjoyable, useful/useless, harmful/harmless. The alpha coefficients for the scenarios were .91 (mid-term exam) and .93 (Valentine).

Subjective norms for each scenario were measured in a global fashion. Normative beliefs and motivations to comply were assessed non-contiguously in the questionnaire with respect to "most people who are important to me". Consistent with the TRA, normative beliefs were combined with motivations to comply to obtain a measure of subjective norms.

Intentions were measured by 3 items for each scenario: "I intend to—", "I will try to—" and "I will make an effort to—". The first item was anchored by "definitely do/definitely do not"; the second and third items by "definitely will/ definitely will not". The alpha coefficients were .96 (mid-term exam) and .97 (Valentine).

Perceived financial control was measured by 4 items: "how much financial control do you have over spending —"; "If I want to, I could easily afford—"; "For me to spend—"; and "My personal income permits me to easily spend—". For the mid-term exam scenario, each item continued as "$10-$25 on celebrating the completion of mid-term exams by going out to dinner, a sporting event, or a rock concert." For the Valentine's day scenario, the items continued as "in the range of $25-$50 on buying dinner/a present as a Valentine's day gift." The 7-point scales were anchored by "complete control/very little control," "extremely likely/extremely unlikely," "easy/difficult," "strongly agree/strongly disagree," respectively. The first three items were adapted from Ajzen and Madden (1986); the last item was created for this study to tap into the affordability and income aspect more directly. An exploratory factor analysis using varimax rotation resulted in a single factor solution for both the scenarios. The first item was found to load weakly (.490 for mid-term, .531 for Valentine) in comparison to the other items, all of which had loadings between .651 and .915. The first item was thus dropped from the scale for both scenarios. The alpha coefficients of the remaining three items were .78 (mid-term exam) and .84 (Valentine).

Behavior self-reports (taken at time 2) were coded as 1 if the subject reported performance of the behavior and 0 if s/he reported the behavior was not performed.

RESULTS

The results are presented by scenario for the hypotheses. Data were analyzed by means of hierarchical regression. For the prediction of intention, attitude and subjective norm were entered in the first step (model 1) to test the TRA. In the second step, perceived financial control was added to the predictors in model 1, resulting in the TPB (model 2). Since behavior is a dichotomous variable, the behavioral data were analyzed by means of logistic regression. Intention as the sole predictor of behavior was entered in the first step to test the TRA (model 1). In the second step, perceived financial control was added, resulting in model 2.

The Inexpensive Scenario

Predicting intentions. The results for prediction of intention are shown in Table 1. It was hypothesized that the inclusion of perceived financial control would add explained variance over and above that provided by attitude and subjective norm in predicting intention. As can be seen from model 1, attitude (b=.58, p<.01) and subjective norm (b=.11, ns) resulted in an R^2 of .39. The inclusion of perceived financial control (model 2) resulted in a significant effect (b=.24, p<.01) and increased the R^2 to .44. The variance explained by model 2 is significantly greater than that explained by model 1 (F=13.3 (1,149), p<.01). (The formula for testing R-square difference between two models is given in Cohen and Cohen, 1975). These results support hypothesis 1.

Predicting behavior. Out of the 117 subjects available at time 2, 37 (31.6%) reported celebrating the completion of mid-term exams by going out to dinner, a sporting event, or a rock concert. The results for prediction of behavior are shown in Table 2. In logit analysis, the significance of a set of k independent variables is determined by a likelihood-ratio (LR) test. The LR test is the counterpart of the F-test in analysis of variance or regression analysis. This involves computing a LR statistic as follows. First, the model is estimated by constraining and not constraining the impact of the set of k independent variables to zero. Then, corresponding log-likelihood (LL) values denoted as L_1 and L_2, the LR statistic is computed as $2(L_2 - L_1)$ and is chi-square distributed with k degrees of freedom. It was hypothesized that perceived financial control would add no variance beyond that explained by intention in predicting behavior for the inexpensive scenario. Consistent with hypothesis 2, the addition of perceived financial control (model 2) did not add variance to the prediction of behavior beyond that accounted for by intention. This can be seen from the non-significant beta coefficient for perceived financial control and a non-significant LR.

The Relatively-Expensive Scenario

Predicting intentions. The results pertaining to the prediction of intention are shown in Table 3. It was hypothesized that perceived financial control would add variance beyond that provided by attitude and subjective norm in predicting intention. As can be seen from model 1, attitude (b=.41, p<.01) and subjective

TABLE 1
Predicting intentions: Celebrating mid-term exams

	b	R^2	R^2 increment[a]
Model 1: TRA			
Attitude	.58***	.39	M2-M1: .05**
Subjective norm	.11		
Model 2: TPB[b]			
Attitude	.54***	.44	M3-M2: .03**
Subjective norm	.10		
Pfc	.24***		
Model 3: TPB with Interactions			
Attitude	.10	.47	M3-M1: .08**
Subjective norm	.48*		
Pfc	-.36		
Pfc * Attitude	.91**		
Pfc * Subjective norm	-.43		

*** $p < .001$
** $p < .05$
* $p < .10$
[a] M1=model 1, M2=model 2, M3=model 3
[b] Pfc=perceived financial control

TABLE 2
Predicting behavior: Celebrating mid-term exams

	beta	LL	LR[c]
Model 1: TRA			
Intention	.18***	-63.6	M2-M1: 0.8
Model 2: TPB			
Intention	.18**	-63.2	M3-M2: 0.0
Pfc	.05		
Model 3: TPB with Interactions			
Intention	.15	-63.2	M3-M1: 0.8
Attitude	.03		
Pfc * Intention	.00		

*** $p < .001$
** $p < .05$
* $p < .10$
[c] LR = 2(LLm2 - LLm1), distributed chi-square with 1 d.f.

Note: Standardized betas are reported in predicting intentions, and unstandardized in predicting behavior.

norm (b=.34, p<.01) resulted in a R^2 of .39. Consistent with hypothesis 1, the inclusion of perceived behavioral control (model 2) resulted in a significant coefficient (b=.27, p<.01) and increased the R^2 to .45. The variance explained by model 2 is significantly greater than that explained by model 1 (F=16.3 (1,149), p<.01).

Predicting behavior. Out of the 117 subjects available at time 2, 73 (62.4%) reported going out to dinner or having bought a present for someone, while 44 (37.9) reported not having done either. Additionally, out of the 72 that had a significant other, 62 (62.07%) engaged in the behavior, while 10 did not. The results pertaining to the prediction of behavior are shown in Table 4. It was hypothesized that perceived financial control would add variance beyond that explained by intention. The inclusion of perceived financial control (beta=.09, p<.10) added to the prediction of behavior vis-a-vis intention alone (Chi-sq.=3.4; 1 df., p<.10). Thus, the data support hypothesis 2.

DISCUSSION

Predicting Intention

It was hypothesized that perceived financial control would add explained variance to the prediction of intention over and above that furnished by the traditional constructs in the TRA. Consistent with this hypothesis, perceptions of financial control were found to contribute to the prediction of intentions for both the inexpensive and the relatively-expensive scenarios. Thus, perceived financial

TABLE 3
Predicting intentions: Valentine's Day Gift

	b	R2	R2 increment
Model 1: TRA			
Attitude	.41***	.39	M2-M1: .06**
Subjective norm	.34***		
Model 2: TPB			
Attitude	.37***	.45	M3-M2: .02
Subjective norm	.27***		
Pfc	.27***		
Model 3: TPB with Interactions			
Attitude	.16	.47	M3-M1: .08**
Subjective norm	.58**		
Pfc	.05		
Pfc * Attitude	.45		
Pfc * Subjective norm	-.38		

*** p < .001
** p < .05
* p < .10

TABLE 4
Predicting behavior: Valentine's Day Gift

	beta	LL	LR
Model 1: TRA			
Intention	.24***	-54.3	M2-M1: 3.4*
Model 2: TPB			
Intention	.21***	-52.6	M3-M2: 6.0**
Pfc	.09*		
Model 3: TPB with Interactions			
Intention	-.09	-49.6	M3-M1: 9.4**
Pfc	-.14		
Pfc * Intention	.02**		

*** p < .001
** p < .05
* p < .10

Note: Standardized betas are reported in predicting intentions, and unstandardized in predicting behavior.

control serves a motivational function in forming intentions—the higher the financial control, the higher the likelihood of a person intending to perform the focal behavior.

Ajzen also expects interactions between perceived behavioral control and attitude and/or subjective norms. According to Ajzen and Madden (1986), "—perceived behavioral control is a necessary, but not a sufficient condition for the formation of intention to perform a behavior. Besides believing that one *could* perform the behavior, one must also be inclined to do so for other reasons. These considerations imply the possibility that perceived behavioral control affects intention in interaction with attitude and subjective norm" (page 459, emphasis original). Thus, for the consumption context, this expectation was tested by adding the interaction terms of perceived financial control with attitude and subjective norms to the variables in model 2 which resulted in model 3. For the midterm exam scenario (model 3, table 1), the perceived financial control x attitude interaction is significant (b=.91, p<.05). In addition, R^2 increased from .44 (model 2) to .47 (model 3); this increase is statistically significant (F=4.2 (2,147), p<.05). This shows that the effects of attitude and perceived financial control on intention are best explained by their interaction: simply stated, intention is highest when both attitude and perceived financial control are high.

The possibility of an interaction effect was also tested for the Valentine's day scenario. Here, perceived financial control combined with attitude and subjective norm in an additive manner to predict intention. The interaction terms were not significant (model 3, table 3). When the interaction terms were added, it is interesting to note that the only significant effect was that of subjective norms. This is most likely due to the nature of the context. According to Ajzen (1991), the relative importance of attitudes, subjective norms, and perceived behavioral control in predicting intention will vary across contexts. Ajzen notes that out of 16 empirical tests of the TPB conducted to date, the effect of subjective norms was mixed across contexts, perhaps because personal considerations were more important than social pressures for the behaviors considered in those studies. In a gift-giving scenario like Valentine's day, social norms might be expected to exert greater pressure on consumers' intentions (Netemeyer et al. 1993).

Predicting Behavior

It was hypothesized that perceived financial control would have a direct and independent influence in predicting behavior for the more expensive Valentine's day scenario, but would make little or no contribution for the less costly, mid-term scenario. The results confirm these expectations.

Ajzen also posits an interaction between intention and perceived behavioral control for the prediction of behavior (Ajzen 1985; Ajzen and Madden 1986). According to Ajzen (1991), "the assumption is usually made that motivation and ability interact in their effects on behavioral achievement" (page 183). Thus, in the consumption context, financial control is a necessary condition when purchasing expensive items and reflects the ability component required for purchase; intention reflects the motivational component. To test for the interaction effect, the interaction between intention and perceived financial control was added to the variables in model 2, resulting in model 3. In the mid-term exam scenario, the intention x perceived financial control interaction was not significant. This result supports the TPB, since the consumption of an inexpensive product is under the volitional control of subjects —when this is the case, the TRA is sufficient to predict behavior.

However, perceived financial control and intention interacted to predict behavior in the Valentine's day scenario. It can be seen from model 3 (table 4), that the interaction is significant (beta=.02, p<.05), and the likelihood ratio (LR) test reveals that the fit of model 3 improves beyond model 2 (Chi-sq.=6; 1 df, p<.05). This implies that the likelihood of performance of a focal behavior will be greatest when a person possesses both ability and motivation. In the present study this translates to: the likelihood of purchase of a relatively-expensive item is greatest when financial control and intention are both strong.

According to Ajzen (1991), though interactions are intuitive and are hypothesized, it is puzzling that they rarely emerge. He reports that out of the 12 empirical tests of version 2 of the TPB, 7 hypothesized interactions, but only 1 study (Schifter and Ajzen 1985) evidenced a marginally significant interaction (p<.10) between intention and perceived behavioral control. In fact, because of no empirical support for the interaction between perceived behavioral control and intention, Doll and Ajzen (1992) are considering dropping this expectation from the theory altogether. The results of our study suggest that the interaction hypothesis should be retained in the TPB.

Limitations and Suggestions for Future Research

The present study operationalized perceived behavioral control as perceived financial control with the assumption that problems of control in consumption contexts are most likely to be problems of financial constraints. Future research should also consider factors such as lack of time, location etc. that hamper purchase. In addition, future research should measure both perceived financial control and the more global perceived behavioral control in the same study to examine whether perceived financial control performs better than perceived behavioral control in consumption contexts. Indirect support for perceived financial control comes from Netemeyer et al. (1993) who also tested the TPB in a Valentine's day gift giving context and examined gift items falling in various price ranges. They used the global perceived behavioral control construct and did not find any support for the hypothesis that perceived behavioral control has a direct effect on behavior. The authors suggest that the perceived behavioral control construct may not have captured financial constraints adequately.

While the TPB was supported by our data, more research needs to be done to explain the additive and interactive effects obtained. We are not able to offer any reasons as to why we obtained interactions while prior research has not. Future research should examine when can we expect additive versus interactive effects and vice-versa and what the additive and interactive effects imply about consumer decision processes.

REFERENCES

Ajzen, Icek (1985), "From Intentions to Actions: A Theory of Planned Behavior," in *Action-control: From Cognition to Behavior*, eds., J. Kuhl and J. Beckman (pp.11-39). Heidelberg: Springer.

Ajzen, Icek (1991), "The Theory of Planned Behavior," *Organizational Behavior and Human Decision Processes*, 50, 179-211.

Ajzen, Icek and Martin Fishbein (1980), *Understanding Attitudes and Predicting Social Behavior*, Englewood and Cliffs, NJ: Prentice-Hall.

Ajzen, Icek and Thomas J. Madden (1986), "Prediction of Goal-Ddirected Behavior: Attitudes, Intentions, and Perceived Behavioral Control," *Journal of Experimental Social Psychology*, 22, 453-474.

Bagozzi, Richard P. (working paper), "On the Neglect of Volition in Consumer Research: A Critique and Proposal," University of Michigan Graduate School of Business Administration, Ann Arbor, MI 49109.

Bagozzi, Richard P. and Paul R. Warshaw (1990), "Trying to Consume," *Journal of Consumer Research*, 17, 126-140.

Bonfield, E.H. (1974), "Attitude, Social Influence, Personal Norm, and Intention Interactions as related to Brand Purchase Behavior," *Journal of Marketing Research*, 11, 379-389.

Cohen, Jacob and Patricia Cohen (1975), *Applied Multivariate Regression/ Correlation Analysis for the Behavioral Sciences*, John Wiley & Sons, NY.

Doll, Jorg and Icek Ajzen (1992), "Accessibility and Stability of Predictors in the Theory of Planned Behavior," *Journal of Personality and Social Psychology*, 63, 754-765.

Fishbein, Martin and Icek Ajzen (1975), *Belief, Attitude, Intention and Behavior: An Introduction to Theory and Research*. Reading, MA: Addison-Wesley.

Greene, W.H. (1990), *Econometric Analysis*, New York: Macmillan.

Hartwick, Jon (1983). Attitudes and Purchase Intentions: Headaches for Fishbein and Ajzen? Paper presented at the annual convention of the American Psychological Association, Anaheim, CA.

Kuhl, J. (1985), "Volitional Aspect of Achievement Motivation and Learned Helplessness: Toward a Comprehensive Theory of Action Control," in *Progress in Experimental Personality Research (Vol. 13)*, ed. B.A. Maher, New York: Academic Press.

Liska, A.E. (1984), "A Critical Examination of the Causal Structure of the Fishbein/Ajzen Attitude-Behavior Model," *Social Psychology Quarterly*, 47, 61-74.

Madden, Thomas J., Pamela Scholder Ellen and Icek Ajzen (1992), "A Comparison of the Theory of Planned Behavior and the Theory of Reasoned Action," *Personality and Social Psychology Bulletin*, 18, 3-9.

Miniard, Paul W., Carl Obermiller and Thomas J. Page (1982), "Predicting Behavior with Intentions: A Comparison of Conditional versus Direct Measures," in *Advances in Consumer Research* (Vol. 9, pp. 461-464), ed. Andrew A. Mitchell, Ann Arbor, MI: Association for Consumer Research.

Netemeyer, Richard G., J. Craig Andrews and Srinivas Durvasula (1993), "A Comparison of Three Behavioral Intention Models: The Case of Valentine's Day Gift-Giving," unpublished manuscript, Marketing Department, Lousiana State University at Baton Rouge.

Ryan, Michael J. (1982), "Behavioral Intention Formation: A Structural Equation Analysis of Attitudinal and Social Influence Interdependency," *Journal of Consumer Research*, 9, 263-278.

Sarver, V.T. Jr., (1983), "Ajzen and Fishbein's "theory of reasoned action": A Critical Assessment," *Journal for the Theory of Social Behavior*, 13, 155-163.

Schifter, Deborah E. and Icek Ajzen (1985), "Intention, Perceived Control, and Weight Loss: An Application of the Theory of Planned Behavior," *Journal of Personality and Social Psychology*, 49, 843-851.

Sheppard, Blair H., Jon Hartwick and Paul R. Warshaw (1988), "The Theory of Reasoned Action: A Meta-Analysis of Past Research with Recommendations and Modifications for Future Research," *Journal of Consumer Research*, 15, 325-343.

Triandis, Harry C. (1977), *Interpersonal behavior*, Monterey, CA: Brooks/Cole.

Warshaw, Paul R. (1980), "A New Model for Predicting Behavioral Intentions: An Alternative to Fishbein," *Journal of Marketing Research*, 17, 153-172.

Warshaw, Paul R.and Fred D. Davis (1984), "Self-Understanding and the Accuracy of Behavioral Expectation," *Personality and Social Psychology Bulletin*, 10, 111-118.

Warshaw, Paul R. and Fred D. Davis (1985), "Disentangling Behavioral Intention and Behavioral Expectation," *Journal of Experimental Social Psychology*, 21, 213-228.

Warshaw, Paul R., Blair H. Sheppard and Jon Hartwick (forthcoming), "The Intention and Self-Prediction of Goals and Behavior," in *Advances in Marketing Communication*, ed., R.P. Bagozzi, Greenwich, CT:JAI Press.

The Effects of Country of Origin, Brand, and Price Information: A Cognitive-Affective Model of Buying Intentions

Wai-Kwan Li, University of Illinois, Urbana-Champaign
Kent B. Monroe, University of Illinois, Urbana-Champaign
Darius K-S Chan, University of Illinois, Urbana-Champaign

ABSTRACT

The present study examines the effects of three extrinsic cues, country of origin, brand, and price information, on buying intentions. The results indicate that these cues affect perceived quality in a similar fashion. However, while price and expected price have direct effects on liking and perceived value, country of origin and brand information have no significant direct effect on these two variables. More importantly, a proposed cognitive-affective model of buying intentions is supported across the two products studied, and has more explanatory power than a cognitive model of buying intentions.

Currently, globalization effects of business firms have brought about important changes in the manufacturing locations of products. Along with these changes, an important issue is whether buyers' evaluations of a product are influenced by knowing the country in which it is manufactured. Recent research has provided some evidence that country of origin, brand name, and price information affect product evaluations and buying intentions (Bilkey and Nes 1982; Ozsomer and Cavusgil 1991; Monroe 1973; Rao and Monroe 1989; Dodds, Monroe, and Grewal 1991). Although these three extrinsic cues have attracted significant research attention, little research has been done to compare whether they affect product evaluations and buying intentions in a similar fashion, or in different ways. Therefore, the first research issue of the present study is to explore *how* these three extrinsic cues affect product evaluations and buying intentions.

In general, researchers have assumed that consumers are rational, and therefore the measurements of product evaluations are essentially cognitively oriented (an example is available in the Appendix of Dodds, Monroe, and Grewal 1991). However, Zajonc and Markus (1982) have argued that, in addition to cognitive factors, affective factors also play an important role in preferences. They illustrated this argument by a food preference example:

"Dog meat is a delicacy in some parts of East Asia, but few Americans would find it appetizing... Most Americans like corn, but in various countries corn has been thought suitable only for pigs."

Recently, Cohen and Areni (1991) proposed a dynamic model of affect in consumer behavior. Essentially, the model describes the interactions between affect and the cognitive system across three phases, which can affect consumers' behaviors.

Recognizing affect is an important component in consumers' preferences, we will extend the cognitively oriented models of buying intentions to a cognitive-affective model of buying intentions, and examine the predictive power of the extended model.

The Cognitive Models of Buying Intentions

Effects of extrinsic cues. Scitovszky (1945) noticed that consumers might use price as a surrogate of product quality, if they had difficulties in evaluating the product. Based on this notion, Monroe (1979), and Monroe and Krishnan (1985) proposed a conceptual model describing the relationships among price, perceived quality, perceived sacrifice, perceived value, and willingness to buy. Recently, Zeithaml (1988), and Dodds, Monroe, and Grewal (1991) extended the model to include brand name and store name (Figure 1A).

In the Dodds et al. (1991) study, price had a positive effect on perceived quality, but a negative effect on perceived value, while the overall effect on willingness to buy was positive. Moreover, a favorable brand name and store name had positive effects on perceived quality. Consistent with these findings, the meta-analysis conducted by Rao and Monroe (1989) suggested that both price and brand name have positive effects on perceived quality. Turning to the country of origin effects, two comprehensive reviews (Bilkey and Nes 1982; Ozsomer and Cavusgil 1991) have consistently concluded that a favorable country of origin image has a positive effect on perceived quality.

Based on these empirical findings, it is logical to hypothesize that (Figure 1B):

H1a: As price increases, buyers' perceptions of quality increase.

H1b: When buyers' perceptions of brand name are more favorable, their perceptions of quality are higher.

H1c: When buyers' perceptions of country of origin are more favorable, their perceptions of quality are higher.

H1d: As price increases, buyers' perceptions of value declines.

H1e: When buyers' perceptions of quality increase, their perceptions of value increase.

H1f: When buyers' perceptions of value increase, their willingness to buy increase.

Effects of reference price. The existence of the concept of reference price is well-documented in the pricing literature. Essentially, it refers to an internal price to which consumers compare the observed prices (Monroe, Grewal, and Compeau 1991). One suggested operationalization is that it is an "expected price" (Winer 1988). By comparing the observed price with the expected price, consumers judge whether the product being considered is of high or low perceived value-for-money. More concretely, if a consumer has an expected price of $199, and the observed price is $250, s/he may judge the product as expensive. In another case, if his/her expected price is $299, with the same observed price, s/he probably will judge the product as not expensive. Therefore, *ceteris paribus*, the higher the expected price, the higher the perceived value-for-money. Incorporating this construct in the present model, we hypothesize that:

H1g: For a given observed price, when the expected price is higher, buyers' perceptions of value are greater.

The Affective Component in Buying Intentions

Although affect is identified as an important antecedent of preferences, its relationships with other cognitive antecedents of

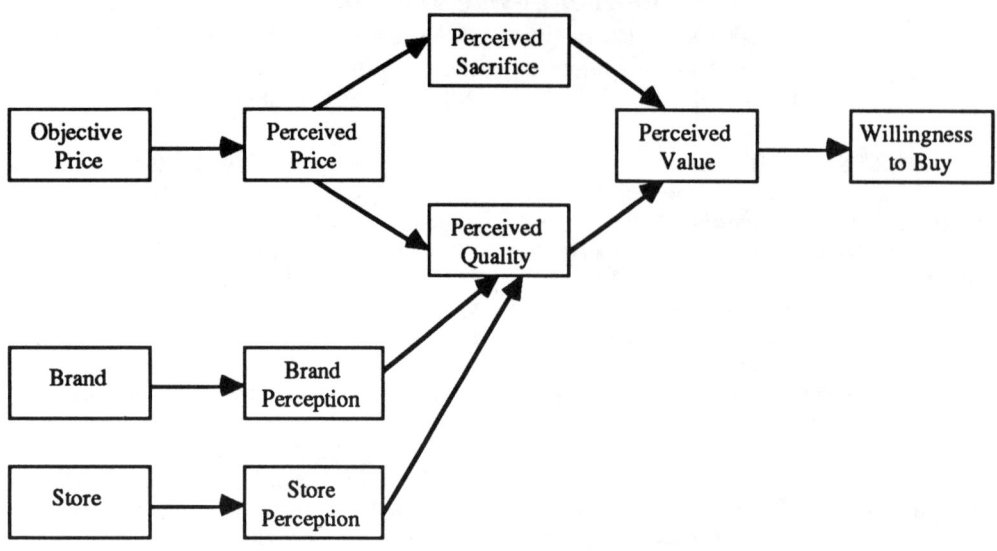

FIGURE 1A
Extended Model Proposed by Dodds et al. (1991)

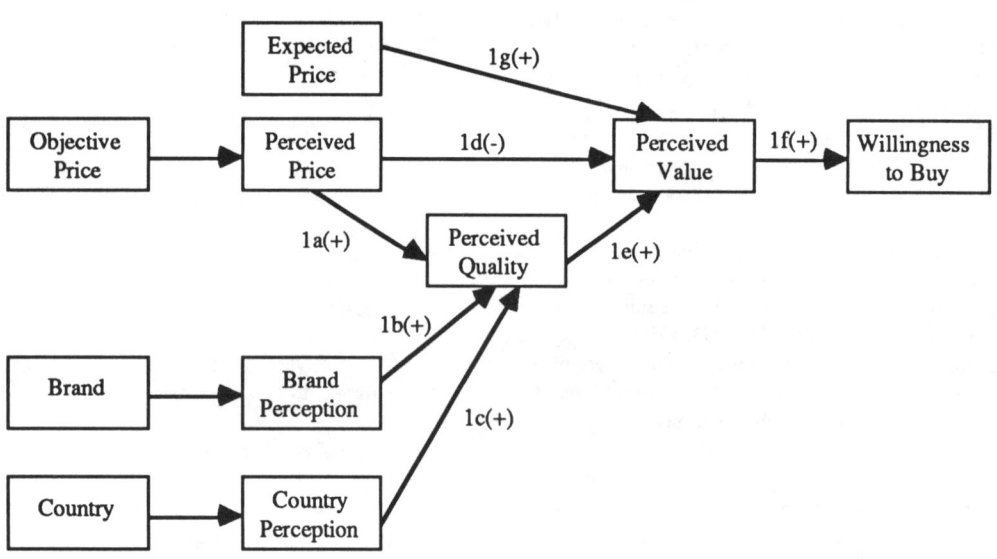

FIGURE 1B
Cognitive Model of Buying Intentions

preferences are unclear. According to the traditional approach, the affect component is influenced by a cognitive component (Zajonc and Markus 1982). For example, before you like a Honda, you must know what it is. In contrast, Zajonc (1980) also suggested that affective reactions can precede cognitive reactions. In this situation, the cognitive reactions perhaps serve as a justification for liking. For example, you like blue, therefore you may evaluate a blue shirt favorably.

Recently, Cohen and Areni (1991) argued that affect can be elicited automatically, as well as after some cognitive processes. In addition, an affective response can influence the subsequent cognitive responses. More concretely, imagine a baby powder advertisement, the audience may elicit some positive affective reactions automatically when the happy babies appear in the advertisement. According to Cohen and Areni's model, these reactions are the first phase affective responses, which may occur before any cognitive reactions. As the advertisement moves on, the audience receives the message about the hygienic feature of the product. This advertisement message may lead to some positive affective reactions. These reactions are the second phase affective responses, which occur after some cognitive reactions. After watching the advertisement, the audience may continue their elaborative interpretation. This elaborative interpretation, a cognitive response, may be affected by the phase two affective responses; however, it may also elicit phase three affective reactions.

The Cognitive-Affective Model of Buying Intentions

Using in-depth interviews, Li and Monroe (1992) reported that country of origin could play two roles in product evaluations, namely, signalling and attribute roles. Specifically, the signalling role of country of origin information suggests that consumers use it as a signal to infer whether a country possesses the necessary skills in manufacturing a product (a cognitive response). Notice that this is a *cognitive* product evaluation process.

On the other hand, the attribute role of country of origin refers to the liking effect on product evaluations. For example, consumers may like a product more (an affective response) if it is from their home countries, which is an *affective* product evaluation process.

If country of origin can elicit both cognitive and affective responses, it is likely that price and brand name can also induce these two types of responses. For instance, people may infer a high price product, or a national brand product, is of high quality (cognitive responses). Alternatively, they may simply like expensive products more, or like and be loyal to a certain brand (affective responses).

First phase affective responses. It should be noted that the affective responses elicited directly from extrinsic cues (some external stimulus) correspond to the first phase affective responses in Cohen and Areni's (1991) model. Therefore, we hypothesize that (see Figure 2A):

H2a: As price increases, buyers' liking (first phase) toward a product increase.

H2b: When buyers' perceptions of brand name are more favorable, their liking (first phase) toward a product is greater.

H2c: When buyers' perceptions of country of origin are more favorable, their liking (first phase) toward a product is greater.

Second phase affective responses. By definition, the second phase affective responses occur after some cognitive responses, that were induced by some external stimulus. As stated in hypotheses 1a to 1c, the three extrinsic cues will trigger some cognitive responses, such as perceptions of quality. Since a consumer should like a product of high quality more than a product of low quality, liking should be positively influenced by perceived quality. Hence we hypothesize (see Figure 2B):

H2d: When buyers' perceptions of quality are more favorable, their liking (second phase) toward a product is greater.

In addition, consumers may compare the observed price with their internal expected prices. If their expected price is greater than the observed price, then the perceived good deal will elicit some positive affective responses. Therefore, we hypothesize (see Figure 2B):

H2e: For a given observed price, when the expected price is higher, buyers' liking (second phase) toward a product is greater.

H2f: For a given expected price, when the observed price is higher, buyers' liking (second phase) toward a product is lower.

Third phase affective responses. As the cognitive process continues, consumers may evaluate the perceived value of a product. This cognitive response may then elicit the third phase affective responses. Therefore, we expect (see Figure 2C):

H2g: As buyers' perceptions of value increases, their liking (third phase) toward a product is greater.

Effects of affective responses on cognitive responses. According to Cohen and Areni's (1991) model, an affective response can also activate some cognitive responses, because consumers may want to justify their preferences by some subsequent cognitive responses (see also Zajonc 1980). Based on this argument, if a consumer likes a product, s/he may justify this preference by considering the product is of higher quality, or is of higher value-for-money. To further extend this reasoning, the affective responses may directly influence one's buying intentions. It should be pointed out that an affective response can only affect the *subsequent* (but not the preceding) cognitive responses. That is, the first phase liking may affect the subsequent perceptions of quality; however, the second and third phases liking cannot influence the preceding perceptions of quality. Hence, we hypothesize:

H2h: As buyers' liking (first phase) toward a product increases, their perceptions of quality increase (see Figure 2A).

H2i: As buyers' liking (first or second phase) toward a product increases, their perceptions of value increase (see Figures 2A and 2B).

H2j: As buyers' liking (first, second, or third phase) toward a product increases, their willingness to buy increase (see Figures 2A, 2B and 2C).

It should be noted that buyers' liking toward a product can occur in the first, second, or third phase. However, since little research has been done in this area, which phase of liking may occur remains an empirical question. Moreover, since we will measure liking only once in the experiment described below, the liking measurement can only represent the affective response which is the strongest one among the three phases. Therefore, we expect that the affective responses described in either (1) phase 1 (hypotheses 2a, 2b, 2c, 2h, 2i, and 2j), or (2) phase 2 (hypotheses 2d, 2e, 2f, 2i, and 2j), or (3) phase 3 (hypotheses 2g, and 2j), will be supported.

METHOD

To investigate these hypotheses, price, brand and country of origin information were provided to subjects with short product descriptions about two electronic products (CD stereo system, and coffeemaker). We conducted a pilot study and a main study.

Pilot Study

In the pilot study, 82 subjects[1] were asked to suggest a price (that they would expect to see in the marketplace) for a coffeemaker and a CD stereo system. These products were described as either with well-known (Sony and Toshiba) or unknown brand names (Mishita and Yichiban), and manufactured in a favorable (Japan) or an unfavorable (Mexico) country. Pictures of the two products were provided in order to make the stimuli more concrete.

The major purposes of the pilot study were to obtain the expected price of the products, as well as to verify the effectiveness

---

[1] A total of 18 subjects were screened out due to the following reasons. First, subjects who suggested a price that was beyond $\pm$ 3 standard deviations were regarded as outliers and therefore screened out. Second, subjects who could not recognize the brand as a Japanese brand were discarded. Third, foreign students were also screened out, since they might not be familiar with the market price.

FIGURE 2A
Cognitive-Affective Model of Buying Intentions (Phase 1)

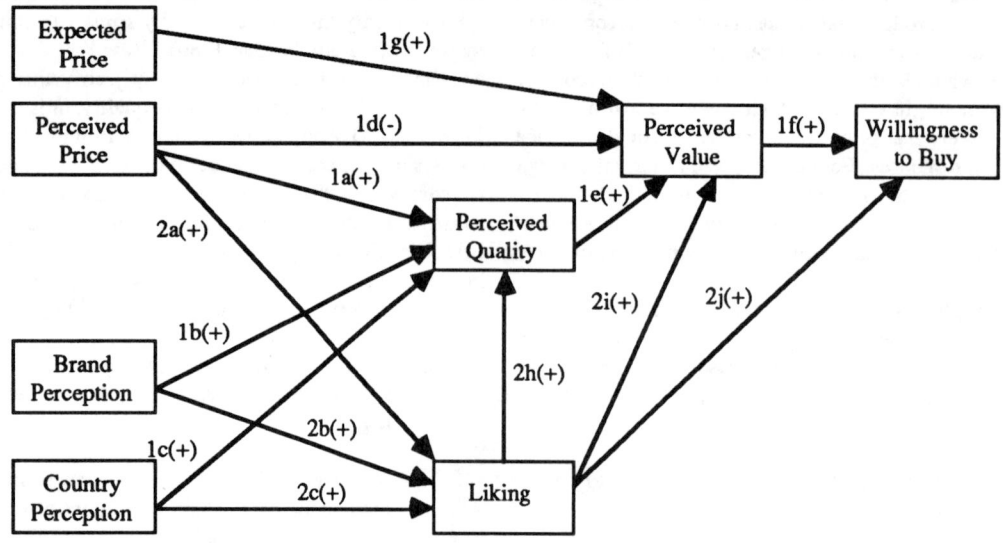

FIGURE 2B
Cognitive-Affective Model of Buying Intentions (Phase 2)

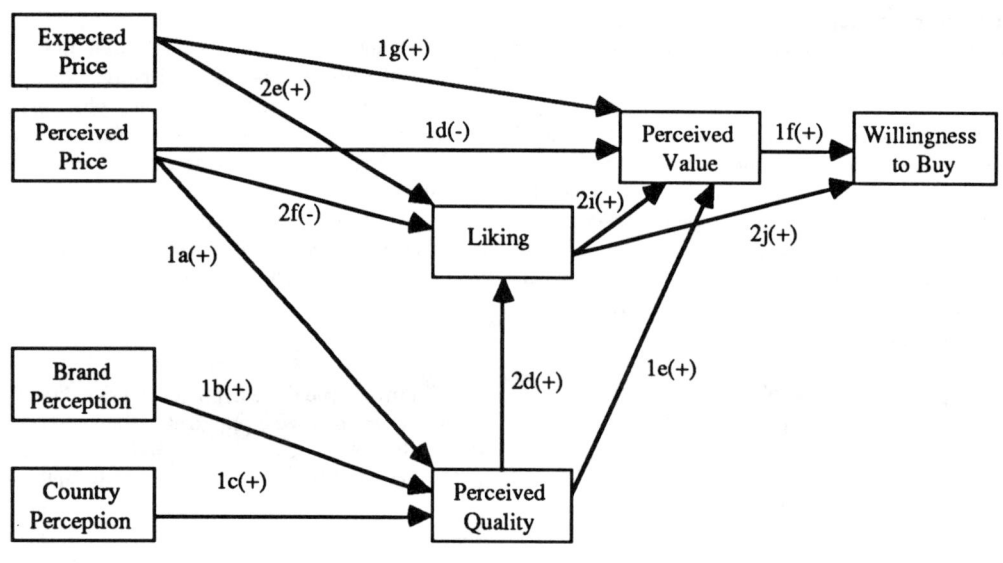

of the selected countries and brand names. This information was later used as the price, country of origin, and brand manipulations for the main study.

Based on the results of the pilot study, the average expected price for the CD stereo system was $399, and for the coffeemaker was $69. These two prices were used as the medium price levels of the two products in the main study. The lowest expected prices suggested by subjects for the CD stereo system and coffeemaker were $179 and $29, respectively, and were used as the low price levels of the two products. These two prices were $220 and $40 lower than the average prices. To obtain a symmetrical manipulation, $619 (i.e., $399+$220) and $109 (i.e., $69+$40) were set as the high price levels for the main study. Also, the known brand was perceived as of higher quality than the hypothetical unknown brand ($X=8.00$ vs. 5.18, $F(1,38)=78.73$, $p<.01$, for CD stereo system; $X=6.70$ vs. 4.93, $F(1,29)=14.04$, $p<.01$, for coffeemaker). In addition, products from Japan were perceived to be of higher quality than products from Mexico ($X=7.62$ vs. 4.08, $F(1,59)=161.93$, $p<.01$, for CD stereo system; $X=6.71$ vs. 4.60, $F(1,57)=65.48$, $p<.01$, for coffeemaker).

Main Study

In the main study, price, brand, and country of origin information were manipulated; cognitive product evaluations (perceived quality, perceived value) and affective product evaluation (liking), buying intentions and expected prices for the two products were measured.

Design. The main study was a 2 (Japan vs. Mexico) x 2 (known vs. unknown brand) x 3 (low, medium, high price level) between-subjects factorial design, with replication across two products. Again, the brands used were either real well-known Japanese brand names (Sony, Toshiba) or hypothetical unknown brand names that

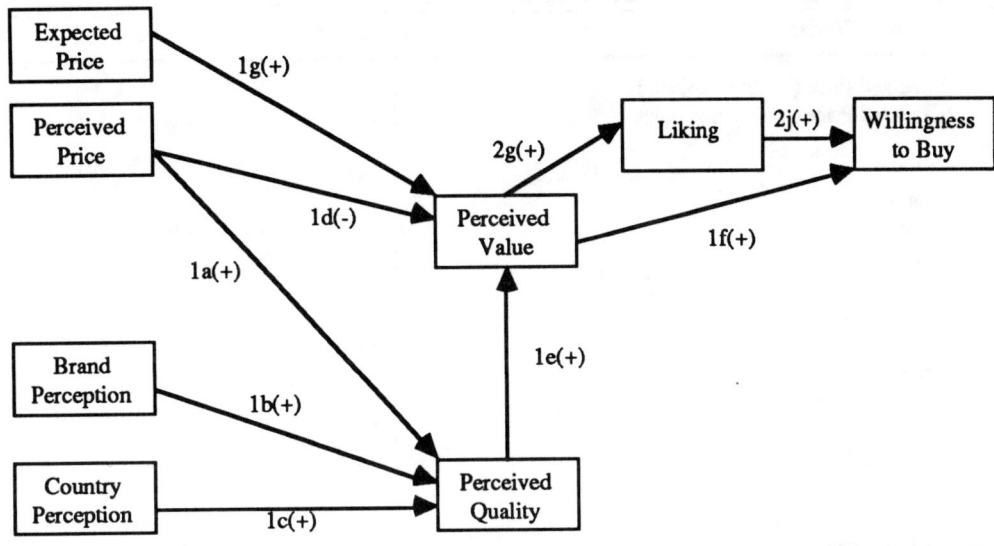

FIGURE 2C
Cognitive-Affective Model of Buying Intentions (Phase 3)

appeared to be Japanese (Mishita, Yichiban). To ensure subjects would be able to perceive them as Japanese brand names, subjects were explicitly told that the brands are "famous manufacturers in Japan" for well-known brands; and just "manufacturers in Japan" for unknown brands. As in the pilot study, pictures of the products were provided with the product descriptions to make the stimuli more concrete.

Sample. A total of 134 students in an introductory business course at a major mid-western university participated in this study. However, a total of eight subjects were screened out because their expected price of the products were located out of the ± 3 standard deviation range. A total of 126 usable cases were used in the following data analyses.

Dependent measurements. First, subjects were asked to suggest an expected price (a specific price point or a price range, if they wished) for each product described. Then, after reading the information about the Japanese brands, they were asked to suggest an expected price for each product again. The objective of this second measure was to detect the effect of knowing the brand's country of origin on expected price, if there was any. Third, subjects were asked to evaluate the products' quality, value, liking, and buying intentions. Each construct was measured by 5 items, on 9-point semantic differential scales. Fourth, demographics such as gender, education level, and subjects' nationality were recorded.

Manipulation checks. Subjects were asked to evaluate the perceived quality of the two products from the two countries, as well as of different brand names using 9-point scales (ranging from very poor to very good). Since hypothetical brand names were used here, subjects were allowed to use 0 to represent they really had no idea about the perceived quality. Subjects were also asked to evaluate the level of technology necessary to manufacture the two products. Nine-point scales, ranged from "not at all" to "requires a lot", were used.

RESULTS

Manipulation Checks

All the manipulations were successful. First, products from Japan were perceived as of significantly higher quality than products from Mexico ($X=7.95$ vs. 3.84, $F(1,108)=409.13$, $p<.01$, for CD stereo system; $X=7.37$ vs. 4.25, $F(1,104)=213.38$, $p<.01$, for coffeemaker). Second, products of the known brand were perceived as of higher quality than products of unknown brand ($X=7.87$ vs. 4.76, $F(1,62)=113.12$, $p<.01$, for CD stereo system; $X=6.50$ vs. 4.65, $F(1,59)=35.05$, $p<.01$, for coffeemaker). Finally, subjects perceived the level of technology required in manufacturing a CD stereo system to be higher than that for coffeemaker ($X=7.61$ vs. 5.42), $F(1,124)=298.63$, $p<.01$).

Reliability Checks

The Cronbach's alpha for the five items measuring perceived quality, perceived value, liking, and buying intentions, for both products, ranged from .90 to .94, suggesting these items were highly internal-consistent. Therefore, the average ratings of the 5 items of each variable were used to represent the variables.

Country of Origin, Brand, and Price Effects on the Dependent Variables

Since there are four dependent variables (perceived quality, perceived value, liking, and buying intentions), a 4-way mixed MANCOVA was performed to reveal all the main and interaction effects (with country of origin, brand, and price being the between-subjects factors; product being the within-subjects factor; and expected price being the covariate). Results reported in Table 1 show that expected price has a significant covariate effect on the dependent variables. Moreover, the results indicate that only the country of origin, brand, price, and product main effects on the four dependent variables were significant, and no interaction effect was significant. Therefore, only main effects will be considered in the subsequent model testing.

Criteria used for Testing Models

LISREL VI's maximum likelihood estimation procedure was used to analyze the four models (Joreskog and Sorbom 1986). The cognitive model (Figure 1B) and the three cognitive-affective models (Figure 2A, 2B, and 2C) were tested by estimating the goodness-of-fit between the hypothesized models and the observed data[2]. Each model was first tested by using coffeemaker as the

---

[2] It should be noted that all four models are viable. Our objective is to identify the model that best fit with the data, among the four models. It is not our intention to challenge the cognitive model with three different competing explanations.

TABLE 1
MANCOVA Results of the Main Study

Source of Variance	F-value**	p-value
Expected Price (Within-subjects)	5.69*	.000
Expected Price (Between-subjects)	9.12	.000
COO	6.14*	.000
Brand	5.00*	.000
Price	27.69	.000
Product	7.02*	.000
COO x Brand	1.00*	.411
COO x Price	1.85	.069
Brand x Price	.29	.968
Product x Price	.81	.597
Product x Brand	2.36*	.058
Product x COO	.96*	.435
COO x Price x Product	.64	.745
COO x Brand x Price	1.86	.066
Brand x Price x Product	1.25	.272
COO x Brand x Product	2.18*	.076
COO x Brand x Price x Product	1.23	.283

Note: ** denotes df(8,220) unless otherwise stated.
* denotes df(4,109).

product, and replicated by using CD stereo system as another product.

Several indices were considered when assessing the likelihood that the data fit the hypothesized models. They include goodness-of-fit statistics, (i.e. the overall chi-square measure, the goodness-of-fit index, and the adjusted goodness-of-fit index), the root-mean-square residual (RSR), and the percentage of variances of buying intentions being explained by the model.

Testing the Cognitive and Cognitive-Affective Models of Buying Intentions

The LISREL results of all four models, for both products are reported in Table 2. First, the goodness-of-fit statistics (X^2, GFI, AGFI) suggest that both the cognitive model and the cognitive-affective model for the second phase fit the data adequately, but the cognitive-affective models for the first and the third phases do not. Second, the RSR residuals for all four models reflect that the hypothetical covariance matrices do not deviate substantially from the observed covariance matrices. Third, among the two adequately fitted models, the cognitive-affective model for the second phase has higher predictive power on buying intention than the cognitive model. To sum up, the results suggest that the cognitive-affective model for the second phase fits best with the data. The path coefficients of the two adequately fitted models are reported in Figures 3A and 3B.

DISCUSSION

Extrinsic Cues

The results from MANCOVA and LISREL analyses revealed some interesting findings about the three extrinsic cues. First, all three extrinsic cues affected the perceived product quality, which implies that subjects did rely on these extrinsic cues to make quality evaluations. Second, among the three extrinsic cues, while price of the product had significant direct effects on liking and perceived value, brand and country of origin had no significant direct effects on them[3]. This finding suggests that price was the major consideration in subjects' product evaluations, although country of origin and brand name might have some indirect effects via perceived quality. However, since this finding may be limited to the student sample used, future research should validate the present finding using a different sample of subjects.

Expected Price

The results concerning expected price provided another interesting line of research. First, the MANCOVA results indicated that expected price had a significant influence on product evaluations. The LISREL analyses clarified that expected price significantly influenced liking and perceived value, but not perceived quality. Moreover, the LISREL results suggest that expected price and price together influenced both liking and perceived value of the product. This finding is consistent with the transaction value literature that consumers compare their internal reference price with the external observed price to evaluate the transaction value (Thaler 1985; Monroe, Grewal, and Compeau 1991). The liking here probably represents the subjects' positive affective responses towards the good deal. Future research should explore if country of origin, or

[3]It is possible that the coupling of brand and country of origin information (e.g. Sony and Mexico) earned little credibility, which made brand and country of origin have no direct effect on liking and perceived value. Future research should measure information

TABLE 2
LISREL Results for the Four Models of Buying Intentions

Criteria	Cognitive Model	C-A* Model Phase 1	C-A model Phase 2	C-A model Phase 3
Product: Coffeemaker				
χ^2 (df)	6.38 (8)	15.74 (9)	10.82 (10)	20.21 (13)
p-value	.605	.072	.372	.090
GFI	.986	.970	.979	.963
AGFI	.951	.880	.926	.900
RSR	.033	.050	.036	.053
% of Variance explained	47.9	62.5	63.7	63.6
Product: CD Stereo System				
χ^2 (df)	10.61 (8)	21.14 (9)	12.62 (10)	58.93 (13)
p-value	.225	.012	.246	.001
GFI	.977	.962	.976	.912
AGFI	.921	.847	.913	.755
RSR	.033	.052	.024	.097
% of Variance explained	64.0	76.2	77.5	77.5

Note: * C-A is the abbreviation of Cognitive-Affective Model.

brand names, affect consumers' expected price, which in turn may affect perceived value or even buying intentions.

Cognitive versus Cognitive-Affective Models of Buying Intentions

It is interesting to compare the cognitive model of buying intentions (Figure 3A) with the cognitive-affective model of buying intentions for the second phase (Figure 3B). First, the data confirmed all seven paths of the cognitive model, in terms of statistical significance as well as predicted directions, which explained 47.9% to 64.0% of the variance in buying intentions, for coffeemaker and CD stereo system, respectively. This result replicated the findings reported in the literature (for example, Dodds et al. 1991; Zeithaml 1988; Rao and Monroe 1989). Second, the results also indicated that the cognitive-affective model for the second phase fits the data very well. All 12 paths, except one, were statistical significant with the expected direction. The only non-significant one was the perceived quality- perceived value path, which suggests that perceived quality had no direct effect on perceived value. However, the significant perceived quality-liking, and liking-perceived value paths suggest that perceived quality had an indirect effect on perceived value, and was mediated by liking. This finding reveals that it is important to include an affective component in the buying intention model. This model explained 63.6% and 77.5% of the variance in buying intentions, for coffeemaker and CD stereo system, respectively. This pattern of results suggested that the cognitive-affective model not only can postulate the specific relations among the various cognitive and affective components, but also seems to be a better predictor of buying intentions, explaining an additional of 13.5% to 15.7% of the variance in buying intentions.

Further, the present findings also indicate that liking is similar in strength with perceived value in influencing buying intentions (path coefficients being .44 vs. .50 for coffeemaker, and .41 vs. .61 for CD stereo system). This result implies that the "affective" component is almost as important as the "cognitive" component in influencing buying intentions, which until recently has been ignored in buying intention studies. Inspired by this finding, future research on product evaluations and buying intentions should pay more attention to the affective component in addition to the cognitive component.

Another interesting issue remaining unanswered is why the cognitive-affective model for phase 1 and 3 is not supported, but that for phase 2 is supported. We speculate that it is due to the products (coffeemaker and CD stereo system) used in this study. The products considered in this study are neither extremely "affective" nor "cognitive", therefore they may provide little support for the cognitive-affective models of phase 1 (affective responses occurred first) and phase 3 (cognitive responses occurred first). It would be interesting to replicate this study by using affective products (e.g. perfume, wedding rings) and cognitive products (e.g. computers, dictionaries), and see if the cognitive-affective models for phase 1 and phase 3 will be supported.

To conclude, the proposed cognitive-affective model of buying intention (phase 2) is generally supported across two products. It is found that the three extrinsic cues affect perceived quality in a similar fashion. However, while price and expected price have direct effects on liking and perceived value, country of origin and brand name do not have a direct significant effect on them. Furthermore, the effect of perceived quality on perceived value is mediated through liking. Finally, liking toward a product and perceived value seem to be of similar importance in predicting buying intention.

REFERENCES

Bilkey Warren J. and Erik Nes (1982), "Country-Of-Origin Effects on Product Evaluation," *Journal of International Business Studies*, 13(spring/summer), 89-99.

456 / The Effects of Country of Origin, Brand, and Price Information: A Cognitive-Affective Model of Buying Intentions

FIGURE 3A
Results for the Cognitive Model of Buying Intentions

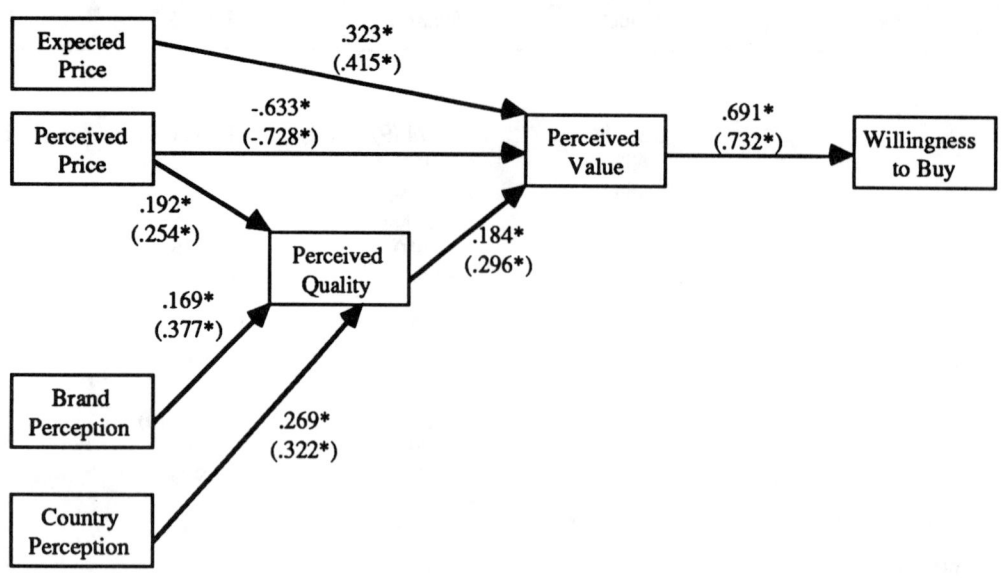

FIGURE 3B
Results for the Cognitive-Affective Model of Buying Intentions

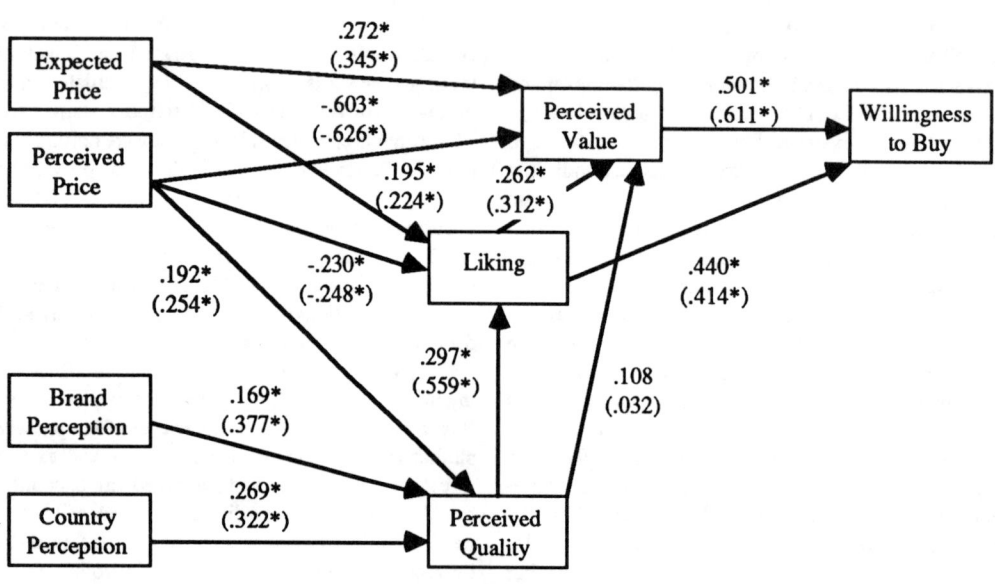

NOTE: * denotes p<.05; entries are path coefficients for coffeemaker and CD stereo system (in parentheses)
For clarity, factor correlations between the independent variables were omitted.

Cohen, Joel B. and Charles S. Areni (1991), "Affect and Consumer Behavior," in *Handbook of Consumer Behavior*, eds Thomas S. Robertson and Harold H. Kassarjian, Prentice Hall, NJ, 188-240.

Dodds, William B., Kent B. Monroe and Dhruv Grewal (1991), "Effects of Price, Brand, and Store Information on Buyers' Product Evaluations," *Journal of Marketing Research*, 28(August), 307-19.

Joreskog, Karl and Dag Sorbom (1986). *LISREL VI: Analysis of Linear Structural Relationships by Maximum Likelihood and Least Square Methods.* Mooresville, IN: Scientific Software, Inc.

Li, Wai-kwan and Kent B. Monroe (1992), "The Role of Country Of Origin Information on Buyers' Product Evaluations: An Indepth Interview Approach," in *AMA Educators' Proceedings: Enhancing Knowledge Development in Marketing*, Volume 3, eds. Robert P. Leone and V. Kumar, Chicago, 274-280.

Monroe, Kent B. (1973), "Buyers' Subjective Perceptions of Price," *Journal of Marketing Research*, 10(February), 70-80.

Monroe, Kent B., Dhruv Grewal, and Larry D. Compeau (1991), "The Concept of Reference Prices: Theoretical Justifications and Research Issues," Working paper, University of Illinois.

Monroe, Kent B. and R. Krishnan (1985), "The Effect of Price on Subjective Product Evaluations," in *Perceived Quality: How Consumers View Stores and Merchandise*, eds. Jacob Jacoby and Jerry C. Olson, Lexington, MA, 209-232.

Ozsomer, Aysegul and S. Tamer Cavusgil (1991), "Country-Of-Origin Effects on Product Evaluations: A Sequel to Bilkey and Nes Review," in *AMA Educators' Proceedings: Enhancing Knowledge Development in Marketing*, Volume 2, eds. Mary Gilly et al., Chicago, 269-277.

Rao, Akshay R. and Kent B. Monroe (1989), "The Effect of Price, Brand Name, and Store Name on Buyers' Perceptions of Product Quality: An Integrative Review," *Journal of Marketing Research*, 26(August), 351-7.

Scitovszky, Tibor (1945), "Some Consequences of the Habit of Judging Quality by Price," *Review of Economic Studies*, 12(Winter), 100-105.

Thaler, Richard (1985), "Mental Accounting and Consumer Choice," *Marketing Science*, 4(Summer), 199-214.

Winer, Russell S. (1988), "Behavioral Perspective on Pricing: Buyers' Subjective Perception of Price Revisited," in T. M. Devinney, ed., *Issues in Pricing: Theory and Research*, Lexington, MA: Lexington Books, pp.35-58.

Zajonc, Robert B. (1980), "Feeling and Thinking: Preferences Need No Inferences," *American Psychologist*, 35 (February), 151-175.

Zajonc, Robert B. and Hazel Markus (1982), "Affective and Cognitive Factors in Preferences," *Journal of Consumer Research*, 9(September), 123-131.

Zeithaml, Valarie A. (1988), "Consumer Perceptions of Price, Quality, and Value: A Means-End Model and Synthesis of Evidence," *Journal of Marketing*, 52 (July), 2-22.

The Role of Hispanic Ethnic Identification On Reference Group Influence

Cynthia Webster, Mississippi State University
James B. Faircloth III, Mississippi State University

ABSTRACT

This paper seeks to discover if Hispanic consumers' perceptions of reference group influence vary according to the extent of ethnic identification. Significant differences in perceptions are found for each of the three dimensions and for most of the items comprising reference group influence. For instance, there is a significant positive relationship between ethnic identification and the likelihood of being affected by both utilitarian and value-expressive reference group influence. The majority of these differences remain after possible social class effects are removed.

INTRODUCTION

The Hispanic[1] community has rapidly come to represent one of the most important consumer markets in the United States. The population of this market is projected to grow by 40 percent during the 1990s to 29.7 million. Current projections indicate that by 2010 this segment could approximate the size of the African-American population (Exter 1991). Business Week (1992) estimates by the year 2050 Hispanics will constitute fully 21 percent of the populace and comprise the largest American minority group. The dramatic population growth has enhanced the economic clout of Hispanics, who had disposable income of $200 billion in 1992, representing growth of 138 percent since 1980 (Business Week 1992). Few would argue these are not significant numbers to marketers.

The primary concern of marketers will be to better understand the nature of this market and how best to meet the needs of the burgeoning population. It is herein suggested that the key to thriving in the Hispanic market is to understand the nature of their ethnic identification and how it affects consumer behavior. It is further proposed that the Hispanic ethnic community, far from being a mere membership group, is the key reference group for many, particularly those demonstrating strong ethnic identity. If this is the case, understanding how strength of ethnic identification is influenced by the Hispanic community as a reference group for consumer behavior should aid marketers. Thus, the purpose of the current research is to examine the relationship between strength of Hispanic ethnic identification and susceptibility to empirically determined forms of Hispanic reference group influence while controlling for the effect of social class.

LITERATURE REVIEW

Ensuing is a brief discussion of the theoretical support for this study. The conceptual literature review begins with a discussion of ethnic identity, is followed by an overview of antecedent works on reference group influence, and finally, concludes with supporting research tying the two topics together.

---

[1] "Hispanic" will be used in this paper to represent persons from Mexico, Central America, South America, and the Caribbean. Although Hispanics from these regions are diverse in many ways, they exhibit many similarities. These similarities include shared frustrations, aspirations, attitudes, traditions, and beliefs (Loza 1988). Mexican-Americans, the population for this study, is considered highly representative of Hispanics in general. Approximately 60 percent of all U.S. Hispanics are Mexican-Americans (Engel et al. 1990).

Ethnic Identification

When groups of individuals of different cultures come into direct or indirect continuous contact and new common attitudes, norms, values, social and work activities, thinking patterns, and self-identification arise from the old culture, acculturation is said to have occurred (Andreasen 1990; Berry 1980; Gordon 1964; Marin et al. 1989; Padilla 1980; Penaloza 1989). Ethnic identity—a related concept—is present when an ethnic group considers itself, part of, but different from the larger population. This focus on ethnic identity, also called ethnicity, was the subject of Max Weber's (1961) classic work on such dimensions of the construct as: a sense of common custom, language, religion, values, morality, and etiquette. A plethora of ethnic identity measurements have been tried: language use (e.g. Kim, Laroche, and Joy 1990; Massey and Mullan 1984); country of origin (Gurak and Fitzgerald 1982); spouse's ethnic identity and social interaction (e.g., Driedger 1975); religion (e.g., Hirschman 1981); parent's ethnic identity (e.g., O'Guinn and Faber 1985); paternal ancestry (Alba and Moore 1982); and subjective measures of self-identification (Hirschman 1981). These ethnic identity suppositions will be shown to be critical elements of the following reference group construct.

Reference Group Influence and Concept Integration

Reference group influence, first noted by Hyman in 1942 (Witt 1970) and the subject of many definitions through the years, is customarily seen to embrace the use of groups as an anchoring point or frame of reference for individuals facing decisions (Mowen 1993; Shibutani 1955; Witt 1970). Representative of these various definitions is one proposed by Merton suggesting, reference groups are, "groups which the individual takes as a frame of reference for self-evaluation and attitude formation" (Witt 1970). It has been suggested that group (reference) influence has seven determinants (Witt 1970): dimensions of reference behavior, bases of social power, susceptibility of individuals to group influence, reference group relevance to a particular decision, group cohesiveness, attraction of individual to group, and status of group. This study will be principally concerned with the determinants of susceptibility to group influence and cohesiveness.

Many past reference group researchers have focused on the various classifications of reference groups (Bourne 1956; Mellott 1983; Newcomb 1943). Other research has concentrated on the type of reference group influence (Deutsch and Gerard 1955; French and Raven; Kelly 1952; Park and Lessig 1977). These trailblazing works allow current studies to proceed to more intensive application of consumer behavior theory in actual market segments.

In a study of cross-cultural and intergenerational influences on purchasing of public/private and luxury/necessity goods, Childers and Rao (1992) found that distinctions exist in different cultures regarding consumer behavior and reference group use. This same research proposed the reference group construct as a more reliable predictor of group influence than group membership. Another study developed a scale to determine the susceptibility of individuals to conform to others' expectations for purchasing decisions (Bearden, Netemeyer, Teel 1989).

Wicklund and Duval (1971) demonstrated that reference groups help individuals establish a self-identity. Other articles have examined the effect of group cohesiveness on reference group influence. Shaw (1971) studied how communications and individual interactions affect group cohesiveness and found, the greater the group cohesiveness, the more influential reference groups are in a consumer's behavior. According to Stafford (1966), the most cohesive groups are attractive to their members and reference group cohesiveness influences an individual's brand preference. Shibutani (1955) writes that conformity to group norms "...depends upon one's relationship and personal loyalty to others who share that outlook".

Expanding upon his theory of group conformity, Shibutani (1955) elaborated on a concept of "social worlds" that identifies an interesting relationship with reference group influence. He suggests modern societies develop communication channels that serve needs of particular portions of a community. These channels tend to insulate segments of the population from the general population, resulting in greater identification and solidarity within the effected groups. He indicates the underworld, ethnic minorities, and social elites are representative of the groups inclined to evolve these communication channels and develop higher group identity.

Past research has demonstrated differences between Hispanics who strongly identify with their ethnic reference group and those who do not. Strong identifiers have more children, greater family stability, stronger father roles, and more extended kinship systems (Sturdivant 1973). Despande et al. (1986) concluded that intensity of ethnic affiliation, not ethnic membership, is the superior predictor of consumer behavior, and established that strong Hispanic identifiers are more likely to purchase nationally advertised brands, have greater brand loyalty, purchase prestige products, and more inclined to buy products advertised to Hispanics than weak identifiers. Webster (1992) has shown that the intensity of Hispanic ethnic identity influences the level of purchasing information search and indicates a tendency to seek product information from family members and coworkers. Research to date has not established the role strength of ethnic identity plays in reference group influence, the focus of this empirical research.

RESEARCH JUSTIFICATION

Research evidence on reference groups purports: (1) they are better predictors of consumer behavior than group membership; (2) the more cohesive a reference group is the more influence it exerts on individuals; (3) consumer related differences exist between strong and weak Hispanic identifiers; and (4) consistent use of the Spanish language to communicate tends to create a Hispanic 'social world'. Therefore, a legitimate case can be made for the efficacy of examining the effect of ethnic identity on the various forms of reference group influence. Reference group influence will be evaluated using a construct developed by Park and Lessig (1977) that considers: (1)Informational influences-perception that the reference group has knowledge of a purchasing decision; (2) Value-expressive influences-how much the reference group enhances an individual's self-concept; and (3) Utilitarian influences-how much an individual is expected to comply with expectations of a reference group.

Thus, the primary purpose of this empirical study is to increase our understanding of both the Hispanic market and reference group influence by testing hypotheses concerning whether or not differences in reference group influence are due to Hispanic ethnic identification or whether they are possibly due to social class effects.

HYPOTHESES

The preceding discussion on Hispanic consumer behavior and reference group influence leads to the following hypotheses:

H1: The strength of Hispanic ethnic identity has a significant effect on reference group influence.

H2: The strength of Hispanic ethnic identity has a significant effect on reference group influence while controlling for the effects of social class.

H3: The strength of Hispanic ethnic identity has a significant effect on the degree of reliance on informational influence.

H4: The strength of Hispanic ethnic identity has a significant effect on the degree of reliance on utilitarian influence.

H5: The strength of Hispanic ethnic identity has a significant effect on the degree of reliance on value-expressive influence.

METHOD

The sample consists of Hispanic adult consumers chosen from the San Antonio metropolitan area. This bilingual city is the nation's ninth largest and is comprised of 53.9% Hispanic and 37.9% Anglo ethnic origin (Strategy Research 1991). Sample members were chosen from ten of the metropolitan area's 99 zip code areas; seven of which were selected at random. The remaining three were selected by judgment after examining detailed census statistics to yield a representative set of areas by varying both proportions of Spanish- and English-speaking residents and median family income levels.

Carefully-instructed interviewers delivered the questionnaires to a representative sample of households in their zones, using detailed street maps. At most six questionnaires were delivered to any one block, and an attempt was made to cover most of each geographical zone. The sampling process was completed in two weeks, including afternoons, evenings, and weekend days. Each interviewer carried both Spanish and English language versions of the questionnaire. Most interviewers were bilingual, and those most fluent in Spanish were assigned to predominantly Spanish zones. After explaining the purpose of the study, agreement of one adult member of the household was secured. To help determine the level of thought given to responding to the scale items, the interviewer stayed with the respondent during questionnaire completion. Eleven questionnaires were later omitted due to obvious respondent carelessness while addressing the items. The response rate, 74%, did not significantly vary among the groups by city area. The final sample was composed of 167 usable questionnaires.

Respondents' level of reference group influence was measured by using Park and Lessig's (1977) scale of the construct. This scale has fourteen items to measure the informational, utilitarian, and value-expressive dimensions of reference group influence. Each scale item was followed by a seven-point scale with the endpoints anchored with "Strongly Agree" and "Strongly Disagree." Demographic information such as age, education, and occupation was collected for husband and wife, as well as combined family income and number of children. The occupation and education information was collected in a manner that facilitated the calculation of Hollingshead's Two-Factor Index of Social Position (Hollingshead and Redlich (1958). As language spoken at home has long been associated with ethnic identification (McArthur 1984), it is used in the current study. Though the association between ethnic identity and language spoken at home is not perfect, it has been used in many studies(see, for example, Massey and Mullan 1984 and Hazuda et al. 1988), and is considered a generally reliable indicator of ethnic identification (Keefe and Padilla 1987; Olmedo and Padilla 1978; Ortiz and Arce 1984; Padilla 1980; Samora and Deane 1956; Tharp et al. 1968). In fact, Marin et al. (1989) identifies language as "the strongest aspect of this complex phenomenon that has been empirically tested." The final sample of 167 respondents is comprised of 53 (31.7%) Hispanics who speak English mainly at home (low-Hispanic identifiers), 68 (40.7%) Hispanics who speak English and Spanish equally at home (bilinguals), and 46 (27.5%) Hispanics who speak Spanish mainly at home (high-Hispanic identifiers).

Hierarchical M/ANOVAs were used to test the hypotheses. This hierarchical approach is appropriate when two factors (e.g., ethnic identification and social class) are correlated and where unequal cell sizes exist. It does not assume linear relationships between ethnic identification and social class, as would ANOVA. This approach also allows for the testing of the effect of ethnic identification alone before controlling the effects of social class, as well as after controlling for this factor. By using the test-retest approach with a 14-day interval, the questionnaire was considered to be reliable ($r = .92$). The Pearson's product moment correlation here indicates a high correlation or consistency between the first and second administrations of the instrument.

RESULTS

The data in the Table reveal the group means for the three Hispanic groups based on ethnic identification and F tests for the items comprising the three types of reference group influence. The first column of F values (FE) presents the F values for a single factor design testing for the effects of ethnic identification alone. The second column of F values ($F_{E/SC}$) presents the conditional F values on the effect of ethnic identification after controlling for possible social class effects.

An examination of both the univariate and multivariate results in the Table indicate that ethnic identification has a significant effect on each of the three types of reference group influence, thus supporting H1. Significant multivariate tests were discovered for the conditional tests after controlling for possible social class effects, which is consistent with H2. These findings imply that differences exist with respect to the likelihood of reference group influence which are not attributable to social class.

Informational influence. The F values and cell means in the Table reveal that the high-Hispanic identifiers, as compared with the Hispanics in the other two groups, appear more likely to seek brand-related information from others (friends, neighbors, etc.) who have reliable information and to perceive that observation of experts' behavior influences their brand choice. On the other hand, this same group of Hispanics appear significantly less likely to seek information from those who work with the product as a profession. Hispanic ethnic identification does not have a significant effect on two of the informational influence items. All of these findings give mixed support for H3.

Since the pattern of findings for utilitarian and value-expressive influence is similar, the findings for these two types of influence will be presented as a unit.

Utilitarian and value-expressive influence. The F values in the Table indicate that ethnic identification has a significant effect on each one the four items comprising utilitarian influence and on four of the five items comprising value-expressive influence. As previously stated, each one of these values remains significant even after possible social class effects are removed. For each of these eight items, the high-Hispanic identifiers, as compared to the Hispanics in the two other groups, would seem to be impacted more by these two types of reference group influence. Thus, H4 and H5 both receive overwhelming support.

The cell means in the Table indicate that Hispanics, in general, do not perceive themselves to be heavily impacted by informational influence (most Xs < 4.00). The one exception to this generalization is the seeking of information from close others. On the other hand, the utilitarian and value-expressive cell means indicate that Hispanics perceive themselves to be heavily impacted by these two types of reference group influence (all Xs > 4.00).

The bilingual couples, or those with a moderate degree of ethnic identification, tend to have reference group influence patterns between the other two Hispanic groups. In each one of the univariate cases where ethnic identification was found to have a significant effect on reference group influence, bilinguals fall between the two other groups. This supports the traditional model of assimilation (Gordon 1964) and the linear, bi-polar model of ethnic identification. In other words, there appears to be a linear pattern of change as the consumer moves away from the behavioral patterns of the Hispanic culture and moves toward the behavioral patterns of the U.S. culture.

CONCLUSIONS

This study examined the impact of Hispanic ethnic identification on Park and Lessig's (1977) three types of reference group influence after controlling for social class effects. In all but one case the group means for strong ethnic identifiers was found to be higher than the other two groups. In general, mixed support was received for the effect of ethnic identification on informational influence. Strong ethnic identifiers emerged more likely to seek advice or help from personal acquaintances or from disinterested experts (i.e. unbiased), but only equally likely to rely on experts who work directly in the product area.

High ethnic identifiers seem significantly more likely to be subject to utilitarian or value-expressive influence than bilinguals or low identifiers. Particularly important is the tendency of high identifiers to be influenced by close acquaintances and/or family members' expectations for the appropriate brand selection. Recognition of this influence should assist in the development of Hispanic marketing strategies.

Support was also forthcoming for value-expressive influence for high identifiers. All but one of the items was found greater for this group. These results suggest high Hispanic identifiers place greater emphasis on the personal statement made by product consumption than the other two Hispanic groups. Status brands are seen as important symbols of personal expression for high identifiers.

Finally, evidence suggests that Hispanics who are not high ethnic identifiers are more likely to be assimilated into prevailing U.S. cultural and behavioral patterns. Clearly this suggests that marketers would be ill advised to treat Hispanics as a homogeneous market.

REFERENCES

Alba, Richard D. and Gwen Moore (1982), "Ethnicity in the American Elite," *American Sociological Review*, 47 (June) 373-382.

Andreasen, Alan R. (1990), "Cultural Interpenetration: A Critical Research Issue for the 1990s," in *Advances in Consumer Research*, Vol 17, eds. Marvin E. Goldberg, Gerald Gorn, and Richard Pollay, Provo, UT: Association for Consumer Research, 847-849.

Bearden, William O., Richard G. Netemeyer, Jessee E. Teel (1989), "Measurement of Consumer Susceptibility to Interpersonal Influence," *Journal of Consumer Research*, 15(March) 473-481.

Berry, John W. (1980), "Acculturation as Varieties of Adaptation," in *Acculturation: Theory, Models and Some New Findings*, ed. Amado M. Padilla, Boulder, CO: Westview Press, 9-26.

TABLE
MANOVA on Reference Group Influence[a]

	English (n=53)	Bilingual (n=68)	Spanish (n=46)	F_E[b]	$F_{E/SC}$[c]
Informational Influence					
Seek information about various brands from an association of professionals or independent group of experts	1.32	1.47	1.68	0.92	0.90
Seek information from those who work with the product as a profession	2.83	2.60	2.28	2.46[d]	2.11
Seek brand-related information from those friends, neighbors, relatives, or work associates who have reliable information	5.44	5.89	6.02	2.64[d]	2.60[d]
Selected brand is influenced by observing a seal of approval of an independent testing agency (i.e., Good Housekeeping)	1.46	1.20	1.23	0.48	0.54
Observation of experts' behavior (e.g., type of car which police drive) influences brand choice	2.33	3.00	4.02	6.21[e]	5.88[e]
Wilks' Lambda				.829[d]	.886[d]
Utilitarian Influence					
Brand selection is influenced by the expectations/preferences of fellow work associates	4.54	4.68	5.17	3.18[d]	2.77[d]
Brand selection is influenced by the expectations/preferences of close friends	4.19	5.03	5.60	6.54[e]	4.95[d]
Brand selection is influenced by the expectations/preferences of family members	4.22	4.48	4.89	3.34[d]	3.08[d]
Brand selection is influenced by the desire to satisfy the expectations of others	4.47	4.69	5.01	2.59[d]	2.39[d]
Wilks' Lambda				.816[d]	.838[d]
Value-Expressive Influence					
The purchase/use of a particular brand will enhance others' image of me	5.15	5.39	5.89	3.40[d]	3.11[d]
Those who purchase/use status brands possess the characteristics I would like to have	4.92	5.47	6.02	4.39[d]	4.41[d]
Often feel that it would be nice to be like the type of person which ads show using a particular brand	5.67	6.22	6.38	3.36[d]	3.33[d]
People who purchase a particular brand (e.g., Mont Blanc) are admired/respected by others	5.62	5.90	6.17	2.42[d]	2.35[d]
The purchase of a particular brand helps me show others what I am, or would like to be	4.86	5.11	5.13	0.58	0.64
Wilks' Lambda				.803[d]	.808[d]

[a] Influence was measured with a seven-point scale where 1 = Strongly Agree and 7 = Strongly Disagree.
[b] F_E denotes the single factor design testing only for the effects of ethnic identification on reference group influence.
[c] $F_{E/SC}$ denotes the effect of ethnic identification on reference group influence while controlling for the effects of social class.
[d] $p \leq .05$
[e] $p \leq .01$

Bourne, Francis S. "Group Influence in Marketing and Public Relations," *Some Applications of Behavioral Science Research*, in Renis Likert and Samuel P. Hayes, Jr. (eds.) Paris: UNESCO, 1957, in *Classics in Consumer Behavior*, ed. Louis E. Boone (1977), Tulsa, OK: Petroleum Publishing Company, 211-235.

Business Week (1992), "A Spicier Stew in the Melting Pot," (December 21), 29-30.

Childers, Terry L. and Akshay R. Rao (1992), "The Influence of Familial and Peer-based Reference Groups on Consumer Decisions," *Journal of Consumer Research*, 19 (September), 198-211.

Deshpande, Rohit, Wayne D. Hoyer, and Naveen Donthu (1986), "The Intensity of Ethnic Affiliation: A Study of the Sociology of Hispanic Consumption," *Journal of Consumer Research*, 13 (September), 214-220.

Deutsch, M., and H. B. Gerard (1955), "A Study of Normative and Informational Social Influences Upon Individual Judgement," *Journal of Abnormal and Social Psychology*, 51:629-36, in *Social Psychology: Sociological Perspectives*, eds, Morris Rosenberg and Ralph H. Turner (1981), New York: Basic Books, Inc., Publishers, 70.

Driedger, L. (1975), "In Search of Cultural Identity Factors: A Comparison of Ethnic Students," *Canadian Review of Sociology and Anthropology*, 12 (May), 150-161.

Engel, James F., Roger D. Blackwell, and Paul Miniard (1990) *Consumer Behavior*. Chicago: The Dryden Press.

Exter, Thomas (1991), "One Million Hispanics Club," *American Demographics*, 13 (February), 59.

French, J. Jr. and B. Raven, "The Bases of Social Power," in Dorwin Cartwright and Alvin Zander (eds.), *Group Dynamics: Research and Theory*, (Second Edition), 607-623, in *Group Influence on Consumer Brand Choice*, Robert E. Witt (1970), The University of Texas: Bureau of Business Research.

Gordon, M. (1964), *Assimilation in America Life*. London: Oxford University Press.

Gurak, Douglas T. and Joseph P. Fitzgerald (1982), "Intermarriage Among Hispanic Ethnic Groups in New York City," *American Journal of Sociology*, 87 (January), 921-934.

Hazuda, Helen P., M. P. Stern, S. M. Haffner (1988), "Acculturation and Assimilation Among Mexican Americans: Scales and Population Based Data," *Social Science Quarterly*, 69 (September), 687-706.

Hirschman, Elizabeth C. (1981), "American Jewish Ethnicity: Its Relationship to Some Selected Aspects of Consumer Behavior," *Journal of Marketing*, 45 (Summer), 102-110.

Hollingshead, August B. and Frederick C. Redlich (1958), *Social Class and Mental Illness*, New York: Wiley.

Hyman, H. (1942), "The Psychology of Status," *Archives of Psychology*, No. 269, 1-95. in Robert E. Witt (1970), *Group Influence on Consumer Brand Choice*, The University of Texas: Bureau of Business Research.

Keefe, Susan E., Amado M. Padilla (1987), *Chicano Ethnicity*, Albuquerque: University of New Mexico Press. 8, 42.

Kelly, H. H. (1952), "Two Functions of Reference Groups," in *Readings in Social Psychology*, eds. G. E. Swanson, T. M. Newcomb, and E. L. Hartley, New York: Holt, Rinehart and Winston, in *Social Psychology: Sociological Perspectives*, eds. Morris Rosenberg and Ralph H. Turner (1981), New York: Basic Books, Inc., Publisher, 68.

Kim, Chankan, Michel Laroche, and Annamma Joy (1990), "An Empirical Study of Ethnicity on Consumption Patterns in a Bi-Cultural Environment," *Advances in Consumer Research*, 17, Marvin E. Goldberg, Gerald Gorn, and Richard Pollay, eds., Ann Arbor, MI: Association for Consumer Research, 839-846.

Loza, Enrique (1988), "Business, Amigo? No! Amigo Business? Si!" *Public Relation Journal*, 44, 6:8-10.

Marin, Gerardo, Barbara Van Oss Marin, Regina Otero-Sabogal, Fabio Sabogal, and Eliseo J. Perez-Stable (1989), "The Role of Acculturation in the Attitudes, Norms, and Expectancies of Hispanic Smokers," *Journal of Cross-Cultural Psychology*, 20 (4), 399-415.

Massey, Douglas, and Brendan P. Mullan (1984), "Processes of Hispanic and Black Spatial Assimilation," *American Journal of Sociology*, (89) 836-73.

McArthur, Edith (1984), "What Language Do You Speak?," *American Demographics*, 6 (October), 32-33.

Mellot, Douglas W. (1983), *Fundamentals of Consumer Behavior*, Tulsa, OK: PennWell Publishing Company.

Mowen, John C. (1993), *Consumer Behavior*, New York: Macmillan Publishing Company.

Newcomb, T. M. (1957), *Personality and Social Change: Attitude Formation in a Student Community*, New York: Holt, Rinehart and Winston. in *Social Psychology: Individuals, Groups, Societies*, eds. John W. McDavid and Herbert Harari, New York: Harper & Row, Publishers, Incorporated, 239-240.

O'Guinn, Thomas C. and Ronald J. Faber (1985), "New Perspectives on Acculturation: The Relationship of General and Role Specific Acculturation with Hispanics' Consumer Attitude," *Advances in Consumer Research*, M. S. Holbrook and E. C. Hirschman eds., 12, 113-117,

Olmedo, Esteban L., Amado M. Padilla (1978), "Empirical and Construct Validation of a Measure of Acculturation for Mexican Americans," *Journal of Social Psychology*, 105, 179-187.

Ortiz, Vilma, Carlos H. Arce (1984), "Language Orientation and Mental Health Status Among Persons of Mexican Descent," *Hispanic Journal of Behavioral Sciences* (6) 127-143.

Padilla, Amado M. (1990), *Acculturation: Theory, Models, and Some New Findings*, Boulder, CO: Westview Press.

Park, C. Whan and V. Parker Lessig (1977), "Students and Housewives: Differences in Susceptibility to Reference Group Influence," *Journal of Consumer Research*, 4 (September), 102-110.

Penaloza, Fernando (1986), "Mexican Family Roles," *Journal of Marriage and the Family*.

Samora, Julian, William N. Deane (1956), "Language Usage as a Possible Index of Acculturation," *Sociology and Social Research* (40) 307-311.

Shaw, Marvin E. (1971), *Group Dynamics: The Psychology of Small Group Behavior*, New York: McGraw Hill, in *Consumer Behavior: Basic Findings and Management Implications*, Gerald Zaltman and Melanie Wallendorf (1979), New York: John Wiley & Sons.

Shibutani, Tamotsu (1955), "Reference Groups as Perspectives," *American Journal of Sociology*, Vol. 60 (May), 560-569 in *Perspectives in Consumer Behavior*, eds. Harold H. Kassargian and Thomas S. Robertson, Glenview, Ill: Scott Foresman and Company, 299-309.

Stafford, James E. (1966), "Effects of Group Influences on Consumer Brand Preferences," *Journal of Marketing Research*, III (February), 68-75, in *Consumer Behavior: Selected Readings*, ed. James F. Engel (1968), Homewood, Ill: Richard D. Irwin, Inc.

Strategy Research Corporation (1991), *The 1991 San Antonio Hispanic Market*, Lo Nuestro.

Sturdivant, Frederick D. "Subculture Theory: Poverty, Minorities, and Marketing." in *Consumer Behavior: Theoretical Sources*, Scott F. Ward and Thomas S. Robertson, eds. Englewood Cliffs, NJ: Prentice-Hall, 1973.

Tharp, Roland G., Arnold Meadow, Susan G. Lennhoff, Donna Satterfield (1968), "Changes in Marriage Roles Accompanying the Acculturation of the Mexican-American Wife," *Journal of Marriage and the Family* (30) 404-412.

Weber, Max (1961), "Ethnic Groups." *Theory of Society*. Talcott Parsons et al., New York: Free Press, 301-309. Translated by Ferdinand Kolegar, From Max Weber 1947. "Enstehung ethnischen Gemeinsamkeitsglaubens. Sprach und Kultgemeinschaft," in Wirtschaft und Gesellschaft, Tulbingen: J.C.B. Mahr, 234-240.

Webster, Cynthia (1992), "The Effects of Hispanic Subcultural Identification on Information Search Behavior," *Journal of Advertising Research*, (September/October) 54-62.

Wickland, R.A. and S. Duval (1971), "Opinion Changes and Performance Facilitation as a Result of Self Awareness," *Journal of Experimental Social Psychology*, 319-342, in *Social Psychology*, Robert C. Williamson, Paul G. Swingle, and Stansfeld Sargent (1982), Itasca, ILL: F. E. Peacock Publishers, Inc. 357

Witt, Robert E. (1970), *Group Influence on Consumer Brand Choice*, The University of Texas: Bureau of Business Research.

Predicting Buyers' Selection of Interpersonal Sources: The Role of Strong Ties and Weak Ties

Pamela Kiecker, Texas Tech University
Cathy L. Hartman, Utah State University

ABSTRACT

The construct of social support is used to explore buyers' motivation for selecting interpersonal sources. The paper reports a study of buyers and purchase pals (interpersonal sources operating at the point-of-purchase) that examined (1) the strength of ties in buyer-pal relationships and (2) buyers' perceptions of the type of social support provided by purchase pals. Findings suggest that the type of interpersonal source selected for support can be predicted by the strength of tie between the buyer and the source.

INTRODUCTION

Numerous studies have shown that buyers employ others as interpersonal sources of information and/or support in their decision making processes (e.g., Assael, Etgar, and Henry 1983; Midgley 1983; Furse, Punj, and Stewart 1984; Price and Feick 1984; Sanders 1985; Hartman and Kiecker 1991). The individuals that buyers use as sources form a diverse set and serve a variety of functions. Examples include the fashion expertise offered by paid wardrobe consultants (Solomon 1987), automobile recommendations provided by insurance agents (Formisano, Olshavsky, and Tapp 1982), and information regarding product innovations from opinion leaders and early adopters of new products (Arndt 1967; Engel, Kegerreis, and Blackwell 1969). Price and Feick (1984) found substantial evidence of the use of interpersonal sources, where 91% of the respondents in their study reported they are likely to use knowledgeable friends, relatives, or acquaintances as information sources.

Buyers vary in terms of their relationships with the various individuals providing them with information and support. For example, wardrobe consultants and insurance agents likely represent weak ties, while close friends and relatives represent strong ties. It also is likely that buyers' selection of a particular source will depend on the nature of their relationship with these individuals, as well as the specific decision task at hand. Buyers' selection of interpersonal sources is explored in this study by focusing on the buyer's purchase decision at the point of sale. By virtue of this focus, we examine relationships between buyers and purchase pals, where the term "purchase pal" is used to specify *"individuals who accompany buyers on their shopping trips in order to assist them with their on-site purchase decisions"* (Hartman and Kiecker 1991, p. 462).

This research uses the construct of social support to explore buyers' motivation for selecting particular individuals as purchase pals. We begin by providing a brief review of the literature on social support and interpersonal sources. We then report the research methods and findings of a study that examined (1) the strength of ties in buyer-pal relationships and (2) buyers' perceptions of the type of social support provided by purchase pals. These findings suggest that the type of interpersonal source selected for support can be predicted by the strength of tie between the buyer and the source.

LITERATURE REVIEW

Social Support

Individuals are generally motivated to seek support for a reason. That is, supportive interactions generally are meaningful and positive for recipients (see Cobb 1976; Caplan 1976; House 1981; Moss 1973; Tolsdorf 1976). While it is likely that supportive interaction also benefits the provider, specific definitions and functions provided in the literature have generally focused on the benefits for the recipient. Central to most conceptualizations of support is the notion of uncertainty reduction. That is, supportive communication can be seen to help people by decreasing the anxiety and stress caused by unknown situations. By reducing perceptions of uncertainty, supportive communication helps the receiver develop a sense of control over potentially stressful circumstances. According to Eyres and MacElveen-Hoehn (1983, p. 3), support occurs when "information and resources from others in the environment . . . minimize the perception of threat, maximize actual and perceived mastery, and facilitate direct action and anticipatory modes of coping."

Extending the notion of social support to buyers' purchase decisions, the experience of uncertainty and ambiguity in the context of a purchase situation motivates buyers to seek the support of others. The information provided by others might include product attributes, prices, distribution outlets, and available alternatives; support may be derived from others' product expertise and negotiation skills.

The dyadic relationship involved in the giving and receiving of support occurs in a socially constructed network of both strong ties and weak ties. Tie strength is indicated by several variables, including the importance attached to social relations, frequency of social contact, and types of social relations (Granovetter 1973; 1982; Weimann 1983). Support from so-called "weak ties" may be provided by buyers' acquaintances, co-workers, or others in the community whom they may not know well but who are able to help because of some generalized cultural or role expectation. Those individuals closest to buyers (i.e., close friends and family members whom buyers know at a psychological level) represent "strong ties." Their support helps buyers because they can discriminate buyers' distinctive needs and, based on this information, determine what is (and is not) effective for them. In other words, individuals representing close ties have the requisite knowledge for understanding buyers' unique perspectives and can use this knowledge to assist them.

The manner in which uncertainty is reduced by the use of strong and weak ties varies. In the close relationships formed by strong ties, uncertainty is reduced via extensive exchanges of personal information, similarities, and interaction with the other person's network (e.g., Berger and Calabrese 1975; Parks and Adelman 1983). Social comparison theory suggests that buyers are most likely to choose "co-oriented peers"—those whose outlook and values they consider to be similar to their own—for comparisons. (It also is likely that those who are perceived as similar in terms of outlook and values will be the same people selected as close friends and spouses). Marketing research that supports this hypothesis includes a study of women's choice of cosmetics. Moschis (1976) found that women were more likely to seek information about product choices from similar friends and to trust the judgments of similar others. This same relationship also was found for evaluations of men's suits and coffee (Burnkrant and Cousineau 1975). Similarly, Brown and Reingen (1987) found individuals more likely to use homophilous ties (than heterophilous ties) for word-of-mouth referrals.

In contrast to strong ties, individuals representing weak ties are detached from the center of the individual's social circle. Consequently, they are unlikely to transmit information back to the individual's primary network of strong ties. In the matter of risk reduction, this distance enhances perceived anonymity and allows people to seek information and support without having to deal with the uncertainty of how those in primary relationships might respond. Weak ties also make it easier for the individual to experiment with new behaviors and new identities without being held accountable by those one sees more regularly. Further, because of their relative detachment from strong ties in a network, weak ties serve to extend the range of information to which the individual has access. These factors have lead researchers to acknowledge the *strength* of weak ties in social networks (e.g., Granovetter 1973).

This literature base suggests that the selection of an interpersonal source will depend, at least in part, on the strength of the tie between the buyer and the source. The following section reviews the relevant literature on interpersonal sources in order to place the role of tie strength within the general literature on buyers' selection of sources. Special attention is given to the limited research that has specifically examined purchase pals as interpersonal sources.

Interpersonal Sources

Previous research examining interpersonal sources indicates that buyers use purchase pals to reduce the risk and uncertainty they associate with the shopping task. For example, Bell (1967) found buyers with little confidence in their car buying talents were likely to use personal friends and acquaintances for product information, while Midgley (1983) identified men's use of their spouses to increase their confidence in clothing purchases. In another study, Sanders (1985) recognized the role of interpersonal sources in the reduction of risk for tatoo consumers.

Research also has shown that buyers' selection of a purchase pal depends on the type of risk associated with the decision process. For example, Kiecker and Hartman (1993) found that buyers who perceive *social/psychological risks* to be associated with a product purchase are more likely to use family members whom they have known for a significant period of time as purchase pals; when buyers perceive *functional risks* to be associated with product purchases, they are more likely to use non-family members whom they have known for less time (fewer than three years).

Other studies indicate that the selection of a particular purchase pal might be influenced by the buyer's perception of the source's credibility. For example, Furse, Punj, and Staelin (1984) found individuals selected as purchase pals were perceived by buyers to be more knowledgeable and experienced than themselves. They suggest that purchase pal assisted-shoppers appear willing to substitute the expertise of purchase pals for their own perceived lack of expertise. And, as indicated above, the type of information or expertise varies by the type of pal. When buyers require information on the *performance or technical aspects* of a product, acquaintances or casual friends are likely to be selected as purchase pals. When buyers require information on the *psychosocial aspects* of a product, close friends or relatives are likely to be selected as purchase pals (Cox 1968).

There also is evidence that buyers' selection of purchase pals depends upon personal characteristics of the buyer. For example, Bell (1967) found the selection of close friends and relatives versus acquaintances varied by buyers' levels of general and specific self-confidence. Those buyers who are quite confident in most areas of their lives, but are uneasy about their car buying abilities, most frequently used casual friends or acquaintances as purchase pals. In this case it seems those individuals who lack specific self-confidence are likely to seek information from sources they perceive to be more objective and, perhaps, more accurate as to the performance of the automobile than close friends or family members might be. Similarly, Punj and Staelin (1983) found consumers to use "expert" friends to help them in their automobile purchase decision.

Taken together, the literature examining social support and interpersonal sources suggests that the strength of tie between buyers and purchase pals can be used to predict the type of purchase pals buyers will seek out for information and support in their decision making. The following section sets forth the general predictions suggested by previous research.

RESEARCH PROPOSITION

Although this study was conducted on a largely exploratory basis, the general proposition suggested by previous research is that buyers will select interpersonal sources that represent (1) strong ties when the information/support required is largely symbolic and based on a psycho-social understanding of the buyer and the buyer's needs, and (2) weak ties when the information/support required is largely functional and based on product and/or marketplace expertise.

METHOD

In order to explore the role of strong ties and weak ties in buyers' selection of interpersonal sources, a quota sample of 84 shopping dyads in a large northwestern city was surveyed. The sample was drawn from a variety of retail outlets, including major downtown stores, regional shopping areas, specialty shopping centers, and individual, free-standing stores. Respondents were selected to represent four different dyad types. These included (1) female buyer/female pal, (2) male buyer/male pal, (3) male buyer/female pal, and (4) female buyer/male pal.

Interviewers were familiarized with the shopper-consultant literature and participated in a training session. They were instructed to identify shopping dyads and request that the buyer answer several questions regarding the objective of the shopping trip. Characteristics of the sample are presented in Table 1.

The survey included open-ended questions about the buyers' experience. To investigate the strength of tie between the buyer and the pal, buyers were asked to indicate (1) the type of social relationship they had with the pal (categories were: parent, sibling, spouse, close friend, boy/girlfriend, neighbor, colleague, classmate, and mere acquaintance), and (2) the length of time they had known the pal. To identify the types of social support provided by pals, buyers were asked to describe the role of the pal in the decision process, specifically in terms of the information and/or support buyers believe the pals provide. The content of buyers' responses to this question was analyzed. General procedures paralleled those suggested in the literature (e.g., Krippendorff 1980). Three independent judges were used to categorize responses and the judgments of the three were compared to determine interrater reliability. Interrater reliability rates ranged from 0.90 to 0.97. Reported results reflect the subset of responses categorized the same way by all three judges. Results from both questions are reviewed in the following section.

RESULTS

Types of Social Relationships

Table 2 provides a summary of the buyer-pal relationships as described by the buyers sampled. The table is broken down by the (1) gender dyad type (i.e., same gender and mixed gender dyads), (2) strength of the tie between the buyer and the pal (strong versus weak), and (3) length of the buyer-pal relationship (greater than

TABLE 1
Characteristics of the Sample (n=84)

AGE	% OF SAMPLE
less than 21 years	18
22 - 24 years	26
25 - 29 years	17
30 - 35 years	15
36 - 45 years	6
46 - 60 years	11
more than 60 years	6
refused	1

MARITAL STATUS	
single	67
married	32
refused	1

EDUCATIONAL LEVEL	
less than High School	11
High School Diploma	25
some college	14
4-year college/university degree	46
refused	4

INCOME	
less than $25,000	40
$25,000 - $39,999	25
$40,000 - $59,999	19
$60,000 or greater	4
refused	12

GENDER	
male	54
female	46

three years versus less than three years). The relationships classified as strong ties, consistent with the literature, include those between buyers and family members (parents and their children, siblings, spouses), boyfriends and girlfriends, and close friends of the same gender. The relationships classified as weak ties include those between buyers and mere acquaintances, classmates, work colleagues, and neighbors.

Across all gender dyad types, a greater percentage of the dyads are strong ties. Interestingly, *every* mixed gender dyad involved a strong tie, and *more than 80 percent* of the female-female dyads involved a strong tie, while *just over half* of the male-male dyads involved strong ties. The majority of strong ties also are long-term relationships, while weak ties more often are short-term relationships. Considering the few cases that are exceptions, the data on length of relationship among strong ties show that the short-term relationships were isolated among close friends and boyfriends-girlfriends. The same data for weak ties show the few long-term relationships to be among work colleagues and neighbors.

Types of Social Support by Strength of Ties

Table 3 reports the findings on type of social support provided by purchase pals. In total, 11 different types of social support were identified via content analysis. These include a variety of activities, representing both functional tasks (e.g., providing information regarding product features, prices, retail outlets, etc.) and symbolic tasks (e.g., providing moral support, increasing buyer's confidence in the decision, determining the suitability of the product for the buyer). The table displays the number of buyers reporting that pals were used for each type of support and for both strong and weak tie relationships.

Tests of differences between strong and weak ties for each type of support involved tests of proportions. The results of these analyses show significant differences in the type of support provided by the strength of ties between the buyer and the pal for 9 of the 11 types of support identified. Strong ties are more likely to be used by buyers seeking moral support for their decisions, determining the appropriateness or suitability of the product for the buyer, and making the actual purchase decision. In contrast, weak ties are more likely to be used by buyers requiring negotiation skills and information on product features, prices, and location of retail stores. Generally, the pattern of the significant findings provides support for the research proposition. The implications of these findings and conclusions drawn from the study's results are discussed in the final section.

TABLE 2
Nature of Buyer-Pal Relationships

STRONG TIES	F-F[1]	M-M[2]	F-M/M-F[3]
mother-daughter	35%	—	—
father-son	—	21%	—
father-daughter	—	—	14%
sister-sister	16%	—	—
brother-brother	—	8%	—
sister-brother	—	—	8%
husband-wife	—	—	50%
close friends	32%	25%	—
boyfriend-girlfriend	—	—	28%
Length of Relationship			
less than three years	12%	26%	21%
greater than three years	88%	74%	79%
WEAK TIES			
acquaintances	—	4%	—
classmates	6%	13%	—
work colleagues	—	29%	—
neighbors	11%	—	—
Length of Relationship			
less than three years	92%	73%	—
greater than three years	8%	27%	—

[1] female buyer-female pal
[2] male buyer-male pal
[3] female buyer-male pal/male buyer-female pal

IMPLICATIONS AND CONCLUSIONS

There is considerable evidence in the literature that buyers' use interpersonal sources for information and support. The data reported here suggest that the nature of the information and support provided by sources varies by the strength of the tie between the buyer and source. Based on these findings, it is possible to predict buyers' selection of specific interpersonal sources on the basis of tie strength. As shown in this study, the support provided by strong ties is of a generally symbolic or psycho-social nature. Accordingly, strong tie support is likely to depend upon the source's familiarity and understanding of the *buyer's* individual characteristics and needs. For example, in order to determine the appropriateness or suitability of a product for the buyer, the pal needs to know his or her personal tastes and preferences, individual "style," and/or values and lifestyle.

In contrast, support provided by weak ties was found to be more functional. It includes objective information that is more likely to rely on the *source's* abilities and know-how, based on specific product experiences and general knowledge of the marketplace. Unlike the support provided by strong ties, weak tie support is largely independent of the personal characteristics of the buyers receiving the support. For example, when providing buyers with information on product features and prices, sources rely on their own knowledge and expertise and are likely to recommend products based on their own tastes and preferences, or recommendations from third parties or nonpersonal sources.

The two types of support for which no significant differences were found between strong and weak ties were (1) identifying and (2) evaluating product alternatives. Hindsight suggests that the objectives used in identifying alternatives and the specific criteria used in their evaluation are more discriminating than the tasks, per se. That is, *both* symbolic and functional roles may come into play in identifying and evaluating alternatives depending upon the objective(s). Based on the findings for other types of support, strong ties are likely to identify alternatives that they deem appropriate for the buyer, and evaluate them on the basis of perceived suitability for the buyer. Weak ties, in contrast, are likely to identify alternatives they believe to be the best, cheapest, fastest, or most functional (based on objective criteria) and evaluate them against an objective standard or personal goal.

Adopting the view that social support is a determinant of source selection suggests that not all interpersonal sources are "created equal." That is, the variety of all possible roles and functions of sources requires a diverse set of skills, abilities, knowledge, and experience, as well as different types of relationships to the support recipient. Knowing more about these roles and functions is likely to increase our general understanding of buyers' selection and use of interpersonal sources. Since this study's focus is on the role of purchase pals at the point-of-purchase, future research might investigate the role of sources in buyers' information search prior to visiting the retail outlet or in post-purchase evaluations. It is likely that the type of support provided by

TABLE 3
Types of Social Support by Strength of Tie[1]

TYPES OF SOCIAL SUPPORT	STRONG	WEAK	t-value[2]
providing moral support for decisions/increasing buyer's confidence in the decision	67	0	8.18a
making purchase decision	18	2	3.58a
determining appropriateness/suitability of product for buyer	21	8	2.41a
evaluating product alternatives	22	18	.98
identifying product alternatives	22	29	-.63
negotiating terms of sale	10	18	-1.51c
providing information on retail stores (e.g., image, location, quality)	17	28	-1.64c
finding bargains/better deals	10	22	-2.12b
providing price information	11	28	-2.72a
constraining price paid by buyer	4	19	-3.13a
providing product information (e.g., benefits, features, quality)	14	39	-3.43a

[1] Some respondents indicated more than one type of social support.
[2] a $p < .01$
b $p < .05$
c $p < .10$

interpersonal sources other than purchase pals also varies by strength of tie.

Of particular interest would be the type of social support provided by professional service providers across a variety of goods and services (e.g., real estate agents, stockbrokers, hospital personnel, retail salesclerks). These individuals, who represent occupations that promote social support through the roles and contexts in which they operate professionally represent weak ties of a different type than those studied here. Currently, we know little about the relationship between professional service providers and social support of consumers, specifically in terms of marketing implications for service providers and psychosocial outcomes for consumers (e.g., service satisfaction). Additional research in this area is recommended.

One final and perhaps more tertiary issue raised by the findings is that of gender. Data reported here suggest there may be gender differences in the strength of ties between buyers and sources. As noted above, a smaller percentage of strong ties were found between male-male dyads (54%) than between both female-female (83%) and mixed gender dyads (100%). It seems reasonable to suggest that (1) buyers' needs and (2) sources' abilities to provide different types of support both vary by gender. Therefore, gender dyad type also may be useful in predicting buyers' selection of particular sources. Future research might concentrate on this issue.

REFERENCES

Arndt, Johan (1967), "Role of Product-Related Conversations in the Diffusion of a New Product," *Journal of Marketing Research*, 4 (August), 291-295.

Assael, Henry, Michael Etgar, and Michael Henry (1983), "The Dimensions of Evaluating and Utilizing Alternative Information Sources," working paper, New York University.

Bell, Gerald D. (1967), "Self-Confidence and Persuasion in Car Buying," *Journal of Marketing Research*, 4 (February), 46-52.

Berger, C. R., and Calabrese, R. J. (1975), "Some Explorations in Initial Interaction and Beyond: Toward a Developmental Theory of Interpersonal Communication," *Human Communication Research*, 1, 99-112.

Brown, Jacqueline J. and Peter H. Reingen (1987), "Social Ties and Word-of-Mouth Referral Behavior," *Journal of Consumer Research*, 3 (December), 350-362.

Burnkrant, Robert and Alain Cousineau (1975), "Informational and Normative Social Influence in Buyer Behavior," *Journal of Consumer Research*, 2 (December), 206-215.

Caplan, G. (1976), "The Family as a Support System," in G. Caplan & M. Killilea (eds.), *Support Systems and Mutual Help*, 19-36. New York: Grune & Stratton.

Cobb, S. (1976), "Social Support as a Moderator of Life Stress," *Psychosomatic Medicine*, 38, 300-314.

Cox, Donald F. (1968), "Consumer Decision Processes—Risk Taking and Information Handling in Consumer Behavior," *Public Opinion Quarterly*, 68 (Fall), 453-466.

Engel, James F., Robert J. Kegerreis, and Roger D. Blackwell (1969), "Word-of-Mouth Communications by the Innovator," *Journal of Marketing*, 33 (July), 15-19.

Eyres, S. J., and MacElveen-Hoehn, P. (1983, April), "Theoretical Issues in the Study of Social Support," presented at the conference on *Social Support: What Is It?* Seattle, WA.

Formisano, Roger A., Richard W. Olshavsky, and Shelley Tapp (1982), "Choice Strategy in a Difficult Task Environment," *Journal of Consumer Research*, 8 (March), 474-479.

Furse, David M., Girish N. Punj, and David W. Stewart (1984), "A Typology of Individual Search Strategies Among Purchasers of New Automobiles," *Journal of Consumer Research*, 10 (March), 417-431.

Granovetter, M. S. (1973), "The Strength of Weak Ties," *American Journal of Sociology*, 78, 1360-1380.

_____ (1982), "The Strength of Weak Ties: A Network Theory Revisited." In P. V. Marsden and N. Lin (eds.), *Social Structure and Network Analysis*, Newbury Park, CA: Sage, 105-130.

Hartman, Cathy L. and Pamela L. Kiecker (1991), "Marketplace Influencers at the Point of Purchase: The Role of Purchase Pals in Consumer Decision Making," *1991 AMA Summer Educators' Conference Proceedings*, American Marketing Association, 461-469.

House, J. S. (1981). *Work Stress and Social Support*. Reading, MA: Addison-Wesley.

Kiecker, Pamela and Cathy L. Hartman (1993), "Purchase Pal Use: Why Buyers Choose to Shop with Others," *1993 AMA Winter Educators' Conference Proceedings*, American Marketing Association, 378-384.

Krippendorff, Klaus (1980). *Content Analysis: An Introduction to Its Methodology*, Beverly Hills, CA: Sage Publications, Inc., 39-60.

Midgley, David F. (1983), "Patterns of Interpersonal Information Seeking for the Purchase of a Symbolic Product," *Journal of Marketing Research*, 20 (February), 74-83.

Moschis, George P. (1976), "Social Comparison and Informal Group Influence," *Journal of Marketing Research*, 13 (August), 237-244.

Moss, G. E. (1973). *Illness, Immunity and Social Interaction*. New York: John Wiley.

Parks, M. R. and Adelman, M. B. (1983), "Communication Networks and the Development of Romantic Relationships: An Expansion of Uncertainty Reduction Theory," *Human Communication Research*, 10, 55-79.

Price, Linda L. and Lawrence F. Feick (1984), "The Role of Interpersonal Sources in External Search: An Information Perspective," in *Advances in Consumer Research*, Thomas C. Kinnear (ed.), Provo, UT: Association for Consumer Research, 250-253.

Punj, Girish N. and Richard Staelin (1983), "A Model of Consumer Information Search Behavior for New Automobiles," *Journal of Consumer Research*, 9 (March), 366-380.

Sanders, Clinton R. (1985), "Tattoo Consumption: Risk and Regret in the Purchase of a Socially Marginal Service," in *Advances in Consumer Research*, Elizabeth C. Hirschman and Morris B. Holbrook (eds.), Provo, UT: Association for Consumer Research, 17-22.

Solomon, Michael R. (1987), "The Wardrobe Consultant: Exploring the Role of a New Retailing Partner," *Journal of Retailing*, 63 (Summer), 110-128.

Tolsdorf, C. C. (1976), "Social Networks, Support, and Coping: Exploratory Study," *Family Process*, 15, 407-417.

Weimann, Gabriel (1983), "The Strength of Weak Conversational Ties in The Flow of Information and Influence," *Social Networks*, 5, 245-267.

Cohort Generational Influences on Consumer Socialization

Aric Rindfleisch, University of Wisconsin-Madison

ABSTRACT

Consumer researchers have long recognized the pervasive influence that social structural variables have on consumer socialization. However, they have largely ignored the role of history in defining generational distinctions among consumers born in different eras. This paper introduces consumer researchers to the concept of cohort generations, and presents a conceptual model of their role in consumer socialization. To explore this model, the paper profiles five year subsets of two of America's most noteworthy generations, the Baby Boomers born between 1950-1955, and the Baby Busters born between 1965-1970, and offers a set of empirically testable propositions of both direct and indirect socialization effects of their generational membership.

Over the past twenty years, consumer researchers have devoted a considerable amount of effort to gain a better understanding of how people learn to participate effectively as consumers in the marketplace. Consumer socialization researchers have suggested that consumer-related skills, knowledge, attitudes and behavior are both directly and indirectly influenced by a broad range of social structural variables such as social class, race and gender (Moschis 1987; Moschis and Churchill 1978). These variables define the social environment in which consumer learning occurs, and place a consumer within a social unit whose members tend to exhibit relatively homogeneous patterns of consumer behavior (Moschis 1987).

In defining the social setting in which consumer learning takes place, consumer researchers have largely ignored the potential influences that cohort generation membership may have on consumer socialization. A *cohort generation* is a group of persons born during a limited span of years who share a common and distinct social character shaped by their shared experiences through time (Mannheim 1952; Marias 1970). Unlike *family generations*, which are based on biological lineages, *cohort generations* are based on shared historical experiences.

The concept of cohort generations as groups of coevals sharing a unique location in the stream of history has intrigued philosophers and scientists over the past two hundred years, and can be found in the writings of Auguste Comte, John Stuart Mill and Karl Mannheim (Marias 1970). Despite its long history, the cohort generation is a concept that has lingered in intellectual obscurity, and is given only cursory attention by most social scientists. Part of the problem lies in the nature of the concept itself. Most generational writings are multidisciplinary, being employed by political scientists to account for intergenerational shifts in political values (Inglehart 1981), by sociologists to examine patterns of family planning (Hill 1970), by psychologists to understand the impact of historical influences on human development (Schaie et al. 1973), and by marketers to explain beverage consumption trends among consumers of various ages (Rentz and Reynolds 1991; Rentz et al. 1983).

The objective of this paper is to draw attention to this fairly neglected aspect of consumer research by offering both a conceptual framework and a specific set of propositions suggesting how consumer socialization may differ among Americans belonging to different cohort generations. This paper first provides a more detailed elaboration of the important distinctions between family and cohort generations, and introduces a conceptual model of the role of cohort generations in consumer socialization. After laying this conceptual foundation, it then profiles five year subsets of two of America's best known generations, the Baby Boomers and the Baby Busters. Along with these generational profiles, a set of empirically testable propositions suggest how these two generations directly and indirectly impact the consumer socialization of their members. This paper concludes with a discussion of theoretical implications and research design issues to help guide future research.

THE PHENOMENA OF GENERATIONS

The terms "cohort" and "generation" are often confused by social scientists, the mass media and the general public (Jaworski and Sauer 1985). Therefore, before developing an explanation of cohort generational influences, it is necessary to first define the terms family generation, cohort generation and cohort.

A *family generation* is the set of children born to a mother and father. The family generation has traditionally been viewed as a thirty year time period because thirty years is considered the average span between the birth of an individual and the birth of his or her offspring (Strauss and Howe 1991). Consumer skills, knowledge, attitudes and behavior are transmitted between family generations, and family members are influential socialization agents (Moschis 1987). However, family generational influences are limited within the confines of the kinship group and generally have a marginal impact on the socialization of persons outside of the family unit (Jaworski and Sauer 1985).

A *cohort generation* refers to a group of persons born during a specific span of time who share a unique character created by their common age location in history (Mannheim 1952). The length of a cohort generation has been arbitrarily estimated to range anywhere from 15 to 33 years (Strauss and Howe 1991). Unlike a family generation, which acts as a socialization agent, a cohort generation is a social structural variable akin to social class, race or gender (Mannheim 1952; Ryder 1965). According to Ryder (1965):

> As a minimum, the cohort is a structural category with the same kind of analytic utility as a variable like social class. Conceptually the cohort resembles most closely the ethnic group: membership is determined at birth, and often has considerable capacity to explain variance, but need not imply that the category is an organized group (p. 847).

Like these other social structural variables, a cohort generation defines the environment in which consumer socialization occurs and locates a person within a specific social grouping whose members share a distinctive social character (Ryder 1965). For reasons of conceptual parsimony, this paper discusses generational membership in terms of an aggregate of all persons born during a specific time period. However, within each cohort generation important differences in socialization processes and outcomes are likely to exist among consumers differentiated by other critical social structural variables such as sex, race and social class (Mannheim 1952; Riley et al. 1988). In fact, any given generation may contain several distinct "generational units" whose members develop a shared identity by responding in a similar manner to common historical events (Mannheim 1952). For example, during the late 1960s and early 1970s the upper middle class antiwar activist and the working class Vietnam foot soldier represented two separate generational units within the Baby Boom generation.

A *cohort* is a group of individuals born within the same time interval (Ryder 1965). The key distinction between cohorts and cohort generations lies in the processes used to identify them. Cohorts are arbitrarily specified groups that are usually defined based on data availability considerations. For example, demographers often examine cohorts in ten year intervals based on data from decennial censuses. Cohort generations are cohorts that are defined based on a theory of how individuals at different stages of life are influenced by important historical and social events (Strauss and Howe 1991).

The Status of Cohort Generations in Consumer Research

While a number of consumer researchers have examined the socialization influence of family generations (Moschis 1987), the study of cohort generations has been largely ignored in socialization studies as well as in many other areas of consumer research. Although a few consumer researchers have acknowledged the importance of cohort influences (e.g. Belk 1986, 1985; Holbrook and Schindler 1992; Schaninger and Danko 1993), few systematic explorations of cohort phenomena have appeared in the *consumer behavior* literature. Rentz and his colleagues have introduced and demonstrated the utility of cohort analysis techniques, but do not discuss the broader issue of cohort generations (Rentz and Reynolds 1991; Rentz et al. 1983; Reynolds and Rentz 1981). Hill and his colleagues (Hill 1980) have conducted an extensive study of the consumption patterns of three *family* generations (e.g. grandparents, parents and adult children) which provides a number of interesting empirical findings and theoretical implications. Unfortunately, this study also confounds the aforementioned distinction between family and cohort generations. The most extensive conceptual treatment of various cohort-related issues to appear in the consumer behavior literature is Jaworski and Sauer's (1985) review of cohort analysis, cohort adaptation and cohort variation. Although Jaworski and Sauer provide a lucid elaboration of the distinctions between cohorts and (family) generations, their discussion excludes any mention of cohort generations.

Jaworski and Sauer also refer to the scarcity of cohort-related studies, and offer a number of reasons why the cohort perspective has not gained much attention from consumer researchers. Their list of potential limiting factors include the convenience of simply explaining age-related differences as age effects, and the fact that the cohort perspective does not fit in well with the psychological orientation of most consumer researchers. While these issues may be key contributing factors, the biggest blockade to research interest appears to be the abstractness and atheoretical nature of most generational writings. As Strauss and Howe (1991) put it, "The cohort generation has been confined by experts to the shadow world of unproven hypothesis" (p. 440). The paucity of tenable cohort-based theories can be directly attributed to what Mannheim (1952) termed "the problem of generations."

The Problem of Generations

The problem of generations has plagued generation theorists for over a hundred years (Marias 1970). This "problem" refers to the difficulty that generation theorists have had in defining generations and developing this fuzzy concept into a concrete theory (Marias 1970). The problem of generations appears to center around three principle questions: (1) how long is a generation, (2) when does an old generation end and a new one begin, and (3) what sort of impact does a generation have on the socialization of its members? Since any propositions regarding generational influences must be based on answers to these queries, the first two questions are specifically addressed below, and the last question is the central topic addressed in the rest of this paper.

How Long is A Generation? Unlike family generations, whose length can be easily determined by chronological age, cohort generations have an indeterminate length (Mannheim 1952). Various generation theorists have estimated the length of a generation to be anywhere from 15 to 33 years (Strauss and Howe 1991). While few agree on the exact length, most agree that the duration of a cohort generation should be linked to stages of life rather than family genealogy (Marias 1970, Ryder 1965). Strauss and Howe (1991) explain:

> Parents give birth to children at widely differing ages, and children intermarry with other families with equally wide birth distributions. Each chain of parent-to-child lineage produces a single thread of *family time*, but combining millions of such threads produces no single rope of *social time* (p. 60).

Generation theorists, much like consumer socialization researchers, are proponents of the notion that socialization processes differ among individuals occupying various stages of life (Marias 1970; Moschis 1987; Strauss and Howe 1991). These stages define the key social roles that individuals play as they move through time. Strauss and Howe (1991), for example, specify four phases of life: youth (central role: dependence), rising adulthood (central role: activity), midlife (central role: leadership), and elderhood (central role: stewardship). Since both generation theorists (Mannheim 1952; Marias 1970) and consumer socialization researchers (Moschis 1987; Ward 1974) recognize the critical importance of early life experiences, the propositions advanced in this paper place emphasis on consumer socialization occurring from childhood through early adulthood.

When Do Generations Begin and End? Most generation theorists believe that cohort generations form around traumatic historical events and sweeping social changes such as wars, revolutions or spiritual movements (Mannheim 1952; Marias 1970; Ryder 1965; Strauss and Howe 1991). Since these events affect people quite differently according to their stage of life, they serve as generational dividers and give each generation a distinctive character (Marias 1970; Strauss and Howe 1991). For example, the Vietnam War had a much different type of socialization effect on the cohort of 1950 (many of whom fought in it, demonstrated against it, or tried to avoid it), than it did on the cohort of 1965 (most of whom may only remember glimpses of it on television) (Mills 1987). Although these monumental historical events will affect the socialization of persons at any age, both generation theorists (Mannheim 1952; Ryder 1965) and developmental psychologists (Cavanaugh 1990) suggest that they have their greatest impact on individuals in their formative years (adolescence through early twenties). The theoretical importance of early life experiences is supported by a broad range of empirical research ranging from Schuman and Scott's (1989) finding that adolescence and early adulthood is the primary period for the imprinting of important historical events, to Holbrook and Schindler's (1991) discovery that the development of musical tastes peaks around age 24. Therefore, although consumer socialization is a continuous process, "early socialization seems to carry greater weight than later socialization" (Inglehart 1981, p. 881).

A CONCEPTUAL MODEL OF GENERATIONAL INFLUENCES

The figure depicts a conceptual model of the impact of cohort generational influences on consumer socialization. This model, which is adapted from a widely accepted general model of consumer socialization (Moschis and Churchill 1978), portrays the process of consumer socialization in terms of its antecedent vari-

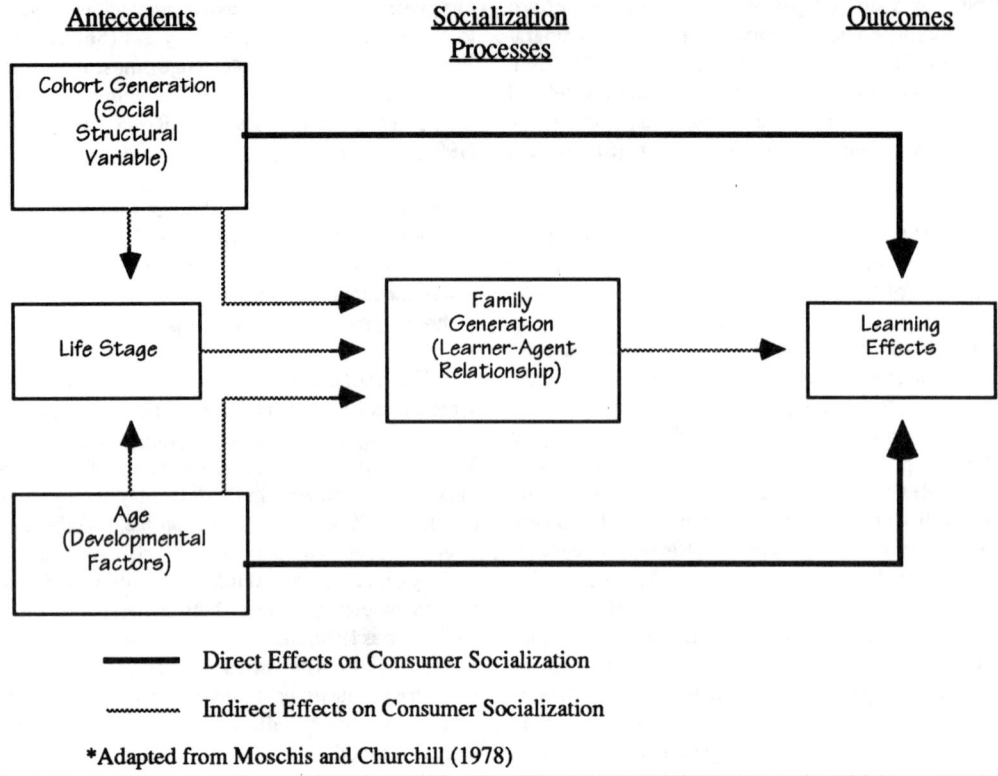

FIGURE
Conceptual Model of Generational Influences on Consumer Socialization*

——— Direct Effects on Consumer Socialization

﹍﹍﹍ Indirect Effects on Consumer Socialization

*Adapted from Moschis and Churchill (1978)

ables, socialization processes, and outcomes. Since the general model is fully described by Moschis and Churchill (1978), the discussion of this adapted model will focus on, (1) the indirect and direct effects of cohort generations on consumer socialization, and (2) this model's unique separation of life stage and age.

Just like any other social structural variable, cohort generations have both direct and indirect effects on socialization outcomes. These outcomes, or learning effects represent the specific consumer attitudes, behavior, skills and knowledge that individuals acquire via the socialization process (Moschis 1987).

Indirect Effects of Cohort Generations

The indirect effects of cohort generations are mediated via their impact on learner-agent relationships, and include such learning effects as the degree to which a child's requests influence family purchasing decisions, and the propensity to model parental consumption behavior (Moschis 1987). In addition to family generations, other important socialization agents include peers, school and the mass media (Moschis 1987). Generation theorists posit that generational membership plays a key role in defining learner-agent relationships (Strauss and Howe 1991). For example, in 1970, only 10% of all births were to unmarried women, by 1990, this figure rose to 25% (Ahlburg and De Vita 1992). Since the vast majority of these single parent families are headed by women, the consumption patterns of America's youngest generation should exhibit much weaker paternal influences compared to previous generations.

Direct Effects of Cohort Generations

Direct effects of cohort generations on consumer socialization represent unmediated outcomes of generational membership, and include such learning effects as materialism and dysfunctional consumer behavior (Moschis 1987). According to generation theorists, consumer attitudes and behaviors may be influenced by generational membership (Ryder 1965). For example, Baby Boomers may be less materialistic than Baby Busters because they were socialized during an era in which materialism symbolized a form of social oppression (Light 1988).

Cohort Generation Effects on Consumer Life Stage

In contrast to consumer socialization researchers, who treat life stage primarily as a biological variable and largely ignore historical influences (Moschis 1987), generation theorists, developmental psychologists and age sociologists suggest that an individual's life cycle is strongly influenced by both developmental factors (age) and generational membership (Cavanaugh 1990; Riley et al. 1988; Strauss and Howe 1991). Although many aspects of the human life cycle are clearly linked to developmental factors, cohort generations play an important part in defining the social roles that are enacted at various ages. For example, as the American Civil War drew to a close, the Confederate Army conscripted many children in their early teens to bolster their sagging ranks (Strauss and Howe 1991). Undoubtedly, the major roles (soldier, defender and hero) that these children fulfilled were much different than the roles played by the majority of today's adolescents. According to Riley et al. (1988), each cohort generation follows a unique life course pattern and different cohorts "age" in different ways.

GENERATIONAL PROFILES AND PROPOSITIONS

The cohort generations selected for study include the two generations commonly known as the post-World War II Baby Boom generation and the succeeding Baby Bust generation. These two generations were selected based on both their familiarity and their significant marketplace presence (Herbig et al. 1993). In order to avoid the problem of generations described earlier, it is necessary to define both the length of each generation and their point of demarcation.

How long are the Baby Boom and Baby Bust generations? The answer to this question is hardly clear-cut. According to demographers, the Baby Boom generation includes those individuals born during the years 1946-1964 (Light 1988; Mills 1987). Throughout this 19 year period, annual births averaged more than four million and the total fertility rate remained over three births per woman in every year except 1946 (Bouvier 1980). These Boomers are immediately followed by a significantly smaller Baby Bust generation, starting in 1965, and ending in the early 1980s. During this period, the total fertility rate dropped to less than two births per woman, and annual births averaged only three and a half million (Bouvier 1980). Since these guidelines are based on a demographic measure (fertility) rather than historical events, they are useful in defining cohorts, but not generations (Howe and Strauss 1993).

The cohort generation perspective on this issue is represented by Strauss and Howe (1991), who posit that the Baby Boom generation includes persons born between 1943 and 1960, while the Baby Bust generation includes those born between 1961 and 1981. These dates are based on extensive historical analysis, which links the separation of these two generations to the traumatic social events and changing values and norms during the late 1960s and early 1970s (Yankelovich 1981).

Ultimately, the exact dates of either generation is an empirical issue that is yet unresolved. Therefore, in order to avoid the danger of over-generalization, this paper offers profiles and propositions directed towards the Boomers born between 1950 and 1955, and the Busters born between 1965 and 1970. Hopefully, these attenuated five year subgroups will enhance the predictive validity of these propositions by minimizing the variance within each generation while maximizing the variance between generations.

In searching for a dividing line between these two generations, all signs point to America's "Consciousness Revolution" of the late 1960s and early 1970s (Howe and Strauss 1993; Light 1988). Traumatic historical events during this period include the heaviest fighting of the Vietnam War, massive student demonstrations and protests, the Apollo space missions, rapid expansion of the civil rights and feminist movements, the assassinations of Martin Luther King, Jr. and Robert Kennedy, and Woodstock (World Almanac 1991). During this period, America was redefining its attitudes towards women, minorities, sex, education, government and almost every other facet of social life (Gottlieb 1987). Gottlieb (1987) refers to this period as experiencing, "the disintegration of a culture" (p. 38). During the late 1960s and early 1970s, the Boomers were adolescents and young adults who witnessed or participated in many of these events, while the Busters were children or yet unborn with little or no memory of this period. Hence, these two generational subgroups clearly represent two points lying on different sides of this monumental social divide.

Since any attempt to profile a social unit as large and diverse as a generation within the confines of a few pages is likely to be shallow and incomplete at best, the following profiles and propositions represent only a brief outline of a few indirect and direct generational influences that are likely to have important effects on the learning outcomes of consumer socialization.

Indirect Influences: Profiles and Propositions

Family/Peer Influences. Perhaps the sharpest distinction between these two generations lies in their childhood and early family experiences. The 1950-1955 Baby Boom cohort members were born and spent most of their childhood during what Light (1988) refers to as, "a period of profoundly pro-child social values" (p. 24). Many Baby Boomers were nurtured in the traditional American two-parent family in which dad was the breadwinner and mom was the homemaker (Ahlburg and De Vita 1992). Only 2% of all Boomers attended institutional child care, and as of 1960, less than 23% of all children lived with one divorced parent (World Almanac 1991).

In contrast, the Baby Busters born between 1965 and 1970 were much more likely to be brought up in a non-traditional household. America's divorce rate doubled between 1965 and 1975 (Howe and Strauss 1993), and as of 1980, 42% of all children lived with one divorced parent (World Almanac 1991). In conjunction with this increasing divorce rate, a growing number of women sought work outside of the home, and by the mid 1970s, the dual worker family replaced the traditional breadwinner/homemaker as America's dominant family model (Ahlburg and De Vita 1992). The Busters became America's first "latchkey" children, and had to learn to fend for themselves during the "Me Decade" of the 1970s (Herbig et al. 1993; Howe and Strauss 1993). All of these factors point to a generation faced with a confusing mix of parental consumption role models and a much lower degree of parental guidance in consumption matters compared to Boomers. Therefore,

P1: Baby Busters are less likely than Baby Boomers to model themselves after parental consumption patterns.

Faced with absentee fathers, working mothers and an adult-oriented society, many Baby Busters turned to their peers for increased guidance and dependence (Gross and Scott 1990). This shifting of socialization influence is in line with the generational supposition that a decline in family-based influence is compensated for by other socialization agents such as school or peers (Ryder 1965). In addition, consumer socialization researchers such as Moschis (1987) suggest that peer and family influences are negatively related, and that peer influence is greater among persons who have received little parental attention. Hence,

P2: Baby Busters are more likely than Baby Boomers to model themselves after peer consumption patterns.

Mass Media Influences. According to Moschis (1987), social structural variables influence the effects of mass media on consumer socialization. Although the Boomers are America's first television generation, it is the Busters who perfected television watching into an artform, and to whom the television was a surrogate for absentee parents (Gross and Scott 1990). While many Boomers spent relatively little time watching television during their early childhood, it is estimated that the average Buster spent close to 5,000 hours in front of the television before reaching the age of five (Howe and Strauss 1993). According to one survey, Baby Busters spent more time watching television than interacting with their parents (Gross and Scott 1990). Furthermore, the reduction in parental guidance suggests that television images and messages were able to exert a direct influence on many young Busters with little adult intervention. In addition to watching more television compared to Boomers, Busters also saw a higher percentage of commercials as the number of network advertisements increased 119% between 1967 and 1981 (Light 1988). Although increased exposure could possibly lead to greater cynicism toward advertising, many contemporary advertising critics believe that advertising's pervasive, repetitive and professionally crafted seductions lull consumers into an "intellectual submission (that) seems almost inescapable" (Pollay 1986, p. 26). Thus,

P3: Baby Busters are more likely than Baby Boomers to use television advertisements in making consumption decisions.

In conjunction with watching more television, Busters spent less time reading than their Boomer counterparts (Howe and Strauss 1993). This decline in reading is symptomatic of the larger educational malaise that afflicted many Busters. Uncompetitive teacher salaries, unsuccessful school reforms and declining educational standards resulted in an inferior education for many Baby Busters. Evidence of the decline in Buster academic achievement is well-documented (Howe and Strauss 1993). For example, the mean SAT scores for the high school class of 1968 was over 950, while mean scores for the class of 1983 dipped below 900 (Howe and Strauss 1993). The combination of increased television viewing and declining educational attainment suggests that Busters are less attuned to print media compared to their Boomer counterparts. Therefore,

P4: Baby Busters are less likely than Baby Boomers to use print advertisements in making consumption decisions.

Direct Influences: Profiles and Propositions

Materialism. Materialism is defined as, "The importance a consumer attaches to worldly possessions" (Belk 1985, p. 265). Compared to Baby Boomers, the Baby Bust generation appears to be much more pragmatic, pro-business and materialistic (Herbig et al. 1993; Light 1988). Pollay (1986) suggests that one of the cultural consequences of modern advertising is the deification and reinforcement of a materialistic lifestyle. Considering the vast number of consumption-oriented messages that Busters have been exposed to during their formative years, it is not surprising that they are often characterized as, "very acquisition minded and conditioned to expect instant gratification in every aspect of their lives" (Herbig et al. 1993). According to UCLA's annual survey of American college freshman, Busters are noticeably more materialistic compared to their Boomer predecessors:

In the clearest split between the 1960s and the 1980s, students of today are much more concerned with making money than with developing a meaningful philosophy of life. The number who place money as their top priority has grown 30% over the past two decades, while the search for meaning has dropped 40 percent (Light 1988, p. 31).

Howe and Strauss (1993) suggest that this distinct generational split in materialistic attitudes can be linked to the economic conditions of each generation's childhood. While the Boomers of 1950-1955 were born into and raised during a time of economic abundance which allowed them to think about such lofty motives as tolerance and free expression, the Busters of 1965-1970 were raised during a time of oil crises, stagflation and recession (Herbig et al. 1993). Unlike many young Boomers coming-of-age in the late 1960s, who rejected materialism and saw it as the basis for social oppression, the Buster experience is quite the opposite. Furthermore, for many Busters the dramatic fall of communism in the late 1980s may have reinforced the value of capitalism and a materialistic lifestyle. Hence,

P5: Baby Busters are more materialistic than Baby Boomers.

Dysfunctional Consumption Behaviors. Dysfunctional consumer behavior refers to consumption behavior that result in negative outcomes to the consumer, to others or to society. Examples of dysfunctional consumer behavior include shoplifting and compulsive consumption (Hirschman 1992; Moschis 1987). The combination of decreased parental contact, lower educational attainment, increased television viewing and higher materialistic attitudes paints a rather negative picture of the Baby Bust generation. According to Howe and Strauss (1993), Baby Busters are the most incarcerated generation in American history and carry many of their early pathologies of neglect with them. It is estimated that one out of every seven Busters will contemplate suicide and that one in 40 will attempt it (Herbig et al. 1993).

Compared to the Boomers of 1950-1955, the Busters of 1965-1970 face lower real incomes, occupy lower-skilled jobs, and have a lower chance of ever owning a home (Gross and Scott 1990). According to consumer socialization research, persons with lower educational attainment, children from disadvantaged socioeconomic backgrounds and males raised in fatherless families are more likely to engage in dysfunctional consumer behavior (Moschis 1987). Furthermore, consumers with addictive-compulsive personalities are often raised in broken families, exhibit a high degree of impulsiveness, and have a strong need for immediate gratifications (Hirschman 1992). Therefore,

P6: Baby Busters are more likely than Baby Boomers to engage in dysfunctional consumer behavior.

DISCUSSION

Theoretical Implications

The concept of cohort generations holds a number of important theoretical implications for consumer researchers. First of all, since cohort generations are defined by historical events, the concept forces researchers to adopt a longer-term perspective, and to consider the role of history in shaping consumer behavior. All too often, consumer researchers may be guilty of what Riley et al. (1988) labels the "life-course fallacy." This fallacy refers to research that overlooks the possibility that cross-sectional studies among persons of various ages may contain variance due to differences in both age *and* cohort generational membership (Riley et al. 1988). This life course fallacy may be one reason why consumer researchers have been unable to develop a consumer/family life cycle model that holds up over time (Schaninger and Danko 1993). Most life cycles are developed using cross sectional data of consumers of different ages at a specific point in time. This type of data confounds age, period and cohort effects, and results in a life cycle that no one has ever lived (Ryder 1965). Therefore, any life cycle model should account for generational differences in consumer roles. Cohort generational differences may also provide new insights into other age-related areas such as adolescent and elderly consumer research.

As discussed throughout this paper, cohort generations present a new conceptual variable that may help researchers gain a better understanding of consumer socialization processes and outcomes. Like most social structural variables, cohort generations will most likely account for only part of the variance in any particular study. However, this does not reduce their importance in consumer behavior. As a minimum, researchers conducting studies among persons of widely different ages should at least control for the possibility of generational influences, because failing to do so may lead to false conclusions (see Rentz and Reynolds 1991 for an example).

Cohort generations also force researchers to question the way the world is defined for them. The terms Baby Boom and Baby Bust are frequently employed by the mass media, social scientists and the general public. However, as shown earlier, the dates associated with these generations are defined by demographic measures that have little direct linkage to historical events. In fact, many persons born in the early 1960s feel more like Busters than Boomers (Gross and Scott 1990). The generational perspective allows researchers to think about cohort generations in a more analytical and critical manner.

Research Design Issues

This paper's propositions offer researchers a starting point for further exploration of this intriguing concept. Unfortunately, as with most any cohort-based investigation, these six propositions could be explained in terms of either historical (cohort generation) or developmental (age) effects. For example, empirical support for P1 could be explained as either evidence for a generational shift in parental modelling or a general tendency for young adults to rebel against parental influence. Since it is widely recognized that simple cross-sectional designs do not allow researchers to untangle these two intertwined effects, many researchers advocate the use of longitudinal, mixed, or sequential designs (Cavanaugh 1990; Schaie et al. 1973). Unfortunately, even these more "advanced" designs are severely limited by a number of practical (e.g. a large investment in time and energy) and methodological (e.g. linear dependency between age, cohort and period effects) issues (Cavanaugh 1990; Glenn 1976; Riley et al. 1988; Rodgers 1982).

Since traditional research designs have been found lacking, a few researchers have begun to look for alternative means of exploring generational phenomena (Cavanaugh 1990; Riley et al. 1988). Many of these alternative techniques such as naturalistic inquiry and historical analysis are also gaining increased acceptance among consumer researchers. A less well known but quite promising alternative methodology is to simply replace chronological age with direct measures of the theoretical variables it indirectly represents (Riley et al. 1988; Rodgers 1982). For example, in their study of alumni values ten years after college, Hoge and Hoge (1984) specify age effects as an indirect indicant of both occupational and family-related influences. This innovative technique is based on a well accepted premise among age researchers that chronological age is little more than an index of an individual's level of biological, psychological and social development (Bengtson and Lovejoy 1973; Cavanaugh 1990), According to Bengtson and Lovejoy (1973):

> It is obvious that years since birthdate is only a rough indicator of what age really means - the culmination of events (biological, psychological, and social) as they have impinged on an individual's life (p. 891).

The substitution of chronological age for more direct measures has been successfully employed in a number of empirical studies by both developmental psychologists and generation researchers (Riley et al. 1988; Rodgers 1982). Since biological age differences between twenty five (e.g. Busters) and forty year olds (e.g. Boomers) are believed to be relatively minimal (Cavanaugh 1990), a direct measure which focuses on psychological and/or social age, such as the one offered by Bengtson and Lovejoy (1973), presents a viable and innovative means of exploring these propositions by allowing researchers to more precisely assess cohort generational influences by removing the variance due to developmental effects. Currently, this technique appears to represent the most appropriate solution to the problem of generations that has plagued researchers over the past hundred years (Riley et al. 1988).

Summary

Cohort generations represent a potentially important but largely neglected social structural variable which may directly and indirectly influence consumer attitudes, behavior, skills and knowledge. Any cohort generation research effort must answer three primary questions: (1) how long is a generation, (2) when does an old generation end and a new one begin, and (3) what sort of impact does a generation have on the socialization of its members? This paper's brief generational profiles and propositions are a modest attempt to answer these questions and stimulate future cohort generation research. The concept of cohort generations presents researchers with a unique and fresh perspective of the impact of historical events and social change upon consumers born in different eras.

REFERENCES

Ahlburg, Dennis A. and Carol J. De Vita (1992), "New Realities of the American Family," *Population Bulletin*, 47 (August).

Belk, Russell (1986), "Yuppies as Arbiters of the Emerging Consumption Style," in *Advances in Consumer Research*, 13, ed. Richard J. Lutz, Provo, UT: Association for Consumer Research, 514-519.

_____ (1985), "Materialism: Trait Aspects of Living in the Material World," *Journal of Consumer Research*, 12 (December), 265-280.

Bengtson, Vern L. and Mary Christine Lovejoy (1973), "Values, Personality and Social Structure: An Intergenerational Analysis," *American Behavioral Scientist*, 16 (July/August), 880-912.

Bouvier, Leon F. (1980), "America's Baby Boom Generation: The Fateful Bulge," *Population Bulletin*, 35 (April).

Cavanaugh, John C. (1990), *Adult Development and Aging*, Belmont, CA: Wadsworth Publishing Company.

Glenn, Norval D. (1976), "Cohort Analysts' Futile Quest," *American Sociological Review*, 41, 900-905.

Gottlieb, Annie (1987), *Do You Believe in Magic?: The Second Coming of the Sixties Generation*, New York: Times Books.

Gross, David M, and Sophrina Scott (1990), "Proceeding with Caution," *Time*, July 16, 56-62.

Herbig, Paul, William Koehler and Ken Day (1993), "Marketing to the Baby Bust Generation," *Journal of Consumer Marketing*, 10 (1), 4-9.

Hill, Reuben (1970), *Family Development in Three Generations*, Cambridge, MA: Schenkman Publishing Company.

Hirschman, Elizabeth C. (1992), "The Consciousness of Addiction: Toward a General Theory of Compulsive Consumption," *Journal of Consumer Research*, 19 (September), 155-179.

Hoge, Dean R. and Jann L. Hoge (1984), "Period Effects and Specific Age Effects Influencing Values of Alumni in the Decade After College," *Social Forces*, 62 (June), 941-962.

Holbrook, Morris B. and Robert M. Schindler (1989), "Some Exploratory Findings on the Development of Musical Tastes," *Journal of Consumer Research*, 16 (June), 119-124.

Howe, Neil and Bill Strauss (1993), *13th Gen: Abort, Retry, Ignore, Fail?*, New York: Vintage Books.

Inglehart, Ronald (1981), "Post-Materialism in an Environment of Insecurity," *American Political Science Review*, 75 (December), 880-900.

Jaworski, Bernard and William J. Sauer (1985), "Cohort Variation," in *Advances in Consumer Research*, Vol. 12, ed. Elizabeth Hirschman and Morris Holbrook, Provo, UT: Association for Consumer Research, 32-36.

Light, Paul C. (1988), *Baby Boomers*, New York: W.W. Norton & Company.

Mannheim, Karl (1952), "The Problem of Generations," in *Essays on the Sociology of Knowledge*, ed. Paul Keczkemeti, New York: Oxford Univ. Press, 276-322.

Marias, Julian (1970), *Generations: A Historical Method*, University, AL: University of Alabama Press.

Mills, D. Quinn (1987), *Not Like Our Parents*, New York: William Morrow.

Moschis, George P. (1987), *Consumer Socialization: A Life-Cycle Perspective*, Lexington, MA: Lexington Books.

_____, and Gilbert A. Churchill, Jr. (1978), "Consumer Socialization: A Theoretical and Empirical Analysis," *Journal of Marketing Research*, 15 (November), 599-609.

Pollay, Richard W. (1986), "The Distorted Mirror: Reflections on the Unintended Consequences of Advertising," *Journal of Marketing*, 50 (April), 18-36.

Rentz, Joseph O. and Fred D. Reynolds (1991), "Forecasting the Effects of an Aging Population on Product Consumption: An Age-Period-Cohort Framework," *Journal of Marketing Research*, 28 (August), 355-360.

_____, Fred D. Reynolds and Roy G. Stout (1983), "Analyzing Changing Consumption Patterns with Cohort Analysis," *Journal of Marketing Research*, 20 (February), 12-20.

Reynolds, Fred D. and Joseph O. Rentz (1981), "Cohort Analysis: An Aid to Strategic Planning," *Journal of Marketing*, 45 (Summer), 62-70.

Riley, Matilda White, Anne Foner and Joan Waring (1988), "Sociology of Age," in *Handbook of Sociology*, ed. Neil Smelser, Newbury Park, CA: Sage, 243-290.

Rodgers, Willard L. (1982), "Estimable Functions of Age, Period and Cohort Effects," *American Sociological Review*, 47 (December), 774-787.

Ryder, Norman B. (1965), "The Cohort as a Concept in the Study of Social Change," *American Sociological Review*, 30 (December), 843-861.

Schaie, K. Warner, Gisela V. Labouvie and Barbara U. Buech (1973), "Generational and Cohort-Specific Differences in Adult Cognitive Functioning," *Developmental Psychology*, 9 (2), 151-166.

Schaninger, Charles M. and William D. Danko (1993), "A Conceptual and Empirical Comparison of Alternative Household Life Cycle Models," *Journal of Consumer Research*, 19 (March), 580-594.

Schuman, Howard and Jacqueline Scott (1989), "Generations and Collective Memories," *American Sociological Review*, 54 (June), 359-381.

Strauss, William and Neil Howe (1991), *Generations*, New York: Quill.

Ward, Scott (1974), "Consumer Socialization," *Journal of Consumer Research*, 1 (September), 1-16.

World Almanac (1991), *The World Almanac and Book of Facts 1992*, New York: Pharos Books.

Yankelovich, Daniel (1981), *New Rules: Searching for Self-Fulfillment in a World Turned Upside Down*, New York: Random House.

A Conceptual Model of the Role of Situational Type on Consumer Choice Behavior and Consideration Sets

Indrajit Sinha, University of Michigan[1]

ABSTRACT

Although prior research has identified the significant role of situational or contextual factors in consumer behavior, its exact nature and process have only recently begun to be closely examined. This paper integrates the findings obtained so far and provides a taxonomy of consumer situations, suggesting that situational variables affect consumer decision-making mostly in ad-hoc situations. It also develops a conceptual framework by advancing that in common situations, consideration sets are retrieved from memory, whereas goal-derived categories mediate the relationship between situational factors and choice in ad-hoc situations. Several propositions that describe the effect of situations on choice are outlined and future research implications of this paper are identified.

Despite the pervasive role of situational or contextual factors in everyday consumer choice and decision-making as highlighted by the studies of a few early researchers, only recently has empirical work again begun to explicitly address this area (e.g Ratneshwar and Shocker 1991; Warlop and Ratneshwar 1993; Graonic and Shocker 1993). Prior research has investigated the influence of situational variables in consumer behavior (Belk 1974a, 1974b, 1975b; Lutz and Kakkar 1975; Park, Iyer, and Smith 1989; Sandell 1968), in the area of choice behavior and attitude (Fennell 1978; Bearden and Woodside 1978; Miller and Ginter 1979), segmentation by usage situation (Dickson 1982), and substitutability-in-use given contextual cues (Srivastava, Alpert and Shocker 1984). Even as the early studies demonstrated the all-encompassing role of situational variables, and stated the need to better examine their nature and effect, the lack of a clear direction and well-developed theory has thwarted concerted empirical progress in this area. Nonetheless, it is clear that situational factors affect consumer behavior and decision-making in various ways in everyday life. A typical consumer shopping for clothes may buy a set of shorts and T-shirts for use around the home, a new suit for use in the office, or a pair of dressy trousers for social events. A person looking for a fast-food restaurant may normally drive to a nearby McDonald's if he (or she) were on his (her) own; but in a specific situation, he (she) may have to accommodate a friend who prefers Wendy's. An average American family may prefer to have chicken or pork on normal situations at home; but they absolutely need to eat turkey on Thanksgiving. Other examples abound that indicate that, apart from individual and brand characteristics, situations do, in a large part, dictate buying and consumption behavior. The impact of situational factors on choice behavior, and, more specifically, on the formation of consideration sets is the focus of this paper.

I may note at the outset that I prefer to use the terms situations and situational factors to the extant and popular construct, *usage-context*. While the latter is perhaps more descriptive, it does not capture all instances where a *situational* effect has been said to occur on consumer choice. For instance, it has been shown that a consumer shopping in an unfamiliar store is greatly influenced by the global situational factor of store knowledge (Park, Iyer, and Smith 1989) in his or her choice outcomes - here usage-context is not especially meaningful.[2]

As noted before, although earlier empirical studies have determined the situational variation of brand choice behavior (Belk 1974a, 1974b, 1975a; Bishop and Witt 1970; Miller and Ginter 1979; Sandell 1968), only a few have attempted to address the question of *how* situations affect choice behavior, or sought to examine the relationship between situational factors and choice set formation in consumer purchase scenarios (e.g. Warlop and Ratneshwar 1993; Graonic and Shocker 1993). This issue assumes greater importance in the light of a lack of well-understood and acceptable theory in situation research. Consequently, this paper seeks to fulfill three objectives: *one*, to provide an integrative review of the existing literature and to propose a typology of situations that may serve to explain choice; *two*, to develop a conceptual framework that accounts for the relationship between situational factors and consideration set formation; and *three*, to outline some meaningful research propositions drawn from this framework that may be investigated in a more formal empirical setting.

In this context, it may be recalled that Barsalou (1983, 1985) introduced the notion of goal-derived categories like *things to eat on a diet* which are different from common taxonomic categories like birds and mammals. Goal-derived categories have been the focus of considerable interest in categorization research, but their role in choice behavior and consumer decision-making has not been adequately emphasized. Only recently, a few researchers have sought to establish that goals are basic to consumer choice and goal-derived categories may well describe the effect of usage-context on formation of consideration sets (Park and Smith 1989; Huffman 1993; Warlop and Ratneshwar 1993). Intuitively, this seems logical since goal-derived categories are established in memory (or created *ad-hoc*) to fulfil certain goals or ideals (Barsalou 1985), which may be prompted by specific situations. For instance, in a given situation, an individual looking for something to eat under a busy schedule, may access a goal-derived category of *ways to get a quick food-item*, which may include a visit to the vending machine around the corner, calling a pizza delivery service, or a quick walk to a fast-food restaurant across the street. These non-comparable alternatives will form the consideration set for the person in that situation.

In subsequent sections, I shall closely look at the constructs that are in the domain of this paper: situational variables, goal-derived categories, and consideration sets. I shall suggest a possible taxonomy of consumer situations, present appropriate propositions and develop a conceptual framework that integrates the major concepts in a meaningful relationship, and finally identify some future research implications.

ROLE OF SITUATIONS

Although earlier research in buyer behavior emphasized the individual and personality variables like motives, satisfaction, and predisposition (Howard and Sheth 1967), the need to better examine the situational context was unmistakably articulated. Engel, Kollat, and Blackwell (1969) called for the consideration of both

---

[1] The author would like to express his sincere appreciation of the helpful suggestions of Youjae Yi and three anonymous reviewers.

[2] Usage context is perhaps equivalent to *task-definition*, which is one of several situational factors under Belk's taxonomy, outlined later.

individual and situational factors in order to explain consumer choices. Similarly, Belk (1975b) suggested that consumer behavior may be a function of the interaction between the individual and the situation. Despite the unfailing direction of consumer choice literature biased toward the investigation of the individual (cognitive and affective) factors, a few substantive papers also examined the situational role. For instance, Sandell (1968) presented subjects with ten beverages which they rated in different situations (e.g., when alone, feeling sleepy in the afternoon, reading a newspaper in the morning) using a seven-point scale from "extremely willing (to try)" to "extremely unwilling". The findings established that a person's choice is highly dependent on the situation. Similar experiments were done by Bishop and Witt (1970) and Belk (1974a, 1974b).

Lutz and Kakkar (1975) investigated the replicability of the Mehrabian and Russell (1974) framework involving pleasure, arousal, and dominance (PAD) in consumption situations. The authors obtained PAD measures for situations like the following: "you are planning a party for a few close friends and are wondering what to have around to snack on" or "you are at the grocery store when you get an urge for a between-meal snack". Research on usage situation has focused on substitutability (Srivastava 1981) and market segmentation (Abell 1980; Dickson 1982; Srivastava et al. 1984). An example cited is that consumers may use instant coffee while in a hurry and regular ground coffee when entertaining. Similarly, inquiry into motivational objectives has enabled the understanding of the distinctions among the heavy beer drinker who seeks to "escape", another heavy drinker who seeks "social accommodation", the athlete who drinks beer to quench his (her) thirst, and the young college party-goer. Demby (1968) undertook a study of the alcoholic beverages market and identified usage situations (e.g. theater, restaurant, travelling, after sport) that impact on consumption.

Miller and Ginter (1979) identified situational variation in brand choice and attitude. This paper was one of the first to consider the role of situations on choice decisions and attitudinal results (see also Bearden and Woodside 1978); however, the authors focused more on the nature of attribute importance and perceptions across situations than on the decision-making process. The authors chose the product category of fast-food restaurants (hamburger places) like Arby's, Borden Burger, Hungry Herman's, and McDonald's and provided the subjects with four distinct situational conditions: lunch on a weekday, snack during a shopping trip, evening meal when rushed for time, and evening meal with the family when not rushed for time. Miller and Ginter found that inclusion of situation specific measures increased the ability of the model to predict subsequent brand choice behavior.

The debate on objective versus psychological situation (see Belk 1975a; Lutz and Kakkar 1975) and lack of a clear direction caused situation research to remain in stasis for quite some time - only recently interest has again surged as the focus of studying the effect of situations on consumer choice behavior has appropriately shifted from the "is" to the "how" question. Thus, while it is universally acknowledged that contextual factors like time, place, interpersonal expectations, and task definition affect choice, the inquiry is now on the intervening processes. As mentioned earlier, recent papers have provided support for the notion that consumer behavior is largely purposive and that goals are integral to every choice situation (Bettman and Sujan 1987; Park and Smith 1989; Huffman 1993; Park 1993). This view can, of course, be rightly traced to the ancient Aristotelian dictum that human nature is essentially *teleological* (see Blanshard 1961). In this context, Barsalou's (1985) concept of goal-derived categories has been proposed as mediating the effect of usage context on consideration set formation. Park and Smith (1989) demonstrated how consumer choice process can work in a top-down, goal-driven manner that results in the inclusion and within-product processing of noncomparable product alternatives as suggested by Barsalou's theory. Warlop and Ratneshwar (1993) provided subjects with both familiar and unfamiliar usage situations and examined choice processes through verbal protocol analysis. Their results indicate that in familiar situations, subjects recalled the product alternatives almost immediately while indicating established categorical structures associated with the corresponding usage situations (see also Ratneshwar and Shocker 1991) and strong memory effects. In contrast, in unfamiliar situations a top-down, goal-driven process seemed to occur that indicated the mediation of an ad-hoc goal-derived category. Similarly, Graonic and Shocker (1993) established the importance of goals and goal-derived categories in consumer decision making. The conceptual framework outlined in this paper is directly supported by the results reported by these authors.

DEFINITION AND TAXONOMY

Belk (1975b) defined a situation simply as a locus in time and space. For our purpose, it shall suffice to describe a situation as an agglomeration of ecological factors (time, place, social setting, task objectives) that are relatively transient both in nature and effect and thus distinct from enduring individual and brand characteristics, and that affect subject behavior either by themselves or in conjunction with other (personal and object) factors. More particularly, in purchase scenarios, choice may be seen as a function of individual factors like attitude and knowledge, brand characteristics like marketing mix variables, and above-mentioned situational variables.

Belk (1975b) provided a definitive structure for classifying these situational variables by proposing that any situation may be defined by five constituent factors such as follows: (1) a physical context consisting of geographic and institutional location, sights, sounds, and aroma; (2) a social context defined by interpersonal roles and expectations; (3) a temporal context defined by time of day, day of week, season, etc.; (4) a task definition described by overall subject intentions; and finally, (5) by the antecedent conditions subsuming miscellaneous residual or "carried-over" effects from a prior state, like a bad headache, having little money in pocket, being in a good mood, etc.

A useful observation to state *a priori* is that, by its definition, a situation and its constituent variables (like time, social nature, task definition, etc.) will define every setting. Thus, it is important to identify when situational factors assume a greater role in decision-making than personal variables like attitudes or motives, and brand-based attributes. Efforts at taxonomy in situation research have focused on classifying situational variables (e.g. Belk 1975b) or on developing *product-specific* situational taxonomies (e.g. Srivastava et al. 1984). A more fruitful exercise may be to examine if the situations *in general* possess a typology. One meaningful way to classify situations may be based on the level of consumer familiarity with them. Prior studies have established that consumer familiarity with choice situations may determine their adopted choice strategy (Bettman and Sujan 1987; Park and Smith 1989). Further, Warlop and Ratneshwar (1993) found that consumers demonstrated different processes in eliciting choice alternatives in familiar versus unfamiliar situations. The former are called "common" situations here and the latter "ad-hoc" situations. Reasons for the use of this particular terminology will become transparent later.

TABLE 1
Major Characteristics of Situational Types

Characteristics	Situational Type	
	Common	Ad-hoc
Examples:	Regular grocery shopping	Shopping in an unfamiliar store
Factor dominance:	Individual and brand	Situational factors are important
Frequency of experience	High	Low
Cognitive Effort Required	Generally low	Generally high, but depends on constraints
Nature of Goal-derived category in choice	Stored	Ad-hoc

Proposition 1: Consumer situations may be classified as being one of two general types: common situations and ad-hoc situations. Each situational type possesses unique characteristics that defines the differential role of situational factors relative to those of individual and/or object (brand) factors. Also, depending on the underlying type, the consumer choice process will be different.

1) *Common situations*: These are the routine and habitual scenarios that typically arise in daily life. These situations offer a neutral or minimal influence in the decision-making context, thereby allowing individual or brand characteristics to predominate in the choice process. Thus, when researchers emphasize the cognitive aspects of decision-making by focusing on the roles of choice heuristics, prior knowledge, and memory (e.g. Bettman, Johnson, and Payne 1991), they most likely assume that individuals are operating within common situations. In some common situations, choice may be characterized by a seeming automaticity, when the consumer may seek to conserve his (her) cognitive resources. An example of a common situation is grocery shopping activity which may involve little variation in the choices made by a consumer per week. Individual factors like preferences, attitude toward the brand, and brand-based factors such as price, packaging, and quality may significantly impact decision-making. Although situational factors are less important in these situations, there are nonetheless several instances (e.g. normative situations, discussed later) where even in common situations, situational variables will have some, albeit moderate, impact.

2) *Ad-hoc situations*: Ad-hoc situations are unfamiliar or less frequently experienced situations that are not as well-defined and as predictable as common situations. Sometimes these situations occur unexpectedly and affect the decision process drastically, but at other times these situations may be anticipated and may result in high-involvement decision-making. All the same, ad-hoc situations are encountered less frequently, and the role of situational factors is more pronounced than in common situations. High-risk, high-involvement ad-hoc situations such as buying a new car may demand considerable decision-making on the part of the consumer. In such instances, all three factors: individual, brand, and situational may play a role. To use the grocery shopping example further, a scenario when the consumer is shopping in an unfamiliar store or is shopping under time-pressure may constitute an ad-hoc situation. Park, Iyer, and Smith (1989) examined the effects of these factors: store knowledge and time pressure on grocery shopping behavior. Using verbal protocols, their study determined that these two factors significantly influenced brand and product switching and purchase volume deliberation.

A subset of both common and ad-hoc situations are normative situations, in which subjects frame their behavior pattern to meet the expectations of significant other(s), i.e. they encumber the subject to make decisions that are culturally expected or socially popular. Thus, both common and ad-hoc situations can be high or low on the normative dimension. While in common situations with low normative influence, the effect of situational factors may be low as compared to those of individual and brand variables, in common situations with high normative influence, situational factors play a more important role. For instance, a Thanksgiving dinner may unmistakably be seen as a *common* normative situation (since it is familiar to many subjects), associated with traditional food choices, whereas a regular dinner may be perceived as a common situation with low normative influence. An example of an *ad-hoc* normative situation is one's first day at work, which may induce one to dress such as "to make a good impression." Traditional gift-giving situations may be construed of as classic normative situations. In the purchase context, if the consumer is shopping in preparation for a visit by his (or her) mother, then his (her) choice process will be dictated by certain social norms pertaining to the anticipated visit, such as buy what she (the mother) likes. Other examples of normative effects on situational choice behavior are the traditional choice of "strawberries and cream" as the preferred food-item in a Wimbledon match, the purchase of a hot-dog during a baseball game, and wearing a dark-blue suit and striped tie for a formal job interview.

Table 1 lists the characteristics of the two major situational types. The issue of choice in the two situational types will be explicated in a later section. At this point, it may be useful to recapitulate that it has been suggested that situational factors are less important (compared to individual and brand variables) in common versus ad-hoc situations. Further, within common situations, those with low normative influence have lower situational effect than in those with high normative influence. Now, since the inherent basis of the taxonomy is consumer familiarity, it is possible that if ad-hoc situations, which are initially unfamiliar to subjects, are experienced very frequently, they would cease to remain so and instead they will presently become common situations. In other words, the dominant situational effect underlying ad-hoc situations will give way to more individual and object dominance.[3] Consider the example cited earlier: while one's first day at work is clearly an ad-hoc situation, in due course, going to work will become a common situation. This notion has major implications in the context of choice behavior and consideration set formation and will be addressed in the following section. Therefore, this idea may be formalized into our second proposition.

Proposition 2: Ad-hoc situations can evolve into common situations, if continually experienced over a period of time.

CHOICE PROCESSES

Consideration sets (cf. evoked sets, choice sets) have a long and venerable history in consumer behavior research. A consideration set is simply a cluster of brands that a consumer will retrieve from memory and/or the external environment, and deliberate on, prior to a buying decision. Consumer decision-making will thus involve the brand-consideration stage (when brands are retrieved) and the brand-evaluation stage when consumers use various decision-rules to determine the optimal choice (Nedungadi 1990). The consideration set is widely acknowledged as a useful construct in explaining consumer decision-making (Hauser and Wernerfelt 1990; Howard and Sheth 1967). For example, Hauser (1978) reported that seventy-eight percent of the explainable variation across consumers was attributable to whether the brand was included in the consideration set. In earlier research, the consideration set was thought to be a static construct (Howard and Sheth 1967). For instance, consumers were supposed to have the same few brands for evaluation and choice in regular purchase situations. Only recently has the set been correctly recognized as being dynamic and subject to variation across individuals (Hauser and Wernerfelt 1990) and situations (Miller and Ginter 1979), also as explicated in this paper.

As noted earlier, recent findings in consumer choice research have indicated that goals are antecedent to almost every consumer purchase situation (Bettman and Sujan 1987; Park and Smith 1989). Goals, in turn, may arise in the context of certain situations, i.e. distinct combinations of certain situational variables (Huffman 1993; Park 1993). This notion is also supported by Fennell (1978) who proposed that usage situations may be seen as being the cause of every consumer purchase problem. Note that there may be a multiplicity of goals even in a single choice situation. A consumer looking to buy a new car may seek to obtain one that is a) roomy and spacious for the whole family, b) that is also powerful, c) not too expensive, and d) has a good resale value. Hence, given that goals are fundamental to the choice problem, it is possible then that the consideration set will consist of a set of alternatives that fulfill the accomplishment of the salient goal(s) - in other words, the consideration set will map the corresponding goal-derived categories. The inclusion of the notion of goal-derived categories is particularly useful since it broadens the definition of the consideration set by facilitating the inclusion of disparate, i.e. noncomparable products in the consideration set, as is true in real-life. It may be recalled that Barsalou (1985) suggested that items which defy the "correlational structure of the environment" (i.e. that have dissimilar attributes) may be included in a common goal-derived category if they fulfill the accomplishment of the corresponding ideals. Results from the exploratory study by Warlop and Ratneshwar (1993) provide support for this theory. For instance, the authors report that when asked to name snack items that might be eaten "shortly after a workout or an aerobics class when you know that you will be meeting some friends in a couple of hours", one subject named TCBY yogurt, watermelon, Snickers bar, crackers and cheese, and slices of bread. None of these alternatives may be said to be truly comparable with another but are included in a common consideration set because of their relevance to the stated goal.

Given the taxonomy proposed earlier, how does the choice process operate in common versus ad-hoc situations? Can we expect that the process described above should work in both these instances, or are the processes inherently different? This is the question that I address below.

1) Choice process in Common situations:

Despite the importance of top-down, goal-driven choice process outlined earlier, it is apparent that in many everyday familiar buying situations, called "common situations" here, a consumer may not actively perform a belabored deliberation of various brands, and may habitually choose the brand that he or she normally buys. For instance, on a grocery shopping trip, a consumer may frame the choice problem simply as buying Liquid Tide detergent, Cheerios cereal, Tropicana Premium orange juice, Campbell chicken-noodle soup, etc. Unless the store has been remodeled (leading to an ad-hoc situation), grocery shopping in many cases may simply be an exercise in visual detection of the desired brands and picking these from the shelves. Thus, as illustrated in Figure 1, in common situations, situational factors (along with individual characteristics) *directly* elicit the choice alternatives in the consideration set, without an apparent mediation of goals and goal-derived categories. Now, it was proposed earlier that goals are antecedent to every choice problem - if so why does the abovementioned goal-derived category-mediated process does not happen in case of common situations? Since common situations, by definition, have been frequently encountered earlier, subjects may already be in possession of well-developed categorical structures associated with the specific situations, which are also well-established in memory (Ratneshwar and Shocker 1991). The specific situation may only serve to cue the retrieval of the *stored* goal-derived category and thus elicit the consideration set. Recall that Barsalou (1983, p. 224, italics mine) advanced that "some ad-hoc categories may be processed so *frequently* that their category concepts, concept-to-instance associations, and instance-to-concept associations all become well-established in memory. At this point, these categories are no longer ad-hoc..., their representations in memory are much more like those of common categories."

If the situational factors merely cue the consideration set in memory, the choice process in common situations should indicate the eliciting of *specific* brands, thus requiring low cognitive deliberation, and also should display significant memory effects, and should have low goal salience. Recent results from Warlop and Ratneshwar (1993) provide support to all of these conclusions. This leads me to suggest the following proposition:

Proposition 3: In common situations, the choice process will indicate a) directly eliciting specific brands in the consideration set; b) choice deliberation will be low; c) eliciting of alternatives will demonstrate strong memory effects; and d) few goals, if any, will be salient indicating the mediation of *stored* goal-derived category in choice.

---

[3] By dominance of factors is meant that these factors account for a significant amount of variance in predicting choice behavior.

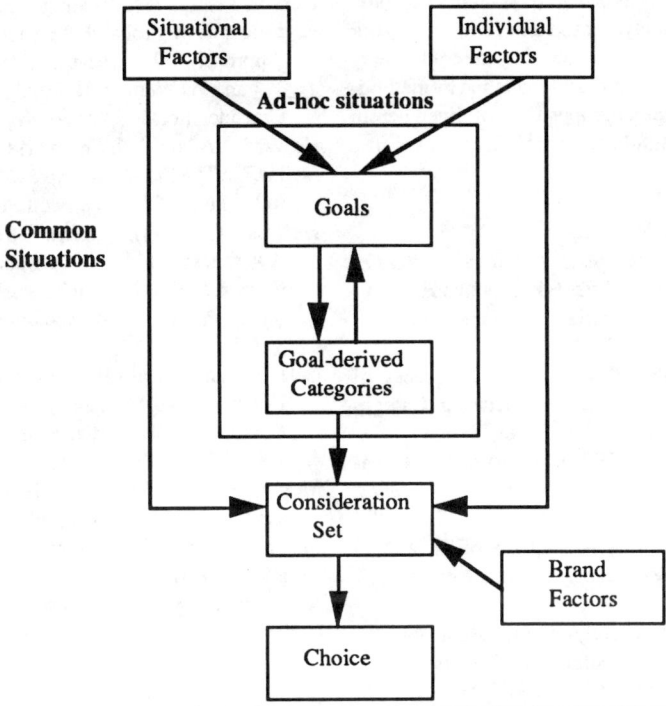

FIGURE
A Situational Conceptual Model

2) Choice process in Ad-hoc situations:

In ad-hoc situations, where situational factors may assume as much or even greater importance than individual and brand characteristics, the choice-process will be altered. It may be seen that, by definition, these situations arise infrequently, the individual must perforce invest much more cognitive resources than that required in common situations. This choice-process may be thought of as follows (see Figure 1). First, these situations will lead to the creation of certain goals or ideals, and the subjects will frame the choice problem in the context of meeting these preset goals. The resulting consideration set will indicate the mediation of the corresponding goal-derived categories.

In typical high-involvement ad-hoc situations like buying a new car, individual and brand characteristics play a significant role. But, all too often the effect of situational factors is misunderstood or even ignored. In reality, situational variables often have a major impact on the choice processes involved in ad-hoc situations and the consequent consideration sets reflect the aforementioned mediation of goal derived categories. This may be observed in the following example of a consumer who is considering buying a new car.

Consider the *antecedent conditions* for the prospective auto-buyer be defined by the fact that he is a young single with some money to spend, *geographic factor* being that he lives in Florida, and the *task objective* being to buy an sporty vehicle. Then one appropriate consideration set may consist of LeBaron convertible, Ford Laredo, Toyota Celica, and an Isuzu Trooper. The relevant category here may be *moderately priced sporty vehicles that are good in a warm weather context*.

The fact that these somewhat disparate vehicles are included in a common consideration set emphasizes the likely mediation of a goal-derived category. Thus, in contrast to common situations, goals will be highly salient in the choice process for ad-hoc situations. Further, it is possible that consideration set formation may be the result of an *iterative*, recursive process (indicated by the bidirectional arrows) in which the deliberation of the categories may consist of matching product attributes with initial goals and returning to editing/redefining the goals or creating new ones; then generating alternatives again, and so on. Support for this notion is evinced in the verbal protocol of subjects reported by Warlop and Ratneshwar (1993). Given an ad-hoc situation: snack that you may eat at home shortly before a date, subject responses clearly indicated this iterative attribute-goal matching and goal-editing process. This is an interesting phenomenon that has not been adequately researched (Park 1993). The above discussion yields the final proposition.

Proposition 4: In ad-hoc situations, the choice process will a) indicate the mediation of several situation-specific goals and corresponding goal-derived categories; b) cognitive deliberation will be higher; and c) subject will indicate an iterative goal-creation/editing and attribute-matching process resulting in the eliciting of choice alternatives.

FUTURE RESEARCH IMPLICATIONS

The role of goals in consumer choice process has only recently begun to be investigated in earnest. Goals arise in a specific situational context and, as this conceptual paper has outlined, are especially salient in ad-hoc situations. As of now, empirical studies have been largely exploratory, thus affording opportunities for useful confirmatory approaches. This paper has sought to offer a conceptual framework that may be utilized in some future inquiry. Secondly, it is genuinely felt that research in choice modeling needs to account for the disparate nature of the alternatives available to the consumer at every choice situation. As explicated here, the notion of goal-derived categories may serve to fill the needed missing link. Oftentimes marketing practitioners unwittingly homogenize the consideration sets in their survey instrument design, and thus neglect to incorporate other noncomparable yet eminently viable alternatives. Finally, this paper is aimed at rekindling interest among marketing researchers in the broad and potentially rich field of situation research. Unfortunately, for too long, empirical work involving situational factors has been hampered by the controversy involving 'objective' versus 'subjective' situations and by methodological constraints. The conceptual propositions outlined herein may lead to developing meaningful and testable hypotheses in a more formal research setting.

REFERENCES

Abell, D.F. (1980), *Defining the Business: The Starting Point of Strategic Planning*, Englewood Cliffs, NJ: Prentice Hall.

Barsalou, L.W. (1983), "Ad-hoc Categories," *Memory and Cognition*, 11 (3), 211-227.

_____ (1985), "Ideals, Central Tendency, and Frequency of Instantiation as Determinants of Graded Structure in Categories," *Memory and Cognition*, 11 (4), 629-648.

Bearden, W.O. and A.G. Woodside (1978), "Consumption Occasion Influence on Consumer Brand Choice," *Decision Sciences*, 9, 273-284.

Belk, R.W. (1974a), "An Exploratory Assessment of Situational Effects in Buyer Behavior," *Journal of Marketing Research*, 11 (May), 156-163.

_____ (1974b), "Application and Analysis of the Behavior Differential Inventory for Assessing Situational Effects in Consumer Behavior," in Scott Ward and Peter Wright (eds.), *Advances in Consumer Research*, Vol. 1, Urbana: Association for Consumer Research, 1974b.

_____ (1975a), "The Objective Situation as a Determinant of Consumer Behavior," in Mary Jane Schlinger (ed.), *Advances in Consumer Research*, Vol. 2, Chicago: Association for Consumer Research, 427-437.

_____ (1975b), "Situational Variables and Consumer Behavior," *Journal of Consumer Research*, 2 (December), 157-154.

Bettman, J.R. and M. Sujan (1987), "Effects of Framing on Evaluation of Comparable and Noncomparable Alternatives by Expert and Novice Consumers," *Journal of Consumer Research*, 14 (September), 141-154.

_____, E.J. Johnson, and J.W. Payne (1991), "Consumer Decision Making," in *Handbook of Consumer Behavior*, Thomas S. Robertson and Harold H. Kassarjian (eds.), Englewood Cliffs, New Jersey: Prentice Hall, 50-84.

Bishop, D.W. and P.A. Witt (1970), "Sources of behavioral variance during leisure time," *Journal of Personality and Social Psychology*, 16, 352-360.

Blanshard, B. (1961), *Reason and Goodness*, London: George Allen & Unwin Ltd.

Demby, E.H. (1968), "The Creative Consumer, A Report on Psychographics," Paper presented to the Market Research Station, American Marketing Association Conference (November).

Dickson, P.R. (1982), "Person-Situation: Segmentation's Missing Link," *Journal of Marketing*, 46 (Fall), 56-64.

Engel, J.F., D.T. Kollat, and R.D. Blackwell (1969), "Personality Measures and Market Segmentation," *Business Horizons*, 12 (June), 61-70.

Fennell, G. (1978), "Consumers' Perceptions of the Product-Use Situation," *Journal of Marketing*, 42 (April), 38-47.

Graonic, M.D. and A.D. Shocker (1993), "On the Transferability of Feature/Level Preferences Across Competing Brands Serving the Same Purpose," in *Advances in Consumer Research*, Vol. 20, Leigh McAlister and Michael L. Rothschild (eds.), Provo, UT: Association for Consumer Research, 389-394.

Hansen, F. (1972), *Consumer Choice Behavior*, New York: The Free Press.

Hauser, J.R. (1978), "Testing the Accuracy, Usefulness, and Significance of Probabilistic Models: An Information Theoretic Approach," *Operations Research*, 26 (May/June), 406-421.

_____ and B. Wernerfelt (1990), "An Evaluation Cost Model of Consideration Sets," *Journal of Consumer Research*, 16 (March).

Howard, J.A. and J.N. Sheth (1967), "A Theory of Buyer Behavior," in *The Great Writings in Marketing*, Howard A. Thompson (ed.), Tulsa, OK: Pennwell Publishing Co., 215-241.

Huffman, C. (1993), "Context Effects on Consumer Goals, Brand Awareness, and Decision-Making," in *Advances in Consumer Research*, Vol. 20, Leigh McAlister and Michael L. Rothschild (eds.), Provo, UT: Association for Consumer Research, 375-376.

Lutz, R.J. and P. Kakkar (1975), "The Psychological Situation as a Determinant of Consumer Behavior," in *Advances in Consumer Research*, Vol. 2, M.J. Schlinger (ed.), Association for Consumer Research, 439-453.

Mehrabian, A. and J.A. Russell (1974), *An Approach to Environmental Psychology*, Cambridge: M.I.T. Press.

Miller, K.C. and J.L. Ginter (1979), "An Investigation of Situational Variance in Product Choice Behavior and Attitude," *Journal of Marketing Research*, 16 (February), 111-123.

Nedungadi, P. (1990), "Recall and Consumer Consideration Sets: Influencing Choice without Altering Brand Evaluations," *Journal of Consumer Research*, 17 (December), 263-276.

Park, C.W. (1993), "Context Effects on Consumer Choice, Brand Awareness and Decision Making," in *Advances in Consumer Research*, Vol. 20, Leigh McAlister and Michael L. Rothschild (eds.), Provo, UT: Association for Consumer Research, 395.

_____ and D.C. Smith (1989), "Product-Level Choice: A Top-Down or Bottom-Up Process," *Journal of Consumer Research*, 16 (December), 289-299.

_____, E. Iyer, and D.C. Smith (1989), "The Effect of Situational Factors on In-Store Grocery Shopping Behavior: The Role of Store Environment and Time Available for Shopping," *Journal of Consumer Research*, 15 (March), 422-433.

Ratneshwar, S. and A.D. Shocker (1991), "Substitution In Use and the Role of Usage Context in Product Category Structures," *Journal of Marketing Research*, 28 (August), 281-295.

Sandell, R.G. (1968), "Effects of Attitudinal and Situational Factors on Reported Choice Behavior," *Journal of Marketing Research*, 4 (August), 405-408.

Srivastava, R.K. (1981), "Usage-Situational Influences on Perceptions of Product Markets: Theoretical and Empirical Issues," in *Advances in Consumer Research*, 8, Kent Monroe (ed.), Chicago: Association for Consumer Research, 106-111.

_____, M.I. Alpert, and A.D. Shocker (1984), "A Customer-oriented Approach for Determining Market Structures," *Journal of Marketing*, Vol. 48 (Spring), 32-45.

Warlop, L. and S. Ratneshwar (1993), "The Role of Usage Context in Consumer Choice: A Problem Solving Perspective," in *Advances in Consumer Research*, Vol. 20, Leigh McAlister and Michael L. Rothschild (eds.), Provo, UT: Association for Consumer Research, 377-382.

Alternative Models of Cognitive Processes Underlying Consumer Reactions to Conjunction Categories

Moonkyu Lee, University of Colorado at Denver
Francis M. Ulgado, Georgia Institute of Technology

ABSTRACT

The effects of consumers' category knowledge on evaluations of products have been intensively studied in consumer behavior over the past few years. However, few studies to date have closely investigated how consumers make their evaluations of a product that belongs to a category, called a *conjunction category*, defined by two simple categories, the implications of which are often inconsistent with each other. Based on the existing literature, this research develops and tests alternative models of consumer evaluation of a conjunction category. The results of the research suggest that, when consumers are given two category labels of a product as well as specific attribute information, they select either one of the categories and use it as the basis for their overall evaluation of the product. Implications of the results for consumer information processing as well as for marketing strategy are discussed.

INTRODUCTION

The use of category knowledge to make an evaluation of an object is well-established in social psychology (Brewer 1988; Fiske and Neuberg 1990; Fiske and Pavelchak 1986; Lingle and Ostrom 1981) and in consumer behavior (Boush and Loken 1991; Lee forthcoming; Meyers-Levy and Tybout 1989; Sujan 1985; Sujan and Bettman 1989). Since the multiattribute models of product evaluation have been dominant in consumer behavior (see Shocker and Srinivasan 1979, and Wilkie and Pessemier 1973 for a review of multiattribute models), it is certainly an intriguing and challenging notion that consumers do not always rely only on the product information given during the situation at hand when evaluating a product; they can and do use their pre-existing knowledge about the product. The existing literature describes the evaluation process as a matching process - matching between category knowledge and target information at hand. Applied to the product evaluation situation, the literature implies that that when the product information matches the prior knowledge and expectations about the product category, the affect associated with the category is directly transferred to the final evaluation of the product (*category-based* or *top-down process*); when the information does not match the category knowledge, evaluations of specific attributes of the product are integrated into the final evaluation (*piecemeal* or *bottom-up process*; Fiske and Neuberg 1990; Fiske and Pavelchak 1986; Sujan 1985).

However, most of the studies in the area focused on conditions under which only one category label was available with some attribute information. For example, Fiske et al. (1987) examined situations where people made evaluations of others with their job category labels (e.g., doctor, artist, etc.) and some specific trait information which was either consistent or inconsistent with the labels. In a similar vein, Sujan (1985) investigated product evaluation situations where consumers were given product category labels (i.e., a 35 mm SLR versus a 110 camera) and some specific feature information. Thus, an important question yet to be answered is: How do consumers react to a more complex category defined by the intersection of two simpler categories? An issue of particular interest is how they react to a complex category from two simple categories that are inconsistent with each other.

Such complex categories have been termed *conjunction* or *intersection* categories (Hastie, Schroeder, and Weber 1990; Kunda, Miller, and Claire 1990; Murphy 1988; Smith, Osherson, Rips, and Keane 1988). A conjunction category consists of more than one "ingredient category" which can be represented as a single lexical or idiomatic item (Murphy 1988). A *Polo* t-shirt sold at $30 can be an example of a conjunction category, which is composed of two ingredient categories, one implying the brand name (*Polo*) and the other, the price ($30).

Consumers' reactions to conjunction categories have important strategic implications for marketers. Many types of strategic changes for an existing product can create conjunction categories. Consider an example of a bi-national product: a *Honda* made in Mexico. In this case, the image associated with the brand name, *Honda* does not easily match the country image. Suppose *Rolex* watches are sold through discount stores such as *K-Mart* or *Target*. Obviously, in this case, the general impression implied by the brand and the image of the stores are not compatible, either. Such examples of conjunction categories in the marketplace are countless. However, little is known about cognitive processes underlying evaluations of conjunction categories.

Based on past literature, this study develops some alternative hypotheses regarding how consumers deal with the inconsistency created by conjunction categories. An experiment is then conducted to examine a situation where two ingredient category labels of a product are available as well as specific attribute information. The purpose is to investigate the reasoning process mediating consumers' responses to the dilemmas posed by conjunction categories.

THEORETICAL BACKGROUND

Categorization literature provides important insights into cognitive processes underlying product evaluations (Cohen and Basu 1987; Fiske and Neuberg 1990; Fiske and Pavelchak 1986; Smith and Medin 1981). Categories are defined as cognitive structures which contain instances that are perceived similar or equivalent (Mervis and Rosch 1981; Smith and Medin 1981). Over time and through experience, people develop categories of objects in an effort to organize and understand them. More importantly, people also develop (1) a set of expectations about the features of a typical category member with respect to a particular category, which is termed *category schema* or *category knowledge*, and (2) an affective reaction to the category, called *category affect* (Mandler and Parker 1976; Fiske and Pavelchak 1986; Fiske and Neuberg 1990). For example, suppose a consumer has a predefined category of a *Sony* stereo color TV set. The product schema, in this case, would involve the consumer's expectations about what features an average member of that category has to offer (e.g., stereo sound system, multi-color system, etc.) as well as what levels of performance it has to provide along those feature dimensions (e.g., good sound quality, good picture quality, etc.). In this sense, a category schema is often thought of as a bundle of expectations about the attributes of the category prototype, which is organized under a *category label* (a *Sony* stereo color TV set in this example). In addition, it is assumed that an overall affective reaction to the category (e.g., good, bad, etc.) is developed and associated with the category.

Generally, in the product domain, it is believed that the most basic types of categories chronically accessible to consumers in product evaluation situations include brand name, price, country-

TABLE 1
Predicted Effects of Ingredient Categories and Attributes Under Alternative Hypotheses

Hypothesis	Category Effect	Attribute Effect
Category Integration Hypothesis	significant main effects for category 1 and for category 2; nonsignificant interaction between the two categories	nonsignificant attribute effect evidenced by the piecemeal response and correlation measures
Subtyping Hypothesis	significant main effect for either one of the ingredient categories; nonsignificant interaction between the two categories	nonsignificant attribute effect evidenced by the piecemeal response and correlation measures
Piecemeal Elaboration Hypothesis	nonsignificant main effects for category 1 and for category 2; nonsignificant interaction between the two categories	significant attribute effect evidenced by the piecemeal response and correlation measures

of-origin, and name of the store where the product is available, as a considerable amount of literature provides evidence of their effects on product evaluations (see Zeithaml 1988, and Rao and Monroe 1989 for a review; also see Bilkey and Nes 1982 for a review of the literature on country-of-origin effects). These are called *extrinsic cues* of a product since they are product-related, but not physical or intrinsic attributes of the product (Olson 1977). It is assumed that these extrinsic cues serve as category labels which are used to organize and understand the remaining product attributes.

As mentioned earlier, the use of category schema to make an evaluative judgment of a product is well-documented in consumer behavior (e.g., Sujan 1985; Sujan and Bettman 1989). However, few studies to date have examined conditions where consumers encounter an intersection category made from two simple categories that are either consistent or inconsistent with each other. The literature on categorization and on impression formation suggests at least three alternative models that could account for processes mediating evaluations of conjunction categories. These models are described in the sections that follow.

Category Integration Hypothesis

Consider a situation where a consumer is trying to evaluate an automobile branded *Honda* and made in Mexico. Apparently, the two ingredient category labels, the brand name and the country-of-manufacture, are inconsistent with each other. The consumer may have a favorable image of *Honda* products while s/he may have a moderately unfavorable impression of the products manufactured in Mexico. Concerning this case, the social judgment literature and the information integration paradigm (Anderson 1970, 1974, 1981; Bettman, Capon, and Lutz 1975; Lynch 1985; Shanteau and Ptacek 1983; Troutman and Shanteau 1976) suggest one possible hypothesis: the consumer uses some type of integration rule that would combine the affect associated with one category with that associated with the other into an overall affective reaction to the conjunction. This is termed category integration hypothesis in this study. Among a variety of integration rules that can be used, past empirical research has generally provided support for linear, adding and averaging types of integration rules. Although providing a complete description of adding and averaging integration rules is beyond the scope of the study (see Anderson 1974, for a review of the integration rules), some measures should be clarified that allow us to detect whether a consumer actually uses the integration rules in the evaluation situation. The literature suggests that, if a consumer indeed uses a linear integration rule to make an overall evaluation of a conjunction category, a factorial plot of the observed responses should exhibit parallelism, evidenced by a statistically significant main effect of one ingredient category, a significant main effect of the other, and a nonsignificant interaction between the two categories on the evaluation of the conjunction in an analysis of variance model (Anderson 1981; Lynch 1985). Under the information integration rules, there can be a special case where a zero weight is assigned to either one of the ingredient categories. In that case, the main effect of the category will become nonsignificant. This type of case will be dealt with separately in the next section because the underlying process can be different from the one hypothesized here.

The category integration hypothesis implies that the evaluative implications of the two simple categories are combined into the final judgment of the intersection category. The possible occurrence of integration of product attribute information into the overall evaluation of the conjunction category is explored in the third hypothesis discussed below. The predicted effects of element categories and attributes on dependent measures suggested by the category integration hypothesis are summarized in Table 1.

Subtyping Hypothesis

Consider again the same example given above: a *Honda* automobile made in Mexico. Fiske and her colleagues suggest that when the object being evaluated does not find the best-fitting category, it can be subtyped on the basis of the current categories (Fiske and Neuberg 1990; Fiske and Pavelchak 1986). The subtyping would entail accessing a category at the level subordinate to either one of the ingredient categories. Thus, the present product can be subtyped into either a category of "basically *Honda* automobiles, but manufactured in Mexico" or one of "essentially Mexican-made automobiles, but branded *Honda*."

Although the subtyping phenomenon has been observed in some studies (see, e.g., Fiske et al. 1987 and Sujan 1985), any predictions about their evaluative outcomes have not been made nor tested. It is postulated that, to the extent that a subtype is formed on the basis of its superordinate category, the direction and the extremity of the evaluation of the subtype would be consistent with those of the affect associated with the original category. In the present example, the automobile could be evaluated on the basis of either the *Honda* or the Mexican-made automobile category depending on which of the two is more salient and, thus, used for the subtyping. Consequently, only one of the two ingredient categories becomes relevant to the final evaluation of the conjunction category. What determines the relative salience of the element categories is certainly an important issue if not a primary concern of the present study. It can be anything which expedites category accessibility, e.g., physical manifestation, temporal primacy, contextual novelty, and so forth. More generally, the relative salience of the categories should depend on the cognitive category structure, i.e., which category is located at a higher level in the hierarchy of categories.

To summarize, the subtyping hypothesis implies that a consumer uses only one of two ingredient categories to make an evaluation of the conjunction category. Accordingly, the hypothesis would be supported by a significant main effect of one of the two ingredient categories, a nonsignificant main effect of the other, and a nonsignificant interaction between the two categories on the evaluation of the conjunction category in an analysis of variance design. It is assumed that the evaluative implications of specific attributes are not yet determined nor integrated into the overall evaluation of the conjunction category. Thus, the effects of product attribute information on the overall evaluation would be nonsignificant. The implications of the subtyping hypothesis are summarized in Table 1.

Piecemeal Elaboration Hypothesis

The final hypothesis is suggested by the possibility that the ingredient category labels are ignored; instead, the specific product attributes are elaborated upon. This process entails an effortful integration of available information in an attribute-by-attribute fashion. The rationale behind the hypothesis is that the two element categories, when contradictory to each other, lose their diagnosticity to the evaluation. The categorization literature suggests that when a category label becomes irrelevant to the evaluation task, a piecemeal or an attribute-by-attribute evaluation process is used (Fiske et al. 1987; Fiske and Neuberg 1990; Fiske and Pavelchak 1986; Pavelchak 1989; Sujan and Bettman 1989).

There are several process/outcome measures that have been used to detect piecemeal processes (see Boush and Loken 1991, Lee forthcoming, Fiske et al. 1987, and Sujan 1985, for the different measures). Among them, verbal protocol and correlation measures are used in this research. It is expected that if a consumer indeed engages in piecemeal processing, s/he will generate more thoughts and verbalizations related to product attributes (called *piecemeal responses*) than if s/he does not. As a result, there will be a high positive correlation between the overall evaluation of the conjunction category and the attribute evaluations. Table 1 shows the predicted effects of the ingredient categories and those of the attributes on the overall evaluation of the conjunction category for the piecemeal elaboration hypothesis.

METHOD

An experiment was conducted to find out how consumers deal with inconsistency created by conjunction categories. Subjects were given specific attribute information about products under two ingredient category labels which were either consistent or inconsistent with each other. Brand name and country-of-manufacture were the selected levels of ingredient categories in the study. Subjects reactions to the conjunction categories were measured. More details about the experiment are described below.

Pretests

For a successful manipulation of consistency between two ingredient categories, it was critical to select product classes that were well-known to the population under study. A pretest was conducted to choose appropriate product categories for the experiment. Ninety-four students at a major metropolitan state university completed a questionnaire asking about their levels of familiarity with several product classes. It was found that TV sets and athletic shoes were the ones that they were most familiar with.

Another pretest was conducted with 82 students to determine brand names and countries-of-manufacture that were associated with either favorable or unfavorable image. The students were asked to list the best and the worst brand names in each of the product classes as well as the best and the worst countries that would manufacture each of the products. The results showed that *Sony* was perceived to be the best and *Emerson*, the worst brand name in the TV set category; Germany was perceived to be the best and Taiwan, the worst country that would manufacture TV sets. The results also revealed that *Nike* was seen as the best and *Converse*, the worst brand name in the athletic shoe category; the U.K. was regarded as the best, and Mexico, the worst country that would manufacture athletic shoes.

The stimulus materials were constructed for the main study on the basis of these brand and country names representing either favorable or unfavorable category image as well as 9 pieces of attribute information, drawn from *Consumer Reports*. The pieces of attribute information were put together such that they varied in terms of favorableness and relevance to the evaluation task. The intent was to ensure that the overall configuration of the information was not suggestive of any particular direction on the favorableness and relevance dimensions, and thus, to create evaluation situations that were closer to reality. The attribute information used for the study is presented in Appendix.

Design and Procedure

Based on pretest results, two levels of brand name (favorable vs. unfavorable) were crossed with two levels of country-of-manufacture (favorable vs. unfavorable). Each subject evaluated two products, a TV set and a pair of athletic shoes, with brand name and country information. Thus, the design was a 2 (ingredient category 1: brand name) X 2 (ingredient category 2: country-of-manufacture) X 2 (product) factorial design, with brand and country names as between subject factors and product as a within subject factor. The same attribute information was given within the same product conditions.

A total of 93 students enrolled in business courses participated in the experiment. They were randomly assigned to each of the experimental conditions; cell sizes ranged from 22 to 25. At the beginning of each session, they were told the study was designed to measure their perceptions and feelings about international products. They were first asked to give their best estimates of the average prices of the products under study. They were also asked to provide their perception of the brand names and the countries-of-manufacture on 9-point bipolar scales ranging from "very bad" to "very good." Then, under a brief scenario (starting with "Suppose you run into the following brand name of a product manufactured in the following country...") they were given stimulus information (A *Sony* TV set manufactured in Taiwan, for instance, and its specific attribute information), and asked to read the information with the purpose of forming an evaluation of the product. After

APPENDIX
Attribute Information Used for the Study

TV Sets

- Standard size
- High Definition with sharp pictures
- No on-screen display of channel
- Hi-fi sound system
- Standard rectangular shape
- Background noise at high volumes
- Multi-function remote control
- Six month warranty period
- Occasional reflection of room lighting on screen

Athletic Shoes

- Modern style and color
- Good ankle support
- Single stitching
- Air-cushioned sole
- Manufactured by a new technology
- Limited variety in size and design
- Versatility (i.e., good for running as well as walking)
- Lasts one and a half years on the average
- Looks heavy or bulky

---

reading it, they rated the quality of the product on a 9-point bipolar scale ranging from "very bad" to "very good." They also indicated their importance weights for each of the attributes (on 9-point scales from "not-at-all important" to "very important"), their likings for the attributes (on 9-point scales from "strongly like" to "strongly dislike"), and their overall impression of all the attributes considered in totality (on a 9-point scale from "strongly like" to "strongly dislike). They were then asked to write down all the thoughts and ideas that they experienced while reading the description. It was requested that they report all thoughts no matter how simple, complex, relevant, or irrelevant they might seem. Finally, subjects were debriefed and thanked.

RESULTS

The success of the manipulations of brand and country levels was checked through a 2 (brand name) X 2 (country-of-manufacture) analysis of variance procedure for each of the product classes. For the TV set category, the main effect for brand name on brand perception reached significance in the expected direction ($F(1,92) = 194.83, p < .000$; Ms = -1.34 vs. 3.08), and the main effect for country name on country perception was also significant ($F(1,92) = 33.29, p < .000$; Ms = -1.17 vs. 1.09). In addition, for the athletic shoe category, there was a significant main effect for brand name on brand perception ($F(1,92) = 139.31, p < .000$; Ms = -.94 vs. 3.24) as well as a significant main effect for country name on country perception ($F(1,94) = 97.88, p < .000$; Ms = -1.13 vs. 1.94), both in the expected direction. Thus, the manipulation worked as intended.

The data were analyzed through a 2 (brand) X 2 (country) analysis of variance procedure performed for each of the two product classes. Subjects' estimates of average prices of the products were used as a covariate in the analysis. Table 2 shows the mean ratings of product evaluations across the conditions. For the TV set category, a significant main effect was found for brand name ($F(1,92) = 81.86, p < .000$). However, neither the main effect for country information nor the brand X country interaction effect reached significance ($F(1,92) = .26, p > .61$ and $F(1,92) = .05, p > .82$ for the two effects, respectively). The data for the athletic shoe category revealed the same pattern of results. While the main effect for brand name was found to be significant ($F(1,92) = 63.39, p < .000$), the main effect for country name and the interaction effect between brand and country name were not ($F(1,92) = 1.24, p > .26$ and $F(1,92) = 3.05, p > .08$ for the two effects, respectively). For both of the product classes examined in the experiment, only the main effect for one ingredient category, brand name, was significant.

Additional tests were performed to see whether the product attribute information influenced the overall evaluations of the conjunction categories. The expectation was that, if the attribute information played any role in resolving the inconsistency created by the conjunction categories, more attribute-oriented thoughts, or piecemeal responses, would be generated under the conditions involving the inconsistency, i.e., the favorable brand/unfavorable country and unfavorable brand/favorable country conditions. Thus, the expectation would be supported by a statistically significant brand X country interaction effect on piecemeal responses in the current analysis of variance design. Subjects' retrospective verbal protocols were coded into four categories: brand-oriented thoughts (e.g., "*Sony* makes good electronic products." in the T.V. set category), country-oriented thoughts (e.g., "I am not sure if T.V. sets made in Taiwan last long."), attribute-oriented or piecemeal thoughts (e.g., "Background noise from a T.V. set can be annoying."), and other thoughts (e.g., "There is too much violence on T.V."). Two independent judges coded the verbalizations into the four categories and their initial agreement was 86%. Any disagreement was resolved by discussion. Among the types of thoughts generated, the attribute-oriented or piecemeal thoughts accounted for a dominant portion of the total thoughts generated; they averaged a frequency of 3.52 per subject (or 61% of total thoughts) for the TV set category and a frequency of 2.95 per subject (or 57% of total thoughts) for the athletic shoe category. However, the results

TABLE 2
Cell Means for the Dependent Measure

Product Evaluation[a]	TV Set			
	Unfavorable Brand		Favorable Brand	
	Unf. Country	Fav. Country	Unf. Country	Fav. Country
	-1.14	-1.05	1.80	2.04

Product Evaluation[a]	Athletic Shoes			
	Unfavorable Brand		Favorable Brand	
	Unf. Country	Fav. Country	Unf. Country	Fav. Country
	-.68	-.92	1.71	2.82

[a] measured on a 9-point bipolar scale with -4 = "very bad" and +4 = "very good"

of the analysis of variance procedure showed that the brand X country interaction was not significant on piecemeal responses ($F(1,89) = 1.68, p > .20$ for the TV set category; $F(1,89) = 2.71, p > .10$ for the athletic shoe category). In addition, the correlations between the overall evaluations and the attribute evaluations were not significantly greater than zero in any of the conditions in the study, which suggests that the evaluative implications of the product attributes were not determined, nor considered (if determined), in making an overall evaluation of the products.

DISCUSSION

The pattern of results, considered in totality, is compatible with that implied by the subtyping hypothesis. It seems that the categories identified with the brand names dominated and incorporated the categories implied by the country-of-manufacture information. Apparently, the products were subtyped within the categories defined by the brand names.

It is somewhat surprising that the attribute information, despite its availability, did not have any effects on evaluation of the conjunction categories. There are at least two possible explanations for the nonsignificant attribute effect. The first possibility is concerned with general cognitive category structure. In this research, it was assumed that the category identified with brand name and that implied by country-of-manufacture are at the same level in the product category structure in consumers' memory. However, as the data suggest, the brand name category might be at a higher level in the hierarchical structure of categories, and thus, might have been able to take a dominant position when it was presented with the country-of-manufacture information. The second possibility is that the attribute information was read, but used only to make a confirmation check on the brand category membership of the product. An interesting point to be made here is that despite the availability of the same attribute information across different conditions, only the brand name effect was found to be significant. This implies that the same attribute information was interpreted either positively or negatively depending on the favorableness of the brand names. This type of phenomenon has been observed in consumer information processing research and elsewhere (e.g., Deighton 1984; Gilovich 1981). According to the literature, consumers' expectation about a product has a profound effect on their subsequent interpretation and evaluation of the product information. In the present study, it is speculated that the brand names created expectations, which served as a hypothesis, and the subjects selectively processed the attribute information in a manner supporting the hypothesis.

The results of the present study have an important implication for marketers who make strategic changes, e.g., change of price, channel outlet, location of plant etc. for their current product. Marketers who make such changes can often anticipate whether these changes will induce favorable or unfavorable reactions from consumers. Then, the most important objective of their communication strategy should be to emphasize desirable changes and/or to de-emphasize undesirable changes. The results of the study suggest that a company can downplay the change by reminding consumers of the brand name and the specific attributes of the product through an effective promotion campaign. As an example of a company that actually puts the idea into practice, *Sony* emphasizes its established brand name (e.g., the "It's a *Sony*" slogan) and the innovative product features, while the product could very well be made in countries outside Japan.

The present study has taken an initial step toward understanding cognitive processes underlying the resolution of conflicting categories in the product domain. It has examined a situation where product attribute information is available as well as two simple category labels. Thus, the generalizability of the study results is limited to such a situation. Future extensions of the study would be to investigate situational and individual differences in processing conjunction categories.

REFERENCES

Anderson, Norman H. (1970), "Functional Measurement and Psychological Judgment," *Psychological Review*, 77, 153-170.

_____ (1974), "Information Integration Theory: A Brief Summary," in *Contemporary Developments in Mathematical Psychology* (Vol. 2), ed. David H. Krantz, R. Duncan Luce, Richard C. Atkinson, and Patrick Suppes, San Francisco: W.H. Freeman, 236-305.

_____ (1981), *Foundations of Information Integration Theory*, New York: Academic Press.

Bettman, James R., Noel Capon, and Richard J. Lutz (1975), "Cognitive Algebra in Multivariate Attitude Models," *Journal of Marketing Research*, 12 (May), 151-164.

Bilkey, Warren J. and Erik Nes (1982), "Country-of-Origin Effects on Product Evaluations," *Journal of International Business Studies*, 13 (Spring/Summer), 89-99.

Boush, David M. and Barbara Loken (1991), "A Process-Tracing Study of Brand Extension Evaluation," *Journal of Marketing Research*, 28 (February), 16-28.

Brewer, Marilynn B. (1988), "A Dual-Process Model of Impression Formation," in *Advances in Social Cognition*, ed. Thomas K. Srull and Robert S. Wyer Jr., Hillsdale, NJ: Erlbaum, 1-36.

Cohen, Joel B. and Kunal Basu (1987), "Alternative Models of Categorization: Toward a Contingent Processing Framework," *Journal of Consumer Research*, 13 (March), 455-472.

Deighton, John (1984), "The Interaction of Advertising and Evidence," *Journal of Consumer Research*, 11 (December), 763-770.

Fiske, Susan T., and Steven L. Neuberg (1990), "A Continuum of Impression Formation, From Category-based to Individuating Processes: Influence of Information and Motivation on Attention and Interpretation," *Advances in Experimental Social Psychology*, 23, 1-74.

———, Steven L. Neuberg, Ann E. Beattie, and Sandra J. Milberg (1987), "Category-based and Attribute-based Reactions to Others: Some Informational Conditions of Stereotyping and Individuating Processes," *Journal of Experimental Social Psychology*, 23, 399-427.

——— and Mark A. Pavelchak (1986), "Category-based versus Piecemeal-based Affective Responses: Developments in Schema-Triggered Affect," in *The Handbook of Motivation and Cognition: Foundations of Social Behavior*, ed. Richard M. Sorrentino and E. Tory Higgins, New York: Guilford Press, 167-203.

Gilovich, Thomas (1981), "Seeing the Past in the Present: The Effect of Associations to Familiar Events on Judgments and Decisions," *Journal of Personality and Social Psychology*, 40, 5, 797-808.

Hastie, Reid, Colin Schroeder, and Renee Weber (1990), "Creating Complex Social Conjunction Categories from Simple Categories," *Bulletin of the Psychonomic Society*, 28, 3, 242-247.

Kunda, Ziva, Dale T. Miller, and Theresa Claire (1990), "Combining Social Concepts: The Role of Causal Reasoning," *Cognitive Science*, 14, 551-577.

Lee, Moonkyu (forthcoming), "Informational and Motivational Influences on Consumer Evaluations of Line and Brand Extensions," *Journal of Business and Psychology*.

Lingle, John H. and Thomas M. Ostrom (1981), "Principles of Memory and Cognition in Attitude Formation", in *Cognitive Responses in Persuasion*, ed. R. E. Petty, T. M. Ostrom, and T. C. Brock, Hillsdale, NJ: Erlbaum, 399-420.

Lynch, John G., Jr. (1985), "Uniqueness Issues in the Decompositional Modeling of Multivariate Overall Evaluations: An Information Integration Perspective," *Journal of Marketing Research*, 22, 1-19.

Mandler, Jean M. and Richard E. Parker (1976), "Memory for Descriptive and Spatial Information in Complex Pictures," *Journal of Experimental Psychology: Human Learning and Memory*, 2 (January), 38-48.

Mervis, Carolyn B. and Eleanor Rosch (1981), "Categorization of Natural Objects," *Annual Review of Psychology*, 32, 89-115.

Meyers-Levy, Joan and Alice M. Tybout (1989), "Schema Congruity as a Basis for Product Evaluation," *Journal of Consumer Research*, 16 (June), 39-53.

Murphy, George L. (1988), "Comprehending Complex Concepts," *Cognitive Science*, 12, 529-562.

Olson, Jerry C. (1977), "Price as an Information Cue: Effects in Product Evaluation," in *Consumer and Industrial Buying Behavior*, ed. Arch G. Woodside, Jagdish Sheth, and Peter D. Bennett, NY: North Holland Publishing Company, 267-286.

Rao, Akshay R. and Kent B. Monroe (1989), "The Effect of Price, Brand Name, and Store Name on Buyers' Perceptions of Product Quality: An Integrative Review," *Journal of Marketing Research*, 26 (August), 351-357.

Shanteau, James, and C. H. Ptacek (1983), "Role and Implications of Averaging Process in Advertising," in *Adverting and Consumer Psychology*, ed. L. Percy and A. G. Woodside, MA: Lexington Books, 149-68.

Shocker, Alan D. and V. Srinivasan (1979), "Multiattribute Approaches for Product Concept Evaluation and Generation: A Critical Review," *Journal of Marketing Research*, 16 (May), 159-180.

Smith, Edward E. and Douglas L. Medin (1981), *Categories and Concepts*, Cambridge, MA: Harvard University Press.

———, Daniel N. Osherson, Lance J. Rips, and Margaret Keane (1988), "Combining Prototypes: A Selective Modification Model," *Cognitive Science*, 12, 485-527.

Sujan, Mita (1985), "Consumer Knowledge: Effect on Evaluation Strategies Mediating Consumer Judgment," *Journal of Consumer Research*, 12 (June), 31-46.

——— and James R. Bettman (1989), "The Effect of Brand Positioning Strategies on Consumers' Brand and Category Perceptions: Some Insights from Schema Research," *Journal of Marketing Research*, 26 (November), 454-467.

Troutman, C. Michael and James Shanteau (1976), "Do Consumers Evaluate Products by Adding or Averaging Attribute Information?" *Journal of Consumer Research*, 3 (September), 101-106.

Wilkie, William L. and Edgar A. Pessemier (1973), "Issues in Marketing's Use of Multiple-Attribute Attitude Models," *Journal of Marketing Research*, 10 (November), 428-441.

Zeithaml, Valarie A. (1988), "Consumer Perceptions of Price, Quality, and Value: A Means-End Model and Synthesis of Evidence," *Journal of Marketing*, 52 (July), 2-22.

Consumption Schemata: Their Effects on Consumer Decision Making

Albert Wenben Lai, University of Wisconsin-Madison

ABSTRACT

Consumers usually use an assortment of products to satisfy a need and obtain utility from the constellation of products in use holistically. Their consumption schema includes two parts: the theme of the consumption and the expectations about their product constellation. A model for product choice is proposed, based on the assumption that consumers use consumption schemata to develop choice strategies.

INTRODUCTION

Consumers usually use an assortment of commodities, instead of isolated ones, to satisfy a need. For example, to furnish a dining room, a typical household uses a table, chairs, lighting, carpet, drapes, and other accessories. In food consumption, consumers who enjoy peanut butter sandwiches are likely to use jelly along with their peanut butter. Despite this, consumer decision making research usually analyzes buying choice at the level of isolated products or brands (Wells 1993), negating the fact that products are used in combination with other products. Whatever the particular attributes of an individual product that may lure potential consumers, the product's meaning will only be fully grasped by researchers when they consider how consumers will actually use or consume that product.

In consumption settings where multiple products are needed, the constellation of products forms a "consumption system" (Boyd and Levy 1963). When considering buying one or several items for that system, the buyers may apply choice strategies (Wright 1975) developed from the complementary interrelationships of the commodities. Starting from the idea that systematic patterns of consumption mediate consumer decision strategies, this paper introduces the construct of consumption schema and presents a model of consumer buying decisions from a new analytical approach.

SYSTEMATIC VIEWS OF CONSUMPTION

The concept of multiple-product consumption and the systematic interrelationships among products in satisfying consumers' needs was first proposed by Boyd and Levy (1963). Boyd and Levy maintained the importance of a comprehensive analysis of consumers' consumption activities in planning effective marketing strategies. They defined a consumption system as "the way a purchaser of a product performs the total task ... that he or she is trying to accomplish when using the product—not baking a cake, but preparing a meal" (Boyd and Levy 1963, pp. 129-130).

Underlying this systematic view of consumption are at least three concepts critical to analysis of consumer behavior. First, the systematic view looks beyond purchase behavior to use behavior, including consumption evidence, to interpret consumer decision making. Second, the systematic view emphasizes the dynamic interrelations between the products that comprise a consumption system: "The use behavior for a particular product is bound to be affected not only by ... the task to be performed with the use of that product but also by the related products and their use behaviors that make up the total consumption system" (Boyd and Levy 1963, p. 130). Third, it analyzes products not as isolated products entering into the consumption system, but rather in terms of the way these products are combined.

Surprisingly, few consumer choice researchers have followed Boyd and Levy's systematic view of consumption. However, some related research is found in the literature on consumption situation.

Srivastava (1981) proposes that the anticipated use, the functions to be served, and the consumption context of a product influence consumers' choices among products/brands. Although it takes a systematic view of consumption, however, this usage-situation influence approach focuses on matching the requirements of the usage-situation and the attributes of the products in consideration. This approach consequently induces an analytical approach centered on the substitution-in-use (SIU) of products (Ratneshwar and Shocker 1991). As Solomon (1983) points out, conventional marketing research has paid much more attention to the substitutability of products than to their complementarity, and the SIU approach is no exception: it does not deal directly with the aspects of complementarity-in-use of products that is at the core of the systematic approach.

Applying a systematic approach to product symbolism consistency, Solomon (1983) claims that consumers employ product constellations in "setting the stage" for the social roles they play. Product constellations occur, that is, because individuals use entire complements of products to play their social roles. The products unified in a constellation all carry social role information. Levy (1981), in his seminal work illustrating the mythology of food consumption in Western culture, also claims that consumption of products has consistent social meaning. However, Levy approaches the systematic meanings of products and related consumption activities from a global perspective (i.e., the mythology of food consumption in the culture as a whole), while Solomon (1983) examines the symbolic meaning of product complements from a local perspective (i.e., the symbolic interactionism between individuals assuming social roles).

McCracken (1988) also claims that "the consumer goods in any complement are linked by some commonality or unity" (P. 119). He refers to the patterns of consistency in product complements as "Diderot unities," in honor of the eighteenth-century French observer (Denis Diderot, 1713-1784) who first documented these product unities. McCracken asserts that "Diderot unities are well known to and daily exploited by advertisers, designers of all kinds, and, of course, the individual consumer, but they are less well understood by social scientists" (p. 119).

STRATEGIES OF PRODUCT CHOICE

Consumers often adopt simplifying strategies to make their product choice decisions, either because the capacity of human information-processing is limited (Bettman 1979) or because the cost of thinking too high (Shugan 1981). Many studies reveal that consumers who are trying to simplify problems use only simple heuristics in making decisions (Wright 1974). In particular, consumers prefer direct (or concrete and meaningful) to indirect information.

As Wright (1975) has pointed out, changes in the definition of the choice problem (or in its framing) can alter dramatically the consequent steps involved in choosing. And, hence, the outcomes of choice can be different, even if the consideration sets are the same. For example, selecting a chair to accompany a particular study desk and selecting chairs for a dining table are two different problems of chair choice. Therefore, the decision process and the evaluation tactics may be different and so the outcomes, even though consumers face the same set of alternative chairs.

Consumer psychology researchers have conceptualized two types of thinking approaches which consumers may apply to

FIGURE 1
A Framework of Consumption Schema: Dining Room Furnishings

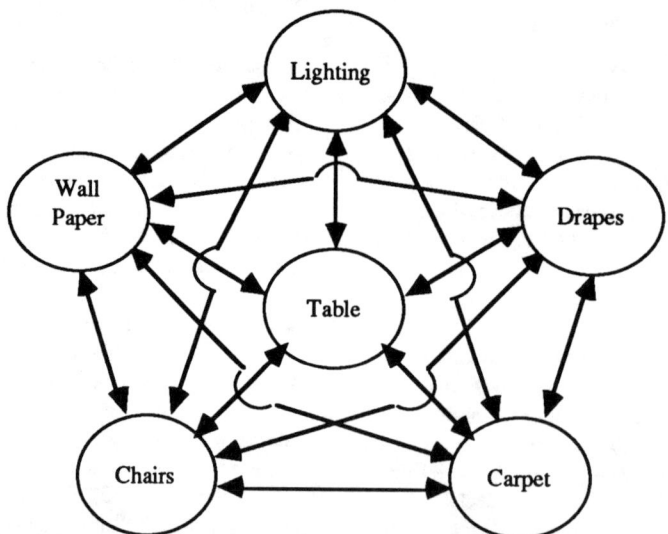

formulate a problem and then compose their choice strategies: 1) conceptually driven and 2) data-driven (Bettman 1979). In conceptually driven methods, also called top-down approaches, consumers' thinking is guided by concepts or images at a higher level than the choice objects. In data-driven methods, or bottom-up approaches, consumers' reactions to choice problems are based only on the features and clues in the choice objects themselves. From them, consumers try to develop a meaningful pattern so a decision can be made. Applying this idea of two archetypal thinking approaches, Hauser (1986) suggested that people use an "agenda" in decision making to economize the cost of thinking. Theoretically, the agenda can be top-down, bottom up, or mixed. However, the cost of thinking in a bottom-up approach is far greater than that of thinking top-down, although the expected payoff of a bottom-up approach is also greater in some situations (Hauser 1986).

It may be safe to say, then, that consumers tend to use their ideas and experiences in daily life to recognize and frame product choice problems, since consumers' experiences, beliefs, and ideas about products in daily life are convenient and direct helps (or influences) in making product choices. Choice strategies that consumers derive from their daily episodic memory (Ashcraft 1989), from their cultural mythology of product and consumption (Levy 1981), or from the ideas systematically represented in their cognitive structure (Crocker 1984) are imagistic and holistic in nature.

CONSUMPTION SCHEMATA

Researchers in cognitive and social psychology propose that people mentally represent their ideas and beliefs in cognitive structures called schemata (Crocker 1984). In other words, consumers use a network structure to organize and represent their knowledge about the meanings of products. A related concept, directly germane to consumption activity, is that of cognitive scripts (Abelson 1976). Over time, that is, consumers organize and represent their knowledge about consumption events and the behavior into scripts they apply in specific cases. Although the schemata and scripts are separable aspects of mental representation, however, they are not exclusive. It can be assumed that the representation processings of semantic memory (general knowledge) and of episodic memory (experiential knowledge) are coexistent and facilitate each other (Ashcraft 1989). Therefore, scripts can be considered as sequential schemata that represent consecutive activities of events.

Beginning with the idea of the cognitive schema, this paper proposes that consumers may acquire cognitive structures to represent various product constellations they use in satisfying needs in daily life. These cognitive structures about specific product complements organize and represent information (or personal cognition) about interrelationships among the complementary products, the temporal sequence of the consumption activity, the cultural value and meanings of the commodities, and personal preferences and affective associations. This paper uses the term *consumption schema* to refer to this cognitive structure from and through which product complements and relevant personal ideas are represented to meet consumer needs.

Figure 1, as an example, presents a brief framework of consumption schema concerning dining room furnishings. A typical American house will need a table, chairs, lighting, carpet, drapes, wall paper, and other accessories to furnish a dining room. This constellation of complementary commodities coexists in use, while a structure of personal ideas and related thoughts about their consumption is represented in users' minds, consciously or unconsciously.

In summary, a consumption schema, by definition, has two parts: the themes (or main ideas) of the consumption activity and consumers' expectations about product constellations and their interrelationships. A consumption schema does not necessarily refer to a representation of the supreme state of consumption in satisfying a need that the consumer can imagine. Rather, a consumption schema can be viewed as a goal state of consumption in meeting a need that the consumer will expect or design within a particular environment.

The Subschemata

As we can experience or certainly observe in a modern civilization, people's operations to meet daily needs in living, such as food, shelter, clothes, transportation and recreation, are rather sophisticated. In addition to the various and delicate tools people use, the processes of the consumption are themselves circuitous and of multiple steps (or parts). From a purely functional view point, we can observe several required functions in these multiple-step (or part) processes. For example, to provide a place for dining at home, the dining room needs many furnishings and other accessories. In short, consumers acquire a consumption schema to meet a need in daily life. And, this consumption schema can be partitioned into subordinate structures, based on the multiple-step nature of the consumption process.

These subordinate structures making up a consumption schema can be referred to as *subschemata*. In a subschema, one or several commodities are put in use as one or several functions are required. For example, in the subschema of sitting in a consumption schema of dining room furnishings, the function of seating is required and a set of chairs is included.

Although subschemata can operate and be represented separately, their contents are subject to the influences of other subschemata within the same consumption schema. In the case of dining room furnishings, the function of seating and the chairs can operate independently, but the particular set of chairs to be used and how they fit into the dining room are influenced by the theme of the broader consumption schema and other objects of furnishings in it.

In summary, the following are first two basic propositions concerning consumer behavior in a model based on consumption schema:

P1: To satisfy a need, people acquire a consumption schema about it, which comprises both the theme of the consumption and their expectations about the complementary products to be used.

P2: A consumption schema can be partitioned into subschemata with requisite functions fulfilled through represented products.

The function that a subschema assumes usually can be performed in different ways (or by alternative products). A method to perform the required function (or functions) is referred to as a *mode* for that subschema. A mode for subschema consists of the way the required function (or functions) is performed and of the product (or the complementary products) to be used. For example, classic style chairs and modern fashion chairs are two different modes for the subschema of sitting in dining room furniture. Different brands of the same product-type, usually with different attributes and/or with particular social meanings, will be discriminated as different modes in the model.

Compatibility and Complementarity

When a consumer tries to combine a product constellation and to construct from it a meaningful pattern according to a consumption schema, some principles regulate the selection of the mode (of a product or products) for each subschemata. This paper assumes that consumers obtain utility holistically, from a product constellation based on a consumption schema rather than from the individual products separately. The dimensions of compatibility and complementarity between products are assumed to be critical considerations in the product choice. Many dimensions of complementarity and compatibility are possible, including functional exhaustivity, operational connectivity, aesthetic coherence, meaning-role consistency, hedonistic value, memorial symbolism, and affective association. The selection from among these dimensions depends on the theme of the consumption and on expectations about the product constellation to be used. The following examples define some interrelational dimensions between products.

Functional exhaustivity suggests that products are chosen and combined in such a way that the required functions of a consumption activity are complete fulfilled. Using the example of dining room furnishings, light fixtures with adjustable illumination, a table with extendible flaps, and chairs adaptable to a child's need to sit at the dining table may all be selected to fulfill the many functions expected by the consumer.

Operational connectivity suggests that the operation (or the physical shapes of the products and their positions in the layout) of a subschema is smoothly connected (or in coherence) with other subschemata. For the dining room furnishing example, a cupboard for dining accessories and small end tables may be arranged to allow smooth setting up and serving.

Aesthetic coherence relates to the sense of beauty or to personal expression. This dimension is very subjective and idiosyncratic. Nevertheless, consumers' preference for a product constellation may be derived mainly from it. For the dining room furnishing example, lighting, table, chairs, and carpet may be required to match a personally-felt aesthetic preference.

Meaning-role consistency refers to the perceived coherence between the cultural meanings of products and the social roles which the consumers assume (Solomon 1983). Based on the concepts of symbolic interactionism and reflexive self-evaluation, Solomon claims that consumers select products which correspond to the selves they "play." For dining room furnishings, particular levels of quality (e.g., prestigious brands) of dining accessories, lighting systems, tables, and chairs may be required to be consistent with a consumer's status.

Consumers may not require that two subschemata be absolutely compatible (or consistent) with each other in every qualitative dimension. Consumers may only require that the degree of compatibility among some dimensions reaches certain satisfactory levels. This notion of a satisfactory degree of compatibility is in harmony with the idea that consumers may be satisfiers instead of utility maximizers (Bettman et al. 1991).

In summary, the following are other basic propositions of the model.

P3: The relevant dimensions of compatibility and complementarity between subschemata in a consumption schema are the main sources from which consumers obtain utility of products.

P4: Consumers require that some dimensions of compatibility and complementarity between modes (products) for the subschemata reach acceptable levels.

The present model only deals with bilateral relationships between subschemata, assuming that no trilateral or more complex, relationship is substantial. When the degrees of compatibility in every relevant dimension between subschemata reach the acceptable levels, the product constellation is said to be *in coherence* for the consumer according to his consumption schema. Further, the present model proposes that the theme of a consumption schema, perception of the compatibility, and the acceptable levels of compatibility are not invariant over time. They may change in response to changes in a consumer's situation.

Costs and Benefits Evaluation

In a consumption schema, the relevant dimensions of compatibility which prescribe the coherence between subschemata only focus on the qualitative aspects of products and their cultural meanings. However, being compatible in the qualitative attributes and cultural meanings may not necessitate that the products will be chosen by the consumers. Consumers may encounter more than one product constellation satisfactory to them in the dimensions of

FIGURE 2
The Framework of Holistic Product Choice Strategy Based on Consumption Schema

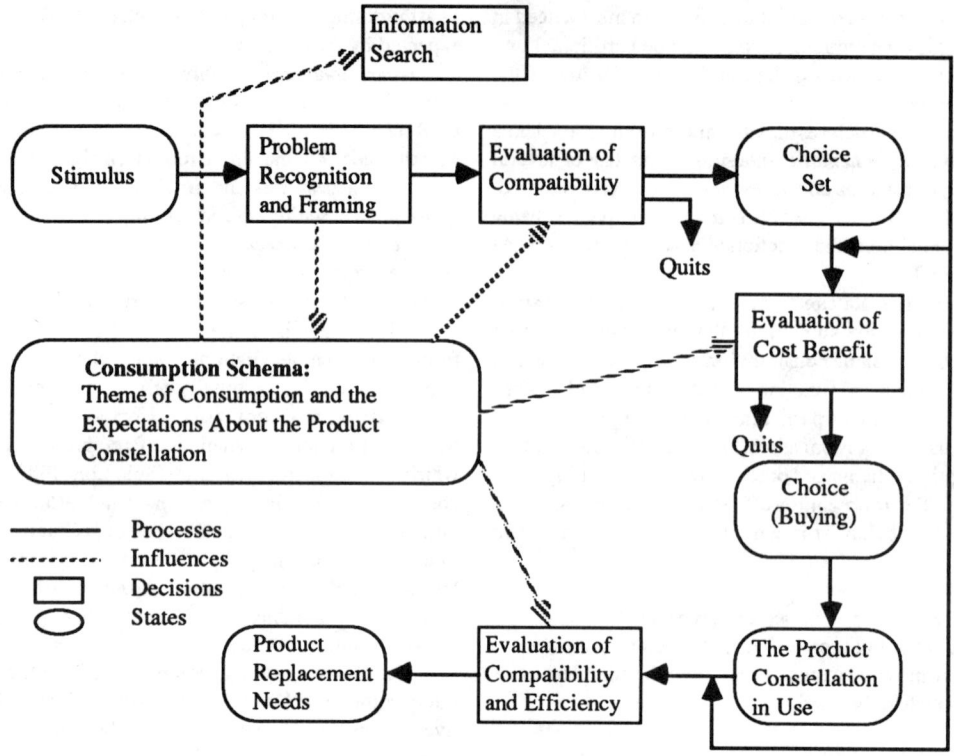

compatibility. Remember that the principle of compatibility is applied on a satisfactory-nonsatisfactory basis, not on a maximization basis. In this case, the principle of compatibility alone does not completely explain consumer decisions. In an other case, consumers may find only one product constellation satisfactory to them, but even assuming adequate financial capacity a purchase may not follow. These cases imply that other types of evaluation, different from the principle of compatibility and complementarity, are also at work in mediating consumer product choices.

Consumers may apply costs-and-benefits evaluation to a product constellation, when the costs are "significant" to them, or when the principle of compatibility and complementarity is exhausted. To solve this problem, the idea of "economic efficiency" is adopted in the present model. The economic-efficiency calculation that evaluates the benefits of a product constellation against its costs is referred to as *costs-and-benefits evaluation*. For example, facing several sets of dining room furnishings products which all are in coherence according to his consumption schema, the consumer may resort to costs-and-benefits evaluation to choose among them. In summary, costs-and-benefits evaluation is the next step following the evaluation on compatibility and complementarity among products.

In the model, the relevant costs of a product constellation are money and time, while human energy anticipated in the consumption is considered trivial. Since the value perception of time and money vary among people, objective amounts of money and time have to be transferred to a subjective scale to be "meaningful" to individual consumers. Consequently, the outcome of cost-and-benefit evaluation must be converted to a subjective scale also. In other words, consumers' subjective perceptions, not objective measurements, are the basis of cost-and-benefit evaluation.

Consumers may acquire their satisfactory levels of cost-and-benefit efficiency by screening product constellations. However, when several product constellations are satisfactory in terms of cost-and-benefit efficiency, consumers may compare between them and rank their standings in efficiency. In this case, the product constellation that maximizes efficiency will be chosen.

P5: Consumers choose the product constellation that has the highest and satisfactory level of cost-and-benefit efficiency.

THE FRAMEWORK OF HOLISTIC PRODUCT CHOICE STRATEGY

Figure 2 presents a framework of product choice strategy based on the construct of consumption schema. This framework summarizes the product choice process and the influence of a consumption schema and depicts how the product choice model works. A consumption schema, again, consists of two parts: the theme of the consumption and expectations about the product constellation. Consumers consult it as a holistic strategy for decision making concerning new product acquisition and "old" product replacement. The consumption schema dictates the whole range of the product choice process, from problem recognition to the post-purchase evaluation.

For illustrating the framework, let's suppose that a hypothetical consumer is considering buying a set of furnishings to furnish his dining room. The consumer recognizes and frames his problem of dining room furnishings by his consumption schema about it, which expresses his life style and various characteristics of his family.

After the decision is framed, effective actions can be undertaken in searching for product information and prospective products. Information search problems, such as what style of furniture, where to search, and how much information, require consulting the consumption schema. When information and prospective products are found, the consumer next has to find acceptable product constellations among the many he may encounter in the market. This process of elimination is carried out by evaluating of compatibility, through which the consumer deliberates on his theme of dining room furnishings and on the relevant dimensions of compatibility and complementarity among the products. If after an evaluation of compatibility the consumer finds no assortment of dining room furnishings in the market acceptable to him, the process ends. If the consumer finds some acceptable assortment of furnishings, then a choice set for further consideration has been established.

For selecting among the acceptable product constellations remaining in the choice set, the consumer then shifts the criteria of decision to the evaluation of costs-and-benefits. The consumption schema still directs the costs-and-benefits evaluation, since the "benefits" can be derived from the prospective product combinations only by consulting the consumption schema. If no product constellation in the choice set is satisfactory, the process ends. If the consumer finds some (or even one) product constellation satisfactory, then the most satisfactory product constellation in terms of the costs-and-benefits evaluation is purchased.

After the purchases are made and the product constellation is put into use, the consumer continues to evaluate the products. The post-acquisition evaluation occurs most intensively when the consumer's consumption schema shifts, or when his perception of product compatibility and complementarity changes. Nevertheless, the same principles of compatibility and costs-and-benefits based on the consumption schema are also applied in the post-acquisition evaluation. If, through this evaluation, the product constellation in use is found out-of-coherence or unsatisfactory, the need to replace the "obsolete" items in it emerges. Then, a process of product choice to form a new product constellation, according to the consumption schema, begins anew.

CONCLUSION

This paper has sketched a model of holistic product choice strategy for consumer decision making, based on the construct of consumption schemata. The model has several advantages, compared to traditional models. First, the model explains well how the Diderot effect (McCracken 1986) works—in particular, why and how a replacement of one piece of furniture in a study room may induce gradually the demand to replace other items. This advantage originates from its premises that consumers obtain utility from product constellations and by consulting their consumption schemata, not from individual products alone. Second, the model captures the reality of consumers' two-step evaluations in making product choice decisions. It indicates that the process by which prospective products are included in a choice set for further consideration is different from that used to make a final choice from the choice set. Both mechanisms are indispensable for a sound model of consumer product choice. Furthermore, the two processes should apply consistently to the same choice strategy. Third, the model applies directly to the phenomenon of consumers' evaluation of products-in-use, up to now largely ignored in the literature. The model explicates parsimoniously both the processes of product-replacement decision within an existing system and of adopting a new products system.

How consumers actually specify their consumption schemata is critical in observing their decision behavior. Theoretically, consumption schemata can be specified at different levels of aggregation on consumption activities, as long as utilities can be perceived separately by consumers.

The examples of consumption schema in this paper only relate to products used coexistently. However, on some consumption occasions, complementary goods are related sequentially. Although these products are sequentially arranged in operation, however, perceptions about product assortments for a sequential operation are represented in a "coexistent" product constellation in consumers' minds. In sequential product constellations, the pattern of interrelationships between the products will reflect the characteristics of their sequence (e.g., operational connectivity will be highlighted).

The concept of consumption schema applies the ideas of complementarity and compatibility within product constellations. However, this paper does not assert that every consumption choice by consumers is consistent with their consumption schemata. Frequently, consumers follow product-constellation patterns that are not in accord with their own expectations. A "non-satisfactory" situation may occur when none of the products available in the marketplace is satisfactory, consumers meet their needs by choosing the "best" available, still perhaps by using the choice strategies based on their consumption schemata. Furthermore, consumption in a "non-satisfactory" situation can occur for many other reasons. Income constraints may limit the range of a consumer's choice. Moreover, even with an affordable income, various priorities for resources (time, money, and human energy) allocation may also cause consumers to stay with their incumbent non-satisfactory product constellation. However, when it becomes feasible, consumers may try to upgrade the commodities they use, consulting their consumption schemata.

REFERENCES

Abelson, Robert P. (1976), "Script Processing in Attitude Formation and Decision Making," in *Cognition and Social Behavior*, eds. John S. Carroll and John W. Payne, Hillsdale, NJ: Erlbaum, 33-45.

Ashcraft, Mark H. (1989), *Human Memory and Cognition*, Glenview, IL: Scott and Foresman.

Bettman, James R. (1979), *An Information Processing Theory of Consumer Choice*, Reading, MA: Addison-Wesley.

_____, Eric J. Johnson, John W. Payne (1991), "Consumer Decision Making," in *Handbook of Consumer Behavior*, eds. Thomas S. Robertson and Harold H. Kassarjian, Englewood Cliffs, NJ: Prentice-Hall, 50-84.

Boyd, Harper W. and S. J. Levy (1963), "New Dimension in Consumer Analysis", *Harvard Business Review*, 41 (November-December), 129-140.

Crocker, Jennifer (1984), "A Schematic Approach to Changing Consumers' Beliefs," in *Advances in Consumer Research*, Vol.11, ed. Thomas C. Kinnear, Provo, UT: Association for Consumer Research, 472-477.

Hauser, John R. (1986), "Agendas and Consumer Choice," *Journal of Marketing Research*, 23 (August), 199-212.

Levy, Sidney J. (1981), "Interpreting Consumer Mythology: A Structural Approach to Consumer Behavior," *Journal of Marketing*, 45 (Summer), 49-61.

McCracken, Grant (1986), "The Role of Product as Social Stimuli: A Symbolic Interactionism Perspective," *Journal of Consumer Research*, 10 (December), 319-329.

_____ (1988), *Culture and Consumption: New Approaches to the Symbolic Character of Consumer Goods and Activities*, Bloomington, IN: Indiana University Press.

Ratneshwar, S. and Allan D. Shocker (1991), "Substitution in Use and Role of Usage Context in Product Category Structures," *Journal of Marketing Research*, 28 (August), 281-295.

Shugan, Steve M. (1980), "The Cost of Thinking," *Journal of Consumer Research*, 7 (September), 99-111.

Solomon, Michael R. (1983), "The Role of Product as Social Stimuli: A Symbolic Interationism Perspective," *Journal of Consumer Research*, 10 (December), 319-329.

Srivastava, Rajendra K. (1981), "Usage-Situational Influences on Perceptions of Product Markets: Theoretical and Empirical Issues," in *Advances in Consumer Research,* vol.8, ed. Kent Monroe, Chicago: Association for Consumer Research, 106-111.

Wells, William D. (1993) "Discovery-oriented Consumer Research," *Journal of Consumer Research*, 19 (March), 489-504.

Wright, Peter (1974), "The Harassed Decision Maker: Time Pressures, Distractions, and the Use of Evidence," *Journal of Applied Psychology*, 59, 555-561.

_____ (1975), "Consumer Choice Strategies: Simplifying Vs. Optimizing," *Journal of Marketing Research*, 12 (February), 60-67.

Innovations in Defining and Measuring Brand Image
Martin S. Roth, Boston College

The purpose of this session was to present new and innovative research in conceptualizing and measuring brand image. Brand image can be defined as the meaning consumers develop about the brand as a result of the firm's marketing activities. Thus brand image encompasses the holistic interpretation consumers have about a brand, and the meaning, or personal relevance, they ascribe to it. Understanding and managing brand images are thus central to the satisfaction of customer needs. For managers, measuring brand image is important both for determining the brand's position vis-a-vis competitors, and to insure that target markets internalize the brand's marketing cues in the manner intended by management.

The first paper by George Zinkhan and Penelope Prenshaw examined consumer images of the "good life," and how these related to brand names. Data collected across multiple countries was presented. The paper "Good Life Images and Brand Name Associations: Evidence from Asia, America, and Europe" is in the *Conference Proceedings*.

The second paper by Marty Roth reported findings of a study investigating the effectiveness of brand image research techniques and formats. Four research techniques (free association, brand personality, brand symbols, and brand personification) and two formats (moderated focus groups and surveys) were compared for their ability to elicit brand image information. Data was collected for two products — Reebok athletic shoes and Haagen-Dazs ice cream. Elicitations were examined across multiple image dimensions (e.g., features and benefits, uniqueness, usage occasions). The imagery information elicited was then related to purchase intentions and purchase frequency. Results were presented showing that research techniques vary in their ability to capture various dimensions of brand images, and that some imagery dimensions are more effective than others in explaining consumer purchase intentions and product usage frequency. Taken together, the results provided insights into selecting research techniques and formats for capturing the most meaningful image perceptions consumers possess about brands.

The third paper by Robin Higie and Gerald Zaltman showed an application of the Zaltman Metaphor Elicitation Technique for capturing brand images. The paper described the ten steps used to incorporate visual and verbal information into mental maps representing how consumer think and feel about brands. Their paper "Using the Zaltman Metaphor Elicitation Technique to Understand Brand Images" appears in the *Conference Proceedings*.

A concluding discussion by Susan Nelson highlighted the practical applications of the three research projects. In particular, increased client and research supplier attention to brand image, brand equity, and corporate identity issues reinforced the importance of the research presented. Suggestions for continued theory development, method advancements, and practical applications were offered.

Good Life Images and Brand Name Associations: Evidence from Asia, America, and Europe

George M. Zinkhan, University of Houston
Penelope J. Prenshaw, University of Houston[1]

ABSTRACT

Consumers' descriptions of the good life frequently contain visions of material possessions, including both general product categories and specific brand names. In this study, we investigate the link between good life visions and brand name images in three different cultures: Spain, Taiwan, and the United States. We find only minimal support for the cultural differences which we had predicted, based upon Hofstede's theory of cultural values. Especially in Spain and in the U.S., we find evidence that the brand names for luxury products (including automobiles and electronics) are strongly linked to this universal notion of "the good life."

INTRODUCTION

What's in a name? More specifically, what's in a brand name? A brand name serves a variety of purposes for both the firm and the consumer (Meyers-Levy 1989). More than just a label, a brand name is a complex symbol providing a variety of associations for the consumer (Zinkhan and Martin 1987). Such associations go beyond simple product inferences and evaluations; and brand names can serve a valuable social function by promoting feelings of group affiliation through brand identification (Friedman 1991).

A main purpose of this study is to determine the extent to which brand names are associated with good life images. In U.S. advertising, everything from cars to beer to yogurt to clothing claim to provide the purchaser with aspects of the good life. In fact, critics of advertising claim that advertising encourages consumers to value products not only as ends in themselves but more importantly as means for acquiring love and friendship (Schudson 1984). Leiss, Kline, and Jhally (1986) put a more positive spin on advertising effects and describe consumer products as symbols with attached meanings for defining what is valued.

The concept of the "good life" exists in many languages (e.g., "la dolce vita," "le bon vie"); but how it is conceived (and defined) varies from culture to culture. Among the formal definitions which have been proposed are Belk and Pollay's (1985) distinction between one view which focuses on material possessions and a second view which emphasizes the cultivation of spiritual rewards. The objective of this paper is to combine the two concepts of brand name and good life. Specifically, an attempt is made: (a) to determine what brand names (if any) are associated with the good life; and (b) to examine cultural differences between good life visions (in terms of brand names mentioned). That is, are there differences across cultures that determine whether brand names are used more frequently in descriptions of the good life? To examine these cultural differences, student essays from three countries (U.S., Spain, and Taiwan) are analyzed. These countries are selected so as to provide representative responses from three different continents. In their essays, respondents are asked to describe what the good life is to them.

BRAND NAME AND IMAGE

Images play an important role in influencing the way that consumers respond to products and services. Similarly, brand name plays a key role in consumer decision making, often through decision-making heuristics or through inferences about quality. In this sense, brand name is one way that brand image is communicated to consumers. From a consumer's point of view, a set of brand name associations may represent an accumulation of knowledge about the brand along with accompanying emotions and affect (Zinkhan and Martin 1987).

Several studies have examined the association sets accompanying brand names and the effect these associations have on brand preference (LeClerc, Schmitt and Dube-Rioux 1989), brand memory (Meyers-Levy 1989), and brand name attitude (Zinkhan and Martin 1982, 1987). The view underlying this research is that, through semantic associations in memory, a brand name can trigger a variety of inferences, which in turn can influence preference, memory, or attitude.

Park, Jaworski and MacInnis (1986) categorized brand images according to the needs brands fulfill for the consumer. For example, a brand with a functional image focuses on solving consumption-related problems (e.g., the images associated with a vacuum cleaner). Symbolic brands fulfill needs associated with self-enhancement, role position, group membership, or ego-identification (e.g., the images associated with automobiles). Brands may also portray an experiential image which provides consumers with pleasure, variety, and/or stimulation (e.g., food products). Hence, a brand name (and its associated image) provides consumers with a multitude of attached meanings (Dobni and Zinkhan 1990).

THE GOOD LIFE

A key question in consumer behavior research is: "Why do people buy what they do?" There are many possible approaches for answering this question. One approach is to develop metaphors, and one promising metaphor which has been proposed is "the good life" (Belk and Pollay 1985). Many consumers strive to achieve or maintain the good life; but visions of the good life are culturally determined; and such good life visions depend upon the values within a culture (Tuan 1986). Further, depending on a culture's value orientations, good life images may be expressed through demand for certain products and/or services (O'Shaughnessy 1987).

If we accept that a relationship exists between cultures and visions of the good life, then we must accept that differences in cultures translate to differences among individuals' visions of the good life. Further, values which are implicit in a culture will affect individuals' good life visions and thus may be linked to demand for specific products, services, or brands.

OVERVIEW OF STUDY

Two research questions are examined in this preliminary investigation of good life visions. First, the analysis attempts to determine which specific brand names consumers link with the notion of good life. Second, we investigate differences in cultures (defined by value orientations) which influence the appearance of brand names in good life descriptions. In order to explore these questions, data were collected from students in three cultures: U.S., Spain, and Taiwan.

The conceptual framework to guide this investigation is derived from the work of Hofstede (1980), who empirically derived four value dimensions from a large-scale study of 116,000 subjects in fifty countries. Hofstede (1980) focused on societal differences by investigating cultural values, and he derived four value dimensions of national culture which are defined as societal norms

---

[1] The authors would like to acknowledge the University of Houston via the Limited Grant-in-Aid program for financial support related to this project.

TABLE 1
Hypotheses and Results

Hypotheses	Value Dimension and Relationship to Frequency of Brand-Name Mentions	Hofstede Prediction of Country Order[a]	Results
One	High Uncertainty Avoidance Leads to More Brands Mentioned	U.S. (46) Taiwan (69) Spain (86)	Not Supported by Essay One Not Supported by Essay Two Supported by Essay Three
Two	High Power Distance Leads to More Brands Mentioned	U.S. (40) Spain (57) Taiwan (58)	Not Supported by Essay One Opposite Results for Essay Two Supported by Essay Three
Three	High Individualism Leads to Few Brands Mentioned	U.S. (91) Spain (51) Taiwan (17)	Not Supported by Essay One, Two or Three
Four	High Masculinity Leads to More Brands Mentioned	Spain (42) Taiwan (45) U.S. (62)	Not Supported by Essay One, Two, or Three

[a]Low to high frequency of brand name mentions; Hofstede scores are in parentheses.

(system of values) shared by the majority of the middle class within a society. Hofstede's value dimensions have been used to understand other aspects of consumer behavior (e.g., tipping behavior) across cultures (Lynn, Zinkhan, and Harris 1993).

It follows, then, that variations in value dimensions should explain variations in individuals' good life visions, as well as the frequency with which brand names are mentioned in descriptions of the good life. Following a brief description of Hofstede's four value dimensions, hypotheses are derived, based on cultural differences described by Hofstede.

HYPOTHESES

Hofstede's first value dimension, "uncertainty avoidance," describes how individuals deal with uncertainty. A culture's score on the "uncertainty avoidance" dimension reflects individuals' need for security and their willingness to accept change and take risks. Uncertainty avoidance provides guidance in dealing with anxiety about the future and the reflects the desire to provide protection (via technology, rules or laws, and religion). Many times consumers are unable to differentiate products on the basis of their physical characteristics. In judging between competitors, consumers rely on a brand's reputation as an assurance that the product meets certain standards (e.g., "you can trust Woolite for all you fine washables," Zikmund and d'Amico 1993). In brief, branding provides a way for consumers to reduce risk by capitalizing on their prior consumption experiences associated with specific brands. It follows, then, that cultures scoring high on the "uncertainty avoidance" dimension should mention brand names more frequently than those cultures scoring lower on this dimension. Thus, we hypothesize (via H1 in Table 1) that respondents from cultures with the highest "uncertainty avoidance" score will mention brand names most frequently in their descriptions of the good life; see Table 1 for a complete summary of the four hypotheses proposed in this study.

Hofstede's second dimension, "power distance," consists of values concerning the desirability or undesirability of social inequality (including the notions of dependence versus interdependence, and the exercise of power). The issue involved relates to areas such as prestige, wealth, status, and power. In high power-distance cultures, the powerful strive to appear as powerful as possible. In contrast, in low power-distance cultures, power holders are somewhat embarrassed by power and attempt to underplay power appearances. Value-expressive brands help individuals communicate their values (Munson and Spivey 1981). Similarly, brands positioned to maintain the exclusivity of the brand can communicate to others the status, prestige, and role position of the brand-user. Individuals in high power-distance cultures are eager to express their position in society; thus, we would expect those cultures scoring high on the "power-distance" dimension to mention brand names more frequently than those cultures scoring lower on this dimension. In turn, we hypothesize that respondents from cultures with high "power-distance" scores will mention brand names more frequently in their descriptions of the good life than will respondents from cultures with low "power-distance" scores (see H2 in Table 1).

Hofstede's "masculinity" dimension explains cultural variation based on the dominant sex-role patterns in societies. The main issue is the extent to which biological differences between the sexes have implications for societal roles. In this regard, cultures with high masculinity scores show greater differences in values between men and women. For example, cultures scoring high on the masculinity dimension illustrate an achievement ideal, have a money and "things" orientation, and view performance and growth as important. In brief, members of a high masculinity culture value material possessions more than those in a low masculinity culture. Thus, we expect those cultures scoring high on the "masculinity" dimension to mention brand names more frequently than those cultures scoring lower on this dimension. Therefore, we hypothesize that respondents from cultures with the highest "masculinity" score will mention brand names most frequently in their descriptions of the good life (again, see Table 1 for a summary of the hypotheses and predictions).

The final dimension described by Hofstede, "individualism," describes the relationship between the individual and the collective or group. The cultural value reflected by low "individualism" places greater emphasis on a "we" consciousness, a collectivity orientation, and belonging, where identity is based in the social system. The values in highly "individualistic" cultures highlight individual decision making and personal freedom so that one's identity is based on the individual. This emphasis on individualism leads to greater optimism and high levels of confidence in one's own ability.

Friedman (1991) describes brand name usage as facilitating group affiliation, such that those who share a brand identification feel a sense of community. Marketing practice reflects this trend through "affinity marketing," where consumers are encouraged to express their loyalty to a group (e.g., a college) through the

TABLE 2
Good Life Results With No Brand Prompt (Essay One)

Sample	Autos	Newspaper Magazines	Food Clothing Luxury Goods	Travel Entertain	Other	Total Brands Mentioned
US n = 106	9 (8.5%)	5 (4.7%)	0	2 (1.9%)	1 (.94%)	17 (16.04%)
Spain n = 101	3 (2.97%)	0	3 (2.97%)	2 (1.98%)	0	8 (7.92%)
Taiwan n = 51	4 (7.84%)	0	0	0	0	4 (7.84%)

[a] Cell entries indicate the number of respondents who mentioned a specific brand name when describing a good life vision. Percentages are in parentheses.

purchase of a specific brand (e.g., American Express credit cards); see Zinkhan, Hong, and Lawson (1990) for a more complete discussion of affinity marketing and cultural values.

In summary, we expect individuals from those cultures which score higher on the "individualism" dimension to mention brand names less frequently than individuals from those cultures scoring lower on this dimension. Therefore, we hypothesize that respondents from cultures with the highest "individualism" scores will mention brand names least frequently in their descriptions of the good life.

METHOD

Essays

On three different days, respondents wrote one-page essays to describe their good life visions. Essay One asked subjects to respond to this question: "What is the good life to you?" Thus, respondents were not specifically prompted to think about brand names in essay one. Essay Two questioned respondents about their good life visions (as they related to material aspects) by providing a products and services prompt. That is, respondents were asked to list the products and services which they associated with the good life. Again, the instructions for Essay Two do not explicitly encourage respondents to think of or list specific brand names. Finally, Essay Three asked respondents to list the brand names which they associated with the good life.

Brand names which are mentioned by consumers in Essay One are expected to be strongly linked to visions of the good life, as these brands emerge with only minimal prompting. For all practical purposes, the phrase, the "good life," is the only prompt which is used in Essay One. The Essay Two prompt is a little more specific in that it directs subjects' thoughts toward material things (i.e., products and services). Thus, brand names which emerge in response to the Essay Two question are also strongly linked to consumers' good life visions.

Sample

In order to examine our research questions, respondents were drawn from three different countries: Spain, the U.S., and Taiwan. As well as representing three continents, these countries represent an old-world western culture (Spain), a new-world western culture (US), and an old-world eastern culture (Taiwan). Respondents were surveyed in two waves. During the first wave, respondents from all three cultures answered Essays One and Two. During the second wave, respondents from the U.S. answered Essays Two and Three; respondents from Spain answered only Essay Three. Thus, for Essay Two, the U.S. sample size is larger due to the number of respondents who participated in the second wave in America. For Essay Two, the Spanish and Taiwanese sample sizes decrease slightly, due to respondents' absence during administration of the second essay.

Coding

These three essays were content analyzed. The content analysis focused on brand name counts (e.g., number of BMWs mentioned). Coding instructions with product and service categories were devised, and two graduate students performed the coding.

RESULTS

Cultural Patterns

The results for the four hypotheses related to cultural values are summarized in Table 1. Almost none of Hofstede's predictions are supported. The individualism hypothesis (H3) and the masculinity hypothesis (H4) are not supported by the results associated with any of the three essays. Essays One and Two provide no support for the Uncertainty Avoidance (H1) and Power Distance (H2) hypotheses. For example, as shown in Table 2, U.S. (16%) respondents were most likely to mention a brand name in response to Essay One (as predicted by the Masculinity dimension). However, this difference is not statistically significant (chi square=4.15, df=2, $p<.2$). Taiwanese (7.84%) and Spanish (7.92%) were less likely than their U.S. counterparts to mention a specific brand name.

With respect to Essay Two, U.S. respondents were again the most likely to mention a brand name (average number of brands mentioned per respondent equals 1.12). Spanish respondents also mentioned a large number of brand names (approximately one name mentioned for each respondent); in contrast, Taiwanese subjects mentioned almost no brand names in response to a "product prompt." Again, as summarized in Table 1, this pattern of brand name mentions matches almost none of Hofstede's predictions (as deduced by us here). The one exception is that the masculinity dimension does predict that U.S. respondents will mention more brand names than their Spanish counterparts; and this expectation is confirmed in Essay Two ($t=1.97$, df=256, $p<.05$).

The Essay Three results do provide support for hypotheses one and two. Spain is higher than the U.S. on both uncertainty avoidance (H1) and power distance (H2); and, as predicted by these two hypotheses, the Spanish subjects mentioned more brand names (16.05 on average) than their American counterparts (13.26). This difference is statistically significant ($t=2.71$, df=114, $p<.05$), thus providing support for H1 and H2.

TABLE 3
Brand Names Mentioned With No Prompt (Essay One Results)

Brand Names	US	Spain	Taiwan
BMW	4	1	2
Porsche	2	1	
Lamborghini	1		
Mercedes	1	1	1
Audi			1
Toyota	1		
Webster	3		
Wall Street	2		
University of Houston	1		
Men's Club	1		
River Oaks Country Club	1		
DuPont		1	
Coca-Cola		1	
Armani		1	
Metropolitan		1	
La Scala of Milan		1	

TABLE 4
Brand Names Mentioned With Product and Service Prompt (Essay Two Results) [a]

Sample	Autos		Electronics		Luxury Goods	
US	Mercedes	18	Macintosh	4	Rolex	4
	BMW	11				
	Porsche	11				
	Toyota	6				
	Honda	6				
	Ferrari	4				
	Acura	4				
	Jaguar	4				
	Chevy	4				
	Corvette	3				
	Ford	3				
Spain	Porsche	10	Sony	3		
	Ferrari	8				
	Mercedes	5				
	BMW	4				
	Jaguar	3				

[a] Only those brand names with three or more mentions are listed.

Specific Brand Names Mentioned

Specific brand names mentioned are shown in Table 3 (for Essay One) and in Table 4 (for Essay Two). Essay One provides no prompt for either product or brand; so the specific brands which show up in Table 3 can be construed as being very powerful, in the sense that respondents view these brands as being strongly connected to their vision of the good life. Across the three cultures, more than half the brands (53.6%) mentioned in Essay One are automobiles (e.g., BMW, Porsche, Mercedes). All but one of the automobiles is manufactured in Europe; and interestingly, this pattern holds true across all three cultures.

Table 4 summarizes the brand names most frequently mentioned in response to a product and service prompt. Here again, subjects were not specifically asked to think about brand names; but they were provided with a cue to think in a "materialistic fashion" (i.e., to think about products and services which might be linked to the good life). Once again, automobiles are the brands most closely associated with the good life. European brands are most common (both among American and Spanish respondents). Asian brands (e.g., Toyota, Honda, Acura) are second most popular with U.S. respondents; but U.S. respondents also mention some North American automobile brands (e.g., Chevy, Corvette, Ford). Electronics (e.g., Macintosh, Sony) and luxury brands (i.e., Rolex) are also mentioned in the Spanish and U.S. samples. Taiwanese subjects listed too few brand names in response to Essay Two to be summarized in Table 4, which only lists those brand names that received 3 or more mentions.

DISCUSSION

We have made some progress toward understanding the brand names associated with good life visions in three cultures. Of all product categories, automobiles are most often associated with the good life. Other material possessions mentioned are all products of the industrial and information revolutions, including electronics equipment and watches. Taiwanese are much less likely to mention a specific brand name, following indirect prompts, than their counterparts in the U.S. or Spain. Unfortunately, we do not have data at this time to investigate Taiwanese brand mentions following a specific request to list brand names. However, we predict that Taiwanese are less materialistic than are Spanish and American consumers. This is born out by the content of the Taiwanese essays (Essays One and Two). To a large extent, Taiwanese respondents discussed the political situation in their country and were very concerned about the natural environment (e.g., the importance of avoiding problems associated with air and water pollution). Hofstede's Masculinity dimension also supports this prediction that Taiwanese would be less materialistic than Americans.

To a large extent, we find very little support for the four hypotheses derived from Hofstede's theory. In total, we test the hypotheses three times each, for a total of twelve tests. Only two of these tests fully support the hypotheses (H1 and H2). From this perspective, the Uncertainty Avoidance and the Power Distance dimensions appear to be the most promising for understanding consumer good life visions across cultures.

To some degree, the failure of the hypotheses is linked to the relatively weak predictions associated with Taiwanese respondents. Perhaps a different sort of cultural theory is required to explain Asian good life visions. Or, alternative interpretations of Hofstede's theory may be possible. For example, it could be argued that consumers express their individualism by purchasing unique brands (such as Rolex watches or Armani suits or a Porsche automobile). The kinds of brands which are associated with good life visions are certainly not brands for the herd (i.e., brands for the collective). Under this argument, the predictions forthcoming from Hofstede's Individualism dimension are fully supported by the Essay Two results. Since Hofstede's values were originally validated in a work setting (rather than in an consumer setting), it is important to allow for adjustments when applying this theory to consumer behavior contexts.

REFERENCES

Belk, Russell W. and Richard W. Pollay (1985), "Images of Ourselves: The Good Life in Twentieth Century Advertising," *Journal of Consumer Research*, 11, (March) 887-897.

Csikszentmihalyi, Mihaly and Eugene Rochberg-Halton (1981), *The Meaning of Things: Domestics Symbols and the Self*, Cambridge: Cambridge University Press.

Dobni, Dawn and George M. Zinkhan (1990), "In Search of Brand Image: A Foundation Analysis," in Marvin E. Goldberg, Gerald Gorn, and Richard W. Pollay, eds., *Advances in Consumer Research*, Vol 17, Provo, UT: Association for Consumer Research, 110-119.

Friedman, Monroe (1991), *A Brand New Language: Commercial Influences In Literature And Culture*, New York: Greenwood Press.

Hofstede, Geert (1980), *Cultural Consequences: International Differences in Work-Related Values*, Abridged Edition, Newbury Park, CA: Sage Publications.

Leclerc, France, Bernd H. Schmitt and Laurette Dube-Rioux (1989), "Brand name a la francaise ? Oui, but for the right product!" in Thomas K. Srull, ed., *Advances in Consumer Research*, Vol 16, Provo, UT: Association for Consumer Research, 253-257.

Leiss, W., S. Kline, and S. Jhally (1986), *Social Communication In Advertising*, Toronto: Methuen.

Lynn, Mike, George M. Zinkhan, and Judy Harris (1993), "Consumer Tipping: A Cross-Country Study," *Journal of Consumer Research*, 19 (December).

Meyers-Levy, Joan (1989), "The Influence of a Brand Name's Association Set Size and Word Frequency on Brand Memory," *Journal of Consumer Research*, 16, (September) 197-207.

Munson, J.A. and W.A. Spivey (1981), "Product and Brand-User Stereotypes Among Social Classes," *Journal of Advertising Research*, 21 (4) 37-48.

O'Shaughnessy, John, *Why People Buy*, New York: Oxford University Press.

Park, C. Whan, Bernard J. Jaworski and Deborah J. MacInnis (1986), "Strategic Brand Concept-Image Management," *Journal of Marketing*, 50, (October) 135-145.

Schudson, M. (1984), *Advertising, the Uneasy Persuasion*, New York: Pantheon.

Tuan, Yi-Fu (1986), *The Good Life*, Madison: The University of Wisconsin Press.

Zikmund, William G. and Michael d'Amico (1993) *Marketing*, St. Paul, MN: West Publishing Group.

Zinkhan, George M., Jae W. Hong, and Robert Lawson (1990), "Achievement and Affiliation Motivation: Changing Patterns in Social Values as Represented in American Advertising, *Journal of Business Research*, 20, 135-143.

Zinkhan, George M. and Claude R. Martin, Jr. (1982), "The Attitudinal Implications of a New Brand's Name," *Advances in Consumer Research*, IX, 467-471.

Zinkhan, George M. and Claude R. Martin, Jr. (1987), "New Brand Names and Inferential Beliefs: Some Insights on Naming New Products," *Journal of Business Research*, 15, 157-172.

Using The Zaltman Metaphor Elicitation Technique to Understand Brand Images

Robin Higie Coulter, University of Connecticut
Gerald Zaltman, Harvard University

Understanding consumers' interpretations of brand image has become increasingly important as firms have attempted to boost brand equity. Our paper introduces the Zaltman Metaphor Elicitation Technique, discusses its theoretical grounding, and examines its use as a tool for investigating brand image management activities.

INTRODUCTION

COKE...NIKE...TIDE...LEVI'S...CREST...The shelves of stores and homes alike are lined with these and other brand names. Since the 1950s, companies have assigned brand names to their products as a means of differentiating them from the competition, and for several decades consumer researchers have studied brand names, brand extensions, and more recently, brand equity. The basis for the research lies in the meaning of the brand - its brand image. Recently, Biel (1993) suggested that brand image is composed of the image of (1) the provider (eg., manufacturer), (2) the user, and (3) the product, itself. Reynolds and Gutman (1984) use their means-end chain framework in proposing that brand image is a synthesis of product attributes, consumer consequences and personal values. Farquhar and Herr (1993) discuss the types of associations that brands evoke, including specific product attributes, customer benefits, usage situations and other summary evaluations. After an extensive review, Dobni and Zinkhan (1990) conclude that brand image is the consumer's subjective interpretation of a brand that is formed by marketing activities and context variables. If we think more about COKE, NIKE, TIDE and other brand names, we realize that they are, in fact, the embodiment of the product, the user, the producer, the marketer, and the use situation.

As firms attempt to develop and sustain stronger brands and build brand equity to maintain a competitive advantage in the marketplace, understanding customers' perceptions becomes increasingly important. Dobni and Zinkhan (1990) review a variety of approaches to assessing brand image, noting that the trend has been toward using quantitative methods. Qualitative procedures, including having customers' engage in thought listing procedures, describe a brand's personality, and define "what the brand thinks of you, as the customer" also have been used in brand image studies (Blaxton 1993; Boivin 1986; Durgee and Stuart 1987) and brand extension studies (Aaker and Keller 1990; Park, Milberg and Lawson 1991). Most of these research techniques rely on verbal communication to obtain customer information. Research on communication, however, suggests that over 80 percent of all human communication is nonverbal, and Biel (1993, p.73) notes that "brand images have a strong nonverbal component." Thus, there appears to be an imbalance between how customers think and communicate about brands and how researchers access customers' thinking.

Our purpose is to introduce the Zaltman Metaphor Elicitation Technique, a research tool that uses visual and sensory images to help better understand the meaning of brands.

Briefly, the Zaltman Metaphor Elicitation Technique (ZMET) employs qualitative methods to elicit the metaphors, constructs and mental models that drive customers' thinking and behavior, as well as quantitative analyses to provide data for marketing mix decisions and segmentation strategies. The Kelly Repertory grid and laddering techniques are integral components of the technique, as are visual (eg., photographs) and other sensory images that consumers provide. The constructs elicited during the interviews are aggregated to produce a consensus map which represents most of the thinking of most people most of the time. In addition, consumers use digital imaging techniques to produce summary images of their thinking.

To begin, we provide a literature review on nonverbal communication and metaphors and briefly discuss the asymmetry between how consumers' think about and experience brands and how most market research data are collected. Next, we define the ZMET steps that have been tested and provide an illustration of the technique's use to study brand images. Finally, we discuss the use of ZMET for understanding an array of brand image issues.

BACKGROUND

Nonverbal Communication

Mehrabian (1971) reports that approximately 93 percent of the meaning contained in any message is nonverbal (including paralanguage) and that only seven percent is contained in verbal language. Birdwhistell (1970) notes that no more than 30 percent of the meaning in a social exchange is conveyed by words. Other evidence indicates that most communication occurs nonverbally (Knapp 1980; Seiter 1988; Weisner 1988). As we noted, the rule of thumb among communications specialists is that about 80 percent of all human communication is nonverbal, and much of the meaning of verbal language also is determined by nonverbal cues. Further, research reinforces the idea that nonverbal communication is dominant (Montagu 1986; Stoller 1989; Howes 1991), and when there is an apparent contradiction, nonverbal cues tend to be believed over verbal ones (Knapp 1980, p. 86). Additionally, visual representations are processed differently than verbal messages and hence are not subject to the same logical scrutiny and counterarguing (Biel 1993). As a consequence, the images and information are more likely to be internalized, with the increased potential of affecting attitudes and behavior.

Metaphors

"The essence of a metaphor," according to Lakoff and Johnson, "is understanding and experiencing one kind of thing in terms of another" (1980, p. 5). It is only through their metaphors that we can better understand customer thinking and behavior and thus develop and market successful brands, goods and services. Even behavior and thoughts are themselves metaphors for one another. Many metaphors are mental images, and as discussed, the majority of these are visual (Arnheim 1969; Kosslyn et al., 1990).

Discussions of imagery and its relevance to advertising, marketing and consumer research that have implications for branding can be found in Lutz and Lutz 1977, 1978; Rossiter 1982; Rossiter and Percy 1978; MacInnis and Price 1987; and Bone and Ellen 1992.

Customer and Firm Metaphors. Understanding customers' metaphors (or knowledge representations) related to a brand and how these metaphors interact with those of the manufacturing firm or advertising agency is important. For customers, metaphors about a brand are found in their images, which may be visual, verbal, mathematical, and musical, among other forms. These images contain a customer's experience, understanding, and memory —in short, their knowledge— about the type of packaging, where the brand can be purchased, and the advertising campaign, for example.

Biel (1993) reminds us that when thinking of brands, visual representations often come to mind. This is particularly the case for well-developed brands. For example, upon hearing "Keebler," Keebler elves might come to the mind's eye, and "McDonald's" may generate a picture of the golden arches. Less well-defined brands are likely to spawn a more diverse set of images.

Because a firm's or ad agency's metaphors about a brand are conveyed in the form of various marketing mix decisions, including advertising, product and package design, product concepts, and distribution channels, these metaphors need to contain components that are both similar and dissimilar to their customers' metaphors. The similarities are necessary because customers are predisposed to find their own metaphors in advertising, the design of a product, or a store setting, for example. Thus, when marketer communications are congruent with customer-generated images, customers are more likely to attend to, process, and comprehend the observed information. The dissimilarities are also necessary; they create a degree of tension that attracts attention and sets the foundation for message comprehension. Creative staffs and product design staffs play a particularly important role in providing the creative "dissimilarities" component.

Pictures as Metaphors and Basic Concepts. Because much communication is nonverbal, pictures can serve as entry points for exploring other customer concepts (Weisner 1988; Ball and Smith 1992). Pictures typically represent basic concepts, which contain extensive information or defining attributes, and people usually recognize such concepts first. After customers recognize basic concepts, then they can infer or identify associated higher-order concepts (Smith 1988; Rosch 1978). For example, the concept of "Hershey's kiss" has more defining characteristics than the higher order concept of "chocolate." The concept of "Hershey's kiss" contains more information, is more readily recognized and is a more efficient way to begin processing information than the concept of "chocolate."

Because pictures are so basic, information-rich and attribute-laden, they can be associated with multiple related higher-order constructs. Pictures represent a natural and efficient way for customers to start communicating higher-order constructs. In fact, some clinical psychologists use a client's photographs as a central part of the therapeutic counselling process (Entin 1981; Krauss and Fryrear 1983; Weisner 1988).

Seeing the Voice of the Customer

As noted, most market research methodologies such as questionnaires and personal and group interviews rely on verbal forms of communication to elicit information. Given the prominence of nonverbal communication, an asymmetry exists between how market research data typically are collected and how customers usually think about and experience their worlds. A better understanding of customers' perceptions requires the use of research tools which engage customers' nonverbal and especially visual "channels" of thought and communication. In this section, we briefly review the literature relevant to photographs and other visual stimuli as research tools and as important components in marketing communications.

Gombrich, Hochberg and Black (1972) provide an excellent discussion of how pictures represent people and things, and about the representation of people and things in pictures. Given the expressive power of pictures, it is not surprising that photography as a research tool has been growing. Excellent discussions of the use of this tool in sociology, psychology, and anthropology can be found in Bateson and Mead 1942; Wagner 1979; Becker 1980; Collier and Collier 1986; Denzin 1989; Ziller 1990; and Ball and Smith 1992. Additionally, Denzin (1989) provides a good discussion of the validity and reliability issues concerning the use of film and photography generally as sociological research tools.

Consumer behavior researchers also have employed photographs as stimuli to elicit consumers' thought processes and/or develop theories relevant to their work. Work by Heisley and Levy (1991) entailed their taking photographs of people and interviewing those people about the content of the photographs. Holbrook (1987), taking on the roles of the researcher and subject simultaneously, took photographs of artifacts around his home and "interviewed himself," asking about the meaning of the pictures. More recently, Wallendorf and Arnould (1991) and their co-investigators did content analyses of photographs of Thanksgiving events to understand the rituals associated with the holiday. The very productive Consumer Odyssey project also made extensive use of still and video images (Belk, Wallendorf and Sherry 1989).

Researchers investigating advertising have examined the visual component of ads, and the interaction between the visual and verbal components. The pictorial content of advertisements has received attention by Rossiter (1982), Edell and Staelin (1983), and Mitchell (1986), for example. Studies have substantiated that pictorial ad stimuli are recalled better than verbal ad stimuli and result in more favorable product beliefs and brand attitudes (Lutz and Lutz 1977; Mitchell and Olson 1981). Childers and Houston (1984) note that pictorial ad content is more effective in delayed recall. Other research has demonstrated that semantically discrepant pictures and words can be combined in a way that yields better recall than that for semantically consistent pictures and words (Houston, Childers and Heckler, 1987). In a recent follow-up, Unnava and Burnkrant (1991) found that when verbal information was low in imagery, the inclusion of pictures consistent with the information increased recall of verbal information on both immediate and delayed post tests. When verbal information was high in imagery, adding pictures did not affect recall of verbal information. In addition, Miniard et al. (1991) discuss the imagery-evoking ability of pictures in ads and subjects' subsequent processing of information in the ad.

Summary

Several important points can be drawn from the literature. First, nonverbal communication is more prevalent than verbal communication. Second, visual images are entry points for accessing people's knowledge structures. Third, photography is a powerful tool for accessing consumers' visual images. Fourth, research documents the importance of visual images in marketing communications. Finally, most market research tools rely on verbal communication. Based upon these factors, we developed ZMET, a methodology that relies on visual and other sensory images to elicit customers' metaphors and constructs.

IMPLEMENTATION OF THE ZALTMAN METAPHOR ELICITATION TECHNIQUE

The Procedure

A total of 25 customers typically are recruited to participate in a project. After qualifying for participation in a project (based on screeners), customers are given a set of instructions and guidelines about the research topic, eg., a brand name, a service concept, product use, or product design. They are instructed to take photographs and/or collect pictures from magazines, books, newspapers or other sources that indicate what the topic means to them. Customers are provided with a camera, and a personal interview is scheduled approximately seven to ten days hence. The personal interview involves a guided conversation which we believe yields more valid, more reliable and, importantly, more relevant insights than traditional structured interview approaches (see McCracken 1988; Mishler 1986).

EXHIBIT 1
Core Steps Tested

Step 1. **Storytelling.** Customer describes the content of each picture.

Step 2: **Missed Images.** Customer describes the pictures he/she was unable to obtain and explains their relevance.

Step 3: **Sorting Task.** Customer sorts his/her pictures into meaningful piles.

Step 4: **Construct Elicitation.** A modified version of the Kelly Repertory Grid technique and the laddering technique are used to elicit basic constructs and their relationships. Customers' pictures serve as stimuli.

Step 5: **Most Representative Picture.** Customer indicates the picture that is most representative.

Step 6: **Opposite Images.** Customer describes pictures that represent the opposite of the task, for example, "what is *not* Nike."

Step 7: **Sensory Images.** Descriptions are elicited of what does and does not describe the taste, touch, smell, sound, color and emotion of the concept being explored.

Step 8: **The Mental Map.** Customer creates a map or a causal model using the constructs that have been elicited.

Step 9: **The Summary Image.** Customer, with assistance from a technician, creates a summary image using digital imaging techniques.

Step 10: **Consensus Map.** Researcher creates a map or causal model involving the most important constructs.

Customer Control over Stimuli

Because ZMET has customers collect their own pictures, the customers (not the researchers) are in control of the stimuli used in the guided conversation. Customer control has a number of benefits. First, customer-generated pictures are especially meaningful because what the eye perceives when it is encoding a sequence of information over time, including the viewing of a static image such as a magazine ad or a point-of-purchase promotion, is guided by existing customer knowledge, beliefs, or expectations. Second, requiring customers to collect the stimuli increases the likelihood of uncovering important, but previously unconsidered customer issues.

In addition to using photographs and pictures as stimuli to elicit constructs, ZMET relies on verbalization to establish and record images the customer wanted to collect but was unable to do so because of time or geographic constraints. The technique also uses an image bank created by the researchers. Other image capture techniques are also effective and the best combination of techniques will vary with the product-usage situation, the target audience, and the theme and objective of the research. Additionally, ZMET makes extensive use of nonvisual sensory images.

The Guided Conversation

The personal (one-on-one) interview or conversation with each customer takes approximately two hours, and it is audiotaped. The conversation focuses primarily on the images customers bring to the interview. During our initial R&D, we examined twelve topic areas, ranging from the meaning of snack foods to the meaning of a specific corporate image. The conversation guidelines include 9 steps, and the input from these steps serve as data for the researchers developing the consensus map. Exhibit 1 describes each step.

INVESTIGATING BRAND IMAGE USING ZMET

Several researchers have discussed a variety of components related to brand image and the interrelationships among these components. Recall, for example, that Reynolds and Gutman (1984) suggested images can be thought of in terms of product features or attributes that yield consequences (benefits or risks), which in turn facilitate values or end-states. Both Reynolds and Gutman, and more recently, Farquhar and Herr (1993) suggested that the aggregation of individual means-end chains results in a network consisting of the brand and its associates (eg., usage situations, product attributes, customer benefits and values). Moreover, the image that a person has about a brand consists of both verbal and nonverbal representations (Biel 1993). These, in turn, are best expressed via verbal and nonverbal channels, respectively. Nonetheless, most research that studies consumers' images of brands typically uses verbal research methods, and thus misses a great deal of what constitutes the individual's brand image.

The purpose of ZMET is to elicit metaphors and constructs and to establish relationships among the constructs using both verbal and nonverbal stimuli. Therefore, we suggest that ZMET is an efficient and effective means for understanding brands. To give the reader a clearer understanding of how ZMET can facilitate the understanding of brand image issues, we herein discuss the details of an interview with Alice, one of the customers who we asked to take and/or collect pictures of what "Tide" meant to her.

Alice, a young mother, collected 14 images. After completing Step 1 (storytelling about each picture), the interviewer asked Alice if there were any pertinent images that she had not been able to collect (Step 2). Alice indicated that she would have liked to take a photograph of a pig sty, noting that she wondered if "Tide" would be able to "clean a dirty pig." In Step 3, Alice sorted her images into three groups: comfort, freshness, drudgery.

In Step 4, the interviewer randomly selected three of Alice's pictures, and asked her, "How are any two of these three pictures similar to each other and different from the third." This surfaced two constructs: unpleasantness and freshness. The interviewer, using the laddering process, helped to elicit additional constructs and their relationships. After Alice's explanation, the interviewer continued to randomly select three pictures and question Alice until no new constructs were elicited.

EXHIBIT 2
Alice's "Tide" Triad

Unpleasantness

Freshness

Exhibit 2 illustrates one of Alice's triads. She indicated that the top picture represented "unpleasantness" and the bottom two pictures represented "freshness." Alice's picture of "two friends making ugly faces" described "unpleasantness." Her comments were "Tide means doing the laundry. It's time consuming and the laundry facilities are not well-maintained. Plus, it's always a hassle to find quarters. I really don't like to do laundry." Clearly, Alice's commentary related to this triad indicated that she associated the brand with the product use situation. Alice then described "freshness": "Using Tide gets my clothes clean and smelling very fresh. I feel more comfortable and refreshed in my clean clothes." Using the laddering process, the interviewer elicited the additional constructs of "makes me feel confident" (self-confident) and "tells people what kind of person I am" (self-image). In this latter case, Alice's comments focused on customer benefits and values.

Continuing with Step 5, Alice indicated that the picture that most represented "Tide" to her was her picture of the sunrise (shown in Exhibit 5). She reported that the sunrise contained several meanings: freshness (as in the smell of her clothing after using "Tide"), brightness (as in the colors of her clothes after using "Tide"), calm or peacefulness (knowing that "Tide" cleaned her clothes put her at ease), and accomplishment (a new day to get things done).

When the interviewer asked Alice what images conveyed the *opposite* of her image of "Tide" (Step 6), she responded with images

EXHIBIT 3
Alice's Sensory Images

Taste:	oysters (Liquid Tide), but not peanuts
Smell:	a cool rain, but not perfume
Touch:	a kitten, but not burlap
Sound:	a train whistle, but not a timid mouse
Color:	orange, but not black
Emotion:	calm, but not nervous

of a bottle of acid ("'Tide' is strong, but not harmful") and a porcupine ("'Tide' leaves clothes feeling soft, not harsh").

In Step 7, the interviewer asked Alice about other nonvisual sensory images of "Tide." Alice's responses are listed in Exhibit 3.

In Step 8, the interviewer reviewed all of the constructs that Alice had discussed and asked her if they were accurate representations of what she meant, and if any important ideas were missing. Then Alice created a map showing constructs and relationships she saw as related to "Tide" (See Exhibit 4). Alice "walked" the interviewer through her map, noting that "'Tide' brings laundry to mind, and when I think of laundry, I think that it's expensive, time consuming and unpleasant. All of it is very aggravating. Also, when I think of 'Tide', I think of a strong and dependable detergent - a detergent that cleans my clothes leaving them soft and fresh. Knowing that 'Tide' gets my clothes clean means I don't have any worries. Because my clothes are clean and fresh I feel refreshed, and because my clothes are clean and soft I feel comfortable. I feel more self-confident when I'm comfortable and refreshed, and I look better to other people. Finally, even though 'Tide' is strong, it is environmentally friendly, and that's important for the water and the health of Americans."

Alice, with the help of a technician, used digital imaging techniques to create her summary image of "Tide" in Step 9. Her digital image consisted of components of five of her pictures and visually depicted her story about "Tide." Exhibit 5, Alice's digital image, "shows my two baskets of laundry... and how I feel about doing laundry...I don't like to do it! You have to separate clothes and find lots of quarters. It takes forever to do laundry in my apartment building - someone's always forgetting to take care of their clothes. The picture also shows a sunrise which means freshness to me - a new day. If you look in the tree, you'll see a teddy bear - he represents how my clothes feel after they are washed in 'Tide', soft and comfortable. The teddy bear is holding a rose to let you know my clothes smell good when washed with 'Tide'."

ZMET Data Compilation

ZMET produces several types of information, including a consensus map, visual and sensory dictionaries, animated vignettes and a set of digital images. After completion of the interviewing, typically consisting of 20 to 25 interviews, a consensus map is developed which represents (a) most of the thinking of (b) most people (c) most of the time. Producing the map involves several

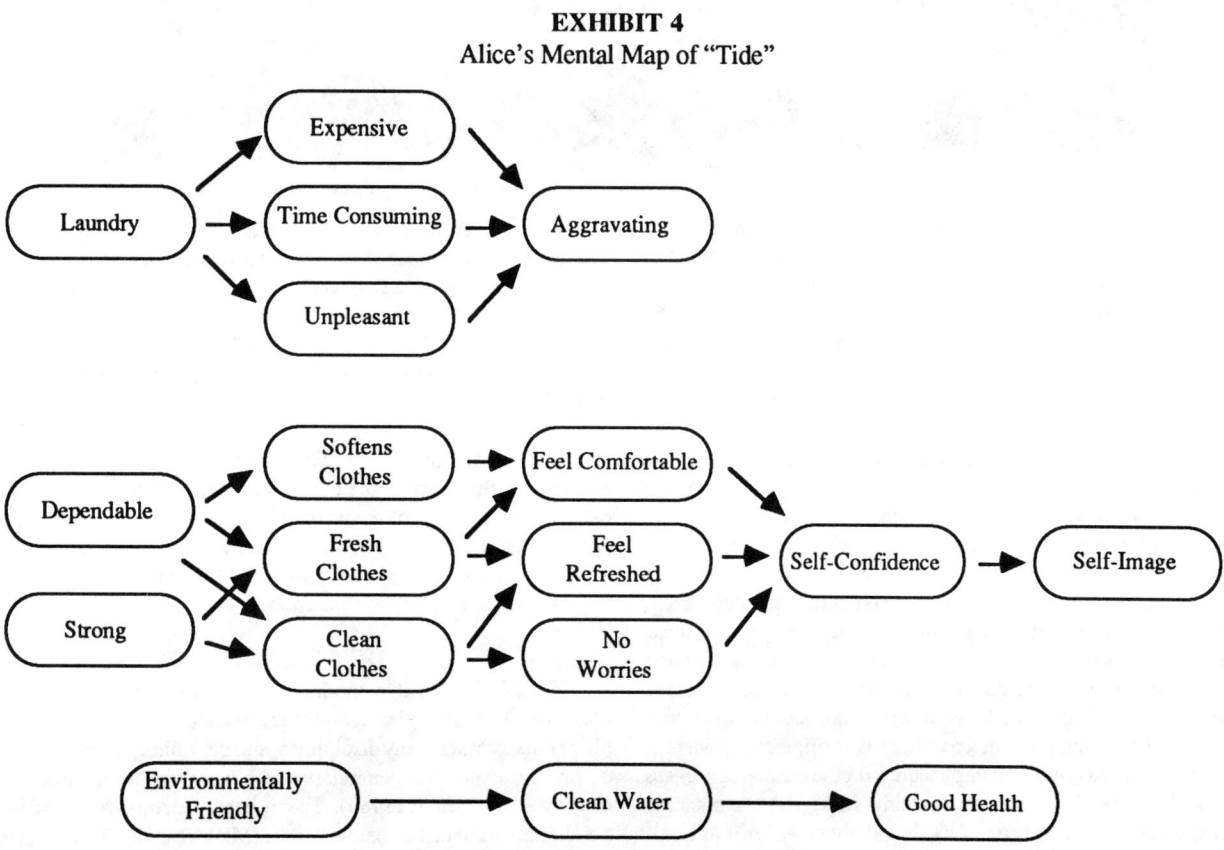

EXHIBIT 4
Alice's Mental Map of "Tide"

EXHIBIT 5
Alice's Digital Image of "Tide"

steps. First, each interview transcript (selected randomly) is systematically examined, and the elicited constructs and the number of new constructs added by each additional customer are recorded. The construct list then is refined and condensed through content analysis. Finally, the researchers aggregate the data across customers and then assess the relationships (as given by respondents) among the pertinent constructs. (For a discussion of meta-ethnographic synthesis techniques, see Noblit and Hare, 1988.) The result is a consensus map which diagrammatically illustrates the linkages among the elicited constructs. These linkages are the reasonings which connect the constructs.

Our R & D objectives for the "Tide" application did not require many interviews; hence, we did not develop a consensus map. However, consensus maps contain three types of constructs. First, some constructs are originating points in a reasoning process, these constructs lead to other constructs. Other constructs are destination or ending points in a reasoning process. Still other constructs serve as transmitters or linkages between originator and receiver constructs. Knowing the status of a construct as an originator, transmitter, or receiver has important implications for the use of a consensus map and the development of marketing strategies. A manager interested in a particular construct should not consider it in isolation, but also should be aware of the constructs that causally precede and follow it. A number of analytical tools and associated software are available to analyze network patterns among constructs and extract still more information from the consensus map.

In addition to the consensus map, ZMET produces nonverbal sensory dictionaries to accompany each construct in the consensus map. These user-friendly dictionaries are made up of the pictures and sensory data that different customers use to convey the constructs. The dictionaries provide a basis for gaining visceral or empathic feelings about the customers, because the relevance of each image to a particular construct is described in the customer's voice. Further, customers' digital images provide visual images that integrate their important constructs. Many images also convey the reasonings connecting constructs.

DISCUSSION

ZMET is a hybrid methodology grounded in a broad body of literature. The use of photography as a research tool has a fifty year history that crosses many disciplines, and the validity and reliability of photography as a general research tool has been discussed extensively by Denzin (1989). The in-depth personal conversation has significant merit in its own right (Mishler 1986; McCracken,

1988), and other research conducted by Griffin and Hauser (1992), Silver and Thompson (1991), Robinson (1991) and Fern (1982) suggests the efficacy of personal interviews compared with focus groups. The validity and reliability of the Kelly Repertory Grid and laddering technique as means for eliciting constructs are well established (Kelly 1973; Gutman 1982; Reynolds and Gutman 1988).

To-date, our R & D with ZMET involving over 400 interviews has yielded some important insights. First, nearly all participants regardless of demographic characteristics, such as educational or occupational experience, successfully engage in all steps. Steps 7, 8 and 9 which *a priori* might seem difficult because the tasks are unfamiliar, are undertaken quite readily.

Second, considerable interviewing practice is required to conduct the interview. Each step can be introduced in different ways and individual differences among customers may call for somewhat different approaches. Third, interviews average about two hours, a considerable amount of time to spend with a single customer discussing a very specific topic. This time frame affords an opportunity to learn not only about people's initial thoughts (much as might be obtained by a structured questionnaire or focus group), but also about the deeper meaning of a topic. At the same time, the interviewers must be sensitive to the issue of customer fatigue. Finally, after the interview, participants are given a follow-up survey (and a self-addressed stamped envelope) which assesses their experiences with ZMET. Typically, we get a response rate of at least 80 percent, and the participants indicate that the entire procedure, from taking/collecting images to the completion of their digital image, is enjoyable, interesting and involving.

FUTURE RESEARCH

ZMET has the potential for understanding many aspects of brand image management. First, as we have seen with the "Tide" example, ZMET can be useful in eliciting and understanding the sensory metaphors associated with brand images. These metaphors potentially are useful in a variety of marketing mix decisions, including developing advertising strategies, determining the shape and type of packaging, and selecting distribution channels. The information also might be useful for examining possible brand extensions. A dual application of ZMET would be needed - one investigating the current brand image and a second examining the potential extension. Researchers then could examine the two maps to determine their image-congruity. Similar maps imply that the prospective extension would be compatible with the existing brand image, whereas dissimilar maps may be a sign that consumers would have difficulty integrating the extension into their current knowledge structure. ZMET also is valuable for brand repositioning. Again, a dual application would be needed, the first to assess the current brand image and the latter to assess an "ideal" product image. Examining the parallels and gaps between the two maps would surface issues or components of image that warrant alteration. Implementing only the latter application, i.e., the "ideal" product image, would be worthwhile in establishing a new brand.

Conducting ZMET for multiple target audiences can establish each segment's consensus map. As a consequence, the marketing group would be able to determine whether a single strategy or multiple strategies were needed to communicate to the groups. We are currently investigating the segmenting of markets by decomposing a consensus map, i.e., considering whether all participants have the same mental model or if there are distinct clusters of respondents who have unique brand association networks. Finally, a dual application directed at corporate image and the brand image would provide information about their image-congruity. Clearly, there are numerous issues related to brand image and other facets of consumer behavior and marketing that could be addressed with ZMET.

KEY REFERENCES
Please contact the first author for a complete reference list.

Biel, Alexander L. (1993), "Converting Image Into Equity," in *Brand Equity & Advertising: Advertising's Role in Building Strong Brands*, eds. David A. Aaker and Alexander L. Biel, Hillsdale, NJ: Lawrence Erlbaum Associates, Publishers, 67-82.

Blaxton, Max (1992), "Beyond Brand Personality: Building Brand Relationships," in *Brand Equity & Advertising: Advertising's Role in Building Strong Brands*, eds. David A. Aaker and Alexander L. Biel, Hillsdale, NJ: Lawrence Erlbaum Associates, Publishers, 113-124.

Collier, John, Jr. and Malcolm Collier (1986), *Visual Anthropology: Photography as a Research Method*, Revised and expanded edition. Albuquerque, NM: University of New Mexico Press.

Denzin, Norman K. (1989), *The Research Act: A Theoretical Introduction to Sociological Methods*, 3rd ed. Englewood Cliffs, NJ: Prentice Hall, Chapter 9.

Dobni, Dawn and George Zinkhan (1990), "In Search of Brand Image: A Foundation Analysis," in *Advances in Consumer Research*, Vol. 17, eds. Marvin E. Goldberg, Gerald Gorn and Richard W. Pollay. Provo, UT: Association for Consumer Research, 100-119.

Farquhar, Peter H. and Paul M. Herr (1993), "The Dual Structure of Brand Associations," in *Brand Equity & Advertising: Advertising's Role in Building Strong Brands*, eds. David A. Aaker and Alexander L. Biel, Hillsdale, NJ: Lawrence Erlbaum Associates, Publishers, 263-277.

Knapp, M. (1980), *Essentials of Nonverbal Communication*, New York, NY: Holt, Rinehart and Winston.

Kosslyn, Stephen M. and Oliver Koenig (1992), *Wet Mind: The New Cognitive Neuroscience*, NY: The Free Press.

Lakoff, George and Mark Johnson (1980), *Metaphors We Live By*, Chicago: The University of Chicago Press.

Mehrabian, Albert (1971), *Silent Messages*, Belmont, CA: Wadworth, 42-47.

Mishler, Elliot G. (1986), *Research Interviewing: Context and Narrative*, Cambridge, MA: Harvard University Press.

Stoller, Paul (1989), *The Taste of Ethnographic Things: The Senses in Anthropology*, Philadelphia: The University of Pennsylvania Press.

Wagner, Jon, ed. (1979), *Images of Information: Still Photography in the Social Sciences*, Beverly Hills, CA: Sage Publications.

The Dark Side of Consumer Behavior: Empirical Examinations of Impulsive and Compulsive Consumption

Brian Wansink, Dartmouth College

Whereas much of the investigation into consumer behavior examines purposeful choice behavior intended to optimize consumer utility, there is also a darker side to consumer behavior. This deals with the impulsive and compulsive behaviors that can influence both the purchase of products and the consumption of them. In mild forms, such behaviors include eating bouts or shopping sprees. In more extreme forms, they include pathological forms of binge eating or serious patterns of overspending.

As pointed out by Meryl Gardner and Christine Wright-Isak, common elements exist between the *compulsive* aspects of consumption (eating bouts and binging) and the *impulsive* aspects of it (impulse buying). Three different sets of studies and three different methodologies are used to triangulate on the commonalities which exist between these compulsive and impulsive aspects of consumption.

Brian Wansink ("Antecedents and Mediators of Eating Bouts") suggests that the cues (internal or external) which stimulate an eating bout dramatically affect one's perception toward that eating bout. The results of his studies indicate that when an eating bout is stimulated by external cues (such as visual salience), perceptions of the food's versatility, perishability, and nutritional value mediate the volume of the food that is eaten. In contrast, eating bouts which are stimulated by internal cues (such as moods, emotions, and cravings) are unaffected by these factors.

A measure validation study by Wendy Martin, Seungoog Weun and Sharon E. Beatty ("Validation of an Impulse Buying Tendency Scale") suggests how such impulsive and compulsive behaviors can be measured. Though this scale is developed and validated in the context of shopping behaviors, the resulting scale contains variables that can be used across many consumption contexts.

The third set of studies ("Two Forms of Compulsive Consumption: Comorbidity Between Compulsive Buying and Binge Eating") exemplifies the interdisciplinary theme of all the studies that have been discussed. This work by Ronald J. Faber, Gary A. Christenson and James Mitchell involves quasi-experimental designs which explicitly show the conceptual synergies between compulsive eating and impulsive buying. Results from their first study indicate that binge eaters may be more likely to demonstrate compulsive buying symptoms than non binge eaters. Using a separate set of subjects, their second study used scales and retrospective reports to confirm this finding. Consistent with their first set of findings, compulsive buyers were shown to have demonstrated a greater predisposition toward binge eating.

The findings from all three of these sets of studies can be interpreted in light of the biopsychosocial model of compulsive or excessive behaviors. This model assumes that a number of compulsive, addictive and impulsive behaviors are related and that all of these behaviors have multiple causes.

An Examination of the Effects of Context-Induced Mood States on the Evaluation of a "Feel-Good" Product: The Moderating Role of Product Type and the Consistency Effects Model

John Hadjimarcou, Kent State University
Lawrence J. Marks, Kent State University

ABSTRACT

This study examines the effects of context-induced mood states on evaluation, cognitions of favorable and unfavorable attribute information, and purchase intentions of a "feel-good" product. The consistency effects model is used to predict and interpret incongruency effects of negative mood states on product evaluations, cognitions, and purchase intentions taking into account the moderating role of product type. Findings indicate that the integration of product type (i.e., a "feel-good" product) and the consistency effects model can adequately account for the majority of the effects observed in the study. Implications for advertising strategy are discussed and further research suggestions are offered.

INTRODUCTION

The literature in social psychology and in marketing has assembled a plethora of findings suggesting strong evidence for the existence of mood effects on various aspects of behavior (e.g., Isen 1970), cognition (e.g., Isen et al. 1978; Bower 1981; Bower, Gilligan, and Monteiro 1981), and judgments of familiar and unfamiliar stimuli (e.g., Isen et al. 1978; Johnson and Tversky 1983). In general, people in positive moods have strong tendencies to provide positive evaluations and act in positive ways while people in negative moods tend to do the reverse (Clark and Isen 1982). While the findings for positive moods are rather robust, negative moods effects have been less predictable (Isen 1984; Gardner 1985). In some cases, negative mood states result in negative evaluations and actions (the congruency effect) and in other cases they have positive results (an "incongruency" effect). Although advertisers keep mood contexts in mind when developing their advertising strategies and media planning (Goldberg and Gorn 1987), a limited understanding of incongruency effects may lead to the use of inappropriate advertising strategies with costly implications. Thus, greater understanding of such effects is warranted by researchers and practitioners.

Research in social psychology provides several plausible arguments that attempt to reconcile the "incongruency" effects evoked by negative mood states, especially with regard to altruistic behavior (e.g., Cialdini, Darby, and Vincent 1973; Carlson and Miller 1987). In a marketing context, Kamins, Marks and Skinner (1991) drew on this research to explain the positive effects of negative moods by using a "consistency effects model." They found that consistency between a mood state (either positive or negative) and the affective tone of a stimulus (advertisement) can lead to favorable evaluations, higher purchase intentions, and better recall of favorable information. Additionally, Gardner and Scott (1990) proposed using product type as a moderator of mood effects. Gardner (1992) found that for some products (mood-ameliorating products) negative mood states may lead to *more* favorable brand evaluations than do positive mood states.

The purpose of the present study is to combine the moderating effect of product type with the consistency effects model to more fully explain incongruency effects. Specifically, we will examine the case where inconsistency between mood and stimuli produces favorable product evaluations as predicted by the moderating role of product type (i.e., a "feel-good" product). Additionally, we will show that the "consistency effects model" accurately predicts cognitions and purchase intentions of a "feel-good" product. The paper begins with a review of the literature and the conceptual foundations of our study. Following the development of the hypotheses, we describe the study methods, processes, and analysis of the data. Finally, we report the results and briefly discuss implications for future research.

PAST RESEARCH AND CONCEPTUAL FOUNDATIONS

There is considerable evidence suggesting that mood states influence judgments, behavior, and recall of information in a mood congruent direction. In particular, using mood congruency theory, researchers agree that subjects processing information in a positive mood state rate ambiguous stimuli as more pleasant (Isen and Shalker 1982), concentrate on positive rather than negative self-relevant information (Mischel, Ebbesen, and Zeiss 1973), and reward themselves more generously (Mischel, Coates, and Raskoff 1968) than those in either a neutral or negative mood state. Further, Bower, Gilligan and Monteiro (1981) examined the impact of mood on cognitions and concluded that subjects were more likely to recall information congruent with their mood at encoding.

In a marketing context, studies have found that subjects processing information in a positive mood are more likely to provide more positive brand attitudes (e.g., Isen et al. 1978; Batra and Stayman 1990). Positive mood states have also been linked to higher levels of persuasion, especially with regard to advertising claims (Batra and Stayman 1990). Similarly, Goldberg and Gorn (1987) reported that viewers who watched commercials during a happy television program were more likely to provide positive cognitive responses and perceive the commercials as more effective than those who watched the commercials in the context of a sad program.

While the congruent effects of positive moods have been substantiated in literature, the influences of negative mood states have been less predictable (Clark and Isen 1982; Isen 1984; Gardner 1985). For example, some researchers have found that being in a negative mood state increases one's antisocial behavior (Moore, Underwood and Rosenhan 1973). At the same time, others have reported that some negative feelings increase prosocial behavior (see Clark and Isen 1982 for an excellent review of the various findings).

In contrast with the predictions of congruency theory, Srull (1983) found a mood "incongruency" effect while investigating the amount of positive and negative information recalled from negative and positive ads. Subjects in a negative mood recalled positive ad information better while subjects in a positive mood had better recall of negative ads. As mentioned earlier, Kamins, Marks, and Skinner (1991) reported incongruency effects with regard to evaluations, cognitions and purchase intentions. Similarly, Gardner (1992) observed mood incongruency effects upon the evaluation of a "mood-ameliorating" product. The latter two studies are examined in greater detail later in this section.

In summary, past research focusing on mood states and consumer behavior has reinforced the notion that consumer product evaluations and recall of ad and/or product related information are significantly affected by the consumer's subjective mood. In many cases, mood congruency theory accurately predicts the impact of positive mood states upon salient consumer behavior variables.

However, there appears to be inadequate attention given to the conflicting effects of negative mood states on consumer behavior variables.

The incongruency effects associated with negative mood states have been investigated extensively in social psychology, especially in the context of altruistic behavior. For example, Cialdini, Kenrick, and Baumann (1981) advance the idea that individuals in a sad mood strive to inhibit this mood by engaging in mood elevating behavior. One way to achieve this is to engage in altruistic behavior because interest in the welfare of others tends to relieve the feeling of sadness (Cialdini et al. 1987). Similarly, Thompson, Cowan, and Rosenhan (1980) argue that people who feel sad because of the misfortunes of others may increase their helping of others as a means of alleviating their own negative feelings.

In marketing, two general perspectives have been advanced to address this phenomenon. First, Kamins, Marks, and Skinner (1991) employed social psychology research to develop and test the "consistency effects model." According to this conceptualization, a directional congruity (consistency) between the mood experienced by an individual and the affective tone of the stimulus will lead to favorable effects even if both are negative. In fact, the authors found that when sad (as well as happy) mood states are *matched* by an advertisement's affective tone subjects provide more favorable attitudes toward the ad, fewer unfavorable cognitions and higher intentions to use the advertised service than when the affective tones of the mood and the stimulus were incongruent. However, this model alone did not account for the fact that some stimuli, even though directionally inconsistent in affective tone with an individual's subjective mood, may still lead to favorable evaluations. Second, Gardner and Scott (1990) proposed "product type" (i.e., "feel- good" product, "feel-bad" product, "try-not-to-feel" products, and "no-feel" products) as a moderating influence on the relationship between mood and product evaluations and use. Using this notion, Gardner (1992) found that, for some "feel-good" products (i.e., those which consumers associate with good experience and which they may use to alleviate a bad mood), brand attitude is *more* favorable for subjects in negative moods than in positive moods. It may be possible that the combination of product type with the consistency effects model may be able to account for cases where inconsistency between mood and stimuli produces positive results.

HYPOTHESES

Given the previous discussion on the moderating role of product type on mood effects, we developed the following hypothesis:

H_1: Subjects in a negative context-induced mood will provide more favorable global attitudes and global evaluations of a "feel-good" product than will subjects in a positive context-induced mood.

The "consistency effects model" suggests that the consistency between the mood induced and the stimulus' affective tone will result in more favorable cognitions, and higher purchase intentions. Thus, considering the happy or positive affective tone associated with a "feel-good" product, we hypothesize:

H_2: Subjects in a positive context-induced mood who are exposed to a "feel-good" product will recall more favorable attribute information and less unfavorable attribute information than those in a negative context-induced mood.

H_3: Subjects in a positive context-induced mood who are exposed to a "feel-good" product will provide higher purchase intention for the product than those in a negative context-induced mood.

METHODOLOGY

The Product

Gardner and Scott (1990) define "feel-good" products as those associated with positive usage experiences which "may be used to alleviate negative moods or to accentuate positive ones" (p. 586). They suggest examples of "feel-good" products and/or activities include cigarette smoking, alcohol consumption, television viewing, and eating cookies. Gardner (1992) used an advertisement for cookies as a "feel-good" product.

In this study, an advertisement for a digital audio tape (DAT) player was used. Such products are often associated with happy music and so happy mood states (cf. Clark and Isen 1982). Indeed, a survey of 18 students from the same population as the experimental study revealed that "listening to happy music" and "going out to drink" were the two most common mood elevating activities performed when they were upset or depressed.

Design and Procedure

Subjects were 77 undergraduate students enrolled in marketing courses at a major midwestern university. All subjects were asked to participate in the study on a voluntary basis and received extra credit in their class for their participation. The subjects were told that they would be participating in two separate studies because of time constraints and the need to collect the data before the end of the semester.

Similar to Batra and Stayman (1990) and Gardner (1992) the experiment was conducted using two separate research assistants in an attempt to mask the connection between the two studies. In addition, the two separate survey instruments were printed on different colored paper using two different font formats. Later informal debriefing of the subjects revealed that the participants actually saw no connection between the two studies.

As mentioned above, the experiment involved two phases. The first phase involved the manipulation of context induced-mood states. This was coined as the "empathy" study. During this stage, the subjects were randomly assigned to one of two experimental groups. After completing an informed consent form, thirty-four subjects were asked to read a "happy" story, whereas thirty-three subjects were asked to read a "sad" story.

Both stories were selected from a total of 12 stories pretested at an earlier time using 115 subjects similar to the ones participating in this study. All stories were generated from actual stories found in popular magazines. After reading the stories, pretest subjects were asked to respond to Peterson and Sauber's (1983) MSF (Mood Short Form) scale developed to assess an individual's mood state. The two stories ultimately chosen for the current experiment were those eliciting the most happy and sad mood states in our pretest subjects. In particular, the happy story described how a middle-aged doctor saved the life of his long-lost early childhood friend who had leukemia, without either of the two gentlemen initially realizing their early childhood ties. The story becomes extremely happy when both eventually get to know each other again. The story designed to elicit a sad mood dealt with a pregnant woman's battle with cancer. She ultimately gives birth to a healthy baby boy, despite the massive chemotherapy treatments she receives during her pregnancy. Soon after the birth she also finds out that her cancer is in full remission. Unfortunately, both her husband and baby boy are later involved in a deadly automobile accident.

After reading the story, the subjects were asked to record their feelings and thoughts regarding the story. As in Gardner (1992), this was done to accentuate the story's impact on the subjects' mood states. They were then asked to respond to the MSF scale along with other independent measures to be explained in detail later in this section.

The second phase of the experiment was conducted immediately following the completion of the "empathy" study. Another researcher asked the participants to complete a second informed consent form and briefly explained the purpose of the study. During this phase the subjects were first asked to read information about a new digital audio tape player (code named DAT-111) soon to be introduced in the market. Specifically, the subjects were instructed to "... imagine that you are actually in the market to buy the DAT player ... try to get an idea of what it would be like and of its quality ... try to form as clear an impression of the product as you can. Later, we will be asking you to evaluate the DAT player and its features, and also whether you would purchase it..." The information consisted of five distinct sentences describing favorable attributes about the product (e.g., it comes with many accessories), five sentences describing neutral attributes (e.g., pushing on the door ejects the tape), and five sentences describing unfavorable attribute information (e.g., average sound quality of 4.2 on a scale of 1 to 10). The attribute information was arranged in random order and presented in a format similar to that found in *Consumer Reports*.

All 15 attributes were derived from a total of 22 attributes pretested at an earlier time. More specifically, 105 undergraduate students from the same population in which the main study was conducted were asked to evaluate all 22 attributes in terms of their favorableness on a seven-point Likert-type scale (1-Very unfavorable to 7-Very favorable), and importance in a purchase decision (1-very unimportant to 7-very important). Based on these results, the attribute information was placed into three distinct groups; i.e., from most favorable to neutral and least favorable. In addition, information was chosen that was considered more or less equally important to the subject population. This was done to avoid biasing for or against any discrete attribute information. In other words, we wanted each piece of attribute information to be given approximately equal chance of being chosen regardless of mood state. As such, a total of three groups of attribute information, each consisting of 5 pieces of equally important information were selected. Consequently, the product could not be clearly evaluated as either positive or negative, but was otherwise regarded as ambiguous in terms of its overall appeal. This also implies that the ad was strictly "informational" or fact-based.

In order to ensure that the evaluations and cognitions did not simply reflect information in short-term working memory, a distractor task was introduced prior to administering the dependent measures. The subjects were simply asked to "... list the classes they were currently enrolled in as well as those they had last semester." Immediately following the distractor task, the participants completed global attitude and global evaluation scales, and were asked to recall and list as much of the attribute information as they could remember. They were then asked to report their purchase intentions. Both phases of the experiment took a total of approximately 25 minutes to complete.

Measures

Mood. To assess the success of the manipulation, mood states were measured using Peterson and Sauber's (1983) four-item scale. Subjects were asked to indicate their feelings on the following five-point Likert-type scales (1-Strongly agree to 5-Strongly disagree): "At this moment I feel edgy or irritable," "For some reason, I am not very comfortable right now," "As I answer these questions, I feel very cheerful," and "Currently I am in a good mood." Consistent with the pretest results, subjects who read the story designed to induce a happy mood were significantly happier (average=2.27) than those who read the sad story (average=3.56, p<.001). The Cronbach's alpha coefficient of reliability for this four component measure of mood was .83.

Global Attitude and Global Evaluation. Global attitude toward the DAT was measured as an average of four seven-point bipolar items (bad-good, unpleasant-pleasant, unagreeable-agreeable, unsatisfactory-satisfactory; alpha=.91). The items used are similar to Marks and Kamins (1988). In addition, the respondents were asked to evaluate the DAT on one seven-point dependent measure (extremely low appeal-extremely high appeal) representing global evaluation of the DAT.

Free Recall. Subjects were asked to reproduce the product attribute information as completely and accurately as possible. Responses were rated by two judges who were blind to the experimental hypotheses. Judges' ratings ranged from 0 (no recall) to 2 (perfect recall) for each of the five positive, neutral, and negative attributes listed in the ad. The two judges agreed on 94 percent of the ratings; disagreements were resolved by a third judge. The mean number of positive and negative attributes recalled was used in the analysis.

Purchase Intentions. Purchase intentions were measured as an average of two five-point Likert-type scales (Definitely will buy - definitely will not buy; definitely like to have-definitely not like to have; alpha=.73; Jamieson and Bass 1989).

RESULTS

The results were analyzed using independent t-tests to make comparisons between the two experimental groups; i.e., between the subjects in the positive mood condition and the subjects in the negative mood condition. Findings provide support for H1: global attitude toward the DAT (a "feel-good" product) was significantly more favorable for subjects in the negative mood condition (average=3.83) than those in the positive mood condition (average=3.17; p<.004). Similarly, relative to subjects in a positive mood those in a negative mood provided a more favorable global evaluation of the product (2.79 vs. 3.44; p<.005).

Findings lend partial support for H2. Specifically, subjects in a positive context-induced mood recalled significantly more positive (favorable) information (average=4.42) than those in a negative context-induced mood (average=2.94, p<.004). However, both groups recalled about the same amount of negative (unfavorable) information (6.48 vs. 6.50, p>.97).

As predicted by Hypothesis 3, subjects in a positive mood provided higher purchase intentions (average=3.91) than subjects in a negative mood (average 3.53, p<.05).

DISCUSSION AND CONCLUSIONS

This study integrates the consistency effects model and product type to explain the incongruency effects sometimes evident in the evaluation of affect-laden stimuli (e.g., "feel-good" products) by subjects in negative mood states. Considered together, the results of the present study indicate that while evaluations of a product with positive connotations are more favorable when subjects are in a negative mood at the time of stimulus exposure, recall of favorable information and purchase intentions are higher when subjects are in a positive mood at exposure time.

Why should the subjects in a negative mood have *more* positive attitudes and global evaluations than those in a positive mood? These results are explained by the mood management perspective advanced by Gardner and Scott (1990). This perspective suggests that the overriding goal of people while in a negative mood is to use any means possible to elevate their mood. Thus, regardless of task, the current negative mood state amplifies the desirability of a future positive mood state (cf. Axelrod 1963). One way to reach a positive mood goal is to use a "feel-good" product and thoughts about how such products will enhance moods may lead to "overevaluations" of the favorableness of the product (Gardner and Scott 1990). In comparison, the maintenance of positive mood by those already experiencing one is not as urgent or overriding. As such, their evaluations will be less strongly influenced by their mood.

Given the positive affective tone of a "feel-good" product, the findings are generally in line with the consistency effects model. To further explicate, we have shown that the consistency between the product's positive affective tone and the subjects' positive mood state resulted in better recall of favorable information and higher purchase intentions. Nonetheless, one would normally expect cognitions and purchase intentions to be consistent with attitudes and global evaluations. There is a simple explanation for the apparent asymmetry hypothesized and observed in this study. Isen (1989) advances the view that memory structures for positive and negative mood states may be different. Specifically, the structure associated with positive mood is "relatively broad and extensive," whereas that associated with negative mood "may be smaller, narrower, less well interconnected with other material, and more specific to the particular state induced or even the way in which it was induced" (Isen 1989, p.103). Thus, positive mood states facilitate the encoding *and* retrieval of congruent information, whereas negative moods may constrain such memory tasks for either congruent or incongruent information. Consequently, subjects in a positive mood state are expected to recall more congruent information (i.e., favorable information). Further, if we correctly assume that subjects in a positive mood state are likely to recall more favorable information, then purchase intentions, which immediately followed the free recall task, should reflect the differences in recall between positive and negative mood subjects. Indeed, the results indicate that those subjects providing better recall of favorable information also gave higher purchase intentions for the product under scrutiny. However, recall of unfavorable information was found to be equal regardless of mood valence. While this finding cannot be readily explained by the theoretical underpinnings examined and/or developed in this study, it can be attributed, in part, to the exact nature of the negative/unfavorable attribute information included in the ad. Despite our intentions to make all attribute information similar in importance, the subjects in the main study may have found the negative information as more relevant or important. This, in turn, may have lead to the higher recall scores witnessed in this experiment. It remains for further research to assess whether the consistency effects model holds in the case when the subjects are in a negative mood and the product has negative connotations.

Several limitations may compromise the generalizability of the present findings. First, the use of two specific stories to induce the desired mood states does not imply that other contexts, or even other stories, can evoke similar moods. Therefore, evidence across studies using different contexts to manipulate mood should provide results that are either consistent or inconsistent with the findings of this study. Similarly, different kinds of positive and negative moods should be employed to test the prescribed hypotheses. Also, *all* "feel-good" products may not lead to similar results. Thus, additional research may be necessary to examine the effects of various product types as well as other products that fall within the "feel-good" category. Such research may give us new insights concerning the degree to which product type influences evaluations. Finally, the study did not involve the manipulation of the affective tone of the ad. Past research indicates that the ad's affective tone may interact with context-induced mood to influence salient dependent measures (Gardner 1992). It would be useful to include such manipulations in future research.

The findings of the study have interesting implications for advertising strategy and media planning. Specifically, the results suggest that it is important for advertisers to consider not only the type of mood consumers may be in when they view an ad or a product, but the product type as well. Also, in testing ads, it is worthwhile to note that a single advertising exposure may lead to more favorable product evaluations but not to higher purchase intentions due to the interaction of mood and product type. Additionally, the results indicate that advertising for "feel-good" products may lead to more favorable product evaluations if they are placed in a negative mood-inducing context. This provides additional evidence that advertisers need not be unduly concerned about placing advertising in negative mood inducing situations.

REFERENCES

Axelrod, Joel N. (1963), "Induced Moods and Attitudes Toward Products," *Journal of Advertising Research*, 3(June), 19-24.

Batra, Rajeev and Douglas M. Stayman (1990), "The Role of Mood in Advertising Effectiveness," *Journal of Consumer Research*, 17(September), 203-214.

Bower, Gordon (1981), "Mood and Memory," *American Psychologist*, 36(2), 129-148.

_____, Stephen Gilligan, and Kenneth Monteiro (1981), "Selectivity of Learning Caused by Affective States," *Journal of Experimental Psychology: General*, 110(December), 451-473.

Carlson, Michael and Norman Miller (1987), "Explanation of the Relation Between Negative Mood and Helping," *Psychological Bulletin*, 102(July), 91-108.

Cialdini, Robert B., Betty L. Darby and Joyce E. Vincent (1973), Transgression and Altruism: A Case for Hedonism," *Journal of Experimental Social Psychology*, 9(November), 502-516.

_____, Douglas T. Kenrick, and Donald J. Baumann (1981), "Insights from Sadness: A Three-Step Model of the Development of Altruism as Hedonism," *Developmental Review*, 1, 207-223.

_____, Mark Schaller, Donald Houlihan, Kevin Arps, Jim Fultz, and Arthur L. Beaman (1987), "Empathy-Based Helping: Is It Selflessly or Selfishly Motivated?," *Journal of Personality and Social Psychology*, 52(April), 749-758.

Clark, Margaret and Alice Isen (1982), "Toward Understanding the Relationship Between Feeling States and Social Behavior," in *Cognitive Social Psychology*, eds. Albert Hastorf and Alice Isen, New York:Elsevier/North-Holland, 73-108.

Gardner, Meryl P. (1985), "Mood States and Consumer Behavior: A Critical Review," *Journal of Consumer Research*, 12(December), 281-300.

_____ and John Scott (1990), "Product Type: A Neglected Moderator of the Effects of Mood," in *Advances in Consumer Research*, Vol. 17, eds. Goldberg, Marvin E., Gerald J. Gorn, and Richard W. Pollay, 585-589.

_____ (1992), "Responses to Emotional and Informational Appeals: the Moderating Role of Context-Induced Mood States," in *Advertising and Consumer Psychology*, eds. E. Clark, T. Brock, and D. Stewart, Hillsdale, N.J.: Lawrence Erlbaum, Inc.

Goldberg, Marvin E. and Gerald J. Gorn (1987), "Happy and Sad TV Programs: How They Affect Reactions to Commercials," *Journal of Consumer Research*, 14(December), 387-403.

Isen, Alice (1970), "Success, Failure, Attention, and Reaction to Others: The Warm Glow of Success," *Journal of Personality and Social Psychology*, 15(4), 294-301.

_____, Thomas Shalker, Margaret Clark, and Lynn Karp (1978), "Affect, Accessibility of Material in Memory, and Behavior: A Cognitive Loop?," *Journal of Personality and Social Psychology*, 36(January), 1-12.

_____, and Thomas Shalker (1982), "The Effect of Feeling State on Evaluation of Positive, Neutral, and negative Stimuli: When You 'Accentuate the Positive,' Do You 'Eliminate the Negative'?" *Social Psychology Quarterly*, 45(1), 58-63.

_____ (1984), "Toward Understanding the Role of Affect Cognition,: in *Handbook of Social Cognition*, eds. Robert Wyer, Jr. and Thomas Srull, Hillsdale, NJ: Lawrence Erlbaum, 179-236.

_____ (1989), "Some Ways in Which Affect Influences Cognitive Processes: Implications for Advertising and Consumer Behavior," in Patricia Cafferata and Alice Tybout eds., *Cognitive and Affective Responses to Advertising*, Lexington,Mass.:Lexington Books,102-106.

Jamieson, Linda F. and Frank M. Bass (1989), "Adjusting Stated Intention Measures to Predict Trial Purchase of New Products: A Comparison of Models and Methods," *Journal of Marketing Research*, 26(August), 336-345.

Johnson, Eric and Amos Tversky (1983), "Affect Generalization, and the Perception of Risk," *Journal of Personality and Social Psychology*, 45(1), 20-31.

Kamins, Michael A., Lawrence J. Marks, and Deborah Skinner (1991), "Television Commercial Evaluation in the Context of Program Induced Mood: Congruency Versus Consistency Effects," *Journal of Advertising*, 20(June), 1-14.

Marks, Lawrence J., and Michael A. Kamins (1988), "The Use of Product Sampling and Advertising: Effects of Sequence of Exposure and Degree of Advertising Claim Exaggeration on Consumers' Belief Strength, Belief Confidence, and Attitudes," *Journal of Marketing Research*, 25(August), 266-281.

Mischel, W., Brian Coates, and Antonette Raskoff (1968), "Effects of Success and Failure on Self-Gratification," *Journal of Personality and Social Psychology*, 10(4), 381-390.

_____, Ebbesen, E., and A. Zeiss (1973), "Selective Attention to the Self: Situational and Dispositional Determinants," *Journal of Personality and Social Psychology*, 27, 129-142.

Moore, Bert, Bill Underwood, and D.L. Rosenhan (1973), "Affect and Altruism," *Developmental Psychology*, 8(1), 99-104.

Peterson, Robert A., and Matthew Sauber (1983), "A Mood Scale for Survey Research," in *AMA Educators' Proceedings*, eds. Patrick Murphy et al., Chicago, IL: American Marketing Association, 409-414.

Srull Thomas (1983), "Affect and memory: The Impact of Affective Reactions in Advertising on the Representation of Product Information in Memory," in *Advances in Consumer Research*, Vol. 10, eds. Richard Bagozzi and Alice Tybout, Ann Arbor, MI: Association for Consumer Research, 520-525.

Thompson, William C., Claudia L.Cowan, and David L. Rosenhan (1980), "Focus of Attention Mediates the Impact on Altruism," *Journal of Personality and Social Psychology*, 38(February), 291-300.

The Influence of Mood and Gender on Consumers' Time Perceptions

James J. Kellaris, University of Cincinnati
Susan Powell Mantel, University of Cincinnati

ABSTRACT

This study explores the subjective experience of time passage as a function of mood and gender. Because consumers often hear music used as a "time filler," we manipulated instrumental background music in a lab experiment to induce mood states in male and female listeners. Gender was found to moderate the influence of mood on event duration estimates. Specifically, event durations were underestimated to a greater extent by females in less (versus more) positive mood states. We discuss potential commercial applications of our findings and develop directions for future consumer research on time perception.

INTRODUCTION & BACKGROUND

The experience of time pervades every aspect of human life (Bergadaà 1990), including consumptive activities. Although time is measured objectively, its passage is experienced subjectively (Hornik 1984). Under some circumstances, the disparity between objective "clock time" and perceived time can be wide. As we will discuss later, this subjective distortion can have interesting theoretic implications and important commercial consequences.

Time perception may be influenced by internal states induced by external stimuli (Levin and Zakay 1989). For example, drugs that increase (or decrease) mental activity have been shown to cause an overestimation (or underestimation) of elapsed time (Fraisse 1963). In addition, research has shown that time perceptions can be influenced by individual characteristics that moderate the impact of internal states (Block 1990).

Psychological research has suggested two processes that may underlie time perception: amount of information processed and allocation of attentional resources. Several researchers (Block 1990; Block 1989; Levin and Zakay 1989; Ornstein 1969) have explored time perception from an information processing perspective. This stream of research suggests that variation in the amount of information processed, stored, and subsequently retrieved from a time period can influence the estimation of the interval's duration. If a subject can recall more things happening during a time interval, s/he will infer more elapsed time. Zakay (1989) suggests that subjects who allocate more attention to processing stimulus events will have a reduced capacity to attend to their "internal clock;" thus, their estimates of lapsed time will be less accurate. As a subject becomes more involved in a processing task, less attention is paid to the passage of time. Hence time estimation will rely more on inferences based on the amount of information encountered/processed/stored/retrieved from the time interval, and less on a cognitive timer. Internal states such as mood should influence attention and information processing, and thus time perceptions.

Mood

There are two predominant theories concerning the influence of mood (or emotion) on memory. Leventhal (1981) advocates a theory of emotion that holds that the human mental structure uses two separate, parallel systems to process information: one emotional and one cognitive. Thus, emotionally charged information may be stored twice within the mental structure; once within the emotional system and once within the cognitive system. Ger (1989), on the other hand, represents the storage of emotional and cognitive information onto separate "nodes" within one mental structure. In either case, research suggests that emotion can influence the organization, storage, and retrieval of cognitive information (Isen 1989; Ger 1989; Matlin 1989) and thus, should affect time perceptions.

The "Pollyanna Principle" states that pleasant information is typically processed, stored, and recalled more efficiently than less pleasant information (Matlin 1989). In general, mood states tend to influence behavior, judgment, and recall; however, negative mood states tend to have more multifarious effects than positive moods (Gardner 1985). According to Gardner's review, one might expect positive affect generated by external stimuli to enhance recall of information, while less positive affect might decrease coding and storage of information. Therefore, with less information stored during a time interval in which less positive affect is experienced, a shorter duration estimate can be expected (Kellaris and Kent 1992).

Gender Differences

Several studies have investigated gender differences in time perception. Two studies found that men estimate short time intervals more accurately than women (e.g., Rammsayer and Lustnauer 1989; Krishnan and Saxena 1984). In addition, Krishnan and Saxena's results indicate that females tend to underestimate the time interval as compared to males. The observed effect was explained from a socialization perspective: males tend to learn time-consciousness as a result of their social and work experiences, which historically have involved more structured scheduling and greater time-pressures.

Gender has also been found to interact with mood to influence behavior (Maccoby and Jacklin 1974; Cox and Kellaris 1988) and memory (Clark and Teasdale 1985). Specifically, Clark and Teasdale found that women are more likely than men to recall pleasant words when in a happy mood and less likely to recall pleasant information when in a depressed mood. Several explanations for the interaction of mood and gender have been suggested. Clark and Teasdale use an associative network model to explain the gender difference and suggest that women may have stronger links between mood and cognitive nodes in memory, either because they are used more frequently or more intensely. An alternative explanation of mood-gender interaction is proposed by Rothkopf and Blaney (1991). The authors suggest that mood congruent recall requires at least some awareness of one's own mood state. Further, women are purportedly more likely to be aware of (and effected by) their own mood state in recall of information. In general, the psychological literature suggests that gender differences may have both a main effect on perceived time and a moderating effect on mood's influence.

The exploratory study reported in this paper manipulates mood via background music in ads (Alpert and Alpert 1989) and measures gender to assess the main and interactive effects of these two variables on time perception. Because mood effects are often ambiguous or inconsistent across studies, we cannot state *a priori* expectations concerning a main effect of mood on time perception. We can, however, anticipate a main effect of gender on the estimation of event durations based on the psychological literature. Specifically, females should underestimate time intervals to a greater extent than males. In addition, because gender and mood have been shown to exert an interactive influence on recall (which may be antecedent to time inferences), it is expected that females

TABLE 1
Variance Analysis (ANOVA) On Duration Estimates

Source of Variation	MS	F	d.f.	p
A: Mood	35.74	.32	1,109	n.s.
B: Gender	482.76	4.29	1,109	.041
A X B Interaction	1030.18	9.16	1,109	.003
Error	112.44			

will attribute longer durations to stimulus events that elicit a more positive mood, and shorter durations under less positive mood. Further, since males are less likely to be aware of (and effected by) their own mood states, it is expected that their time estimates will remain relatively invariant across mood states.

METHOD

Our experiment explored the influence of music-induced mood and gender of listener on time perceptions using a 2 (less/more positive mood) by 2 (male/female) between-subjects design. Subjects were exposed to simulated radio ads that contained mood-inducing background music and provided a deceptive premise for the experimental task. Perceived time passage, measured retrospectively as estimates of ad durations, was the dependent variable. The procedure involved randomly assigning subjects to treatments, exposing them individually to test ads via headsets, and asking them to complete a brief, self-administered questionnaire.

Subjects

One hundred fourteen undergraduate students were recruited from a subject pool at a large midwestern university. Subjects were naive to the purpose of the study. Extra course credit was offered as an incentive to participate. The gender distribution was about 66% male, 34% female. Ages ranged from 18 to 42 years, with a median age of 21. Complete responses were obtained from all but four of the subjects for a final sample size of one hundred ten (N=110).

Stimuli

A set of simulated radio ads were created to manipulate mood. Listening to ads also provided a deceptive premise for the mood-induction procedure. To create the stimuli, we wrote ad copy for two fictitious restaurants: a Chinese restaurant, and an elegant British-American restaurant. The copy for each restaurant ad was as similar as possible, containing about one hundred words, the name of the restaurant followed by a slogan, and other information designed to be affectively neutral. Each ad was read by the same announcer, recorded on the same equipment under identical conditions, and lasted for exactly 32 seconds.

Brief excerpts of instrumental music were selected to manipulate mood. The music was "mixed" with ad copy in a sound studio to create a set of twelve test ads. Twenty-five student subjects listened to and rated the mood of the ads in a pretest. We retained the highest and lowest rated ads for each restaurant. This stimulus construction procedure resulted in a set of multiple test ads for each level of mood. Multiple exemplars were used within each cell to increase construct validity (Cook and Campbell 1979).

Procedure

Subjects were processed individually in a listening lab. The purpose of the study was not disclosed. Subjects were told only that they would be hearing a radio ad about which they would be asked some "opinion questions." Subjects did not anticipate the time estimate measure. Printed instructions reminded subjects that they would be hearing a radio ad, that they should not look at the questions until the ad has stopped playing, and that they should begin answering the questions when the ad is over.

Measures

The dependent variable was perceived duration of the ad, measured retrospectively. Instructions preceding the time estimation measure read as follows: "Radio ads typically last anywhere from 10 seconds to over 45 seconds. Since many ads are read 'live' on the air, they often last for some odd duration (as opposed to TV ads which normally last for exactly 30 seconds). How long did the ad that you just heard seem to last? Please be as precise as possible, even if you are not certain." The estimate item was "I estimate that the ad lasted for _____ seconds." This type of open-ended item is commonly used in time perception research in psychology (e.g., Block 1990; Fraisse 1984; Levin and Zakay 1989) and, recently, in consumer research (Kellaris and Altsech 1992; Kellaris and Kent 1992).

The questionnaire also contained demographic items (i.e., sex, age), and a multi-item seven-point semantic differential scale to facilitate post-test manipulation and confounding checks. The mood scale was preceded by the prompt "The music made me feel." The scale items were "good/bad," "pleased/displeased," "happy/sad," and "positive/negative." A composite scale was formed by summing and averaging the items (Cronbach's alpha=.86).

RESULTS

Manipulation/Confounding Check

Variance analysis (ANOVA) examined the impact of the treatment variables on the manipulation check measure. We found a significant main effect of the mood treatment on the mood manipulation check scale ($F(1,109)=7.4$, $p<.01$), with no main or interactive effect involving gender. This provides evidence of a successful manipulation that is unconfounded with gender (Perdue and Summers 1986).

Effects on Perceived Time

Time estimates ranged from 5 to 60 seconds, with an average estimate of about 27 seconds (median=25 sec.) across all conditions. This is consistent with previous research that found duration

FIGURE 1
Interactive Effect of Mood and Gender on Duration Estimates

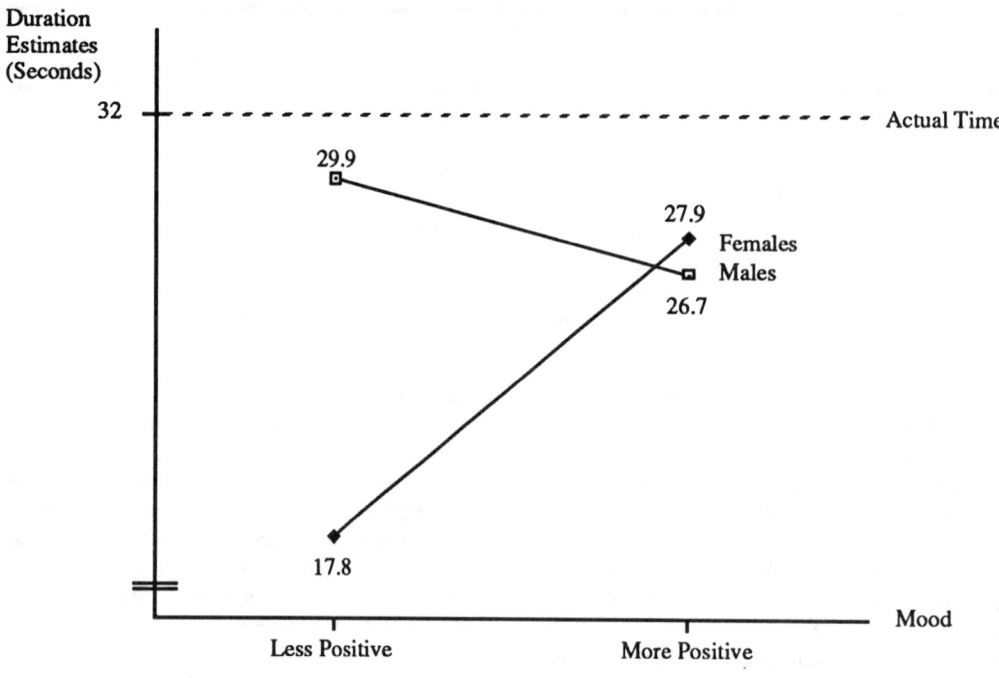

estimates to vary widely about a slightly underestimated central tendency (e.g., Fraisse 1984). ANOVA results are summarized in Table 1.

Variance analysis found a significant main effect of gender on perceived duration ($F(1,109)=4.29, p<.05$). The group mean duration estimate is 28.4 seconds for males, and 24.1 seconds for females. The magnitude of the effect was estimated as $\omega^2=.03$ (see Keppel 1982, p. 92 for a discussion of effect size interpretation).

The two-way interaction of mood and gender was also statistically significant ($F(1,109)=9.16, p<.003$), with an effect size of $\omega^2=.07$. This interaction is illustrated in Figure 1.

The duration estimates of males and females differed statistically under the less positive mood condition ($t=3.54, p<.001$), but not under the more positive mood condition ($t=-.35$, n.s.). A significant difference was observed between mood groups among females ($t=-2.94, p<.006$), but not among males ($t=1.02$, n.s.).

Comparisons with Clock Time

Comparing subjects' duration estimates to actual clock time, we found a general tendency to underestimate retrospectively the passage of time ($t=-3.55, p<.001$). This tendency was observed across mood conditions for both male ($t=-2.95, p<.01$) and female ($t=-4.43, p<.001$) subjects, and under both less ($t=-3.55, p<.001$) and more ($t=-3.48, p<.001$) positive mood states across genders.

However, comparing mean duration estimates separately for each cell of our 2 X 2 design with clock time, we found statistical differences between perceived and real time in only two cells: among females in the less positive mood group ($t=-6.76, p<.001$), and among males in the more positive mood group ($t=-3.29, p<.01$). The duration estimates of females in more positive moods and males in less positive moods did not differ statistically from clock time.

DISCUSSION

Our experimental findings suggest that both gender and its interaction with mood can influence consumers' time perceptions. The data supported our expectation that males would produce more accurate time estimates, whereas females tended to perceive shorter, less accurate durations. Further, while both genders tended to underestimate the duration of a stimulus event (test ad) in relation to clock time, the pattern of time estimates varied systematically across mood conditions, although mood had no apparent influence on time perceptions independently of gender.

Females' time estimates were significantly different for the less versus more positive mood conditions while the males' responses were relatively invariant across mood conditions. Perhaps, as suggested by Rothkopf and Blaney (1991), the female subjects were more affected by their mood state than their male counterparts due to greater self-awareness. This greater self-awareness would not necessarily be detected in our post-test manipulation check of mood state, which should have induced self-awareness *post hoc* in both males and females by asking them to recall their feelings at the time of exposure. We must commend testing of the self-awareness explanation to future research.

It is interesting to note that although the males' responses were statistically invariant across mood conditions, the direction of mean duration estimates was negative (i.e., males in good moods estimated the event duration to be about two seconds shorter). Based on the "mood preservation hypothesis" (people in good moods avoid activities that would result in loss of good mood), we speculate that the males in less (versus more) positive mood states may have been slightly more motivated (or less demotivated) to process the information they encountered (Isen 1989).

For the women, the shorter time estimates associated with the less positive mood condition suggests that time does not necessarily fly when they are having fun. This result, although inconsistent with popular wisdom, is consistent with prior mood/music research in consumer behavior (Kellaris and Kent 1992). This finding is also consistent with at least two process explanations. Women may be more likely to *store* a larger quantity of information about positively valenced stimulus events (Rothkopf and Blaney 1991). Alternatively, women may have stronger links between mood and cognitive nodes in memory and thus can *retrieve* more stored information when they are in positive moods (Clark and Teasdale 1985). No matter the underlying process, our data suggest that mood has a greater influence on the temporal experience of female (versus male) subjects.

Although these results should be considered preliminary, with reliability subject to future replication, we believe that they provide an interesting, initial demonstration of principles that eventually may be used in practical contexts.

Commercial Applications

There are many circumstances under which marketers may wish to diminish consumers' perceptions of time passage. For example, consumers may grow impatient and annoyed during long waits in check-out lines or other queues, while waiting for tables at a busy restaurant, while placed on "hold" when phoning a business, or while the viewing of a program is interupted with a commercial. Dissatisfaction may be mitigated by "shrinking" the perceived duration of the delay. Our study provides a preliminary glimpse into how such diminution of time can be achieved by manipulating moods with music.

Specifically, our findings suggest that music designed to elevate customers' moods may be counter-productive among females. Elevating moods may actually increase the accuracy of their time perceptions, such that they experience the full duration of a delay. Music that provides a distraction without inducing an elevated mood should be used when time diminution is a goal.

There are also circumstances under which marketers may wish to augment the perceived passage of time. For example, once restaurant patrons are seated at a table, "expanding" time perceptions may lead to quicker table turn-over without making customers feel rushed. Although we did not observe systematic over-estimation of time under the conditions in this study, our findings suggest the general possibility that music can be used to alter temporal perception. Future research should investigate conditions that lead to time augmentation.

Limitations & Future Research

The findings of this study should be interpreted cautiously given the preliminary nature of the study. Although the results are consistent with previous research, the use of student subjects and a forced exposure condition may have influenced responses in ways that are difficult to evaluate. Additional research is needed to assess the extent to which these lab findings generalize to other groups of consumers and natural settings.

Future exploration of time perception should be of ample interest to consumer researchers and marketing practitioners alike. Of particular interest are the process mechanisms underlying temporal perception. Because our findings are consistent with several explanations, we must commend the investigation of underlying psychological processes to future research.

Conclusion

In sum, this study has examined the influence of music-induced mood and gender on time perception. We found potentially consequential gender differences, and developed tentative commercial applications. We believe that a better understanding of factors that influence consumers' time perceptions eventually may allow marketers and service providers to mitigate negative consequences of time passage (e.g., delays in service) by engineering environmental stimuli such as music to diminish the perception of time passage.

REFERENCES

Alpert, Judy I. and Mark I. Alpert (1989), "Background Music as an Influence in Consumer Mood and Advertising Responses," *Advances in Consumer Research*, 16, 485-491.

Bergadaà, Michelle M. (1990), "The Role of Time in the Action of the Consumer," *Journal of Consumer Research*, 17, 289-302.

Block, Richard A. (Ed.) (1990), *Cognitive Models of Psychological Time*, Hillsdale, NJ: Erlbaum.

Block, Richard A. (1989), "Experiencing and Remembering Time: Affordances, Context, and Cognition," in I. Levin and D. Zakay (Eds.), *Time and Human Cognition: A life Span Prospective*, Amsterdam: North-Holland, 333-363.

Cook, Thomas D. and Donald T. Campbell (1979), *Quasi-Experimentation: Design and Analysis Issues for Field Settings*, Chicago, IL: Rand McNally.

Cox, Dena S., and James J. Kellaris (1988), "The Effect of Mood and Gender on Perceived Likelihood of Making Unplanned Purchases," in L. Alwitt, ed., *Proceedings of the Division of Consumer Psychology*, Washington, D.C., American Psychological Associaiton, 14-16.

Clark, David M. and John D. Teasdale (1985), "Constraints on the Effects of Mood on Memory," *Journal of Personality and Social Psychology*, 48:6, 1595-1608.

Fraisse, Paul (1963), *The Psychology of Time*, Greenwood Press Publishers, Westport, Conneticut.

Fraisse, Paul (1984), "Perception and Estimation of Time," *Annual Review of Psychology*, 35, 1-36.

Gardner, Meryl Paula (1985), "Mood States and Consumer Behavior: A Critical Review," *Journal of Consumer Research*, 12(December), 281-300.

Ger, Guliz (1989), "Nature of Effects of Affect on Judgment: Theoretical and Methodological Issues," in *Cognitive and Affective Responses to Advertising*, ed. Patricia Cafferata and Alice M. Tybout, Lexington, Massachusetts: D.C. Heath Company, 263-275.

Hornik, Jacob (1984), "Subjective vs. Objective Time Measures: A Note on the Perception of Time in Consumer Behavior," *Journal of Consumer Research*, 11, 615-618.

Isen, Alice M. (1989), "Some Ways in Which Affect Influences Cognitive Processes: Implications for Advertising and Consumer Behavior," in *Cognitive and Affective Responses to Advertising*, ed. Patricia Cafferata and Alice M. Tybout, Lexington Massachusetts: D.C. Heath and Company, 91-117.

Kellaris, James J., and Moses B. Altsech (1992), "The Experience of Time as a Function of Musical Loudness and Gender of Listener," in J. Sherry and B. Sternthal, eds., *Advances in Consumer Research*, Vol. 19, Provo, UT: Association for Consumer Research, 725-729.

Kellaris, James J., and Robert J. Kent (1992), "The Influence of Music on Consumers' Temporal Perceptions: Does Time Fly When You're Having Fun?" *Journal of Consumer Psychology*, 1, 4, 365-376.

Keppel, Geoffrey (1982), *Design & Analysis — A Researcher's Handbook*, 2nd ed., Englewood Cliffs, NJ: Prentice-Hall.

Krishnan, Lila and Neelaksh Kumar Saxena (1984), "Perceived Time: Its Rela-tionship with Locus of Control, Filled Versus Unfilled Time Intervals, and Perceiver's Sex," *The Journal of General Psychology*, 110, 275-281.

Leventhal, Howard (1982), "The Integration of Emotion and Cognition: A View from the Perceptual-Motor Theory of Emotion," in *Affect and Cognition: The Seventeenth Annual Carnegie Symposium on Cognition*, eds. Margaret Sydnor Clark and Susan T. Fisk, Hillsdale, NJ: Lawrence Eribaum, 121-156.

Levin, Iris and Daniel Zakay (Eds.) (1989), *Time and Human Cognition*, Advances in Psychology series # 59, Elsevier Science Publishers, North-Holland.

Maccoby, Eleanor Emmons and Carol Nagy Jacklin (1974), *The Psychology of Sex Differences*, Stanford, CA: Stanford University Press.

Matlin, Margaret W. (1989), *Cognition*, Chicago: Holt, Rinehart, and Winston, Inc.

Ornstein, Robert E. (1969), *On the Experience of Time*, New York, NY: Penguin Books.

Perdue, Barbara C., and O. John Summers (1986), "Checking the Success of Manipulations in Marketing Experiments," *Journal of Marketing Research*, 23, 317-326.

Rammsayer, Thomas and Sebastian Lustnauer (1989), "Sex Differences in Time Perception," *Perceptual and Motor Skills*, 68, 195-198.

Rothkopf, Jeffrey S. and Paul H. Blaney (1991), "Mood Congruent Memory: The Role of Affective Focus and Gender," *Cognition and Emotion*, 5:1, 53-64.

Zakay, Daniel (1989), "Subjective Time and Attentional Resource Allocation : An Integrated Model of Time Estimation," in I. Levin and D. Zakay (Eds.), *Time and Human Cognition: A Life Span Prospective*, Amsterdam: North-Holland, 365-398.

Phenomenological Insights in Mood and Mood-Related Consumer Behaviors
Jacqueline J. Kacen, University of Illinois at Urbana-Champaign

ABSTRACT

Individuals' mood states have been found to affect sociability, self-concept, recall, evaluations, judgments and risk taking. However, mood effects on consumer behaviors are largely unknown. This paper reports the findings of an exploratory study into individual experiences of mood and subsequent mood-related behaviors. Data were collected in multiple, depth interviews and analyzed by a constant comparative method revealing insights into the lived meaning of mood. Distinguishing aspects of moods and behaviors prompted by moods are identified and directions for future research are suggested.

INTRODUCTION

Early work by Tompkins (1970) held that feelings are the primary motivators of human behavior. Others have identified "experiential" and hedonic aspects of consumption (Ahtola 1985; Holbrook and Hirschman 1982; Venkatraman and MacInnis 1985). This approach to consumer behavior holds that emotional desires dominate utilitarian motives in the consumer choice process in some instances (Etzioni 1988; Hirschman and Holbrook 1982). Weinberg and Gothwald (1982) found that emotions are a key ingredient in stimulating impulse purchases. Langer (1983) has suggested that difficult economic conditions may increase consumers' needs for treats and emotional charges. One way to explore this idea of emotional or mood-driven consumer behaviors is to examine, from an in-depth phenomenological perspective, individual's experiences of mood and the activities and behaviors associated with these moods.

The objectives of the study reported here were to 1) explore the context and phenomenology of mood through individual depth interviews, and 2) identify patterns of consumer behavior linked to good and bad mood states. This paper begins with a discussion of the theoretical foundations underlying the concept of mood and its effects on sociability, evaluations, judgments, and behavior. The research method is then described. The results of the interviews are presented, interpreted and integrated into a discussion of "mood management" theory. The paper concludes with suggestions for further research.

CONCEPTUAL BACKGROUND

Mood has been described as a particular state of mind or feeling that is theoretically associated with personality and the temporary internal state of an individual in a particular environment (Peterson and Sauber 1983). Moods have also conceptualized as subjectively perceived feeling states that are transient, omnipresent and easily influenced by little things (Gardner 1985; Gardner and Vandersteel 1984). They are contrasted with feeling states that are relatively stable and permanent such as optimistic or pessimistic personality dispositions (Westbrook 1980) and are distinct from feelings directed toward a specific object (e.g., the affective component of brand attitude; see Gardner 1985).

Moods are also distinct from emotions which have generally been conceptualized as more intense states of arousal (Wessman and Ricks 1966). However, moods can also be intense and arousing (Morris and Reilly 1987). What distinguishes moods from emotions is that the latter have an object reference (Ewert 1970) and their effects create a state of awareness which may redirect attention to the source of the emotion (Gardner 1985; Simon 1967). Moods, on the other hand, are more unfocused and pervasive feeling states that provide a general context for thought (Simon 1982) and a general "tuning" of the organism (Scherer 1986). They are best described as temporary, affect-laden feeling states that are ubiquitous in nature.

Motivational Role of Mood

Isen (1984, 1985) has suggested that we are generally motivated to maintain, even prolong, pleasant moods but attempt to terminate unpleasant ones. This interpretation, grounded in social learning theory (e.g., Bandura 1977, Mischel 1973) and the principle of self-regulation (Carver and Scheier 1981), holds that individuals who are feeling good will try to maintain this state (mood maintenance); individuals who are feeling badly will engage in acts to improve their mood (mood repair). It has been found that individuals try to resist negative moods and may engage in behaviors or psychological processes that seek to terminate unpleasant mood states (Schwarz and Clore 1983).

Carver and Scheier's (1981, 1990) model proposes that self-regulation processes involve comparing one's current state with a goal or standard. If there is a discrepancy, one may either adjust one's behavior to meet the standard or, if one expects to fail, abandon attempts to meet it. Disruptions or failures in the pursuit of one's goals activate processes of self-regulation, which require focusing attention on the self (Pyszczynski and Greenberg 1987). An experience of failure "signals a need for self-regulation" (Greenberg and Pyszczynski 1986, p. 1041). Negative feelings may warn that something is wrong and that one must attend to the self in order to surmount the failure or to adjust one's standards (Wood, Saltzberg, and Goldsamt 1990). The findings from research on compulsive buying indicates that the alleviation of negative feelings appears to be the primary motivation for this behavior (Faber, O'Guinn, and Krych 1987; O'Guinn and Faber 1989).

Positive feelings may also encourage self-focus as a means of prolonging the good mood (Greenberg and Pyszczynski 1986; Wicklund 1975). However, affect-control processes are likely to be more urgent when we are sad than when we are happy because we try to keep negative feelings away (Isen 1984, 1985). Sadness may be more salient (i.e., more novel and preoccupying) than happiness and therefore more likely to prompt attention (Isen 1984; Wood et al. 1990). Further, controlling negative feelings requires more effort since it involves trying to change our emotional state rather than merely prolonging our current state; this may induce more self-focus (Wood et al. 1990).

Mood and Consumer Behavior

Consumer behavior involves the acquisition, consumption and disposition of a variety of goods and services. Inherent in this is making choices about which products to acquire, consume, and dispose of. These choices likely are affected by our moods, and our efforts to manage them.

Moods are accompanied by thoughts and feelings that tend to facilitate and extend the mood experience (Clark and Isen 1982; Cohen 1990; Zillmann 1988; Zillmann and Bryant 1985). Engaging and absorbing activities that share a behavioral affinity to the current mood state perpetuate the prior mood because they revive mood-maintaining cognitions (cf. Zillmann 1979). Revival is due to the fact that behaviorally related affective reactions share associative networks (Anderson and Bower 1973; Isen 1984). Activities that lack similarity with the mood experience in which they intervene tend to disrupt and impair the mood maintaining looping in and rehearsing of thoughts related to the particular mood experience, thus diminishing the intensity of the mood and fostering its termination (Zillmann and Bryant 1985; see also Kendall and Hollon 1979).

Negative moods create unpleasant feelings that must be disposed of. This can be done by acquiring something that has more positive self-enhancing properties. Since products "enabl[e] the consumer to appropriate the world of his or her desires" (Churchill and Wertz 1985), purchasing a product with positive attributes may help to overcome a negative mood. Alternatively, bad moods may involve consuming more positive stimuli (e.g., television programs, the sights and sounds of a shopping mall). Consumption of these stimuli can distract attention away from negative feelings and allow refocusing on more pleasant things. Disposition behavior (e.g., cleaning) may be a kind of cleansing ritual, a way of removing the negative and beginning anew (cf. Young 1991). Thus, consumer activities and behaviors that enable us to eliminate our unpleasant feelings, refocus on more positive stimuli, and restore our self-image will likely be pursued when we are in a bad mood.

Positive moods are likely to encourage more acquisition and consumption behaviors. Individuals in a good mood tend to be more generous to themselves (Mischel, Coates, and Raskoff 1968; Underwood, Moore, and Rosenhan 1973) and to others (Isen 1970). Engaging in pleasant activities (e.g., eating, shopping, visiting with friends) will prolong a good mood. Activities with negative connotations (e.g., watching a depressing movie) will probably be avoided.

It is likely that individuals engage in self-regulatory mood-management processes and have devised strategies for coping with unpleasant moods and for prolonging pleasant moods. By exploring individuals' phenomenological experiences of pleasant and unpleasant moods, and the means (i.e., the acquisition, consumption and disposition behaviors) by which they manage these experiences, it is possible to come to a greater understanding of consumers' mood-related behaviors.

METHOD

Twelve depth interviews were conducted as part of this study. The overall objective of the interviews was to gain a richer, deeper insight into behaviors which arise as a result of "good" or "bad" moods as experienced by individuals. The development of an understanding of individuals' experiences of mood, as expressed by the informants, was an integral goal of the research. An additional goal was the identification of consumer behaviors designed to manage an individual's moods. Existential phenomenology offers a perspective and methodology to achieve these goals by focusing on a person's experiences as they are lived in a social context (Thompson, Locander, and Pollio 1989; Valle and King 1978). The interviews were conducted to answer two questions: "How do individuals experience good moods and bad moods?" and "Do they have strategies (e.g., do they engage in specific behaviors) to manage their moods?"

The 12 informants (six men and six women) interviewed for this study were all undergraduates at a large midwestern university who received course credit for their participation. All were single, middle class, and ranged in age from 19 to 24. The interviews were audiotaped and lasted approximately one hour. Before beginning, informants were told that the purpose of the interview was to gain insight into individuals' experiences of different moods. Each interview began with the question "Tell me about a time recently when you were in a bad mood." After a detailed discussion of bad mood experiences (approximately 30 minutes into the interview) informants were asked to describe a recent good mood experience. All other questions emerged spontaneously from the ensuing dialogue. (Bad mood experiences were discussed first so that the interview ended on a positive note.)

This unstructured approach allows for more rapid development of rapport, maximizes informants' opportunities to introduce topics in a manner comfortable to them, and lets informants develop the discussion at their own pace (Schouten 1991). All informants were readily able to recall several recent good and bad mood experiences.

Analysis was an iterative process of transcribing, coding and categorizing the data (cf. McCracken 1988; Miles and Huberman 1984). Data of apparent thematic similarity were identified throughout the transcription process, highlighted and coded with key words. Coded data were compared and contrasted, producing a few broad categories which were further sorted and clustered to yield the principal themes (cf. Mick and DeMoss 1990; Schouten 1991; Young 1991).

FINDINGS

Bad Moods: Sources and Effects

Bad moods generally arose from disruptions or failures in the pursuit of informants' goals (cf. Pyszczynski and Greenberg 1987) leading to feelings of powerlessness and loss of self-esteem. Among the students interviewed in this study, many bad moods came about due to poor academic performance, or problems with social relationships. Concern with grades was mentioned by nearly all the participants:

> I took the conflict exam that we had. [My professor] said that the conflict wasn't going to be any harder, and in my opinion it wound up being a lot harder. I was very depressed because I didn't do that good on it. (Michelle)

Roommates and significant others were also the basis for many bad moods. Desmond's arguments with his girlfriend leave him in a bad mood:

> It's frustrating. It's hard to really express what I'm thinking or feeling without her taking it the wrong way. I feel that anything I could do would be useless. (Desmond)

Feeling a lack of control over things, e.g., unresolved issues involving social relationships or academic responsibilities, or external pressures related to work load and academic performance, produced feelings of apprehension and frustration.

> I have a lot of stress right now because I have a bunch of papers and quizzes this week and next week. I feel like I don't have enough time to finish it all. I get mad because I don't have enough time. I can't do things as well as I'd like to, and I'm just getting totally stressed because I don't have enough time to do everything. (Pam)

The negative feelings induced by a bad mood often reduced self-confidence and led to more focusing on the self:

> I just go to my room. Stay distant from people. Maybe clean it up. Go through my checkbook. If something's really bothering me, I'll be thinking about that. (Janet)

This self-focusing resulted in an inability to concentrate on other things (especially school work), and often led to a loss of energy, a lack of effort and conscientiousness toward (school) work, antisocial tendencies, or a heightened sensitivity toward negative things (criticism, bad news, etc.)

> I guess when I get in a bad mood I'm more quiet. I keep to myself more. I stay in my room and don't want to be bothered....I'm unproductive when I'm in a bad mood....I just can't study as I should, or just don't feel like doing anything. (Scott)

Bad Moods: Mood-Managing Strategies

Two principle themes emerged from an analysis of the strategies adopted to overcome negative feelings: escape and control behaviors. Escape activities improve a negative mood by changing one's attentional focus.

> Usually if I'm in a bad mood I read *People*, or some kind of magazine like that. I actually like to read the *Enquirer* too and stuff like that, just because it's something that's totally outside of my everyday life...something entertaining just to set everything else aside and maybe lift my spirits a little....But just reading the stuff like things about Oprah getting married and just...maybe reading about other people's problems helps too....Some guy could be losing $20 million in a lawsuit and I can see that as being more of a problem than me not getting an A in Finance...(Troy)

Activities like reading, watching tv, or listening to music provide a sense of escape by refocusing the mind on different (usually happier) things - in effect, pushing away negative thoughts.

> If I'm feeling mopey, I won't do much of anything. I won't do homework. I'll sit on the couch and watch junk tv. I won't watch 'Nature' and 'Discovery' where I actually have to learn something, think about something. I just want to be bombarded by what's on the screen. Maybe I'll read a novel, like Stephen King or John Grisham. (Bill)

Sometimes the escape activity requires a *physical* escape like shopping or going to the movies. Shifting to a new environment allows individuals in a bad mood to leave their negative feelings behind and focus on different (more positive) stimuli.

> A lot of times actually when I get depressed I feel like going shopping....Sometimes I'll find myself going to the mall just to spend money when I'm in a bad mood. I don't know, for some reason, spending money, not a lot but a small amount, for some reason it makes me feel better....Actually, I can remember one time where I just went and bought some earrings. Just something small. But it just made me feel better to have something new....Maybe like, that I could get on and not worry about this, I have something new. I should forget about the old things and start doing new things instead. (Pam)

"Working out" was an often cited mood-management strategy. Exercise provides escape by 1) refocusing attention on more intense *physical* sensations which can overpower the unwanted *emotional* sensations, and 2) providing a release for negative feelings.

> I'll go and work out, exercise....It kind of clears your mind because you're able to - even though your thoughts are still with you, you can concentrate on something else... (Tracy)

Writing letters and talking with friends or family works analogously by allowing negative feelings to "escape" through communication channels.

> It gets it off my chest...that always helps talking to my roommates.... We start talking about one thing and it just leads to another, and pretty soon we're just talking, hanging out, tripping out, laughing and my girlfriend is not even on my mind anymore. (Desmond)

Control behaviors are designed to overcome negative feelings like powerlessness by demonstrating one's dominance over something.

> I really like classical music. And playing it is even better. Because you're the one who's controlling it. It makes you feel like you're in power, in control. (Sarah)

Cleaning, driving, or playing a musical instrument are all empowering activities that provide a sense of mastery over the physical environment. Control over the *physical* helps bring one's *emotional* state under control.

> It's just driving and being by myself and looking at things that you don't get to see every day. I'd go down by the river, something like that, just drive by.... Driving's probably a good way to get rid of stress or something, at least for a while, because for me it was like being in control. (Troy)

Cleaning one's room or one's apartment can also be seen as a physical manifestation of "straightening up" the thoughts and feelings in one's head. Such organizing refocuses attention, provides a physical release for the feelings created by the negative mood, and restores one's sense of order, direction and control.

> Usually if I'm in a really bad mood, I'll clean my room, you know, just to get.... I'll feel like I've got to get some organization in my life. I'll clean up my room, maybe throw away some papers that I have everywhere across the room. (Michelle)

Analysis of the data reveals that most negative mood behaviors are pursued as solitary activities. Due to diminished self-esteem and self-confidence, most individuals choose to be alone when they are in a bad mood, at least initially. However, while bad moods encourage "nesting" instincts and the pursuit of solitude, there is also a need to release the negative feelings, which may sometimes involves communicating with a close "other."

> When I have a problem, and I want to get rid of the feeling or whatever, I'd rather talk to somebody about it. Which is usually my girlfriend or my parents. And it's kind of like, through talking they put in their advice or their input and it kind of helps put things in perspective or make things not seem as bad. (Scott)

Further, bad moods can encompass a variety of feelings and effects. There is a difference, for example, in the energy one feels when one is frustrated versus when one is depressed. This has an effect on the mood-managing activities chosen, as revealed by Bill. When he's "mopey," he "won't do much of anything" but when in irritated or frustrated moods:

> I work them off. I do homework. I clean the apartment. I'll go for a jog. Just anything to keep busy. Because if I sit there, it's just going to get worse....I'll just focus on that. Anything just to distract me. (Bill)

Similarly, Josie likes to listen to music when she's in a bad mood. But there is different music for different bad moods:

> When I'm in a bad mood, I'll listen to music. Classic rock like the Police, the Rolling Stones. If I'm really really upset, then I put the Scorpions on.... Maybe it's the beat. Maybe it corresponds with your heartbeat. You just concentrate on the beat and you forget what you're upset about. [If I'm depressed] I put on the really sad stuff.... Just the songs that have emotion in them. I guess maybe it's the things they are singing about, and you just let that emotion ride out its course, then you're fine. (Josie)

In sum, negative moods seem to arise from disruptions in the pursuit of goals which activates self-regulatory processes. Individuals first engage in self-focusing to try to understand their feelings, and then pursue activities that allow the negative feelings to dissipate and/or restore self-esteem (cf. Swann, Pelham, and Krull 1989). Pleasant, or more positive, activities disrupt the negative thoughts and feelings that accompany a bad mood and help to terminate it. The activities chosen depend on the nature of the mood. Arousing negative moods (e.g., frustration, irritation) create excess negative energy that must be eliminated, often through physical activities (exercise, cleaning). Depressive moods sap energy and result in more sedentary activities (watching television).

Good moods: Sources and Effects

Not surprisingly, good moods were prompted by things which made informants feel good about themselves, things that confirmed self-worth and matched expectations of achievement of a personal goal or standard (cf. Carver and Scheier 1981).

> Yesterday after I worked out - it was a good workout, nice, hard, you know, burned the muscles - and I ran home and I made it all the way home. Not easily, but I wasn't hurting. So I was just elated. It was like, "Yes! I did it!" (Desmond)

Some sources of good moods mentioned by the participants included academic successes, feeling cared about and wanted, accomplishing a personal goal, pleasurable social events (vacations, visiting family and friends, parties) and feeling free from responsibilities, time pressures and (school) work. For example, John feels "in a good mood during vacations, when I get to see [old] friends."

In contrast to negative moods, positive moods led to heightened self-esteem, more self-confidence, greater sociability, and more energy.

> My personality improves, I guess, when I'm in a good mood. I'm more open to other people as far as conversation or laughing along with somebody, something like that. When I'm in a good mood I usually want to do something. Rather than sit there and be in a good mood, I'd rather be sharing my good mood with the world, so to speak....Because usually when I get in a good mood I have extra energy for some reason. So I want to burn the energy off or, I don't know, do something rather than just sit there. (Scott)

Good moods also reduced worrying, and increased the propensity for (slight) risk-taking (cf. Isen and Patrick 1983).

> I guess sometimes when I'm in a good mood, I may take more risks....I may call somebody up that I haven't talked to for a long time or something....One time I called somebody that I'd had a fight with a while ago and I was afraid to do it, but I was in a good mood so I was like, "well, I'll take this chance and I'll try it." (Pam)

Consistent with prior findings (Mischel et al. 1968; Underwood et al. 1973), when in a good mood, informants were generous to themselves, and more willing to try new things.

> When I'm in a good mood [at the grocery store] I like to try something new. When I'm in a bad mood, I just don't want to try anything. I get the old stuff. Because you're just like an old person, you don't want to do anything. You don't want to think. So I just get something I always get. But sometimes when I'm in a good mood I try to get something new. (Wilson)

Good Moods: Mood-Management Strategies

Positive moods generally create a desire to "share the good mood with the world." In contrast to bad moods, good moods encourage the pursuit of social activities: team sports, or going out with friends.

> In a good mood, I'm more apt to do things that I normally don't do. Like maybe go out with a group of friends or something.... Out to eat maybe. Or over to somebody's house. Maybe play basketball with some friends. (Troy)

Engaging in activities with friends that are inherently enjoyable prolongs the good mood. Social activities also confirm one's sense of self-worth and feelings of being loved. Good moods increase self-confidence which encourages more risk-taking behavior: "it's like there's nothing I can't handle. Nothing I can't achieve" (Desmond).

SIGNIFICANCE OF MOOD FINDINGS

It is clear from these interviews that moods do affect our acquisition, consumption, and disposition behaviors. Individuals do engage in self-regulatory behaviors and do have a variety of mood-managing strategies that prolong their pleasant moods and help to alleviate their unpleasant ones. The chosen activities affect mood by perpetuating or interrupting the mood experience.

The unpleasant feelings that accompany a negative mood can be eliminated by acquiring something new, like a pair of earrings. Having something new represents a fresh start, a rebirth and helps us to "forget about the old things and start doing new [more positive] things" (Pam). Consumption of pleasantly engaging stimuli such as television programs, magazines, books, movies or the sights and sounds of a shopping mall distract us from our negative feelings and provide a happier, more positive focus. As an acquisition and consumption behavior, exercise provides new physical sensations, enhanced capabilities (we are stronger, faster, leaner) and an improved self-image while "consuming" negative energies. Disposition behavior - throwing out papers or other personal items - may be a kind of cleansing ritual, a way of throwing out the old, negative self and getting a fresh start. Exercise allows us to literally dispose of negative feelings by "sweating them away." Similarly, "disposing" of negative feelings may be done through letter writing or confiding in a close friend.

Good mood consumer behaviors are much more social and generally entail engaging in acquisition and consumption behaviors in the pursuit of a good time. These can include shopping, going out to eat, or calling friends. We may buy things simply because we are feeling more generous toward ourselves. Consumption of food and drink in a public restaurant/bar provides a social atmosphere which prolongs the good mood by reaffirming our social ties and our sense of being loved.

Interestingly, some consumer behaviors are both good mood and bad mood behaviors. We may choose to go shopping or to the movies when we are in a good mood *and* when we are in a bad mood. However, the purpose and the experience is different when the behavior is pursued to relieve a bad mood or to maintain a good mood.

> When I go [to the movies] when I'm in a good mood it is just to enjoy the movie. And just enjoy myself. But if I go for a bad mood it's probably just to get away from other things. So it may not even be a movie that I necessarily want to see...it's just a way of getting away from things that are bothering me now. (Troy)

Typically, when we're in a bad mood we engage in solitary activities because we are focused on ourselves, on restoring our self-esteem, on regaining control of our environment (cf. Wood et al. 1990). The intent is escape, relief of negative feelings, or control. On the other hand, if we are in a good mood, we may engage in the same behavior, but it will be with friends, and the emphasis will be on the social aspect of the activity. The shops we go into or the movie we see will be of secondary importance to the people who are with us. With good mood behaviors, the intent is to prolong the mood by sharing it with others.

CONCLUSIONS, LIMITATIONS AND DIRECTIONS FOR FURTHER RESEARCH

This study illustrates the central role that mood can play in individual consumer behaviors. It describes the events and experiences which lead to different moods, and the resulting behaviors aimed at managing these feelings and maintaining or restoring self-esteem. The principal mood-managing consumer behaviors discovered in this study include shopping, exercise, reading, driving, cleaning, writing letters, watching television, going out with friends, and talking to loved ones. Escape and control activities help to eliminate negative feelings and restore self-esteem by interrupting negative thoughts and providing a sense of mastery over the environment. Socially oriented behaviors prolong positive moods by affirming social likability, and hence, self-worth.

However, the "self context" of the study participants is important to a discussion of the findings. Sears (1986) has argued that college students have less formulated senses of the self, stronger cognitive skills, stronger tendencies to comply with authority and more unstable peer group relationships. These characteristic tendencies were clearly evident in the interview transcripts. Additionally, since achievement is an expected behavior in a college setting (Frieze, Sales, and Smith 1991), it is possible that the informants exhibited more concern with achievement than they would have in other situations.

Further, one of the central factors affecting the context of one's life is where one is in the life cycle. The self changes in predictable ways at different life stages (Frieze et al. 1991). Accordingly, one's self-concept changes also, and is dependent upon how well one handles those issues that are most important to psychological growth and well-being during any given life stage. The mood experiences and effects described by the students in this study unquestionably reflect their current life stage concerns. The findings expressed here, therefore, may not be generalizable beyond a college student population.

Nevertheless, moods and mood management strategies bear further examination. The informants were, admittedly, extremely homogeneous. Depth interviews with individuals in other stages of life who have different concerns (see Frieze et al. 1991) as well as a wider range of adults encompassing more diverse racial, cultural, and socioeconomic backgrounds is needed to compare and extend the findings from this study. Since moods seem to arise from things that facilitate or disrupt the pursuit of one's goals, it is likely that the moods of adults in different life stages will be prompted by things which affect their self-concept as determined by the life concerns with which they are faced. With a larger sample of individual moods and mood-related actions, better insights into mood and its motivational role in consumer behavior can be obtained.

Since affective factors have been recognized as important - if not primary (see, e.g., Tompkins 1970; Zajonc 1984) - motivators of behavior, the relationship between mood and mood-related behaviors is a significant one. This study makes a modest contribution toward understanding that relationship.

REFERENCES

Ahtola, Olli T. (1985), "Hedonic and Utilitarian Aspects of Consumer Behavior," in *Advances in Consumer Research*, Vol. 12, ed. Elizabeth C. Hirschman and Morris B. Holbrook, Provo, UT: Association for Consumer Research, 7-10.

Anderson, John R. and Gordon H. Bower (1973), *Human Associative Memory*, Washington, DC: Winston.

Bandura, Albert (1977), "Self Efficacy: Toward a Unifying Theory of Behavioral Change," *Psychological Review*, 84 (March), 191-215.

Cantor, Nancy, Julie K. Norem, Paula M. Niedenthal, Christopher A. Langston, and Aaron M. Brower (1987), "Life Tasks, Self-Concept Ideals, and Cognitive Strategies in a Life Transition," *Journal of Personality and Social Psychology*, 53 (December), 1178-1191.

Carver, Charles S. and Michael F. Scheier (1981), *Attention and Self-Regulation: A Control Theory Approach to Human Behavior*, New York: Springer-Verlag.

_____ and Michael F. Scheier (1990), "Principles of Self-Regulation: Action and Emotion," in *Handbook of Motivation and Cognition*, Vol. 2, ed. E. Tory Higgins and Richard M. Sorrentino, New York: Guilford Press, 3-52.

Clark, Margaret and Alice M. Isen (1982), "Toward Understanding the Relationship Between Feeling States and Social Behavior," in *Cognitive Social Psychology*, ed. Albert Hastorf and Alice M. Isen, New York: Elsevier/North Holland, 73-108.

Cohen, Joel B. (1990), "Attitude, Affect, and Consumer Behavior," in *Affect and Social Behavior*, ed. Bert S. Moore and Alice M. Isen, New York: Cambridge University Press, 152-206.

Churchill, Scott D. and Frederick J. Wertz (1985), "An Introduction to Phenomenological Psychology for Consumer Research: Historical, Conceptual, and Methodological Foundations," in *Advances in Consumer Research*, Vol. 12, ed. Elizabeth C. Hirschman and Morris B. Holbrook, Provo, UT: Association for Consumer Research, 550-555.

Etzioni, Amitai (1988), "Normative-Affective Factors: Toward a New Decision-Making Model," *Journal of Economic Psychology*, 9 (June), 125-150.

Ewert, Otto (1970), "The Attitudinal Character of Emotion," in *Feelings and Emotions*, ed. Magda B. Arnold, New York: Academic Press, 233-240.

Faber, Ronald J., Thomas C. O'Guinn, and Raymond Krych (1987), "Compulsive Consumption," in *Advances in Consumer Research*, Vol. 14, ed. Melanie Wallendorf and Paul F. Anderson, Provo, UT: Association for Consumer Research, 132-135.

Frieze, Irene, Esther Sales, and Christine Smith (1991), "Considering the Social Context in Gender Research," *Psychology of Women Quarterly*, 15 (September), 371-392.

Gardner, Meryl Paula (1985), "Mood States and Consumer Behavior: A Critical Review," *Journal of Consumer Research*, 12 (December), 281-300.

_____ and Marion Vandersteel (1984), "The Consumer's Mood: An Important Situational Variable," in *Advances in Consumer Research*, Vol. 11, ed. Thomas C. Kinnear, Ann Arbor, MI: Association for Consumer Research, 525-529.

Greenberg, Jeff and Tom Pyszczynski (1986), "Persistent High Self-Focus After Failure and Low Self-Focus After Success: The Depressive Self-Focusing Style," *Journal of Personality and Social Psychology*, 50 (May), 1039-1044.

Hirschman, Elizabeth C. and Morris B. Holbrook (1982), "Hedonic Consumption: Emerging Concepts, Methods and Propositions," *Journal of Marketing*, 46 (Summer), 92-101.

Holbrook, Morris B. and Elizabeth C. Hirschman (1982), "The Experiential Aspects of Consumption: Consumer Fantasies, Feelings, and Fun," *Journal of Consumer Research*, 9 (September), 132-140.

Isen, Alice M. (1970), "Success, Failure, Attention and Reaction to Others: The Warm Glow of Success," *Journal of Personality and Social Psychology*, 15 (August), 294-301.

_____ (1984), "Toward Understanding the Role of Affect in Cognition," in *Handbook of Social Cognition*, ed. Robert Wyer, Jr. and Thomas Srull, Hillsdale, NJ: Lawrence Erlbaum, 179-236.

_____ (1985), "Asymmetry of Happiness and Sadness in Effects on Memory in Normal College Students," *Journal of Experimental Psychology: General*, 114 (September), 388-391.

_____ and Robert Patrick (1983), "The Effect of Positive Feelings on Risk-Taking: When the Chips are Down," *Organizational Behavior and Human Performance*, 31 (April), 194-202.

Kendall, Philip C. and Steven D. Hollon, eds. (1979), *Cognitive-behavioral Interventions: Theory, Research, and Procedures*, NY: Academic Press.

Langer, Judith (1983), "Treats and Luxuries: Marketing in Hard Times," *Marketing Review*, 38 (December/January), 31-37.

McCracken, Grant (1988) *The Long Interview*, Newbury Park, CA: Sage.

Mick, David Glen and Michelle DeMoss (1990), "To Me from Me: A Descriptive Phenomenology of Self-gifts," in *Advances in Consumer Research*, Vol. 17, ed. Marvin Goldberg et al., Provo, UT: Association for Consumer Research, 677-682.

Miles, Matthew B. and A. Michael Huberman (1984), *Qualitative Data Analysis: A Sourcebook of New Methods*, Beverly Hills, CA: Sage.

Mischel, Walter (1973), "Toward a Cognitive Social Learning Reconceptualization of Personality," *Psychological Review*, 80 (July), 252-283.

_____, Brian Coates, and Antonette Raskoff (1968), "Effects of Success and Failure on Self-gratification," *Journal of Personality and Social Psychology*, 10 (December), 381-390.

Morris, William N. and Nora P. Reilly (1987), "Toward the Self-regulation of Mood: Theory and Research," *Motivation and Emotion*, 11 (September), 215-249.

O'Guinn, Thomas C. and Ronald J. Faber (1989), "Compulsive Buying: A Phenomenological Approach," *Journal of Consumer Research*, 16 (September), 147-157.

Peterson, Robert A. and Matthew Sauber (1983), "A Mood Scale for Survey Research," in *AMA Educators' Proceedings*, ed. Patrick Murphy, Chicago, IL: American Marketing Association, 409-414.

Pyszczynski, Tom and Jeff Greenberg (1987), "Self-regulatory Preservation and the Depressive Self-focusing Style: A Self-awareness Theory of the Development and Maintenance of Depression," *Psychological Bulletin*, 102 (July), 122-138.

Scherer, Klaus R. (1986), "Emotion Experiences Across European Cultures: A Summary Statement," in *Experiencing Emotion: A Cross-Cultural Study*, ed. Klaus R. Scherer et al., Cambridge, England: Cambridge University Press, 173-189.

Schouten, John W. (1991), "Selves in Transition: Symbolic Consumption in Personal Rites of Passage and Identity Reconstruction," *Journal of Consumer Research*, 17 (March), 412-425.

Schwarz, Norbert and Gerald Clore (1983), "Mood, Misattribution, and Judgments of Well-being: Informative and Directive Functions of Affective States," *Journal of Personality and Social Psychology*, 45 (September), 513-523.

Sears, David O. (1986), "College Sophomores in the Laboratory: Influences of a Narrow Data Base on Social Psychology's View of Human Nature," *Journal of Personality and Social Psychology*, 51 (September), 515-530.

Simon, Herbert A. (1967), "Motivational and Emotional Controls of Cognition," *Psychological Review*, 74 (January), 29-39.

_____ (1982), "Affect and Cognition: Comments," in *Affect and Cognition*, ed. Margaret S. Clark and Susan T. Fiske, Hillsdale, NJ: Erlbaum, 333-342.

Swann, William B., Jr., Brett W. Pelham, and Douglas S. Krull (1989), "Agreeable Fancy or Disagreeable Truth? Reconciling Self-enhancement and Self-verification," *Journal of Personality and Social Psychology*, 57 (November), 782-791.

Thompson, Craig J., William B. Locander, and Howard R. Pollio (1989), "Putting Consumer Experience Back into Consumer Research: The Philosophy and Method of Existential-Phenomenology," *Journal of Consumer Research*, 16 (September), 133-146.

Tompkins, Silvan S. (1970), "Affect as the Primary Motivational System," in *Feelings and Emotions*, ed. Magda B. Arnold, NY: Academic Press, 101-110.

Underwood, Bill, Bert S. Moore, and D. L. Rosenhan (1973), "Affect and Self-Gratification," *Developmental Psychology*, 8 (March), 209-214.

Valle, Ronald and Mark King (1978), "An Introduction to Existential-Phenomenological Thought in Psychology," in *Existential-Phenomenological Alternatives for Psychology*, ed. Ronald Valle and Mark King, New York: Oxford University Press, 6-17.

Venkatraman, Meera P. and Deborah J. MacInnis (1985), "The Epistemic and Sensory Exploratory Behaviors of Hedonic and Cognitive Consumers," in *Advances in Consumer Research*, Vol. 12, ed. Elizabeth C. Hirschman and Morris B. Holbrook, Provo, UT: Association for Consumer Research, 102-107.

Weinberg, Peter and Wolfgang Gothwald (1982), "Impulsive Consumer Buying as a Result of Emotions," *Journal of Business Marketing*, 10 (March), 43-57.

Wessman, Alden E. and David F. Ricks (1966), *Mood and Personality*, New York: Holt, Rinehart & Winston.

Westbrook, Robert A. (1980), "Intrapersonal Affective Influences on Consumer Satisfaction with Products," *Journal of Consumer Research*, 7 (June), 49-54.

Wicklund, Robert A. (1975), "Objective Self-Awareness," in *Advances in Experimental Social Psychology*, Vol. 8, ed. Leonard Berkowitz, Orlando, FL: Academic Press, 233-275.

Wood, Joanne V., Judith A. Saltzberg, and Lloyd A. Goldsamt (1990), "Does Affect Induce Self-focused Attention?" *Journal of Personality and Social Psychology*, 58 (May), 899-908.

Wood, Joanne V., Judith A. Saltzberg, John M. Neale, Arthur A. Stone, and Tracy B. Rachmiel (1990), "Self-focused Attention, Coping Responses, and Distressed Mood in Everyday Life," *Journal of Personality and Social Psychology*, 58 (June), 1027-1036.

Young, Melissa Martin (1991), "Males, Females, and Possession Disposition," in *Gender and Consumer Behavior*, ed. Janeen Arnold Costa, Salt Lake City, UT: University of Utah Printing Service, 105-114.

Zajonc, Robert B. (1984), "On the Primacy of Affect," *American Psychologist*, 39 (February), 117-23.

Zillmann, Dolf (1979), *Hostility and Aggression*, Hillsdale, NJ: Lawrence Erlbaum.

_____ (1988), "Mood Management: Using Entertainment to Full Advantage," in *Communication, Social Cognition and Affect*, ed. Lewis Donohew et al., Hillsdale, NJ: Lawrence Erlbaum, 147-171.

_____ and Jennings Bryant (1985), "Affect, Mood and Emotion as Determinants of Selective Exposure," in *Selective Exposure to Communication*, ed. Dolf Zillmann and Jennings Bryant, Hillsdale, NJ: Lawrence Erlbaum, 157-190.

Mood Effects in Consumer Behavior: A Unifying Theme
Ronald C. Goodstein, University of California, Los Angeles

INTRODUCTION

An accepted principle in our field is that both affective and cognitive reactions to marketing stimuli influence consumer behavior. In recent years Zajonc and Markus (1982) challenged consumer researchers to consider both types of reactions in understanding consumers. Since that time researchers have investigated many different aspects of affect and how they influence attitudes and behavior. For instance, studies have examined how feelings (e.g., Aaker and Stayman 1989; Edell and Burke 1987), moods (e.g., Batra 1986; Kahn and Isen 1993), general affect (e.g., Machleit, Allen, and Madden 1993), and attitude transfer (e.g., MacKenzie, Lutz, and Belch 1986) impact attention, persuasion, and behavior. Unfortunately, one cannot make generalized conclusions about the influence of affect on behavior because the findings in these areas often disagree. The three investigations of mood presented in this session provide a good example of this conflict in that they all come to different conclusions about mood's effect on consumer behavior.

The paper by Hadjimarcou and Marks (1993) conceptualizes mood as a *pre-existing state* that subjects bring to the ad processing domain. They believe that "the overriding goal of people while in a negative mood is to use any means possible to elevate their mood." This mood management perspective is based on the premise that consumers in a negative mood will be motivated to process ad information in hopes of improving their current mood. Motivation will be reflected by higher evaluations of the advertised product, relative to those in a positive mood. Those in a positive mood will be less motivated to process the information, and their evaluations will be less strongly influenced by their mood. The authors find that evaluations of a "feel-good" (mood elevating) product are more favorable for subjects in a negative mood relative to those in a positive mood, supporting the mood management hypothesis. This indicates deeper processing for subjects in a negative mood.

The experimental work presented by Kellaris and Mantel (1993) views mood as an *affective reaction* to an advertisement. The theoretical approach is similar to that proposed by Batra (1986) in that "ads are not merely liked or disliked; they also generate moods and make us feel a certain way." Using time perceptions as an indicator of processing intensity, they find that for women "time does not necessarily fly when they are having fun." That is, more intensive processing (i.e., longer) was associated with positive moods than with negative moods for female participants. This evidence counters the traditional mood preservation hypotheses (Isen 1989, cited in Kellaris and Mantel 1993)[1] which predict that subjects in a positive mood will avoid processing in order to maintain their current, positive mood state.

Finally, Kacen (1993) conceptualizes moods as emotional states that are *precursors to further activities and behaviors* directed toward managing the mood. This work provides an in-depth, phenomenological perspective of individuals' experiences of mood and the behaviors associated with moods. The methodology employed is unstructured depth interviews with 12 subjects which were transcribed, coded, and categorized. The findings indicate that negative moods are managed by refocusing attention on new activities, while positive moods are managed by either not refocusing attention or by engaging in mood congruent activities. Here, the answer to whether positive versus negative moods motivate more intensive processing is, "it depends." These results agree with the mood management discussion offered by Isen (1993) in that negative moods motivate consumers to refocus attention and positive moods will either motivate or fail to motivate refocusing attention depending on the affect associated with the new activity.

In summary, the papers presented in this session agree that feelings (moods) are primary motivators of behavior (cf. Tompkins 1970), but they disagree on whether moods are pre-existing states or reactions to stimuli. The also disagree on the exact nature of the relationship between mood and behavior. Rather than providing a detailed critique of each of the papers, this paper investigates whether these disparate findings can be integrated within a single framework. My discussion will attempt to reconcile these differences by emphasizing the importance of the source of the mood, i.e., its cause. While other frameworks might be used to explain this phenomenon, and while acknowledging that the relationship between moods and behavior is quite complex, the goal here is to offer one idea for simplifying the relationship.

THE DEBATE IN PSYCHOLOGY

That moods affect behavior is very clear, the question that remains is how they affect behavior. Mackie and Worth (1989, 1991) show that people are motivated to prolong a positive mood and therefore, have little motivation to process additional information. This may either be due to the fact that refocusing attention risks loss of the positive mood state or that the complex memory structures associated with positive moods allow little capacity for additional processing (Mackie and Worth 1989). Regardless of why, this research concludes that positive moods discourage processing of incoming information.

Other research in the domain, however, makes the opposite conclusion. Happy, positive moods are more likely to encourage processing of persuasive messages (Janis, Kaye, and Kirschner 1965). Further, when the mood evoked from stimulus processing is positive (cf. Batra 1986), people are more likely to approach that stimulus further (e.g., Fiske 1982; Zajonc 1980). Yet, current research again indicates that positive affect (mood) is accompanied by the use of more heuristic (versus systematic) processing strategies (Forgas and Bower 1987).

The debate also occurs in the realm of negative moods and affect. When the affect associated with a stimulus is negative, individuals are more likely to avoid further processing (Zajonc 1980). This is true even when the affect is evoked automatically upon categorizing the stimulus (Fiske 1982). Other psychologists find that negative affect (mood) motivates more extensive processing since people are compelled to terminate negative moods (Isen

---

[1] Isen has traditionally been cited for initiating support for the mood preservation hypothesis. In recent discussions, however, Isen (1993) has stated that this is an incorrect attribution to her work. In fact, positive moods may give rise to more creative and flexible processing of new, positively valanced material (Kahn and Isen 1993). When presented with negatively valanced material, consumers may ignore the information in order to avoid negative thinking, especially when in a positive mood (Kahn and Isen 1993). Although this latter statement agrees with the mood preservation hypothesis, note that this is predicted only for negatively valanced material. It is inconsistent to say that subjects in a positive mood will *always* avoid processing (mood preservation); it is more consistent to say they will avoid processing if the affect related to that processing is negative.

1985). People inhibit the continuation of sad (negative) moods by engaging in mood elevating behaviors (refocusing, Cialdini, Kenrick, and Baumann 1981).

THE DEBATE IN CONSUMER BEHAVIOR

It is hardly surprising to find that the debate over mood effects exists in the domain of consumer behavior. For instance, negative moods often create situations that many consumers wish to avoid (Batra and Stayman 1990). Many consumers increase their shopping (product search), purchasing, and consuming of products in order to terminate a negative mood (e.g., Churchill and Wertz 1985; O'Guinn and Faber 1989). Mood-ameliorating products appear to be approached more often by consumers experiencing a negative mood (Gardner 1992). However, negative moods evoked during a consumption experience are sometimes likely to inhibit processing. For example, negatively valanced schema affect appears to curtail ad processing (Goodstein 1993).

In the consumer domain positive moods (affect) have been associated with more flexible and sustained information processing (e.g., Aaker, Stayman, and Hagerty 1986; Edell and Burke 1987; Goodstein 1993). Positive affect associated with unconditioned stimuli also leads to more attention paid to a conditioned brand (Janiszewski and Warlop 1993). Finally, positive moods evoked by advertisements tend to lead to greater processing and persuasion (Batra 1986; Batra and Ray 1986; Edell and Burke 1987). Alternately, consumer research illustrates that positive moods may inhibit processing. This may be due to mood-protection mechanisms (Swinyard 1993) such as biased (heuristic) processing of incoming material (Batra and Stayman 1990) or avoidance of cognitive elaboration (Isen and Levin 1972).

ONE POSSIBLE RESOLUTION

Although moods can be differentiated along many dimensions such as valence, intensity, source, etc., I believe that one way to unify many of the findings discussed in consumer research is to investigate the source of mood more rigorously. In particular, I suggest that moods formed prior to exposure (pre-states) are qualitatively unlike moods formed during stimulus exposure (reactions). The primary distinction between the two is that pre-states are generalized affect without focus and reactions are object oriented (cf. Clore and Ortony 1983).

As a pre-state, moods function as general, nonspecific positive or negative input (Frijda 1986). As a reaction, moods evolve with specific signalling functions about particular environmental occurrences (Frijda 1986). Stated more simply, mood has been conceptualized as an affective *predisposition* that is unrelated to the stimulus at hand (cf. Gardner 1985). Alternately, mood has also been conceptualized as an affective *reaction* with a known cause, namely the stimulus at hand (e.g., Batra and Stayman 1990).

I believe that consumers are motivated to achieve and maintain a positive mood state regardless of its source. The general effect of moods on processing, however, will depend directly on the source of the mood. When the mood's source is a predisposition, then processing of an additional stimulus (e.g., an advertisement) is likely to be avoided to sustain the current mood. When the mood's source is a reaction, then processing is likely to continue since the stimulus itself is the source of the positive affect. Conversely, when the predisposition is negative, consumers will process the stimulus in order that they might achieve a more pleasant affective state. When the source is negative, they are likely to cease processing of the current stimulus for the same reason. Let me use the papers presented in this session to illustrate these propositions.

Hadjimarcou and Marks manipulate mood by having subjects read either a happy or sad story before exposure to an ad for a "feel good" product. The study reveals that ad processing was more intense for the subjects that read the sad story (negative mood). Apparently processing the ad allowed subjects the possibility of achieving a more positive mood. Those reading the happy story (positive mood) processed the ad in a more cursory manner in order to sustain their prior mood.

Although Kacen did not manipulate moods, she did have subjects recall a positive and negative mood experience. After evoking this general mood, she then asks her respondents to identify behaviors used to manage their moods. In the negative case, most respondents tend to engage in activities meant to alter their moods in a more positive direction. In the positive case they tend to either continue in current activities or engage in mood congruent activities. Presumably, the desire to end in a more positive state was the commonalty, perhaps explaining why many similar behaviors (e.g., shopping, eating) are described as relating to both subjects in positive and negative moods.

Kellaris and Mantel manipulate mood by including either positive or negative background music in a radio advertisement. The mood evoked is measured by answering the question, "The ad made me feel..." Clearly, the mood is an affective *reaction* to the ad. Recall that more intensive processing was associated with positive moods than with negative moods for female participants. When the source evoked positive affect it was approached to maintain the positive experience, when negative it was avoided in order to terminate the negative mood.

The distinction between moods as a predisposition versus as a reaction can be used to explain more general affective consequences in consumer behavior as well. For instance, when moods are manipulated via an unrelated story (predisposition), subjects in a positive mood process ads seen later in a more heuristic, i.e., more cursory, manner (Batra and Stayman 1990). Similarly, subjects viewing a more interesting (positively evaluated) television program allocate less attention to an ad embedded in that program (Soldow and Principe 1981). These studies demonstrate that consumers have little motivation to process persuasive stimuli when they are already in a positive mood. Negative predispositions have received much less attention in the consumer literature.

Positive affect generated as a reaction to a stimulus motivates more extensive processing. Upbeat and warm feelings evoked in response to an ad yield greater ad involvement (Edell and Burke 1987). Positive schema triggered affect for advertisements is related to greater motivation to process the ad (Goodstein 1993). Negative stimulus generated affect reduces ad processing (Edell and Burke 1987; Goodstein 1993).

In summary, consumers are motivated to attain positive affective states and avoid negative affective states. This holds regardless of whether the mood state is developed *prior to* or *during* stimulus exposure. However, the means of achieving the desired state depends upon whether the mood was pre-existing or was a reaction to the stimulus. To sustain a positive mood developed prior to stimulus exposure may mean limiting processing of incoming information. Yet, increasing processing could prolong a positive mood if the stimulus was the source of the mood. Likewise, a consumer motivated to terminate a negative mood is apt to process a new stimulus if the mood was pre-existing. However, a consumer is likely to limit processing if the stimulus was the cause of the negative mood. This proposition can integrate the findings of the three studies presented in this session, and might be an interesting area for future research.

REFERENCES

Aaker, David A. and Douglas M. Stayman (1989), "What Mediates the Emotional Response to Advertising? The Case of Warmth," in P. Cafferata & A.M. Tybout (eds.), Cognitive and Affective Responses to Advertising, Lexington, MA: Lexington Books, 287-303.

_____, _____, and Michael R. Hagerty (1986), "Warmth in Advertising: Measurement, Impact, and Sequence Effects," Journal of Consumer Research, 12 (March), 365-381.

Batra, Rajeev (1986), "Affective Advertising: Role, Process, and Measurement," in R.A. Peterson, W.D. Hoyer, & W.R. Wilson (eds.), The Role of Affect in Consumer Behavior, Lexington, MA: Lexington Books, 53-85.

_____, and Michael L. Ray (1986), "Affective Responses Mediating Acceptance of Advertising," *Journal of Consumer Research*, 13 (September), 234-249.

_____, and Douglas M. Stayman (1990), "The Role of Moods in Advertising Effectiveness," *Journal of Consumer Research*, 17 (September), 203-214.

Churchill, Scott D. and Frederick J. Wertz (1985), "An Introduction to Phenomenological Psychology for Consumer Research: Historical, Conceptual, and Methodological Foundations," in *Advances in Consumer Research*, E. Hirschman & M. Holbrook (eds.), 12, Provo, UT: Association for Consumer Research, 550-555.

Cialdini, Robert B., Douglas T. Kenrick, and Donald J. Baumann (1981), "Transgression and Altruism: A Case for Hedonism," *Journal of Experimental Social Psychology*, 9 (November), 502-516.

Clore, Gerald and Andrew Ortony (1983), "The Cognitive Causes of Emotion," paper presented at the Nags Head Conference on Emotion, Stress, and Conflict, Nags Head, NC.

Edell, Julie A. and Marian C. Burke (1987), "The Power of Feelings in Understanding Advertising Effects," *Journal of Consumer Research*, 14 (December), 421-433.

Fiske, Susan T. (1982), "Schema-Triggered Affect: Applications to Social Perception," in *Affect and Cognition: The 17th Annual Carnegie Symposium on Cognition*, Margaret S. Clark and Susan T. Fiske, eds., Hillsdale, N.J.: Lawrence Erlbaum Associates, 55-78.

Forgas, Joseph P. and Gordon H. Bower (1987), "Mood Effects on Person-Perception Judgments," *Journal of Personality and Social Psychology*, 53 (1), 53-60.

Frijda, Nico H. (1986), *The Emotions*, London, England: Cambridge University Press.

Gardner, Meryl P. (1985), "Mood States and Consumer Behavior: A Critical Review," *Journal of Consumer Research*, 12 (December), 281-300.

_____ (1992), "Responses to Emotional and Informational Appeals: The Moderating Role of Context-Induced Mood States," in *Advertising and Consumer Psychology*, E. Clark, T. Brock, & D. Stewart (eds.), Hillsdale, NJ: Lawrence Erlbaum.

Goodstein, Ronald C. (1993), "Category-based Applications and Extensions in Advertising: Motivating More Extensive Ad Processing," *Journal of Consumer Research*, 20 (June), 87-99.

Hadjimarcou, John and Lawrence J. Marks (1993), "An Examination of the Effects of Context-Induced Mood States on the Evaluation of a 'Feel-Good' Product: The Moderating Role of Product Type and the Consistency Effects Model," paper presented at The Association for Consumer Research Conference, Nashville, TN.

Alice, M. Isen (1985), "Asymmetry of Happiness and Sadness in Effects on Memory in Normal College Students," *Journal of Experimental Psychology: General*, 114 (September), 388-391.

_____ (1989), "Some ways in Which Affect Influences Cognitive Processes: Implications for Advertising and Consumer Behavior," in P. Cafferata & A.M. Tybout (eds.), *Cognitive and Affective Responses to Advertising*, Lexington, MA: Lexington Books, 91-117.

_____ (1993), "Comments during Discussion of 'Mood Effects,'" competitive paper session at The Association for Consumer Research Conference, Nashville, TN.

_____ and Paula F. Levin (1972), "The Effect of Feeling Good on Helping: Cookies and Kindness," *Journal of Personality and Social Psychology*, 21 (3), 384-388.

Janis, Irving L., Donald Kaye, and Paul Kirschner (1965), "Facilitating Effects of 'Eating While Reading' on Responsiveness to Persuasive Communication," *Journal of Personality and Social Psychology*, 1 (2), 181-186.

Janiszewski, Chris and Luk Warlop (1993), "The Influence of Classical Conditioning Procedures on Subsequent Attention to the Conditioned Brand," *Journal of Consumer Research*, 20 (September), 171-189.

Kacen (1993), Phenomenological Insights into Mood and Mood-Related Consumer Behaviors," paper presented at The Association for Consumer Research Conference, Nashville, TN.

Kahn, Barbara E. and Alice M. Isen (1993), "The Influence of Positive Affect on Variety Seeking among Safe, Enjoyable Products," Journal of Consumer Research, 20 (September), 257-270.

Kellaris, James J. and Susan Powell Mantel (1993), "The Influence of Mood and Gender on Consumers' Time Perceptions," paper presented at The Association for Consumer Research Conference, Nashville, TN.

Machleit, Karen A., Chris T. Allen, and Thomas J. Madden (1993), "The Mature Brand and Brand Interest: An Alternative Consequence of Ad-Evoked Affect," *Journal of Marketing*, 57 (October), 72-81.

MacInnis, Deborah J., Christine Moorman, and Bernard J. Jaworski (1991), "Enhancing and Measuring Consumers' Motivation, Opportunity, and Ability to Process Brand Information From Ads," *Journal of Marketing*, 55 (October), 32-53.

MacKenzie, Scott B., Richard J. Lutz, and George E. Belch (1986), "The Role of Attitude toward the Ad as a Mediator of Advertising Effectiveness: A Test of Competing Explanations," *Journal of Marketing Research*, 23 (May), 130-143.

Mackie, Diane M. and Leila T. Worth (1989), " Processing Deficits and the Mediation of Positive Affect in Persuasion," *Journal of Personality and Social Psychology*, 57 (1), 27-40.

_____ and _____ (1991), "Feeling Good, but Not Thinking Straight: The Impact of Positive Mood on Persuasion," in Emotion and Social Judgment, J.P. Forgas (ed.), Oxford: Pergamon, 201-219.

O'Guinn, Thomas C. and Ronald J. Faber (1989), "Compulsive Buying: A Phenomenological Approach," *Journal of Consumer Research*, 16 (September), 147-157.

Soldow, Gary F. and Victor Principe (1981), "Response to Commercials as a Function of Program Context," *Journal of Advertising Research*, 21 (2), 59-65.

William R. Swinyard (1993), "The Effects of Mood, Involvement, and Quality of Store Experience on Shopping Intentions," *Journal of Consumer Research*, 20 (September), 271-280.

Tompkins, Silvan S. (1970), "Affect as the Primary Motivational System," in *Feelings and Emotions*, M.B. Arnold (ed.), New York: Academic Press, 101-110.

Zajonc, Robert B. (1980), "Feeling and Thinking: Preferences Need No Inferences," *American Psychologist*, 35, 151-175.

_____ and Hazel Markus (1982), "Affective and Cognitive Factors in Preferences," *Journal of Consumer Research*, 9 (September), 123-131.

The Effects of the New Food Labels on Consumer Decision Making
Gary T. Ford American University

In December 1992, the Food and Drug Administration (FDA) announced new regulations governing food labels, which provide consumers with much more information about a food's nutritional value, standardize adjectival descriptors such as "light" or "low in sodium" and place strict limitations on health claims about a food and a specific disease, such as between calcium and osteoporosis. The new labels affect over 300,000 consumer products and represent the most sweeping changes ever made in the type of nutrition and health information that both must be, and cannot be, provided to consumers. In order to begin understanding the effects of the new labels, this special session included three empirical papers concerning the effects of the new food labels and the relationship between knowledge of diet/disease relationships and behavior.

Alan Levy, Chief of the Consumer Studies Branch at the Food and Drug Administration, presented a paper titled, "Antecedents of Dietary Consumption Behavior." The paper was based on three-day dietary intake of a nationally representative sample of 1,894 American consumers. A LISREL modelling approach was used to investigate the relationship between food intake and cognitive variables. Results indicate that awareness of diet disease relationships, beliefs that diets can affect one's health, and concern about specific dietary risk factors are the most important mediators of the effects of SES and health status on food intake.

Gary T. Ford, Manoj Hastak and Anusree Mitra, all of American University and Debra J. Ringold of the University of Baltimore, presented "Health Claims in the Presence of Consistent and Inconsistent Nutrient Information: A Laboratory Investigation." The objective of this study was to determine whether health claims concerning diet-disease relationships interact with or are independent of subsequent processing of detailed nutrition information. A two ("Does your heart good" health claim vs. no health claim) by two (nutrition information which is consistent with the claim vs. inconsistent) by two (absolute vs. adjectival nutritional format) factorial design was used. Key results indicate health claims and nutrition information have independent effects, and that respondents can detect when a health claim is partially contradicted by detailed information on the product label. Products that make health claims are rated significantly more "heart healthy" than those without the claim regardless of the nutrition information provided or the format used.

Sandra Burke of Georgetown University presented "The Case of the Implied Nutrient Claim: Can Context Influence the Meaning of the Ingredient Statement." The purpose of this pilot study was to investigate consumer reactions to presentation format and symbol usage in conjunction with ingredient statements. A three (starburst symbol vs. banner symbol vs. no symbol) by two (high vs. low knowledge of the importance of the ingredient for good nutrition) design was used. No statistically significant differences were found on the key dependent measures of overall brand evaluation and attribute importance.

Alan Andreasen of Georgetown University provided discussant remarks.

Assessing Viewer Judgement of Advertisements and Vehicles: Scale Development and Validation

Tammi S. Feltham, Wilfrid Laurier University[1]

ABSTRACT

Lack of a common scale in marketing communications research hinders comparability among studies. This paper reports the development of a theory driven, bi-polar adjective scale, the Persuasive Discourse Inventory (PDI), which captures the fundamental elements of ads and/or media vehicles. If used, this inventory would foster greater comparability across studies.

INTRODUCTION

Marketing communications researchers use various scales to describe the stimuli in their work. Examples include descriptions of ad content as "image" or "reason-why" (Aaker and Brown 1972), "humorous" or "non-humorous" (Murphy, Cunningham and Wilcox 1979), "thinking" or "feeling" (Golden and Johnson 1983), "cognitive" or "affective" (McClung, Park and Sauer 1985), "emotional" or "factual" (Liu and Stout 1987), and "happy" or "sad" (Goldberg and Gorn 1987). Examples of vehicle editorial environment descriptions include "prestigious" or "expert" (Aaker and Brown 1972), "drama" or "game show" (Wise, Brown, and Cox 1975), "documentary", "action/adventure", or "situation comedy" (Murphy et al. 1979), "cognitive" or "affective" (Park and McClung 1986), and "happy" or "sad" (Goldberg and Gorn 1987). Researchers and practitioners cannot arrive at reliable conclusions about the theory under investigation when the descriptions of the stimuli used vary from study to study. This non-uniformity leads to a situation where conclusions as to the effect of particular stimuli (for example: humorous ads) must be based on an assumption that the stimuli used in numerous investigations are comparable.

Diverse measures of stimuli in marketing communication research raise several problems. Firstly, when discussing the effect that a characteristic of a stimulus (i.e., humorous ads) has on a theoretical measure, it is difficult to know whether discrepant findings between studies are due to different measures or different behaviours. When different measures are used, how does a researcher know that the same phenomenon has been tested from one study to the next? Secondly, a problem may arise when measures employ single-item scales (and do not report reliability and validity testing results). Single-item scales lack richness of description, may not adequately capture the characteristics of the ads or vehicles, and may have low reliability. Thirdly, diverse measures obscure theoretical insights and explanations which might otherwise become apparent if all studies used a common method for describing and measuring ads and vehicles. Fourthly, current scales are descriptive rather than theoretically based. Thus a general, valid, multi-item, theory-based scale to measure ads and vehicles is needed.

To address these problems, this article develops and validates the Persuasive Discourse Inventory (PDI). This inventory contributes to marketing communication research by providing a standard classification structure for ad and vehicle stimuli which is comprehensive in nature. The PDI is based on the theory of *Rhetoric* (Aristotle 1984), wherein Aristotle discussed a tri-partite concept of a persuasive message. The three elements of the PDI, *ethos*, *pathos*, and *logos*, provide a common ground and basis of understanding across many disciplines. The PDI may provide comparability among studies, flexibility across diverse applications, quantitative measurability, and consistency to marketing communications research.

DEFINING PERSUASIVE DISCOURSE

In the *Rhetoric*, Aristotle stated: "Of the proofs which are furnished through the instrumentality of the speech itself, ... there are three kinds, one residing in the character [*ethos*] of the speaker, the second in the feelings and emotions [*pathos*] produced in the audience, and the third, which is proof in its proper sense, logical, direct proof [*logos*], in the speech itself" (1867, Book I, Chapter II, ll. 1356^{a}1-4).

There is support for using Aristotle's writings as a basis for studying persuasive messages: "Aristotle discussed the processes of attitude change at considerable length.... His distinction, in the *Rhetoric*, between ethos, pathos, and logos as alternative processes for changing attitudes has been frequently elaborated in subsequent centuries" (McGuire 1969, p. 200). For example, extensive work on the three components was undertaken by the Yale group (Hovland, Janis and Kelley 1953; Hovland et al. 1957; Hovland and Weiss 1951).

The Persuasive Discourse perspective, as developed in this paper, is based on the theory of *Rhetoric* (Aristotle 1984). When applied to marketing stimuli, the theoretical components of the PDI (*ethos*, *pathos*, and *logos*) provide a thorough description of the constituent properties of the ads and vehicles used.

Ethos Appeals

In Aristotle's *Rhetoric*, *ethos* refers to "persuasive appeals that concentrate on the source rather than the message" (McGuire 1969, p. 200). The source effects literature has investigated issues which fall within the definition of *ethos*. Source characteristics research deals with the credibility and attractiveness of the spokesperson in a persuasive message. Attributions about the characteristics of a source can influence evaluations of an advertising message (positive correlation) (Chaiken 1979; Cooper and Croyle 1984; Percy 1983). Source credibility effects for vehicles have been found to be consistent with the effects found for ads (Andreoli and Worchel 1978; Wegner et al. 1981).

Pathos Appeals

Studies of advertising effects which have examined emotional or affective appeals fall within the definition of *pathos*. Several advertising and media studies have found an impact of mood states on the formation of consumer attitudes (Clark 1982; Isen 1984; Isen et al. 1978). Goldberg and Gorn (1987) defined vehicles as "happy" or "sad" and found that those watching the happy program rated the commercials as more effective, and had better recall than those watching the sad program. Research on the processes involved in emotional advertising has focused on the classification of emotion (Holbrook and O'Shaughnessy 1984; Stout and Leckenby 1986), and how emotion influences the persuasion process (Mitchell 1983, 1986a, 1986b; Mitchell and Olson 1981; Ray and Batra 1983).

---

[1] The author thanks S. J. Arnold, Queen's University, and the anonymous ACR reviewers for their insightful comments; and the Wilfrid Laurier University Post-Doctoral Research Fellowship for financial assistance.

Logos Appeals

Plato used *logos* in the sense of giving an account, and Aristotle used it as reason, or rationality (Peters 1967, p. 111). The philosophical dictionary terms used to define *logos* include account, reason, definition, and rational faculty (Peters 1967, p. 110). *Logos* appeals have been defined as reasoned discourse by Knepprath and Clevenger (1965, p. 152) who state that reasoned discourse "is a name given to the manner of putting words and ideas together in such a way that conclusions seem to follow." Cronkhite (1964, p. 16) defined a logical argument as the induction of audience perception of a relationship between concepts. McGuire (1969, p.202) considered as logical "those appeals which argue for the truth of a given belief by presenting evidence." In investigating rational ads, Pallak, Murroni, and Koch (1983, pp. 138-139) found that positive "product/message-oriented thoughts" were predictive of product evaluations. A *logos* appeal, whether in a vehicle or an ad, appears to provide evidence or information about a concept (*i.e.*, a product) from which a consumer can form and evaluate beliefs.

Separability of Persuasive Discourse Constructs

While *ethos* appeals concentrate on the source of the message, *pathos* and *logos* appeals persuade by focusing attention on the message content (Rosenthal 1966). While marketing studies commonly examine the previously defined concepts of *pathos* and *logos* as opposite ends of a continuum (Goldberg & Gorn 1987; Golden & Johnson 1983; Holbrook 1978; McClung et al. 1985; Park & McClung 1986), there is precedent for treating these constructs separately. These factors most likely do not represent two ends of a continuum; they are two distinct dimensions (Knepprath and Clevenger 1965; McGuire 1969; Percy 1983; Pallak et al. 1983).

There is also precedent for treating *logos* and *ethos* (as defined in the PDI) as separable. Pallak et al. (1983) found that source effects due to the expertness or attractiveness of the communicator had no significant effect on the evaluation of the product when the message was rationally based. It seems that "students in the rational-message conditions thought about the content of the message," as opposed to thinking about the communicator (p. 135). They concluded that the rational advertisements were processed systematically, based on the message content.

PERSUASIVE DISCOURSE SCALE DEVELOPMENT[2]

Stimuli selection

A three part, bi-polar adjective, Persuasive Discourse scale was developed based on the above definitions of *ethos*, *pathos*, and *logos*. Television was chosen as the medium for scale development and validation, although it is assumed that the final PDI will apply to radio and print studies (confirmation awaits further testing). Multiple scenes from a single movie were used for the program stimuli because of the wide range of *ethos*, *pathos*, and *logos* found in dramatic presentations (while attempting to decrease the variability of characters and settings across stimuli conditions, *i.e.*, hold extraneous characteristics constant). Commercials considered for the study were chosen from the product categories of wrist watches, candy, photography equipment, coffee and pain relievers. The criterion for choosing the commercials was that the advertised products be of interest to an adult population. In addition, no commercial had been aired in the previous five years and no commercial was distinguished by any unusual exposure history.

---

[2]For complete results and tables, contact the author.

Item generation

Once a pool of commercials and film clips was gathered, scale items were generated. The objective was to develop a valid and reliable scale for differentiating vehicles and advertisements on the dimensions of *ethos*, *pathos*, and *logos*. Items were generated from a lexicon of philosophical terms (Peters 1967), an encyclopedia of philosophy (Kerferd 1967), speech communication literature (Cronkhite 1964; Knepprath and Clevenger 1965; Rosenthal 1966), and consultation with colleagues for each of the *ethos*, *pathos*, and *logos* dimensions.

Data collection

A questionnaire was developed from the item pool using seven point bi-polar adjective scales. The resulting questionnaire was administered to a convenience sample of nineteen adult volunteers (mean: 42.3 years, median: 35 years, range: 24 to 72 years). Volunteers were told they would see a series of movie clips and television commercials which they would be asked to rate on the basis of the scale items listed on the questionnaire. Procedurally, they viewed a video stimulus, the tape was paused, and they then filled out the scale items for that stimulus. The next clip or ad was played, the tape paused, and so on through sixteen stimuli (five movie clips, then eleven ads).

Measure Purification

The pool of seventeen persuasive discourse scale items were subjected to an internal validity analysis, based on performance across the sixteen media and ad stimuli. Individual scale items were examined for correlation to total score for each related component variable, i.e., E1, E2, E3, E4, E5 to Ethos (summation of *ethos* scores on items E1 through E5); L1, L2, L3, L4, L5, L6 to Logos (same procedure as Ethos); and P1, P2, P3, P4, P5, P6 to Pathos (same procedure as Ethos). The objective was to establish that each item contributed to the same component concept, "thereby establishing the homogeneity or internal consistency of the component variables" (Seymour and Lessne 1984, p. 813). The average correlation matrix revealed that scale items had item-to-total correlation coefficients ranging from 0.63 to 0.91.

While the subscales of the PDI (Ethos, Pathos, Logos) measure three separate and distinct aspects of the test stimuli as shown by item-to-total correlations, it was discovered that the *ethos* of the ads tended to follow the *logos* levels. The nature of advertising would support a positive correlation between Logos and Ethos; if a person/message is seen as convincing, informative, and logical, then it is also seen as believable, credible, and trustworthy.

An examination of the PDI scale scores for each program and ad revealed that each subscale component (Ethos, Pathos, and Logos) differentiated among the sixteen ad and program test stimuli. The scores for Ethos were distributed fairly evenly across the range of the Ethos subscale from 14.7 to 29.5 (possible range 5 to 35); *i.e.*, the test stimuli were perceived to vary in terms of their *ethos* content. Likewise, the scores for the Pathos subscale ranged from 13.2 to 33.4 (possible range 7 to 49), and the Logos subscale ranged from 16.7 to 33.2 (possible range 5 to 35).

The recommended measure of internal consistency of a set of items is provided by coefficient alpha. According to Churchill (1979, p. 68) it "*absolutely* should be the first measure one calculates to assess the quality of the instrument. . . . Thus, a low coefficient alpha indicates the sample of items performs poorly in capturing the construct which motivated the measure". Reliability analysis (coefficient alpha) was run for Ethos, Logos, and Pathos for each of the sixteen stimuli. The average coefficient alphas over the sixteen stimuli were 0.8903 for Ethos (range: 0.6092 to 0.9819), 0.8593 for Logos (range: 0.3994 to 0.9819), and 0.8215

Exhibit 1
Persuasive Discourse Inventory Questionnaire

Please check the box which you feel best describes the commercial you just saw. If you check a box nearest the word at either end, it means you think the commercial was very much like that word. If you check the box in the middle, it means that you think the commercial was not like either of the words.

not knowledgeable	☐ ☐ ☐ ☐ ☐ ☐ ☐	knowledgeable
not trustworthy	☐ ☐ ☐ ☐ ☐ ☐ ☐	trustworthy
is stimulating	☐ ☐ ☐ ☐ ☐ ☐ ☐	is not stimulating
rational	☐ ☐ ☐ ☐ ☐ ☐ ☐	not rational
is stirring	☐ ☐ ☐ ☐ ☐ ☐ ☐	is not stirring
unbelievable	☐ ☐ ☐ ☐ ☐ ☐ ☐	believable
does not reach out to me	☐ ☐ ☐ ☐ ☐ ☐ ☐	reaches out to me
not informative	☐ ☐ ☐ ☐ ☐ ☐ ☐	informative
touches me emotionally	☐ ☐ ☐ ☐ ☐ ☐ ☐	does not touch me emotionally
logical	☐ ☐ ☐ ☐ ☐ ☐ ☐	not logical
reliable	☐ ☐ ☐ ☐ ☐ ☐ ☐	unreliable
is not moving	☐ ☐ ☐ ☐ ☐ ☐ ☐	is moving
dependable	☐ ☐ ☐ ☐ ☐ ☐ ☐	undependable
affects my feelings	☐ ☐ ☐ ☐ ☐ ☐ ☐	does not affect my feelings
credible	☐ ☐ ☐ ☐ ☐ ☐ ☐	not credible
deals with facts	☐ ☐ ☐ ☐ ☐ ☐ ☐	does not deal with facts
is not exciting	☐ ☐ ☐ ☐ ☐ ☐ ☐	is exciting

---

for Pathos (range: 0.5915 to 0.9684). While Nunnally (1967, p. 226) suggests that increasing reliabilities beyond 0.80 is probably wasteful, using the correlation matrix and coefficient alpha scores, the PDI scale items were revised by dropping a poorly performing Logos item and replacing several poorly performing Pathos items with new items. Additional data was then collected.

Reliability assessment with new data

According to Churchill (1979), the next step in assessing reliability of a measure is to collect additional data because "coefficient alpha does not adequately estimate, . . . errors caused by factors external to the instrument, such as differences in testing situations and respondents over time" (p. 70). The second test consisted of seven commercials and three movie clips. Procedures were the same as in the first data collection period. The second test was conducted among volunteers from four introductory marketing classes (n= 25, 19, 15, and 20 respectively). To check for scale item order effects, the instrument items were ordered in two ways and both versions distributed equally in each session. An example of the instrument is found in Exhibit 1. The purpose of this test was to replicate and refine the scale items. The average correlation matrix (to examine item-to-total, inter-item, and cross-correlations) was calculated. Reliability analysis (coefficient alpha) was conducted on the three scales of Ethos, Pathos, and Logos. Examination of the two forms of the instrument for each of the sessions revealed no significant differences in mean responses due to scale item presentation order. Scale item order was, therefore, ignored in further analyses.

Examination of the average correlation matrix, summing over nine vehicles and ads (commercial one served to introduce participants to the task), revealed that the adjustments to the PDI scale items improved the subscale inter-item correlations, while retaining low cross-correlations among the Ethos, Pathos, and Logos scales. The average correlation of items-to-total for the Pathos scale was .79. The Ethos and Logos scale items' inter-item correlations fell from those recorded in earlier testing. However, the cross-correlations between Ethos and Logos also declined (desirable). The average correlation of items-to-total for the Ethos scale was .78. The average correlation of items-to-total for the Logos scale was .74.

To further examine the internal reliability of the Ethos, Pathos, and Logos subscales, coefficient alpha was calculated. Reliability scores averaged across nine stimuli were .83 for the Ethos scale (range: 0.6736 to 0.9167); .79 for the Logos scale (range: 0.5903 to 0.8893); and .89 for the Pathos scale (0.8173 to 0.9671). Coefficient alpha scores fell slightly for the Ethos and Logos subscales and improved for the Pathos subscale (note the previous adjustment of items and new sample of ads/programs rated). In general, the reliabilities are acceptable and stable across situations.

Additional replications were conducted with volunteers from an MBA marketing class (n = 15) and volunteers from a local choir (n = 7). These sessions supported the findings of the four introductory marketing sessions for a population with an older age range.

The final format of the PDI contains seventeen items; five for Ethos, five for Logos, and seven for Pathos (Exhibit 2).

CONCLUSIONS

This paper develops and validates a 7 point bi-polar adjective scale, the PDI, based on Aristotle's Rhetoric. The use of this multi-item, theoretically based scale allows for greater comparability, providing the potential for greater insight both within and across studies and for a common measurement standard for media research. Field tests in upcoming research projects are planned to further validate the scale.

In particular, these tests will examine the convergent and discriminant validity of the PDI scale to ensure that the scale is validly measuring the theoretical components of a persuasive communication. The development of the PDI to this point leaves certain questions unanswered. For example, does the PDI capture figurative elements of language in ads and programs, and executional dimensions such as vividness?

EXHIBIT 2
Persuasive Discourse Inventory

Ethos scale items: Ethos = E1 + E2 + E3 + E4 + E5 (range: 5 - 35)
    E1) unbelievable / believable
    E2) not credible / credible
    E3) not trustworthy / trustworthy
    E4) unreliable / reliable
    E5) undependable / dependable

Logos scale items: Logos = L1 + L2 + L3 + L4 + L5 (range: 5 - 35)
    L1) not rational / rational
    L2) not informative / informative
    L3) does not deal with facts / deals with facts
    L4) not knowledgeable / knowledgeable
    L5) not logical / logical

Pathos scale items: Pathos = P1 + P2 + P3 + P4 + P5 + P6 + P7 (range: 7 - 49)
    P1) does not affect my feelings / affects my feelings
    P2) does not touch me emotionally / touches me emotionally
    P3) is not stimulating / is stimulating
    P4) does not reach out to me / reaches out to me
    P5) is not stirring / is stirring
    P6) is not moving / is moving
    P7) is not exciting / is exciting

Note. This scale was developed as a seven point bi-polar adjective instrument. The scale may be broken into three constituent parts to measure the *ethos*, *logos*, or *pathos* content of a vehicle or an advertisement.

While each of the three subscales, Ethos, Pathos, and Logos can be used independently, the greatest potential benefit lies in using the entire PDI scale to choose the ads and programs used in research. With a more comprehensive characterization available, regardless of the theory being tested or the phenomenon under investigation, additional insights may materialize and some of the data limitations of current research may be avoided.

The PDI can provide additional control over ad and program stimuli used in many consumer studies. For example, the researcher could use the PDI to select ads with the characteristic of interest, high *pathos*, while measuring and controlling the levels of *ethos* and *logos*. A specific area which lends itself well to the use of the PDI is the influence of program context on advertising effectiveness. In this area, the issue of defining congruity between an ad and a program is important; the PDI would provide a standard definitional base for defining/matching congruent ads and programs.

REFERENCES

Aaker, David A. and Phillip K. Brown (1972), "Evaluating Vehicle Source Effects," *Journal of Advertising Research*, 12 (August), 11-16.

Andreoli, Virginia and Stephen Worchel (1978), "Effects of Media, Communicator, and Message Position on Attitude Change," *Public Opinion Quarterly*, 42 (Spring), 59-70.

Aristotle (1867), *Rhetoric*, trans. E. M. Cope, in *An Introduction to Aristotle's Rhetoric*, Cambridge: Macmillan and Co.

Aristotle (1984), *Rhetoric*, trans. W. Rhys Roberts, in *The Complete Works of Aristotle: The Revised Oxford Translation*, ed. Jonathan Barnes. Bollingen Series LXXI, 2. Princeton, New Jersey: Princeton University Press.

Chaiken, Shelly (1979), "Communicator Physical Attractiveness and Persuasion," *Journal of Personality and Social Psychology*, 37, 1387-1397.

Churchill, Gilbert A. Jr. (1979), "A Paradigm for Developing Better Measures of Marketing Constructs," *Journal of Marketing Research*, XVI (February), 64-73.

Clark, Margaret (1982), "A Role for Arousal in the Link Between Feeling States, Judgments, and Behavior," in *Affect and Cognition*, eds. Margaret Clark and Susan Fiske. Hillsdale, NJ: Erlbaum, 263-289.

Cooper, Joel and Robert T. Croyle (1984), "Attitudes and Attitude Change," *Annual Review of Psychology*, 35, 395-426.

Cronkhite, Gary Lynn (1964), "Logic, Emotion, and the Paradigm of Persuasion," *Quarterly Journal of Speech*, L, 13-18.

Goldberg, Marvin E. and Gerald J. Gorn (1987), "Happy and Sad TV Programs: How They Affect Reactions to Commercials," *Journal of Consumer Research*, 14 (December), 387-403.

Golden, Linda L. and Keren A. Johnson (1983), "The Impact of Sensory Preference and Thinking Versus Feeling Appeals on Advertising Effectiveness," in *Advances in Consumer Research, Volume X*, eds. Richard P. Bagozzi and Alice M. Tybout. Ann Arbor, MI: Association for Consumer Research, 203-208.

Holbrook, Morris B. (1978), "Beyond Attitude Structure: Toward the Informational Determinants of Attitude," *Journal of Marketing Research*, XV, 545-556.

Holbrook, Morris B. and John O'Shaughnessy (1984), "The Role of Emotion in Advertising," *Psychology & Marketing*, 1 (Summer), 45-64.

Hovland, Carl I., Irving L. Janis, and Harold H. Kelley (1953), *Communication and Persuasion*, New Haven: Yale University Press.

———, Wallace Mandell, Enid H. Campbell, Timothy Brock, Abraham S. Luchins, Arthur R. Cohen, William J. McGuire, Irving L. Janis, Rosalind L. Feierabend, and Norman H. Anderson (1957), *The Order of Presentation in Persuasion*, New Haven: Yale University Press.

——— and Walter Weiss (1951), "The Influence of Source Credibility on Communication Effectiveness," *Public Opinion Quarterly*, 15 (Winter), 635-650.

Isen, Alice M. (1984), "The Influence of Positive Affect on Decision Making and Cognitive Organization," in *Advances in Consumer Research: Volume XI*, ed. Thomas C. Kinnear. Provo, UT: Association for Consumer Research, 534-537.

Isen, Alice M., Margaret Clark, Thomas E. Shalker, and Lynn Karp (1978), "Affect, Accessibility of Material in Memory and Behavior: A Cognitive Loop?" *Journal of Personality and Social Psychology*, 36, 1-12.

Kerferd, G. B. (1967), "Logos," *The Encyclopedia of Philosophy, Volume 5*, ed. Paul Edwards. New York: Macmillan Publishing Co., Inc. & The Free Press.

Knepprath, Eugene and Theodore Jr. Clevenger (1965), "Reasoned Discourse and Motive Appeals in Selected Political Speeches," *Quarterly Journal of Speech*, LI, 152-156.

Liu, Scott S. and Patricia A. Stout (1987), "Effects of Message Modality and Appeal on Advertising Acceptance," *Psychology & Marketing*, 4(3), 167-187.

McClung, Gordon W., C. Whan Park, and William J. Sauer (1985), "Viewer Processing of Commercial Messages: Context and Involvement," in *Advances in Consumer Research, Volume XII*, eds. Elizabeth C. Hirschman and Morris B. Holbrook. Provo, UT: Association for Consumer Research, 351-355.

McGuire, William J. (1969), "The Nature of Attitude and Attitude Change," *The Individual in a Social Context*, Vol. III of *The Handbook of Social Psychology*, eds. Gardner Lindzey and Elliot Aronson, 2nd ed. Reading, MA: Addison-Wesley, 136-314.

Mitchell, Andrew A. (1983), "The Effects of Visual and Emotional Advertising: An Information-Processing Approach," *Advertising and Consumer Psychology*, eds. Larry Percy and Arch G. Woodside. Lexington, Massachusetts: Lexington Books, D.C. Heath and Company, 197-217.

——— (1986a), "Some Issues Surrounding Research on the Effects of 'Feeling Advertisements'," *Advances in Consumer Research*, Vol. XIII, ed. Richard J. Lutz. Provo, UT: Association for Consumer Research, 623-628.

——— (1986b), "The Effect of Verbal and Visual Components of Advertisements on Brand Attitudes and Attitude Toward the Advertisement," *Journal of Consumer Research*, 13 (June), 12-24.

——— and Jerry C. Olson (1981), " Are Product Attribute Beliefs the Only Mediator of Advertising Effects on Brand Attitude?" *Journal of Marketing Research*, 18, 318-332.

Murphy, John H., Isabella C.M. Cunningham, and Gary B. Wilcox (1979), "The Impact of Program Environment on Recall of Humorous Television Commercials," *Journal of Advertising*, 8 (2), 17-21.

Nunnally, Jum C. (1967), *Psychometric Theory*, New York: McGraw-Hill Book Company.

Pallak, Suzanne R., Enid Murroni, and Juliann Koch (1983), "Communicator Attractiveness and Expertise, Emotional Versus Rational Appeals, and Persuasion: A Heuristic Versus Systematic Processing Interpretation," *Social Cognition*, 2, 122-141.

Park, C. Whan and Gordon W. McClung (1986), "The Effect Of TV Program Involvement On Involvement With Commercials," in *Advances in Consumer Research, Volume XIII*, ed. Richard J. Lutz. Provo, UT: Association for Consumer Research, 544-548.

Percy, Larry (1983), "A Review of the Effect of Specific Advertising Elements upon Overall Communication Response," in *Current Issues & Research in Advertising*, 6, 77-118.

Peters, F. E. (1967), *Greek Philosophical Terms: A Historical Lexicon*, New York: New York University Press.

Ray, Michael L. and Rajeev Batra (1983), "Emotion and Persuasion in Advertising: What We Do and Don't Know About Affect," *Advances in Consumer Research: Vol. X*, eds. Richard P. Bagozzi and Alice M. Tybout. Ann Arbor, MI: Association for Consumer Research, 543-547.

Rosenthal, P. I. (1966), "Concept of Ethos and the Structure of Persuasive Speech," *Speech Monographs*, 33, 114-126.

Seymour, Daniel and Greg Lessne (1984), "Spousal Conflict Arousal: Scale Development," *Journal of Consumer Research*, 11 (December), 810-821.

Stout, Patricia A. and John D. Leckenby (1986), "Measuring Emotional Response to Advertising," *Journal of Advertising*, 15, No. 4, 35-42.

Wegner, Daniel M., Richard Wenzlaff, R. Michael Kerker, and Ann E. Beattie (1981), "Incrimination Through Innuendo: Can Media Questions Become Public Answers?" *Journal of Personality and Social Psychology*, 40, 822-832.

Wise, Gordon L., Herbert E. Brown, and Myron K. Cox (1975), "The Effect of Program Type and Other Variables in Reaching the Daytime Television Viewer with Advertising Messages," *Journal of Advertising*, 4 (3), 41-46.

An Examination of the Psychometric Properties of a Conservation-Oriented Consumption Scale

Katryna Malafarina, University of Minnesota
Jeff Jass, University of Minnesota

ABSTRACT

Due to increased academic focus on measuring attitudes and behaviors concerning energy conservation matters, the psychometric properties of a "Conservation-Oriented Consumption" scale (Allen, Calantone and Schewe, 1982) are assessed. A review of the development of the current measure reveals the basis for a four factor conceptualization ("general feelings of effectiveness", "perceived change in consumption", "perceptions of others" and "locus of blame") of conservation-oriented consumption proposed by Allen et al. The present study supports a three factor solution and demonstrates the reliability, discriminant and construct validity of the scale.

In his State of the Union Address on February 15, 1993, President Clinton gave Americans a prelude to his proposed economic plan in which the public discovered that they may be subjected to a broad-based energy conservation tax which would impact all forms of energy, including petroleum, natural gas, coal, hydroelectricity and nuclear power. One implication of this proposed tax is the need for Americans to conserve energy in many areas of life; from home heating to gas consumption. This issue, once a hot topic for researchers in marketing in the late 1970's and early 1980's, is once again attracting interest within the field (Malafarina and Loken 1993).

With these factors in mind, it appears to be an appropriate time to revitalize the impact that research in marketing exercises in this area. Several methodological alternatives, including experimentation and survey research, are available in accomplishing this objective. When the latter route is chosen, it is critical for the administered tests to exhibit acceptable levels of reliability and validity.

This study recognizes the importance of solid measurement practices if this area of marketing is to be revitalized successfully. Malafarina and Loken (1993) conducted a content analysis of social marketing studies (half of which related to environmental and energy conservation issues) and determined that the area is underdeveloped in terms of methodology. This study evaluates the reliability, discriminant validity and convergent validity of a scale created by Allen, Calantone and Schewe (1982) which assesses consumers' attitudes toward energy conservation through the construct "conservation oriented consumption". This scale was chosen for two reasons. First, academic literature dealing with measurement of energy conservation topics is quite limited. The "conservation oriented consumption scale" was one of the few pieces which reported its actual scale and fully described the conceptualization behind the scale. Second, the scale is an extension of an empirically tested scale created by Allen (1982). The second scale (Allen, Calantone and Schewe 1982) replicated the findings from the first scale (Allen 1982) and furthermore created new items which tapped an additional construct.

This paper will briefly review the literature addressing energy issues. Next, the "conservation oriented consumption" scale will be described and the theory behind it will be explored. Furthermore, the psychometric properties of the scale will be assessed. Finally, the relevance of the scale in relation to academic pursuits will be discussed.

LITERATURE REVIEW

Many studies were conducted a decade ago assessing varying aspects of consumers' attitudes and interests toward energy conservation. The December, 1981 issue of the Journal of Consumer Research was devoted entirely to studies addressing energy conservation and the environment. Other studies in marketing literature have included analyzing energy consumption patterns by the stage of the family life cycle (Fritzsche 1981), using the Fishbein-Ajzen model to predict home energy conservation (Seligman, Hall and Finegan 1982) and assessing public policies on energy conservation (Rudelius, Weijo and Dodge 1984).

Two interesting results can be explicated from these studies. First, the extent to which an individual accepts personal responsibility for conserving energy is an important factor influencing attitudes and behavior (Allen, Callentone and Schewe 1982; Allen 1982; Awad et al 1982 and Ellen, Wiener and Cobb-Walgren 1991). Second, conservers and nonconservers do not share the same attitudes and beliefs (Seligman, Hall and Finegan 1982; Allen 1982; Allen, Callentone and Schewe 1982).

Development of Conservation-Oriented Consumption Scale

The scale utilized by Allen, Calantone and Schewe (1982) in their study measuring international consumers' Conservation-Oriented Consumption is composed of four unique dimensions: "Perceived Change in Consumption" (PCC), "General Feelings of Effectiveness" (GFE), "Locus of Blame" (BLAME) and "Perceptions of Others" (OTHERS). Previous research has identified these factors as strong indicators of Socially Conscious Consumption (SCC) (Kinnear et.al 1974; Webster 1975; Allen and Dillon 1979; Allen 1982; Millstein 1977; Yankelovich 1974). An examination of these earlier studies provides insight into the focus of the current measure of interest.

Perceived Consumer Effectiveness

Berkowitz and Lutterman (1968) define a Socially Responsible Person as one who participates in community activities, strives to meet her obligations, possesses the ideals of the American core culture and feels unalienated from society. In their study the authors attempt to create an understanding of the construct "Social Responsibility" by reporting a number of behavioral and attitudinal correlates to their "Social Responsibility Scale" (SRS). Their results demonstrate the measure's ability to identify subjects possessing traditional, conservative American ideals. Of particular interest is the socially responsible citizen's belief that his individual actions influence events in the community as a whole. Persons possessing social responsibility hold fast to the belief that their own actions influence their surrounding community. This concept is reflected in later work as Perceived Consumer Effectiveness.

Attempting to improve upon this research, Kinnear, Taylor and Ahmed (1974) implement their "Index of Ecological Concern" to explore the characteristics of consumers that contribute to socially conscious purchasing patterns. Ecological concern is operationally defined as consisting of two dimensions: Buyers' attitudes must express concern for the ecology while purchase behavior must be consistent with maintenance of the environment

(Kinnear and Taylor 1973). Perceived Consumer Effectiveness, defined as the extent to which the respondent believes that an individual consumer can be effective in pollution abatement, is found to be a powerful indicator of ecological concern. "Those who felt strongly that consumers could be useful in pollution abatement demonstrated higher than average concern...as consumers perceive that individuals can be increasingly effective in pollution abatement, they will show more concern for the ecology" (Kinnear et. al. 1974, p. 22). Consumers who felt that individual action was influential in the broader arena exhibited greater concern for the issue at hand.

In his conceptualization of the Socially Conscious Consumer, Webster (1975) departs from the "traditionally" responsible citizen depicted in the Social Responsibility Scale (Berkowitz and Lutterman 1968). According to Webster, a Socially Conscious Consumer is one who "takes into account the public consequences of his or her private consumption or who attempts to use his or her purchasing power to bring about social change" (p.188). Perceived Consumer Effectiveness is envisioned in this study as an attitudinal variable. High levels of PCE reflect an attitude held by individuals who view the world as an interconnected system where the actions of one person have an influence on the entire system. Perceived Consumer Effectiveness demonstrates a significant influence on the behavioral construct SCC: Individuals scoring high on Perceived Consumer Effectiveness reported participating in more socially conscious behaviors than subjects exhibiting low PCE. In addition, Webster (1975) offers a full description of the Socially Conscious Consumer, profiling the group's characteristics beyond PCE. These consumers are accepting of the views of others, are engaged in behavior that is somewhat counter to social norms, are somewhat insensitive to social pressures and are willing to engage in purchase behavior that may not be popularly accepted but is consistent with their own ideas of responsibility. It is argued that while the social responsibility scale identifies traditional social values, the socially conscious consumption measure taps "modern" consumer values. It is interesting to note that "perceived consumer effectiveness" is the only researched construct to demonstrate a significant relationship with both of these measures. Because of its focus on actual behavior, Webster (1975) recommends that subsequent research concentrate on examining the dimensions of socially conscious consumption.

In accord with the recommendation of Webster (1975), Scott (1977) continues the stream of research focusing on socially conscious consumption. She does, however, introduce an additional dimension into the conceptualization of the construct. Arguing that traditional persuasive messages may produce only marginal changes in perceived consumer effectiveness, Scott (1977) introduces self-perception based strategies into the SCC arena. Specifically, Scott demonstrates the effectiveness of the foot-in-the-door technique in influencing both verbal and overt socially conscious behavior. Subjects who agreed to display a "Conserve Resources-Recycle" sign in their window were more likely to perform a subsequent envelope-addressing task. The importance of this study lies in the reconceptualization of PCE as a self-perception variable.

Self Perception and Conservation Issues

Self-Perception theory is an attributional approach to understanding attitudes. Bem (1972) originally discussed the theory, stating that to the extent that external causes for an act are absent, the individual engaged in the act will infer his attitude toward the topic on the basis of his behavior.

Belk, Painter and Semenik (1981) also demonstrate that if consumers display an internal locus of control (a belief in personal responsibility for their lives) rather than an external locus of control (a belief that chance or others control their lives) they generally display more ecological activism. The overall perspective from these two studies is that if a consumer believes individuals have the ability to solve energy problems, then they are more likely to report positive attitudes towards energy conservation.

Allen (1982) suggests that energy related issues may represent a situation where consumers are highly receptive to self-perception based labeling approaches. In his study those exposed to an attribution message perceived they had made more changes in their consumption to help with the energy problem than those in the persuasive condition. These results support a viewpoint in which PCE incorporates a self-perception dimension.

Allen and Dillon (1979) incorporate both a self-perception view and the more traditional conceptualization of Perceived Consumer Effectiveness in their scale measuring socially conscious consumption. Rather than suggesting that the reconceptualized interpretation of PCE may in fact be an entirely unique construct, Allen and Dillon propose a dual-dimensional model of Perceived Consumer Effectiveness. One dimension, "perceived change in consumption" (PCC), is envisioned as the self-perception component of PCE as it measures an "individual's self-perceptions that he/she has made in consuming and using products as a response to a specific social problem" (Allen and Dillon 1979, p. 551). It is argued that socially conscious consumers are more likely to perceive that they have changed their consumption habits in order to help alleviate the social problem. The second PCE dimension, here labeled "concern and effectiveness", measures an individual's general attitude of concern about a given social issue, as well as the person's own feelings of effectiveness in responding to the problem. (Allen 1982 subsequently labels this dimension "general feelings of effectiveness".) This dimension corresponds to the conceptual definitions applied to the entire construct, perceived consumer effectiveness, as envisioned by Kinnear et. al (1974) and Webster (1975).

Allen and Dillon (1979) constructed a measure of PCE from a pool of thirty-six items believed to tap the various dimensions of socially conscious consumption. Using factor analysis with Varimax rotation the item pool was reduced to a manageable fifteen item scale. Four factors were generated from the analysis: OTHERS (25%), BLAME (16.2%), PCC (12.6%) and Concern and Effort (8.4%) (numbers in parentheses reflect percentage of common variances). The "perceptions of other" (OTHERS) construct is based on an argument presented by Yankelovich (1974). In his study Yankelovich posits a model that outlines five stages of concern individuals experience when considering social issues that have cost consequences. A person at the fourth stage is concerned about the relevant issue yet will fail to take action if it is perceived that others are not acting in a responsible way. Similarly, Belk, Painter and Semenik (1981) report that individuals are more likely to conserve energy if they believe that other individuals are also conserving energy. The "perception of others" construct, therefore, identifies subjects' outlook concerning how others consume in socially conscious manners.

The "locus of Blame" (BLAME) construct is adopted from a study completed by Milstein (1977). Reporting results from a number of focus groups, Milstein concludes that consumers do not make increased efforts at energy conservation due to skepticism and cynicism. He reports that approximately 67% of subjects surveyed blame either big business, Politicians or the government for any energy problems. Allen and Dillon (1979) and Allen et. al (1982) reason that to the extent that individuals blame these parties for creating the energy problem, they are not likely to consume in an energy conscious way.

In a later study, Allen (1982) reports results from a factor analysis with Varimax rotation for a similar twelve item scale measuring socially conscious consumption. In this paper, Allen adheres to his conceptualization of perceived consumer effectiveness by including both PCC and GFE in his scale. He also replaces BLAME with an additional "Others" construct. The factors, labels, eigenvalues and percent of variance explained are reported as follows (Factor, label, Eigenvalue, % of Variance): *1*, GFE, 2.364, 19.7%; *2*, OTHERS, 1.934, 16.1%; *3*, Others must act, 1.19, 9.9%; *4*, PCC, 1.02, 8.5%.

This latter study more convincingly supports the proposition suggested by past research that perceived consumer effectiveness is strongly tied to SCC (28% of variance explained by PCE in 1982 study versus 12.5% in 1979 study).

Projective Techniques

Because energy consciousness is deemed as "politically correct", many individuals will respond to measures with a positive bias which may not reflect their true attitudes. Therefore, scales measuring energy conservation attitudes should try to incorporate items which may indirectly assess consumers' attitudes so that they will respond with their true attitudes and not those deemed as socially desirable. These types of items can be obtained through projective techniques and are included on this scale.

Although Allen, Calantone and Schewe (1982) do not mention projective techniques specifically, we believe they do play a role in two of the subscales: Locus of Blame and Perception of Others. Projective techniques are often used in measurements designed to assess responses which may have social implications (Aaker and Day 1986). If individuals believe that a response may reflect upon their self image in some manner or that giving a certain response may be deemed socially appropriate, they may not give accurate answers. Third person techniques are particularly useful for revealing true attitudes (as compared to socially desirable ones). "Third person techniques usually ask what friends, neighbors or the average person would think about a particular situation. The researcher can then observe, to some extent, the respondent's projection of their own attitudes onto the third person, thus revealing more of their "true feelings" (Aaker and Day 1986). The Perception of Others subscale is particularly subject to this type of technique.

The Conservation Oriented Consumption Scale

The preceding logic provides the basis for the conceptualization of the measure examined in this study (Allen et. al. 1982). The four identical factors utilized by Allen and Dillon (1979) (GFE, PCC, OTHERS, and BLAME) are presented as indicators of conservation-oriented consumption (a new label for socially conscious consumption). In addition, the dual-dimensional structure of perceived consumer effectiveness is adhered to. Seventeen items are included in the measure with six items measuring GFE (G1 - G6), two measuring PCC (P1 and P2), five tapping BLAME (B1 - B5) and four measuring OTHERS (O1 - O4). Alpha coefficients are reported for the four unique samples drawn for the study as an indication of reliability. Alpha's ranged from .65 to .69 for GFE, .42 to .48 for BLAME, and .43 to .60 for OTHERS. These coefficient values are offered as indicating an acceptable level of reliability for the scales.

EMPIRICAL MEASUREMENT ANALYSIS

Sample

The Conservation Oriented Consumption scale (Allen et. al. 1982) as well as the convergent and discriminant scales (Awad et. al. 1982) were administered to 192 undergraduate and graduate business students: 143 undergraduates and 49 graduates. A one-way ANOVA with unequal sample sizes was conducted to ensure that the respondents were similar in their responses. An overall F-test revealed that the null hypothesis was non-significant, indicating that the sample means were equal and that subjects' responses could be viewed as equivalent. Because the p-value approached significance (p=.051), orthogonal contrasts were run on the classes to determine if there were any differences between graduate and undergraduate students or between undergraduate classes.

No significant differences were found between the four undergraduate classes, but a slight significant difference was found between the graduate and undergraduate classes. Specifically, the graduate classes had a slightly higher mean then the undergraduate classes on the overall scale. It was hypothesized that the differences in mean score were due to the age difference in the students. The older (graduate) students are likely to have more experience with energy consumption behaviors and more awareness of energy conservation issues. To examine these possibilities, we conducted a discriminant analysis on the following: awareness of a potential gas tax in the state, awareness of a possible energy conservation tax, purchase experience with compact refrigerators, purchase experience with microwave ovens and purchase experience with new or used cars. The authors anticipated that there might be some potential differences between graduate and undergraduate students and therefore included questions assessing these five items at the end of the questionnaire. The two analyses pertaining to potential taxes were conducted solely to determine whether or not there were any significant differences between students in their knowledge of related energy issues. The three questions relating to purchase behaviors were analyzed solely to determine whether any significant differences existed in experience with purchasing products that are affected by consciousness of their impact on energy conservation (ie-larger cars consume more gas than do smaller cars and different appliances vary in the level of electricity they consume). Two significant differences were obtained; graduate students indicated a higher level of awareness than did undergraduates and also had greater purchase experience with microwave ovens. Additionally, a one-way ANOVA was conducted on both the discriminant and convergent scales (to be discussed later) between all the classes and no significant differences were obtained. Because the sample was relatively equivalent, the sample was randomly split to conduct an exploratory and confirmatory factor analysis. Although there is a slight difference between undergraduates and graduates, this issue is not a problem since both groups are still represented in each sample.

Reliability

Several methods exist for estimating reliability including, test-retest, equivalent forms and split-halves. We chose to examine reliability through split halves, using Cronbach's Alpha as a measure of reliability. Coefficient Alpha is "the expected correlation of one test with another test of the same length when the two tests purport to measure the same thing" (Nunnally1978, p.215). From table 2, alpha's appear to be reasonable (Nunnally 1978) and are equal to, and often greater than, the coefficients reported by Allen. This provides substantial evidence for the reliability of the scale. (Note the items included in particular runs, however, and how alpha values changed).

Item-to-total correlations and inter-item correlations

Item-to-total correlations were examined to determine which items could potentially be dropped from the scale. On an initial analysis, it was apparent that items B1 and B3 (the first and third statements on the BLAME scale) should be dropped from the scale because their Item-to-total correlations were -.3199 and -.1859,

TABLE 1
Conservation Oriented Consumption (Allen, Calantone, and Schewe, 1982)

1. Perceived Consumer Effectiveness (PCE)

  A. General Feelings of Effectiveness (GFE)
  G1.Energy is not my problem because there is simply nothing I can do about it.
  G2.Energy conservation is good for the country.
  G3.I am not really concerned about our nation's energy problem.
  G4.I am not going to reduce the amount of energy that I use as long as others are allowed to continue to waste energy.
  G5.Individuals like myself have no influence over what the government does about the energy problem.
  G6.People who conserve energy are helping the country reduce the severity of the energy problem.

  B. Perceived Change in Consumption (PCC)
  P1.I've changed the way I purchase and use products as a result of the nation's energy problem.
  P2.When I buy products, I seldom consider how my use of them will contribute to reducing the nation's energy problem.

2. Locus of Blame (BLAME)
  B1.Political considerations have played too strong a role in setting energy policy for the nation.
  B2.Environmental groups create unnecessary roadblocks for those trying to solve social problems like energy.
  B3.We need more government regulations designed to force businesses and individuals to conserve energy.
  B4.One of the causes of the energy problem has been too much interference by the government in the operations of companies that supply energy.
  B5.The government should decrease its control over the management and operations of utility companies.

3. Perceptions of Others (OTHERS)
  O1.Most people are not willing to make sacrifices to conserve energy.
  O2.The only reason people conserve energy is to save money.
  O3.Most people ignore the nation's energy problem when it comes to their day-to-day lives.
  O4.Most people have made some changes in the way they live in an effort to help reduce the severity of the nation's energy problem.

TABLE 2

	Coefficient Alpha		
	Run 1*	Run 2	Run3
Overall Scale	.6923	.7849	.7931
GFE subscale	.6625	.6625	.6625
PCC subscale	.7959	.7959	.7959
BLAME subscale	-.1884	.4809	.5555
OTHERS subscale	.6411	.6411	.6411

  * Run 1: included B1-B5; Run 2: included B2, B4 and B5; Run 3: included B4 and B5

respectively. Additionally, the "Alpha if Item-deleted" column on the analysis indicated that alpha would be increased if these items were dropped. Furthermore, an analysis of the correlation matrix revealed consistently low or negative correlations with these items. A second reliability analysis was then run, eliminating items B1 and B3, which increased alpha to .7849. An analysis of the output indicated that B2 (second statement on the BLAME scale) could also be dropped due to low Item-to-total correlations and an indication that alpha would be increased if the item were deleted. This item was dropped and another reliability run was conducted which further increased alpha to .7931. In addition to these empirical indicators, we referred back to the theory establishing the BLAME construct for further direction. From examination of the theory, the items, and the responses, it was concluded that subjects may not have comprehended the wording of these items. The reliability analysis, therefore, identified items B1, B2 and B3 as possible items to be excluded. Items G2 (second item on the GFE scale) and item O1 (first item on the OTHERS scale) could have potentially been deleted due to low Item-to-Total correlations and low inter-item correlations, but were retained due to their consistency with the theoretical basis (Nunnally, 1978).

Structure of Scale-Exploratory Analysis

To conduct our exploratory stage of factor analysis, we used two extraction methods; Alpha and Principal Axis Factoring (PAF). These two methods were chosen from the available methods because both are good methods for assessing the underlying dimensions of a scale. Varimax rotation was used for both factoring methods (Kim 1975).

Six factors were identified from the initial factor run that exhibited eigenvalues greater than one. Because six factors were not consistent with the theory and because an analysis of the factor

TABLE 3

	Discriminant		Convergent	
	Run1 *	Run2	Run1	Run2
Overall Scale	-.3791	-.3462	.1393	.1773
GFE subscale	-.4676	-.4676	.1789	.1789
PCC subscale	-.2921	-.2921	.2246	.2246
BLAME subscale	-.1722	-.1384	-.2087	-.1104
OTHERS subscale	-.0836	-.0836	.1077	.1077

*Run 1: with B1-B5 included; Run 2: without B1, B2 and B3

loadings revealed no consistent pattern of interpretation, we forced an additional run to four factors. These runs revealed that the factor loadings could still not be interpreted in accordance with theory. In fact, no meaningful interpretation was possible with the loadings. B1, B2 and B3 in particular demonstrated no underlying commonality amongst themselves or with the other BLAME items. For instance, in a four factor PAF solution B1 loaded on factor four, B2 loaded on factor two, and B3 loaded on factor one. Consistent with our reliability analysis, factor analysis recommends that these items be eliminated from the scale. Subsequent analyses were run without these items.

At this point the authors examined the theory underlying the scale and concluded that the problem with the factor analysis may have been due to the two PCE subscales. As previously discussed, Allen and Dillon (1979) were the first researchers to propose this two-dimensional view of perceived consumer effectiveness. Additionally, only work completed by Allen and his colleagues (Allen et. al, 1982; Allen, 1982) supports this conceptualization. From our analysis, we decided to run another factor analysis with three factors. When we ran this factor analysis, our loadings produced meaningful interpretations: All of the items loaded clearly onto theoretically expected factors. From this analysis we concluded that only three factors were meaningful and that the PCE scale could not be delineated into two subscales. The three factor solution is further explained when one considers the two item construction of the PCC subscale. Additional indicators are recommended for this construct. The PCE items loaded on the first factor, the BLAME items loaded on the third factor and the OTHERS items loaded on the second factor. The following results from a factor analysis restricted to three factors and utilizing PAF extraction and Varimax rotation exemplify our findings. Results are reported as follows (Factor number, label, Eigenvalue, % of Variance explained): **1**, PCE, 3.51, 25.1%; **2**, OTHERS, .9, 6.4%; **3**, BLAME, .77, 5.5%.

As our results indicate, the PCE factor exhibits the largest Eigenvalue. Consistent with previous research, PCE is determined to be a powerful indicator of socially conscious consumption.

Validity of the Scale

We specifically addressed construct validity, discriminant validity and convergent validity. Construct validity concerns a hypothesized relationship between a measure of a construct and a particular observable variable (Nunnally 1978). Peter (1981) further states that "if a construct were hypothesized to have three dimensions, a factor analysis of a purported measure of the construct which produces three meaningful factors could be interpreted as supportive evidence of construct validity." Our factor results support the conceptualization of PCE as a single dimensional construct. While Allen et. al purport that PCE contains two dimensions, our results suggest that PCC and GFE are too closely related to be considered separate entities. Construct validity is established for this conceptualization (Webster, 1975; Kinnear et. al, 1974) of the latent variable.

Discriminant validity reflects the extent to which the measure is unique and not a reflection of other variables and is determined by low correlations between the measure of interest and other measures that are not measuring the same variable or concept (Campbell and Fiske 1959). Discriminant validity was assessed through correlations with a Cynicism and a Home Economics scale created by Awad et al. (1982). The Awad et al scale was used for validation purposes for two reasons. First, as mentioned previously, there is a paucity of reported scales dealing with energy conservation attitudes. Although some scales have been used to measure energy consumption patterns by stage of family life cycle (Fritzche 1981), scales such as this were not appropriate for validation purposes because they did not specifically deal with attitude measurement. The Awad et al scale was intentionally designed to measure attitudes. Second, on a conceptual basis, the Awad et al. scale could be divided into subscales to use for both discriminant and convergent validity. In Awad et al.'s study, cynicism and home economics were shown to be negatively related to energy conservation. Table 3 displays the correlations between the portions of the Allen et. al scale and the discriminant and convergent scales. As is evidenced, support for discriminant validity is established.

Convergent validity measures the degree to which attempt to measure the same concept using two or more different measures yield the same results and is determined by high correlations between the measures (Campbell and Fiske 1959). Convergent validity was assessed through correlations with two scales created by Awad et al (1982): Concern for Supply and Avowal of Social Norms. Both of these scales were shown to be positively related to energy conservation.

As is made apparent by the above low correlations between scales, convergent validity was not established. Although convergent validity was not established, an analysis of the "Concern for Supply" scale and the "Avowal of Social Norms" scale (Awad et. al. 1982), provides a few explanations for the current results. First, Awad et al. initially administered the scale to individuals in association with five specific behaviors: use of air conditioning, use of washer/dryer, use of dishwasher, use of heating and use of lights. For example, the statement "I am always careful about my use of electricity" was rated five times, once for each type of behavior. Subjects in this sample were only given the statement to rate once, and the subject was left to interpret the meaning of the behavior. Therefore, the subject may have viewed this statement as reflecting a "general" behavior or may have viewed the statement in relation to only one specific behavior such as using the dishwasher. This type of interpretation could have occurred for any of the three "Avowal of Social Norms" questions. Since the scale was initially meant to assess specific behaviors, any misinterpretation of the question could lead to lower convergent validity.

TABLE 4

Scale	Discriminant Validity Correlation	Convergent Validity Correlation
Overall Scale	-.4671	.2525
PCE	.3552	.2951
OTHERS	-.1406	.1505
BLAME	-.0095	-.0095

Second, the items in the "Concern for Supply" scale use terminology which may confuse the subjects. For example, subjects could respond to this statement, "The most important reason for conserving electricity is to be sure there will be an adequate supply for our children" in several ways, depending upon their interpretation of the salient aspects of the statement. If a subject believes that ensuring an "adequate supply for our children" is an important, but not *the* most important reason for conserving energy, the subject would tend to disagree with this statement while in fact he/she may still believe that we need to maintain the supply for the future. Additionally, simply replacing "for our children" with "for ourselves in the future" could have an impact on how people respond to this question. The other two statements have similar problems in that while a subject may have a concern for supply, the subject's focus may be on concern for supply on a personal basis and not as a concern for future generations.

These three items seem to intertwine the aspects of concern for supply and future generations and ignore aspects related to concern on a more individual basis. Although the correlations from this study are positive, which is consistent with the positive relation Awad et al. found, they are not sufficiently large enough to justify convergent validity. The previous analysis of the individual items, however, demonstrates how wording in the Awad et. al scale may have produced our low correlations.

Confirmatory Factor Analysis

The second set of data were used to confirm the results of the exploratory stage. Comparable results were achieved using this split sample technique. The following output summaries detail the properties of the refined conservation-oriented consumption scale (without items B1, B2 and B3). Scale reliability is reported as follows (Scale items, coefficient alpha): Overall scale, .8069; PCE, .8167; BLAME, .6945; OTHERS, .6974.

It is apparent from the results that coefficient alpha for the overall and subscales increased over the exploratory analysis results, providing further evidence for the reliability of the scale.

Maximum Likelihood is the most common confirmatory factor analysis approach (Stewart 1981) and was therefore used for confirmatory purposes. The three factor model was supported, with every item loading on the same factor as in the exploratory analysis (PCE-factor 1; OTHERS-factor 2; BLAME-factor 3). One difference was noted, however. In this confirmatory run OTHERS was identified as the factor explaining the greatest percentage of variance. Results are reported as follows (Factor number, label, eigenvalue, % of variance explained): *1*, PCE, 1.415, 10.1%; *2*, OTHERS, 3.5, 25%; *3*, BLAME, 1.31, 9.4%. Noticeably stronger Eigenvalues are produced in this run for OTHERS and BLAME than in the exploratory stage.

The convergent and discriminant validity tests support the results from the exploratory analysis. Discriminant validity is established while no support is forwarded for convergent validity (Table 4).

Conclusion

As conservation issues receive greater attention by the government, the media and academia, these topics will increasingly influence the products consumers purchase and the services they use. Measures such as Allen, Callantone and Schewe's (1982) scale measuring conservation-oriented consumption will prove useful in monitoring these shifting attitudes. We believe the scale to be relevant due to increased interest in the area on the part of marketing researchers and because of the salience of energy issues in the minds of American citizens produced, in part, by the recent passage of Clinton's budget plan which includes a 4.3 cent gas tax.

Anticipating the potential resistance to the new tax, Clinton has emphasized that Americans should be willing to accept personal environmental responsibility for their individual actions. However, Ellen, Wiener and Cobb-Walgren (1991) report that consumers high in PCE do not favor government intervention. This would seem to pose a conflict for Clinton, which could explain why Clinton has emphasized that Americans should take personal responsibility for actions. By focusing on the voluntary aspect of energy conservation in a positive manner, resistance to intervention may be dispelled (Ellen, Wiener, and Cobb-Walgren, 1991). Allen, Calantone and Schewe (1982) have identified a dimension, "perceived consumer effectiveness" (PCE) as an indicator related to personal responsibility. Whereas personal responsibility merely reflects an individual's willingness to accept accountability, PCE reflects a more active construct in which an individual not only takes responsibility, but also acts on it (Ellen, Wiener and Cobb-Walgren 1991). This construct (PCE) should help researchers and practitioners in determining which consumers will believe that their actions can make a difference and who should then behave proactively on their energy conservation concerns.

The present study contributes to this stream of research on conservation oriented consumption by providing an empirical test of several psychometric properties of Allen, Calantone and Schewe's (1982) measure of PCE and presenting evidence for reliability, construct validity and discriminant validity. While we feel that the study does not provide overwhelming evidence for these properties, it does support the use of the scale in the following areas: (1) it provides further evidence for the construct PCE, (2) it enhances the reliability of the scale from the findings of Allen et. al (1982), and (3) it provides evidence for the discriminant capabilities of the scale.

This study additionally supports the use of projective techniques in scales. Although Allen, Calantone and Schewe did not initially emphasize this aspect of their scale, it can be seen that the inclusion of these items accounted for a significant proportion of the variance.

This study does, however, recognize the need for additional empirical investigations concerning this measure. Future research may assume four distinct challenges. First, because the current results differ in regards to the dimensionality of PCE, future research may wish to further investigate the construct in an effort to establish its dimensionality (uni-dimensional versus two-dimensional). Secondly, an attempt to assess the nomological validity of conservation-oriented consumption should be examined in future work. Additionally, it is recommended that this scale be used to assess consumers' attitudes concerning potential energy conservation programs. Through these efforts stronger evidence for construct validity may be established for this measure. Finally, it is hoped that researchers examining other socially related issues will contribute to this area of scholarship in marketing by developing reliable and valid measures.

REFERENCES

Aaker, David A and George J. Day, (1986), *Marketing Research*, John Wiley and Sons, Inc: New York, 126-130.

Allen, Chris T. (March 1982). "Self-perception based strategies for stimulating energy conservation". *Journal of Consumer Research*. 8: 381-390. 5

Allen, Chris T., Roger J. Calantone and Charles D. Schewe (1982). "Consumers' attitudes about energy conservation in Sweden, Canada, and the United States, with Implications for policymakers," *Journal of Marketing and Public Policy*. 1: 57-67.

Allen, Chris T., William Dillon (1979). "On Receptivity to Information Furnished by the Public Policymaker: The Case of Energy", in *1979 Educator's Proceedings*, Chicago, IL: American Marketing Association. pp. 550-556.

Anderson, Thomas W. and William Cunningham (1972). "The Socially Conscious Consumer," *Journal of Marketing*. 36: 23-31.

Awad, Ziyad A., Roger H. Johnston, Jr., Shel Feldman, and Michael V. Williams. (1982) "Customer attitude and intentions to conserve electricity," *Advances in Consumer Research*. 10: 652-654.

Bem, Daryl J, (1972), "Self Perception Theory," in *Advances in Experimental Psychology*, ed. Leaonard Berkowitz, New York, N.Y.: Academic Press. pp 1-62.

Berkowitz, Leonard and Kenneth Lutterman (1968), "The Traditional Socially Responsible Personality," *Public Opinion Quarterly*, 32: 169-85.

Campbell, Donald T. and Donald W. Fiske, (March 1959) "Convergent and Discriminant Validation by the Multitrait-Multimethod Matrix," *Psychological Bulletin*, 56: 100-122.

Ellen, Pam S., Joshua L. Wiener, and Cathy Cobb-Walgren, (1991) "The Role of Perceived Consumer Effectiveness in Motivating Environmentally Conscious Behaviors," *Journal of Public Policy and Marketing*, 10(2): 102-117.

Fritzsche, David J. (1981) "An analysis of energy consumption patterns by stage of family life cycle," *Journal of Marketing Research*. 18: 227-232.

Kim, Jae-On, "Factor Analysis," *SPSS Statistical Package for the Social Sciences*, Second Edition, (1975) New York: McGraw Hill, Chapter 24.

Kinnear, Thomas, James R. Taylor and Sadrudin A. Ahmed (1974), "Ecologically Concerned Consumers: Who are They?," *Journal of Marketing*, 38: 20-24.

Malafarina, Katryna and Barbara Loken, (1993), "Progress and Limitations of Social Marketing: A Review of Empirical Literature on the Consumption of Social Ideas ", *Advances in Consumer Research*, forthcoming.

Milstein, Jeffrey S. (1977) "Attitudes, Knowledge, and Behavior of American Consumers Regarding Energy Conservation with some Implications for Governmental Action", *Advances in Consumer Research* Vol. 4, pp. 315-321.

Nunnally, Jum (1978), *Psychometric Theory*, New York: McGraw Hill.

Peter, Paul J. (1981), "Construct Validity: A Review of Basic Issues and Marketing Practices," *Journal of Marketing Research*, 18, 133-145.

Rudelius, William, Richard Weijo and Gary Dodge (1984), "Marketing energy conservation to homeowners: an action program from public policy research," *Journal of Public Policy and Marketing*. 3: 149-166.

Rummel, R.J. (1970), *Applied Factor Analysis*, Evanston: Northwestern University Press.

Scott, Carol, A. (1977), "Modifying Socially-Conscious Behavior: The Foot-in-the-Door Technique", *Journal of Consumer Research*. 4: 156-64.

Seligman, Clive, Don Hall, and Joan Finegan (1982), "Predicting home energy consumption: an application of the Fishbein-Ajzen model," *Advances in Consumer Research*. 10: 645-651.

Stewart, David W. (1981), "The Application and Misapplication of Factor Analysis in Marketing Research", *Journal of Marketing Research*. 18: 51-62.

Webster, Frederick E. (1975), "Determining the Characteristics of the Socially Conscious Consumer", *Journal of Consumer Research*. 2: 188-196.

Yankelovich, Daniel (1974), "How Opinion Polls Differ from Social Indicators," in *Social Indicators and Marketing*, Chicago: American Marketing Association, 54-66.

Socially Desirable Responses in the Measurement of Need for Cognition

James M. Hunt, Temple University
Karen M. Stevens, Temple University
Anindya Chatterjee, Temple University
Jerome B. Kernan, George Mason University[1]

ABSTRACT

Two studies suggest that subjects may feign a high need for cognition (NC) in a socially-desirable effort to appear "smart." In one study, the need for cognition scale (Cacioppo and Petty 1982; Cacioppo, Petty, and Kao 1984)—both long and short versions—was found to be correlated significantly with the social desirability scale (Crowne and Marlowe 1964). In a second, the scale was assessed experimentally by manipulating the motivational set under which subjects completed it. Findings revealed that subjects given normal instructions: (1) scored higher in NC than those instructed to "downplay" their intelligence in completing the scale; and (2) scored no higher or lower than subjects instructed to "demonstrate" their intelligence. In that NC is a key concept in Petty and Cacioppo's (1986) elaboration likelihood model (ELM), caution would seem appropriate when the NC scale is employed, particularly in those settings associated with cognitive achievement.

Attitude theory and research has been profoundly influenced by the elaboration likelihood model of Petty and Cacioppo (1986). This model (ELM) has both enhanced and refined traditional thinking about the attitude construct by providing valuable insights from the area of social cognition. Not only does the model prescribe a rich network of factors and responses, but it also encourages creative approaches to the dynamics of attitude processes.

Among other things, the Petty and Cacioppo model shows how individual difference variables affect a person's susceptibility to persuasive stimuli. One of these variables, need for cognition (Cacioppo and Petty 1982), is the focus of our concern. More specifically, Cacioppo, Petty, and Morris (1983) have demonstrated rather convincingly that an individual's need for cognition can influence the intake and use of information contained in persuasive messages. Their principal finding—embedded in the ELM—is that people with a high need for cognition are more likely to process message argumentation actively, whereas those who are low in this need will focus on the peripheral elements of the presentation (e.g., source attractiveness). Cacioppo and Petty (1982; Cacioppo, Petty, and Kao 1984) use a need for cognition scale (NCS), which they developed based on the work of Cohen (1957; Cohen, Stotland, and Wolf 1955). Our concern arises from the scale's possible transparency (cf. Cacioppo and Petty 1982). Accordingly, we offer two studies designed to ascertain whether the NCS produces an independent assessment of a subject's need for cognition, or whether that scale presents a confound with social desirability (Crowne and Marlowe 1964)—in effect, subjects (particularly students) attempting to appear more studious than they are in reality. In that NCS scores are typically used as a blocking factor (both *a priori* and *ex post*) in ELM-related studies, this concern is far from being an idle one.

BACKGROUND

As initially presented by Cacioppo and Petty (1982), the concept of need for cognition (NC) is defined as an individual's "tendency to engage in and enjoy thinking" (p. 116). The authors note that this conceptualization follows from the work of Cohen (1957; Cohen, Stotland, & Wolf 1955), who viewed this need as one's need for cognitive clarity (Cohen 1964). Cohen (1957) was able to demonstrate that a high need for cognitive clarity seems to be associated with greater attention to a persuasive message as well as a greater desire or ability to organize the information contained in that message. Presumably, such processing on the part of these message recipients facilitates message retrieval, thereby influencing post-message attitude. Since Cohen left no documentation as to how he measured the need he studied, Cacioppo and Petty (1982) undertook a series of studies aimed at developing a measuring instrument. The objective of this work was to develop a need for cognition scale that would "distinguish between individuals who dispositionally tend to engage in and enjoy effortful analytic activity and those who do not" (Cacioppo et al. 1983, p. 806).

Cacioppo and Petty's original work produced an instrument containing 34 opinion statements. Response to each item was measured on a 5-point bipolar scale ranging from "extremely uncharacteristic of me" to "extremely characteristic of me." In subsequent research, this instrument was reduced to 18 items by the authors (Cacioppo, Petty, & Kao 1984). Results from the latter effort indicated the two versions to be closely correlated ($r=0.95$). Both versions have been shown to have a high reliability as measured by Cronbach's alpha (.91 for the longer version and .90 for the shorter). In both cases, factor analysis of the items has revealed a structure with one dominant factor, explaining from 27% (long version) to 37% (short version) of the variance.

Cacioppo and Petty have employed their scale to observe how personality can systematically influence the intake of persuasive communication and the resulting formation of attitudes. Typically, they have manipulated subjects' issue-related thoughts by exposing them to either a strong set of arguments (those that produce more positive than negative issue-related thoughts) or a weak set (those that produce more negative thoughts). The usual finding obtained by these authors (see Haugtvedt, Petty, Cacioppo, and Steidley 1988) is that greater effects occur for subjects who are high in NC than for those who are low in NC. Presumably, this is a result of greater motivation to process on the part of high NC subjects.

A second common finding of Cacioppo and Petty's work—couched in their ELM—involves the manipulation of peripheral (to the central arguments of the message) persuasion cues. For instance, the authors (Haugtvedt et al. 1988) have manipulated subjects' attraction to the message source—either positive or negative. The usual finding is that low NC subjects are more responsive to this manipulation than are high NC subjects when post-message attitude is used as the response variable. Since low NC subjects supposedly engage in less active message processing, they are thought to rely more on simple heuristics such as using peripheral cues to form issue-related attitudes.

One of Cacioppo and Petty's (1982) stated concerns with their NCS was that it might be confounded with social desirability, or "the disposition to respond in a socially desirable manner" (Crowne

---

[1] This research was supported by a Faculty Senate Grant, Temple University. An earlier version of the first of the two studies reported here can be found in James M. Hunt, Anindya Chatterjee and Jerome B. Kernan (1993), *Perceptual and Motor Skills*, 77 (August), 95-98.

and Marlowe 1964, p.10). This concern is particularly acute for any scale purported to measure the value individuals place on thinking. For this reason, Cacioppo and Petty (1982, Study 3) tested for the presence of a relationship between need for cognition and social desirability as measured by the Crowne-Marlowe scale. Results indicated this relationship to be nonsignificant ($r=.08$, $N=104$). Although the NCS is somewhat transparent, the authors tentatively concluded that the scale is not confounded by respondents' efforts to convey favorable impressions when their responses are anonymous.

STUDY 1

In light of Cacioppo and Petty's stated concern regarding the potential transparency of the NCS, we first assessed its relationship to social desirability in an associative study carried out in an academic environment (where the appropriateness of establishing a contemplative facade should be relatively strong). Inasmuch as this study was designed to explore a broad set of issues dealing with personality, cognitive style, and generalized values, need for cognition was only one of several variables we studied. To ensure an unbiased assessment, we first estimated the association of each measure and need for cognition.

Subjects

One-hundred-fifty-six students from a large Eastern university agreed to participate in a survey for extra credit in various courses. Sixty-three of them were undergraduates, 93 were graduate students. Most (95%) were business majors. Average age was 26 years. Sixty-seven were female, 89 male.

Materials and Procedures

Subjects were asked to complete a battery of six questionnaires over two sessions. Administration of the social desirability and need for cognition scales took place during the second session, which was conducted after the close of class. In all, five groups of 12 to 41 students participated. At the beginning of each session, respondents were told that they would be participating in a study of general opinions and attitudes, that their responses would be held in confidence, and that their identity would remain unknown to the researchers. (To assure anonymity over both sessions, respondents were identified only by number). Immediately following these instructions, test booklets were distributed. The NCS was distributed first, followed by the Crowne-Marlowe (1964) social desirability scale. The NCS distributed was the longer 34-item (1982) scale, but both it and the shorter 18-item version (Cacioppo et al. 1984) were used in analyses. At the conclusion of subjects' last session, they were thanked and dismissed. Debriefing took place after all groups had been run.

Results

Our results regarding the properties of the NCS parallel those of Cacioppo and Petty discussed above. Alpha coefficients were .89 for the longer version and .88 for the shorter one. Correlation between both versions of the scale was .95 ($p=.001$). Factor analysis, in which a maximum likelihood extraction procedure was used, confirmed Cacioppo and Petty's (1982) finding that one factor was dominant in explaining scale variance (32.6%). Eigenvalues indicated that each of the other factors explained only a small proportion of the remaining variance. Our results also parallel Cacioppo et al. (1984) in that all but one of the original items loaded heavily (.43 to .73) on the first factor. In contrast to Cacioppo and Petty, however, we found a direct relationship between need for cognition and social desirability. Correlation coefficients were .24 ($p<.01$) for the longer NCS and .19 ($p<.02$) for the shorter version. It appears as though the transparent nature of the NCS did encourage, however slightly, some biasing of responses. In elaborating this relationship through regression analysis, we found both age and class status (undergraduate vs. graduate) interacted with NCS in a positive manner. As age—$F_{1,150}=9.45$, $p<.01$—and class standing—$F_{1,150}=11.84$, $p<.01$—increased, social desirability biased NCS scores more. These predictive alliances would be expected if NCS is confounded with social desirability in the first place. Graduate students, who are generally older, are also more socialized with academic values. As a consequence, they would be more disposed to "highlight" their cognitive skills. Of course, it also could be argued that as people age, they simply become more cognitively motivated.

Discussion

Our initial evidence suggests the possibility, albeit slight, that subjects' perceived need to give socially desirable answers may bias NCS. Apparently, NCS scores are explained, at least in part, by subjects' belief that it is socially advantageous to appear deliberative or contemplative. Although tentative, these findings reinforce Cacioppo and Petty's caution regarding the potentially transparent nature of their scale. Both the validity and utility may be jeopardized, particularly when administered in contexts involving cognitive achievement. Despite anonymously responding to our questionnaire outside of class, our subjects still seem to have associated the task with their academic environment. To the extent that such associations are made, NCS scores become biased measures of individual differences in cognitive need. We recognize, of course, that our correlations are relatively small; however their significance gives pause for concern. Why our results depart from those reported by Cacioppo and Petty is not readily apparent. Perhaps our student subjects were more "tied" to their academic surroundings. Alternatively, maybe they were *less* focused on academic achievement since they were required to complete a number of other questionnaires.

STUDY 2

Given the possibility that the NCS is confounded by social desirability, a second study was undertaken to assess the explanation that individuals attempt to project a studious facade, particularly in settings associated with cognitive performance. Our tack was to have subjects *simulate* (based on the instructions they received) the test behavior we ascribed to those scoring "high" vs. "low" on the NCS. That is, subjects simulated extreme levels of social desirability. We hypothesized differences in NCS results between these groups, but no difference between the "high NC simulators" and a control group given normal instructions.

Subjects

Fifty evening students completed a questionnaire for extra course credit. Thirty-four were MBA students, 16 were undergraduate marketing students. Average age was 30. Twenty-three were female, 27 male.

Materials and Procedures

In an administered procedure, all subjects were asked to complete the long version of the NCS after the closing of class. Each was randomly assigned to one of three treatment groups, constituted by the instructions given. This assignment produced a "high NC simulator group," a "low NC simulator group," and a "usual instruction" control group. Instructions to the high simulator group read: "Please answer these questions as though you want to demonstrate your ability to act intelligently and to be contemplative and methodical." Instructions to the low simulator group were identical to those received by the high group with the exception of these words: "Please answer these questions as though you want to downplay your ability to act intelligently and to be contemplative and methodical." Instructions to the control group read: "Please answer these questions as honestly as possible." The experimenter ensured that all subjects understood their instructions. After completing the questionnaire, subjects were asked what they thought the study was about and whether they could guess the hypothesis. Debriefing occurred the following week.

Results

As in Study 1, analysis of both NCS scales indicated that a single factor dominated the explanation of variance (.47 for the long version and .55 for the short one), with each additional factor contributing little to the explanation. Alpha coefficients for both versions of the scale were .98. Two analyses of variance were run on subjects' NCS scores, one for each version of the scale. Cell sizes were 16 per instruction group. (Of the 50 original subjects, two were dropped from analysis due to incomplete questionnaires.) Our results do not support an NCS free of confound; analyses revealed a significant difference across the three experimental groups, for both the long and short versions of the NCS. For the long version, cell means were: 139 ($S.D.$=12.3) for the high NC simulator group, 133 ($S.D.$=13.2) for the control group, and 105 ($S.D.$=34.7) for the low NC simulator group. The statistical difference produced across these conditions ($F_{2,45}$=9.91, p<.001) was due to the low NC simulator group (Sheffe's test, p=.05), which scored below the control group and the high NC simulator group. For the short NCS, cell means were: 74 ($S.D.$=6.9) for the high NC group, 73 ($S.D.$=7.6) for the controls, and 56 ($S.D.$=20.3) for the low NC group—$F_{2,45}$=8.88, p<.001. These differences were a result of the low scores of the low NC group (p=.05). No evidence of demand characteristics was present; none of our subjects was able to guess the study's purpose or hypothesis. Further, it appears that all subjects made a conscientious effort to complete the questionnaire according to instructions. The significantly lower means in the low NC simulator group attest to an effective experimental manipulation. Indeed, the comments of several subjects from the low NC simulator group are noteworthy; these people mentioned that they had difficulty in "downplaying" their cognitive ability, which may explain the larger standard deviations for that group. If this was the case, our results are conservative ones.

Discussion

Our second study implies that people completing the NCS under what can be described as normal test instructions/conditions (our control subjects) react to that scale in the same way they would have had they assumed a socially desirable facade (our high NC simulator group). If this is so, then the transparency of the NCS poses a serious problem. We realize that drawing conclusions from the null hypothesis is always a tenuous proposition, at best. And we should make mention that our failure to find significant differences between the controls and high NC subjects might be due to a "ceiling effect"—a possibility for which we have no data. Nevertheless, when considered in conjunction with our first study, these experimental results caution against the unrestricted use of the NCS.

SUMMARY DISCUSSION

Succinctly stated, the results of our research show little support for the notion that Cacioppo and Petty's (1982) NCS produces an unbiased measure of need for cognition. According to other studies (Cacioppo and Petty 1982; Cacioppo et al. 1984), the magnitude of correlation between NCS scores and social desirability should not have reached statistical significance. In our first study, however, it did. Although the coefficients were relatively small in magnitude, they were significant. Apparently, our subjects responded to the NCS in a manner that reflected their desire to give socially propitious answers, to appear analytical or otherwise "smart." The greater this desire, the higher the NCS. Support for this interpretation also comes from our analysis involving age and level in school (undergraduate or graduate). As age and level increased, so did the *relationship* between social desirability and NCS. This would be expected if one assumes that older/graduate students are more apt to judge themselves on the basis of cognitive endeavor—i.e., they are more socialized with academic values. As a result, when given a questionnaire that is a transparent measure of those values, these students will likely respond in a manner that mirrors those "socially desirable" values.

The results we obtained in our second study follow nicely the results we obtained from the first one. Based on the earlier study, we had reasoned that if NCS is an unbiased measure of NC (i.e., the scale is unconfounded with respect to social desirability), then its product should be independent of manipulations that encourage subjects to adopt a "studious" facade in completing the scale. Our data did not show this to be the case, however. Subjects who completed the NCS under normal instructions and circumstances responded to the scale in the same way as those who had been instructed to "demonstrate" their cognitive ability. Notwithstanding a possible ceiling effect, this finding implies that the NCS produces scores that are confounded with subjects' desires to exhibit their intellectual prowess.

Thus, both our studies suggest that the NCS is confounded by a form of social desirability. However, this apparent confound is not an entirely unique one, nor is it necessarily a serious one. It is well known that self-report measures can be clouded by socially desirable responding (Crowne and Marlowe 1964). However, a more insidious type of problem could arise when the NCS is used in conjunction with other variables that involve cognitively oriented tasks. This can be seen in the ELM research designs employed by Cacioppo and Petty (1982; Cacioppo et al. 1983; Cacioppo et al. 1986; Haugtvedt et al. 1988; Haugtvedt and Petty 1992). A common objective of their work is to study how individual differences can predict the likelihood that recipients of persuasive communication will extract and cognitively elaborate on the information contained in that communication. To operationalize the ELM framework, subjects are sometimes partitioned *a priori* into either a high or low level of need for cognition based on NCS scores. This blocked factor is then crossed experimentally with an argument quality factor, which is made up of either strong or weak persuasive information. Results from this design typically demonstrate that subjects who are high in NC process the issue-relevant information more actively than do those who are low in NC. Evidence of this processing difference is normally presented in terms of attitudinal or memory differences between the two types of subjects. High NC subjects exhibit a greater cognitive and attitudinal sensitivity to the argument quality manipulation than do low NC subjects. Presumably, high NC subjects' elevated sensitivity is a reflection of their more elaborate message processing. Although we do not dispute the general conclusions drawn from Cacioppo and Petty's studies, we note the possible confound that their research design produces if an association exists between the NCS and social desirability. If NCS really captures individuals' desire merely to *appear* cognitively astute, as such an association would imply, then the degree to which NC affects the elaboration of persuasive information is indeterminate. It would be unclear whether (and to what extent) subjects' responses to their cognitive task were a result of a chronic NC or an acute need to present a cerebral facade. The greater the latter, the more likely persuasive information would be elaborated by subjects—but not for the hypothesized reason. Subjects assigned to the high NC group by virtue of their NCS score might exhibit a greater sensitivity to information cues simply as a result of their desire to appear contemplative, and *not* because of any inherent cognitive need. In short, demand characteristics present an alternative explanation to NC where social desirability has not been ruled out.

A confounded NC measure also could bring about an undesirable interaction between the pre-measured NCS and ELM subjects' subsequent exposure to cognitively oriented treatments. If subjects are required to complete a NCS prior to their exposure to such treatments, they could easily become sensitized to the cognitive demands of the persuasive task. Their desire to appear thoughtful would heighten their attention to the quality of the arguments contained in the experimental stimuli and both internal and external validity would be threatened.

Finally, we emphasize the apparent role played by age in the NCS-social desirability relationship. Our data suggest that the older the student, the greater the "temptation" of social desirability. This should be expected, inasmuch as most of our older subjects were MBA students who identify with middle- to upper-level management mentalities. Cognitive achievement is highly salient for such people, particularly when they are cast into a highly competitive academic environment. All this tells us nothing about the social approval proclivities of experimental subjects older than graduate students, however. One can speculate, but the self-presentation tendencies of, say, middle aged or elderly people are not well understood. But typical ELM experiments use college students and other young adults as subjects, hence the limited age range for which we do have data is probative.

To summarize, our results echo the expressed concerns of Cacioppo and Petty (1982) regarding the potential transparency of their NCS. A confound seems to exist between that scale and people's tendency to respond in a socially desirable way. Age of subject (over a relevant range) appears to accentuate this confound. Of course these findings are tentative and limited to academic settings in which administered questionnaires are used. Moreover, we recognize that none of these conclusions proceeds from a comprehensive replication of any of Cacioppo and Petty's individual studies (cf. Rosenthal 1991). Certainly, a better understanding of the relationship between the focal variables would emerge from such a study. Nevertheless, our findings counsel against the indiscriminate use of the NCS in any setting that is likely to emphasize cognitive skill. The cumulative contribution of the ELM paradigm has been substantial because the model is sound conceptually and because its tests have been executed with skill and care. We wish merely to emphasize what Cacioppo and Petty (1982) recognized about their NCS at the outset—that its use requires *particular* care.

REFERENCES

Cacioppo, John T. and Richard E. Petty (1982), "The Need for Cognition," *Journal of Personality and Social Psychology*, 42 (January), 116-131.

_____, Richard E. Petty and Chuan F. Kao (1984), "The Efficient Assessment of Need for Cognition," *Journal of Personality Assessment*, 48 (June), 306-307.

_____, Richard E. Petty, Chuan F. Kao and Regina Rodriguez (1986), "Central and Peripheral Routes to Persuasion: An Individual Difference Perspective," *Journal of Personality and Social Psychology*, 51 (November), 1032-1043.

_____, Richard E. Petty and Katherine J. Morris (1983), "Effects of Need for Cognition on Message Evaluation, Recall, and Persuasion," *Journal of Personality and Social Psychology*, 45 (October), 805-818.

Cohen, Arthur R. (1957), "Need for Cognition and Order of Communication as Determinants of Opinion Change," In Carl I. Hovland (ed.), *The Order of Presentation in Persuasion* (pp. 79-97), New Haven, CT: Yale University Press.

_____ (1964), *Attitude Change and Social Influence*, New York: Basic Books.

_____, E. Stotland and D. Wolfe (1955), "An Experimental Investigation of Need for Cognition," *Journal of Abnormal and Social Psychology*, 51 (September), 291-294.

Crowne, Douglas P. and David Marlowe (1964), *The Approval Motive*, New York: Wiley.

Haugtvedt, Curt, Richard E. Petty, John T. Cacioppo and Theresa Steidley (1988), "Personality and Ad Effectiveness: Exploring the Utility of Need for Cognition," In Michael Houston (ed.), *Advances in Consumer Research*, (Vol. 15, pp. 209-212), Provo, UT: Association for Consumer Research.

_____ and Richard E. Petty (1992), "Personality and Persuasion: Need for Cognition Moderates the Persistence and Resistance of Attitude Change," *Journal of Personality and Social Psychology*, 63 (August), 308-319.

Hovland, C. I. and Janis, I. L., eds. (1959), *Personality and Persuasibility*, New Haven, CT: Yale University Press.

Petty, Richard E. and John T. Cacioppo (1986), *Communication and Persuasion: Central and Peripheral Routes to Persuasion*, New York: Springer-Verlag.

Rosenthal, Robert (1991), "Replication in Behavioral Research," In J. W. Neuliep (ed.), *Replication Research in the Social Sciences*, (pp. 1-30), Newbury Park, CA: Sage.

Comments on Scale Development and Testing
Thomas J. Page, Jr., Michigan State University

INTRODUCTION

The three papers all deal with some aspect of scale development or testing. The paper by Feltham attempts to develop a new scale for classifying stimuli into consistent categories. The papers by Malafarina & Jass and Hunt et al examine the validity of existing scales. In general, the papers represent a good combination of the different steps that need to be carried out in developing and using scales in research projects. The comments presented here will attempt to summarize the major points of the session and also make some suggestions for future research concerning the specific papers.

MAJOR POINTS OF THE SESSION

There are two points that readers of the three papers should come away with after reading them. The first is Feltham's point concerning generalizable conclusions. Her point is that we cannot make any generalizable conclusions about a theory unless we have some degree of certainty about the methods used to test it. For example, one study may call a construct humor, another may call it warmth, and still another may call it emotion, and yet they may all be talking about the same stimulus. This lack of consistency severely hinders the discipline's ability to make generalizations about a particular theory.

In addition to restricting the generalizability of results, this inconsistency is often evoked to explain unexpected results. Frequently, researchers testing a particular theory may arrive at results that are not consistent with either the theory or previous research in the area. One popular method of explaining the discrepant results is to claim that their stimuli were somehow slightly different from those used in other studies. While this may indeed be the case, it would certainly be desirable to have a method that can at least reduce some of this ambiguity. Thus, the attempt by Feltham to develop a method of dealing with this problem is certainly a step in the right direction.

The second major point of the session comes from the two papers that examine the validity of existing scales. Too often, researchers just blindly accept the validity of an existing scale without giving any thought as to how potential problems with the scale may affect their research. Obviously, problems with the dimensionality of a scale as uncovered by Malafarina and Jass, or problems with discriminant validity as found by Hunt et al, could seriously affect the results of a particular study. Just because there are a lot of published studies using a particular scale does not preclude the possibility that it will occasionally demonstrate undesirable psychometric properties. Thus, authors should, whenever possible, examine such characteristics as discriminant and convergent validity, and dimensionality of the scales they are using in their research. This does not mean that wholesale revamping of a scale should be carried out every time it used, but if a particular scale seems to have undesirable properties in a particular case, the researchers need to take into account how they may affect their results, and perhaps consider using a different scale.

COMMENTS ON INDIVIDUAL PAPERS

The paper by Feltham represents a good first step in developing a method of classifying stimuli so that generalizations can be made across studies. As the author states, though, there is still a lot of work to be done. In particular, the convergent and discriminant validity of the three categories needs to be established. Also, there is a need for some sort of independent verification that the stimuli being classified into a certain category are actually logical, emotional, or posses a particular source characteristic. Once this has been accomplished, using larger sample sizes, the classification scheme will be very useful.

Malafarina & Jass present a very good literature review of work in the area of consumer conservation. They demonstrate that some of the sub-scales of the Conservation-Oriented Consumption Scale have low coefficient alphas. They also demonstrate that the scale fails to achieve convergent validity with the Concern for Supply and Avowal of Social Norms scales. This may indeed represent a problem with the scale, but it may also be due to other causes. For example, the Avowal of Social Norms scale and the Concern for Supply Scale may not be highly correlated with each other. If this is the case, they would not demonstrate convergent validity with the Conservation-Oriented Consumption Scale. Also, if different scales were used to assess convergent validity, the Conservation-Oriented Consumption Scale might have achieved an accpetable level. Nevertheless, this paper does point out the need to critically examine a scale before using it in one's research.

Hunt et al are concerned about the transparency of the Need For Cognition Scale. In particular, the second study provided some very provocative results. Specifically, they showed that a control group's responses were not significantly different from a group that was told to deliberately attempt to display their intelligence in responding to the Need for Cognition Scale. This is taken as evidence that the scale may indeed be susceptible to social desirability effects. This is a very intriguing result. However, before condemning the Need For Cognition Scale, some more work needs to be done. The authors need to show that their manipulation was indeed manipulating social desirability and not just telling people to respond differently to the scale. This is particularly important in this case since telling someone to downplay or display their intelligence in responding to the scale is a bit transparent in itself. However, if a series of studies along these lines demonstrate consistent findings, then the Need for Cognition Scale may need to be reexamined in terms of its validity.

Consumers' Response to Waiting Time: New Segmentation Bases Are Required for Service Industries

Marie Marquis, Université du Québec à Montréal
Laurette Dubé, Université de Montréal
Jean-Charles Chebat, Université du Québec à Montréal

ABSTRACT

The objective of this research was to investigate the effect of two individual characteristics namely the circadian orientation and Type A/B behavior pattern on consumers' responses to waiting time in service settings. A first exploratory study (n=34) showed that both characteristics induced differences in consumers' emotional responses and tolerance level to delays. In study 2, taxonomic analyses were used to demonstrate that consumers could be empirically segmented according to their circadian orientation. Implications for segmentation strategy in service industries are discussed.

INTRODUCTION

In our post-modern society, time has become one of consumers' scarcest resources. As a result, the amount of time used and saved in purchasing and consuming products and services is now a critical factor in consumer choice (Kaufman et al. 1991; Marmorstein et al. 1992). In services, consumers' concern for saving time has not only involved design modifications but has also forced many industries such as banking and supermarkets to deliver services around the clock (Kelley 1989). Just think about products such as eyeglasses or rolls of film for which the processing time has been cut from days to minutes.

Yet, no systematic attempt has been made to categorize consumers on the basis of their reaction to time. Pinpointing time-related preferences of segments of consumers and designing products or services accordingly may well be a neglected weapon to gain a competitive edge in service industries. In this paper, we focus on consumers' reactions to waiting time in services. We investigated two individual characteristics -circadian orientation and Type A/B behavior pattern - whose effects are likely to influence consumers' response to waiting time. We first provide the theoretical rationale for these effects and then report a study that provides preliminary evidence. Finally, in a second study, segments of consumers presenting different circadian orientations are empirically identified using taxonomic methods.

REVIEW OF THE LITERATURE

Individual differences in consumers' response to waiting time

Among the many individual differences that have been studied in psychology and consumer behavior, we have selected circadian orientation and Type A/B behavior pattern. Both characteristics have been shown to influence variables such as cognitive performance (Horne et al. 1980; Juszczak and Andreassi 1987; Matthews 1982), arousal (Matthews 1988), mood (Patkai 1971; Strube and Lott 1984), and time perception (Burnam et al. 1975; Thor 1962). According to recent psychological theories about memory for temporal information and duration estimation, these variables may be mediators of consumers' response to waiting time (Block 1989; Zakay 1989; see Zakay and Hornik 1991 for an application of these theories to consumers' response to waiting). Thus, both circadian orientation and Type A/B behavior pattern are most likely to impact on consumers' response to waiting time. In this section, we briefly review findings on circadian orientation and Type A/B behavior that bear on consumers' response to waiting time.

Circadian orientation

A number of studies in chronobiology have demonstrated the impact of circadian cycles on individuals. Circadian cycles refer to the day-night cycles that create, within each individual, an internal rhythm, called circadian clock. This phenomenon has been a topic of interest in various disciplines mainly because of its stability and influence (Aschoff 1984). These cycles can be predict, occur at regular intervals and have an impact on human behavior during day and night. Influences on physiological functions such as body temperature or basal metabolism have been demonstrated (Aschoff 1984, 1989).

However, results of many research have shown that circadian cycles were not affecting everyone at the same time of the day. Interindividual differences, called circadian orientation, were recognized and further operationalized in the concept of Morning and Evening types. More specifically, studies have indicated arousal peak level differences related to Morning/Evening types. The Morning type energetic peak, called arousal acrophase, would be somewhere between the morning and the beginning of the afternoon while the Evening type acrophase would be somewhere between the end of the afternoon and the beginning of the evening (Akerstedt and Froberg 1976; Foret et al. 1982; Kerkhof 1985; Matthews 1988; Patkai 1971). In relation with time estimation, it has also been demonstrated that Evening and Morning types estimation of small time intervals (less than 2 minutes) fluctuated according to the time of the day (Thor 1962).

Type A/B behavior pattern

The construct of Type A/B behavior pattern has been introduced by Friedman and Rosenman in studies in which the role of specific behavior patterns was related to the development of coronary heart disease(Jenkins et al. 1979). The most critical characteristics of Type A individuals are competitiveness, achievement striving, aggressiveness and easily aroused hostility. Type As also show a sense of time urgency. Individuals who exhibit a Type B behavior pattern are described as being more relaxed and having an easy-going life-style (Jenkins et al. 1979).

Type As' concern for time urgency has been said to be the only evident behavior present in all Type As (Mueser et al. 1987). These individuals are impatient, constantly struggle to achieve more in less time and are continually striving to avoid loss of control over their environment (Krantk et al. 1974). With respect to time perception, Burnam et al. (1975) conducted a study in which Type As and Type Bs were required to read aloud a technical article during 60 seconds. Type As underestimated the passage of the minute (52.6 sec.) while Type Bs overestimated the same interval (75.0 sec.). However, neither Warner and Block (1984) nor Retzlaff (1982) obtained results to confirm these findings. Different time periods and level of activity during the experiment may explain the different results (Retzlaff 1982; Warner and Block 1984).

The association of time urgency with Type As has also been explored in a study in which the perceived appropriateness of time adjectives was examined (Mueser et al. 1987). The study revealed that Type As rated low speed and energy adjectives as inappropriate time descriptors while Type Bs rated them as appropriate time descriptors.

In sum, past research on both circadian orientation and on Type A/B behavior pattern suggests that individuals presenting different levels of these characteristics are likely to differ in their tolerance level and emotional responses when facing an unexpected waiting time. An exploratory study was conducted to investigate these issues.

STUDY 1

Overview

The study was designed as a preliminary test of the effect of circadian orientation and Type A/B behavior pattern on consumers' response to waiting. Subjects were asked to indicate their emotional responses and tolerance levels to scenarios of unexpected delays. Their individual circadian orientation and behavior pattern were assessed with standardized tools.

Method

Subjects were 34 undergraduate anglophone students in an eastern Canadian Business School. They participated in the study on a voluntary basis. The study was presented as part of a research on consumers' individual characteristics and was conducted in a group session at 10:15 a.m.

Independent variables

Circadian orientation: The Smith et al. (1989) morningness questionnaire including 13 items was used to classify subjects as Morning or Evening types. This latest english version of morningness questionnaire is a composite scale that includes the best of three previous morningness questionnaires (Folkard et al. 1979; Horne and Ostberg 1976; Torsvall and Akerstedt 1980). A median split on the total score was used to identify Morning and Evening types.

Type A/B behavior pattern: Following Matthews(1982), Strube et al(1986) and Feather and Volkmer(1988), subjects were classified as Type As or Type Bs on the basis of the short form of the student version of the Jenkins Activity Survey(SJAS). The SJAS version has been modeled after the adult version (Zyzanski and Jenkins 1970) to suit an academic context(Glass 1977). A slightly modified short form of the SJAS was used. This short form of the SJAS is limited to the speed/impatience and hard-driving/competitive factors. It has been found to give a satisfactory internal consistency, an excellent test-retest reliability (Yarnold et al. 1986) as well as a criterion-related validity (Yarnold et al. 1987).

Dependent variables

Emotional response to delays: Subjects were asked to imagine that they were waiting in situations commonly encountered in service settings. Because it could be assumed that our subjects would have had a reasonable amount of personal experience with such situations, they were likely to be reliable informants of their behavior in similar real-life situations (Schmitt, Dubé, Leclerc 1992). For *situation specific responses,* subjects were asked to imagine themselves in the following situations: having missed a bus, being unable to get a cab, waiting for a phone call. On a 9-point scale, they were asked to indicate how upsetting they found each of these situations (1=not at all, 9=very upsetting). For *general emotional response,* subjects were asked to indicate how angry they were when they have to face unexpected delays in general (1=not at all, 9=very angry).

Tolerance to unexpected delay: Subjects were asked to imagine having dinner at a restaurant and to indicate how they would react to an unexpected delay in the service. The following scenario was given:

"Suppose you are in a restaurant and you are told that you have to wait for fifteen minutes before you will be seated. How soon after the end of the expected delay will you get restless?"

Subjects indicated their responses to this pre-process delay in minutes. Because consumers' responses to waiting time have been shown to vary as a function of the phase in the service delivery process (Dubé, Schmitt and Leclerc 1989, 1991), we also ask subjects to indicate their reactions to a 15 minutes delay occurring as they were waiting for the main course (within-process) and for the check (post-process).

Results

Reliability of the scales

The alpha coefficient for the 13-items circadian orientation scale was 0.81. The alpha coefficient for the overall SJAS scale was 0.72 (15 items). Alpha coefficients were also computed for the speed/impatience subscale (alpha=0.69, 4 items) and for the hard-driving/competitive subscale (alpha=0.81, 5 items).

The three emotional responses to waiting times presented a good reliability (alpha= 0.73) and an average score was computed. The three items related to the tolerance to unexpected delay presented an alpha coefficient of 0.75. An average score was also computed.

Effects of circadian orientation and behavior pattern

In order to investigate the effect of the two personality characteristics on consumers' response to waiting time, a series of mean comparisons (t-test with pooled variance estimate) were conducted on the three dependent variables (emotional responses to specific situations, general emotional response, and tolerance to unexpected delay) between sub-groups formed for each characteristic. For Type A/B behavior pattern, sub-groups were formed for the overall scale and also for sub-scales of speed/impatience and hard-driving/competitive. Means are presented in Table 1 for circadian orientation and Type A/B behavior pattern classified on the speed/impatience sub-scale.

Effect of circadian orientation: Results show that individuals with an Evening type orientation demonstrated a more negative emotional response when they encountered unexpected waiting time in service situations (M:Morning= 5.00; M:Evening= 6.14; T[32]=2.22; $p<.05$).

With respect to the amount of time they could tolerate an unexpected delay before getting upset, Evening and Morning types did not differ significantly although differences tend to appear at the post-process phase (M:Morning=5.77 min.; M:Evening=7.82 min.; $p<0.3$). Interestingly, for Morning types, tolerance to waiting time varied as a function of the phase of the process. They were willing to wait a shorter period of time when the unexpected delay occurred at the post-process phase (5.77 min.) than when it occurred at the pre-process (10.35 min.) or in-process phase (9.82 min.)(mean comparisons: post and pre-process: T[16]= 3.12; $p<.05$; post and in-process:T[16]= 2.43; $p<.05$). The same trend was observed for the Evening type although the differences did not reach significance level (all $ps > 0.3$).

Effect of Type A/B behavior pattern: Means comparisons for subjects classified as Type A/B on the basis of the overall SJAS scale and on the hard/driving competitive sub-scale did not show any significant differences in consumers' response to waiting time. However, individuals categorized as Type A or B on the basis of the speed/impatience sub-scale did show important differences in the dependent variables. Type As were significantly more upset than Type Bs when facing unexpected delay in specific service delivery environments (Type A= 6.10; Type B= 5.09; T[32]= -1.94; $p<0.07$).

TABLE 1
Emotional responses and tolerance to waiting time as a function of circadian orientation and Type A/B behavior pattern

	Circadian orientation		Behavior pattern	
	Morning	Evening	Type A	Type B
Emotional responses				
situation specific	5.00a	6.14b*	6.10a	5.09b**
general response	5.18a	5.24a	5.75a	4.72b**
Tolerance				
overall	8.65^a	8.80^a	7.06^a	10.20^{b**}
pre-process	10.35^a	9.29^a	8.44^a	11.06^a
within-process	9.82^a	9.29^a	7.00^a	11.83^{b*}
post-process	5.77^a	7.82^a	5.75^a	7.72^a

Note: Comparisons are made rowwise within each individual characteristic for means with different subscripts.
* Means with different subscripts are significantly different at $p < 0.05$
** Means with different subscripts are significantly different at $p < 0.10$

Type As also indicated that their usual emotional reaction to unexpected delay was significantly more negative than Type Bs (Type A= 5.75; Type B= 4.72; T[32]= -1.84; $p<0.08$).

With respect to their tolerance level to unexpected delay, across all three phases of the process, Type As were willing to wait for a shorter period of time than Type Bs (Type A= 7.06 min; Type B= 10.20 min.; T[32]= 2.00; $p<0.06$). When separate analyses were conducted for the three different phases of the service process, Type As were significantly less tolerant than Type Bs only at the within-process phase (Type A= 7.00 min.; Type B= 11.83 min.; T[32]=2.29; $p<0.05$). Finally, we found that both Type As and Type Bs manifested significant differences in their tolerance level to unexpected delay as a function of the phase of the process in which they occur. At a marginal level, Type As were less tolerant to delays in the post-process (5.75 min.) than in the pre-process phase (8.44 min.)(mean comparisons: T[15]= 1.76; $p<.10$). Type Bs were also less tolerant in the post-process phase (7.72 min.) compared to the within-process (11.83 min.)(mean comparisons: T[17]= 2.61; $p<.05$) or pre-process phase (11.06 min.)(mean comparisons: T[17]=2.20; $p<.05$).

Discussion

The results of this first study suggest that consumers presenting different circadian orientation and type of behavior pattern would respond differently to waiting situations. Type A/B behavior pattern induced differences in both emotional and tolerance responses to waiting. Individuals who scored high on the speed/impatience subscale responded more negatively to unexpected delay and they would wait a shorter period of time before getting upset. Further research should replicate these effects and investigate their underlying mediators.

Turning to circadian orientation, Evening type individuals, compared to Morning types, demonstrated a more negative emotional response to unexpected delay. Does this effect reflect a more general negative affective state for Evening type or is it related to the time of the day when the study was conducted (10:15 a.m.)? Kleitman (1963) has suggested that Evening types may, in general, be in a more negative affective state due to the fact that their diurnal rhythm of sleep and wakefulness does not conform to the habits of the majority of the population. Patkai (1971) also found that a series of negative feelings (gloomy, morose, dispirited) were reported only by Evening types. However, in Patkai's study, Evening types expressed these negative feelings only when the reports were made in the morning. In our study, even though we did not manipulate the time of the day when the delay occurred, it may be that subjects naturally took into account the actual time when they completed the questionnaire. This could explain why significant effect were found only for situation-specific measures. Further research should systematically investigate the effect of circadian orientation on consumers' reactions to unexpected delays occurring at different times of the day.

In sum, the results of this study suggest that both circadian orientation and Type A/B behavior may be valuable segmentation bases for service industries. If these preliminary results on time related differences among consumers are confirmed, service providers may seek to redesign part of their service operations to suit specific needs and wants of the target segments. Moreover, specific training programs could be planned to help contact personnel to recognize patterns of behavior expressed by each segment and to adopt appropriate roles during the individual service encounter. Service industries might also adapt their communication strategy with messages emphasizing time concern attributes (time saving procedures, round the clock service, home service, etc.) or emotional response to delay. Thus, it would become important to empirically identify segments on the basis of these two characteristics. In study 2, we used taxonomic analyses to classify segments of consumers presenting different circadian orientations.

STUDY 2

Overview

This second experiment was part of a larger project on service quality in the banking industry. Subjects were asked to complete the Smith et al. (1989) questionnaire on circadian orientation. They were classified as being either Morning or Evening type using cluster and discriminant analyses.

Method

Subjects were 219 undergraduate francophone students in an eastern Canadian Business School who volunteered for the study. Subjects were run in groups of 20 to 30 in a class setting. The study was presented as a research on consumer behavior in banks. The english version of the scale was translated in french and validated using back translation. It was completed by the subjects at the

TABLE 2
Means of individual items of the circadian orientation scale for each cluster - Study 2

	Cluster 1	Cluster 2
1. Rising time without constraints *	2.31	3.19
2. Bed time without constraints *	2.32	2.93
3. Ease to get up	2.07	2.81
4. Morning alertness	2.11	2.68
5. Morning feeling of tiredness	2.30	2.94
6. Physical performance (7 - 8 a.m)	2.51	3.23
7. Evening hour of tiredness *	2.93	3.15
8. Preferred time for intellectual test	2.32	3.41
9. Self perception of M/E type	1.70	3.00
10. Rising hour preference	1.60	2.67
11. Pleasantness with 6:00 a.m. rising	1.95	2.86
12. Time required to recover	3.35	3.68
13. Self perception of M/E activity	1.80	3.04

Note: Means are presented prior to data standardization. Standardized means are significant at $p < 0.0005$ for each variable except for the item # 7.
* Items measured on 5-point scale. Otherwise items were measured on 4-point scale.

TABLE 3
Predicted vs observed categorization as a function of circadian orientation - Study 2

		Predicted group membership	
Actual groups	n	Group 1 Evening	Group 2 Morning
1 (Evening)	78	77 / 98.7%	1 / 1.3%
2 (Morning)	134	13 / 9.7%	121 / 90.3%

beginning of the experimental session. Half of the subjects completed the questionnaire at 10:00 a.m. and the other half at 7:00 p.m.

Analysis

As a statistical method of classification, cluster analysis has been used in marketing to create market segments or groups of subjects along several personality and decision behavior characteristics (Punj and Stewart 1983). Quick Cluster analysis was conducted on measures of circadian orientation collected with the Smith et al. instrument, specifying that two clusters of subjects were to be found.

The 13 items of the scale were considered to be interval-scale measures. Standardized scores were computed to allow for comparison between 4 and 5-point scales. The cluster analysis retained 212 subjects and classified 65 individuals in the first cluster and 147 in the second. The interpretation of the means of the independent variables indicated that the first cluster included the Evening types and the second cluster included the Morning types (Table 2).

To validate the cluster solution, analysis of variance and discriminant analysis were conducted (Klastorin 1983). The analysis of variance confirmed that variable means were statistically different between each cluster for 12 of the 13 variables ($p<0.005$).

Prior to conducting the discriminant analysis, the correlation matrix was examined and showed that correlations among the variables were low to moderate, the largest correlation coefficient being 0.55. The Box's M test confirmed the equality of the group covariance matrices (Box-M= 90.294; $p< 0.05$). A stepwise method based on Mahalanobis' distance selected 10 variables to be included in the discriminant function (Norusis 1990). The function discriminated significantly between the two groups (chi-squared= 201.77; df= 10; $p<0.0005$) and correctly classified 93.87% of the subjects (Table 3). Results of study 2 confirmed the capacity of the Smith et al. questionnaire to classify segments of consumers upon their circadian orientation.

CONCLUSION

Results of Study 1 suggest that specific circadian orientation or behavior pattern induce different responses to waiting. Furthermore, Study 2, demonstrated that segments of consumers presenting different circadian orientation can be empirically identified. These time related segmentation variables may help service operations position themselves on innovative bases, focusing on attributes that are particularly critical for different consumer markets.

Further research should provide a more precise understanding of how consumers react to waiting in service delivery environments and could also correlate these individuals characteristics to other aspects of consumer behavior in services. Such studies would enlarge our very limited knowledge in the specific area of consumer behavior in the service industries.

REFERENCES

Akerstedt, T. and J.E. Froberg (1976), "Interindividual Differences in Circadian Patterns of Catecholamine Excretion, Body Temperature, Performance, and Subjective Arousal," *Biological Psychology*, 4, 277-292.

Aschoff, Jurgen (1989), "Temporal Orientation: Circadian Clocks in Animals and Humans," *Animal Behavior*, 37, 881-896.

Aschoff, Jurgen (1984), "Circadian Timing," *Annals New York Academy of Sciences*, 423, 442-468.

Block, R.A. (1989), "Experiencing and Remembering Time: Affordance, Context and Cognition" in I. Levin and D. Zakay (eds.) *Time and Human Cognition: A Life Span Perspective*, Amsterdam, North Holland.

Burnam, A., Pennebaker, J.W. and D.C. Glass (1975), "Time Consciousness, Achievement Striving, and the Type A Coronary-Prone Behavior Pattern," *Journal of Abnormal Psychology*, 84(1), 76-79.

Dubé, L., Schmitt, B.H., Leclerc, F.(1991), "Consumers' affective Responses to Delays at Different Phases of a Service Delivery" *Journal of Applied Social Psychology*, 20, 810-820.

Dubé, L., Schmitt, B. H., Leclerc, F. (1989), "When Delays Affect the Perception of Service Quality," in Srull T.K. *Advances in Consumer Research*, 16 (ed.), Ann Harbor, MI: Association for Consumer Research, 112-125.

Feather, N.T. and R.E. Volkmer (1988), "Preference for Situations Involving Effort, Time Pressure, and Feedback in Relation to Type A Behavior, Locus of Control, and Test Anxiety," *Journal of Personality and Social Psychology*, 55(2), 266-271.

Folkard, Simon et al. (1979), "Towards a Predictive Tools of Adjustment to Shift Work," *Ergonomics*, 22, 79-91.

Foret, Jean et al. (1982), "Sleep Schedules and Peak Times of Oral Temperature and Alertness in Morning and Evening 'types'," *Ergonomics*, 25, 821-827.

Glass, D.C. (1977). *Behavior patterns, stress, and coronary disease*. Hillsdale, N.J. Erlbaum.

Horne, J.A. et al. (1980), "Circadian Performance Differences Between Morning and Evening 'types'," *Ergonomics*, 23 (1), 29-36.

Horne, J.A. and O. Ostberg (1976), "A Self-Assessment Questionnaire to Determine Morningness-Eveningness in Human Circadian Rhythms," *International Journal of Chronobiology*, 4, 97-110.

Jenkins, C.D., Zyzanski, S.J. and R.H. Rosenman (1979). *Jenkins Activity Survey*. The Psychological Corporation, 31 p.

Juszczak, N.M. and J.L. Andreassi (1987), "Performance and Physiological Responses of Type A and Type B Individuals During a Cognitive and Perceptual-Motor Task," *International Journal of Psychophysiology*, 5, 81-89.

Kaufman, C.F. et al. (1991), "Exploring More than 24 Hours a Day: A Preliminary Investigation of Polychronic Time Use," *Journal of Consumer Research*, 18 (december), 392-401.

Kelley, Scott W. (1989), "Efficiency in Service Delivery : Technological or Humanistic Approaches?," *The Journal of Services Marketing*, 3 (summer), 43-50.

Kerkhof, Gerard A.(1985), "Inter-Individual Differences in the Human Circadian System : A Review," *Biological Psychology*, 20, 83-112.

Klastorin, T.D. (1983), "Assessing Cluster Analysis Results," *Journal of Marketing Research*, 20 (february), 92-98.

Kleitman, N. (1963). *Sleep and Wakefulness*. Chicago. Univer. Chicago Press.

Krantz, D.S., Glass, D.C. and M. L. Snyder (1974), "Helplesness, Stress Level, and the Coronary-Prone Behavior Pattern," *Journal of Experimental Social Psychology*, 10, 284-300.

Marmorstein, H. et al. (1992), "The Value of Time Spent in Price-Comparison Shopping: Survey and Experimental Evidence," *Journal of Consumer Research*, 19 (june), 52-61.

Matthews, Gerald (1988), "Morningness-Eveningness as a Dimension of Personality: Trait, State, and Psychophysiological Correlates," *European Journal of Personality*, 2, 277-293.

Matthews, Karen A. (1982), "Psychological Perspectives on the Type A Behavior Pattern," *Psychological Bulletin*, 91 (2), 293-323.

Mueser, K.T., Yarnold, P.R. and F.B. Bryant (1987), "Type A Behavior and Time Urgency: Perception of Time Adjectives," *The British Psychological Society*, 267-269.

Norusis, Marija J. (1990). *SPSS Advanced Statistics Student Guide*. Marketing Department, SPSS Inc, Chicago.

Patkai, Paula (1971), "Interindividual Differences in Diurnal Variations in Alertness, Performance, and Adrenaline Excretion," *Acta physiol. scand.*, 81, 35-46.

Punj, G. and D.W. Stewart (1983), "Cluster Analysis in Marketing Research: Review and Suggestions for Application," *Journal of Marketing Research*, 20 (may), 134-148.

Retzlaff, Paul D. (1982), "Verbal Estimation, Production, and Reproduction of Time Intervals by Type A Individuals," *Perceptual and Motor Skills*, 55, 331-334.

Schmitt, B. H., Dubé, L. and F. Leclerc (1992), "Consumers' Reactions to Delay while Waiting in Queues: Individual Costs and Moral Outrage as Determinants of Affective and Behavioral Responses," *Journal of Personality and Social Psychology*

Smith, Carlla S., Reilly, C. and K. Midkiff (1989), "Evaluation of Three Circadian Rhythm Questionnaires With Suggestions for an Improved Measure of Morningness," *Journal of Applied Psychology*, 74 (5), 728-738.

Strube, M.J. et al. (1986), "Self-Schematic Representation of Type A and B Behavior Patterns," *Journal of Personality and Social Psychology*, 51(1), 170-180.

Strube, M.J. and C.L. Lott (1984), "Time Urgency and the Type A Behavior Pattern: Implications for Time Investment and Psychological Entrapment," *Journal of Research in Personality*, 18, 395-409.

Thor, Donald H. (1962), "Diurnal Variability in Time Estimation," *Perceptual and Motor Skills*, 15, 451-454.

Torsvall, L. et Akerstedt, T. (1980), "A Diurnal Type Scale," *Scandinavian Journal of Work and Environmental Health*, 6, 282-290.

Warner, D.J. and R.A. Block (1984), "Type A Behavior and Temporal Judgment," *Bulletin of the Psychonomic Society*, 22(3), 163-166.

Yarnold, P.R., F.B. Bryant and L.G. Frimm (1987), "Comparing the Long and Short Forms of the Student Version of the Jenkins Activity Survey," *Journal of Behavioral Medicine*, 10 (1), 75-90.

Yarnold, P.R., Mueser K.T., Grau B.W. and L.G. Grimm (1986), "The Reliability of the Student Version of the Jenkins Activity Survey," *Journal of Behavioral Medicine*, 9 (4), 401-414.

Zakay, D. (1989), "Subjective Time and Attentional Resource Allocation: An Integrated Model of Time Estimation" in I.Levin & D. Zakay (eds.) *Time and human cognition a lifespan perspective* pp. 365-377, Elsevier Science Publishers.

Zakay D., and J. Hornik (1991), "How Much Time Did you Wait in Line? A Time Perception Perspective" in (eds Chebat J.C. and V. Venkatesan) *Time and Consumer Behavior,* Montreal.

Zyzanski, S.J. and Jenkins C.D. (1970), "Basic Dimensions Within the Coronary-prone Behavior Pattern," *Journal of Chronical Disease,* 22, 781-795.

The Effect of Arousal Seeking Tendency on Consumer Preferences for Complex Product Designs

Dena Cox, Indiana University
Anthony Cox, Indiana University

ABSTRACT

Research and theory concerning consumers' arousal seeking tendency (AST) would seem to suggest that high-AST consumers should prefer products with visually complex designs. However, the only previous study to examine how AST moderates preferences for complex, meaningful objects (Furnham and Bunyan 1988) found the exact opposite to be true. The present study re-examines this issue, while addressing some of the methodological problems of the Furnham and Bunyan study. Yet once again our results are contrary to those predicted in the arousal seeking literature. We conclude by discussing possible interpretations of this anomalous finding, and issues for future research.

In recent years, there has been a growing recognition among consumer researchers that many important consumer behaviors (e.g., reactions to fashion and decorative products, music, and advertisements) are affected by consumers' aesthetic or hedonic preferences (e.g. Sewall 1978, Hirschman and Holbrook 1982, Bell, Holbrook and Solomon 1991). This recognition has in turn stimulated experiments aimed at understanding how consumers' aesthetic preferences are affected by the design of marketing stimuli. For example, Bell, Holbrook and Solomon examined how consumer preferences for ensembles of furniture were affected by the consistency of styling within these ensembles, and Cox and Cox (1988) examined how the visual complexity of advertisements moderated the impact of repetition on consumer preferences for those advertisements.

Much of this research on consumer aesthetic preferences has been influenced by basic work in "experimental aesthetics," and especially by the research of Daniel Berlyne (e.g. Berlyne 1968, 1970; Berlyne and Lawrence 1964). Berlyne and his colleagues posited that humans' aesthetic preferences were a function of a stimulus' "arousal potential," which in turn was largely determined by its "collative properties;" e.g., its complexity, novelty and incongruity. According to Berlyne, aesthetic preference is related to a stimulus' arousal potential in an inverted-U shaped pattern, in which the most preferred stimuli are those which are *moderately* novel and complex, and therefore moderately arousing. In contrast, Berlyne's research suggests, subjects tend to dislike stimuli that are either too simple and familiar (which elicit a negative "tedium" response) or too complex and novel (which raises subjects' arousal beyond the optimal, preferred level).

While the above researchers have been examining how humans' aesthetic preferences are affected by a *stimulus'* arousal potential, other researchers, working virtually independently, have been studying a seemingly related phenomenon: *individual differences* in subjects' preferred or optimum arousal level. This personality trait has been variously termed "Sensation Seeking" (e.g., Zuckerman, Kolin and Zoob 1964) "Optimal Stimulation Level" (e.g. Raju 1980) and "Arousal Seeking Tendency" (Mehrabian and Russell 1973). A good description of this proposed construct is provided by Mehrabian and Russell (1973, p. 315):

"An individual's preference for an environment is closely related to his preferred arousal level: Some persons characteristically prefer calm settings, whereas others actively seek to increase their arousal by selecting novel, complex, or unpredictable situations."

In a recent article, Steenkamp and Baumgartner (1992) present both a literature review and original research examining the relationship between arousal seeking tendency and a variety of consumer behaviors: e.g., risk-taking, willingness to use a new brand, and information search. Surprisingly, however, they note that no study has examined the relationship between consumers' arousal seeking tendency, and their reactions to the collative properties (e.g., complexity, novelty) of marketing stimuli. In their discussion of future research, Steenkamp and Baumgartner (1992, p. 446) state:

"...we feel that some areas of exploratory behavior offer especially great potential for future research...particularly the effect of OSL [optimum stimulation level] on consumer responses to collative properties of stimuli. This is an important field of inquiry, and little experimental research is available. For example, one would expect that consumers with high OSL's would have greater preferences for complex, ambiguous or novel ads than consumers with lower OSL's. Furthermore, research on the relation between collative properties and consumer responses...may also be fruitfully employed to understand consumer reactions to other types of stimuli such as aesthetic objects."

The present study will seek to address this gap in the literature; i.e., we will examine whether consumers' aesthetic preferences for products that vary in their collative properties are moderated by consumers' measured Arousal Seeking Tendency. The particular collative property we will examine will be stimulus complexity, since this variable is most clearly operationalized in the work of Berlyne et al.

Since Berlyne's research indicates that complex stimuli tend to be more arousing than simple stimuli, one would logically expect that subjects scoring high on arousal seeking would be more likely to prefer complex stimuli than would low arousal seekers. However, only one study has examined this hypothesis directly, and it yielded somewhat ambiguous results. Furnham and Bunyan (1988) presented subjects with four types of paintings: abstract paintings of high and low visual complexity, and representational paintings of high and low complexity. After exposure to the paintings, subjects expressed their preferences, and then completed Zuckerman's Sensation-Seeking scale. The authors found that, among the abstract paintings, preferences followed exactly the pattern one would predict based on Berlyne's theory: the higher subjects' sensation-seeking scores, the more likely they were to prefer the complex paintings. However among the representational paintings, the results were somewhat surprising: preferences for the simple/representational paintings were not significantly correlated with sensation-seeking, and preferences for the complex/representational paintings were *negatively* correlated with subjects' sensation-seeking scores (r=-.33). Since complex stimuli are typically more arousing (Berlyne 1968, 1970) the results regarding the representational stimuli seem contrary to what one would expect based on Berlyne's theory.

In contemplating these results, it is important to note that most of Berlyne's research on collative variables has tended to employ abstract, meaningless stimuli (e.g. abstract line drawings, black and white grids, etc.) while most marketing stimuli (e.g. advertisements) tend to present representational depictions of recognizable objects (e.g., a product). Thus it would seem particularly relevant to consumer research to determine whether these seemingly anomalous findings for representational stimuli are a bona fide, replicable phenomenon, or are somehow an artifact of the particular experiment reported by Furnham and Bunyan.

Unfortunately, a straightforward interpretation of Furnham and Bunyan's findings is somewhat hampered by some methodological problems in their experiment. First, while the authors employed "experts" to help classify the paintings as either simple or complex, they apparently performed no manipulation checks to confirm that subjects perceived them as such, nor did they measure any other perceived differences among the purportedly complex and simple stimuli (e.g., was each set of paintings perceived as equally novel? Were there confounds between the paintings' complexity and their artistic style? For example, all five of the abstract/simple paintings were by Mark Rothko, who has a very bold, distinctive style). Second, there was no effort in the Furnham and Bunyan study to control for subjects' knowledge of paintings in general, nor their prior exposure to these particular paintings. Third, the experiment employed a within-subjects design, in which all subjects apparently saw the paintings in the same order, suggesting a potential confound of stimulus effects and order effects. Finally, Furnham and Bunyan employed Zuckerman's sensation-seeking scale, which some researchers have criticized for reliability problems, and proneness to producing anomalous results (see Mehrabian and Russell 1973; Steenkamp and Baumgartner 1992).

Thus our study will address some of these methodological difficulties, while examining the following research question:

Will subjects scoring high on Arousal Seeking Tendency be more likely to prefer depictions of visually complex product designs than subjects scoring low on Arousal Seeking Tendency?

METHOD

The design of our experiment addressed some of the methodological problems of the Furnham and Bunyan study: we employed a between subjects design, manipulation and confounding checks for complexity, controls for prior product knowledge, and an arousal-seeking scale that is widely viewed as more reliable than that used by Furnham and Bunyan. Specifically, our study employed a 2 x 2 between subjects design with two levels of product design complexity (simple and complex) and two levels of the measured variable, Arousal Seeking Tendency (AST) (low and high). We also employed multiple operationalizations of each level of product complexity to increase the construct validity of this manipulation (Cook and Campbell, 1979), using women's fashion products as the stimuli.

Subjects

Subjects were recruited from undergraduate business classes at a large Midwestern University. As an incentive to participate, subjects' names were placed in a lottery to win a Sony compact disc player. After excluding thirteen cases with excessive missing data, and selecting subjects scoring in the top or bottom third of the Arousal Seeking Tendency scale (discussed below) 343 subjects provided the data for this study. Subjects' ages ranged from 19 to 41, with a median age of 20. The sample intentionally included both female (35%) and male (65%) subjects. While men do not typically purchase female fashions, male opinions of fashion attractiveness are rated as extremely important to females in this age group (see, e.g., Reynolds and Wells 1977) and thus are likely to exert an indirect influence on purchase behavior. The impact of gender on subjects' judgments in discussed in the Results.

Stimuli and Pretests

The stimuli were professionally prepared drawings of fashion apparel. Fashion is a product for which consumer aesthetic response is very important (Sewall 1978) and which can believably be presented in a wide variety of designs. A total of forty-two dress styles were initially designed, which were intended to vary on perceived complexity as defined by Berlyne and Lawrence (1964) (having many heterogeneous elements, irregular in arrangement). The styles varied in their complexity of both shape (some had many complex embellishments, while others were very simple) and fabric (some fabrics were very simple, such as a solid shade; others had complex prints such as an irregular arrangement of circles and rectangles).

Next, the initial set of product designs was pretested to gauge subjects' perceptions of their complexity and to ensure that the complexity manipulation was not confounded with perceived novelty (another collative variable that might have been a confound in the Furnham and Bunyan study) or overall likability.

The pretests were conducted among a total of 421 undergraduate students, using measures modelled after Cox and Cox (1988). Perceived complexity was measured on two 7-point semantic differential scales anchored by "complicated-simple" and "not complex-complex" (1 scored as simple, 7 scored as complex). The coefficient alpha for this scale was 0.85. Perceived novelty was measured on five, 7-point semantic differential scales anchored by "new-old," "original-unoriginal," "unusual-common," "familiar-novel," and "typical-atypical." The coefficient alpha for this scale was 0.81. Stimulus likability was measured by three 7-point semantic differential scales anchored by "bad-good," "pleasant-unpleasant," and "likable-not likable." This scale's coefficient alpha was 0.89.

From these pretests, six product designs were found to meet our criteria. The mean perceived complexity of the three simple designs ($\bar{X}=2.60$) was significantly lower than that of the three complex designs ($\bar{X}=5.95$; t=10.2; p<.001), with all three complex designs ($\bar{X}_4=6.18, \bar{X}_5=5.20, \bar{X}_6=5.60$) being rated substantially higher than all three simple designs ($\bar{X}_1=1.78, \bar{X}_2=2.83, \bar{X}_3=2.20$). The mean liking of the simple designs ($\bar{X}=4.17$) did not differ significantly from that of the complex designs ($\bar{X}=4.27$). Finally, the mean perceived novelty of the simple designs ($\bar{X}=5.01$) was not significantly different from the mean of the complex designs ($\bar{X}=4.87$). All designs were perceived as at least moderately novel, with means ranging from 4.47 to 5.25 on the 1-7 point scale.

After pretesting, the six stimulus product designs were placed in the context of advertisements for a fictitious retail store.

The finished ads, like many fashion ads, were very simple. They contained minimal copy (the headline and store location information) and no product related copy. Aside from the variations in dress design, all of the experimental ads were identical on all other factors: store name, type, letter size, as well as the model, her accessories, her facial expression, etc. Each subject was exposed to only one of the six target stimuli, presented along with several unrelated "filler" ads within an experimental booklet.

Procedure

The booklets were randomly distributed to volunteer subjects within three large classes. Subjects were told that we were interested in their thoughts about some advertisements. Subjects were also told that we would be asking different people different questions due to the limited time period. This was done to help mask any demand artifacts about the target ad.

Subjects were given 20 seconds to view each ad in the booklet. (Pretests indicated that most subjects' attention seemed to wander after about a 20 second exposure to these ads). Subjects were instructed not to look back at any previous advertisements (compliance with this request was confirmed by experimenter observation of the subjects). After this task, subjects were asked to write all of the brand, store or manufacturer names that they could recall. Next, they were presented with a list of product categories and asked to place checks by those depicted in the preceding ads. These tasks were designed to disguise the true purpose of the study, as well as provide a slight delay before measurement. Next, subjects viewed a picture of the target product design and were asked to rate its visual appeal, and its visual complexity. They viewed another product and were asked similar questions about this product. Next, subjects completed the forty-item Arousal Seeking Tendency scale, and demographic questions.

Measures

Consumer liking of the product designs' visual appeal was measured by averaging six 7-point scales, anchored by "bad-good," "pleasant-unpleasant", "likable-not likable," "flattering-unflattering," "unattractive-attractive," and "stylish-not stylish." The first three adjective pairs were taken from Cox and Cox (1988), and the last three were designed to be specifically relevant to fashion. The polarity of some adjectives was reversed to avoid acquiescence bias, and then recoded before being combined into a mean score. This scale had a coefficient alpha of 0.92. *Perceived Complexity* was measured using two 7-point scales, anchored by "complex-not complex" and "complicated-simple." This scale had a coefficient alpha of 0.92.

Arousal Seeking Tendency (AST) was measured using Mehrabian and Russell's (1973) arousal seeking tendency scale. This summed scale asks subjects to provide 9-point agree-disagree ratings of 40 different statements related to arousal seeking (e.g., "I like to experience novelty and change in my daily routine" and "shops with thousands of exotic herbs and fragrances fascinate me".) Because we were interested in extreme effects, those scoring in the top and bottom thirds of this scale were used in the ANCOVA. We chose to use this particular measurement instrument for several reasons. First, as noted by Raju (1980), this scale taps a wider variety of arousal seeking behaviors than some of the alternatives, including several consumption-related behaviors. Second, as demonstrated both by Mehrabian and Russell (1973) and by Steenkamp and Baumgartner (1992), the AST scores well on a variety of tests of reliability and validity. Finally, the AST is fairly easy to administer.

The coefficient alpha of the AST scale in this study was 0.89, which is very consistent with past studies (e.g., Steenkamp and Baumgartner 1992).

Product-Category Knowledge was measured by asking "In general, would you say that you are knowledgeable about current fashions?" to which subjects responded on a seven-point scale ranging from "not at all knowledgeable" to "very knowledgeable."

RESULTS

Subjects' preferences regarding the fashion stimuli were analyzed using a 2 x 2 ANCOVA, with product design complexity (2 levels; high and low) as a manipulated factor, and Arousal seeking tendency (2 levels; top 1/3 and bottom 1/3) as a measured factor. A manipulation check confirmed that the mean perceived complexity of the "complex" designs (5.34) was significantly higher than that of the "simple" designs (2.88; p less than .001). Gender was included in the analysis as a covariate since (given the nature of the product category) we expected that there might be gender differences in the ratings of the stimuli.

The results of the ANCOVA are shown in the Table. As can be seen, arousal seeking had no main effect on product preferences, but dress complexity did (p<.013). This finding cannot be interpreted in a straightforward manner, since, as expected, there was a significant interaction between complexity and arousal seeking (F=5.73; d.f.=1, 338; p<.017). Figure 1 shows this interaction. As can be seen, the effect is contrary to what one would expect given the theories of Berlyne (1968, 1970) and Mehrabian and Russell (1973), but consistent with the results Furnham and Bunyan (1988) obtained for representational stimuli: Subjects with high arousal seeking tendencies preferred the simple product designs to the complex designs, while the low arousal seeking subjects rated both the low and high complexity dress designs the same ($\overline{X}_{low}$ =3.84, $\overline{X}_{high}$ =3.80).

As discussed earlier, we also measured subjects' self-reported *fashion knowledge*. Since several of the items in the AST scale measure interest in changes in one's environment and novel sensory experiences, one might expect AST to be positively correlated with fashion knowledge. Furthermore, since people with different levels of fashion knowledge may tend to view particular styles differently, we wanted to make sure that the apparent interaction of *AST* and design complexity was not actually an interaction between *fashion knowledge* and design complexity. Our analysis did confirm that AST was positively correlated with fashion knowledge (r=.228). However, when fashion knowledge was included as a covariate in the ANCOVA, the interaction between AST and complexity was essentially unaltered (p=.016). Thus, even after controlling for subjects' self-reported fashion knowledge, our original findings hold.

DISCUSSION

This study examines the moderating effect of consumers' arousal seeking tendency (AST) on their preferences for complex and simple product designs. Our data analysis revealed that AST does interact with product complexity, but the pattern of the interaction is the *opposite* of what one would expect based on the literature on arousal-seeking tendency (e.g., Mehrabian and Russell 1973; Steenkamp and Baumgarten 1992): High arousal-seeking consumers actually preferred the simple products to the complex products.

One previous study (Furnham and Bunyan 1988) examined the interactive impact of AST and stimulus complexity on the liking of meaningful objects (representational paintings), and they also obtained findings which appeared contrary to conventional arousal-seeking theory. Initially, we had speculated that Furnham and Bunyan's anomalous findings might have resulted from several methodological problems in their experiment (e.g., the absence of manipulation and confounding checks, possible order effects, their measure of arousal-seeking, failure to control for subjects' prior knowledge of this stimulus category). However, even when we addressed these methodological problems in our own experiment, we obtained results very similar to those of Furnham and Bunyan.

In trying to make sense of these anomalous findings, several potential issues come to mind. The first involves a reassessment of what is actually measured by the AST or Sensation-Seeking instru-

TABLE 1
Analysis of Variance in Product Preference

Source of Variation	Sum of Squares	d.f.	Mean Square	F	Sig. of F
Covariate					
Sex	9.32	1	9.32	4.45	0.36
Main Effects					
Arousal-seeking	.002	1	.002	.001	.976
Complexity	12.99	1	12.99	6.197	.013
2 Way Interactions					
Arousal-seeking X Complexity	12.01	1	12.01	5.73	.017
Explained	34.36	4	8.59	4.1	.003
Residual	708.36	338	2.096		
Total	**724.79**	**342**	**2.172**		

ments. In initiating this investigation, we (like Furnham and Bunyan) accepted the traditional view that these instruments measure a *general* tendency toward "Arousal Seeking" or "Sensation Seeking;" thus it seemed reasonable to expect that subjects scoring highly on these scales would prefer stimuli with *any* arousing attribute, whether it be stimulus complexity, novelty, etc. However, if one examines the specific items included in these scales (particularly Mehrabian and Russell's AST scale) one cannot help but notice that a very large number of these items appear to measure respondents' preference for *novelty or change*, and *none* directly mentions preference for *complexity*. For example, the forty AST items include multiple mentions of the words "change," "new," and "unpredictable," as well as the words "strange," "weird," "unfamiliar," "surprises," and "novelty;" however neither "complex," "complicated," nor any close synonyms, are mentioned in the AST items. Probably the statement most closely related to the complexity construct is "Shops with thousands of exotic herbs and fragrances fascinate me." This raises the possibility that the AST, rather than tapping into all types of arousal-seeking tendency, is primarily a measure of *novelty*-seeking, and has little relevance to subjects' preference for complexity. This would help explain why our high-AST subjects did not tend to prefer the complex designs.

If, in addition, the simple designs were seen as more novel than the complex designs, then this might explain why the high-AST (i.e., high-novelty-seeking) respondents tended to prefer the simple designs. This might be a plausible interpretation of the Furnham and Bunyan results, since (as mentioned earlier) they did not control for the perceived novelty of their paintings. However, in our study, the pretests indicated no significant differences in perceptions of novelty between the complex and simple products; thus we must look for constructs other than complexity *or* novelty to help explain our results.

One such construct, which has recently received considerable attention in the field of experimental aesthetics, is stimulus *prototypicality*. Several recent studies (e.g. Hekkert and van Wieringen 1990; Martindale, Moore and West 1988) suggest that while complexity and other collative variables may be the most important determinants of preferences for the abstract/meaningless stimuli typically employed by Berlyne and his colleagues, preferences for meaningful stimuli are largely determined by stimulus *prototypicality*, or the extent to which stimuli are seen as "typical" or "classic" examples of a particular category of objects. (For example, even though robins and penguins are both birds, robins are likely to be viewed as more *prototypical*, since they possess more of the attributes normally associated with the category "bird:" smallness, chirping, ability to fly, etc.) In one study, Hekkert and van Wieringen (1990) found that while preferences for abstract paintings were an inverted-U function of their complexity (as would be predicted by Berlyne) preferences among representational works bore little relation to complexity, but exhibited a monotonically positive relationship to their prototypicality.

How might this relate to our research? It is conceivable that our complex and simple designs may have differed in their degree of perceived prototypicality (e.g., as "dresses," or "garments"), and that this difference may have elicited different reactions from the high and low AST subjects. For example, it may be that the complex designs contained more of the elements typically associated with dresses (e.g. pleats, fabric ornamentation, etc.) and thus were viewed as more prototypical; the simple dresses, being less prototypical, may have stimulated more arousal (see e.g., Mandler 1982), making them more preferable to the high AST subjects. However, without further experimentation, this interpretation is simply speculation.

It is clear that future research is needed on the relationships between arousal-seeking tendency, product design characteristics and consumers' aesthetic preferences. While the relationships between these variables might appear to be straightforward from a reading of the literature on arousal seeking (e.g. Steenkamp and Baumgartner 1992), both our study and Furnham and Bunyan's obtained results that are not readily explained by that literature. Future research should attempt to operationalize the construct "product design prototypicality," to examine the impact of prototypicality on consumers' aesthetic preferences, and to explore its possible interactions with consumer arousal-seeking tendency. In addition, future studies of aesthetic preference should include explicit measures of subjects' arousal states, so that the presumed

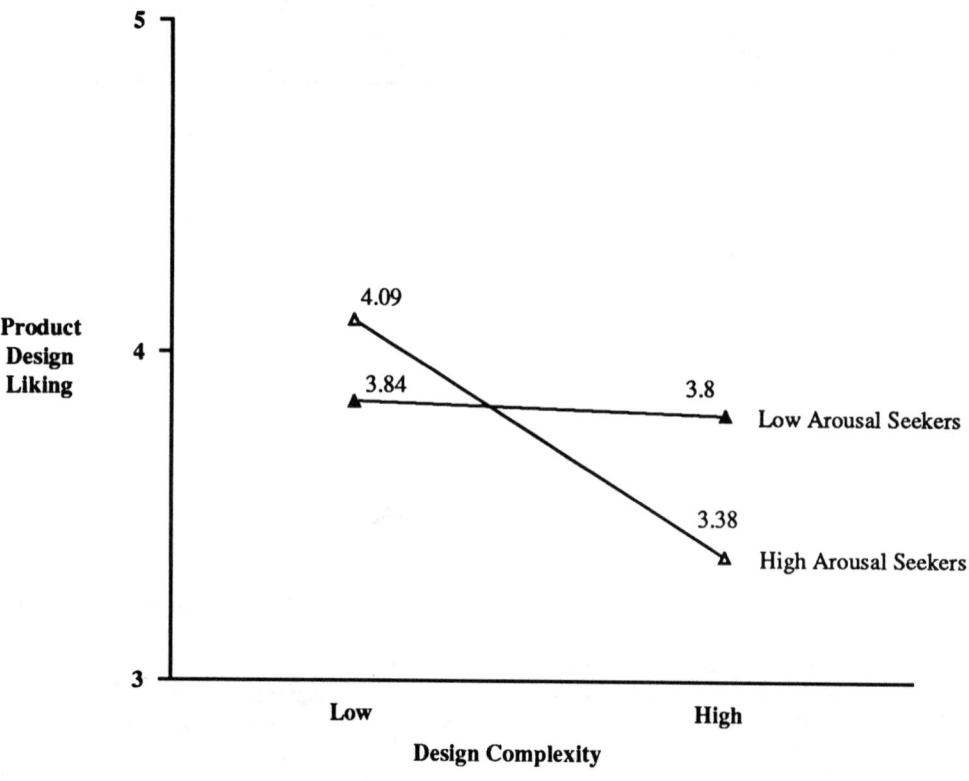

FIGURE 1
The Effect of Design Complexity and Arousal Seeking on Product Design Liking

role of arousal as a mediator of design preferences can be confirmed (or refuted) directly, rather than assumed, based on Berlyne's theory. In general, while the work of Berlyne and his associates offers many insights into human preferences for abstract visual stimuli, there is a great need for more research into the formation of consumers' aesthetic preferences for products and other meaningful stimuli.

REFERENCES

Bell, S., M. Holbrook and M. Solomon (1991), "Combining Esthetic and Social Value to Explain Preferences for Product Styles with the Incorporation of Personality and Ensemble Effects," *Journal of Social Behavior and Personality*, 6(6), 243-274.

Berlyne, D.E., and G. Lawrence (1964), "Effects of Complexity and Incongruity Variables on GSR, Investigatory Behavior and Verbally Expressed Preference," *Journal of General Psychology*, 71, 21-45.

Berlyne, D.E. (1968), "The Motivational Significance of Collative Variables," in R. Abelson, et al., eds., *Theories of Cognitive Consistency*, Chicago, IL.: Rand McNally, 275-288.

Berlyne, D.E. (1970), "Novelty, Complexity and Hedonic Value," *Perception and Psychophysics*, 8(Nov.), 279-286.

Cook, T. and D. Campbell (1979), *Quasi-Experimentation: Design and Analysis Issues for Field Settings*, Chicago, IL.: Rand McNally.

Cox, D. and A. Cox (1988), "What Does Familiarity Breed? Complexity as a Moderator of Repetition Effects in Advertisement Evaluation," *Journal of Consumer Research*, 15, 111-116.

Furnham, A. and M. Bunyan (1988), "Personality and Art Preferences," *European Journal of Personality*, 2, 67-74.

Hekkert, P. and C. van Wieringen (1990), "Complexity and Proto- typicality as Determinants of the Appraisal of Cubist Paintings," *British Journal of Psychology*, 81, 483-495.

Hirschman, E. and M. Holbrook (1982), "Hedonic Consumption: Emerging Concepts, Methods and Propositions," *Journal of Marketing*, 46(3), 92-101.

Mandler (1982), "The Structure of Value: Accounting for Taste," in *Affect and Cognition*, M. Clark and S. Fiske eds., Hillsdale N.J.: Erlbaum.

Martindale, C., K. Moore, and A. West (1988), "Relationship of Preference Judgments to Typicality, Novelty, and Mere Exposure," *Empirical Studies of the Arts*, 6(1), 79-95.

Mehrabian, A. and J. Russell (1973), "A Measure of Arousal Seeking Tendency," *Environment and Behavior* 5(3) (Sept.), 315-333.

Raju, P. (1960) "Optimum Stimulation Level: Its Relationship to Personality, Demographics, and Exploratory Behavior," *Journal of Consumer Research*, 7(Dec.), 272-282.

Schierman, M. and G. Rowland (1985), "Sensation Seeking and Selection of Entertainment," *Personality and Individual Differences*, 6, 599-603.

Sewall, M. (1978). "Market Segmentation Based on Consumer Ratings of Proposed Product Designs," *Journal of Marketing Research* 15 (Nov.), 557-564.

Smith S. and T. Myers (1966), "Stimulation Seeking Behavior and Extraversion," *Acta Psychologica* 32, 269-280.

Steenkamp, J. and H. Baumgartner (1992), "The Role of Optimum Stimulation Level in Exploratory Consumer Behavior," *Journal of Consumer Research*, 19(Dec.), 434-448.

Venkatraman, M. and D. MacInnis (1985), "The Epistemic and Sensory Exploratory Behaviors of Hedonic and Cognitive Consumers," in *Advances in Consumer Research*, 12, eds. Elizabeth Hirschman and Morris Holbrook, Provo, UT.: Association for Consumer Research, 102-107.

Wahlers, R., M. Dunn and M. Etzel (1986), "The Congruence of Alternative OSL Measures with Consumer Exploratory Behavior Tendencies," in *Advances in Consumer Research*, 13, ed. Richard Lutz, Provo, UT.: Association for Consumer Research, 398-402.

Whitfield, T. and P. Slatter (1979), "The Effects of Categorization and Prototypicality on Aesthetic Choice in a Furniture Selection Task," *British Journal of Psychology*, 70, 65-75.

Zuckerman, M., A. Kolin, L. Price and I. Zoob (1964), "Development of a Sensation Seeking Scale," *Journal of Consulting Psychology* 28, 477-482.

Zuckerman, M., S. Schultz, and T. Hopkins (1967), "Sensation Seeking and Volunteering for Sensory Deprivation and Hypnosis Experiments," *Journal of Consulting Psychology*, 31, 358-363.

Judging the Attractiveness of Product Design: The Effect of Visual Attributes and Consumer Characteristics

Molly Eckman, Colorado State University
Janet Wagner, University of Maryland

ABSTRACT

The objective of this study was to explore aesthetic aspects of product design. Judgments of the attractiveness of men's tailored clothing were analyzed, focusing on the effects of visual attributes and consumer characteristics. An individual-subject analysis of variance, based on a conjoint model with interactions, showed that consumers' judgments were affected by visual attributes and configurations of visual attributes. Consistent with aesthetic theory, the most important main effect was one dimension of silhouette—jacket length. The most important interaction effect was between jacket width and jacket pattern. Judgments of attractiveness differed by age, with older consumers evaluating visual attributes differently from younger consumers.

More than a decade has passed since Holbrook (1981) issued his seminal "Aesthetic Imperative." In that document, Holbrook challenged consumer researchers to change their focus from utilitarian to aesthetic attributes of products. Despite the widespread use of measurement techniques, based on information processing theory, which are well-suited to the study of aesthetic attributes (Berlyne 1971), there continues to be little research on the aesthetic aspects of consumption. Following Holbrook and his colleagues, the purpose of our research was to explore the aesthetic aspects of product design. We chose apparel as the vehicle for our study, for two reasons. First, the aesthetic attributes of apparel are often major factors in consumer choice. Second, apparel is an important means of visual communication, conveying information on individual creativity as well as reference group membership (Holman 1981). The rules of visual communication are not as well-defined as those of verbal communication. Nevertheless, aesthetic theory suggests that some visual attributes have more influence than others on how consumers evaluate product design.

In this research, we applied conjoint analysis, a research technique commonly used to study the processing of information on utilitarian attributes of products, to study how consumers evaluate aesthetic attributes. Our results demonstrate how conjoint analysis might be applied in evaluating the design of new products and suggest how consumer decision-making models might be modified to better accommodate aesthetic judgments.

Aesthetics and Design

Aesthetics is the study of artistic phenomena. While the term "aesthetics" is associated with all the fine arts—music, literature, dance, painting and sculpture—it is usually used in reference to the visual arts. As such, aesthetics is often extended to the design of everyday objects, such as apparel, that are consumed visibly.

A design is a unique combination of visual elements—line, space, shape, light, color and pattern. For centuries, philosophers and aestheticians have debated how the elements of design relate to one another in determining the attractiveness of an object. Historically, line has been considered the definitive design element, interacting with space to create visual attributes of objects, such as silhouette, shape and pattern. Of the visual attributes, aestheticians believe silhouette to be most important, because it "frames" an object in its surroundings. Line also interacts with color, to emphasize or deemphasize silhouette and shape (DeLong 1987). According to the noted aesthetician Bell (1914), the interaction of line and color is the most important determinant of "significant form"—a visual image that people find attractive.

The extensive conceptual work on how visual elements affect consumer preferences for design, there has had little research to either support or refute it. In view of that void, the first objective of our study was to determine whether or not the visual attributes—silhouette, color, shape and pattern—differ in their impact on consumers' judgments of the attractiveness of design. We advanced the following hypothesis:

H1: The visual attributes of design differ in their effect on how consumers judge the attractiveness of products.

Consumer Characteristics and Processing Visual Information

Models of consumer decision-making suggest that strategies consumers use to process information may be affected by personal characteristics, such as age, sex and involvement. Consumers of different ages have had different experiences that may affect their preferences for visual information. Similarly, males and females have different culturally-based experiences, and may judge visual information differently.

Due to their reliance on student samples, consumer researchers have neglected the effect of age on most aspects of consumer decision-making (Wells 1993). An exception is the work of Holbrook and Schindler (1989), who recruited subjects ranging in age from 18-86 from local church groups, to study the relationship between age and preferences for an aesthetic product—popular music. The results of an OLS regression analysis showed that adult consumers preferred music popular when they were in their teens or early twenties. Holbrook and Schindler suggested extending their research to consumer preferences for other aesthetic products, including apparel.

Holbrook (1986) explored how sex and personality affect preferences for men's apparel. Forty-two female and 22 male M.B.A. students evaluated a set of 32 black-and-white drawings of men's suits. The results of a canonical correlation analysis showed that visually-oriented women tended to prefer solid jackets, verbally-oriented women preferred plaid jackets, and men, in general, disliked any combination of visual attributes that clashed.

Models of consumer decision-making suggest that consumers are more involved with some products than others. In research on involvement in women's apparel, Fairhurst, Good and Gentry (1989) compared the performance of standard fashion involvement scales to Zaichowsky's (1985) Personal Involvement Inventory (PII). The PII was superior in validity and equivalent in reliability. In the consumption of any product, involvement may affect the extent and rigor with which consumers process information. However, previous research on involvement has focused on the processing of verbal, as opposed to visual information.

Given the conceptual and empirical evidence we have cited, the second objective of our research was to explore the effect of personal characteristics—age, sex and involvement—on the processing of visual information by consumers.

We advanced the following hypotheses:

H2: Older consumers will judge the attractiveness of products differently from younger consumers.

H3: Females will judge the attractiveness of products differently from males.

H4: Consumer judgements of the attractiveness of products will differ by level of involvement.

The Processing of Visual Information and Research Methodology

According to Holbrook and Moore (1981a), progress toward understanding the aesthetic aspects of consumption has been hindered by reliance on the additive model of information processing. In that model, it is assumed that consumers process information in a linear manner. The additive model is well-suited to the analysis of information on utilitarian attributes, which is easily presented in verbal protocols. However, the additive/verbal paradigm may not be as well-suited to the analysis of aesthetic attributes, for two reasons. First, visual attributes of design are presented more effectively in pictorial stimuli. Second, the Gestalt principle suggests that visual attributes of a design may be processed configurationally, rather than linearly. To capture the configurative aspects of a design, it is necessary to extend the conventional conjoint model to include interaction terms.

Holbrook and Moore (1981b) compared the processing of information on sweaters presented in pictorial and verbal stimuli, using a conjoint model with interaction terms. While more main effects were observed for the pictorial than the verbal stimuli, no differences were observed in the number of interaction effects. The strength of the most powerful main effect was compared to that of the most powerful interaction effect, based on Hays' (1988) omega-squared values. The results offered support for configurality in the processing of both visual and verbal information.

In this research, we analyzed the effect of visual attributes on consumers' judgments of the attractiveness of men's tailored clothing. Subjects in four age groups judged the attractiveness of 32 designs presented in pictorial form. Their judgment strategies were analyzed using a conjoint model with interactions. By using a conjoint model, we were able to explore the relative importance of individual visual attributes and selected configurations of visual attributes.

METHODOLOGY

Stimuli

Stimuli were colored line drawings of men's tailored jacket and trouser combinations, presented on a male figure. The same figure was used throughout, to control for the effect of body type on the subjects' responses. All designs were based on a classic rectangular silhouette. Drawings were rendered by a professional artist, then photographed and converted into slides. The jacket and trouser combinations were developed using a 2^8 fractional factorial design (Hahn and Shapiro 1966: Appendix I, plan 7b), making it possible to analyze main effects for eight visual attributes and six interactions. Each visual attribute was presented at two levels. Levels were chosen by reviewing trade publications and the fashion press to determine what silhouettes, colors, and patterns were likely to be on the market when the study was conducted. Spring 1991, when the data were collected, was marked by a continuation of the conservative look of the 1980's concurrent with a return to the flamboyance of the 1960's. The most important trend in silhouette was long, wide jackets worn with wide trousers. Short jackets with high drops[1] and no lapels were new. Fashionable colors included blues and greens and plaids were becoming popular. The eight visual attributes and corresponding levels of the jacket and trouser combinations included two dimensions of jacket silhouette: width (wide or narrow) and length (long or short); jacket drop (high or low); jacket neckline (lapels or no lapels); jacket color (blue or olive); jacket pattern (plaid or solid); trouser width (wide or narrow); and trouser color (blue or olive).[2] The six interactions involved one dimension of silhouette —jacket width—in conjunction with jacket drop, neckline, color and pattern, and trouser width and color. The 16 designs were fully replicated, to test for consistency in aesthetic judgments. Eight filler designs were included to disguise the intent of the study and reduce subject monotony. Both the original slides and the replicates were randomized.

A data collection book was compiled for each subject. The first page included instructions. The core of the booklet was a series of 100 millimeter continuous ratings scales with end points labeled "very unattractive" and "very attractive". A fashion involvement questionnaire (based on Zaichowsky's (1985) PII) and a set of demographic questions appeared at the end of the booklet.

Sample

The sample was convenient, purposive and stratified. Subjects were recruited from local religious organizations, restricted to Episcopalian, Presbyterian, Unitarian, and Jewish, to control for the effect of socioeconomic status[3]. Participating organizations were located in the suburbs of a large metropolitan area on the East Coast. Members were offered a $10 donation to their religious group as inducement to participate. Our goal was to collect data from 20 males and 20 females in each of four age groups: 20-24, 31-35, 44-48, and 56-60. Each of the three older groups was composed of individuals who were 20-24 years of age during one of the post World War II peaks in fashion trends, including the "Edwardian Dandy" (1955), the "Peacock Revolution" (1967) and the "Return of Conservatism" (1980) (Paoletti 1991). The fourth group, composed of individuals 20-24 years old at the time of the study, was intended as a point of comparison. Unfortunately, we found it difficult to recruit males, particularly in the older groups. Consequently, there were only 19 males in the 31-35 age group and 14 males in the 56-60 age group. Data were collected from 172 subjects. Four sets of results were unusable, leaving a total sample of 168 subjects.

Procedure

Data were collected either before or after meetings or services to minimize inconvenience to participants. Subjects were divided into small groups of all males or all females, and were seated at tables in front of a screen, with the data collection booklets face down in front of them. Subjects were thanked for volunteering and asked to turn their booklets over. Instructions printed on the first page of the data collection booklet were then read aloud to them.

---

[1] "Drop" is the distance between the base of the neck and the first button.

[2] The levels were reviewed by three professors of design to ensure that they represented meaningful differences.

[3] Previous research by Gockel (1969) and Goldstein (1969) suggests that members of these four religious groups are similar in socioeconomic status. The trickle-down theory of fashion adoption, consumer decision-making models, and conventional market segmentation strategies in the fashion industry suggest that consumers in a given socioeconomic group may use similar judgment strategies.

TABLE 1
Number of Main Effects and Average Omega-Squared Values for Each Visual Attribute
(n=168)

Visual Attribute	Number of Main Effects	Average Omega-Squared Value
Jacket length	69	.109
Jacket pattern	49	.067
Drop	39	.054
Neckline	34	.049
Jacket width	27	.030
Trouser width	24	.028
Jacket color	23	.028
Trouser color	20	.027

p<.05

Slides were projected on the screen for 15 seconds each.[4] To evaluate each design, subjects placed a mark on the corresponding rating scale. After half the data collection sessions, the order of the slides was changed. When the slide portion of data collection was finished, subjects completed the fashion involvement questionnaire and the set of demographic questions.

Responses were analyzed using an individual-subject analysis of variance, which allowed us to identify attributes and interactions affecting subjects' aesthetic judgments, and assess their relative importance, using Hays' (1988) omega-squared values. A 4 (Age) x 2 (Sex) x 3 (Involvement) x 2^8 post hoc ANOVA performed on the average omega-squared values was used to assess the effect of age, sex and involvement on subjects' aesthetic judgments.[5] Post hoc Tukey tests were used to identify differences among the groups in the relative importance of visual attributes.

RESULTS

Description of Sample

Most subjects were married, had attended college, were employed in professional, technical or managerial jobs, and reported salaries greater than $50,000. Chi-squares used to test for differences in socioeconomic status[6] showed no significant differences among subjects in the four religious groups.

Visual Attributes Affecting Aesthetic Judgments

Main Effects. The results of the individual-subject ANOVA are summarized in Table 1. Jacket length was the visual attribute appearing to most often affect the subjects' aesthetic judgments, followed by jacket pattern, drop and neckline. Visual attributes with fewer effects included jacket width, trouser width, jacket color, and trouser color.

The average omega-squared values in Table 1 show a pattern similar to the main effects, in that jacket length, with an omega-squared value of .109, was the dominant element, followed by jacket pattern, with an omega-squared value of .067. Drop and neckline were next in importance, followed by jacket width, trouser width, jacket color, and trouser color.

Interaction Effects. The results presented in Table 2 show that the dominant interaction effect was that of jacket width and jacket pattern, which affected the judgments of 78 subjects and yielded an average omega-squared value of .138. The remaining interaction effects had little influence, as demonstrated by the few significant effects and low average omega-squared values.

Differences among the Visual Attributes. The results of the post hoc ANOVA showed that the visual attributes differed in importance (F=12.86; p≤.0001). Ensuing Tukey tests confirmed that jacket length was the most important visual element, followed by jacket pattern (p≤.01). No differences were observed in relative importance among the other attributes.

Differences by Age, Sex and Involvement. The results of the post hoc ANOVA showed a significant interaction (F=2.71; p≤.001) between the visual attributes and age, indicating that the visual attributes were used differently by subjects in the four age groups. Ensuing Tukey tests showed that jacket length was more important to subjects in the two older groups (ages 56-60 and 44-48) than to subjects in the youngest group (age 20-24) (p≤.05). A similar difference was observed between subjects in the 44-48 age group and those in the 31-35 age group (p≤.01). No interaction effects were observed between the visual attributes and either sex or involvement. However, a significant interaction was observed among the four groups of variables—visual attributes, age, sex, and involvement. The post hoc Tukey tests showed that jacket length was more important to high involvement males, age 56-60 and medium involvement females, age 44-48 than to subjects in other categories.

DISCUSSION

In this research, we explored aesthetic aspects of the consumption of product design, focusing on consumer judgments of the attractiveness of men's tailored clothing. Our results were consistent with Hypothesis 1, in showing that the visual attributes differed in their effect on judgments of attractiveness. The most important single attribute was jacket length, lending credibility to the fundamental, but hitherto untested, tenet of aesthetics that line is the definitive visual element. The marginal means showed that the majority of subjects (94 percent) for whom jacket length was significant preferred the longer silhouette. Principles of proportion (see Davis 1987) suggest that a rectangular silhouette, such as that created by the long jacket, is more interesting and attractive than a square silhouette, such as that created by a short jacket.

Next to jacket length, pattern was the most important visual attribute. However, the importance of pattern stemmed from

---

[4] Pretesting showed that 15 seconds was sufficient time for subjects to make their judgments.

[5] Zaichowsky (1991) suggested dividing the sample into three groups, based on involvement scores; twenty-five percent were treated as high involvement, 50% as medium involvement and 25% as low involvement.

[6] Socioeconomic status was evaluated using occupation as a proxy.

TABLE 2
Number of Significant Effects and Average Omega-Squared Values for Interaction of Jacket Width and Other Visual Attributes
(n=168)

Interaction	Number of Interaction Effects	Average omega-squared value
Jacket width* jacket pattern	78	.138
Jacket width* jacket color	16	.024
Jacket width* trouser color	12	.018
Jacket width* neckline	10	.020
Jacket width* drop	7	.017
Jacket width* trouser width	2	.015

p<.05

dislike of the plaid. The marginal means showed a majority of subjects (96%) preferred the solid jacket. Preference for the solid jacket was part of an overall tendency for subjects to prefer conventional attributes (e.g., longer jacket, solid color) to those that were more newer (e.g., short jacket, plaid).

The majority of interaction effects were of relatively little importance. However, the interaction between jacket width and pattern was an exception, yielding more significant effects and a larger omega-squared value than any of the individual attributes. This result lends support to the Gestalt principle that visual attributes may be processed as configurations. The marginal means showed that the majority (74 percent) of subjects preferred the conventional narrow jacket and solid color. However, 24 percent preferred the more newer square jacket in the plaid. The meager effect of the jacket width/color interaction casts doubt on Bell's (1914) assertion that the relationship between line and color is a critical determinant of "significant form."

Our results support Hypothesis 2, in showing that judgment strategies differ by age of the consumer. This result is consistent with models of consumer decision-making and previous research (Holbrook and Schindler 1989) showing that age is related to preferences for music, another aesthetic product. Our results are also consistent with conceptual work in design (DeLong 1987; Sproles 1979) suggesting that consumer judgments of attractiveness differ by age. Although models of consumer decision-making and the results of previous research led us to hypothesize that judgments of attractiveness would differ by sex (Holbrook 1986) and involvement, neither hypothesis was supported.

It is important to interpret our results in light of limitations inherent in our study. Our research was limited to one product category—men's tailored clothing. Clearly, this type of research should be extended to other product categories to test the generalizability of the results. Our research was also limited to upper middle class consumers. However, diffusion theory suggests that members of the upper middle class are often early adopters of new products. Thus, their judgments of aesthetic attributes may be useful in gauging the potential for widespread adoption of new products.

CONCLUSION

In this research, we studied consumers' judgments of the aesthetic attributes of product design. Our results have both conceptual and methodological implications. In the conceptual domain, our results contribute to the development of aesthetic theory, in showing that the visual attributes of design differ in their effect on those judgments, with silhouette dominating. Our results also lend support to the Gestalt principle that visual attributes may be processed as configurations, as suggested by the relatively large jacket width/pattern interaction. In the methodological domain, our results demonstrate the potential usefulness of conjoint analysis in evaluating the potential acceptance of new product design.

The aesthetic aspects of consumption represent a fascinating, yet undeveloped research area. Given the pervasive effect of design on products in our culture, the processing of information on aesthetic attributes holds enormous promise for consumer researchers.

REFERENCES

Bell, Clive (1914), "Art as Significant Form," in *Aesthetics*, eds. (1989) George Dickie, Richard Sclafani and Ronald Robin, NY: St. Martins Press.

Berlyne, D.E. (1971), *Aesthetics and Psychobiology*, New York: Meredith Corporation.

Davis, Marian L. (1987), *Visual Design in Dress*, 2nd. ed., Englewood Cliffs, NJ: Prentice-Hall Inc.

DeLong, Marilyn Revell (1987), *The Way We Look*, Ames, IA: Iowa State University Press.

Fairhurst, Ann E., Linda K. Good and James W. Gentry (1989), "Fashion Involvement: An Instrument Validation Procedure", *Clothing and Textiles Research Journal*, 7 (Spring), 10-14.

Gockel, Galen (1969), "Income and Religious Affiliation: A Regression Analysis," *The American Journal of Sociology*, 74 (May), 632-649.

Goldstein, Sidney (1969), "Socioeconomic Differentiation Among Religious Groups in the United States", *The American Journal of Sociology*, 74 (May), 612-631.

Hahn, G. and S. Shapiro (1966), "A Catalog and Computer Program for the Design and Analysis of Orthogonal Asymmetric Fractional Factorial Designs," Report No. 66-C-165, General Electric Corporation, Schednectady, NY.

Hays, William (1988), *Statistics*, 4th ed., New York: Holt, Rhinehart and Winston.

Holbrook, Morris B. (1986), "Aims, Concepts and Methods for the Representation of Individual Differences in Esthetic Responses to Design Features," *Journal of Consumer Research*, 13 (3), 337-347.

_____ (1981), "The Esthetic Imperative in Consumer Research," in *Symbolic Consumer Behavior*, eds. Elizabeth C. Hirschman and Morris B. Holbrook, Provo, UT: Association for Consumer Research, 36-37.

_____ and William B. Moore (1981a), "Cue Configurality in Esthetic Responses," in *Symbolic Consumer Behavior*, eds. Elizabeth C. Hirschman and Morris B. Holbrook, Provo: UT: Association for Consumer Research, 16-25.

_____ (1981b), "Feature Interactions in Consumer Judgments of Verbal Versus Pictorial Presentations," in *Journal of Consumer Research*, 8 (June), 103-113.

_____ and Robert M. Schindler (1989), "Some Exploratory Findings on the Development of Musical Tastes," *Journal of Consumer Research*, 16 (June), 119-124.

Holman, Rebecca H. (1981), "Apparel as Communication," in *Symbolic Consumer Behavior*, eds. Elizabeth C. Hirschman and Morris B. Holbrook, Provo, UT: Association for Consumer Research, 36-37.

Paoletti, Jo B. (1991), Associate Professor, Department of American Studies, University of Maryland, Personal Communication, June 15.

Sproles, George B. (1979), *Fashion*, Minneapolis: Burgess Publishing Company.

Wells, William D. (1993), "Discovery-oriented Consumer Research," *Journal of Consumer Research*, 19 (March), 489-504.

Zaichowsky, Judith L. (1985), "Measuring the Involvement Construct," *Journal of Consumer Research*, 12 (December), 341-352.

_____ (1991), Personal Communication, November 19.

Ethical Issues in Consumer Research
Jacob Jacoby, New York University

Dictionaries define ethics as "a set of moral principles ... of right and wrong behavior." We focused on "right and wrong" as these surface in consumer research and involve consumer researchers.

Holbrook (1993) outlined philosophical perspectives regarding ethics and provided a four-celled framework for considering ethics in the consumer context. Crossing consumers vs. researchers with actions "done to" vs. "taken by" individuals, activities falling within each cell were discussed (see accompanying paper).

Olson discussed deception and use of debriefing to "handle" problems created by deception (see Toy, Olson and Wright, 1993). A framework was presented that distinguishes between deceptions creating false self-relevant beliefs (more serious ethical problems) vs. beliefs unrelated to self (less serious ethical problems), and between intended and unintended deception effects. Olson then described considerations for deciding whether to use deception in consumer research and how applying alternative ethical perspectives for analyzing the effects of deception can lead to different conclusions. He finished by offering several recommendations, including considering alternatives to deception.

Jacoby (1993) outlined ACR's history re: establishing an ethics committee (see Friedman, 1977a,b; Jacoby, 1977). Citing a 1992 survey commissioned by the AAAS showing that "27% of the respondents said they had personally encountered the fabrication, falsification or theft of research in the past decade," Jacoby asked: "What makes us believe things are any different in consumer research?" After conducting an exercise revealing substantial audience agreement on what constituted unethical behaviors among consumer researchers, Jacoby asked: "What would happen if an ACR member violated these understandings?" His answer: "As things stand now, absolutely nothing." He then described filing a formal complaint of plagiarism with the ACR Executive Committee in 1992, only to be told they could not hear the matter, as ACR had not established procedures for doing so. Apparently, as ACR has neither developed nor adopted any professional standards of conduct, anything goes. Concluding, Jacoby noted that, in the absence of checks and balances, there is potential for ACR (and committees acting as executives of ACR) to act unethically.

As Chairman of the Professional Standards Task Force established in 1993 to examine ACR's role vis-a-vis ethics, Smith (1993) presented the report he delivered to ACR's Board of Directors. His committee identified three relevant sets of issues: ACR members (1) in relation to research subjects and research beneficiaries; (2) in relation to each other; and (3) as ACR executives. Weighing the pros and cons of taking action, this committee recommended that ACR move forward to develop a Code of Ethics and form an ethics committee. Smith reported that the Board of Directors voted down these recommendations.

William Wilkie, the "Discussant," commented on the presentations, then opened the session to discussion. Among the audience, there was general recognition that, as part of their maturation and development, organizations purporting to represent scholarly disciplines develop formal mechanisms to govern and police the ethical issues surrounding their discipline. There was general consensus that, as the organization purporting to be the voice of consumer research, the time was ripe for such action within ACR.

REFERENCES

Friedman, Peter Monroe (1977) "ACR Standards for Professional Conduct in Consumer Research: Can we get there from here?" In William D. Perrault, Jr. (ed.) *Advances in Consumer Research*, Vol. IV, 254-55.

Friedman, Peter Monroe (1977) "Establishing Standards for Professional Conduct in Consumer Research: A Suggested Role for the Association for Consumer Research." In William D. Perrault, Jr. (ed.) *Advances in Consumer Research*, Vol. IV, 261.

Holbrook, Morris B. (1993) "Ethics in Consumer Research: An Overview and Prospectus" In Chris T. Allen and Deborah Roedder John (eds.) *Advances in Consumer Research*, Vol. XXI, 1994.

Jacoby, Jacob (1977) "History and Objectives Underlying the Formation of ACR's Professional Affairs Committee." In William D. Perrault, Jr. (ed.) *Advances in Consumer Research*, Vol. IV, 256-57.

Jacoby, Jacob (1993) "Ethical Issues in Consumer Research: Selected Remarks."

Smith, Craig (1993) "Ethics and ACR: An Initial Report to the ACR Board of Directors from the ACR Professional Standards Task Force."

Toy, Daniel, Jerry Olson and Lauren Wright (1993) "The Role of Deception and Debriefing in Consumer Research." Working Paper Series in Marketing Research, Pennsylvania State University, University Park, PA. 16802

Ethics in Consumer Research: An Overview and Prospectus

Morris B. Holbrook, Columbia University[1]

ABSTRACT

This paper develops a general conceptualization and typology of ethical issues in consumer research so as to identify four primary areas of concern: (A) Marketing Ethics, (B) Ethics in Marketing Research, (C) Consumer Ethics, and (D) Ethics in the Review Process. These four areas appear to have attracted different degrees of interest in the past. Hence, the paper argues (A) that questions of marketing ethics have been well explored; (B) that issues concerning scientific misconduct are helpfully addressed by the other papers in the present special topic session; (C) that emerging aspects of consumer ethics require more systematic conceptual development and empirical investigation; and (D) that ethical problems with the review process deserve increased attention.

INTRODUCTION

One approaches the topic of ethics in consumer research with trepidation. Though issues concerning ethics–distinguishing Good from Bad, pursuing Right versus Wrong, judging objects according to their Worth or Value–are as old as philosophy itself, ethics appears to be one of those areas in which knowledge does not so much progress as move in ever-widening circles that eventually return every investigator to the place where he or she began, a position characterized by deep doubts and unresolved uncertainties. Thus–with rare exceptions–we approach ethical issues in consumer research armed with no proven arsenal of scientific procedures, no instruments with accepted validity, no rigorously standardized tests, no generally accepted criteria. Instead, the main investigative tools we can bring to the task at hand are a little detachment and a lot of humility.

This essay applies a bit of abstract logical reasoning to the task of developing a conceptualization and typology of ethical issues in consumer research. Toward that end, I shall describe a general scheme for the demarcation of ethical issues pertaining to Character, Deontology, and Teleology. I shall illustrate that scheme by showing how it organizes the differences among nine types of ethical conduct of relevance to marketing. I shall then consider the ethical issues that arise in consumer research–proposing a typology to describe four aspects that appear to be logically distinct. These four logical types of ethical issues in consumer research have attracted different degrees of interest in the past. Hence, I shall indicate which areas have already received attention, which have begun to emerge, and which remain in a state of neglect.

THE DEMARCATION OF ETHICS: VIRTUE, JUSTICE, AND MORALITY

At the level of ordinary language or linguistic usage, everybody knows that *Ethics* studies the "right" or "good" (Edel 1973, p. 173); that it concerns "morality, moral problems, and moral judgments" (Frankena 1973, p. 4); that it seeks "a method that will specify the conditions that any good ethical decision should meet" (Donaldson and Werhane 1989, p. 1); and that it evaluates "whether actions are right or wrong, good or bad" (Smith 1993, p. 13). Yet even these commonplace observations raise potent terminological and conceptual questions that we must address before proceeding farther. For example, what is the difference between "right" and "good"? What distinguishes "ethical" from "moral"? What contrasting views apply to the "conditions" for "good ethical decisions"?

In answer to such questions, extending the reviews just cited, I propose the conceptual demarcation shown in Table 1.

Briefly, this scheme suggests a chain of effects in which Person→Act→Result. Contrasting philosophical perspectives emphasize different steps in this chain. Those emphasizing the *Person* concern themselves with *character* (e.g., Hobbes) and focus on individual *dispositions* or traits as reflections of one's potential for humanity according to what is considered "Natural." Those emphasizing the *Act* concern themselves with *deontology* (e.g., Kant) and focus on *principles* as represented by various juridical rules, duties, or maxims for doing what is "Right." Those emphasizing *Result(s)* concern themselves with *teleology* (e.g., Bentham or Mill) and focus on the *consequences* as in a goal-seeking utilitarian pursuit of the greatest general "Good."

Further, various facets of ethical inquiry–Virtue, Justice, and Morality–appear to emphasize contrasting aspects of the possible *correspondences* or *matches* among Persons, Acts, and Results. Thus, in referring to a correspondence between Character (the Natural) and Deontology (the Right), we speak of *Virtue* (e.g., the Stoics); for example, a person displays virtue via a disposition to behave according to certain principles. When Deontology (the Right) aligns with Teleology (the Good), we speak of *Justice* (e.g., Plato); for example, in a just society, the juridical principles that guide behavior produce beneficent consequences. Finally, when a match occurs between Character (the Natural) and Teleology (the Good), we speak of *Morality* (e.g., Aristotle); for example, we regard a person who seeks the welfare of others as displaying high morals.

ILLUSTRATION: TYPES OF ETHICAL CONDUCT

Besides the benefits of whatever conceptual clarification it might contribute, the scheme just proposed alerts us to a wider range of ethical issues than we might otherwise tend to notice in any given situation. Suppose, for example, that–with respect to each perspective (Nature, Deontology, Teleology)–we follow Etzioni (1988) by recognizing three possible contrasting orientations: Inward Looking (toward the Self or "I"); Outward Looking (toward Others or "We"); and Inward-Outward Looking (toward the Self-Other Interaction or "I&We"). A simple cross-classification of Perspectives against Orientations suggests the types of ethical conduct found in Table 2.

To flesh out Table 2 with some concrete examples, I have borrowed from a list of principles that "most people associate with ethical behavior" developed by the Josephine Institute and reported by Smith and Quelch (1993, p. 694). Specifically, after combining "Concern" and "Loyalty," the typology covers nine of the eleven ethical principles in Josephine's list and omits only the two of least salience (Reputation and Accountability). More importantly, the proposed scheme suggests an approach to *deriving* the relevant ethical principles according to a more clearly articulated conceptual structure.

---

[1] The author thanks Peter Paulis and Alex Simonson for their helpful suggestions. He also gratefully acknowledges the support of the Columbia Business School's Faculty Research Fund.

TABLE 1
A Conceptual Scheme for the Demarcation of Ethics

	Person →	Act →	Result
Perspective	Character	Deontology	Teleology
Exponent	Hobbes	Kant	Bentham/Mill
Focus	Dispositions	Principles	Consequences
Terminology	"Natural"	"Right"	"Good"

TABLE 2
Types of Ethical Conduct (With Examples of Valued Behavior)

Orientation	Nature	Deontology	Teleology
Inward (Self)	Integrity	Excellence	Fairness
Outward (Other)	Honesty	Law-Abiding	Respect
Inward-Outward (Self-Other)	Trustworthiness	Leadership (Role Model)	Concern/ Loyalty

TABLE 3
A Typology of Ethical Issues in Consumer Research

	Reactive (Done To)	Active (Done By)
Consumers	(A) Marketing Ethics	(C) Consumer Ethics
Researchers	(D) Ethics in the Review Process	(B) Ethics in Marketing Research

A TYPOLOGY OF ETHICAL ISSUES IN CONSUMER RESEARCH

Our focus on ethics in *consumer research* entails aspects of primary relevance to (1) *consumers* and (2) *researchers*. Further, the type of issue under investigation might regard the consumer or researcher as relatively more (a) *reactive* (things *done to* the individual) or (b) *active* (things *done by* the individual). Hence, combining these two simple dichotomies in all four possible ways creates the typology shown in Table 3.

Table 3 suggests four key areas of interest concerning the role of ethical issues in consumer research. I have labelled these from "A" to "D" in what I take to be their (descending) frequency of appearance in our literature. Accordingly, in what follows, I shall describe each briefly and shall suggest that some have already received much of the attention they deserve whereas others remain in a state of chronic neglect.

(A) MARKETING ETHICS (WHAT IS DONE TO CONSUMERS)

Questions of *marketing ethics* arise when ordinary producers (IBM, GM, GF, P&G, NBC, or RJR) come to market with conventional consumer products (PS1s, Pontiacs, Sanka, Tide, "Saturday Night Live," or Uptown). Given the imperatives of the profit motive–as blessed by our capitalistic free-enterprise system–such marketing activities often raise ethical questions. Various ethical approaches have evolved toward resolving some of these issues. Those with a *deontological* flavor emphasize *obeying rules* or *following principles* (such as the legal requirements passed by congress or the regulatory guidelines promulgated by various government agencies). Those with a more *teleological* viewpoint emphasize the *consequences* of business practices for customers, competitors, employees, the environment, or society as a whole and adopt such positions as the "simple idea" (perhaps *too* simple) that "companies are required not to do harm" (Beim 1993, p. 1). Hunt and Vitell (1986) have proposed a general descriptive (as opposed to prescriptive) theory of marketing ethics that combines the deontological and teleological perspectives and that has received some empirical support (Hunt and Vitell 1993). Attempts to combine alternative frameworks prescriptively have appeared in the work of, among others, Laczniak (1983) and Fritzsche (1985).

The subtle and challenging questions that arise in marketing ethics have begun to receive much of the attention they deserve. Conspicuous examples include the growing body of empirical and

TABLE 4
The Military Model Versus the Marketing Orientation

	Military Model	Marketing Orientation
Target	Compet'rs = Enemies	Customers = Friends
Purpose	Destroy Target	Appeal to Target
Tools	Sales Promotions, Price Cuts, False Ads	Product Design, Channels, Valid Ads
Attitude	War/Hatred	Peace/Love

legal studies of deceptive advertising (Preston 1993), the emerging focus on the normative implications of philosophical underpinnings (Laczniak 1983), attempts to propose and test descriptive models (Hunt and Vitell 1986, 1993), work on the formulation of social policy (Andreasen 1991), the general books on marketing ethics (Laczniak and Murphy 1985), the encouragement of various "new emerging paradigms" (Ray 1991), and the burgeoning interest in such ethically concerned publications as the *Journals* of *Macromarketing, Consumer Affairs, Public Policy and Marketing,* or *Business Ethics.* In particular, the recent compendium by Smith and Quelch (1993) has admirably covered the ethical aspects of *Product Management* (safety or health hazards, pollution or waste, misleading labels or packages, targeting or excluding disadvantaged groups); *Pricing* (collusion, predation, discrimination, gouging); *Advertising* (deception, targeting children, stereotypes, materialism), *Personal Selling* (bribes, lies, unfair practices, disguises or posing as researchers); and *Channels* (push money or slotting allowances, coercive tactics, intrusive direct marketing, redlining or excluding the disadvantaged). To these, Fritzsche (1985) adds a treatment of ethical issues in Multinational Marketing (harmful or dangerous exports, bribes or payoffs, dumping, gray markets). Hence, while applauding the scholarly work aimed in these specific directions, one feels little need to argue further for the already well-accepted importance of such concerns.

More generally, however, we might pause to recommend a change in the main metaphor or guiding narrative by which we represent the nature of marketing to ourselves. Inspired by the increased pace of international competition at the global level, thinkers in our field have begun increasingly to use military rhetoric (Kotler 1991) and to adopt a vocabulary of marketing warfare (Ries and Trout 1986). Such metaphorical narratives may capture some sense of the competitive threats from abroad and the need for strong tactical responses. Nevertheless, this militaristic rhetoric fundamentally misconstrues the nature of the marketing orientation and is ethically dangerous. Thus, Table 4 contrasts the (questionably ethical) military model with the (ethically appealing) marketing orientation. Under "marketing warfare," the purpose is to destroy the competitive target, viewed as an enemy, just as an army fires weapons at its adversaries and drops bombs on its opponents. By contrast, the more pacifist marketing orientation views the customer as the primary target of interest, where the purpose is not to destroy but rather to please this target to the greatest extent possible by designing, distributing, and describing an offering with maximum appeal. In this, the ethically preferable marketing orientation revives a theme from the 1960s: Make Love, Not War.

(B) ETHICS IN MARKETING RESEARCH (WHAT IS DONE BY RESEARCHERS)

By contrast, issues of *ethics in marketing research* arise when researchers (academicians, consultants, market-research specialists, ad-agency employees) pursue self-interested concerns (publish or perish, billable hours, profit maximization, winning the account) that may clash with the needs of those (a) undergoing or (b) sponsoring the investigations in question. Here, we encounter the needs (a) to protect customers or competitors against untoward research practices and (b) to preserve the integrity of findings intended to offer growth in knowledge, helpful inputs into managerial decisions, or valid guidance on social issues.

Other fields of inquiry have demonstrated a profound concern for ethical issues raised by scientific misconduct. As vividly illustrated by the troubled adventures of Professors Pons and Fleishmann or Doctors Imanishi-Kari and Baltimore (Goodstein 1991), alarmed colleagues and vigilant reporters stand ready to pounce on any situation that prompts even mild suspicion of fraud, falsification, or fabrication (the three F's) or of prevarication, plagiarism, or profiteering (the three P's). Thus, a thriving literature exists to deplore *Betrayers of the Truth* (Broad and Wade 1982), *ProfScam* (Sykes 1988), and *Stealing Into Print* (LaFollette 1992).

The situation appears somewhat different, however, when one looks at the issue of scientific misconduct in the field of consumer research. Here, we have isolated examples of attempts to address the general relevance of ethics in marketing research (Tybout and Zaltman 1974) or to develop the appropriate ethical codes (Castleberry and French 1987; Smith and Quelch 1993, p. 146; Tull and Hawkins 1985, p. 58). These contributions reflect a consensus on the respondent's rights to anonymity or confidentiality, to peace of mind or safety, to candor or openness, and to freedom of choice or informed consent; conversely, they reflect agreement on strictures against practices deemed hurtful to customers in collecting data (spying or invasions of privacy, physical harm or psychological stress, deception or misrepresentation, coercion or trickery) or to competitors in gathering marketing intelligence (deceit, bribes, espionage, theft). But we have not yet developed a scholarly tradition of work directed toward the more refined and sophisticated guidance of research practice, especially with respect to the aforementioned three F's and P's. Fortunately, judging from their titles, it appears that the presentations in this special topic session by Jacoby and by Toy, Wright, and Olson will move toward addressing some of these important issues.

TABLE 5
A Typology of Value in the Consumption Experience

		Extrinsic	Intrinsic
Self-Oriented	Active	Efficiency (O/I)	Play (fun)
	Reactive	Excellence (quality)	Aesthetics (beauty)
Other-Oriented	Active	Politics (success)	Ethics (virtue, justice, morality)
	Reactive	Esteem (reputation)	Spirituality (faith)

(C) CONSUMER ETHICS (WHAT IS DONE BY CONSUMERS)

The area of *consumer ethics* concerns the issues that arise when ordinary consumers (housespouses, children, pets) acquire, use, and dispose of conventional consumer products (canned tuna, military toys, flea collars). Such aspects of consumption raise a host of ethical questions related to the potential for Consumer *Mis*behavior that have attracted scattered attention from those studying socially responsible consumption in general (Leigh et al. 1988) or such more specific phenomena as self-restraint (Horowitz 1985), voluntary simplicity in conserving energy (Leonard-Barton 1981), customer boycotts (Smith 1990), ethical investing (Irvine 1987), compulsive consumption (O'Guinn and Faber 1989), or the dark side of consumer behavior (Hirschman 1991). However, with rare exceptions, general treatments of consumer ethics have remained few and far between (Marks and Mayo 1991; Muncy and Vitell 1992). One such effort by Cooper-Martin and Holbrook (1993) presents an empirical exploration of the dimensions underlying an MDS space intended to capture the differentiating aspects of ethical consumption.

Problems due to the neglect of consumer ethics resemble those that confront us in trying to understand issues that pertain to quality. Specifically–as in the case of quality–we appear unlikely to resolve questions concerning consumer ethics until we place them into their context within the overall nature and general types of *customer value*. Toward that end, I have elsewhere proposed a definition of customer value as *an interactive relativistic preference experience* and have suggested that the various types of customer value differ on three key dimensions: (1) *Extrinsic* (prized as a means to an end) versus *Intrinsic* (appreciated for its own sake as an end in itself); (2) *Self-* versus *Other-Oriented*; and (3) *Active* versus *Reactive* (Holbrook 1993). The resulting typology appears in Table 5.

This is not the place to rehearse the subtleties involved in discriminating among the eight types of customer value shown in Table 5. However, I might pause to emphasize that–beyond the validity of the typology in depicting aspects of value that arise in consumption experiences–the nature of consumer ethics has certain key properties that deserve careful empirical investigation in their own right. Specifically, as conceptualized here, this type of customer value is (1) *intrinsic* (pursued for its own sake as an end in itself with "virtue" regarded as "its own reward"); (2) *other-oriented* (done *not* for my sake, for its effect on me, or for how I shall react–but *rather* done for *their* sake, for its effect on *them*, or for how *they* will react); and (3) *active* (in the sense that it involves some manipulation of the environment rather than just some passive or reactive response–as in the difference between "works" and "faith"). Hence, the scope for ethical consumption includes such intrinsic, other-oriented, active value as found in "green" purchases, charitable donations, and buying animal-safe products; whereas the potential for unethical consumption includes consuming activities that hurt others as in pollution, pornography, prostitution, drugs, or other forms of crime.

(D) ETHICS IN THE REVIEW PROCESS (WHAT IS DONE TO RESEARCHERS)

A final set of ethical issues concerns the *review process* at our major journals (as well as in evaluations for hiring or promotions). I have commented previously on "Sadomasochism in the Review Process" (Holbrook 1986) and shall not rehearse this theme here except to note its potential ethical implications. Specifically, those concerned with the ethics of science in general have pointed to what may be a fundamental corruption inherent in the nature of the review process that characterizes journals from our own field in particular.

For example, in a penetrating review of LaFollette's *Stealing Into Print* (1992), Goodstein (1992) launches a brief but scathing attack on what he regards as "the most important problem" (p. 1503). Here, (1) Goodstein refers to a physics journal "so prestigious that many researchers feel their jobs...depend on their publishing...in it." Ironically, (2) this prestige results from a self-fulfilling prophesy of doom in which "it rejects a majority of the papers submitted to it." (3) Such rejection decisions are made by editors who lack the time or ability to read or comprehend the papers evaluated "because they are greatly overworked and because nobody can understand more than a tiny fraction of the articles published by the journal, much less those submitted to it." (4) The editors therefore rely on referees who are (a) protected by anonymity to secure their cooperation ("If the judgment is wrong or unfair, ...the author won't know who wrote the report") and (b) inevitably biased ("The referees [play] a high-status game in which the authors are usually known personally to them and are often competitors"). Clearly, (5) this procedure would be a prescription for disaster *if* these referees happened to be "guided by self-interest, professional jealousy, or other unethical motives"; Goodstein argues that such pressures toward unethical conduct *do* occur because "nearly all referees have had their ethical standards corroded by themselves being victims of unfair referees' reports in the past when they were authors." Thus, (6) Goodstein concludes that the review process is "a system in which misconduct is almost inevitable." To which (7) he adds: "And yes, ...I think misconduct does happen, quite a lot."

A sober look at the intermingled fields of marketing and consumer research strongly suggests that our disciplines suffer from the problems identified by Goodstein. Specifically, (1) our tenure and promotion committees also count publications in the most prestigious journals; (2) these journals must reject most of the papers submitted (around 85 percent in most cases); (3) our editors are overworked and underpaid; (4) they must therefore rely on the advice of reviewers who are anonymous but potentially competing; (5) these reviewers have themselves been victims of unfairness in the review process; (6) they may therefore engage in unethical behavior (such as giving an unfavorable review to a paper that they know meets the standards for acceptable scholarship or dragging out the revision process so long as to debilitate a rival author); (7) this unethical conduct colors the review process in our discipline by feeding back on itself in a vicious cycle when a wronged author in turn becomes a reviewer of someone else's work. (For further discussion of this vicious cycle, see the chapters in Cummings and Frost 1985 by Staw, p. 103; Graham and Stablein, p. 139; Pondy, p. 210; Toffler, p. 587.) Like Goodstein, I hasten to add that ethical lapses happen in our review processes *not* because they are run by bad people but because we have created a *bad system*. I also hasten to add that I am *myself* part of that system and am therefore as guilty as anybody else. But–after blaming the system and confessing complicity–I must still insist that, if we ever want the system to work in an ethically acceptable way, *we must fix it*.

Probably, we all have our own opinions on how the review process could be improved. My own number one priority–which seems quite consistent with Goodstein's perceptive analysis–is to remove the protective veil of anonymity by insisting on signed reviews. This recommendation parallels those offered in more general contexts by Frost and Taylor (Ch. 2 in Cummings and Frost 1985), by Morgan (Ch. 3 in Cummings and Frost 1985), by Chubin and Hackett (1990), and by Lock (1991). In my view, few reviewers would write the kinds of reviews they do if their names appeared at the bottom. If true, this says something profoundly disturbing about the nature of our review process and the unethical depths to which it has sunk.

CONCLUSION

In essence, I have served up a smorgasbord of ethical concepts and related issues of concern to consumer researchers. Some of these have already received wide attention–such as the nature of marketing ethics and the metaphorical movement toward making love instead of war. Others have begun to attract greater interest, as in the case of scientific misconduct, explored in this special topic session by Jacoby and Toy et al. Still others await more systematic development along the lines suggested by work recently devoted to preliminary treatments of customer value in general and consumer ethics in particular. And some issues invite exploration but remain neglected–in part, perhaps, because they raise such potentially disturbing questions.

In this latter connection, I think especially of the ethical quandaries posed by the nature of the review process at our major journals of marketing and consumer research. Without great cynicism, we might view that process as one that conserves scarce journal space by using up vast quantities of the editors', the reviewers', and (especially) the authors' time. But loss of time is synonymous with death. And unjust or involuntary cause of death spells murder. And this means that, as currently conducted, the review process often comes dangerously close to violating one of our most sacred ethical commandments: Thou Shalt Not Kill.

REFERENCES

Andreasen, Alan R. (1991), "Consumer Behavior Research and Social Policy," in *Handbook of Consumer Behavior*, Englewood Cliffs: Prentice-Hall, 459-506.

Beim, David O. (1993), "A Short Course in Business Ethics," Working Paper, Columbia Business School.

Broad, William and Nicholas Wade (1982), *Betrayers of the Truth*, New York: Simon & Schuster.

Castleberry, S. B. and W. A. French (1987), "Reviewing the MRA's Code of Ethics," *Journal of Data Collection*, 27, 42-48.

Chubin, Daryl E. and Edward J. Hackett (1990), *Peerless Science*, Albany: SUNY Press.

Cooper-Martin, Elizabeth and M. B. Holbrook (1993), "Ethical Consumption Experiences and Ethical Space," in *Advances in Consumer Research*, Vol. 20, 113-118.

Cummings, L. L. and Peter J. Frost (ed. 1985), *Publishing in the Organizational Sciences*, Homewood: Irwin.

Donaldson, Thomas and Patricia H. Werhane (1989), "Introduction to Ethical Reasoning," in *Case Studies in Business Ethics*, ed. T. Donaldson, Englewood Cliffs: Prentice-Hall, 1-13.

Edel, Abraham (1973), "Right and Good," in *Dictionary of the History of Ideas*, Vol. 4, ed. P. P. Wiener, New York: Scribner's, 173-187.

Etzioni, Amitai (1988), *The Moral Dimension: Toward a New Economics*, New York: The Free Press.

Frankena, W. K. (1973), *Ethics*, Englewood Cliffs: Prentice-Hall.

Fritzsche, David J. (1985), "Ethical Issues in Multinational Marketing," in Laczniak and Murphy (1985), 85-96.

Goodstein, David (1991), "Scientific Fraud," *The American Scholar*, 60 (Autumn), 505-515.

_____ (1992), "Travails of Publishing," *Science*, 258 (November 27), 1503-1504.

Hirschman, Elizabeth C. (1991), "Secular Mortality and the Dark Side of Consumer Behavior," in *Advances in Consumer Research*, Vol. 18, 1-4.

Holbrook, M. B. (1986), "A Note on Sadomasochism in the Review Process," *Journal of Marketing*, 50 (July), 104-108.

_____ (1993), "The Nature of Customer Value," in *Frontiers in Service Quality*, ed. R.T. Rust and R.L. Oliver, Thousand Oaks: Sage, 21-71.

Horowitz, Daniel (1985), *The Morality of Spending*, Baltimore: Johns Hopkins University Press.

Hunt, Shelby D. and Scott J. Vitell (1986), "A General Theory of Marketing Ethics," *Journal of Macromarketing*, 6, 5-16.

_____ and _____ (1993), "The General Theory...," in Smith and Quelch (1993), 775-784.

Irvine, William B. (1987), "The Ethics of Investing," *Journal of Business Ethics*, 6, 233-242.

Kotler, Philip (1991), *Marketing Management*, Englewood Cliffs: Prentice-Hall.

Laczniak, Gene R. (1983), "Frameworks for Analyzing Marketing Ethics," *Journal of Macromarketing*, 3 (Spring), 7-18.

_____ and Patrick E. Murphy (ed. 1985), *Marketing Ethics*, Lexington: D. C. Heath.

LaFollette, Marcel C. (1992), *Stealing Into Print*, Berkeley: University of California Press.

Leigh, James H., Patrick Murphy, and Ben M. Enis (1988), "A New Approach to Measuring Socially Responsible Consumption Tendencies," *Journal of Macromarketing*, 8 (Spring), 5-20.

Leonard-Barton, Dorothy (1981), "Voluntary Simplicity Lifestyles and Energy Conservation," *Journal of Consumer Research*, 8 (December), 243-252.

Lock, Stephen (1991), "The State of Peer Review," in *Peer Review in Scientific Publishing*, Chicago: Council of Biology Editors, 27-31.

Mark, J. Paul (1987), *The Empire Builders*, New York: Morrow.

Marks, Lawrence J. and Michael A. Mayo (1991), "An Empirical Test of a Model of Consumer Ethical Dilemmas," in *Advances in Consumer Research*, Vol. 18, 720-728.

Muncy, James A. and Scott J. Vitell (1992), "Consumer Ethics," *Journal of Business Research*, 24 (June), 297-311.

O'Guinn, Thomas C. and Ronald J. Faber (1989), "Compulsive Buying," *Journal of Consumer Research*, 16 (Sept.), 147-157.

Preston, Ivan L. (1993), "Relating Research on Deceptiveness Law to Ethics in Advertising," in Smith and Quelch, 662-671.

Ray, Michael L. (1991), "The Emerging New Paradigm in Business," in *New Traditions in Business*, ed. J. Renesch, San Francisco: Sterling & Stone, 32-45.

Ries, Al and Jack Trout (1986), *Marketing Warfare*, New York: New American Library.

Smith, Craig (1990), *Morality and the Market*, London: Routledge.

——— (1993), "Ethics and the Marketing Manager," in Smith and Quelch (1993), 3-34.

——— and John A. Quelch (ed. 1993), *Ethics in Marketing*, Boston: Irwin.

Sykes, Charles J. (1988), *ProfScam*, Washington, D.C.: Regnery Gateway.

Tull, Donald S. and Del I. Hawkins (1985), "Ethical Issues in Marketing Research," in Laczniak and Murphy (1985), 55-70.

Tybout, Alice M. and Gerald Zaltman (1974), "Ethics in Marketing Research," *Journal of Marketing Research*, 11, 357-368.

Coming of Age in a Material World: Juvenile Delinquency and Adolescent Angst

Debra Lynn Stephens, Villanova University
Ronald Paul Hill, Villanova University

INTRODUCTION

The transition from childhood to adulthood is a major rite of passage in all cultures, one that involves a significant change in status and role behaviors (Wright 1991). In many cultures, adolescents develop new identities by emulating adult behavior. In America, however, youths "have difficulty finding a preordained place in the social unit (Lipsitz 1977, p. 5). Instead of providing a clear path into adulthood, our culture supplies adolescents with a long period of emphasis on self-definition, with expectations of "open choice" and with the possibility of social mobility.

While most individuals are able to confront this challenge and construct the self as a positive, functioning adult member of the community, there are many in our society who fail to move successfully into adult roles, and end up engaging in antisocial or criminal behaviors. According to Lipsitz (1977), one possible explanation is that delinquent youths bear the additional burdens of geographic mobility and/or lack of opportunity because of their poverty and lack of education. Thus, violent and illegal acts become a way of gaining revenge against a society that is, in effect, a prison for these youths. For example, stealing may be viewed as an alternative preferable to employment at a low level service job that provides limited opportunities for advancement or higher income (National Commission on Youth 1980).

The purpose of this paper is to compare the portrayal of juvenile delinquents by film makers with consumer research findings about such youths (Hill 1992). The research findings suggest that delinquents lack positive role models, and live in a violent and unsupportive world. Thus, they prefer to "live for today" by acquiring money and possessions, typically by unlawful means. Their usage and disposition of these material goods demonstrate the importance of wealth as a status maker in their communities. Together, the films selected for this study represent a historical portrayal of these types of troubled youth—middle-class youths lacking any competent and empathic adult guidance (*Rebel Without A Cause*), disadvantaged white youths who are propelled into juvenile delinquency by circumstances beyond their control (*The Outsiders*), and inner-city blacks who must struggle just to stay alive (*Boyz N The Hood*). Below, each film will be discussed and its portrayal of juvenile delinquents is compared with the consumer research findings.

Rebel Without A Cause

This film was directed by Nicholas Ray and starred James Dean as the proverbial "good kid gone bad." Jim sees his father as ineffectual and weak, and his mother as a domineering "bitch." Arrested on drunk and disorderly charges, Jim confronts his parents when they come to the police station to secure his release:

Father, flustered, explaining to police officer: "We just moved here, y'understand, and th-the kid hasn't got any friends, y'understand, and we moved into a–"

Jim, shouting to be heard above his father: "Tell the man why we moved here, Dad."

Father: "Will you hold it?"

Jim (low and bitter): "You can't protect me."

This dialogue poignantly expresses the relationship "dance" Jim and his father are stuck in: that of a father who, while he loves his son, feels unwilling or unable to offer the boy any guidance; and a son who, while he loves his father, does not respect him and feels compelled to punish him for his incompetence as a parent.

Thus, Jim, like the youths in the Hill study, lacks a strong father figure to turn to for guidance and to emulate. The other two protagonists in *Rebel* also lack effective fathers: Judy's father is cold and rejecting, while John's (Plato's) is absent. Unlike the real delinquents, however, none of the protagonists has an especially warm, loving mother. Indeed, Plato's mother is hardly there for him: he declares at one point in the film that she took the money that had been earmarked for his psychotherapy, and used it to pay for her trip to Hawaii.

The initial dialogue between Jim and his father at the police station goes on to illustrate the most striking difference between the youths in *Rebel* and those interviewed by Hill: the former neither suffer material deprivation, nor do they seem to value material goods.

Father (on the defensive): "Do you mind if I try [to protect you]? Do you have to slam the door in my face? I'm trying to get to him what happened. Don't I buy you everything you want? A bicycle, you got a bicycle, a car..."

Jim (sarcastically): "You buy me many things, you've bought me many things."

Father (pleading): "Not just things, we give you love and affection, don't we?"

Jim's comments indicate that he sees material possessions as poor substitutes indeed for the parental empathy and guidance he so desperately needs. The real juveniles, in contrast, equate money and what it can buy with power and freedom from the harsh, impoverished environment in which they are struggling to survive—psychologically as well as physically.

Jim, Judy, and Plato appear to be suffering from "love deprivation" at least as much as the delinquents in the Hill study. The deprivation experienced by the film protagonists is eloquently conveyed in the following dialogue, which occurs when Plato, pretending to be a real estate agent, "shows" an abandoned mansion to Jim and Judy, who are pretending to be typical upper middle-class newlyweds:

Jim: "You see, we're newlyweds..."

Judy: "Yes! Oh no, there's just one thing. What about—"

Plato: "Children? Right this way.... You see, we really don't encourage them. They're so noisy and troublesome. Don't you agree?"

Judy: "Oh, yes, yes, and so terribly annoying when they cry. Oh, yes, I don't know what to do when they cry, do you, Dear?"

Jim: "Drown them, like puppies!"

John (leading the other two to an empty swimming pool): "As you see, the nursery's far away from the rest of the house....

You'll find that this is a wonderful arrangement. They can carry on and you'll never even notice. In fact, if you lock them in, you'll never have to see them again!"

Judy: "Much less talk to them!"

Jim: "*Talk* to them? Nobody *talks* to children!"

Judy: "No, they just tell them."

As for school and community support for the *Rebel* youths, it appears that the protagonists have given up on adults, viewing them either with contempt (as Jim sees his father) or with despair, as evidenced in Plato's comment to the juvenile counselor at the police station, where he has been brought for shooting some puppies: "Nobody can help me." It is clear that for these adolescents, good intentions on an adult's part do not cut it. In the Hill study, there is far more evidence that support is simply not forthcoming from schools and community. While both film and reality portray a lack of subjectively perceived adult support, in the film, adults try to help and fail, but in reality the adult community displays massive indifference—or inertia—when it comes to helping troubled youths find their way.

Like the real delinquents, those in *Rebel* turn to each other for support and guidance. And, like the real juveniles, the price of belonging to a peer group is to engage in high-risk behaviors—for the former, stealing, selling drugs, and fighting, and for the latter, fighting and "chickie runs": to gain acceptance by his peers in a new town, Jim is forced to participate in a contest in which two youths drive their cars toward a bluff, and the one who jumps out of his car first is a chicken. While no one enjoys these contests, as Jim's opponent puts it, "We've got to do somethin.'" This youth dies in his attempt to outlast Jim in a chickie run.

But peers in *Rebels* (also like those in the real world, according to Hill's study), do provide one another with emotional and physical support, to the best of their ability. For example, in the jail scene referred to above, Jim observes Plato and his guardian (the housekeeper) in an exchange, and attempts to help, though Plato is a stranger to him:

Plato's guardian, concerned: "You shiverin', John, are you cold?"

Plato continues to sit with his head bowed.

Jim takes off his jacket and offers it to Plato: "Want my jacket—want my jacket? It's warm..."

Plato's guardian takes the jacket and attempts to place it on Plato's shoulders, but he shakes his head, almost imperceptibly, so she gives it back to Jim.

At the film's conclusion, when Plato, wielding a loaded gun, breaks into a building seeking refuge from the police pursuing him, Jim and Judy go after him, and the ensuing dialogue reflects the trust that Plato now feels for Jim:

Jim: "Are you cold? Here (offering Plato his jacket), it's warm. Here's my jacket—it's warm."

Plato: "Can I keep it?"

Jim: "Well, what do you think?"

Plato puts on the jacket, wrapping himself in it.

In the ensuing gun battle between Plato and the police, Plato tragically dies. Before Plato's body is taken away on a stretcher, Jim, weeping, stoops over his lost friend and zips up the jacket, murmuring to himself, "He's always cold."

The Outsiders

This film was directed by Francis Ford Coppola and starred several members of the Hollywood "brat pack," including Patrick Swazy and Rob Lowe. In contrast to the adults in *Rebel Without a Cause*, those in *The Outsiders* are not even well-intentioned but ineffectual—in fact, the only adults shown are trigger-happy policemen and parents who are too busy fighting with each other to even notice whether their son is home or not. This dearth of adult support seems even more extreme than that for the juveniles in the Hill study.

The protagonists in *The Outsiders* are "greasers"—working-class youths who both hate and envy the "soces"—their upper middle-class cohorts. The difference in status becomes abundantly clear in a scene in which two greasers—Johnny and Pony Boy—are saying good bye to the two "soc" girls they've just met at a drive-in movie:

Sherry (to Pony Boy): "If I see you in school and I don't say Hi, please don't take it personal, ok?"

Pony Boy: "Yeah, I know."

Sherry: "Really—you're a nice boy an' everything, but—"

Pony Boy: "It's ok."

The greasers, trapped by their social and economic circumstances, forced to defend a title and a way of life that they find repugnant, resemble the real juveniles in their reverence for material possessions, as the following dialogue poignantly illustrates:

(In this scene, Johnny and Pony Boy are sitting before a fire they've built for warmth in a vacant lot, talking about the group of soces they've just had a run-in with.)

Johnny (with admiration and longing): "Man, that was a tough car, huh—Mustangs, they're tough."

Pony Boy (bitterly): "Big-time soces, all right. It's always the same."

Johnny (starts to cry): "I can't take much more of this. I-I-I'll kill myself or somethin'."

Pony Boy (goes to Johnny and puts an arm around his shoulders): "Johnny, c'mon, you don't want to kill yourself..."

Johnny (with an edge of desperation): "I've gotta do somethin'. Seems like it must be someplace without greasers, soces—must be someplace just plain ordinary people—just people..."

Like the real juveniles, the outsiders try to give one another support and guidance not available elsewhere, as we see later on in the scene in the lot:

Johnny (to Pony Boy): "You better get home, all right? I'm gonna stay all night out here. Who'd care, anyway?"

Pony Boy: "All right. If you get cold, come on over to my house."

Later in the film, it becomes necessary for Johnny and Pony Boy to hide from the police, because Johnny has killed a soc who was trying to drown Pony Boy. They go to their friend Dally for guidance, and he instructs them to hop a freight to an abandoned church, and provides them with a gun. After their first night at the church, Johnny goes shopping for provisions, returning with a surprise for Pony Boy:

Johnny (taking items from bag): "...a loaf of bread, a week's supply of baloney here, peanut butter—"

Pony Boy (peeks into the bag and retrieves a paperback book): "*Gone With the Wind*! Johnny, how'd you know I always wanted *Gone With the Wind*?"

Johnny: "I remembered you sayin' somethin' about it once...me an' you went to see that movie, remember? Thought maybe you could read it out loud, help kill time."

Pony Boy (places a hand on Johnny's shoulder): "Thanks a lot, Johnny."

Later in the course of events, Johnny and Pony Boy display true heroism when they are on an outing with Dally, who has come to check on them in their hide-out. The two fugitives see a church going up in flames, find out from the adults outside it that a number of small children are still trapped inside, and go in after them. Johnny is severely burned, and is lying in the hospital when the following scene takes place:

(Pony Boy and his friend Two-Bit are out walking when they are accosted by a group of soces, one of whom wants to talk to Pony Boy out of earshot of the others.)

Randy: "I couldn't tell this to anyone else. My friends would think I's off my rocker or somethin'. Y'know that friend of yours, the one that got burned, he might die?"

Pony Boy: "Yeah..."

Randy (referring to a "rumble" that will be held that night—a regularly scheduled fight between the greasers and soces): "Tonight—people get hurt in rumbles, maybe even killed, right? (begins to cry noiselessly) You can't win, you know that, don't cha? Doesn't matter if you whip us tonight, you'll still be where you were before, at the bottom. And we'll still be the lucky ones, at the top, with all the breaks. Doesn't matter, greasers'll still be greasers, and soces'll still be soces. Doesn't matter. (pulls himself together) Anyway, thanks, greaser."

Randy begins walking back to his friends, but turns back toward Pony Boy: "Hey, I didn't mean that, I meant 'thanks, kid.' "

Pony Boy: "Been nice talkin' to you, Randy. My name's Pony Boy."

Ironically, Randy's manner perpetuates the very injustices he appears to abhor. And to his way of thinking, even heroism cannot change a greaser's social status; he sees no possibility of change.

But Johnny, who dies in the end, leaving Pony Boy a note stuck between the pages of their copy of *Gone With the Wind*, has a very different vision:

Pony Boy— I asked the nurse to give you this book so you could finish it. It was worth saving those little kids. Their lives are worth more than mine. They have more to live for. Tell Dally I think it's worth it....There's still a lot of good in the world. Tell Dally, I don't think he knows.

The note never reaches Pony Boy; he is killed by police while trying to help Dally escape from the scene of a robbery he has committed in his despair and rage over Johnny's death. This tragic irony, we would—and do, on occasion—see played out by today's troubled, trapped youths.

Boyz 'N the Hood

This film, directed by John Singleton, looks at the inertia and impotence of black youths in South Central Los Angeles. Like *The Outsiders*, these adolescents face a day-to-day environment devoid of any form of family or community support, and they must negotiate their way through a violent network of armed gang members, drug dealers, and trigger-happy police. The hero of the film, played by Cuba Gooding, Jr., stands in stark contrast to the typical juvenile, for he is employed, eschews drugs, respects his girlfriend, and listens to his father.

Trey, the hero, is fortunate enough to have a strong, wise, and loving father;

"You know, Trey, you may think I'm bein' hard on you right now. But I'm not. What I'm doin' is I'm tryin' to teach you how to be responsible. It's like your little friends across the street, they don't have anybody to show them how to do that, they don't. You gonna see how they end up, too."

And after an attempted break-in, Trey and his father have the following conversation about black-on-black violence:

Father: "Somebody must've been prayin' for that fool, 'cause I swear I aimed right for his head."

Trey: "You shoulda blew it off."

Father: "Don't say that. Don't say that. Just woulda been contributin' to killin' another brother."

The black policeman who comes out to their house to get an account of the crime expresses a very different view:

"Y'know, it's too bad you didn't get'm. Be one less nigger out on the streets we'd have to worry about."

Trey's "little friends across the street" are as deprived of love and guidance as Trey is enriched with it. The message that Ricky, Chris, and Doughboy get from their mother, who is raising them alone, is very clear:

"You ain't shit, you don't do shit, and you ain't gonna amount to shit."

The fact that Trey has a strong father figure sets him apart from the juveniles in the Hill study. While his friends resemble the latter in that their fathers are absent, their mother is hardly the loving but permissive type described by Hill as typical of the delinquents' mothers.

As for support from the community and the schools, there is none in evidence. The only school scene in the film gives eloquent evidence that the schools offer these youths nothing relevant or helpful. In this scene, Trey's (white) teacher holds forth about the first Thanksgiving to a group of youngsters who are growing up in a war zone, and some of whom have seen their own siblings or parents murdered. The film closely parallels the reality in this respect; it is all too easy to understand why inner-city youths are dropping out of school in droves.

In *Boyz*, we see little about the importance of material possessions in acquiring status. What becomes poignantly obvious early on, though, is that stealing is the only way in which many of the youths depicted can obtain anything of their own. In one instance, Trey and his father return from a fishing outing just in time to see Ricky led away in handcuffs because he was caught stealing from a local retailer. Ironically, during their outing, Trey and his father had discussed the importance of *asking* rather than *stealing*. It is safe to assume that his friends' mother never engaged her sons in such a discussion about right and wrong, respect and disrespect.

Trey's father is clearly a stronger influence on Trey than are his peers. But Ricky is torn between the lifestyles of his brothers, one of whom has been partially paralyzed by a bullet, and a desire to make something of himself. He has his first child when he is 16 or so; the child crawls into the livingroom while a recruiter for the USC football team sits talking with Ricky about what he would like to major in in college. A few months later, Ricky and Trey are walking home from a local market, when Ricky is gunned down by two youths who were angry about something he had said to them. It is Ricky's single-minded attention to finding out which number is on his lottery ticket that prevents his noticing his pursuers closing in on him.

Trey's father makes sense of this violence in a way that makes us as marketers feel every bit as guilty as those who pull the trigger:

> Speaking of crack, he says: "It wasn't a problem till it was in Iowa, and it showed up on Wall Street, where there are hardly any black people....Why is it that there's a gun shop on almost every corner in this community? For the same reason that there's a liquor store on almost every corner in the black community. Why? They want us to kill ourselves."

This film and the Hill study give us a clear message that many of us do not wish to hear: what is happening in our inner cities is *everyone's* problem—and we owe it to ourselves, our communities, and our children to get busy searching for solutions.

REFERENCES

Hill, Ronald Paul (1992), "Transition in Turmoil: When Becoming an Adult Involves Criminal Behavior," in *Advances in Consumer Research*, John Sherry and Brian Sternthal, eds. Provo, UT: Association for Consumer Research, 399-401.

Lipsitz, Joan (1977), *Growing Up Forgotten*, Lexington, MA: Lexington Books.

National Commission on Youth (1980), *The Transition of Youth to Adulthood: A Bridge Too Long*, Boulder, Westview Press.

Wright, Newell D. (1991), "The Role of Consumption in the Transition from Pre-Adult to Adult," working paper, Virginia Polytechnic Institute and State University.

Women As Commodities: Prostitution as Depicted in *The Blue Angel*, *Pretty Baby*, and *Pretty Woman*

Elizabeth C. Hirschman, Rutgers University
Barbara B. Stern, Rutgers University

INTRODUCTION

Consumer research has recently been confronted by two significant challenges. The first came in the form of an Association for Consumer Research (ACR) Fellows Address (Rogers 1987), two ACR Presidential Addresses (Andreasen 1993; Hirschman 1991b) and several articles published in the *Journal of Consumer Research* (e.g., Murray and Ozanne 1991; Wells 1993) that called upon consumer researchers to attend more closely to *social issues* relevant to consumption. The common theme across these diverse writings is that consumer research can and should increase its commitment to furthering social welfare. Concurrent with this has come a burgeoning demand to examine *sexism* as a clear and present danger to the field (e.g., Holbrook 1990; Stern 1991, 1993; Hirschman 1991b, 1993; Bristor and Fischer 1991, 1993). Framed from a feminist perspective, these latter papers called attention to both omissions and commissions in consumer research that acted to mute or distort women's voices. The present inquiry seeks to address both of these challenges by examining an aspect of the dark side of consumer behavior that is, and always has been, bound-up closely with sexism as a social issue—prostitution.

Feminist critiques point out that at the present time as well as in most past eras, prostitutes have been viewed as *profane commodities* (Belk, Wallendorf, and Sherry 1989). They serve no familial function, and fulfill neither the domestic nurturance nor reproductive roles usually assigned to women. Instead, prostitutes' social and economic value lies in their provision of a sexual service to men. They are, in modern terms "sex workers" (Lewin 1992, B16), women those humanity is derogated by reduction to their sexual parts (Bullough 1974; Perkins and Bennett 1985). In essence, a prostitute is a *sexual commodity*, a bundle of product attributes whose primary role is to serve as an object or product consumed by men.

In the present inquiry, we examine cultural attitudes toward the commoditization of women as prostitutes in three motion pictures. Following the perspectives of Barthes (1964, 1972, 1983), Metz (1974) and Baudrillard (1968, 1981), our research views motion pictures as vehicles of popular culture that carry and communicate consumption ideology. It is assumed that the beliefs and values semiotically encoded within the narrative are representative of the culture that produces and consumes them (cf. Levi-Strauss 1965, 1966). This line of reasoning has been well developed in consumer research since 1986, when two articles (Holbrook and Grayson 1986; Mick 1986) introduced the method of *semiotics* to the field. Since that time, several articles (Hirschman 1988, 1990; Holbrook 1988, Holbrook, Bell and Grayson 1989; McCracken 1989; Scott 1990; Stern 1989) and conference presentations or programs (Umiker-Sebeok 1987; 1993) have broadened the application of semiotics to a wide variety of cultural *texts* (Holbrook and O'Shaughnessy 1988) including motion pictures, television shows, television commercials, print advertisements, magazines, plays, and autobiographies.

Our present interest in motion pictures as vehicles of consumption ideology (see Eagleton 1991) stems from this medium's widely recognized impact as a socializing agent for consumers (see O'Guinn, Faber and Rice 1985). Feminists in particular have been cognizant of film's power as a vehicle for both encoding and enforcing society's views of 'women's place.' As de Lauretis (1984, p.4) writes: " The alliance of feminism, semiotics and film is of long standing. In cinema the stakes for women are especially high. The representation of woman as spectacle—body to be looked at, place of sexuality, and body of desire—so pervasive in our culture, finds in narrative cinema its most complex expression and widest circulation."

Our analysis uses the perspective of feminist film theory (see e.g., Kaplan 1983; Penley 1989; Tseelon and Kaiser 1992). From this vantage point, the analysis seeks to counteract the masculinist bias that defines a prostitute as a passive object or image, that which is "to-be-looked-at," consumed (Mulvey 1975), and ultimately discarded. This use of the prostitute as the object of male desire can be found in art (e.g., Berger 1972; Betterton 1985) and in advertising (e.g., Myers 1989), as well as in film (e.g., Kuhn 1982, 1985). As Tseelon and Kaiser (1992, p. 120) observe, within such ideological vehicles, the prostitute is an "enigmatic threat to be idolized or destroyed." Following Kaplan (1983, p. 18), "Our task, then, in looking at Hollywood films is to unmask the images, the *sign* of woman [as prostitute], to see how the meanings that underlie the codes function."

THE PROSTITUTE IN LITERATURE

The images of prostitutes in film derive from a long history of earlier texts—poems, plays, and novels that commodify prostitutes as a subordinate group even within the larger group of women, itself subordinate to men. Virtually all of these images are reductive, defining a prostitute not as a complete human being, but as merely a collection of sexual parts. The terms used to signify a female prostitute indicate that she is a thing rather than a person—an entity limited to her sexual role. Descriptors are synonyms derived from her working hours ("lady of the evening"), working conditions ("street walker"), body parts ("piece of ass"), and anatomical resemblances to animal life ("beaver," "pussy").

These modes of expression reveal the socially reified view of the prostitute as an *object*—a signifier denoting the patriarchal judgment of prostitution as a typically deviant or "other" (de Beauvoir 1953) human behavior characteristic of women. This view has found expression in the literary canon, where up until the recent past, the prostitute has been depicted primarily by male writers. Their focus has been on the psychology of the individual prostitute, rather than on the holistic view of the sociology of prostitution that embraces the consumer as well as the consumed (Horn and Pringle 1984). Because the prostitute has been almost exclusively a masculine literary creation, male writers have created limited fictional roles for prostitutes, usually depicting them as stereotypes rather than as individualized human beings. Further, the study of prostitution in literature—until the advent of feminist scholarship in the 1970's—has also been shaped by an androcentric perspective concentrated on the masculine literary response to images of prostitution (Hapke 1989). In consequence, there has been very little research from the woman's perspective on "literary works about women paid for sexual services" (Hapke 1989, p. 5).

Feminist literary critics started to examine the image of the prostitute in literature from a female point of view during the 1970's. This stream of research extends to the study of prostitutes in films, where the cinematic portrayal of women has begun attracting research attention from feminist film critics (Jacobs 1991, Kaplan 1980). Thus, the images of prostitution in film occupy a central space in the transition from literary texts to consumption lore.

FOUR ARCHETYPES OF PROSTITUTES AS CONSUMED COMMODITIES

The ideological conflicts and ambiguities expressed in the literature on prostitution are far from resolved. However, images of prostitutes do cluster into several archetypes of the prostitute as a commodified object (Horn and Pringle 1984). The archetypes differ because the female prostitute in literature and film exists largely as a projection of male fantasy and thus is depicted as an embodiment of the different female types desired by different men. Our present typology of prostitutes is derived from Horn and Pringle's (1984) nine-category typology, itself based upon fictional works—mainly British, American, and Continental plays and novels—written by male writers and written about by male critics. These works have entered the literary canon—a generally accepted body of literature deemed worthy of scholarly attention—by means of literary criticism, in which interpretation has also been male-dominant up until the present generation.

The Horn-Pringle methodology is inductive, in that it surveys an entire domain and then derives categories from exemplars observed within that domain. In literary criticism, this method is a traditional one dating back to Aristotle (Fergusson 1961), whose *Poetics* draws general principles of tragedy from the extant Greek tragedies with which he was familiar. A modern example of inductive criticism is Frye's *Anatomy of Criticism* (1973), in which a schema for sorting texts into categories is developed by examining the textual universe available to the scholar. Thus, we follow literary tradition and rely upon Horn and Pringle's data and methods for discerning archetypes of the prostitute in fictional works.

However, we have modified and updated the Horn and Pringle typology by condensing their original nine archetypes into a more parsimonious set of four relevant to cinematic texts. Film is a new art form that both reshapes traditional literary archetypes and adds a postmodern feminist perspective (DeLauretis 1984; Kaplan 1983; Kuhn 1982; Mayne 1985; Penley 1988). Thus, while we begin with a historical typology, we adapt it to suit contemporary data and current ideological influences. This type of analysis can be viewed as *interpretive cluster analysis*, for our interpretation of the underlying structure of each film was used to categorize or cluster it within a general literary schema derived from prior prostitution narratives. In this approach, the films are 'mapped onto' categories of prostitution believed to reflect overarching cultural beliefs and values regarding prostitutes, such as how prostitutes behave; how they look and dress; and what outcomes occur in their lives.

Four Quadrants

The dialectical dimensions for the proposed typology are Good versus Evil and Punished versus Unpunished. They relate to two key elements of drama—character and plot. These elements are essential to drama, the category into which all films fall, for they are performances designed to be viewed. Character and plot are intertwined, for in most western literature the notion of "character in action" prevails—that is, the action of plot is rooted in the nature of the characters, and what the character *is* determines what happens to him or her. The typology expresses a bipolar opposition of Good versus Evil that refers to the prostitute's *character*—character is composed of the traits, behaviors, and motivations of the central figure. The other bipolar opposition—Punished versus Unpunished—refers to the *plot* of the text; it defines the outcome of the action and summarizes what happens to the character.

It is important to note that these are orthogonal constructs, because Goodness and Evil as marks of character do not necessarily determine the prostitute's fate in our texts. That is, evil prostitutes may be portrayed as living happily ever after, and good ones may be shown to suffer horrible lives and painful deaths. The importance of this tenuous relationship between character and plot derives from the lack of moral geometry that is characteristic of the literature on prostitution from which these cinematic images flow. From a feminist point of view, the underlying male-dominance in the images of prostitutes is evident in mismatches between character and plot. The "rules" of dramatic structure are suspended when prostitution is the subject, and outcomes need not be firmly tied to sound dramatic architecture.

The defining criteria of each quadrant are described below:

I. Evil-Unpunished

The archetype of the evil but unpunished prostitute termed *Evil Eve* is traceable to the Biblical figure of Eve as portrayed in misogynistic early Christian literature. In such texts, the dramatic emphasis is placed on the coexistence of seductive and evil traits in the same woman. The woman further exhibits cynicism and world-weariness in conjunction with great physical beauty. She is a coquettish moody seductress whose narcissism brings men sorrow; her destruction of the men she attracts is depicted as almost accidental or careless. The Evil Eve figure is a survivor, despite her evil ways. She remains alive at the end of the narrative and no punishment is meted out to her. In literature, Manon (Prevost 1731; Puccini 1893) is an early example of this archetype—a flirtatious and emotionally unstable woman who seduces men, bringing them momentary happiness but eventual sorrow. Her story has been popular; it was first told in novel form by Abbe Prevost (*Manon Lescaut*, 1731), and later turned into two operas—Massenet's *Manon* (1885) and Puccini's *Manon Lescaut* (1893). In the present inquiry, this archetype is represented by the character of Lola Lola in the film *The Blue Angel* (1929).

II. Good-Unpunished

There are three subtypes represented in this quadrant, each representing variations on the oppositional theme of Good—Unpunished characters. The first is termed the *Whore-with-a-heart-of-gold* and is derived from the Romantic tradition that emphasized the innate goodness of humanity. A second subtype is termed the *Saved Sinner* and is derived from Christian doctrine originating in the forgiveness of the prostitute Mary Magdalene. In these texts, the prostitute is redeemed through a conversion process set in motion by others. Typically, the person responsible for initiating the prostitute's salvation risks his own reputation on her behalf.

The third subtype is labeled the *Material Girl* and is traceable to the Marxist/Socialist view of capitalist society. Here the text emphasizes the prostitute's economic motivation—the necessity for her to earn a living. The text also serves a larger metaphorical function of indicting capitalist society as one in which most persons are prostituted in various ways. At the narrative's conclusion, the prostitute is saved by means of her own efforts. A literary example is Shaw's Mrs. Warren, in *Mrs. Warren's Profession* (1894). Within the present inquiry, this subtype is portrayed by means of the character of Vivienne in *Pretty Woman* (1991).

III. Good-Punished

This archetype is labeled the *Hapless Harlot* and is traceable to the advent of Realism in the modern novel. Here, the text's focus is upon social forces that drive individuals into prostitution. Often the narrative centers around an innocent child who is seduced, abandoned, and left to a life of misfortune and poverty. Both young men and young women are depicted as becoming prostitutes through this process. In these narratives the life of the prostitute is shown to be degrading rather than glamorous, and typically, even if the victim is rescued from the profession, his/her life is portrayed as forever damaged. Literary works depicting this archetype include Charles Dickens' Little Emily in *David Copperfield* (1849-1850). The character of Violet in *Pretty Baby* (1977) exhibits this pattern in the present study.

IV. Evil-Punished

The fourth quadrant includes texts in which the prostitute is depicted as evil and punished as a result. Termed the *Bitch Whore* archetype, this character is derived from the early Christian view of pagan goddesses as seductresses who led their lovers to ruin and death. Such evil women were to be punished by horrible deaths—disease, disfigurement, or murder. Characters in this category are often shown to be vengeful creatures who direct their anger at all men or society at large. A literary example is Emile Zola's Nana in *Nana* (1880). Although we did not include this archetype in our present film sample, this character type is recognizable as Tralala in Hubert Selby's *Last Exit to Brooklyn* (1957). Tralala dies as a result of gang rape, and represents but one of many prostitutes whose death becomes the climax of violent pornographic films. This archetype is most evident in pornography, where the implicit misogynistic desire to inflict pain upon women often culminates in torture and murder.

Cinematic Examples. As noted, the present inquiry examines three American films dealing with prostitution, which span a time period from 1929 (*The Blue Angel*) to 1991 (*Pretty Woman*). As described previously, our inquiry focuses on these selected exemplars in conformance to the conventions of inductive criticism. The films in our sample were chosen as representative examples of prostitution in American motion pictures, but obviously are not intended to constitute a complete universe of all possible ways that prostitution has been portrayed cinematically. The use of exemplars to discuss cultural archetypes in film follows Denzin's (1991) cinematic analysis of alcoholism. As in Denzin's analysis, we focus attention upon films that have received significant critical acclaim and/or substantial commercial success.

1. Evil-Punished: "Evil Eve"

An early and iconic cinematic depiction of the Evil Eve archetype is found in Marlene Dietrich's portrayal of "Lola Lola" in *The Blue Angel* (1929). This archetype embodies cultural beliefs regarding the prostitute's cruelest and most evil manifestation—as a seductress who leads her lovers to ruin and death. This type of prostitute is portrayed as having few redeeming moral qualities; the core of her being is the *projection* of beauty, for she attracts lovers not by what she is, but by what she *appears* to be. Her ability to convey sensuality is a cover for underlying moral viciousness, but the mask is so artistically wrought that her lovers fail to see beneath it. (Motion picture synopsis available from authors).

Lola Lola is a glamorized version of Evil Eve, the alluring singer/performer who enchants and then destroys Dr. Rath. Her sexual power is signalled by her costume, for one of the hallmarks of prostitution is clothing designed to reveal the merchandise. Since clothing is a status-marker denoting women's social position, as de Beauvoir pointed out, it is "only the prostitute, functioning exclusively as an erotic object, who displays herself as this and no more (1953, p. 592)." However, the effect of the provocative clothing not only reveals the body but also hides the soul—that fundamental kernel of evil at the heart of Evil Eve. From a misogynistic perspective, whenever women become sexually visible, they are potentially dangerous.

Lola Lola further personifies the ambiguous association between entertainment, beauty, and sexual pleasure, for her talent is intertwined with her stage seductiveness. She acquires value as a unique product by offering her special singing talent to the audience, thus showing herself as more humanized than the mere display of flesh captured by her pictures would suggest. She exists more in the realm of "art" than that of pornography (de Beauvoir 1953), and in this she resembles the Greek *hetera* or the Japanese *geisha*—the woman who treats not only her body but also her entire personality as capital to be exploited. Like those prostitutes, less tainted by misogyny than later Western ones, Lola Lola is *in control*. Her sole motive is profit: she sells her singing talent (her stage self) and her visual image (pornographic pictures). Thus, she commoditizes herself, and in so doing, perverts her talent in order to enslave men and to satisfy her need for comfort, security, and power.

In the text, Lola Lola is portrayed as a dangerous woman *because* she is a successful woman. She succeeds in making her own money and thus gains economic independence in her life outside of the traditional bounds of marriage. She earns a living as does a man, is uninhibited in her behavior and conversation, and consumes alcohol and cigarettes openly. When she marries Rath, she exhibits male sex role prerogatives: first by seducing him, then by supporting him, and finally by discarding him for a younger partner. Rath's decline is traced by his loss of money, social position, self respect, and ultimately, life itself.

The narrative uses semiotic markers to reinforce the danger of thus sex role reversal, one that portends disaster for any man captivated by Lola Lola's siren song. The black musical doll is a symbol of her figurative emasculation of Rath in their first sexual act, a humiliation that is prefigured when Rath awakens holding the doll. It foreshadows his eventual loss of manhood, for in this era—recall that the film was made at the end of the 1920's—black men were viewed stereotypically as phallic symbols reputed to possess large sex organs and innate musical ability, coupled with a passive nature that required a master's strong will to control. The doll stands for what patriarchal society most fears and despises—a man reduced to sexual slavery who has become a woman's toy.

The narrative shows death to be Rath's fate followed by Lola Lola is continued seductive activities after she has destroyed him. In the last scene, she is shown singing a reprise of "Falling in Love Again" at the same cabaret where she first met him. At the narrative's end, Lola Lola goes unpunished—she is depicted as unrepentant, unchanged in her wanton ways, and, by implication destined to enslave other men in the future.

2. Good-Unpunished: "The Whore-With-A-Heart-of-Gold"

Unlike Evil Eve who goes unpunished because she is a misogynistic proof of women's wicked ways, the whore-with-a-heart-of-gold goes unpunished because she is innately good. She is a popular literary archetype, found in Dickens's *Oliver Twist* (1837-1838), George Moore's *Esther Waters* (1894), and William Saroyan's *The Time of Your Life* (1939). The most popular stereotypes emphasize materialism, sentimentality, and salvation of the sinner, three perennially popular motifs in Western literature.

In the material girl subtype, the emphasis is less on sentimentality than on *materialism*. This subtype is exemplified in *Pretty Woman* (1990), where Vivienne is an updated version of the whore-with-a-heart-of-gold. During the 1980s, materialism became a dominant cultural theme (Hirschman 1988) as this narrative exemplifies. (Motion picture synopsis available from authors).

Vivienne exemplifies the prostitute gifted with innate good character, and consumption serves as the vehicle by which her goodness is made manifest in the film. We are shown that she is a good person despite her messy exterior (e.g., safety pins hold her costume together) because she is quick to learn how to consume properly. Edward begins her education in consumption by hiring her as an employee; they make a business deal in which her services are given in exchange for his money. She then turns to a surrogate mentor, the hotel manager, for consumption lessons, and he teaches her what to wear on an elegant dinner date and how to eat at a fine restaurant. Edward takes charge of the practical application of her schooling in actual consumption scenes. The scene in which Edward accompanies her on a shopping spree on Rodeo Drive portrays the revenge of the disempowered. It is Vivienne's empowerment through money that hints at the financial prostitution at the heart of the capitalist system.

Edward expresses the notion of society as a whorehouse when he points out that although a woman who has no money and has to sell her body to pay the rent is called a prostitute, the same woman *with* money can elicit prostitute-like behavior from others. He later makes a second comparison of prostitution to corporate takeovers, when he says, "We both screw people for money." However, feminists would note that the male/female power difference in economic terms is hardly comparable, for Edward is rich, male, and in control of substantial capital resources, while Vivienne is poor, female, and driven to sell herself to gain access to these resources. The difference is that Edward has the power to cause others to prostitute themselves, while Vivienne has only the power to prostitute herself.

Despite her brief foray into prostitution, Vivienne further displays her moral integrity and essential goodness by declining to become Edward's mistress. She knows that a mistress is still a prostitute, albeit one with a less precarious lifestyle. The film turns sentimental when Edward becomes the prince and rescues Vivienne by proposing marriage, but it does not end with a wedding scene. The reason is that the text's focus is more on material well-being and self-help than on romantic rescue. Before the final scene, Vivienne gives evidence of rescuing herself by planning to finish high school, training for a job, and the most important indicator of her high moral character by rescuing others. She saves her friend Kit from a life on the street and Edward from a life of empty greed. Like many works with materialism as the theme, *Pretty Woman* ends with a social program for ensuring economic success that goes beyond the vague prescription for marital happiness in sentimental fiction.

3. Good-Punished: "The Hapless Harlot"

In contrast to the good unpunished prostitute, the hapless harlot is society's victim—a good person punished by the society that spawned and then spurned him/her. This archetype is often exemplified by a child prostitute, a youngster who has been seduced and abandoned and whose loss of virginity leads to life on the streets. Stephen Crane's Maggie (*Maggie, A Girl of the Streets*, 1893), for example, becomes a prostitute after having been seduced and then thrown out by her family, and Dickens's Little Emily (*David Copperfield*, 1849-1850) is also the victim of a male seducer. In twentieth century literature, it is important to note that young men as well as young women can be seduced and then discarded, often falling into a life of prostitution as a result of their loss of innocence.

Novels with the hapless harlot as the leading character are in the realistic tradition, usually detailing the political and economic conditions that produce society's victims. This archetype is especially prevalent in modern novels from Spain and Latin America that focus on the social forces driving impoverished lower-class men and women into prostitution. In cultures where a small elite class rules a huge underclass, victimized children are often forced by poverty into a profession presented as degrading rather than as glamorous. Unlike the whore-with-a-heart-of-gold, the hapless harlot is unable to transform an unsatisfactory life into a tolerable one. Even if rescued from prostitution, s/he has insufficient reserves of strength left upon which to draw. Since the novels presenting this archetype focus on the social milieu more than on the characters themselves, the hapless harlot is often depicted with more detailed context than character revelation, unlike the other archetypes.

The importance of context is evident in the story of Violet, the child prostitute in *Pretty Baby*. The film is based on a factual story about Hilaire Bellocq, a noted photographer of New Orleans prostitutes in the early 1900's. (Motion picture synopsis available from authors).

Violet's story brings the institution of white female slavery into the 20th Century. She is shown as a child shaped by her environment and warped by maternal in-attention. Although Hannie claims that she wants to be "respectable," she willingly participates in the sale of her virginal daughter, viewing her as another source of income. Bellocq, the photographer, is an enigmatic figure, ambiguous in his feelings for Violet. Although she is only a child, he loves her as one would an adult woman (rather than as a parent would love a daughter), yet he does not express his love in any overtly sexual way.

The scene most evocative of what prostitution means to women is the sale of Violet's virginity to the highest bidder. She is brought into the viewing room on a litter, decorated like a mannequin in a store window. The bidding for her replicates that of slave auctions a century before the date of the film. The man who buys her rapes her brutally, but Violet is committed to a life of prostitution, evidenced when she smiles beguilingly at the next customer. The text's externalized view of Violet emphasizes her commodity status, for there is no indication of how she feels—only how she is viewed by her purchasers. Ironically, at the close of the film, Violet's stepfather records one final image of her on film. Although dressed in expensive and conservative clothes, the direct gaze of Violet's eyes betrays the sexualized and commoditized self beneath the prim exterior. There is no innocence here.

Of the three films discussed, *Pretty Baby* is perhaps the most troubling, both in its fictional content and in its real-life production. Child prostitution, from a behavioral perspective, is the most destructive manifestation of the commoditization of human beings. Occurring as it does during the young person's early years of identity formation, it can prevent the individual from ever achieving a sense of wholeness and self-worth. And it can serve to distort the individual's ability to construct intimate—as opposed to merely sexual—relationships with others. Given this, the production of *Pretty Baby* constituted a symbolic act of child prostitution for its central actress, Brooke Shields, who was only 11 1/2 at the time of the filming. Depicted virtually nude in several scenes with her suitor (Keith Carradine), mouthing lines such as "Where'd you get that thing" to male actors playing customers, and being seen *as* a prostitute by millions of audience members replicated in real life that which was being depicted as fiction on the screen.

DISCUSSION

The commoditization of women as prostitutes has been practiced from the earliest recorded history to the present day. In the present analysis, we have extended the literary portrayal of the prostitute to the American cinema, where iconic images of what prostitutes *are* and what they *become* have shaped the popular view of their role in American society since the late 1920's. From the man-eating Lola Lola of *The Blue Angel* (1929) to the redemptive Vivienne in *Pretty Woman* (1990), the depiction of prostitution has influenced our collective ideology of women's roles as subject and object, as person and product, and as predator and victim.

The cinematic portrayal of women as prostitutes—as cultural commodities—holds a mirror up to the reflected (and refracted) images of women in American society. From the militant feminist cultural perspective, *all* women may be seen as commercialized commodities, taught from childhood to groom themselves to obtain men's approval, in order to become quite literally the objects of male desire. Cinematic images of painted and packaged prostitutes coexist with advertising images of painted and packaged "models" whom women are taught to view as aspirational referents. Further, just as Vivienne recognized that she was in a very competitive business, so too do most women learn about sexual competition in the marriage market, using their beauty and their bodies to attract men as mates.

The cinematic depiction of prostitution also throws into sharp relief the roles of women as *sacred* and *profane* commodities in American culture (see Belk, et al 1989; Hirschman 1988). This dialectic informs all three of the films in this paper, in terms of the iconic tension between two conceptions of women's roles—that of pure, virtuous vessel serving as the privatized domestic nurturer of hearth and home versus that of rampant, wanton sexual predator destroying the men who seek her out. Sacred whores, such as Vivienne of *Pretty Woman*, we are taught, deserve salvation. They need only to be rescued by "good men" to find their salvation in marriage and motherhood. In contrast, profane whores have lost so much of their female virtue and have become so masculinized by their exposure to the secular pleasures of the world (e.g., alcohol, tobacco, fornication) that they are unsalvageable. They are left to destroy the men who try to save them (e.g., Lola Lola) or to be destroyed (e.g., Violet in *Pretty Baby*).

The consumption of these cinematic images has a powerful effect on women's—and men's—images of themselves, their roles, their *place*. Our intent has been to illustrate that as we consume media texts, so also do they consume us, by shaping our views of who and what we are.

REFERENCES

Barthes, Roland (1983), *The Fashion System*, New York: Hill and Wang.

Barthes, Roland (1972), *Mythologies*, New York: Hill and Wang.

Barthes, Roland (1964), *Elements of Semiology*, London: Cape.

Baudrillard, Jean (1981), *For a Critique of the Political Economy of the Sign*, St. Louis: Telos.

Baudrillard, Jean (1968), *Les Systémes des Objets*, Paris: Gallimard.

Belk, Russell, Melanie Wallendorf, and John Sherry (1989), "The Sacred and the Profane in Consumer Behavior: Theodicy on the Odyssey,", 16 (June), 1-38.

Berger, J. (1972), *Way of Seeing*, London: BBC and Penguin.

Betterton, R. (1985), "How Do Women Look? The Female Nude in the Work of Suzanne Valadon," *Feminist Review*, 19, 3-24.

Bullough, Vern L. (1974), *The Subordinate Sex: A History of Attitudes Toward Women*, Baltimore: Penguin Books.

DeLauretis, Teresa (1984), *Alice Doesn't: Feminism, Semiotics, Cinema*, Bloomington: Indiana University Press.

Eagleton, Terry (1991), *Ideology*, London: Verso.

Fergusson, Francis, trans. (1961), *Aristotle's Poetics*, New York: Hill and Wang.

Hapke, Laura (1989), *Girls Who Went Wrong: Prostitutes in American Fiction, 1885-1917*, Bowling Green, OH: Bowling Green State University Popular Press.

Hirschman, Elizabeth C. (1993), "Ideology in Consumer Research: A Marxist and Feminist Critique, 1980 and 1990," *Journal of Consumer Research*, 19 (March), 537-556.

Hirschman, Elizabeth C. (1991a), "A Feminist Critique of Marketing Theory: Toward Agentic-Communal Balance," in Janeen A. Costa (ed.), *Gender and Consumer Behavior*, Salt Lake City: University of Utah Press, 324-340.

Hirschman, Elizabeth C. (1991b), "Secular Mortality and the Dark Side of Consumer Behavior: Or How Semiotics Saved My Life," in Rebecca Holman and Michael R. Solomon (eds.), *Advances in Consumer Research*, Vol. 18, Association for Consumer Research: Provo, UT, 1-6.

Hirschman, Elizabeth C. (1990), "Secular Immortality and the American Ideology of Consumption," *Journal of Consumer Research*, 17 (June), 31-42.

Hirschman, Elizabeth C. (1988), "The Ideology of Consumption: A Structural-Syntactical Analysis of *Dallas* and *Dynasty*," *Journal of Consumer Research*, 15 (December), 344-359.

Holbrook, Morris B. (1988), "An Interpretation: *Gremlins* as Metaphors for Materialism," *Journal of Macromarketing*, 8 (Spring), 54-59.

Holbrook, Morris B., Stephen Bell, and Mark W. Grayson (1989), "The Role of the Humanities in Consumer Research: Close Encounters and Coastal Disturbances, in *Interpretive Consumer Research*, E. C. Hirschman (ed.), Provo, UT: Association for Consumer Research, 29-47.

Holbrook, Morris B. and Mark W. Grayson (1986), "The Semiology of Cinematic Consumption: Symbolic Consumer Behavior in *Out of Africa*," *Journal of Consumer Research*, 13 (December), 374-381.

Holbrook, Morris B. and John O'Shaughnessy (1988), "On the Scientific Status of Consumer Research and the Need for an Interpretive Approach to Studying Consumer Behavior, *Journal of Consumer Research*, 15 (December), 398-402.

Horn, Pierre L. and Mary Beth Pringle (1984), "Introduction," in *The Image of the Prostitute in Modern Literature*, eds. Pierre L. Horn and Mary Beth Pringle, New York: Frederick Ungar Publishing Co., 1-7.

Jacobs, Lea (1991), *The Wages of Sin: Censorship and the Fallen Woman Film, 1928-1942*, Madison, WI: The University of Wisconsin Press.

Kaplan, E. Ann (1983), *Women and Film: Both Sides of the Camera*, New York: Routledge.

Kaplan, E. Ann (1980), "Introduction," *Women in Film Noir*, ed. Ann Kaplan, London: British Film Institute, 1-5.

Kuhn, A. (1982), *Women's Pictures: Feminism and Cinema*, London: Routledge.

Levi-Strauss, Claude (1966), *The Savage Mind*, London: Weiderfeld and Nicholson.

Levi-Strauss, Claude (1965), "The Structural Study of Myth," in *Myth: A Symposium*, ed. Thomas A. Sebeok, Bloomington, IN: Indiana University Press, 81-106.

Lewin, Tamar (1992), "Furor on Exhibit at Law School Splits Feminists," *The New York Times Law*, (Nov. 13), p. B16.

Mayne, J. (1985), "Feminist Film Theory and Criticism," *Signs: Journal of Women in Culture and Society*, 11 (1), 81-100.

McCracken, Grant (1989), "Who is the Celebrity Endorser: Cultural Foundations of the Endorsement Process," *Journal of Consumer Research*, 16 (December), 310-321.

Metz, Christian (1974), *Film Language: A Semiotics of the Cinema*, trans. Michael Taylor, New York: Oxford University Press.

Mick, David Glenn (1986), "Consumer Research and Semiotics: Exploring the Morphology of Signs, Symbols, and Significance," *Journal of Consumer Research*, 13 (September), 196-213.

Mulvey, Laura (1975), "Visual Pleasure and Narrative Cinema," *Screen*, Vol. 16, No. 3, 6-18.

Murray, Jeff B. and Julie L. Ozanne (1991), "The Critical Imagination: Emancipatory Elements in Consumer Research," *Journal of Consumer Research*, 18 (September), 129-144.

Myers, K. (1989), "Towards a Feminist Erotica," in R. Betterton (ed.), *Looking On: Images of Femininity in the Visual Arts and the Media*, London: Pandora, 189-202.

O'Guinn, Thomas C., Ronald J. Faber, and Marshall Rice (1985), "Popular Film and Television as Consumer Acculturation Agents: America 1900 to the Present," in *Historical Perspectives in Consumer Research: National and International Perspectives*, Chin Tiong Tan and Jagdish N. Sheth (eds.), Singapore: Association for Consumer Research, 297-300.

Penley C. (1989), "The Future of an Illusion," *Film, Feminism and Psychoanalysis*, Minneapolis: University of Minnesota Press.

Perkins, Roberta and Garry Bennett (1985), *Being a Prostitute*, Sydney: Allen and Unwin.

Pomeroy, Sarah B. (1975), *Goddesses, Whores, Wives, and Slaves: Women in Classical Antiquity*, New York: Schocken Books.

Scott, Linda M. (1990), "Understanding Jingles and Needledrop: A Rhetorical Approach to Music in Advertising," *Journal of Consumer Research*, 17 (September), 223-236.

Stern, Barbara B. (1993), "Feminist Literary Criticism and the Deconstruction of Ads: A Postmodern View of Advertising and Consumer Responses," *Journal of Consumer Research*, 19 (March), 556-566.

Stern, Barbara B. (1991), "Deja Vu: Feminism Revisited," in Janeen A. Costa (ed.), *Gender and Consumer Behavior*, Salt Lake City: University of Utah Press, 341-349.

Stern, Barbara B. (1989), "Literary Criticism and Consumer Research," *Journal of Consumer Research*, 16 (December), 322-334.

Tseelon, Efrat and Susan B. Kaiser (1992), "A Dialogue with Feminist Film Theory," in *Studies in Symbolic Interaction*, Vol. 13, 119-137.

Umiker-Sebeok, Jean (1993), *Marketing and Semiotics, Vol. II*, Bloomington, IN: Indiana University Press.

Umiker-Sebeok, Jean (1987), *Marketing and Semiotics: New Directions in the Study of Signs for Sale*, Berlin, West Germany: Mouton de Gruyter.

Wells, William (1993), "Discovery Oriented Consumer Research," *Journal of Consumer Research*, 19 (March), 489-504.

The Influence of Affective Context on Advertising Effectiveness

Douglas M. Stayman, Cornell University

Traditional approaches to affect in advertising have focused on affect as a mediator. That is, advertisements have been seen as influencing feeling responses which, in turn, influence relevant outcomes. This approach is exemplified by the stream of research on the influence of feelings on ad attitudes. In contrast, recent research has suggested the importance of the affective context in which stimuli are experienced to how those stimuli are interpreted and acted upon. This approach treats affect as a moderator, influencing processing of the ad and thus the impact of the ad on variables such as cognitive responses which then influence ad outcomes. This special topic session included papers focusing on different aspects of this moderation role of affect as a context variable for ad processing.

The first paper, by Douglas Stayman, explored the mechanism underlying the influence of affect on the processing of information in advertisements. The paper contrasted two explanations for why affect might lead to reduced (peripheral) processing, reduced capacity or motivation, with a third explanation of an influence of affect, that affect does not necessarily influence the *extent* to which information is processed systematically (the amount of processing), but rather the *way* that the information is interpreted (the type of processing).

The research first replicated Batra and Stayman (*JCR* 1990), who found an interaction between affect and argument strength consistent with a capacity or motivation explanation (less difference between strong and weak arguments in the positive affect versus control condition). However, Batra and Stayman used attribute importance as the manipulation of argument strength. This research extended their study in also manipulating the logical consistency of the arguments used. When specious arguments are used as the weak argument manipulation, the Batra and Stayman interaction is not replicated. The paper argues that this finding is inconsistent with either a capacity or motivation explanation and provides further support for the view that affect influences persuasion through influencing the way that information in messages is interpreted, rather than how extensively it is processed.

The second paper, by Karen France, Reshma Shah, and C.W. Park, considered the impact of specific program induced emotions at varying levels of intensity on the evaluation and memory of embedded advertisements. They suggest that positive emotion inducing programs facilitate ad evaluation and memory due to the cue accessibility hypothesis, while negative emotion inducing programs debilitate ad evaluation and memory due to distraction effects. Furthermore, they suggest that highly intense positive emotions elicited by television programs do not further facilitate ad effectiveness when compared to programs eliciting lower intensity positive emotions. Highly intense negative emotions, however, further debilitate ad effectiveness when compared to programs that elicit negative emotions at lower levels of intensity.

With a 2 x 2 full-factorial, between-subjects design, this study considered the impact of high and low emotional valence at high and low levels of felt emotional intensity on commercial effectiveness, specifically ad evaluation and memory. A pod of commercials was embedded in each program segment. Commercial effectiveness was assessed with multiple dependent measures (e.g., attitude toward the ad, attitude toward the brand, attention, distraction, and recall of ad message content). The paper on which this abstract is based is published elsewhere in this volume.

The third paper, by Meryl Gardner and David Schumann, expanded the role of affect related to advertising to the impact on consumption and post consumption, with specific emphasis on comparison standards used in (dis)confirmation judgments. The paper gave a conceptual framework for investigating the role of affect as it concerns advertising and satisfaction and the types and features of comparison standards used. The features discussed included nature, level, framing and perceptual distinctiveness. In addition, "mood management" as concerns product expectancies and subsequent evaluation were discussed. Finally, the role of other related mediators and moderators was presented.

The concluding discussion by Paul Miniard brought out some of the complexities and difficulties in researching the influence of affect, including some suggestions for further research into these effects.

The Impact of Emotional Valence and Intensity on Ad Evaluation and Memory

Karen Russo France, West Virginia University
Reshma H. Shah, University of Pittsburgh
C. Whan Park, University of Pittsburgh

ABSTRACT

This study examines the impact of specific program-induced emotions at varying levels of intensity on the memory for and evaluation of embedded advertisements. Consistent with previous research, we found that a positive emotion-inducing program facilitates ad evaluation while a negative emotion-inducing program debilitates ad evaluation. Furthermore, we found that highly intense positive emotions elicited by a television program do not further facilitate ad evaluation when compared to programs eliciting lower intensity positive emotions. Highly intense negative emotions, however, further debilitate ad evaluation when compared to programs that elicit negative emotions at lower levels of intensity. Ad memory was not significantly impacted by the television program's emotional valence or intensity. We offer several processing explanations for these findings.

Given a television program's ability to induce valenced affective states (Averill 1969, Axelrod 1963, Gardner and Wilhelm 1987, Goldberg and Gorn 1987, Gouaux 1971, Gouaux and Summers 1973, Mattes and Cantor 1982, Pavelchak, Antil, and Munch 1988), a relevant area of research might consider the impact of these varying emotions on viewers' reactions to commercials embedded in a program. Although previous research has considered the dichotomous effect of positive and negative program-induced moods (c.f. Goldberg and Gorn 1987), it has neglected the array of differentially valenced emotions. In general, previous research has supported the hypothesis that positive program-elicited moods enhance commercial effectiveness whereas negative ones debilitate effectiveness. These findings have been applied to ad placement by managers who want viewers to be in a generally positive state when their advertisement is aired (Schultz 1979, Schwerin 1958).

The present research argues that examining the impact of positive and negative feeling states may be appropriate when studying the impact of moods which are milder in intensity than emotions (Cohen and Areni 1991, Clark and Isen 1992, Gardner 1985). However, the simple distinction between positive/negative moods may not be adequate to explain the role of different types of program-induced *emotions* on commercial effectiveness. Emotions are more stimulus specific than moods, comprise more of a cognitive interface than moods, and tend to interrupt goal-directed activities (Cohen and Areni 1991, Clark 1982). Moreover, unlike moods, emotions may vary greatly in their intensity level (Mehrabian and Russell 1973). Thus, emotions may impact commercial effectiveness differently than do moods. Specifically, differences in commercial effectiveness may be more pronounced at lower levels of emotional intensity than at higher levels. At lower levels of emotional intensity, the impact of valence may be more pronounced; whereas higher levels of emotional intensity may tend to disrupt or interfere with ongoing attention and processing of embedded ads, thereby diminishing the impact of emotional valence.

The current study examines the impact of specific program-induced emotions at varying levels of intensity on the processing and evaluation of embedded advertisements. In pursuing these research issues, this study replicates and extends the work of Goldberg and Gorn (1987). We use Goldberg and Gorn's (1987) study as a benchmark for the following reasons: (1) it was the first study available that offered a specific mood-based explanation (cue-accessibility) for the impact of program-induced emotions on ad effectiveness, (2) it did not examine the impact of emotional intensity which may prove to have a differential impact on processing (Mehrabian and Russell 1973), and (3) while Goldberg and Gorn rely on the cue accessibility explanation, their cognitive response data reveal that other mechanisms may also operate. We test some of these other explanations. The present study is, thus, designed to shed light on some of the unresolved issues raised by Goldberg and Gorn, and to further extend findings of previous program-context effects research.

THEORY AND HYPOTHESES

While much of previous program-context effects research has examined the impact of positive/negative program-induced moods on commercial effectiveness, it may be more appropriate to examine the impact of program-induced emotions. Although researchers have found differences to exist between moods and emotions, these two terms have been used interchangeably in affect research, with little consideration given towards their unique differences. There has been an implicit assumption in previous research that the effects of emotions may be understood to operate similarly to moods on ad effectiveness. This assumption is evident in the Goldberg and Gorn study which utilized a mood-based explanation—the cue accessibility hypothesis—to predict the impact of positive and negative emotions (i.e. happy and sad) on commercial effectiveness.

According to the cue accessibility hypothesis, programs that elicit positive/negative affective states prime similarly valenced material stored in memory. In other words, an affective state may influence one's evaluations of stimuli because material stored in memory that is congruent with that feeling state will be more accessible, and consequently more likely to come to mind than it would at another time (Clark 1982, Clark and Isen 1982, Isen 1984, Isen 1975, Isen, Shalker, Clark, and Karp 1978). Previous research has found cue accessibility to operate in the case of positive emotions, but has neglected to examine whether it operates in the case of negative emotions (Clark 1982, Clark and Isen 1982, Isen 1984, Isen 1975, Isen, Shalker, Clark, and Karp 1978).

In the context of television commercials, consumers are likely to have an array of stored memories regarding brands and products. Therefore, affectively positive responses elicited by a television program would increase the accessibility of positive material stored in memory regarding the advertised brand, product, or product category. Goldberg and Gorn (1987) find support for the cue accessibility hypotheses in that the happy television program tended to lead to greater perceived commercial effectiveness, more affectively positive cognitive responses, and somewhat better recall than the sad television program. The cue accessibility hypothesis also predicts better recall in the case of positive programs since positive affective states lead to broader, more integrated cognitive categories (Isen et al. 1978, Isen 1984). These larger, well-integrated categories enhance information processing and memory through a spreading activation process. Positive affective states also tend to increase the extent of information processing (Hoffman 1986, Mamo 1990), thereby potentially increasing recall (Isen, Daubman, and Gorgoglione 1984).

Negative emotions may operate differently than positive emotions. Since negative emotions tend to induce more thought (Clark 1982, Goldberg and Gorn 1987), subjects may be distracted from attending to and processing embedded advertisements. When negative emotions are elicited by a television program, particularly from a negative program that is issue-oriented, it is likely that a viewer will be distracted from processing ad information. For example, in the Goldberg and Gorn (1987) study, 54 percent of those viewing the negative program reported still thinking about the program as they viewed the advertisement compared to only 21 percent who viewed the positive program. Thus, in the case of negative emotions, we would expect ad evaluation and memory to decrease not because of cue accessibility, but rather due to distraction/interference.

In light of the above discussion, we hypothesize that:

H1: *A positive emotion-inducing program facilitates ad memory and evaluation while a negative emotion-inducing program debilitates ad memory and evaluation.*

Clark (1982) proposes a link between arousal (emotional intensity) and affect valence. Specifically, experiencing intense emotions in the present will help to prime material previously stored in memory linked with the level of intensity. To the extent that a program induces strong emotional intensity, it facilitates retrieval of similarly valenced thoughts related to the brand, product, or product category. The greater the emotional intensity a person experiences with a specific emotion, the more intense the priming of similarly valenced material from memory, and consequently, the stronger the influence on brand evaluations. The cue accessibility hypothesis predicts that emotions, as a stronger form of moods, may better facilitate retrieval of similarly valence memories than do moods. While this may be a reasonable assumption for lower intensity emotions, the same may not hold for higher intensity emotions.

A great deal of research in psychology and consumer behavior has found a disruptive influence on information processing resulting from higher levels of emotional intensity (Eysenck 1976, 1982, Hasher and Zacks 1979, Park and Young 1986, Pavelchak, Antil and Munch 1988, Sanbonmatsu and Kardes 1988). Similarly, intense emotions resulting from program viewing may decrease one's motivation to attend to and process ad information (Bryant and Comisky 1978, Kennedy 1971, Soldow and Principe 1981, Television Audience Assessment 1984, Thorson and Oberman 1985, Thorson and Reeves 1986). Viewers' ongoing program-related thoughts may distract them from paying attention to the information presented in the advertisement.

As noted earlier, negative emotions tend to involve more issue-oriented thought. As such, higher intensity negative emotions should lead to increased interference/distraction. Positive emotions, on the other hand, tend to involve less program-oriented thought and, thus, should not disrupt processing of embedded commercials to the same extent as negative emotions. However, when the emotions felt during a television program are intensely positive, their impact on ad effectiveness is not clear. The cue accessibility hypothesis predicts that ad evaluation should be more favorable. According to this hypothesis, we may expect that strong positive emotions elicited by the program may, in fact, facilitate retrieval of similarly positive memories regarding the advertised brand, product, or product category. This should increase ad evaluation. However, other research on emotional intensity has demonstrated that intense emotions tend to distract viewers, thereby decreasing processing of subsequent stimuli. This should, in turn, decrease ad evaluation. Expecting the possible presence of both explanations, we propose that stronger positive emotions do not facilitate ad effectiveness to a greater degree than lower intensity positive emotions. From this discussion, it is hypothesized that:

H2: *More intense negative emotions elicited by a television program decrease ad memory and evaluation; whereas more intense positive emotions elicited by a television program do not facilitate ad memory and evaluation when compared to lower intensity positive emotions.*

METHODOLOGY

Design and Subjects:

To test the impact of program valence and intensity on advertisement effectiveness, a 2 X 2 full-factorial design was used in which program emotional valence (positive or negative) and felt emotional intensity (low or high) were manipulated between subjects. A total of 89 Masters of Business Administration students at a large, eastern university were recruited as subjects. Subjects represented a diverse group in terms of age, sex, and occupation.

Program and Advertisement Selection:

The two programs that were used to operationalize emotional valence and intensity were selected through expert judgement and several rounds of pretesting (see discussion below). The movies chosen for this study were *Dirty Dancing* (positive valence) and *Midnight Express* (negative valence). The stimuli for the current study were similar to those used in the Goldberg and Gorn (1987) study in that the negative program tended to induce more program-related thoughts in the elicitation of emotion while the positive program did not. It was necessary to use stimuli similar to that used by Goldberg and Gorn to test the competing hypotheses proposed.

A series of informal pretests, with approximately five subjects per cell, were conducted prior to the main pretest. During these informal pretests, subjects viewed the program segments and then completed a series of questions regarding the valence and intensity of emotions elicited by the program. Also, to ensure that the sequence of rearranged segments did not undermine understanding of the movie's plot, these subjects were questioned about the flow of the programs. After each informal pretest, the movies were re-edited in order to ensure that the programs varied along the appropriate dimensions.

The final version of the program stimuli was edited to approximately eleven minutes in duration and was pretested to ensure continuity as well as the intended manipulations. We manipulated emotional intensity at high and moderate levels of intensity since a low level of emotional intensity would decrease subject's involvement with the stimuli. Therefore, in this paper, we refer to low and high levels of intensity in a relative sense. To induce high levels of positive emotions, scenes from *Dirty Dancing* that included upbeat music and/or those in which the characters were portrayed as experiencing positive emotions (e.g., happiness, warmth, excitement) were used. Low intensity positive emotions were elicited with scenes that were void of music and in which the characters were experiencing less intense levels of positive emotions. Inducing high levels of negative emotions was accomplished with scenes from *Midnight Express* which were very graphic (e.g., a fight between two prison inmates) and/or portrayed the characters as experiencing intensely negative emotions (e.g., despair, loneliness, anger). Low intensity negative emotions were elicited with scenes in which there was less violence and in which the characters experienced less intense levels of negative emotions.

In addition to selecting various scenes from each movie, instructions to the subjects were used to induce different levels of felt emotional intensity. Subjects in the high emotional intensity condition were told that it was important for them to try to experience the emotions of the main character(s) as it was relevant to the completion of a questionnaire following the viewing. Subjects in the low emotional intensity condition were directed only to try to gain an understanding of the movie's contents. Finally, so as not to confound program involvement with emotional intensity, subjects in both the low and high emotional intensity groups were asked to pay close attention to the movie segments and were told they would be questioned on what they had viewed.

Advertisements were selected on the basis of two criteria: (1) they had to be unfamiliar to the subjects, and (2) they had to be generally positive in affect. As indicated by previous research, it was important to use commercials with which the subjects were unfamiliar to ensure no effects of ad memory on advertisement evaluation. Also, since advertisements are, in most cases, positive in nature (Batra and Ray 1986), it was necessary to use ads that met this criteria so as to not cause subjects to focus an unusual amount of attention on the advertisements. A non-local commercial for *Meritor Bank* was selected as the target commercial. A second commercial, for *Gorton's Fish*, was used as a filler.

Program and Advertisement Pretest:

To assess the extent to which the program segments varied along the critical dimensions, 68 subjects similar in profile to those used in the main study participated in a pretest. The pretest confirmed that the programs manipulated both emotional valence and level of intensity in the intended direction. Emotional responses to the program were measured via a sixteen-item, nine-point, semantic differential scale (1="felt not at all," 9="felt very strongly") that was modified from Edell and Burke (1987). Positive emotion items included: happy, hopeful, amused, cheerful, warmhearted, enthusiastic, lively, and energetic. Negative emotion items consisted of: angry, sad, apprehensive, anxious, distressed, depressed, disgusted, and offended. Composite scores were created by combining positively (negatively) valenced emotion dimensions. Cronbach's alpha reliabilities equaled 0.96 and 0.93 for the positive and negative composite scores, respectively. Results strongly suggest that subjects felt positive emotions when viewing the positive programs ($X_{low-pos}=5.28, X_{high-pos}=6.80, X_{low-neg}=2.12, X_{high-neg}=2.06; F=128.53, p=0.00$) and felt negative emotions when viewing the negative programs ($X_{low-pos}=2.20, X_{high-pos}=2.78, X_{low-neg}=4.45, X_{high-neg}=6.27; F=56.34, p=0.00$). A larger mean on the positive (negative) composite score indicates that the respondents felt positive (negative) emotions more intensely when viewing the program segment.

A composite measure, "NETMOVIE", was calculated by subtracting the mean score of the negative emotional scales from the mean score of the positive emotional scales. As such, NETMOVIE may be used to assess both emotional valence and emotional intensity. That is, the larger the NETMOVIE score, the more intensely felt were the positive emotions; whereas, the smaller the NETMOVIE score, the more intensely felt were the negative emotions. Means on NETMOVIE for *Midnight Express* were -2.28 and -4.18 for low and high emotional intensity, respectively; while, means for *Dirty Dancing* were 3.41 and 4.79 for low and high emotional intensity, respectively. In the case of *Dirty Dancing* we find an increase in NETMOVIE from low to high levels of intensity, while a decrease is found for *Midnight Express*. A main effect of emotional valence on NETMOVIE ($F=172.85, p=0.00$) and a valence x intensity interaction ($F=8.86, p=0.00$) were obtained.

Since NETMOVIE was calculated by subtracting the mean of negative emotion scores from the mean of the positive emotion scores, the significant interaction effect indicates that both emotional intensity and valence were successfully manipulated.

Subjects were asked to assess the degree to which they found the program to induce emotions while also provoking a great deal of program-related thought by indicating their agreement on three, nine-point scales ranging from "Disagree" (1) to "Agree" (9). The scales assessed the degree to which subjects felt the programs (1) compelled one to think about the issues of right or wrong, (2) made one think about the issues raised in the segment, (3) could be characterized as being heavy and thought-provoking. On all of these scales, subjects indicated that they found the versions of *Dirty Dancing* (positive program) to be less thought provoking than *Midnight Express (negative program)* (See Table 1).

Finally, pretest results revealed that *Midnight Express* and *Dirty Dancing* differed in terms of both familiarity ($F=9.59, p=0.00$) and involvement ($F=5.11, p=0.03$). Familiarity was measured on a nine-point scale ranging from 1 (Very Unfamiliar) to 9 (Very Familiar). Similarly, involvement was assessed on a nine-point scale with end anchors ranging from "Uninvolved" (1) to "Involved" (9). Subjects tended to be more familiar with *Dirty Dancing*; whereas, they found *Midnight Express* to be more involving. While the intention was to control involvement through the experimental instructions, it appears that the *Midnight Express* stimuli created higher levels of felt involvement. Therefore, familiarity and involvement are used as covariates in analyzing the data for the main experiment.

A second pretest of twenty-five students was conducted to assess the target commercial used in our study. Pretest results revealed that subjects found the Meritor Bank commercial to be positive in nature (composite mean of eight, nine-point positive emotion scales $X=4.9$). Subjects also felt very few negative emotions while watching this commercial (composite mean of eight, nine-point negative emotion scales=2.5). Moreover, subjects evaluated the Meritor Bank commercial positively based on the composite mean for two, nine-point scales (1="Dislike" to 9="Like", and 1="Negative" to 9="Positive") ($X=6.24$). Additionally, subjects were unfamiliar with the Meritor Bank commercial ($X=2.16$ on a nine-point scale ranging from (1) Unfamiliar to (9) Familiar).

Experimental Procedure

The experiment was conducted during class time. The experimenter introduced him/herself and stated in the cover story that this was a research experiment being conducted by faculty members who were interested in assessing how people process television programs. Subjects were then told that they would be viewing a videotape of *Dirty Dancing [Midnight Express]*. Following this brief introduction, the experimenter distributed instruction sheets and read them aloud while the subjects were asked to read along. To substantiate the cover story and to better approximate a realistic viewing environment, subjects were instructed to "pay as much *attention*" as they could to the movie. However, it was thought that subjects might become suspicious about the true intent of the study for the following two reasons: (1) the appearance of commercials in the program, and (2) for anyone familiar with the movies, the rearranged sequence of the movie. To reduce demand effects, subjects were told that the movie they would be watching was edited in order to be aired on television in another part of the country. Thus, subjects were led to expect some changes in movie sequence and the appearance of commercials.

After the instructions were read, subjects watched a videotape of one of the two versions of either *Midnight Express* or *Dirty*

TABLE 1
Means

Measure	DD - Low	DD - High	ME - Low	ME - High	F	p
(1) compelled one to think about the issues of right or wrong	3.31	5.75	7.17	7.86	34.53	0.00
(2) made one think about the issues raised in the segment	3.5	5.75	6.22	7.55	18.69	0.00
(3) could be characterized as being heavy and thought-provoking	2.25	4.42	7.39	7.91	102.5	0.00

Scale Values ranged from 1 (Agree) to 9 (Disagree)

NOTE: DD = Dirty Dancing
ME = Midnight Express

Dancing. The videotapes were prepared with the commercials embedded at the end of the program segment. Immediately following exposure to the programs, subjects completed the questionnaire booklet.

Experimental Measures

Respondents' evaluations of advertisements were inferred from measures of attitude toward the ad (A_{AD}) and attitude toward the brand (A_{BR}). Advertisement processing was assessed through measures of ad recall, attention to the ad, and distraction from it. *Ad attitudes* were measured on a two-item, nine-point semantic differential scale with anchors ranging from "Dislike" to "Like" and "Negative" to "Positive". *Brand attitudes* were measured using a two-item, nine-point semantic differential scale that asked subjects to indicate whether they found the advertised product or service to be "Bad" or "Good" and "Unappealing" or "Appealing". The A_{AD} and A_{BR} scales described below, were computed by the average of the summated items. Attention to the ad was assessed by asking subjects to indicate their level of attention to the ad on a scale ranging from 1 (Very Little) to 9 (Very Much). The degree to which subjects found the programs to distract them from paying attention to the ad was assessed on a nine-point scale ranging from 1 (Movie Did Not Distract Me) to 9 (Movie Distracted Me). Finally, direct measures of recall of the brand name and advertised product were taken.

RESULTS

Manipulation Checks

The manipulation checks of the selected programs yielded results that were highly consistent with those found in the pretest. The composite measure of program valence and intensity, NETMOVIE, revealed a main effect of emotional valence ($F=253.14$, $p=0.00$) and a significant emotion by intensity interaction ($F=13.54$, $p=0.00$). Means on NETMOVIE were as follows: *Dirty Dancing* $X_{low}=2.30$, $X_{high}=3.80$; *Midnight Express* $X_{low}=-2.84$, $X_{high}=-4.52$.

Hypotheses Testing

Hypothesis 1 predicts that a program that elicits positive emotions facilitates ad memory and evaluation; whereas a negative program decreases ad memory and evaluation. In terms of A_{AD}, we found a significant main effect of valence ($p=0.00$); whereas, emotional intensity and the interaction effect were not significant ($p=0.11$ and $p=0.80$, respectively). In other words, A_{AD} was significantly decreased when the ad was embedded in the negative ($X=4.21$) as compared to the positive program ($X=6.17$; $F=10.78$, $p=0.00$); thus supporting Hypothesis 1. A similar decrease resulted on A_{BR} from the positive to the negative program ($X_{pos}=6.32$, $X_{neg}=4.79$ respectively; $F=12.13$, $p=0.00$). The negative program distracted subjects from paying attention to the ad ($X=6.26$) more so than the positive program ($X=4.11$; $F=16.26$, $p=0.00$). Likewise, subjects paid more attention to the commercial when it was embedded in the positive program ($X=6.87$) than when it was embedded in the negative program ($X=5.58$; $F=6.54$, $p=0.01$). However, as was found by Goldberg and Gorn (1987), recall of the advertised brand names and product was not significantly impacted by valence of the television program. These results are consistent with the findings of previous research regarding the facilitating effects of positive programs on ad effectiveness.

According to Hypothesis 2, more intense negative programs should decrease ad evaluation and memory more so than less intense negative emotions; whereas more intense positive emotions should not facilitate ad evaluation and memory. In the case of negative emotions, we found directional support for this hypothesis in that A_{AD} was somewhat lower for the high intensity condition as compared to the low intensity condition ($X_{low}=4.70$, $X_{high}=3.69$; $t=1.52$, $p=0.07$, one-tailed). The impact on A_{BR} did not, however, significantly differ between the two programs ($X_{low}=4.98$, $X_{high}=4.60$; $t=0.71$, $p=0.2$, one-tailed). Additionally, ad processing was reduced as indicated by a decrease in attention paid to the ad when it was embedded in the high intensity negative program ($X=5.05$) when compared to the low intensity negative program ($X=6.09$; $t=1.75$; $p=0.04$, one-tailed). Respondents also reported that the highly intense negative programs distracted them from thinking about the commercial ($X_{low}=5.36$, $X_{high}=7.19$, $t=2.47$, $p=0.00$, one-tailed). However, brand and product recall were not impacted by the level of emotional intensity. Therefore, these results did not support Hypothesis 2 in the case of negative emotions.

In the case of positive emotions, we found no significant differences on A_{AD} ($t=1.27$, $p=0.21$) between the low intensity ($X=6.63$) and high intensity ($X=5.85$) conditions. Similar results were found for A_{BR} ($X_{low}=6.29$, $X_{high}=6.33$; $t=0.09$, $p=0.93$). Subjects indicated that they paid equal attention to the advertisement in both the low ($X=7.32$) and high intensity ($X=6.56$) conditions ($t=1.54$, $p=0.13$). Moreover, respondents were not differentially distracted from thinking about the ad in the low ($X=3.95$) versus high intensity ($X=4.22$) conditions ($t=0.39$, $p=0.7$). Recall of the brand and product also were unaffected by the intensity of the positive emotions. These results support our contention that high intensity positive emotions do not facilitate ad effectiveness when compared to low intensity positive emotions. Overall, Hypothesis 2 is, thus, partially supported.

DISCUSSION

This study examined the impact of program induced emotions and their intensity on advertising effectiveness. Consistent with previous research, the results show that positive programs facilitate ad effectiveness whereas, negative programs are found to be debilitating. Moreover, the results of the current study suggest that when emotional intensity (low and high) is introduced, highly intense positive programs tend not to further facilitate ad effectiveness in comparison with low intensity positive programs. In the case of negative programs, high levels of emotional intensity did not significantly debilitate ad effectiveness when compared to lower levels. While these results constitute important findings in the area of advertising research, they also offer several important implications for future research.

First, the results of the present study did not support Hypothesis 2. Specifically, in the case of negative programs, although we found a significant increase in distraction from and decrease in attention to the ad, from low to high levels, standard levels of significance on A_{AD}, A_{BR} and recall were not obtained. A_{AD} and A_{BR} may not have differed between the high and low negative intensity conditions since 1) the experimental commercial (see the liking rating in the methods section) was highly well liked and 2) the advertised product (free checking) was likely to be appealing to respondents, thereby further augmenting respondent's liking of the commercial. Moreover, to the extent that a commercial captures a viewer's attention, the impact of program emotional intensity may be lessened. The commercial, with its humor, was able to draw audience attention despite interference from the program, thereby mitigating the expected distraction effects. Additionally, since this study was conducted in an experimental setting, recall may not have been affected by emotional intensity as respondents might have been sensitive to questions asking them to recall specific details of the experimental stimuli.

Second, since we used stimuli similar to that used by Goldberg and Gorn (1987), this study also has a confound between program valence and the amount of issue-oriented thinking. *Midnight Express*, the negative program, induced more issue-oriented thought than the positive program, *Dirty Dancing*. Additionally, these programs tapped into specific types of emotions (e.g., warmhearted and disgusting). Perhaps varying emotions impact ad processing and evaluation differentially. For example, the impact of excitement might be markedly different from the impact of warmheartedness. Similarly, a negative emotion such as sadness may impact ad effectiveness differently than anger. These limitations should be addressed in future research which replicates and extends the present study through the use of programs that induce different degrees of thought and tap into different positive and negative emotions.

Third, while the present study specified two possible mechanisms (cue accessibility and distraction) that explain the impact of emotional valence and intensity on ad effectiveness, other mechanisms may also have been operating. Specifically, as noted earlier the degree of issue-oriented thinking associated with a particular program was proposed to affect an audience's attention to the program. Issue-oriented thinking might also activate alternative processing mechanisms. This may be particularly true in the case of negative emotions, which as discussed earlier, tend to elicit issue-oriented thought more so than do positive programs.

One additional mechanism alluded to, but not tested in the present study is processing capacity resource constraints. This mechanism may decrease one's *ability* (versus their motivation) to process ad information when the majority of processing resources are devoted to the program. Eysenck (1976, 1982) and Hasher and Zacks (1979) explain that stimuli that is very affectively involving (i.e. higher in emotional intensity) interferes with the viewer's ability to encode ad information because the program may preempt some of the resources needed to process ad information. Schumann and Thorson (1990) discuss this phenomenon in terms of a "processing activity ratio." That is, if processing activity, or the amount of program-generated processing, favors the program, it is predicted that memory for the advertisement will be damaged. Future research may examine the impact of processing capacity and other explanations for the impact of program emotions and intensity on ad effectiveness. Finally, this study did not consider the dynamic relationship among mechanisms. For example, addressing the questions of when does one mechanism dominate the others, or when do mechanisms become complementary to one another, is important for advertisers in helping to alleviate the problems associated with negative emotion inducing programs.

REFERENCES

Averill, James R. (1969), "Autonomic Response Patterns During Sadness and Mirth," *Psychophysiology*, 5 (4), 399-414.

Axelrod, Joel N. (1963), "Induced Moods and Attitudes toward Products," *Journal of Advertising Research*, 3 (2), 19-24.

Batra, Rajeev and Michael L. Ray (1986), "Affective Responses Mediating Acceptance of Advertising," *Journal of Consumer Research*, 13 (September), 234-249.

Bryant, Jennings and Paul W. Comisky (1978), "The Effect of Positioning a Message Within Differentially Cognitively Involving Portions of a Television Segment on Recall of the Message," *Human Communications Research*, 5 (1), 63-75.

Clark, Margaret S. (1982), "A Role for Arousal in the Link between Feeling States, Judgments, and Behavior," in *Affect and Cognition: The Seventeenth Annual Carnegie Symposium on Cognition*, eds. M.S. Clark and S.T. Fiske, Hillsdale, NJ: Lawrence Erlbaum Associates, 263-290.

Clark, Margaret S. and Alice M. Isen (1982), "Toward Understanding the Relationship Between Feeling States and Social Behavior," in *Cognitive Social Psychology*, eds., A.H. Hastorf and A.M. Isen, New York, NY: Elsevier North Holland, Inc., 73-108.

Cohen, Joel B. and Charles S. Areni (1991), "Affect and Consumer Behavior," in *Handbook of Consumer Behavior*, eds. T.S. Robertson and H.H. Kassarjian, Englewood Cliffs, NH: Prentice Hall.

Edell, Julie A. and Marian Chapman Burke (1987), "The Power of Feelings in Understanding Advertising Effects," *Journal of Consumer Research*, 14 (December), 421-433.

Eysenck, Michael W. (1982), *Attention and Arousal: Cognition and Performance*, New York, NY: Springer-Verlag.

Gardner, Meryl Paula (1985) "Mood States and Consumer Behavior: A Critical Review," *Journal of Consumer Research*, 12 (December), 281-300.

Gardner, Meryl Paula and Frederick O. Wilhelm, Jr. (1987) "Consumer Responses to Ads with Positive vs. Negative Appeals: Some Mediating Effects of Context-Induced Mood and Congruency Between Context and Ad," in *Current Issues and Research in Advertising*, eds. J.H.Leigh and C.R. Martin, JR. Ann Arbor, MI: University of Michigan Press.

Goldberg, Marvin E. and Gerald J. Gorn (1987), "Happy and Sad TV Programs: How They Affect Reactions to Commercials," *Journal of Consumer Research*, 14 (December), 387-403.

Gouaux, Charles (1971), "Induced Affective States and Interpersonal Attraction," *Journal of Personality and Social Psychology*, 20 (1), 37-43.

Gouaux, Charles and Karen Summers (1973), "Interpersonal Attraction as a Function of Affective State and Affective Change," *Journal of Research in Personality*, 7, 254-260.

Hasher, Lynn and Rose T. Zacks (1979), "Automatic and Effortful Processes in Memory," *Journal of Experimental Psychology: General*, 108 (3), 356-388.

Hoffman, Martin L. (1986), "Affect, Cognition, and Motivation," in *Handbook of Motivation and Cognition*, eds. R.M. Sorrentino and E.T. Higgins, New York, NY: The Guilford Press, 244-280.

Isen, Alice M. (1984), "The Influence of Positive Affect on Decision Making and Cognitive Organization," in *Advances in Consumer Research*, Vol 11, ed., T. Kinnear, Provo, UT: Association for Consumer Research, 534-537.

Isen, Alice M. (1970), "Success, Failure, Attention, and Reactions to Others: The Warm Glow of Success," *Journal of Personality and Social Psychology*, 15, 294-301.

Isen Alice M., Kimberly A. Daubman, and Joyce M. Gorgoglione (1987) "The Influence of Positive Affect on Cognitive Organization," in *Aptitude, Learning and Instruction: Conative and Affective Processes*, eds., R.E. Snow and M.J. Farr, Hillsdale, NJ: Erlbaum.

Isen, Alice M., Thomas E. Shalker, Margaret Clark, and Lynn Karp (1978), "Affect, Accessibility of Material in Memory, and Behavior: A Cognitive Loop?" *Journal of Personality and Social Psychology*, 36 (1), 1-12.

Kennedy, John R. (1971), "How Program Environment Affects TV Commercials," *Journal of Advertising*, 11 (1), 33-38.

Mamo, Haim (1990), "Emotional States and Decision Making,' in *Advances in Consumer Research*, Vol 17, eds. M.E. Goldberg, G. Gorn, and R.W. Pollay, Provo, UT: Association for Consumer Research, 577-584.

Mattes, John and Joanne Cantor, (1982), "Enhancing Responses to Television Advertisements via the Transfer of Residual Arousal from Prior Programming," *Journal of Broadcasting*, 26 (2), 553-566.

Mehrabian, Albert and James A. Russell (1973), "A Measure of Arousal Seeking Tendency," *Environment and Behavior*, 5 (3), 315-333.

Park, C.W. and S. Mark Young (1986), "Consumer Response to Television Commercials: The Impact of Involvement and Background Music on Brand Attitude Formation," *Journal of Marketing Research*, 23 (February), 11-24.

Pavelchak, Mark A., John H. Antil, and James M. Munch (1988), " The Super Bowl: An Investigation into the Relationship Among Program Context, Emotional Experience, and Ad Recall," *Journal of Consumer Research*, 15 (December), 360-367.

Sanbonmatsu, David M. and Frank R. Kardes (1988), "The Effects of Physiological Arousal on Information Processing and Persuasion," *Journal of Consumer Research*, 15 (December), 379-385.

Schultz, D. E. (1979), "Media Research Users Want," *Journal of Advertising Research*, 19, 13-17.

Schwerin, Horace A. (1958), "Do Today's Programs Provide the Wrong Commercial Climate?" *Television Magazine*, 15 (8), 90-91.

Soldow, Gary F. and Victor Principe (1981), "Response to Commercials as a Function of Program Context," *Journal of Advertising Research*, 21 (2), 59-65.

Television Audience Assessment, Inc. (1984), "Commercial Effectiveness and Viewers' Involvement with Television Programs: A Literature Review," Cambridge, MA: Television Audience Assessment, Inc.

Thorson, Esther and Heiko Oberman (1985), "Program Involvement and the Processing of Television Commercials," Paper presented at the Association for Education in Journalism and Mass Communication Annual Conference, Memphis, August.

Thorson, Esther and Bryon Reeves (1986), "Effects Over-Time Measures of Viewer Liking and Activity During Programs and Commercials on Memory for Commercials," in *Advances in Consumer Research*, Vol 13, ed. R. Lutz, Provo, UT: Association for Consumer Research.

Individual and Situational Influences on Purchase Goal Specification
Stephen J.S. Holden, Ecole Supérieure de Sciences Economiques et Commerciales

Goals in consumer decision processes represent a critical, but much neglected issue in consumer research. The focus on goals is motivated by a fundamental belief that a better understanding of consumer choice processes must take into account the factors influencing goal specification and the influences of goals themselves.

Huffman presented research on some external and internal influences on goal formation. She examined the influence of two external factors on goal formation: amount of external information provided (about features of the product) and the nature of the wording (experiential versus regular feature wording). Experiential wording links a stated product feature to a user-experience (e.g. a 30 foot cord allows the user to vacuum two rooms from one power point). Also examined was an internal factor, namely, the influence of imaging by the consumer on goal formation. The major measures of goal formation were feature listing, importance ratings of features, and remembering and picturing past experiences. Increasing the amount of external information provided to subjects led to an increase in the degree to which they remembered and pictured prior experiences, and led to an increase in the number of features listed as important to choice. While, the provision of experiential feature wording did not lead to increases in remembering and picturing of prior experiences, it led to increases in the rated importance of features identified. Imaging, an internal factor, failed to interact with experiential wording as was expected.

Ratneshwar, Pechmann and Shocker presented research extending the notion of consumer consideration sets as goal-derived categories. Specifically, they examined how one generic need can lead to the formation of consideration sets comprising products from different nominal product categories (i.e. noncomparable alternatives). Focusing on the generic need for a snack, Ratneshwar et al. examined the influence of both an individual level goal ("health" measured two weeks before the study) and a situational goal ("cool down" manipulated by a situation of a mild spring day versus a hot summer day) on consideration and choice in a stimulus-based task. In the stimulus-based set, there were two nominal categories (granola bars and ice creams). The major dependent variable was an across-category consideration measure developed by the authors. The first finding was that goal ambiguity (where both the "health" goal and the "cool down" goal are low in salience) and goal conflict (where both goals are high in salience) leads to greater across-category consideration. That is, the consideration sets under these circumstances are more likely to include alternatives from different nominal categories. The second finding was that under situations of goal ambiguity, there was likely to be greater use of externally provided features.

Walker and Houston explore the different goal structures underlying individual versus situational involvement. Using a greeting card decision, the influence of two different situations (wedding card and thinking-of-you situation reflecting high and low involvement respectively) and measured individual involvement effects on the means-end goal structures was measured. Using a novel adaptation of the means-end chaining technique, the major dependent measures were the content (elements) and the structure (relationships between elements) of means-end decision maps. In terms of content, under higher levels of involvement (individual and/or situational), more abstract, self-related goals appeared to dominate. However, goal structure (relationships, complexity, and integration) was apparently unaffected by the nature of individual and situational involvement.

Meyer, as discussant, initiated a discussion about the value of goals to the consumer decision-making models. One issue was that goals may be powerful predictors of individual behavior; however, due to their idiosyncratic nature, they may be of little value in predicting aggregate behavior.

The papers collectively offer a number of contributions to the study of goals. First, the session highlights the interplay of goals and decisions as a dynamic process. Goals both influence the decision process (Ratneshwar et al.) and are themselves influenced and determined by the decision process (Huffman; Walker and Houston). Second, goals may be a function of both internal, individual factors as well as external, contextual factors. Finally, the three papers represent the considerable range of methodologies that may be applied to the study of goals in the consumer decision process. In particular, Ratneshwar et al. and Walker and Houston each introduce innovative methodologies to the study of goals.

Compulsive Buying Tendency as a Predictor of Attitudes and Perceptions

Allison Magee, Arizona State University

ABSTRACT

Compulsive buying is a phenomenon with serious societal and personal consequences. An exploratory study using scenarios of consumer's purchasing behavior tested whether compulsive buying tendency influences identification and perceptions of others' behavior. Empirical findings show the compulsive buying tendency predicted identification with others' buying behavior. The findings also support the greater the compulsive buying tendency, the more likely one would permit the use of credit cards for purchases. However, the greater the compulsive buying tendency, the more likely one is to view dysfunctional behavior as appropriate was not supported by the findings. The discussion highlights implications.

INTRODUCTION

When the going gets tough, the tough go shopping.
I can't be out of money, I still have checks.
I'd rather be at the mall.
Born to shop.
Shop until you drop.

The bumper stickers and slogans abound. It is commonplace in our society to make light of people who frequently shop and buy. However, for many Americans the process of shopping and buying has caused their lives to go out of control. Much like substance abusers, they get a "high" by buying items and are unable to control their behavior. These people are called compulsive buyers and it is estimated that fifteen million Americans suffer from this phenomenon (Arthur 1992).

Consumer researchers have been exploring this phenomenon in an effort to describe, explain, and identify it. Psychology has given us answers concerning the origins of the phenomenon. We now know that compulsive buying is a behavioral disorder that causes an individual to continually make purchases regardless of financial, social, or psychological consequences (Damon 1988; Faber 1992; Krueger 1988; Faber and O'Guinn 1992; Scherhorn 1990, Valence et al. 1988). Compulsive buying is the result of dysfunction in any or all of the following processes: heredity, family of origin, psychological, and society (Damon 1988, Faber 1992, Hirschman 1992; Scherhorn 1990; Valence et al. 1988). Compulsive buying is distinguished from functional buying by the following characteristics: the items are not bought for their intrinsic value, there is denial to the negative consequences of the actions, it is disruptive to the individual's life, repeated failures in attempts to control the behavior, and a urge or drive to buy (Faber, O'Guinn, and Krych 1987; Krueger 1988; O'Guinn and Faber 1989; Valence et al. 1988).

It has been proposed that the socio-cultural environment is one of the many factors in the creation of compulsive buyers (Damon 1988; Faber 1992; Hirschman 1992; Valence et al. 1988). People's perceptions of what is appropriate and inappropriate behavior are based on societal, cultural, and individual norms. During the socialization process, consumers learn what is acceptable and unacceptable. If one's socialization process has been dysfunctional, that is, dysfunctional behavior has been modeled to the individual, that person will "grow up" believing the dysfunctional behavior is "normal." Furthermore, if the socio-cultural environment is conducive to this type of dysfunctional behavior, the individual's norm becomes reinforced.

While the literature recognizes the presence and importance of the socio-cultural environment in compulsive buying, none of the literature focuses on how its characteristics shape people's attitudes towards buying behavior. If social norms play an important part in encouraging compulsive buying, it stands to reason that the creation of compulsive buyers will influence society and individuals' attitudes and norms. This paper reports a study which explores the degree to which compulsive buying tendency influences attitudes toward buying/purchasing behavior. The paper is divided into three parts: the first part deals with the literature on compulsive buying and what has been found about the phenomenon, the second part details the study and its results, and in the third part, implications are discussed.

REVIEW OF THE LITERATURE

Compulsive buying had been recorded in the early 1900's by psychiatrists. However, it was not until the late 1980's that compulsive buying began to receive much attention. All of the compulsive buying research has centered on defining and explaining the phenomenon. Faber and O'Guinn (1988) derived their definition from the much broader category of compulsive consumption. They defined compulsive consumption "as a response to an uncontrollable drive or desire to obtain, use, or experience a feeling, substance or activity that leads an individual to repetitively engage in a behavior that will ultimately cause harm to the individual and/or to others."

That led to the description of compulsive buying as "chronic, repetitive purchasing that becomes a primary response to negative events or feelings (O'Guinn and Faber 1989)." d'Astous (1990) provides a less extreme definition of compulsive buying "as a generalized urge to buy in the consumer population and that individuals who are extremely high on this factor may be called compulsive buyers." d'Astous suggested that by dichotomizing consumers into two categories, compulsive or not compulsive, that we were missing much of the phenomenon. By ignoring what lies between compulsive and functional, we may be overlooking information that would help us to better understand the phenomena and its origins. First, there is much evidence to support d'Astous's idea of a generalized urge. For example, a barrage of advertising messages constantly and strongly encourage consumers to buy and to use credit. Our country's burgeoning federal deficit portrays our culture's receptiveness to debt and overspending. The increase in credit card debt, often incurred by compulsive buyers, over the last 20 years is associated with the growth in the federal deficit. Second, this definition portrays buying or purchasing behavior on a continuum with compulsive buying occupying one end and functional purchasing at the other.

Nataraajan and Goff (1991) also view purchasing behavior on a continuum. They described a continuum as based on motive and control. Thus, compulsive buyers are those who are high on motive and low on control. Our cultural norms that encourage purchasing behaviors affect the motivational component.

Several empirical studies have yielded interesting findings about factors related to compulsive buyers. Consistent with the work of Moschis and Churchill (1978), O'Guinn and Faber (1989, 1992) found that compulsive buyers tend to be younger. However, Scherhorn et al. (1990) did not find age to be a significant factor. O'Guinn and Faber (1989, 1992) have also found that women tend to score higher as compulsive buyers. This is supported by d'Astous (1990) and Scherhorn et al. (1990). Compulsive buyers have also been found to have lower self-esteem (O'Guinn and Faber 1989).

Not much has been written in our literature about the various components that make up the socio-cultural environment factor that contributes to compulsive buying. Valence et al. (1988) suggests that it has three components: culture, commercial environment, and advertising. Probably the best treatment of this comes from the popular press, in a book by therapist Janet Damon titled *Shopaholics* (1988). In it, Damon looks are three aspects that have contributed to the creation of compulsive buyers in our society. She cites the breakdown of family and community, advertising messages, and that spending has become a form of worship in our society. These all combine to create an environment that reinforces one's beliefs, attitudes, and personal norms that overspending and excess buying is acceptable.

O'Guinn and Faber (1989) suggest that how society views compulsive behavior will have implications for society's perception of the consequences, the amount of self-control a person is expected to have with respect to purchasing, and the appropriate treatment of the compulsive behavior.

Perceptions of Appropriate Behavior

Based on these findings, people differ in their degree of compulsive buying tendency. These differences are derived from socialization experiences, all within the context of a culture that is permissive about buying and spending behaviors.

Compulsive buyers are those who have an uncontrollable urge to repetitively engage in the act of buying and have been taught dysfunctional norms. They learn that this dysfunctional behavior is "normal" and perceive their own and other's behavior accordingly. Therefore, compulsive buyers may view certain purchasing behaviors differently than people who are less compulsive. They may be more apt to view dysfunctional purchasing behaviors "normal" and identify with those exhibiting this behavior. The forms the basis for the first hypothesis.

H1: The greater the tendency toward compulsive buying, the more likely one will identify with the dysfunctional purchasing behavior of others.

It also stands to reason that if a person views their own behavior as appropriate even though it may not be, that they will tend to judge others exhibiting the same purchasing behavior as behaving appropriately. This yielded the second hypothesis:

H2: The greater a person's compulsive buying tendency, the more likely the person is to view the dysfunctional purchasing behavior of others as appropriate.

Past research has shown a correlation between compulsive buyers and irrational credit card usage (d'Astous 1990) as well as the fact that compulsive buyers are likely to own more credit cards than normal consumers (O'Guinn & Faber 1989). These results tend to indicate that compulsive buyers are more likely to condone the use of credit cards for purchases whether it is appropriate or not. This formed the third hypothesis:

H3: The greater the compulsive buying tendency, the more likely a person would be more permissive in the use of credit cards.

METHODOLOGY

Instrument

A questionnaire was devised composed of three parts. Only minimal information was provided to the subjects. Subjects were informed that their help was needed in providing answers and opinions for a study being done on purchasing and spending habits. Conditions of anonymity and confidentiality were stated in addition to being expressed on the cover sheets of the questionnaire. The terms "compulsive" as well as "compulsive buying" were never mentioned, as it was thought that this might sensitize the subjects.

The first part solicited personal and demographic information. This information was used to describe the sample and to analyze for differences due to age or sex.

The second part of the survey contained the Faber and O'Guinn (1992) clinical screener for compulsive buying. The scale measures a person's capacity for compulsive buying on seven items. Items are scored using a five point Likert scale. Faber and O'Guinn (1992) report an alpha of .95 and the scale to be unidimensional.

In the third part of the questionnaire, the respondent was presented with one of two scenarios, as a projective device to elicit respondent's perceptions of certain purchasing behaviors. The two conditions, labeled Consumer A and Consumer B, were randomly assigned to subjects. Forty-nine subjects received the Consumer B scenario and 45 received Consumer A.

In the two conditions, the subject read about a "recent graduate" who had not yet found a job. In both cases, the protagonist received a credit card through the mail. Neither the sex, age, marital status, nor race of the consumer was mentioned to allow the respondent to project his/her self into the scenario. The two conditions were manipulated with respect to credit card usage. Scenario A portrays relatively dysfunctional purchasing behavior. Consumer A uses a credit card heavily and does not have the income to pay off the purchases. In the other condition, Consumer B is more responsible. He or she makes similar purchases but uses cash from savings and demonstrates the activities of budgeting and comparison shopping.

Following the scenario, the subject was asked how much they identified with the consumer in the scenario. The item was a 7 point Likert scale ranging from strongly identify to do not identify at all. Next, the subject was asked to rate the consumer on a ten-item bipolar adjective "responsibility" scale. These ten items were designed to capture the subject's projection of how responsible they viewed the actions of the consumer. The ten items were comprised of various synonyms for the word responsibility. All ten items used a 7 point Likert scale. As an additional indicator of perceptions, subjects were also asked to what extent they agreed with the various behaviors exhibited by the consumer in the scenario. To operationalize permissiveness concerning credit card usage, one question asked the respondent to indicate how much the consumer should use the credit card. The item was based on a 7 point Likert scale anchored at one end by the credit card's limit and at the other end by none at all.

Two open-ended questions completed the questionnaire. These questions prompted the subject to describe the consumer as well as to relate their thoughts on what happened next in the scenario.

Pretesting

A pretest showed that the questions were understandable. Upon debriefing, none of the pretest subjects indicated that they were aware of what the researchers were trying to accomplish.

TABLE 1
Regression Analysis Results

Hypothesis Tested	Equation	F	p	Standardized Regression Coefficient	r^2
Hypothesis One: Identification					
Entire sample	2.97-.46(CBT)	17.64	p<.001	-0.403	.162
Scenario A	2.26-.55(CBT)	18.24	p<.001	-0.55	.303
Scenario B	3.60-.38(CBT)	6.25	p<.05	-0.342	.117
Hypothesis Two: Responsibility					
Entire Sample	33.63-.53(CBT)	0.35	p=.557	-0.061	.004
Scenario A	25.15+.19(CBT)	0.06	p=.814	0.036	.001
Scenario B	41.4-1.03(CBT)	0.73	p=.397	-0.123	.015
Hypothesis Three: Use of Credit Card					
Entire Sample	2.76-.26(CBT)	9.53	p<.05	-0.306	.094
Scenario A	2.69-.41(CBT)	16.15	p<.001	-0.522	.273
Scenario B	2.83-.14(CBT)	1.13	p=.29	-0.153	.024
Age predicting CBT					
Entire Sample	-1.41+.06(age)	11.09	p<.01	0.329	.109

Note: CBT=compulsive buying score

Sample

The questionnaire was administered to a convenience sample of 95 respondents. Of the 95, 94 questionnaires were returned, yielding a return rate of 98.8%. The sample was comprised of college students from five upper level marketing classes at a large Southwestern university and various respondents from the community. Fifty-two or 55.3% were male and 44.7% or 42 were female. The mean age of the sample was 26.75. Seventy-nine point eight percent of the sample was under the age of thirty.

RESULTS

On the compulsive buying scale, the mean score was .142. The scores ranged from -4.19 to 3.30. Faber and O'Guinn (1992) classify compulsive buyers as those who score less than or equal to -1.34. Fifteen or 16% of the respondents fell into this range.

A factor analysis was performed on the ten item responsibility scale. All items loaded on one factor with values of .70 or higher and were retained for analysis. Coefficient alpha was an acceptable .94 for the ten items.

Hypothesis Testing

Regression analysis was used to test the hypothesis of whether compulsive buyers identified more with the consumers than people who were not as compulsive. The compulsive buying score was used to predict to what extent the respondent identified with the consumer in the scenario. The analysis was conducted first for the entire sample and then by condition. The regression equation was significant. Table 1 summarizes the results of this analysis. Compulsive buying tendency does predict the respondent's identification with the consumer portrayed in the scenario.

Analyzing by condition, the compulsive buying tendency predicted the respondent's identification with the consumer for each scenario. Results are reported in Table 1.

The second hypothesis proposed that compulsive buying tendency would predict the respondent's rating of the scenario on the responsibility scale. Regression analysis did not confirm this hypothesis. See Table 1 for results. Furthermore, it was found to be non-significant in an analysis by condition. Compulsive buying score did not predict the perceived responsibility of the scenarios' consumers. However, Consumer B was perceived as more responsible than A, thus affirming that the manipulation was effective. See Table 2 for results.

The third hypothesis proposed that compulsive buying tendency would predict how much the respondent would allow the consumer to charge on the credit card. The regression equation was significant and the results are reported in Table 1. Compulsive buying tendency predicted how much the respondents allowed the consumer to use the credit card. An analysis by condition yielded slightly different results. For the more dysfunctional scenario, compulsive buying tendency predicted how much the respondent would allow the consumer to use the credit card. However, for the more "appropriate" consumer, compulsive buying tendency did not predict how much the respondent would allow the consumer to use the credit card. Results are reported in Table 1.

Open Ended Responses

Two open-ended questions asked the respondents to describe what happened next in the scenario and to describe the consumer. The answers were coded by the researcher and several themes identified. Three categories describing the endings to the scenario were determined: positive consequences (e.g. got a good job, paid off bills), negative consequences (e.g. went bankrupt, credit rating declined, took a job beneath standards), and neutral consequences. Two main categories described the consumers: irresponsible (e.g. doesn't think about consequences, immature, spontaneous) and responsible (e.g. plans ahead, reliable, careful). Two judges were then asked to recode the data using the new categories. The interjudge reliability rating was an acceptable 86.4%. An anova analysis showed the endings proposed for consumer A were significantly different from consumer B. Table 2 reports the results. Thus,

TABLE 2
Anova Analysis Results

Dependent Variable	Means		Anova		
	A	B	F	p	n
Scenario Ending	1.28	1.75	9.02	p<.01	91
Consumer Description	1.10	1.36	8.62	p<.01	86
Responsibility	25.27	41.65	46.91	p<.001	89

Note: For scenario ending, Negative consequences=1, Positive consequences=2, Neutral=3; For consumer description, Irresponsible=1, Responsible=2.

respondents viewed Consumer A's behavior as having more negative consequences than Consumer B's behavior. An anova analysis also showed that the descriptions for Consumer A were significantly different from Consumer B. These results are reported in Table 2. However, looking at each consumer separately, it was found that descriptions of Consumer B revealed a responsible/irresponsible dichotomy.

Additional Findings

Past research has found that age and sex may be important factors in determining one's compulsiveness (d'Astous and Tremblay 1988; Moschis and Churchill 1978; O'Guinn and Faber 1989, 1992; Scherhorn et al. 1990). Through regression analysis, age was found to be a significant factor in predicting one's compulsiveness. See Table 1 for results. Consistent with previous research (d'Astous and Tremblay 1988; O'Guinn and Faber 1989), the younger a respondent, the higher his or her compulsive buying score. There may be some limits to this finding. Sampling procedures yielded a relatively young sample. Since age can be a predictor of compulsiveness, future research may want to utilize purposeful sampling procedures to avoid imbalances in the age factor. An analysis was performed to check for a interaction between age and the the manipulation of low/high responsibility. The results were non-signficant indicating there was no interaction present.

With regards to sex, an anova was performed. For this sample, there is no significant difference between genders for the compulsive buying score. The F value (1,92) was 2.28 for p=.135. An analysis was performed to check for a interaction between sex and the the manipulation of low/high responsibility. The results were non-signficant indicating there was no interaction present. These results do not support the previous findings of d'Astous and Tremblay (1988), O'Guinn and Faber (1989), and Scherhorn et al. (1990). One explanation may be that this study's sample was not self-selected unlike previous research. O'Guinn and Faber (1989) suggest that women are more likely to seek help concerning personal issues and would be more aware of compulsive buying. They attribute their finding that women score higher as compulsive buyers to methodological artifact.

Summary

The empirical findings showed that compulsive buyers are more likely to identify with the dysfunctional purchasing behavior of others. The study also found that the greater a person's compulsive buying tendency, the more they condone the use of a credit card for purchases. The study did not support the hypothesis that the greater a person's compulsive buying tendency, the more likely the person is to view dysfunctional purchasing behavior as appropriate. Supporting previous work, age was found to be a predictor of one's compulsive buying tendency. However, the study did not confirm that sex was a predictor of one's compulsive buying tendency.

DISCUSSION

This study was concerned with to what degree one's compulsiveness influence's one's perceptions of what is appropriate and inappropriate behavior. While the study showed that a relationship exists between one's compulsiveness and how one identifies with and perceives others' behavior, there are several limitations to it. The use of such a relatively young sample when age has been shown to be a predictor of compulsiveness may have biased the results. Second, different results may be obtained if different scenarios are utilized. Finally, a univariate analysis may provide only part of the picture. Future research should include multivariate analysis to draw a more complex picture.

The results of the study support the use of the scenarios as stimuli to elicit respondents' attitudes and perceptions toward compulsive buying. As a projective device, the scenarios provide a way to portray compulsive buying without having to label it as such and thus, biasing responses. Other types of dependent measures might be used to determine the different types of attitudes that people hold.

In contrast to previous research, sex was not found to be a significant factor in determining compulsive buying score. More work should be conducted to investigate this relationship.

Based on the study's findings, it would appear that a person's compulsive buying tendency is related to his/her identification with, and attitudes towards, dysfunctional buying behavior. Additionally, the study suggests that the greater a person's compulsive buying tendency, the more permissive their attitude toward dysfunctional buying behavior. This has many implications for society. First of all, if society is helping to create an environment that enables compulsive buying, and since it has been shown that compulsive buyers have more permissive attitudes towards dysfunctional behavior, societal norms and attitudes may be modified over time to reflect this dysfunctional orientation. Thus, societal attitudes and norms could become more permissive over time, thus creating even a more friendly environment for this phenomenon.

The study did not confirm the hypothesis that the greater a person's compulsive buying tendency, the more likely they are to view others' dysfunctional purchasing behavior as appropriate. However, this is consistent with the idea that compulsive buying is a compulsion and not a permanent inability to distinguish between appropriate and inappropriate purchasing behavior. This is especially salient for those developing treatment programs for compulsive buyers as it indicates that rehabilitation is possible.

The lighthearted vein in which society treats the phenomenon of compulsive buying may reinforce the attitudes held by those afflicted. The humorous manner in which the town drunk was portrayed in the fifties and sixties (e.g. Otis on the Andy Griffith Show) is an excellent example of society reinforcing denial. If we are laughing at it, most likely there are those who will feel they do not have a problem.

This study explored the influence of compulsive buying tendency on identification with and perceptions of others' buying behaviors. By studying these implications, we will gain much needed knowledge. The time is ripe for research in this area as concern over the federal deficit has people questioning our cultural values. Compulsive buying is a phenomenon that has and will continue to seriously affect our society.

REFERENCES

Arthur, Caroline (1992), "Fifteen Million Americans Are Shopping Addicts," *American Demographics*, (March), 14-15.

d'Astous, Alain (1990), "An Inquiry into the Compulsive Side of "Normal Consumers"", *Journal of Consumer Policy* 13(March), 15-32.

_____, and S. Tremblay (1988), "The Compulsive Side of 'Normal' Consumers: An Empirical Study," in *Marketing Thought and Practice in the 1990's*, eds. G.J. Avlonitis, N.K. Papvasiliou, and A.G. Kouremenos, Athens: The Athens School of Economics and Business Science, pp. 657-669.

Damon, Janet (1988). *Shopaholics*. Los Angeles, CA: Price Stern Sloan,Inc.

Faber, Ronald J. (1992), "Money Changes Everything: Compulsive Buying From A Biopsychosocial Perspective," *American Behavioral Scientist*, 35(July), 809-819.

_____ and Thomas C. O'Guinn (1988), "Compulsive Consumption and Credit Abuse, "*Journal of Consumer Policy*, 11, 97-109.

_____ and Thomas C. O'Guinn (1992), "A Clinical Screener for Compulsive Buying," *Journal of Consumer Research*, 19(December), 459-469.

_____, Thomas C. O'Guinn, and Raymond Krych (1987), "Compulsive Consumption," in *Advances in Consumer Research*, Vol. 14 eds. Melanie Wallendorf and Paul Anderson, Provo, UT: Association for Consumer Research, 132-135.

Hirschman, Elizabeth C. (1992), "The Consciousness of Addiction: Toward a General Theory of Compulsive Consumption," *Journal of Consumer Research* 19(September), 155-179.

Krueger, David W. (1988), "On Compulsive Shopping and Spending: A Psychodynamic Inquiry," *American Journal of Psychotherapy*, 42(October), 574-584.

Moschis, George and Gilbert A. Churchill (1978), "Consumer Socialization: A Theoretical and Empirical Analysis," *Journal of Marketing* (Summer), 40-48.

Nataraajan, Rajan and Brent G. Goff (1991), "Compulsive Buying: Toward A Reconceptualization," Special Issue: To have possessions: A handbook on ownership and property. *Journal of Social Behavior and Personality*, 6(6), 307-326. 14(December), 189-199.

O'Guinn, Thomas C. and Ronald J. Faber (1989), "Compulsive Buying: A Phenomenological Exploration," *Journal of Consumer Research*, 16(September), 147-157.

Scherhorn, Gerhard (1990), "The Addictive Trait in Buying Behavior," *Journal of Consumer Policy*, 13(March), 33-52.

_____, Lucia A. Reisch, and Gerhard Raab (1990), "Addictive Buying in West Germany: An Empirical Study," *Journal of Consumer Policy*, 13(December), 355-388.

Valence, Gilles, Alain d'Astous, and Louis Fortier (1988), "Compulsive Buying: Concept and Measurement, " *Journal of Consumer Policy*, 11(September), 419-433.

Neuroticism, Affect and Postpurchase Processes

Todd A. Mooradian, The College of William and Mary
James M. Olver, The College of William and Mary

ABSTRACT

Recent research in psychology has shown that enduring personality *traits* predict transient affective *states*; specifically, neuroticism predicts negative affect. Additionally, recent consumer research has shown that postpurchase processes are related not only to cognitive assessments of the consumption experience but also to consumption-based affect. This research proposes and tests a model in which neuroticism, a fundamental and enduring personality trait, predicts negative affective states which, in turn, predict consumer satisfaction, complaint behavior, and negative word-of-mouth. The results begin to integrate important recent advances in the understanding of personality and emotions into the consumer behavior domain.

INTRODUCTION

"My headset's too tight. When are we going to eat? My seat's too small. How much further?"
— The Whiners, from Saturday Night Live

Every marketing manager has encountered Mr. or Mrs. Whiner—no matter what product is provided, it just isn't good enough. There is always something to complain about and nothing makes them happy.

This paper presents and tests a theoretical model which seeks to understand the Whiners and other *consumers with a propensity to be dissatisfied*. In doing this, we integrate emerging literature on personality traits and emotions from psychology with recent consumer research efforts relating affective experiences to postpurchase processes, including consumer satisfaction, complaint behavior and negative word-of-mouth. Although previous research linking personality and consumer behavior has been disappointing, this research offers promising results and shows that, by including major intervening systems such as affect, consumers' behaviors may be shown to have relatively robust relationships with enduring individual traits and dispositions. Initially, the relevant literatures from personality psychology and consumer behavior are reviewed. We then present a model linking one widely-accepted personality construct, neuroticism, to consumer satisfaction, complaint behavior and negative word-of-mouth. Thus, this paper contributes both a specific understanding of the relationship between neuroticism and consumption and, more generally, a promising framework for integrating personality with consumer behavior *via fundamental intervening systems*, such as affect.

LITERATURE REVIEW

Personality

Overview. Debate over two central issues—whether traits can predict behaviors, and the fundamental structure of personality—has dominated personality scholarship over the past several decades. However, it appears that preliminary consensus may be emerging. As of the late 1960s, decades of personality and attitude research had failed to empirically identify robust relationships between traits and behaviors. Mischel (1968) concluded that "highly generalized behavioral consistencies have not been demonstrated, and the concept of personality traits as broad response predispositions is thus untenable" (p. 146). He introduced the disparaging term "the personality coefficient" to describe "...the correlation between .20 and .30 which is found persistently when virtually any personality dimension... is related to almost any conceivable external criterion" (1968, page 78). Since this discouraging review, researchers have made meaningful advances toward explaining the poor empirical results and toward developing improved procedures and methods for identifying relationships. Ajzen (1988) has presented an excellent review of these advances and concludes that "while measures of behavioral dispositions cannot be used indiscriminately, when appropriately employed they yield highly valuable information... people are quite consistent in the patterns of behavior they exhibit" (page 150).

During this same period, a second important question in the personality literature has been: what are the basic personality dimensions? Literally hundreds of personality traits have been proposed. Five fundamental traits—extraversion, neuroticism, agreeableness, conscientiousness and openness—were identified as early as 1961 (Tupes and Christal 1961) and have been more generally agreed upon in the past half decade (McCrae and John 1992). Two of these, extraversion and neuroticism, have been linked theoretically and empirically with the experience of emotions. Neuroticism in particular has been so closely linked with negative affect that some researchers have labeled it *negative affectivity*: "the disposition to experience aversive emotional states" (Watson and Clark 1984).

Neuroticism and Affect. Of the "Big Five" personality factors, there is probably the least controversy about the definition of neuroticism (N), which has been variously labeled *negative affectivity, emotionality, stability-instability, trait anxiety, adjustment, well-being, stress-reaction,* or *psychasthenia* (Watson and Clark 1984; McCrae and John 1992; Eysenck and Eysenck 1975). Regardless of the label, neuroticism "represents individual differences in the tendency to experience distress, and in the cognitive and behavioral styles that follow from this tendency. High N scorers experience chronic negative affects and are prone to the development of a variety of psychiatric disorders" (McCrae and John 1992).

A large and growing number of studies have correlated personality traits and affective states. Further, neuroticism has been shown to predict, via the mediating system of affect, such diverse outcomes as health complaints, perceived stress and daily social activities, subjective well-being, and minor daily illnesses (see Larsen and Ketelaar 1991 for a thorough review).

At least two explanations can be hypothesized for the relationship between personality and negative affect: a *temperamental* theory posits that neurotics are more likely to experience negative affect *in a given situation*; the alternative *instrumental view* holds that neurotics may place themselves in more adverse life situations (and therefore experience more negative affect). Larsen and Ketelaar (1991) found support for the temperamental perspective, drawing on theory developed by Eysenck (1967) and expanded by Grey (1981, 1987) which proposes that neurotics are more likely to focus on *punishment signals* (negative aspects of given situations) while extraverts attend more to *reward signals* (positive aspects of situations).

In summary, an emerging body of evidence indicates that neuroticism is a fundamental structure of personality that predicts the experience of negative affect. Further, affect has been shown to mediate the effects of neuroticism on various behavioral outcomes. The neuroticism-negative emotions relationship has been found in both correlational and experimental studies, suggesting that the relationship is robust. To date, neuroticism has not been linked with consumption-based affect or to consumer behavior outcomes.

Personality and Consumer Behavior. In 1991, Kassarjian and Sheffet declared: "An overview of the studies on personality effects can be summarized by the single word 'equivocal'" (page 281). Generally, their review indicates that most reported studies in consumer behavior which have included personality have found the .20 to .30 range of correlations bemoaned by Mischel, above. "A few studies indicate a strong relationship between personality and aspects of consumer behavior, a few indicate no relationship, and the great majority indicate that if correlations do exist they are so weak as to be questionable or perhaps meaningless" (Kassarjian and Sheffet 1991, page 291).

Sparks and Tucker (1971) did identify canonical roots relating personality *profiles* with *patterns* of purchases. Similarly, Alpert (1972) used canonical correlation to relate personality profiles with the relative importance placed on product attributes (in three product categories: residences, automobiles and movies). These studies suggest that, while *specific* consumer behaviors may not be predictable with *individual* personality traits, personality does relate with aggregated behaviors and with cognitive criteria in more complex patterns.

Kassarjian and Sheffet (1991) identified several shortcomings of consumer behavior research on personality which presumably explain many of the disappointing findings. A major weakness pointed out in their review was *the compatibility of the traits and behaviors*: "...instruments originally intended to measure gross personality characteristics such as sociability, emotional stability, introversion, or neuroticism have been used to make predictions of the chosen brand of toothpaste or cigarettes" (Kassarjian and Sheffet 1991, page 292). Kassarjian and Sheffet call for marketing and consumer behavior to conceptualize and develop measures for personality traits which *should* predict specific consumer behaviors: "If neuroticism and sociability are not relevant personality variables, then perhaps such terms as risk aversion, status seeking, and conspicuous consumption can be used. Personality variables that in fact are relevant to the consumer model need to be theorized and tests developed and validated" (page 292). This criticism is certainly valid; it is similar to the 'principle of compatibility' from attitudes theory, which asserts that broad attitudes cannot be expected to predict narrowly defined and measured behaviors. However, an alternative solution may be to use 'gross personality traits,' such as those in the five-factor model explicated above, to predict *gross consumer constructs*, such as affective experiences or attitudinal states, which may mediate the effects of personality on more specific consumer behaviors. This would similarly satisfy the requirement for compatibility. The research reported here takes exactly such an approach to the personality—consumer behavior relationship.

Affect and Postpurchase Processes in Consumer Behavior

Satisfaction. Day summarized a consensus conceptualization of satisfaction as "the consumer's response in a particular consumption experience to the evaluation of the perceived discrepancy between prior expectations (or some other norm of performance) and the actual performance of the product as perceived after its acquisition" (1984, p. 496). This definition captures the dominant, highly cognitive *confirmation/disconfirmation model* within which much of the study of satisfaction has been framed. While this model has received strong empirical support (e.g., Oliver 1980; Tse and Wilton 1988), in the absence of affective considerations it may offer an incomplete description of the antecedents of satisfaction and postpurchase processes.

Affect in Consumer Research. In the last decade, affect has emerged as an important construct in the marketing literature, paralleling an increased focus on affect in psychology and social psychology. A great deal of research on affect in consumer behavior has focused on two central areas. The first of these has been *conceptualizing and measuring* affect and related constructs, including moods, feelings, emotions, evaluations and arousal (e.g., Gardner 1985; Aaker, Stayman and Vezina 1988). The second major focus has been toward examining affect as a mediating system in attitudes and advertising effects (e.g., Edell and Burke 1987; Allen, Machleit and Kleine 1992). A few studies have focused on *affect in consumption experiences* (Westbrook 1987; Dube-Rioux 1988; Westbrook and Oliver 1991). This consumption-based affect is the focus of the research reported in this paper.

Consumption-Based Affect and Postpurchase Processes. Westbrook and Oliver (1991) defined consumption-based emotion as:

> ...the set of emotional responses elicited specifically during product usage or consumption experiences, as described either by the distinctive categories of emotional experience and expression (e.g., joy, anger, and fear) or by the structural dimensions underlying emotional categories, such as pleasantness/unpleasantness, relaxation/action, or calmness/excitement... Consumption emotion is distinguished from the related affective phenomenon of mood (Gardner 1985) on the basis of emotion's relatively greater psychological urgency, motivational potency, and situational specificity (page 85).

Holbrook specified consumption-based affect as a major component in the tripartite model of consumption experiences: cognition, affect and behavior (Holbrook 1986; Holbrook and Hirschman 1982). Havlena and Holbrook (1986) examined the affective component of consumption and noted that, although some products are more associated with positive or negative emotions than others, "...emotional aspects of consumption experiences occur to a greater or lesser degree in almost all consuming situations" (page 395). Several studies have found significant relationships between consumption-based affect and postpurchase attitudes and behavior (see Westbrook 1987; Allen, Machleit and Kleine 1992; Westbrook and Oliver 1991; Dube-Rioux 1989).

Consumption-based affect has emerged as a major component in consumption experiences that often reduces to a two-dimensional framework, positive and negative affect. The Differential Emotions Scale (DES) has been shown to be a valid measure of consumption-based affect. Further, consumption-based affect has been shown to predict significant and unique variance in postpurchase processes including consumer satisfaction, consumer complaint behavior, and consumer word-of-mouth behaviors.

Consumer Complaint Behavior. Consumer complaint behaviors are conceptualized as "a set of multiple (behavioral and nonverbal) responses, some or all of which are triggered by perceived dissatisfaction with a purchase episode" (Singh 1988). Singh (1988, 1990) has reviewed the literature on consumer complaint behavior and its relationship to consumer satisfaction/dissatisfaction thoroughly. Westbrook (1987) found that consumption-based affect predicted consumer complaint behavior (directed at the seller) and word-of-mouth behaviors.

Negative Word-of-Mouth. Word-of-mouth behaviors have been shown to strongly influence purchase behavior (Swan and Oliver 1989; Price and Feick 1984; Arndt 1967). Previous studies have linked consumer satisfaction and dissatisfaction to word-of-mouth behavior (Richins 1983; Swan and Oliver 1989). Richins

FIGURE 1
Hypothesized Model

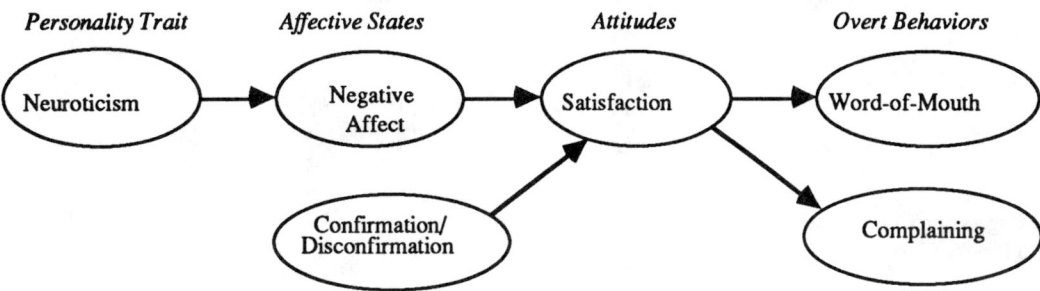

specifically linked dissatisfaction with negative word-of-mouth (1983). Hence, negative word-of-mouth is a second influential overt behavioral outcome of consumer dissatisfaction.

The Model

Personality has been shown to predict affective experiences and those affective experiences have been linked with specific behaviors. In particular, neuroticism has emerged as a fundamentally affective disposition, linked to a host of affective experiences and outcomes. This research is based on the proposition that neuroticism may predict the experience of negative consumption-based affect, an important mediating system explaining consumer satisfaction, consumer complaint behavior and negative word-of-mouth. The first hypothesis to be tested in this research is that neuroticism will predict negative consumption-based affect. Next, we test whether negative consumption-based affect will predict consumer satisfaction with that consumption object *beyond that explained by confirmation/disconfirmation of expectations*. The third hypothesis is that consumer satisfaction with the product will predict complaint behavior and negative word-of-mouth. Together, these postulates lead to the hypothesized model shown in Figure 1. Note that this model links personality traits, which have only been 'equivocally' related to consumer outcomes in previous research, to overt and observable consumer behaviors via the mediating mechanism of consumption-based affect.

METHOD

Subjects in our study were undergraduate students enrolled in upper level marketing classes at an Eastern university. Data was collected in two administrations, the first during class time, the second as a take-home survey. Of 70 students in the initial pool, 40 returned usable, complete questionnaires for both parts of the data collection. The product category selected for this research was cars, a product that may be expected to invoke meaningful affective experiences and variance across subjects on the postpurchase processes of interest (Westbrook 1987). An in-class poll indicated that a large majority of the students owned their own automobiles.

Neuroticism was measured early in the Fall, 1992 semester using the Eysenck Personality Questionnaire (EPQ; Eysenck and Eysenck 1975). This measure has been widely used and validated in the personality literature, and more specifically has been employed in several studies exploring the neuroticism-negative affect relationship (e.g., Larsen and Ketelaar 1991). Following Westbrook (1987), consumption-based affect was measured using the six DES subscales relevant to postpurchase processes: anger, disgust, contempt, interest, joy and surprise. The DES-III version of the scale, which presents each item in the form of a phrase, was employed (Allen, Machleit and Marine 1988; Allen, Machleit and Kleine 1992). Consumer satisfaction was measured using the 'delighted-terrible' (D-T) and the circles items (Andrews and Withey 1976; Westbrook 1987). Disconfirmation of expectations were measured regarding benefits, problems and overall performance using items from Westbrook (1987; see Oliver 1980). Negative word-of-mouth was measured using three self-report frequency items addressing conversations which involved: "something you do not like about your car," "a problem you had with your car," and "a problem you had with your car dealership." Complaint behavior was measured using Richins' (1982) Guttman-type scale (as adapted by Bearden and Teel 1983; cf. Singh 1988, 1990). The coefficient of reproducibility was 0.965. Cronbach's α for the DES-III subscales were all over .80 with the exception of CONTEMPT (.69); alphas for the 7-item disconfirmation scale, the 2-item satisfaction measure and the three item negative word-of-mouth measure were .90, .89 and .60, respectively. These latter measures (consumption-based affect, disconfirmation, satisfaction, complaint behavior and negative word-of-mouth) were included in a single questionnaire which was distributed during and returned to class late in the same semester, approximately three months after the initial (EPQ) data collection.

RESULTS

We attempted to replicate Westbrook's confirmatory factor analysis using the six DES-III scales attributing causal agency to the stimulus (i.e., ANGER, DISGUST, CONTEMPT, SURPRISE, INTEREST, and JOY). Due in part to the small sample employed, measures of sampling adequacy for JOY and INTEREST (.33 and .36, respectively) were too low to justify confirmatory factor analysis (Kim and Mueller 1983). The three measures that clearly relate to negative activity—ANGER, DISGUST and CONTEMPT—loaded .83, .80, .51, respectively, on a single principal component accounting for 53 percent of the variance in these measures. The regression score for this component is used as a measure of negative affectivity in the analyses that follow.

The model depicted in Figure 1 was tested with a series of nested, stepwise regression equations. Variables with hypothesized direct effects were entered in step 1; variables thought to impact each dependent variable only indirectly through mediating constructs were then entered in blocks to test for unexpected direct effects. Inter-item correlations and stepwise regression results are presented in the Table below, with order of entry in the regressions reading from left to right. The enduring trait neuroticism (NEUROT) is a significant predictor of negative affective experiences (N.AFFECT). That is, there is a fundamental and enduring characteristic of the subjects which predicts the degree of negative emotions they will or will not experience with the product during consumption experiences. Further, our results support the negative

TABLE
Measure Intercorrelations and Regression Results

CORRELATIONS	NEUROT	DISCON	N.AFFECT	SATISF	NEG.WOM
DISCON	-.09				
N.AFFECT	.48[a]	-.31[b]			
SATISF	-.21	.78[a]	-.50[a]		
NEG.WOM	-.18	-.27[b]	.07	-.34[b]	
COMPLAIN	.02	-.51[a]	.19	-.58[a]	.25

Standardized Regression Coefficients
(R^2 Change in Blocks [ ])

D.V.	SATISF	DISCON	N.AFFECT	NEUROT	R^2
N.AFFECT				.48[b]	.23
SATISF		.70[a]	-.28[b,d]	[.000]	.68
NEG.WOM	-.33[c]	[	.012]	[.053]	.11
COMPLAIN	-.58[a]	[	.017]	[.013]	.34

[a] Significant at $p < .001$.
[b] Significant at $p < .01$.
[c] Significant at $p < .05$.
[d] R^2 change after entry of DISCON significant at $p < .01$

impact of disconfirmation (DISCON) on satisfaction.[1] Importantly, negative affect explains *unique* variance in satisfaction not accounted for by these cognitive processes (semipartial correlation significant at $p < .01$). NEUROT did *not* predict significant variance in satisfaction after entering DISCON and N.AFFECT, suggesting that the effect of neuroticism on postpurchase processes is mediated by the intervening affective system.

Finally, satisfaction is a significant explanator of two overt behavioral responses: negative word-of-mouth (N.WOM) and complaint behaviors (COMPLAIN). No causally antecedent measures contributed significant unique variance beyond their impact through the mediating effect of satisfaction.

CONCLUSIONS

Contribution. This paper has reviewed important advances in the study of personality and has found support for a model linking neuroticism, affect, and consumer behaviors. It contributes some specific understanding of consumers and their relationships with products, and more generally, an approach to studying such relationships. We not only show that the neuroticism trait predicts how consumers will interact with products, we also demonstrate the value of examining cognition *and affect* as mediators of personality-consumer behavior relationships. At the most basic level, this research offers a theoretically-based model of personality-consumer behavior association which is *not* equivocal, but in fact explains important differences in how consumers respond to products.

The link between personality, specific affective responses, satisfaction, and behavior (particularly in the form of complaining and negative word-of-mouth) is important for managers to understand. Meeting or exceeding "normal" product or service quality standards may *not* be sufficient to satisfy all consumers. Marketers who hope to avoid consumer dissatisfaction and its negative outcomes need to understand why dissatisfaction occurs: is it the product/service, or is it the customer?

Larsen and Ketelaar (1991) suggest that neurotic consumers will be more likely to focus on negative, *punishment signals*, while extraverts tend to focus on *reward signals*. If so, then efforts to provide positive signals (e.g., special sales or attractive displays) will *not* compensate for unintended negative signals (such as product defects, slipshod service or frequent out-of-stocks) because different personality types attend to each. Savvy marketers may wish to pay particular attention to minimizing potential punishment signals because neurotic consumers may be a disproportionately important source of negative word-of-mouth that "infects" other customers.

Future Research. Future research should examine whether our findings generalize to larger and more diverse populations. The model should also be extended to incorporate relationships between *extraversion and positive affect*, which have also been linked in prior research (e.g., Larsen and Ketelaar 1991). Although we measured extraversion and positive affect, the observed relationships were insignificant (albeit in the predicted direction). A larger, consumer sample may well produce significant results.

Future research should also relate personality traits and affective experiences to other behavioral outcomes of interest to marketers. For example, Larsen and Ketelaar found support for a temperamental view of the relationship between personality and affect. Previous research (e.g., Edell and Burke 1987) has linked emotional responses to advertising effects. It may be profitable to examine the effects of neuroticism (and extraversion) on feeling responses to advertising.

REFERENCES

Aaker, David A., Douglas M. Stayman and Richard Vezina (1988), "Identifying Feelings Elicited By Advertising," *Psychology and Marketing*, 5 (Spring), 1-16.

Ajzen, Icek (1988), *Attitudes, Personality and Behavior*. Chicago, Il: The Dorsey Press.

---
[1] Note that disconfirmation and negative affect are correlated. It is likely that disconfirmation contributes to negative affect.

Allen, Chris T., Karen A. Machleit and Susan Schultz Kleine (1992), "A Comparison of Attitudes and Emotions as Predictors of Behavior at Diverse Levels of Behavioral Experience," *Journal of Consumer Research*, 18 (March), 493-504.

_____, _____ and Susan S. Marine (1988), "On Assessing the Emotionality of Advertising via Izard's Differential Emotions Scale," in *Advances in Consumer Research*, Vol. 15, ed. Michael J. Houston, Provo, UT: Association for Consumer Research, 226-231.

Alpert, Mark I. (1972), "Personality and the Determinants of Product Choice," *Journal of Marketing Research*, 9 (February), 89-92.

Andrews, Frank M. and Steven B. Withey (1976), *Social Indicators of Well-Being*, New York: Plenum Press.

Arndt, John (1967), "Role of Product-Related Conversations in the Diffusion of a New Product," *Journal of Marketing Research*, 4 (August), 291-295.

Bearden, William O. and Jesse E. Teel (1983), "Selected Determinants of Consumer Satisfaction and Complaint Reports," *Journal of Marketing Research*, 20 (Feb), 21-28.

Day, Ralph L. (1984), "Modeling Choices Among Alternative Responses to Dissatisfaction," in *Advances in Consumer Research*, Volume 11, Thomas C. Kinnear, (ed), Ann Arbor, MI: Association for Consumer Research, 496-499.

Dube-Rioux, Laurette (1990), "The Power of Affective Reports in Predicting Satisfaction Judgments," in *Advances in Consumer Research*, Volume 17, Marvin E. Goldberg, Gerald Gorn and Richard W. Pollay (eds), Provo, UT: Association for Consumer Research, 571-576.

Edell, Julie A. and Marian Chapman Burke (1987), "The Power of Feelings in Understanding Advertising Effects," *Journal of Consumer Research*, 14, 3 (December), 421-433.

Eysenck, H. J. (1967), *The Biological Basis of Personality*, Springfield, IL: Charles C Thomas.

_____ and S. B. G. Eysenck (1975), *Manual of the Eysenck Personality Questionnaire*, San Diego: Educational and Industrial Testing Service.

Eysenck, S. B. G., H. J. Eysenck and Paul Barrett (1985), "A Revised Version of the Psychoticism Scale," *Personality and Individual Differences*, 6, 1, 21-29.

Gardner, Meryl P. (1985), "Mood States and Consumer Behavior: A Critical Review," *Journal of Consumer Research*, 12, 281-300.

Grey, J. A. (1981), "A Critique of Eysenck's Theory of Personality," in H. J. Eysenck (Ed.), *A Model for Personality*, New York: Springer, 246-276.

_____ (1987), "Perspectives on Anxiety and Impulsivity: A Commentary," *Journal of Research in Personality*, 21, 493-509.

Havlena, W. J. and M. B. Holbrook (1986), "The varieties of consumption experience: comparing two typologies of emotion in consumer behavior," *Journal of Consumer Research*, 13(December), pp. 394-404.

Holbrook, M. B. (1986), "Emotion in the consumption experience: toward a new model of the human consumer," in Peterson, Hoyer, and Wilson (eds.), *The Role of Affect in Consumer Behavior*, Lexington, Mass: Lexington Books, 17-52.

_____ and E. C. Hirschman (1982), "The experiential aspects of consumption: consumer fantasies, feelings, and fun," *Journal of Consumer Research*, 9 (Sept), 132-140.

Kassarjian, Harold H. and Mary Jane Sheffet (1991), "Personality and Consumer Behavior: An Update," in Harold H. Kassarjian and Thomas S. Robertson (Eds.), *Perspectives in Consumer Behavior*, 4th Ed., Englewood Cliffs, NJ: Prentice Hall, 281-303.

Kim, Jae-On and Charles W. Mueller (1978), *Factor Analysis: Statistical Methods and Practical Issues*, Sage University Paper series on Quantitative Applications in the Social Sciences, 07-014, Beverly Hills and London: Sage Publications.

Larsen, Randy J. and Timothy Ketelaar (1991), "Personality and Susceptibility to Positive and Negative Emotional States," *Journal of Personality and Social Psychology*, 61, 1, 132-140.

McCrae, Robert R. and Oliver P. John (1992), "An Introduction to the Five-Factor Model and Its Applications," *Journal of Personality*, 60, 2 (June, 175-215.

Mischel, Walter (1968), *Personality and Assessment*, New York: Wiley.

Oliver, Richard L. (1980), "A Cognitive Model of the Antecedents and Consequences of Satisfaction Decisions," *Journal of Marketing Research*, 17 (November), 460-469.

Price, Linda L and Lawrence F. Feick (1984), "The Role of Interpersonal Sources in External Search: An Informational Perspective," in Thomas C. Kinnear (ed.), *Advances in Consumer Research, Vol. 11*, Provo, UT: Association for Consumer Research, 250-255.

Richins, Marsha L. (1982), "An Investigation of Consumers' Attitudes Toward Complaining," in Andrew A. Mitchell (ed.), *Advances in Consumer Research, Vol. 9*, Provo, UT: Association for Consumer Research, 502-506.

_____ (1983), "Negative Word-of-Mouth by Dissatisfied Customers: A Pilot Study," *Journal of Marketing*, 47 (Winter), 68-78.

Singh (1990), "A Typology of Consumer Dissatisfaction Response Styles," *Journal of Retailing*, 66, 1 (Spring), 57-99.

_____ (1988), "Consumer Complaint Intentions and Behavior: Definitional and Taxonomical Issues," *Journal of Marketing*, 52, 1 (January), 93-107.

Sparks, David L. and W.T. Tucker (1971), "A Multivariate Analysis of Personality and Product Use," *Journal of Marketing Research*, 8 (February), 67-70.

Swan, John E. and Richard L. Oliver (1989), "Postpurchase Communications by Consumers," *Journal of Retailing*, 65, 4 (Winter), 516-533.

Tse, David K. and Peter C. Wilton (1988), "Models of Consumer Satisfaction: An Extension," *Journal of Marketing Research*, 25, May, 204-212.

Tupes, E. C. and R. E. Christal (1961), *Recurrent Personality Factors Based on Trait Ratings* (USAF ASD Technical Report No. 61-97), Lackland Air Force Base, TX: U.S. Air Force.

Watson, David, Clark, L.A., and Tellegen, A. (1988), "Development and Validation of Brief Measures of Positive and Negative Affect: The PANAS Scales," *Journal of Personality and Social Psychology*, 54, 6, 1063-1070.

_____ and Auke Tellegan (1984), "Toward a Consensual Structure of Mood," *Psychological Bulletin*, 98, 2, 219-235.

_____ and Clark, L.A. (1984), "Negative Affectivity: The Disposition to Experience Aversive Emotional States," *Psychological Bulletin*, 96, 3, 465-490.

Westbrook, R. A. (1987), "Product/consumption-based affective responses and postpurchase processes," *Journal of Marketing*

Research, 24(August), pp 258-270.

_____ and Richard L. Oliver (1991), "The Dimensionality of Consumption Emotion Patterns and Consumer Satisfaction," *Journal of Consumer Research*, 18 1 (June), 84-91.

Anxiety Associated with Social Issues: The Development of a Scale to Measure an Antecedent Construct

Trina Sego, University of Texas at Austin
Patricia A. Stout, University of Texas at Austin

ABSTRACT

Emotional response to issue-related advertisements is generally studied by manipulating emotional appeals in advertisements and measuring aggregate effect on subjects. Such an approach overlooks individual response based on chronic emotional states associated with the social issues presented in the ads. In this paper, we introduce the first stage in a program of research which aims to examine how anxiety, as a chronic emotional state directed at an issue, affects how individuals respond to messages about the issue. Specifically, we develop a measure of issue-related anxiety and examine its relationship to reported behavioral intent. Results suggest that at least two dimensions of issue-related anxiety associated with AIDS and recycling are negatively related to intent to communicate about and to support those social issues.

INTRODUCTION

Educational messages sponsored by groups advocating awareness of various social causes are common. Undoubtedly, individuals sometimes respond to these messages with feelings of guilt or anxiety driven by the seriousness of the consequences associated with the issues. Often, this anxiety is further heightened by the use of "fear appeals" in advertising messages.

The "fear appeals" literature, while inconclusive, suggests that responses characterized by high degrees of anxiety hinder persuasion. The issue itself, independent of the "appeal" used in the message, may stimulate some feelings of anxiety and therefore affect response to the message.

In this exploratory study, we examine feelings associated with two social issues, AIDS and recycling. Specifically, we develop a measure of issue-related anxiety and examine its relationship to intent to communicate about and to support those social issues.

BACKGROUND

While consumer behavior researchers have shown an active interest in emotional responses to advertisements (e.g., Agres, Edell and Dubitsky 1990), most studies ignore antecedent conditions which might affect individuals' responses. Some researchers recognize that antecedent emotional states, particularly mood, can affect response to messages (Batra and Stayman 1990; Gardner 1985; Gardner and Hill 1988).

Moods are general and pervasive feeling states which *are not* directed toward specific objects (Gardner and Hill 1988). In this paper, we are interested in chronic feeling states which *are* directed toward specific objects. In particular, we are interested in anxiety because of its relevance to social issues and the degree of research attention the construct has received in psychology (see Zuckerman 1976). Because we assume that prior experience is a powerful influence on such states, the emphasis here is on measurement rather than manipulation of feelings.

Responses characterized by anxiety have long been studied within the "fear appeals" literature, where studies often examine social issues rather than products (see Rotfeld 1988; Sutton 1982). Research in this tradition generally takes a message-centered approach (focusing on messages that provoke anxiety) rather than a person-centered approach (focusing on the effects of anxiety based on individuals' experiences). Thus previous research fails to acknowledge that the individual has a history of emotional experiences related to social issues.

Anxiety which is directed toward specific issues, AIDS and recycling, is examined here. These issues were selected because they are timely and are likely to elicit different degrees of anxiety. Research examining responses of fear or anxiety to messages about environmental issues is scarce and warrants greater attention (Hine and Gifford 1991). Similarly, consumer researchers continue to call for additional research related to AIDS (Cooper-Martin and Stephens 1990; Hill 1989). Few studies examine anxiety as a variable in response to AIDS messages (Hill 1988; Stout 1990), and existing studies fail to account for individuals' previous experiences.

RESEARCH QUESTIONS

This study will focus on four research questions, including the following:

Question 1: What are the underlying dimensions of issue-related anxiety?

Analyses of general anxiety scales often reveal cognitive and somatic dimensions (Delmonte and Ryan 1983; Schalling, Cronholm and Asberg 1975; Schwartz, Davidson and Goleman 1978; see also Kellner 1988). The cognitive dimension typically represents worry and preoccupation while the somatic dimension represents physical symptoms such as a perspiration or nausea.

Many anxiety scales are said to have other dimensions. For example, the Symptom Rating Test is associated with four dimensions: anxiety, depression, somatic symptoms, and inadequacy (Kellner and Sheffield 1973). The Hopkins Symptom Checklist is associated with nine factor analytically validated subscales, of which the "anxiety" and "somatic" subscales are popularly used (Derogatis, Lipman and Covi 1976; Kellner and Uhlenhuth 1991). While the present study is exploratory, we expect that analysis of issue-related anxiety items may reveal cognitive and somatic factors.

Question 2: What is the relationship between issue-related anxiety and issue-related behavioral intentions?

As previously noted, the "fear appeals" literature, although inconclusive, suggests that high anxiety may discourage individuals from paying attention to a persuasive appeal, or from acting upon it (Sutton 1982). Behavioral intentions are operationalized here as intent to communicate about a social issue and intent to support a social issue. We expect that issue-related anxiety will be negatively related to these intentions.

Question 3: What is the relationship between emotional response associated with an issue and issue-related behavioral intentions?

Research on emotion in the consumer behavior literature has focused primarily on the use of emotion to create favorable brand attitudes through transfer of affect from attitudes toward the ad (Holbrook and O'Shaughnessy 1984; Holbrook and Batra 1987;

Stayman and Aaker 1988), and only incidentally on behavioral intentions. Little research on emotional response and social issues exists outside of the fear appeals literature (Rotfeld 1988). Emotion typically encompasses a range of different feelings, including fear or anxiety (Izard 1977; Plutchik 1980). We expect that issue-related anxiety and emotional response are two different constructs and that emotional response will have only a weak role in predicting behavioral intentions (Stout and Leckenby 1986; 1988).

Question 4: How does the ability of issue-related anxiety to predict behavioral intentions compare to the ability of emotional response items to predict behavioral intentions?

Issue-related anxiety is a more specific construct than emotional response and as such could have more or less predictive power. Issue-related anxiety might have less predictive power because it measures only one emotion rather than several dimensions of emotional experience. However, issue-related anxiety might have more predictive power in situations where anxiety is a particularly relevant emotion. We expect that anxiety is particularly relevant to the social issues studied here, and that issue-related anxiety will be a stronger predictor of behavioral intentions than emotional response will be.

METHODOLOGY

Subjects and Procedure

A total of 103 undergraduates (44 percent male, 55 percent female) participated in the study in exchange for extra course credit. Each respondent answered all items for two issues, AIDS and recycling, resulting in a total of 206 observations for each item (issues were rotated to control for order effects). Students were considered an appropriate sample because they tend to be at moderate risk for exposure to AIDS (Edgar, Freimuth and Hammond 1988), and because they have expressed concern for the environment and will have much influence on environmental issues in their lifetimes (Buttel 1979; Dunlap, Gale and Rutherford 1973).

Respondents were told they were participating in a research project asking their feelings, opinions and behavior in general and related to certain social issues. Respondents completed the questionnaire at their own pace, which took approximately 10-15 minutes.

Independent Measures

Current state of anxiety, issue-related anxiety, and issue-related emotional responses were measured as independent measures. Current state of anxiety was assessed using the 20-item state anxiety form from Spielberger's (1983) State-Trait Anxiety Inventory (STAI). Items were scored using a four-point scale (1=not at all, 4=very much so). The STAI is widely used and considered reliable (Levitt 1980).

Issue-related anxiety was measured using fifteen Likert items (1=strongly agree, 5=strongly disagree). Some items were developed by adapting items from existing scales, including Taylor (1953), Cattell and Scheier (1963), Kellner and Sheffield (1973), and Spielberger (1983), which are used to assess general and clinical anxiety. Such scales are widely available; however, items had to be adapted to measure issue-related anxiety (for reviews of anxiety scales, see Kellner and Uhlenhuth 1991; Thompson 1989).

Many items from existing scales were not applicable because they contained clinical terms, they were not adaptable to Likert scaling, their wording seemed cliched or dated (e.g., "I am often afraid that I am going to blush" Taylor 1953), they were too general ("feeling inferior to other people" Kellner and Sheffield 1973), or they lacked face validity ("I am inclined to let my actions get swayed by jealousy" Cattell and Scheier 1963). Items dealing with cognition, negative affect, arousal, physiological symptoms, and general statements about anxiety were included in the questionnaire.

The respondent's emotions about the issue were measured using eighteen semantic-differential items developed by Russell, Ward, and Pratt (1981). The scale, which is designed to measure three dimensions of emotion (i.e., pleasure, arousal and dominance), was developed using multidimensional scaling techniques, and has been applied in studies on environmental psychology (Russell 1989; Russell, Ward, and Pratt 1981). Sample items include word pairs like "happy-unhappy" (to measure the pleasure dimension), "stimulated-relaxed" (to measure arousal), and "controlling-controlled" (to measure dominance).

Data on knowledge about each issue, sexual behavior, recycling behavior, the degree to which respondents consider the issue a personal threat as well as a threat to society, and demographics were also collected. An open-ended question asked respondents to recall incidents related to the social issue.

Dependent Measures

Intentions to communicate about and to support the issues were measured using Likert scales (5=strongly agree, 1=strongly disagree). Intent to communicate was measured by two items: "I try to avoid conversation about AIDS [recycling]" and "I always pay attention to reports about AIDS [recycling] in the newspaper and on television." The former item was reverse coded. Behavioral intention was measured by one item: "I intend to take actions to combat AIDS [support recycling]."

RESULTS

A state anxiety score was calculated for each individual based on responses to Spielberger's State Anxiety Inventory using the procedures outlined in Spielberger (1983). This score provides a baseline measure of respondents' current levels of general anxiety. The means (and standard deviations) for state anxiety scores found for females and males are 43.53 (11.20) and 42.57 (14.28) respectively.

Spielberger (1983) reports scores (and standard deviations) for female and male college students of 38.76 (11.95) and 36.47 (10.02) under normal circumstances. He reports that mean scores for female and male college students under exam conditions (when students are anxious about exams) of 60.51 and 54.99. State anxiety scores found here appear to be slightly high for normal conditions, but not as high as scores expected for exam conditions.

To examine the underlying dimensions of issue-related anxiety, the fifteen issue-related anxiety items were analyzed using principal components analysis, with varimax rotation, retaining factors with eigenvalues greater than 1.00. The analysis resulted in four factors, labeled "uncomfortable," "tense," "rational," and "decisive" (see Table 1).

The first factor, "uncomfortable," explained nearly 23 percent of the variance. Items about discomfort and irritation loaded positively on this factor.

The second factor, "tense," explained 22 percent of the variance. Items such as those describing felt anxiety and physiological symptoms loaded positively on this factor.

The third factor, "rational," explained nearly 10 percent of the variance. Items such as those describing rationality and energy when dealing with the issue loaded positively on this factor.

The fourth factor, "decisive," explained nearly 10 percent of the variance, and was the most difficult to interpret. An item about difficulty in thinking and deciding about the issue loaded negatively

TABLE 1
Factor Loadings of Issue-Related Anxiety Items

	Factors and Factor Loadings			
	Uncomfortable	Tense	Rational	Decisive
The situation surrounding [issue] makes me uncomfortable.	**.825**	.204	.117	-.122
Discussing or thinking about [issue] makes me irritable.	**.780**	.203	-.195	.146
Sometimes I feel restless or jittery about problems associated with [issue].	**.734**	.386	.136	-.049
When I think about [issue], sometimes I feel tense.	**.679**	.459	-.080	.089
I get over-excited or "rattled" when I talk to others about [issue].	**.579**	.334	-.122	.453
I often feel anxious about [issue].	.195	**.788**	-.109	.088
I sometimes feel physical symptoms of nervousness or anxiety, such as "butterflies in my stomach," or rapid heartbeat, when I think about [issue].	.325	**.766**	-.184	.105
Sometimes I get so worried about [issue] that I lose my appetite.	.208	**.744**	-.139	.117
Sometimes I think about [issue] and I cannot get it out of my head.	.306	**.711**	.264	-.064
I worry a lot about problems associated with [issue].	.345	**.515**	.495	.028
I am able to think about problems associated with [issue] in a rational manner.	.112	-.162	**.698**	.158
I always have enough energy when faced with problems associated with [issue].	-.214	.125	**.503**	.370
I am usually steady and relaxed when I think about or discuss [issue].	-.364	-.363	**.480**	-.093
I have difficulty thinking clearly or deciding what to do about [issue]	.134	.056	-.220	**-.705**
When I think about [issue], I become excited.	.364	.199	.503	**.638**
Eigenvalues	3.366	3.302	1.490	1.364
Percent Variance Explained	22.440	22.014	9.936	9.091

on the factor (-.705), while an item about becoming excited about the issue loaded positively on the factor (.638).

Mean factor scores and standard deviations for each issue are presented in Table 2. According to the results of t-tests comparing these scores, the mean scores for the two issues differed significantly on only two factors: "uncomfortable" and "rational." This suggests that respondents associated AIDS with significantly less "uncomfortable" feelings and significantly less "rational" feelings than they associate with recycling.

A series of regression analyses used as predictors the state anxiety scores and four factor scores from the issue-related anxiety items (see Table 3). First, regression analyses were performed separately for each issue, which generated some differential results (available from the first author upon request). Then, the analyses

TABLE 2
t-tests Assessing Differences In Mean Factor Scores For AIDS and Recycling

Factor	AIDS Mean (Standard Deviation)	Recycling Mean (Standard Deviation)	t-value	p-value
Uncomfortable	-.273 (1.093)	.318 (.715)	-4.545	.001*
Tense	-.083 (1.103)	.084 (.882)	-1.182	.238
Rational	-.365 (.939)	.368 (.926)	-5.572	.001*
Decisive	.120 (1.014)	-.100 (1.014)	1.564	.119

*Indicates significance at or beyond the .05 level.

were performed with items pooled across issues in order to increase generalizability of the findings.

The regression equation predicting reported likelihood of conversing about the issue was significant (R^2=.190, p=.001). Three independent variables, "tense" (p=.009), "rational" (p=.001) and "decisive" (p=.001), were significant. This suggests that individuals who reported being less "tense," more "rational," and less "decisive" about a social issue were more likely to report a high likelihood of conversing about the issue.

The regression analysis predicting reported likelihood of attending to media reports about the issue was also significant (R^2=.214, p=.001). All five independent variables, state anxiety (p=.008), "uncomfortable" (p=.006), "tense" (p=.014), "rational" (p=.020) and "decisive" (p=.001), were highly significant. This suggests that individuals who reported being in a more anxious state and who reported being less "uncomfortable," less "tense," less "rational," and less "decisive" about a social issue were more likely to report a high likelihood of attending the media reports about the issue.

The regression analysis predicting reported behavioral intent to take action to support the issue was significant (R^2=.155, p=.001). Two independent variables, "tense" (p=.001) and "decisive" (p=.004), were highly significant. This suggests that subjects who reported being less "tense" and less "decisive" about a social issue were more likely to report strong intent of taking action to support recycling.

The emotional response scale was factor-analyzed (principal components analysis, varimax rotation, minimum eigenvalue=1.00), resulting in four factors. As expected, the first three factors represented pleasure (variance explained=27.7 percent), arousal (variance explained=14.3 percent) and dominance (variance explained=14.1 percent) (Russell, Ward and Pratt 1981). Only two items loaded significantly on the fourth factor (variance explained=7.3 percent). The item with the highest loading on the fourth factor, "autonomous-guided," may have been confusing to undergraduate respondents. (Complete factor loadings are available from the first author upon request.)

The factor scores for four emotional response factors were then used in a series of regression analyses to predict behavioral intent (see Table 3). The dimensions of the emotion scale proved significant predictors of reported likelihood of conversing about the issue (R^2=.049, p=.039), reported likelihood of attending to media reports about the issue (R^2=.051, p=.032) and reported intent to support the issue (R^2=.047, p=.047). However, the strength of the relationship between the emotion dimensions and the dependent variables is weak as evidenced by the small R^2. The predictive power of issue-related anxiety appears to exceed that of emotional response.

State anxiety was not included in the regression equation with emotional response items since the antecedent state of anxiety is not theoretically applicable to the emotional response model. The analogous antecedent state of mood was not measured in this study. Two additional regression analyses were performed using as predictors issue-related anxiety without state anxiety, and the dimensions of emotional response with state anxiety, to allow direct comparison of the two affective measures with and without the antecedent state anxiety. State anxiety did not greatly contribute to the predictive power of the emotional response items. In predicting intent to support the issue, the dimensions of emotional response without state anxiety performed better than the same equation including state anxiety (complete results are available from the first author).

In addition, items measuring the perceived threat to self, perceived threat to society, age, sex, marital status, and ethnicity were added to the issue-related anxiety regression analysis. While these items increased the R^2 (by an average .053 for R^2 and .029 for adjusted R^2), none of these additional variables were significant predictors of all three dependent variables. The added variables also had little effect on the significance or directionality of the other independent variables (complete results are available from the first author).

DISCUSSION AND CONCLUSIONS

In this exploratory study, we report the first stage in a program of research which aims to examine how anxiety, as a chronic affective state directed at an issue, relates to how individuals respond to messages about the issue. Of the factors which emerged from the factor analysis of issue-related anxiety items, all four were significant predictors of likelihood to attend to media reports about social issues, while three were significant predictors of likelihood to converse about social issues. Two factors were significant predictors of intent to support social issues.

The factor labeled "tense" was a significant predictor of all three dependent variables. Similar to somatic dimensions found in other studies of anxiety, this factor represents symptoms such as "butterflies in my stomach" and loss of appetite associated with anxiety (Delmonte and Ryan 1983; Schalling, Cronholm and Asberg 1975; Schwartz, Davidson and Goleman 1978). The results suggest that an absence of such symptoms is related to a higher reported likelihood of conversing about an issue, reported likelihood of attending media reports about an issue, and reported intent to support an issue.

The factor labeled "rational" resembles a cognitive dimension that has emerged in other anxiety studies (Schalling, Cronholm and Asberg 1975; Schwartz, Davidson and Goleman 1978). This factor, which represents the lack of ability to think rationally and steadily relative to an issue, was a significant predictor of two of the three dependent variables. These results suggest that individuals who report an ability to think rationally about an issue are less likely to

TABLE 3
Results of Regression Analyses Using State Anxiety and Issue-related Anxiety to Predict Intent To Converse, to Attend to Media Reports, and to Support Issue

Standardized Regression Coefficients (p value)

Dimensions of Issue-related Anxiety as Predictors

Independent Variables	Reported Likelihood of Conversing About Issue	Reported Likelihood Of Attending To Media Reports About Issue	Reported Intent To Support Issue
State Anxiety	.025 (.701)	.172 (.008)*	-.084 (.203)
Uncomfortable	.037 (.567)	-.177 (.006)*	-.124 (.062)
Tense	-.171 (.009)*	-.196 (.002)*	-.318 (.001)*
Rational	.303 (.001)*	-.149 (.020)*	-.008 (.900)
Decisive	-.254 (.001)*	-.292 (.001)*	-.190 (.004)*
R-square (prob.)	.190 (.001)*	.214 (.001)*	.155 (.001)*
Adj. R-square	.170	.194	.134

Dimensions of Emotion Response as Predictors

Independent Variables	Reported Likelihood of Conversing About Issue	Reported Likelihood Of Attending To Media Reports About Issue	Reported Intent To Support Issue
Pleasure	.167 (.017)*	-.126 (.070)	.104 (.136)
Arousal	0 (1.00)	.188 (.007)*	.153 (.028)*
Dominance	.142 (.041)*	.010 (.888)	.072 (.299)
Autonomous	-.036 (.036)	-.012 (.858)	-.088 (.205)
R-square (prob.)	.049 (.039)*	.051 (.032)*	.047 (.047)*
Adj. R-square	.030	.032	.028

*Indicates significance at or beyond the .05 level.

attend to media reports about that issue, but more likely to converse about the issue.

The factor labeled "decisive" explained little variance in the item responses, but was a significant predictor of all three dependent variables. Decisiveness and arousal associated with an issue appears to discourage individuals from conversing about an issue, attending to media reports about an issue, and intending to support an issue. Although results for this factor were not as expected, they are consistent with traditional consumer behavior theory which would suggest that decisiveness, in many situations, would not lead to information search (Solomon 1992). The ambiguity of the factor analysis results and the general measure of intent to support the issue may also have influenced the overall results.

The factor labeled "uncomfortable" accounted for a substantial amount of the variance of responses to issue-related anxiety items, but was a significant predictor of only one dependent measure. The authors suspected that the "uncomfortable" factor might be associated with a general societal concern (rather than perceived threat to self) that is not strongly related to action. However, the addition of items about perceived social threat and perceived personal threat to the regression equations did not affect the direction or significance of the other variables, including "uncomfortable."

Relative to emotional response, issue-related anxiety appears to be a stronger predictor of intent to communicate about and to support social issues. In research situations where a specific feeling (e.g., anxiety) is expected to be relevant, use of a measure that better captures that particular feeling may be a more fruitful approach than use of an emotional response scale (such as those that tap the pleasure-arousal-dominance dimensions).

As with all research studies, the methodology applied here suffers from some limitations. For example, the three dependent variables were each measured using a single item, and intention measures were not time-specific. Future studies will correct these limitations as well as employ larger samples, use more diverse social issues, and examine test-retest reliabilities. In addition, the results presented here offer only correlational evidence; no directionality can, in fact, be determined.

Despite its limitations, these results are a promising first step in a program of research which aims to examine how issue-related anxiety affects individual response to messages about social issues. The results suggest that antecedent affective states may have a powerful effect on response to messages. Future research should continue to address the role of antecedent affective states.

The findings reported here further suggest that campaign planners should take great care when designing messages about social issues such as AIDS and environmentalism. Antecedent feelings associated with the issue, in addition to those provoked by the message appeal, may lead to negative response. The results reported here offer a possible explanation for the contradictory findings evident in the "fear appeals" literature.

REFERENCES

Agres, S. J., J. A. Edell and T. M. Dubitsky (Eds.) (1990), *Emotion in Advertising: Theoretical and Practical Explorations.* Westport CT: Quorum Books.

Batra, Rajeev and Douglas M. Stayman (1990), "The Role of Mood in Advertising Effectiveness," *Journal of Consumer Research*, 17, 203-214.

Buttel, F. H. (1979), "Age and Environmental Concern: A Multivariate Analysis," *Youth and Society*, 10, 237-256.

Cattell, R. B. and I. H. Scheier (1963). *Handbook for the IPAT Anxiety Scale*. Champaign, IL: Institute for Personality and Ability Testing.

Cooper-Martin, Elizabeth and Debra L. Stephens (1990), "AIDS Prevention through Consumer Communication: Ideas from Past and Current Research," In *Advances in Consumer Research*, Vol. 17, Eds. Marvin E. Goldberg, Gerald Gorn and Richard W. Pollay, Chicago: Association for Consumer Research, 288-293.

Delmonte, M. M. and G. M. Ryan (1983), "The Cognitive-Somatic Anxiety Questionnaire," *British Journal of Clinical Psychology*, 22, 209-212.

Derogatis, L. R., R. S. Lipman and L. Covi (1976), "An Outpatient Psychiatric Rating Scale," In *ECDEU Assessment Manual for Psychopharmacology*, Rockville, MD: U.S. Department of Health, Education, and Welfare, 320.

Dunlap, R. P., R. P. Gale, and B. M. Rutherford (1973), "Concern for Environmental Rights among College Students," *American Journal of Economics and Sociology*, 32, 45-60.

Edgar, Timothy, Vicki S. Freimuth and Sharon L. Hammond (1988), "Communicating the AIDS Risk to College Students: The Problem of Motivating Change," *Health Education Research*, 3, 59-65.

Gardner, Meryl P. (1985), "Mood States and Consumer Research: A Critical Review," *Journal of Consumer Research*, 12, 281-300.

Gardner, Meryl P. and Ronald P. Hill (1988), "Consumers' Mood States: Antecedents and Consequences of Experiential versus Informational Strategies for Brand Choice," *Psychology and Marketing*, 5, 169-182.

Hill, Ronald P. (1988), "An Exploration of the Relationship between AIDS-related Anxiety and the Evaluation of Condom Advertisements," *Journal of Advertising*, 17, 35-42.

Hill, Ronald P. (1989), "The Growing Threat of AIDS: How Marketers Must Respond," *Journal of Health Care Marketing*, 9, 5-12.

Hine, Donald W. and Robert Gifford (1991), "Fear Appeals, Individual Differences, and Environmental Concern," *Journal of Environmental Education*, 23, 36-41.

Holbrook, Morris B. and Rajeev Batra (1987), "Assessing the Role of Emotions as Mediators of Consumer Responses to Advertising," *Journal of Consumer Research*, 14, 404-420.

Holbrook, Morris B. and John O'Shaughnessy (1984), "The Role of Emotion in Advertising, *Psychology and Marketing*, 1, 45-64.

Holbrook, Morris B. and Richard A. Westwood (1989), "The Role of Emotion in Advertising Revisited," In *Cognitive and Affective Responses to Advertising*, Eds. Patricia Cafferata and Alice M. Tybout, Lexington, Mass.: Lexington, 353-372.

Izard, Carroll E. (1977), *Human Emotions*, New York, NY: Plenum.

Kellner, Robert (1988), "Anxiety, Somatic Sensations and Bodily Complaints," In *Handbook of Anxiety, Vol. 2: Classification, Etiological Factors and Associated Disturbances*, Ed. R. Noyes, M. Roth and G. D. Burrows, New York: Elsevier Sciences, 213-237.

Kellner, Robert and Brian F. Sheffield (1973), "A Self-Rating Scale of Distress," *Psychological Medicine*, 3, 88-100.

Kellner, Robert and Eberhard H. Uhlenhuth (1991), "The Rating and Self-rating of Anxiety," *British Journal of Psychiatry*, 159, 15-22.

Levitt, E. E. (1980), *The Psychology of Anxiety*, Hillsdale, NJ: Erlbaum.

Plutchik, Robert (1980), *Emotion: A Psychoevolutionary Synthesis*, New York: Harper and Row.

Rotfeld, H. J. (1988), "Fear Appeals and Persuasion: Assumptions and Errors in Advertising Research," *Current Issues and Research in Advertising*, 11, 21-40.

Russell, J. A. (1989). Measures of Emotion. In *Emotion: Theory, Research, and Experience*, Eds. R. Plutchik and H. Kellerman, San Diego: Academic, 83-111.

Russell, J.A., L. M. Ward, and G. Pratt (1981), "The Affective Quality Attributed to Environments: A Factor Analytic Study," *Environment and Behavior*, 13, 259-288.

Schalling, D., B. Cronholm and M. Asberg (1975), "Components of State and Trait Anxiety Related to Personality and Arousal," In *Emotions: Their Parameters and Measurement*, Ed. L. Levi, New York: Raven, 603-617.

Schwartz, G., R. Davidson and D. Goleman (1978), "Patterning of Cognitive and Somatic Processes in the Self-regulation of Anxiety," *Psychosomatic Medicine*, 40, 321-328.

Solomon, Michael R. (1992), *Consumer Behavior: Buying, Having, and Being*, Boston: Allyn and Bacon.

Spielberger, Charles D. (1983), *Manual for the State-Trait Anxiety Inventory (Form Y)*, Palo Alto, CA: Consulting Psychologists Press, Inc.

Stayman, Douglas M. and David Aaker (1988), "Are All the Effects of Ad-Induced Feelings Mediated by Aad?" *Journal of Consumer Research*, 15, 368-373.

Stout, Patricia (1990), "Positive and Negative Emotional Responses to Threat Appeals in AIDS Messages," Paper presented at the conference of the International Communication Association, Dublin, Ireland.

Stout, Patricia A. and John D. Leckenby (1986), "Measuring Emotional Response to Advertising," *Journal of Advertising*, 15, 35-42.

Stout, Patricia A. and John D. Leckenby (1988), "The Nature of Emotional Response of Advertising: A Further Examination," *Journal of Advertising*, 17, 53-57.

Sutton, S. B. (1982), "Fear-arousing Communications: A Critical Examination of Theory and Research," In *Social Psychology and Behavioral Medicine*, Chichester, England: John Wiley & Sons, 303-337.

Taylor, J. A. (1953), "A Personality Scale of Manifest Anxiety," *Journal of Abnormal and Social Psychology*, 48, 285-290.

Thompson, Chris (1989), "Anxiety," In *The Instruments of Psychiatric Research*, Ed. Chris Thompson, Chichester, England: John Wiley & Sons, 127-155.

Zuckerman, Marvin (1976), "General and Situation-specific Traits and States: New Approaches to Assessment of Anxiety and Other Constructs," In *Emotions and Anxiety: New Concepts, Methods, and Applications*, Eds. M. Zuckerman and C. D. Spielberger, Hillsdale, NJ: Lawrence Erlbaum, 133-174.

AUTHOR INDEX

Aaker, Jennifer 139
Abeele, Piet Vanden 226
Allen, Douglas E. 70
Alwitt, Linda F. 95
Anderson, Paul F. 70
Andreasen, Alan R. 254
Anglin, Linda K. 126
Areni, Charles S. 337
Auchinachie, Lisa 153
Babin, Barry J. 406
Babin, Laurie A. 406
Baer, Robert 399
Bagozzi, Richard P. 8
Bailey, James R. 437
Baker, Stacey Menzel 169
Banarjee, Bobby 147, 292
Barone, Michael J. 299
Bates, Myra Jo 30
Baumgartner, Hans 138
Beltramini, Richard F. 218
Berger, Ida E. 95
Bickart, Barbara 329
Billings, Robert S. 437
Block, Lauren G. 252
Bloom, Diane L. 387
Bloom, Paul N. 387
Brian Wansink, ... 508
Brooker, George 286
Brown, Christina L. 291
Brown, Steven P. 218, 353
Burns, Alvin C. 98
Caudill, Eve M. 213
Celsi, Richard L. 51
Chakraborty, Goutam 23
Chan, Darius K-S 449
Chatterjee, Anindya 543
Chattopadhyay, Amitava 224
Chebat, Jean-Charles 548
Chen, Hong C. 181
Claxton, Reid P. 141, 422
Compeau, Larry D. 115
Costa, Janeen Arnold 372
Costley, Carolyn L. 79
Coulter, Robin Higie 276, 501
Cowley, Elizabeth J. 58
Cox, Anthony 554
Cox, Dena 554
Cox, K. Chris 337
Denton, Frank 132
Desai, Kalpesh Kaushik 436
deTurck, Mark A. 208
Dhar, Ravi 24
Dolstra, Jamie 165
Doran, Kathleen Brewer 318
Dubé, Laurette 15, 548
Eckman, Molly 560
Eisner, Ellen J. 387
Englis, Basil G. 97, 374
Escalas, Jennifer Edson 304
Faircloth, III, James B. 458

Feltham, Tammi S. 531
Fischer, Eileen 137
Fiske, Carol A. 43
Fitzsimons, Gavan J. 252
Ford, Gary T. 530
Forkin, Frank 412
Foxall, Gordon R. 312
France, Karen Russo 583
Freitas, Anthony 165
Fullerton, Ronald A. 418
Gainer, Brenda 137
Gentry, James W. 30
Gibson, Rhonda 282
Goodstein, Ronald C. 526
Graeff, Timothy R. 201
Granbois, Donald H. 41
Griffin, Mitch 406
Gross, Barbara L. 120
Gulas, Charles 292
Hadjimarcou, John 509
Harris, William D. 181
Hartman, Cathy L. 464
Haugtvedt, Curtis P. 234
Heath, Chip 119
Heckler, Susan E. 140
Heisley, Deborah 253
Henderson, Caroline M. 86
Hill, Donna J. 399
Hill, Ronald Paul 13, 572
Hirschman, Elizabeth C. 576
Hoch, Stephen J. 224
Holbrook, Morris 566
Holden, Stephen 589
Holt, Douglas 64, 65
Hoyer, Wayne D. 436
Hunt, James M. 543
Iyer, Easwar 292
Jacoby, Jacob 565
Janiszewski, Chris 329
Jass, Jeffrey 536
Johar, Gita Venkataramani 96
Joiner, Christopher 188
Jones, David B. 141
Jorgensen, Brian K. 348
Joy, Annamma 153
Kacen, Jacqueline J. 519
Katrichis, Jerome M. 412
Kellaris, James J. 514
Kennedy, Patricia F. 169, 365
Kernan, Jerome B. 543
Kiecker, Pamela 464
Konkel, Mark 412
Krish, Rajan 255
Lacher, Kathleen T. 354
Lai, Albert Wenben 489
Lee, Angela Y. 270
Lee, Moonkyu 483
Lepisto, Lawrence R. 126
Li, Wai-Kwan 449
Loken, Barbara 188

Lowrey, Tina M.	25
Luebbehusen, Lisa A.	43
MacLachlan, Douglas L.	225, 226, 582
Magee, Allison	590
Malafarina, Katryna	536
Maloy, Kate	13
Manning, Kenneth C.	299
Mantel, Susan Powell	514
Marks, Lawrence J.	509
Marquis, Marie	548
Martin, Jr., Claude R.	380
Martin, Mary C.	365
Martins, Marielza	75
Mayhew, Glen	224
Mayo, Michael	343
McIntyre, Roger P.	141
McKeage, Kim	147
McMullen, James S.	175
Menon, Geeta	379
Milbourne, Constance C.	159
Miniard, Paul W.	299
Mitchell, Deborah J.	330
Mittal, Banwari	256
Mittal, Vikas	412
Mittelstaedt, Robert	427
Miyazaki, Anthony D.	43
Monroe, Kent B.	75, 449
Mooradian, Todd A.	595
Moore, David J.	181
Moorman, Christine	12
Morris, Jon D.	175
Morwitz, Vicki G.	379
Mulvey, Michael S.	51
Munch, James M.	343
Murray, Jeff B.	422
Neslin, Scott A.	224
Nowlis, Stephen M.	139
O'Curry, Suzanne	119
Oliver, Richard L.	16
Olson, Jerry C.	51, 201
Olver, James M.	595
Otnes, Cele	25, 158, 159
Page, Jr., Thomas J.	547
Park, C. Whan	583
Patterson, Maggie Jones	13
Paul, Pallab	255
Pavia, Teresa	195
Peltier, James W.	244
Pennell, Greta E.	97, 359
Petty, Richard E.	234
Prenshaw, Penelope J.	496
Rachlin, Robert A.	208
Rindfleisch, Aric	470
Rose, Randall L.	299
Roth, Martin	495
Rucker, Margaret	165
Ruth, Julie	159
Sahni, Arti	442
Sarigollu, Emine	224
Sayre, Shay	109
Schibrowsky, John A.	244
Schulz, Steve	427
Searls, Kathleen	65
Sego, Trina	601
Seiders, Kathleen	79
Sewall, Murphy A.	276
Shah, Reshma H.	583
Shimp, Terence A.	1
Simmons, Carolyn J.	96
Sinha, Indrajit	477
Smith, Stephen M.	234
Sojka, Jane	392
Spangenberg, Eric	392
Spiggle, Susan	35
Spotts, Harlan	238
Srivastava, Joydeep	255
Stephens, Debra Lynn	572
Stern, Barbara B.	576
Stevens, Karen M.	543
Stewart, David W.	310
Stout, Patricia A.	601
Strahilevitz, Michal Ann	233
Stuenkel, Kathleen	126
Sujan, Harish	435
Sutton, Sharyn M.	387
Thompson, Craig J.	104
Toncar, Mark	343
Ulgado, Francis M.	483
Urbany, Joel E.	43
VanderVeen, Steven	331, 332
Vanhuele, Marc	264
Venkatesh, Alladi	323
Viswanathan, Madhubalan	397
Wagner, Janet	560
Walker, Beth A.	51
Walsh, Patricia Ann	35
Wells, William D.	375
West, Patricia M.	291
Wheatley, John J.	286
Williams, Laura A.	98
Winer, Russell S.	224
Witkowski, Terrence H.	251
Wittmayer, Cecelia	427
Wright, Alice	23
Yi, Huiuk	282
Young, Melissa J.	208
Zaltman, Gerald	501
Zillmann, Dolf	282
Zinkhan, George M.	496
Zolner, Kyle	25
Zwick, Rami	435